MEDICAL LAW

WITHDRAWN

Text, Cases, and Materials

FOURTH EDITION

Emily Jackson

WITHDRAWN

OXFORD

UNIVERSITY PRESS

OXFORD
UNIVERSITY PRESS

Great Clarendon Street, Oxford, OX2 6DP,
United Kingdom

Oxford University Press is a department of the University of Oxford.
It furthers the University's objective of excellence in research, scholarship,
and education by publishing worldwide. Oxford is a registered trade mark of
Oxford University Press in the UK and in certain other countries

First edition 2006
Second edition 2009
Third edition 2013
Impression: 1

Published in the United States of America by Oxford University Press
198 Madison Avenue, New York, NY 10016, United States of America

British Library Cataloguing in Publication Data
Data available

Library of Congress Control Number: 2016931925

ISBN 978–0–19–874350–7

Printed in Great Britain by
Bell & Bain Ltd., Glasgow

NEW TO THIS EDITION

- Coverage of important new cases in all chapters, including *Montgomery and Lanarkshire Health Board, Cheshire West and Chester Council v P, Doogan v Greater Glasgow and Clyde Health Board, R (Nicklinson) v Ministry of Justice,* and *Aintree University Hospitals Foundation Trust v James.*

- Coverage of the implementation of the Health and Social Care Act 2012.

- A new section on public health law.

- Description and analysis of the considerable body of Mental Capacity Act case law since the third edition.

- Coverage of the implications of the *Cheshire West* decision for the Deprivation of Liberty Safeguards (DoLS), and the Law Commission's proposals for replacing DoLS.

- Coverage of the EU General Data Protection Regulation.

- Coverage of the EU Clinical Trials Regulation.

- Coverage of the Human Fertilisation and Embryology (Mitochondrial Donation) Regulations 2015.

- Description and analysis of the recent case law on surrogacy, and the implications of overseas surrogacy arrangements.

ACKNOWLEDGEMENTS

We are grateful to the following for permission to reproduce copyright material and commercial documents:

Crown copyright material is reproduced under Class Licence Number C2006010631 with the permission of the Controller of HMSO and the Queen's Printer for Scotland. Parliamentary copyright material is reproduced with the permission of the Controller of Her Majesty's Stationery Office on behalf of Parliament.

Cambridge University Press: extract from Bernard Williams, *Making Sense of Humanity and Other Philosophical Papers* (CUP: Cambridge, 1995).

Crown: extracts from Data Protection Act 1998 Schedules 1–3 and Human Fertilisation and Embryology Act 2008 section 54.

Crown Prosecution Service: extract from DPP Policy for Prosecutors in Respect of Cases of Encouraging or Assisting Suicide (CPS, 2010).

England and Wales Court of Appeal: extract from *Parkinson v St James and Seacroft University Hospital NHS Trust* [2001] EWCA Civ 530; *Nicklinson v Ministry of Justice* [2013] EWCA Civ 961; and *R (on the application of Tracey) v Cambridge NHS Foundation Trust* [2014] EWCA Civ 822.

England and Wales Court of Protection: extract from *M v N* [2015] EWCOP 76.

High Court of Justice of England and Wales (EWHC): extracts from Eleanor King J, *An NHS Trust v DE* [2013] EWHC 2562 (Fam); *Re JA (A Minor) (Medical Treatment: Child Diagnosed with HIV)* [2014] EWHC 1135 (Fam); *W v M (An Adult Patient)* [2011] EWHC 1197 (Fam); *Re G (Surrogacy: Foreign Domicile)* [2007] EWHC 2814 (Fam); and *Stone v South East Coast Strategic Health Authority* [2006] EWHC 1668 (Admin).

House of Lords (UKHL): extracts from *Campbell v MGN (Mirror Group Newspapers)* [2004] UKHL 22; *R (on the application of Quintavalle) v Secretary of State for Health* [2003] UKHL 13; *Rees v Darlington Memorial Hospital NHS Trust* [2003] UKHL 52 and *R (on the application of Purdy) v Director of Public Prosecutions* [2009] UKHL 45.

Incorporated Council of Law Reporting for England and Wales (ICLR): extracts from the Law Reports: Appeal Cases (AC), King's Bench Division (KB), and Queen's Bench Division (QB).

Jordan Publishing Ltd: extract from Family Law Report: *Re A (Children) (Conjoined Twins: Surgical Separation)* [2001] 1 FLR 267. The Family Law Reports are published under the Family Law imprint.

Northern Ireland's Queen Bench: extract from The Northern Ireland Human Rights Commission's Application [2015] NIQB 96.

Nuffield Council on Bioethics: extracts from 'Human bodies: donation for medicine and research' (2011) available at http://www.nuffieldbioethics.org/donation.

Oxford University Press Journals: extract from Medical Law Review: Lord Woolf: 'Are the Courts Excessively Deferential to the Medical Profession?', 9 Medical Law Review 1 (2001).

Supreme Court of the United Kingdom: extracts from: *Montgomery v Lanarkshire Health Board* [2015] UKSC 11; *Cheshire West and Chester Council v P* [2014] UKSC 19; *Rabone v Pennine Care NHS Foundation Trust* [2012] UKSC 2 and *R (Nicklinson and Another) v Ministry of Justice* [2014] UKSC 38.

Sweet & Maxwell Ltd: extract from Criminal Law Review: case report: *R (on the application of Smeaton) v Secretary of State for Health* [2002] Crim LR 664.

Every effort has been made to trace and contact the copyright holders but this has not been possible in all cases. If notified, the publisher will undertake to rectify any errors or omissions at the earliest opportunity.

CONTENTS

1   AN INTRODUCTION TO BIOETHICS   1

2   THE PROVISION OF HEALTH CARE SERVICES: THE NHS, RESOURCE ALLOCATION, AND PUBLIC HEALTH   35

3   MEDICAL MALPRACTICE   119

4   CONSENT I: UNDERSTANDING   189

5 | CONSENT II: CAPACITY AND VOLUNTARINESS   234

6 | MENTAL HEALTH LAW   320

7 CONFIDENTIALITY 389

8 GENETIC INFORMATION 440

9 CLINICAL RESEARCH 474

10   THE REGULATION OF MEDICINES   539

11 ORGAN TRANSPLANTATION   588

12 EMBRYO AND STEM CELL RESEARCH   660

13   ABORTION   698

14   LIABILITY FOR OCCURRENCES BEFORE BIRTH   760

17 END-OF-LIFE DECISIONS 912

TABLE OF CASES

TABLE OF LEGISLATION

*Page references in **bold** indicate that the text is reproduced in full.*

TABLE OF UK STATUTORY INSTRUMENTS

*Page references in **bold** indicate that the text is reproduced in full.*

TABLE OF TREATIES, CONVENTIONS AND EUROPEAN LEGISLATION

Page references in **bold** *indicate that the text is reproduced in full.*

1

AN INTRODUCTION
TO BIOETHICS

CENTRAL ISSUES

1. Conventional medical ethics focused on the individual doctor–patient encounter. Bioethics' remit is much broader, encompassing the dilemmas new technologies may raise for society.

2. Religious perspectives on bioethics tend to be less individualistic than secular approaches. Few now believe that modern medicine 'usurps God's will'. Instead, medical progress is, within limits, supported by most religious bioethicists.

3. There is a difference between utilitarian and deontological reasoning. A utilitarian is concerned with an action's consequences, whereas deontological reasoning prioritizes respect for a person's rights. Virtue ethics involves working out what a 'virtuous' person would do in a particular situation.

4. The 'principlist' approach lays out four top-down principles: autonomy, beneficence, non-maleficence, and justice, which can be used to explain what is at stake in medical dilemmas. In contrast, casuistry involves bottom-up reasoning by analogy, taking previous cases as a starting point.

5. A feminist ethic of care rejects the individualistic model of patient autonomy, and places more emphasis upon interdependence and relationships.

6. Arguments from 'human dignity' or respect for the 'sanctity of human life' have particular resonance in the medical context, but their meaning is opaque.

7. Slippery slope claims are often essentially empirical claims, and effective regulation might be the best way to accommodate them.

1 INTRODUCTION

The purpose of this chapter is to provide an introduction to bioethical reasoning. The words 'ethics' and 'morality' derive from the Greek (*ethos*) and Latin (*mores*), meaning 'customs'. In their ordinary usage, the words have slightly different connotations. 'Morality' often implies a restrictive code of conduct, setting out the difference between right and wrong. 'Ethics' refers to the systematic analysis of what it means to lead a decent life. Medical ethics is a branch of applied ethics, and it is principally concerned with how we should go about resolving difficult questions that arise from the practice of medicine.

As we shall see throughout this book, it is impossible to study medical law without confronting complex ethical dilemmas, such as:

- Is it acceptable to withdraw life-prolonging treatment from a patient in a minimally conscious state?
- Should parents be allowed to choose their children's sex?
- What, if anything, would be wrong with paying someone to 'donate' one of their kidneys?
- Should an anorexic teenager be force-fed?
- What limits, if any, should be placed upon women's access to abortion?
- Should euthanasia be legalized?

It would be difficult to work out the appropriate legal response to such questions without also considering their ethical implications. While this is principally a book about medical law, it would be artificial to draw a sharp distinction between medical law and ethics. Rather, throughout this book we will be considering how law should respond to some complex ethical dilemmas.

This opening chapter attempts to summarize various ways in which we might go about resolving, or at least discussing, these ethical problems. We begin by looking at what we might mean by 'medical ethics' and the more recent term 'bioethics'. Next, we consider several different types of ethical reasoning: from religious bioethics to a feminist ethic of care.

When justifying a preference for a particular outcome in the field of medical law and ethics, it is common for people to appeal to the dangers of the 'slippery slope', or to ground their argument in the need to respect 'human dignity', or to have respect for the 'sanctity of human life'. We briefly consider what these claims might involve. We conclude by looking at changing attitudes towards the human body within medical law and ethics.

2 BIOETHICS

Medical ethics has a very long history; the Hippocratic oath dates back to the fifth century BCE. Conventional medical ethics is concerned with the ethics of good medical practice: that is, with what it means to be a good doctor. Ethical rules or codes of conduct, like the Hippocratic oath, were guidelines that the medical profession imposed upon itself in order to ensure that doctors' behaviour towards their colleagues and their patients met appropriate standards of moral decency. The vantage point was therefore that of the doctor himself: how the doctor should obtain consent; when a doctor can breach his duty of confidentiality; and so on. Until comparatively recently, medical practice was strongly paternalistic: doctors were under a duty to act in their patients' best interests, but it was doctors (as opposed to the patients themselves) who decided what those interests were.

In the next extract Susan Sherwin argues that conventional medical ethics tended to marginalize both the patient's perspective and the broader social causes of ill health.

Susan Sherwin[1]

Until very recently, conscientious physicians were actually trained to act paternalistically toward their patients, to treat patients according to the physician's own judgement about what would be best for their patients, with little regard for each patient's own perspectives or preferences. The problem with this arrangement, however, is that health care may involve such intimate and central aspects of a patient's life—including, for example, matters such as health, illness, reproduction, death, dying, bodily integrity, nutrition, lifestyle, self-image, disability, sexuality, and psychological well-being—that it is difficult for anyone other than the patient to make choices that will be compatible with that patient's personal value system . . .

A striking feature of most . . . discussions about patient autonomy is their exclusive focus on individual patients; this pattern mirrors medicine's consistent tendency to approach illness as primarily a problem of particular patients . . . Within the medical tradition, suffering is located and addressed in the individuals who experience it rather than in the social arrangements that may be responsible for causing the problem. Instead of exploring the cultural context that tolerates and even supports practices such as war, pollution, sexual violence, and systemic unemployment—practices that contribute to much of the illness that occupies modern medicine—physicians generally respond to the symptoms troubling particular patients in isolation from the context that produces these conditions.

Heather Draper and Tom Sorrell argue that medical ethics has also ignored the obligations of patients.

Heather Draper and Tom Sorrell[2]

In comparison to what it asks of doctors, mainstream medical ethics makes very few demands of patients, and these usually begin and end with consent. Traditionally medical ethics has asserted that, as autonomous agents, competent patients must be allowed to decide for themselves the course of their medical treatment, and even whether to be treated at all. . . . Little or nothing is said about what kinds of decisions patients ought to make. Nor is much said about their responsibilities for making good rather than bad decisions. Indeed . . . mainstream medical ethics implies that a competent patient's decision is good simply by virtue of having been made by the patient . . .

In welfare states, discussion about the use of limited resources extends naturally to a consideration of whether citizens have some sort of moral obligation, other things being equal, to limit their demands on these resources. If the answer is 'Yes', then there may be a civic obligation to follow preventive health measures recommended by one's doctor. If one is advised to stop smoking or over-eating, and one disregards that advice, so that one's condition deteriorates to the point that expensive treatment is required to keep one alive, one may be doing something doubly wrong—breaking obligations to oneself and breaking civic obligations not to use public resources unnecessarily . . .

In short, there are duties not to use health services casually. . . . Someone who indulges their hypochondria by frequent visits to the GP, or who summons an ambulance after getting sunburn; someone who knowingly presents himself at an emergency room with nothing more than severe indigestion; or who calls out a doctor because he needs a prescription that could be filled in office hours next day; all of these patients do something morally wrong, wrong primarily because they have taken away time and resources better spent on more urgent cases.

[1] 'A Relational Approach to Autonomy in Healthcare' in Susan Sherwin (ed), *The Politics of Women's Health: Exploring Agency and Autonomy* (Temple UP: Philadelphia, 1998) 19–47, 21.

[2] 'Patients' responsibilities in medical ethics' (2002) 16 Bioethics 335–51.

Bioethics is a much newer discipline and its remit is much wider. The term was first used in the twentieth century, and it is concerned with the life sciences in general, not just with the doctor–patient encounter. Rapid technological progress poses some complex dilemmas, particularly at the beginning and end of life, which have implications beyond how a doctor should treat his patient. For example, once it became possible to (a) perform organ transplants, and (b) keep a patient's heart beating after death, it was necessary to ask whether 'brain-dead' but still breathing patients were a legitimate source of organs for transplantation.

In the next extract, Helga Kuhse and Peter Singer reflect upon the origins and remit of bioethics, suggesting that it was also a response to the rise of patient autonomy, and the decline of medical paternalism.

Helga Kuhse and Peter Singer[3]

Since the 1960s, ethical problems in health care and the biomedical sciences have gripped the public consciousness in unprecedented ways. In part, this is the result of new and sometimes revolutionary developments in the biomedical sciences and in clinical medicine . . . Another factor has been a growing concern about the power exercised by doctors and scientists, which shows itself in concern to assert 'patients' rights' and the rights of the community as a whole to be involved in decisions that affect them. This has meant greater public awareness of the value-laden nature of medical decision-making, and a critical questioning of the basis on which such decisions are made . . .

It was in the climate of such new ethical issues and choices that the field of inquiry now known as 'bioethics' was born. . . .

. . . Bioethics, on the other hand, is a more overtly critical and reflective enterprise. Not limited to questioning the ethical dimensions of doctor–patient and doctor–doctor relationships, it goes well beyond the scope of traditional medical ethics in several ways. First, its goal is not the development of, or adherence to, a code or set of precepts, but a better understanding of the issues. Second, it is prepared to ask deep philosophical questions about the nature of ethics, the value of life, what it is to be a person, the significance of being human. Third, it embraces issues of public policy and the direction and control of science.

In the next extract, Daniel Callahan and Bruce Jennings argue that the focus of bioethics is becoming broader still, as it moves away from its initial focus on patient autonomy and high-tech medicine, towards much wider public health considerations.

Daniel Callahan and Bruce Jennings[4]

When the field of bioethics emerged in the late 1960s and early 1970s, it represented a significant broadening of medical ethics. It moved the subject beyond the doctor–patient relationship and medical professionalism into the new territory of, among other things, organ transplants, genetics, reproductive biology, and resource allocation. But little attention was paid by bioethics in its early years to the distinctive ethical problems inherent in public health.

---

[3] 'What is Bioethics? A Historical Introduction' in Helga Kuhse and Peter Singer (eds), *A Companion to Bioethics* (Blackwell: Oxford, 1998) 3–11.

[4] Daniel Callahan and Bruce Jennings, 'Ethics and public health: forging a strong relationship' (2002) 92 American Journal of Public Health 169–76.

That is perhaps not surprising. Bioethics received its initial stimulus from the abuses of human subjects research, the emergence of the patients' rights movement, and the drama of high-technology medicine. . . . In early bioethics, the good of the individual, and particularly his or her autonomy, was the dominant theme, not population health. . . .

For its part, bioethics has become restless for change, and it is particularly looking for a value orientation that may bring it into closer proximity with public health. There has always been an undercurrent of resistance to the individualistic, autonomy-driven mainstream orientation within bioethics . . . But the obvious need for universal health care, the persistence of racial and ethnic disparities in health status, and the importance of background social and economic factors have caught the eye of many. A shift of direction in the field of bioethics was called for, and it has already begun.

3 HOW SHOULD WE MAKE DIFFICULT ETHICAL DECISIONS?

Many people have 'gut feelings' or intuitive reactions to ethical dilemmas. It is very common for people to react to a controversial new technique, such as human cloning, by saying: 'I just think it's wrong.' There are those who believe that what might be called the 'yuck factor' in fact embodies some deep, inner wisdom. This idea is most closely associated with Leon R Kass, whose controversial article 'The Wisdom of Repugnance' admits that '[r]evulsion is not an argument', but goes on to say that,

In crucial cases, however, repugnance is the emotional expression of deep wisdom, beyond reason's power fully to articulate it . . . We are repelled by the prospect of cloning human beings not because of the strangeness or novelty of the undertaking, but because we intuit and feel, immediately and without argument, the violation of things that we rightfully hold dear.[5]

John Harris is one of this article's most strident critics.

John Harris[6]

George Orwell once memorably referred to this reliance on intuition as use of 'moral nose'; as if one could simply sniff a situation and detect wickedness. The problem is that nasal reasoning is notoriously unreliable, and olfactory moral philosophy, despite valiant efforts of Kass and others, has done little to refine it or give it a respectable foundation. We should remember that in the recent past, among the many discreditable uses of so-called 'moral feelings', people have been disgusted by the sight of Jews, black people and, indeed, women being treated as equals and mixing on terms of equality with others. In the absence of convincing arguments, we should be suspicious of those who use nasal reasoning as the basis of their moral convictions.

Our gut instincts tend to be immediate, unreasoned responses, and while they will often inevitably form the starting point for our analysis of an issue, on their own there is no reason

---

[5] Leon R Kass, 'The wisdom of repugnance' (1997) 216 The New Republic 22.

[6] John Harris, *Enhancing Evolution: The Ethical Case for Making Better People* (Princeton UP: Princeton, 2007) 130.

why anyone else should be persuaded by them. In order to convince others, it is necessary to point to some coherent reasoning or moral principles that explain or justify our position.

In short, we need to find some mechanism for resolving ethical dilemmas that goes beyond an appeal to our 'gut instincts'. As we will see in the following sections, bioethicists are interested in working out what this mechanism should be.

(a) RELIGIOUS BIOETHICS

The comprehensive rejection of medical expertise on religious grounds is now rare; more commonly, some people's religious beliefs inform their anxiety about modern medicine's power to create and to destroy life. Within a secular and culturally diverse society, religion tends to be regarded as a matter of private faith. As a result, while religious leaders' pronouncements on bioethical issues may be of central importance to the adherents of particular religions, and will often determine how they approach their own personal medical dilemmas, it is less clear what role they should have in shaping public policy.

In the next extract, Daniel Callahan regrets the 'secularization' of bioethics and suggests that because all religions have a long and rich history of grappling with questions that are of central importance to medical law and ethics—such as the meaning of life and death— religious perspectives might be a particularly useful resource for the comparatively new secular discipline of bioethics.

Daniel Callahan[7]

> The net result of this narrowing of philosophy and the disappearance or denaturing of religion in public discourse is a triple threat. It leaves us, first of all, too heavily dependent upon the law as the working source of morality. The language of the courts and legislatures becomes our only shared means of discourse. That leaves a great number fearful of the law (as seems the case with many physicians) or dependent upon the law to determine the rightness of actions, which it can rarely do since it tells us better what is forbidden or acceptable, than what is commendable or right.
>
> It leaves us, secondly, bereft of the accumulated wisdom and knowledge that are the fruit of long-established religious traditions. I do not have to be a Jew to find it profitable and illuminating to see how the great rabbinical teachers have tried to understand moral problems over the centuries. Nor will Jews find it utterly useless to explore what the popes, or the leading Protestant divines, have had to say about ethics. . . .
>
> It leaves us, thirdly, forced to pretend that we are not creatures both of particular moral communities and the sprawling inchoate general community that we celebrate as an expression of our pluralism. Yet that pluralism becomes a form of oppression if, in its very name, we are told to shut up in public about our private lives and beliefs and talk a form of what Jeffrey Stout has called moral Esperanto.

There are clearly important differences both between and within religions. Within Christianity, for example, views on the moral status of the embryo—and hence the legitimacy of abortion and embryo research—differ markedly. Nevertheless, a number of similarities between religious approaches to bioethics might be identified. First, religious bioethics tend to emphasize the intrinsic rightness or wrongness of a particular course of action, and

---

[7] 'Religion and the secularization of bioethics' (1990) 20 Hastings Center Report 2–4.

be less swayed by pragmatic or consequentialist arguments. In relation to euthanasia, for example, a religious perspective would concentrate upon the legitimacy or otherwise of bringing about another person's death, rather than the practical difficulties in setting up an effective regulatory regime.

Secondly, religions tend to share two principal moral concerns: (a) love for one's neighbour (almost every religion contains some version of the Golden Rule: that you should treat your neighbour as you would want to be treated yourself); and (b) a sense of awe and respect for 'God's creation', and especially for human life, through what we might call the 'sanctity principle'.

In the next extract, Hazel Markwell and Barry Brown describe how a belief in the sanctity of life informs Roman Catholic responses to a wide variety of bioethical questions.

Hazel Markwell and Barry Brown[8]

Fundamental to Catholic bioethics is a belief in the sanctity of life: the value of a human life, as a creation of God and a gift in trust, is beyond human evaluation and authority. God maintains dominion over it. In this view, we are stewards, not owners, of our own bodies and are accountable to God for the life that has been given to us.

But while many religions share a belief in the sanctity of life, and hence in the wrongness of killing, what this means in practice can vary dramatically. The Roman Catholic view that a new human person exists from conception has resulted in an absolute prohibition of abortion, and condemnation of its social causes, such as sexual permissiveness. In the Episcopal Anglican tradition, there is no consensus, and for many abortion is viewed as a matter of individual conscience. Jewish bioethics does not regard the fetus as having the same status as the pregnant woman, and hence the morality of abortion depends upon whether there is sufficient cause to justify the taking of fetal life. In some schools of Buddhism, the sanctity of life is not necessarily confined to human life.

Applied to medicine, however, all religious perspectives are less individualistic than secular bioethics and start from the premise that life is a gift, which is not ours to destroy. Taken together, this means that religious bioethics tend to place less emphasis on patient autonomy.

Thirdly, the idea that life is a gift raises the question of how far man should be allowed to interfere with the natural order. Answers have varied dramatically—from the idea that modern medicine is frustrating God's will, to the more progressive (and much more common) view that man's quest for knowledge, and hence medical progress, is itself part of God's creation. Paul Badham explains this shift, from a Christian perspective.

Paul Badham[9]

[M]edical ethics provides the largest number of instances where Christians today almost unanimously accept as good practices which their predecessors in the faith regarded as evil. For many centuries Christians forbade the giving of medicine, deeming it equivalent to the practice of sorcery. The practice of surgery, the study of anatomy and the dissection of corpses for

---

[8] 'Bioethics for clinicians: Catholic bioethics' (2001) 165 Canadian Medical Association Journal 189–92, 189.

[9] 'Theological Examination of the Case for Euthanasia' in Paul Badham and Paul Ballard, *Facing Death: An Interdisciplinary Approach* (Cardiff University of Wales Press: Cardiff, 1996) 101–16, 103.

medical research were all at one time firmly forbidden. Later the practices of inoculation and vaccination faced fierce theological opposition. Indeed in 1829 Pope Leo XII declared that whoever decided to be vaccinated was no longer a child of God; smallpox was a judgement of God, vaccination was a challenge to heaven. For similar reasons the initial use of quinine against malaria was denounced by many Christians. The introduction of anaesthesia and, above all, the use of chloroform in childbirth were seen as directly challenging the biblical judgement that, because of their inheritance of the guilt of Eve's original sin, all women must face the penalty that 'in pain you shall bring forth children'. Consequently the use of chloroform in childbirth was vigorously attacked from public pulpits throughout Britain and the United States . . .

The root objection to all the medical practices mentioned above was the belief that the duty of human beings was to submit in patience to what God had willed. All innovations in medical practice were initially seen as implying a lack of faith and trust in God's good purposes. Doctors were accused of 'playing God', of being unwilling to accept that God knows what is right for a particular person, of prying into sacred mysteries and areas of God's own prerogative. Yet gradually all mainstream Christian churches have modified their teaching, and the formerly criticized activity of the doctor has itself come to be seen as itself a channel of God's love and the vehicle of his providence.

Judaism has a long tradition of accepting medical interventions. The conviction that one's body belongs to God translates into a duty to care for it. Not only is there an emphasis on preventative medicine—such as an interest in hygiene and diet—but also, as Glick explains, within Judaism the treatment of illness is obligatory, on the part of both physicians and their patients.

Shimon Glick[10]

Consonant with the high priority given to life, the Jewish tradition, unlike Anglo-Saxon law, requires the physician to respond to any patient's call for help . . . But just as the physician is obligated to render care, so too, the seeking of care by the patient is mandatory. The reason for this obligation is that, in our Jewish tradition, man does not possess title to his life or his body. Man is but the steward of the divine possession which he has been privileged to receive. The terms of that stewardship are not of man's choice, but are determined by God's commands. We forbid suicide and require man to take all reasonable steps to preserve life and health. When beneficence conflicts with autonomy, the former is given precedence by Judaism, a view clearly in conflict with the modern Western consensus. While such a violation of autonomy for the patient's good is not enforceable in our modern pluralistic societies, it has full sanction in the Jewish tradition, and Jewish courts may enforce medical treatment when unequivocally indicated.

In the deliberations as to permissibility of a given act, its being 'natural' or 'unnatural' plays little role. In our tradition, the world is regarded as a deliberately unfinished product placed in the trust of man—himself a finite and imperfect being. Man is expected, indeed commanded . . . to engage in completing . . . the work of the Creator . . .

Healing the ill . . . is therefore not only theologically acceptable, but is mandated. This eagerness to modify Nature, together with the great value placed on human life, contributed to the exalted place occupied by the healing profession in Jewish tradition.

[10] 'A View from Sinai: A Jewish Perspective on Biomedical Ethics' in Edmund Pellegrino, Patricia Mazzarella, and Pietro Corsi (eds), *Transcultural Dimensions* (University Publishing Group: Frederick, MD, 1992) 73–82.

Mainstream Muslim theologians agree that technological intervention in nature, so long as its purpose is to improve human welfare, does not contravene the prohibition against altering God's creation. Indeed, it has been argued that scientific research is protected by the *Shari'a*, and that medicine is a religious duty in every community. Indeed, Sahin Aksoy suggests that the duty to help others, if it lies in one's capacity, is so strong that it might encompass an obligation to ensure an adequate supply of organs for transplantation.

Sahin Aksoy[11]

In Islamic law, a person is obliged to act, if the action is in his capacity. It is a crime (that one can be held responsible for) to do something which is forbidden to do, or not to do something which is commanded. If someone dies in a neighbourhood due to hunger or cold, the people of the neighbourhood who are able to take care of him are held responsible and are punished for this 'inaction' or 'non-action'. It is especially important when it is a matter of life and death . . .

At the First International Conference on Islamic Medicine, it was agreed that the donation of body parts is a social obligation, of the kind classified in Islamic law as *fard al-kifâya* . . . This means the community is under a collective obligation to find the right organs for transplantation in order to preserve the lives and health of its sick members. If a sick person dies while awaiting a transplant, the society as a whole carries some responsibility for that.

Preventative medicine—through the *Shari'a*'s rulings on hygiene and self-restraint—is encouraged. The Islamic Code of Medical Ethics, for example, states that:

The natural prophylaxis against some diseases rests in the revival of such religious values as chastity, purity, self-restraint, and refraining from advertly or inadvertently inflicting harm on self or others. To preach these values is preventative medicine and therefore lies within the jurisdiction and obligation of the medical profession.[12]

But while most religions embrace medical interventions that treat disease and relieve suffering, religious traditions have varying concerns about interventions that go beyond this. Below, for example, Damian Keown, Mohamad Abdalla, and Lisa Soleymani Lehmann describe Buddhist, Muslim, and Jewish approaches to enhancement.

Damian Keown[13]

The Buddhist view has always been that the clarity of mind and intellectual lucidity needed to attain nirvana is best achieved through natural methods, and that the primary technique for obtaining clarity of insight is through meditation. Buddhism would, therefore, tend to see artificial enhancement of the kind described as a temporary 'quick fix' rather than a permanent solution to the underlying problems. Furthermore, while palliation of emotional

---

[11] 'Some principles of Islamic ethics as found in Harrisian philosophy' (2010) 36 Journal of Medical Ethics 226–9.

[12] Issued by the International Organisation of Islamic Medicine (later called the Islamic Organisation of Medical Sciences) in 1981.

[13] 'Religious perspectives on the use of psychopharmaceuticals as an enhancement technology' (2014) 53 Journal of Religion and Health 1440–55.

symptoms may not be harmful in the short term, it can lead to dependency and undermine the achievement of a more permanent solution. Buddhist psychology detects a cyclic pattern in such conditions and observes that unless the causal sequence is permanently reset, the effects will recur indefinitely. What is needed, therefore, is insight into the underlying causes giving rise to these unsatisfactory states of mind, and this insight, it is believed, can be attained only through deep reflexion and analysis of the kind facilitated by meditative practice.

Mohamad Abdalla[14]

Islam, as a religion and a way of life, does not condemn the use and application of medicine and medical technologies in seeking cures for physical illness. There is ample textual and historical evidence to demonstrate this. However, reliance on these is not sufficient to attain happiness and more fulfilling and productive lives. To do so, it is necessary to resort to a process of purification of the self that aims to rid it of unquantifiable diseases such as jealousy, malice, hatred, and arrogance. A failure to do this can essentially lead to a false sense of happiness.

Lisa Soleymani Lehmann[15]

[H]uman beings are mandated to complete God's creation. These sources provide a foundation for Judaism to embrace the use of scientific knowledge and technology to improve the world. From this perspective, Judaism would allow the use of psychopharmaceuticals for the purpose of achieving our full human potential and our God-given task of improving the world. Although most authorities within Judaism generally have a positive view of scientific advancement, the implications of using psychopharmaceuticals for both the individual and society must be considered. The decision to support the use of these drugs for enhancement needs to be weighed against the potential harm to individuals and to society . . . The permissibility of using psychopharmaceuticals to enhance ourselves is dependent on a case-by-case analysis of the risks and benefits of using these medications to individuals and to society.

Fourthly, religious bioethics tend to adopt a normative approach to ethical dilemmas. Whereas secular bioethicists might accept that there is no right answer to a particularly controversial ethical question, a person reasoning from a faith perspective would be more likely to take a strong normative position that a practice either is or is not acceptable. Fifthly, religious perspectives on ethical dilemmas often consist in the interpretation of past authority, and are always to some extent constrained by the written or oral teachings or texts of the particular tradition.

(b) SECULAR BIOETHICS

If secular bioethics is not looking for the right answer to a difficult ethical dilemma, what is it doing? One possibility might be that reasoned argument and deliberation is the most rational way to resolve difficult questions. In the next extract, Dan Brock argue that the requirement to give reasons, or to justify one's moral views, is an especially important feature of ethical reasoning.

[14] Ibid.   [15] Ibid.

Dan W Brock[16]

> [M]oral judgments are unlike some judgments of taste and moral disagreements are unlike some disagreements over matters of taste, because moral judgments must be backed by reasons. If you like vanilla ice cream and I like chocolate, we can just accept this as a difference in taste—there is no correct preference about flavours of ice cream, and if asked why I prefer chocolate, I may be able to repeat only that it tastes better to me. Unlike matters of taste, moral judgments, for example, about whether voluntary euthanasia is wrong, must be backed with reasons . . . [T]he very process of having and offering reasons for our moral judgments is the principal feature distinguishing morality from mere expressions of simple taste or preference.
>
> Because the principal role of moral judgments is to guide action . . . moral judgments are subject to a special worry. The worry is that they may be no more than a hodgepodge of thinly veiled rationalizations and biases reflecting our own self-interest, prejudices, and arbitrary preferences. General moral principles or theories can help allay this worry by explaining these judgments: they are shown to fit, and to be derivable and made from, a coherent, unified moral conception. We come to see that our particular moral judgments have a coherent identifiably moral source, heretofore likely only implicit, and are not merely a cover for our prejudices and self-interest.

(1) Moral Theories

The question of how we should go about resolving complex ethical dilemmas has formed the basis of moral philosophy for thousands of years. There is insufficient space here to describe fully the extensive and rich philosophical literature from which medical ethics has borrowed, but three different traditions are worth noting, and are explained in more detail below.

First, teleological (from the Greek *telos*: consequences) theories judge the rightness or wrongness of an action in terms of its consequences. So to argue that legalizing euthanasia might damage the doctor–patient relationship would be an example of consequentialist or teleological reasoning. Utilitarianism—or the idea that we should act so as to maximize the amount of pleasure or happiness within society—is the most well-known teleological theory.

Secondly, deontological (from the Greek *deontos*: duty) theories, in contrast, insist that the intrinsic rightness or wrongness of an action does not depend upon its consequences, but rather upon whether it is consistent with certain basic moral principles. An example might be basing an argument for the legalization of euthanasia upon the principle that we should respect the autonomous decisions of competent adults. The writings of the philosopher Immanuel Kant (1724–1804), and especially his well-known injunction not to treat others as a means to an end, are often used as an example of deontological moral theory.[17] In short, as Matti Häyry has pointed out, the utilitarian places the concepts of 'good and bad' before the ideas of 'right and wrong', whereas the Kantian does the opposite.[18]

Thirdly, virtue ethics are derived from Ancient Greek moral philosophy, and in particular the writings of Aristotle, with its emphasis upon human flourishing. Virtue ethics are concerned not only with good outcomes, but also with the character or motivation of the individual: a person acts virtuously if they do the right thing for the right reason.

---

[16] 'Public Moral Discourse' in LW Sumner and Joseph Boyle (eds), *Philosophical Perspectives on Bioethics* (University of Toronto Press: Toronto, 1996) 271–96.

[17] I Kant, *Groundwork of the Metaphysics of Morals* (1785).

[18] 'Utilitarianism and Bioethics' in Richard E Ashcroft et al (eds), *Principles of Health Care Ethics*, 2nd edn (Wiley: Chichester, 2007) 57–64.

(a) Utilitarianism

Utilitarianism emerged as a secular alternative to Christian ethics in the late eighteenth and early nineteenth centuries through the work of Jeremy Bentham and later John Stuart Mill, whose father was one of Bentham's pupils. According to utilitarianism, morality lies not in religious obedience, but in the maximization of human welfare. Because the pleasure and wellbeing of each human being matters equally, utilitarianism is essentially egalitarian.

A utilitarian is interested in the consequences of an action, rather than whether it is intrinsically either right or wrong. An example might be the question of whether we should keep our promises. A utilitarian would say that there can be both good and bad consequences from keeping a promise. When the good consequences outweigh the bad consequences, it will be right to keep the promise; when the reverse is true, the promise should be broken. The problem with this is that it ignores the fact that simply having made a promise to another person is, in itself, a good reason to keep it.

A variation on utilitarianism, called 'rule utilitarianism', provides a partial solution to some of the defects of utilitarianism. A rule utilitarian would not ask, on a case-by-case basis, which action will maximize welfare, but rather which general rules will, on the whole, lead to the best consequences. When deciding whether doctors should respect patient confidentiality, for example, a strict utilitarian would answer: 'it depends'. Sometimes it will be a good idea to keep patient information secret, but at other times it might not. This case-by-case approach would require doctors to predict the consequences of both revealing and not revealing every single piece of information they hold about each of their patients. This would clearly be an unmanageable task, which would itself have negative consequences because the health service would grind to a halt. So, a rule utilitarian might say that it is sensible to impose a general duty on doctors to respect their patients' confidentiality.

Another problem with strict utilitarianism is its quantitative approach to welfare. It is the total aggregate of wellbeing that matters, not any particular individual's welfare. If killing one healthy person would enable us to transfer her organs into five patients who would otherwise die, might a utilitarian have to conclude that this would be the right thing to do? Again, rule utilitarianism might offer a way to avoid this unpalatable conclusion: applying the principle that doctors should 'above all do no harm' will, in general, tend to have better consequences than allowing doctors to kill their patients in order to save other people's lives.

It is also necessary to work out what counts as 'utility'. While good health is clearly welfare-maximizing, it is not the only thing that matters. Indeed, many of us have dietary and other preferences that may be positively harmful to health. Do we maximize utility by eating only low-fat food and spending every evening at the gym, or by eating things we enjoy and going to the pub with friends?

Utilitarianism, as Kevin Wildes explains, also depends upon the existence of a mechanism through which different outcomes can be ranked; otherwise it would be impossible to tell whether consequence A is preferable to consequence B.

Kevin Wildes[19]

The appeal to the consequences of one's decisions brings no more success [in resolving moral controversies], because it faces the problem of how to assess and evaluate different consequences. For example, some believe that living somewhat longer as a result of

---

[19] 'Particularism in Bioethics: Balancing Secular and Religious Concerns' (1994) 53 Maryland Law Review 1220, 1228.

chemotherapy is a better consequence, even with the side effects, than dying. Yet for others, living a life unimpaired by treatment is a more important outcome than extending the length of life. To make a judgment among consequences one needs an agreed-upon method by which to rank the outcomes. Therefore a consequentialist must build in some presuppositions about the assessment and ranking of values, both to evaluate possible outcomes of ethical choices and to know which outcomes are more desirable and should be given priority.

(b) Kantianism

The aspect of Kant's philosophy that we are particularly interested in is his 'Categorical Imperative'. Kant gives four formulations of the Categorical Imperative, two of which are worth singling out here:[20]

(a) Act only on that maxim whereby you can at the same time will that it should become a universal law.

(b) So act as to treat humanity, whether in your own person or in that of any other, never solely as a means but always also as an end.

The first imperative requires us to act consistently and justly. The latter (which is more commonly cited by medical ethicists) demands that we do not ever treat another person—or allow ourselves to be treated—purely in order to satisfy another's purposes.

Both are negative tests for actions: that is, they tell us what we must not do: do not act inconsistently, and do not use another person solely for one's own ends. It would also, as John Rawls has pointed out, be 'a serious misconception to think of the Categorical Imperative procedure as an algorithm intended to yield, more or less mechanically, a correct judgement'.[21] Rather, Rawls suggests that the point of the categorical imperative may simply be to inculcate 'a form of moral reflection that could reasonably be used to check the purity of our motives'.[22]

In the next extract, Onora O'Neill argues that Kant was interested in 'principled autonomy', or the giving of reasons that others might understand.

Onora O'Neill[23]

Autonomy in thinking is no more—but also no less—than the attempt to conduct thinking (speaking, writing) on principles on which all others whom we address could also conduct their thinking (speaking, writing). Autonomy in action is also no more—but also no less—than the attempt to act on principles on which all others could act . . .

So 'self-legislation' is not a mysterious phrase for describing merely arbitrary ways in which a free individual might or might not act. It is the basic characteristic of ways of thinking or willing that are conducted with sufficient discipline to be followable or accessible to others. Such ways of thinking and acting must be lawlike rather than lawless, and will thereby be in principle intelligible to others, and open to their criticism, rebuttal or reasoned argument.

In contrast, Barbara Secker is concerned that Kantian autonomy, with its emphasis upon independence and rationality, asks too much of patients.

---

[20] Immanuel Kant, *Groundwork of the Metaphysics of Morals* (1785).

[21] John Rawls, *Lectures on the History of Moral Philosophy* (ed Barbara Herman) (Harvard UP: Cambridge, MA, 2000) 166.

[22] Ibid, 148.   [23] *Autonomy and Trust in Bioethics* (CUP: Cambridge, 2002).

Barbara Secker[24]

This idealistic concept [of autonomy] is of little practical relevance in health contexts where patients, on the whole, bear little resemblance to the Kantian free, independent, exclusively rational individual . . . However, patients frequently are in vulnerable positions, are unable to act on their decisions, and require that positive measures be taken on their behalf. . . .

If we appeal to the Kantian view (based on an ideal of the self as independent and exclusively rational), very few, if any, patients will be regarded as autonomous. Actual patients are likely to be dependent or interdependent, and their decision-making capacity is not always based (exclusively) on reason.

My second concern is that Kantian autonomy appears to place a premium on independence. . . . [I]f autonomy is morally valuable, and if autonomy is associated with independence, then dependence is regarded as morally inadequate and, consequently, those who are dependent are devalued. . . . The nature of patienthood, however, is partially characterized by dependency of one kind or another.

So is the ethical practice of medicine principally deontological or utilitarian? The short answer is that it is both: individual doctors must prioritize the needs and rights of their patients, whereas, as Garbutt and Davies explain, the National Health Service (NHS) must try to do the most good with finite resources.

Gerard Garbutt and Peter Davies[25]

Historically, medicine has described itself, and been described by others, in terms of the interaction of the doctor, the patient and the disease. The transactions between patient and doctor have been private clinical and commercial transactions, and as such have been guarded by privacy and confidentiality. The ethics of such relationships are intrinsically on a deontological footing—they are about how one person should treat another.

This deontological basis of medical care is strongly buttressed by professional codes such as the General Medical Council's (GMC) good medical practice and its starting premise, 'You must make care of the patient your first concern.' Note the key point here that it is the individual patient who is the focus of attention, and not the wider needs of the healthcare system or the country's economy.

These individual doctor–patient interactions are nestled within a larger payment system that provides the financial and other resources within which these interactions can occur . . . In modern complex healthcare systems such as the UK NHS the needs of the system, in terms of its survival as a coherent entity, are rapidly becoming as large as those of the patients in the consulting room. This larger system is unavoidably utilitarian, having to make the best use it can of finite resources . . . .

[T]here is a tension between the deontology of individual doctor–patient interactions and the utilitarian nature of the NHS as a payment system that exists to enable the delivery of medical services to patients. At root what we see with this question is the old tension between the need to balance overall system resources with the demands of any one individual patient.

[24] 'The appearance of Kant's deontology in contemporary Kantianism: concepts of patient autonomy in bioethics' (1999) 24 Journal of Medicine and Philosophy 43–66.

[25] 'Should the practice of medicine be a deontological or utilitarian enterprise?' (2011) 37 Journal of Medical Ethics 267–70.

(c) Virtue ethics

Interest in virtue ethics, which derives from Ancient Greek philosophy, has emerged in reaction to perceived disadvantages with the minimal ethical content of most moral theories. A virtue ethicist is interested not in whether an act is permissible, but whether it would be the right thing to do.

A central feature of virtue ethics is its rejection of the idea that patient autonomy is an absolute or overriding virtue. This means that the fact that an individual wants to do something is not, in itself, a reason for thinking it would be the right thing to do. For example, in relation to euthanasia, Philippa Foot has argued that simply wanting to die is not enough to make death a good thing for a person.[26] Rather, causing a person's death could only be virtuous if her life now lacks the most basic human goods.

In Chapter 13, we will encounter Rosalind Hursthouse's argument that the morality of a woman's decision to have an abortion depends upon the character she manifests in electing to terminate a new human life.[27] According to Hursthouse, parenthood is intrinsically good and so a woman who fails to appreciate this, and seeks an abortion for a trivial reason has not reflected with due seriousness, and has therefore not made a virtuous decision. In contrast, a woman who knows that she would be unable to provide her child with a decent life may have acted virtuously in terminating an unwanted pregnancy.

If acting out of self-interest is not virtuous, what is? According to virtue ethicists, virtues are the character traits necessary for human flourishing, such as honesty, compassion, kindness, justice, and courage. While compiling a list of virtues may be comparatively straightforward, this does not necessarily help us to make difficult decisions because different virtues may point in different directions. For example, in deciding which patient should have priority for an available bed, should a non-urgent patient who has already waited for six months be given priority, or should the bed always go to the patient with the most immediately pressing need? The virtues of fairness and compassion are relevant here, but they do not tell us what to do.

Or, let us imagine that a doctor is advising a couple on the chance that their second child would have the same inherited condition as their first. Genetic tests have revealed that the husband could not be the first child's father. Does the doctor act virtuously by being honest with the husband? Or would a virtuous person reveal this information only to the wife? Or not at all?

It has also been pointed out that virtuous people will sometimes act wrongly, despite their good intentions. Robert Veatch, for example, is 'concerned about well-intentioned, bungling do-gooders'.[28] A doctor who withholds a diagnosis of terminal cancer from her patient may be acting out of compassion, but this would almost always be the wrong thing to do.

(2) Principlism and its Critics

Moral philosophy can be a helpful way of framing medical dilemmas, but it will seldom provide clear answers for doctors faced with difficult choices. For example, a doctor might be told that: 'A utilitarian would do X, and a Kantian would do Y', which might be interesting, but is not terribly helpful.

A more practical way to decide medical questions was set out in Tom Beauchamp and James Childress's groundbreaking book *Principles of Biomedical Ethics*, now in its seventh edition.

---

[26] 'Euthanasia' (1977) 6 Philosophy and Public Affairs 85–112.

[27] 'Virtue theory and abortion' (1991) 20 Philosophy and Public Affairs 223–46.

[28] Robert Veatch, 'The danger of virtue' (1988) 13 Journal of Medicine and Philosophy 13.

Beauchamp and Childress distilled four basic principles—autonomy, non-maleficence, beneficence, and justice—from 'the most general and basic norms of the common morality'.

(a) The word *autonomy*—from the Greek *autos* (self) and *nomos* (rule)—initially referred to the self-rule of independent cities. It has since been extended to mean self-governance, and encompasses a cluster of interests such as liberty, privacy, and freedom of choice. In relation to medicine, respect for autonomy means giving competent adults the right to make decisions about their medical treatment.

(b) *Non-maleficence*, or the duty to 'above all do no harm' (*primum non nocere*) has its origins in the Hippocratic oath. This principle captures the idea that doctors should never use their medical training for immoral purposes, such as torture. While it would be difficult to find anyone who thought that it was acceptable for doctors to be involved in torture, in other cases there may be disagreement over what counts as 'harm'. For example, some would argue that it is this principle which prohibits medical participation in euthanasia, whereas others would argue that by bringing an end to a patient's suffering, euthanasia can prevent the greater harm of a protracted and distressing death.

(c) *Beneficence* refers to the obligation to act for the benefit of others. Since acting to benefit the patient is a primary goal of medicine, beneficence has been seen by some as its foundational value. It is, however, important to distinguish between what one might call the Hippocratic duty of beneficence: that is, the doctor's duty to act in their patient's interests, and 'social' beneficence, which might refer to a wider duty to help others whenever one can. This distinction helps to illuminate the fact that socially beneficent actions may be discretionary: I do not have an obligation to donate one of my healthy kidneys to a stranger. In contrast, Hippocratic duties of beneficence, such as the duty of care health care professionals owe to their patients, are mandatory.

(d) *Justice* is often interpreted to mean that we should treat like cases alike. But, of course, this depends upon being able to tell when cases are either 'like' or 'unlike'. When allocating lungs for transplant, do we act justly by making non-smokers a lower priority than smokers (that is, are these 'unlike' cases?), or should the only relevant criteria be clinical need, in which case the smoker and the non-smoker are 'like' cases? In relation to health care, it is seldom possible to give every patient immediate access to the best medical treatment, so justice instead demands that we ration scarce resources fairly and transparently.

Aside from 'justice', the principles' focus is upon the individual doctor–patient encounter, thus missing the wider implications many bioethical dilemmas have for society as a whole. As a result, Amitai Etzioni has suggested the addition of a fifth principle, that of the 'common good'.

Amitai Etzioni[29]

[I]t is important to note that even the nuanced and enriched set of normative principles developed by Beauchamp and Childress does not include a concept of the common good, above and beyond the concept of justice—for instance, conditions under which individuals have to accept various sacrifices for the good of all. A thicker definition would include common goods that command our moral respect, such as the protection of the environment, basic research,

---

[29] 'Authoritarian versus responsive communitarian bioethics' (2011) 37 Journal of Medical Ethics 17–23.

homeland security and public health. These kinds of concerns that Gostin—and communitarians more generally—have about preventing the spread of infectious diseases, responding to bioterrorist attacks, protecting the environment, balancing preventive and acute medical treatments, and determining the extent to which one can foster or force limits on individual choices for the public good, do not find a comfortable home in the most widely followed bioethical texts. Hence, concern for the common good, responsive communitarians would argue, should be added to the already existing core values on which bioethics draws.

These four (or five, if we include the common good) principles are more 'user-friendly' than abstract moral philosophy, but they nevertheless borrow from the traditions we considered in the previous sections. Respect for patient autonomy might be described as a deontological principle because it is regarded as valuable, irrespective of the consequences of the patient's decision. Beneficence and non-maleficence are plainly consequentialist principles, which require us to take into account possible benefits and harms. Virtue ethicists would be principally concerned with the virtues of 'doing good' (beneficence) and acting justly.

While there are those who believe in 'single principle' approaches—a libertarian, for example, believes that actions are right if, and only if, they respect a person's autonomy—most people accept that all of these principles may have a role to play in medical decision-making. In fact, commonly more than one principle will be relevant. Sometimes they will pull in the same direction: for example, in respecting a patient's autonomy, a doctor will often also be doing good—a doctor will act beneficently by telling the patient the truth, respecting her privacy, and facilitating autonomous decision-making.

At other times, the principles may come into conflict with each other. Many of the medical dilemmas we consider in this book could be framed as a clash between two or more of these basic principles. It might even be argued that the reason why some questions are difficult is precisely because they are cases in which principles that most of us accept are in tension with each other. Consider assisted suicide: the principle of autonomy might suggest that a competent patient's wish to die should be respected. Against this, the principle of non-maleficence might be invoked to say that doctors must not actively help patients to die.

Hence, while the principlist approach might enable us to describe a moral dilemma as a conflict between competing principles, and work out what important values are at stake, it will seldom tell us what to do. Rather, when principles conflict there is no escaping the need to decide which factor is more important in the particular circumstances. One solution might be to rank the principles, but any hierarchy requires justification that cannot be provided by the principles themselves. If, for example, we want to say that autonomy should take priority over beneficence, either in general, or in a particular case, then we need to explain why.

In the next extract, Tom Beauchamp and James Childress explain that the principlist approach requires what they describe as further 'specification' and 'balancing'.

Tom L Beauchamp and James F Childress[30]

Our four clusters of principles do not constitute a general moral theory. They provide only a framework for identifying and reflecting on moral problems. The framework is spare, because prima facie principles do not contain sufficient content to address the nuances of many moral circumstances. We therefore need to examine how to specify and balance these abstract principles. . . .

---

[30] *Principles of Biomedical Ethics*, 7th edn (OUP: Oxford, 2013).

Specification is a process of reducing the indeterminateness of abstract norms and providing them with action guiding content. For example, without further specification, 'do no harm' is an all-too-bare starting point for thinking through problems, such as assisted suicide and euthanasia. It will not adequately guide action when norms conflict. . . .

Principles, rules and rights require balancing no less than specification. We need both methods because each addresses a dimension of moral principles and rules range and scope, in the case of specification, and weight or strength, in the case of balancing. Specification entails a substantive refinement of the range of scope of norms, whereas balancing consists of deliberation and judgment about the relative weights or strength of norms. Balancing is especially important for reaching judgments in individual cases, and specification is especially useful for policy development.

Etzioni suggests that autonomy is frequently likely to come into contact with his additional 'common good' principle, and that the best way to resolve these dilemmas is on a case-by-case basis: if the interference with autonomy is slight and the common good is strong, then the common good should win out. If, on the other hand, the sacrifice of autonomy is substantial and the gains to the common good are marginal, then autonomy should be the trumping principle. But, of course, this does not help us to make a decision when the interference with autonomy and the gains to the common good are either equally substantial, or equally slight.

Whether an interference with autonomy is substantial or slight might also be a matter of opinion. For example, when the ban on smoking in public places in the UK was set to be extended to high-security hospitals, some in-patients claimed that the interference with the freedom to smoke in what was effectively their home represented a violation of their human right to a private and family life. The Court of Appeal disagreed:[31] 'Preventing a person smoking does not, at any rate in the culture of the United Kingdom, generally involve such adverse effect upon the person's "physical or moral integrity" . . . as would amount to an interference with the right to respect for private or home life within the meaning of Art.8.' Of course, the Court of Appeal's decision that Article 8 was not engaged was determinative, but the claimants undoubtedly found the interference with their autonomy substantial, going so far as to claim that 'the smoking ban made their lives intolerable'.

While it has undoubtedly been hugely influential, Beauchamp and Childress's approach is not without its critics. In the next extract, K Danner Clouser and Bernard Gert argue that, rather than clarifying difficult questions, principlism can be unsystematic and misleading.

K Danner Clouser and Bernard Gert[32]

We believe that the 'principles of biomedical ethics' approach is mistaken and misleading. Principlism is mistaken about the nature of morality and is misleading as to the foundations of ethics . . . Our bottom line, starkly put, is that 'principle', as conceived by the proponents of Principlism, is a misnomer and that 'principles' so conceived cannot function as they are in fact claimed to be functioning by those who purport to employ them. At best, 'principles' operate primarily as checklists naming issues worth remembering when considering a biomedical moral issue. At worst 'principles' obscure and confuse moral reasoning by their failure to be guidelines and by their eclectic and unsystematic use of moral theory . . .

---

[31] *R (on the application of G) v Nottinghamshire Healthcare NHS Trust* [2008] EWHC 1096 (Admin).
[32] 'A critique of principlism' (1990) 15 Journal of Medicine and Philosophy 219–36.

Taking what is properly the moral ideal of helping others (and hence not morally required), and lumping it under a 'principle' of beneficence along with genuine duties (which are required), eg, the duty of health care professionals to help their patients, leads to confusion and misunderstanding. The confusion basically results from treating beneficence as if it were morally required just as noninterference with the freedom of others is morally required.

The appeal of principlism is that it makes use of those features of each ethical theory that seems to have the most support. Thus, in proposing the principle of beneficence, it acknowledges that Mill was right in being concerned with consequences . . . In proposing the principle of autonomy, it acknowledges that Kant was right in emphasising the importance of the individual person . . . But there is no attempt to see how these different concerns can be blended together as integrated parts of a single adequate theory, rather than disparate concerns derived from several competing theories.

(3) Casuistry

While philosophers and ethicists are accustomed to discussing general and abstract principles, clinicians tend to be more interested in cases. This has contributed to renewed interest in casuistry, or case-based reasoning, a tradition which has its origins in Roman Catholic theology.

In casuistry, instead of starting with broad, abstract principles (a top-down approach), we instead begin with our response to concrete cases and reason by analogy (a bottom-up approach). This is, as John Arras points out, similar to the judiciary's incremental development of the common law.

John D Arras[33]

Developed in the early Middle-Ages as a method of bringing abstract and universal ethico-religious precepts to bear on particular moral situations, casuistry has had a chequered history. In the hands of expert practitioners during its salad days in the sixteenth and seventeenth centuries, casuistry generated a rich and morally sensitive literature devoted to numerous real-life ethical problems, such as truth-telling, usury, and the limits of revenge. By the late seventeenth century, however, casuistical reasoning had degenerated into a notoriously sordid form of logic-chopping in the service of personal expediency. To this day, the very term 'casuistry' conjures up pejorative images of disingenuous argument and moral laxity.

In spite of casuistry's tarnished reputation, some philosophers have claimed that casuistry, shorn of its unfortunate excesses, has much to teach us about the resolution of moral problems in medicine. . . .

Contrary to deductivist ethical theories, wherein principles are said to preexist the actual cases to which they apply, the new casuistry contends that ethical principles are 'discovered' in the cases themselves, just as common law legal principles are developed in and through judicial decisions on particular legal cases . . . Rather than stemming originally from some ethical theory, such as Utilitarianism, these principles are said to emerge gradually from reflection upon our responses to particular cases.

In the next extract, Albert Jonsen argues that no moral dilemma is entirely novel, and that it therefore makes sense to look at how similar dilemmas have been resolved in the past.

[33] 'Getting down to cases: the revival of casuistry in bioethics' (1991) 16 Journal of Medicine and Philosophy 29–51.

Albert R Jonsen[34]

> No ethical problem is completely unprecedented. Regardless how novel, it bears some resemblance to problems that are more familiar. The more familiar ones will often be ones for which resolutions have been offered and sometimes accepted. Thus, one compares the new case with the more familiar one. That comparison almost always involves seeking for the similarities and differences in circumstance. . . . In this view, ethical reasoning is primarily reasoning by analogy, seeking to identify cases similar to the one under scrutiny and to discern whether the changed circumstances justify a different judgement in the new case than they did in the former.

While it is obviously important to draw upon past experience when addressing novel dilemmas, several problems with casuistry have been identified. First, even if we believe that our intuitions will sometimes embody universally valid moral judgements—an example might be condemnation of Nazi doctors' abuse of research subjects during the Second World War—these are the exception rather than the norm. It is also not clear that our intuitive response to black-and-white cases actually helps us very much when we are faced with more finely balanced moral choices. For example, we can all agree that it would be wrong to kill disabled children. But how does that assist us when we are faced with the more nuanced question of whether it could ever be right to withdraw life-sustaining medical treatment from a permanently and profoundly incapacitated neonate? Some would say that the cases are the same and neither course of action should be permitted, while others would point to important differences between the two cases.

Secondly, case-based reasoning will only yield a definite answer if there is some consensus upon what counts as a relevant similarity. Is abortion relevantly similar to murder (the deliberate killing of a person), or is it relevantly similar to contraception (allowing women to control their reproductive capacity)? Without underlying agreement on certain fundamental moral questions, casuistry provides us with little concrete guidance.

Thirdly, the analogy with the common law is imperfect. The common law contains a system of binding precedent, and identifies individuals (ie judges) whose interpretation of previous cases is authoritative. In the field of bioethics, even if we could identify moral 'experts' to adjudicate on competing interpretations of previous authority, there is no reason why anyone else should be bound by their interpretation.

Fourthly, it is not clear how we can be guided by decisions in previous cases unless those decisions are distilled into some sort of general principle. We could, for example, say that depriving someone of their liberty is wrong, but we might also be able to think of exceptional circumstances in which detention might be justified, perhaps because someone suffers from such a serious mental illness that she would otherwise pose a serious risk of harm to herself, or others. So we distil from these cases the general principle that compulsory detention will be legitimate only in order to prevent a serious risk of harm.

On the other hand, even if casuistry—like principlism—cannot tell us what to do when faced with a difficult dilemma, it is important to recognize the role cases play in modern bioethics. In the previous section, we saw that there will often be a conflict between, say, autonomy and non-maleficence. At a high level of abstraction, it is impossible for us to tell which should take priority. In the context of a real case, however, it may be possible to

---

[34] 'Casuistry: an alternative or complement to principles?' (1995) 5 Kennedy Institute of Ethics Journal 237–51.

reason why, in this particular case, there are grounds for thinking that autonomy (or non-maleficence) is more important.

So, for example, in Chapter 5 we will encounter the case of E, a teenager who wanted to refuse a blood transfusion. Without greater detail than this, it is impossible to tell whether the priority should be to respect E's wishes or to act in his best interests. For example, we need to know more about E's age, and reasoning capacity, and it will be helpful to consider how similar cases were decided in the past. In practice, decision-making in a case like this will be guided not only by principles, but also by careful analysis of the facts in individual cases.

In addition to real cases, bioethicists tend to make extensive use of imagined cases, or thought experiments. Judith Jarvis Thomson's classic essay on abortion (extracted in Chapter 13) asks the reader to imagine that they wake up to discover that a world-famous violinist has been attached to their body, and that he needs to be wholly dependent upon them for a further nine months. In the context of the acts/omissions distinction, James Rachels has asked us whether there is a moral difference between Smith, who drowns his cousin, and Jones, who has the same intention, but finds that at the critical moment, the cousin bangs his head and drowns anyway.[35]

Are these hypothetical examples useful? On the one hand, if they are too fantastical, their relevance to real cases may be tenuous, at best. On the other hand, they may offer a fresh lens from which to view a moral problem that has, as Adrian Walsh puts it, 'become stale'.[36] The point of Thomson's violinist analogy is not necessarily to claim that an unwanted pregnancy is exactly the same as waking up attached to a world-famous violinist, but rather it is intended to prompt us to identify salient similarities and differences between these cases.

(4) Feminism

There is no single 'feminist' approach to bioethics. At the risk of drastic oversimplification, three different approaches might be identified.

First, liberal feminists' principal focus is on gender inequality. For example, in Judith Jarvis Thomson's essay on abortion, the point of her—at first sight bizarre—analogy between an unwanted pregnancy and finding that one's body is necessary to support the life of a famous violinist, is that the former is an experience which only women can experience, while the latter (hypothetical) experience is gender neutral. If, Thomson reasons, we can agree that it would clearly be unreasonable to expect a person to give up his body for nine months to support the violinist, then we ought to be able to agree that it is unreasonable to expect women to exercise a similar degree of self-sacrifice in relation to an unwanted pregnancy.

Another example of inequality, which we explore in more detail in Chapter 9, is women's traditional exclusion from clinical trials, due both to their fluctuating hormonal cycles, and the possibility of pregnancy. Systematic exclusion of women from clinical trials means that medicines are not as safe or as effective when taken by female patients. Liberal feminists are concerned to identify this sort of inequality in order to put in place practical measures to promote fair and equal treatment.

A second feminist approach is concerned primarily with oppression, and how practices may, perhaps unwittingly, contribute to, or exacerbate, existing systems of oppression. As we see in Chapter 15, feminists were initially among the fiercest critics of reproductive technologies, arguing that (male) scientists and doctors were essentially experimenting on

---

[35] James Rachels, 'Active and passive euthanasia' (1975) 292 New England Journal of Medicine 78–80.

[36] Adrian Walsh, 'The Use of Thought Experiments in Health Care Ethics' in Richard E Ashcroft et al (eds), *Principles of Health Care Ethics*, 2nd edn (Wiley: Chichester, 2007) 177–83.

women's bodies and exploiting women's desire for children by persuading them to consent to dangerously untested new treatments. Now that *in vitro* fertilization (IVF) has become a routine medical treatment, feminist criticism is more muted; however, this sort of feminist analysis has been evident in relation to compensated egg donation. Some feminists have criticized payments to egg donors on the grounds that they exploit vulnerable women, who may be more likely to volunteer to undergo the uncomfortable and not entirely risk-free process of ovarian stimulation and egg collection.

The third feminist approach represents the most direct challenge to bioethics itself. What we might call the 'ethics of care' emerged as a result of some feminists' dissatisfaction with conventional medical ethics. First, as we have seen, traditional medical ethics focused upon the proper conduct of the medical profession, which was, until comparatively recently, heavily male-dominated. Women, on the other hand, are disproportionately represented among patients. Their reproductive capacity, their role as principal carers for both children and the elderly, and their greater life expectancy combine to make women more frequent users of medical services than men. Women are also more likely to be employed in health services as carers, either as nurses (whose role used to be confined to carrying out doctors' orders) or as auxiliary staff.

When medical ethicists focus upon the dilemmas facing doctors, they are ignoring the equally important ethical issues that are encountered by carers, nurses, and patients. In the late 1990s, for example, anthropologist Rayna Rapp documented the moral dilemmas pregnant women faced in relation to the decision to use new prenatal testing techniques, such as amniocentesis. These patients were, she argued, 'moral pioneers . . . forced to judge the quality of their own fetuses, making concrete and embodied decisions about the standards for entry into the human community'.[37]

Secondly, drawing on the influential and controversial work of psychologist Carol Gilligan, feminist theorists have argued that abstract moral reasoning, and in particular, an emphasis on individualistic values such as autonomy, are distinctively 'male'. Women's existence, according to this analysis, is characterized by connections with others, especially through pregnancy and child-rearing, and this leads them to value relationships more highly than individual autonomy.

Carol Gilligan[38]

> The psychology of women that has consistently been described as distinctive in its greater orientation toward relationships and interdependence implies a more contextual mode of judgment and a different moral understanding. Given the differences in women's conceptions of self and morality, women bring to the life cycle a different point of view and order human experience in terms of different priorities.

A third and related point is that the dominant principle of medical ethics, namely patient autonomy, presupposes an independent, largely self-sufficient individual who is able to weigh information in order to reach a rational decision about his medical treatment. Yet, of course, few patients meet this exacting standard. Illness commonly creates dependency and vulnerability. And in any event, a model of moral reasoning which privileges the rational, self-directed individual relies on a partial and inaccurate understanding of what it is to be human.

---

[37] *Testing Women, Testing the Fetus: The Social Impact of Amniocentesis in America* (Routledge: New York, 1999) 3.
[38] *In a Different Voice* (Harvard UP: London, MA, 1982) 22.

All of us were completely dependent on others at the beginning of our lives, and most of us will spend some time unable to function independently before we die. An ethic of care takes for granted the inevitability of dependency and the importance of social context. As Rogers et al explain, although there are some sections of society which are especially vulnerable, none of us is actually invulnerable to ill health or bad luck.

Wendy Rogers, Catriona Mackenzie, and Susan Dodds[39]

We have argued that, rather than vulnerability being a property of only those people who fall into the category 'vulnerable groups' or 'vulnerable populations,' all human life is characterized by vulnerability, and that specific factors exacerbate the vulnerability of specific individuals and groups. A focus on vulnerability highlights our common humanity and offers grounds for solidarity. As biological and social beings, we share much vulnerability—to ill health, to bad luck, to natural and human-generated disasters, and so forth. Although these and other vulnerabilities are not equally distributed, none of us is invulnerable; we all have some experience and understanding of what it is to feel vulnerable. . . .

Just as we share much vulnerability, it is also the case that our social practices and institutions can ameliorate vulnerabilities and can help foster resilience. Rather than simply drawing attention to our shared vulnerability to harm, a fuller account of vulnerability can attend to the social practices (such as education, health promotion, access to the range of social services and legal protections) that can promote our well-being and capacities for agency, while reducing vulnerability to need, ill health, or exploitation. Linking vulnerability to vital needs and to flourishing provides an additional and cogent moral reason for action on health inequalities.

In the next extract, Jonathan Herring explains that because caring has traditionally been women's work, it has been systematically undervalued and largely ignored by medical ethicists. This is a mistake, not least because without the efforts of informal and unpaid carers—whose care has been valued at over £110 billion per year, more than the entire NHS budget—the health service, not to mention social care services, would be unsustainable.

Jonathan Herring[40]

Caring is a gendered activity. It is seen as 'women's work' and as such is ignored in the 'male gaze'. I mentioned earlier the enormous economic value of care and yet it is not given the respect or recognition that other higher profile 'economically productive' activities have. By describing care work as 'voluntary' and 'informal' it is marginalised as unimportant. Hence, the professional doctor–patient relationship is subject to careful and extensive legal regulation and is dealt with at length in the court reports and the wider media. The carer–patient relationship, of greater significance to many patients, is ignored. This all has the impact of care work being unvalued and unnoticed. All of this is convenient to a society in which 'men's' work goes rewarded and valorised, while 'women's' work is invisible and unrecognised. The lack of respect owed to caring has played a significant role in the unequal economic position of women.

---

[39] 'Why bioethics needs a concept of vulnerability' (2012) 5 International Journal of Feminist Approaches to Bioethics 11–38.
[40] 'Where are the Carers in Healthcare Law and Ethics?' (2007) 27 Legal Studies 51–73.

Under an ethic of care the practice of caring would be hugely valued within society. Carers would, far from being hidden, come to represent a norm. Social structures and attitudes would need to be set up to encourage and enable caring. This would require adequate remuneration of carers: not the payment of benefits of the kind paid to those 'unable to work', but payment acknowledging the key role they play. Work would need to be done to ensure that the burden of caring did not fall on the few but was shared across the community.

The feminist ethics of care has its critics, however. In the following extract, Helga Kuhse questions whether it can replace ethical principles and reasoned argument.

Helga Kuhse[41]

Is ethics gendered? Do women and men approach ethics differently? The answer of many thinkers has been 'yes'. Rousseau thought that abstract truths and general principles are 'beyond a woman's grasp . . .; woman observes, man reasons'. Schopenhauer bluntly proclaimed: 'the fundamental fault of the female character is that it has no sense of justice'. This 'weakness in their reasoning faculty', Schopenhauer continued, 'also explains why women show more sympathy for the unfortunate than men' . . . Freud believed that 'for women the level of what is ethically normal is different from what it is in men'. Women, he wrote, 'show less sense of justice than men'. On these views, then, men and women not only approach ethics differently, but insofar as women were thought to lack a head for abstract principles, and a sense of justice, their ethical approach was also regarded as somewhat defective and inferior to that of men . . .

There is [a] school of thought that holds that traditional male thinkers, while wrong on much else, were right . . . that women and men do approach ethics differently. This school of thought rejects the idea that women are *incapable* of abstract, principled thinking; rather, and much more fundamentally, it claims that principled ethical thinking is not the only valid (or best) approach to ethics. There is, according to this view, an alternative 'female' approach to ethics which is based not on abstract 'male' ethical principles or wide generalisations, but on 'care', that is, on receptivity and responsiveness to the needs of others . . .

If women . . . excessively devalue reasoned argument, if they dismiss ethical principles and norms and hold that notions of impartiality and universalizability have no place in a female ethics of care, then they will be left without the theoretical tools necessary to condemn some actions or practices, and to defend others. Bereft of a universal ethical language, women will be unable to participate in ethical discourse.

Rather than seeing an ethic of care as an alternative to norms like justice and impartiality, perhaps it would be more useful to regard it as a necessary supplement. An ethic of care, just like the principlist approach discussed previously, will rarely dictate a solution to a difficult dilemma, such as which patient should get the only available intensive care bed. Instead, it is a useful reminder that patients are not, in fact, solitary autonomous individuals, making rational and self-interested decisions entirely divorced from the interests of others and the social context that has shaped them.

[41] 'Clinical ethics and nursing: "yes" to caring, but "no" to a female ethics of care' (1995) 9 Bioethics 207–19.

(c) COMMON JUSTIFICATORY STRATEGIES

(1) Human Dignity; the Sanctity of Human Life and Playing God

A common response to novel or controversial medical techniques—such as euthanasia, cloning, and abortion—is to argue that they interfere with human dignity; or that they are at odds with the sanctity of human life; or that they would involve human beings 'playing God'. International agreements on biomedicine have also emphasized the importance of respect for human dignity: the preamble to the Council of Europe's Convention on Human Rights and Biomedicine requires signatories 'to take such measures as are necessary to safeguard human dignity and the fundamental rights and freedoms of the individual with regard to the application of biology and medicine'.

But what do these phrases actually mean? In the next extract, Ruth Chadwick attempts to pin down what might be meant by the expression 'playing God'.

Ruth F Chadwick[42]

[I]t seems clear that the use of the term 'playing God' normally indicates moral disapproval on the part of the speaker, but it is not obvious what is supposed to be bad about taking the decision. Let us consider alternative ways of looking at the question.

(a) God's prerogative

From a religious point of view the objection may be that it is for God to give life and for God to take it away. Such a view notoriously has the difficulty however that it seems to imply the rejection of medicine altogether . . .

(b) Letting nature take its course

Here the playing-God objection is interpreted as a claim that human beings are interfering with the course of nature, and that this is wrong. As such it can be, and has been, fairly easily answered . . . John Stuart Mill points out that it is impossible for humans to let nature take its course because every human action has an impact, however slight, upon nature.

(c) Equality

A third possibility . . . is that the objection expresses an intuition about equality . . . The suggestion may be that human beings have lives that are of equal value and that it is therefore wrong for one set of people to judge that the lives of others are of less value. . . .

(d) Omniscience

A further claim about equality may be involved here. The suggestion would be that one thing that human beings have in common is that their knowledge is limited. Those who take decisions about the quality of the lives of others are aspiring to the kind of omniscience that is simply not available to them . . .

The playing-God objection may be useful, then, in that it reminds us that certain things have unpredictable and possibly disastrous consequences. But it seems doubtful that it can provide a conclusive argument against a certain course of action.

---

[42] 'Playing God' (1989) 3 Cogito 186–93, 188.

In a secular society, what might it mean to say that human life is sacred? In the next extract, Ronald Dworkin suggests that there is a universal, and not necessarily religious, sense of awe at the 'miracle' of human creation.

Ronald Dworkin[43]

Any human creature, including the most immature embryo, is a triumph of divine or evolutionary creation, which produces a complex, reasoning being from, as it were, nothing, and also of what we often call the 'miracle' of human reproduction, which makes each new human being both different from and yet a continuation of the human beings who created it. . . .

The life of a single human organism commands respect and protection, then, no matter in what form or shape, because of the complex creative investment it represents and because of our wonder at the divine or evolutionary processes that produce new lives from old ones, at the processes of nation and community and language through which a human being will come to absorb and continue hundreds of generations of cultures and forms of life and value, and, finally, when mental life has begun and flourishes, at the process of internal personal creation and judgement by which a person will make and remake himself, a mysterious, inescapable process in which we each participate, and which is therefore the most powerful and inevitable source of empathy and communion we have with every other creature who faces the same frightening challenge. The horror we feel in the wilful destruction of a human life reflects our shared inarticulate sense of the intrinsic importance of each of these dimensions of investment.

On the other hand, Peter Singer argues that the 'sanctity of human life', which he condemns as speciesist, derives from a specifically Christian moral tradition.

Peter Singer[44]

People often say that life is sacred. They almost never mean what they say. They do not mean, as their words seem to imply, that all life is sacred. If they did, killing a pig or even pulling up a cabbage would be as contrary to their doctrine as infanticide. So when in the context of medical ethics people talk of the sanctity of life, it is the sanctity of human life that they really mean . . .

[W]hat is the position when we compare severely and irreparably retarded human infants with nonhuman animals like pigs and dogs, monkeys and apes? I think we are forced to conclude that in at least some cases the human infant does not possess any characteristics or capacities that are not also possessed, to an equal or higher degree, by many nonhuman animals. This is true of such capacities as the capacity to feel pain, to act intentionally, to solve problems, and to communicate with and relate to other beings; and it is also true of such characteristics as self-awareness, a sense of one's own existence over time, concern for other beings, and curiosity. . . .

So when we decide to treat one being—the severely and irreparably retarded infant—in one way, and the other being—the pig or monkey—in another way, there seems to be no difference between the two that we can appeal to in defense of our discrimination . . . The doctrine of the sanctity of human life, as it is commonly understood, has at its core a discrimination on the basis of species and nothing else . . .

[T]he intuitions which lie behind [the doctrine of the sanctity of human life] are not insights of self-evident moral truths, but the historically conditioned product of doctrines about

---

[43] *Life's Dominion: An Argument about Abortion and Euthanasia* (HarperCollins: London, 1993) 83–4.
[44] Helga Kuhse (ed), *Unsanctifying Human Life: Essays on Ethics* (Blackwell: Oxford, 2002).

immortality, original sin and damnation which hardly anyone now accepts; doctrines so obnoxious, in fact, that if anyone did accept them, we should be inclined to discount any other moral views he held. Although advocates of the doctrine of the sanctity of human life now frequently try to give their position some secular justification, there can be no possible justification for making the boundary of sanctity run parallel with the boundary of our own species, unless we invoke some belief about immortal souls.

Human dignity is an especially vague and ambiguous concept. In particular, its scope is potentially wider than respect for persons or human rights. We might, for example, be required to treat an embryo or a corpse, neither of which is a person or rights' holder, with dignity. We might not have to behave as though an embryo or a corpse was a human person, but neither are we entitled to use and dispose of them as if they were things.

Deryck Beyleveld and Roger Brownsword have argued that the concept of human dignity has undergone a significant shift in meaning in recent years. Respect for human dignity used to mean promoting autonomous choice, which they describe as 'human dignity as empowerment'. According to Joseph Raz, for example:

Respecting human dignity entails treating humans as persons capable of planning and plotting their future. Thus, respecting people's dignity includes respecting their autonomy, their right to control their future. . . . An insult offends a person's dignity if it consists of or implies a denial that he is an autonomous person or that he deserves to be treated as one.[45]

In recent years, however, Beyleveld and Brownsword suggest that human dignity is instead being invoked in order to restrict individual's choices, which they refer to as 'human dignity as constraint'. This is commonly done by arguing that a controversial medical practice is 'against human nature'.

Deryck Beyleveld and Roger Brownsword[46]

Many persons feel that a number of scientific interventions are 'unnatural', and cite this as the reason why it is wrong to employ them. This reaction may be linked to the idea that such interventions are contrary to dignity by the following reasoning. Dignity is the property by virtue of which human beings have moral rights or moral standing. All human beings have dignity simply by virtue of being human. Dignity is thus an essential part of human nature. Therefore, to act contrary to human nature is to act contrary to human dignity, and it might, then, be alleged that, for example, assisted reproduction itself is against nature; or 70-year-old women bearing children is against nature; or lesbianism is against nature; or men bearing children is against nature. . . .

An attempt to explicate respect for human dignity in terms of human nature is not without its problems even if couched within a framework that links having dignity to being human (in a biological sense) . . . Suppose that it is held that it is unnatural for a lesbian woman to bear a child, or for a man to bear a child. What is meant by saying that it is unnatural? Clearly, it cannot be meant that it goes against the laws of nature. If something is contrary to the laws of nature then it cannot (physically) happen. And, if it is not possible for it to happen then there is no need to prescribe that it ought not to happen or to take steps to prevent it from happening.

[45] Joseph Raz, *The Authority of Law* (OUP: Oxford, 1979) 221.
[46] *Human Dignity in Bioethics and Biolaw* (OUP: Oxford, 2001).

> Perhaps, then, what is meant is that it cannot happen without human intervention. However, there are so many things that cannot happen without human intervention that this threatens to imply that human action itself is contrary to human nature. Certainly, anyone who adopts such a view must, it seems, hold that all medical intervention without which a person would die is contrary to human nature.

Suzy Killmister suggests a third possible meaning for human dignity, namely that it involves the avoidance of humiliation and shame, and ensuring that people's treatment is consistent with standards and values that are, or have been, important to them. To leave a patient in soiled bedsheets, or to force them to sit in a crowded waiting room in a skimpy hospital gown is to fail to treat them with appropriate dignity.

Suzy Killmister[47]

> For most of us, at least part of the trauma of undergoing medical procedures is the shame we experience at having our bodies exposed, the public nature of otherwise deeply private bodily functions, and the childlike dependence to which we are reduced. While such situations are not deliberately inflicted upon the patient, they can nonetheless be experienced as humiliation. This is when the definition of aspirational dignity as the upholding of one's standards becomes crucial. The reason why, for example, being left semi-naked on a hospital trolley is experienced as humili-ation, and thus as a violation of dignity, is that the patient has standards of public decency that they strive to maintain in their daily lives, and which they are here being forced to abandon . . .
>
> Similarly, insufferable pain and loss of control over bodily functions are seen to compro-mise the ability of the individual to maintain the standards that they have sought to uphold throughout their life . . .
>
> The definition of dignity would thus be as follows: dignity is the inherent capacity for upholding one's principles . . . The difference between what autonomy demands and what dignity demands can be drawn out thus: to respect an individual's autonomy requires respect for their self-governance . . . To respect an individual's dignity, meanwhile, requires respect for their self-worth.

(2) The Slippery Slope

Another common objection to controversial medical practices is that they might represent the first step on a slippery slope. This is a consequentialist argument in that it does not appeal to the intrinsic wrongness of a particular technique; rather, as Schauer explains, the fear is that allowing something that may seem fairly innocuous in itself might have unfore-seeable, uncontrollable, or dangerous consequences.

Frederick Schauer[48]

> Sometimes the warning is of 'a foot in the door,' and the British often refer to 'the thin edge of the wedge'. Most commonly we are told to beware of the 'slippery slope'. Yet regardless of the term employed, the phenomenon referred to is the same. The single argumentative

---

[47] 'Dignity: not such a useless concept' (2010) 36 Journal of Medical Ethics 160–4.
[48] 'Slippery Slopes' (1985) 99 Harvard Law Review 361.

claim supported by each of these metaphors, as well as by many others, is that a particular act, seemingly innocuous when taken in isolation, may yet lead to a future host of similar but increasingly pernicious events. But why should this be? What induces people to believe that in some cases neither doctrinal limits nor judicial intervention can prevent the slide down the slippery slope? . . .

As a start we can say that a slippery slope argument necessarily contains the implicit concession that the proposed resolution of the instant case is not itself troublesome. By focusing on the consequences for future cases, we implicitly concede that this instance is itself innocuous, or perhaps even desirable. If we felt otherwise, then we would not employ the slippery slope argument, but would rather claim much more simply that this case, in itself, is impermissible. By implicitly conceding that the instant case is, by itself, unobjectionable, the slippery slope argument directs our attention and our fears to the danger case in the future. It is not permitting the instant case that worries us, but rather the possibility that permitting the instant case will lead to the danger case . . .

Thus, what can distinguish a slippery slope claim from other warnings about the future is the identification of factors increasing the likelihood not only of slippage, but of slippage in the particular direction that takes us from the instant case to the danger case.

In the next extract, Bernard Williams contrasts two different types of slippery slope claims: the 'horrible result' argument and the 'arbitrary result' argument. He also explains that slippery slope arguments do not necessarily justify banning a practice; rather, a different response might be regulation, which draws a line between acceptable and unacceptable practices.

Bernard Williams[49]

First it is worth distinguishing two types of slippery slope argument. The first type—the horrible result argument—objects, roughly speaking, to what is at the bottom of the slope. The second type objects to the fact that it is a slope: this may be called the arbitrary result argument. . . .

All of the arguments that I shall be considering use the idea that there is no point at which one can non-arbitrarily get off the slope once one has got onto it—that is what makes the slope slippery. Arguments that belong to the first type that I have distinguished involve, in addition, the further idea that there is a clearly objectionable practice to which the slope leads. The second type of argument, by contrast, relies merely on the point that after one has got on to the slope, subsequent discriminations will be arbitrary . . .

The first requirement is that it should be probable in actual social fact that such a process will occur. This requires that there should be some motive for people to move from one step to the next. Suppose it is plausible that there will be a slide, and that there will be, at each stage, pressure to take the next step. What follows from that? The slippery slope argument concludes that one should not start, and that the first case should not be allowed, on the ground that after the first step there is nowhere to stop . . .

But there is an obvious alternative. Granted that we are now considering cases in which a definite rule of practice is needed, we have the alternative of drawing a sharp line between cases that are allowed and cases that are not . . . Is drawing a line in this way reasonable? Can it be effective? The answer to both these questions seems to me evidently to be 'Yes, Sometimes' . . .

[49] *Making Sense of Humanity and Other Philosophical Papers* (CUP: Cambridge, 1995) 213–14, 220–1.

[T]he slippery slope argument should be properly understood as in good part an empirical, consequentialist argument . . . Seen in this light, it seems to me that the slippery-slope style of argument can carry weight, and is to be taken seriously; but that, equally, it need not necessarily carry the day, in the sense of proving that the first step should never be taken. We may, instead, take the path of drawing a line, and that is a perfectly reasonable reaction, in the right circumstances, to the challenge that is indeed posed by the slippery slope considerations.

4 THE BODY

In recent years, there has been a great deal of academic interest in 'the body'. For our purposes, two particular themes are worth highlighting. First, in the past medical knowledge about the body was believed to be scientific, and hence neutral and objective. In recent years, however, sociologists have argued that medicine also controls our bodies, by defining illness and abnormality, and by instilling us with a sense of responsibility for the state of our bodies. Secondly, our relationship with our bodies is difficult to classify according to conventional legal norms.

(a) THE SOCIAL CONSTRUCTION OF THE BODY

Medical knowledge decides what counts as an illness. In the nineteenth century, for example, masturbation was believed to be a dangerous illness which produced a cluster of symptoms, including vertigo, headaches, loss of hearing and memory, and which had some very serious long-term consequences, such as heart disease, insanity, blindness, and even death. While this now seems like a comical example of Victorian ignorance and prudery, today other natural processes, such as the menopause, are increasingly treated as 'medical conditions', in need of professional intervention and control.

In the next extract, Deborah Lupton fleshes out the claim that medical knowledge about the body is not neutral, but instead embodies a set of cultural and political assumptions.

Deborah Lupton[50]

Social theorists who are interested in the body and medicine deny that medical knowledge, or indeed any other type of knowledge, can be regarded as neutral, scientific or politically disinterested. Rather, like the body or any other phenomenon, medicine is socially constructed, is mediated through social understandings, and has political effects. For instance, while we may think that the version of the human body presented in a medical textbook is 'scientific truth' and therefore politically neutral, closer examination reveals conventions of representation that support wider sociocultural and political assumptions and objectives. The body in such textbooks is nearly always that of a young white male, suggesting that this type of body is the 'real' or 'normal' human body, against which other bodies (those of women, people of non-white ethnicity, or the elderly) are considered 'abnormal' . . .

[50] 'The Body, Medicine and Society' in John Germow (ed), *Second Opinion: An Introduction to Health Sociology* (OUP: Oxford, 1998) 121–35.

Throughout the history of scientific medicine, medical and public health knowledges have been employed to distinguish and differentiate between 'normal', 'healthy' bodies and those that are regarded as 'abnormal', 'diseased' or 'deviant'. The male European body has been represented as the archetypical normal, healthy body . . . By way of contrast, the female body, the bodies of the working classes or the poor, non-white bodies, and homosexual bodies have been singled out as diseased, passive, contaminating, dirty and lacking self-control. There is a symbiotic relationship, therefore, between identifying the bodies of particular social groups (such as women, non-Whites, the working class, or homosexuals) as being uncontrolled, dirty, and as a result, more susceptible to illness, disease and early death, and the reproduction of the notion that such groups are inferior to the dominant social group (that is, well-off, white, heterosexual men). . . .

Compared with the male body, the female body has been represented as sickly, weak, and susceptible to illness. Women are typically described in the legal, medical and early social scientific literature as possessing problematic and unruly bodies, with their sexual and reproductive capacities requiring constant surveillance and regulation. Particularly in the nineteenth and twentieth centuries, medical assumptions about women—for example, that they were prone to uncontrolled emotional outbursts, which in turn were produced by the uterus, or that their natural place was in the home rather than participating in the public sphere—have contributed to the control of women and their confinement to the domestic sphere.

In the next extract, Bill Hughes argues that the ill and dependent body is increasingly seen as a reflection of the patient's weakness or failure. In part, this is because preventative medicine emphasizes the individual's responsibility for her own health, and may downplay some of the wider social causes of ill health, such as poverty and social inequality.

Bill Hughes[51]

As health maintenance—as opposed to curative—strategies emerge as the priority in contemporary patterns of health care, then responsibility for health shifts from the professional to the lay person . . . There can be no doubt that this apparent democratisation of the relationship between professional and patient suited western governments intent on reducing public expenditure and squeezing the welfare state. The ideas of self care and health maintenance as the responsibility of the lay person rather than the professional became, in the 1980s, important ideological tools in the privatisation of healthcare activities. In the contemporary, secular, deregulated world, a good deal of the policing of human behaviour—which is traditionally invested in the powers of religion and law—is carried out in the name of health . . . Medical knowledge, often in the form of behavioural prescriptions, challenges the population to be healthy, to adopt healthy behaviours and to choose healthy places to live and work.

Disease—in at least some of its manifestations—can now be regarded as a failure of health maintenance, a sign of an improper relationship to one's body and to what one does with it.

(b) DO WE OWN OUR BODIES?

In contemporary bioethics, the question of whether we have rights in our bodies akin to ownership emerges in debates about surrogacy and payment for organ donation. Certainly,

---

[51] 'Medicalized Bodies' in Philip Hancock et al (eds), *The Body, Culture and Society: An Introduction* (Open UP: Milton Keynes, 2000) 12–28.

some of the rights that we have over our bodies look very like property rights: a right to use them, to exclude others, and to be compensated for negligently inflicted damage are all rights that also commonly exist in relation to things that we own. On the other hand, it is less clear whether we possess another right that we would normally associate with ownership, namely the right to transfer for value.

In the next extract, Stephen Munzer argues that while it would not make sense to say that we have full ownership of our bodies, we do possess some limited property rights in them.

Stephen Munzer[52]

[S]ome hold that the body should be thought of as property and emphasize that each person owns or has title to himself or herself. Others maintain that the body ought not to be thought of as property at all, and indeed that it demeans human beings to think of them or their bodies as property. In contrast, the position advocated here is that, insofar as one takes an overall view, people do not own, but have some limited property rights in, their bodies. . . .

It is unhelpful to say that no body rights are property rights. It is also unhelpful to say that all body rights are property rights . . . Since both extreme views should be rejected, one must provide a criterion for classifying some, but not all, body rights as property rights. The most useful criterion is transferability . . .

[O]ne can divide all body rights into personal rights and property rights. Personal rights are body rights that protect interests or choices other than the choice to transfer. Property rights are body rights that protect the choice to transfer . . . One can subdivide property rights in the body into weak and strong varieties. A weak property right involves only a choice to transfer gratuitously. A strong property right involves a choice to transfer for value . . .

[I]t is a mistake to characterize body rights, jointly or individually, as self-ownership. Taken jointly, the body rights of each person amount not to ownership but only to a weaker package of limited property rights. Considered individually, the body rights of each person are not all in the same boat. Most body rights are personal rather than property rights; examples are rights not to be murdered, not to be searched without a warrant or just cause . . . and to exclude others from sexual or other physical contact. Some body rights are property rights—whether weak, such as the right to donate an organ upon death, or strong, such as the right to sell semen; but these weak and strong property rights are neither so numerous nor so central as to establish that persons 'own' themselves.

Against this, Jonathan Herring and P-L Chau argue that a property model is unduly individualistic and misses the interconnectedness of our bodies.

Jonathan Herring and P-L Chau[53]

A property model which conceives of me owning my body promotes a highly individualistic way of conceiving of the body. Arguments in favour of it tend to emphasise the power to

[52] *A Theory of Property* (CUP: Cambridge, 1990).
[53] 'Interconnected, inhabited and insecure: why bodies should not be property' (2014) 40 Journal of Medical Ethics 39–43.

control body parts and exclude others from bodies. . . . However, the use of such approaches overlooks the many complex ways in which bodies are interconnected and interdependent. From our beginnings, in pregnancy the fetus and pregnant woman are in deepest connect. The health and well-being of the fetus can impact on the woman's well-being, and the reverse is true. This interchange is found still after birth through breast feeding. . . .

In relationships of care, the bodies of the carer and the cared for are interdependent. For example, a child is dependent on their carer, and the carer becomes dependent on the child. If the child suffers an infectious childhood illness and is required to remain indoors, in effect this quarantine is imposed on the body of the carer too. If the child will not sleep, nor, in reality, will the parent. This is true not just in child–parent relationships, but in any close relationship involving caring. If, for example, a carer breaks their arm, this has an impact on the person cared for, and of course vice versa. In a relationship involving dependence, an injury to the body of either the carer, or the person cared for, impacts significantly on the other's body.

5 CONCLUSION

In the remainder of this book, we will see that there has been a shift from a paternalistic model of medical decision-making, based upon the idea that 'doctor knows best', towards an autonomy-based model, which assumes that a competent adult patient should have an almost absolute right to refuse medical treatment. It would, however, be a mistake to regard patient autonomy as the overriding value in all medical decision-making. The right to autonomy is a negative right to prevent unwanted intervention, and patients do not have the right to demand access to medical treatment when resources are unavailable; or when treatment would be against the doctors' clinical judgement; or when parliament has decided that the treatment in question is ethically unacceptable and should be legally proscribed (examples include human reproductive cloning and female genital mutilation).

The problem for the law is that there will be very few cases when there is agreement over the legitimacy of controversial medical practices. There will never be any consensus over whether euthanasia should be legalized, for example, or whether it is legitimate to experiment on embryos. In this chapter, we have focused mainly upon how we might go about discussing these questions. We could, for example, look at the consequences of regulating in one way or another. So, in relation to euthanasia, we could ask whether legalization would, on balance, make life better or worse for sick and vulnerable patients. We could also think about what principles might be at stake, and how the tension between autonomy and non-maleficence should be resolved. It might be important to think about what arguments grounded in human dignity or respect for the sanctity of human life mean in this context, and whether there is a slippery slope that either could, or could not, be contained through regulation. None of these considerations can tell us what to do, however, and undoubtedly most of us will also bring our own values and personal experiences to bear on these questions. In relation to euthanasia, for example, someone with strong religious convictions will be influenced by their faith, and someone who has seen a relative die a protracted and painful death may find that that experience shapes their judgement. Our 'gut instincts' will inevitably often provide the starting point for our reasoning process, but it is important to remember that, on their own, there is no reason why anyone else should find them persuasive.

FURTHER READING

Ashcroft, Richard E, Dawson, Angus, Draper, Heather, and McMillan, John R (eds), *Principles of Health Care Ethics*, 2nd edn (Wiley: Chichester, 2007) chs 1, 3, 5, 6, 7, 11.

Beauchamp, Tom L and Childress, James F, *Principles of Biomedical Ethics*, 7th edn (OUP: Oxford, 2013).

Beyleveld, Deryck and Brownsword, Roger, *Human Dignity in Bioethics and Biolaw* (OUP: Oxford, 2001).

Caplan, Arthur L and Arp, Robert (eds), *Contemporary Debates in Bioethics* (Wiley Blackwell: Chichester, 2013).

Harris, John (ed), *Bioethics* (OUP: Oxford, 2001).

Herring, Jonathan, *Caring and the Law* (Hart Publishing: Oxford, 2013) ch 3.

Kuhse, Helga and Singer, Peter (eds), *A Companion to Bioethics* (Blackwell: Oxford, 1998).

O'Neill, Onora, *Autonomy and Trust in Bioethics* (CUP: Cambridge, 2002).

THE PROVISION OF HEALTH CARE SERVICES: THE NHS, RESOURCE ALLOCATION, AND PUBLIC HEALTH

CENTRAL ISSUES

1. The National Health Service (NHS) was set up in 1948 in order to provide health care for everyone in the UK, free at the point of use and funded from general taxation. It has undergone several reorganizations, most recently in 2013, as a result of the Health and Social Care Act 2012. Overall responsibility for the delivery of NHS services lies with NHS England, with most commissioning devolved to Clinical Commissioning Groups. Oversight is provided by several bodies including the Care Quality Commission and the financial regulator, Monitor.

2. Scarce resources are a fact of life in the NHS, and so one of the most important questions it faces is how to allocate those resources fairly. Should the priority be clinical need or maximizing health gains, for example, and is it ever acceptable to take account of the patient's responsibility for their ill health, their age, or public opinion?

3. In England and Wales, the National Institute for Health and Care Excellence (NICE) was set up in order to evaluate whether treatments are cost-effective enough to justify NHS provision. In Scotland, a similar task is performed by the Scottish Medicines Consortium (SMC).

4. If denied treatment, patients can ask for 'exceptional case' funding. Funding decisions are also judicially reviewable. Historically, the judiciary was reluctant to interfere with decisions about the allocation of scarce resources, but more recently, patients have had some success in challenging refusals of exceptional case funding.

5. Patients might wish to seek treatment abroad, and within the EU their right to do so is protected by law. Non-EU citizens have attempted to resist deportation on the grounds that depriving them of medical treatment might amount to inhuman and degrading treatment, and hence violate their human rights. These claims have seldom succeeded.

6. Public Health England has responsibility for the promotion of public health in the UK. Public health is not confined to the provision of medical treatment, but includes all organized measures to prevent disease, promote health, and prolong life in the population as a whole. It involves the recognition that the public's health is improved not just by medical treatment, but also through effective anti-tobacco and anti-obesity policies and by tackling the social determinants of health.

1 INTRODUCTION

In this chapter we examine three complex and politically contentious questions. First, we look at how the NHS is organized; secondly, we consider how resource allocation, or rationing, takes place within the NHS; thirdly, we examine the use of the law to promote public health.

Politicians know that the British public is very attached to the NHS. A former Chancellor of the Exchequer, Nigel Lawson, once said that 'the National Health Service is the closest thing the English have to a religion';[1] and, according to a 2014 Ipsos Mori poll, 52 per cent of the public said that the NHS was what made them most proud to be British (above the royal family at 33 per cent and the BBC at 22 per cent).[2] Successive governments have increased spending on the NHS, but it nevertheless faces a funding crisis. The Chartered Institute of Public Finance and Accountancy predicted that the NHS's overall deficit in 2014–15 would be £2.1 billion, two-and-a-half times 2013–14's record deficit of £820 million.[3] Given an ageing population, and the availability of more and better treatments, the NHS needs substantial increases in spending each year just in order to stand still. In addition, cuts to the social care budget increase costs within the NHS by making it harder to discharge elderly and infirm patients from hospital.[4]

Since the NHS first started treating patients in 1948, demand for health care services has outstripped the NHS's capacity to supply them. If 'tragic choices' are unavoidable, it is important to ensure that they are taken fairly. We therefore consider how we might distinguish between fair and unfair ways to allocate scarce resources. Clearly, the NHS must not discriminate unlawfully when making rationing decisions, but disagreement exists over whether it might sometimes be reasonable to take into account factors such as the patient's responsibility for her own ill health.

Choices about the allocation of resources might be challenged, principally, of course, by dissatisfied patients who believe that they have been unfairly denied access to treatment. Challenges have come from patients who believe that the decision not to fund their treatment was taken unlawfully, and by illegal immigrants or failed asylum seekers who are currently receiving treatment in the UK which would be unavailable to them in their country of origin, and who therefore argue that deporting them might infringe their human rights.

---

[1] *The View from Number Eleven* (Doubleday: London, 1992).
[2] Iain Dale, *The NHS: Things that Need to be Said* (Elliott and Thompson: London, 2015), viii.
[3] CIFPA Briefing, 'The Health of Health Finances' (CIFPA, 2015).
[4] The King's Fund, *Quarterly Monitoring Report* (October 2015).

Finally, it is worth remembering that providing medical treatment to individual patients is only one way to promote the health of the population as a whole. A focus on the public's health might instead emphasize the importance of preventative measures, such as anti-tobacco policies, and lead to concern about the socioeconomic determinants of health. There is a weight of evidence that poverty and inequality are bad for people's health, so concern for public health might extend far beyond what the NHS can achieve, and look instead at the social and economic drivers of ill health.

2 THE MODERN NHS

After the end of the Second World War, a Labour government was elected under Clement Attlee which promised massively to expand welfare provision, and in particular to introduce a national health service. The NHS was set up by the National Health Service Act 1946, and it started treating patients two years later. There continues to be strong public support for the idea of a health care system which is free at the point of use, and which provides everyone with good-quality care. Unlike the privatization of other former state monopolies, like British Telecom, a majority of the public is against the privatization of the NHS.

As a result of devolution, it no longer makes sense to talk about a UK-wide NHS. Instead, health is a devolved matter, and the Scottish parliament and Welsh and Northern Irish assemblies now take their own decisions about funding and the organization of services. This book will focus on the English NHS, but questions of scarcity and the need for rationing are relevant throughout the UK.

In England, the NHS Constitution sets out patients' rights and responsibilities within the NHS. In its latest version, it affirms the principle of a comprehensive health service, free at the point of use, while also stressing the need to make fair and efficient use of finite resources.

The National Health Service Constitution[5]

Principles

1. The NHS provides a comprehensive service, available to all irrespective of gender, race, disability, age, sexual orientation, religion, belief, gender reassignment, pregnancy and maternity or marital or civil partnership status. The service is designed to improve, prevent, diagnose and treat both physical and mental health problems with equal regard. It has a duty to each and every individual that it serves and must respect their human rights. At the same time, it has a wider social duty to promote equality through the services it provides and to pay particular attention to groups or sections of society where improvements in health and life expectancy are not keeping pace with the rest of the population.

2. Access to NHS services is based on clinical need, not an individual's ability to pay. . . .

6. The NHS is committed to providing best value for taxpayers' money and the most effective, fair and sustainable use of finite resources . . .

---

[5] Department of Health, 'The NHS Constitution: The NHS Belongs to Us All' (DH: London, 2015).

(a) SCARCITY

Before the NHS was set up, it had been thought that providing the whole population with free and comprehensive health care, in addition to the other social services which were to be provided through the welfare state, might improve the nation's health, and thus lead to a diminishing demand for health care services. As David Hunter explains:

> the NHS was founded on a fallacy: that there was a finite amount of ill-health in the population which, once removed, would result in the maintenance of health and the provision of health care becoming cheaper as the need for it dropped off. What has happened is that success in health care has resulted in people living longer potentially to be ill more often and therefore consume more resources.[6]

As soon as the NHS started treating patients, it became obvious that the assumption that the costs of care would fall was hopelessly naïve. Three years after the NHS was set up, prescription charges were introduced, leading to the resignation of Aneurin Bevan, the chief architect of the NHS and the first Secretary of State for Health.

Since 1948, successive governments have increased spending on the NHS at above the rate of inflation. The proportion of the UK's gross domestic product (GDP) spent on health doubled from 5 per cent in the 1980s to a highpoint of 9.7 per cent in 2009, falling to 9.1 per cent in 2013.[7] Despite successive governments' commitment to protect NHS expenditure, for a number of reasons there is likely to be continued pressure on stretched NHS resources.

First, life expectancy has increased dramatically since the 1940s, but our success in extending the average lifespan has not been accompanied by the same level of success in reducing the infirmity and morbidity associated with ageing. Hence, extending the period of old age increases demand for health services. It is also the very elderly sector of the population which is increasing most rapidly: by 2035, the proportion of the UK's population who are over 85 years old is predicted to grow from 2 to 5 per cent of the total population.[8]

Secondly, technological and scientific progress has led to the availability of more sophisticated and expensive treatments for a wide variety of conditions. Not only are more options available, but the numbers of us who qualify as patients has also increased with the emergence of treatments for some of the normal consequences of ageing, like the menopause, and for risk factors, such as high cholesterol and high blood pressure.

Thirdly, patients' expectations have risen dramatically. Most of the UK's population has been able to take the NHS's existence, and their right to free, comprehensive health care for granted throughout their lives. We are also becoming less deferential and more demanding; as a result of the internet, patients often will have decided what is wrong with them, and worked out what treatment they need, before they see their GP.

Fourthly, when a service is provided free of charge, there are fewer constraints on demand than when people have to pay for it 'out of pocket'. With no financial disincentives to seeking medical care, people visit their GP for minor complaints that are overwhelmingly likely to clear up by themselves. Demand for 'free' health care services is therefore especially elastic.

---

[6] *Desperately Seeking Solutions: Rationing Health Care* (Longman: London, 1997) 20.
[7] See further http://data.worldbank.org.
[8] Office for National Statistics, *Population Ageing in the United Kingdom, its Constituent Countries and the European Union* (ONS, 2012).

Fifthly, as we see in the next chapter, clinical negligence claims represent a significant and increasing drain on NHS funds. In 2014/15, the NHS Litigation Authority (NHSLA) received 11,497 clinical negligence claims, up from 6,652 in 2009/10; the amount paid out also increased, from £787 million to almost £1.4 billion.[9]

Finally, the problem of health care funding appears to be universal. One study estimated that providing all the health care that could be beneficial to every French citizen would cost five-and-a-half times France's gross national product.[10] If rationing is therefore inevitable, the important task is to ensure that it is done as fairly and, as Alan Maynard explains, as openly as possible.

Alan Maynard[11]

There are two certainties in life: death and scarcity. A long, good-quality life free of pain, disability and distress from birth to death is the exception rather than the rule. Most people confront morbidity over the life-cycle and demand cures and care which are expensive and often of unproven benefit. . . . The policy issue is therefore not whether, but how, to ration access to health and social care. Society and its political representatives are, however, reluctant to confront this reality . . . A health service in 'political denial' stunts the development of socially agreed rationing principles, that are openly discussed and accountably applied, and creates a market of special pleading on both the demand—(for example, patient advocacy groups) and supply side (for example, the pharmaceutical industry). These are organisations with overlapping goals which result in a single demand: spend more!

If rationing is inevitable, it is important to distinguish between the various different levels at which resource allocation decisions are taken. At the macro level, political choices must be made about how much public money should be spent on the NHS, in the light of competing demands upon the nation's resources. Within the health budget, decisions have to be taken about what treatments the NHS will fund. At a national level, the National Institute for Health and Care Excellence (NICE) is responsible for determining whether particular treatments are sufficiently cost-effective to justify NHS funding. As we see in the next section, clinical commissioning groups operate at the local level to decide which treatments to commission for people in their area.

(b) THE ORGANIZATION OF THE NHS

The NHS has undergone many reorganizations since 1948. In 1991, for example, a purchaser/provider split was introduced in order to give fundholders, such as GPs, a stake in ensuring value for money. Because money would no longer be awarded in block grants, but would instead 'follow the patient', hospitals would effectively have to compete for business. The then Conservative government believed that the injection of competition into the NHS would drive costs down and quality up. Similar motivations were behind the more recent reforms, but, as Lindsay Stirton has explained, in practice it has proved difficult to introduce competition into the health service.

---

[9] NHSLA, *Annual Report and Accounts 2014–15* (NHSLA, 2015).

[10] Cited in Richard D Lamm, 'Rationing of Health Care: Inevitable and Desirable' (1992) 140 University of Pennsylvania Law Review 1511, 1512.

[11] 'Ethics and health care "underfunding"' (2001) 27 Journal of Medical Ethics 223–7.

Lindsay Stirton[12]

[S]uccessive reforms of the organisational structure of the NHS have repeatedly aimed towards the same results as earlier ones. For example, the Government's aims in creating NHS Foundation Trusts—including freedom from top-down control, improved responsiveness to patients and local needs, and better management of human resources—were substantially the same as those used to justify the original creation of NHS Trusts. Similarly, the objective of securing GP involvement in commissioning processes has motivated successive rounds of purchasing reform, including the creation of GP fund-holding, their replacement with PCGs/PCTs, the introduction of practice-based commissioning and most recently with the creation of CCGs. Parallels may be drawn with experience in the utilities, where consumers have often shown little interest in 'shopping around' for the best service, and—despite the efforts of regulators to improve standardised provision of information—arguably lack the knowledge to choose between different packages, which are in any case often rapidly changing . . . [A] twenty-year perspective shows just how difficult it is to establish workable competition in health services.

The Private Finance Initiative (PFI), first introduced in the early 1990s, did not just apply to hospitals, but its after-effects have been especially significant within the NHS. PFI involved private capital being used to fund large public projects, such as hospitals, with the buildings then being leased back to the NHS, along with contracts for support services, for 25 or 30 years. Politicians' enthusiasm for PFI is easy to understand: new hospitals (with their obvious appeal to voters) could be built without using or borrowing public money. The downside, of course, was that this was not free money and it has saddled the NHS with considerable debts.

The most recent reorganization started in 2010 with the publication of a White Paper, *Equity and Excellence: Liberating the NHS*, by the then Secretary of State for Health, Andrew Lansley. Despite concerted opposition, this resulted in the Health and Social Care Act 2012 and changes that were, according to the then NHS Chief Executive, David Nicholson, 'so big you can see them from space'.[13]

The activities of the NHS can be split into three: commissioning services, providing them, and monitoring their provision. Commissioning is overseen by the NHS Commissioning Board, now called NHS England. Set up in 2012, it is responsible for allocating resources to all 209 Clinical Commissioning Groups (CCGs); overseeing the activities of CCGs; commissioning primary care and other directly commissioned services; and providing national leadership. The provision of health care throughout the NHS is then monitored by several bodies. The Care Quality Commission inspects services and reports on their quality. Monitor is a financial regulator whose role is to ensure that services are well run and efficient. Monitor can investigate conflicts of interest, and anti-competitive practices.

(1) Clinical Commissioning Groups

CCGs receive £67 billion of NHS England's total budget of £99 billion. They are responsible for commissioning most health care services in their areas, including hospital and community-based health care. All GP practices are members of CCGs. Initially there were 211 CCGs, mergers mean that there are now 209. CCGs are overseen and held to account by NHS England, which also has responsibility for commissioning specialist services that can only

[12] 'Back to the Future? Lessons on the Pro-Competitive Regulation of Health Services' (2014) 22 Medical Law Review 180–99.

[13] Quoted in Chris Ham et al, *The NHS under a coalition government—part one: NHS reform* (King's Fund, 2015).

be provided efficiently and effectively at national or regional level. Until 2015, only NHS England could commission primary care services.

CCGs do not have to commission services from NHS providers, and can instead commission services from 'third sector' (ie charitable) or private providers. Indeed section 75 of the Health and Social Care Act 2012, and Regulations made under it,[14] are specifically intended to prevent anti-competitive practices, so that NHS services do not have 'preferred provider' status. Instead the private sector must be allowed to compete against NHS providers. Although private providers continue to be responsible for a small proportion of NHS services, as Appleby explains, the rate of growth is significant.

John Appleby[15]

Over the seven years since 2006–7, the proportion of NHS patients treated by non-NHS providers has risen from around 0.5% (73 000) to 2.6% (471 000) of all inpatient episodes. . . . For outpatient care, the proportion treated by non-NHS providers has risen faster—from 0.2% (123 000) to 5.5% (4.5 million). . . . If rates of growth since 2006–7 continue over the next 20 years, non-NHS providers could account for one in five of all outpatient attendances and approaching one in 10 inpatient episodes paid for by the NHS.

Does competition from alternative providers always drive up quality? The evidence is mixed. In their study of all providers of primary care services, Greaves et al found that alternative providers in fact provided a worse standard of care on almost all measures.

Felix Greaves et al[16]

Alternative Provider of Medical Services practices performed significantly worse than [traditional GP] practices on 13 of the 17 quality indicators examined in every study year, including all measures of clinical quality. . . .

The results suggest that alternative providers have not been widely contracted to deliver primary care services, making up only 4% of practices since 2004. . . . Practices run by alternative providers supplied consistently worse quality of care than traditional practices—across a broad range of indicators. . . . [O]ur findings provide little support for the hypothesis that increasing plurality of provision has increased quality of care.

The intention behind the Health and Social Care Act 2012 was to delegate more responsibility for rationing decisions to doctors, though it is noteworthy that GPs represented fewer than half of the members of the new CCGs that took on responsibility for commissioning from April 2013.

Nonetheless, GPs undoubtedly have more responsibility over the NHS budget than before. If GPs have financial interests in private providers of care, there may be a risk of perceived or actual conflict of interests. If a CCG is deciding which hospital should be commissioned to provide, say, routine hip replacement surgery and members of that CCG have a financial interest in a local private provider of hip replacement surgery, there is an obvious conflict of

---

[14] National Health Service (Procurement, Patient Choice and Competition) (No 2) Regulations 2013.

[15] 'Paid for by the NHS, treated privately' (2015) 350 British Medical Journal h3109.

[16] 'Performance of new alternative providers of primary care services in England: an observational study' (2015) 108 Journal of the Royal Society of Medicine 171–83.

interest. The risks of conflicts of interest became more acute in 2015 when it became possible for CCGs to choose to take on responsibility for commissioning primary medical services.

A new regulator, Monitor, has the power to ensure that commissioners manage conflicts of interest and that particular interests do not influence their decision-making.[17] Ensuring that this never happens will be difficult, however, given how common these sorts of financial interests are. In 2015, the National Audit Office investigated conflicts of interests in CCGs, and how they are managed.

National Audit Office[18]

Some 1,300 (41%) of clinical commissioning group (CCG) governing body members in position at the time of our analysis in 2014–15 were also GPs, who may, potentially, have made decisions about local health services and have been paid by their CCG for providing them. Non-GP commissioners may also have potential conflicts of interest, for example where have they have financial or other interests in organisations providing locally commissioned health services . . .

During 2014–15, a minority of CCGs had reported they had to manage actual or perceived conflicts of interest. We reviewed CCGs' governing body minutes for April to December 2014. Potential conflicts were declared for agenda items in 22% of CCGs during this period. This related to 75 recorded instances of potential or actual conflicts . . .

We could not always assess from publicly available information how CCGs had managed specific conflicts of interest, which limits local transparency. In the 75 instances of potential or actual conflicts we found from our sample of governing body minutes, the level of detail given about the conflict and how it had been managed varied. In 14 cases the information provided was insufficient for us to assess how the CCG managed the conflict. . . . Where CCGs reported information about their controls for managing risks of conflicts of interest, it showed the adequacy of those controls had varied.

A further difficulty that may result from greater GP involvement in commissioning is that doctors are at the sharp end of rationing decisions, unlike politicians or health service managers. It is not easy for a GP to tell her patients that effective treatment is available, but that it will not be provided because the CCG of which she is a member has decided that it is too expensive.

Catriona Chatfield[19]

The therapeutic relationship between GP and patient is paramount in creating good healthcare: patients must be able to feel that they can trust GPs to look out for their welfare above all other considerations. If a patient knows that their GP is directly determining what local resources will or will not be provided, this severely threatens that relationship. . . .

There is also a real danger that the degree of localisation built into the new model will worsen health inequalities between different areas—and that the increased patient choices it promises will, as ever, benefit the wealthier and more proactive members of society at the expense of the least privileged.

[17] Department of Health, *Securing Best Value for NHS Patients: Requirements for Commissioners to Adhere to Good Procurement Practice and Protect Patient Choice* (DH: London, 2012).

[18] National Audit Office, *Managing conflicts of interest in NHS clinical commissioning groups* (NAO, 2015).

[19] 'Coalition: NHS reform at what cost?', Prospect, 21 April 2011.

Active involvement in rationing, which inevitably means that some patients are denied care because it is too expensive, may be at odds with the medical profession's primary ethical responsibility to make the health of each patient her first concern; as van Delden et al have put it: 'choosing between patients is not their job'.[20]

On the other hand, it could be argued that the 'gate-keeping' role which has long been played by GPs within the NHS is itself a form of rationing. A person's GP should normally be their first point of contact when they feel unwell. If the patient's condition is potentially serious, or requires expert attention, the GP will refer her to an appropriate specialist, usually in a local hospital. Specialist services are therefore only provided to patients whose need for them has been vetted first by their GP, rather than being clogged up by anyone who thinks that they might benefit from an appointment with a consultant. But, as McPake et al explain, 'the mechanism works imperfectly, general practitioners have widely varying rates of referral and large numbers of patients directly attend Accident and Emergency departments for minor complaints that could be dealt with by the GP'.[21]

In the UK, doctors have seldom explicitly acknowledged that they are rationing medical treatment, and instead cost–benefit considerations have been absorbed within their clinical discretion. If a patient is suffering from symptoms which are very likely to be caused by a minor complaint, but there is a remote chance that there might be something seriously wrong, doctors will often adopt a 'wait and see' approach: the patient will be asked to return in a week or two if their symptoms have not improved, even though there is a very small chance that they might benefit from undergoing expensive investigative procedures immediately. Few doctors would see this as rationing, but, as Gillon has explained:

> If one were to take thoroughly to heart the idea that as curative doctors we should never allow concern for cost to others to deflect us from doing whatever we could to benefit our patients, then diagnostic services would be overwhelmed as we tested for rare but possible problems.[22]

(2) Privatization?

In addition to enabling private providers to compete for NHS business, section 165 of the Health and Social Care Act 2012 removed the 'private patient income cap', which had previously limited the proportion of private treatment which could be undertaken by Foundation Trusts to 2 per cent. Now up to 49 per cent of an NHS Foundation Trust's income can come from treating private patients. This gives some overstretched NHS hospitals, especially large and/or specialist hospitals in London, the option of increasing their revenue through expanding their provision of treatment for private patients. The Royal Marsden earns the most from private patients (£76.9 million), followed by Great Ormond

[20] J JM van Delden, A M Vrakking, A van der Heide, and P J van der Maas, 'Medical decision making in scarcity situations' (2004) 30 Journal of Medical Ethics 207–11.

[21] Barbara McPake, Lilani Kumaranayake, and Charles Normand, *Health Economics: An International Perspective* (Routledge: London, 2002) 202.

[22] Raanan Gillon, 'Ethics, Economics and General Practice' in Gavin Mooney and Alistair McGuire (eds), *Medical Ethics and Economics in Health Care* (OUP: Oxford, 1988) 114–34, 128.

Street (£40.9 million) and Royal Brompton & Harefield (£37.5 million).[23] District hospitals do not have the same earning potential. Critics have also been concerned that the expansion of private care within NHS hospitals might mean that NHS patients become second-class citizens within the NHS.[24]

In their review of the reforms effected by the Health and Social Care Act, the King's Fund has concluded that they have not resulted in the privatization of the NHS, as some critics have argued. Nevertheless, the King's Fund found that their complexity, and the fragmentation of structures that has resulted, have been profoundly damaging to the NHS.

The King's Fund[25]

Historians will not be kind in their assessment of the coalition government's record on NHS reform. . . . [T]he reforms have certainly resulted in greater marketisation in the NHS, but claims of mass privatisation were and are exaggerated. Private providers do play a part in providing care to NHS patients, as they have always done, and their share of provision of community and mental health services has somewhat increased. Notwithstanding this, NHS providers continue to deliver the vast majority of care to NHS patients, especially in acute hospital services, and there is little evidence that this will change any time soon. . . .

Arguments about privatisation distract from the much more important and damaging impacts of the reforms on how the NHS is organised and the ability of its leaders to deal with rapidly growing financial and service pressures. By taking three years to dismantle the old structures and reassemble them into new ones, the government took scarce time and expertise away from efforts to address these pressures. Although it is not possible to demonstrate a causal relationship with NHS performance, it seems likely that the massive organisational changes that resulted from the reforms contributed to widespread financial distress and failure to hit key targets for patient care . . .

Nowhere has this been more apparent than at the centre of the system, where the leadership previously provided by the Department of Health has been fractured and distributed between several organisations, each overseeing part of the NHS but none responsible for the whole.

3 DIFFERENT RATIONING STRATEGIES

Before we consider the role of the National Institute for Health and Care Excellence in making rationing decisions for the NHS, we first examine different ways in which rationing might be carried out.

(a) FROM IMPLICIT TO EXPLICIT RATIONING

In the NHS's first few decades, patients tended to assume that decisions about their treatment were taken in their best interests and were unaffected by cost considerations. Rationing was, as Keith Syrett explains, implicit rather than explicit.

---

[23] 'NHS private pay income up 14% in two years', *Health Investor*, 3 August 2015.

[24] John Lister, 'Breaking the Public Trust' in Jacky Davis and Raymond Tallis (eds), *NHS SOS* (Oneworld: London, 2013) 17–37.

[25] Chris Ham et al, *The NHS under a coalition government—part one: NHS reform* (King's Fund, 2015).

Keith Syrett[26]

[F]or many years, rationing in the NHS was not a matter of significant political or public debate. This was in part because lower expectations in the early years of the Service led to acceptance that deficiencies in provision were simply a fact of life. More significantly, most rationing took place under cover of clinical judgment: that is, it was *implicit*, in that 'the reasoning involved [was] not clearly stated to anyone except . . . the person making the decision'. Medical professionals effectively 'converted' political decisions on resource allocation into clinical decisions about treatment by 'internalising' resource limits and providing justification for denial on medical grounds by portraying the decision as optimal or routine in the specific circumstances. Suspicion that such decisions were in reality dictated by resource considerations tended to be minimal because of the existence of high levels of trust between doctors and patients, premised upon the belief that physicians possessed both expertise and access to all medical resources necessary for effective care and that they would act as dedicated patient advocates in attempting to secure these.

Explicit rationing, in contrast, involves being frank with patients. Of course, a patient who learns that she has been denied care because it is too expensive is likely to be upset and frustrated. As a result, there are those who have argued that implicit rationing is 'more conducive to stable social relations and a lower level of conflict'.[27] Implicit rationing works, according to David Mechanic 'because patients trust that doctors are their agents and have their interests at heart'.[28]

Whatever its downsides, most people now accept that explicit rationing should displace the 'benign deceit' of the past.[29] As we see in Chapter 4, patients need access to relevant information in order to make informed choices about their treatment. The existence of an effective treatment which the NHS will not fund is, for many patients, important and relevant information. If you know that potentially effective treatment has been withheld, you might try to pay for it yourself, or seek to challenge the decision.

It could also be argued that the public is now so well informed about the availability of different treatment options, that 'camouflaging' rationing decisions as exercises of clinical judgement is no longer an option. As James Sabin has put it: 'personal computers and the internet drive the nails into the coffin of implicit rationing'.[30]

Transparency about rationing facilitates consistency and public accountability,[31] or what Norman Daniels and James Sabin have referred to as 'accountability for reasonableness'.[32] According to Daniels and Sabin, there are four requirements for reasonable public decision-making:

- Publicity: decisions, and the grounds for making them, must be transparent and open.

- Relevance: decisions must be based upon relevant criteria.

[26] 'Impotence or Importance? Judicial Review in an Era of Explicit NHS Rationing' (2004) 67 Modern Law Review 289–304.

[27] David Mechanic, 'Dilemmas in rationing health care services: the case for implicit rationing' (1995) 310 British Medical Journal 1655–9.

[28] Ibid.   [29] Bill New and Julian LeGrand, *Rationing in the NHS* (King's Fund, 1996) 24.

[30] 'Fairness as a Problem of Love and the Heart: A Clinician's Perspective on Priority Setting' in Angela Coulter and Chris Ham (eds), *The Global Challenge of Healthcare Rationing* (Open UP: Buckingham, 2000) 117–22, 120.

[31] Keith Syrett, *Law, Legitimacy and the Rationing of Health Care* (CUP: Cambridge, 2007) 62–3.

[32] Norman Daniels and James E Sabin, *Setting Limits Fairly—Can We Learn to Share Medical Resources?* (OUP: Oxford, 2000).

- Revision and appeals: there must be a process for challenging decisions, and the possibility of their subsequent revision.
- Enforcement: there must be regulation to ensure compliance with these criteria.[33]

The theory is that, if a rationing decision was based on relevant criteria and sound evidence, and if affected patients have a right of challenge, decisions which are always going to be unpopular may nevertheless secure some level of public legitimacy and social acceptability.

Daniels and Sabin's model is not without its critics, however.[34] It could, for example, be argued that what counts as a relevant criterion is not just a procedural matter. The decision to take into account a person's responsibility for their own ill health, for example, is controversial. Critics have also suggested that Daniels and Sabin should add public participation as a prerequisite of a fair rationing process.[35]

(b) DIFFERENT RATIONING STRATEGIES

The concept of triage (from the French verb *trier*: to sort) emerged on the battlefields of the First World War, when there were insufficient resources to treat every injured soldier. Battlefield triage involves deciding who to treat, based upon both the severity of their injuries and how quickly they might be able to return to active service. If the NHS was overwhelmed with a serious flu pandemic—which might infect more than half of the population—choices akin to battlefield triage might have to be made. Who should have priority for the first doses of the flu vaccine, for example: the nurse who would then be able to care for others, or the sewerage worker who can ensure that the whole population has access to clean water? Although such choices are inevitably difficult, Lomasky points out that decisions taken *in extremis*, when there is little time for reflection, may be less 'dreadful' than the rational, considered choice to treat one patient at the expense of another.

Loren E Lomasky[36]

Two classic examples of triage are the dangerously overloaded lifeboat and the harried medic patching up the wounded on a battlefield. Whatever is done, some salvageable lives will be forfeited. The dreadfulness of these choices though is somewhat softened by the urgency of a crisis: action must be immediate and there is little luxury for reflective deliberation. If called upon to justify his actions, an agent could plead that he was reacting instinctively to the needs of the moment.

Contemporary medical technology is responsible for triage situations of a rather different character. A mechanism is devised that is effective against some previously untreatable condition. Unfortunately, only a small percentage of those afflicted can receive treatment. Who shall be allowed to live? Here decision-makers are dealing with a series of events predictable well in advance. Not enmeshed in a precipitously developing crisis, they are privileged to assume the role of detached administrator. There is, however, a price to be paid for this

---

[33] Ibid.
[34] Alex Friedman, 'Beyond accountability for reasonableness' (2008) 22 Bioethics 101–12.
[35] Ibid.
[36] 'Medical progress and national health care' (1980) 10 Philosophy and Public Affairs 65–88.

relative ease: whatever standards are developed and employed are subject to close scrutiny. Those disfavoured in the selection process are perfectly entitled to ask why . . .

Triage is never unproblematic, but on what basis could a creature of the state adopt any principle of selection? Whoever is excluded can justifiably complain that he is thereby being disadvantaged by the very institution whose special duty is to extend equal protection to all persons.

In the following sections, we examine different criteria that could plausibly be used to ration health care services. We might agree that resources should be allocated fairly, but this just begs the question: what do we mean by fair? Do we treat people fairly when we treat them equally? Or should priority always be given to those in the greatest need? Ought we to ensure that resources are allocated where they will do most good, using cost-effectiveness analysis? We could choose to take an individual's responsibility for their own ill health into account; or their social value, or we could opt for a straightforward free market, in which those who can spend the most have access to the best standard of care. In practice, most people would probably advocate some sort of mixed rationing system, in which a number of different factors are taken into account: for example, an approach based upon the cost-effectiveness of treatment might be supplemented by additional criteria, such as the urgency of clinical need.

Before we assess potentially fair rationing criteria, it is worth pointing out that some obviously unfair grounds for distinguishing between patients might nevertheless carry some weight. First, while it would clearly be unethical to take into account the patient's likeability, in practice doctors are human beings capable of feeling compassion for one patient and exasperation with another. It is probably impossible to guarantee that health care professionals are never prompted to do more for a patient out of personal sympathy.

Secondly, some patients are simply more demanding and assertive than others. A patient who insists upon a second opinion, or who repeatedly telephones a consultant's secretary, may receive care that other patients might not have the confidence or the knowledge to seek out. John Butler interviewed health care professionals about their attitudes to rationing, and concern was expressed about patients' uneven ability to exert pressure upon health care resources.

John Butler[37]

The health visitor was clear about the injustice that could result from rationing by inaccessibility, in which the astute and the persistent were rewarded at the expense of those who lacked the know-how to seek out what they wanted. Those who are put off, she said, will not be the better-educated middle-class families, they will be the poorer families who are under-educated and inarticulate . . .

The surgeon, too, expressed his moral concern at the potential for social bias in the innate responsiveness of the service to the pressure exerted upon it by patients. Those who 'push and shove a bit' will often get the best treatment, but they will not be a cross-section of all those waiting to be seen. He recognized it as wrong (albeit, perhaps, unavoidable) that a class bias will ensue through which cases may not always be seen in the order of their clinical urgency. It was the replacement of need by pressure as the determinant of access to secondary care that he saw as wrong.

---

[37] *The Ethics of Health Care Rationing: Principles and Practices* (Cassell: London, 1999) 230.

(1) Equality

As Amy Gutmann explains, equality of access means that everyone with an equivalent health need should have equivalent access to care.

Amy Gutmann[38]

A principle of equal access to health care demands that every person who shares the same type and degree of health need must be given an equally effective chance of receiving appropriate treatment of equal quality so long as that treatment is available to anyone. . . . The principle requires that if anyone within a society has an opportunity to receive a service or good that satisfies a health need, then everyone who shares the same type and degree of health need must be given an equally effective chance of receiving that service or good.

Equal access also places limits upon the market freedoms of some individuals, especially, but not exclusively, the richest members of society. The principle does not permit the purchase of health care to which other similarly needy people do not have effective access . . . Thus, the rigorous implementation of equal access to health care would prevent rich people from spending their extra income for preferred medical services, if those services were not equally accessible to the poor.

Patients who are alike in relevant ways should therefore be treated alike, and patients who are unlike should be treated differently. But, of course, this just begs the question: what factors justify treating patients similarly, and what factors justify differentiating between them? Is an alcoholic who needs a liver transplant 'like' a non-drinker with a similarly urgent need for a transplant, or does the patient's alcoholism turn these into 'unlike' cases?

In practice, on its own, equality does not tell us very much about how to allocate scarce resources. Instead, it supplements other rationing criteria, such as need or cost-effectiveness, by ensuring that these are employed consistently between patients in order to avoid arbitrary and unfair distribution of resources. As Larry S Temkin explains, because health is so central to our ability to lead a flourishing life, concern for equality might lead us to give particular priority to the least healthy and/or least well off.

Larry S Temkin[39]

We don't merely recognize the sad but inevitable truth that some people are in poor health or receive little or substandard health care and see the pressing need to address the situation; we rankle at the further fact that there is so much undeserved inequality in the distribution of health states and health care. For many, the situation is not merely unfortunate: it is terribly unfair, and this provides significant additional force to the legitimate claims of many living in poor health . . .

Aristotle and Bentham had radically different views about what mattered most about human existence, but both would have agreed that a valuable human existence depends, in fact, on certain basic, fundamental necessities. Minimally, it depends on physical and

---

[38] 'For and against equal access to health care' (1981) 59(4) Milbank Memorial Fund Quarterly/Health and Society 542–60, reprinted in Gregory Pence (ed), *Classic Works in Medical Ethics* (McGraw Hill: Boston, MA, 1998) 367–8.

[39] 'Inequality and Health' in Nir Eyal et al (eds), *Inequalities in Health: Concepts, Measures, and Ethics* (OUP: Oxford, 2013) 13–26.

psychological preservation, which in turn depends on minimum levels of food, shelter, security, freedom from pain, and good health . . . Good health isn't *everything*, but it is a *lot*. Freedom from debilitating illness is more than a necessary precondition to a worthwhile human existence. Arguably, good physical and psychological health constitute a large part of what makes a human life worth living.

(2) Need

At first sight, distributing NHS resources according to need might appear attractively fair and simple. Needs, after all, have much greater moral force than wants or desires. But, as Richard Lamm has put it, 'Medical "need" is an infinitely expandable concept. We need what is available, and in a creative and inventive society such as our own, there is no end to what we can do to treat aging bodies.'[40]

Need could also only operate as a rationing criterion if we were able to construct a hierarchy of needs, so that we could tell whether one patient's need was greater or less than another's. Someone whose life is in danger clearly 'needs' treatment more than someone who will survive without treatment, and so it might be argued that life-saving treatment should always be our first priority. However, this would ignore the question of whether the person could actually benefit from treatment. For example, the life of a patient who is in a permanent vegetative state can be preserved—at enormous cost—for many years. The fact that this sort of treatment will prolong life does not necessarily mean that it should take priority over palliative care, which is not life-extending, but which benefits dying patients by relieving their pain and distress.

Norman Daniels has applied John Rawls' theory of justice to the distribution of health care. Daniels argues that health care is of special importance, and should be regarded as a primary social good, because of its capacity to ensure fair equality of opportunity. Disease and infirmity interfere with a person's range of opportunities. In order to rectify the resulting inequality, priority should be given to those needs which most interfere with 'normal species functioning'. When deciding between competing needs, Daniels argues that we can rank them according to the extent to which normal species function is impaired.

Norman Daniels[41]

What emerges here is the suggestion that we use impairment of the normal opportunity range as a fairly crude measure of the relative importance of health-care needs at the macro level. In general, it will be more important to prevent, cure, or compensate for those disease conditions which involve a greater curtailment of normal opportunity range.

For example, someone with a broken hip will generally have their normal opportunity range restricted more than someone with a disfiguring scar, and hence we might decide that funding hip replacement operations should be a higher priority than cosmetic surgery.

There are, however, several problems with the attempt to prioritize different health needs by the extent to which they interfere with normal species functioning. First, 'normal species

---

[40] Richard D Lamm, 'Rationing of Health Care: Inevitable and Desirable' (1992) 140 University of Pennsylvania Law Review 1511, 1512.

[41] 'Health-care needs and distributive justice' (1981) 10 Philosophy and Public Affairs 146–79.

functioning' may sound like an objective criterion, but it is quite difficult to pin down. It is normal for our bodies to degenerate with age, but we would not want to make the treatment of elderly patients a low priority on the grounds that some degree of ill health is 'normal' for them. Moreover, since normal species functioning depends in part upon the availability of health care services, there may be a degree of circularity in using 'normal functioning' as a criterion for the distribution of health care.

Secondly, in practice it would be extremely difficult to construct an objective, population-wide hierarchy of illnesses and disabilities according to their degree of interference with normal species functioning. For some people, such as surgeons or pilots, losing the sight in one eye could have disastrous consequences, for others its impact might be comparatively slight.

Finally, there would have to be exceptions to Daniels's classification in order to accommodate beneficial treatments that do not attempt to 'restore normal species functioning'. Contraception, for example, does not cure or treat anything; in fact, its purpose is to disrupt normal functioning, yet it is considered such a cost-effective public good that it has always been exempt from the prescription charge.

(3) Maximizing Health Gains

(a) Assessing cost-effectiveness: the QALY

Quality-Adjusted Life Years, known as QALYs,[42] are an attempt to compare the cost-effectiveness of different treatments objectively so that scarce NHS resources 'do as much good as possible'.[43] The point of QALYs, as Alan Williams explains, is that they not only measure the amount of extra life that a treatment might generate, but also its quality; the assumption being that we should divert resources to treatments which are likely to offer people the longest periods of healthy and active life.

Alan Williams[44]

The essence of a QALY is that it takes a year of healthy life expectancy to be worth 1, but regards a year of unhealthy life expectancy as worth less than 1. Its precise value is lower the worse the quality of life of the unhealthy person (which is what the 'quality adjusted' bit is all about). If being dead is worth zero, it is, in principle, possible for a QALY to be negative, i.e. for the quality of someone's life to be judged worse than being dead.

The general idea is that a beneficial health care activity is one that generates a positive amount of QALYs, and that an efficient health care activity is one where the cost per QALY is as low as it can be. A high priority health care activity is one where the cost-per-QALY is low, and a low priority activity is one where cost-per-QALY is high.

There are a number of stages to the use of QALYs. First, QALYs require us to be able to judge quality of life on a scale ranging from 0 (death) to 1.0 (full health). Next, we multiply

---

[42] The QALY scale was first developed in the work of Rosser et al in the 1970s. See further R Rosser and VC Watts, 'The measurement of hospital output' (1972) 1 International Journal of Epidemiology 361–8; R Rosser and P Kind, 'A scale of values of states of illness: is there a social consensus?' (1978) 7 International Journal of Epidemiology 347–58.

[43] Alan Williams, 'Economics, QALYs and Medical Ethics: A Health Economist's Perspective' in Souzy Dracopoulou (ed), *Ethics and Values in Health Care Management* (Routledge: London, 1998) 29–37.

[44] 'The value of QALYs' (1985) 94 Health and Social Service Journal 3.

patients' life expectancy and quality of life scores, both before and after treatment. The difference between these will be the QALY score. So, for example, let us imagine that, without treatment, a patient with condition A has two years of life left, and her quality of life is 0.5. Before treatment, the patient's life contains 1 QALY. If treatment X would give her six years with a quality of life of 1.0, post-treatment, her life contains 6 QALYs. The QALY value of treatment X is therefore 5. The next stage is to calculate the cost per QALY. So let us imagine that treatment X costs £50,000. Since it provides 5 QALYs, the cost per QALY is £10,000. By working out the QALY scores for different treatments, it should be possible to determine which offer the best value for money.

For several reasons, some commentators have challenged the usefulness and fairness of the QALY approach. First, according to the logic of QALYs, the purpose of a health service is to generate the maximum number of quality-adjusted life years at the lowest cost. QALYs therefore assume that society is neutral as to how health benefits are distributed across society, and that it does not matter whether the years of healthy life go to people who are already in good health or to those whose health is poor. In practice most of us would prefer the NHS to fund the treatment of patients with serious conditions, such as cancer and heart disease, in preference to more trivial complaints, such as hay fever or acne, even if these latter treatments are more cost-effective. Our concern is not simply to maximize the aggregate health gain in society at the lowest cost, but rather to ensure that the NHS can help those who are in the greatest need.

Secondly, the emphasis upon maximizing health gains is explicitly utilitarian. QALYs measure units of lifetime, as if they are interchangeable, rather than treating patients as separate individuals who value their own lives, and those of people they love, especially highly. If spending £50,000 on treatment X will enable us to extend patient A's life for five years, while spending £50,000 on treatment Y will only extend patient B's life for one year, it seems clear that treatment X should receive priority over treatment Y. But as John Harris, one of QALYs' most vigorous critics, points out, patient B, who is thereby forced to sacrifice an additional year of life, might not agree.

John Harris[45]

> What matters is that the person is not prepared to agree that his interest in continued life is of less value than that of anyone else, nor that that interest necessarily varies with the quality of his life nor with his life expectancy. In short, if a person wants continued existence, then, in my view, his interest in continued existence is entitled to be treated as on a par with that of anyone else. All people who want to go on living have an interest in continued existence, the value of which can only be determined by themselves.

Simona Giardano explains that while QALYs appear to capture what matters to us—securing the longest life expectancy of the best quality—this is in fact an illusion because 'what matters to people is not "the number of healthy life years the world contains", but the number of healthy years that *they or people they care about* will have'.[46]

Thirdly, it has been suggested that using QALYs to ration treatment will tend to exacerbate existing discrimination against the elderly and the disabled, whose QALY scores are likely to

---

[45] 'Double jeopardy and the veil of ignorance—a reply' (1995) 21 Journal of Medical Ethics 151–7, 151.

[46] 'Respect for equality and the treatment of the elderly: declarations of human rights and age-based rationing' (2005) 14 Cambridge Quarterly of Healthcare Ethics 83–92.

be fairly low because of their reduced life expectancy and/or their lower pre-existing quality of life. People who are unlucky enough to suffer from conditions that are very expensive to treat—and this is usually people with serious illnesses—might fare badly, because the cost per QALY of treating them is likely to be high. This is, in Harris's words, 'a sort of double jeopardy', whereby people who have already been unlucky enough to be seriously ill or disabled will be further disadvantaged when competing for scarce resources.[47]

John Harris[48]

The ageism of QALY is inescapable, for any calculation of the life-years generated for a particular patient by a particular therapy must be based on the life expectancy of that patient after treatment. The older the patient is when treated, the fewer the life-years that can be achieved by the therapy . . . [I]t will usually be more QALY efficient to concentrate on areas of medicine which will inevitably generate more QALYs, neonatal care or paediatrics, for example. And equally, to channel resources away from (or deny them altogether to) areas such as geriatric medicine or terminal care.

This argument has been contested by others, who argue that Harris has overlooked a crucial feature of QALYs, namely, that what is measured is the change in a person's health brought about by an intervention. In order to maximize QALYs, resources should not always be diverted to people whose post-treatment quality of life or life expectancy is greatest, but for whom the QALY gain per pound spent is higher. If I am already fit and healthy, a medical treatment may not alter my QALY score very much, whereas, if my present quality of life is low, my QALY score post-treatment might be much higher. Michael Rawlins and Andrew Dillon—at the time the Chair and CEO of NICE—gave the example of a treatment for osteoporosis, which cost £32,936 per QALY for patients aged 50 years, and £12,191 per QALY for patients aged 70, explaining that 'this occurs because older patients have a greater risk of complications of osteoporosis and thus benefit more'.[49]

Fourthly, the QALY approach may be inconsistent with the principle that people with equal health needs should have equal access to appropriate medical treatment. As Penelope Mullen and Peter Spurgeon explain, if a patient's access to treatment depends upon the costs of treating them, 'systematic discrimination could result against, say, those from ethnic minority groups who require interpreters, those living in poorer housing who might require inpatient stays rather than day surgery and those living in remote, sparsely populated locations'.[50]

Fifthly, when a new treatment is introduced, it may be extremely expensive at first, but its cost may decrease as the technology becomes cheaper, or as the expense of staff training is eliminated. The QALY scale might then discourage innovation in favour of established and currently cheaper treatments, even if there might be cost savings from adopting the new treatment over the longer term.

Sixthly, QALYs assume that it is possible to devise an objective and accurate mechanism for measuring the anticipated length and quality of a person's life. In fact, the medical

---

[47] 'QALYfying the value of life' (1987) 13 Journal of Medical Ethics 117–23, 120.

[48] 'More and Better Justice' in JM Bell and Susan Mendus (eds), *Philosophy and Medical Welfare* (CUP: Cambridge, 1988) 75–96, 80.

[49] 'NICE discrimination' (2005) 31 Journal of Medical Ethics 683–4, 683.

[50] Penelope Mullen and Peter Spurgeon, *Priority Setting and the Public* (Radcliffe Medical Press: Abingdon, 2000).

profession's predictions of life expectancy are unreliable, and speculating about the future quality of a person's life is also inherently uncertain. Treatment outcomes depend upon a wide variety of factors, such as the patient's physical fitness and the quality of aftercare services. Because the QALY calculation is too crude to capture all of the relevant variables, its results will inevitably lack precision.

It could also be argued that it is impossible to reduce such a complex concept as quality of life to a single numerical value between 0 and 1. We would also need to work out who should be charged with making these assessments. Would it be people suffering from the particular illness or disability, or the medical profession, or members of the public? It could be argued that only people who live with a condition can judge its effect on their quality of life, although if a person has been disabled from birth, it may be difficult for them to judge how life with their disability compares to life without. Doctors and members of the public may be able to speculate about the relative inconvenience or distress caused by a range of disabilities, especially if they have experience of caring for someone with a disabling condition, but they do so from a position of relative ignorance.

Moreover, quality of life judgements are inevitably subjective, whereas the QALY scales are supposed to be objective. I might think that depression would be worse than chronic back pain, whereas you might think the opposite. QALY weightings are also arbitrary: they suggest that living for ten years with a quality of life score of 0.9 is equivalent to living for nine years in perfect health. In practice, many of us might prefer a longer life, even if we have to put up with a minor health complaint. At the other extreme, some of us might regard one year of perfect health (1×1), as preferable to spending ten years at death's door (10×0.1), whereas the QALY scale suggests that there is nothing to choose between them.

Using QALYs at the macro level is less problematic, because it would simply involve deciding that treatment X, in general, leads to better patient outcomes, at lower cost, than treatment Y. As John Harris explains, it is at the micro level, when choices have to be made between individual patients, that taking QALYs into account is invidious.

John Harris[51]

There are two ways in which QALYs might be used. One is unexceptionable and useful, and fully in line with the assumptions which give QALYs their plausibility. The other is none of these.

QALYs might be used to determine which of rival therapies to give to a particular patient or which procedure to use to treat a particular condition. Clearly the one generating the most QALYs will be the better bet, both for the patient and for a society with scarce resources. . . .

But whereas it follows from the fact that given the choice a person would prefer a shorter, healthier life to a longer one of severe discomfort, that the best treatment for that person is the one yielding the most QALYs, it does not follow that treatments yielding more QALYs are preferable to treatments yielding fewer QALYs where different people are to receive the treatments. That is to say, while it follows from the fact (if it is a fact) that I and everyone else would prefer to have, say, one year of healthy life rather than three years of severe discomfort, that we value healthy existence more than uncomfortable existence for ourselves, it does not follow that where the choice is between three years of discomfort for me or immediate death on the one hand, and one year of health for you or immediate death on the other, that I am somehow committed to the judgement that you ought to be saved rather than me.

51 'QALYfying the value of life' (1987) 13 Journal of Medical Ethics 117–23, 118.

(b) A wide or narrow interpretation of cost-effectiveness?

When health economists engage in cost-effectiveness analysis of medical treatments, they tend to judge 'effectiveness' according to the extent to which a treatment produces a clinical benefit. It would, however, be possible to broaden the scope of these calculations in several ways.

First, it has been estimated that health services affect only about 10 per cent of the principal indices for measuring health (such as infant mortality, absences through sickness, and life expectancy), while 90 per cent are determined by other factors, such as environment, nutrition, and lifestyle.[52] Could it therefore be argued that the cost-effectiveness of new medical technologies should be judged not only against other medical treatments, but also against social measures, which might in fact lead to greater improvements in health at lower cost? Eliminating child poverty, for example, would be likely to have a dramatic—and quite possibly cost-effective—impact upon health; yet raising welfare payments to poor families does not have the same popular appeal as heroic medical interventions to cure the sick.

In order to engage in a cost–benefit calculation, it is also, of course, necessary to work out what counts as a benefit. Are we concerned only with the health benefit to the patient, or might it be legitimate to take into account other benefits from her successful treatment? Enabling employees to return to work has clear social and economic benefits that, if included in the cost–benefit calculation, might lead us to give priority to the treatment of adults of working age, or to those in full-time employment, or even to those who do especially valuable jobs. Should we take into account whether a patient has dependent children who will benefit from her recovery? In deciding what priority substance abuse treatment programmes should receive, is it relevant that successfully treating drug addiction will not only improve the individual addict's life, but also that of her family and the community in which she lives?

Jonathan Glover argues that, while normally judging patients' social value would be invidious, it will sometimes be legitimate to take into account benefits to third parties, such as dependent children, when deciding which patient to treat.

Jonathan Glover[53]

If there are two people whose lives are in question and we have to choose to save only one, the number of people dependent on them should be regarded as very important. If other things are equal, but one has no family and the other is the mother of several young children, the case against deciding between them randomly is a strong one . . . Refusal to depart from random choice when knowledge about their dependents is available is to place no value on avoiding the additional misery caused to the children if the mother is not the one saved . . .

If we give some weight to the interests of dependents, should we take into account more generalized side effects, such as the relative importance of the contributions to society made by different people? There are good grounds for rejecting this as a general policy. It is a truism that we have no agreed standard by which to measure people's relative contribution to society. How does a mother compare with a doctor or a research scientist or a coal-miner? Any list of jobs ranked in order of social value seems, at least at present, to be arbitrary and debatable. It also seems to introduce the offensive division of people into grades.

---

[52] David J Hunter, *Desperately Seeking Solutions: Rationing Health Care* (Longman: London, 1997) 18.
[53] *Causing Death and Saving Lives* (Penguin: London, 1977) 222–3.

In contrast, John Harris argues that prioritizing those with dependants amounts to offensive discrimination against the childless and friendless.

John Harris[54]

[T]he feeling that it is somehow more important to rescue those with dependents, when elevated to the level of policy, amounts to a systematic preference of those with families over those without . . . Dependence . . . is not simply dependence on parents, and grief and misery are not confined to family relationships. But even if they were, it is unclear that they would constitute adequate reasons for preferring to save one person rather than another. We should not forget that while the bereaved deserve sympathy, by far the greatest loss is to the deceased, and the misfortune of her friends and relations pales into insignificance besides the tragedy to the individual who must die. It seems as obviously offensive systematically to inflict this loss on the childless, and perhaps the friendless, as it would be to grade people in any other way.

Finally, if systematic family preference became overt public policy, it might begin to seem that a relatively cheap form of insurance against a low-priority rating in the rescue stakes would be the acquisition of a family.

It could further be argued that it would in practice be impossible to calculate the wider benefits of treating an individual. How could doctors be expected to predict accurately their patients' likely contribution to society? It might be simple to find out whether a patient has young children, but not all parents actually support and love their children, and some childless people make a hugely positive contribution to children's lives. Giving priority to patients whose loss might cause tangible harm to other people would involve time-consuming and intrusive investigations.

It is also possible that bias, prejudice, and stereotyping might creep into these judgements. Offering priority to people in high-skilled employment may benefit the country as a whole, but it might also turn out to be indirectly discriminatory. On the other hand, where particular types of care, such as treating people for addiction, are likely to have enormously beneficial effects for society, it seems less obviously unjust to use this as an additional reason for diverting funds to this type of treatment. Taking these broader purposes into account when setting health care priorities does not involve claiming that certain people's lives are more valuable than others. Dan Brock therefore argues that taking into account indirect non-health benefits can be legitimate at a macro level, where it does not involve discriminating against particular individuals on account of their relative usefulness.

Dan W Brock[55]

As a rough generalization and all other things being equal, the higher level a macro health care resource allocation or prioritization decision, the more defensible it is to give weight to the indirect non health benefits and costs of alternative resource uses in health care. The closer to micro level choices by health professionals between the needs of their individual patients, the stronger the case that these indirect non health benefits and costs should be ignored on grounds of fairness.

---

54 *The Value of Life* (Routledge: London, 1985) 104–6.
55 Dan Brock, 'Separate spheres and indirect benefits' (2003) 1 Cost Effectiveness and Resource Allocation 4.

While agreeing that social-utilitarian considerations should normally be disregarded, Beauchamp and Childress argue that in an emergency it may be legitimate to take an individual's social worth into account when rationing treatment.

Tom Beauchamp and James Childress[56]

[J]udgements of comparative social worth are inescapable and acceptable in some situations. For example, in an earthquake when some injured survivors are medical personnel who suffer only minor injuries, they justifiably receive priority of treatment if they are needed to help others. Similarly, in an outbreak of infectious disease, it is justifiable to inoculate physicians and nurses first to enable them to care for others. Under such conditions, a person may receive priority for treatment on grounds of social utility if and only if his or her contribution is indispensable to attaining a major social goal. As in analogous lifeboat cases, we should limit judgements of comparative social value to the specific qualities and skills that are essential to the community's immediate protection without assessing the general social worth of persons. If we limit exceptions based on social utility to emergencies involving necessity, they do not threaten the ordinary moral universe or imply the general acceptability of social-utilitarian calculations in distributing health care.

(4) Age

Is it ever acceptable to take into account a patient's age when rationing treatment? We can quickly dismiss the argument that, because they are more likely to suffer from multiple co-morbidities, treating older people might be less cost-effective. It is unfair to make assumptions about older people's frailty; some elderly individuals are extremely fit and active. While age may be one variable that affects prognosis, it is by no means the only or even the most important one. To use sweeping generalizations about a large and diverse section of the population in order to ration services would be arbitrary and unjust.

A more plausible argument in favour of age-based rationing is that an older person is more likely to have had a 'fair innings'. As John Harris explains:

What the fair innings argument needs to do is capture and express in a workable form the truth that while it is always a misfortune to die when one wants to go on living, it is not a tragedy to die in old age; but it is on the other hand, both a tragedy and a misfortune to be cut off prematurely.[57]

But while it is trite to observe that dying in old age is not as tragic as premature death, Harris is clear that this does not justify age discrimination in the distribution of health care resources.

---

[56] *Principles of Biomedical Ethics*, 6th edn (OUP: Oxford, 2008).
[57] John Harris, *The Value of Life* (Routledge: London, 1985) 93.

John Harris[58]

> The systematic disvaluing of the old or those with life-threatening illness might have a corrosive effect on social morality and community relations more generally. It might, for example, lead to an increasing tolerance of the idea that any and all resources, or even care, devoted to the old or those with life-threatening disease was a waste of time, money, and emotion. . . .
>
>   Moreover, once the old, however defined, had been ruled out of account, the middle-aged would become the old. They would after all have greater elapsed time 'in the bank' and shorter life expectancy ahead than the rest of society and the cycle of argument and discrimination would have a tendency to extend indefinitely, a tendency moreover that would be difficult to restrain.

(5) Individual Responsibility for Ill Health?

Many conditions are caused or exacerbated by a patient's own behaviour. Should this be relevant when allocating scarce resources? If an individual is responsible for creating her own need for health care services, should she bear the cost of her treatment, or be a lower priority for NHS care? On the one hand, it might be argued that making access to treatment depend upon whether someone is responsible for her illness could provide a powerful incentive towards healthy behaviour. On the other hand, if the prospect of poor health and premature death does not dissuade someone from engaging in unhealthy activities, it is hardly likely that being a lower priority for NHS care will do so.

  Some commentators, such as Robert Blank, have nevertheless suggested that it is fair and just to take individual responsibility into account when rationing scarce resources:

> [P]eople who try to take care of themselves are helping underwrite the costs incurred by those who fail to do so. Understandably, there is an increasingly vocal demand to shift the monetary burden to those individuals who knowingly take the health risks . . . Considerable initiative for these actions comes from distaste at having to pay for someone else's bad habits.[59]

In practice, however, it would probably be impossible to devise a fair system for attributing responsibility for ill health. First, the obvious examples of smokers, alcoholics, and drug abusers may not attract much public sympathy, but these are not the only sorts of behaviour which may adversely affect one's health. Should we also penalize cyclists whose head injuries were the result of not wearing a helmet; skin cancer sufferers who sunbathed too much when they were young; athletes with sporting injuries; people with type 2 diabetes who used to eat a lot of junk food? The list of people who may have contributed to their own need for health care services is potentially endless.

---

[58] 'The age-indifference principle and equality' (2005) 14 Cambridge Quarterly of Healthcare Ethics 93–9.
[59] Robert Blank, *Rationing Medicine* (Columbia UP: New York, 1988) 199–200.

Secondly, it is questionable whether unhealthy behaviour is always the result of deliberate choice. Very few people actively choose to become alcoholics or drug addicts. Indeed, alcoholism is increasingly regarded as a disease, which may even be triggered by genetic factors that are outside a person's control.[60]

Thirdly, as we see later, smoking, drug use, and poor diet tend to correlate with socio-economic status, hence penalizing people with unhealthy lifestyles would in practice mean that priority for health care services is given to the richest and healthiest sections of society.

Fourthly, at the individual level, it is seldom possible to isolate a single causal factor for ill health. The fact that someone leads a sedentary lifestyle may have contributed to his need for a heart bypass operation, but there are other possible causes. Commonly, genetic predisposition and environmental and lifestyle factors interact with each other to increase someone's susceptibility to a particular disease.

While penalizing patients for their poor health might operate unfairly or be impracticable, it could be argued that someone who costs the NHS a great deal of money as a result of her diet or lifestyle, should take responsibility for the fact that her behaviour has an opportunity cost for others. NHS resources are finite and if someone uses up more than their fair share—perhaps because they get very drunk every Saturday night and routinely end up in their local accident and emergency department, or because they eat so much junk food that they become morbidly obese—there is less left in the 'pot' for other people.

HM Evans, for example, maintains that a sense of social responsibility should persuade us not to squander public resources and disregard the needs of others.

HM Evans[61]

> Public provision of this sort involves mutual benefit and mutual participation: so my own medical treatment is, whatever else it is, liable to be an opportunity cost (however justifiable) in terms of the healthcare needs of others requiring comparable treatment at the time when I am treated. Both in general, and in the specific context of public healthcare provision, I have at least a prima facie moral responsibility to take other people's interests seriously; this implies that I ought not to incur opportunity costs to others avoidably, recklessly or excessively . . .
>
> Second, and as a result, the interests of my 'competitor' co-patients produce in me not merely the negative duties of avoiding either uncivil behaviour or needless waste, but also, provocatively, positive duties to promote my own health and, in the case of illness, to recover as quickly as possible.

The NHS Constitution adopts this approach. It does not advocate the denial of care to people who are responsible for their need for treatment; instead it lists taking care of one's health as one of the obligations patients acquire in return for their rights to NHS care: 'Please recognise that you can make a significant contribution to your own, and your family's, good health and wellbeing, and take personal responsibility for it.'[62]

---

[60] DM Dick and LJ Bierut, 'The genetics of alcohol dependency' (2006) 8 Current Psychiatric Reports 151–7.
[61] 'Do patients have duties?' (2007) 33 Journal of Medical Ethics 689–94.
[62] The NHS Constitution: The NHS Belongs to Us All (DH: London, 2015).

(6) Relevance of Public Opinion

(a) In setting priorities

What role should public opinion play in setting priorities within the NHS? On the one hand, the NHS is funded through taxation, and used by virtually everyone in the country, and so the public, as both taxpayers and service users, has an interest in the distribution of NHS resources. Because depriving citizens of medical treatment on cost grounds is so controversial and potentially divisive, it might also be important to seek public agreement with the principles that inform rationing decisions.

On the other hand, there may be disadvantages in relying too heavily on public opinion. Why should the public have any say over whether treatment for schizophrenia is more or less of a priority than orthopaedic surgery, for example? There is evidence that the public tends to prioritize 'sympathetic' patient groups, such as sick children, and be less keen on funding treatment for drug addicts or people with mental illnesses. 'Rationing by opinion poll' might leave addiction and mental illness inadequately treated, and this would be likely to have negative consequences not only for untreated patients, but also for society as a whole.

In the next extract, Bill New and Julian Le Grand point out that respondents to one-off public opinion surveys are ill-equipped to make complex rationing decisions.

Bill New and Julian Le Grand[63]

[E]ven if perfectly representative samples of the public can be consulted, the legitimacy of their having a direct influence on resource allocation and rationing will still be deeply problematic. The outcome of such exercises will reflect majority opinion and, although it is hard to be sure what that opinion would be, it is likely that the interests of very old, infirm, mentally ill or disabled people will be neglected in favour of the concerns of the majority. High-technology rescue or repair medicine, for example, can easily be conceived as immediately relevant to us all. Furthermore, it is simply naïve to suppose that the lay public have the requisite knowledge to make many decisions which are of a complex, technical nature . . .

Political decision-making—and that is what rationing decisions are—must be open to challenge, scrutiny and debate, and those who make the decisions must bear the responsibility for and deal with the consequences of those decisions . . . Why, for example, should members of the public make considered judgements when they do not face the prospect of being challenged on them, nor of answering for any unfavourable consequences? Accountability would, under these circumstances, be weakened.

(b) The acceptability of incentives

One issue where the question of how much weight we should give to public opinion has been brought into sharp focus is the use of incentives. The problem can be simply stated. If (and this is currently a fairly big 'if') there is clear and compelling evidence that offering financial incentives to people to stop smoking or lose weight would be cost-effective for the NHS, how much weight should we give to the fact that a majority of the public appears to disapprove strongly of this sort of scheme?

In favour of incentives, it is sometimes argued that people would generally prefer not to smoke or be morbidly obese, but the short-term pleasures of smoking and eating chips

63 *Rationing in the NHS: Principles and Pragmatism* (King's Fund, 1996).

make it difficult for them to give up their unhealthy behaviour. Providing a financial reward then helps to align the unhealthy person's short-term interests with her longer term preferences and best interests. Because smoking, drug use, and obesity impose enormous costs on the NHS, it is possible that modest financial incentives could be a cost-effective use of NHS resources. In the next extract, Promberger et al consider how we should balance this with evidence that the public believes that paying drug users, smokers, and obese people 'rewards bad behaviour' and is unfair to those who behave healthily without being 'bribed'.

Marianne Promberger et al[64]

There are several possible reasons why people may find financial incentives less acceptable. It may stem from a violation of a cultural norm, namely the use of money in the relationship between a doctor or healthcare provider and a patient. . . . The perceived unacceptability of financial incentives in the current context may also stem from a marked sense of injustice about offering money, a fungible good, to those who, through their own behaviour, might have avoided this. . . .

Rejection of incentive schemes by the general public could all too easily be seen by politicians as a reason not to introduce them. This conclusion does not follow from our findings. To answer the question as to whether or not incentive schemes should be introduced would require more evidence on their consequences, intended and unintended, as well as in-depth analysis of the associated ethical issues of using incentives in healthcare. . . . It may be the case that the results reported here stem from prejudice and illegitimate value judgements, and should thus not be reflected in policy decisions . . .

Even if a residual disutility for incentives in health contexts stubbornly persists, benefits may be great enough to justify overriding such concerns. At the other extreme, opposition to 'rewarding bad behaviour' might translate into the very tangible consequence of corroding the goodwill, and eroding the good behaviour, of those not rewarded for their virtue.

(7) Ability to Pay

A free market in health care would replace rationing with market forces. People would be free to purchase health care, either at the point of use or through insurance, and services would be available only if there was consumer demand for them. In their favour, market forces might deter inappropriate use of health care services: many of us would make less profligate use of GP services if we were charged £100 per visit. Against this, there are many reasons why a free market in medical treatment is an unattractive proposition.

Most importantly, there would always be people who were unable to afford treatment or insurance, and who would therefore experience unnecessary pain, or die preventable deaths, if society was not prepared to cover the costs of their care. Our consumption of health care resources is generally concentrated in our last years of life, when we are least able to generate additional income. Even allowing for the pooling of risk via insurance, there is an inverse correlation between socioeconomic status and good health. Insurance premiums are set according to risk rather than wealth, so in a free market the cost of insurance would be lowest for the richest and healthiest, and highest for those who are very ill and/or very poor.

---

[64] 'Acceptability of financial incentives to improve health outcomes in UK and US samples' (2011) 37 Journal of Medical Ethics 682–7.

Secondly, although charges might stop people from seeing their GP when there is nothing much wrong with them, people often do not know in advance if their symptoms are trivial or significant. In practice, using charges to discourage the use of services is likely to reduce the chance of early diagnosis, which in turn may make treatment more expensive. As Jeremiah Hurley explains, charging people for health care may turn out to be inefficient and costly.

Jeremiah Hurley[65]

Reduced consumption of effective preventive and therapeutic care can cause people to develop wholly preventable conditions or allow mild conditions to become more serious and expensive to treat than they would be if they were caught early. The ultimate costs to the public health care system across the full range of health services can actually increase as a result of user charges. Limiting the magnitude of user charges in an attempt to reduce these adverse effects unfortunately also limits their revenue potential. Further, equity concerns dictate that low-income individuals either be exempt from charges or be liable for a maximum amount of annual out-of-pocket expenditure. Such provisions require costly administrative mechanisms to assess eligibility and to track expenditures against any specified expenditure limits, and the associated administrative costs can substantially reduce the net revenue gain to the public insurer. In the end, when all effects are properly counted, real financial savings to the system often end up far less than promised.

Thirdly, in general patients do not choose medical treatment, in the same way as they might choose to purchase other goods and services. A free market is supposed to work because consumers are able to exercise choice over their spending: they will only buy those goods or services which they want, and they can select providers who best meet their needs. Patients are unlike purchasers of other consumer goods, however. Efficient markets depend upon informed and discerning consumers, but there is a fundamental information imbalance in the doctor–patient relationship, and patients are unable to exercise much control (other than the straightforward right of refusal) over which treatments they receive.

Fourthly, because few people could afford to pay for acute medical treatment as they need it, and no one would want to face the additional stress of trying to borrow money when they are seriously ill, a free market in health care would tend to operate through insurance. And there are a number of additional specific problems that arise from using private insurance to cover the costs of health care:

- Some health risks will be uninsurable. Many insurance policies exclude certain conditions, such as self-inflicted injuries, drug abuse, HIV/AIDS, or major epidemics. Very elderly people or those with serious conditions may find it very difficult or even impossible to purchase health insurance. There would therefore have to be a state-funded safety net to cover the treatment of risks which private insurance companies choose to exclude from their policies. Thus, the problem of rationing publicly funded care remains.

- When risks are pooled through insurance, low-risk patients will often be charged premiums that appear to be higher than their anticipated benefits, and they may therefore decide not to bother purchasing insurance. As a result, high-risk individuals' premiums will be even higher, and may become unaffordable, thus increasing the proportion

---

[65] 'User charges for health care services: some further thoughts' (2013) 8 Health Economics, Policy and Law 537–41.

of the population that is uninsured and dependent, once again, on the publicly funded safety net.

- Because insurance insulates the patient from the real costs of care, it encourages people to make more use of medical services than they would in a straightforward free market.

- Insurance schemes also tend to give health care providers an incentive to over-treat, and thus waste resources for no additional health gain.

- Finally, the administration costs of a system in which there are multiple private insurers are significantly higher than those of state-run systems. The US spends much more than any other developed country on health, but Americans are not healthier than residents of European countries which spend half as much on their health services. In 2010, the Commonwealth Fund ranked different health care systems. The UK was the most efficient, while the US, despite continuing to spend much more than any other country, 'ranks last or next-to-last on all five dimensions of a high performance health system'.[66]

In the next extract, James Meek spells out some of the downsides of the US insurance-based system.

James Meek[67]

But just paying a premium each month doesn't make healthcare free at the point of delivery. Two standard features of US health insurance are the 'copay', a fee for consultations or drugs, and the 'deductible', an amount the patient is expected to pay before the insurance kicks in, like the excess on car insurance. The lower the premiums, the higher the copays and deductible. Kaiser's Copayment 25 Plan, for instance, costs $487 a month for a 48-year-old living in San Francisco; that's a high premium, and there's no deductible. But every time you see the doctor, you have to pay $25; an ambulance is $100, a month's supply of branded prescription drugs $35; you have to contribute $200 a day for a hospital stay, and so on up to a maximum of $2500 a year. At the other end of the scale, there's a plan that costs $169 a month. That's a bargain if you don't get sick or pregnant (maternity isn't covered). But if you're ill, you have to pay the first $5000 out of your own pocket. After that the copays kick in—$50 to see the doctor, and for hospital treatment, 30 per cent of the actual cost—until you've forked out $7500. As for prescription drugs, you're on your own. . . .

A Harvard-led study found that 62 per cent of all bankruptcies in the United States in 2007 were due to medical bills, an increase of 50 per cent in six years. Most of those affected were well-educated, middle-class homeowners. Astonishingly, three-quarters had had their finances destroyed by medical costs even though they had insurance. In a significant number of cases, it was paying to look after a sick child that bankrupted parents.

Rationing according to the patient's ability to pay might appear to be fundamentally incompatible with the NHS's founding principle that health care should be free at the point of delivery, but it should be noted there are already some health services which are routinely provided in the private sector. Very few adults receive free dental or optical care. Most fertility treatment is provided privately. Working adults in England must pay the prescription charge, and people who need long-term social care often have to contribute towards its cost.

---

[66] Karen Davis, Cathy Schoen, and Kristof Stremikis, *How the Performance of the US Health Care System Compares Internationally: 2010 Update* (Commonwealth Fund: New York, 2010).

[67] 'It's already happened: the NHS goes private' (2011) 33 London Review of Books 3–10.

In 2006, the Health Select Committee looked at the issue of charging in the NHS, and its conclusion was that the 'system of health charges in England is a mess'.

Health Select Committee[68]

Charges for prescriptions and dentistry have been in place for over 50 years and sight tests for almost 20 years. They have not been introduced following detailed analysis of their likely consequences; rather they have come about piecemeal, often in response to the need to raise money. There are no comprehensible underlying principles. The charges remain largely for 'historical' reasons. In recent years, hospital patients and their visitors have also had to pay increasing sums for non-clinical services, such as car parking . . .

There are exemptions, which aim to mitigate the negative effects of charges . . . [But] the system of exemptions is full of anomalies. . . . The system of medical exemptions to the prescription charge is particularly confusing. People with diabetes who require insulin receive free medicines for all conditions while people with diabetes controlled by diet must pay for all their medication.

An increasing proportion of the services routinely provided by the NHS can be purchased privately, and private patients will usually be treated more quickly. Approximately 12 per cent of the UK population is covered by private medical insurance, and people without insurance may choose to pay directly for elective treatment. Although it is by no means the norm, this is clearly rationing according to ability to pay rather than need.

It is also important to remember that a parallel private sector is not a simple 'add-on' to the NHS. Instead, the two interact with each other. The NHS subsidizes the private sector through allowing its employees to carry out private treatment within NHS hospitals, and by permitting NHS consultants to maintain private practices. For some years, NHS trusts have increased capacity by purchasing private sector care for their patients.[69] As we have seen, the Health and Social Care Act 2012 bolsters the private sector's ability to compete for NHS business, and allows NHS Foundation Trusts to increase their income from private patients.

(8) Defining a Package of Care

Another way to ration medical treatment might be to set limits upon which treatments will be funded by the state. A core package of essential services would be provided free of charge, but non-essential services might only be available privately. Rationing policies that exclude particular treatments are open and transparent, and ensure that patients understand the limits of what they can expect from the public health service.

In some other countries, there have been explicit attempts to devise packages of health care services, but these have not been overwhelmingly successful. In New Zealand, the Core Services Committee could not find any treatment or area of service within the current range of provision that could be completely excluded. So, 'in something of an anti-climax, the Committee recommended that "core" be defined as being what was already being provided prior to the reforms'.[70]

---

[68] Third Report 2005/6, available at www.publications.parliament.uk.

[69] Christopher Newdick, *Who Should We Treat? Rights, Rationing and Resources in the NHS*, 2nd edn (OUP: Oxford, 2005) 233.

[70] M Cooper, 'Core Services and the New Zealand Health Reforms' in R Maxwell (ed), *Rationing Health Care* (Churchill Livingstone: London, 1995) 799–807, 805.

Some health authorities in the UK have specified that they will not fund certain procedures such as tattoo removal and sterilization reversal. The reason for identifying low-priority interventions and excluding them from NHS coverage is not that such treatments are ineffective, or that they are a significant drain on NHS resources. In fact, tattoo removal and sterilization reversal cost very little compared with the maintenance of acute health services. A refusal to fund certain procedures may help to clarify what it is reasonable to expect from the NHS, but it will not solve the funding crisis.

Moreover, blanket exclusions are likely to be unfair and unlawful. Tattoo removal may seem trivial, but what if a person was tattooed while he was a prisoner of war? Fairness demands that a ban on funding for marginal procedures can accommodate exceptional cases.

(9) Rationing by Dilution

Rationing by dilution involves offering less care than is ideal; perhaps by carrying out fewer diagnostic tests, or by spending less time with patients. Rationing by delay means that patients have to wait to be treated, perhaps by waiting for an appointment with their GP, or by being put on a waiting list for hospital treatment. Delays in treating patients may reduce demand because some patients will get better while waiting to see a doctor, while others might die.

As Donald Light explains, health services in the UK continue to be available to everyone, but few get immediate access to the best possible treatment.

Donald Light[71]

The NHS already rations on a massive scale. The NHS rations by delay to get on waiting lists, and then on the waiting lists themselves, and then with the further wait after an appointment has been made. It rations by undersupply of staff, doctors, machines, facilities, etc; by undercapitalisation of run down facilities; by dilution of tests done and services received; by discharge earlier than desirable; and by outright denial to even the chance to wait or be undertreated.

McPake et al argue that queuing should be regarded as a rationing device, whereby treatment is rationed 'on the basis of the patient's willingness to allocate time in order to receive a service', but it is, they argue, 'an inefficient and inappropriate rationing mechanism' because its true purpose will generally be to maximize 'the efficiency with which health professionals' time is used', rather than to ensure fair distribution of health care.[72] Alan Williams further argues that a narrow focus on the economic costs of health care misses the fact that there are other costs, such as patients' time, which is currently 'used profligately by the system, as any "free" resource would be'.[73] There is a 'cost' incurred when a patient has to wait for four hours in A&E, but this cost is borne by the patient herself and hence is marginalized in debates about the rationing of NHS resources.

---

[71] Donald W Light, 'The real ethics of rationing' (1997) 315 British Medical Journal 112–15.

[72] Barbara McPake, Lilani Kumaranayake, and Charles Normand, *Health Economics: An International Perspective* (Routledge: London, 2002) 204.

[73] Rudolf Klein and Alan Williams, 'Setting Priorities: What is Holding us Back—Inadequate Information or Inadequate Institutions?' in Angela Coulter and Chris Ham (eds), *The Global Challenge of Healthcare Rationing* (Open UP: Buckingham, 2000) 15–26, 18.

(c) RATIONING IN THE NHS: THE ROLE OF NICE

The National Institute for Health and Care Excellence (NICE) was set up in 1999,[74] in part to make resource allocation decisions in the NHS more explicit and transparent and to address the problem of the 'postcode lottery'. There are a number of different types of NICE guidance, some of which—like its public health and clinical practice guidance—is not mandatory: an example would be its 2015 guideline on preventing dementia which instructs 'Public Health England, NHS England, relevant national third-sector organisations and health and social care commissioners' that they should: 'Make it clear that some common unhealthy behaviours can increase the risk of dementia and that addressing those behaviours will reduce the likelihood of developing dementia and other non-communicable chronic conditions.'[75]

NICE plays a central role in rationing in the UK through its technology appraisals, which assess the clinical and cost-effectiveness of medicines and other treatments in order to determine whether they should be funded by the NHS. CCGs are under an obligation to fund NICE-approved treatments within three months.

(1) NICE's Cost-Effectiveness Appraisals

NICE's appraisals can recommend: (a) the treatment's unrestricted use in the NHS; (b) its restricted or 'optimized' use in a subset of patients only; (c) its use to be confined to clinical trials; or (d) that it should not be used in the NHS. Of the 567 technology appraisals carried out by NICE between 1 March 2000 and 30 September 2015, 62 per cent involved straight-forward approval; 18 per cent of decisions were that the treatment should be available only in certain circumstances; 5 per cent permitted the use of the treatment but only in research; and in 15 per cent of cases, the guidance was that the treatment should not be provided.[76]

NICE's decision-making process is undoubtedly open and transparent: all of NICE's appraisals are available on its website and, before decisions are finalized, there is an opportunity for 'stakeholders'—such as patient groups and the medical profession—to comment upon its draft conclusions. There is also a right of appeal for interested groups, such as drugs manufacturers.

NICE has been open about its use of QALYs, although it has also been clear that they are not the only relevant factor. According to NICE, the general threshold for affordability in the NHS is approximately £20,000 per QALY. If treatments costing less than £20,000 are not to be recommended, reasons should be given; perhaps because there are limitations to the evidence for effectiveness. For treatments which cost between £20,000 and £30,000 per QALY, NICE will consider whether there are considerations which justify recommending the technology, such as the particular needs of the patient group. Costs of more than £30,000 per QALY are generally not acceptable, unless there are other compelling factors in favour of its recommendation.

Researchers at the University of York evaluated NICE's appraisals and found that the NICE's QALY threshold was significantly greater than that of the majority of non-NICE approved treatments within the NHS, which they calculated to be about £13,000 per QALY.[77]

---

[74] Although the acronym has remained the same, NICE's name has changed twice: with first the insertion of the word 'health', and then in 2013 'clinical' was changed to 'care' in order to accommodate NICE's role in providing social care guidance.

[75] NICE, *Dementia, disability and frailty in later life—mid-life approaches to delay or prevent onset* (NICE, 2015).

[76] See further nice.org.uk/news/nice-statistics.

[77] Karl Claxton et al, 'Methods for the estimation of the National Institute for Health and Care Excellence cost-effectiveness threshold' (2015) 19 Health Technology Assessment 14.

They also found that, in fact, NICE routinely approved treatments which cost significantly more than £30,000 per QALY. As a result of both these findings, as Hawkes explains, Claxton et al's study found that NICE appraisals have considerable opportunity costs for other NHS patients.

Nigel Hawkes[78]

NHS outcomes would be better if it refused to fund any drug that cost more than £13000 per quality adjusted life year (QALY). NICE says that its threshold is between £20000 and £30000 per QALY, but on average, Claxton said, the institute approves drugs that cost £40000 per QALY and sometimes as high as £50000.

The York team set out to discover how much a QALY was worth on average across the NHS, by comparing the money spent in 23 different disease areas with the outcomes achieved. . . . The results, . . . showed that in the NHS in England as a whole the average cost per QALY was £12936, a result that showed that the NHS was 'really good value,' Claxton said. This was far below the NICE threshold, meaning that every drug with a cost per QALY greater than that was taking money from other services that could use it more effectively. Outcomes would improve, he said, if all NHS spending on drugs above this level ceased.

For every £10m spent on a new drug that cost £40000 per QALY, 250 QALYs would be gained, but 773 would be lost because the money spent would not be available for other services. The net harm would be 523 QALYs. The Cancer Drugs Fund [see the following section], which lacks any formal threshold, fares even worse. This year (2014–15) it will spend £280m, which will buy, the York team estimates, 4098 QALYs. But the health lost elsewhere will be 21645 QALYs—five times as much.

NICE's appraisals are carried out by scientific and clinical experts, but the views of the public are also taken into account via its Citizens Council. This is a representative sample of UK citizens, to whom questions are referred by NICE. The Citizens Council played an important part in the drawing up of *Social Value Judgements*, a document which sets out the social values which NICE adopts when making decisions. In the following extract, NICE sets out its approach to the questions of whether a person's age or their responsibility for their condition should be relevant.

National Institute for Health and Care Excellence[79]

6.3 Age

There is much debate over whether, or how, age should be taken into account when allocating healthcare resources. The Citizens Council considered that health should not be valued more highly in some age groups than in others; and that social roles at different ages should not affect decisions about cost effectiveness. They said, though, that where age is an indicator of benefit or risk, it can be taken into account.

---

[78] Nigel Hawkes, 'NICE is too generous in approving drugs, analysis says' (2015) 350 British Medical Journal h955.
[79] *Social Value Judgements*, 2nd edn (July 2008).

NICE's general principle is that patients should not be denied, or have restricted access to, NHS treatment simply because of their age. The Institute's guidance should refer to age only when one or more of the following apply.

- There is evidence that age is a good indicator for some aspect of patients' health status and/or the likelihood of adverse effects of the treatment.

- There is no practical way of identifying patients other than by their age (for example, there is no test available to measure their state of health in another way).

- There is good evidence, or good grounds for believing, that because of their age patients will respond differently to the treatment in question.

6.6 Behaviour-dependent conditions

The Citizens Council advised that NICE should not take into consideration whether or not a particular condition was self-induced. It was often impossible, in an individual, to decide whether the condition was dependent on their own behaviour or not; and receiving NHS care should not depend on whether people 'deserved' it or not.

NICE should not produce guidance that results in care being denied to patients with conditions that are, or may have been, dependent on their behaviour. However, if the behaviour is likely to continue and can make a treatment less clinically effective or cost effective, then it may be appropriate to take this into account.

(2) NICE and End-of-Life Medicines

NICE's QALY thresholds have meant that many drugs that are capable of extending the life of cancer patients for a relatively short period of time have been judged too expensive. As a result, in January 2009, NICE issued supplementary guidance, to apply to patients with less than two years to live, where the medicine is capable of extending life by at least three months. In such cases, and provided the estimates of life expectancy are robust, the Appraisals Committee is invited to give 'greater weight to QALYs achieved in the later stages of terminal diseases'.

National Institute for Health and Clinical Excellence[80]

2 Criteria for appraisal of end of life treatments

2.1 This supplementary advice should be applied in the following circumstances and when all the criteria referred to below are satisfied:

2.1.1 The treatment is indicated for patients with a short life expectancy, normally less than 24 months and;

2.1.2 There is sufficient evidence to indicate that the treatment offers an extension to life, normally of at least an additional 3 months, compared to current NHS treatment, and;

2.1.3 The treatment is licensed or otherwise indicated, for small patient populations.

---

[80] *Appraising Life-Extending, End of Life Treatments* (NICE, 2009).

Wider access to expensive cancer drugs may appear to be good for patients, but, as Raftery points out, making exceptions for some patient groups will have an opportunity cost for others.

James Raftery[81]

The main attraction of the cost per QALY measure is its universal applicability. Making an exception for any group—such as, life-extending treatments for terminally ill patients—limits that universality and sets a precedent for other groups. In addition, setting the threshold higher for some groups within a fixed overall budget results in other patient groups being denied treatment.

Marissa Collins and Nicholas Latimer estimated that this new guidance cost the NHS an additional £549 million in its first two years alone.

Marissa Collins and Nicholas Latimer[82]

Between January 2009 and December 2011, NICE's appraisal committee discussed 24 interventions to determine if they met the end of life criteria. Fourteen interventions met the criteria, of which nine were approved for NHS use . . . The additional cost to the NHS of providing the new interventions analysed between 2009 and 2011 is over £549m a year.

Our analysis shows that use of NICE's end of life criteria has resulted in substantial QALY losses. We have assumed that the cost of end of life drugs is met entirely through displacement of other services or treatments in the NHS. Although we do not know whether this has been the case, as the NHS budget is under increasing strain, it seems reasonable to assume that disinvestment will be required. To put the losses into context, the £549m that we estimated has been spent on the nine end of life treatments each year is more than the £505m it cost to provide dialysis for the 21 544 patients with kidney failure in England in 2009.

In addition to NICE's special end-of-life criteria, in 2011 the government set up a new cancer drugs fund (CDF). The CDF was intended to make an additional £280 million available each year to cover drugs not (yet) approved by NICE, or where NICE had recommended only restricted access.[83]

It might be thought that the public would be likely to support the priority given to end-of-life drugs in general, and cancer drugs in particular, but Linley and Hughes' survey of 4,118 adults did not bear this out, finding instead that respondents would prioritize treatments for severe or untreatable conditions.

---

[81] 'NICE and the challenge of cancer drugs' (2009) 338 British Medical Journal 67.

[82] 'NICE's end of life decision making scheme: impact on population health' (2013) 346 British Medical Journal f1363.

[83] Department of Health, *The Cancer Drugs Fund: Guidance to Support Operation of the Cancer Drugs Fund in 2011–12* (DH: London, 2011) para 4.1.

Warren G Linley and Dyfrig A Hughes[84]

Our study suggests, all else being equal, that severity of disease, diseases for which no other available treatments exist (representing unmet needs) and medicines that reduce reliance on informal carers (representing wider societal benefits) are supported by society as valid NHS resource prioritisation criteria . . .

Although disease severity and significant innovation were supported in our study, we observed no compelling evidence for the three other prioritisation criteria we explored (disadvantaged populations, children and patients at the end-of-life) . . .

On the basis of the anticipated annual costs (8000 QALYs) and returns (4000 QALYs) of the CDF, the government assumes society values health benefits to cancer patients at least twice as highly, all else being equal, than benefits to patients suffering other conditions. There was no robust empirical evidence in support of this assumption when the CDF was introduced and our study now provides empirical evidence to refute this assumption.

Alan Maynard and Karen Bloor are blunt in their criticism of the cancer drugs fund.

Alan Maynard and Karen Bloor[85]

This is an inequitable and inefficient scheme. It is inefficient because pharmaceuticals are financed regardless of whether they meet an appropriate cost-QALY threshold, subverting NICE processes. It is inequitable because it discriminates against other diseases which may be equally in need of additional funding. . . . Government continues to subvert the efficiency of technology appraisal work carried out by NICE in order to subsidise industry. Does this benefit the UK taxpayer and NHS patients? Or does government tacitly wish to tax the NHS with high pharmaceutical prices of sometimes inefficient drugs and, in so doing, increase the wealth of industry?

In 2015, the National Audit Office published an investigation into the cancer drugs fund's first five years of operation.[86] It found that the Department of Health had not collected data on the outcomes for patients who had received non-NICE approved drugs via the fund. It also found that the fund had spent £968 million, and that in 2013–14 and 2014–15 NHS England had overspent the allocated budget for the fund by 35 per cent, thus reducing the funds available for other treatments. The National Audit Office also reported that 51 per cent of patients whose treatment was funded by the CDF were receiving drugs that NICE had explicitly rejected as insufficiently cost-effective; others were receiving drugs that had not yet been appraised. Routine bypassing of NICE evaluations via the fund had, according to the National Audit Office, become part of 'mainstream cancer care'.

---

84 'Societal views on NICE, cancer drugs fund and value-based pricing criteria for prioritising medicines: a cross-sectional survey of 4118 adults in Great Britain' (2013) 22 Health Economics 948–64.

85 Alan Maynard and Karen Bloor, 'Regulation of the pharmaceutical industry: promoting health or protecting wealth?' (2015) 108 Journal of the Royal Society of Medicine 220–2.

86 National Audit Office, Investigation into the Cancer Drugs Fund (NAO, 2015).

National Audit Office[87]

> By the end of March 2015, 74,380 cancer patients had been approved to receive cancer drugs paid for by the Fund. The number of cancer patients approved for funding increased by about 30% each year between 2011–12 and 2014–15. Although the Fund was introduced as a temporary measure, it has become part of mainstream cancer services. In 2014–15, the number of patients approved for funding was about 19% of all cancer patients who started a new chemotherapy treatment.

The future of the CDF is uncertain. As the National Audit Office explains: 'All parties agree that the Fund is not sustainable in its current form.'[88] In 2015, NHS England proposed that the fund should become a 'managed access' fund. It would pay for promising new drugs, but only *before* NICE had appraised them. It would therefore no longer fund drugs that NICE had rejected as insufficiently cost-effective. At the time of writing, NHS England is consulting upon these proposals, with the aim of implementing new arrangements in 2016.

(3) 'Top-Up' Payments

Complex issues arise when a patient wants to continue to receive NHS care, but also wants to pay 'top-up' fees for a part of their care—an expensive cancer drug, for example—which NICE has not recommended for NHS provision. We can see examples of patients who did just this in the *Rogers* and the *Otley* cases, which we consider later in this chapter.

Until recently, the general principle was that a patient could not be an NHS patient and a private patient during the same course of treatment. This meant that some patients were told that if they wanted to pay for one aspect of their care privately, they must opt out altogether, and pay for all of their treatment themselves. Some patients might be able to find a few thousand pounds for an expensive new medicine, but very few would be able to pay for all of the costs of caring for them in hospital.

On the one hand, it seems unfair to banish a patient from the NHS just because she wishes to pay for a medicine that the NHS will not fund. On the other hand, permitting NHS patients to buy additional medicines means that the standard of care NHS patients receive may depend upon their ability to pay, which appears to contradict one of the NHS's founding principles.

In 2008, the first National Clinical Director for Cancer, Mike Richards, produced a report on access to medicines in the NHS, which directly considered the question of top-up fees. These should be permitted, Richards recommended, but only if the privately purchased medicine is administered separately, ideally in non-NHS premises. The Department of Health accepted Richards's recommendation that purchasing additional private services should not exclude a patient from receiving NHS care, and specified that the private treatment must be delivered separately, in order to avoid the NHS subsidizing private treatment.

Department of Health[89]

> 4.1 This guidance establishes that, where a patient opts to pay for private care, their entitlement to NHS services remains and may not be withdrawn.

---

[87] Ibid.   [88] Ibid.

[89] *Guidance on NHS Patients Who Wish to Pay for Additional Private Care—A Consultation* (DH: London, 2008).

4.2 Patients may pay for additional private healthcare while continuing to receive care from the NHS. However, in order to ensure that there is no risk of the NHS subsidising private care:

- Private and NHS care should be kept as clearly separate as possible.

- Private care should be carried out at a different time and place. A different place would include the facilities of a private healthcare provider, or part of an NHS organisation which has been designated for private care, including amenity beds.

Where an NHS hospital contains a private ward, it may be relatively easy—if clinically unnecessary—to move a patient to another part of the hospital for delivery of the privately purchased medicine. But not all NHS hospitals contain private facilities, and so, in order to avoid subjecting patients to unnecessary and disruptive journeys, areas in NHS hospitals can be designated as temporarily 'private' while the privately purchased medicine is provided. Essentially this means labelling one part of an NHS ward 'private' for a short period of time while an NHS patient receives the privately funded medication.

(4) NICE and Innovative Medicines

Between 2010 and 2014, the coalition government had signalled that it intended to change the way in which NICE worked, by moving to a system of 'value-based pricing', later described as 'value-based assessment'. The intention was to tweak QALY thresholds so that they are higher for medicines that treat diseases with a greater 'burden of illness', for example because of unmet need or particular severity, and for medicines that can demonstrate greater therapeutic innovation or wider societal benefits. The theory was that pharmaceutical companies would then orient their research towards medicines likely to produce the greatest value for patients, because value-based pricing would make them more profitable.

In practice, this is more complicated than the government had assumed, not least because evidence of a drug's value to patients will be patchy at launch. Evidence gathered after a medicine has been in use for a while may reveal that the initial assessment of the drug's value was wrong.[90] In addition, as Paulden et al point out, unless NICE also takes into account the opportunity cost to other patients of increasing the QALY threshold for some drugs, it would be valuing some patients' health more than others.

Mike Paulden et al[91]

NICE has repeatedly privileged the identified beneficiaries of treatment over those bearing the opportunity cost. As a result, NICE may recommend a treatment which displaces more QALYs than it gains in the very patients whose health it ostensibly values more. This may create the perception that NICE does not value the special value considerations per se, but only if doing so favours the adoption of a new technology. Such an approach would be ethically untenable as well as manifestly incompatible with NICE's previous basic equity position and the terms of reference provided by the Department of Health. This raises the broader issue of whether NICE's revealed values are defensible—specifically, valuing the health of some patients more than others.

[90] J Cairns, 'Providing guidance to the NHS: The Scottish Medicines Consortium and the National Institute for Clinical Excellence compared' (2006) 76 Health Policy 134–43.

[91] 'Some inconsistencies in NICE's consideration of social values' (2014) 32 PharmacoEconomics 1043–53.

Instead of moving to value-based assessment, NICE has decided that any changes to its methods 'need to be made as part of a wider review of the innovation, evaluation and adoption of new treatments (including those for cancers) involving patients, people working in or with the NHS, the life sciences industries and health researchers'.

As part of this process, the government set up the Accelerated Access Review, which is due to report in 2016 on how to speed up the use of data in order to ensure that patients can access new medicines more quickly. NICE itself has set up the Office of Market Access, which will work with industry in order to speed up the adoption of new medicines, devices, and diagnostics by the NHS. The Early Access to Medicines Scheme (EAMS) was set up in 2014, and it aims to give patients with life-threatening or seriously debilitating conditions access to medicines that do not yet have a marketing authorization when there is a clear unmet medical need. Under the scheme, the Medicines and Healthcare products Regulatory Agency (MHRA) will give a scientific opinion on the benefit/risk balance of the medicine, based on the data available when the EAMS submission was made. If potential benefit is demonstrated to the MHRA's satisfaction, a company will be able to market the product. The first medicine to be approved through this scheme was a novel cancer drug to treat melanoma, pembrolizumab (marketed as Keytruda), which can be provided by the NHS to patients who have not benefited from other therapies, provided that the manufacturer supplies it at an agreed discount.

(5) Evaluating NICE's Effectiveness

There have been several criticisms of NICE over the past 16 years. First, the status of NICE guidance is ambiguous. Directions issued in January 2002 instructed health authorities that any treatments which have been approved by NICE should normally be available to patients within three months.[92] And the NHS Constitution states that: 'You have the right to drugs and treatments that have been recommended by NICE for use in the NHS, if your doctor says they are clinically appropriate for you.' As this statement makes clear, however, while CCGs may be under a duty to fund NICE-recommended treatments, doctors are not under a duty to prescribe them. The question of what treatment is appropriate for a particular patient remains a matter of clinical discretion, although obviously in fulfilling their duty of care, doctors would be expected to have regard to relevant guidance.

Secondly, despite the quasi-mandatory status of NICE technology appraisals, extra money is not put aside to fund their implementation, and so CCGs must find the resources to pay for NICE-approved technologies and treatments from elsewhere in their budgets. Different CCGs will choose to make savings in different ways, resulting in a new 'postcode lottery', as the cuts necessary to implement NICE's recommendations are made unevenly. Paradoxically, in order to fund NICE recommendations, CCGs might restrict access to treatments which are, in fact, more cost-effective than those recommended by NICE, but which have not been formally appraised.

NICE is not a budget holder and does not have to decide which treatments should be paid for by the NHS. Rather, it looks at different treatments in isolation, and decides

---

[92] *Directions to Health Authorities, Primary Care Trusts and NHS Trusts in England* (DH: London, 11 December 2001).

whether they meet some threshold level of cost-effectiveness. It therefore cannot tell whether the treatments it recommends are more or less cost-effective than the majority of treatments, which have not had their cost-effectiveness investigated.

Thirdly, implementation of NICE guidance remains variable.[93] There is also some confusion between technology appraisals, which must be implemented and clinical guidelines, which CCGs are supposed to work towards, but which are not mandatory. The House of Commons Health Select Committee drew attention to this problem.

House of Commons Health Select Committee[94]

It appears that patients and the public are sometimes not aware that only approved technology appraisals are mandatory and that the NHS is not under any obligation to implement other types of guidance within a specific timeframe. This is partly because of the terminology used by NICE: the term 'guidance' is commonly employed for all types of advice given by the Institute, and does not differentiate between that which is obligatory and that which is not. This has led to confusion about the status of the different types of guidance issued by NICE, and elevated expectations among patients of the type of treatment that they will receive. For example, in vitro fertilisation (IVF) is the subject of a clinical guideline. NICE recommended that PCTs should provide three cycles of IVF to eligible patients. Many patients therefore believe that the NICE guideline means that they should have access to three cycles of IVF through the NHS.

The Committee questioned the logic of this differential status of guidelines and appraisals: 'it seems illogical that technology appraisals must be implemented while eminently sensible elements of clinical guidelines are not obligatory'.

Fourthly, NICE's 'topic selection' process is not random, but rather is intended to ensure that NICE issues guidance on novel or expensive treatments in a rolling programme of appraisals, decided upon in collaboration with the Horizon Scanning Research and Intelligence Centre at the University of Birmingham. It would, of course, be impossible to subject every available medical procedure to the sort of rigorous assessment carried out by NICE, and it is sensible for NICE to concentrate upon evaluating the cost-effectiveness of expensive new treatments. But when coupled with the duty to fund NICE recommendations, the result of this prioritized review may be that only certain patient groups benefit from the requirement to fund NICE-approved treatments. This skews funding towards new and expensive medicines for acute illness, and away from low-tech interventions and preventative and primary care. It also means that NICE has spent more time evaluating new medicines, at the expense, perhaps, of promoting disinvestment from cost-ineffective existing medicines.

Rooshenas et al observed CCG meetings and found multiple barriers to disinvestment, not least because so much of the CCGs' time was taken up with implementing NICE recommendations.

---

[93] Trevor A Sheldon et al, 'What's the evidence that NICE guidance has been implemented? Results from a national evaluation using time series analysis, audit of patients' notes, and interviews' (2004) 329 British Medical Journal 999.

[94] 'National Institute for Health and Clinical Excellence: First Report of Session 2006–07', paras 289–90.

Leila Rooshenas et al[95]

Discussions of new opportunities for disinvestment were largely absent from observed commissioning group meetings, which largely focused on new investments. Interviews and observed meetings revealed practical and ideological barriers to disinvestment, including an absence of guidance and capacity to engage in disinvestment, difficulties in collaboration, reluctance to engage in explicit rationing, and a perceived lack of central/political support. . . .

[W]e found little evidence of tools to support disinvestment decision-making. Our study showed the direct and indirect consequences of not having a clear disinvestment process—both in terms of identifying worthwhile opportunities for disinvestment, and implementing proposals as policy . . .

Despite general consensus that disinvestment is a cornerstone to sustaining some health systems, disinvestment in practice is imbued with difficulties. A lack of guidelines and capacity make it difficult to engage in disinvestment. Furthermore, 'disinvestment' is a poorly demarcated term that sparks a range of different understandings. First steps towards advancing the disinvestment agenda should consider providing a clear definition of the term, and developing specific tools and guidelines to support decision-makers.

In response to the concern that it should do more to promote disinvestment, NICE has set up a 'do not do' database, which contains a long list of recommendations, extracted from its guidance and appraisals, about treatments that should not be provided. Examples include the recommendation that pharmacological interventions to aid sleep should not be prescribed, unless sleep problems persist despite following a sleep plan; that antidepressants should not be provided to patients suffering from mild depression; and that antibiotics should not be provided in a range of specific cases.

Fifthly, giving 'interested parties'—such as patient groups and the pharmaceutical industry—a right to make representations and a right of appeal has led to the criticism that NICE might be too easily swayed by powerful lobbying groups. There is then the danger that certain diseases and treatments will receive preferential treatment over other conditions which may be just as deserving, but which lack skilled and powerful advocates.

Sixthly, despite its commitment to open and transparent decision-making, in practice NICE often withholds the evidence upon which its appraisals are based because pharmaceutical companies have specified that the relevant information was supplied in confidence.

4 CHALLENGING RATIONING DECISIONS

(a) JUDICIAL REVIEW

As we saw earlier, one requirement of Daniels and Sabin's 'accountability for reasonableness' is that rationing decisions should be open to challenge. Judicial review is available to scrutinize the legality but not the merits of decisions taken by public authorities, such as CCGs or NICE.

A patient who believes that a CCG has wrongly deprived her of treatment can apply for judicial review, but only on the grounds that the CCG had acted illegally, unfairly, or

---

[95] '"I won't call it rationing …": an ethnographic study of healthcare disinvestment in theory and practice' (2015) 128 Social Science & Medicine 273–81.

disproportionately and irrationally. A patient could also apply for judicial review of a decision on the grounds that it infringed her rights under the Human Rights Act 1998.

It is noteworthy that there were no challenges to NHS funding decisions in the first 30 years of the NHS's existence. As we saw earlier, implicit rationing meant that in the past patients were seldom aware that treatment was rationed. In addition to being better informed, patients' expectations are now higher, and they are more willing to complain.

Initially, however, the judiciary was what can only be described as extremely hostile to actions brought against struggling health authorities. *R v Central Birmingham Health Authority, ex parte Collier* involved a four-year-old boy who had had a number of unsuccessful heart operations, and was in desperate need of open heart surgery. Despite being placed at the top of the waiting list, the operation was postponed several times because of a shortage of both beds and nurses. His father applied for judicial review, but the Court of Appeal rejected his application as 'wholly misconceived'.

R v Central Birmingham Health Authority, ex parte Collier[96]

Sir Stephen Brown

I am bound to say that, whilst I have for my part every sympathy with the position of Mr Collier and his family and can understand their pressing anxiety in the case of their little boy, it does seem to me unfortunate that this procedure has been adopted. It is wholly misconceived in my view. The courts of this country cannot arrange the lists in the hospital, and, if it [sic] is not evidence that they are not being arranged properly due to some unreasonableness in the *Wednesbury* sense on the part of the authority, the courts cannot, and should not, be asked to intervene.

The decision in *Collier* has been sharply criticized by Newdick as 'one of the most unsatisfactory cases ever to have emanated from the Court of Appeal in England'.

Christopher Newdick[97]

The case is unsettling because neither the applicant nor the court appeared to know how, or why, facilities could not be made available for this undeniably urgent operation. On any Hippocratic assessment of the case, its merits could hardly have been greater: the case was urgent, surgery was life-saving and well-understood, and the prospects of success were good. How could any reasonable system of priorities sensibly have abandoned such a deserving case?

The first judicial review case to attract much media attention was the 'Child B' case, or *R v Cambridge Health Authority, ex parte B.*[98] Jaymee Bowen, who was ten years old, had developed acute myeloid leukaemia. Consultants at Addenbrooke's Hospital in Cambridge, and at the Royal Marsden Hospital in London agreed that the only possible treatment (intensive chemotherapy and a second bone marrow transplant) would be unlikely to succeed and was

---

[96] Unreported, 6 January 1988.

[97] 'Public health ethics and clinical freedom' (1998) 14 Journal of Contemporary Health Law and Policy 335, 354.

[98] [1995] 1 WLR 898.

not in her best interests. Her father sought second opinions from other doctors in the UK and in the US. Treatment in the US would have been prohibitively expensive, but he did find one doctor at the Hammersmith Hospital in London who was prepared to treat his daughter privately, and he sought an extra-contractual referral from Cambridge and Huntingdon Health Authority to pay for the £75,000 treatment. His request was refused, not because the treatment was too expensive but because her doctors believed that it would be ineffective and inappropriate. Jaymee's father then applied for judicial review of this decision. At first instance, in *R v Cambridge District Health Authority, ex parte B (No 1)*, Laws J called upon the health authority to justify its decision by explaining the priorities which had led it to refuse to fund Child B's treatment.

R v Cambridge District Health Authority, ex parte B (No 1)[99]

Laws J

[W]here the question is whether the life of a ten year old child might be saved, by more than a slim chance, the responsible authority must in my judgment do more than toll the bell of tight resources. They must explain the priorities that have led them to decline to fund the treatment.

Later the same day, in *R v Cambridge Health Authority, ex parte B*, the Court of Appeal overturned his judgment on the grounds that the health authority had acted rationally and fairly, and that court intervention in such a case would be misguided.

R v Cambridge Health Authority, ex parte B[100]

Sir Thomas Bingham MR

I have no doubt that in a perfect world any treatment which a patient, or a patient's family, sought would be provided if doctors were willing to give it, no matter how much it cost, particularly when a life was potentially at stake. It would however, in my view, be shutting one's eyes to the real world if the court were to proceed on the basis that we do live in such a world. It is common knowledge that health authorities of all kinds are constantly pressed to make ends meet. They cannot pay their nurses as much as they would like; they cannot provide all the treatments they would like; they cannot purchase all the extremely expensive medical equipment they would like; they cannot carry out all the research they would like; they cannot build all the hospitals and specialist units they would like. Difficult and agonising judgments have to be made as to how a limited budget is best allocated to the maximum advantage of the maximum number of patients. That is not a judgment which the court can make.

The Child B case attracted a great deal of media interest—*The Sun*'s headline was 'Condemned by Bank Balance' and the *Daily Mail*'s was 'Sentenced to Death'. As a result, an anonymous private benefactor came forward to pay for Jaymee Bowen's treatment. The consultant who had agreed to treat Jaymee privately decided against a second bone marrow transplant, and

---

[99] The Times, 15 March 1995.   [100] [1995] 1 WLR 898.

instead gave her an experimental treatment, known as a donor lymphocyte infusion. Jaymee survived for a few more months and died the following year.

One of the reasons for the courts' reluctance to interfere with funding decisions is that they are not in a position to know about the other—possibly more compelling—claims upon the NHS's scarce resources. If funds are diverted to patient A, there may not be enough to pay for the treatment of patients B, C, or D, none of whom has been represented before the court. This point was emphasized by Lord Donaldson MR in *Re J (A Minor)*:[101]

> I would stress the absolute undesirability of the court making an order which may have the effect of compelling a doctor or health authority to make available scarce resources (both human and material) to a particular child, without knowing whether or not there are other patients to whom those resources might more advantageously be devoted.

More recently, there have been a number of cases in which the courts have found that health authorities have acted unlawfully when deciding not to fund particular treatments. In *R v North West Lancashire Health Authority, ex parte A*, the health authority had adopted a restrictive referral policy for transsexuals seeking gender reassignment surgery at the country's only specialist Gender Identity Clinic at Charing Cross Hospital in London. Three applicants who had had their requests for extra-contractual referrals turned down applied for judicial review. Auld LJ agreed that health authorities were entitled to make lists of treatments which were and were not a priority, and he agreed that it would 'make sense' to give gender reassignment surgery a lower priority than treatment for cancer, heart disease, or kidney failure. But he found that the policy did not make adequate provision for an individual's exceptional circumstances to be taken into account, and that the policy should be reformulated in order to (a) acknowledge properly that transsexualism is an illness, and (b) make effective provision for exceptions in individual cases.

R v North West Lancashire Health Authority, ex parte A[102]

Auld LJ

It is natural that each authority, in establishing its own priorities, will give greater priority to life-threatening and other grave illnesses than to others obviously less demanding of medical intervention ... In my view, a policy to place transsexualism low in an order of priorities of illnesses for treatment and to deny it treatment save in exceptional circumstances such as overriding clinical need is not in principle irrational, provided that the policy genuinely recognises the possibility of there being an overriding clinical need and requires each request for treatment to be considered on its individual merits ...

The authority should reformulate its policy to give proper weight to its acknowledgement that transsexualism is an illness, apply that weighting when setting its level of priority for treatment and make effective provision for exceptions in individual cases from any general policy restricting the funding of treatment for it.

---

[101] [1992] 4 All ER 614.   [102] [2000] 1 WLR 977.

In practice, of course, it is possible that the health authority could still refuse to fund these applicants' gender reassignment surgery, while satisfying the Court of Appeal that it was not operating a blanket ban by offering them reasons for its decision. Could it then be argued that the practical consequence of the decision in *NW Lancashire* is not to ensure that patients actually receive treatment, but instead to offer them a personalized justification for the refusal to treat them? In Derek Morgan's words: 'The right to health care becomes in fact a right to transparency about the tragic choices that are being negotiated.'[103]

Of course, the reasons given for refusing treatment must be defensible. In *R (on the application of Rose) v Thanet Clinical Commissioning Group*, a CCG had refused to fund oocyte preservation for a woman with Crohn's disease who was about to undergo treatment that would leave her infertile. One of the reasons it gave was that it disagreed with NICE's updated guideline on the effectiveness of oocyte preservation. Jay J found that Thanet CCG was not obliged to follow the NICE guideline, but that it could not legitimately disagree with NICE's evaluation of the scientific evidence.

R (on the application of Rose) v Thanet Clinical Commissioning Group[104]

Jay J

The extent of the public law obligation is to have regard to the relevant NICE guideline and to provide clear reasons for any general policy that does not follow it....

The Defendant has no compliance obligation as such, but the issue in the instant case is whether CCGs may legitimately disagree with NICE on matters concerning the current state of medical science. NICE's view is that the evidence base supports the effectiveness of oocyte cryopreservation, and the CCG's sole basis for not following the NICE recommendation is that it disagrees. No basis or reasoning on grounds of exceptionality has been put forward. In my judgment the Defendant could have found other reasons for not following the NICE recommendation, but not this one. It follows that the new ART policy is unlawful.

R v North and East Devon Health Authority, ex parte Coughlan is an exceptional case in which the applicant was entitled to more than defensible reasons for a rationing decision. Miss Coughlan had been seriously injured in a road traffic accident in 1971. She was tetraplegic and required constant care. In 1993, she and seven other seriously disabled patients were moved to Mardon House, a purpose-built unit, which they were assured would be their 'home for life'. In 1996, the health authority recommended that Mardon House should be closed, and alternative arrangements made for her care.

Miss Coughlan applied for judicial review. The Court of Appeal found that the patients had a legitimate expectation not only to be treated fairly by the health authority, but also to the substantive benefit of a home for life in Mardon House. Frustrating that expectation would be so unfair that it would amount to an abuse of power. Lord Woolf even suggested that a failure to honour the substantive promise made to the applicant was 'equivalent to a breach of contract in private law'.

---

[103] *Issues in Medical Law and Ethics* (Cavendish: London, 2001) 58.
[104] [2014] EWHC 1182 (Admin).

R v North and East Devon Health Authority, ex parte Coughlan[105]

Lord Woolf MR

[T]he cheaper option favoured by the health authority misses the essential point of the promise which had been given.... The health authority's undertaking to fund her care for the remainder of her life is substantially different in nature and effect from the earlier promise that care for her would be provided at Mardon House. That place would be her home for as long as she chose to live there.

We have no hesitation in concluding that the decision to move Miss Coughlan against her will and in breach of the health authority's own promise was in the circumstances unfair. It was unfair because it frustrated her legitimate expectation of having a home for life in Mardon House.

It is important to remember that one of the reasons for treating public law differently from private law is that public authorities have a duty to balance competing claims upon their resources. The health authority's evidence to the Court of Appeal stated that Mardon House had become 'a prohibitively expensive white elephant' which 'left fewer resources available for other services'. Of course, keeping one's promises is important, but if maintaining Mardon House might jeopardize the health authority's ability to offer services to other patients, whose interests were not represented in this case, could it be argued that the Court of Appeal strayed into judging the merits, as opposed to the legality, of the decision?

Against this, Paul Craig and Søren Schønberg have suggested that the Court of Appeal in *Coughlan* rightly separated two different exercises of power by the health authority: the promise to Miss Coughlan and the policy decision to close Mardon House. Craig and Schønberg agree that the policy change was not irrational in the *Wednesbury* sense, but instead the breach of promise amounted to an abuse of power.[106]

In recent years, there have been several cases in which patients have challenged funding decisions concerning expensive cancer drugs. In the first case, *R (Ann Marie Rogers) v Swindon Primary Care Trust and the Secretary of State*, Ms Rogers suffered from stage 1 breast cancer. She had had a mastectomy, and, as a result of her son's research on the internet, she asked to be tested for HER2 breast cancer, which could apparently be treated with a new drug, Herceptin, which was as yet unlicensed for use in patients like Ms Rogers and which had not been appraised by NICE.

Ms Rogers tested positive for HER2. Her consultant, Dr Cole, asked Swindon PCT if Ms Rogers could pay for Herceptin, while remaining an NHS patient. Its response was that she could not. Ms Rogers paid for two doses of Herceptin herself, but she was unable to pay for the whole course of treatment. The PCT's policy was not to fund the 'off-licence' prescription of drugs, unless the patient's case was exceptional. It therefore conducted an 'exceptional case review' of Ms Rogers' circumstances, and decided that, because she was in the same position as other sufferers of stage 1 breast cancer, her case could not be considered exceptional.

Ms Rogers sought judicial review of this decision on the grounds that it was arbitrary and hence irrational. The Court of Appeal overturned the first instance judge's rejection of Ms Rogers case, and found that the PCT had acted irrationally. Because all women with stage 1 breast cancer were in the same situation as Ms Rogers, the PCT's 'exceptionality' review procedure was meaningless.

---

[105] [2001] QB 213.
[106] 'Substantive Legitimate Expectations after *Coughlan*' (2000) Public Law 684–701.

R (Ann Marie Rogers) v Swindon Primary Care Trust and the Secretary of State[107]

Sir Anthony Clarke MR (giving the judgment of the Court)

The essential question is whether the policy was rational; and, in deciding whether it is rational or not, the court must consider whether there are any relevant exceptional circumstances which could justify the PCT refusing treatment to one woman within the eligible group but granting it to another. And to anticipate, the difficulty that the PCT encounters in the present case is that while the policy is stated to be one of exceptionality, no persuasive grounds can be identified, at least in clinical terms, for treating one patient who fulfils the clinical requirements for Herceptin treatment differently from others in that cohort ...

If that policy had involved a balance of financial considerations against a general policy not to fund off-licence drugs not approved by NICE and the healthcare needs of the particular patient in an exceptional case, we do not think that such a policy would have been irrational....

The non-medical personal situation of a particular patient cannot in these circumstances be relevant to the question whether Herceptin prescribed by the patient's clinician should be funded for the benefit of the patient. Where the clinical needs are equal, and resources are not an issue, discrimination between patients in the same eligible group cannot be justified on the basis of personal characteristics not based on healthcare.

For these reasons we have reached the conclusion that the policy of the PCT is irrational. Here the evidence does not establish the possibility of there being relevant clinical circumstances relating to one patient and not another and, in the case of personal characteristics, there is no rational basis for preferring one patient to another.

Note that the Court of Appeal specifically ruled out using 'non-medical' or personal circumstances as a reason to distinguish between different patients. In deciding whether a woman's case was 'exceptional', non-clinical considerations—the example he gave was a patient who had to care for a disabled child—had to be treated as irrelevant. Swindon PCT had said that its decision was not based upon cost. This was because the then Secretary of State for Health, Patricia Hewitt, had stated publicly that PCTs should not refuse to fund Herceptin on cost grounds. If the PCT had cited cost as a reason not to fund Herceptin for Ms Rogers, ironically the Court of Appeal admitted that they would have been on stronger ground.

In the next extract, Keith Syrett argues that the *Rogers* case is not, as some commentators have suggested, 'a landmark victory for an individual over a health trust ... [and] an important step forward for "patient power"', but rather that it demonstrates that if PCTs are honest about the scarcity of resources, they will have a much wider discretion to fund, or not fund, expensive treatments.

Keith Syrett[108]

[I]t is submitted that it is most useful to read the case as a judicial exhortation to PCTs to be transparent as to the part played by financial considerations in making difficult choices on the availability of treatments and services for the population which they serve.

---

[107] [2006] EWCA Civ 392.

[108] 'Opening Eyes to the Reality of Scarce Health Care Resources? *R (on the application of Rogers) v Swindon NHS Primary Care Trust and Secretary of State for Health*' (2006) Public Law 664–73.

Provided that cost plays a part in the decision-making of a PCT and it is acknowledged as pertinent, a court will allow the PCT considerable scope to do as it pleases, subject only to intervention where the policy adopted is egregious in the extreme (such as funding Herceptin only to women with red hair) or where it fails to admit of the possible relevance of exceptional individual circumstances . . . However, if the PCT has sufficient funds available for treatment or if, like Swindon PCT, it purports as such, the court will scrutinise the decision-making process much more closely to ensure that any policy or decision to deny access to treatment can be *properly justified* to disappointed patients (and the wider public) *by reference to clinical factors*, since it is to be expected that the PCT will meet all clinical needs if it is operating under no resource constraints.

In *R (on the application of Otley) v Barking and Dagenham NHS Primary Care Trust*,[109] the health authority again operated an 'exceptionality policy', which this time was held to be lawful. What was not lawful, however, was its application to Ms Otley, who was suffering from metastatic colorectal cancer, and tumours in her liver. Ms Otley had responded poorly to chemotherapy. Her sister discovered the existence of a new drug, Avastin, on the internet. Avastin was licensed in the US and in many European countries, but not in England and Wales. It cost between £1,000 and £1,500 per cycle.

Ms Otley paid for five cycles of Avastin, which she took in combination with other drugs. Her response was excellent: there were minimal side effects; she felt much better; and the tumours appeared to have shrunk. Ms Otley's doctor applied to her local PCT to fund a further five prescriptions of Avastin. The application was refused and Ms Otley applied for judicial review of that decision.

Mitting J found that while 'the policy is entirely rational and sensible', its application to Ms Otley's case was irrational. The panel had failed to take into account the fact that there were no other options available to Ms Otley. Ms Otley was young and fit; she could not tolerate other drugs; she appeared to have benefited from Avastin and had suffered no side effects. Resource considerations could not be a decisive factor in Ms Otley's case because the anticipated outlay—of another five cycles of Avastin—would be relatively modest and certainly would not jeopardize the trust's capacity to provide care for other patients. According to Mitting J, 'on any fair minded view of the exceptionality criteria identified in the critical analysis document, her case was exceptional'.

In *R (Murphy) v Salford Primary Care Trust*, another case in which a patient challenged the refusal to pay for an expensive new cancer drug, this time for the treatment of renal cancer, Burnett J set out the principles to be applied in these cases.

R (Murphy) v Salford Primary Care Trust[110]

Burnett J

The legal principles that are in play are not controversial:

a. When an NHS body makes a decision about whether to fund a treatment in an individual patient's case it is entitled to take into account the financial restraints on its budget as well as the patient's circumstances.

---

[109] [2007] EWHC 1927 (Admin).   [110] [2008] EWHC 1908 (Admin).

> b. Decisions about how to allocate scarce resources between patients are ones with which the Courts will not usually intervene absent irrationality on the part of the decision-maker. There are severe limits on the ability of the Court to intervene.
>
> c. The Court's role is not to express opinions as to the effectiveness of medical treatment or the merits of medical judgment.
>
> d. It is lawful for an NHS body to decide to decline to fund treatment save in exceptional circumstances, provided that it is possible to envisage such circumstances.

Seven grounds were put forward as to why Ms Murphy's case should be treated as exceptional, such as the fact that she also suffered from breast cancer, which excluded her from a clinical trial of this new drug, and that she had had mental health problems. The panel considered each of these factors individually, and none was judged sufficient to mark Ms Murphy out as an exceptional case. Burnett J decided that, in addition to their individual consideration, they should also have looked at Ms Murphy's case 'in the round': 'As a matter of general principle when considering a series of factors which might inform the overall decision, it is of course necessary to look at them individually ... But having looked at all factors individually, it seems to me that it is necessary to consider them in the round.' Burnett J therefore quashed the original decision and remitted it back to the Commissioning Panel, which could, of course, come to the same decision again, provided that before doing so it considered Ms Murphy's circumstances 'in the round'.

In *R (on the application of Ross) v West Sussex Primary Care Trust*,[111] the judge found that the PCT's exceptionality review process was unlawful because it had required Mr Ross to prove that his case was unique. As Judge Grenfell explained: 'the Review and Appeal Panels [fell] into error simply on the ground that they clearly thought that, because other patients could find themselves in the Claimant's position, therefore, he did not come within the exceptionality [policy]'.

While it might be clear that a patient's situation does not have to be unique in order for her to be judged exceptional, as Ford explains in the next extract, exceptionality remains a rather fuzzy concept: if a patient might be more likely to benefit from treatment, that could be relevant, but not decisive; her social circumstances should not normally be relevant; and her prognosis might or might not be a factor.

Amy Ford[112]

> If we take the five cancer patients who sought judicial review of the funding decisions made by their respective PCTs, Ann Rogers, Linda Gordon, Victoria Otley, Jean Murphy, and Colin Ross, and apply the criteria outlined above to them, using the information available to us in the court reports about their circumstances, the manifest lack of objectivity in the concepts that emerges, aside from the suggestion that social circumstances can be disregarded, means that each individual could be determined to be both exceptional and unexceptional, depending on how the criteria are interpreted . . .
>
> In the absence of clear legal criteria on the determination of exceptionality, reaching decisions which are robust enough to withstand judicial review is challenging and PCTs are exposed to the risk of costly legal action. Furthermore, the money and time spent by PCTs on defensive legal action cannot be invested in improving clinical care. Clinicians are left

---

[111] [2008] EWHC 2252 (Admin).
[112] 'The Concept of Exceptionality: A Legal Farce?' (2012) 20 Medical Law Review 304–36.

bewildered as to why some seemingly very similar patients are deemed exceptional, when others are not. The process of applying for funding on the basis of exceptional circumstances creates unrealistic expectations for patients, fuelled by media hype and indirect marketing by pharmaceutical companies. In addition, seeking recourse in the courts is not an option easily accessible to all, further increasing inequities between patients.

It continues to be difficult to prove that an exceptionality review policy and the way it is implemented is irrational, especially given the cost constraints under which the NHS must operate. In *R (on the application of C) v Berkshire West Primary Care Trust*, the Court of Appeal was adamant that neither the trust's policy of treating breast augmentation surgery as a 'non-core' treatment for gender identity disorder, nor its decision that C was not an exceptional case, was irrational.

R (on the application of C) v Berkshire West Primary Care Trust[113]

Hooper LJ

The appellant in this case was seeking NHS funding for a surgical operation where the PCT had reasonably concluded (as the judge found and was, in my view, entitled to find) that there was an absence of evidence that it was likely to be clinically effective to improve the appellant's health.... I understand why the appellant feels aggrieved that the respondent funds the core gender reassignment procedures outlined in the Policy, notwithstanding the absence of evidence of limited clinical effectiveness, but does not also fund breast augmentation surgery for persons like the appellant ... But the answer in law to that feeling is that the respondent, in exercising its statutory responsibilities, has to make very difficult choices as to what procedures to fund and not to fund and the choice made in this case is not irrational.

In addition, it is worth stressing that a finding that there was a procedural irregularity in the operation of an exceptional review process is not the same thing as a decision that funding must be made available. In *R (on the application of Gordon) v Bromley NHS Primary Care Trust*,[114] Ouseley J agreed with Linda Gordon that the basis for the PCT's rejection of her application to be provided with a short trial of Tarceva—a treatment for the second or third line treatment of lung cancer—was not wholly clear: the PCT appeared to believe that they had been asked to fund a two-month trial, when in fact only one further month's funding was needed in order to work out whether Ms Gordon would be likely to benefit. Ouseley J stressed, however, that a properly explained decision might still be to refuse funding:

I emphasise that the claimant may well find it impossible to challenge a refusal of further funding, even on a trial basis, if the decision is explained and grapples with the relevant issues ... I ... make it clear so that the claimant, whose life is on any view tragically short, does not have unrealistic expectations as a result of the modest success which she has achieved here.

(b) THE HUMAN RIGHTS ACT 1998

A patient who is denied access to medical treatment might try to invoke the Human Rights Act 1998 in order to challenge the decision. If a patient is denied treatment which might

---

[113] [2011] EWCA Civ 247.   [114] [2006] EWHC 2462 (Admin).

save her life, would it be possible to argue that her right to life, protected under Article 2, has been violated? Article 2 not only obliges public bodies to refrain from deliberately taking its citizens' lives, but it can also sometimes require them to take adequate measures to protect life. Patients will not generally be able to use Article 2 to force health authorities to fund treatment, however. The European Court of Human Rights (ECtHR) has generally been slow to interfere with resource allocation decisions within public services, and has been clear that the right to life 'must be interpreted in a way which does not impose an impossible or disproportionate burden on the authorities'.[115]

Nevertheless, in exceptional circumstances, it might be possible to challenge a refusal to provide potentially life-saving measures on human rights grounds. One such exceptional case was *Savage v South Essex Partnership NHS Foundation Trust*,[116] in which the House of Lords found that, where a mentally ill patient was a known suicide risk, there was an obligation, under Article 2, to do all that could reasonably be expected in order to prevent that risk materializing. The duty to provide services under Article 2 was triggered, according to Baroness Hale, by 'a "real and immediate risk to life" about which the authorities knew or ought to have known at the time'.

If sufficiently serious, could a denial of medical treatment amount to 'inhuman or degrading treatment', prohibited under Article 3? At first instance in *R (on the application of Watts) v Bedford Primary Care Trust*, discussed further in Section 4(e), Munby J rejected the claim that having to wait a year for a hip replacement operation, with all the pain and suffering to be endured in the meantime, might amount to a breach of Article 3.

R (on the application of Watts) v Bedford Primary Care Trust[117]

Munby J

Article 3 is not engaged unless the 'ill-treatment' in question attains a minimum level of severity and involves actual bodily injury or intense physical or mental suffering. However that is not this case. Making every allowance for the constant pain and suffering that the claimant was having to endure—and I do not seek in any way to minimise it—the simple fact in my judgment is that nothing she had to endure was so severe or so humiliating as to engage Article 3.

In contrast, in *Price v United Kingdom*, the prison authority's inadequate treatment of a four-limb-deficient thalidomide victim with numerous health problems amounted to a violation of Article 3.

Price v United Kingdom[118]

Judgment of the ECtHR

There is no evidence in this case of any positive intention to humiliate or debase the applicant. However, the Court considers that to detain a severely disabled person in conditions

---

[115] *Osman v United Kingdom* (Case 87/1997/871/1083) [1999] 1 FLR 193.   [116] [2008] UKHL 74.
[117] [2003] EWHC 2228 (Admin).   [118] (2001) 34 EHRR 1285.

> where she is dangerously cold, risks developing sores because her bed is too hard or unreachable, and is unable to go to the toilet or keep clean without the greatest of difficulty, constitutes degrading treatment contrary to Article 3.[119]

There have also been attempts to argue that a refusal to fund treatment might amount to unlawful interference with a patient's private and family life, and hence breach Article 8. In *R (on the application of Condliff) v North Staffordshire Primary Care Trust*,[120] Mr Condliff's PCT had a policy only to fund gastric band operations for patients whose body mass index (BMI) was greater than 50. Mr Condliff was morbidly obese and suffered from a range of associated health problems, but because his BMI was 43, he did not fit within the PCT's policy. He made an individual funding request (IFR) on the grounds that his was an exceptional case. The PCT's individual funding request policy specified that the patient's case could only be considered exceptional for clinical reasons. Social factors, such as the patient's family circumstances, were irrelevant. An appendix to the policy explained why:

> If, for example, treatment were provided which had the effect of keeping someone in paid work, this would tend to discriminate in favour of those of working age and against the retired. If a treatment were provided differentially to patients who were carers this would tend to favour treatment for women over men. If treatment were provided in part on the basis that a medical condition had affected a person at a younger age than that at which the condition normally presents, this would constitute direct age discrimination.

Mr Condliff argued that the failure to fund his gastric band operation was having a devastating effect on his private and family life—his wife had to deal with the consequences of his incontinence throughout the night, for example—and that this should have been taken into account. At first instance, and on appeal to the Court of Appeal in *R (on the application of Condliff) v North Staffordshire Primary Care Trust*, Mr Condliff's claim was refused.

R (on the application of Condliff) v North Staffordshire Primary Care Trust[121]

Toulson LJ

The PCT has grappled with the difficult ethical and practical questions involved in setting its IFR policy. In arriving at that policy the PCT has struck what it considers to be a fair balance between the interests of individuals and the community (for example, whether patients who are carers should have priority over others) and a fair balance between different patients with similar health conditions....

Nothing in the authorities therefore leads me to conclude that the policy of the PCT, properly understood, is to be regarded as showing a lack of respect for Mr Condliff's private and family life, so as to bring article 8 into play. If, however, article 8 is applicable, there were legitimate equality reasons for the PCT to adopt the policy that it did and its decision was

---

[119] [2003] EWHC 2228 (Admin).
[120] [2011] EWCA Civ 910.   [121] [2011] EWCA Civ 910.

> well within the area of discretion or margin of appreciation properly open to it ... The sad fact remains that the PCT on proper medical advice does not consider his condition to be exceptional for someone with his diabetes, obesity and co-morbidities.

Mr Condliff subsequently submitted a successful IFR request, this time presenting fresh evidence that his clinical circumstances were exceptional, on the grounds that he would benefit more from this operation than other comparable patients.

Regardless of the usefulness or otherwise of Convention rights to patients who wish to challenge rationing decisions, the Human Rights Act 1998 has undoubtedly led to a greater emphasis upon the proportionality of decisions to restrict access to medical treatment. In the next extract, Keith Syrett explains how a shift from *Wednesbury* unreasonableness to proportionality, as the standard of scrutiny, makes it easier to challenge decisions of public bodies successfully, because it necessarily requires the decision-maker to give reasons.

Keith Syrett[122]

> [In *Collier*] the Court took the view that judicial intervention was only permissible if the decision was 'unreasonable' in the so-called *Wednesbury* sense, that is that it was 'so unreasonable that no reasonable authority could ever have come to it'. Under this test, a public body is under no obligation to explain the decision reached unless the applicant for judicial review can make a case for its irrationality. This represents a much less searching standard of scrutiny than other public law principles, notably proportionality, which requires a court to assess the balance struck between competing interests by the decision-maker and the relevant weight accorded to interests and considerations. Necessarily, in undertaking scrutiny according to this latter standard, a court will be required to examine the justifications put forward by the decision-maker as to why it has favoured one interest over another, so that it can establish that interference with the latter is not disproportionate.

(c) JUDICIAL REVIEW CLAIMS AGAINST NICE

As a public body, NICE's decisions can be subject to judicial review, but given the expertise of those responsible for its technology appraisals, the openness and transparency of its processes, and its active involvement of stakeholders, it would be hard to establish procedural impropriety. Nevertheless, there have been a handful of applications for judicial review of NICE decisions, most of which have come from the pharmaceutical industry, and most of which have involved technical issues about the use of data and access to modelling assumptions.[123]

In the first judicial review application against one of its decisions, *Eisai Ltd v National Institute for Health and Clinical Excellence*, the manufacturer of donepezil (brand name Aricept) challenged the decision of NICE's appeal panel, and NICE's subsequent guidance—that Aricept should not be funded for patients in the earlier stages of Alzheimer's disease (AD)—on the grounds of procedural unfairness, discriminatory effects, and irrationality.

---

[122] *Law, Legitimacy and the Rationing of Health Care* (CUP: Cambridge, 2007) 166–7.

[123] See, eg, *R (on the application of Bristol-Myers Squibb) v National Institute for Health and Clinical Excellence* [2009] EWHC 2722 (Admin) and *Servier Laboratories v National Institute for Health and Clinical Excellence* [2010] EWCA Civ 346.

At first instance, Eisai succeeded only on the discrimination aspect of their claim. Mini mental-state examinations, used to judge AD's severity, produced inaccurate results in non-native English speakers and people with learning difficulties, and hence breached NICE's obligations under equality law. Eisai then appealed successfully to the Court of Appeal on the grounds of procedural fairness. Their claim was that, by giving them access to 'read only' versions of NICE's economic modelling formulae, it was impossible for them to check or comment upon the reliability of NICE's calculations. In *Eisai Ltd v National Institute for Health and Clinical Excellence*,[124] the Court of Appeal held that 'procedural fairness does require release of the fully executable version of the model'.

Giving Eisai access to the functional version of the modelling tool does not alter the judgement that Aricept's cost per QALY for patients with mild AD is too great to justify NHS provision. In August 2009, after the Court of Appeal's decision, NICE reiterated that for people with mild AD, Aricept's cost per QALY ranged from £56,000 to £72,000, and this was still too high to make Aricept cost-effective.[125] The following year NICE changed its mind on Aricept and two similar drugs, however, citing new evidence of the drugs' effectiveness. There had not been a new landmark study, and NICE itself had described the evidence base as 'disappointing'. Nevertheless, by adjusting its calculations to give more weight to the costs of caring for someone with AD, the cost per QALY was reduced to £30,000 and NHS provision was judged acceptable.[126]

There has been one case in which patients have sought to challenge a NICE patient care guideline. In *R (on the application of Fraser) v National Institute for Health and Clinical Excellence*,[127] two patients who had been diagnosed with Myalgic Encephalomyelitis (ME) claimed that NICE had acted irrationally by giving too little consideration to pharmaceutical treatments for ME, and had prioritized instead psycho-social treatments, such as cognitive behavioural therapy and graded exercise therapy. They advanced a number of grounds for this claim, many alleging bias or conflict of interest on the part of NICE's expert advisers. All were rejected, and the court also noted that legal proceedings of this type might serve as a disincentive to health care professionals from involving themselves in NICE's decision-making processes in the future.

(d) BREACH OF STATUTORY DUTY

The National Health Service Act creates a duty on the part of the Secretary of State, which is now shared with NHS England, and with CCGs.

National Health Service Act 2006 sections 1 and 3, as amended

1 Secretary of State's duty to promote health service

(1) The Secretary of State must continue the promotion in England of a comprehensive health service designed to secure improvement—

(a) in the physical and mental health of the people of England, and

(b) in the prevention, diagnosis and treatment of illness...

---

[124] [2008] EWCA Civ 438.

[125] Zosia Kmietowicz, 'NICE decision on dementia drugs was based on "common sense" not evidence, expert says' (2010) 341 British Medical Journal 5642.

[126] Ibid.   [127] [2009] EWHC 452 (Admin).

(4) The services so provided must be free of charge except in so far as the making and recovery of charges is expressly provided for by or under any enactment, whenever passed …

1H …

(2) The [National Health Service Commissioning] Board is subject to the duty under section 1(1) concurrently with the Secretary of State [except in relation to that part of the health service which is provided for the purpose of protecting the public in England from disease or other dangers to health, or which is provided for the purpose of improving public health.] …

3(1) A clinical commissioning group must arrange for the provision of the following to such extent as it considers necessary to meet the reasonable requirements of the persons for whom it has responsibility:

(a) hospital accommodation,

(b) other accommodation for the purpose of any service provided under this Act,

(c) medical, dental, ophthalmic, nursing and ambulance services,

(d) such other services or facilities for the care of pregnant women, women who are breastfeeding and young children as the group considers are appropriate as part of the health service,

(e) such other services or facilities for the prevention of illness, the care of persons suffering from illness and the after-care of persons who have suffered from illness as the group considers are appropriate as part of the health service,

(f) such other services or facilities as are required for the diagnosis and treatment of illness.

Notice, however, that the statutory duty under the National Health Service Act is to *promote* rather than to *provide* a comprehensive health service. In *R v North and East Devon Health Authority, ex parte Coughlan*, Lord Woolf was clear that the duty to promote a comprehensive NHS was very far from a duty to ensure that the service was comprehensive.

R v North and East Devon Health Authority, ex parte Coughlan[128]

Lord Woolf

The truth is that, while [the Secretary of State] has the duty to continue to promote a comprehensive free health service and he must never, in making a decision under section 3, disregard that duty, a comprehensive health service may never, for human, financial and other resource reasons, be achievable.

Under the National Health Service Act there is no penalty or remedy prescribed for breach of the duties imposed upon the Secretary of State. And in the context of other social services, the House of Lords has confirmed that the purpose of legislation is to benefit society as a whole, rather than to offer remedies to individual citizens.[129] In *Re HIV Haemophiliac Litigation*,[130] Rougier J had held that it was plain that parliament did not intend there to be a

---

128 [2001] QB 213.
129 See, eg, the comments of Lord Browne-Wilkinson in *X v Bedfordshire County Council* [1995] 3 All ER 353.
130 (1998) 41 BMLR 171.

cause of action for any member of the public affected by breach of the duties in the National Health Service Act, and this was upheld by the Court of Appeal. Ralph Gibson LJ stated that he shared 'the judge's view of the apparent nature of the duties imposed by the 1977 Act. They do not clearly demonstrate the intention of parliament to impose a duty which is to be enforced by individual civil action.'

In contrast to the National Health Service Act, a rather more specific obligation is imposed on health authorities by section 117(2) of the Mental Health Act 1983: 'It shall be the duty of the district health authority … to provide … after-care services for any person to whom this section applies.' This is a duty to provide, rather than to promote aftercare. Nevertheless, the courts have been reluctant to find health authorities liable to individual patients for failing to make appropriate provision. In *Clunis v Camden and Islington Health Authority*, the Court of Appeal rejected Clunis's claim that the health authority might be liable for breach of the statutory duty to provide him with appropriate aftercare services.

Clunis v Camden and Islington Health Authority[131]

Beldam LJ

The primary method of enforcement of the obligations under section 117 is by complaint to the Secretary of State. No doubt, too, a decision by the district health authority or the local social services authority under the section is liable to judicial review at the instance of a patient … [But] the wording of the section is not apposite to create a private law cause of action for failure to carry out the duties under the statute.

(e) SEEKING TREATMENT ABROAD

Could a patient who has been denied treatment in the UK, or who wants to avoid UK waiting lists, seek reimbursement for treatment abroad? Article 49 of the EC Treaty prohibits restrictions on the freedom to provide and receive services within the EU, and the European Court of Justice (ECJ) has held that this applies to publicly funded medical treatment.[132] But while Article 49 may enable patients to seek treatment in other Member States, it does not give them the right to be reimbursed for that treatment.

Member States are entitled to decide whether to authorize reimbursement for treatment abroad. The UK is under no obligation to reimburse patients for treatment that is not available within the NHS. Reimbursement cannot be refused, however, if the treatment is normally provided by the NHS, but the patient is unable to access it 'within the time normally necessary for obtaining the treatment in question in the Member State of residence, taking account of his current state of health and the probable course of the disease'.[133] Patients cannot expect the NHS to pay for treatment abroad just because they will not be treated immediately in the UK. It is only where the waiting time amounts to 'undue delay' that there may be an obligation to fund treatment which the patient receives in another Member State.

The question of whether or not European law entitles a patient on an NHS waiting list to be reimbursed for treatment in another Member State arose for the first time in the UK in *R (on the application of Watts) v Bedford Primary Care Trust and Another*.[134] Yvonne Watts

---

[131] *Clunis v Camden and Islington Health Authority* [1998] QB 978.
[132] Case C-158/96 *Kohll v Union de Caisses de Maladie* [1998] ECR I-1931.
[133] Article 22 of Council Regulation No 1408/71.
[134] *R (on the application of Watts) v Bedford Primary Care Trust and Another* [2004] EWCA Civ 166.

had undergone a hip replacement operation in France in order to avoid the NHS waiting time of approximately one year. Her local NHS trust had refused to fund the operation, and she challenged this decision, arguing that it was contrary to her free movement rights under EU law. The critical question was whether the waiting list for surgery meant that Ms Watts was subject to 'undue delay'. The Court of Appeal asked for further clarification from the ECJ on a number of questions, among them:

> Is the United Kingdom National Health Service entitled to refuse to authorise a patient's treat-ment in another Member State if it reasonably judges that to do so in the particular and similar cases would dislocate its system of administering priorities through waiting lists?

There are, as Gareth Davies explains, good reasons why the NHS might fear the consequences of a wide-ranging right to be reimbursed for treatment abroad.

Gareth Davies[135]

> The Member States' central fear is that patients going abroad, usually to avoid waiting lists, will result in higher costs. Not only will the national authorities lose their control over the rate of treatment, and hence spending, but they will also be left with possibly half-empty institutions. These cannot simply be closed down, because maintaining the national medical infrastructure is a matter of strategic and public health importance. Therefore the state will be forced to operate an inefficient system, adding an extra burden to its budget.

In *R (on the application of Watts) v Bedford Primary Care Trust and Another*,[136] the ECJ decided that, while NHS patients are entitled to undergo treatment in another Member State, they cannot expect the NHS to pay for it unless they have received prior authorization. Refusal to grant prior authorization could not be justified generically by the need for resource planning in the NHS. Instead, it would be necessary to carry out an objective medical assessment of the patient's medical condition; the history and probable course of his illness; the degree of pain he was in and/or the nature of his disability. Where the delay arising from waiting lists exceeded an acceptable time, having regard to an objective medical assessment of the patient's circum-stances, the NHS should not refuse to pay for treatment abroad. Although this may seem like a patient-friendly decision, it ignores the public health dimensions of resource allocation and, as Newdick explains, it is more likely to benefit relatively fit and affluent patients.

Chris Newdick[137]

> [A] plausible public health response [to the unequal burden of ill health suffered by the poor-est in society] is to shift the distribution of health resources away from acute care in hospitals and toward health promotion and preventive care in the community (especially for children).

---

[135] 'Health and Efficiency: Community Law and National Health Systems in the Light of Müller-Fauré' (2004) 67 Modern Law Review 94–107.

[136] Case C-372/04 [2006] All ER (D) 220 (May).

[137] 'Promoting Access and Equity in Health: Assessing the National Health Service in England' in Colleen M Flood and Aeyal Gross (eds), *The Right to Health at the Public/Private Divide: A Global Comparative Study* (CUP: Cambridge, 2014) 107–28.

The advantage will be less morbidity and mortality overall, but the downside is that waiting times for hospital treatment may increase. . . .

By contrast, the ECJ has created a substantive right. Once the conditions of access are satisfied (i.e., 'normal treatment' and 'reasonable time'), the patient may seek treatment elsewhere in the EU, pay for it there, and seek reimbursement from their health authority at home. This has implications for the ethical integrity of national systems. It undermines the democratic right of parliaments to manage health care and threatens the legitimacy of national priority setting . . . The ECJ's approach is to re-divert resources from the 'public health' policy and give it back to litigants seeking hospital treatment . . . The ECJ did not consider—and may not have understood—that by 'favoring' patients who are relatively fit and able to travel and who need acute hospital care, it risks ignoring poorer members of society who cannot afford to pay for their care and those in need of preventive care.

An EU Directive on access to cross-border health care provision within Europe came into force in 2013,[138] and was implemented in the UK by amendments to the National Health Service Act 2006. As established in the *Watts* case, Member States are entitled to require prior authorization in order to manage the potential outflow of patients. Prior authorization can be refused on safety grounds, or, under section 6BB(5)(d) of the National Health Service Act 2006, if the treatment could be provided in the UK 'within a period of time that is medically justifiable, taking into account the patient's state of health at the time ... and the probable course of [his] medical condition'. In determining whether the period of time is 'medically justifiable', under section 6BB(6) the Secretary of State can take into account:

(a) the patient's medical history;

(b) the extent of any pain, disability, discomfort, or other suffering that is attributable to the medical condition to which the service is to relate;

(c) whether any such pain, disability, discomfort, or suffering makes it impossible or extremely difficult for the patient to carry out ordinary daily tasks; and

(d) the extent to which the provision of the service would be likely to alleviate, or enable the alleviation of, the pain, disability, discomfort, or suffering.

In order to discourage 'health tourism', patients who receive treatment overseas are to be reimbursed only at the rates payable for that treatment in their home country, meaning that if the treatment costs more in the country where treatment is sought, the patient must pay the difference.

(f) THE RIGHTS OF NON-RESIDENTS

Under section 175 of the National Health Service Act 2006, only those who are 'ordinarily resident' in the UK have the right to free health care. Whether or not someone has a British passport is irrelevant. The question of whether a failed asylum seeker could be 'ordinarily resident' in the UK came before the court in *R (on the application of YA) v West Middlesex University Hospital NHS Trust*. At first instance, Mitting J had held that until removal directions were set, a failed asylum seeker had the same immigration status as a person whose asylum claim had yet to be determined. This meant that they could be 'ordinarily resident in the UK', and hence entitled to receive free NHS treatment.

---

[138] Directive of the European Parliament and the Council on the application of patients' rights in cross-border healthcare (2011/24/EU).

In *R (on the application of YA) v West Middlesex University Hospital NHS Trust*, the Department of Health successfully appealed to the Court of Appeal, which relied upon *obiter* comments in an earlier immigration case to establish, first, 'if [the person's] presence in the country is unlawful, for example in breach of the immigration laws, he cannot rely on his unlawful residence as constituting ordinary residence', and, secondly, that there is a 'principle of public policy that the *propositus* [person immediately affected] cannot profit from his unlawful act'.

R (on the application of YA) v West Middlesex University Hospital NHS Trust[139]

Ward LJ

[T]he Secretary of State's duty ... is to continue the promotion in England of a comprehensive health service designed to secure improvement in the health 'of the people of England'. Note that it is the people *of* England, not the people *in* England, which suggests that the beneficiaries of this free health service are to be those with some link to England so as to be part and parcel of the fabric of the place. It connotes a legitimate connection with the country ... This strongly suggests that, as a rule, the benefits were not intended by Parliament to be bestowed on those who ought not to be here ...

Failed asylum seekers ought not to be here. They should never have come here in the first place and after their claims have finally been dismissed they are only here until arrangements can be made to secure their return, even if, in some cases, like the unfortunate YA, that return may be a long way off.

The National Health Service (Charges to Overseas Visitors) Regulations 2015 set out when overseas visitors should and should not be charged for NHS services. Regulation 3 specifies that the NHS must charge and recover payment for relevant services, unless the case falls into one of the exceptional cases, when no charge is payable.

Unless the person has travelled to the UK for the purpose of seeking that treatment, regulation 9 provides that no charges are made for accident and emergency services (but only before someone becomes an inpatient); family planning services (which do not include termination of pregnancy); treatment for sexually transmitted diseases; and treatment for a list of specified diseases where treatment will protect public health, including TB, leprosy, rabies, malaria, and HIV (HIV was added to this list as a result of evidence that antiretroviral medication substantially reduced the risk of onward transmission).

The Department of Health has issued guidance on the 2015 Regulations which spells out when treatment should be given without first seeking payment, but which also specifies that attempts should usually be made to recover the costs of that treatment.

Department of Health[140]

8.2 Relevant NHS bodies must also ensure that treatment which is immediately necessary is provided to any person, even if they have not paid in advance. Failure to provide immediately necessary treatment may be unlawful under the Human Rights Act 1998. Urgent treatment should also always be provided to any person, even if deposits have not been secured.

---

[139] [2009] EWCA Civ 225.
[140] *Guidance on Implementing the Overseas Visitors Hospital Charging Regulations 2015* (DH: London, 2015)

Non-urgent treatment should not be provided unless the estimated full charge is received in advance of treatment . . .

8.4 Immediately necessary treatment is that which a patient needs:

- to save their life; or

- to prevent a condition from becoming immediately life-threatening; or

- promptly, to prevent permanent serious damage from occurring . . .

8.7 Urgent treatment is that which clinicians do not consider immediately necessary, but which nevertheless cannot wait until the person can be reasonably expected to return home. . . .

8.8 For urgent treatment, relevant NHS bodies are strongly advised to make every effort, taking account of the individual's circumstances, to secure payment in the time before treatment is scheduled. However, if that proves unsuccessful, the treatment should not be delayed or withheld for the purposes of securing payment.

8.9 Treatment is not made free of charge by virtue of being provided on an immediately necessary or urgent basis. Charges found to apply cannot be waived and if payment is not obtained before treatment then every effort must be made to recover it after treatment has been provided.

In practice, NHS hospitals are not used to charging people for their care, and the systems may not be in place to ensure that ex-patients are chased for their debts. A report commissioned by the Department of Health in 2013 found that: 'Overall, the indications are that Trusts collect about 15% of the sums that are potentially chargeable to non-EEA patients (excluding irregular migrants).'[141]

A different issue arises when a failed asylum seeker or other illegal immigrant is desperately ill and facing deportation to a country where they will not receive the care that they need. On a number of occasions, the courts have been asked to consider whether deportation in such cases could amount to inhuman and degrading treatment, and hence be a violation of Article 3.

In *D v United Kingdom*,[142] D, who was due to be deported to St Kitts after his release from prison, was suffering from HIV/AIDS. His illness was at a very advanced stage, and death was imminent. Deportation to St Kitts would mean that D would not have access to treatment, including palliative care, and his death was therefore likely to be painful and distressing. The ECtHR decided that 'in the very exceptional circumstances of this case and given the compelling humanitarian considerations at stake, it must be concluded that the implementation of the decision to remove the applicant would be a violation of Article 3'.

Subsequent cases have fleshed out when a patient's circumstances will be sufficiently 'exceptional' to make deportation a breach of Article 3. The bar is a very high one, as we can see from *N v Secretary of State for the Home Department*.[143] N was a Ugandan citizen whose application for asylum had been refused. N had been diagnosed with advanced HIV/AIDS, and as a result of the treatment she had received in the UK, her condition had stabilized. N had a good chance of surviving for decades if treatment continued; without treatment, N would be unlikely to live for more than two years. N claimed that forcing her to return to Uganda would amount to inhuman and degrading treatment. The House of Lords dismissed her appeal on the grounds that her case was not sufficiently exceptional.

N then took her case to the ECtHR. In *N v United Kingdom*, a majority in the ECtHR agreed with the House of Lords that N's case did not meet the high exceptionality threshold set by *D v United Kingdom*.

---

[141] *Quantitative Assessment of Visitor and Migrant Use of the NHS in England: Exploring the Data* (DH: London, 2013).

[142] (1997) 24 EHRR 423.   [143] [2005] UKHL 31.

N v United Kingdom[144]

Judgment of the ECtHR

The decision to remove an alien who is suffering from a serious mental or physical illness to a country where the facilities for the treatment of that illness are inferior to those available in the Contracting State may raise an issue under Article 3, but only in a very exceptional case, where the humanitarian grounds against the removal are compelling. In the *D* case the very exceptional circumstances were that the applicant was critically ill and appeared to be close to death, could not be guaranteed any nursing or medical care in his country of origin and had no family there willing or able to care for him or provide him with even a basic level of food, shelter or social support.

   The Court does not exclude that there may be other very exceptional cases where the humanitarian considerations are equally compelling. However, it considers that it should maintain the high threshold set in *D v the United Kingdom*....

   Advances in medical science, together with social and economic differences between countries, entail that the level of treatment available in the Contracting State and the country of origin may vary considerably. While it is necessary, given the fundamental importance of Article 3 in the Convention system, for the Court to retain a degree of flexibility to prevent expulsion in very exceptional cases, Article 3 does not place an obligation on the Contracting State to alleviate such disparities through the provision of free and unlimited health care to all aliens without a right to stay within its jurisdiction. A finding to the contrary would place too great a burden on the Contracting States.

In addition to the high exceptionality threshold, there are two particular factual difficulties that affect failed asylum seekers suffering from HIV/AIDS. First, the disease is so common in some parts of the world, and treatment so inadequate, that proving that anyone's circumstances are exceptional is, almost by definition, impossible. In *ZT v Secretary of State for the Home Department*,[145] a case involving a woman with HIV/AIDS facing deportation to Zimbabwe, the Immigration Appeal Tribunal had held that:

[T]he claimant's situation is far from exceptional. It is certainly not unique. On the contrary, it is estimated that one-third of the adult population of Zimbabwe is now infected with HIV and/or AIDS. Whilst the situation which would face the claimant on return to Zimbabwe is undoubtedly a grim and distressing one, it is not one which is exceptional.

When this case reached the Court of Appeal, Sedley LJ admitted that the ubiquity of suffering from HIV/AIDS makes the exceptionality requirement almost impossible to satisfy.

ZT v Secretary of State for the Home Department[146]

Sedley LJ

If HIV were a rare affliction, readily treatable in the UK but not treatable except for the fortunate few in many other countries, the courts would have little hesitation in holding

---

144 Application no 26565/05 (2008).
145 [2005] EWCA Civ 1421. See also *BK (Zimbabwe) v Secretary of State for the Home Department* [2008] EWCA Civ 510.
146 [2005] EWCA Civ 1421.

removal of sufferers to such countries to be inhuman treatment contrary to Article 3. It is the sheer volume of suffering now reaching these shores that has driven the Home Office, the Immigration Appellate Authority and the courts to find jurisprudential reasons for holding that neither Article 3 or Article 8 can ordinarily avail HIV sufferers who face removal.

Secondly, *D v United Kingdom* is treated as the paradigm example of an 'exceptional' case, and yet, as Palmer points out, treatment options for HIV/AIDS have improved dramatically since D's case was decided. If the critical factor which marked D's case out was his imminent death, the existence of antiretroviral drugs which enable HIV/AIDS sufferers to lead much longer and healthier lives again makes it virtually impossible for someone currently receiving effective treatment to fit within the *D v United Kingdom* exception.

Stephanie Palmer[147]

The Strasbourg jurisprudence concerning the expulsion of aliens with HIV/AIDS has been shown to be unsatisfactory because of the medical advances in the treatment of this disease. The question in *D* concerned the particular circumstances of his inevitable death. In contrast, the seminal issue in N' s case concerned the length and quality of her life and whether there is a positive obligation on the state to sustain her medical treatment on a long-term basis.

In *GS (India) v Secretary of State for the Home Department*, six claimants were seeking to challenge their deportation on the grounds that they would be at risk of an early death if deported. Five of the claimants were suffering from end-stage kidney disease; the sixth was at an advanced stage of HIV/AIDS. None of their claims succeeded under Article 3. It was not enough to show that a claimant would suffer gravely if deported, it also had to be shown, as Laws LJ, put it, 'that the impugned state should be held responsible for his plight'.

GS (India) v Secretary of State for the Home Department[148]

Underhill LJ

The starting point as regards this part of the claim must be that, as the European Court of Human Rights has repeatedly affirmed, article 3 does not confer on a person who is liable to removal the right to remain in the territory of a contracting state in order to benefit from medical treatment which would not be available to him in the state to which he is returned. To put it another way, the returning state cannot be regarded as having responsibility for the inadequacy of the healthcare system in the country of return or, therefore, for the suffering which the person who is returned may undergo as a result of that inadequacy.… [T]hat principle applies even where the life of the person removed would be 'significantly shortened' by the inability to access treatment.

---

[147] 'AIDS, Expulsion and Article 3 of the European Convention on Human Rights' (2005) 5 European Human Rights Law Review 533–40.
[148] [2015] EWCA Civ 40.

In this case, the claimants had also attempted to resist deportation through Article 8 (see later in this section). Such claims are also usually unsuccessful. In *Bensaid v United Kingdom*, B, an Algerian national, had been receiving NHS treatment for schizophrenia. He was due to be deported, and he claimed that his removal would violate his rights under Article 3 and Article 8. The ECtHR held that B failed to meet the high threshold required by Article 3 because treatment was available in Algeria, albeit not as conveniently as in the UK. His removal would not breach Article 8, because the disruption of relationships he had formed in the UK was found to be justifiable under Article 8(2).

Bensaid v United Kingdom[149]

Judgment of the ECtHR

Even assuming that the dislocation caused to the applicant by removal from the United Kingdom where he has lived for the last eleven years was to be considered by itself as affecting his private life, in the context of the relationships and support framework which he enjoyed there, the Court considers that such interference may be regarded as complying with the requirements of the second paragraph of Article 8, namely as a measure 'in accordance with the law', pursuing the aims of the protection of the economic well-being of the country and the prevention of disorder and crime, as well as being 'necessary in a democratic society' for those aims.

This was followed by the House of Lords in *R (on the application of Razgar) v Secretary of State for the Home Department (No 2)*.[150] R was an Iraqi of Kurdish origin who had been refused asylum in Germany. R resisted removal from the UK on the ground that it would violate his human rights under Article 8, because he was receiving psychiatric treatment for depression and post-traumatic stress disorder. The House of Lords found that it would be possible to rely on Article 8 to resist removal if removal would damage a person's mental health, but that the threshold was again very high, amounting to, according to Lord Bingham, 'something very much more extreme than relative disadvantage'. Indeed, Baroness Hale's judgment started with the observation that 'it is not easy to think of a foreign health care case which would fail under article 3 but succeed under article 8'.

Unsurprisingly, therefore, in *GS (India) v Secretary of State for the Home Department*, following *Bensaid* and *Razgar*, five of the six claimants' Article 8 claims were also dismissed (in the sixth case, the Secretary of State had accepted that it is arguable that the Upper Tribunal had failed adequately to consider GM's Article 8 claim, and the case was remitted back by consent for redetermination).

GS (India) v Secretary of State for the Home Department[151]

Underhill LJ

First, the absence or inadequacy of medical treatment, even life-preserving treatment, in the country of return, cannot be relied on at all as a factor engaging article 8: if that is all there is, the claim must fail. Secondly, where article 8 is engaged by other factors, the fact

---

[149] (2001) 33 EHRR 10.   [150] [2004] UKHL 27.   [151] [2015] EWCA Civ 40.

that the claimant is receiving medical treatment in this country which may not be available in the country of return may be a factor in the proportionality exercise; but that factor cannot be treated as by itself giving rise to a breach since that would contravene the 'no obligation to treat' principle.

5 PUBLIC HEALTH

(a) WHAT IS PUBLIC HEALTH LAW?

Public health law is concerned not with the medical treatment of individual patients, but instead with measures that benefit the health of the public as a whole. This involves monitoring the public's health, and designing interventions in order to reduce the overall burden of disease, disability, and premature mortality within the population. A wide variety of interventions might help to improve the health of the public, including vaccination programmes; sex education; needle-exchange programmes; fluoridation of tap water; safe cycle lanes; and encouraging people to stop smoking, drink less, and reduce their sugar intake.

Public health interventions might or might not benefit a particular individual. A good example is the mandatory wearing of seat belts, a policy that has significantly reduced deaths from road traffic accidents. I might never be involved in a crash in which wearing a seat belt saves my life; indeed, I might be involved in a crash in which wearing a seat belt fails to save my life. But regardless of whether or not I will ever benefit from wearing a seat belt, it is very clearly in the interests of the population as a whole that everyone wears a seat belt when driving.

Public health interventions thus save 'statistical lives', rather than heroically rescuing specific individuals. As Bayer et al explain: 'This creates a political problem because public health officials cannot claim credit for rescuing identifiable persons—credit that has a powerful appeal in a culture of individualism.'[152] Geoffrey Rose further points out that because even the most effective public health measures may offer little in the short term for a particular person, it can be hard to motivate the individual subject: 'Mostly people act for substantial and immediate rewards, and the medical motivation for health education is inherently weak. Their health next year is not likely to be much better if they accept our advice or if they reject it.'[153]

Earlier in this chapter, we considered the funding of expensive cancer drugs, whereas a public health approach to cancer would focus instead on the fact that 35 per cent of all cancers are attributable to 'modifiable risk factors',[154] including 'tobacco use; alcohol consumption; unhealthy diets and physical inactivity; infections; occupational exposures, such as asbestos; and environmental factors, such as radiation and chemical pollution'.[155] Public health interventions are directed towards reducing exposure to these risk factors.

In relation to smoking, for example, hardly anyone starts smoking in adulthood. Unless teenagers continue to start to smoke, the tobacco industry's consumers will eventually die out. As a result, the industry is dependent upon persuading teenagers to smoke, while

---

152 'Introduction' in Ronald Bayer et al (eds), *Public Health Ethics* (OUP: Oxford, 2007) 27–31.
153 Geoffrey Rose, 'Sick Individuals and Sick Populations' in Ronald Bayer et al (eds), *Public Health Ethics* (OUP: Oxford, 2007) 33–43.
154 Otis W Brawley, 'Avoidable cancer deaths globally' (2011) 61 CA: A Cancer Journal for Clinicians 67–8.
155 Robert Beaglehole, Ruth Bonita, and Roger Magnusson, 'Global cancer prevention: an important pathway to global health and development' (2011) 125 Public Health 821–31.

public health policies are intended to make starting smoking seem expensive, inconvenient, and unattractive. To this end, the World Health Organization's *Framework Convention on Tobacco Control* sets out a range of regulatory measures, from higher taxes to plain packaging, that states should implement in order to discourage young people from taking up smoking.

Responsibility for public health was delegated to local government in 2013, with support from Public Health England (PHE), an Executive Agency of the Department of Health. PHE is charged with bringing together evidence on public health and supporting local government, via its Health and Wellbeing Boards, to protect the public's health. It also has a role in preparing for public health emergencies, such as flu pandemics. In October 2014, PHE set out its seven priorities: tackling obesity, reducing smoking, reducing harmful drinking, ensuing every child has the best start in life, reducing dementia risk, tackling antimicrobial resistance, and reducing tuberculosis.[156]

PHE publishes extraordinarily detailed annual health profiles for each region in the country. These set out health inequalities both within each area, and across the UK, and, as a result, they make for sobering reading. For example, in the London Borough of Camden in 2015: 'Life expectancy is 11.4 years lower for men and 8.9 years lower for women in the most deprived areas of Camden than in the least deprived areas.'[157] In Blackpool: '29.5% of adults are classified as obese, worse than the average for England.... Estimated levels of adult excess weight, smoking and physical activity are worse than the England average. Rates of sexually transmitted infections and people killed and seriously injured on roads are worse than average.'

PHE also regularly publishes *Health Matters*, a source of 'facts, figures and evidence of effective (and cost-effective) interventions to tackle major public health problems'. Its first version contained information about smoking, as part of its campaign 'to see a tobacco-free generation by 2025'.[158]

Public Health England[159]

Despite a continuing decline in smoking rates, nearly 1 in 5 adults still smoke and there are around 90,000 regular smokers aged between 11 and 15. . . . Smoking causes 17% of all deaths in people aged 35 and over . . .

Smoking and the harm it causes aren't evenly distributed. People in more deprived areas are more likely to smoke and are less likely to quit. . . . Men and women from the most deprived groups have more than double the death rate from lung cancer compared with those from the least deprived. Smoking is twice as common in people with longstanding mental health problems.

There are relatively high smoking levels among certain demographic groups, including Bangladeshi, Irish and Pakistani men and among Irish and Black Caribbean women. Smoking in pregnancy increases the risks of miscarriage, stillbirth or having a sick baby, and is a major cause of child health inequalities. At the time of their babies' birth, over 1 in 4 pregnant women are recorded as smokers in Blackpool, but fewer than 2 in 100 in the London Borough of Westminster.

---

[156] Public Health England, *From evidence into action: opportunities to protect and improve the nation's health* (PHE, 2014).
[157] Public Health England, *Health Profiles* (PHE, 2015).
[158] Public Health England, *Health matters: smoking and quitting in England* (PHE, 2015).
[159] Ibid.

As we see later, health interventions are not the only way to improve the public's health, as a result, both the National Audit Office and the King's Fund have argued that, to be more effective, PHE needs to have a greater cross-departmental role.[160]

The King's Fund[161]

Public Health England needs to urgently offer its expertise to other government departments—for free if necessary—to ensure that the impacts of wider government actions adequately take into account impacts on inequalities in health. More broadly, a mechanism such as the sub-committee on public health needs to be brought back into the centre of government to adequately assess and hold to account wider government actions on inequalities in health, as policies are developed. If austerity is the only game in town, it needs to be managed in a way that minimises its effects on inequalities in health—that is not currently happening. . . .

The persistence of low life expectancy in some areas means that the state, centrally and locally, has not tackled inequalities in health adequately. Inequalities in health are not self-correcting, and the role of wider determinants, lifestyles and services need to be addressed together rather than in isolation from—or in opposition to—each other.

(b) PUBLIC HEALTH INTERVENTIONS

If some of the biggest gains to the public's health might come from lifestyle changes, what is the role of the state in enabling and/or persuading people to lead healthier lives? If changes in behaviour can prevent ill health and premature death, are paternalistic measures justifiable, or should we be wary of the 'nanny state' telling us how to lead our lives? Public health advocates would argue that this way of framing the issue is misconceived, and that unhealthy behaviour may not be the result of autonomous choice. Nevertheless, resistance to top-down legislative interventions had led to interest into whether it might be preferable to 'nudge' people into healthier behaviour.

Of course, some unhealthy behaviours, such as illegal drug use, are against the law. Using the criminal law to prohibit practices that are bad for people's health might seem like an especially tough and uncompromising way to influence behaviour. In reality, however, illegality tends to make drug taking even more risky; it is, for example, not uncommon for illicit drugs to be 'bulked out' or cut with poisonous substances. A 'harm reduction' approach would instead accept that people are likely to take drugs anyway, and would focus instead on ways to make drug use safer, perhaps by providing access to clean needles.

Finally, and most radically, if the most accurate predictors of future ill health and low life expectancy are absolute poverty and relative inequality, might economic redistribution be justifiable on health grounds?

(1) Paternalism?

Some public health measures, such as minimum unit alcohol pricing and bans on smoking in public places, are intended to restrict people's 'freedom' to harm themselves. At first sight, this might appear to be contrary to John Stuart Mill's harm principle.

---

[160] National Audit Office, *Public Health England's grant to local authorities* (NAO, 2014).

[161] David Buck and David Maguire, *Inequalities in life expectancy: changes over time and implications for policy* (King's Fund, 2015).

John Stuart Mill[162]

That the only purpose for which power can be rightfully exercised over any member of a civilized community, against his will, is to prevent harm to others. His own good, either physical or moral, is not a sufficient warrant. He cannot rightfully be compelled to do or forbear because it will be better for him to do so, because it will make him happier, because, in the opinion of others, to do so would be wise, or even right . . . The only part of the conduct of anyone, for which he is amenable to society, is that which concerns others. In the part which merely concerns himself, his independence is, of right, absolute. Over himself, over his own body and mind, the individual is sovereign.

Matti Häyry is concerned not only with the paternalism of public health interventions, but also with the surveillance of the population that would be a necessary part of measuring their success.

Matti Häyry[163]

The emphasis on longer lives can be counterproductive if the extended length of lives is treated as a goal in itself, as opposed to being a means to happiness, responsibility or flourishing. . . . The emphasis on 'fewer diseases' can have similar effects, as people may value their self-made lifestyle choices more than disease prevention, when these conflict with each other . . .

When public health is promoted by studying the conditions of longer and healthier lives, individuals, groups and communities will be placed under a magnifying glass for extended durations. This means constant surveillance, probable intrusions into people's private lives and possible leaks of sensitive information. . . .

Furthermore, when public health is promoted by 'implementing policies and measures', this is often carried out without consulting the people and communities. The upshot of this is that, at best, benevolent paternalistic control is imposed on people's lives, without their consent or against their will, or that, at worst, detrimental procedures are launched in the name of the common good or public interest.

It is also not uncommon for those who are against public health measures to make slippery slope claims. As David Resnik puts it: 'today trans fats; tomorrow hot dogs'.

David Resnik[164]

I argue that while trans fat bans may help to improve public health, they represent a worrisome policy trend, because they open the door to further restrictions on food. Though few people will mourn the loss of artificial trans fats from restaurant food, the issue here is much larger than that. At stake is a freedom that most of us exercise every day but often take for granted: the freedom to choose what we eat. . . . Today, trans fats; tomorrow, hot dogs. . . . Emboldened by victories against trans fats, health advocates could go after red meats, processed meats, sugared drinks, and other unhealthy foods.

---

[162] *On Liberty* (John W Parker and Son: London, 1859) 21–2.
[163] 'Public health and human values' (2006) 32 Journal of Medical Ethics 519–21.
[164] 'Trans fat bans and human freedom' (2010) 10 American Journal of Bioethics 27–32.

Richard Epstein also makes a slippery slope claim through contrasting the 'old' public health—such as clean air legislation—with the new public health, which, he argues, wrongly categorizes obesity and smoking as 'epidemics' in order to justify intrusive state action.

Richard Epstein[165]

The old public health established the principle that epidemics offer strong reason for decisive public intervention, whether by quarantine, vaccination, or the creation of public sewers and waste disposal systems. Today, the new public health uses the term 'epidemic' to justify state regulation to limit tobacco consumption or control obesity, even though these activities do not pose risks of communicable disease or any other form of recognizable externalities (*pace* secondhand smoke) to other individuals. . . .

[T]he designation of obesity as a public health epidemic is designed to signal that state coercion is appropriate, and it is just that connection that is missing. Education and persuasion, yes—but these can be supplied by private institutions and foundations without government coercion or participation . . .

One fashionable proposal is to think of a 'fat tax' that might be levied on certain foods. But taxes of this sort are highly problematic because of the imperfect fit between the incidence of the tax and its social objectives. Thus, a tax on certain kinds of goods strikes all consumers of that product no matter what their individual health profiles. The person who counts calories and exercises faithfully is now penalized because she chooses to eat a cream pie as part of a sound overall diet.

The 'nanny state' is an especially powerful metaphor commonly invoked in order to criticize public health interventions. As Roger Magnusson explains, it is effective not just against freedom-limiting measures, but has even been used to criticize 'talking down' to people by giving them more information.

Roger Magnusson[166]

The metaphor has force because it associates government action with a fussing, over-bearing nanny who intrudes into the private lives of citizens and treats them as infants who cannot be trusted to make their own decisions. . ...

Nanny state theorists have become experts in framing health interventions as insults to the dignity and intelligence of ordinary people. This helps to explain why the nanny state critique applies not only to interventions that truly restrict the freedom of individuals (e.g. smoke-free laws), but to non-coercive, information-based interventions—like health warnings, and clearer nutrition labelling—that are aligned with the values of consumerism: informed choices and personal responsibility . . .

No one wants to be told that the government believes they are too stupid to decide what food to buy, or that they are 'helpless automatons manipulated into consuming whatever big corporations choose to produce'. Ironically, it is this same, treasured sense of self-sufficiency that makes nanny state name-calling a powerful ally as the tobacco, alcohol and processed food industries seek to maintain market share and their influence over consumer purchasing patterns.

[165] 'Let the shoemaker stick to his last: a defense of the "old" public health' (2013) 46 Perspectives in Biology and Medicine S138–S159.
[166] 'Case studies in nanny state name-calling: what can we learn?' (2015) 129 Public Health 1074–82.

Critics of public health policies, like Snowdon, tend to characterize the sorts of behaviour that pose a risk to health as entirely self-regarding actions.

Christopher Snowdon[167]

Matters that are routinely described as 'public health issues'—most notably, drinking, smoking and eating—are matters of private, not public, behaviour. Aside from instances of excessive alcohol consumption leading to public disorder, these personal habits should barely feature on the radar of a liberal democracy. . . .

   Is a greater risk of diabetes a price worth paying for enjoying an excess of high-calorie food? Is a greater risk of liver disease a price worth paying for years of beer-guzzling? Is a greater mortality risk a price worth paying for a lifetime's smoking? Who is to draw the line? The mandarins of 'public health' would draw it as near to zero as is politically feasible, but in an enlightened society the judgement can only be made by the one person who bears all the risk and enjoys all the benefits: the individual.

On the other hand, it could be argued that someone who becomes seriously ill as a result of exercising his freedom to smoke, drink, and live on junk food does not do so in isolation from those who will bear the burdens and the costs of his care. As Mary Ann Glendon has put it: 'the independent individualist, helmetless and free on the open road, becomes the most dependent of individuals in the spinal injury ward'.[168]

Framing restrictions upon what can be sold to consumers as an interference with their freedom to choose also misses the point that large corporations already restrict our choices. As Freudenberg and Galea put it: 'no consumer ever entered a restaurant demanding a portion of trans fats. Rather, food companies constrain consumer options through decisions made primarily to increase profits.'[169] The tobacco industry, for example, has criticized restrictions upon people's 'freedom' to smoke, whereas it could be argued that a significant interference with freedom comes from 'big tobacco' and its effective marketing techniques.

Smoking is addictive. It is clearly not impossible to stop smoking, but people often find it difficult. For many smokers, buying a packet of cigarettes is not an autonomy-enhancing expression of free will, but rather a burden of habit and addiction. Of course, that is not true of the first cigarettes that someone smokes, but, as Goodin points out, this will usually have been when they were a young teenager.

Robert E Goodin[170]

There might have been consent in the very first instance—in smoking your first cigarette. But once you were hooked, you lost the capacity to consent in any meaningful sense on a continuing basis. . . . [T]o consent implies the possibility of doing otherwise; and addiction substantially deprives you of the capacity to do other than continuing smoking. . . . A vast

---

[167] 'The Disease of Public Health', Spiked, 28 October 2013.

[168] Mary Ann Glendon, *Rights Talk: The Impoverishment of Political Discourse* (The Free Press: New York, 1991).

[169] Nicholas Freudenberg and Sandro Galea, 'The impact of corporate practices on health: implications for health policy' (2008) 29 Journal of Public Health Policy 86–104.

[170] 'No Smoking: The Ethical Issues' in Ronald Bayer et al (eds), *Public Health Ethics* (OUP: Oxford, 2007) 117–26.

majority of smokers began smoking in their early to middle teens . . . The crux of the matter, then, is just this: being below the age of consent when they first began smoking smokers were incapable of meaningfully consenting to the risks in the first instance. Being addicted by the time they reached the age of consent, they were incapable of consent later, either.

It could also be argued that freedom of choice is autonomy-enhancing only if a person has a range of valuable options from which to choose. The freedom to choose to work in a dangerous workplace, if there are no other options, is not an example of an individual being sovereign over himself. In the next extract, Lawrence Gostin suggests that it makes no sense to reify individual freedom of choice.

Lawrence O Gostin[171]

It is false to believe that a small limit on unfettered choice matters more to individuals, families, and communities than the crushing burdens of disease, suffering, and early death. When we recognize that the disproportionate burdens of diabetes and cardiovascular disease rest on society's poorest and most vulnerable people, a *failure* to act has deep moral dimensions.

The life choices of the disadvantaged are already severely constrained by their physical environments and socioeconomic status. To ignore the burdens of suffering from ill health, and fail to take known effective action, is far more morally culpable than a miniscule limit on their 'choice' to eat an artificial, palpably harmful additive ingredient.

Gostin and Gostin further argue that 'hard' paternalism, in the form of effective public health laws, is sometimes justifiable, in part in order to increase someone's range of choices in the future.

Lawrence O Gostin and Kieran G Gostin[172]

If the collective benefits are high and the individual burdens are low, the rhetorical assertion that a policy is paternalistic should not operate as a political trump. Public health paternalism that markedly improves health and well-being within the population offers a 'broader freedom'. This term is used advisedly to mean that when people have better opportunities for health and longevity, and live in more vibrant, productive communities, they have enhanced prospects for life and a wider range of choices for now and into the future . . .

When a person becomes seriously ill or disabled, the adverse effects on his or her autonomy, let alone full enjoyment of life, are palpable. This does not even take into account the losses that accrue to society when countless people develop preventable injuries and diseases due to their own activities.

It is also clear that not all choices are equally central to one's ability to be the author of one's own life plan. Interfering with someone's freedom to marry or start a family is rather different from reducing the salt content of junk food. As James Wilson explains, 'if a government passed a law on avowedly paternalistic grounds mandating that prepackaged meals could not contain more than a certain percentage of salt, few people would be worried they had

[171] 'Trans fat bans and the human freedom: a refutation' (2010) 10 American Journal of Bioethics 33–4.
[172] 'A broader liberty: JS Mill, paternalism and the public's health' (2009) 123 Public Health 214–21.

thereby been deprived of the ability to author their own life, given the ready availability of salt cellars'.[173]

A further consequence of the neo-liberal emphasis upon freedom of choice is, as the next two extracts explain, that individuals have no one but themselves to blame for their poor choices.

Janet Hoek[174]

Neo-liberal discourse presents people who smoke, or who consume too much alcohol or food, as making informed choices to engage in actions with harmful consequences, lacking in personal responsibility, or both. Tobacco companies thus currently claim that people who smoke have made informed and free choices, knowing the health risks they face. . . .

The reasoning represented in these arguments relies on three important assumptions. First, it assumes individuals can access accurate and balanced information relevant to their decisions Second, it assumes people make rational and informed decisions, having undertaken a thoughtful appraisal of the risks and benefits associated with different options. Third, it assumes individuals can predict, understand and accept the consequences of actions they take. Each of these assumptions re-locates responsibility for harm away from product manufacturers and marketers to individual consumers.

Alistair Wardrope[175]

By emphasizing the causal connection between individual behaviours and health outcomes, individual responsibility for health is rendered most salient; illness then comes to be seen as 'self-inflicted' and thus worthy of blame. If individual behaviour is emphasized as causally explanatory of health problems, then such health problems may be treated as evidence of irresponsible, weak-willed, lazy or otherwise deviant behaviour; these characteristics then stereotype individuals suffering from such health problems, with resulting stigmatization.

Given that, on average, the poorest in society lead the unhealthiest lives, stigmatizing people who have 'chosen' to smoke or eat unhealthily in practice means further castigating the most disadvantaged in society.

Bruce G Link and Jo C Phelan[176]

[T]hroughout history, socioeconomic status has had a robust association with disease and death: people with greater resources of knowledge, money, power, prestige, and social connections are generally better able to avoid risks and to adopt protective strategies. As

---

[173] James Wilson, 'Why it's time to stop worrying about paternalism in health policy' (2011) 4 Public Health Ethics 269–79.

[174] 'Informed choice and the nanny state: learning from the tobacco industry' (2015) 129 Public Health 1038–45.

[175] 'Relational autonomy and the ethics of health promotion' (2015) 8 Public Health Ethics 50–62.

[176] 'Stigma and its public health implications' (2006) 367 The Lancet 528–9.

stigma places people at a substantial social disadvantage with respect to these resources, it increases their exposure to risks and limits access to protective factors, potentially adding to their burden of disease or disability.

In their 2007 report on public health, the Nuffield Council on Bioethics (NCOB) attempted to steer a middle course between the liberal 'harm principle' starting point and the recognition that restrictions upon freedom in order to protect public health can sometimes be justifiable. The NCOB set out a 'stewardship' model, with what they described as an 'intervention ladder'. On this model, public health interventions require justification, and the greater the interference with a person's freedom, the stronger the justification would have to be.

Nuffield Council on Bioethics[177]

Our proposed 'intervention ladder' suggests a way of thinking about the acceptability and justification of different public health policies. The least intrusive step is generally 'to do nothing', or at most monitor the situation. The most intrusive is to legislate in such a way as to restrict the liberties of individuals, the population as a whole, or specific industries. In general, the higher the rung on the ladder at which the policy maker intervenes, the stronger the justification has to be. A more intrusive policy initiative is likely to be publicly acceptable only if there is a clear indication that it will produce the desired effect, and that this can be weighed favourably against any loss of liberty that may result.

1. Do nothing or simply monitor the current situation.

2. Provide information. Inform and educate the public, for example as part of campaigns to encourage people to walk more or eat five portions of fruit and vegetables per day.

3. Enable choice. Enable individuals to change their behaviours, for example by offering participation in a NHS 'stop smoking' programme, building cycle lanes, or providing free fruit in schools.

4. Guide choices through changing the default policy. For example, in a restaurant, instead of providing chips as a standard side dish (with healthier options available), menus could be changed to provide a more healthy option as standard (with chips as an option available).

5. Guide choices through incentives. Regulations can be offered that guide choices by fiscal and other incentives, for example offering tax-breaks for the purchase of bicycles that are used as a means of travelling to work.

6. Guide choice through disincentives. Fiscal and other disincentives can be put in place to influence people not to pursue certain activities, for example through taxes on cigarettes, or by discouraging the use of cars in inner cities through charging schemes or limitations of parking spaces.

7. Restrict choice. Regulate in such a way as to restrict the options available to people with the aim of protecting them, for example removing unhealthy ingredients from foods, or unhealthy foods from shops or restaurants.

8. Eliminate choice. Regulate in such a way as to entirely eliminate choice, for example through compulsory isolation of patients with infectious diseases.

[177] *Public health: ethical issues* (NCOB, 2007).

(2) 'Nudge'

Cass Sunstein and Richard Thaler's influential book *Nudge* adopts a non-paternalistic approach, which is four rungs up the Nuffield Council's intervention ladder. They have called their approach 'libertarian paternalism',[178] while others have described it as the 'psychological state'.[179] Instead of direct regulatory interventions—such as placing limits on the sugar content of food—the 'nudge' approach instead relies upon designing 'choice architecture' in order to prompt people to make healthier choices for themselves. As Sunstein and Thaler put it: 'To count as a mere nudge, the intervention must be easy and cheap to avoid. Nudges are not mandates. Putting the fruit at eye level counts as a nudge. Banning junk food does not.'[180]

Nudge theory recognizes that we do not always make considered choices, and it exploits our tendency to make decisions quickly and intuitively. When we order a large portion of chips, if this is the default option, it is not because we have weighed up carefully the pros and cons of eating a large portion of chips, it is *because* it is the default option.

Cass Sunstein and Richard Thaler[181]

Our emphasis is on the fact that in many domains, people lack clear, stable or well ordered preferences. What they choose is strongly influenced by the details of the context in which they make their choices, for example, default rules, framing effects (that is the wording of possible options), and starting points . . .

Libertarian paternalism is a relatively weak and non-intrusive type of paternalism, because choices are not blocked or fenced off. In its most cautious forms, libertarian paternalism imposes trivial costs on those who seek to depart from the planner's preferred option. But the approach we recommend nonetheless counts as paternalistic, because private and public planners are not trying to track people's anticipated choices, but are self-consciously attempting to move people in welfare promoting directions.

In the UK, the government has shown considerable interest in nudge theory and the possibility of using 'non-regulatory' ways to effect behavioural change. In 2010, it set up the Behavioural Insights Team, known as the 'nudge unit', which first operated within the Cabinet Office, and now describes itself as a 'social purpose company'. Drawing on 'ideas from the behaviour science literature', one of its purposes is to enable people to make better choices for themselves. It evaluates different interventions in order to see what works and what does not work. For example, it recently found that including the costs of a missed appointment in an appointment reminder text message reduced the number of missed appointments by 3 per cent.[182]

The obesity epidemic is unlikely to be solved by putting fruit at eye level, and some would argue that instead of tweaking individual's choices, it might be more effective to target the food industry, and place legal restrictions upon what they are allowed to sell and where.

---

[178] *Nudge: Improving Decisions About Health, Wealth, and Happiness* (Penguin: London, 2009).

[179] Rhys Jones, Jessica Pykett, and Mark Whitehead, *Changing Behaviours: On the Rise of the Psychological State* (Edward Elgar: Cheltenham, 2013).

[180] Richard H Thaler and Cass R Sunstein, *Nudge: Improving Decisions About Health, Wealth and Happiness* (Penguin: New York, 2008) 6.

[181] 'Libertarian Paternalism is not an Oxymoron' (2003) 70 University of Chicago Law Review 1159–202.

[182] Michael Hallsworth et al, 'Stating appointment costs in SMS reminders reduces missed hospital appointments: findings from two randomised controlled trials' (2015) 10 PLoS ONE e0137306.

Of course, these sorts of restrictions are unpopular with large corporations, and it is therefore unsurprising that the food industry has been a strong supporter of the government's interest in non-regulatory measures to tackle obesity.

The House of Lords Select Committee on Science and Technology evaluated non-regulatory ways to change behaviour, and concluded that, in isolation, such measures were unlikely to be effective. For example, it pointed out that the campaign to nudge people into fastening their seat belts every time they get into their cars ('clunk click every trip'), accompanied a change in the law, and that without legislation it is unlikely that this 'nudge' would have been effective.

House of Lords Science and Technology Select Committee[183]

In general, the evidence supports the conclusion that non-regulatory or regulatory measures used in isolation are often not likely to be effective and that usually the most effective means of changing behaviour at a population level is to use a range of policy tools, both regulatory and non-regulatory. Given that many factors may influence behaviour, this conclusion is perhaps unsurprising . . .

We therefore urge ministers to ensure that policy makers are made aware of the evidence that non-regulatory measures are often not likely to be effective if used in isolation and that evidence regarding the whole range of policy interventions should be considered before they commit to using non-regulatory measures alone.

More specifically, Allen et al evaluated the difference between regulatory and non-regulatory measures to reduce consumption of trans fats, and found, unsurprisingly, that a total ban would be much more effective than either better labelling or a partial ban (in restaurants and fast-food outlets).

Kirk Allen et al[184]

A total ban on trans fatty acids in processed foods might prevent or postpone about 7200 deaths (2.6%) from coronary heart disease from 2015-20 and reduce inequality in mortality from coronary heart disease by about 3000 deaths (15%). Policies to improve labelling or simply remove trans fatty acids from restaurants/fast food could save between 1800 (0.7%) and 3500 (1.3%) deaths from coronary heart disease and reduce inequalities by 600 (3%) to 1500 (7%) deaths, thus making them at best half as effective. . . . The sum of all savings for the total ban would be about £297m . . . , while for other policies the best estimates would lie in the range of £80–147m.

Of course, the state does not have a monopoly on nudging people into making particular decisions, and the imperceptible manipulation of choice is not always motivated by concern for public health. As Meredith Stark and Joseph Fins point out, computer algorithms use the data we put into search engines and social media in order to produce targeted advertising, which may unwittingly steer us towards particular health choices.

---

[183] *Behaviour Change*, 2nd Report of Session 2010–12.

[184] 'Potential of trans fats policies to reduce socioeconomic inequalities in mortality from coronary heart disease in England: cost effectiveness modelling study' (2015) 351 British Medical Journal h4583.

Meredith Stark and Joseph J Fins[185]

Imagine an individual searches for information on a painful arthritic knee. Having typed keywords into a search engine, browsed various websites, and joined the arthritis group of a social networking site, the individual begins to see, on the margins of various web pages, advertisements for a specific brand of pain reliever. Perhaps the ads even tout the suitability of that brand for arthritic pain. Soon ads are displayed for a nearby orthopedic practice and associated surgical center, the leading regional provider of knee replacements. . . .

From other ads now displayed, the patient even knows the brand name of a leading type of artificial joint and why that brand is best . . . In discussions with the surgeon at the center, the patient conveys her choice, and the physician incorporates these strong patient preferences into his treatment recommendation, as this is clearly an informed patient who has researched and thought comprehensively about all of the various options. Or has she?. . .

Intrusion in and appropriation of the space afforded patients to be more active participants in healthcare decisions are perhaps all the more paradoxical, as the availability of these online tools ostensibly should function to increase autonomy, allowing individuals more access to information and more input into health decisions. Instead, owing to intricate means of behavioral targeting, these strategies may be lulling individuals into a sense of informed decision-making while actually directing them toward specified outcomes, in a manner that thwarts voluntariness, engineers choice, and surreptitiously exploits decisional vulnerabilities.

(3) Harm Reduction

Although its potential remit is much wider, a harm reduction approach to public health came to prominence as a result of the HIV/AIDS pandemic. The spread of HIV/AIDS can be prevented by condom use and clean needles. In countries where prostitution and heroin use are illegal, providing condoms and sexual health advice to sex workers, and clean needles and/or methadone to heroin users, involves the recognition that the criminalization of these practices is not going to prevent them, and that it is preferable instead to reduce the risk of harm they pose to individuals.

Harm reduction programmes are accepted as best practice by the World Health Organization and UNAIDS, and there is now a weight of evidence that they work.[186] They do, however, face resistance from those who believe that distributing syringes, or providing safe places for the injection of drugs, enables illegal drug use. In the next extract, Bela Fishbeyn uses Russia as an example of the ideological rejection of a harm reduction approach to heroin addiction.

Bela Fishbeyn[187]

Many countries have, at one point or another, enacted drug policies that are influenced by ideology instead of evidence, including the depiction of drug use as a character flaw or moral weakness . . . Policies grounded in ideology that focus on eradication as the goal often lead

---

[185] 'Engineering medical decisions' (2013) 22 Cambridge Quarterly of Healthcare Ethics 373–81.

[186] See, eg, Cecile M Denis et al, 'Impact of 20 years harm reduction policy on HIV and HCV among opioid users not in treatment' (2015) 146 Drug & Alcohol Dependence e261.

[187] 'When ideology trumps: a case for evidence-based health policies' (2015) 15 The American Journal of Bioethics 1–2.

to the misapplication of criminal law, arbitrary health policies, and, as a result, can negatively impact the health of not only that specific population but that of society as well. . . .

The success of substitution therapy, primarily in the form of methadone, has been widely studied in a variety of countries and exhaustive empirical data supports its multi-faceted success . . . Despite these positive results, methadone—and indeed every other form of substitution therapy—is illegal or unavailable in some countries, including Russia.

This resistance to a proven successful and inexpensive health policy has left Russia with one of the fastest growing epidemics in the world, with injecting drug use accounting for close to 70% of new HIV infections. Russia also happens to be one of the world's top consumers of heroin, with . . . over 2.5 million injecting opiate users, totaling about 2.29 per cent of the county's population—more than any other country in the world. Yet the implementation of harm reduction measures continues to be controversial in Russia and almost all treatment options for Russia's injecting drug users are abstinence-oriented. Russian physicians themselves were amongst the strongest agents behind the resistance to substitution therapy, arguing that offering methadone is merely 'substituting one drug for another'.

A harm reduction approach might also be used to challenge laws which exacerbate risks to health. For example, the illegality of homosexual sex in 75 countries makes HIV transmission in those countries more, rather than less, likely.

Jorge Saavedra, Jose Antonio Izazola-Licea, and Chris Beyrer[188]

Most obviously, where same-sex behavior is criminalized, [men who have sex with men] remain hidden, they will be very cautious or refuse to get an HIV test, even if they feel they need it, and those seeking to reach them with services, from condoms and lubricants to education and treatment outreach, can be harassed for supporting illegal activities. A recent example is from Nepal, where police have beaten peer outreach workers for attempting to distribute condoms.

In countries where homosexuality is legal, commentators have sought to challenge the criminalization of HIV transmission on similar grounds, namely that it will discourage testing and hence make transmission more, rather than less, likely.

Matthew Weait[189]

It is also the case that HIV epidemics are driven largely by undiagnosed infection, not by people who are diagnosed positive—and criminal law generally only addresses those who know their status because it is concerned not only with agents' actions and their consequences, but with those who may reasonably be treated as having acted in a sufficiently blameworthy way. . . . [C]riminalisation may lead people to believe that new partners will explicitly disclose their HIV positive status to avoid liability, leading to a false sense of security and heightened risk-taking. . . . [T]here is evidence that criminalisation complicates in an unhelpful way the

---

[188] 'Sex between men in the context of HIV: the AIDS 2008 Jonathan Mann Memorial Lecture in health and human rights' (2008) 11 Journal of the International AIDS Society 9.

[189] 'Unsafe law: health, rights and the legal response to HIV' (2013) 9 International Journal of Law in Context 535–64.

relationship between patients and health-care workers. Finally, criminal cases more often than not lead to lurid, inaccurate and sensationalist reporting in the popular media—more often than not, these days, the only kind of reporting there is about HIV—and give the impression that people living with the virus are 'monsters', 'murderers' and 'assassins' bent on harming and killing others. Nothing, of course, could be further from the truth but these stories reinforce the stigma and fear surrounding HIV. This does absolutely nothing to encourage people to test regularly and to know their status—a precondition for accessing treatment, and so guaranteeing their own health and reducing the risk of onward transmission to others.

A harm reduction approach to public health is not limited to preventing HIV transmission. For example, as Lawrence Gostin and Aliza Glasner explain, there is currently considerable debate over whether e-cigarettes are an effective harm reduction technique.

Lawrence O Gostin and Aliza Y Glasner[190]

Public health advocates have debated whether e-cigarettes are effective harm reduction tools or offer a pathway to smoking. By delivering nicotine and mimicking oral inhalation, e-cigarettes could reduce dependency on combustible cigarettes and prevent relapse. Alternatively, e-cigarettes could become a gateway to smoking by exposing young people to the world of nicotine and relegitimizing tobacco use in society. Probably both scenarios are true: e-cigarettes can help older, entrenched smokers to quit smoking, whereas younger nonsmokers could transition from electronic to combustible cigarettes once they are addicted to nicotine.

(4) The Social Determinants of Health

Life expectancy varies dramatically both between and within countries. Average life expectancy in Nigeria is 52 years; in Japan it is 83 years. A girl born in Richmond, Surrey can expect to live for 15 more years in good health than a girl born in Manchester.[191] Women in the UK live to 82, on average; unless they are homeless, when average female life expectancy is 43. On average, people who suffer from mental illness die 15–20 years earlier than those who do not.[192] Importantly, however, it is not just that poverty and disadvantage are associated with ill health. As Michael Marmot has explained:

the social gradient in health is not confined to those in poverty. It runs from top to bottom of society, with less good standards of health at every step down the social hierarchy. Even comfortably off people somewhere in the middle tend to have poorer health than those above them.[193]

In the 1960s, Michael Marmot and colleagues carried out a study that has become known as Whitehall I, in which they tracked the mortality rates of 18,000 male British civil

---

[190] 'E-cigarettes, vaping, and youth' (2014) 312 Journal of the American Medical Association 595–6.

[191] Centre for Local Economic Strategies, *Due north: report of the inquiry on health equity for the north* (CLES, 2014).

[192] Public Health England, *From evidence into action: opportunities to protect and improve the nation's health* (PHE, 2014).

[193] 'Introduction' in Michael Marmot and Richard Wilkinson, *Social Determinants of Health*, 2nd edn (OUP: Oxford, 2005).

servants.[194] The men were put into one of four categories, depending upon their occupational status: senior administrators (that is, people at the top of the civil service such as permanent secretaries); professionals and executives; clerical (that is, people who dealt with paperwork); and 'other' (which included messengers and porters).

Across all causes of death, those with higher occupational status had lower percentages of deaths. Even amongst affluent individuals, higher social status was associated with better health outcomes. For example, in Whitehall I, the percentage in each group dying of heart disease between 1967 and 1977 was: senior administrator = 2.16 per cent; professional/executive = 3.58 per cent; clerical = 4.90 per cent; other = 6.59 per cent. For lung cancer, the respective percentages were: 0.35, 0.73, 1.47, 2.33. A second Whitehall II study included women and the results were the same.[195] Multiple studies since, including Sir Douglas Black's 1980 report *Inequalities in Health* (known as the Black Report) and its 1987 update, Margaret Whitehead's *The Health Divide*, have established unequivocally that 'the risk of death is greater for lower socio-economic groups at all stages of the life course and for all causes of death'.[196]

The evidence suggests that there are three drivers of this social gradient in health: social status, social affiliations, and stress in early life.

Richard Wilkinson[197]

Social status is linked to health not simply through the direct physical effects of exposure to better or worse material conditions. It is also a matter of position in the social hierarchy, people's experience of superior and dominant status versus inferior and subordinate status, coupled with processes of stigmatization and exclusion of those nearer the bottom of the hierarchy. . . .

The second group of psychosocial risk factors are those connected with social affiliations and involvement. . . . [S]ocial affiliations of almost any kind are protective of health. Close 'confiding' relationships, social support, friendship networks, and involvement in wider community life, all seem beneficial. Apparently confirming these connections, hostility and 'negative' relationships have been shown to be harmful to health . . .

The third important category of psychosocial influences on health were those occurring in early life. . . . People who were smaller as babies are, for instance, more likely to suffer from heart disease, diabetes, and stroke in later life. Although low birth weight was initially thought to reflect poor nutrition in pregnancy, it now looks as if it is more likely—at least in the rich countries—to reflect the effect of maternal stress . . . in the developing foetus . . . [T]here is also good evidence that stress and lack of stimulation in early childhood compromises future health.

Jonathan Wolff fleshes out some of the reasons why a supportive social network might lead to better health outcomes.

---

[194] M G Marmot et al, 'Employment grade and coronary heart disease in British civil servants' (1978) 32 Journal of Epidemiology and Community Health 244–9.

[195] M G Marmot et al, 'Health Inequalities among British civil servants: the Whitehall II study' (1991) 337 The Lancet 1387–93.

[196] Michael P Kelly, 'The Development of an Evidence-Based Approach to Tackling Health Inequalities in Britain' in Amanda Killoran, Catherine Swann, and Michael P Kelly (eds), *Public Health Evidence: Tackling Health Inequalities* (OUP: Oxford, 2006) 41–62.

[197] Richard Wilkinson, 'Ourselves and Others—For Better or Worse: Social Vulnerability and Inequality' in Michael Marmot and Richard Wilkinson, *Social Determinants of Health* (OUP: Oxford, 2005).

Jonathan Wolff[198]

One possibility is simply that having people around you helps you talk through your problems and seek solutions. Another is that regular contact with others reduces stress. But here is another possibility. A supportive social network helps you rest. This could be important. Very often someone in recovery from an illness will need to take some rest to allow the body's natural healing processes to come into effect. But to a mother with young children and no family around her to help, what does it mean to be ordered to rest? Or a self-employed small business person? Or someone on a low wage with no sick pay and an unsympathetic employer? Rest could be impossible, or lead to even more serious problems.

In 2008, Sir Michael Marmot was asked by the then Secretary of State for Health to propose evidence-based strategies for addressing health inequalities in England. In the 2010 Marmot Review, he pointed out that the social gradient in health has an economic as well as a human cost.

The Marmot Review[199]

The benefits of reducing health inequalities are economic as well as social. The cost of health inequalities can be measured in human terms, years of life lost and years of active life lost; and in economic terms, by the cost to the economy of additional illness. If everyone in England had the same death rates as the most advantaged, people who are currently dying prematurely as a result of health inequalities would, in total, have enjoyed between 1.3 and 2.5 million extra years of life. They would, in addition, have had a further 2.8 million years free of limiting illness or disability. It is estimated that inequality in illness accounts for productivity losses of £31–33 billion per year, lost taxes and higher welfare payments in the range of £20–32 billion per year, and additional NHS healthcare costs associated with inequality are well in excess of £5.5 billion per year. If no action is taken, the cost of treating the various illnesses that result from inequalities in the level of obesity alone will rise from £2 billion per year to nearly £5 billion per year in 2025.

It is not just absolute poverty that is associated with worse health outcomes, but relative inequality. On this point, Kate Pickett and Danny Dorling suggest that the Marmot Report did not go far enough.

Kate E Pickett and Danny Dorling[200]

We suggest that a major (but significant) problem with the UK Marmot Review is that it fails to deal with the need to reduce inequality by focusing on the top end of the social hierarchy, as well as the bottom. Although the Review calls for the establishment of a 'minimum income for healthy living', there is no suggestion that a maximum income or a constraint on the ratio of top-to-bottom incomes in institutions would also help reduce inequalities, and so improve the health and well-being of the population as a whole. . . . We suspect that more

---

[198] 'How should governments respond to the social determinants of health?' (2011) 53 Preventive Medicine 253–5.

[199] *Fair Society, Healthy Lives* (Institute of Health Equity, 2010).

[200] 'Against the organization of misery? The Marmot Review of health inequalities' (2010) 71 Social Science & Medicine 1231–3.

radical policy measures were not proposed because the political climate in Britain across the mainstream party spectrum, whilst accepting the rhetoric of 'fairness', is actually diffident in its support for the policies needed to create more equality.

There is a great deal of evidence that improving people's environment and life chances, and reducing inequality, have measurable effects on their health. The World Health Organization has suggested that action is needed under three broad headings:

World Health Organization[201]

- Improve the conditions of daily life—the circumstances in which people are born, grow, live, work, and age.
- Tackle the inequitable distribution of power, money, and resources—the structural drivers of those conditions of daily life—globally, nationally, and locally.
- Measure the problem, evaluate action, expand the knowledge base, develop a workforce that is trained in the social determinants of health, and raise public awareness about the social determinants of health.

Tackling the social determinants of health is difficult, however, because they are so diffuse and varied. Action is needed across almost all central and local government departments: employment, education, transport, and urban planning, as well as health and welfare. Even if the evidence is overwhelming, Carey and Crammond found that politicians may nevertheless need to be persuaded that any policy intervention will result in an immediate gain that will play well with voters. In their interviews with policy-makers, one explained that:

[Just because] something might be printed in the New England Journal of Medicine, or the Lancet or the BMJ . . . it wouldn't get the time of day unless it was accompanied by market research that showed what the impact of that would be in marginal seats.[202]

In the next extract, Jonathan Wolff proposes a policy that might have a positive impact upon one of the social determinants of health, and which might even be cost-effective, but which is unlikely to play well with politicians.

Jonathan Wolff[203]

If it is true that chronic stress is detrimental to health, then it is incumbent on us to think who in UK society is under the greatest chronic stress and to consider what could be done about it. . . . I conjecture that one very vulnerable group in this respect are people commonly known as 'benefit cheats'. I am not here referring to those involved in significant fraud, but rather

---

[201] *Closing the gap in a generation: health equity through action on the social determinants of health* (WHO: Geneva, 2008).

[202] Gemma Carey and Brad Crammond, 'Action on the social determinants of health: views from inside the policy process' (2015) 128 Social Science & Medicine 134–41.

[203] 'How should governments respond to the social determinants of health?' (2011) 53 Preventive Medicine 253–5.

those in receipt of benefit who also do a relatively small amount of cash in hand work in order to do such things as have a night out once a week or to buy birthday or Christmas presents for their children. For people who would much rather simply have a decently paying job, the stress of being on the wrong side of the law must be significant. And it may well contribute to stress related disorders and hence the social gradient of health. An enlightened policy would be to allow those in receipt of benefits to earn some money without needing to declare it for tax or benefit assessment purposes. Now it may be that this would not actually cost the Treasury anything, and might even reduce the need for some categories of bureaucrats, but if it does cost money a bid could be made to the Department of Health, under its social determinants support budget.

Critics like Mark A Rothstein have been concerned about the potential reach of public health policy, once all of the social, political, economic, and cultural determinants of health are taken into account.

Mark A Rothstein[204]

Just because war, crime, hunger, poverty, illiteracy, homelessness, and human rights abuses interfere with the health of individuals and populations does not mean that eliminating these conditions is part of the mission of public health. . . . It is incongruous to embrace the broadest meaning of public health at the same time that our legal system and public health infrastructure are based on a narrow definition of public health jurisdiction, authority, and remedies. . . . The broad power of government to protect public health includes the authority to supersede individual liberty and property interests in the name of preserving the greater public good. It is an awesome responsibility, and therefore it cannot and must not be used indiscriminately.

As we saw earlier, commentators who accuse public health interventions of being unduly paternalistic often individualize the problem of health inequalities, by maintaining that the solution is for individuals to improve their own health, rather than for the state to attempt to improve their material conditions. So, for example, rates of smoking in lower socioeconomic groups are much higher than in more affluent groups. Should we therefore blame poor individuals for not taking better care of their own health, or should we try to understand the reasons why, as Killoran et al explain, 'smokers living with multiple disadvantage are an extremely hard target group for smoking cessation activities'?

Amanda Killoran, Lesley Owen, and Linda Bauld[205]

Such communities are characterized by a lack of social mobility and a fatalistic attitude: 'an overwhelming lack of self-belief, self esteem and hope'. There is no culture of quitting, and smoking is perceived to be the norm. Although the risks of smoking are known, these seem minor compared with other difficulties such as low income and debt, low educational achievement

---

[204] Mark A Rothstein, 'Rethinking the meaning of public health' (2002) 30 Journal of Law, Medicine and Ethics 144–9.

[205] 'Smoking Cessation: An Evidence-Based Approach to Tackling Health Inequalities' in Amanda Killoran, Catherine Swann, and Michael P Kelly (eds), *Public Health Evidence: Tackling Health Inequalities* (OUP: Oxford, 2006) 341–6.

and lack of job opportunities, and physical and mental health problems. Most postpone quitting until a point when life is more under control, but have little confidence that this point will ever be reached. The findings indicate that most low-income smokers require a dramatic and sustained upturn in personal circumstances for smoking cessation to be a viable option.

Ironically, health education campaigns tend to be most successful among groups who are already comparatively healthy. As Shah et al point out, this may lead to a tension between maximizing public health, which can be achieved at relatively low cost by improving the health of the most advantaged, and reducing health inequalities, which will require greater expenditure for less overall gain.

Koonal K Shah et al[206]

[P]ublic health interventions that produce overall health improvement often exacerbate relative health differences between the most and least advantaged groups in society. . . .

It is often the case that public health programmes tend to benefit individuals who are already quite healthy, and therefore result in increased health inequalities. This is true of smoking cessation services, for example, which in the past have been found to be least likely to attract people from sectors of the population where smoking rates are high. . . . For example, suppose the targeted programme has a cost per QALY gained of £15,000, but spending the same amount of money on a universal version of the programme (which mainly benefits more advantaged individuals) would be associated with a cost per QALY gained of £10,000. In this case, it would be possible to increase population health by approving a universal version of the programme rather than the targeted version. The decision to spend money on the targeted intervention is then an *implicit* decision to depart from 'a QALY is a QALY is a QALY' and to give greater weight to the health gains for the disadvantaged population.

While eradicating social disadvantage might be the only way to eliminate relative health inequalities, targeting spending on health care in the most disadvantaged areas appears to be effective in reducing absolute inequalities. Between 2001 and 2011, a health inequalities component was incorporated into the NHS allocation formula in order to allocate more resources to deprived areas. Barr et al found that it reduced mortality rates, and that the return from every pound spent in a deprived area was greater than in more affluent areas.

Ben Barr, Clare Bambra, and Margaret Whitehead[207]

The policy of allocating greater NHS resources to more deprived areas led to a reduction in absolute health inequalities in mortality amenable to healthcare. Investment of NHS resources in more deprived areas was associated with a greater improvement in outcomes than investment in more affluent areas. Our study suggests that any change in resource allocation policy that reduces the proportion of funding allocated to deprived areas may reverse this trend and widen geographical inequalities in mortality from these causes.

---

[206] 'NICE's social value judgements about equity in health and health care' (2013) 8 Health Economics, Policy and Law 145–65.

[207] 'The impact of NHS resource allocation policy on health inequalities in England 2001–11: longitudinal ecological study' (2014) 348 British Medical Journal g3231.

NHS England has continued to use a funding formula which allocates additional funding to deprived areas, and indeed there is now a statutory obligation to have regard to the need to reduce health inequalities.

Health and Social Care Act 2012 section 1C

In exercising functions in relation to the health service, the Secretary of State must have regard to the need to reduce inequalities between the people of England with respect to the benefits that they can obtain from the health service.

Of course, while this might look progressive, 'having regard to the need to reduce inequalities' does not require specific action or set a specific target for the reduction or elimination of health inequalities. The scope of section 1C is also limited; it refers only to inequalities in access to *health care services*. As we have seen, the social determinants of health inequalities go far beyond differential access to NHS services. As Alex Scott-Samuel and Katherine Elizabeth Smith point out, political action on health inequalities has tended to focus on 'downstream' solutions, despite a lack of evidence that they will work, while failing to address the 'upstream' causes of inequality.

Alex Scott-Samuel and Katherine Elizabeth Smith[208]

While it can be politically expedient for governments to make commitments to reducing health inequalities, they cannot, within current political, social and economic norms, realistically propose actions which evidence suggests will substantially reduce them—such as tackling power inequalities, social status and connections, or class inequality. In this context, policy actors and researchers working in the United Kingdom have devised a parallel fantasy world in which proximal, downstream, easily tackled exposures are posited as potential solutions to health inequalities. This is, we argue, a 'utopian' exercise in the sense that this word is traditionally understood; an impossible dream in which the long-established social gradient in health is gradually flattened via a series of downstream interventions and policies which, for the most part, focus on trying to change behaviours that affect health outcomes, particularly in poorer communities, rather than trying to change the social and economic environments which inform people's circumstances and decision-making.

6 CONCLUSION

In the UK, we are, as our politicians realize, very attached to the principle of universal access to free health care. At the same time, few of us are willing to pay much higher rates of income tax. Given an ageing population, there will never be sufficient funds to eliminate the need to make tough choices about the allocation of scarce resources. It is also important to recognize that there are limits to what the NHS can achieve, given the extent to which our health is affected by our environment, lifestyle, income, and social status.

---

[208] 'Fantasy paradigms of health inequalities: utopian thinking?' (2015) 13 Social Theory & Health 418–36.

At the time of writing, it is too early to offer a definitive evaluation of the reforms introduced by the Health and Social Care Act 2012. However, as Donaldson et al point out, reform itself is always costly.

Cam Donaldson, Rachel Baker, and Neil McHugh[209]

> The usual response of governments to resource crises is to reform the health care system. However, it could be argued that all such reforms (continually) do is to create new entities to manage scarcity without facing up to the need to develop people and processes for doing this. Also, reform, in and of itself, is costly.

It is certainly noteworthy that senior members of the Conservative government have since queried the wisdom of such a massive and expensive reorganization. According to a 2014 article in *The Times*,

> David Cameron did not understand the controversial reforms and George Osborne regrets not having prevented what Downing Street officials call a 'huge strategic error'. . . . One senior cabinet minister told *The Times*: 'We've made three mistakes that I regret, the first being restructuring the NHS. The rest are minor'.[210]

FURTHER READING

Carey, Gemma and Crammond, Brad, 'Action on the social determinants of health: views from inside the policy process' (2015) 128 Social Science & Medicine 134–41.

Evans, HM, 'Do patients have duties?' (2007) 33 Journal of Medical Ethics 689–94.

Eyal, Nir et al (eds), *Inequalities in Health: Concepts, Measures, and Ethics* (OUP: Oxford, 2013).

Ford, Amy, 'The Concept of Exceptionality: A Legal Farce? (2012) 20 Medical Law Review 304–36.

Gostin, Lawrence O and Gostin, Kieran G, 'A broader liberty: JS Mill, paternalism and the public's health' (2009) 123 Public Health 214–21.

Ham, Chris et al, *The NHS under a coalition government—part one: NHS reform* (King's Fund: London, 2015).

Hoek, Janet, 'Informed choice and the nanny state: learning from the tobacco industry' (2015) 129 Public Health 1038–45.

Magnusson, Roger, 'Case studies in nanny state name-calling: what can we learn?' (2015) 129 Public Health 1074–82.

Newdick, Christopher, 'Judicial Review: Low-Priority Treatment and Exceptional Case Review' (2007) 15 Medical Law Review 236–44.

---

[209] 'The Economics of Proper Medical Treatment' in Sara Fovargue and Alexandra Mullock (eds), *The Legitimacy of Medical Treatment: What Role for the Medical Exception?* (Routledge: Abingdon, 2015) 183–96.

[210] Chris Smyth, Rachel Sylvester, and Alice Thomson, 'NHS reforms our worst mistake, Tories admit', *The Times*, 13 October 2014.

Newdick, Christopher, 'Promoting Access and Equity in Health: Assessing the National Health Service in England' in Colleen M Flood and Aeyal Gross (eds), *The Right to Health at the Public/Private Divide: A Global Comparative Study* (CUP: Cambridge, 2014) 107–28.

Scott-Samuel, Alex and Smith, Katherine Elizabeth, 'Fantasy paradigms of health inequalities: utopian thinking?' (2015) 13 Social Theory & Health 418–36.

Shah, Koonal K et al, 'NICE's social value judgements about equity in health and health care' (2013) 8 Health Economics, Policy and Law 145–65.

Stirton, Lindsay, 'Back to the Future? Lessons on the Pro-Competitive Regulation of Health Services' (2014) 22 Medical Law Review 180–99.

Syrett, Keith, 'Health technology appraisal and the courts: accountability for reasonableness and the judicial model of procedural justice' (2011) 6 Health Economics, Policy and Law 469–88.

Thaler, Richard H and Sunstein, Cass R, *Nudge: Improving Decisions About Health, Wealth and Happiness* (Penguin Books: New York, 2008).

Weait, Matthew, 'Unsafe law: health, rights and the legal response to HIV' (2013) 9 International Journal of Law in Context 535–64.

Wolff, Jonathan, 'How should governments respond to the social determinants of health?' (2011) 53 Preventive Medicine 253–5.

3

MEDICAL MALPRACTICE

CENTRAL ISSUES

1. Patients whose medical treatment goes wrong may wish to bring an action in negligence. For private patients, the implied contractual term that the doctor will exercise reasonable care and skill is indistinguishable from the doctor's duty of care in the tort of negligence.

2. Establishing that a doctor owes her patient a duty of care is straightforward. More complex issues arise when the claim is that a doctor's negligence resulted in her patient injuring someone else.

3. According to the *Bolam* test, as modified by *Bolitho*, the doctor will not be found to have acted negligently if she has acted in accordance with a practice accepted as proper by a responsible body of medical opinion, provided that that opinion is capable of withstanding logical analysis.

4. Having established that the doctor has breached her duty of care, the claimant must prove that this breach caused her injuries. This may be difficult in clinical negligence cases because, in most cases, the patient is already ill, and so there may be at least two possible causes of her deterioration.

5. There is a great deal wrong with the clinical negligence system: it is costly and inefficient, and few claimants succeed. More importantly still, it helps to foster a 'blame culture', which may make learning from mistakes less likely.

6. Other ways to deal with poor medical practice exist. In rare cases, doctors might face prosecution for gross negligence manslaughter. More commonly, a doctor's 'fitness to practise' might be investigated by the General Medical Council. It is also possible for patients to complain about their care via the NHS complaints system.

1 INTRODUCTION

In this chapter, we consider the law's response to medical treatment that has gone wrong. It has tended to be assumed that people who have been injured as a result of poor medical treatment will want financial compensation. In practice, evidence suggests that an explanation, an apology, and reassurance that the incident will not be repeated are more important to patients. In one study of people affected by medical injuries, 60 per cent wanted an apology, explanation, or inquiry into the cause of the incident; only 11 per cent thought that financial compensation was the most appropriate response.[1]

Negligence also has a rather narrow focus upon personal injury. Unless the patient has suffered physical injury or a recognized psychiatric illness, it is impossible to bring an action in negligence. The tort of negligence is therefore ill equipped to deal with some of the poor care and patient suffering that was identified in Sir Robert Francis QC's report into failings at Mid-Staffordshire NHS Foundation Trust,[2] such as leaving patients unwashed, with inadequate access to food, drink, toilet facilities, and clean sheets.

Despite its limited scope and its failure to offer patients their preferred remedies, the volume of clinical negligence cases has increased dramatically—by as much as 1,200 per cent—over the past 30 years.[3] We begin this chapter by looking briefly at the possibility of an action for breach of contract, before exploring the different stages involved in a clinical negligence claim. In recent years, there has been a great deal of criticism of the way in which medical mishaps are handled. The clinical negligence system costs the NHS millions of pounds each year. It has also been blamed for fostering a 'blame culture', which makes learning from mistakes less likely, and fails to provide patients with apologies and explanations.

Negligence is not the only way to address inadequate care, and so we also consider the NHS complaints system; the possibility of disciplinary action by the General Medical Council (GMC); and the circumstances in which a doctor might be prosecuted for gross negligence manslaughter.

In this chapter, our focus is mainly upon doctors' mistakes, rather than those of other health care workers. This is partly because doctors are principally responsible for patient care, and hence responsible when something goes wrong, and partly because the bulk of litigation has been against the medical profession, rather than nurses or other health care professionals.

It should also be noted that two 'special cases' in the tort of negligence are dealt with elsewhere in this book: the question of liability for failing to provide sufficient information to patients, and the possibility of liability for occurrences before birth, are covered in Chapters 4 and 14 respectively.

2 BREACH OF CONTRACT

If health care is provided in the private sector, the patient will have a contract with her doctor and/or with the clinic or hospital where she receives treatment. The nature of these contracts varies. For example, a patient may make an agreement directly with a doctor, who will then arrange for the patient's admission, or alternatively the patient's agreement may be made with a hospital, which then employs a doctor to provide the necessary services. The terms of contracts for private health care will also differ: for example, some may contain a term that specifies the identity of the treating doctor.

Contracts for private health care obviously include terms that are implied by statute: under sections 4 and 9 of the Supply of Goods and Services Act 1982, medical devices must be of satisfactory quality and fit for their purpose. Statutory limits on the use of exclusion

---

[1] *Making Amends: A Consultation Paper Setting Out Proposals for Reforming the Approach to Clinical Negligence in the NHS* (DH: London, 2003) 75.

[2] The Mid Staffordshire NHS Foundation Trust Public Inquiry (DH: London, 2013).

[3] Vivienne Harpwood, *Medicine, Malpractice and Misapprehensions* (Routledge-Cavendish: Abingdon, 2007) 2.

clauses also apply; for example, it is not possible to exclude or restrict liability for death or personal injury caused by negligence.[4]

It is possible, if unlikely, that a contract could contain an express term guaranteeing the outcome of the procedure. Few doctors would ever choose to give such a warranty, however, and the courts would be very unlikely to imply such a term into a contract for health care services. In *Thake v Maurice*, a failed sterilization case, Neill LJ stated:

> I do not consider that a reasonable person would have expected a responsible medical man to be intending to give a guarantee. Medicine, though a highly skilled profession, is not, and is not generally regarded as being, an exact science. The reasonable man would have expected the defendant to exercise all the proper skill and care of a surgeon in that speciality; he would not in my view have expected the defendant to give a guarantee of 100% success.[5]

The Court of Appeal did accept that there might be some circumstances in which a guarantee of success might reasonably be inferred. Nourse LJ gave the example of an operation to amputate a limb. A patient who goes into hospital to have her right leg amputated could reasonably expect that the operation will remove her right rather than her left leg. Such cases are likely to be rare, and more commonly, a reasonable person could not expect a doctor to guarantee a successful outcome.

In *Thake v Maurice* the Court of Appeal held that the patient's contract contained an implied term that the doctor would exercise reasonable care and skill. In practice, this is indistinguishable from the duty to take reasonable care in the tort of negligence, owed by all doctors to their patients. Because the vast majority of malpractice claims are brought in negligence, it is within our discussion of clinical negligence actions that we flesh out what is meant by 'reasonable care and skill'.

3 NEGLIGENCE

In order to succeed in an action in negligence, the claimant must establish that:

(a) she is owed a duty of care by the defendant (this will usually be the treating doctor, and her employer will be vicariously liable. GPs are a special case, and are sued personally, though they will be insured by a medical defence union); and

(b) the defendant breached that duty by failing to exercise reasonable care; and

(c) the breach of duty caused the claimant's injuries, and that those injuries are not too remote.

Finally, there are a number of defences which may be available to the defendant. Let us examine each of these stages in turn.

(a) THE EXISTENCE OF A DUTY OF CARE

The existence of a duty of care within the doctor–patient (or nurse–patient) relationship can generally be taken for granted. It is a well-established duty situation, and it is inconceivable

---

[4] Unfair Contract Terms Act 1977, s 2(1).   [5] *Thake v Maurice* [1986] QB 644.

that a doctor, or other health care worker, who had made a mistake during medical treatment would attempt to argue that she did not owe her patient a duty of care. The duty will be to exercise reasonable care and skill in diagnosis, advice, and treatment. Provided that the doctor committed the tort in the course of her employment—which will invariably be the case in clinical negligence cases—her employer will be vicariously liable for her negligence.

In three situations, however, the question of the existence of a duty of care is slightly more complicated.

(1) When Does the Doctor–Patient Relationship Come into Being?

There are times when the question of whether a particular individual was the doctor's patient at the relevant time is not straightforward. Because a doctor is under no legal obligation to treat a 'stranger', it is important to know when the transition from 'stranger' to 'patient' takes place. The common law position is that a duty of care is imposed upon the doctor once she has assumed responsibility for the patient's care.

In hospitals, the duty may arise as soon as the patient presents herself for treatment, before she is actually seen by a doctor. This was the case in *Barnett v Chelsea and Kensington Hospital Management Committee*. After drinking tea later discovered to have contained arsenic, three men had started vomiting and attended the casualty department of the defendant's hospital. The nurse telephoned Dr Banerjee, who was on duty at the time, and he told her to tell the men to go home and call their own doctors. The men died hours later from arsenic poisoning. One of the men's widows brought an action in negligence. Nield J held that Dr Banerjee had owed the men a duty of care, which he had breached by failing to examine them himself. (Later in this chapter we will see that this action failed on the question of causation.)

Barnett v Chelsea and Kensington Hospital Management Committee[6]

Nield J

I have no doubt that Nurse Corbett and Dr. Banerjee were under a duty to the deceased to exercise that skill and care which is to be expected of persons in such positions acting reasonably . . . Without doubt Dr. Banerjee should have seen and examined the deceased. His failure to do either cannot be described as an excusable error as has been submitted, it was negligence. It is unfortunate that Dr. Banerjee was himself at the time a tired and unwell doctor, but there was no-one else to do that which it was his duty to do.

The doctor's duty of care will arise only when she knows of the patient's need for medical services. For some patients, such as those over the age of 75, who must be offered an annual consultation, a GP's duty of care might extend to seeking out the patient, but normally it is only when the patient requests the doctor's assistance that the duty of care comes into being.

(2) Who Else Might Owe Primary Duties of Care to Patients?

In addition to being vicariously liable for its employees' negligence, might an NHS body owe a primary duty of care to patients to ensure that they receive adequate treatment? In

[6] [1969] 1 QB 428.

Wilsher v Essex AHA, for example, the Court of Appeal was of the view that the health authority owed patients a duty of care to provide properly skilled medical staff, and an adequately equipped hospital.

Wilsher v Essex AHA[7]

Sir Nicolas Browne-Wilkinson V-C

In my judgment, a health authority which so conducts its hospital that it fails to provide doctors of sufficient skill and experience to give the treatment offered at the hospital may be directly liable in negligence to the patient . . .

   Claims against a health authority that it has itself been directly negligent, as opposed to vicariously liable for the negligence of its doctors, will, of course, raise awkward questions. . . . Should the authority be liable if it demonstrates that, due to the financial stringency under which it operates, it cannot afford to fill the posts with those possessing the necessary experience? But, in my judgment, the law should not be distorted by making findings of personal fault against individual doctors who are, in truth, not at fault in order to avoid such questions.

An obvious problem in relation to this primary duty is that scarce resources are the norm in NHS hospitals. Courts may be prepared to impose some minimum standard of care, but they are generally reluctant to interfere with policy decisions about the allocation of limited resources. In *Bull v Devon AHA*, for example, the Court of Appeal drew a distinction between the hospital's duty to provide minimally adequate treatment, for which it could be liable in negligence, and its freedom to choose how to organize its services within the limited funds available to it.

   Mrs Bull had brought an action against Devon Health Authority on behalf of her severely handicapped son, one of twins, who had been injured as a result of a delay in the registrar's arrival while she was in labour. The system for urgently summoning an obstetrician had broken down, and there was a delay of about an hour before the registrar arrived. The health authority argued that such a delay was unavoidable because the hospital operated on two sites. The Court of Appeal rejected this, and held that the system failed to provide an acceptable level of care.

Bull v Devon AHA[8]

Dillon LJ

Obviously, there are highly specialised medical services which a district hospital does not have the equipment to provide and does not hold itself out as ready to provide. But this case is not about highly specialised services like that. The Exeter City Hospital provides a maternity service for expectant mothers, and any hospital which provides such a service ought to be able to cope with the not particularly out of the way case of a healthy young mother in somewhat premature labour with twins.

---

[7] [1987] QB 730.   [8] [1993] 4 Med LR 117 (CA).

So while Mrs Bull was not entitled to expect that an obstetrician would be available imme-diately, waiting for an hour fell below the minimum standard of care that the hospital was under a duty to provide. If, say, the registrar had arrived within 15 minutes, Mrs Bull's action would probably have failed.

In *Garcia v St Mary's NHS Trust*, it had taken 30 minutes for the on-call cardio-thoracic registrar to arrive at Mr Garcia's bedside, after he lost consciousness following cardiac sur-gery, and this delay was held not to be negligent.

Garcia v St Mary's NHS Trust[9]

Judge Shaun Spencer

I take the view that the whole system obviously has to be framed to deal with that which is reasonably foreseeable. I do not take the view that the whole system has to be framed to deal with the possibility that a rare occurrence will happen, and by rare the figure mentioned is one in a thousand . . . I am fortified in my conclusion that the two surgeons, who know hospitals far better that I do, regard the time taken and the system as reasonable, despite the outcome which affects Mr Garcia.

Rather than relying upon a hospital's primary duty to provide adequate treatment, it will usually be more straightforward for an injured patient to bring an action in negligence against an individual employee, whose employer will then be vicariously liable.

The primary duty to provide adequate treatment might be more significant, however, when, as is increasingly common, a patient's NHS treatment is being provided in a private hospital. In such cases, the Clinical Commissioning Group which commissioned the treat-ment will continue to owe a primary duty to arrange adequate care, even though it is not the individual doctor's employer. Of course, there will normally be an arrangement with the private hospital to indemnify the NHS against liability, but the patient herself will be able to sue the NHS commissioning body.

Re HIV Haemophiliac Litigation[10] was an unusual case in which patients sought to argue that the Secretary of State for Health was in breach of his duty of care to them. The patients were haemophiliacs who had received transfusions with HIV-contaminated blood products. They brought an action against the Secretary of State for Health for fail-ing to warn patients of the risks of contamination. The Court of Appeal held that the case could proceed to trial because there was at least an arguable case, but the case was then settled.

A relationship of proximity between the Secretary of State for Health and individual patients would undoubtedly be exceptional. Although there was no full hearing in this case, haemophiliac patients are unusual because there are relatively few of them, and they are likely to need at least one blood transfusion during their lifetime. They are a small group of patients, known in advance to have a need for blood products.

More commonly, there will be no relationship of proximity between the Secretary of State for Health and individual patients. For example, in *Danns v Department of Health*,[11] Mr and Mrs Danns unsuccessfully brought an action against the Department of Health for failure to take steps to disseminate new findings about the reversibility of vasectomy to the 1.5 million people estimated to be relying upon vasectomies as their only method

---

[9] [2006] EWHC 2314 (QB).   [10] (1998) 41 BMLR 171.   [11] [1998] PIQR P226.

of birth control. The Court of Appeal found that the Department of Health could not owe Mr and Mrs Danns a duty of care because it was not in a sufficient relationship of proximity with them.

(3) Could Health Care Workers Ever Owe Non-Patients a Duty of Care?

Usually, the only person likely to be injured by a doctor's mistake is the patient herself. In the next sections, we consider four scenarios in which a third party might seek to claim that they were owed a duty of care by a health care professional:

- wrongful pregnancy;
- psychiatric injury;
- failure to prevent the patient from causing harm;
- medical examinations.

(a) 'Wrongful pregnancy'

Where a sterilization operation has been carried out negligently, or a patient has been given negligent advice about its success, it is, as we see in Chapter 14, possible to recover damages in tort for the pain and discomfort associated with pregnancy and childbirth. These are suffered only by women. If a man's sterilization has failed, the 'damage' is therefore suffered not by the patient himself, but by a third party. She will generally only be able to recover damages if she was within the doctor's contemplation at the time of the operation, because she was the patient's wife or partner.

In *McFarlane v Tayside Health Board*,[12] a case we consider in Chapter 14, the male patient was married and his wife was in a sufficiently proximate relationship with her husband's doctors. In contrast, in *Goodwill v BPAS*, the court decided that a doctor carrying out a vasectomy does not owe a duty to all of his patient's future sexual partners.

Goodwill v BPAS[13]

Peter Gibson LJ

The defendants were not in a sufficient or any special relationship with the plaintiff such as gives rise to a duty of care. I cannot see that it can properly be said of the defendants that they voluntarily assumed responsibility to the plaintiff when giving advice to Mr MacKinlay. At that time they had no knowledge of her, she was not an existing sexual partner of Mr MacKinlay but was merely, like any other woman in the world, a potential future sexual partner of his, that is to say a member of an indeterminately large class of females who might have sexual relations with Mr MacKinlay during his lifetime.

(b) Psychiatric injury

It is possible that someone close to the patient might suffer psychiatric injury as a result of witnessing negligent medical treatment. In such cases, the third party is described as a secondary victim, and the limiting principles developed in *Alcock v Chief Constable of South*

---

[12] 2000 SC (HL) 1.   [13] [1996] 1 WLR 1397.

Yorkshire[14] and *White v Chief Constable of South Yorkshire*[15] apply. In short, the claimant must have a close relationship with the primary victim; she must be close in time and space to the incident; she must witness it, or its immediate aftermath, with her unaided senses; and she must suffer a recognizable psychiatric illness, such as post-traumatic stress disorder (PTSD) as a result.[16]

In *Sion v Hampstead Health Authority*,[17] a father had stayed in hospital with his son, who had been injured in a motorbike accident. His son lapsed into a coma and died 14 days later. The father alleged that the hospital treating him had been negligent, and claimed damages for his own psychiatric illness. His claim was dismissed by the Court of Appeal on the grounds that, as Staughton LJ explained, there had been:

> no sudden appreciation by sight or sound of a horrifying event. On the contrary, the report describes a process continuing for some time, from first arrival at the hospital to the appreciation of medical negligence after the inquest. In particular, the son's death when it occurred was not surprising but expected.

In contrast, in *North Glamorgan NHS Trust v Walters*, a mother whose newborn baby's death was the result of the defendant's negligence, and who witnessed his distressing final 36 hours, was said to have suffered the requisite 'shock'.

North Glamorgan NHS Trust v Walters[18]

Ward LJ

In my judgment on the facts of this case there was an inexorable progression from the moment when the fit occurred as a result of the failure of the hospital properly to diagnose and then to treat the baby, the fit causing the brain damage which shortly thereafter made termination of this child's life inevitable and the dreadful climax when the child died in her arms. It is a seamless tale with an obvious beginning and an equally obvious end. It was played out over a period of 36 hours, which for her both at the time and as subsequently recollected was undoubtedly one drawn-out experience . . . The necessary proximity in space and time is satisfied. The assault on her nervous system had begun and she reeled under successive blows as each was delivered.

Walters is, however, an unusual case. It was distinguished in *Liverpool Women's Hospital NHS Foundation Trust v Ronayne*, in which the claimant had observed a rapid deterioration in his wife's condition after she was readmitted to hospital following a negligently performed hysterectomy. Mr Ronayne claimed that he had suffered PTSD as a result. The Court of Appeal unanimously held, first, that there was not the necessary element of suddenness, but instead a gradual realization of the seriousness of his wife's condition and, secondly, that what the claimant had seen was not sufficiently horrifying.

---

[14] [1992] 1 AC 310.   [15] [1999] 2 AC 455.

[16] Both *Alcock* and *White* arose out of the Hillsborough stadium disaster in 1989, and involved claims brought by friends or relatives (*Alcock*) and policemen (*White*).

[17] *Sion v Hampstead Health Authority*, The Times, 10 June 1994.   [18] [2002] EWCA Civ 1792.

Liverpool Women's Hospital NHS Foundation Trust v Ronayne[19]

Tomlinson LJ (with whom Sullivan and Beatson LJJ agreed)

Having been told of the severity of his wife's condition and that she was being administered a cocktail of antibiotics, it cannot in my judgment be said that what thereafter occurred had the necessary element of suddenness.

Furthermore what the Claimant saw on these two occasions was not in my judgment horrifying by objective standards. Both on the first occasion and on the second the appearance of the Claimant's wife was as would ordinarily be expected of a person in hospital in the circumstances in which she found herself. What is required in order to found liability is something which is exceptional in nature. On the first occasion she was connected to monitors and drips. The reaction of most people of ordinary robustness to that sight, given the circumstances in which she had been taken into the A & E Department, and the knowledge that abnormalities had been found, including a shadow over the lung, necessitating immediate exploratory surgery, would surely be one of relief that the matter was in the hands of the medical professionals, with perhaps a grateful nod to the ready availability of modern medical equipment. The same is more or less true of her swollen appearance on the second occasion.... I can readily accept that the appearance of Mrs Ronayne on this occasion must have been both alarming and distressing to the Claimant, but it was not in context exceptional and it was not I think horrifying in the sense in which that word has been used in the authorities. Certainly however it did not lead to a sudden violent agitation of the mind, because the Claimant was prepared to witness a person in a desperate condition and was moreover already extremely angry.

Psychiatric injury might also be caused to non-patients by the communication of traumatic information. It would be difficult to fit this within the *Alcock* criteria: the claimant is supposed to have witnessed the shocking event with her unaided senses, as opposed to just being told about it. Nevertheless, if information is communicated negligently, might it be possible for a relative to claim that she is a primary victim, and hence that the distinction between physical and psychiatric injury is less important?

At first sight, this might seem improbable, given that it has generally been assumed that primary victims must have been physically endangered by the defendant's negligence. In *Page v Smith*,[20] for example, Lord Lloyd said that to be a primary victim, the claimant had to be 'within the range of foreseeable physical injury'. A different approach was, however, adopted in *Farrell v Avon Health Authority*.[21] When the claimant arrived at the hospital following the birth of his son, he was wrongly informed that he had died, and was given a dead baby to hold for 20 minutes. He was then told that there had been a mistake, and his son was in fact alive and well. Bursell J held that the claimant was a primary victim because he was directly involved in the traumatic incident, and he was therefore able to recover for his PTSD.

In the next extract, Paula Case discusses some of the special problems facing relatives seeking to claim for psychiatric illnesses triggered by their relatives' negligent medical treatment.

---

[19] [2015] EWCA Civ 588.   [20] [1996] AC 155.   [21] (2000) 2 LGLR 69.

Paula Case[22]

> The relative is unlikely to witness at first hand the 'sudden shocking event' currently required by English law as, unlike the typical accident environment, the hospital is a highly controlled space where the family's view of tragedy is often occluded by the intervention of hospital personnel . . .
>
> The claimant will generally not witness the moment of their relative's demise and may rely on viewing the deceased's body after death as the 'shocking event' which caused the harm. Where the relative is absent during the events which caused the death of the deceased, an attempt to rely on identification of the body after death as the 'shocking event' is likely to fail . . . In *Alcock*, their Lordships agreed that secondary victims must demonstrate that their injury be caused by a 'sudden appreciation by sight or sound of a horrifying event which violently agitates the mind'.
>
> The sudden shocking event requirement presents particular problems in hospital cases, because it might be argued by defendants that the 'suddenness' of the shocking event is negated by the reasons that brought the MAV [medical accident victim] to hospital. In other words, the probability of deterioration is known merely by the fact that the MAV was in hospital.

Jyoti Ahuja further argues that the law's limiting criteria bear no resemblance to evidence of what is especially traumatic for bereaved relatives. In fact, coming upon the immediate aftermath and seeing it with one's unaided senses may make someone *less* likely to suffer serious psychological harm.

Jyoti Ahuja[23]

> The proximity requirement views trauma as resulting primarily from the sight of the mutilated body of the loved one, and assumes that the pain is less when the body is not witnessed. This is, however, contrary to research evidence. Studies suggest that bereaved relatives who are denied the choice to view the body of their loved one may suffer more than those who were given the opportunity. . . . Recovery has been found to be especially hard when the body of the loved one is never found . . . The law, paradoxically, might deny recovery to those who possibly suffer the greatest distress . . .
>
> Imagined images may often be worse than reality. . . . Contrary to judicial assumptions, it does not appear that those who hear about the death from another source are spared much of the emotional pain that those who see it.

Rachael Mulheron has also pointed out that the need for the claimant to have suffered a 'recognizable psychiatric illness' is problematic because diagnostic categories are designed in order to plan treatment, rather than to allocate blame.

---

[22] 'Secondary Iatrogenic Harm: Claims for Psychiatric Damage Following a Death Caused by Medical Error' (2004) 67 Modern Law Review 561–87.

[23] 'Liability for Psychological and Psychiatric Harm: The Road to Recovery' (2015) 23 Medical Law Review 27–52.

Rachael Mulheron[24]

> The diagnostic classifications were not intended or approved for legal (forensic) use, but were designed for research and clinical diagnostic purposes, as DSM-IV itself points out: 'When the DSM-IV categories, criteria, and textual descriptions are employed for forensic purposes, there are significant risks that diagnostic information will be misused or misunderstood. These dangers arise because of the imperfect fit between the questions of ultimate concern to the law and the information contained in a clinical diagnosis'. . . .
>
> For one thing, clinically speaking, an accurate diagnosis (say, whether a patient has a depressive episode or a mixed anxiety and depressive disorder) is important when planning *treatment*; but from a litigious point of view, the emphasis is different, because the court is seeking to ascertain whether the claimant has suffered any *compensable damage*.

(c) Failure to prevent the patient from causing harm

There are a number of ways in which patients who are not offered proper advice or treatment might pose a risk to others. First, if a doctor realizes that her patient is unfit to drive, she is under a duty both to tell her not to drive and to inform the Driver and Vehicle Licensing Agency. If she instead does nothing, it is foreseeable that a third party might be injured as a result. Secondly, patients with infectious diseases pose a risk to third parties, hence a doctor's negligent failure to diagnose her patient's condition, or to offer her appropriate advice or treatment might put others at risk. Thirdly, if a doctor does not 'section' a psychiatric patient whom she believes to be likely to harm someone else (see further Chapter 6), it is foreseeable that a third party might be hurt. In these situations, could a doctor owe foreseeably injured non-patients a duty of care?

It is important to remember that in such cases the doctor has not directly caused the claimant's injury; rather, she would be being sued for an omission, or a failure to prevent harm from occurring. As a result, a three-stage test applies: (1) the claimant's injury must be foreseeable; (2) there must be a proximate relationship between the claimant and the doctor; and (3) the imposition of a duty must be fair, just, and reasonable.[25] While it might be relatively straightforward to establish foreseeability, proving that there is a sufficient relationship of proximity, and that imposing a duty of care would be fair, just, and reasonable, will often be much more problematic.

The question of whether doctors might be under a duty to protect a member of the public from a dangerous psychiatric patient arose in *Palmer v Tees Health Authority*.[26] A man who had a long history of psychiatric problems abducted, sexually assaulted, and murdered a four-year-old girl, Rosie Palmer. Rosie's mother claimed that the defendant health authority's medical staff had failed to diagnose that there was a real, substantial, and foreseeable risk that this man would commit serious sexual offences against children, and that the defendants should therefore be liable for her daughter's death, and for her own PTSD and pathological grief reaction.

It was not disputed that the injuries to Rosie and her mother might have been foreseeable; but the judge held that there was not a relationship of sufficient proximity between the health authority and Rosie Palmer, and that it was not fair, just, and reasonable to impose

---

[24] 'Rewriting the Requirement for a "Recognized Psychiatric Injury" in Negligence Claims' (2012) 32 Oxford Journal of Legal Studies 77–112.

[25] *Caparo v Dickman* [1990] 2 AC 605.   [26] [1999] Lloyd's Rep Med 351 (CA).

a duty of care upon the defendants. Mrs Palmer's appeal to the Court of Appeal was dismissed, Stuart Smith LJ pointing out that where a future victim was not identifiable, it would in practice be impossible to protect them from harm:

> An additional reason why in my judgment in this case it is at least necessary for the victim to be identifiable (though as I have indicated it may not be sufficient) to establish proximity, is that it seems to me that the most effective way of providing protection would be to give warning to the victim, his or her parents or social services so that some protective measure can be made. . . .

There have been no cases in which claimants have sued medical professionals or their employers for failure to prevent a patient from causing injuries through dangerous driving or infectious disease. It is, however, likely that the courts would find that injuring other road users or infecting close contacts were foreseeable consequences of the failure to provide reasonable care to the patient, but that it would be much more difficult to establish the requisite proximity.

In the case of infectious disease, unless both the claimant's existence and her risk of infection were known to the doctor, it would be difficult to argue that there was a sufficiently proximate relationship. Even if the claimant was identifiable in advance as someone likely to be infected by the patient, perhaps because the doctor knew about their sexual relationship, other considerations, such as the duty to protect patient confidentiality (considered in Chapter 7), might mean that it would not be fair, just, or reasonable to impose a duty to protect the claimant from infection.

(d) Medical examinations

Finally, it is clear that a doctor who has been employed to carry out a medical examination on behalf of a third party owes a duty of care to the person who is examined. In *D v East Berkshire Community Health NHS Trust*,[27] the Court of Appeal held that a doctor examining a child where there is a suspicion that the child has been abused undoubtedly owes the child a duty of care. The case then went to the House of Lords, on the question of whether the doctor in such circumstances might also owe a duty of care to the parents. In *JD v East Berkshire Community Health NHS Trust* the House of Lords decided that this would create an unacceptable conflict of interest, and so any duty of care is owed to the child alone.

JD v East Berkshire Community Health NHS Trust[28]

Lord Rodger

The duty to the children is simply to exercise reasonable care and skill in diagnosing and treating any condition from which they may be suffering. In carrying out that duty the doctors have regard only to the interests of the children. Suppose, however, that they were also under a duty to the parents not to cause them psychiatric harm by concluding that they might have abused their child. Then, in deciding how to proceed, the doctors would always have to take account of the risk that they might harm the parents in this way. There would be not one but two sets of interests to be considered. Acting on, or persisting in, a suspicion of abuse might well be reasonable when only the child's interests were engaged,

---

[27] *D v East Berkshire Community Health NHS Trust* [2003] EWCA Civ 1151.
[28] [2005] UKHL 23.

but unreasonable if the interests of the parents had also to be taken into account. Of its very nature, therefore, this kind of duty of care to the parents would cut across the duty of care to the children.

(b) BREACH

(1) What is the Standard of Care?

Having established (usually straightforwardly) that she was owed a duty of care, the next stage for a claimant in a negligence action is to prove that the doctor breached her duty of care. In order to work out whether there has been a breach, it is necessary to establish what standard of care could reasonably have been expected. In ordinary tort actions, defendants are judged by what is known as the 'reasonable man' test, but clearly this does not mean that the doctor's skill is judged by what it would be reasonable to expect from the 'man on the Clapham omnibus'. Rather, the doctor must meet the standard of care that can be expected from a doctor 'skilled in that particular art':[29] a GP must act as a reasonable GP; a neurosurgeon as a reasonable neurosurgeon, and so on. If a GP were to attempt a specialist procedure, such as anaesthesia, she would be judged by the standard of a reasonable anaesthetist. If the GP is unable to meet this standard, she might be found negligent for undertaking treatment beyond her competence.

The standard of care will be judged at the time when the alleged negligence occurred. If the claimant was injured during childbirth 20 years ago but only now brings an action for her injuries, the obstetrician will be judged by the standards of reasonable and responsible obstetric care 20 years ago. In *Roe v Minister of Health*,[30] heard in 1954, the defendants had administered contaminated anaesthetic to the claimant in 1947, but at that time the particular risk of contamination was unknown. The Court of Appeal found that there had been no negligence, Denning LJ, as he then was, famously saying 'We must not look at the 1947 accident with 1954 spectacles.' In 1951, a leading textbook had warned against the practice that led to the accident in *Roe*, and Denning LJ therefore went on to say:

If the hospitals were to continue the practice after this warning, they could not complain if they were found guilty of negligence. But the warning had not been given at the time of this accident. Indeed, it was the extraordinary accident to these two men which first disclosed the danger. Nowadays it would be negligence not to realise the danger, but it was not then.[31]

The central problem in judging the standard of care is that reasonable doctors within the same area of expertise may disagree. If differences of medical opinion are inevitable, how can the court decide which view should be preferred? As many law students will recall, the answer to this question has been dominated by the *Bolam* test, now qualified by the *Bolitho* gloss.

(a) The Bolam *test*

In *Bolam v Friern Hospital Management Committee*, John Bolam, who was suffering from depression, was advised by a consultant at the defendants' hospital to undergo electroconvulsive therapy (ECT). He was not warned that ECT carried a small risk of fracture, nor

---

[29] *Bolam*, see the following section.   [30] [1954] 2 QB 66.   [31] Ibid.

was he physically restrained or given relaxant drugs. As a result, Mr Bolam sustained a fractured hip. At the time, medical opinion varied, both as to the desirability of warning patients of the risk of fracture associated with ECT, and as to whether it was appropriate to use relaxant drugs and physical restraint.

Bolam v Friern Hospital Management Committee[32]

McNair J (in his direction to the jury)

The test is the standard of the ordinary skilled man exercising and professing to have that special skill. A man need not possess the highest skill at the risk of being found negligent. It is well established law that it is sufficient if he exercises the ordinary skill of an ordinary competent man exercising that particular art. . . .

A doctor is not guilty of negligence if he has acted in accordance with a practice accepted as proper by a responsible body of medical men skilled in that particular art . . . Putting it the other way round, a doctor is not negligent, if he is acting in accordance with such a practice, merely because there is a body of opinion that takes a contrary view. At the same time, that does not mean that a medical man can obstinately and pig-headedly carry on with some old technique if it has been proved to be contrary to what is really substantially the whole of informed medical opinion. Otherwise you might get men today saying: 'I don't believe in anaesthetics. I don't believe in antiseptics. I am going to continue to do my surgery in the way it was done in the eighteenth century.' That clearly would be wrong.

Although *Bolam v Friern Hospital Management Committee* was itself only a first instance decision, and one of the last medical negligence cases to come before a jury, McNair J's '*Bolam* test' has subsequently been approved by the House of Lords.[33]

The *Bolam* test appears to treat medical negligence differently from most other negligence actions. When deciding whether an employer or a driver has been negligent, the standard of care is set by the court using the device of the reasonable man. When the defendant is a doctor, however, the standard of care has historically been set by other doctors, via the *Bolam* test. This judicial deference to medical opinion may have been partly due to the complexity of medical evidence, but might also be explained by a sense of professional solidarity, and by the high regard in which the medical profession has conventionally been held.

Maynard v West Midlands RHA, a case in which a patient sought to challenge her doctor's decision to carry out an invasive test for Hodgkin's disease, offers a good example of the judiciary's obvious reluctance to question the evidence of a 'responsible' medical practitioner.

Maynard v West Midlands RHA[34]

Lord Scarman

I have to say that a judge's 'preference' for one body of distinguished professional opinion to another also professionally distinguished is not sufficient to establish negligence in a practitioner whose actions have received the seal of approval of those whose opinions,

---

[32] [1957] WLR 582.
[33] In *Whitehouse v Jordan* [1981] 1 WLR 246 and *Maynard v West Midlands* [1984] 1 WLR 634.
[34] [1984] 1 WLR 634.

truthfully expressed, honestly held, were not preferred. . . . For in the realm of diagnosis and treatment negligence is not established by preferring one respectable body of professional opinion to another.

In *Maynard*, notice that Lord Scarman suggests that the courts should defer to the opinions of expert witnesses if they are 'truthfully expressed, honestly held', which implies that the court should scrutinize the credibility of witnesses, rather than the content of their evidence. For many years doctors were therefore able to escape liability if they could find one or more respectable expert witnesses prepared to say that they would have acted in the same way.

There had, however, been one notable exception to the court's apparent reluctance to review the substance, as opposed to just the credibility, of expert evidence. In *Hucks v Cole*, a case decided in 1968 but not widely reported until 1994, the Court of Appeal had rejected the evidence of the defendant's four expert witnesses, and found that the doctor's failure to prescribe penicillin to a woman with a septic finger, who was at special risk because she was about to give birth, was negligent.

Hucks v Cole[35]

Sachs LJ

Despite the fact that the risk could have been avoided by adopting a course that was easy, efficient and inexpensive, and which would have entailed only minimal chances of disadvantages to the patient, the evidence of the four defence experts to the effect that they and other responsible members of the medical profession would have taken the same risk in the same circumstances has naturally caused me to hesitate considerably on two points. Firstly, whether the failure of the defendant to turn over to penicillin treatment during the relevant period was unreasonable. On this, however, I was in the end fully satisfied that . . . failure to do this was not merely wrong but clearly unreasonable. The reasons given by the four experts do not to my mind stand up to analysis. . . .

Doctor Cole knowingly took an easily avoidable risk which elementary teaching had instructed him to avoid; and the fact that others say they would have done the same neither ought to nor can in the present case excuse him in an action for negligence however sympathetic one may be to him.

(b) Bolam + Bolitho: *a less deferential approach?*

Then in 1997, in *Bolitho v City and Hackney Health Authority*, the House of Lords adopted a more robust, and potentially less deferential, version of the *Bolam* test. Patrick Bolitho, who was two years old, had been admitted to hospital suffering from breathing difficulties. His condition deteriorated, and he suffered a cardiac arrest, leading to brain damage and subsequently to his death. The on-duty paediatric registrar did not see him, but even if she had, she said that she would not have intubated him. Intubation was the only procedure that could have prevented respiratory failure, but it was not without risks.

The expert witnesses for each side expressed diametrically opposed views about whether a failure to intubate was reasonable. On the facts, the House of Lords held that the registrar

[35] [1993] 4 Med LR 393.

had not breached her duty of care, but the case is important for Lord Browne-Wilkinson's comments on the circumstances in which the court would be likely to decide that there had been negligence, despite the evidence of expert witnesses who agreed with the defendant's course of action.

Bolitho v City and Hackney Health Authority[36]

Lord Browne-Wilkinson

In the vast majority of cases the fact that distinguished experts in the field are of a particular opinion will demonstrate the reasonableness of that opinion. In particular, where there are questions of assessment of the relative risks and benefits of adopting a particular medical practice, a reasonable view necessarily presupposes that the relative risks and benefits have been weighed by the experts in forming their opinions. But if, in a rare case, it can be demonstrated that the professional opinion is not capable of withstanding logical analysis, the judge is entitled to hold that the body of opinion is not reasonable or responsible.

I emphasise that, in my view, it will very seldom be right for a judge to reach the conclusion that views genuinely held by a competent medical expert are unreasonable. The assessment of medical risks and benefits is a matter of clinical judgment which a judge would not normally be able to make without expert evidence. . . . It is only where a judge can be satisfied that the body of expert opinion cannot be logically supported at all that such opinion will not provide the bench mark by reference to which the defendant's conduct falls to be assessed.

I turn to consider whether this is one of those rare cases. Like the Court of Appeal, in my judgment it plainly is not.

Following *Bolitho*, then, the views of expert witnesses must not only be honestly and sincerely held, but must also be 'capable of withstanding logical analysis'. What does this mean in practice?

As an initial caveat, it is still by no means easy to prove that a doctor, whose conduct has been endorsed by other expert witnesses, was in fact negligent. In *Wisniewski v Central Manchester Health Authority*,[37] there was disagreement between the expert witnesses over the reasonableness of the defendant's failure to carry out a procedure to detect whether the baby's umbilical cord was wrapped around his neck during childbirth. Brooke LJ explained that:

Hucks v Cole itself was unquestionably one of the rare cases which Lord Browne-Wilkinson had in mind. . . . In my judgment the present case falls unquestionably on the other side of the line, and it is quite impossible for a court to hold that the views sincerely held by Mr Macdonald (an eminent consultant and an impressive witness) and Professor Thomas cannot logically be supported at all.

Nevertheless, there have now been a sufficient number of judgments which have invoked, either implicitly or explicitly, the *Bolitho* gloss for it to be worth questioning whether it would still be accurate to describe these cases as 'rare'.[38]

---

[36] [1998] AC 232.

[37] *Wisniewski v Central Manchester Health Authority* [1998] Lloyd's Rep Med 223 (CA).

[38] Rachael Mulheron, 'Trumping *Bolam*: A Critical Legal Analysis of *Bolitho*'s "Gloss"' (2010) 69 Cambridge Law Journal 609–38.

Essentially, the *Bolam + Bolitho* test for the standard of care in negligence is now a two-stage one. First, the court must ask whether the doctor acted in accordance with responsible medical opinion—which might be established through expert medical testimony. If she did not, she would have been found negligent according to the traditional *Bolam* test. An example of straightforward *Bolam* negligence is *Fallon v Wilson*. This was a case in which a premature baby, Alice Fallon, who had only just been discharged from hospital, was taken to see her GP for a repeat prescription. While in Dr Wilson's consulting room, Alice's condition markedly deteriorated. Despite this, Dr Wilson just advised her mother to take her home and keep her warm. Although there was some dispute over what actually happened in Dr Wilson's consulting rooms, expert evidence was that—if Alice's mother's account was correct—the right response would have been to refer Alice to hospital immediately. Alice was taken home but soon afterwards stopped breathing and was then taken straight to hospital. Had Dr Wilson's failure to refer her to hospital immediately amounted to a breach of his duty of care? Once Eady J had established that, on certain important matters of fact, Alice's mother's account was correct, he found that Dr Wilson had not acted as a reasonable GP.

Fallon v Wilson[39]

Eady J

On 15 January 1997, however, at some point between 17.00 and 17.30, he was called upon to make a judgment in a busy surgery on limited information and in the light of his long experience. I regret to say, however, that in making that judgment he fell short of the standard to be expected of a competent practitioner in the situation that confronted him. It was an inadequate response to advise merely that Alice should be kept warm.

I find in the light of the evidence that she should have been referred to hospital straight away and that, accordingly, there was a breach of duty on the Defendant's part . . . There would be a low threshold for referral in the case of a premature baby—and, in particular, a baby who had been born at 27 weeks and had still by the time of the consultation not reached the equivalent of full term.

If, however, the doctor did act in accordance with a body of responsible medical opinion, that is not now the end of the matter, and the claimant has a second opportunity to prove that the doctor was negligent if she can establish that this body of medical opinion is 'not capable of withstanding logical analysis'.

So what does this mean in practice? Most obviously, and following on from the earlier case of *Hucks v Cole*, it will be relatively straightforward for the court to determine that expert evidence 'does not withstand logical analysis' when the doctor failed to do something—such as take a simple precaution or examine the patient—in circumstances when it would be obvious to a lay person that they should have done so. For example, in *Reynolds v North Tyneside Health Authority*,[40] Gross J found that the failure to examine the claimant's mother properly during childbirth—which led to the claimant's asphyxia, and resulting cerebral palsy—was a case in which the court should be prepared to disregard expert witnesses who claimed that they would have acted in the same way as the treating doctor, on the grounds that their opinion 'was unreasonable, irresponsible, illogical and indefensible'.

Similarly, in *Marriott v West Midlands RHA*, Mr Marriott had suffered a head injury and had been unconscious for 20–30 minutes. During the following week he had been lethargic,

---

[39] [2010] EWHC 2978 (QB).   [40] [2002] Lloyd's Rep Med 459.

had suffered from headaches, and had had no appetite. His GP, Dr Patel, attended him but did not think there was anything wrong with him. Four days later, Mr Marriott's condition deteriorated. He lost consciousness, and was left permanently disabled. One expert witness supported Dr Patel's judgement, while another claimed that it had been negligent not to refer Mr Marriott back to hospital. Since it would seem blindingly obvious that doctors should be concerned about symptoms reported by someone who has recently suffered a head injury, the Court of Appeal decided that the evidence given by the expert witness who defended the doctor's conduct could not be logically supported.

Marriott v West Midlands RHA[41]

Beldam LJ

The judge then identified the area of disagreement which lay, she said, in the element of discretion which a reasonably prudent doctor would exercise whether or not to advise readmission to hospital.

'Furthermore, whilst a Court must plainly be reluctant to depart from the opinion of an apparently careful and prudent general practitioner, I have concluded that, if there is a body of professional opinion which supports the course of leaving a patient who has some 7 days previously sustained a severe head injury at home in circumstances where he continues to complain of headaches, drowsiness etc, and where there continues to be a risk of the existence of an intracranial lesion which could cause a sudden and disastrous collapse, then such approach is not reasonably prudent. It may well be that, if in the vast majority of cases, the risk is very small. Nevertheless, the consequence, if things go wrong, are disastrous to the patient. In such circumstances, it is my view that the only reasonably prudent course in any case where a general practitioner remains of the view that there is a risk of an intracranial lesion such as to warrant the carrying out of neurological testing and the giving of further head injury instructions, then the only prudent course judged from the point of view of the patient is to re-admit for further testing and observation.' . . .

It was open to the judge to hold that, in the circumstances as she found them to have been, it could not be a reasonable exercise of a general practitioner's discretion to leave a patient at home and not to refer him back to hospital. Accordingly, I would dismiss the appeal.

In the next extract, Lord Woolf (writing extra-judicially) suggests that there has, since *Bolitho*, been a trend away from the excessive deference of the past, and he explores some of the reasons for this shift.

Lord Woolf[42]

[U]ntil recently the courts treated the medical profession with excessive deference, but recently the position has changed. It is my judgment that it has changed for the better . . . What is it that has caused the change? I would identify the following causes:

[41] [1999] Lloyd's Rep Med 23.
[42] 'Are the Courts Excessively Deferential to the Medical Profession?' (2001) 9 Medical Law Review 1–16.

First, today the courts have a less deferential approach to those in authority. The growth in judicial review has resulted in the judiciary becoming accustomed to setting aside decisions of those engaged on behalf of the Crown in public affairs, from a Minister of the Crown downwards. By comparison the medical profession and the Health Service were small beer.

Secondly, while there has been the huge growth in the scale of litigation, including actions brought against hospital trusts and the medical profession, the proportion of successful medical negligence claims in England is put at only 17 per cent. The courts became increasingly conscious of the difficulties which bona fide claimants had in successfully establishing claims.

Thirdly, there had developed an increasing awareness of patients' rights. The public's expectations of what the profession should achieve have grown . . . The move to a rights-based society has fundamentally changed the behaviour of the courts.

Fourthly, the 'automatic presumption of beneficence' has been dented by a series of well-publicised scandals . . .

Fifthly, our courts were aware that courts at the highest level of other Commonwealth jurisdictions, particularly Canada and Australia, were rejecting the approach of the English courts. They were subjecting the actions of the medical profession to a closer scrutiny than the English courts . . .

Sixthly, medical negligence litigation was revealed as being a disaster area. The Health Service and the insurance industry had to be required to change their approach to handling litigation. They appeared to consider that every case was worth fighting . . . The annual cost of medical negligence litigation is estimated to be at least equivalent to building, running and staffing one new hospital annually. The litigation was particularly bitter and often singularly unproductive . . .

Seventhly, recently a series of cases have come before the courts that raised fundamental questions of medical ethics. . . . The courts, having had to struggle with issues such as these, were prepared to adopt a more proactive approach to resolving conflicts as to more traditional medical issues.

Eighthly, a final influence that will be of increasing importance and probably played a part in the case of some of the factors I have already mentioned was first the proposal for and subsequently the incorporation into English domestic law of the European Convention of Human Rights.

(c) The role of guidelines

In England, the NHS Litigation Authority (NHSLA, whose role we consider later) operates a Clinical Negligence Scheme for Trusts (CNST), which sets its own approved risk management standards. The CNST operates as a quasi-insurance system for NHS providers, including since 2013 independent sector providers of NHS care, and it offers discounted premiums in return for compliance with the NHSLA risk management standards.

In addition, the Royal Colleges of Medicine routinely issue best practice guidance, and the National Institute for Health and Care Excellence (NICE, whose role we considered in the previous chapter) has developed treatment protocols for a number of conditions. Unsurprisingly, given the wealth of evidence of best practice that now exists, courts increasingly rely on professional guidance when determining the standard of care.

This does not mean that any health care professional who deviates from clinical guidance will be found to have been negligent if something goes wrong, however. Guidelines are, by definition, not mandatory. Nevertheless, as we can see from the following case, they will often form a useful starting point. In *C v North Cumbria University Hospitals NHS Trust*, a midwife was found not to have been negligent in delivering a second dose of a drug used to stimulate contractions during a difficult delivery.

C v North Cumbria University Hospitals NHS Trust[43]

Green J

[The guidelines] are not merely informal documents produced by manufacturers. They are intended to be relied upon and should accordingly carry considerable weight in favour of a midwife who acts consistently with them. In particular the guidance represents a balancing of risks and benefits such that if the guidelines are adhered to then that is inherently likely to reflect a properly balanced (reasonable) decision....

In conclusion my view is that *prima facie* a midwife who acts in accordance with the guidelines should be safe from a charge of negligence. However, in the present case since it is common ground that in some regards the guidelines are not satisfactory I do not decide this case upon the basis that adhering to guidelines is sufficient. I consider that the fact that Midwife Bragg acted in accordance with the guidelines is a factor militating against negligence but I also assess Midwife Bragg's conduct against the benchmark of the other surrounding facts and circumstances.

In the next extract, Margaret Brazier and José Miola argue that increased availability of professional guidance, coupled with the decision in *Bolitho*, indicate that the courts may be not only more willing to challenge medical evidence, but also will be better equipped to do so.

Margaret Brazier and José Miola[44]

Most importantly, *Bolitho* has been decided at a time when other developments also point to a revolution in the way medical malpractice is judged. Medicine itself is changing with practitioners increasingly evaluating their own practice and seeking to develop evidence-based medicine. The traditional guardians of clinical standards, the Royal Colleges of Medicine, have over the last decade become more and more proactive, issuing guidelines about good practice with reference to treatments and procedures . . .

The judge confronted by individual experts who disagree about good practice will in certain cases be able to refer to something approaching a 'gold standard' . . . The judge will have access to material, independent of the particular dispute before him, enabling him to assess the logic of the parties' cases. *Bolitho*, plus more ready access to clinical guidelines, suggests a more proactive role for judges assessing expert evidence. . . . *Bolitho* demands that doctors explain their practice. Doctors themselves are developing tools which will enable judges to review those explanations.

In contrast, Ash Samanta et al set out some limitations to an approach which Harvey Teff has described as 'a new kind of medical paternalism—"*the guideline knows best*"'.[45]

---

43 [2014] EWHC 61 (QB).

44 'Bye-Bye *Bolam*: A Medical Litigation Revolution?' (2000) 8 Medical Law Review 85–114.

45 'Clinical Guidelines, Negligence and Medical Practice' in Michael Freeman and Andrew Lewis (eds), *Current Legal Issues: Law and Medicine*, vol 3 (OUP: Oxford, 2000) 67–8, 79.

Ash Samanta et al[46]

There is always a need for flexibility in patient care, and although guidelines are designed to promote best practice, in any given clinical episode, the slavish adherence to guidelines may not be the best practice for that particular patient. In medical practice, many situations arise where the art of identifying patient problems and the application of clinical acumen to individual patients' needs remain removed from the science and technological advances of the discipline . . . Additionally, guidelines are only as good as the underlying empirical evidence and the appropriateness of the conclusions reached on the basis of synthesis of evidence. The validity of guidelines may be undermined by weak research data as well as confounding factors and biases emanating from misconceptions, personal experiences and beliefs of the developers.

(2) Is the Standard of Care Fixed?

The standard of care in tort law is objective. Many law students will recall the case of *Nettleship v Weston*,[47] in which a learner driver was found negligent for failing to meet the standard of care that would be expected of a reasonably experienced driver. Does this mean that the standard of care in medical negligence is fixed and objectively determined, or might it vary according to the circumstances? In the next sections, we briefly consider whether it would be reasonable to expect a lower standard of care in four different situations:

- if resources are scarce;
- if the doctor is treating the patient in an emergency;
- if the doctor is inexperienced; or
- if the doctor is practising alternative medicine.

(a) Scarce resources

As we saw in the previous chapter, the NHS often cannot provide an optimum standard of care. This political reality makes judging the standard of care in negligence difficult: if less than perfect care is inevitable, how do courts tell when treatment has failed to meet an acceptable standard?

In *Knight v Home Office*,[48] insufficient resources did not offer a complete defence to an allegation of negligence, but were nonetheless relevant to the standard of care a mentally ill prisoner could expect in the hospital wing of Brixton prison. Failure to put him on continuous observation meant that he had the opportunity to hang himself. Pill J decided that the prison doctors had not been negligent, because limited resources meant that they were unable to offer the same standard of care as a specialist psychiatric hospital.

On the other hand, in *Brooks v Home Office*,[49] Garland J held that a remand prisoner with a high-risk pregnancy was entitled to the same standard of care as any other pregnant woman. There had been a five-day delay in seeking specialist advice when a scan revealed

---

[46] 'The Role of Clinical Guidelines in Medical Negligence Litigation: A Shift from the *Bolam* Standard' (2006) 14 Medical Law Review 321.
[47] [1971] 2 QB 691.   [48] [1990] 3 All ER 237.
[49] *Brooks v Home Office* [1999] 2 FLR 33 (QBD).

that one of the prisoner's twins was not growing normally. Garland J held that this fell below the standard of care that could reasonably be expected:

> I cannot regard Knight as authority for the proposition that the plaintiff should not, while detained in Holloway, be entitled to expect the same level of antenatal care, both for herself and her unborn infants, as if she were at liberty, subject of course to the constraints of having to be escorted and, to some extent, movement being retarded by those requirements.

In this case, however, because a two-day delay before admission to hospital would have been acceptable, and the baby had died within that period, the doctor's breach of duty had not caused the baby's stillbirth.

Recall the cases of *Bull v Devon AHA*[50] and *Garcia v St Mary's*,[51] discussed earlier, in which it was clear that, while hospitals do not have to ensure that they provide for every possible eventuality, a certain minimum standard of care should be met, regardless of financial constraints. Let us take the common example of having to wait to be treated in a busy accident and emergency department. It would not be negligent to expect someone with a minor injury to wait for a few hours, but a similar failure to attend to someone who had had a heart attack would fail to meet this basic minimum standard of care.

In *Mulholland v Medway NHS Foundation Trust*, Anthony Mulholland claimed that there had been a negligent failure to refer him for tests that would have led to earlier diagnosis of his brain tumour. Green J held that the practitioners in a busy A&E department did not have the luxury of time, and that, in the circumstances, it had not been negligent to rely upon the conclusions of Mr Mulholland's GP and the stroke team.

Mulholland v Medway NHS Foundation Trust[52]

Green J

In forming a conclusion about the conduct of a practitioner working within triage within an A&E Department context cannot be ignored. The assessment of breach of duty is not an abstract exercise but one formed within a context—which here is that of a busy A&E where the task of the triaging nurse is to make a quick judgment call as to where next to send the patient. The A&E department was busy seeing up to 200 patients per day. There is no opportunity for a triage nurse to devote a great deal of time to the taking of a detailed history or the performance of an extensive diagnosis.... The reasonable nurse is one who operates in a busy A&E which has a procedure which the nurse will follow for streaming and which does not contemplate an exhaustive diagnosis being formed ...

[D]octors in A&E do not have the luxury of long and mature consideration. They take decisions at short notice in a pressurised environment. They cannot (ordinarily) consult the country's leading experts at the drop of a hat having given those experts months or even years to prepare their expert opinions. If Dr Chong had been given the week off in order to research Mr Mulholland's case she might, just possibly, have listed a Jacksonian seizure on her list of possible causes. But in my judgment the standard of care owed by an A&E doctor must be calibrated in a manner reflecting reality. It was not, in the circumstances confronting her, negligent of Dr Chong to omit this sort of specialised neurological condition from her assessment.

---

[50] [1993] 4 Med LR 117 (CA).   [51] [2006] EWHC 2314 (QB).   [52] [2015] EWHC 268 (QB).

(b) Emergencies

In an emergency, it might be difficult for doctors to provide the same standard of care as might normally be expected. Following a major disaster, such as a bomb blast, hospitals may be overwhelmed with casualties. Off-duty doctors in the UK are not under a legal duty to offer assistance if they come upon a medical emergency, but a failure to assist in an emergency might prompt disciplinary action by the General Medical Council. GMC guidance on the duties of a doctor states that: 'You must offer help if emergencies arise in clinical settings or in the community, taking account of your own safety, your competence and the availability of other options for care.'[53] If a doctor does stop at the scene of an accident, the lack of equipment will inevitably compromise the standard of care that she can provide. In such circumstances, would it be reasonable to expect a lower standard of care than normal?

Once a doctor has undertaken to offer care to an injured person, she undoubtedly assumes a duty of care towards her. But since what is expected of doctors is reasonable care, it is appropriate to take into account the surrounding circumstances. It would clearly not be reasonable to expect a doctor who is treating patients at the scene of an accident to provide the level of care that would be available in a well-equipped intensive care unit.

(c) Inexperience

Should a doctor's inexperience affect the standard of care that can reasonably be expected of her? On the one hand, doctors have to learn by experience, and it would seem harsh for junior doctors to be liable in negligence for their inability to reach the standard of care that would be expected from an experienced doctor. But, on the other hand, if the standard of care were to fluctuate according to the doctor's experience, patients would be well advised to refuse to be treated by anyone who is inexperienced, and the system through which junior doctors learn 'on the job' would break down.

This issue arose in *Wilsher v Essex AHA*, where a baby was deprived of oxygen after a junior doctor mistakenly inserted a catheter into a vein rather than an artery. Although the junior doctor was ultimately exonerated because he had taken the reasonable step of asking a registrar for assistance, a majority of the Court of Appeal held that the standard of care should not be lower for inexperienced doctors.[54]

Wilsher v Essex AHA[55]

Glidewell LJ

In my view, the law requires the trainee or learner to be judged by the same standard as his more experienced colleagues. If it did not, inexperience would frequently be urged as a defence to an action for professional negligence.

If this test appears unduly harsh in relation to the inexperienced, I should add that, in my view, the inexperienced doctor called on to exercise a specialist skill will, as part of that skill, seek the advice and help of his superiors when he does or may need it. If he does seek such help, he will often have satisfied the test, even though he may himself have made a mistake.

[53] *Good Medical Practice* (GMC: London, 2013) para 26.

[54] It was only on the issue of causation that appeal was made to the House of Lords, and this judgment is considered later. It is the Court of Appeal judgment in *Wilsher* which determined whether the junior doctor had breached his duty of care.

[55] [1987] 1 QB 730.

(d) Complementary and alternative medicine

How should the courts determine the standard of care that can reasonably be expected of a practitioner of complementary or alternative medicine? Should a Chinese herbalist be judged against the reasonable practitioner of Chinese herbal medicine, or should he be expected to meet the same standard of care as an orthodox clinician? Interestingly, there have been virtually no cases brought by patients who claim that they have been injured as a result of alternative therapies. This is not necessarily because such treatments are safe; rather, it is possible that patients who believe that they have been left worse off after resorting to alternative medical treatments are less likely to complain, and may be reluctant to consult a conventional doctor about their symptoms.

The issue has arisen only once in the UK. In *Shakoor v Situ*, Mr Situ, a practitioner of traditional Chinese herbal medicine, had been consulted by Abdul Shakoor about a skin condition for which the only orthodox medical treatment was surgery. After taking nine doses of the herbal remedy, Mr Shakoor suffered acute liver failure and died. It had been established that, on the balance of probabilities, his death was probably caused by the remedy, but Bernard Livesey QC rejected his widow's claim that Mr Situ had been negligent.

Shakoor v Situ[56]

Bernard Livesey QC

The Chinese herbalist . . . does not hold himself out as a practitioner of orthodox medicine. More particularly, the patient has usually had the choice of going to an orthodox practitioner but has rejected him in favour of the alternative practitioner for reasons personal and best known to himself and almost certainly at some personal financial cost . . . The decision of the patient may be enlightened and informed or based on ignorance and superstition. Whatever the basis of his decision, it seems to me that the fact that the patient has chosen to reject the orthodox and prefer the alternative practitioner is something important which must be taken into account. Why should he later be able to complain that the alternative practitioner has not provided him with skill and care in accordance with the standards of those orthodox practitioners whom he has rejected?

On the other hand, it is of course obviously true to say that the alternative practitioner has chosen to practice in this country alongside a system of orthodox medicine and must abide by the laws and standards prevailing in this country . . .

Accordingly, a claimant may succeed in an action against an alternative practitioner for negligently prescribing a remedy either by calling an expert in the speciality in question to assert and prove that the defendant has failed to exercise the skill and care appropriate to that art . . . Alternatively, the claimant may prove that the prevailing standard of skill and care 'in that art' is deficient in this country having regard to risks which were not and should have been taken into account.

In short, there are two ways in which a claimant might establish negligence on the part of an alternative medical practitioner. First, she could prove that the defendant did not meet the standard of care of a reasonable practitioner of that particular 'art'. Secondly, even if the defendant did act as a reasonable alternative practitioner, it would still be open to the claimant to establish that the prevailing standard of care in that 'art' is itself deficient, on the grounds that it fails to take proper account of published evidence of toxicity.

[56] [2001] 1 WLR 410.

(3) Proof of Breach

It is for the claimant to prove on the balance of probabilities that the defendant has breached her duty of care. The maxim *res ipsa loquitur* (the thing speaks for itself) allows the courts, in certain circumstances, to draw an inference that the defendant was negligent. An example might be if a surgical instrument is left inside the patient's body after surgery. It would be difficult to think of circumstances in which this had occurred, but no one had breached their duty of care towards the patient. Similarly, if a patient went into hospital in order to have her cancerous right kidney removed, and her healthy left kidney was removed instead, again the inference might reasonably be drawn that the surgeon had been negligent.

Essentially, then, *res ipsa loquitur* is just an elaborate way of saying that there will occasionally be circumstances in which a judge would be entitled to find that the defendant had been negligent without the need for expert witnesses to establish that the defendant's actions fell below the appropriate standard of care. It does not reverse the burden of proof, such that it is for the defendant to prove that she was not negligent, rather it applies in simple and unusual cases where negligence can be inferred by a lay person, from the facts themselves.

Hobhouse LJ's judgment in *Ratcliffe v Plymouth and Torbay Health Authority* offers a helpful explanation of the limited application *res ipsa loquitur* is likely to have in actions against doctors. Mr Ratcliffe had undergone an operation on his ankle, and had been given a spinal anaesthetic to relieve post-operative pain. The operation itself was a success, but Mr Ratcliffe was left with a serious neurological defect, causing severe pain, a total loss of sensation in his leg and penile numbness. He contended that this raised an inference that the spinal anaesthetic had been given negligently. His claim was dismissed by Mantell J, and the Court of Appeal dismissed his appeal.

Ratcliffe v Plymouth and Torbay Health Authority[57]

Hobhouse LJ

Res ipsa loquitur is no more than a convenient Latin phrase used to describe the proof of facts which are sufficient to support an inference that a defendant was negligent and therefore to establish a prima facie case against him. . . . The burden of proving the negligence of the defendant remains throughout upon the plaintiff. The burden is on the plaintiff at the start of the trial and, absent an admission by the defendant, is still upon the plaintiff at the conclusion of the trial . . . The plaintiff may or may not have needed to call evidence to establish a prima facie case. The admitted facts may suffice for that purpose . . . In practice, save in the most extreme cases of blatant negligence, the plaintiff will have to adduce at least some expert evidence to get his case upon its feet. . . .

Res ipsa loquitur is not a principle of law: it does not relate to, or raise, any presumption. It is merely a guide to help to identify when a prima facie case is being made out.

In *Lillywhite v University College London Hospitals' NHS Trust*,[58] a case we consider again in Chapter 14, a professor of obstetrics had viewed a fetal scan and recorded the presence of brain structures which were not, in fact, there. While not formally applying the maxim of *res ipsa loquitur*, Latham LJ held that the court was required 'to focus

[57] [1998] Lloyd's Rep Med 168.   [58] [2005] EWCA Civ 1466.

with some care on the explanation given by a defendant to displace that which would otherwise be the inevitable inference from the claimant's case that negligence has been established'.

(c) CAUSATION

Once a claimant has established that the doctor has breached her duty of care, she still has to prove that it was this breach of duty that caused her injuries. In practice, causation poses particular difficulties in medical negligence actions because there may be at least two possible causes of the patient's injury: the doctor's actions and the patient's pre-existing condition. Where there are multiple possible causes, proving causation on the balance of probabilities is especially problematic. The patient's health may have deteriorated even if the care she received was non-negligent, which means that often what has been lost is the *chance* of being restored to full health. The courts are then forced to speculate about what might have happened if the doctor had not breached her duty of care.

(1) The 'But For' Test

The standard test for causation is often referred to as the 'but for' test: but for the defendant's negligence, would the claimant have suffered this injury? This means that the claimant must show that their injury was caused by the doctor's negligence, rather than something that would have happened anyway. It is not enough to show both that the doctor breached her duty of care, and that the claimant's health has deteriorated; rather, there must be a causal link between the two.

The application of the 'but for' test was straightforward in *Barnett v Chelsea and Kensington Hospital Management Committee*, the case we considered earlier involving a man who had died from arsenic poisoning after being sent home unexamined from the hospital's casualty department.

Barnett v Chelsea and Kensington Hospital Management Committee[59]

Nield J

There has been put before me a timetable which, I think, is of much importance. The deceased attended at the casualty department at 8.05 or 8.10am. If Dr Banerjee had got up and dressed and come to see the three men and examined them and decided to admit them, the deceased could not have been in bed in a ward before 11am. I accept Dr. Goulding's evidence that an intravenous drip would not have been set up before 12 noon . . .

If the principal condition is one of enzyme disturbance—as I am of the view that it was here—then the only method of treatment which is likely to succeed is the use of the specific or antidote which is commonly called BAL [dimercaprol]. Dr Goulding said this in the course of his evidence:

The only way to deal with this is to use the specific BAL. I see no reasonable prospect of the deceased being given BAL before the time at which he died . . .

[59] [1969] 1 QB 428.

> I regard that evidence as very moderate, and that it might be a true assessment of the situation to say that there was no chance of BAL being administered before the death of the deceased.

The simplicity of the application of the 'but for' test in *Barnett* is the exception rather than the rule, however, and proving causation is often more problematic. Not only may there be more than one possible cause of the patient's injuries, but also it is not always possible to be certain what the outcome would have been if the patient had been properly treated.

In *Wilsher v Essex AHA*,[60] there were five possible causes of Martin Wilsher's near blindness, one of which was the fact that he had negligently been given excess oxygen on two occasions. The House of Lords found that he had failed to prove that it was the excess oxygen that caused his injuries. Lord Bridge stated that:

> [W]hether we like it or not, the law, which only Parliament can change, requires proof of fault causing damage as the basis of liability in tort. We should do society nothing but disservice if we made the forensic process still more unpredictable and hazardous by distorting the law to accommodate the exigencies of what may seem hard cases.

Loss of a chance cases arise when the doctor's breach of duty deprives the patient of the opportunity of recovery. In *Hotson v East Berkshire AHA*, Stephen Hotson, then 13 years old, had injured his hip in a fall. He was taken to hospital, where his injury was not correctly diagnosed, and he was sent home. After five days of severe pain, Stephen was taken back to hospital, where a proper diagnosis was made and he was given emergency treatment. He was, however, left permanently disabled.

At the trial, the judge found that even if Stephen's injury had been diagnosed and treated immediately, there was still a 75 per cent risk of his disability developing, but that the breach of duty had turned that risk into an inevitability, thus denying him a 25 per cent chance of a good recovery. The judge awarded him 25 per cent of the full value of the damages awardable for the claimant's disability. The Court of Appeal upheld the judge's decision, but the health authority successfully appealed to the House of Lords.

Hotson v East Berkshire AHA[61]

Lord Ackner

I have sought to stress that this case was a relatively simple case concerned with the proof of causation, on which the plaintiff failed, because he was unable to prove, on the balance of probabilities, that his deformed hip was caused by the authority's breach of duty in delaying over a period of five days a proper diagnosis and treatment. Where causation is in issue, the judge decides that issue on the balance of the probabilities. . . .

Once liability is established, on the balance of probabilities, the loss which the plaintiff has sustained is payable in full. It is not discounted by reducing his claim by the extent to which he has failed to prove his case with 100% certainty.

According to *Hotson*, the court must be satisfied that it is *more likely than not* that the claimant's injuries would have been avoided if the doctor had not been negligent. If there

---

[60] [1988] 1 AC 1074.   [61] [1987] 1 AC 750.

is a 55 per cent chance that the patient would have made a complete recovery if she had received non-negligent treatment, she can recover in full, whereas if there is a 45 per cent chance of recovery, her claim fails because she has not proved on the balance of probabilities that her injuries were caused by the defendant's negligence.

The problem with framing the issue in this way is that the courts are engaged in an inevitably hypothetical inquiry about what *might have happened* if the doctor had not acted as she did, and this sort of speculation is not well suited to precise quantification in percentage terms.

In *Hutchinson v Epsom and St Helier NHS Trust*,[62] the question for the judge was whether a heavy drinker would have stopped drinking if he had been told he had end-stage liver disease. On the evidence of his wife, the judge found that he would have done. For obvious reasons, it is impossible to judge the truth or falsity of this finding.

In the non-medical case of *Fairchild v Glenhaven Funeral Services*,[63] the House of Lords adopted a rather more flexible approach to causation, and compensated employees for the lost chance of not contracting mesothelioma from exposure to asbestos. At the same time, the House of Lords suggested that clinical negligence cases were different, and should be governed by the more restrictive approach to causation in *Wilsher*. As Lord Hoffmann explained:

> [T]he political and economic arguments involved in the massive increase in the liability of the National Health Service . . . are far more complicated than the reasons . . . for imposing liability upon an employer who has failed to take simple precautions.

Certainly in *Gregg v Scott*, a case in which a GP's failure to diagnose a lymphoma (a type of cancer) and refer Malcolm Gregg to a specialist, reduced his chance of survival from 42 to 25 per cent, a majority of the House of Lords confirmed that *Fairchild* did not affect the requirement that the claimant must prove causation on the balance of probabilities.

Gregg v Scott[64]

Lord Hoffmann

In effect, the Appellant submits that the exceptional rule in Fairchild should be generalised and damages awarded in all cases in which the defendant may have caused an injury and has increased the likelihood of the injury being suffered. . . .

  It should first be noted that adopting such a rule would involve abandoning a good deal of authority. . . . Furthermore, the House would be dismantling all the qualifications and restrictions with which it so recently hedged the Fairchild exception. There seem to me to be no new arguments or change of circumstances which could justify such a radical departure from precedent . . .

  [A] wholesale adoption of possible rather than probable causation as the criterion of liability would be so radical a change in our law as to amount to a legislative act. It would have enormous consequences for insurance companies and the National Health Service . . . I think that any such change should be left to Parliament.

---

[62] [2002] EWHC 2363 (QB).   [63] Applied in *Barker v Corus* [2006] UKHL 20.
[64] [2005] UKHL 2.

Lord Phillips

Under our law as it is at present, and subject to the exception in Fairchild, a claimant will only succeed if, on balance of probability the negligence is the cause of the injury. If there is a possibility, but not a probability, that the negligence caused the injury, the claimant will recover nothing in respect of the breach of duty. . . .

The complications of this case have persuaded me that it is not a suitable vehicle for introducing into the law of clinical negligence the right to recover damages for the loss of a chance of a cure. Awarding damages for the reduction of the prospect of a cure, when the long term result of treatment is still uncertain, is not a satisfactory exercise. Where medical treatment has resulted in an adverse outcome and negligence has increased the chance of that outcome, there may be a case for permitting a recovery of damages that is proportionate to the increase in the chance of the adverse outcome. That is not a case that has been made out on the present appeal.

It is worth noting the final paragraph in this extract from Lord Phillips's judgment. On a different set of facts, Lord Phillips implies that he would not, in principle, be hostile to such claims. This is especially important in the light of the powerful speeches from the two dissenting judges, Lord Hope and Lord Nicholls since it suggests that the majority in the House of Lords in *Gregg v Scott* was not necessarily averse to a more flexible approach to proof of causation.

Lord Nicholls (dissenting)

A patient is suffering from cancer. His prospects are uncertain. He has a 45% chance of recovery. Unfortunately his doctor negligently misdiagnoses his condition as benign. So the necessary treatment is delayed for months. As a result the patient's prospects of recovery become nil or almost nil. Has the patient a claim for damages against the doctor? No, the House was told. The patient could recover damages if his initial prospects of recovery had been more than 50%. But because they were less than 50% he can recover nothing.

This surely cannot be the state of the law today. It would be irrational and indefensible. The loss of a 45% prospect of recovery is just as much a real loss for a patient as the loss of a 55% prospect of recovery. In both cases the doctor was in breach of his duty to his patient. In both cases the patient was worse off. He lost something of importance and value. But, it is said, in one case the patient has a remedy, in the other he does not.

This would make no sort of sense. It would mean that in the 45% case the doctor's duty would be hollow. The duty would be empty of content. . . . It cannot be right to adopt a procedure having the effect that, in law, a patient's prospects of recovery are treated as non-existent whenever they exist but fall short of 50%. If the law were to proceed in this way it would deserve to be likened to the proverbial ass . . . The present state of the law is crude to an extent bordering on arbitrariness. It means that a patient with a 60% chance of recovery reduced to a 40% prospect by medical negligence can obtain compensation. But he can obtain nothing if his prospects were reduced from 40% to nil. This is rough justice indeed.

More recently in *Bailey v Ministry of Defence*, the claimant Grannia Bailey had aspirated her own vomit and suffered a cardiac arrest while receiving in-patient care following an operation to remove a gall stone. Her claim was that this only happened because her negligent post-operative care had left her too ill and weak to prevent herself from reacting normally when she vomited. The Court of Appeal held that in cases of cumulative causes, it was sufficient to establish that the first defendant's lack of care had made a material contribution to the weakness of her condition, which led to her cardiac arrest and subsequent brain damage.

Bailey v Ministry of Defence[65]

Waller LJ

In my view one cannot draw a distinction between medical negligence cases and others. I would summarise the position in relation to cumulative cause cases as follows. If the evidence demonstrates on a balance of probabilities that the injury would have occurred as a result of the non-tortious cause or causes in any event, the claimant will have failed to establish that the tortious cause contributed. Hotson's case exemplifies such a situation. . . . In a case where medical science cannot establish the probability that 'but for' an act of negligence the injury would not have happened but can establish that the contribution of the negligent cause was more than negligible, the 'but for' test is modified, and the claimant will succeed.

The instant case involved cumulative causes acting so as to create a weakness and thus the judge in my view applied the right test, and was entitled to reach the conclusion he did.

Bailey is a complex case, but it is different from *Hotson* and *Gregg*. In those cases, the patient had a pre-existing condition or illness that was not adequately treated. In both cases, medical experts agreed that adequate treatment would, on the balance of probabilities, not have avoided the eventual damage, and hence could not be considered to have caused it. In *Bailey*, Ms Bailey's weakness, which made her unable to react normally to vomiting, had two causes, one tortious (her inadequate treatment) and one non-tortious (pancreatitis). The difficulty was that it was impossible to tell the exact contribution of both causes.

If medical experts could have been certain, on the balance of probabilities, that Ms Bailey's pancreatitis would *on its own* have caused her to be so weak that she was likely to inhale her own vomit, then her inadequate treatment would not have caused her weakened state. Since that was not possible, and it was clear that her inadequate treatment had materially contributed to her weakened state, it also materially contributed to her inability to react normally to vomiting, and therefore was a cause of her injuries.

As Janet Smith, writing extra-judicially, explains, this benefits claimants (and disadvantages defendants) where there is evidential uncertainty:

This passage [from Waller LJ's judgment] draws attention to the disadvantage which defendants face where the claimant's medical condition is not well understood. As I have said, in *Hotson*, the claimant would have succeeded in full if the doctors had not been able to assess the contributions made by the two causative factors. But the doctors could, so the 'but for' rule had to be satisfied. In *Bailey*, the claimant succeeded in full because the doctors could not assess the contributions. So the 'but for' rule was modified.[66]

---

[65] [2008] EWCA Civ 883.
[66] 'Causation—The Search for Principle' (2009) 2 Journal of Personal Injury Law 101–13.

It is also worth noting that Waller LJ suggests that causation in medical negligence cases should not be treated differently from other negligence claims, whereas, as we saw earlier, the House of Lords has previously maintained that there might be important policy reasons for distinguishing between them.

Bailey was followed in *Canning-Kishver v Sandwell & West Birmingham NHS Trust*,[67] a case in which the nursing staff in a neonatal intensive care ward were found to have been in breach of their duty of care by not summoning a doctor urgently when a very premature baby's heart and respiratory rates dropped dramatically. As a result of this delay, the baby suffered a cardiac collapse and had to undergo drastic resuscitation. It was not wholly clear whether the permanent brain injury suffered by the baby was caused by this delay or by her extreme prematurity. Nevertheless, and explicitly following *Bailey v Ministry of Health*, Sir Christopher Holland was satisfied that, despite not being likely to succeed according to the 'but for' test, causation was established:

> The evidence does not establish on balance of probabilities that Ayesha's brain injury arose simply from her immaturity. That cannot be excluded as a possibility but there is nothing that suggests that that non-tortious cause was probable . . . All that said, the fact of residual possibilities militates against success for Ayesha by reference to a 'but for' test. However, I am entitled to find—and I do find—that on balance of probabilities the contribution of the collapse occasioned by the breach of duty constituted a contribution to the atrophy of the cerebellum that was more than negligible so that the claim succeeds.

The case of *Gouldsmith v Mid Staffordshire General Hospitals NHS Trust* raises a different sort of 'loss of a chance' question. At first instance, the judge found that it had been negligent not to refer the patient, who suffered from lesions on her left hand, to a specialist hospital. Mrs Gouldsmith had established that most but not all specialists would be likely to have operated on her hand, and that operating would have avoided the subsequent amputation of her fingers. At first instance, the judge found that she had not proved, on the balance of probabilities, that if she had been referred to a specialist hospital, she would have had this operation.

By a majority, the Court of Appeal disagreed. They found that having established that most specialists would have operated prima facie justified the conclusion that the specialist to whom the respondents should have referred her would be likely to have done so. It was not necessary for the claimant to prove that the specialist would have, in fact, operated, but just that it was more likely than not that she would have done.

Gouldsmith v Mid Staffordshire General Hospitals NHS Trust[68]

Pill LJ

[H]er establishment of the fact shifted the evidential burden of proof on to the respondents. It was open to them to have countered, had they had the material with which to do so, with evidence that the reference would be likely to have been to a particular specialist who would not have operated on the appellant. In the absence of credible evidence of that character the answer to the first question proffered on behalf of the appellant should have secured judgment for her.

---

[67] [2008] EWHC 2384 (QB).   [68] [2007] EWCA Civ 397.

An even more complex issue arose in *Wright v Cambridge Medical Group*.[69] The defendant GP practice admitted negligence in failing to see a baby, who was in fact suffering from an undiagnosed super-infection, and refer her to hospital, following the mother's description of her symptoms on the telephone. They claimed, however, that the negligent failure to refer Clarice Wright to hospital immediately did not cause her injury because, even if she had been promptly referred, she would, in any event, not have been treated properly at the hospital, and therefore would still have suffered the permanent damage to her hip which was caused by the inadequately treated infection. When Clarice was eventually admitted to hospital two days after the telephone call, a catalogue of errors meant that she was not immediately treated with appropriate antibiotics, leading the first instance judge, Mackay J, to conclude that:

> The compelling criticisms of the performance of [the paediatric] unit through [the] period 9–21 April 1998 make it impossible for me to find as a fact that it is more likely than not that if [the claimant] had been placed in their hands during the evening of 15 April she would have been so treated as to avoid permanent damage to her hip.

At first instance, Mackay J had held that it was for the claimant to prove that she would have been treated non-negligently if she had been admitted to hospital on 15 April, but the Court of Appeal found that he had misdirected himself, and that a claimant did not have to prove that an earlier referral would have led her to have been competently treated. As Lord Neuberger MR explained:

> However, once the claimant established that (i) she could and should have been referred to the Hospital on 15 April, and (ii) she would not have suffered the damage now complained of had she been so referred and been treated competently at the Hospital, she had the benefit of a presumption that she would have been competently treated thereafter. In the absence of evidence to the contrary, the court will assume that professional and other service providers would have or have performed their functions competently.

All three members of the Court of Appeal agreed that the judge had been wrong to direct himself that the burden of proof had shifted to the claimant to prove that she would have been properly treated, had she been referred to hospital on the 15th rather than the 17th of April. At this point, however, their reasoning diverged.

A majority decided that Clarice had succeeded in proving that the delay in referral caused her permanent injury, but the two majority judgments differed. Despite claiming that he was not deciding this as a 'loss of a chance' case, Lord Neuberger MR argued that:

> it seems to me that, in a case where a doctor has negligently failed to refer his patient to a hospital, and, as a consequence, she has lost the opportunity to be treated as she should have been by a hospital, the doctor cannot escape liability by establishing that the hospital would have negligently failed to treat the patient appropriately, even if he had promptly referred her. Even if the doctor established this, it would not enable him to escape liability, because, by negligently failing to refer the patient promptly, he deprived her of the opportunity to be treated properly by the hospital.

[69] [2011] EWCA Civ 669.

Also finding for Clarice, Smith LJ argued that the delayed referral shortened the period available to treat her effectively, and thereby reduced the hospital's 'margin for error'. Hence—although she admitted that the case was 'very close to the line'—Clarice's permanent injury was not too remote from the original negligence:

> I think that the crucial point is the extent to which the GP's negligence shortened the period available to the hospital to provide effective treatment and increased the risk that she would suffer permanent harm . . . It was still possible for the team to treat her successfully but they had a much reduced opportunity and a much reduced margin for error.

Elias LJ dissented on the grounds that, if Clarice had been properly treated when she was eventually referred to hospital, on the 17th rather than the 15th April, permanent injury to her hip would have been avoided. The doctor's duty was to present the patient to a specialist in time to be properly treated, and although there was clearly culpable delay, he had nevertheless done that. Elias LJ therefore found that it would be 'unjust to make him liable for the hospital's negligent treatment'.

A key problem for the Court of Appeal was that this action was brought only against the GP practice, rather than—as would have been more sensible—joining the hospital as defendants. This was a case in which there were two successive instances of negligence—the late referral and the subsequent inadequate treatment in hospital. If Clarice had sued both tortfeasors, they might have been left to fight out or agree their respective contribution to her loss between themselves. By suing only the GP practice, Clarice ran the risk of losing altogether, and while she won in the Court of Appeal, it does seem a little unfair to hold the GP practice wholly, as opposed to partly, responsible for the inept treatment she later received in hospital.

(2) Remoteness

There is another hurdle to overcome once a claimant has succeeded in proving factual causation: it is also necessary to establish that the type of damage is not too remote. According to the *Wagon Mound*[70] test for remoteness, the type of damage must be foreseeable, although its extent, and the manner in which it occurred, need not be. Normally in clinical negligence cases the type of damage will be some sort of physical injury, which is obviously a foreseeable consequence of negligent medical care. As a result, there are few medical cases where remoteness has been an issue.

One exception is *R v Croydon Health Authority*.[71] The claimant had undergone a pre-employment chest X-ray, and the radiographer failed to alert her to an abnormality (primary pulmonary hypertension or PPH), which would be exacerbated by pregnancy. She argued that if she had known that she had PPH, she would not have become pregnant. The Court of Appeal dismissed her claim for the costs arising from the birth of her child because, as Kennedy LJ held:

> The damage was, as is sometimes said, too remote. The chain of events had too many links. . . . We understand that the radiologist never actually saw the plaintiff, and he probably knew very little about her except her age. He would no doubt have accepted that, in so far as he failed to observe an abnormality which could have affected her fitness for

---

[70] [1961] AC 388.   [71] (1997) 40 BMLR 40.

work as an employee of the health authority in the immediate future, that was something for which he should be held accountable, but her domestic circumstances were not his affair.

In *Page v Smith*,[72] a non-medical case, the House of Lords held that provided physical injury was foreseeable, the defendant might also be liable if the claimant suffers psychiatric injury as a result of her negligence. Hence, if it is foreseeable that a doctor's negligence will physically injure her patient, the doctor could be liable if the patient suffers psychiatric injury, even if no physical injury results. This was the issue in *The Creutzfeldt-Jakob Disease Litigation; Group B Plaintiffs v Medical Research Council*, where the claimants were children of short stature who had taken part in a clinical trial of a type of human growth hormone (Hartree HGH). They subsequently learned that this might have infected them with Creutzfeldt-Jakob disease (CJD), the human form of BSE or mad-cow disease. On a trial of the preliminary issues, Morland J held that it might be possible to recover damages for the psychiatric injury that had been caused by this knowledge.

The Creutzfeldt-Jakob Disease Litigation; Group B Plaintiffs v Medical Research Council[73]

Morland J

I am satisfied that when the defendants breached their duty of care to them by being responsible for injecting them with potentially lethal Hartree HGH they should have reasonably foreseen that, if deaths occurred from CJD caused by HGH contaminated with the CJD agent, some of the recipients of that HGH, including some of normal phlegm and ordinary fortitude, might well suffer psychiatric injury on becoming aware of the risk to them. . . . The defendants as tortfeasors committed a wrong upon the Group B plaintiffs by imperilling their lives from a terrible fatal disease. It was reasonably foreseeable that, if the worst fears were realised and deaths from CJD occurred, Hartree HGH recipients, both those of normal fortitude and those more vulnerable, might suffer psychiatric injury.

A further dimension to remoteness is the question of whether an intervening act or decision has broken the chain of causation. If a psychiatric patient who was known to be at risk of taking her own life succeeds in committing suicide as a result of a negligent failure to keep her under appropriate surveillance, has the chain of causation been broken by the patient's own action in deliberately taking her own life? In *Kirkham v Chief Constable of Greater Manchester*,[74] the court rejected the claim that the deceased's suicide had been a *novus actus* on the grounds that it was the very act that the defendants had been under a duty to prevent.

Where there was no prior indication that a patient was at risk of committing suicide, her actions would be more likely to break the chain of causation. In *Hyde v Tameside AHA*,[75] the claimant was being treated in a general hospital for a physical disability. He subsequently jumped out of a window, leaving him permanently disabled. The Court of Appeal held that the hospital staff were not on notice that he was a suicide risk, and hence they were not under a duty to prevent him from attempting to commit suicide.

---

[72] [1996] AC 155.   [73] [2000] Lloyd's Rep Med 161.   [74] [1990] 2 QB 283.
[75] The Times, 15 April 1981.

(d) DEFENCES

There are several possible defences to a claim in negligence. A partial defence would exist if the patient had been contributorily negligent. Under section 1 of the Law Reform (Contributory Negligence) Act 1945, damages can be reduced in proportion to the extent of the claimant's responsibility for her injuries. Contributory negligence usually has little role to play in clinical negligence cases, however. Doctors' responsibility for medical treatment means that, if something goes wrong, it is unlikely to be regarded as the patient's fault.

An alarming, although ultimately unsuccessful, attempt was made in *St George v The Home Office*[76] to invoke the claimant's 'fault' in becoming addicted to drugs and alcohol as a reason to reduce his damages. Despite knowing that Ryan St George was at risk of seizures due to withdrawal from heroin and alcohol, prison staff had negligently allocated him a top bunk. Ryan suffered a seizure and fell out of his bunk, suffering head injuries which resulted in brain damage. At first instance, his damages were reduced by 15 per cent, on the grounds that he was partly at fault because his addiction was the result of his own lifestyle decisions. This was overturned by the Court of Appeal, on the grounds that, the claimant's fault in becoming addicted in his teens could not be regarded as a 'potent cause' of the head injuries he sustained as a result of his negligent treatment in Brixton prison. As Dyson LJ explained:

> The judge recognised that the analogy that he gave . . . of a person wandering abroad in a drug-induced state of intoxication walking into the path of a negligently driven car was very far from being perfect. I respectfully consider that this is not a good analogy at all. In my judgment, the fault of such a person (negligently walking into the path of a car) is a potent cause of the injury which he sustains in the accident. The fault (walking in the road in a drug-induced state of intoxication) is closely connected in time and place with the accident which is caused then and there by a combination of the negligence of the claimant and the defendant.
>
> There is a far closer analogy with the case of a claimant who seeks medical treatment for a condition from which he is suffering as a result of his own fault and sustains injury as a result of negligent treatment. Examples of such a condition are lung cancer caused by smoking or cirrhosis of the liver caused by excessive consumption of alcohol.

Dyson LJ acknowledged that, if accepted, the idea that one's fault in needing health services might reduce the damages awarded for negligent medical treatment could apply to anyone who is negligently treated for a condition which may be partly the result of her own behaviour. As we saw in the previous chapter, this is potentially a very long list indeed. It would mean, for example, that a smoker with cancer who underwent botched surgery might have their damages reduced because they were responsible for their need for surgery, or a rock climber having an operation for a complex fracture might receive less compensation if they were given the wrong dose of general anaesthetic.

Where the patient was wholly responsible for her injuries, this may simply lead to a finding that the doctor had not been negligent at all. In *Venner v North East Essex Health Authority and Another*,[77] a woman who was about to undergo a sterilization operation was advised to come off the contraceptive pill, but to take other contraceptive precautions prior to the operation. Before the operation she was asked whether there was any chance that she could be pregnant, to which she answered 'no', despite the fact that she and her husband had had unprotected sexual intercourse. She was in fact pregnant when the operation took place, and

[76] [2008] EWCA Civ 1068.   [77] The Times, 21 February 1987.

subsequently gave birth to a healthy child. Tucker J found that there had been no negligence, and the patient herself—a mature woman who understood the likelihood of conception—was responsible for her pregnancy.

The defence of *volenti non fit injuria*[78] is extremely unlikely to affect clinical negligence claims. It is difficult to imagine a case in which the patient could be said to have voluntarily assumed the risk of being injured by their doctor's negligence.

There have been cases where the defence of illegality (or *ex turpi causa non oritur actio*[79]) has been raised. In *Clunis v Camden and Islington Health Authority*, a man with mental health problems who had killed a fellow Tube passenger argued that the health authority had failed to treat him with reasonable care and skill, and that if they had, he would have been sectioned and would not have killed Jonathan Zito. The Court of Appeal applied the defence of illegality to reject his claim.

Clunis v Camden and Islington Health Authority[80]

Beldam LJ

In the present case the plaintiff has been convicted of a serious criminal offence. In such a case, public policy would in our judgment preclude the court from entertaining the plaintiff's claim unless it could be said that he did not know the nature and quality of his act, or that what he was doing was wrong . . . The court ought not to allow itself to be made an instrument to enforce obligations alleged to arise out of the plaintiff's own criminal act and we would therefore allow the appeal on this ground.

(e) LIMITATION PERIODS

Most personal injury cases must be brought within three years either of the date when the injury occurred, or the date when the patient realized, or should have realized, that she might be able to sue.[81] If the patient dies as a result of her injuries, her relatives have three years from the date of death, or from the date when they realize, or should have realized, that an action could be brought.[82] Section 14 of the Limitation Act sets out when this three-year period starts to run:

Limitation Act 1980 section 14

14(1) . . . references to a person's date of knowledge are references to the date on which he first had knowledge of the following facts—

   (a) that the injury in question was significant; and

   (b) that the injury was attributable in whole or in part to the act or omission which is alleged to constitute negligence . . . ; and

   (c) the identity of the defendant; and

---

[78] This translates as 'to a willing person, no injury is done', and means that there is no liability when an injured person 'volunteered' to run the risk.

[79] This means 'from a dishonourable cause an action does not arise', and means that actions can be barred by the claimant's illegal behaviour.

[80] [1988] QB 978 (CA).   [81] Limitation Act 1980, ss 11(4) and 14(1).   [82] Ibid.

(d) if it is alleged that the act or omission was that of a person other than the defendant, the identity of that person and the additional facts supporting the bringing of an action against the defendant. . . .

(2) For the purposes of this section an injury is significant if the person whose date of knowledge is in question would reasonably have considered it sufficiently serious to justify his instituting proceedings for damages.

One of the problems section 14 presents in medical cases is that it may be particularly difficult for an individual to determine whether their injury was 'attributable in whole or in part to the act or omission which is alleged to constitute negligence'. Medical treatment is not always successful, and so an individual whose condition deteriorates may have just been unlucky. It is not necessary for the claimant to know that their injuries are due to negligence: rather, time starts to run when they could be said to have constructive knowledge of the possibility of litigation.

In *Forbes v Wandsworth Health Authority*, Mr Forbes had had an unsuccessful operation on his left leg in October 1982. As a result, he had to have his leg amputated. In June 1991 he consulted a solicitor. Advice from a vascular surgeon obtained in October 1992 suggested that the amputation could have been avoided. In December 1992, Mr Forbes issued proceedings against the defendant health authority. At first instance, the judge held that his action was not time-barred because he had no reason to suspect or think that the removal of his leg was due to the act or omission of the defendant. Before the health authority's appeal was heard by the Court of Appeal, Mr Forbes died. By a majority, its appeal was allowed.

Forbes v Wandsworth Health Authority[83]

Stuart-Smith LJ

It seems to me that where, as here, the plaintiff expected or at least hoped that the operation would be successful and it manifestly was not, with the result that he sustained a major injury, a reasonable man of moderate intelligence, such as the deceased, if he thought about the matter, would say that the lack of success was 'either just one of those things, a risk of the operation or something may have gone wrong and there may have been a want of care; I do not know which, but if I am ever to make a claim, I must find out'.

In my judgment, any other construction would make the 1980 Act unworkable since a plaintiff could delay indefinitely before seeking expert advice and say, as the deceased did in this case, I had no occasion to seek it earlier. He would therefore be able, as of right, to bring the action, no matter how many years had elapsed. This is contrary to the whole purpose of the 1980 Act which is to prevent defendants being vexed by stale claims which it is no longer possible to contest.

In *Whiston v London Strategic Health Authority*, the claimant suffered from cerebral palsy as a result of oxygen deprivation during childbirth. Until early adulthood, he was relatively unimpaired by his condition, obtaining a PhD and regular employment. His condition then worsened and by 2005, when he was 31, the deterioration had become significant. At that point, he discussed with his mother, a trained nurse, the circumstances of his birth—in which a junior doctor had persisted for too long with a forceps delivery with the wrong type

[83] [1997] QB 402 (CA).

of forceps—and in 2006, 32 years after his birth, he brought an action alleging that his injuries were caused by his negligent delivery.

The Court of Appeal found that his claim was statute-barred. The claimant had known for most of his life that his disabilities were the result of his birth, and the Court of Appeal found that a reasonable person would, when his condition deteriorated, have asked his mother about the circumstances of his birth, and discovered then that there might have been a question over the conduct of the junior doctor.

Whiston v London Strategic Health Authority[84]

Dyson LJ

I take into account the fact that a person who suffers from a disability at birth is more likely to be accepting of his disability (because he has never known anything different) than a person who suffers an injury during adult life. But where the disability becomes more serious as he becomes an adult and he knows that the disability is in some way related to the circumstances of his delivery (rather than, say, the result of some genetic disorder), it seems to me that there comes a time when a reasonable person would want to know about the circumstances of his birth which have given rise to the problem. There comes a time when the reasonable person in the circumstances of the claimant would ask his mother, particularly since she is a nurse and a trained midwife. As a reasonable person, the claimant would have known that she would be able to answer his questions. In these circumstances . . . I have concluded that the claimant had constructive knowledge of the facts which he discovered from his mother in 2005 no later than when he was in his early twenties, say in about 1998.

A finding that a claim is statute-barred is not necessarily the end of the matter, however. Section 33 of the Limitation Act 1980 gives the court discretion to extend the limitation period where it would be equitable to do so. In deciding whether to exercise this discretion, the court has to balance the degree to which the statutory limitation period prejudices the claimant, with the degree to which an extension of that period would prejudice the defendant. The court will have regard to a number of factors, such as the reasons for the delay and the conduct of both parties. In *Forbes v Wandsworth Health Authority*,[85] the court declined to exercise its discretion, in part because Mr Forbes was now dead, which meant that 'the potential damages recoverable for the benefit of the estate of the deceased are significantly less than they would have been if the deceased were still alive', and in part because there was only a 'modest' chance of his case succeeding.

In contrast, in *Whiston* the court balanced the disadvantage to the defendant hospital in trying to defend a stale claim, by which time some relevant notes would have been destroyed, with the disadvantage to the now very seriously disabled claimant.

Dyson LJ

The practical consequences of his current condition are that his mobility is severely restricted (he uses a wheelchair outside his home) and he is dependent on his mother for most of the practicalities of day to day life. He has considerable speech difficulties

---

[84] [2010] EWCA Civ 195.   [85] [1997] QB 402 (CA).

> and cannot write (although he can and does use a computer/email to communicate). He is now only able to work intermittently from home. He lives in accommodation provided by the local authority which has, to some extent, been adapted. His parents are in their 60s (his mother is 68) and they will not be able to provide him with care and assistance for much longer.
>
> In these circumstances, I accept the submission of Mr Havers that any damages awarded to the claimant will be substantial. If he is not permitted to pursue this claim, he will therefore lose all prospect of his future needs being properly provided for and all prospect of recovering compensation for the loss of the substantial earnings that, but for his disability, he is likely to have achieved. . . . I am satisfied that, despite the fact that the allegations of negligence relate to what happened in September 1974, it would be equitable to allow this claim to proceed.

The existence of this overarching discretion, and the courts' application of it, suggests that the more substantial the claimant's injury, the more likely it is that the court will find that this outweighs the disadvantage to the defendants of having to defend a claim based on events that took place many years ago.[86] As Richard Lewis explains, section 33 is an example of the balance the law on limitation strikes between the need for finality and the interests of justice.

Richard Lewis[87]

> There is general agreement over the aims of the law of limitation. First, it provides finality so that sooner or later an incident or transgression which might have led to a claim can be safely treated as closed by all concerned. Secondly, it gives defendants a degree of protection from stale claims which they can no longer properly contest. And thirdly it provides an incentive to plaintiffs to commence proceedings without delay. This is closely related to the need to protect defendants from old claims but goes further in that it also recognises that the trial of disputes on complete or unreliable evidence is prejudicial to the public interest in the proper administration of justice. These objectives must of course be balanced against the interests of plaintiffs and the law now attaches very great weight to the need to give injured persons a fair chance to commence proceedings.

For children and adults who lack capacity, the limitation period does not begin to run until or unless they gain capacity.[88] In such cases, it is obviously possible to bring an action many years after the alleged negligent act, when evidence as to the precise circumstances which led to the claimant's injuries may no longer be reliable.

4 PROBLEMS WITH CLINICAL NEGLIGENCE

For several reasons, set out in the following sections, there is widespread dissatisfaction with the clinical negligence system.

---

[86] See also *Smith v Leicestershire Health Authority* [1998] Lloyd's Rep Med 77.
[87] 'The Limitation Period in Medical Negligence Claims' (1998) 6 Medical Law Review 62–98, 64.
[88] Limitation Act 1980, s 28.

(a) COSTS TO THE NHS

In 2014/15, the NHSLA received 11,497 clinical negligence claims, up from 6,652 in 2009/10. The amount paid out also increased, from £787 million to almost £1.4 billion, of which a significant proportion (50 per cent, for claims worth less than £100,000) is spent on legal costs. Claimants' legal costs for lower value claims are, according to the NHSLA, 'disproportionate and excessive': in claims where compensation is less than £10,000, claimant lawyers (on average) recover three times more than that in costs.[89]

Regardless of how deserving individual claimants' cases might be, diverting scarce NHS funds to the payment of damages and lawyers' fees reduces the amount of money available for patient care. As Alan Merry and Alexander McCall Smith explain:

> If damages become payable, then that means that there is a correspondingly reduced amount available for the maintenance of wards and equipment, the purchase of drugs or the provision of treatment. A medium-sized award, therefore, may be crudely translated into ten fewer hip replacements.[90]

In the following extract, John Harris suggests that victims of medical negligence should compete for scarce NHS funds according to ordinary rationing criteria, in the same way as patients, rather than, as happens now, being given absolute priority.

John Harris[91]

> In most healthcare systems the need to prioritise patients for care and to ration the resources available is now well recognised. . . . However, one group of claimants for health-care resources have been guaranteed top priority for receipt of funds available for health care—victims of medical accidents. This fact has been scarcely noted and its justice seldom questioned. . . .
>
> If people who need treatment to save their life can be told that scarcity of resources does not allow them to be treated, why, equally, should not people who need legal redress and compensation (out of the same limited pot of money) be told that the resources necessary to fund the professional help and compensation that they need are either exhausted or committed to those with a greater need? . . .
>
> If public resources available for patient care are to be cash limited and patients forced to compete for priority within those limits, why should not the same be true of access to litigation and compensation? Why, in short, are some victims of medical accidents given priority over the victims of all other types of accidents, injuries, and illnesses? . . .
>
> I think it plausible to insist that the health related needs of victims of medical accidents or negligence compete on at least an equal footing with other such needs rather than having automatic and absolute priority.

---

[89] NHSLA, *Annual Report and Accounts 2014–15* (NHSLA, 2015).
[90] *Errors, Medicine and the Law* (CUP: Cambridge, 2001) 212.
[91] 'The injustice of compensation for victims of medical accidents' (1997) 314 British Medical Journal 1821.

(b) FAILURE TO PROVIDE REMEDIES TO INJURED PATIENTS

As we have seen, proving breach of duty and causation are formidable obstacles, and most patients who seek compensation receive nothing.[92] For the majority of claimants, stressful and expensive litigation will end in disappointment. Research appears to indicate that even where claimants are awarded damages, many remain dissatisfied because they have not been given an explanation, an apology, or reassurance that the same thing will not happen again.[93]

According to the NHSLA, 60–70 per cent of claims do not proceed beyond initial contact with a solicitor or disclosure of medical records and 30 per cent of claims which are formally pursued are abandoned by the claimant.[94] Moreover, many patients who have suffered injury as a result of their medical treatment never even consider litigation. Some patients may not realize that they are eligible to bring a claim. Others, as Linda Mulcahy explains, may decide that the difficulties of pursuing a legal action outweigh the small chance of receiving compensation:

> Patients may also *choose* not to make a complaint or clinical negligence claim . . . for some, avoiding disputes is a positive and rational choice. Asked why they had not voiced their dissatisfaction, this subset said they had other priorities, wished to put negative experiences behind them or avoid confrontation.[95]

The fear that doctors might not apologize to patients in case this might be used against them in court has been addressed by introducing a statutory duty of candour. The statutory duty of candour was set out in regulation 20 of the Health and Social Care Act 2008 (Regulated Activities) Regulations 2014 and came into force towards the end of 2014.

Health and Social Care Act 2008 (Regulated Activities) Regulations 2014 regulation 20

1. Registered persons must act in an open and transparent way with relevant persons in relation to care and treatment provided to service users in carrying on a regulated activity.

2. As soon as reasonably practicable after becoming aware that a notifiable safety incident has occurred a registered person must—

   (a) notify the relevant person that the incident has occurred in accordance with paragraph (3), and

   (b) provide reasonable support to the relevant person in relation to the incident, including when giving such notification.

3. The notification to be given under paragraph (2)(a) must—

   (a) be given in person by one or more representatives of the registered person,

---

[92] NHSLA Claims Factsheet.

[93] Linda Mulcahy, *Disputing Doctors: The Socio-Legal Dynamics of Complaints about Medical Care* (Open UP: Maidenhead, 2003) 96.

[94] Department of Health, Full Regulatory Impact Assessment NHS Redress Act (DH: London, 2006).

[95] Linda Mulcahy, *Disputing Doctors: The Socio-Legal Dynamics of Complaints about Medical Care* (Open UP: Maidenhead, 2003) 64–6.

(b) provide an account, which to the best of the registered person's knowledge is true, of all the facts the registered person knows about the incident as at the date of the notification,

(c) advise the relevant person what further enquiries into the incident the registered person believes are appropriate,

(d) include an apology, and

(e) be recorded in a written record which is kept securely by the registered person.

4. The notification given under paragraph (2)(a) must be followed by a written notification given or sent to the relevant person containing—

(a) the information provided under paragraph (3)(b),

(b) details of any enquiries to be undertaken in accordance with paragraph (3)(c),

(c) the results of any further enquiries into the incident, and

(d) an apology....

5. In relation to a health service body, 'notifiable safety incident' means any unintended or unexpected incident that occurred in respect of a service user during the provision of a regulated activity that, in the reasonable opinion of a health care professional, could result in, or appears to have resulted in—

(a) the death of the service user, where the death relates directly to the incident rather than to the natural course of the service user's illness or underlying condition, or

(b) severe harm, moderate harm or prolonged psychological harm to the service user.

The Care Quality Commission has issued guidance to NHS providers on what the duty of candour requires of them.

Care Quality Commission[96]

- Providers must promote a culture that encourages candour, openness and honesty at all levels. This should be an integral part of a culture of safety that supports organisational and personal learning. There should also be a commitment to being open and transparent at board level or its equivalent, such as a governing body.

- Providers should have policies and procedures in place to support a culture of openness and transparency, and ensure that all staff follow them.

- Providers should take action to tackle bullying and harassment in relation to duty of candour, and must investigate any instances where a member of staff may have obstructed another in exercising their duty of candour.

- Providers should have a system in place to identify and deal with possible breaches of the professional duty of candour by staff who are professionally registered, including the obstruction of another in their professional duty of candour. This is likely to include an investigation and escalation process that may lead to referral to their professional regulator or other relevant body.

- Providers should make all reasonable efforts to ensure that staff operating at all levels within the organisation operate within a culture of openness and transparency, understand

---

[96] *Regulation 20: Duty of candour: information for all providers: NHS bodies, adult social care, primary medical and dental care, and independent healthcare* (CQC, 2015).

> their individual responsibilities in relation to the duty of candour, and are supported to be open and honest with patients and apologise when things go wrong.
>
> - Staff should receive appropriate training, and there should be arrangements in place to support staff who are involved in a notifiable safety incident.
>
> - In cases where a provider is made aware that something untoward has happened, they should treat the allegation seriously, immediately consider whether this is a notifiable safety incident and take appropriate action.

In 2015, the General Medical Council and the Nursing and Midwifery Council issued a joint statement on the Professional Duty of Candour. This sets out in considerable detail what is expected of health care professionals, for example by giving guidance on how to say sorry to patients.

General Medical Council and Nursing and Midwifery Council[97]

> 16. We do not want to encourage a formulaic approach to apologising since an apology has value only if it is genuine. However, when apologising to a patient, you should consider each of the following points.
>
>   (a) You must give patients the information they want or need to know in a way that they can understand.
>
>   (b) You should speak to patients in a place and at a time when they are best able to understand and retain information.
>
>   (c) You should give information that the patient may find distressing in a considerate way, respecting their right to privacy and dignity.
>
>   (d) Patients are likely to find it more meaningful if you offer a personalized apology—for example 'I am sorry . . .'—rather than a general expression of regret about the incident on the organisation's behalf. This doesn't mean that we expect you to take personal responsibility for system failures or other people's mistakes.
>
>   (e) You should make sure the patient knows who to contact in the healthcare team to ask any further questions or raise concerns. You should also give patients information about independent advocacy, counselling or other support services‡ that can give them practical advice and emotional support.

It remains to be seen whether, as Christopher Mellor suggests, one practical result of clinicians having to admit to patients, or relatives, that something has gone seriously wrong with their treatment might be an increase in clinical negligence claims.

Christopher Mellor[98]

> [T]he practical effect in many cases will be that healthcare providers will be required to tell patients/patients families, that they believe they have caused serious injury or death. Whilst it is recommended that such notification should not amount to an admission of liability, it

---

[97] *Openness and honesty when things go wrong: the professional duty of candour* (GMC and NMC, 2015).

[98] 'A duty of candour: a change in approach' (2014) 20 Clinical Risk 36–46.

will obviously have an influence on subsequent negligence claims. Furthermore, the fact that the duty will arise in the absence of any complaint being made, or any litigation being commenced, adds further to its novelty. It could effectively amount to a statutory duty that requires a potential defendant to inform a potential claimant that they may have a claim: that very notion obviously seems entirely anomalous in an adversarial system of law.

(c) A COMPENSATION CULTURE?

Despite the low chance of success and dissatisfaction with available remedies, patients have been increasingly willing to sue when their medical treatment goes wrong, leading to fears that we are moving towards a US-style 'compensation culture'. This is thought to have two negative consequences for the NHS. First, as we have seen, it means that money that could be spent on patient care is diverted towards litigation, in which the principal beneficiaries may be lawyers.

Secondly, it is feared that the threat of litigation may persuade doctors to practise what is known as 'defensive medicine'. This means doctors choosing treatment which is legally safest, rather than that which is in the best interests of their patients. An example might be the high caesarean delivery rates in the US, prompted by obstetricians' fear of litigation if something goes wrong during a natural delivery. Obstetricians in the US are, on average, sued three times in their careers, and their insurance premiums are very high indeed.

It is not, however, clear that doctors are primarily motivated by a desire to avoid litigation. As Baroness Hale said in *Gregg v Scott*:[99] 'of course doctors and other health care professionals are not solely, or even mainly, motivated by the fear of adverse legal consequences. They are motivated by their natural desire and their professional duty to do their best for their patients.'

Furthermore, as Michael Jones points out in the next extract, the claim that fear of being sued might prompt doctors to practise defensive medicine is difficult to evaluate, because it is not clear that there is anything necessarily wrong with taking a cautious approach, and indeed it will sometimes be the right thing to do.

Michael Jones[100]

The increase in medical malpractice litigation over the last 15 or 20 years has been accompanied by claims that, in response to the threat of litigation, doctors now practise defensively. This involves undertaking procedures which are not medically justified but are designed to protect the doctor from a claim for negligence. The most commonly cited examples are unnecessary diagnostic tests, such as X-rays, and unnecessary caesarean deliveries. However, applying the *Bolam* test, a reasonable doctor would not undertake an *unnecessary* procedure and so a doctor could not avoid a finding of negligence by performing one. In fact, to the extent that the procedure carries some inherent risk, a practitioner acting in this way may increase his chances of being sued. Moreover, there is little clear understanding within the medical profession of what the term 'defensive medicine' means. 'Defensive' may mean simply treating patients conservatively or even 'more carefully', and this begs the question whether that treatment option is medically justified in the patient's interests. Nonetheless,

---

[99] [2005] UKHL 2.
[100] 'Breach of Duty' in Andrew Grubb with Judith Laing (eds), *Principles of Medical Law*, 2nd edn (OUP: Oxford, 2004) 369–441.

the courts have apparently acknowledged the existence of the phenomenon of defensive medicine, despite the fact that there is virtually no empirical, as opposed to anecdotal evidence of such practices in this country.

Despite doubts over whether defensive medicine exists and whether it is always necessarily a bad thing, the Compensation Act 2006 was in part directed at the perceived problem of excessively risk-averse behaviour.

Compensation Act 2006 section 1

1. A court considering a claim in negligence or breach of statutory duty may, in determining whether the defendant should have taken particular steps to meet a standard of care (whether by taking precautions against a risk or otherwise), have regard to whether a requirement to take those steps might—

   (a) prevent a desirable activity from being undertaken at all, to a particular extent or in a particular way, or

   (b) discourage persons from undertaking functions in connection with a desirable activity.

In the next extract, Kevin Williams suggests that the 'problem' of defensive medicine, and other risk-averse practices arising from fear of litigation, is a media-driven 'urban myth', and he argues that section 1 of the Compensation Act provides a 'phoney' solution to a non-existent problem.

Kevin Williams[101]

The fact that there may be no objective proof that we live in an increasingly 'blame and sue' society is beside the point when an 'urban myth' to the contrary is said to have taken hold . . .

Crucially, section 1 is unlikely to reduce fear of litigation, defensive practices or the number of frivolous claims; nor is it likely to cause socially valuable activities, such as volunteering, to increase. Unless it is read as a tacit invitation to judges to raise the height of the breach barrier, section 1 looks like a strongly media-driven phoney solution to a phoney problem.

The claim that doctors might not act in the best interests of their patient as a result of a fear of litigation was also behind the Access to Medical Treatments (Innovation) Bill, first introduced into the House of Lords by Lord Saatchi, after the death of his wife from cancer, and reintroduced into the House of Commons in late 2015.

The Bill presupposes that some terminally ill patients are deprived of treatments that might save their lives because doctors fear being sued in negligence. There is, however, no evidence that this has ever happened, and indeed medical research charities, the GMC, the BMA, and medical defence unions have been clear that it has not. In Chapter 9, when we consider clinical research, we look at the case of *Simms v Simms*, which confirms that when a patient's condition is desperate, a doctor might act reasonably in giving her a drug that is

---

[101] 'Politics, the Media and Refining the Notion of Fault: Section 1 of the Compensation Act' (2006) 4 Journal of Personal Injury Law 347.

not yet licensed for use. Reasonable doctors need not fear litigation from innovating. On the other hand, the Bill might give immunity from future liability in negligence to 'quacks' who 'innovate' with alternative treatments for cancer. Given that removing the possibility of litigation against doctors is *all* that the Bill would accomplish—that is, it would not provide additional funding for expensive cancer drugs—Miola is clear that it does not enhance patients' rights, but instead, and paradoxically, it takes them away.

José Miola[102]

Therefore, the Bill does not give doctors access to any drugs or medication that they cannot currently access. Nor does it allow doctors to use any unlicensed drugs that they are not currently allowed to use. It does not provide any additional funding for innovative treatment or access to drugs. Indeed, the MIB does not permit doctors to do anything at all beyond what they can already currently do. The only thing that it does is prevent the patient from being able to sue if the doctor complies with the process outlined in the Bill and the patient is injured. In this regard, it is not a Bill that gives patients any 'rights'. Instead, it removes those rights in return for a hope that doctors, unencumbered by the fear of litigation, will innovate in a positive way and speed-up breakthroughs in diseases such as cancer . . .

  With cancer in particular, there are many bodies that claim to provide alternatives to conventional therapies such as chemotherapy, and many of these have been criticized as irresponsible by the medical community. . . . Such practitioners may either convince the patient to forego regular therapies or provide treatments that, in some cases, may actively harm the patient. Again, any treatment would be 'innovative' under the Bill and therefore potentially receive protection.

The so-called 'compensation culture' has also been blamed for the emergence of Claims Management Companies (CMCs). These are organizations which encourage people to bring personal injury claims, through high-pressure sales techniques, like cold-calling and sending unsolicited text messages. The Compensation Act 2006 attempted to regulate CMCs by controlling advertising and setting up a mandatory authorization scheme for CMCs, administered by the Claims Management Regulation unit, within the Ministry of Justice.

  Since 2013, it has been an offence for CMCs to pay or receive payment for referrals of personal injury cases.[103] This will radically affect their business, because selling on personal injury claims to solicitors, described here by the House of Commons Health Select Committee, was essentially their core business:[104]

CMCs operate by collecting claims, assessing their contestability and likely value and then either charging a fee to individual personal injury lawyers or to practices for claims that are passed on to them. CMCs sometimes hold auctions for batches of claims of a particular type. This can lead to a situation where CMCs sell claims to the highest bidder and not to the best qualified solicitor.

As a result of these changes, there are now fewer CMCs—1,752 in 2014/15, compared with 2,693 in 2012/13.

---

[102] 'Bye-bye *Bolitho*? The curious case of the Medical Innovation Bill' (2015) 15 Medical Law International, online 15 September 2015.

[103] Legal Aid, Sentencing and Punishment of Offenders Act 2012, s 56.

[104] Sixth Report 2010/12.

(d) WHAT ABOUT OTHER PEOPLE WITH DISABILITIES?

Finally, it is worth remembering that most people who live with serious illness and disability will not receive any damages at all. Only those who can prove that another's negligence caused their ill health will receive generous financial assistance with the costs of their care. To illustrate this, compare the results in two cases in which babies suffered cerebral palsy as a result of something going wrong during their births. In one case, where negligence was successfully established, Leo Whiten received £5,685,507.79 in damages to compensate him for his cerebral palsy.[105] In contrast, failure to prove that the oxygen deprivation that caused Jack Jones's cerebral palsy was the result of negligence meant that he received nothing at all.[106]

The needs of these brain-damaged babies do not depend upon whether or not their disabilities were caused by negligence during childbirth. It is often said that tort law serves two purposes, compensation and deterrence. If we are principally concerned with compensating the victims of medical accidents, a social security system, or welfare state, which allocates resources according to need might then be fairer than the tort of negligence. Of course, such a system would not deter negligent behaviour, but at the same time, is it really plausible to argue that what motivates obstetricians to deliver babies safely is fear that the NHSLA might have to settle a large claim on their behalf?

It is not just the expense, inconvenience, and unfairness of negligence claims that has come under attack. Even more importantly, as we see in the next section, it is increasingly recognized that the clinical negligence system may work against ensuring that mistakes are not repeated.

5 LEARNING FROM MISTAKES

If adverse events result from human error, the tort system is not an effective way to ensure that such errors are not repeated. The deterrent effect of tort law is fairly weak when damages are not paid by the individual who has been found to be at fault. Even if doctors do fear being sued for the damage it might do to their reputation, paradoxically the most egregious examples of negligence will be settled quickly and quietly by the doctor's employer.

Furthermore, as Alan Merry and Alexander McCall Smith put it: 'A point which is often misunderstood is that human error, being by definition unintentional, is not easily deterred.'[107] Most doctors will have prescribed or administered the wrong drug, or the wrong dose of a drug, to a patient at some point in their career. Usually, these mistakes are harmless and may go unnoticed. If the patient dies or is injured as a result, the doctor (or in practice, her employer) may be sued for negligence. Alan Merry and Alexander McCall Smith describe this as 'outcome bias', whereby culpability depends on the consequences of an action, rather than upon its blameworthiness.[108] A system of deterrence built upon such haphazard foundations is unlikely to work. Instead, a more effective way to prevent human error is to anticipate likely mistakes, such as drug administration errors, and to design systems intended to minimize the risk materializing.

Medical mishaps are common: it has been estimated that 10 per cent of hospital inpatient admissions result in an adverse event.[109] Many of these have serious consequences: one study

---

[105] *Whiten v St George's Healthcare NHS Trust* [2011] EWHC 2066 (QB).
[106] *Jones v North West Strategic Health Authority* [2010] EWHC 178 (QB).
[107] *Errors, Medicine and the Law* (CUP: Cambridge, 2001) 2.   [108] Ibid, 46–7.
[109] Department of Health Expert Group, *An Organisation with a Memory* (DH: London, 2000) viii.

found that one-third of adverse events led to moderate or great disability, or death.[110] And as many as 70 per cent of adverse incidents are preventable.[111]

Historically, there has been a difference between the NHS and other high-risk activities, such as the aviation industry,[112] where human error is anticipated, and non-punitive reporting systems are used to ensure that learning from mistakes is the norm. Open reporting of adverse incidents helps medical staff to learn from them, but the adversarial negligence system has traditionally provided disincentives to admitting mistakes.

Over the past 15 years, there has been a trend towards open reporting. This began with *An Organisation with A Memory*, in which the Department of Health's Expert Group contrasted a person-centred approach to mistakes (like the clinical negligence system) where the emphasis is upon discovering who was at fault, and a systems approach, which assumes that humans are fallible and that errors are inevitable. The problem with the person-centred approach is that by trying to apportion individual blame, systemic reasons for adverse events may be missed, and effective learning hampered.

Department of Health Expert Group[113]

- Human error may sometimes be the factor that immediately precipitates a serious failure, but there are usually deeper, systemic factors at work which if addressed would have prevented the error or acted as a safety-net to mitigate its consequences . . .

- There is evidence that 'safety cultures', where open reporting and balanced analysis are encouraged in principle and by example, can have a positive and quantifiable impact on the performance of organisations. 'Blame cultures' on the other hand can encourage people to cover up errors for fear of retribution and act against the identification of the true causes of failure . . .

- Human error is commonly blamed for failures because it is often the most readily identifiable factor operating in the period just prior to an adverse event. Yet two important facts about human error are often overlooked. First, the best people can make the worst mistakes. Second, far from being random, errors fall into recurrent patterns. The same set of circumstances can provoke similar mistakes, regardless of the people involved. Any attempt at risk management that focuses primarily upon the supposed mental processes underlying error (forgetfulness, inattention, carelessness, negligence, and the like) and does not seek out and remove these situational 'error traps' is sure to fail.

A further recommendation from the Expert Group relates to the importance of reporting not only adverse events themselves, but also near misses. If data is only gathered when serious harm has resulted, this risks 'skewing learning towards a very small cross-section of accidents'.[114] In the aviation industry, for example, pilots are under a duty to report near

---

[110] Charles Vincent et al, 'Adverse events in British hospitals: preliminary retrospective record review' (2001) 322 British Medical Journal 517–19.

[111] Department of Health Expert Group, *An Organisation with a Memory* (DH: London, 2000) 26.

[112] Although compared with the NHS, the aviation industry is relatively low risk. The Chief Medical Officer as he then was, Sir Liam Donaldson, estimated that the odds of dying as a result of hospital treatment are 33,000 times that of dying in an air crash: Vivienne Harpwood, *Medicine, Malpractice and Misapprehensions* (Routledge-Cavendish: Abingdon, 2007) 38.

[113] *An Organisation with a Memory* (DH: London, 2000) viii–ix, 21, available at www.gov.uk/government/organisations/department-of-health.

[114] Ibid, 39.

misses since these are likely to yield information that could help to ensure that a similar mistake, which might on another occasion cause a serious accident, is not repeated.

The Bristol Royal Infirmary Inquiry began as a public inquiry into the abnormally high death rate for paediatric cardiac surgery at Bristol Royal Infirmary, but its final report included some damning conclusions about the NHS's response to adverse events, and boldly claimed that clinical negligence should be abolished.

Bristol Royal Infirmary Inquiry[115]

Chapter 26

35 Ultimately, we take the view that it will not be possible to achieve an environment of full, open reporting within the NHS when, outside it, there exists a litigation system the incentives of which press in the opposite direction. We believe that the way forward lies in the abolition of clinical negligence litigation, taking clinical error out of the courts and the tort system. It should be replaced by effective systems for identifying, analysing, learning from and preventing errors along with all other sentinel [adverse] events.

The crucial point is that instead of expecting medical staff to be infallible, it is more realistic to assume that mistakes are inevitable, and to try to build protections into the system to anticipate them and minimize their impact. To take a mundane example, the designers of word-processing packages take it for granted that users are likely to close documents without remembering to save their work. As a result, prompting mechanisms are built into computer software to remind users that they might want to save documents before closing them, and back-up documents are generated automatically.

In relation to medical practice, a systems approach might involve practices such as ensuring that different drugs do not have confusingly similar packaging, or that drugs with similar names are not stored together. The Chief Pharmaceutical Officer's Report, *Building a Safer NHS for Patients: Improving Medication Safety*,[116] lays out a number of strategies for reducing medication errors, such as automatic double-checking by a second person in high-risk situations; checking medication with patients and carers at the time of administration; and special wristbands for patients with known allergies.[117]

In the fertility sector, particular interest in avoiding adverse incidents was generated after a case in which a woman's eggs were fertilized with the wrong man's sperm.[118] Human fallibility means that the risk of this sort of mistake cannot be eliminated, but it can be reduced. As a result, there are now witnessing requirements to ensure that at least two people confirm the patient's identity. Rather than just relying upon the patient's name as an identifier, additional information such as their date of birth and hospital number must also be recorded, in order to reduce the likelihood of error when different patients with similar names are being treated at the same time.

In recent years, there has been considerable progress in improving open reporting of adverse incidents. Set up in 2001, the National Patient Safety Agency (NPSA) runs a mandatory reporting system. In 2004, the NPSA launched the national reporting and learning

---

[115] *Learning from Bristol: The Report of the Public Inquiry into Children's Heart Surgery at the Bristol Royal Infirmary 1984–1995* (Cm 5207, 2001).

[116] (DH: London, 2004).

[117] *Building a Safer NHS for Patients: Improving Medication Safety* (DH: London, 2004) 9.

[118] *Leeds Teaching Hospital NHS Trust v A* [2003] EWHC 259 (QB).

system (NRLS). In addition to extracting information from existing local risk management systems, NHS employees are also able to report patient safety incidents anonymously and directly through an online form. The NRLS encourages open reporting of 'all patient safety' incidents, including 'those that caused no harm or minimal harm to patients' and 'near misses'.

When reporting to the NRLS began, the total number of adverse incidents reported in England and Wales in the first quarter was 158. At the time of writing, 434,881 incidents had been reported in the NRLS's most recent three-month reporting period.[119] The total number of incidents reported in its first decade of operation was 10,809,052. Superficially, this might look disastrous—as though there has been an exponential rise in adverse events in the last 12 years—but, in reality, it suggests that non-punitive reporting is working, and that the NHS is in a much better position to learn from errors than it was a decade ago. Having gathered information about incidents—an example might be a patient identification error resulting from two patients having the same hospital number—the NPSA issues alerts and workbooks to ensure that all other NHS bodies are able to learn from them.[120]

Openness about mistakes is also important for patients who have been the victims of medical mishaps, who, as we have seen, are often more interested in an explanation and an apology than they are in financial compensation. Indeed, litigation appears to be more likely where patients believe that there has been a cover-up, or that a mistake has gone unacknowledged. Vincent et al's study of the motivations of litigants found that the decision to take legal action was determined not only by the original injury, but also by insensitive handling and poor communication afterwards. Patients who had decided to sue were seeking greater honesty; an acknowledgement of the severity of the trauma they had suffered; and assurances that lessons had been learned from their experiences: 'Communication assumes a special importance when things have gone wrong. Patients often blame doctors not so much for the original mistakes, as for a lack of openness or willingness to explain.'[121]

In the next extract, Martin Smith and Heidi Foster argue that the disclosure of medical mistakes is justified by a variety of different types of ethical reasoning (which we considered in Chapter 1).

Martin Smith and Heidi Foster[122]

Pertaining to rights-based reasoning, honest and candid communication followed by apology are a sign and a support of patients' rights to respectful treatment and care, and to self-determination. . . .

A consideration of professional virtues or character traits also supports the general principle of disclosing mistakes with forthrightness . . . The virtue of truthfulness is ultimately essential for an effective professional–patient relationship because relationships cannot endure failures of truthfulness for long. . . .

Finally, in ethically evaluating disclosure of mistakes from a consequentialist perspective, consideration needs to be given to the harms and benefits to all 'parties' who stand to be

---

[119] See further www.npsa.nhs.uk/nrls/reporting/.   [120] See further ibid.

[121] C Vincent, 'Why do people sue doctors? A study of patients and relatives taking legal action' (1994) 343 The Lancet 1609–13, 1613.

[122] 'Morally managing medical mistakes' (2000) 9 Cambridge Quarterly of Healthcare Ethics 38–53.

harmed or benefited by disclosure and apology . . . On the harm side of the ledger, disclosure is not always a benign activity. Patients can be emotionally fragile or in the middle of life-threatening situations; a disclosure of a mistake at that moment, similar to the giving of 'bad news' in such situations, could be detrimental to patient welfare and best interests. If mistakes are disclosed, patients or families might worry unnecessarily about other aspects of their care, and such worry might cause stress, discourage patients from seeking necessary care, and lead them to reject beneficial interventions in the future . . . Also in the current climate of healthcare, professionals could have their reputations, careers, livelihoods, referrals, staff privileges, and future employment opportunities jeopardized if they disclose a serious mistake.

On the benefit side of disclosure, patients . . . who have greater clarity and understanding of the medical situation may make better healthcare decisions . . . Honest disclosure can provide them with explanations and understanding . . . , give consolation that lessons have been learned, promote acceptance and closure about what transpired, and eliminate lawsuits filed to find out what really happened. . . .

But while a 'systems' approach to error is widely endorsed, in the next extract Quick argues that eliminating blame and individual accountability may have its dangers.

Oliver Quick[123]

The focus on systems also risks diluting the notion of individual professional responsibility that has been central to medical autonomy and accountability . . .

In the medical context, if blaming the system becomes the default response, to what extent will this shelter the incompetent or poor performer? Sir Donald Irvine, president of the GMC during the turbulent times of the Bristol affair, warned against this over-emphasis on the system which may mask individual failings. A recent example of this followed a surgeon's conviction for manslaughter with the judge remarking that:

> It was not your fault that you were allowed to go on operating, subject to restrictions, for another two years. Much of the evidence of these events was known at the time and the balance of the evidence was easily discoverable had it occurred to anyone making elementary inquiries.

As comments such as this become a more common reaction to error, it is worth questioning whether this drift towards blaming others and organisations risks underplaying the ethics of individual conscience.

6 REFORMING CLINICAL NEGLIGENCE

There have been a number of attempts to improve the functioning of the clinical negligence system. The National Health Service Litigation Authority (NHSLA) was set up in 1995, and it has encouraged the earlier admission of liability, and the provision of explanations and apologies. This led to reductions in the time taken to settle claims: new cases now take, on average, 1.31 years to settle, compared with 5.5 years in 1999/2000.[124] The

---

123 'Outing Medical Errors: Questions of Trust and Responsibility' (2006) 14 Medical Law Review 22, 41–2.
124 NHSLA, *Annual Report 2014–15* (NHSLA, 2015).

NHSLA uses a specialized panel of solicitors and, since 2014, has run its own mediation service.

Reforms to the civil justice system mean that parties are now given incentives to settle actions quickly. Where a case does go to court, pre-trial agreements to determine what the court will be asked to decide are now encouraged, and the court has a more proactive role in case management. Civil Procedure Rules emphasize that expert witnesses' primary duty is to assist the court to determine the truth, and not to offer partisan evidence to support one party's point of view, and in straightforward cases, the judge can appoint a single expert. Where more experts are used, they may be invited to submit a joint report.

The Clinical Negligence Scheme for Trusts (CNST), administered by the NHSLA, was set up in 1995 in order to help NHS trusts fund litigation by pooling resources, so that one high-value case does not bankrupt an NHS provider. As a condition for discounted premiums, it requires the development of clinical incident reporting systems and compliance with its risk management standards.

Because the NHSLA defends every negligence action against NHS providers, it is a 'super repeat player' in the clinical negligence system. In the next extract, Linda Mulcahy suggests that it should be more open about its litigation strategy.

Linda Mulcahy[125]

If we are to have confidence in the fairness of this new landscape, it is important for the Litigation Authority to be more transparent about its case management strategy. The absence of detailed information is likely to promote concerns that cases which have the potential to be most problematic in terms of setting negative precedents for the Authority are being settled while those with precedent setting potential which might favour NHS Trusts are those most likely to be pursued to appeal. The provision of information about litigation strategy and the characteristics of cases that are settled would provide much welcomed transparency in this new era of the super repeat player. The new focus on the collective interest in data contained in clinical negligence claims should allow us to pose new questions about the ways in which public authorities are managing claims and promoting the public interest by prompting public adjudication.

As we see later, the NHS complaints system has also been reformed recently. Unfortunately, however, the complaints and the claims systems still largely operate independently of each other, with patients having to choose whether to lodge a complaint or to pursue a claim. It would perhaps make more sense to have a single-track system, providing all patients with an explanation, apology, and assurance that steps have been taken to avoid repetition.

In its review of the clinical negligence system, the previous Labour government was not persuaded to move towards a no-fault compensation scheme. Although such schemes also exist in Denmark, Sweden, and Finland, and to a limited extent in France, the most well-known example is in New Zealand where a no-fault scheme has been in place since 1972.

Although removing the need to prove fault would simplify and speed up the process of compensation, the problem of establishing causation remains, and in medical cases, this

---

[125] 'The Market for Precedent: Shifting Visions of the Role of Clinical Negligence Claims and Trials' (2014) 22 Medical Law Review 274–90.

is a significant obstacle. It also means that arbitrary lines continue to be drawn between patients who are eligible for compensation because they can prove that their injuries were caused by a medical mishap, and those who cannot. As we have seen, the needs of a brain-damaged baby are the same, regardless of whether her injuries were caused by asphyxia at birth or a congenital disability. A no-fault compensation scheme would continue to distinguish between patients on grounds other than need.

Indeed, precisely because 'no fault' schemes must distinguish between medical mishaps and injuries that happen in the ordinary course of things, it is, as Manning points out in the context of the New Zealand scheme, difficult to eliminate considerations of negligence:

Joanna M Manning[126]

Lapsing into negligence thinking seems to arise particularly in respect of omissions and failures in the treatment process, such as misdiagnoses or delayed diagnoses, failures to give treatment or timely treatment, failure to refer to a specialist or hospital or to give the proper information to enable informed consent to be given. The theory is that ACC [Accident Compensation Corporation] no longer makes a positive finding of fault on behalf of a health professional or organization. But, in order to assess and determine whether there has been such a failure, the focus, including in the expert clinical advice, remains fixed on what a practitioner or service should have done in the relevant circumstances according to current guidelines and standards of accepted practice . . .

What was not anticipated at the time of the reform was how difficult it is to actually achieve the elimination of fault. Even though the courts and ACC are no longer making formal findings of individual and organizational fault in resolving treatment injury claims, they are continuing to make findings of negligence as part of the reasoning process in certain kinds of treatment injury claim.

No-fault schemes may be cheaper to administer, but they are also likely to attract higher numbers of claims. In New Zealand, for example, the proportion of the population making claims each year is more than double that in England. As a result, the Chief Medical Officer estimated that a no-fault scheme would be unaffordable for the NHS, costing as much £4 billion each year.[127]

Despite this, in Scotland, the No Fault Compensation Review Group, chaired by Sheila McLean, recommended that the Scottish government should implement a no-fault system of compensation.

No Fault Compensation Review Group[128]

The potential benefits of a no fault approach would be that:

- More people would obtain compensation, because of the removal of the requirement to prove fault;

---

[126] 'Plus ça change, plus c'est la même chose: negligence and treatment injury in New Zealand's accident compensation scheme' (2014) 14 *Medical Law International* 22–51.

[127] *Making Amends: A Consultation Paper Setting Out Proposals for Reforming the Approach to Clinical Negligence in the NHS* (DH: London, 2003).

[128] *Reports and Recommendations*, vol 1 (Scottish Government, 2011).

- Compensation could be awarded much more quickly, because:
  - o There is no need to prove fault;
  - o Care needs could be met by a guarantee of ongoing care provision by the state;
  - o The award could be made by administrative means or tribunal, rather than following an adversarial process;
  - o Money currently leaving the NHS would be retained in the system, thus improving NHS resources overall;
  - o There may be a considerable saving in legal fees.

Following a consultation process, in which significant concerns were raised about the overall costs of such a scheme, the Scottish Government nevertheless decided to 'proceed with caution'.

The Scottish Government[129]

6.10.10 Given the complexity of the issues and the potential costs we will proceed with caution to:

- Explore the scope, shape and development of a no-fault compensation in Scotland for injuries resulting from clinical treatment and the subsequent introduction of such a scheme. This will involve further detailed work especially in relation to projected cost and eligibility criteria; and

- consider how the scheme could more effectively contribute to patient safety, learning, improvement and how it links with and supports safe disclosure of adverse events and aligns with the complaints and claims procedure.

In England and Wales, however, having rejected both the status quo and a move towards a no-fault compensation system, the then government's preferred solution was the NHS Redress Act, which received Royal Assent in 2006 but which was never implemented in England.

The Welsh Assembly has issued its own NHS Redress (Wales) Measure, which led to the National Health Service (Concerns, Complaints and Redress Arrangements) (Wales) Regulations 2011. If there is 'qualifying liability in tort', the responsible body may offer compensation (up to a limit of £25,000); or a contract for care and treatment; an apology; an explanation; and a report on action taken to prevent recurrence of the event. If the offer is accepted, the complainant waives the right to bring civil legal proceedings.

One possible weakness of the Welsh scheme is that it retains the need to establish clinical negligence, and delegates this complex task to NHS staff. From the patient's point of view, there is now a unified system for reporting incidents, complaints, and claims, which reduces complexity, and may additionally mean that what starts as a 'complaint' actually leads to the payment of compensation. As Vivienne Harpwood points out, the amount paid out in compensation has increased, but costs have been reduced.

---

[129] Consultation Report—Consultation on recommendations for no-fault compensation in Scotland for injuries resulting from clinical treatment (Scottish Government, 2014).

Vivienne Harpwood[130]

> An increase of up to 60 per cent in the number of complaints about healthcare throughout Wales was reported soon after the scheme was introduced . . . Anecdotal evidence suggests that the duty on Health Boards to offer compensation when it is determined that a qualifying liability exists, has already resulted in a rise in compensation payments to claimants . . . However, there is evidence that costs have been substantially reduced in respect of lower value clinical negligence claims, a factor which might balance out the rise in compensation payments to some extent.

In his report into reform of the funding of the civil justice system, Lord Justice Jackson argued in favour of the resurrection of the NHS Redress Scheme,[131] but this seems to have fallen on deaf ears, and at the time of writing it looks unlikely that an NHS Redress Scheme will be set up in England. The most likely reason is that by making it easier to claim, it would be likely to bring new claims into the system and might therefore cost more than the clinical negligence system.

The Department of Health had predicted that the increase in the number of cases might be as high as 43 per cent, although it also envisaged that opportunistic claims will easily be rejected, and in the longer term, it expected to see substantial savings in legal costs.[132] Nevertheless, Department of Health economists estimated that, even with a payout cap of £20,000, the financial effect of the scheme would be likely to range from a saving of £7 million to a cost of £48 million.[133] Given the latter possibility, it is unsurprising that it has not seen the light of day.

Instead, in 2011 the coalition government consulted on proposals, first mooted by Lord Young,[134] to set up a similar system to the current Road Traffic Accidents Personal Injury (RTA PI) Scheme to cover lower value (ie less than £25,000) clinical negligence claims.[135] The RTA PI scheme essentially has three stages:

- Stage 1—the claimant solicitor completes the claim notification form and sends it to the insurer who may admit/deny liability.

- Stage 2—if liability is admitted, the claimant obtains a medical report and a settlement is negotiated.

- Stage 3—if the parties cannot agree a settlement, an application is made to court for a quantum hearing.

There are a number of difficulties with this proposal, not least the fact that establishing both liability and causation in clinical negligence cases is much more complex than in road traffic accidents. In the next extract, Emma Cave additionally points out that there may be some risk in English patients having access to a weaker form of redress than patients in Wales and Scotland.

---

[130] 'Clinical Negligence and Poor Quality Care: Is Wales "Putting Things Right"?' in Pamela Ferguson and Graeme Laurie (eds), *Inspiring a Medico-Legal Revolution: Essays in Honour of Sheila McLean* (Ashgate: Aldershot, 2015) 139–53.

[131] The Rt Hon Lord Justice Jackson, *Review of Civil Litigation Costs, Final Report* (TSO: London, 2010) ch 23, paras 7 and 8.

[132] Ibid, ch 23, paras 7 and 8.   [133] Ibid.

[134] HM Government, Lord Young, *Common Sense, Common Safety* (Cabinet Office: London, 2010) 23.

[135] Ministry of Justice, *Solving Disputes in the County Courts: Creating a Quicker, Simpler and More Proportionate System* (2011), available at www.justice.gov.uk.

Emma Cave[136]

The necessity to ensure that redress is 'joined-up' is receiving inadequate attention. In this time of austerity measures, the focus is naturally on cutting costs, but losing sight of adequate access to justice will itself prove costly. Advances made in relation to the complaints process and professional regulation are limited by the adverse effects clinical negligence has on the doctor patient relationship. Where financial compensation is barred by virtue of limitations on legal aid and civil law reform, more pressure will be placed on the complaints system and professional regulation to deliver appropriate sanction, communication and correction. If Scotland adopts a no fault system and the redress scheme in Wales proves effective, the dichotomy in access to justice will be sorely felt in England. The CMO recommended a comprehensive package of reforms to effect a culture change in the NHS. The government is steering an altogether steadier course, prioritising the reduction of costs to the NHS. A low value, fast track scheme would reduce costs, but a failure to serve the interests of patients will result in a lack of confidence not merely in the process of restoration, but in other aspects of NHS redress.

7 THE NHS COMPLAINTS SYSTEM

Patients who are dissatisfied with their medical treatment, who are ineligible, unable, or unwilling to bring an action in negligence may nevertheless want to complain about the care that they have received. The Patient Advice and Liaison Service (PALS) was set up in order to listen to patients' concerns, and to offer information and support. PALS officers are available in all hospitals and they will liaise with others in order to try to resolve problems before a formal complaint is made.

If informal resolution does not succeed, there is then a two-stage process for formal complaints. Local resolution is the first and usually the only stage—only two per cent of complaints progress beyond the local resolution stage. Complaints can be resolved locally through a report which sets out how the complaint was considered, the conclusions reached, and, if relevant, a remedial action plan. An Independent Complaints Advocacy Service (ICAS) exists to ensure that complainants have access to support in articulating their concerns and in navigating the complaints system.

The volume of formal complaints has risen dramatically in recent years. In 2014/15 a total of 205,000 written complaints were received, up from 131,022 in 2007/8.[137] This figure, while high, is probably an underestimate of patient dissatisfaction, however. It appears that most dissatisfied patients do not, in fact complain.

House of Commons Health Select Committee[138]

The 'toxic cocktail' of service users reluctant to complain and providers reluctant to listen must be avoided at all costs, as it inevitably leads to a spiral of decline in service quality.

---

[136] Emma Cave, 'Redress in the NHS' (2011) 27 Journal of Professional Negligence 138–57.

[137] Health and Social Care Information Centre, *Data on Written Complaints in the NHS 2014–15* (HSCIC, 2015).

[138] Health Select Committee Fourth Report of Session 2014–15, *Complaints and Raising Concerns.*

Patients must be empowered to give constructive feedback on services which they believe are substandard. Anna Bradley, Chair of Healthwatch England, told us that:

> One in three [patients and carers] says that they have had personal experience, or know someone who has had personal experience, of a really quite serious incident, but only half of them have done anything about it . . . One in four of them says they did not do anything about it because they did not think anyone would be interested. Three in five said they did not know how to do anything about it. One in two said no one would do anything about it anyway and they did not trust that they would get a decent response. As we also know, very many people . . . just feel too vulnerable.

As this shows, the complaints process is seen as complex and difficult to navigate, and can prove off-putting.

If people are not satisfied with the way a local NHS body has dealt with their complaint, the next stage is to complain to the Health Service Ombudsman. A complaint to the Ombudsman has to be made within a year from when the patient became aware of the events that are the subject of the complaint, and the patient must show that she has suffered some hardship or injustice.

In practice, the vast majority of complaints that the Ombudsman receives are not fully investigated, often because local resolution has not been exhausted. It is not usually possible to obtain damages, although in rare cases (generally fewer than ten per year) where the there is proof of financial loss, the Ombudsman may order some financial payment.

In 2014–15, the Ombudsman carried out 1,652 investigations, compared with 852 in 2013–14. This may sound like a large number of complaints but it should be put into the context of the volume of NHS activity: on average the Ombudsman investigates 6.2 complaints for every 100,000 clinical episodes in each acute trust. Less than half (44 per cent) of complaints against acute hospital trusts were upheld.

Some of the most commonly cited reasons for complaints were receiving an adequate apology (34 per cent), poor communication (31 per cent), and that the response to the original complaint was wrong or incomplete (24 per cent). Staff attitude was a factor in 21 per cent of cases. The Ombudsman has also found that the number of complaints varies considerably between different trusts. This should not be taken as a measure of hospital performance, however, partly because of the different work undertaken by different hospitals, and partly because 'some NHS organisations have better information for patients about making a complaint and encourage learning from complaints'.[139] A high number of complaints may indicate that the hospital has a proactive attitude towards learning from mistakes.

Following Robert Francis QC's report into failings at Mid-Staffordshire hospital (see Section 9), the government asked Ann Clywd MP and Professor Tricia Hart to conduct a detailed review of complaints handling in the NHS and make recommendations for improvement. They found that patients and their relatives found it difficult to complain and that, far from valuing complaints, some NHS hospitals appeared to want them to 'go away'.

---

[139] Parliamentary and Health Service Ombudsman, *Complaints about acute trusts 2014–15* (PHSO, 2015).

Ann Clwyd and Tricia Roberts[140]

People expressed their, fear that their, or their relative's, care might get worse if they were to complain. They also felt intimidated by the power of professionals or institutions; the complexity of the system and the feeling that nothing will happen—that all their effort will prove to be worth nothing. There is also a strong sense that people who are less able (or feel less able) do not complain . . .

People were often unhappy that their concerns were not addressed on the spot by staff. Had they been resolved then, people would not have had to make a formal complaint. People also complained that insufficient attempts had been made to understand their complaint or to assess how serious it was . . .

Delays were one of the main causes of dissatisfaction. People felt that only their unremitting efforts would keep a complaint from lapsing; and that, whatever the rhetoric the hospital did not welcome the complaint and would prefer it went away . . .

People said they felt isolated or 'out-gunned' by a powerful and monolithic organisation.

In response, the Department of Health set up a Complaints Programme Board (CPB) in order to improve complaints handling in the NHS, and one outcome has been that, since 2014, how an organization handles complaints has been a mandatory key line of inquiry in Care Quality Commission inspections. Indeed, the CQC has said that how an NHS body responds to complaints is a proxy for whether it is a well-run organization:

Complaints handling is an excellent proxy for an open, transparent and learning culture that we would expect to see in well-led organisations . . . A service that is safe, responsive and well-led will treat every concern as an opportunity to improve. It will encourage its staff to raise concerns without fear of reprisal. It will respond to complaints openly and honestly.[141]

Despite this recent focus upon complaints as an opportunity to learn, there is still room for improvement. In its 2014–15 report on Complaints and Raising Concerns, the House of Commons Health Select Committee recommended a single complaints gateway, and that trusts should be required to set out publicly what they have learned from patient complaints:

We recommend that Trusts be required to publish at least quarterly, in anonymised summary form, details of complaints made against the Trust, how the complaints have been handled and what the Trust has learnt from them . . .

We agree that the onus should be on the system to help a complainant. People should not be forced to search out the most appropriate way to raise concerns. . . . We recommend that the complaints system be simplified and streamlined by establishing a single 'branded' complaints gateway across all NHS providers. This should be available online, but not exclusively so.[142]

8 PROFESSIONAL REGULATION

The GMC is the medical profession's regulatory body (the Nursing and Midwifery Council fulfils a similar role in relation to nurses). Doctors can only practise medicine in the UK if

---

[140] *A Review of the NHS Hospitals Complaints System Putting Patients Back in the Picture* (DH: London, 2013).

[141] Care Quality Commission, *Complaints Matter* (CQC, 2014).

[142] Health Select Committee Fourth Report of Session 2014–15, *Complaints and Raising Concerns*.

they are registered with the GMC. In cases of seriously poor practice, a patient (or another health care professional) might report a doctor to the GMC. The GMC can investigate if a doctor's fitness to practise is impaired, as a result of misconduct, deficient performance, criminal conviction, ill health, or the decision of another health care regulator (an example might be a decision of the Human Fertilisation and Embryology Authority that a clinician has failed to fulfil her obligations under the Human Fertilisation and Embryology Act 1990).

Fitness to practise and interim order panel hearings are now conducted independently of the GMC by the Medical Practitioners Tribunal Service (MPTS). If a doctor's fitness to practise is found to be impaired, she can be erased ('struck off') or suspended from the medical register, or conditions may be imposed upon her practice, such as a requirement that she refrains from carrying out a particular procedure. In 2014, the MPTS held 237 fitness to practise hearings, in which 71 doctors were erased from the register; 86 were suspended; conditions were imposed in 22 cases; warnings given in 10; and 37 cases resulted in a finding of no impairment. There were 571 interim order panel hearings in 2014; 102 of which led to temporary suspension and 350 to conditions being placed upon the doctor's practice.[143]

In *McCandless v General Medical Council*, the appellant had been struck off the medical register, and appealed to the Privy Council (which at that time was responsible for hearing appeals from GMC decisions), arguing that 'serious professional misconduct' implied that the conduct had to have been morally blameworthy. The appellant admitted that he had been negligent, but said that an honest mistake could not amount to serious professional misconduct. The Privy Council disagreed.

McCandless v General Medical Council[144]

Lord Hoffmann

[T]he possible penalties available to the committee, which used to be confined to the ultimate sanction of erasure, have been extended to include suspension and the imposition of conditions upon practice. This suggests that the offence was intended to include serious cases of negligence ... [T]he public has higher expectations of doctors and members of other self-governing professions. Their governing bodies are under a corresponding duty to protect the public against the genially incompetent as well as the deliberate wrongdoers.

'Seriously deficient performance' is a relatively new ground for suspension or conditional registration.[145] It is defined as 'a departure from good professional practice, whether or not it is covered by specific GMC guidance, sufficiently serious to call into question a doctor's registration'. This definition is rather circular and question-begging: performance is seriously deficient when it is a departure from good practice serious enough to call into question a doctor's registration. It is, however, clear that it is not necessary to prove that a patient has been harmed by the doctor's 'seriously deficient performance'.

Since 2003, appeals against Fitness to Practise Panel decisions have been to the High Court. The Court of Appeal in *Fatnani v General Medical Council* was clear that such appeals should not be an occasion for re-sentencing: that is, it is not for the court to substitute its view as to the appropriate punishment for a doctor whose practice amounted to serious professional misconduct.

---

143 GMC, *Fitness to Practise Annual Statistics Report 2014* (GMC: London, 2015).
144 [1996] 1 WLR 167.   145 Introduced by the Medical (Professional Performance) Act 1995.

Fatnani v General Medical Council[146]

Laws LJ

As it seems to me the fact that a principal purpose of the Panel's jurisdiction in relation to sanctions is the preservation and maintenance of public confidence in the profession rather than the administration of retributive justice, particular force is given to the need to accord special respect to the judgment of the professional decision-making body in the shape of the Panel . . .

[T]he High Court will correct material errors of fact and of course of law and it will exercise a judgment, though distinctly and firmly a secondary judgment, as to the application of the principles to the facts of the case.

As part of a raft of reforms instituted in response to the perceived failings of the regulation of the medical profession highlighted by the case of Harold Shipman,[147] section 29 of the National Health Service Reform and Health Care Professions Act 2002 gives the Council for Healthcare Regulatory Excellence the power to appeal against the decisions of fitness to practise panels on the grounds of 'undue leniency'. Because fitness to practise panels are concerned with preserving public confidence in the medical profession, as well as with patient safety, a punishment might be judged unduly lenient if it focused only upon whether the doctor continued to pose a risk to patients, and did not give sufficient attention to public interest considerations.

A similar provision exists in relation to nurses' registration, and in *Council for Healthcare Regulatory Excellence v Nursing and Midwifery Council*,[148] the Court of Appeal held that the fitness to practise panel of the Nursing and Midwifery Council had given too much weight to Nurse Grant's remorse and insight into her failings, and insufficient weight to the need to uphold public confidence in the nursing profession. Grant had acted insensitively and in a bullying way towards patients and colleagues over a prolonged period of time—including being rude and insensitive to a woman who had had to deliver her baby after its death *in utero*. Unlike a case in which the health care professional's performance was clinically deficient, where remedial action may mean that their fitness to practise is no longer impaired by the time of the hearing, in cases of egregious conduct towards patients, the need to preserve confidence in the profession may result in finding that their fitness to practise is impaired, regardless of any remedial action taken in the meantime.[149]

Also in response to the case of Harold Shipman, when the GMC had been alerted to a police investigation but had said that it had no powers to alter Dr Shipman's registration unless or until he was convicted, section 41A of the Medical Act 1983 provides for the making of interim orders to suspend registration or make it subject to conditions 'for the protection of the public' or where this would be 'otherwise in the public interest'. These interim orders can be made initially for up to 18 months, but with court approval they are renewable indefinitely. There has been a dramatic rise in the use of interim orders in recent years: only four were made in the 16 years from 1980 to 1996, while in 2014 alone, 571 doctors appeared before Interim Orders Panel hearings, 18 per cent of whom received interim suspensions and 61 per cent interim conditions.

---

[146] [2007] EWCA Civ 46.

[147] Dr Shipman was found guilty of 15 murders in 2000, but it is believed that he almost certainly murdered more than 250 of his patients.

[148] [2011] EWHC 927 (Admin).

[149] See further Paula Case, 'The public interest in a finding of impairment' (2011) 27 Journal of Professional Negligence 177–80.

Paula Case's analysis of all interim orders made in a nine-month period in 2009 found that in 44 per cent of cases, the interim sanction was more draconian than the final one, suggesting that sometimes the pre-trial process is effectively part of the punishment.[150] She also draws attention to a tension within section 41A, which is thus far unresolved in the case law. On the one hand, if the justification for making an interim order is the need to protect the public, the bar might be set quite high, with orders only being made if the health care professional poses a risk to patients. Yet, on the other hand, if the justification is that the order is 'otherwise in the public interest', reputational risk to the profession might be sufficient, and the bar might be set much lower.

In *Yeong v General Medical Council*—a case in which a doctor had had a sexual relationship with a patient, and tried to argue that the fact that the Interim Order Panel had not ordered full suspension cast doubt upon the decision of the fitness to practise panel (FTPP) to do so—Sales J took the former approach, emphasizing that interim orders should principally be used to deal with immediate risk to patients.

Yeong v General Medical Council[151]

Sales J

[T]he role of the Interim Orders Panel at the interim hearing stage is very different from the role of the FTPP at the final hearing. It will not typically be appropriate for the Interim Orders Panel at the interim stage (ie before a full hearing on the merits) to impose sanctions on grounds based simply on the importance in the public interest of maintaining clear standards of behaviour, as distinct from dealing with an immediate risk posed by a practitioner in relation to his treatment of patients . . . Therefore, the absence of sanction imposed by the Interim Orders Panel does not indicate that the FTPP was wrong to impose the sanction of suspension after the full hearing at the end of the disciplinary process.

Conversely, in relation to two doctors who had been involved in the case of Baby P, a toddler who had died after suffering horrifying neglect and abuse, lengthy interim orders were made, Case suggests, solely to promote public confidence. The orders were made 'under the watchful eye of the media', but there was no suggestion of 'dishonesty, criminal offences, or of posing a risk to patients which could not be addressed by imposing conditions on their registration'.

In the following extract, Case argues that there is a further danger that 'protecting the public interest' may elide into promoting public confidence in the regulator itself. Given the profound consequences interim suspension has for individual doctors, it is questionable whether these should ever be made in order to promote confidence in the muscularity of professional regulation.

Paula Case[152]

A construction of interim suspension powers which envisage their use as a tool for protecting public confidence has serious implications for the doctor concerned . . . [T]here is

---

[150] Paula Case, 'Putting Public Confidence First: Doctors, Precautionary Suspension, and the General Medical Council' (2011) 19 Medical Law Review 339–71.

[151] [2009] EWHC 1923 (Admin).

[152] Paula Case, 'Putting Public Confidence First: Doctors, Precautionary Suspension, and the General Medical Council' (2011) 19 Medical Law Review 339–71.

> something instinctively problematic about applying an *interim* sanction on the grounds of protecting the profession's reputation. . . .
>
> The danger which accompanies the assumption that confidence in the profession and in its regulator are co-extensive, is that self-preservation strategies of the regulator can masquerade as attempts to build confidence in the profession . . . What is . . . questionable is whether the 'public interest' should include bolstering the reputation of *the regulator* at significant expense.

Historically, doctors were admitted to the medical register on qualification, and no further checks were made, unless the doctor's performance gave rise to concern. Since 2005, in order to retain their licence to practise, doctors have to 'revalidate', by demonstrating that they remain up to date and fit to practise. Doctors must now prove that their own practice over the previous five years has been in line with the principles set out in the GMC's guide to the duties of a doctor, *Good Medical Practice*. This means routinely collecting and keeping data and information drawn from their day-to-day medical practice. The GMC also demands evidence of participation in an internal appraisal scheme. This process became more formal in 2009, when in addition to being registered, doctors have to hold a licence to practise, which must be renewed annually.

In addition to professional regulation, the National Clinical Assessment Service (NCAS), now a part of the NHSLA, was set up in 2001 to support the NHS in dealing with doctors and dentists whose performance gives cause for concern. The NCAS provides advice about the local handling of cases, and can carry out clinical performance assessments of individual practitioners. In 2014–15, it received 927 new referrals and carried out 68 assessments. Where the assessment reveals that the practitioner's performance could be improved, the NCAS will put in place an action plan. In the most serious cases, practitioners can be suspended or excluded from work.

9 WHISTLEBLOWING

Other health care workers will often be better placed than patients to spot unusually poor results, or inadequate care. The GMC's guide to good medical practice states that doctors must take steps to protect patients where they suspect a colleague may be unfit to practise (a similar duty is placed on nurses by the Nursing and Midwifery Council[153]).

General Medical Council[154]

> 25c If you have concerns that a colleague may not be fit to practise and may be putting patients at risk, you must ask for advice from a colleague, your defence body or us. If you are still concerned you must report this, in line with our guidance and your workplace policy, and make a record of the steps you have taken.

---

[153] *Raising and Escalating Concerns: Guidance to Nurses and Midwives* (NMC, 2015).
[154] *Good Medical Practice* (GMC: London, 2013).

In practice, however, it is often difficult for doctors and nurses to raise concerns about colleagues' poor performance. Stephen Bolsin, the 'whistleblower' who reported his doubts about the practice of paediatric cardiac surgery at the Bristol Royal Infirmary was ostracized by the medical establishment, and eventually emigrated to Australia.

The Public Interest Disclosure Act 1998 is supposed to protect employees who have disclosed information in the public interest from dismissal and victimization, and NHS trusts are under a duty to investigate staff concerns, and to guarantee that staff who raise concerns responsibly and reasonably will be protected against victimization. It is, however, unclear whether this has removed all of the powerful cultural and institutional barriers to open reporting. Indeed, a 2013 survey of over 800 hospital doctors found that 46 per cent were fearful of the personal consequences of raising concerns.

Zosia Kmietowicz[155]

Nearly a third of respondents (31%) admitted to having witnessed incidents of poor care of patients that they did not report but that they now wished they had. When asked why they had not reported the incident, 67% said that they were worried they would not be supported by their trust's management, 48% were worried they would not be supported by their colleagues, and 49% feared the effect that raising concerns might have on their career.

In his inquiry into poor patient care at Mid-Staffordshire Hospital—thought to have led to between 400–1,200 unnecessary patient deaths[156]—Robert Francis QC expressed concern that health care professionals who had tried to raise concerns about practices within the hospital had been discouraged from doing so.

Robert Francis QC[157]

A study of the experiences of those involved in these three episodes arising out of raising serious concerns is not encouraging. It must not be forgotten what pressures can be applied to deter staff from coming forward, and how little it can take to dissuade nervous individuals from pursuing matters. Any failure to go the extra mile to protect and respect those who raise genuine concerns has to be seen against a national background, in which there are frequent reports of injustices being perpetrated against whistle-blowers. How many such reports are correct is not in point: staff locally will see in every failure to take the appropriate and expected steps internally as reinforcement of what they read happening elsewhere.

And in their 2015 report on Complaints and Raising Concerns, the House of Commons Health Select Committee recommended that efforts should be made to identify and apologize to NHS staff who have suffered as a result of raising concerns.

---

[155] 'Half of English hospital doctors fear raising concerns, finds survey' (2013) 347 British Medical Journal f7053.

[156] Tony Delamothe, 'Repeat after me "Mid-Staffordshire"' (2010) 340 British Medical Journal 132.

[157] *Robert Francis Inquiry report into Mid-Staffordshire NHS Foundation Trust* (DH: London, 2011) para 193.

Health Select Committee[158]

> 114. The failure to deal appropriately with the consequences of cases where staff have sought protection as whistleblowers has caused people to suffer detriment, such as losing their job and in some cases being unable to find similar employment. This has undermined trust in the system's ability to treat whistleblowers with fairness. This lack of confidence about the consequences of raising concerns has implications for patient safety.
>
> 115. We expect the NHS to respond in a timely, honest and open manner to patients, and we must expect the same for staff. We recommend that there should be a programme to identify whistleblowers who have suffered serious harm and whose actions are proven to have been vindicated, and provide them with an apology and practical redress.

10   THE CRIMINAL LAW

In extreme cases, if a patient's death is caused by a doctor's gross negligence, a conviction for manslaughter is possible, although, as Hannah Quirk points out, these cases are not straightforward.

Hannah Quirk[159]

> White-collar crime, committed by 'a person of respectability and high social status in the course of his occupation; has long presented difficulties for the police. 'White-coat' suspects present even greater challenges—not only do they possess professional status and special-ist expertise in the subject under investigation, but they usually have no malicious intention, have not acted for personal gain and often arouse sympathy. Prosecutors are aware that 'judges and juries do not like having these cases (particularly involving doctors) in front of them'. . . . Another challenge in bringing medical manslaughter charges is that 'prosecutors, judges and juries all struggle with the ill defined concept of gross negligence.'

As Quirk indicates, it is not easy to work out when negligence should be considered gross. In *R v Adomako*, the defendant had been the anaesthetist during an eye operation, and had failed to notice that the tube from the ventilator had become disconnected. The patient suffered a cardiac arrest and died. The House of Lords held that negligence is 'gross' when it is so bad that it should be criminal.

R v Adomako[160]

Lord Mackay

> The jury will have to consider whether the extent to which the defendant's conduct departed from the proper standard of care incumbent upon him, involving as it must have done a risk of death to the patient, was such that it should be judged criminal.

---

[158] Health Select Committee Fourth Report of Session 2014–15, *Complaints and Raising Concerns.*

[159] 'Sentencing White Coat Crime: The Need for Guidance in Medical Manslaughter Cases' (2013) 11 Criminal Law Review 871–88.

[160] [1995] 1 AC 1.

> It is true that to a certain extent this involves an element of circularity, but in this branch of the law I do not believe that is fatal to its being correct as a test of how far conduct must depart from accepted standards to be characterised as criminal. This is necessarily a question of degree and an attempt to specify that degree more closely is I think likely to achieve only a spurious precision. The essence of the matter, which is supremely a jury question, is whether, having regard to the risk of death involved, the conduct of the defendant was so bad in all the circumstances as to amount in their judgment to a criminal act or omission.

The circularity of this definition was challenged unsuccessfully in *R v Misra*. Two junior doctors had failed to notice obvious symptoms of infection in a patient who had just undergone routine surgery. By the time the infection was diagnosed, the patient had suffered toxic shock syndrome, which caused his death. The doctors were convicted of gross negligence manslaughter. They appealed against their convictions on human rights grounds: first, they claimed that the definition of gross negligence manslaughter—according to which it is for the jury to decide, after the event, if it is so bad as to be criminal—involves retrospective criminalization, which is prohibited by Article 7 and, secondly, that it additionally breaches the right to a fair trial (Article 6). The Court of Appeal dismissed their appeals.

R v Misra[161]

Judge LJ

In our judgment the law is clear. . .✱The jury concluded that the conduct of each appellant in the course of performing his professional obligations to his patient was 'truly exceptionally bad', and showed a high degree of indifference to an obvious and serious risk to the patient's life✱Accordingly, along with the other ingredients of the offence, gross negligence too, was proved. In our judgment it is unrealistic to suggest that the basis for the jury's decision cannot readily be understood.

Despite judicial confidence in the clarity of the definition of gross negligence manslaughter, it has been suggested that the vagueness, circularity, and possible subjectivity of the need to establish that what the defendant did was 'so bad as to be criminal', or 'truly exceptionally bad', has the potential to operate unfairly. Moreover, because there can only be a prosecution if the patient dies as a result of the gross negligence, it will fail to capture a doctor who has behaved 'truly exceptionally badly', but where fortuitously, or as a result of the skill and dedication of other doctors,[162] the patient did not die. Given that a truly exceptionally bad doctor has to also be unlucky in order to face prosecution, this may weaken any deterrent effect of the threat of criminal sanctions. As Margaret Brazier and Amel Aghrani put it: 'Any deterrent effect of the criminal law would be much greater if it embraced gross negligence causing serious injury and not only fatal errors'.[163]

In the next extract, Oliver Quick draws upon his interviews with Crown Prosecutors to argue not that gross negligence should be extended, but rather that gross negligence manslaughter should be abolished.

---

[161] [2004] EWCA Crim 2375.   [162] *Kay v Ayrshire and Arran Health Board* [1987] 2 All ER 888.
✱[163] Margaret Brazier and Amel Alghrani, 'Fatal medical malpractice and criminal liability' (2009) 25 Journal of Professional Negligence 51–67.

Oliver Quick[164]

[S]everal reasons for principle and practice point to its abolition. First, the offence is too broad for prosecutorial judgment to be consistently applied, and this translates into particular harshness for those operating in error-ridden activities who are exposed to risk of prosecution by virtue of their socially vital work, and often at the mercy of moral luck. An analysis of the interview responses suggests that no meaningful hierarchy of seriousness is adopted in relation to classifying errors as gross. Respondents struggled to pin down their understanding of the term gross, often initially relying on gut instinct . . .

The statistics show that a disproportionate number of non-white practitioners figure in medical manslaughter prosecutions. This is a troubling finding and one that may be understood with reference to a number of sociological explanations, such as the training and language skills of overseas-trained practitioners, as well as their ability to gain employment and superior supervision in better performing hospitals. The high number may also be related to racist attitudes that creep into the decisions to complain about and consider investigating individuals in the first place.

More recently, Quick has advocated replacing gross negligence manslaughter with an offence based on subjective recklessness:

In short, recklessness works. The (very few) cases which lead to conviction are classic subjective recklessness. . . . To summarise, we could say the following: where a doctor has special knowledge that certain procedures carry with them certain risks, and fails to investigate those risks without justification, criminal responsibility can be properly attributed on the basis of recklessness.[165]

In recent years, there has been an increase in the number of prosecutions against doctors for manslaughter.[166] This is almost certainly not because there has been a dramatic increase in instances of gross negligence. Rather, more plausible explanations are an increased tendency to involve the police, and greater willingness on the part of the Crown Prosecution Service to prosecute doctors, perhaps because it perceives that juries have become more likely to convict.[167]

It is also now possible to prosecute NHS bodies under the Corporate Manslaughter and Homicide Act 2007, though as yet there have been no such prosecutions. Invoking the cases of Dr Ubani, who was exhausted, stressed, and working as a locum on his first shift in England, and who accidentally administered ten times the recommended dose of diamorphine to a patient, and Dr Ramnath who, 'in the pressure cooker' atmosphere of a busy intensive care unit, had injected her patient with a lethal injection of adrenalin, Brazier and Alghrani suggest that corporate manslaughter might sometimes be more appropriate than prosecution of the incompetent doctor.

---

[164] 'Prosecuting "Gross" Medical Negligence: Manslaughter, Discretion and the Crown Prosecution Service' (2006) 33 Journal of Law and Society 421–50, 449.

[165] 'Medicine, Mistakes and Manslaughter: A Criminal Combination?' (2010) 69 Cambridge Law Journal 186–203.

[166] RE Ferner and SE McDowell, 'Doctors charged with manslaughter in the course of medical practice' (2006) 99 Journal of the Royal Society of Medicine 309–14.

[167] Ibid.

Margaret Brazier and Amel Alghrani[168]

There is no evidence that either Dr Ubani or Dr Ramnath, or the many other doctors and nurses convicted of manslaughter, acted with any intent to cause harm. These two high profile cases help us by their very facts. At first sight both errors were crass. Establishing liability in tort for clinical negligence would be simple, and the degree of negligence is high on any scale of poor practice. Yet other factors played a key part in the events that ended with a patient's death and criminal convictions for the doctors. Any 'system' that permitted an exhausted doctor with poor English and a lack of familiarity with medical practice in the UK to treat patients looks defective. A hospital that failed to notice the stress affecting Dr Ramnath, failed in its duty to her and the patient. And so many would ask should it be the relevant NHS Trusts that face prosecution for corporate manslaughter?

Although corporate manslaughter has not so far been used against the NHS, there have been prosecutions under the Health and Safety at Work Act 1974. In *R v Southampton University Hospital Trust*,[169] the Trust pleaded guilty to failing to discharge the duty imposed on it by the Health and Safety at Work Act to people other than employees. This case followed the successful prosecution of two junior doctors in *R v Misra*, discussed earlier. In addition to the doctors' own gross negligence, there had also been serious failures in their supervision. Initially, the Trust was fined £100,000, but this was reduced on appeal to £40,000, in part to reflect the fact that rapid steps had been taken to put proper systems in place after these failures had been identified.

Gross negligence manslaughter was of little use in tackling some of scandalously poor care Robert Francis QC had found at Mid-Staffordshire NHS Foundation Trust.

Robert Francis QC[170]

The first inquiry heard harrowing personal stories from patients and patients' families about the appalling care received at the Trust. On many occasions, the accounts received related to basic elements of care and the quality of the patient experience. These included cases where:

- Patients were left in excrement in soiled bed clothes for lengthy periods.
- Assistance was not provided with feeding for patients who could not eat without help.
- Water was left out of reach.
- In spite of persistent requests for help, patients were not assisted in their toileting.
- Wards and toilet facilities were left in a filthy condition.
- Privacy and dignity, even in death, were denied.
- Triage in A&E was undertaken by untrained staff.
- Staff treated patients and those close to them with what appeared to be callous indifference.

---

[168] Margaret Brazier and Amel Alghrani, 'Fatal medical malpractice and criminal liability' (2009) 25 Journal of Professional Negligence 51–67.

[169] [2006] EWCA Crim 2971.

[170] *Robert Francis Inquiry report into Mid-Staffordshire NHS Foundation Trust* (DH: London, 2013).

Alghrani et al explain why a new offence of wilful neglect might be of more practical use than gross negligence.

Amel Alghrani et al[171]

> Wilful neglect is a conduct crime rather than a result crime (meaning that it need not be shown that tangible injury was caused). The chance element that arises with gross negligence manslaughter, where liability depends on there being a provable death, is absent. It would mean that there would not be the current discrepancy whereby a doctor who finds himself in a difficult situation makes a badly negligent error may find himself facing a manslaughter charge, yet a professional who persistently neglects a patient with no justification or excuse need not fear the criminal law.

A criminal offence of wilful neglect by care workers (which includes anyone who provides health care) and care providers was introduced by the Criminal Justice and Courts Act 2015.

Criminal Justice and Courts Act 2015 sections 20 and 21

20 Ill-treatment or wilful neglect: care worker offence

(1) It is an offence for an individual who has the care of another individual by virtue of being a care worker to ill-treat or wilfully to neglect that individual.

(2) An individual guilty of an offence under this section is liable—

(a) on conviction on indictment, to imprisonment for a term not exceeding 5 years or a fine (or both);

(b) on summary conviction, to imprisonment for a term not exceeding 12 months or a fine (or both).

21 Ill-treatment or wilful neglect: care provider offence

(1) A care provider commits an offence if—

(a) an individual who has the care of another individual by virtue of being part of the care provider's arrangements ill-treats or wilfully neglects that individual,

(b) the care provider's activities are managed or organised in a way which amounts to a gross breach of a relevant duty of care owed by the care provider to the individual who is ill-treated or neglected, and

(c) in the absence of the breach, the ill-treatment or wilful neglect would not have occurred or would have been less likely to occur.

As Karen Yeung and Jeremy Horder explain, the point of creating a criminal offence of wilful neglect is not principally to regulate the practice of medicine, but rather to send a strong message that the mistreatment of vulnerable patients is unacceptable.

---

[171] 'Healthcare scandals in the NHS: crime and punishment' (2011) 37 Journal of Medical Ethics 230–2.

Karen Yeung and Jeremy Horder[172]

[T]he criminal law's role in this context is not to play a frontline part in deterring and coercing people into complying with proper standards of behaviour. Rather, its central function applies only to the worst kinds of unacceptable ill-treatment. When it is used against such serious wrongdoers, the criminal law carries a uniquely symbolic and expressive significance that is lacking when less draconian regulatory instruments, or civil liability, are used. A criminal conviction amounts to a public proclamation that the conduct in question is seriously wrongful and worthy of condemnation and punishment, whether or not it leads directly to a substantial improvement in healthcare quality. In light of the appalling failures of care evidenced by the Francis Report, there is no doubt that the criminal law could properly have been invoked, not primarily because it will deter such failures of care in the future, but because it is the most powerful and important social institution through which we hold to account, and express public censure of, those who have mistreated others in a wholly unacceptable and highly culpable way.

11 CONCLUSION

It is commonly said that tort law serves two purposes: compensation and deterrence. In the context of medical negligence, we have seen, first, that it does not offer an efficient compensation scheme for patients who suffer injury or damage as a result of negligent treatment and, secondly, that it does not effectively deter poor practices or encourage good ones. Worse still, not only is tort law costly and inefficient, but it may actually contribute towards poor care by inhibiting the open reporting of errors, which is, of course, the best way to ensure that they are learned from, rather than repeated.

Whether or not an NHS Redress Scheme or another fast-track scheme would improve matters is open to question. Lower administration costs and lower awards may be offset by increases in the number of claims. The need to establish that there has been a serious shortcoming in NHS care means that it will still be necessary to blame an individual doctor, or other health care provider.

Any redress scheme which singles out victims of negligence will continue to distinguish between people whose illnesses or disabilities can be attributed to the fault of another in NHS care, and those who have become unwell or disabled as a result of natural processes. In 1970, with the first publication of *Accidents, Compensation and the Law*, Patrick Atiyah drew attention to the unfairness of drawing a distinction between individuals with identical needs in this way, and his remarks undoubtedly remain pertinent today.

Patrick Atiyah[173]

Why, for example, should a child born disabled as a result of negligence on the part of the doctor who delivered the child be entitled to substantial compensation from the tort system, while the child born with similar congenital disabilities receives no common law

---

[172] 'How can the criminal law support the provision of quality in healthcare?' (2014) 23 British Medical Journal Quality & Safety 519–24.

[173] Peter Cane, *Atiyah's Accidents, Compensation and the Law*, 8th edn (Butterworths: London, 1993) 331–2.

damages? . . . It has been suggested that the view that brain-damaged babies deserve more generous compensation than the congenitally disabled is rooted in the desire for accountability, not compensation. More generally, it might be argued that compensating victims of human causes at a higher level than victims of natural causes is a way of giving effect to notions of personal responsibility: a person should be required to pay compensation for injuries if, but only if, that person was in some sense responsible for the disabilities . . .

Nevertheless, if compensation for disabilities was paid by individuals, the argument based on personal responsibility might have some force. However, we have seen that most tort compensation is not paid by individuals, but by insurers, corporations and the government, and in this light it is less clear why tort-type benefits should only be available to those injured by human action. On the whole, those disabled people who can recover tort damages . . . are much better provided for than those disabled people who must rely on social security benefits alone. Can this be justified in the light of the fact that the tort system and the social security system are, in effect, both financed by the public at large?

FURTHER READING

Ahuja, Jyoti, 'Liability for Psychological and Psychiatric Harm: The Road to Recovery' (2015) 23 Medical Law Review 27–52.

Alghrani, Amel et al, 'Healthcare scandals in the NHS: crime and punishment' (2011) 37 Journal of Medical Ethics 230–2.

Case, Paula, 'Putting Public Confidence First: Doctors, Precautionary Suspension and the General Medical Council' (2011) 19 Medical Law Review 339–71.

Farrell, Anne-Maree and Devaney, Sarah, 'Making Amends or Making Things Worse? Clinical Negligence Reform and Patient Redress in England' (2007) 27 Legal Studies 630–48.

Harris, John, 'The injustice of compensation for victims of medical accidents' (1997) 314 British Medical Journal 1821.

Health Select Committee, Fourth Report of Session 2014–15, *Complaints and Raising Concerns* (TSO: London, 2015).

Merry, Alan and McCall Smith, Alexander, *Errors, Medicine and the Law* (CUP: Cambridge, 2001).

Miola, José, 'Bye-bye *Bolitho*? The curious case of the Medical Innovation Bill' (2015) 15 Medical Law International, online 15 September 2015.

Newdick, Christopher, 'NHS Governance after *Bristol*: Holding On, or Letting Go?' (2002) 10 Medical Law Review 111–13.

Quick, Oliver, 'Medicine, Mistakes and Manslaughter: A Criminal Combination?' (2010) 69 Cambridge Law Journal 186–203.

4

CONSENT I: UNDERSTANDING

CENTRAL ISSUES

1. If a patient has capacity, treatment should not take place without her informed consent. The difficult question is working out exactly how much information patients need in order to be properly or adequately 'informed'.

2. A failure to inform the patient 'in broad terms' about the medical treatment she is about to receive could lead to an action in battery.

3. More usually, a patient who claims to have been inadequately informed might bring an action in negligence, claiming that the failure to warn her about a particular risk was a breach of the doctor's duty of care to inform her about material risks.

4. Information is material if a reasonable person in the patient's position would be likely to attach significance to the

risk, or the doctor should reasonably be aware that the particular patient would be likely to attach significance to it.

5. Causation raises particular difficulties in 'informed consent' cases. This is because the patient has to prove that, if she had been told about the risk which has now materialized, she would have refused to undergo the treatment. This is a speculative inquiry, in which the patient has the benefit of hindsight.

6. In practice, professional guidance appears to impose more onerous duties of information disclosure upon doctors than tort law, but because a 'reasonable doctor' will follow professional guidelines, these more stringent standards might be indirectly incorporated into the doctor's duty of care.

1 INTRODUCTION

One of the first principles of medical law is that patients with capacity must give consent to their medical treatment. Touching a person without her consent—however benevolently—is prima facie unlawful. For consent to be valid, it must be given voluntarily, by someone who has the capacity to consent, and who understands what the treatment involves. We deal with the issues of capacity and voluntariness in the next chapter. Here we are concerned with the question of how much information must be provided to patients before they consent to medical treatment.

We begin by considering the ethical justifications for informing patients about their medical treatment. We then turn to explore how the law protects patients' interests in information disclosure. Both battery and negligence suffer from defects, although a recent Supreme Court case has both clarified and enhanced the standard of care which patients can expect. We then explore some alternatives to the law of tort, and conclude by considering the patient-centred guidance produced by the medical profession.

2 WHY INFORM PATIENTS?

In the past, doctors were under no duty at all to provide patients with information about their prognosis, or the advantages and disadvantages of different treatments. On the contrary, the assumption was that a doctor would exercise his customary care and skill in deciding what treatment was best for his patient. The Hippocratic oath assumes that treatment decisions are for the doctor alone:

> I swear by Apollo and Aesculapius that I will follow that system of regimen which according to my ability and judgment I consider for the benefit of my patients.[1]

Indeed, Hippocrates even enjoined physicians to take positive steps to conceal information from their patients:

> Perform [your duties] calmly and adroitly, concealing most things from the patient while you are attending to him . . . turning his attention away from what is being done to him; . . . revealing nothing of the patient's future or present condition.[2]

Until relatively recently, it was thought that informing patients about a poor prognosis, possible side effects, or the availability of alternative treatments would be likely to cause distress and confusion, and hence might jeopardize the patient's recovery. Keeping patients in ignorance, and maintaining their trust and hope through the illusion of medical certainty was especially important given that most of the available treatments were largely ineffective, and any reported improvements resulted from the placebo effect. Silence and at times deception were intended to benefit patients by maintaining their belief in the possibility of a cure.

Occasionally providing information was judged to be in a patient's best interests: when surgical procedures were carried out without anaesthesia, for example, it was important for patients to prepare themselves for the infliction of excruciating pain. In the 1767 case *Slater v Baker and Stapleton*,[3] a surgeon had, without the patient's consent, re-fractured his leg and placed it in an experimental apparatus to stretch and strengthen it during healing. The failure to seek consent before re-fracturing a patient's leg amounted to professional misconduct, in part because 'It is reasonable that a patient should be told what is about to be done to him, that he may take courage and put himself in such a situation as to enable him to undergo the operation.'

---

[1] Hippocrates, 'Oath of Hippocrates' in *1 Hippocrates* 299–301 (trans WHS Jones) (Heinemann: London, 1962).

[2] Hippocrates, *Decorum* (trans W Jones) (Harvard UP: Cambridge, MA, 1967) 267.

[3] 2 Wils KB 359, 95 ER 850 (1767).

It was not until the twentieth century that patients were thought to be in need of information in order to exercise some control over their treatment. In part, this was a result of the growing importance of the principle of patient autonomy, considered in Chapter 1. It was also thought, as Michael Jones explains, that giving patients information might help to redress the imbalance of knowledge and power within the doctor–patient relationship.

Michael Jones[4]

It is a trite observation that the doctor–patient relationship involves a major imbalance of power, some of which stems from social norms—patients expect to be at a disadvantage, because of their lack of knowledge, their lack of training, and sometimes because we want to believe desperately that the doctor is all knowing and all powerful and therefore will definitely make the correct diagnosis and provide a complete cure. Although some of this disparity is inherent in most professional–client relationships those relationships are not generally conducted when the client is ill (and on occasion when the client is at the disadvantage of being naked, apart from a flimsy robe). Part of the imbalance between doctor and patient is due to the patient's lack of information, and, on one view, it is the function of the law to redress the imbalance by providing patients with the 'right' to be given that information, or perhaps more accurately imposing a duty on doctors to provide it.

Of course, while it is true that there is an information imbalance in the doctor–patient relationship, doctors are not always omniscient and all-powerful. In addition to the problem of false positives and false negatives, and the inevitability of human error, medical knowledge itself is often uncertain and tentative. Telling patients the truth may sometimes involve the doctor explaining what is not known, and what is uncertain.

There is often more than one option for a patient faced with a particular diagnosis. Since few treatments have no risks or side effects, it may be necessary to weigh the advantages and disadvantages of different treatment options, as well as the possibility of doing nothing. Doctors' special skill may enable them to diagnose a patient's condition and to carry out medical procedures, but it does not give them the ability to decide which treatment best accommodates the patient's own priorities. On the contrary, as Harry Lesser explains, the patient herself is the only person with the expertise necessary to make a judgement about the tolerability of side effects and adverse consequences. Following a diagnosis of breast cancer, for example, a choice between chemotherapy and mastectomy is best made by the patient herself, in the light of her doctor's advice about side effects and likely success rates.

Harry Lesser[5]

[T]here is not always a medically best course of action, for two reasons. One is that medicine has at least three aims—to prolong life, to remove obstacles to a person's physical and mental functioning and to relieve suffering. Very often these three all come together . . . But this is not always so; if, for example, the choice is to relieve pain at the cost of leaving patients feeling 'woozy' and confused, or to help them to be mentally alert at the cost of appreciable

---

4 'Informed Consent and Other Fairy Stories' (1999) 7 Medical Law Review 103–34, 129.

5 'The Patient's Right to Information' in Margaret Brazier and Mary Lobjoit (eds), *Protecting the Vulnerable: Autonomy and Consent in Health Care* (Routledge: London, 1991) 150–60.

physical pain, then there is no 'better' course of action, even medically, except in terms of the individual patient's preference, whichever it may be: it is honourable to choose alertness and the price of physical suffering, but in no way dishonourable to choose the reverse . . .

[D]octors' expertise enables them to know the possible consequences of various alternatives and to have some idea of their likelihood; but there is still no right answer to the question which alternative is best, which risks are worth taking and which are not, except in terms of what the patient chooses.

The Hippocratic principle that the doctor decides which treatment the patient receives has thus been replaced by a *partnership* model of decision-making, in which both the doctor and the patient have specialist knowledge which must be shared in order to ensure that the patient makes the best possible decision *for herself*. The doctor is a source of information and expert advice, but the ultimate decision is for the patient.

Applying some of the concepts explored in Chapter 1, there are both deontological and consequentialist justifications for the twin elements of informed consent: (a) to seek the patient's consent prior to treatment; and (b) to ensure that the patient has sufficient information about the proposed treatment. The deontological justification is obviously respect for patient self-determination and bodily autonomy: the patient has the right to choose what is done to her body, and in order to exercise this choice, she needs information about what the doctor is proposing to do.

The consequentialist justification for informed consent would instead emphasize the beneficial consequences that flow from involving patients in medical decision-making. Giving patients control over the care that they receive may lead to better outcomes: for example, patients might be more likely to comply with a treatment regime that they have chosen for themselves.

While it is clearly important to give patients enough information to enable them to make informed decisions about their medical treatment, several criticisms might be made of the concept of 'informed consent'. First, the expression 'informed consent' itself is both ambiguous and misleading. It is not entirely clear whether the word 'informed' refers to the doctor's conduct (has she informed the patient?) or the patient's state of mind (is the patient informed?). Has consent been 'informed' if information has been provided, regardless of whether the patient has in fact read, listened to, or understood anything? Or must the consent itself have been 'informed' by the patient's consideration of all relevant information?

The rather confusing implication of the phrase 'informed consent' is that consent is either informed or uninformed, when in fact this is not a binary question, and instead the important issue is working out *how much* information patients need in order to be adequately—though probably not fully—informed. PDG Skegg has suggested that:

It is regrettable, although entirely understandable, that it was not the expression 'sufficiently informed consent' which became so common. This would have alerted users to the fact that there is an issue of how informed it is necessary to be, in the context and for the purpose in question.[6]

In short, to say that consent should be 'informed' does not tell us how much information should be provided. It is, in practice, difficult for doctors to work out prospectively how

---

[6] 'English Medical Law and "Informed Consent": An Antipodean Assessment and Alternative' (1999) 7 Medical Law Review 135–65, 138.

much disclosure is necessary in order to avoid liability in negligence. As a result of this uncertainty, there is a danger that doctors might feel obliged to disclose too much information to patients.

Presenting patients with lengthy and complex consent forms may inhibit rather than promote genuine communication between doctors and their patients. There is, for example, some evidence that patients' understanding of consent forms is inversely related to their length. To take a mundane example, we all know that the longer the 'terms and conditions' on a website, the more likely we are to click that we have read them when we have not. Information overload could also prompt patients to attach disproportionate importance to a very remote risk, and, as a result, refuse treatment that is overwhelmingly likely to be both safe and successful.

Giving patients detailed information about every risk associated with a treatment, and ensuring that they have understood it, would take time, and therefore cost money. If doctors had to disclose everything, scarce NHS resources might be diverted to lengthy consent procedures, when it could have been spent on providing more or better medical treatment.

In practice, the process of obtaining patient consent for invasive treatments and diagnostic procedures is commonly limited to one or two encounters before the procedure takes place, when the doctor offers the patient some information about its risks and benefits, before asking the patient to sign a consent form. This model of decision-making can be unsatisfactory for two reasons.

First, it sits uneasily with the reality of medical treatment, which will rarely involve one single decision, but rather a series of decisions taken as more information becomes available about the patient's condition. Consent forms exacerbate the false perception that consent is a one-off event, rather than a process that takes place over time. A doctor's duty to communicate effectively with her patients may be especially important *during* treatment, and should not be confined to some brief bureaucratic ritual when the patient is first admitted to hospital. In their interviews with health care professionals, Heywood et al found that many of them perceived the consent form to have been driven by lawyers, and believed that it hampered rather than enhanced informed decision-making.

Rob Heywood et al[7]

[T]he medical practitioners within the study seem to suggest the process has become too formalised and bureaucratic. They perceive the most important basis for consent as being an ethical imperative grounded in the wishes and needs of the patient, which is about more than obtaining a signature on a form. They suggest there is a danger that lengthy and elaborate forms detract from the consent process itself, a process which should discuss the treatment, its risks and benefits.

Concerns were raised over problems with bureaucracy and 'red-tape' in the consent process. The feeling was that this is driven by 'the law'. The contention is grounded in the fact that both doctors and patients involved in the consent process may be happy to proceed with treatment based on the fact that there is a signature on a form. A signature is certainly not conclusive evidence that any discussion whatsoever has taken place between the doctor and the patient about the proposed procedure.

[7] Rob Heywood et al, 'Informed Consent in Hospital Practice: Health Professionals' Perspectives & Legal Reflections' (2010) 18 Medical Law Review 152–84.

Secondly, although patients are free to withdraw their consent at any point, some may wrongly believe that signing a consent form binds them to its contents. In fact, there is no need for consent to any sort of medical treatment to be in writing (aside from specific statutory exceptions, contained in the Mental Health Act 1983 and the Human Fertilisation and Embryology Act 1990). As the Department of Health's guidance makes clear:

> The validity of consent does not depend on the form in which it is given. Written consent merely serves as evidence of consent: if the elements of voluntariness, appropriate information and capacity have not been satisfied, a signature on a form will not make the consent valid.[8]

In other contexts, a person who signs a document will usually have made a binding commitment to fulfil their side of the bargain, so it is unsurprising that many patients do not understand that their right to refuse treatment persists throughout their care.

In their small empirical study of patients' perceptions of the consent process, Rob Heywood, Ann Macaskill, and Kevin Williams discovered that, while patients valued openness and good communication, and thought that this helped people to cope with bad news and to prepare themselves for treatment and its aftermath, they did not think this had anything to do with the consent process, which they instead regarded as a non-optional precondition for access to medical treatment.

Rob Heywood, Ann Macaskill, and Kevin Williams[9]

> Few patients mentioned or even implied that consent was about their right to self-determination. Instead it seems to be viewed as a means to an end; something that is *necessary* and that they have to do in order to get to the next stage, treatment . . .
>
> Despite patients looking favourably on openness and disclosure, there is evidence to suggest that any information provided is not used in the decision-making process and that patients make their decision long before they reach the 'consenting stage'. In other words, the patients in this study failed to make the link between the actual signing of the consent form and the information that was given to them in order that they could make an informed choice. The legal rules governing consent and information disclosure attempt to protect patient autonomy and redress the imbalance of power in the doctor–patient relationship. However, the patients in this study were not predominantly concerned with these factors, or at least they did not perceive them as the most important basis for disclosure. They failed to make the link between *information disclosure* and the *consent process* and did not relate consent to any notions of self-determination. Instead the importance they attached to pre-operative information was the way in which it enhanced coping mechanisms and the recovery process.

In their survey of 732 patients who had undergone obstetric surgery within the previous month, Akkad et al found similar levels of confusion about the purpose of the consent forms that they had signed.

---

[8] Department of Health, *Reference Guide to Consent for Examination or Treatment* (DH: London, 2009).
[9] 'Patient perceptions of the consent process: qualitative inquiry and legal reflection' (2008) 24 Journal of Professional Negligence 104–21.

Andrea Akkad et al[10]

[M]ost participants (646, 88%) believed it was a legal requisite to sign a consent form before surgery. A fifth (20%) did not know whether they could change their mind after they had signed the form, and 118 (16%) incorrectly thought that signing a consent form removed their right to compensation. . . . One in 10 patients reported that they did not know what they agreed to when they signed the consent form. . . . Almost half of all participants (46%) believed that the main function of signing the consent form was to protect the hospital from litigation, and two thirds (68%) thought it gave doctors control over what happened . . .

Many patients did not see written consent as functioning primarily in their interests nor as a way of making their wishes known. As suggested in previous work, many thought the primary function of the form was to protect the hospital.

Misunderstandings about the consent process are especially common in preventative screening programmes. When invited to participate in screening—such as triennial cervical smear tests or annual mammograms for women over the age of 50—many people think that they have been 'called in' for testing, rather than being asked if they wish to be screened. It is often assumed that screening is self-evidently beneficial, and that there is no need to weigh up the risks and benefits. While people appreciate being offered a leaflet that explains what is going to happen, they do not understand that its purpose is to enable them to evaluate the pros and cons of consenting to be screened.[11]

This may be exacerbated by the way in which information is provided. In their analysis of the leaflets provided to UK patients invited to take part in routine breast screening Gøtzsche et al found that they overemphasized the benefits of screening and downplayed the existence of what are, in fact, significant risks.

Peter C Gøtzsche et al[12]

No mention is made of the major harm of screening—that is, unnecessary treatment of harmless lesions that would not have been identified without screening . . . It is in violation of guidelines and laws for informed consent not to mention this common harm, especially when screening is aimed at healthy people . . . Another harm is false positive diagnoses. . . . We now know that the psychosocial strain of a false alarm can be severe and may continue after women are declared free from cancer . . . A third harm is caused by radiotherapy of overdiagnosed women.

If 2000 women are screened regularly for 10 years, one will benefit from the screening, as she will avoid dying from breast cancer. At the same time, 10 healthy women will, as a consequence, become cancer patients and will be treated unnecessarily. These women will have either a part of their breast or the whole breast removed, and they will often receive radiotherapy and sometimes chemotherapy. Furthermore, about 200 healthy women will experience a false alarm. The psychological strain until one knows whether it was cancer, and even afterwards, can be severe.

---

[10] 'Patients' perceptions of written consent: questionnaire study' (2006) 333 British Medical Journal 528.

[11] Wenche Osterlie et al, 'Challenges of informed choice in organised screening' (2008) 34 Journal of Medical Ethics e5.

[12] 'Breast screening: the facts—or maybe not' (2009) 338 British Medical Journal b86.

It is certainly true that simply providing patients with information does not ensure that they have understood it. Not only is risk inherently difficult to understand, but, as Onora O'Neill points out, illness may undermine an individual's capacity to digest information.

Onora O'Neill[13]

A person who is ill or injured is highly vulnerable to others, and highly dependent on their action and competence. Robust conceptions of autonomy may seem a burden and even unachievable for patients; mere choosing may be hard enough. And, in fact, the choices that patients are required to make are typically quite limited. It is not as if doctors offer patients a smorgasbord of possible treatments and interventions, a variegated menu of care and cure. Typically a diagnosis is followed with an indication of prognosis and suggestions for treatment to be undertaken. Patients are typically asked to choose from a smallish menu—often a menu of one item—that others have composed and described in simplified terms. This may suit us well when ill, but it is a far cry from any demanding exercise of individual autonomy.

Neil Levy and Arthur Caplan would go further and suggest that we need more robust assistance in order to make good decisions for ourselves, especially when we are ill and tired. Levy argues that our reasoning suffers from multiple pathologies and should not be taken at face value by clinicians, while Caplan suggests that there is nothing wrong with health care professionals giving strong and authoritative advice.

Neil Levy[14]

First, patients may be asked to make a series of decision. When they do so, they can be expected to suffer decision fatigue and a consequent decline in the quality of their judgements. Second, and more pervasively, almost by definition the context in which informed consent is sought is a stressful one. The cognitive resources of patients can be expected to be at a low ebb in these circumstances: because they may be overwhelmed with information and because (obviously) the decision is a significant one, which will be found stressful by all patients. . . .

Since we know that human beings, unaided, are subject to a dizzying variety of pathologies of reasoning, I hold that we ought not to expect patients to make crucial decisions unaided. Rather they should be helped and supported to make good decisions, and sometimes this help should come in the form of confrontation. We should tell patients when we think their decisions are distorted by cognitive illusions or when they are misapplying their values. We should do these things in the service of promoting their values and their conception of the good. To refrain from doing these things is not to respect autonomy, it is to decrease it.

[13] *Autonomy and Trust in Bioethics* (CUP: Cambridge, 2002) 38–9.
[14] 'Forced to be free? Increasing patient autonomy by constraining it' (2014) 40 Journal of Medical Ethics 293–300.

Arthur L Caplan[15]

Autonomy often does not work in healthcare. Our brains are not designed to let us act upon it. . . . [W]e bring too much affect and magical thinking along with us as subject or patient; and our basic memory and perceptual skills fail us when the topic is who is going to stick a needle in our arm or give us a brand new pill in our life-and-death fight against cancer. . . .

There is nothing wrong with healthcare providers strongly suggesting a course of care, raising their voice so that you hear their message about health promoting activities, or telling you what they would do if it was their mother in that bed.

Strongly suggesting a course of prevention, care or palliation in the face of a patient's expression of a different choice may be paternalistic but it is a projection of what is good based not upon the doctor's values but upon expertise and experience. Both ought to count in resolving choices in healthcare settings. Autonomy, if it is to be taken seriously, ought to be able to stand up to the professional's vigorously expressed fact-based opinion about what is best.

3 LEGAL PROTECTION FOR PATIENTS' INTERESTS IN INFORMATION DISCLOSURE

In this section we consider what legal claim is appropriate when consent has not been properly informed. Does a lack of adequate information vitiate the patient's consent altogether, in which case the claim would be for unlawful touching or battery? Or is the provision of information part of the doctor's ordinary duty of care, meaning that a failure to offer adequate information might ground an action in negligence? In the UK, the duty to obtain the patient's consent prior to treatment is protected by the tort of battery, while the duty to ensure that the patient has been given enough information (whatever that might mean) is treated as an aspect of the doctor's ordinary duty of care.

An action in battery will be successful only if the patient did not consent to the medical treatment that she received. Given that obtaining consent prior to treatment is routine, it would be most unusual for a patient not to be told what is going to happen to her, and actions in battery are rare. The courts have been reluctant to find that a failure to give the patient information about risks or alternatives invalidates the patient's consent, which means that most cases involving allegations of inadequate disclosure are brought in negligence.

An action in negligence is possible only if damage was caused by the doctor's breach of duty. Patients who have been inadequately informed prior to treatment can bring an action in negligence only if they happen to have suffered injury as a result of the doctor's failure to disclose a piece of information. As we see later, this means that tort law covers a small subset of cases of inadequate disclosure.

(a) BATTERY

Trespass to the person can be both a tort (battery) and a crime (assault). The patient's consent will absolve a medical practitioner from liability in battery for unlawful touching as long as the consent is 'real', and to be real, the patient must have been told what the doctor

---

[15] 'Why autonomy needs help' (2014) 40 Journal of Medical Ethics 301–2.

is planning to do. If a patient consented to a completely different procedure, an action in battery is possible: if, for example, a patient consents to the removal of her appendix, but the doctor removes her womb as well, then because she did not consent to a hysterectomy, she would be likely to have an action in battery, as well as in negligence.

Trespass to the person can also be a criminal offence. In *R v Tabassum*,[16] T—who had no medical qualifications at all—was convicted of indecent assault after he persuaded several women to consent to him showing them how to carry out breast self-examination. Each complainant said they had consented only because they thought that T was medically qualified. The Court of Appeal upheld his conviction on the grounds that 'consent was given because they mistakenly believed that the defendant was medically qualified ... and that, in consequence, the touching was for a medical purpose. As this was not so, there was no true consent'.

In contrast, in *R v Richardson*,[17] a dentist continued to treat her patients after her registration had been suspended. Her patients were not mistaken as to her identity, because she had treated them before, but they wrongly assumed she was entitled to practise dentistry. According to the Court of Appeal, 'either there is consent to actions on the part of a person in the mistaken belief that he or they are other than they truly are, in which case it is assault or, short of this, there is no assault'. Because 'the complainants were fully aware of the identity of the appellant', the Court of Appeal quashed her conviction.

The advantage of an action in battery is that it is not necessary to establish that any physical harm has been caused by the inadequate disclosure. As we see later, causation represents an obstacle to many claimants' actions in negligence because of the need to prove that proper disclosure would have prompted the patient to reject the treatment. Instead, following a successful action in battery, a patient can be compensated for the dignitary harm of being treated without valid consent.

Patients who are inadequately informed about an alternative treatment option will only be able to recover in negligence if the treatment that they received goes wrong and they suffer physical injury as a result. Yet the patient's right to make an informed choice about which therapeutic option is best for them may have been infringed even if their treatment does not cause them physical injury. (Indeed it may be that this requires recognition of a new 'harm', interference with autonomy, discussed further in Section 3(b)3(a).)

It is no defence to a charge of battery that the doctor was acting in the best interests of her patient, or that she exercised all reasonable care and skill. Evidence of accepted medical practice is also irrelevant: if the failure to provide information to a patient vitiates their consent, the fact that the defendant can point to other doctors who would have acted in the same way will not absolve her of responsibility. There could also be no 'therapeutic privilege' (discussed later) if the cause of action is battery rather than negligence. If certain information is necessary for consent to be real, the doctor cannot claim exemption from the need to disclose it because disclosure might cause the patient distress or anxiety.

There has been little enthusiasm on the part of the judiciary for using the tort of battery in order to protect patients' interests in information disclosure. Provided that the patient agreed to the procedure that was in fact carried out, her consent will be effective and there could be no action in battery. The leading case is *Chatterton v Gerson*, in which Bristow J held that consent would be real as long as the patient had been informed 'in broad terms' about the nature of the procedure.

In order to treat Miss Chatterton's chronic pain, the defendant doctor operated to block a sensory nerve. His and Miss Chatterton's accounts of what information was provided

---

[16] [2000] 2 Cr App R 328 (CA).   [17] 43 BMLR 21 (CA).

differed. Dr Gerson said his normal practice was to explain to patients before the operation that it would result in numbness, and that it might involve temporary loss of muscle power. Miss Chatterton claimed not to have been so warned. She lost sensation in her right leg, and claimed that her consent to the operation was vitiated by Dr Gerson's failure to tell her about this risk.

Chatterton v Gerson[18]

Bristow J

In my judgment what the court has to do in each case is to look at all the circumstances and say 'Was there a real consent?' ... In my judgment once the patient is informed in broad terms of the nature of the procedure which is intended, and gives her consent, that consent is real, and the cause of the action on which to base a claim for failure to go into risks and implications is negligence, not trespass. Of course if information is withheld in bad faith, the consent will be vitiated by fraud. Of course if by some accident, as in a case in the 1940s in the Salford Hundred Court where a boy was admitted to hospital for tonsillectomy and due to administrative error was circumcised instead, trespass would be the appropriate cause of action against the doctor, though he was as much the victim of the error as the boy. But in my judgment it would be very much against the interests of justice if actions which are really based on a failure by the doctor to perform his duty adequately to inform were pleaded in trespass.

In *The Creutzfeldt-Jakob Disease Litigation*, the claimants had been treated with Human Growth Hormone (HGH), which had been extracted from pituitary glands that had been unlawfully harvested from dead bodies. They argued that they gave consent on the understanding that the drug had been lawfully prepared, and that this consent was vitiated by the fact that the pituitaries had been unlawfully harvested. May J dismissed their claim.

The Creutzfeldt-Jakob Disease Litigation[19]

May J

There is assault and battery when there is physical violation of a person's body without true consent. There is true consent when a person consents to the nature of the act done. There is no English law doctrine of informed consent and a person may succeed in a claim for failure to inform or warn only if the failure alleged amounts to negligence. To frame such a claim in battery is not only deplorable but insupportable in law.

Judicial hostility to the use of battery in medical cases flows from the connotations of a charge of battery. A doctor who fails to tell a patient about a small risk inherent in a proposed treatment does not intend to injure her. Because a battery will also often be an assault, judges have been reluctant to criminalize by association well meaning but misguided decisions to withhold information from patients.

---

[18] [1981] QB 432 (QBD).
[19] *The Creutzfeldt-Jakob Disease Litigation* [1995] 54 BMLR 1 (QBD).

In *Wells v Surrey AHA*,[20] a sterilization operation was first suggested to the claimant after she had gone into labour, and the operation was performed at the same time as a caesarean section. The court found that the doctor had been negligent in failing to give the claimant 'proper advice' about sterilization. Given the circumstances in which her consent was obtained, it is hard to believe that the claimant had understood the implications of the operation to which she consented. Despite this, the court held that her consent had been real. Gerald Robertson suggests that the only explanation for this is 'that the court was struggling to avoid the conclusion that the doctor was guilty of the tort of battery'.[21]

There have been a handful of successful cases, however. In *Appleton v Garrett*, a dentist had deliberately carried out extensive and wholly unnecessary dental treatment for personal financial gain, and had been struck off as a result. His intentional and fraudulent wrongdoing may have helped to persuade the court to find him liable for battery rather than negligence.

Appleton v Garrett[22]

Dyson J

The evidence undoubtedly establishes that none of these eight plaintiffs was given any information on which to base a suitably informed consent. None was told why Mr Garrett was of the view that massive restorative treatment was required, often on perfect teeth. Typically, the plaintiff went for a normal routine check-up, and was subjected to the course of treatment without any explanation at all ... I am quite satisfied that the failure to inform in these eight cases was not mere negligence and that Mr Garrett withheld information deliberately and in bad faith. The scale of the unnecessary treatment was so great that it must have been obvious to him that it was indeed unnecessary. The radiographs that he took before he embarked on the treatment showed in many cases that the teeth in these young plaintiffs were free from caries and were in what has been described as 'virgin condition'. Much of the treatment on these teeth was considerable in its scope and extent....

I conclude therefore that Mr Garrett deliberately embarked on large-scale treatment of these plaintiffs which he knew was unnecessary and that he deliberately withheld from them the information that the treatment was unnecessary because he knew that they would not have consented had they known the true position.... I find, therefore, that none of the plaintiffs consented, at any rate to the treatment of those teeth that required no treatment, and that, at least in relation to those teeth, the tort of trespass to the person has been made out.

In the next extract, Ian Kennedy suggests that a broader application of the tort of battery might better protect patients' interests in information disclosure.

Ian Kennedy[23]

[P]atients' interests could well be better protected if the tort of battery were held to have a wider application. In particular, questions of what has come to be known as 'informed

---

[20] The Times, 29 July 1978.

[21] 'Informed Consent to Medical Treatment' (1981) 97 Law Quarterly Review 102–26, 123.

[22] 34 BMLR 23 (QBD).

[23] 'The Fiduciary Relationship and its Application to Doctors' in P Birks (ed), *Wrongs and Remedies in the Twenty-First Century* (Clarendon Press: Oxford, 1986) 111–40.

consent' could well be differently analysed and decided. A patient may have consented on the 'nature and purpose' test, but the information provided by the doctor may be so inadequate, in that it failed to respect the patient's right to know, so as to be able to choose, that the consent should be regarded as entirely invalid. Such an extension of the tort of battery would restore the law's protection of the symbolic harm represented by the complaint that the patient's right to know was not respected.

Battery has its limitations, however. Medical treatment can only amount to battery if there has been some sort of physical contact between doctor and patient. Of course, there are many medical decisions which do not involve touching, and these would be unaffected by a more robust application of the tort of battery. The prescription of medicines, for example, does not involve any physical contact, and so a patient who is inadequately informed about a drug's side effects could not bring an action in battery.

(b) NEGLIGENCE

Before we come to the standard 'failure to warn' negligence action, it is worth briefly mentioning that it is possible that the failure to obtain consent could also amount to negligence. *Border v Lewisham and Greenwich NHS Trust* was an unusual case in which, at first instance, the judge had accepted the claimant's evidence that the doctor did not discuss whether to insert a cannula (an intravenous tube) into her left arm. As she had put it: 'he just went, "I don't have any choice", bang, in it went without me having any more to say'.

Immediately before inserting the cannula, the claimant had told Dr Prenter that she had recently undergone a procedure which made it risky to cut her left arm. Despite finding that she had not given consent to its insertion, the judge went on to consider whether inserting the cannula had been the right thing to do. Because the claim had not been framed as one of trespass to the person at trial, the Court of Appeal's hands were tied, on the grounds that 'different findings of fact might have emerged if the claim [of trespass] had been included at the outset'. Nevertheless, the Court of Appeal were clear that a finding that the doctor had inserted a cannula without the patient's consent amounted to a breach of his duty of care, and the case was remitted back to the trial judge on the question of causation.

Border v Lewisham and Greenwich NHS Trust[24]

Richards LJ

[I]t seems to me to be open to the claimant to contend on the appeal that the finding that the procedure was carried out without the claimant's consent should have led the judge to find a breach of duty on the part of Dr Prenter even though that was not the way the claimant's case was being advanced at trial. And if the contention is open to the claimant, it must succeed. A finding of absence of consent to the insertion of the cannula leads inexorably in this case to a finding of breach of duty in inserting it.

More usually in negligence actions, the patient's consent will have been sufficiently informed to avoid a charge of battery, but the patient might instead claim that the doctor's failure to

---

[24] [2015] EWCA Civ 8.

disclose information about a risk associated with treatment amounted to negligence. As we saw in the previous chapter, there are three stages to an action in negligence. First, the defendant must owe the claimant a duty of care; secondly, he must breach that duty; and, thirdly, the breach must have caused the claimant's damage.

(1) The Duty of Care

At the outset it is worth noting, as Andrew Grubb explains, that liability for the failure to disclose information amounts to a duty to act positively, rather than to refrain from causing harm. Such duties are exceptional in English law, and generally require special justification.

Andrew Grubb[25]

[I]t is immediately apparent that if the patient is entitled to be informed, the doctor is under a duty to provide the information. To so assert, however, is to place on the doctor a duty of affirmative action. It is trite law that English law regards such a duty as exceptional. While it is one thing to expect people to refrain from careless behaviour, English law, with its aversion to the 'officious intermeddler', will not ordinarily impose a duty to do something on behalf of another. The first step, therefore, is to examine the legal basis for the doctor's duty to inform a patient, so as to obtain valid consent to treatment.

One well-established ground on which a duty to inform could be based would be to find that, as between the doctor and the patient, there exists a 'special relationship', giving rise to a duty to act. The traditional example is the parent–child and, by extension, the teacher–child relationship. In effect, therefore, the duty is derived from the status of the parties. The common law has not, however, regarded the doctor–patient relationship as falling into the category of special relationships. . . .

So, where does the duty come from? Curiously, when the English courts very belatedly got round to examining whether a doctor is under a duty to inform a patient, the legal-technical difficulties involved in actually finding some juristic basis for a duty of affirmative action were largely ignored. Instead, the general duty of care owed by a doctor to a patient was interpreted as extending not only to acts but also omissions, in this case the failure properly to inform.

Despite this ambiguity, it is now accepted that one aspect of a doctor's duty of care to her patients is to provide them with information. The chief problem has then been working out when the doctor has breached this duty. How much information is required in order to fulfil the doctor's duty of care?

(2) The Standard of Care: From *Sidaway* to *Montgomery*

(a) Sidaway *to* Chester

It is sometimes forgotten that the *Bolam*[26] case itself involved a doctor's failure to warn the patient about the risks involved in electroconvulsive therapy, and to advise him that these might be minimized by the use of restraints or muscle relaxants. In a less famous passage

---

[25] 'Consent to Treatment: The Competent Patient' in Andrew Grubb with Judith Laing (eds), *Principles of Medical Law*, 2nd edn (OUP: Oxford, 2004) 179–80.

[26] *Bolam v Friern Hospital Management Committee* [1957] WLR 582.

from his direction to the jury, McNair J suggested that the doctor might act properly in withholding information about a risk that he considers to be 'minimal'.

Bolam v Friern Hospital Management Committee[27]

McNair J

You have to make up your minds whether it has been proved to your satisfaction that when the defendants adopted the practice they did (namely, the practice of saying very little and waiting for questions from the patient), they were falling below a proper standard of competent professional opinion on this question of whether or not it is right to warn. Members of the jury, though it is a matter entirely for you, you may well think that when dealing with a mentally sick man and having a strong belief that his only hope of cure is ECT treatment, a doctor cannot be criticized if he does not stress the dangers which he believes to be minimal involved in that treatment.

Now of historical interest, the first House of Lords case to consider the question of how much information patients should be given before consenting to medical treatment was *Sidaway v Board of Governors of the Bethlem Royal Hospital and the Maudsley Hospital*.

Mrs Sidaway had complained that she had not been told about an operation's small risk—estimated to be between 1 and 2 per cent—of damage to her spinal column. She claimed that if she had been warned, she would not have had the operation. This risk had in fact materialized, and Mrs Sidaway was now seriously disabled. The House of Lords unanimously rejected Mrs Sidaway's claim that the failure to warn her of this risk had been negligent. They were also agreed that the duty to disclose information is part of the doctor's ordinary duty of care. There were, however, marked differences in their approaches to determining the relevant standard of care.

Sidaway v Board of Governors of the Bethlem Royal Hospital and the Maudsley Hospital[28]

Lord Scarman

Ideally, the court should ask itself whether in the particular circumstances the risk was such that this particular patient would think it significant if he was told it existed. I would think that, as a matter of ethics, this is the test of the doctor's duty. The law, however, operates not in Utopia but in the world as it is: and such an inquiry would prove in practice to be frustrated by the subjectivity of its aim and purpose. The law can, however, do the next best thing, and require the court to answer the question, what would a reasonably prudent patient think significant if in the situation of this patient ... The test of materiality is whether in the circumstances of the particular case the court is satisfied that a reasonable person in the patient's position would be likely to attach significance to the risk. Even if the risk be material, the doctor will not be liable if upon a reasonable assessment of his patient's condition he takes the view that a warning would be detrimental to his patient's health.

---

[27] [1957] WLR 582. [28] [1985] AC 871.

Lord Diplock

[W]hen it comes to warning about risks, the kind of training and experience that a judge will have undergone at the Bar makes it natural for him to say (correctly) it is my right to decide whether any particular thing is done to my body, and I want to be fully informed of any risks there may be involved of which I am not already aware from my general knowledge as a highly educated man of experience, so that I may form my own judgment as to whether to refuse the advised treatment or not. No doubt if the patient in fact manifested this attitude by means of questioning, the doctor would tell him whatever it was the patient wanted to know …

To decide what risks the existence of which a patient should be voluntarily warned and the terms in which such warning, if any, should be given, having regard to the effect that the warning may have, is as much an exercise of professional skill and judgment as any other part of the doctor's comprehensive duty of care to the individual patient, and expert medical evidence on this matter should be treated in just the same way. The *Bolam* test should be applied.

Lord Bridge (with whom Lord Keith agreed)

[T]he issue whether non-disclosure in a particular case should be condemned as a breach of the doctor's duty of care is an issue to be decided primarily on the basis of expert medical evidence, applying the *Bolam* test…. I am of opinion that the judge might in certain circumstances come to the conclusion that disclosure of a particular risk was so obviously necessary to an informed choice on the part of the patient that no reasonably prudent medical man would fail to make it. The kind of case I have in mind would be an operation involving a substantial risk of grave adverse consequences, as, for example, the ten per cent risk of a stroke from the operation which was the subject of the Canadian case of *Reibl v Hughes*.

Lord Templeman

There is no doubt that a doctor ought to draw the attention of a patient to a danger which may be special in kind or magnitude or special to the patient … Whenever the occasion arises for the doctor to tell the patient the results of the doctor's diagnosis, the possible methods of treatment and the advantages and disadvantages of the recommended treatment, the doctor must decide in the light of his training and experience and in the light of his knowledge of the patient what should be said and how it should be said. At the same time the doctor is not entitled to make the final decision with regard to treatment which may have disadvantages or dangers. Where the patient's health and future are at stake, the patient must make the final decision.

According to Lord Diplock, the *Bolam* test applied to all aspects of a doctor's duty of care, and he saw no reason to treat advice differently from diagnosis and treatment: the doctor's disclosure should therefore be judged by its conformity with responsible medical practice. At the other extreme, Lord Scarman argued that the doctor's duty of disclosure arose from the patient's 'basic human right' to make her own medical decisions. The test should therefore be what the prudent patient, in this patient's position, would want to know.

Falling somewhere in between are the judgments of Lord Bridge, with whom Lord Keith agreed, and Lord Templeman, all of whom supported a modified *Bolam* test. Disclosure was 'primarily a matter of clinical judgment', but in certain circumstances, the judge might conclude that a risk ought to have been disclosed even if there was a body of responsible medical opinion that would not have warned the patient of it.

Four years later, the Court of Appeal in *Gold v Haringey Health Authority*[29]—a case involving a doctor who had not warned his patient about the failure rate of female sterilization—adopted a rather surprising interpretation of the judgments in *Sidaway*. Despite the views of Lords Bridge, Keith, and Templeman (that is, the majority), that it would be negligent not to warn a patient of a risk which was either 'substantial and grave' or 'special', not to mention Lord Scarman's radical embrace of the doctrine of informed consent, the Court of Appeal in *Gold* simply stated that the House of Lords in *Sidaway* had applied the *Bolam* test. The only judgment referred to was that of Lord Diplock, whose straightforward application of *Bolam* did not represent the more nuanced approach of the majority.

In *Pearce v United Bristol Healthcare NHS Trust*, the Court of Appeal appeared to move closer to the 'reasonable patient' test in determining whether the 0.1–0.2 per cent risk of stillbirth associated with waiting for a natural birth should have been disclosed to a pregnant woman whose baby was two weeks overdue, and who had begged to have her labour induced or to undergo a caesarean section. Tina Pearce accepted her consultant's advice to 'let nature take its course', and her baby died *in utero* a few days later.

Pearce v United Bristol Healthcare NHS Trust[30]

Lord Woolf MR

In a case where it is being alleged that a plaintiff has been deprived of the opportunity to make a proper decision as to what course he or she should take in relation to treatment, it seems to me to be the law, as indicated in the cases to which I have just referred, that if there is a significant risk which would affect the judgment of a reasonable patient, then in the normal course it is the responsibility of a doctor to inform the patient of that significant risk, if the information is needed so that the patient can determine for him or herself as to what course he or she should adopt....

Turning to the facts of this case, the next question is, therefore, 'Was there a significant risk? ... [O]n any basis, the increased risk of the stillbirth of Jacqueline, as a result of additional delay, was very small indeed ... Even looked at comprehensively it comes to something like 0.1–0.2%. The doctors called on behalf of the defendants did not regard that risk as significant; nor do I.

There is some ambiguity in Lord Woolf MR's judgment. On the one hand, he advocated disclosure of 'a significant risk which would affect the judgment of the reasonable patient', which looks quite patient-centred. On the other hand, in determining whether the doctors should have disclosed the small risk of stillbirth, he said that '*the doctors* called on behalf of the defendants did not regard that risk as significant, nor do I' (my emphasis). Lord Woolf appeared to rely upon the *doctors'* assessment of whether the risk was 'significant', and not on Tina Pearce's own perception of the significance of a small risk of stillbirth, or the views of a reasonable pregnant woman in Tina Pearce's situation.

Given how traumatic stillbirth is—a woman must go through labour and give birth to what she knows to be a dead baby—it is at least arguable that many pregnant women would be likely to attach significance to even a very small risk of stillbirth. A risk of 0.1–0.2 per cent might sound small, but it translates to one woman in every 1,000 or one woman in every 500, and where the bad outcome is as grave as stillbirth, it is not clear that Woolf LJ's description of it as a 'very, very small additional risk' would be consistent with a 'reasonable patient' test.

[29] [1988] QB 481.   [30] (1998) 48 BMLR 118 (CA).

In their interviews with patients undergoing colonoscopy, for example, Janssen et al found that most of their interviewees considered a 0.01 per cent risk of a serious complication significant enough to warrant disclosure.[31]

Despite this ambiguity, in *Wyatt v Curtis*, a case in which a woman was not warned about the risk of fetal abnormality after she contracted chicken pox during pregnancy, Sedley LJ suggested that Lord Woolf's approach in *Pearce* 'refines' Lord Bridge's judgment in *Sidaway* by explaining that whether a risk is 'substantial' or 'grave' should be assessed from the patient's and not the doctor's point of view.

Wyatt v Curtis[32]

Sedley LJ

Lord Woolf's formulation refines Lord Bridge's test by recognising that what is substantial and what is grave are questions on which the doctor's and the patient's perception may differ, and in relation to which the doctor must therefore have regard to what may be the patient's perception. To the doctor, a chance in a hundred that the patient's chickenpox may produce an abnormality in the foetus may well be an insubstantial chance, and an abnormality may in any case not be grave. To the patient, a new risk which (as I read the judge's appraisal of the expert evidence) doubles, or at least enhances, the background risk of a potentially catastrophic abnormality may well be both substantial and grave, or at least sufficiently real for her to want to make an informed decision about it.

In his judgment in the House of Lords in *Chester v Afshar*, a case we discuss in detail later, Lord Steyn also quoted with approval Lord Woolf's approach in *Pearce*, and said that patients have the 'right' to be informed of 'small but well-established' risks of serious injury.

Chester v Afshar[33]

Lord Steyn

A surgeon owes a legal duty to a patient to warn him or her in general terms of possible serious risks involved in the procedure.... In modern law medical paternalism no longer rules and a patient has a prima facie right to be informed by a surgeon of a small, but well established, risk of serious injury as a result of surgery.

Again, notice that while Lord Steyn explicitly rejects 'medical paternalism' and states that the duty is to warn the patient about 'serious' risks, he does not specify whether seriousness is judged from the patient's or the doctor's perspective.

The move away from *Sidaway* towards a more patient-centred test for the standard of care was continued in the case of *Birch v University College London Hospital NHS Foundation Trust*. Mrs Birch had been warned that there was a 1 per cent risk of stroke associated with catheter angiography, but she was not told that there was an alternative, albeit slightly less exact, diagnostic technique, namely an MRI scan, which carried no

---

[31] NB Janssen et al, 'Under what conditions do patients want to be informed about their risk of a complication? A vignette study' (2009) 35 Journal of Medical Ethics 276–82.

[32] [2003] EWCA Civ 1779.   [33] [2004] UKHL 41.

risk of stroke. After Mrs Birch suffered a stroke, she claimed that the doctor had breached his duty of care by failing to tell her about the comparative risks of angiography versus MRI. The defendant's expert witnesses had argued that the doctor's duty was just to inform Mrs Birch of the risks associated with the catheter angiogram, which he had undoubtedly done. Nevertheless Cranston J agreed with Mrs Birch that this approach was negligent.

Birch v University College London Hospital NHS Foundation Trust[34]

Cranston J

Was it necessary for the defendant to go further and to inform Mrs Birch of comparative risk, how this risk compared with that associated with other imaging procedures, in particular MRI? No authority was cited to this effect but in my judgment there will be circumstances where consistently with Lord Woolf MR's statement of the law in *Pearce v United Bristol Healthcare NHS Trust* the duty to inform a patient of the significant risks will not be discharged unless she is made aware that fewer, or no risks, are associated with another procedure. In other words, unless the patient is informed of the comparative risks of different procedures she will not be in a position to give her fully informed consent to one procedure rather than another.

(b) Montgomery v Lanarkshire

In the years following *Sidaway*, then, English law had been gradually inching towards a more patient-centred test for disclosure. This journey was completed in 2015, when *Sidaway* was overruled by the case of *Montgomery v Lanarkshire Health Board*.[35]

Nadine Montgomery brought an action for damages following the birth of her severely disabled son. Mrs Montgomery suffered from diabetes, and, as a result, was likely to have a larger than normal baby, with a particular concentration of weight at the shoulders. Shoulder dystocia, where the shoulders are too wide to pass through the mother's pelvis without medical intervention, is a particular concern in diabetic pregnancies. Mrs Montgomery had been told that she was having a larger than usual baby, but she was not told about the risk of shoulder dystocia, which was agreed to be 9–10 per cent. The consultant obstetrician and gynaecologist, Dr McLellan, accepted that this was a significant risk, but her practice was not to spend time discussing the risks of shoulder dystocia, in part because the risk of serious damage to the baby was small and in part because patients would then ask for caesarean delivery, which would not be in their interests.

Dr McLellan accepted that Mrs Montgomery had expressed concern about the size of the baby and the risk that it might be too big to be delivered vaginally, but she had not asked 'specifically about exact risks'. In the event, mechanical efforts to deal with Mrs Montgomery's baby's shoulder dystocia led to him suffering profound disabilities, including cerebral palsy. The Supreme Court unanimously held that Dr McLellan's failure to be frank with Mrs Montgomery amounted to a breach of her duty of care.

The Supreme Court's judgment is notable for its wholesale rejection of the reasonable doctor test and its enthusiasm instead for the partnership model of medical decision-making embodied in GMC guidance.

---

[34] [2008] EWHC 2237 (QB).   [35] [2015] UKSC 11.

Montgomery v Lanarkshire Health Board[36]

Lords Kerr and Reid (with whom Lords Neuberger, Clarke, Wilson, and Hodge agreed. Lady Hale added some observations on pregnancy and childbirth, but also said that she 'entirely agreed' with the majority)

Since *Sidaway's* case, however, it has become increasingly clear that the paradigm of the doctor–patient relationship implicit in the speeches in that case has ceased to reflect the reality and complexity of the way in which healthcare services are provided, or the way in which the providers and recipients of such services view their relationship. One development which is particularly significant in the present context is that patients are now widely regarded as persons holding rights, rather than as the passive recipients of the care of the medical profession. They are also widely treated as consumers exercising choices ...

Other changes in society, and in the provision of healthcare services, should also be borne in mind. One which is particularly relevant in the present context is that it has become far easier, and far more common, for members of the public to obtain information about symptoms, investigations, treatment options, risks and side-effects via such media as the internet (where, although the information available is of variable quality, reliable sources of information can readily be found), patient support groups, and leaflets issued by healthcare institutions.... It would therefore be a mistake to view patients as uninformed, incapable of understanding medical matters, or wholly dependent on a flow of information from doctors. The idea that patients were medically uninformed and incapable of understanding medical matters was always a questionable generalisation, as Lord Diplock implicitly acknowledged by making an exception for highly educated men of experience. To make it the default assumption on which the law is to be based is now manifestly untenable.

These developments in society are reflected in professional practice. The court has been referred in particular to the guidance given to doctors by the General Medical Council, who participated as interveners in the present appeal....

In addition to these developments in society and in medical practice, there have also been developments in the law. Under the stimulus of the Human Rights Act 1998, the courts have become increasingly conscious of the extent to which the common law reflects fundamental values.... As well as underlying aspects of the common law, that value also underlies the right to respect for private life protected by article 8 of the European Convention for the Protection of Human Rights and Fundamental Freedoms. The resulting duty to involve the patient in decisions relating to her treatment has been recognised in judgments of the European Court of Human Rights ... as well as in a number of decisions of courts in the United Kingdom....

The social and legal developments which we have mentioned point away from a model of the relationship between the doctor and the patient based on medical paternalism. They also point away from a model based on a view of the patient as being entirely dependent on information provided by the doctor. What they point towards is an approach to the law which, instead of treating patients as placing themselves in the hands of their doctors (and then being prone to sue their doctors in the event of a disappointing outcome), treats them so far as possible as adults who are capable of understanding that medical treatment is uncertain of success and may involve risks, accepting responsibility for the taking of risks affecting their own lives, and living with the consequences of their choices.

[36] [2015] UKSC 11.

In the law of negligence, this approach entails a duty on the part of doctors to take reasonable care to ensure that a patient is aware of material risks of injury that are inherent in treatment ... The doctor's advisory role cannot be regarded as solely an exercise of medical skill without leaving out of account the patient's entitlement to decide on the risks to her health which she is willing to run (a decision which may be influenced by non-medical considerations). Responsibility for determining the nature and extent of a person's rights rests with the courts, not with the medical professions....

It follows that the analysis of the law by the majority in *Sidaway's* case is unsatisfactory, in so far as it treated the doctor's duty to advise her patient of the risks of proposed treatment as falling within the scope of the *Bolam* test ... There is no reason to perpetuate the application of the *Bolam* test in this context any longer.

The correct position, in relation to the risks of injury involved in treatment, can now be seen to be substantially that adopted in Sidaway by Lord Scarman ... An adult person of sound mind is entitled to decide which, if any, of the available forms of treatment to undergo, and her consent must be obtained before treatment interfering with her bodily integrity is undertaken. The doctor is therefore under a duty to take reasonable care to ensure that the patient is aware of any material risks involved in any recommended treatment, and of any reasonable alternative or variant treatments. The test of materiality is whether, in the circumstances of the particular case, a reasonable person in the patient's position would be likely to attach significance to the risk, or the doctor is or should reasonably be aware that the particular patient would be likely to attach significance to it.

The doctor is however entitled to withhold from the patient information as to a risk if he reasonably considers that its disclosure would be seriously detrimental to the patient's health. The doctor is also excused from conferring with the patient in circumstances of necessity, as for example where the patient requires treatment urgently but is unconscious or otherwise unable to make a decision....

Three further points should be made. First, it follows from this approach that the assessment of whether a risk is material cannot be reduced to percentages. The significance of a given risk is likely to reflect a variety of factors besides its magnitude: for example, the nature of the risk, the effect which its occurrence would have on the life of the patient, the importance to the patient of the benefits sought to be achieved by the treatment, the alternatives available, and the risks involved in those alternatives. The assessment is therefore fact-sensitive, and sensitive also to the characteristics of the patient.

Secondly, the doctor's advisory role involves dialogue, the aim of which is to ensure that the patient understands the seriousness of her condition, and the anticipated benefits and risks of the proposed treatment and any reasonable alternatives, so that she is then in a position to make an informed decision. This role will only be performed effectively if the information provided is comprehensible. The doctor's duty is not therefore fulfilled by bombarding the patient with technical information which she cannot reasonably be expected to grasp, let alone by routinely demanding her signature on a consent form.

Thirdly, it is important that the therapeutic exception should not be abused. It is a limited exception to the general principle that the patient should make the decision whether to undergo a proposed course of treatment: it is not intended to subvert that principle by enabling the doctor to prevent the patient from making an informed choice where she is liable to make a choice which the doctor considers to be contrary to her best interests ...

Approaching the present case on this basis, there can be no doubt that it was incumbent on Dr McLellan to advise Mrs Montgomery of the risk of shoulder dystocia if she were to have her baby by vaginal delivery, and to discuss with her the alternative of delivery by caesarean section....

Although [Dr McLellan's] evidence indicates that it was her policy to withhold information about the risk of shoulder dystocia from her patients because they would otherwise request caesarean sections, the 'therapeutic exception' is not intended to enable doctors to prevent their patients from taking an informed decision. Rather, it is the doctor's responsibility to explain to her patient why she considers that one of the available treatment options is medically preferable to the others, having taken care to ensure that her patient is aware of the considerations for and against each of them.

Significantly, the Supreme Court in *Montgomery* went beyond the 'prudent patient test', according to which the doctor should give each patient that information which the reasonable person in the patient's position would want to know.

The prudent (or reasonable) patient test, while an improvement on *Bolam*, might still fail to protect individual patients' interests in information. People have different priorities, beliefs, and family histories, all of which affect the relative importance they attach to the risks and benefits of medical treatment. While all patients want to know about risks that are very likely to materialize or which have potentially grave consequences, lesser risks may be significant to some patients, but not to others. Giving every patient the information which the abstract reasonable patient would consider material might be preferable to the *Bolam* standard, but it would still result in some patients being deprived of information which might be vitally important to them.

Instead the Supreme Court in *Montgomery* acknowledged that people have variable information needs, and it imposed a duty upon doctors to tailor their disclosures according to the individual patient's priorities and concerns:

The test of materiality is whether, in the circumstances of the particular case, a reasonable person in the patient's position would be likely to attach significance to the risk, *or the doctor is or should reasonably be aware that the particular patient would be likely to attach significance to it.* (my emphasis)

As Alexander Capron explains, it is only this subjective test which is capable of adequately protecting patients' interest in information.

Alexander Morgan Capron[37]

The importance of a subjective rather than an objective standard of materiality can be seen by comparing how well each standard would serve the functions of informed consent. For example, a physician-investigator's self scrutiny is likely to be increased if he has to ask, 'Is this procedure right for this patient, based on what I actually know about him or her?' and not on what is known about the 'reasonable patient'.... The requirement that the physician-investigator individualize the informing process is consistent with the obligation to individualize the diagnostic and therapeutic processes.

---

[37] 'Informed Consent in Catastrophic Disease Research and Treatment' (1974) 123 University of Pennsylvania Law Review 340, 416–17.

Within the modern and increasingly impersonal health care system, doctors cannot be expected to know in advance what matters to an individual patient. But the point of this subjective standard of disclosure is that doctors should attempt to discover the patient's particular concerns or priorities through appropriate questioning. As the Supreme Court in *Montgomery* makes clear, this is the approach adopted by GMC guidance.

General Medical Council[38]

4. No single approach to discussions about treatment or care will suit every patient, or apply in all circumstances. Individual patients may want more or less information or involvement in making decisions depending on their circumstances or wishes . . .

28. The amount of information about risk that you should share with patients will depend on the individual patient and what they want or need to know. Your discussions with patients should focus on their individual situation and the risk to them . . .

31. You should do your best to understand the patient's views and preferences about any proposed investigation or treatment, and the adverse outcomes they are most concerned about. You must not make assumptions about a patient's understanding of risk or the importance they attach to different outcomes.

The decision in *Montgomery* has been welcomed by almost all commentators. Rob Heywood, for example, has said that: 'Possibly the most remarkable thing about *Sidaway* is that it was allowed to lurk in the background for so long, and that it took such an inordinate amount of time for the Supreme Court to finally be provided with the opportunity to overrule it.'

Rob Heywood[39]

It goes without saying that what a patient wants and needs in terms of preoperative information is an inherently subjective question. Any set of legal rules designed to give teeth to the right of autonomy must therefore remain sensitive to this issue. . . .

The strength of *Montgomery* lies not in its confirmation of a more appropriate standard of disclosure, but in the manner in which Lord Kerr and Lord Reed reconceptualised the nature of the doctor–patient relationship in the eyes of the law. . . . Will the move away from medical paternalism cause judges to question the appropriateness of *Bolam* in the fields of diagnosis and treatment and perhaps bring *Bolitho* to the fore in terms of a greater willingness to question medical decision-making and expert testimony?

Elspeth Reid does suggest one possible concern, namely that tailoring to the individual patient's intelligence and understanding could mean distinguishing between patients according to the sophistication of their medical knowledge, although it should be noted that this interpretation might be at odds with Lords Kerr and Reid's unqualified statement that 'It would ... be a mistake to view patients as uninformed, incapable of understanding medical matters.'

---

38 GMC, *Consent: Patients and Doctors Making Decisions Together* (2008).
39 'RIP *Sidaway*: patient-oriented disclosure—a standard worth waiting for?' (2015) 23 Medical Law Review 455–66.

Elspeth Reid[40]

One uncomfortable issue left open is how exactly duty is to be tailored to the 'reasonable person in the patient's position'. The Supreme Court specifically noted that Mrs Montgomery was a 'clearly highly intelligent person', a graduate in molecular biology and a hospital specialist in the pharmaceutical industry. Moreover, her mother and sister were both general medical practitioners, and her mother had accompanied her on occasion to the antenatal clinic. The implication was that Mrs Montgomery's understanding of medical risk was more sophisticated than that of the average patient. Is this type of background information now relevant as part of the profile of the 'reasonable person in the patient's position'? If so, is there a lesser duty to disclose to patients with no scientific qualifications and no relatives in the medical profession?

(c) Therapeutic exception

The Supreme Court in *Montgomery* accepted that, in exceptional circumstances, there could be a 'therapeutic exception' to the duty of disclosure. If a doctor believes that a particular piece of information would cause serious harm to the patient, then that information may reasonably be withheld.

Because the therapeutic exception allows the doctor's paternalistic concern for her patient's best interests to trump the principle of patient self-determination, its scope must be tightly circumscribed. In particular, as was the case in *Montgomery*, it is important that information is not withheld just because it might prompt the patient to refuse treatment that the doctor judges to be in her best interests. Instead, doctors can invoke the therapeutic exception only if the patient would suffer physical or mental harm *other than that which the doctor believes would be caused by her decision to refuse to have the treatment in question.* Once again, this is enshrined in the GMC's guidance to doctors:

16 You should not withhold information necessary for making decisions for any other reason, including when a relative, partner, friend or carer asks you to, unless you believe that giving it would cause the patient serious harm. In this context 'serious harm' means more than that the patient might become upset or decide to refuse treatment.[41]

In practice, doctors find it difficult to imagine circumstances in which concern for a patient's welfare could justify non-disclosure. Among Heywood et al's interviewees, 'the legal concept of a therapeutic privilege was largely unrecognised'. Unusually, however, it had been the standard practice of the consultant obstetrician and gynaecologist in *Montgomery* to withhold information about shoulder dystocia from diabetic pregnant women on the grounds that it would be better for women not to have the caesarean sections they would be likely to request if they knew about the risk. The Supreme Court was clear that there was 'no question' of the therapeutic exception applying to Dr McLellan's withholding of information, because it 'is not intended to enable doctors to prevent their patients from taking an informed decision'.

---

[40] 'Montgomery v Lanarkshire Health Board and the Rights of the Reasonable Patient' (2015) 19 Edinburgh Law Review 360–6.

[41] GMC, *Consent: Patients and Doctors Making Decisions Together* (2008).

In her additional remarks, Lady Hale was robust in her criticism of Dr McLellan's decision to withhold information which might encourage a woman to opt for caesarean delivery.

Montgomery v Lanarkshire Health Board[42]

Lady Hale

Dr McLellan ... later expressed the view that 'it's not in the maternal interests for women to have caesarean sections'. Whatever Dr McLellan may have had in mind, this does not look like a purely medical judgment. It looks like a judgment that vaginal delivery is in some way morally preferable to a caesarean section: so much so that it justifies depriving the pregnant woman of the information needed for her to make a free choice in the matter....

A patient is entitled to take into account her own values, her own assessment of the comparative merits of giving birth in the 'natural' and traditional way and of giving birth by caesarean section, whatever medical opinion may say, alongside the medical evaluation of the risks to herself and her baby.... She cannot force her doctor to offer treatment which he or she considers futile or inappropriate. But she is at least entitled to the information which will enable her to take a proper part in that decision.

(d) When and how should information be provided?

The Supreme Court in *Montgomery* was also clear that giving patients information, without trying to ensure that it is comprehensible, is plainly not sufficient. Health care professionals must present information in a way that patients will be able to understand. If the patient cannot understand English, access to translated information, or to an interpreter, might be necessary.

The context in which information is disclosed is also important. However comprehensive the disclosure, giving a patient information about the risks associated with surgery immediately before or after an operation might nevertheless be negligent. In *Lybert v Warrington Health Authority*[43] the surgeon discussed the irreversibility of sterilization, and the risks of failing to achieve sterility immediately after the patient had undergone the operation. The court concluded that the surgeon had been negligent because the warning was not sufficiently emphatic and clear, and because the timing and the conditions in which it was given were inappropriate. It might also be unsatisfactory to delegate the task of informing patients to junior doctors, who may have limited experience of communicating with patients, and who may not be able to answer all the patients' questions.

The central problem is that it is difficult to communicate effectively with patients. Research indicates that patients are seldom able to recall information that has been disclosed to them about their condition and its treatment. It is common for patients to sign consent forms without reading them. Perfect patient comprehension is an unrealistic goal. Again GMC guidance suggests that doctors should actively try to ensure that patients have actually understood the information that has been provided.

---

[42] [2015] UKSC 11.   [43] [1996] 7 Med LR 71.

General Medical Council[44]

> 21. You should check whether the patient needs any additional support to understand information, to communicate their wishes, or to make a decision. You should bear in mind that some barriers to understanding and communication may not be obvious; for example, a patient may have unspoken anxieties, or may be affected by pain or other underlying problems. You must make sure, wherever practical, that arrangements are made to give the patient any necessary support. This might include, for example: using an advocate or interpreter; asking those close to the patient about the patient's communication needs; or giving the patient a written or audio record of the discussion and any decisions that were made . . .
>
> 34. You must use clear, simple and consistent language when discussing risks with patients. You should be aware that patients may understand information about risk differently from you. You should check that the patient understands the terms that you use, particularly when describing the seriousness, frequency and likelihood of an adverse outcome. You should use simple and accurate written information or visual or other aids to explain risk, if they will help the patient to understand.

In *Al Hamwi v Johnston*,[45] counsel for Mrs Al-Hamwi went further and argued that the clinician's duty of care incorporated a duty to ensure that the information given to the patient had been understood. In this case, despite evidence that Mrs Al-Hamwi had received the standard information about the risks of amniocentesis, which include a 1 per cent risk of miscarriage, Mrs Al-Hamwi claimed to have understood the risk to be about 75 per cent. Simon J held that to place doctors under a duty to ensure that the patient has, in fact, understood the information would 'place too onerous an obligation on the clinician'. In the light of the Supreme Court's decision in *Montgomery*, it seems likely that doctors should now take steps to ensure that the patient has understood what they have been told, even if ensuring perfect comprehension remains impracticable.

(e) What was said?

A further practical problem in negligence cases lies in establishing what information was, in fact, disclosed to the patient. Patients are unlikely to have made notes at the time, and many years later may not be able to recall accurately what they were told. Doctors' notes may not record every detail of the conversations they have had with patients, and it is often difficult for doctors to remember exactly what was discussed, particularly if the consultation happened several years ago. The courts will therefore often be faced with two flatly contradictory accounts of what was, and was not, said.

Evidence of a doctor's usual practice will be relevant, though in many cases the judge will simply have to decide who is the more credible witness. In *Chatterton v Gerson*, for example, Bristow J believed the doctor's account of the pre-operation discussions:

> I have come to the conclusion that on the balance of probability Dr Gerson did give his usual explanation about the intrathecal phenol solution nerve block and its implications of numbness instead of pain plus a possibility of slight muscle weakness, and that the plaintiff's recollection is wrong; and on the evidence before me I so find.[46]

---

44 GMC, *Consent: Patients and Doctors Making Decisions Together* (2008).
45 [2005] EWHC 206 (QB).   46 *Chatterton v Gerson* [1981] QB 432.

In contrast, in the first instance decision in *Chester v Afshar*, the trial judge had preferred the claimant's account on the grounds that it had the 'ring of truth and [was] most unlikely to be the result of either invention or reconstruction'.[47]

(f) A duty to answer questions

The Supreme Court in *Montgomery* was critical of Lord Diplock's suggestion in *Sidaway* that an educated and inquiring patient (the example he used was a judge) would receive personalized information because 'the doctor would tell him whatever it was the patient wanted to know'. As Margaret Brazier has pointed out, the educated, middle-class patient, who is not intimidated by a consultant's expertise, would then have access to a subjectively defined, patient-orientated standard of information disclosure, whereas frightened, inarticulate patients would be offered only a more minimal, standardized level of information.

Margaret Brazier[48]

The less articulate, the apprehensive, those who feel socially ill at ease with the consultant, or whose doctors are hard-pressed in inner city clinics, will be hesitant to initiate discussions. Not 'bothering' the doctor is a deeply entrenched tradition in many parts of Britain. It implies that the patient doubts the doctor's skill, raises fears of offending those who are going to care for you, and may just seem plain rude. It does not follow though that the tradition of patient silence implies lack of interest or desire to participate in decision-making if that opportunity is offered by the doctor.

Montgomery places the final nail in the coffin of Lord Diplock's distinction: patients do not have to be able to ask the right questions in order to obtain personalized information. Rather, the doctor may be under a duty to probe the patient's values and preferences in order to find out what matters to her.

Montgomery v Lanarkshire Health Board[49]

Lords Kerr and Reid

The significance attached in *Sidaway* to a patient's failure to question the doctor is however profoundly unsatisfactory. In the first place, as Sedley LJ commented in *Wyatt v Curtis* ..., there is something unreal about placing the onus of asking upon a patient who may not know that there is anything to ask about. It is indeed a reversal of logic: the more a patient knows about the risks she faces, the easier it is for her to ask specific questions about those risks, so as to impose on her doctor a duty to provide information; but it is those who lack such knowledge, and who are in consequence unable to pose such questions and instead express their anxiety in more general terms, who are in the greatest need of information. Ironically, the ignorance which such patients seek to have dispelled disqualifies them from obtaining the information they desire. Secondly, this approach leads to the drawing of excessively fine distinctions between questioning, on the one hand, and expressions of concern falling short of questioning, on the other hand: a problem illustrated by the present case. Thirdly, an approach which requires the patient to question the doctor disregards the social

---

[47] [2002] EWCA Civ 724.
[48] 'Patient Autonomy and Consent to Treatment: The Role of the Law?' (1987) 7 Legal Studies 169–93.
[49] [2015] UKSC 11.

and psychological realities of the relationship between a patient and her doctor, whether in the time-pressured setting of a GP's surgery, or in the setting of a hospital. Few patients do not feel intimidated or inhibited to some degree.

(g) Waiving the right to information?

While some patients seek out as much information as possible, other patients may not want to be told very much at all. People have different ways of coping with illness: some will become experts in their condition and its treatment, while others would prefer not to think about it. When we are ill and in pain, we may not feel able to digest and weigh complex information: it is in practice not uncommon for patients to ask their doctors what they would do if they were in the patients' shoes.

Should the patient have the right to refuse information about a treatment's risks, and to ask the doctor to make a decision on her behalf? Where a patient has a high level of trust and confidence in her doctor, it might be argued that she exercises her own autonomous choice by expressing a preference for the doctor to make the decision for her.

Ulrik Kihlbom[50]

A patient can take an autonomous decision to undergo a medical treatment without having (positive) knowledge of the treatment and risks. . . . Furthermore, if I, as the patient, choose to let you, as the physician, determine my treatment, and I have well founded beliefs that you will choose the treatment that best promote my values, and that the risks of the treatment you will choose, is in accordance with my attitudes towards different kinds of risks, I will exercise my autonomy, not waive my right to exercise it.

Against this, it might be argued that what Kihlbom calls 'negative informed consent' could lead to problems if a patient subsequently wants to claim that, if they had been informed about a particular risk, they would not have consented to treatment. Kihlbom counters that it should be possible for the consent form to record that the patient gave consent to treatment proceeding in the absence of any disclosure of risks or side effects, and that this should absolve the doctor from liability for non-disclosure. On the other hand, the consent form is not a contractual document, and a future court would not be bound by the patient's apparent waiver of her right to information.

More subtly, Neil Manson suggests that even a patient who wants her doctor to decide what treatment would be best for her might nevertheless value the provision of information, not in order to make an informed choice, but because frank and open communication is a sign of respect and trustworthiness.

Neil C Manson[51]

Human beings have a deeply entrenched interest in being respected . . . It should be obvious that the *manner* of informing can show respect (or contempt). . . . The *fact* that a clinician is

---

[50] 'Autonomy and negatively informed consent' (2008) 34 Journal of Medical Ethics 146–9.

[51] 'Why do patients want information if not to take part in decision making?' (2010) 36 Journal of Medical Ethics 834–7.

willing to inform a patient about treatment options may be viewed as indicative of respect (provided it is done so in respectful manner). The clinician treats the patient as someone who is capable of being informed, and who has an interest in being informed. A patient can have an interest in being respected without thereby wanting to make decisions herself . . .

The fact that the clinician is willing to engage in communication may help to inspire confidence in the clinician as a trustworthy agent. . . . The fact that the clinician is willing to talk in detail about the intervention may be taken to be a reasonable, but not infallible, basis for judging that the clinician is honest, open, has 'nothing to hide' and is likely to be trustworthy in other respects. In contrast, evasive speech or trying to steer the patient's questions away from details, may be taken as evidence that the clinician does not give a strong consideration to the patient's interests. . . .

Suppose a patient . . . wants to entirely defer her decision making to a clinician. It is not irrational or irrelevant to seek assurances that the decision will be made in a reasonable way, and the disclosure of information can provide this kind of assurance. That is, a patient can want to be assured that a good decision *will be made* (by someone else) without wanting to make that decision herself.

(3) Causation

In order to succeed in an action in negligence, the claimant must not only prove that the doctor owed her a duty of care which has been breached, but also that damage has been caused as a result. It is only possible to bring an action if the negligent non-disclosure caused the claimant to suffer injury or loss. The claimant who has managed to establish that her doctor was in breach of the duty to give her sufficient information—itself by no means an easy task—therefore has three further obstacles to a successful claim. She must prove that:

(a) she has suffered an injury that has made her worse off than she would have been if the procedure had not been performed; and

(b) her injury is the materialization of the negligently undisclosed risk; and

(c) if she had been informed of this risk, she (or a reasonable patient) would not have consented to the procedure, and so the injury would not have occurred.

(a) Causation in practice

Applying the 'but for' test to disclosure cases means that we need to know whether the injury would have occurred even if the patient had been properly informed. Causation will therefore be established if the claimant can prove that proper disclosure would have led her to refuse the treatment that has resulted in her injury. But, of course, this question is almost impossible to answer. Not only is it a speculative inquiry about what the patient might have done in different circumstances, but also the claimant now has the benefit of hindsight. She now *knows* that a particular remote risk *has* materialized. From her perspective, the 0.1 per cent risk of a bad outcome has ceased to be a remote hypothetical possibility, and has become a 100 per cent certainty. It is therefore likely that her assertions of what she would have done had she known about this risk will be coloured by her knowledge that she is among the unlucky 0.1 per cent of patients.

The 'but for' test would ordinarily require us to ask whether this patient would have refused to be treated if she had been properly informed. If she would have had the treatment anyway, the doctor's breach of duty did not cause her loss. If, on the other hand, she would have refused treatment, and hence avoided exposing herself to the risk that has now materialized, causation is established. Causation is thus normally judged subjectively.

In disclosure cases, concerns about relying too heavily on the patient's hindsight-influenced testimony has led some judges to adopt a hybrid subjective/objective test, such as that employed in *Smith v Barking, Havering and Brentwood Health Authority*, in which Hutchison J suggested that an objective test should be used to 'test' the truth of the patient's assertion from the witness box that she would have refused to have treatment if she had known about the undisclosed risk. If a reasonable patient would have agreed to the proposed treatment even if she had been told about this risk, then the onus would be on the patient to produce some evidence to back up her claim that she would have refused to be treated.

Smith v Barking, Havering and Brentwood Health Authority[52]

Hutchison J

However, there is a peculiar difficulty involved in this sort of case—not least for the plaintiff herself—in giving, after the adverse outcome is known, reliable answers as to what she would have decided before the operation had she been given proper advice as to the risks inherent in it. Accordingly, it would, in my judgment, be right in the ordinary case to give particular weight to the objective assessment. If everything points to the fact that a reasonable patient, properly informed, would have assented to the operation, the assertion from the witness box, made after the adverse outcome is known, in a wholly artificial situation and in the knowledge that the outcome of the case depends upon the assertion being maintained, does not carry great weight unless there are extraneous or additional factors to substantiate it. By extraneous or additional factors I mean, and I am not doing more than giving examples, religious or some other firmly-held convictions; particular social or domestic considerations justifying a decision not in accordance with what, objectively, seems the right one; assertions in the immediate aftermath of the operation made in a context other than that of a possible claim for damages; in other words some particular factor which suggests that the plaintiff had grounds for not doing what a reasonable person in her situation might be expected to have done.

While a patient with unusual religious beliefs might be able to demonstrate that she would not have acted in the same way as a reasonable patient, it will usually be difficult for a claimant to produce evidence to support her assertion that she would have responded idiosyncratically to information about a remote risk. Furthermore, adopting an objective test for establishing causation will enable the doctor to rely on evidence that, even when they have been informed about the risk in question, patients generally consent to treatment, and this sort of solid, empirical evidence may have more sway than the claimant's assertion that she would not have consented if she had known about this risk.

Adopting an objective approach to causation confuses the question of the credibility of the claimant's evidence with its objective reasonableness. A patient is under no duty to make the same decision as a reasonably prudent patient. On the contrary, as we see in the next chapter: 'A mentally competent patient has an absolute right to refuse to consent to medical treatment for any reason, rational or irrational, or for no reason at all, even where that decision may lead to his or her own death.'[53]

[52] (1988) reported [1994] 5 Med LR 285.   [53] *Re MB* (1997) 38 BMLR 175, per Butler-Sloss LJ.

In the next extract, Alexander Capron argues that testing a claimant's evidence against what a hypothetical reasonable person in her situation would have done significantly undermines the patient's right to make foolish or eccentric choices. The credibility of evidence from a patient with peculiar priorities should be assessed in the ordinary way—does the judge believe her account?—rather than against a standard of objective reasonableness.

Alexander Morgan Capron[54]

[T]he patient owes no one a duty to decide prudently or to require for his decision only the facts that an ordinary person would want. . . . An 'individualized test of causation is indicated because informed consent seeks to assure patients the right to make even irrational decisions'. To deny recovery because . . . a reasonable person would not have cared about a certain factor (although . . . the factor did matter to the particular patient-plaintiff) undermines the fundamental purpose of the informed consent rule, the promotion of individual autonomy.

In contrast, in the next extract, Tony Honoré suggests, in the context of discussion of a Canadian 'failure to warn' case, that additional evidence to back up the claimant's assertions of what she would have done if properly warned is necessary in order to discharge the evidential burden of establishing proof of injury.

Tony Honoré[55]

In *Arndt v Smith* a mother sued her physician, who had not warned her that her foetus might be injured as a result of the chickenpox she contracted during her pregnancy. When her daughter was born with a congenital injury attributable to the chickenpox, she claimed the cost of raising the child, alleging that, had she been told of the risk, she would have sought an abortion. . . .

The causal issue in such cases turns on a hypothesis about events that did not happen. Did one non-event—the doctor's failure to warn—cause another non-event—the patient's not deciding to have an abortion? There may be little evidence available apart from that of the patient herself. She, after the event, is almost certain to say that, had she been warned, she would have reached a different decision. Otherwise she would not have sued. But her evidence, however honest, is speculative. We cannot know for certain what we would have done in circumstances with which we were never faced. . . .

Assertions about hypothetical conduct therefore need buttressing by more solid evidence about the plaintiff's temperament and beliefs (how keen was she to have a child? was she pro- or anti-abortion?), how great the risks really were and what medical advice would have been given in the light of them. Evidence of this sort may be termed objective, since it does not turn on the plaintiff's say-so. But to adduce it goes, surely, to the discharge of the evidential burden that lies on the plaintiff on the causal issue.

More recent cases in the UK have appeared to adopt a more straightforwardly subjective test for causation, tempered only by the judge's assessment of the witness's credibility.[56]

---

[54] 'Informed Consent in Catastrophic Disease Research and Treatment' (1974) 123 University of Pennsylvania Law Review 340.

[55] 'Causation and Disclosure of Medical Risks' (1998) 114 Law Quarterly Review 52–5.

[56] See, eg, *O'Keefe v Harvey-Kemble* (1999) 45 BMLR 74 (CA) and *Gowton v Wolverhampton Health Authority* [1994] 5 Med LR 432.

In *Birch v University College London Hospital NHS Foundation Trust*, a case we considered earlier, Cranston J accepted Mrs Birch's evidence that she would have opted for an MRI scan if she had been properly informed about the risk of stroke from catheter angiography.

Birch v University College London Hospital NHS Foundation Trust[57]

Cranston J

To establish liability on the defendant's part, Mrs Birch needs also to demonstrate, on the balance of probabilities, that had she been so informed she would have declined catheter angiography.... In her evidence Mrs Birch said explicitly that if the comparative risks had been explained to her she would have chosen an MRI. I accept that evidence. Mrs Birch struck me as an intelligent and sensible individual, well able to have made that decision ... It is clear to me that had she been given a fair and balanced account in the way I have held was necessary she would have rejected catheter angiography in favour of MRI. In other words, properly informed she would have declined the procedure leading to her stroke.

And in a post-*Montgomery* case, *FM v Ipswich Hospital NHS Trust*, where the issue was again whether a woman would have opted for a caesarean section if she had been given proper information about shoulder dystocia, His Honour Judge McKenna acknowledged that he had to be cautious about evidence given with the benefit of hindsight, but he nevertheless believed that Mr and Mrs M would have sought a caesarean section, despite the doctor's assertion that most patients in their situation would have agreed to vaginal delivery.

FM v Ipswich Hospital NHS Trust[58]

His Honour Judge McKenna

I must however be cautious about placing too much reliance on Mrs M's evidence that she would have opted for a caesarean section. As counsel for the Defendant submitted, she now knows that the alternative of a vaginal birth was in fact what led to F being significantly disabled and it is unrealistic to expect her to be able to set aside that knowledge....

Having carefully considered all the evidence I have come to the conclusion that Mrs M would in fact have opted for a caesarean section even if the advice from the obstetrician would have been to proceed with a vaginal birth....

Mrs M plainly wanted to avoid another traumatic birth like J's at any cost ... It was of course the evidence of Mr Tuffnell that he was able to persuade most of his patients not to elect for caesarean sections in such cases and that therefore his experience was that most patients did not.... [C]rucially in any event, what this court is concerned with is what these particular parents would have done in the particular circumstances of this case.

On the balance of probabilities therefore I conclude that Mrs M, in discussions with the obstetrician following the ultrasound scan, would not have been influenced by statistics but would have put the wellbeing of her baby ahead of herself and elected, and if necessary pushed, for caesarean section.

---

[57] [2008] EWHC 2237 (QB).   [58] [2015] EWHC 775 (QB).

What if the patient can establish that she would not have consented to have this particular treatment at this time if she had been properly informed, but she cannot prove that she would never have undergone the procedure in the future? Here the question of causation becomes especially complicated. Applying the 'but for' test, it could be argued that the patient can establish that the doctor's inadequate disclosure caused her injury: she would not have undergone the operation when she did, and therefore the risk would not have materialized on this occasion. But, on the other hand, she might have undergone the same operation—and been exposed knowingly to an identical risk—at a later date.

This issue first came before the English courts in *Chester v Afshar*,[59] a case in which Mr Afshar, a neurosurgeon, did not warn Miss Chester, who was reluctant to undergo surgery to treat her chronic back pain, that there was a 0.9–2 per cent risk that the operation would cause cauda equina syndrome (a serious condition involving pain, loss of sensation, and bowel and bladder dysfunction). Miss Chester's evidence was that, if she had been warned of this risk, she would not have agreed to have the operation when she did, but would have sought a second opinion, advice on alternatives, and taken more time to think it over. She admitted that she might, nevertheless, have consented to go ahead with the operation at a later date.

By a 3:2 majority the House of Lords applied the reasoning adopted in an earlier, though factually different, Australian case, *Chappel v Hart*,[60] and found that it was not necessary for a patient to prove that she would have refused the operation for the rest of her life if she had been properly advised. Instead, the fact that 'but for' the defendant's negligence, she might nevertheless have been exposed to an identical risk at a later date would only be relevant when quantifying her loss. Normally, of course, the chance that the particular risk would materialize if she had the operation on another occasion would be very small and so any reduction in damages would be likely to be nominal. An exception to this would be if the claimant was especially susceptible to the risk, so that the chance of the same risk materializing in the future would, in fact, be high.

Chester v Afshar[61]

Lord Steyn

[I]t is a distinctive feature of the present case that but for the surgeon's negligent failure to warn the claimant of the small risk of serious injury the actual injury would not have occurred when it did and the chance of it occurring on a subsequent occasion was very small. It could therefore be said that the breach of the surgeon resulted in the very injury about which the claimant was entitled to be warned ...

I have come to the conclusion that, as a result of the surgeon's failure to warn the patient, she cannot be said to have given informed consent to the surgery in the full legal sense. Her right of autonomy and dignity can and ought to be vindicated by a narrow and modest departure from traditional causation principles.

Lord Hope

For some [patients] the choice may be easy—simply to agree to or to decline the operation. But for many the choice will be a difficult one, requiring time to think, to take advice and to weigh up the alternatives. The duty is owed as much to the patient who, if warned, would

---

[59] [2004] UKHL 41.   [60] (1998) 72 AJLR 1344.   [61] [2004] UKHL 41.

> find the decision difficult as to the patient who would find it simple and could give a clear answer to the doctor one way or the other immediately.
>
> To leave the patient who would find the decision difficult without a remedy, as the normal approach to causation would indicate, would render the duty useless in the cases where it may be needed most. This would discriminate against those who cannot honestly say that they would have declined the operation once and for all if they had been warned. I would find that result unacceptable.

The majority in *Chester* admitted to departing from traditional causation principles, in order to ensure that 'due respect is given to the autonomy and dignity of each patient' (per Lord Steyn). The defendant's failure to give Miss Chester information about the risks associated with this operation had deprived her of the opportunity to make a fully informed choice. In a sense, then, it could be argued that the majority found for the claimant not because she had proved that the lack of proper information caused her to be exposed to a risk to which she would not have been exposed if she had been properly informed, but rather because she had been deprived of the right to weigh up the risks in order to make an informed choice.

Underlying the judgments of the majority of the House of Lords was a reluctance to penalize Miss Chester for her honesty in admitting that she could not be certain that she would not have undergone the operation at some point in the future, even if properly warned.

In contrast, in their vigorous dissenting judgments, Lords Bingham and Hoffmann followed the dissenting judgment of McHugh J in *Chappel v Hart*,[62] arguing that Miss Chester had in fact failed the 'but for' test, since the timing of the operation did not affect the risk of injury.

Lord Bingham (dissenting)

[I]n the ordinary run of cases, satisfying the 'but for' test is a necessary if not a sufficient condition of establishing causation. Here, in my opinion, it is not satisfied. Miss Chester has not established that but for the failure to warn she would not have undergone surgery. She has shown that but for the failure to warn she would not have consented to surgery on Monday 21 November 1994. But the timing of the operation is irrelevant to the injury she suffered, for which she claims to be compensated. That injury would have been as liable to occur whenever the surgery was performed and whoever performed it.

Lord Hoffmann (dissenting)

The claimant argued that as a matter of law it was sufficient that she would not have had the operation at that time or by that surgeon, even though the evidence was that the risk could have been precisely the same if she had it at another time or by another surgeon.

In my opinion this argument is about as logical as saying that if one had been told, on entering a casino, that the odds on no 7 coming up at roulette were only 1 in 37, one would have gone away and come back next week or gone to a different casino. The question is whether one would have taken the opportunity to avoid or reduce the risk, not whether one would have changed the scenario in some irrelevant detail. The judge found as a fact that the risk would have been precisely the same whether it was done then or later or by that competent surgeon or by another.

---

[62] [2004] UKHL 41.

It follows that the claimant failed to prove that the defendant's breach of duty caused her loss. On ordinary principles of tort law, the defendant is not liable. The remaining question is whether a special rule should be created by which doctors who fail to warn patients of risks should be made insurers against those risks ...

I can see that there might be a case for a modest solatium in such cases. But the risks which may eventuate will vary greatly in severity and I think there would be great difficulty in fixing a suitable figure. In any case, the cost of litigation over such cases would make the law of torts an unsuitable vehicle for distributing the modest compensation which might be payable.

In the next extracts, Andrew Grubb argues that the majority in *Chester* made the right decision, while Charles Foster agrees with the dissenting judges, and argues that the majority effectively abolished the need for claimants to prove causation.

Andrew Grubb[63]

It is difficult to argue with [the majority's] reasoning. It would undermine the rule and be unjust for a doctor to require a patient to show that she would never have a particular procedure in the future. It is also counterintuitive to think that because the patient may run the risk in the future—by agreeing to and having the procedure—the negligence is not connected to her injury. At worst, she will be exposed to a small risk of injury which is unlikely *then* to eventuate. She had in a real and immediate sense suffered injury that she would not otherwise have suffered. That should be sufficient to establish a causal link.

Charles Foster[64]

This is Alice in Wonderland stuff. Causation is not established but, since it should be, it will be deemed to be. Where a duty exists for some reason that can be described in terms of human rights (and what duty cannot be?) a breach will entitle the claimant to damages on policy grounds, even if causation cannot be proved. The House of Lords has stretched the rules of causation before—notably in *Fairchild v Glenhaven Funeral Services*. But *Chester* goes much further: it abolishes the requirement for causation in any meaningful sense. . . .

The reasoning was, basically: a human right has been breached. That is a bad thing because human rights are important. Therefore, although causation is not really established, we will say that it is. The claimant is therefore entitled, presumably, to damages identical to those that she would have received had she been able to prove that a proper warning would have led her to decline the operation. Surely a more logical thing to do would be to award her the fairly notional damages that she would have got under the European Convention on Human Rights for the article 8 breach she had suffered. Indeed, Lord Hoffmann conceded that 'there might be a case for a modest solatium'.

Causation in consent cases of the *Chester* type has always been difficult to prove. Now it will be easy. Claimants' witness statements will in future, no doubt, say: 'If I had been properly warned, I would have gone off and pondered.' That will be difficult to gainsay.

---

[63] 'Consent to Treatment: The Competent Patient' in Andrew Grubb with Judith Laing (eds), *Principles of Medical Law*, 2nd edn (OUP: Oxford, 2004) 200.

[64] 'It Should Be, Therefore It Is' (2004) 154 New Law Journal 7151.

Kumaralingam Amirthalingam further argues that the decision in *Chester* reflects an increasing tendency to view causation as a matter of moral accountability rather than factual cause.

Kumaralingam Amirthalingam[65]

Recently, causation has transcended its role in attributing causal responsibility and has been used instead to fix liability on a party who, in the court's eyes, ought to have been held accountable even if there were no evidence that that party actually caused the injury. The current mantra is that causation must be seen in the context of the purpose of the law and should not be separated from questions of liability. Effectively, this means that courts may find a defendant causally responsible if at the end of the day, despite the absence of actual evidence of a causal link, it is fair, just and reasonable that the defendant, rather than the plaintiff, should bear the loss. This confuses causation with the broader question of liability, more properly addressed at the duty or remoteness stage.

If Miss Chester's loss is better described as the loss of the right to make an informed choice, rather than exposure to a risk to which she would not have been subjected with proper information, it could be argued that damages should be awarded for this deprivation of autonomy, rather than for the physical injury she suffered.

It is interesting that the majority in *Chester* did not consider the possibility of making a 'conventional award', as the majority of the House of Lords had done in *Rees v Darlington Memorial NHS Trust*[66] (see Chapter 14), for the patient's loss of autonomy. The majority awarded Miss Chester full damages for physical injury, despite the fact that their judgments describe the real loss in this case as the deprivation of the right to make an informed choice. As JK Mason and Douglas Brodie point out, this may mean that Miss Chester was overcompensated.

JK Mason and Douglas Brodie[67]

However, the measure of damages allowed does not, in truth, reflect the loss suffered because, at the end of the day, the loss lay in an invasion of autonomy per se, and an award of full damages can be said to over-compensate. What is, in some ways, surprising is that the solution adopted in *Rees v Darlington Memorial NHS Trust* was not applied here. There, the requirements of distributive justice meant that damages should not be awarded to compensate the plaintiff for the loss that had arisen as the result of a failed sterilisation operation . . . The solution adopted was to award a 'modest' conventional sum by way of general damages to acknowledge the infringement of the plaintiff's autonomy by the fault of the defendant.

The possibility of a conventional award was mentioned by Lord Hoffmann, however, in his dissenting judgment: 'I can see that there might be a case for a modest solatium.' In the end, however, he rejects this solution for two reasons: it would be difficult to settle on an appropriate amount, and, it would not be cost-effective to use litigation in order to pursue what would always be a modest award.

---

[65] 'Medical Non-Disclosure, Causation and Autonomy' (2002) 118 Law Quarterly Review 540–4, 542.
[66] [2003] UKHL 52.
[67] '*Bolam, Bolam*—Wherefore Are Thou *Bolam*?' (2005) 9 Edinburgh Law Review 298–305.

In the next extract, Tamsyn Clark and Donal Nolan explain that the tensions in *Chester* derive precisely from trying to squeeze what is essentially a fairly modest interference with autonomy—namely, being deprived of more time for reflection—into a personal injury tort.

Tamsyn Clark and Donal Nolan[68]

These tensions arise because of a basic lack of fit between a 'duty to disclose' based on a patient's 'right to choose' and a medical negligence framework built around compensation for physical injury. The result is that the 'duty of disclosure' is (in the words of Izhak Englard) 'double-faced':

> Janus-like one face is looking into the direction of patient autonomy; the other face stares into the direction of medical injuries seeking compensation. The result is a strange disharmony in the real world: patient autonomy is sanctioned if a medical accident has happened, and compensation for medical accidents is granted where an infringement of patient autonomy has occurred.

This 'strange disharmony' was all too apparent in *Chester*. The felt need to protect patient autonomy drove the House of Lords to depart from well-established principles that stood in the way of recovery for the claimant's physical injury. However, the result was an award of damages that was both unjust, since the claimant was over-compensated, and incoherent, because it was contrary to a central tenet of negligence doctrine. In our view, *Chester* demonstrates that there is only one way in which the tensions in the law of non-disclosure can be resolved, and harmony restored. This is to break the connection with physical injury, and to give redress for the autonomy violation in its own right.

(b) Additional problems with causation

It is unclear whether the House of Lords' apparent relaxation of causation principles in *Chester v Afshar* will be limited to cases where the patient can establish that she would not have been exposed to the risk at this time, but may have been at a later date, or whether it might have wider application, through which deprivation of the autonomy-based right to make an informed choice, or even the right to have time for reflection before consenting to an operation, becomes the 'gist' of an action in negligence.

In addition to this uncertainty, there are a number of further reasons why causation raises particular difficulties in actions for negligent non-disclosure of information.

First, a successful claim in negligence for failure to disclose a material risk is in practice synonymous with strict liability for medical mishaps. Informed consent therefore becomes a route for patients to seek financial compensation for unfortunate but blameless outcomes. Doctors who exercised all reasonable care and skill in the performance of an operation might be found liable for the consequences of a side effect which they could have done nothing to prevent just because their pre-operation disclosures were inadequate.

As Peter Cane explains, 'whatever the ideological basis of the duty to warn (or, in other words, the interest which it protects), its importance in practice lies in providing a basis for imposing liability for physical injury not caused by negligence'.[69] Gerald Robertson further suggests that this expansion of liability might be a deliberate response to the limits of a fault-based compensation system.

---

[68] 'A critique of *Chester v Afshar*' (2014) 34 Oxford Journal of Legal Studies 659–92.
[69] 'A Warning about Causation' (1999) 115 Law Quarterly Review 21–7, 23.

Gerald Robertson[70]

It is beyond doubt that one effect of the recognition of the doctrine of informed consent is to expand the liability of the medical profession. The explanation for this is quite simple. Courts, particularly in this country, constantly stress the truism that things can go wrong in the course of medical treatment without that treatment having necessarily been performed negligently . . . This means that a large number of patients who suffer injury in the course of medical treatment will, under a fault-based system of compensation such as our own, go without compensation because they are the victims, not of negligent performance of the treatment, but rather of the risks incident thereto. One way in which to remedy this situation, within the present fault-based framework, is to expand liability by making the doctor answerable in damages for failing to warn the patient of these risks prior to undergoing treatment. In this way a greater number of medical accident victims receive compensation, by means of extending the liability of the medical profession beyond the bounds of actual negligent performance of treatment.

Secondly, because the claimant must prove that the inadequate disclosure caused her injury, cases only come before the courts where the patient has not been informed about the risk of an adverse outcome, which has then materialized. Adequate information is not, however, confined to disclosure of risks. In order to exercise meaningful choice, it is important that patients are told about alternatives to the proposed treatment. As Marjorie Maguire Shultz explains, negligently depriving the patient of choices will seldom result in the sort of damage or injury which is recognized in tort law.

Marjorie Maguire Shultz[71]

Thus, a patient not told about a method of sterilization that is more reversible than the one performed may have difficulty convincing a court that nonreversibility is a cognizable physical injury. A patient who alleges that, properly informed, she would have chosen a lumpectomy rather than a radical mastectomy might find it hard, under existing negligence rules, to characterize the successful operation that removed her breast and eradicated her cancer as having 'injured' her. Similarly, the patient with a desire to go home or to a hospice to die, who is instead maintained alive by hospital machinery, might have difficulty establishing 'injury' under definitions of an interest in physical well-being rather than choice.

Some patients might want to know if animal products were used in the preparation of a pharmaceutical product or device. For example, meshes used in surgery may be of animal origin—usually from pigs or cows—and for some patients this will be material information.[72] If the procedure in which an animal-derived product was used was successful, it would only be possible to bring an action in tort for non-disclosure if the patient could establish that they had suffered a recognizable psychiatric injury as a result of discovering that material of animal origin had been left in their body. A vegan or Muslim patient could legitimately believe that their right to make an informed choice had been compromised by non-disclosure of this

---

[70] 'Informed Consent to Medical Treatment' (1981) 97 Law Quarterly Review 102–26.
[71] 'From Informed Consent to Patient Choice: A New Protected Interest' (1985) 95 Yale Law Journal 219.
[72] Muhammad Hanif Shiwani, 'Surgical meshes containing animal products should be labelled' (2011) 343 British Medical Journal 261.

sort of information, but, unless they had suffered a psychiatric injury, tort law would offer no protection of their interest in this information.

Patients might want to know if their doctor is going to benefit financially from their decision to opt for a particular course of treatment. They might want to know how much experience their surgeon has, and her success rates. In the following extract, Frances Miller discusses a particular type of information which might be increasingly important for patients, but which is marginalized by the tort of negligence. As we saw in Chapter 2, rationing of scarce medical resources has become inevitable, and it will not always be possible to provide every patient with the best available treatment. If treatment is withheld on the grounds of cost, are patients entitled to be told that a treatment exists which will not be available to them unless they pay for it privately?

Frances Miller[73]

If physicians withhold the information that potentially beneficial treatment is being denied their patients for economic reasons, they not only usurp the possibility of patient choice or self-help on the matter, but they assume a staggering moral burden. The traditional justification for silence under such circumstances is that it would be cruel and inhumane to tell patients that therapy might help them, but that they have no access to it. One can construct a powerful argument, however, that silence under such circumstances often is not only equally cruel and inhumane, but also morally unacceptable.

Physicians truly are 'playing God' in such circumstances, but they may not have all the facts. Some patients may have their own resources for obtaining medical care about which their doctors are unaware. Others may choose to invest their energies in trying to change rationing policies that affect them detrimentally, rather than passively accepting denial of care as their lot.

Amanda Owen-Smith et al's empirical research found that while most patients did want to know if their care had been rationed, where the withheld treatment was life-saving and unaffordable, this sort of information could be extremely distressing.

Amanda Owen-Smith, Joanna Coast, and Jenny Donovan[74]

Nearly all patients said they wanted to know how financial factors affected their access to healthcare, and this was normally because they wanted to be granted the autonomy to decide whether to contest decision-making or to access care in the private sector. . . .

However, nearly all also acknowledged that it would be very distressing to know about rationing if you were unable to access care through another route, and one patient in this situation regretted having been told. Half of informants felt that explicitness was not the right approach for all patients, and four identified situations where they would not want to know (such as if the treatment was likely to be life-saving, or they were unable to afford treatment in the private sector).

[73] 'Denial of Health Care and Informed Consent in English and American Law' (1992) 18 American Journal of Law and Medicine 37.

[74] 'Are patients receiving enough information about healthcare rationing? A qualitative study' (2010) 36 Journal of Medical Ethics 88–92.

> Knowing what it's like when you're at that point, to be told there is this treatment and be told that we won't get funding for it . . . I think that would probably have made me suicidal. (Pa9)
>
> If it's 20 or 30 thousand a year, no one could keep that up for very long . . . and I think myself I'd rather not know that. (Pa20)

Thirdly, 'cause' appears to have acquired a rather special meaning in failure to warn cases. As Peter Cane has explained, the doctors in these cases rarely 'caused' the injury in question 'in the central sense of the word "cause" as it is used outside the law', because 'failure to warn of a risk does not "cause" the materialization of the risk'.[75] Rather, the injury has usually been caused by an unfortunate and inherently unlikely combination of circumstances, and the doctor simply *created the situation* in which this unusual sequence of events could occur. The question of whether a doctor should be liable for a failure to disclose a risk is more accurately stated as whether she should be liable for creating the situation in which an accidental injury might or (much more likely) might not occur.

(c) MOVING AWAY FROM BATTERY AND NEGLIGENCE

The central problem is that both battery and negligence are imperfect mechanisms for protecting a patient's right to information about their treatment. Battery is inadequate because it will only be relevant where the treatment involves unlawful touching, and in any event the courts have been reluctant to use it in most non-disclosure cases. Despite the new patient-centred approach adopted by the Supreme Court in *Montgomery*, negligence requires proof that the inadequate information caused physical harm, which is seldom the case when a patient is not given enough information. What alternatives might there be?

(1) The New Zealand Code

In the next extract, Joanna Manning describes the system which exists in New Zealand. If a patient wishes to obtain compensation for a doctor's failure to warn her of a particular risk, under the no-fault compensation scheme, it will still be necessary to establish a causal link between the failure to warn and physical injury. However, in addition a Code of Rights offers additional protection to patients' interests in information disclosure, since it is a breach of the Code not to disclose information which the reasonable patient would consider material.

While the Code does not provide financial compensation to patients who have been inadequately informed—which is instead the function of the compensation scheme—it nevertheless places doctors under a robust duty to give patients sufficient information to enable them to make informed choices.

Joanna Manning[76]

> One of the advantages of the Code is its recognition that a consumer is likely to want a wider range of information than about risks in making decisions about treatment. Right

---

[75] 'A Warning about Causation' (1999) 115 Law Quarterly Review 21–7, 23.

[76] 'Informed Consent to Medical Treatment: The Common Law and New Zealand's Code of Patients' Rights' (2004) 12 Medical Law Review 181.

6, in referring to 'the information that a reasonable consumer, in that consumer's circumstances, would expect to receive', recognises that the information patients might need is not confined to information about risks, but extends to other types of information that may be needed to enable them to make an informed decision about their care . . .

In New Zealand, separating compensation for injury from issues of professional accountability has made possible one of the advantages of the Code for complainants—breach of the Code does not depend upon proof of injury, nor of a causal link between any injury suffered and a breach of a Code Right . . . It is not necessary to show that the patient suffered harm as a result of a failure to be sufficiently informed. So, it is strictly irrelevant to whether there has been a breach of Right 6 that the Commissioner finds it probable that, even if the health provider had explained the risks of the procedure, the patient would have gone ahead with it in any event. The patient is entitled to appropriate information irrespective of whether it would have been a determinative factor in the decision to proceed . . . This properly reflects the paramount interest that the duty of disclosure and the concept of informed consent is designed to secure—the individual's autonomy and right to decide in an informed manner, not just the interest in bodily safety.

(2) A Fiduciary Relationship?

If the doctor–patient relationship could be said to be fiduciary in nature, we might have an alternative basis for imposing an obligation on doctors to disclose material information. Since equitable duties of disclosure usually arise in relationships where one party is unusually vulnerable to the other's ability to exercise some discretion or power over her interests, they might seem a promising basis for a more patient-orientated approach to informed consent.

In other countries, there have been times when the courts have categorized the doctor's duty of disclosure as a fiduciary obligation,[77] but there has been little support for this approach among the English judiciary. In *Sidaway* in the Court of Appeal,[78] Dunn LJ said that the fiduciary relationship 'has been confined to cases involving the disposition of property, and has never been applied to the nature of the duty which lies upon a doctor in the performance of his professional treatment of his patient'. In the House of Lords, Lord Scarman was the only Law Lord to consider the possibility of a fiduciary relationship between doctor and patient, and he was similarly dismissive.

Sidaway v Board of Governors of the Bethlem Royal Hospital and the Maudsley Hospital[79]

Lord Scarman

Counsel for the appellant referred to *Nocton v Lord Ashburton* in an attempt to persuade your Lordships that the relationship between doctor and patient is of a fiduciary character entitling a patient to equitable relief in the event of a breach of fiduciary duty by the doctor. The attempt fails: there is no comparison to be made between the relationship of doctor and patient with that of solicitor and client, trustee and cestui qui trust or the other relationships treated in equity as of a fiduciary character.

---

[77] *Miller v Kennedy* 522 P 2d 852 (1974).   [78] [1984] QB 491.   [79] [1985] AC 871 at 884.

It is, however, uncontroversial that the doctor–patient relationship is one of trust and confidence, and, in other contexts, the courts have recognized that it might be fiduciary in character. A presumption of the invalidity of gifts and bequests from patient to doctor, for example, was established in the nineteenth century.[80] There are obligations which doctors owe to their patients—most obviously, the duty of confidentiality—which are equitable in nature, and which arise because equity has acknowledged the special dependency which exists within the doctor–patient relationship. Conceding that fiduciary relationships normally arise only when property interests are at stake, Margaret Brazier has nevertheless argued that 'in a sense the patient does entrust his most precious property, his body and health to the doctor'.[81]

But while an equitable basis for the duty of disclosure might initially appear attractive, there are reasons to be sceptical about whether recognizing a fiduciary relationship would in fact improve patients' access to adequate information. Since the fiduciary's principal obligation is to act in her client's best interests, this might translate into a paternalistic 'doctor knows best' approach to information disclosure. Ian Kennedy goes so far as to describe the 'best interests' test, which would define the fiduciary's duties, as 'the anti-principle, the means whereby courts have handed power to doctors by allowing them to determine what should be done'.[82]

4 GOOD MEDICAL PRACTICE

Until *Montgomery v Lanarkshire*, there appeared to be a gap between tort law's fairly minimal requirements and the codes of practice and guidelines promulgated by the GMC, the British Medical Association,[83] the Royal Colleges, and the Department of Health,[84] which have tended to be much more detailed and expansive. The GMC's guidance on obtaining patients' consent, quoted approvingly by the Supreme Court in *Montgomery*, is explicitly based upon the 'partnership' model of medical decision-making, and advocates a subjective, patient-specific standard of information disclosure:

General Medical Council[85]

> 2 Whatever the context in which medical decisions are made, you must work in partnership with your patients to ensure good care. In so doing, you must:
>
> (a) listen to patients and respect their views about their health
>
> (b) discuss with patients what their diagnosis, prognosis, treatment and care involve
>
> (c) share with patients the information they want or need in order to make decisions
>
> (d) maximise patients' opportunities, and their ability, to make decisions for themselves
>
> (e) respect patients' decisions.

---

80 *Rhodes v Bate* (1866) 1 Ch App 252.
81 'Patient Autonomy and Consent to Treatment: The Role of the Law?' (1987) 7 Legal Studies 169–93, 191.
82 'The Fiduciary Relationship and its Application to Doctors' in Peter Birks (ed), *Wrongs and Remedies in the Twenty-First Century* (Clarendon Press: Oxford, 1986) 111–40, 138.
83 British Medical Association, *Consent Tool Kit*, 5th edn (BMA, 2009).
84 *Reference Guide to Consent for Examination or Treatment* (DH: London, 2009).
85 GMC, *Consent: Patients and Doctors Making Decisions Together* (2008).

3 For a relationship between doctor and patient to be effective, it should be a partnership based on openness, trust and good communication . . .

7 The exchange of information between doctor and patient is central to good decision-making. How much information you share with patients will vary, depending on their individual circumstances. You should tailor your approach to discussions with patients according to:

    (a) their needs, wishes and priorities

    (b) their level of knowledge about, and understanding of, their condition, prognosis and the treatment options

    (c) the nature of their condition

    (d) the complexity of the treatment, and

    (e) the nature and level of risk associated with the investigation or treatment.

8 You should not make assumptions about:

    (a) the information a patient might want or need

    (b) the clinical or other factors a patient might consider significant, or

    (c) a patient's level of knowledge or understanding of what is proposed.

Of course, doctors who fail to follow GMC guidance are not immediately struck off, but the latest guidance robustly states that 'Serious or persistent failure to follow this guidance will put your registration at risk.'[86]

A defect of both tort law and professional guidance is that the 'informed consent' process involves only the health care professional and her patient: a clinician provides information and the patient makes a decision for herself, on her own. In practice, however, we commonly involve those close to us in our medical decisions, and take account of their views. Indeed, Roy Gilbar goes further and suggests that in the majority of cases, relatives' involvement enhances patients' capacity to make informed choices.

Roy Gilbar[87]

In the majority of cases, the involvement of the relatives in the decision-making process helped the patient be more autonomous when she/he had to make a decision. It enabled the patient to be more informed and to consider the various implications of the available options diligently in a focused manner. In the majority of cases, it helped the patient feel more confident and in control of the situation. . . .

In as much as [the patients in this study] quite naturally reacted emotionally to the information they received, they could not absorb the information properly. For them the relatives' presence in the consultation room was essential. Without it, serious legal questions about their ability to make informed decisions might have been raised . . .

Overall, the patients needed their relatives to help them make the decisions and therefore voluntarily involved them in the decision-making process, allowing them to have an impact on it . . .

---

[86] Ibid, 5.
[87] 'Family involvement, independence, and patient autonomy in practice' (2011) 19 Medical Law Review 192–234.

The current case law and guidelines request clinicians to pay attention to family pressure which can amount to undue influence. . . . However, the default legal position should not be confrontational, namely in treating the family as the enemy of the doctor and the patient. On the contrary, it should assume that relatives help the patient make better decisions by considering the various ramifications of each decision together and by reaching decisions that suit the patient's personal and familial circumstances.

5 CONCLUSION

The importance of the recent Supreme Court decision in *Montgomery v Lanarkshire* cannot be overstated. It aligns the standard of care in tort law with professional guidance on consent, and it is now clear that a doctor is under a duty to provide whatever information she should be aware matters to the individual patient. The doctor no longer 'knows best', instead, patients are rights-holders who cannot be assumed to be reliant entirely upon their doctor for medical information. Rupert Jackson, writing extra-judicially, has suggested that the onslaught on *Bolam* will not stop here.

Rupert Jackson[88]

In the latter part of the twentieth century many claimants had their guns trained on *Bolam*. . . . Finally, just a month ago, the invaders captured the citadel. In *Montgomery v Lanarkshire Health Board* the Supreme Court held that the majority in *Sidaway* was wrong. The *Bolam* test did not determine the extent of a doctor's duty to advise. . . . Now that the invaders have broken through the castle walls, they will not stop there. I predict that over the coming years there will be continuous onslaught on *Bolam*. The argument will be that the ordinary principles of tortious liability should apply to the professions in the same way that they apply to everybody else. There is no reason for the courts to accord special protection to the professions. Whether any of those attacks will succeed I do not know and it would be wrong for me, as a judge, to predict.

FURTHER READING

Brazier, Margaret, 'Patient Autonomy and Consent to Treatment: The Role of the Law?' (1987) 7 Legal Studies 169–93.

Caplan, Arthur L, 'Why autonomy needs help' (2014) 40 Journal of Medical Ethics 301–2.

Clark, Tamsyn and Nolan, Donal, 'A critique of *Chester v Afshar*' (2014) 34 Oxford Journal of Legal Studies 659–92.

Heywood, Rob, 'RIP *Sidaway*: Patient-Oriented Disclosure—A Standard Worth Waiting For? *Montgomery v Lanarkshire Health Board*' (2015) 23 Medical Law Review 455–66.

---

[88] 'The Professions: Power, Privilege and Legal Liability', Peter Taylor Memorial Lecture to the Professional Negligence Bar Association, 21 April 2015, paras 4. 11 and 4. 12.

Heywood, Rob, Macaskill, Ann, and Williams, Kevin, 'Patient perceptions of the consent process: qualitative inquiry and legal reflection' (2008) 24 Journal of Professional Negligence 104–21.

Manson, Neil, 'Why do patients want information if not to take part in decision making?' (2010) 36 Journal of Medical Ethics 834–7.

Stapleton, Jane, 'Cause in Fact and the Scope of Liability for Consequences' (2003) 119 Law Quarterly Review 388–425.

5

CONSENT II: CAPACITY AND VOLUNTARINESS

CENTRAL ISSUES

1. The principle of patient autonomy means that a competent adult patient has the right to refuse medical treatment, even if her reasons are bizarre, irrational, or non-existent, and even if her refusal will result in her death.

2. Under the Mental Capacity Act 2005, adults who lack capacity should be treated in their best interests. In Scotland, the Adults with Incapacity (Scotland) Act 2000 applies.

3. Parents normally give consent to their children's medical treatment.

If there is a dispute, or the treatment is controversial, the court has wide powers to authorize the medical treatment of minors in their best interests.

4. Mature minors can acquire the right to consent to treatment, but they do not necessarily have the same right to refuse treatment.

5. The patient's consent must have been given voluntarily: that is, it must not have been vitiated by undue influence or coercion.

1 INTRODUCTION

One of the first principles of medical law is that a competent adult patient must first give consent to medical treatment. As Cardozo J famously said in the US case, *Schloendorff v New York Hospital*:[1] 'Every human being of adult years and sound mind has a right to determine what shall be done with his own body.'

Touching a person without her consent, however benevolently, is prima facie unlawful. For consent to be valid: first, the patient must have the capacity to consent; secondly, her consent must be given voluntarily; and, thirdly she must understand, in broad terms, the nature of the treatment to which she has consented. We consider the first two criteria in this chapter. The question of how much information should be provided to fulfil the third criterion was dealt with in the previous chapter.

---

[1] 105 NE 92 (1914).

Consent has a legal, a moral, and a clinical function. Legally, consent may convert what would otherwise be unlawful touching into lawful conduct. Morally, consent is required in order to respect the patient's right to self-determination. Clinically, a patient's consent will make it easier to treat her, and her cooperation may contribute towards the treatment's success.

Most of this chapter is concerned with what happens when a patient cannot give consent, and because the rules are different, adults and children are dealt with separately. At the end of this chapter, we consider the requirement that the patient's consent must have been given voluntarily, and we briefly examine factors that might undermine the patient's ability to consent freely to medical treatment.

2 THE CONSENT REQUIREMENT

(a) CRIMINAL LAW

It is commonly believed that it is the patient's consent to medical treatment that prevents it from being both a civil wrong and a criminal assault. This is only partially true, because consent cannot offer a defence to the infliction of actual or grievous bodily harm. Some medical procedures, such as taking a patient's blood pressure, will not cause bodily harm, and the patient's consent would therefore offer a defence to what might otherwise be unlawful touching. More invasive treatment, such as surgery, involves cutting the body in a way that could undoubtedly amount to grievous bodily harm. Because consent is not a defence to the bodily harm involved in surgery, something else must explain its lawfulness.

The legality of 'reasonable' and 'proper' surgical procedures does not seem to be in doubt, however. In *Attorney General's Reference (No 6 of 1980)*, the Court of Appeal referred to the accepted legality of, among other things, 'reasonable surgical interference . . . as needed in the public interest'.

Attorney General's Reference (No 6 of 1980)[2]

Lord Lane CJ

Nothing which we have said is intended to cast doubt upon the accepted legality of properly conducted games and sports, lawful chastisement or correction, reasonable surgical interference, dangerous exhibitions, etc. These apparent exceptions can be justified as involving the exercise of a legal right, in the case of chastisement or correction, or as needed in the public interest, in the other cases.

In *R v Brown*, a case in which the House of Lords decided that causing actual bodily harm through consensual sadomasochistic practices was an offence, the Lords agreed that 'proper' medical treatment does not constitute a criminal offence, but as Lord Mustill explains, the patient's consent could not, on its own, explain this exception.

---

[2] *Attorney General's Reference (No 6 of 1980)* [1981] QB 715.

R v Brown[3]

Lord Mustill

Many of the acts done by surgeons would be very serious crimes if done by anyone else, and yet the surgeons incur no liability. Actual consent, or the substitute for consent deemed by the law to exist where an emergency creates a need for action, is an essential element in this immunity; but it cannot be a direct explanation for it, since much of the bodily invasion involved in surgery lies well above any point at which consent could even arguably be regarded as furnishing a defence. Why is this so? The answer must in my opinion be that proper medical treatment, for which actual or deemed consent is a prerequisite, is in a category of its own.

Lord Mustill had made similar remarks a year earlier.

Airedale NHS Trust v Bland[4]

Lord Mustill

[T]here is a point higher up the scale than common assault at which consent in general ceases to form a defence to a criminal charge.... If one person cuts off the hand of another it is no answer to say that the amputee consented to what was done.

How is it that, consistently with the proposition just stated, a doctor can with immunity perform on a consenting patient an act which would be a very serious crime if done by someone else? The answer must be that bodily invasions in the course of proper medical treatment stand completely outside the criminal law. The reason why the consent of the patient is so important is not that it furnishes a defence in itself, but because it is usually essential to the propriety of medical treatment.

At common law, it seems to be well established that, for public interest reasons, rather than because the patient gave consent, 'proper' medical treatment stands completely outside the criminal law.

Of course, the use of qualifying words like 'reasonable' or 'proper' means that not every surgical intervention will satisfy this public interest exception. Female circumcision is specifically proscribed by the Female Genital Mutilation Act 2003, but if it is judged not to be 'reasonable surgical interference', it might also amount to a criminal offence at common law.

Amputating a person's healthy limbs in order to increase her income from begging would not be 'proper' medical treatment. But more complicated is the question of whether it could ever be legitimate to amputate a person's healthy limb when its presence is causing her considerable distress. In 2000 it was revealed that a surgeon in Scotland had performed elective single-leg amputations on two physically healthy individuals who suffered from a rare sort of body dysmorphic disorder, in which the patient wishes to be an amputee.[5] The surgeon involved said that 'at follow up, both patients remain delighted with their new state'.[6]

On the one hand, operating in order to transform a non-disabled individual into a disabled one self-evidently causes grievous bodily harm, and seems manifestly 'unreasonable'. Yet, on the other hand, we now accept as 'reasonable' both gender reassignment surgery and

---

[3] [1994] 1 AC 212.   [4] [1993] AC 789.

[5] Sarah Ramsay, 'Controversy over UK surgeon who amputated healthy limbs' (2000) 355 The Lancet 476.

[6] Ibid.

cosmetic surgery, and, in both cases, the operation alters the patient's physical body so that it better fits her (preferred) body image. In the next extract, Tracey Elliott questions whether a sharp distinction can be drawn between procedures that are generally assumed to be 'proper medical treatment'—such as cosmetic surgery, live organ donation, and gender reassignment surgery—and healthy limb amputation.

Tracey Elliott[7]

As in the case of healthy limb amputation, both live organ donation and gender reassignment surgery invariably involve the removal of healthy body parts. . . . In addition, while it has been argued by some commentators that proper medical treatment 'must serve some therapeutic purpose', live organ donation offers no therapeutic benefits for the donor, and in the case of cosmetic surgery, any therapeutic purpose may be difficult, if not impossible to find. . . . It is perhaps difficult to see how an operation upon a young woman to enlarge her breasts to enormous proportions so that she may become a glamour model or television game show contestant might be said to be in the public interest. . . .

Given that the removal of healthy body parts in gender reassignment surgery in order to treat a severe psychological condition is lawful; might not healthy limb amputation be regarded as being justified upon a similar basis? . . . Cosmetic surgery is lawful in spite of the fact that procedures are frequently undertaken merely to satisfy personal vanity or increase earning potential: aesthetic surgery has become part of a burgeoning 'beauty' industry, in which 'customers' are encouraged to take active steps to modify their bodies to attain or maintain their ideal physical image. If the criminal law has no place in controlling cosmetic surgery performed by qualified surgeons upon competent adults with their consent, why should it have any place in controlling other forms of surgery performed in similar circumstances?

(b) CIVIL LAW

Provided that the patient consented to the treatment she received, there could be no action in tort for unlawful touching. An action in battery would be possible only if the patient can establish that her apparent consent was not 'real', perhaps because she was not told what she was consenting to, or because she was coerced into giving consent. In practice, such actions are rare. As we saw in the previous chapter, very few patients have been able to persuade a court that their apparent consent was defective due to a lack of information and, later in this chapter, it is evident that coercion and undue influence are also unlikely to vitiate a patient's consent.

(c) THE FORM CONSENT SHOULD TAKE

Consent to medical treatment does not need to be in writing. There are a few procedures, such as fertility treatment, where there is a statutory requirement to obtain written consent,[8] but this is exceptional.

---

[7] 'Body Dysmorphic Disorder, Radical Surgery and the Limits of Consent' (2009) 17 Medical Law Review 149–82.
[8] See further Chapter 15.

For most routine medical treatment the patient's consent can be inferred from her behaviour. If I put out my arm to have a blood sample taken, the health care professional can legitimately assume that I am consenting to having a needle stuck into my vein. In most encounters with health care professionals, formal consent procedures are non-existent. Rather, by seeking treatment and complying with instructions, the patient indicates her willingness to be treated.

Where the treatment involves surgery, it is good medical practice, albeit not a legal requirement, to obtain the patient's consent in writing, through her signature on a standard consent form. It is, however, important to remember that the consent form is not a contract between the doctor and her patient. Rather, the patient's consent must be ongoing throughout her treatment, and she is free to withdraw her consent at any time. Signing a consent form does not affect the patient's right to refuse to undergo the procedure.

(d) THE PRINCIPLE OF AUTONOMY

The principle that a competent adult must not be treated without her consent protects both her autonomy and her bodily integrity. As we can see from these extracts from the House of Lords' judgment in *Airedale NHS Trust v Bland*, it is settled law that, if an adult patient has capacity, she has the right to refuse medical treatment, even if this is not in her best interests.

Airedale NHS Trust v Bland[9]

Lord Mustill

If the patient is capable of making a decision on whether to permit treatment, . . . his choice must be obeyed even if on any objective view it is contrary to his best interests.

Lord Goff

[T]he principle of self-determination requires that respect must be given to the wishes of the patient, so that if an adult patient of sound mind refuses, however unreasonably, to consent to treatment or care by which his life would or might be prolonged, the doctors responsible for his care must give effect to his wishes, even though they do not consider it to be in his best interests to do.

Indeed, it is clear from these extracts from the Court of Appeal's judgment in *Re T (Adult: Refusal of Treatment)* that the patient's right of refusal exists regardless of whether her reasons are bizarre, irrational, or non-existent, and whether she might die as a result.

Re T (Adult: Refusal of Treatment)[10]

Lord Donaldson MR

This right of choice is not limited to decisions which others might regard as sensible. It exists notwithstanding that the reasons for making the choice are rational, irrational, unknown or even non-existent.

---

[9] [1993] AC 789.   [10] [1993] Fam 95.

Butler-Sloss LJ

A man or woman of full age and sound understanding may choose to reject medical advice and medical or surgical treatment either partially or in its entirety. A decision to refuse medical treatment by a patient capable of making the decision does not have to be sensible, rational or well-considered.

Staughton LJ

An adult whose mental capacity is unimpaired has the right to decide for herself whether she will or will not receive medical or surgical treatment, even in circumstances where she is likely or even certain to die in the absence of treatment.

In addition to the common law's robust protection of autonomy, the patient's right to make her own medical decisions is also protected by the Human Rights Act 1998. A number of Convention rights might be relevant, but probably the most important is Article 8 (respect for private and family life), which undoubtedly incorporates a right to make important decisions about what happens to one's body.

Respect for patient autonomy is also undoubtedly good medical practice. The British Medical Association, for example, advises doctors that: 'It is well established in law and ethics that competent adults have the right to refuse any medical treatment, even if that refusal results in their death.'[11]

It is therefore settled law that competent adult patients have the right to make irrational and life-threatening decisions to refuse medical treatment (we come back to this in the context of end-of-life decisions in Chapter 17). In Chapter 1, we saw that some commentators have criticized the priority given to autonomy on the grounds that it is an excessively individualistic value. Giving the competent adult patient an absolute right to reject life-saving medical treatment ignores the impact that this might have upon other people, such as her dependent children. The principle of patient autonomy gives the individual a right to make decisions that could have a profoundly negative impact upon those close to her. At times, then, there may be a tension between a patient's *legal* right to determine what is done to her body, and her *moral* obligations to others.

In the next extract, Shimon Glick argues that there might also be dangers in respecting the short-term autonomy of a frightened and distressed patient.

Shimon Glick[12]

[O]ftentimes individuals under acute stress may make hasty tragic decisions which they subsequently, under more careful consideration, regret . . . I would hope that even the most devoted advocates of autonomy might accept the premise that a patient who is frightened and stressed, may not be fully autonomous; his/her refusal should therefore be assigned less weight. It is tragic to accept such a patient's refusal automatically at face value, even if a team of psychiatrists and lawyers judge that person legally competent . . .

---

[11] British Medical Association, *Withholding and Withdrawing Life-Prolonging Medical Treatment: Guidance for Decision Making*, 3rd edn (BMA: London, 2007) para 25. 5.

[12] 'The morality of coercion' (2000) 26 Journal of Medical Ethics 393–5.

In addition, autonomy is of no value to a dead person. By permitting a patient to die avoidably, when it is virtually certain that were he saved against his present protest he would be grateful, one is granting that person his short term 'autonomous' wish while depriving him of his long term autonomy.

(e) PREGNANT WOMEN'S AUTONOMY?

In *Re T (Adult: Refusal of Treatment)*,[13] Lord Donaldson mooted one possible exception to the right to refuse treatment:

The only possible qualification is a case in which the choice may lead to the death of a viable foetus. That is not this case and, if and when it arises, the courts will be faced with a novel problem of considerable legal and ethical complexity.

Later the same year, such a case arose. In *Re S (Adult: Refusal of Treatment)*,[14] Mrs S wanted to refuse a caesarean section on religious grounds (she was a born-again Christian). Her competence was not in doubt. An emergency application was made, and after an *ex parte* hearing lasting less than two hours, Sir Stephen Brown granted a declaration that the operation would be lawful. *Re S* is now of historical interest only, however. In two subsequent cases, the Court of Appeal has confirmed that pregnancy does not diminish the competent adult patient's right to refuse unwanted medical intervention.

In *Re MB (An Adult: Medical Treatment)*, although MB was judged to lack capacity temporarily as a result of her needle phobia, Butler-Sloss LJ referred to *Re S* as 'a decision the correctness of which we must now call in doubt'. Instead, she was emphatic that:

A competent woman who has the capacity to decide may, for religious reasons, other reasons, for rational or irrational reasons or for no reason at all, choose not to have medical intervention, even though the consequence may be the death or serious handicap of the child she bears, or her own death.[15]

A year later, in *St George's NHS Trust v S*, the emergency caesarean section that had been performed upon S against her wishes was held to have been unlawful. Judge LJ defended the pregnant woman's right to refuse treatment that could save her fetus's life, even if her decision might appear to be 'morally repugnant'.

St George's NHS Trust v S[16]

Judge LJ

In our judgment while pregnancy increases the personal responsibilities of a woman it does not diminish her entitlement to decide whether or not to undergo medical treatment. Although human, and protected by the law in a number of different ways ..., an unborn

---

[13] [1993] Fam 95.   [14] [1992] 4 All ER 671.
[15] *Re MB (An Adult: Medical Treatment)* [1997] 2 FLR 426.   [16] [1999] Fam 26.

child is not a separate person from its mother. Its need for medical assistance does not prevail over her rights. She is entitled not to be forced to submit to an invasion of her body against her will, whether her own life or that of her unborn child depends on it. Her right is not reduced or diminished merely because her decision to exercise it may appear morally repugnant.

While the Court of Appeal's judgment in *St George's NHS Trust v S* robustly asserts the primacy of patient autonomy, Thorpe, writing extra-judicially, has suggested that it may in practice be easier for an appellate court to affirm the primacy of autonomy, after the operation has been carried out successfully, than it was for the judge who had to make the decision in the 'heat of the moment', when lives were in immediate danger.

Matthew Thorpe[17]

It is, perhaps, easier for an appellate court to discern principle than it is for a trial court to apply it in the face of judicial instinct, training, and emotion . . . It is simply unrealistic to suppose that the preservation of each life will not be a matter of equal concern to the Family Division judge surveying the medical dilemma. Whatever emphasis legal principle may place upon adult autonomy with the consequent right to choose between treatments, at some level the judicial outcome will be influenced by the expert evidence as to which treatment affords the best chance of the happy announcement that both mother and baby are doing well.

3 INCAPACITY

If a patient has capacity, then, unless she has been sectioned under the Mental Health Act 1983 (see Chapter 6), her refusal of medical treatment is decisive. In contrast, if a patient lacks capacity, she can be treated without consent. It is therefore vitally important to be able to tell whether or not a patient has capacity.

There are two possible approaches to the assessment of capacity: one based upon status and the other upon function:

- According to the *status* approach, some categories of patients lack capacity because of their status (an example would be age), regardless of their actual decision-making ability. On this approach, all under 18s—from babies to mature teenagers—would be treated as though they lacked capacity.

- The *functional* approach instead focuses on the individual's capabilities. On this approach, a child's capacity to make a particular decision would have to be individually assessed. A sensible and mature 14-year-old might be judged to have capacity, while a less mature 15-year-old might not.

The status approach is clearly the simplest—it is more straightforward to find out a child's age than it is to judge her reasoning skills—but, as Ian Kennedy explains, it is the functional approach which best promotes patient self-determination.

---

[17] 'The Caesarean Section Debate' (1997) 27 Family Law 663, 663–4.

Ian Kennedy[18]

The fundamental flaw in the status approach is that it takes no account of the individuality of each person. Respect for autonomy, however, involves respect for each person's individuality. It demands, therefore, that any criterion intended to determine when someone is incapable of being autonomous should, equally, be respectful of that person's individuality. Merely placing him in a class is far too gross a test of incapacity. It denies respect to the individual as an individual, and must therefore be rejected.

English law adopts a combination of the status and the functional approaches to capacity: all adults are presumed to have capacity, and all children under the age of 16 are presumed to lack capacity. Although these presumptions are status-based, they are just starting points that can be rebutted by evidence of the person's actual decision-making capacity. The difference between adults and children is therefore a shift in the burden of proof: evidence must be brought forward to establish that an adult does not have capacity; conversely, it would be for a 15-year-old to establish that she does, in fact, have the capacity to make a particular decision.

There appears to be one exception to this hybrid approach. As we see later, when children want to take certain life-threatening decisions—most commonly to refuse a blood transfusion on religious grounds—it is virtually impossible for them to establish that they are competent, and instead their 'status' as minors appears, in practice, to be decisive.

In reality, of course, capacity is a question of degree. Although patients at either end of the spectrum are easily identified—a permanently comatose patient clearly lacks capacity, whereas it may be obvious that intelligent, articulate university students are able to make their own decisions—towards the middle, as Gunn explains, it may be harder to tell whether someone is able to make decisions for herself.

Michael Gunn[19]

Capacity/incapacity are not concepts with clear a priori boundaries. They appear on a continuum which ranges from full capacity at one end to full incapacity at the other end. There are, therefore, degrees of capacity. The challenge is to choose the right level to set as the gateway to decision-making and respect for persons and autonomy.

Normally, as we know from experience, the question of whether an adult patient has capacity does not arise. Few people reading this book will have undergone a capacity assessment before having given consent to medical treatment.

Questioning a patient's decision-making capacity only tends to happen in two situations. First, if the patient belongs to a group whose members often or normally lack capacity, health care professionals may be alerted to the possibility that she may not be able to consent to treatment. A person suffering from Alzheimer's disease may or may not still have capacity, but the presence of a degenerative brain disorder might lead doctors to question her ability to make decisions. As a result, people suffering from certain mental disorders are more likely to have their capacity assessed, and perhaps also more likely to be found to lack capacity, even though mental disorder and incapacity are not

---

[18] *Treat Me Right* (OUP: Oxford, 1988) 57–8.
[19] 'The Meaning of Incapacity' (1994) 2 Medical Law Review 8.

synonymous with each other, and the presumption of competence applies to mentally disordered adults too.

Secondly, if a patient's doctors believe that her decision is seriously misguided or irrational, they may be more likely to question her capacity. The irrationality of a patient's choice does not justify a finding of incapacity, however. On the contrary, if a patient has capacity, then her decision must be respected regardless of how foolish or irrational it seems to others. But it is probably inevitable that doctors will be more likely to question a patient's capacity when she refuses to agree to treatment that the doctor believes to be in her best interests, than when she agrees with the doctor's recommendation.

Of course, if health care professionals are unlikely to question a patient's decision-making capacity when she has consented to a proposed treatment, the pool of patients who are judged to lack capacity will be smaller than it would be if all patients' decision-making capacity had to be scrutinized. In the study discussed in the next extract, Raymont et al assessed the decision-making capacity of acutely ill medical inpatients, and found that almost half of them lacked capacity, but since none of them had refused treatment, the treating doctors had treated their acquiescence as if it were a valid consent.

Vanessa Raymont et al[20]

Our study suggests that in routine clinical practice, doctors most usually fail to identify that patients with significant cognitive impairment do not have capacity. If we accept that a high proportion of acutely ill medical inpatients do not have mental capacity to make decisions about current treatment, our findings have implications for clinical practice, legislation, and the doctor–patient relationship. The current position is to assume capacity unless there is strong evidence to the contrary. We suspect that a substantial proportion of patients with decisional difficulties place their trust in doctors, and passively acquiesce with treatment plans. Thus, incapacity is frequently overlooked. . . .

However, to accept the passive acquiescence of such patients as evidence of true consent would be dangerous when important and irreversible decisions need to be made. Before making such decisions, the clinician should have considered the possibility that the patient is unable to give valid consent.

Let us now turn to consider how the law treats patients who lack capacity or whose capacity is in doubt. Despite some similarities, there are important differences between the treatment of adults and children, and so we consider them separately.

(a) ADULTS

At the beginning of the twenty-first century, there were several reasons for introducing statutory reform of the law relating to the treatment of adults who lack capacity. The common law framework was believed to be unclear, leaving medical professionals and carers uncertain how to act, and potentially vulnerable to legal challenge. Legal uncertainty was also thought to delay some patients' access to treatment. The number of affected patients was also increasing: in an ageing population, the number of patients who might lack capacity as a result of conditions such as dementia will increase every year.

---

[20] 'Prevalence of mental incapacity in medical inpatients and associated risk factors: cross-sectional study' (2004) 364 The Lancet 1421–7.

The Mental Capacity Act 2005 (MCA) came into force in 2007. The Act covers much more than just the medical treatment of people who lack capacity; the management of their financial affairs and decisions about where they should live also come within its scope. Our discussion will be confined to the MCA's application to decisions about health care.

(1) The 'Principles'

Section 1 of the MCA sets out five statutory principles which capture the most basic and important assumptions underpinning the statutory scheme, namely that people who lack capacity should (a) have their interests protected, and (b) be helped, as far as possible, to make or take part in decisions affecting them.

Mental Capacity Act 2005 section 1

1(1) The following principles apply for the purposes of this Act.

(2) A person must be assumed to have capacity unless it is established that he lacks capacity.

(3) A person is not to be treated as unable to make a decision unless all practicable steps to help him to do so have been taken without success.

(4) A person is not to be treated as unable to make a decision merely because he makes an unwise decision.

(5) An act done, or decision made, under this Act for or on behalf of a person who lacks capacity must be done, or made, in his best interests.

(6) Before the act is done, or the decision is made, regard must be had to whether the purpose for which it is needed can be as effectively achieved in a way that is less restrictive of the person's rights and freedom of action.

The Act's Code of Practice, updated most recently in 2014, sets out how these principles, and the legislative provisions described later, should apply in practice.

The Act applies to people over the age of 16. Young people aged 16 and 17 are in a slightly curious position. The MCA may apply to them, if they lack capacity, but, as we see later, the presumption of capacity that applies to them is slightly different from the more robust presumption which applies to over 18s.

(2) Definition of Incapacity

(a) What is incapacity?

The Act preserves the common law presumption of capacity. Under section 2 of the Mental Capacity Act 2005, there is then a two-stage test for capacity.

Mental Capacity Act 2005 section 2

2 People who lack capacity

(1) For the purposes of this Act, a person lacks capacity in relation to a matter if at the material time he is unable to make a decision for himself in relation to the matter because of an impairment of, or a disturbance in the functioning of, the mind or brain.

(2) It does not matter whether the impairment or disturbance is permanent or temporary.

Under section 2(1), it must first be established that the person is suffering from 'an impairment of, or a disturbance in the functioning of, the mind or brain'. This 'diagnostic threshold' means that someone will not fall within the provisions of the Act unless they are suffering from some sort of mental impairment, which can be either temporary or permanent.

The Code of Practice suggests that a wide variety of conditions will be covered:

Mental Capacity Act Code of Practice

4.12 Examples of an impairment or disturbance in the functioning of the mind or brain may include the following:

- conditions associated with some forms of mental illness
- dementia
- significant learning disabilities
- the long-term effects of brain damage
- physical or medical conditions that cause confusion, drowsiness or loss of consciousness
- delirium
- concussion following a head injury, and
- the symptoms of alcohol or drug use.

The Code of Practice also attempts to address the problem, described previously, of under-diagnosis of incapacity (a) in patients suffering from chronic physical illness, and (b) among patients who agree with a doctor's proposed treatment plan:

Mental Capacity Act Code of Practice

4.26 . . . Temporary factors may also affect someone's ability to make decisions. Examples include acute illness, severe pain, the effect of medication, or distress after a death or shock . . .

4.45 . . . Be aware that the fact that a person agrees with you or assents to what is proposed does not necessarily mean that they have capacity to make the decision.

Once this diagnostic requirement has been satisfied, the second stage is to work out whether the person is able to make a decision for himself. Section 3(1) sets out what is meant by being 'unable to make a decision':

Mental Capacity Act 2005 section 3

3 Inability to make decisions

(1) For the purposes of section 2, a person is unable to make a decision for himself if he is unable—

(a) to understand the information relevant to the decision,

(b) to retain that information,

> (c) to use or weigh that information as part of the process of making the decision, or
>
> (d) to communicate his decision (whether by talking, using sign language or any other means).
>
> (2) A person is not to be regarded as unable to understand the information relevant to a decision if he is able to understand an explanation of it given to him in a way that is appropriate to his circumstances (using simple language, visual aids or any other means).
>
> (3) The fact that a person is able to retain the information relevant to a decision for a short period only does not prevent him from being regarded as able to make the decision.

This second stage is, essentially, a statutory version of the three-stage test at common law, first set out by Thorpe J in *Re C (Adult: Refusal of Treatment)*. C suffered from chronic paranoid schizophrenia. His consultant was of the view that, unless his gangrenous leg was amputated, he had an 85 per cent chance of death. C had said that he would rather die with two feet than live with one. He had delusions that he had had an international career in medicine, during which he had never lost a patient. C's solicitor sought, and was granted, a declaration that no amputation should take place without C's written consent.

Re C (Adult: Refusal of Treatment)[21]

Thorpe J

I consider helpful Dr E's analysis of the decision-making process into three stages:

- first, comprehending and retaining treatment information,
- secondly, believing it and,
- thirdly, weighing it in the balance to arrive at choice.

Applying that test to my findings on the evidence, I am completely satisfied that the presumption that Mr C has the right of self-determination has not been displaced.

The test for capacity is decision-specific: the question is whether the person has the capacity to make a particular decision, rather than being a general judgement about their cognitive ability. A person might have capacity in relation to some decisions, and lack it in relation to others.

Of course, while this functional and decision-specific approach to capacity is autonomy-enhancing, it also means that someone's capacity ought—in theory at least—to be assessed afresh in relation to each decision that arises about their treatment. Not only might this be rather time-consuming, but it also inevitably means that the Act places considerable reliance on the judgement of the person charged with assessing capacity. We return to this point later.

---

[21] [1994] 1 WLR 290. The *Re C* test was approved by the Court of Appeal three years later in *Re MB (An Adult: Medical Treatment)* [1997] 2 FLR 426.

The key test for capacity is whether the person can understand the information that is relevant to the particular decision, retain it, and use it in order to make a choice.

It is sufficient if the person can retain information temporarily. Section 3(3) of the Act specifies that someone who can retain information only for short periods of time should nevertheless be entitled to make their own decisions. This might be particularly important for patients suffering from progressive memory loss: they could be judged to have capacity to make a decision even if they are likely to have forgotten what they have been told a few days later. Moreover, the Code of Practice suggests that efforts should be made to help people to retain information:

> If they have difficulty understanding, it might be useful to present information in a different way (for example, different forms of words, pictures or diagrams). Written information, audio-tapes, videos and posters can help people remember important facts.[22]

The fourth limb of the section 3(1) test—namely that P is not able to communicate his decision—was not mentioned by Thorpe J in *Re C* because it was not an issue in C's case. It was, however, always the case at common law that, for patients who cannot communicate at all, there is no option but to treat them as if they lack capacity. The Code of Practice confirms that this applies only to patients, such as those who are in a coma or suffering from locked-in syndrome, who cannot express a view by even the most minimal means, such as squeezing an arm or blinking an eyelid.[23]

Of course, in order to apply this test, it is necessary to know what is meant by 'information relevant to the decision'. Does a person have to be able to understand, retain, and use complex clinical information, or is it enough that they have a very basic understanding of what is proposed? In *Heart of England NHS Foundation Trust v JB*, Peter Jackson J found that all that was necessary was that JB had a 'broad, general understanding' of the benefits and risks of amputation, rather than a more detailed understanding of the relative risks of different types of amputation.

Heart of England NHS Foundation Trust v JB[24]

Peter Jackson J

[W]hat is in my view required is that she should understand the nature, purpose and effects of the proposed treatment, the last of these entailing an understanding of the benefits and risks of deciding to have or not to have one or other of the various kinds of amputation, or of not making a decision at all.

What is required here is a broad, general understanding of the kind that is expected from the population at large. JB is not required to understand every last piece of information about her situation and her options ... [W]hat is required is an understanding of the nature, purpose and effects of the proposed treatment. In this sense 'the proposed treatment' is surgical treatment for a potentially gangrenous limb, and is not limited to one of the possible operations. Treating each type of amputation as different is an impractical and unnecessary distinction that would diminish the scope of JB's capacity.

---

[22] Mental Capacity Act 2005 Code of Practice para 4. 18.   [23] Para 4. 23.
[24] [2014] EWHC 342 (COP).

In order to protect their autonomy, it is important that patients are not disqualified from making decisions for themselves because they cannot understand all of the possible ramifications of a relatively simple decision. For example, in the case of contraception, it should be enough, as Bodey J explained in *A Local Authority v A*, that a woman understands what a contraceptive injection will involve, rather than needing to have a full understanding of what it would be like for her to have a baby.

A Local Authority v A[25]

Bodey J

Although in theory the 'reasonably foreseeable consequences' of not taking contraception involve possible conception, a birth and the parenting of a child, there should be some limit in practice on what needs to be envisaged, if only for public policy reasons. I accept the submission that it is unrealistic to require consideration of a woman's ability to foresee the realities of parenthood, or to expect her to be able to envisage the fact-specific demands of caring for a particular child not yet conceived (let alone born) with unpredictable levels of third-party support. I do not think such matters *are* reasonably foreseeable: or, to borrow an expression from elsewhere, I think they are too remote from the medical issue of contraception. . .

So, in my judgment, the test for capacity should be so applied as to ascertain the woman's ability to understand and weigh up the immediate medical issues surrounding contraceptive treatment.

This case is also noteworthy for Bodey J's application of section 3(1)(c)—the need for the person to be able to weigh this information as part of the process of making a decision. Mrs A was able to understand the 'proximate medical issues' relevant to the decision about contraception, but she was judged unable to weigh this information, crucially not because the impairment in her brain made this impossible, but because her husband Mr A exercised such overpowering control over her that she was unable to make a choice of her own free will.

Bodey J

To say however that capacity as to contraception exists because Mrs A can understand sufficient (as I find she can) about the medical aspects of it, would be to bypass section 3(1)(c) of the 2005 Act. There must also be the ability to use or weigh that information . . . The question is whether the influence of Mr A over Mrs A has been so overpowering as to leave her unable to weigh up the information and take a decision of her free will . . .

In view of what I find to be the completely unequal dynamic in the relationship between Mr and Mrs A, I am satisfied that her decision not to continue taking contraception is not the product of her own free will . . . [S]he is unable to weigh up the pros and cons of contraception because of the coercive pressure under which she has been placed both intentionally and unconsciously by Mr A. . . I am in no doubt that Mrs A presently lacks capacity to take a decision for herself about contraception.

[25] [2010] EWHC 1549 (Fam).

The problem with this interpretation of section 3(1)(c) is that it suggests that undue influence might not only vitiate consent, but might also justify a decision that someone lacks capacity. Of course, this could only happen to someone who had satisfied the 'diagnostic' threshold of having an impairment or a disturbance of the brain, but nevertheless, the logical consequence of Bodey J's judgment is that someone who might otherwise be judged to have capacity could be found to lack capacity on the grounds that someone else has put them under pressure in relation to that decision.

If someone with borderline capacity does not satisfy the diagnostic threshold, and hence does not lack capacity within the terms of the Mental Capacity Act, that is not necessarily the end of the matter. In *Re L (Vulnerable Adults with Capacity: Court's Jurisdiction)*, the Court of Appeal held that the inherent jurisdiction still existed for 'vulnerable' adults who, while not suffering from mental incapacity within the definition of the Act, were incapacitated from making decisions as a result of 'constraint, coercion, undue influence or other vitiating factors'.

Re L (Vulnerable Adults with Capacity: Court's Jurisdiction)[26]

McFarlane LJ

Where, on a strict mental health appraisal, such an individual does not lack capacity in the terms of the MCA 2005 and therefore falls outside the statutory scheme, but other factors, for example coercion and undue influence, may combine with his borderline capacity to remove his autonomy to make an important decision, why, one may ask, should that individual not be able to access the protection now afforded to adults whose mental capacity puts them on the other side of that borderline?

(b) The right to take unwise or irrational decisions?

While the statutory principles preserve the patient's right to take unwise decisions, there is an ambiguity here. On the one hand, provided that a patient satisfies the test for capacity, it does not matter if the decision she wants to take is irrational or eccentric. On the other hand, it is sometimes difficult to distinguish between a person's bizarre and irrational wishes, which must nevertheless be respected, and a person's inability to use and weigh information, which may mean that they fail section 3(1)(c) of the test for capacity.

When assessing capacity, the critical question is whether someone can make a decision, not whether she can make a sensible or a responsible decision. In *The Mental Health Trust v DD*, one of several Court of Protection decisions concerning DD, a pregnant woman with a complex obstetric history, learning difficulties, and an autistic spectrum disorder, Cobb J explained that he had to 'review with particular care whether DD's decision making is simply "unwise" rather than evidence of her incapacity'. If her decision-making were merely 'unwise', he would 'have no right under the Mental Capacity Act 2005 to intervene'.

---

[26] [2011] EWHC 1022 (Fam).

The Mental Health Trust v DD[27]

Cobb J

Her decision-making is undoubtedly 'unwise', but it is not, in my judgment, just 'unwise'; it lacks the essential characteristic of discrimination which only comes when the relevant information is evaluated, and weighed. I am satisfied that in relation to each of the matters under consideration her impairment of mind (essentially attributable to her autistic spectrum disorder, overlaid with her learning disability) prevents her from weighing the information relevant to each decision.

In contrast, in *Re SB (A Patient) (Capacity to Consent to Termination)*, the treating psychiatrist was adamant that a pregnant woman with bipolar disorder did not have capacity, as a result of her paranoid and persecutory beliefs. As counsel for the NHS Trust put it, she was 'not thinking straight'. Holman J disagreed, and found that even if her reasoning was skewed by paranoia, she was able to make the decision to terminate her pregnancy.

Re SB (A Patient) (Capacity to Consent to Termination)[28]

Holman J

What weighs most significantly with me is that, even if the patient has some skewed thoughts and paranoid or delusional views with regard to her husband and his attitude towards her and his behaviour, she gives many other reasons for desiring a termination....

It seems to me, therefore, that even if aspects of the decision making are influenced by paranoid thoughts in relation to her husband and her mother, she is nevertheless able to describe, and genuinely holds, a range of rational reasons for her decision. When I say rational, I do not necessarily say they are good reasons, nor do I indicate whether I agree with her decision, for section 1(4) of the Act expressly provides that someone is not to be treated as unable to make a decision simply because it is an unwise decision. It seems to me that this lady has made, and has maintained for an appreciable period of time, a decision. It may be that aspects of her reasons may be skewed by paranoia. There are other reasons which she has and which she has expressed. My own opinion is that it would be a total affront to the autonomy of this patient to conclude that she lacks capacity to the level required to make this decision. It is of course a profound and grave decision, but it does not necessarily involve complex issues. It is a decision that she has made and maintains; and she has defended and justified her decision against challenge. It is a decision which she has the capacity to reach. So for those reasons I conclude that it has not been established that she lacks capacity to make decisions about her desired termination.

In *Kings College NHS Foundation Trust v C*, MacDonald J explained that C had sought to live life 'entirely and unapologetically on her own terms; that life revolving largely around her looks, men, material possessions and "living the high life". In particular, it is clear that during her life C has placed a significant premium on youth and beauty and on living a life that, in C's words, "sparkles".'

After taking an overdose of paracetamol, C had suffered kidney failure and wished to refuse dialysis. With dialysis, C would have a good prognosis; without it, she would die. Two experts thought C was unable to weigh information about her prognosis in order to make a

---

[27] [2014] EWCOP 11.   [28] [2013] EWHC 1417 (COP).

choice, and that she therefore lacked capacity to make this decision. MacDonald J disagreed. He found that C did understand and believe her prognosis, it was just that she chose to give it no weight 'within the context of her own values and outlook'. As C had capacity, she had the right to refuse dialysis. C died two weeks later.

Kings College NHS Foundation Trust v C[29]

MacDonald J

[T]he rationale expressed by C for refusing treatment was that she believed she may need dialysis for the rest of her life, saw a bleak future if she could not have a life of socialising, drinking and partying with friends, that getting old scared her both in terms of illness and appearance....

The decision C has reached to refuse dialysis can be characterised as an unwise one. That C considers that the prospect of growing old, the fear of living with fewer material possessions and the fear that she has lost, and will not regain, 'her sparkle' outweighs a prognosis that signals continued life will alarm and possibly horrify many, although I am satisfied that the ongoing discomfort of treatment, the fear of chronic illness and the fear of lifelong treatment and lifelong disability are factors that also weigh heavily in the balance for C. C's decision is certainly one that does not accord with the expectations of many in society. Indeed, others in society may consider C's decision to be unreasonable, illogical or even immoral within the context of the sanctity accorded to life by society in general. None of this however is evidence of a lack of capacity. The court being satisfied that, in accordance with the provisions of the Mental Capacity Act 2005, C has capacity to decide whether or not to accept treatment C is entitled to make her own decision on that question based on the things that are important to her, in keeping with her own personality and system of values and without conforming to society's expectation of what constitutes the 'normal' decision in this situation (if such a thing exists). As a capacitous individual C is, in respect of her own body and mind, sovereign.

Where does this leave the anorexic patient, who chooses to give information about her need for food no weight in relation to her own 'values and outlook'? Anorexia has tended to be treated as a rather special case, in that it is a mental health condition which may interfere with someone's ability to use or weigh information.

Mental Capacity Act Code of Practice

4.21 ... Sometimes people can understand information but an impairment or disturbance stops them using it. ...

4.22 For example, a person with the eating disorder anorexia nervosa may understand information about the consequences of not eating. But their compulsion not to eat might be too strong for them to ignore.

For example, *A Local Authority v E* involved a 32-year-old woman with anorexia whose death was imminent. E was adamant that she did not want to eat or be fed. Despite describing E as being 'fully aware of her situation' and 'intelligent and charming',

---

[29] [2015] EWCOP 80.

Peter Jackson J found that she lacked capacity, and that feeding her against her wishes was in her best interests (we return to Peter Jackson's decision as to E's best interests later).

A Local Authority v E[30]

Peter Jackson J

There is no doubt that E has an impairment of, or a disturbance in the functioning of, the mind or brain in the form of her anorexia. Equally it is clear that in terms of MCA s. 3(1) she can understand and retain the information relevant to the treatment decision and can communicate her decision.

However, there is strong evidence that E's obsessive fear of weight gain makes her incapable of weighing the advantages and disadvantages of eating in any meaningful way. For E, the compulsion to prevent calories entering her system has become the card that trumps all others. The need not to gain weight overpowers all other thoughts.

A particularly clear illustration of the fact that anorexia destroys someone's capacity to weigh information about their need for food comes from the fact that sufferers might have capacity in relation to other decisions, including life and death decisions about medical treatment, and lack capacity only in relation to their anorexia. This was the case in *NHS Trust v L*, as Eleanor King J explained.

NHS Trust v L[31]

Eleanor King J

A sufferer may otherwise appear perfectly rational and may well be able to make appropriate capacitous decisions about a range of issues e.g. relating to financial matters. More specifically in Ms L's case it is agreed that she has capacity to decide whether to take antibiotics for her pneumonia, the antibiotics are not calorific so she is able to make a perfectly rational decision that she needs antibiotics to fight off the infection which would otherwise, in all likelihood, kill her.

Similarly, in *An NHS Trust v X*, Ms X lacked capacity in relation to the treatment of anorexia, while she retained the ability to weigh information in relation to her alcoholism and end-stage cirrhosis of the liver.

An NHS Trust v X[32]

Cobb J

Because Ms X is body dysmorphic she believes she is larger than she is and is unlikely therefore to understand how ill she in fact is. In any event, [Dr Glover] was firmly of the view that

---

[30] [2012] EWHC 1639 (Fam).   [31] [2012] EWHC 2741 (COP).   [32] [2014] EWCOP 35.

Ms X was unable to weigh the relevant information: '... *her ability to weigh the decision in the balance is significantly disturbed by her fear of weight gain. This disturbance is sufficient to render [Ms X] incapacitous with respect to these decisions.*' ... On the evidence which I have heard, I am entirely satisfied that Ms X lacks capacity to litigate and to make decisions about her eating disorder.

Both Dr. A and Dr. Glover were clear in drawing a distinction between Ms X's capacity to make decisions around her eating disorder (anorexia) and her use of alcohol. They both considered that Ms X was able to understand, retain, and crucially weigh up, the decision around drinking; they felt that her drinking was responsive to events—she appeared to be making choices about when to drink, when to drink more, and when to drink less. In particular, Dr. Glover was of the view that Ms X was able to weigh information such as the calorific content of alcohol, and appeared to be aware of the consequences for her liver functioning of continued abusive drinking, including the prospect that it could kill her; Dr. Glover considered that she may limit her alcohol consumption on occasion for this reason. In short, both doctors considered that she had capacity to make decisions about alcohol and I accept these opinions.

It follows that my jurisdiction is limited to making best interests decisions only in relation to the treatment of anorexia nervosa and not in relation to the management or treatment of her alcohol dependence disorder.

In the next extract, John Coggon highlights two issues that flow from the decision-specific test for capacity evident in *An NHS Trust v X*: that it might be difficult to untangle the application of an 'advance decision' if P only had capacity in relation to one of her disorders, and that it illustrates that it may not make sense to refer to the 'competent patient'.

John Coggon[33]

Cobb J, having affirmed her capacity, necessarily finds the advance decision to be valid, notwithstanding that it would have no contemporary application. However, his judgment highlights the complication that although Ms X had capacity in relation to alcohol, she lacked it in relation to her anorexia and conditions arising because of that. A practical difficulty would arise if it were impossible to establish definitively the cause of a particular health problem. Thus, the precise extent to which the advance decision might be binding is to be doubted; we have a situation where the scope of the patient's competence seems quite unclear. . . .

This case provides a clear illustration of how and why 'the competent patient' does not, in truth, exist as a free-standing concept in English mental capacity law. A patient can only be competent in reference to a specific issue. Decision-specific capacity is ignored when universal claims are asserted through the idea of 'the competent patient'.

Heather Draper has pointed out an interesting distinction between chronic undereating usually caused by psychological problems, where a finding of incapacity and the authorization of force-feeding has been relatively straightforward, and chronic overeating, which might similarly be prompted by psychological problems such as low self-esteem,

[33] 'Alcohol Dependence and Anorexia Nervosa: Individual Autonomy and the Jurisdiction of the Court of Protection' (2015) 23 Medical Law Review 659–67.

and which can be similarly life-threatening, but where a diagnosis of incapacity would be unlikely.[34]

Of course, one explanation for this difference is that anorexia is classified as a mental illness in the International Classification of Diseases (ICD-10), whereas extreme gluttony is not, although it should be noted that this classification is not universally accepted, and that, in any event, having a mental illness is not synonymous with lacking capacity.[35] Draper has also contrasted an anorexic's refusal of food with a woman's rejection of radical mastectomy.

Heather Draper[36]

Let us take a step back from the emotionally charged issue of anorexia and consider a parallel case—that of a woman who knows that with a radical mastectomy and chemotherapy she has a good chance of recovering from breast cancer but who refuses to have the operation because, in her opinion, living with only one breast or no breasts at all will be intolerable. She is *also* making a decision based on her perception of her body image and we might think that this is an irrational perception. Nevertheless, operating without her consent is unthinkable.

(c) Equal treatment

Buttressing the presumption of capacity, the Act spells out certain factors which must not be used to ground a finding of incapacity. As we have seen, the fourth principle specifies that: 'a person should not be assumed to lack capacity just because they make an unwise decision', and, according to section 2(3):

Mental Capacity Act 2005 section 2

2(3) A lack of capacity cannot be established merely by reference to—

(a) a person's age or appearance, or

(b) a condition of his, or an aspect of his behaviour, which might lead others to make unjustified assumptions about his capacity.

The intention of this section is clear: to remind health care professionals that they should not rely on stereotypes and assumptions when judging capacity. The use of the word 'merely' is, however, rather odd, since the implication is that a lack of capacity could be established based upon a person's age or appearance, provided that there are other factors which also justify this finding. It could be argued that 'unjustified assumptions about his capacity' should not be relevant at all, rather than being potentially relevant if backed up by other factors.

---

[34] 'Anorexia nervosa and respecting a refusal of life-prolonging therapy: a limited justification' (2000) 14 Bioethics 120–33, 131.

[35] Ibid, 130; Rebecca Dresser, 'Feeding the Hunger Artists: Legal Issues in Treating Anorexia Nervosa' (1984) 2 Wisconsin Law Review 297.

[36] 'Treating anorexics without consent: some reservations' (1998) 24 Journal of Medical Ethics 5–7.

This unfortunate wording is repeated in section 4 when deciding what treatment to offer. The word 'merely' implies that someone's appearance or behaviour could be relevant to the decision as to what is in their best interests, as long as it is not the only factor. A more patient-friendly formulation would simply delete the word 'merely'.

Mental Capacity Act 2005 section 4

4(1) In determining for the purposes of this Act what is in a person's best interests, the person making the determination must not make it merely on the basis of—

(a) the person's age or appearance, or

(b) a condition of his, or an aspect of his behaviour, which might lead others to make unjustified assumptions about what might be in his best interests.

(3) Assisted Decision-Making

The second statutory principle, in section 1(3), provides that 'a person is not to be treated as unable to make a decision unless all practicable steps to help him to do so have been taken without success'. This is bolstered by section 3(2):

Mental Capacity Act 2005

3(2) A person is not to be regarded as unable to understand the information relevant to a decision if he is able to understand an explanation of it given to him in a way that is appropriate to his circumstances (using simple language, visual aids or any other means).

The Code of Practice goes into considerable detail about the support which people might need, and offers guidance on how to maximize their decision-making ability.

Mental Capacity Act Code of Practice

2.7 The kind of support people might need to help them make a decision varies. It depends on personal circumstances, the kind of decision that has to be made and the time available to make the decision. It might include:

- using a different form of communication (for example, non-verbal communication)
- providing information in a more accessible form (for example, photographs, drawings, or tapes)
- treating a medical condition which may be affecting the person's capacity or
- having a structured programme to improve a person's capacity to make particular decisions (for example, helping a person with learning disabilities to learn new skills). . . .

3.10 To help someone make a decision for themselves, all possible and appropriate means of communication should be tried.

- Ask people who know the person well about the best form of communication (try speaking to family members, carers, day centre staff or support workers). They may also know somebody the person can communicate with easily, or the time when it is best to communicate with them.

- Use simple language. Where appropriate, use pictures, objects or illustrations to demonstrate ideas.

- Speak at the right volume and speed, with appropriate words and sentence structure. It may be helpful to pause to check understanding or show that a choice is available.

- Break down difficult information into smaller points that are easy to understand. Allow the person time to consider and understand each point before continuing.

- It may be necessary to repeat information or go back over a point several times.

- Is help available from people the person trusts (relatives, friends, GP, social worker, religious or community leaders)? If so, make sure the person's right to confidentiality is respected.

- Be aware of cultural, ethnic or religious factors that shape a person's way of thinking, behaviour or communication . . .

- If necessary, consider using a professional language interpreter . . .

- Would an advocate (someone who can support and represent the person) improve communication in the current situation?. . .

3.13 . . . Where possible, choose a location where the person feels most at ease. For example, people are usually more comfortable in their own home than at a doctor's surgery.

3.14 . . . Try to choose the time of day when the person is most alert—some people are better in the mornings, others are more lively in the afternoon or early evening. It may be necessary to try several times before a decision can be made.

In an emergency, extensive steps to support the person to make their own decision may not be practicable. The Code suggests that when an urgent decision is required, and 'treatment cannot be delayed while a person gets support to make a decision ... the only practical and appropriate steps might be to keep a person informed of what is happening and why'.[37]

Despite the Act and the Code's emphasis on assisted decision-making, when it considered the law on capacity, as part of its review of the Deprivation of Liberty Safeguards (which we consider in Chapter 6), the Law Commission proposed a further legal process through which people could appoint 'supporters' to help them make decisions for themselves.

Law Commission[38]

12.10 Arguably, the second principle of the Mental Capacity Act already makes adequate provision for supported decision-making. However, the evidence received by the House of Lords committee showed that the Mental Capacity Act principles were not working effectively, and that supported decision-making under the Act was 'rare in practice'. As a result, it concluded that 'supported decision- making, and the adjustments required to enable it, are not well embedded' and that 'a fundamental change of attitudes among

[37] Para 2.9.
[38] *Mental Capacity and Deprivation of Liberty: A Consultation Paper* (Law Commission, 2015).

professionals is needed in order to move from protection and paternalism to enablement and empowerment' . . .

12.12 We provisionally consider that there are a number of clear benefits in introducing a formal legal process in which a person (known as a 'supporter') is appointed to assist with decision-making.

(4) How Should People Who Lack Capacity be Treated?

As at common law, the statutory principles confirm that the treatment of people who lack capacity is governed by a best interests test, and that the 'least restrictive alternative' principle applies.[39]

(a) The least restrictive alternative

When deciding between possible courses of action, there should always be a presumption in favour of the least intrusive one, and consideration should be given as to whether it is necessary to act at all. So, for example, if a woman who lacks capacity cannot cope with her heavy periods, hysterectomy must be an option of last resort, and less intrusive ways to control her menstrual cycle, such as injections or implants, should be tried first.

A Local Authority v K was the first non-therapeutic sterilization case to come before the Court of Protection. K was a 21-year-old woman with Down's syndrome and mild to moderate learning difficulties. Her parents were concerned that as she grew older, they would be able to exercise less control over her behaviour, thus increasing the risk that she might engage in wanted or unwanted sexual activity. A hormonal contraceptive implant had been tried, but its insertion had been traumatic and the hormones had adversely affected K's temperament.

K's parents believed that sterilization would be in her best interests, and they had even considered taking her abroad if it was not possible to sterilize K in the UK. Cobb J found that K lacked capacity, but that sterilization would not be in her best interests because it was not the least restrictive alternative.

A Local Authority v K[40]

Cobb J

[I]t is my judgment that sterilisation would be a disproportionate (and not the least restrictive) step to achieve contraception for K in the future (absent significant change in her circumstances). Plainly risk management is better than invasive treatment, it is less restrictive.... [T]here are less restrictive methods of achieving the purpose of contraception than sterilisation, and that in the event of a need for contraception, these ought to be attempted.

(b) The best interests test

Section 4 sets out the factors to be considered when deciding what is in a person's best interests. It is not an exhaustive list of relevant factors. Rather, the Code makes it clear that the

---

[39] Section 1(5) and (6).   [40] [2013] EWHC 242 (COP).

section 4 'checklist is only the starting point: in many cases, extra factors will need to be considered'.[41]

Mental Capacity Act 2005 section 4

4(2) The person making the determination must consider all the relevant circumstances and, in particular, take the following steps.

(3) He must consider—

    (a) whether it is likely that the person will at some time have capacity in relation to the matter in question, and

    (b) if it appears likely that he will, when that is likely to be.

(4) He must, so far as reasonably practicable, permit and encourage the person to participate, or to improve his ability to participate, as fully as possible in any act done for him and any decision affecting him …

(6) He must consider, so far as is reasonably ascertainable—

    (a) the person's past and present wishes and feelings (and, in particular, any relevant written statement made by him when he had capacity),

    (b) the beliefs and values that would be likely to influence his decision if he had capacity, and

    (c) the other factors that he would be likely to consider if he were able to do so.

(7) He must take into account, if it is practicable and appropriate to consult them, the views of—

    (a) anyone named by the person as someone to be consulted on the matter in question or on matters of that kind,

    (b) anyone engaged in caring for the person or interested in his welfare,

    (c) any donee of a lasting power of attorney granted by the person, and

    (d) any deputy appointed for the person by the court,

as to what would be in the person's best interests and, in particular, as to the matters mentioned in subsection (6).

(i) Temporary incapacity

The 'best interests' test applies to all patients who lack capacity, and this is by no means a homogenous group. Someone who is unconscious when they arrive at A&E after an accident, or a patient who has been anaesthetized, is in a very different position from a patient in a permanent vegetative state. If a patient temporarily lacks capacity, a particularly important factor is that, under section 4(3), regard must be had to whether and when a person might be expected to regain capacity. This means that if the person's incapacity is likely to be short-lived, decisions should only be taken if it would not be possible to wait until she regains capacity: an example might be life-saving surgery carried out on a person who is unconscious after a road traffic accident.

Section 4(3) does not just apply to emergency treatment, however, and is also intended to capture the idea that, if capacity might be regained, consideration must be given to the possibility of delaying making a decision so that the patient can take the decision for herself. For example, a bipolar patient might lack capacity during a manic episode, but be expected to

[41] Para 5.6.

regain it once her condition stabilizes; section 4(3) means that only immediately necessary medical decisions should be taken while she is unwell.

(ii) Relevance of the patient's views

One striking feature of the MCA's best interests checklist is the emphasis it places on the patient's own views and beliefs. Of course, if a patient has never been able to express an opinion, her values may be unknown or non-existent, and the doctor's objective assessment of her clinical interests may take priority. But where there is any evidence of the factors that would matter to the patient herself, then her 'best interests' are not to be judged purely objectively, according to what the doctor believes to be clinically indicated. The Act recognizes that the patient's views and values are relevant to what is best for her.

The Act does not specify what weight should be given to the patient's wishes: they are important, but not necessarily decisive. There is no hierarchy of relevant factors and the weight given to different factors will vary according to the particular case. Nevertheless, Mary Donnelly has suggested that a decision to go against the preference of the person who lacks capacity now requires rigorous justification.

Mary Donnelly[42]

At a practical level, the participation requirement should, at a minimum, necessitate the acknowledgement, if this is the case, that the person lacking capacity has an alternative preference. This in turn should lead to a rigorous scrutiny of the evidence presented in favour of the argument that the decision-maker should act against this preference. It cannot be enough for a decision-maker simply to acknowledge the views of the person lacking capacity before reaching a decision which takes no account of these views.

In recent years, as we see again in Chapter 17 when we look at end-of-life decisions, the courts appear to be placing increasing emphasis upon the need to respect the patient's wishes, despite her lack of capacity. Of course, each decision in the Court of Protection is fact-specific, so comparing one decision in which a person's wishes were disregarded with a decision, in a different case, in which another person's wishes were decisive does not necessarily establish anything other than that the patients' situations were different.

Nevertheless, since the Supreme Court's judgment in *Aintree University Hospitals Foundation Trust v James*,[43] in 2013 (considered in detail in Chapter 17), the patient's wishes and feelings do appear to be carrying considerable weight when determining what is in their best interests. As Baroness Hale put it in her judgment, with which the other Justices agreed: 'The purpose of the best interests test is to consider matters from the patient's point of view … [I]n so far as it is possible to ascertain the patient's wishes and feelings, his beliefs and values or the things which were important to him, it is those which should be taken into account because they are a component in making the choice which is right for him as an individual human being.'

For example, in the pre-*Aintree* decision, *A Local Authority v E*, Peter Jackson J held that force-feeding would be in E's best interests, despite it being contrary to her clearly expressed wishes, and despite the fact that the treatment had only a modest chance of success and would involve 'a wholesale overwhelming of her autonomy' for an extended period of time.

---

[42] 'Best Interests, Patient Participation and the Mental Capacity Act 2005' (2009) 17 Medical Law Review 1–29.

[43] [2013] UKSC 67.

A Local Authority v E [44]

Peter Jackson J

E's wishes and feelings, as described above and written down by her in an attempt to control her treatment, are clear. They are not the slightest bit less real or felt merely because she does not have decision-making capacity. I agree with [counsel] that particular respect is due to the wishes and feelings of someone who, although lacking capacity, is as fully and articulately engaged as E.

E's views are entitled to high respect. She is not a child or a very young adult, but an intelligent and articulate woman, and the weight to be given to her view of her life is correspondingly greater.

I acknowledge the significant risks involved in treatment, not excepting a risk to life. I acknowledge the modest prospects of success and the wholesale and prolonged invasion of E's privacy and self-determination that is proposed. I acknowledge the high chance that, even if short-term progress can made, long-term difficulties will remain. I accept that E may recover capacity only to make a valid advance decision. I accept that a resumption of treatment deprives E of an imminent and relatively peaceful death. These are all weighty factors.

Against them, I place E's life in the other scale. We only live once—we are born once and we die once—and the difference between life and death is the biggest difference we know. E is a special person, whose life is of value. She does not see it that way now, but she may in future. I would not overrule her wishes if further treatment was futile, but it is not. Although extremely burdensome to E, there is a possibility that it will succeed.

Two years after *Aintree*, in *Wye Valley NHS Trust v B*, Peter Jackson J declared that it would not be in the best interests of a man who lacked capacity to amputate his foot against his wishes, despite the fact that, without amputation, Mr B would be likely to die within a few days. Peter Jackson J had visited Mr B in hospital, where he had been adamant that he did not want the operation: 'I don't want it. I'm not afraid of death. I don't want interference. Even if I'm going to die, I don't want the operation.' Peter Jackson J explained why it was important not to discount the beliefs and values of someone who lacked capacity.

Wye Valley NHS Trust v B [45]

Peter Jackson J

Where a patient lacks capacity it is accordingly of great importance to give proper weight to his wishes and feelings and to his beliefs and values. On behalf of the Trust in this case, Mr Sachdeva QC submitted that the views expressed by a person lacking capacity were in principle entitled to less weight than those of a person with capacity. This is in my view true only to the limited extent that the views of a capacitous person are by definition decisive in relation to any treatment that is being offered to him so that the question of best interests does not arise. However, once incapacity is established so that a best interests decision must be made, there is no theoretical limit to the weight or lack of weight that should be given to the person's wishes and feelings, beliefs and values ...

[44] [2012] EWHC 1639 (Fam).   [45] [2015] EWCOP 60.

This is not an academic issue, but a necessary protection for the rights of people with disabilities. As the Act and the European Convention make clear, a conclusion that a person lacks decision-making capacity is not an *'off-switch'* for his rights and freedoms. To state the obvious, the wishes and feelings, beliefs and values of people with a mental disability are as important to them as they are to anyone else, and may even be more important. It would therefore be wrong in principle to apply any automatic discount to their point of view …

Mr B has had a hard life. Through no fault of his own, he has suffered in his mental health for half a century. He is a sociable man who has experienced repeated losses so that he has become isolated. He has no next of kin. No one has ever visited him in hospital and no one ever will. Yet he is a proud man who sees no reason to prefer the views of others to his own. His religious beliefs are deeply meaningful to him and do not deserve to be described as delusions: they are his faith and they are an intrinsic part of who he is. I would not define Mr B by reference to his mental illness or his religious beliefs. Rather, his core quality is his *'fierce independence'*, and it is this that is now, as he sees it, under attack....

I am quite sure that it would not be in Mr B's best interests to take away his little remaining independence and dignity in order to replace it with a future for which he understandably has no appetite and which could only be achieved after a traumatic and uncertain struggle that he and no one else would have to endure. There is a difference between fighting on someone's behalf and just fighting them. Enforcing treatment in this case would surely be the latter.

A few months later, Mostyn J also decided to visit the patient who lacked capacity before making his decision. In *A Hospital NHS Trust v CD*, a case we consider in the next chapter when we look at the Deprivation of Liberty Safeguards, he explained why it had been an enlightening experience.

A Hospital NHS Trust v CD[46]

Mostyn J

I took the view that it would be right if I were to meet CD face to face and I did so at the mental hospital on the first day of the hearing. It was an enlightening experience and one which I would recommend to any judge hearing a similar case. Mr Justice Jackson met Mr B and it is obvious from his judgment that the encounter was critically valuable. The reason it was enlightening for me was that the person I met was different in many respects to the person described in the papers. CD was engaging and polite. She was articulate. She was amusing. She listened carefully to questions and answered them equally carefully. True, there were comments that suggested powerful delusional forces; and Dr FH explained that she was heavily medicated. But even so, the person I met was a world away from the violent sociopath described in the papers.

Although it is clear that the court can accord particular weight to the person's wishes and beliefs, the section 4 checklist gives decision-makers discretion over how much weight they should have in the particular circumstances. In its 2015 report on mental capacity, mentioned earlier, the Law Commission also proposed that, in the absence of good reasons not to follow them, there should be an assumption that the person's wishes and feelings should be determinative.

---

[46] [2015] EWCOP 74.

Law Commission[47]

12.42 However, we are concerned that the law fails to give sufficient certainty for best interest decision-makers on how much emphasis should be given to the person's wishes and feelings. On the one hand, it can be said that there is no hierarchy between the various factors listed in section 4. This was clearly the policy intention behind the legislation. On the other hand, the Supreme Court has clarified in the *Aintree* case that best interests requires consideration of matters from the person's point of view and that the person's wishes and feelings are an important factor, arguably attaching some level of primacy to this factor. Similarly, in some cases the Court of Protection has gone to great lengths to make the decision the person would have wanted. But equally, in other cases, the outcomes have been expressly inconsistent with what the person wants or would have wanted. . . .

12.45 We therefore provisionally propose that section 4 of the Mental Capacity Act should be amended to attach a level of primacy to a person's wishes and feelings. Their precise legal status might range from making them a 'primary consideration' for decision-makers, to simply directing that they be given effect to, unless impractical. We provisionally consider that an intermediate option would be appropriate. Under this approach there would be an assumption that the person's wishes and feelings are determinative as to their best interests, although this assumption could be overridden where there are good reasons to do so.

It should be remembered that patients with capacity do not have the right to demand access to treatment. Similarly, the preferences of a person who lacks capacity, however strongly held, cannot force a doctor to provide treatment contrary to her professional judgement.

For example, in *AVS v NHS Foundation Trust*, the patient had, while competent, executed a lasting power of attorney (discussed later) in favour of his brother and had discussed with him his desire for all possible steps to be taken to prolong his life. The patient suffered from sporadic Creutzfeldt-Jakob disease (sCJD), and was, at the time of the hearing, close to death. His brother had researched the condition on the internet, and had discovered a 2002 paper by a Japanese neuropathologist which appeared to show some success with PPS (Pentosan Polysulphate) in rodents and dogs affected by a similar condition. His brother was adamant that the patient would want to receive this experimental treatment. If his brother had been able to identify a clinician who was willing to carry out PPS treatment, there would have been no issue for the court to decide. Because no clinician willing to provide this treatment could be found, Wall LJ explained that seeking a declaration that it would be in the patient's best interests would not only be academic, but would amount to an abuse of process.

AVS v NHS Foundation Trust[48]

Wall LJ

A declaration of the kind sought will not force the respondent hospital to provide treatment against their clinicians' clinical judgment. To use a declaration of the court to twist the arm of some other clinician, as yet unidentified, to carry out these procedures or to put pressure upon the Secretary of State to provide a hospital where these procedures may be

---

[47] *Mental Capacity and Deprivation of Liberty: A Consultation Paper* (Law Commission, 2015).
[48] [2011] EWCA Civ 7.

undertaken is an abuse of the process of the court and should not be tolerated.... If there are clinicians out there prepared to treat the patient then the patient will be discharged into their care and there would be no need for court intervention. If there is no-one available to undertake the necessary operation the question of whether or not it would be in the patient's best interests for that to happen is wholly academic and the process should be called to a halt here and now.

It is also important to remember that the fact that the court decides that a particular treatment is in a person's best interests does not override clinical judgement. If a court declares that treatment without consent would be in a patient's best interests, it is not ordering that treatment to take place. If the doctors subsequently decide that it would not, in fact, be in the patient's best interests to proceed, the declaration would not force them to do so. A declaration is enabling rather than obligatory.

An NHS Trust v K was a complex case in which the court decided that it would be lawful (but not obligatory) not only to perform a hysterectomy, but also to sedate a 61-year-old woman suffering from a psychotic disorder and schizophrenia, before telling her about the operation. Mrs K suffered from delusions: she was convinced that she did not have cancer, and that she was 20 years old with a boyfriend with whom she was having or would like to have an active sexual relationship.

The operation to treat Mrs K's cancer had a good chance of success, but the risks were greater than normal due to her obesity and other co-morbidities, and to the likelihood of her non-compliance with the post-operative regime. Given Mrs K's opposition to the proposed treatment, Holman J was candid about the fact that the treating clinicians still had to exercise their professional judgement before sedating her and going ahead with the operation: in reality, they had a power of veto over his judgement that the operation was in her best interests. Indeed, Holman J went further and suggested that if her devoted sons also changed their mind about the operation being in their mother's best interests, the operation should not go ahead without further consideration by the court.

An NHS Trust v K[49]

Holman J

No one, nor any court, can order or require any doctor to take any step. The court can only permit it. It follows, of course, as I wish to make crystal clear, that my intended order will permit and render lawful the procedures described, notwithstanding the lack of consent of the patient. Right up to the last moment, however, it must remain a matter for the individual professional judgement of Dr. VB and Mr. J whether they think it justifiable to embark on the sedation, the anaesthesia and the surgery. Each of them has, therefore, a practical power of veto....

I have paid considerable regard to the position and views of the three sons, which I respect. They are not doctors but they know their mother well and each of them would be heavily involved during her recovery and convalescence. I do not make the declarations because they ask me to do so; but I might well have refused to make the declarations if they had raised any reasoned opposition to them.

[49] [2012] EWHC 2922 (COP).

> Circumstances may change. They may reassess issues, such as the mental state of their mother or her likely post-operative compliance. For that reason, although the operation does not require their consent, there must be a temporary brake upon it if any of them notifies the doctors, making reference to the relevant part of the court order, that he no longer considers that the operation should take place. I stress that all these powers of veto or brakes are temporary, not absolute. They would halt the process but would not preclude further consideration by the court (myself if possible) in the light of the changed circumstances.

(iii) Consulting others

Aside from formally appointing someone with a lasting power of attorney, discussed later, under section 4(7) carers and family members must be consulted in order to elicit information about the patient's values and beliefs. A doctor should only proceed without consultation if it would not be 'practicable and appropriate'. In *Winspear v City Hospitals Sunderland NHS Foundation Trust*, a DNACPR (do not attempt cardio-pulmonary resuscitation) notice had been placed upon Carl Winspear's notes at 3 am. It was cancelled when his mother became aware of it, and had no impact on Carl's death later that day, but the failure to consult his mother failed to meet the requirements of section 4(7), and, since it was not in accordance with the law, amounted to a breach of Article 8.

Winspear v City Hospitals Sunderland NHS Foundation Trust[50]

Blake J

In the case of persons who lack capacity, the MCA spells out when and with whom a decision taker must consult; if it is not 'practicable or appropriate' to consult a person identified in s 4(7) before the decision is made or acted on, then there would be a convincing reason to proceed without consultation.

If, on the other hand, it is both practicable and appropriate to consult then in the absence of some other compelling reason against consultation, the decision to file the DNACPR notice on the patient's medical records would be procedurally flawed. It would not meet the requirements of s4(7) MCA; it would accordingly not be in accordance with the law. It would be an interference that is not justified under Article 8(2) for two reasons:

  (i) a decision that is not taken 'in accordance with law' cannot justify an interference with the right to respect afforded under Article 8(1);

  (ii) if consultation was appropriate and practicable there is no convincing reason to depart from it as an important part of the procedural obligations inherent in Article 8.

I can see every reason why a telephone call at 3.00am may be less than convenient or desirable than a meeting in working hours, but that is not the same as whether it is practicable.

There may, of course, be a tension between the duty to consult others and the principle of patient confidentiality, considered in more detail in Chapter 7. The Code of Practice makes it clear that section 4(7) does not suspend the incapacitated person's right to confidentiality,

[50] [2015] EWHC 3250 (QB).

but rather that health care professionals need to balance the duty to consult with the duty to respect confidentiality:

Mental Capacity Act Code of Practice

5.56 Decision-makers must balance the duty to consult other people with the right to confidentiality of the person who lacks capacity. So if confidential information is to be discussed, they should only seek the views of people who it is appropriate to consult, where their views are relevant to the decision to be made and the particular circumstances.

It is possible that family members will disagree about what the patient would have wanted. The Code of Practice advocates trying to reach agreement, involving the person who lacks capacity as far as possible, but ultimately responsibility for deciding what treatment is in a patient's best interests lies with the doctor.[51]

Of course, there will be times when a patient's apparent wishes have to be viewed in the light of the influence others may have over them. This was the case in *A Primary Care Trust v P*, in which P's mother, AH, who was extremely close to her son, held eccentric views on the appropriate treatment of his uncontrolled epilepsy. As a result, Sir Mark Potter P held that it was in P's best interests to be admitted as an inpatient, so that his condition could be assessed in the absence of his mother.

A Primary Care Trust v P[52]

Sir Mark Potter P

The real difficulty in this case has been, and continues to be, that, such is the closeness of the relationship between P and AH, his mother and carer, that . . . there is real and unresolved doubt as to how far P's expressed views as to where, by whom, and in what manner he wishes or is prepared to accept treatment, are his own, and how far they are no more than simple adoption and repetition of his mother's views in a situation where he would otherwise be malleable and co-operative with the attempts of the experts to understand the true aetiology and interrelationship of his various symptoms and to relieve P from what is now largely a wheelchair bound existence.

In order to perform an overall assessment, reach an holistic diagnosis, and set in train an appropriate course of treatment in respect of P's condition, it is necessary for him to be assessed as an in-patient over a substantial period, during which he is seen, observed and treated as an individual patient rather than on the basis of his symptoms and condition as reported or recounted in the presence and under the influence of his mother. This is particularly so because, despite her genuine and praiseworthy concerns, AH holds views which, so far as medical orthodoxy is concerned, are in many respects eccentric, misguided and, in the view of the experts, positively harmful rather than helpful in relation to the diagnosis and treatment of P.

Mary Donnelly has argued that care must be taken to ensure that reports of a person's previously expressed views in fact represent their wishes. Elderly patients, for example, may have made vague and ambiguous statements about not wanting to be a burden, but these may have been prompted by a wish for comfort and reassurance, rather than representing a considered view about their future medical treatment.

---

[51] Para 5.64.   [52] [2008] EWHC 1403 (Fam).

Mary Donnelly[53]

> While the consultative model is a good one, it is important to remember that even close friends or family members cannot always know the past preferences or the relevant beliefs and values of the person lacking capacity. Statements such as 'I would rather die than be dependent' may reflect a desire for reassurance, or may be a result of temporary depression or fear, and may not represent the person's considered views on future care should they lose capacity.

For patients who do not have close friends or family, sections 35 to 37 provide for the appointment of an Independent Mental Capacity Advocate (IMCA) to support and represent them. Under section 37(3), an IMCA must be appointed before a person is given 'serious medical treatment', if no close family member or friend is available to consult about his wishes or feelings. The Mental Capacity Act 2005 (Independent Mental Capacity Advocate) (General) Regulations 2006 set out in detail how and when IMCAs should be appointed, their functions, and their role in challenging decisions. They also define 'serious medical treatment':

Mental Capacity Act 2005 (Independent Mental Capacity Advocate) (General) Regulations 2006 regulation 4

> 4(2) Serious medical treatment is treatment which involves providing, withdrawing or withholding treatment in circumstances where—
>
> (a) in a case where a single treatment is being proposed, there is a fine balance between its benefits to the patient and the burdens and risks it is likely to entail for him,
>
> (b) in a case where there is a choice of treatments, a decision as to which one to use is finely balanced, or
>
> (c) what is proposed would be likely to involve serious consequences for the patient.

The Code of Practice gives some examples of serious medical treatment, including treatment for cancer, electroconvulsive therapy, major surgery, termination of pregnancy, and withholding artificial nutrition and hydration. If the treatment is needed urgently in an emergency, an IMCA need not be appointed, although this should be done for any follow-up serious treatment.

The IMCA is specifically charged with trying to elicit the person's wishes and values, and with ensuring that they have been given all the support they need to be involved in decision-making.

Mental Capacity Act 2005 (Independent Mental Capacity Advocate) (General) Regulations 2006 regulation 6

> 6(5) The IMCA must evaluate all the information he has obtained for the purpose of—
>
> (a) ascertaining the extent of the support provided to P to enable him to participate in making any decision about the matter in relation to which the IMCA has been instructed;

[53] 'Best Interests, Patient Participation and the Mental Capacity Act 2005' (2009) 17 Medical Law Review 1–29.

(b) ascertaining what P's wishes and feelings would be likely to be, and the beliefs and values that would be likely to influence P, if he had capacity in relation to the proposed act or decision;

(c) ascertaining what alternative courses of action are available in relation to P;

(d) where medical treatment is proposed for P, ascertaining whether he would be likely to benefit from a further medical opinion.

(iv) Not just medical best interests

It is evident that the best interests test accommodates factors other than the patient's immediate clinical needs, and can also take account of their emotional and welfare interests, or even, in some cases, the interests of others. The Code of Practice gives an example of taking a blood sample from someone who lacks capacity when investigating a familial genetic predisposition to cancer.

When the Mental Capacity Bill was debated in Parliament, the BMA had raised the question of HIV testing after a health care worker has suffered a needlestick injury. If the patient is found to be HIV positive, the health care worker could receive post-exposure prophylaxis treatment in order to prevent infection. Testing the incapacitated patient will usually also be in her own best interests, so that she can receive treatment. If, however, the patient is unlikely to recover, a blood sample taken for the purposes of HIV testing would not be in her best interests. Instead it might be justified by the claim that the patient herself would, if competent, have agreed to have a blood sample taken in order to protect the health of those treating her.

Perhaps the clearest example of a case in which non-clinical factors have determined the question of whether medical treatment was in a person's best interests was *An NHS Trust v DE*. This was the first case in which a court had declared that it would be in the best interests of a man who lacked capacity to be sterilized. Not only was DE clear that he did not want to have any more children, but also a vasectomy would enable DE to re-establish the independence he had achieved before his girlfriend PQ had become pregnant three years previously. Eleanor King also found that DE would benefit from the relief a vasectomy would bring to his parents, FG and JK, whose anxiety DE found distressing.

An NHS Trust v DE[54]

Eleanor King J

Section 4(6)(c) requires the court to take into account other factors which DE would be likely to consider if he were able to go so; the so called 'substituted judgment' test although it is but one factor with 'best interests' the final test. In this context the court must take into account the Mental Capacity Act Code of Practice para 5.48 which allow actions that benefit other people, as long as they are in the best interests of the person who lacks capacity. DE is very close to his parents; he loves and relies upon them. If they are upset he is upset. The court can take into account the benefits to FG and JK of DE having a vasectomy if it is a factor DE would consider if he had capacity. It is likely that DE would consider the benefit to his parents of relieving them of the anxiety and strain that they have been suffering and of which he has been very conscious....

---

[54] [2013] EWHC 2562 (Fam).

> Such a benefit to the parents would be of significant benefit to DE, not only because he would benefit from them being happier and less anxious, but also because relieved of the anxiety of a second pregnancy, I am satisfied that JK would feel able significantly to relax the level of supervision she felt to be necessary and that, despite her general misgivings about PQ, would once again promote and support the relationship as she did prior to the pregnancy ...
>
> PQ's pregnancy followed by the interim declaration that DE did not have the capacity to consent to sexual relations has had very serious consequences for DE, resulting in his losing, for a period, all autonomy and his being supervised at all times. Whilst there has been some easing of supervision, his life is still very different from his life before XY was born and he is still never alone with PQ....
>
> It is simply stating the obvious to observe that DE's quality of life is incomparably better when he can go and have a coffee in town with PQ or go to the local gym with his friend....
>
> In my judgment DE's hard earned achievements, whether learning to swim by imitation as he can't process spoken instruction, or getting a bus on his own must be treasured, valued and measured in the same terms as the winning of an Iron Man or completing the Paris to Peking rally would be for a person without his disabilities.

In *DE*'s case, there were many factors on the 'benefits' side of the balancing exercise that Eleanor King J undertook, including his wishes and his future freedom of movement. But it is especially interesting that a factor in favour of the operation was that DE was also likely to benefit from the relief it would bring to his parents.

In a pre-Mental Capacity Act case, *Re Y (Mental Patient: Bone Marrow Donation)*, acting as a bone marrow donor to her desperately ill sister was held to be in the best interests of a severely mentally handicapped adult. There could be no possible clinical benefit to Y from undergoing an uncomfortable procedure in order to donate bone marrow to her sister. Rather, the donation would be of immeasurable benefit to Y's mother (who was already in poor health), as well as to her sister, who might otherwise die. Because it would help to maintain her relationships with her mother and sister, the operation was said to be for Y's 'emotional, psychological and social benefit'.

Re Y (Mental Patient: Bone Marrow Donation)[55]

Connell J

Accordingly, it is to the benefit of the defendant that she should act as donor to her sister, because in this way her positive relationship with her mother is most likely to be prolonged. Further, if the transplant occurs, this is likely to improve the defendant's relationship with her mother who in her heart clearly wishes it to take place and also to improve her relationship with the plaintiff who will be eternally grateful to her.

It is doubtful that this case would act as a useful precedent in cases where the surgery involved is more intrusive than in this case, where the evidence shows that the bone marrow harvested is speedily regenerated and that a healthy individual can donate as much as two pints with no long-term consequences at all.

[55] [1996] 2 FLR 787.

Where the proposed procedure would benefit someone else, it is, as the Code of Practice makes clear, especially important to be clear that the purpose of seeking the views of family members is to find out what the person herself would have wanted.

Mental Capacity Act Code of Practice

> 4.49 . . . Family members and close friends may be able to provide valuable background information . . . But their personal views and wishes about what *they* would want for the person must not influence the assessment.

Against this, Jonathan Herring and Charles Foster would contest whether it is either possible or desirable to try to isolate the interests of the person who lacks capacity from those of her family members. Because acting altruistically is fundamentally good, they question whether Connell J needed to establish that donating bone marrow would benefit Y. Rather, they argue that acting altruistically towards people with whom one has relationships is inherently, and not merely instrumentally, part of a person's best interests.

Jonathan Herring and Charles Foster[56]

> If a patient has context—has relationships—she necessarily has obligations to those to whom she relates. . . . Thus acting morally towards others is a central part of ensuring her own best interests . . .
>
> It is morally right to be altruistic, and it is in the best interests of the donor to do the morally right thing. . . . Doing the right thing is an important part of living as a properly oriented human being: it is an important part of human thriving. A judge's job in determining best interests can more accurately be described as maximising the flourishing of the human in question. Flourishing people are altruistic people.

(v) Exceptions to the best interests test

There are two exceptions to the requirement that treatment given to a person who lacks capacity must be in their best interests. First, it is possible for someone who lacks capacity to participate in research, when the purpose is not necessarily to benefit the individual patient. We deal with this issue in Chapter 9.

Secondly, as we see in the following section, valid and applicable advance refusals of treatment are binding and must be complied with, even if they force a doctor to refrain from giving treatment which she believes to be in the patient's best interests. The Code of Practice spells this out.

Mental Capacity Act Code of Practice

> 9.36 Where an advance decision is being followed, the best interests principle does not apply. This is because an advance decision reflects the decision of an adult with capacity who has made the decision for themselves. Healthcare professionals must follow a valid and applicable advance decision, even if they think it goes against a person's best interests.

---

[56] 'Welfare means Relationality, Virtue and Altruism' (2012) 32 Legal Studies 480.

(5) Advance Decisions

Advance decisions (ADs) are defined in section 24.

Mental Capacity Act 2005 section 24

24(1) 'Advance decision' is a decision made by a person ('P'), after he has reached 18 and when he has capacity to do so, that if—

(a) at a later time and in such circumstances as he may specify, a specified treatment is proposed to be carried out or continued by a person providing health care for him, and

(b) at that time he lacks capacity to consent to the carrying out or continuation of the treatment, the specified treatment is not to be carried out or continued.

Section 24(1) specifies that ADs must have been made when an adult had capacity, and must specify which treatment should not be carried out or continued when P lacks capacity. ADs are advance refusals of treatment. An advance request for treatment would be relevant under section 4(6)(a) when deciding what is in a person's best interests, but not decisive.

In line with the first statutory principle, the assumption should be, as the Code of Practice makes clear, that the person did have capacity when she made the advance decision:

Mental Capacity Act Code of Practice para 9.8

9.8 In line with principle 1 of the Act, that 'a person must be assumed to have capacity unless it is established that he lacks capacity', healthcare professionals should always start from the assumption that a person who has made an advance decision had capacity to make it, unless they are aware of reasonable grounds to doubt the person had the capacity to make the advance decision at the time they made it.

In practice, however, if someone suffers from a condition that might have affected their capacity when they made their AD, doubt may be cast on whether or not they had capacity.

In *A Local Authority v E*, for example, E had attempted to execute an AD refusing force-feeding but, despite her psychiatrist's view that she had capacity at the time, Peter Jackson J held that she did not, and hence it was not a binding AD for the purposes of the Act. In E's case, given her long history of anorexia, the presumption of capacity appeared to have been converted into a presumption of incapacity, which could be rebutted only if there had been a thorough capacity assessment when she signed her AD. The subsequent evidence of her consultant psychiatrist was insufficient, instead, according to Peter Jackson J, 'a full, reasoned and contemporaneous assessment evidencing mental capacity to make such a momentous decision would in my view be necessary'.

In the next extract, Rob Heywood reflects upon the fact that the MCA does not require a capacity assessment to have taken place when an AD is made. Although there are good reasons for this omission, it inevitably leaves many ADs vulnerable to subsequent challenge.

Rob Heywood[57]

Amid the range of formalities that were included in the Mental Capacity Act 2005, what mechanisms are in place within the legislation to ensure that a patient is competent at the time they actually draft their advance decision? The answer is, quite simply, none. . . .

The law may have also resisted requiring a formal assessment of capacity for a number of other reasons. First, it would be in direct conflict with the golden thread that runs through the Mental Capacity Act 2005, the presumption of capacity. Requiring an assessment of a patient's capacity by a witness as a prerequisite to validating the advance decision reverses this and works from the starting position that patients are incapable of exercising their right of choice before someone else confirms they are capable of doing so. . . .

[I]t would certainly add a further and perhaps unwelcome layer of complexity to insist that the witness must be a trained professional with expertise in assessing capacity. It stands to reason that this would inhibit access by making the process of creating an advance decision more costly, time-consuming, and bureaucratic. Yet, as the law stands, we are still left with a situation in which the central feature of the advance decision, the feature which gives it teeth, is left untested and this will always render it vulnerable to attack.

Anyone who suffers from a condition which might affect their capacity would therefore be well advised not to rely upon the presumption of capacity, but instead to ensure that a doctor specifically certifies that they have capacity when they make their AD.

With one important exception—refusals of life-saving treatment must be signed and witnessed—there are no particular formalities that have to be satisfied for an advance decision to be valid. In practice, however, it is advisable to put ADs in writing, since this makes it easier to be certain about the person's wishes. Under section 24(2), it is enough for the treatment that P wishes to refuse to be described in layman's terms.

A person can withdraw or alter their AD at any time when he has capacity to do so, and under section 24(4) and (5), withdrawals and alterations do not have to be in writing, although once again certainty will be promoted if the patient has documented any variation or withdrawal.

Section 25(1) specifies that, to be effective, an AD must be both *valid* and *applicable to the treatment*. If a decision is both valid and applicable, then under section 26(1) 'the decision has effect as if he had made it, and had had capacity to make it, at the time when the question arises whether the treatment should be carried out or continued': that is, it is like a contemporaneous refusal and the person can refuse treatment for rational reasons, irrational reasons, or no reasons at all.

(a) Validity

Section 25(2) sets out when an AD will not be valid.

Mental Capacity Act 2005 section 25

25(2) An advance decision is not valid if P—

(a) has withdrawn the decision at a time when he had capacity to do so,

---

[57] 'Revisiting Advance Decision Making Under the Mental Capacity Act 2005: A Tale of Mixed Messages (2015) 23 Medical Law Review 81–102.

(b) has, under a lasting power of attorney created after the advance decision was made, conferred authority on the donee (or, if more than one, any of them) to give or refuse consent to the treatment to which the advance decision relates, or

(c) has done anything else clearly inconsistent with the advance decision remaining his fixed decision.

Hence, to be valid, there must be no evidence that the P has either withdrawn the decision or conferred authority in relation to the relevant treatment on a donee via a lasting power of attorney.

Under section 25(2)(c) the decision is not valid if the P has acted in a way which is 'clearly inconsistent' with the decision. What does this mean? One obvious example might be if someone has explicitly renounced the religious beliefs upon which their previous refusal was based.

Of course, it may be difficult in practice to tell whether a person's subsequent actions are 'clearly inconsistent' with her AD. The Act does not specify whether the actions that invalidate the AD under section 25(2)(c) must have occurred while P had capacity, or whether conduct after capacity was lost could also invalidate an AD. On the one hand, the failure to specify when the 'clearly inconsistent' actions should take place would seem to lead to the conclusion that any inconsistent conduct should invalidate the decision. Yet, on the other hand, section 24(3) specifies that P may withdraw or alter an AD only 'when he has capacity to do so', so it would be odd if someone who lacks capacity could invalidate her previous AD simply by acting inconsistently with it.

The Code of Practice recommends that patients should be advised to regularly review and update their ADs because a recently reviewed decision is more likely to be found valid than if a considerable period of time has elapsed since it was made.

(b) Applicability

Section 25(3)–(6) specifies when an advance decision will not be applicable.

Mental Capacity Act 2005 section 25

25(3) An advance decision is not applicable to the treatment in question if at the material time P has capacity to give or refuse consent to it.

(4) An advance decision is not applicable to the treatment in question if—

(a) that treatment is not the treatment specified in the advance decision,

(b) any circumstances specified in the advance decision are absent, or

(c) there are reasonable grounds for believing that circumstances exist which P did not anticipate at the time of the advance decision and which would have affected his decision had he anticipated them.

An AD will therefore lapse if the person regains capacity. It is also necessary that the AD precisely covers the situation in which the P now finds himself, and that there has not been a change of circumstances which casts doubt upon whether the AD reflects the P's views. An example might be where a patient executes an advance refusal of a particular medication because she finds its side effects intolerable. If, in the mean-time, a new version has been developed which does not have those side effects, there may be reasonable grounds for believing that this would have affected the patient's decision

When deciding whether an AD is applicable, the Code of Practice recommends that health care professionals consider a number of factors.

Mental Capacity Act Code of Practice

9.43 So when deciding whether an advance decision applies to the proposed treatment, healthcare professionals must consider:

- how long ago the advance decision was made, and
- whether there have been changes in the patient's personal life (for example, the person is pregnant, and this was not anticipated when they made the advance decision) that might affect the validity of the advance decision, and
- whether there have been developments in medical treatment that the person did not foresee (for example, new medications, treatment or therapies).

The Code of Practice recommends that, when drawing up an AD, it is important to try to anticipate as many eventualities as possible, in order to avoid doubt about whether it applies in the circumstances that have arisen.

Mental Capacity Act Code of Practice

9.16 It is a good idea to try to include possible future circumstances in the advance decision. For example, a woman may want to state in the advance decision whether or not it should still apply if she later becomes pregnant. If the document does not anticipate a change in circumstance, healthcare professionals may decide that it is not applicable if those particular circumstances arise.

Again, it is advisable for people to regularly update their ADs, in order to minimize the chance that it will have been invalidated by changes in circumstances.

Mental Capacity Act Code of Practice

9.29 . . . Decisions made a long time in advance are not automatically invalid or inapplicable, but they may raise doubts when deciding whether they are valid and applicable. A written decision that is regularly reviewed is more likely to be valid and applicable to current circumstances—particularly for progressive illnesses. This is because it is more likely to have taken on board changes that have occurred in a person's life since they made their decision.

It is unclear whether section 25(4)(c) could apply to a scenario in which a now demented individual appears to be contented and does not want to die, despite having issued an otherwise binding AD refusing life-sustaining treatment. Is the fact that he appears to be happy despite his dementia a circumstance 'which P did not anticipate at the time of the advance decision and which would have affected his decision'? If interpreted in this way, the scope of section 25(4)(c) is potentially extremely broad since it would almost always be possible to argue that the patient issued their AD in a state of relative ignorance about what it would actually be like to be incapacitated.

As well as the practical problem of working out whether the AD covers the circumstances which have arisen and reflects the patient's wishes, some people have suggested that there may be more fundamental problems with respecting ADs made before a person really knows what it would be like to lack capacity.

Rebecca Dresser and Allen Buchanan, for example, have argued that profound incapacity may sever the 'psychological continuity' between the competent individual who issued the AD, and the person who now lacks capacity and requires life support, meaning that the incapacitated person should not necessarily be bound by her previous self's wishes.

Rebecca Dresser[58]

If little or no psychological connectedness and continuity exist between the individual at the two points in time, then there is no particular reason why the past person, as opposed to any other person, should determine the present person's fate.

Allen Buchanan[59]

[The] very process that renders the individual incompetent and brings the advance directive into play can—and indeed often does—destroy the conditions necessary for her personal identity and thereby undercuts entirely the moral authority of the directive . . .

So long as the degree of psychological continuity which we take to be necessary for the preservation of personal identity is present, the advance directive has full moral authority . . . [But] presumably a point is eventually reached at which the degree of psychological continuity between the author of the advance directive and the incompetent individual is so small that the advance directive of the former has no authority at all over the latter.

The idea that the adult who lacks capacity should not be bound by their previously competent self's AD is a controversial one. Ronald Dworkin, for example, has said that ADs express values that we should continue to respect because the person who lacks capacity is not just a collection of current interests, but rather is a person with a past.[60] Similarly, Nancy Rhoden has argued that the 'notion that a person is one person, and one person only, from birth through old age, despite whatever changes and vicissitudes she might undergo' is 'deeply embedded in our culture'.

Nancy K Rhoden[61]

If we are to make decisions about them as persons, we must view them not only as they are in the present, but also as the persons they were—persons who had strong opinions about

---

[58] Rebecca Dresser, 'Life, Death, and Incompetent Patients: Conceptual Infirmities and Hidden Values in the Law' (1986) 28 Arizona Law Review 380–1, 373.

[59] 'Advance directives and the personal identity problem' (1988) Philosophy and Public Affairs 131–54.

[60] Ronald Dworkin, 'Autonomy and the demented self' (1986) 64 Milbank Quarterly 4, 14 (Supp II).

[61] 'Litigating Life and Death' (1988) 102 Harvard Law Review 375, 414.

> how their body, even when insensate, should be treated . . . We must see the person as she, when competent, would have imagined herself after incompetency, rather than viewing her from the outside and as she is now . . .
>
> [A]n entirely present-oriented view is a bad way to view even persons who left no living will; it is unlikely that they would want to be viewed just as a body that can experience only physical sensations . . . Considering the patient only in the immediate present divides the patient from her past, her history, her values, and her relationships—from all those things that make her human.

Let us imagine a practical example. As a healthy university teacher, I may view the prospect of dementia with horror, and I might decide that should I become severely demented, and suffer a life-threatening infection, I would not want to be treated with antibiotics. I might then execute an unambiguous AD to that effect. But what if, once I am demented, I seem to be able to gain pleasure (which previously seemed unimaginable) from my severely impaired existence. Perhaps I spend my days apparently enjoying watching the Teletubbies, as the philosopher and author Iris Murdoch was said to have done.[62] If I develop a serious, but easily treatable infection, should doctors withhold antibiotics, in accordance with my AD?

In the next extract, Inez de Beaufort explains why she would want her previously competent wishes to take priority.

Inez de Beaufort[63]

> For me, the thought of my children spending their precious time visiting me when I do not recognize them is very painful, as is the idea that I know that they would suffer from that situation. Their suffering would, in my view, not be compensated by any interest I have in continuing my life. They will be sad because they knew me as the person I was, and feel powerless in not being able to save me from this fate. The fact that I consider this, and take their future feelings at heart in viewing my possible future is an essential part of me, of who I am and what I value.
>
> When I am demented, I may enjoy the visit of my 'mother' or whomever I think is visiting me, and I may be genuinely pleased about that. But the purpose and point of my AED [advance euthanasia directive] is precisely that I do not want to end up in the situation of someone who cannot be there for her loved ones anymore . . . The argument that you will be another you, and you will experience things differently when you are demented, does not convince me. To the contrary, because what I want to prevent is precisely this fact that I will experience things differently. I do not want to become someone who does not recognize her children anymore even if the demented-me would not suffer from not recognizing them anymore.

If all ADs were subjected to a 'present best interests' review, whereby the AD is not binding if it conflicts with what seems to be in the person's best interests now, there would, as Michalowski points out, be little point in making an AD, since exactly the same decision would be taken in its absence. The main reason for executing an AD is precisely because one fears that decisions taken in the future, which would be governed by the best interests test, might not coincide with how one would want to be treated.

---

62 John Bayley, *Iris: A Memoir of Iris Murdoch* (Abacus: London, 1999).
63 'The view from before' (2007) 7 American Journal of Bioethics 57–8.

Sabine Michalowski[64]

> To disregard the decision made by the competent patient because it violates the general (or one person's) perception of the patient's present interests would mean that the validity of an advance directive is subjected to a 'present best interests' assessment exercised by a third party at the time a treatment decision needs to be made. Advance directives would then no longer be a means by which a patient can ensure that his/her own subjective values govern his/her medical treatment towards the end of life.

The law is clear that valid and applicable ADs do not have to be in P's present best interests, and that they are binding even if they are contrary to unanimous medical opinion about what would now be best for P. In practice, however, because P now lacks capacity, there will often be some room for doubt over whether all of the various requirements are satisfied, and this doubt could be relied upon in order to disregard an AD. In *A Local Authority v A*, Peter Jackson J found that E had lacked capacity when she made her AD, even though there was evidence that could have been relied upon in order to come to a contrary conclusion. In contrast, in *X Primary Care Trust v XB*, despite failing accurately to describe the treatment that XB wished to refuse, Theis J found that his AD was binding. A contrary decision, namely that his AD was not precisely applicable to these circumstances, might also have been open to Theis J.

X Primary Care Trust v XB[65]

Theis J

> In places, the terms of the advance decision that was agreed to by him and signed on his behalf by YB and witnessed by XW and AW are not always clear. But I am satisfied it is more likely than not on the evidence I have read and heard that that does not undermine what XB intended; for example, the term 'non invasive ventilation' was not in fact what XB was having ... He has invasive ventilation, and has had this since 2003. But XW was very clear in his oral evidence that what was being discussed with XB in his presence and what he agreed to was the removal of his 'Nippy' device, which is the invasive ventilation he has had for over eight years.

(c) Advance refusals of life-saving treatment

Section 25(5) and (6) set out additional requirements for advance refusals of life-sustaining treatment. The P must specifically acknowledge that he intends to refuse treatment even if this puts his life at risk; the decision must be in writing and signed by P, or a representative in P's presence, and the signature must be witnessed.

These requirements are important in practice because it is precisely this sort of treatment that most people who seek to make 'living wills' want to refuse. Few people will execute advance decisions in order to refuse mundane or trivial treatments. Rather, a person might want to execute an advance refusal of blood transfusions on religious grounds, or, more commonly, they might want to set out when they wish to stop receiving

---

[64] 'Advance Refusals of Life Sustaining Treatment' (2005) 68 Modern Law Review 958.
[65] [2012] EWHC 1390 (Fam).

artificial nutrition or hydration, or when they do not want to be resuscitated, or to be treated in the event of contracting an infection. In all these cases, they would be refusing life-sustaining treatment and the refusal must therefore be in writing, signed, and witnessed.

Without legal advice, then, it is likely that many advance refusals will be invalid, as was the case in *An NHS v D*.[66] In this case, D, who was now in a permanent vegetative state, had put his wishes in a signed written letter, and they could not have been clearer:

> I refuse any medical treatment of an invasive nature (including but not restrictive to placing a feeding tube in my stomach) if said procedure is only for the purpose of extending a reduced quality of life. By reduced quality of life, I mean one where my life would be one of a significantly reduced quality, with little or no hope of any meaningful recovery, where I would be in a nursing home/care home with little or no independence. Similarly, I would not want to be resuscitated if only to lead to a significantly reduced quality of life.

But since D's signature had not been witnessed, this clear statement of D's wishes was not a binding AD under the Act. In D's case, this did not make much difference in practice, because the fact that he was in a permanent vegetative state meant that the court came to the same decision in his best interests. But because the whole point of making an advance decision is to prospectively refuse treatment which doctors might believe to be in one's best interests, these strict requirements as to witnessing can operate harshly for people who have tried to make unambiguous 'living wills' without legal advice.

(d) Effects of advance decisions

Where there is doubt about the validity or applicability of an advance decision, under section 26(4) an application can be made to the court for a declaration. If the AD is valid and applicable, the court has no power to overrule it. While the court's advice is being sought, under section 26(5) nothing in the AD should prevent the provision of life-sustaining treatment or steps to prevent a deterioration in the P's condition.

An advance decision that is not valid or applicable does not thereby become completely irrelevant, however. In the absence of a binding AD, the doctor will decide what treatment is in the patient's best interests, and if the AD expresses the person's wishes or feelings, it is explicitly relevant to this assessment under section 4(6)(a). The Code of Practice reiterates that a finding that an AD does not apply does not therefore mean that doctors are entitled to provide the treatment it attempted to refuse.

Mental Capacity Act Code of Practice

> 9.45 If an advance decision is not valid or applicable to current circumstances:
>
> - healthcare professionals must consider the advance decision as part of their assessment of the person's best interests if they have reasonable grounds to think it is a true expression of the person's wishes, and

---

[66] [2012] EWHC 885 (COP).

- they must not assume that because an advance decision is either invalid or not applicable, they should always provide the specified treatment (including life-sustaining treatment)—they must base this decision on what is in the person's best interests.

In a case we consider in Chapter 17, *Sheffield Teaching Hospitals NHS Foundation Trust v TH*, TH's preference to have no further treatment was respected even though Hayden J found that 'the stringent requirements of Section 24 are not met', and there was 'no advance decision to refuse treatment here'.

Sheffield Teaching Hospitals NHS Foundation Trust v TH[67]

Hayden J

I am left in no doubt at all that TH would wish to determine what remains of his life in his own way not least because that is the strategy he has always both expressed and adopted.... Privacy, personal autonomy and dignity have not only been features of TH's life, they have been the creed by which he has lived it. He may not have prepared a document that complies with the criteria of section 24, giving advance directions to refuse treatment but he has in so many oblique and tangential ways over so many years communicated his views so uncompromisingly and indeed bluntly that none of his friends are left in any doubt what he would want in his present situation.

Although only advance refusals of treatment can be binding, it is increasingly common for patients nearing the end of life to be encouraged to express their preferences about what should happen to them in their final days and weeks. This sort of advance care planning might include making formal advance decisions to refuse resuscitation, but it could also incorporate positive preferences about what treatments they would like to receive, and where they would like to die. As Carolyn Johnston explains, advance care planning can be beneficial for patients and their families.

Carolyn Johnston[68]

With appropriate training, ACP [advance care planning] is a valuable process for promoting patient-centred care for future treatment. It can be of benefit to the patient, his or her loved ones, and health and care providers. A qualitative study found that patients with end stage renal disease perceived the process of ACP a means of providing hope through provision of information, empowerment and enhancing relationships with staff and loved ones. Patients identify ACP as an important element in a trusting doctor–patient relationship, and evidence shows that ACP and end of life discussions reduce stress, anxiety and depression in surviving relatives. In a study investigating the impact of ACP on end of life care in elderly patients, family members were more likely to be satisfied with the quality of the patient's death from both their own perspective and the perceived perspective of the patient where ACP was used. ACP is associated with fewer hospital admissions from residential care and when undertaken in a hospital

---

[67] [2014] EWCOP 4.
[68] 'Advance Decision Making—Rhetoric or Reality?' (2014) 34 Legal Studies 497–514.

> environment improves treatment in accordance with patient prior wishes. ACP has broader goals than the creation of [advance decisions to refuse treatment] and the discussion with healthcare/trained professionals enables provision of information about realistic healthcare choices.

(6) Avoiding Liability

Normally it will be a doctor (rather than a judge) who decides whether a person lacks capacity and what treatment would be in her best interests. It is, of course, possible that the doctor might get one or both of these decisions wrong. If it turns out that the patient did, in fact, have capacity, has a doctor who mistakenly treated her without consent committed an assault or battery?

According to section 5 of the Act, in order to be protected from a charge of battery or assault, a doctor needs: (a) to take 'reasonable steps' to establish whether the P has capacity; (b) have a 'reasonable belief' that the person lacks capacity; and (c) 'reasonably believe' that the treatment is in P's best interests.

Mental Capacity Act 2005 section 5

5 Acts in connection with care or treatment

(1) If a person ('D') does an act in connection with the care or treatment of another person ('P'), the act is one to which this section applies if—

    (a) before doing the act, D takes reasonable steps to establish whether P lacks capacity in relation to the matter in question, and

    (b) when doing the act, D reasonably believes—

        (i) that P lacks capacity in relation to the matter, and

        (ii) that it will be in P's best interests for the act to be done.

(2) D does not incur any liability in relation to the act that he would not have incurred if P—

    (a) had had capacity to consent in relation to the matter, and

    (b) had consented to D's doing the act.

The MCA Code of Practice makes clear that when judging the reasonableness of a decision-maker's beliefs, health care professionals will be assumed to be more skilled in assessing capacity than informal carers—that is, it will be harder for them to establish that they acted reasonably by wrongly deciding the person lacked capacity. It also specifies that detailed records should be kept.[69]

In the next extract, Mary Donnelly points out that the Act does not contain any formal mechanism to hold assessors of capacity to account. Of course, a disgruntled patient could challenge the decision that they lacked capacity by bringing an action in tort law. But not only does the Act contain protections for doctors who have acted reasonably, it is also important to remember that, given the circumstances of many people with borderline capacity, this sort of 'privatized' enforcement is likely to be ineffective.

[69] Para 6. 33.

Mary Donnelly[70]

Most crucially, the extent to which the MCA provisions will have a real impact on capacity assessment is dependent on whether assessors on the ground are persuaded (or compelled) to comply with them. In this respect, the MCA falls short. The framework includes no mechanisms to monitor the performance of assessors. Thus, monitoring is essentially a private matter, dependent on people either challenging the results of assessments in the Court of Protection or taking tort actions . . . There are two problems with reliance on this kind of private monitoring. First, it requires the person him or herself, or someone acting on his or her behalf, to initiate the legal process. For a person of borderline capacity, this may represent a considerable burden. Secondly, legal actions of this kind are less effective at changing underlying patterns of behaviour than at developing ways to prove compliance with strict legal norms. Thus, the requirement to take practical steps to help the person make the decision could be addressed by a bland recitation of formal steps taken which would do nothing to enhance the actual communication between the parties. . . . The MCA tells assessors what to do but is much more reticent in actually ensuring that they do this.

As we see later, the House of Lords Select Committee on the Mental Capacity Act echoed Donnelly's criticisms of the Act's lack of 'teeth'.

A doctor might also make a mistake in relation to an advance refusal of treatment. A valid and applicable advance refusal of treatment has exactly the same effect as a contemporaneous one, which means that if a doctor wrongly relies on an invalid AD or wrongly treats in the face of a valid AD, the possibility of liability arises. Section 26(2) and (3) provide for exemption from liability in certain circumstances.

Mental Capacity Act 2005 section 26

26(2) A person does not incur liability for carrying out or continuing the treatment unless, at the time, he is satisfied that an advance decision exists which is valid and applicable to the treatment.

(3) A person does not incur liability for the consequences of withholding or withdrawing a treatment from P if, at the time, he reasonably believes that an advance decision exists which is valid and applicable to the treatment.

There is a significant difference between the test for avoiding liability depending upon whether the doctor has wrongly treated despite the existence of a valid AD, or not treated because he was relying on an invalid AD.

If the doctor wrongly fails to comply with a valid AD—that is, he gives treatment that the patient has refused—the doctor will not be liable unless at the time he was 'satisfied' that there was a valid AD in existence. This means doctors will only face liability if they blatantly disregard what they know (or are 'satisfied') to be a valid AD. Hence, if a doctor has any doubts about an AD's validity, it will be relatively straightforward to establish that he was not 'satisfied' that a valid AD existed, and he can therefore ignore it with impunity. It is not necessary for those doubts to be objectively reasonable: if the doctor is not 'satisfied' that it is binding on him, he is not bound.

---

[70] 'Capacity Assessment under the Mental Capacity Act 2005: Delivering on the Functional Approach?' (2009) 29 Legal Studies 464–91.

In contrast, under section 26(3), if a doctor refrains from treating a patient because he wrongly believes her AD is valid, he will avoid liability for any harm caused by his failure to treat provided that he reasonably believed that her AD was valid. Taken together, these provisions suggest that doctors should be wary of complying with ADs where they have any doubts at all about their validity. A doctor could be liable for withholding treatment if his belief in the AD's validity is later judged not to have been reasonable, whereas he will only be liable for ignoring a valid AD if he knowingly disregarded its contents. This would appear to be confirmed by the Code of Practice.

Mental Capacity Act Code of Practice paras 9.57–9.59

9.57 Healthcare professionals must follow an advance decision if they are satisfied that it exists, is valid and is applicable to their circumstances. Failure to follow an advance decision in this situation could lead to a claim for damages for battery or a criminal charge of assault.

9.58 But they are protected from liability if they are not:

- aware of an advance decision, or
- satisfied that an advance decision exists, is valid and is applicable to the particular treatment and the current circumstances.
- If healthcare professionals have genuine doubts, and are therefore not 'satisfied', about the existence, validity or applicability of the advance decision, treatment can be provided without incurring liability.

9.59 Healthcare professionals will be protected from liability for failing to provide treatment if they 'reasonably believe' that a valid and applicable advance decision to refuse that treatment exists. But they must be able to demonstrate that their belief was reasonable (section 26(3)) and point to reasonable grounds showing why they believe this.

In the next extract, Alasdair Maclean argues that giving this protection to doctors who treat a patient despite the existence of a valid AD shows that the MCA's protection of patients' 'precedent autonomy' is trumped by its protection of clinical discretion.

Alasdair Maclean[71]

The statute tries to balance four things: respect for the patient's self-determination, facilitation of healthcare provision, protection of the incompetent adult's welfare and protection of the treating physician. In trying to achieve this balance, the Government has arguably tipped the scale towards protection and facilitation and away from individual autonomy. If the provisions were intended to protect the competent patient's precedent autonomy, then the Act is open to criticism for the resulting vulnerability of advance directives. The Act is arguably most successful in facilitating the provision of healthcare by supporting clinical discretion and protecting the physician who acts in good faith. Thus, the Act provides patients with a trump that only works when healthcare professionals and/or the courts are comfortable with the patient's decision.

---

[71] 'Advance Directives and the Rocky Waters of Anticipatory Decision-Making' (2008) 16 Medical Law Review 1–22.

(7) The Use of Restraint

In exceptional circumstances, it can be legitimate to use force or restraint in order to ensure someone receives medical treatment. Restraining P will not attract liability provided the conditions in section 6(2) and (3) are met:

Mental Capacity Act 2005 section 6

6(2) The first condition is that D reasonably believes that it is necessary to do the act in order to prevent harm to P.

(3) The second is that the act is a proportionate response to—

(a) the likelihood of P's suffering harm, and

(b) the seriousness of that harm.

The Code of Practice makes clear that the onus will be on D to prove that restraint is necessary, and not just convenient.

Mental Capacity Act Code of Practice para 6.44

6.44 Anybody considering using restraint must have objective reasons to justify that restraint is necessary. They must be able to show that the person being cared for is likely to suffer harm unless proportionate restraint is used. A carer or professional must not use restraint just so that they can do something more easily. If restraint is necessary to prevent harm to the person who lacks capacity, it must be the minimum amount of force for the shortest time possible.

In *DH v NHS Foundation Trust*,[72] Sir Nicholas Wall P was impressed with the care that had been taken over the treatment of PS, who needed to undergo treatment for cancer which she was resisting because of her needle and hospital phobia. PS was likely to refuse to attend hospital so the trust had arranged for a consultant anaesthetist to travel with an ambulance crew to PS's home in order to give her a sedative in a soft drink. Sir Nicholas Wall P agreed that, as a last resort, it might be necessary to use force to convey PS to hospital for treatment:

In my judgment, the evidence clearly establishes that it is in the best interests of PS to undergo a hysterectomy and bilateral salpingo-oophorectomy in order to treat her endometrial cancer.... I am further satisfied, given her hospital and needle phobia, that it may well be necessary to sedate PS in order to convey her to hospital.... The need for such sedative treatment will only arise if persuasion fails, and I am accordingly satisfied that it is necessary for the trust to authorise such treatment as being in PS's best interests, and to use force if necessary to sedate her and convey her to hospital.

The 'least restrictive alternative' principle in section 1(6) is relevant here. In authorizing the use of physical restraint in a further case involving DD, a woman for whom pregnancy was

---

[72] [2010] EWHC 1217 (Fam).

extremely risky, Cobb J stressed that it should be used only after less restrictive alternatives had failed.[73]

Mental Health Trust v DD

Cobb J

The issue of forced entry to her home and restrictions on her freedom of movement arise again today as they have arisen on previous occasions. Again, not without considerable reservation, I do nonetheless consider it in DD's best interests that I give authorisation to the Applicant to exercise physical restraint for the purposes of giving DD the relevant contraception injection, by professionals who have received training in the relevant techniques and only as a last resort, where less restrictive alternatives have failed; it is important that at all times the professionals should maintain DD's dignity.

The use of force or restraint also must not interfere with the patient's right, under Article 3 of the Human Rights Act 1998, to be free from inhuman and degrading treatment. In the *Herczegfalvy* case, considered again in the next chapter, force and restraint had been used on a mentally ill patient. The European Court of Human Rights found that this did not breach Article 3 because:

a measure which is a therapeutic necessity cannot be regarded as inhuman or degrading. The Court must nevertheless satisfy itself that the medical necessity has been convincingly shown to exist.

It follows that where treatment is *not* a therapeutic necessity, the use of force might amount to a violation of Article 3.

It will seldom be in the best interests of patients who lack capacity to undergo forced treatment. The harm that might be done by imposing treatment on an unwilling patient may outweigh the clinical benefits of the treatment. This was the case in a pre-MCA case, *Re D*,[74] in which a man who lacked capacity refused to undergo dialysis. Since he refused to keep still, dialysis (which he needed four times a week) could only be provided under general anaesthetic. Given the patient's condition, this would be both impracticable and dangerous. The doctors therefore sought a declaration from the court that it would be lawful not to impose dialysis upon him. Sir Stephen Brown P granted the declaration, finding that it would be in the best interests of the patient, and hence lawful 'not to impose haemodialysis upon him in circumstances in which, in the opinion of the medical practitioners responsible for such treatment, it is not reasonably practicable to do so'.

(8) Proxy Decision-Making

The Mental Capacity Act introduced, for the first time, the possibility of formal proxy medical decision-making for incapacitated adults. This involves the P nominating one or more people, referred to as 'donees', with lasting power of attorney (LPA) who, under section 9(1)(a), will have the authority to make decisions about, among other things, P's personal welfare, or specified matters concerning his personal welfare, if/when he loses capacity. This power undoubtedly extends to taking medical decisions. A donee is only permitted to take decisions about life-sustaining treatment if P has included a clear statement to this effect in the LPA document. Donees do not have a right to take decisions if

---

[73] *Mental Health Trust v DD* [2014] EWCOP 44.　　[74] (1997) 41 BMLR 81.

the P regains capacity, or if she has made a binding advance decision to refuse a particular treatment.

If more than one donee is appointed, the donor can specify, under section 10(4), whether they should act 'jointly' or 'severally' in relation to different decisions. If they are to act jointly, all the donees must agree on every decision; if they can act 'severally', the decision of one donee is sufficient. An LPA could also specify that the donees must agree where a serious medical decision has to be made, but that they could act independently in relation to more trivial decisions. If the LPA does not specify this, and more than one donee is appointed, they will have to act jointly in relation to all decisions.

The power of the donee of an LPA is, under section 9(4), subject to the provisions of the Act. Donees are therefore bound by the requirement to take decisions in P's best interests. It also means that section 4(3) applies, and the donee must take into account whether P is likely to regain capacity in the near future, and, under section 4(6), that the person's past and present wishes and feelings must be considered.

If someone has not nominated a 'donee', their close friends or relatives should be consulted under section 4(7)(e) when assessing their best interests, although their views will be advisory rather than determinative.

There are two potential problems with proxy consent under the MCA, highlighted in the next extract. First, empirical studies suggest that we are not very good at predicting what others would decide, even when we know them very well indeed. Secondly, because a donee does not have the same freedom as the patient to take decisions which conflict with her best interests, they are an imperfect proxy. Anthony Wrigley therefore suggests that proxies are advisers, rather than substitute decision-makers.

Anthony Wrigley[75]

There is evidence to indicate that we are simply not very good at making substituted judgements for other people, not even for close relatives . . . This empirical evidence suggests that as a practical means of extending the autonomous wishes and desires of a patient who now lacks capacity, substituted judgement is an extremely poor method, as it is likely to be unrepresentative and could lead to errors. . . .

The MCA places fairly obvious restrictions on what a proxy can and can't consent to . . . Upon analysis, the MCA has created a situation where lip service is paid to the notion of a proxy consenter, but when the matter is pursued, the ethical and, ultimately, legal status of such a proxy seems diminished to that of an advisor. This should not be taken in a negative light, however, because this role of advisor to a professional medical team is the most useful and morally authoritative role a proxy can take. . . . Ultimately, 'proxy consent' should not be seen as consent at all, but rather 'assistance' to those best placed to judge the patient's best interests.

Under section 16, it is also open to the court to appoint a deputy to make decisions on behalf of an incapacitated person. Section 17(d) specifies that the deputy's powers extend to 'giving or refusing consent to the carrying out or continuation of a treatment by a person providing health care for P', with one important exception: deputies are not able to refuse consent to life-sustaining treatment. The appointment of deputies will be unusual in relation to health

---

[75] 'Proxy consent: moral authority misconceived' (2007) 33 Journal of Medical Ethics 527–31.

care decisions. Section 16(4)(a) provides that 'a decision by the court is to be preferred to the appointment of a deputy to make a decision', and the Code of Practice suggests that the appointment of a deputy will only be appropriate in 'the most difficult cases', perhaps because of a history of serious family disputes.[76]

(9) The Court of Protection

A new specialist court was set up to administer the MCA. Section 15 sets out the powers the Court of Protection has to make declarations.

Mental Capacity Act 2005 section 15

15 Power to make declarations

(1) The court may make declarations as to—

(a) whether a person has or lacks capacity to make a decision specified in the declaration;

(b) whether a person has or lacks capacity to make decisions on such matters as are described in the declaration;

(c) the lawfulness or otherwise of any act done, or yet to be done, in relation to that person.

(2) 'Act' includes an omission and a course of conduct.

Court involvement in decisions about the medical treatment of people who lack capacity is unusual, and in the vast majority of cases, decisions are taken by doctors, in consultation with the patient's relatives. There are, however, a handful of especially controversial medical procedures where court involvement is necessary, even if the doctors and the patient's family agree.

In addition to a non-exhaustive list of treatments that should be brought before the Court in the Code of Practice,[77] the President of the Court of Protection issues Practice Directions on a range of matters, including, in 9E, setting out which matters must be brought before the court for a decision.

Practice Direction 9E (supplementing Part 9 of the Court of Protection Rules 2007)

5. Cases involving any of the following decisions should be regarded as serious medical treatment for the purpose of the Rules and this practice direction, and should be brought to the court:

(a) decisions about the proposed withholding or withdrawal of artificial nutrition and hydration from a person in a permanent vegetative state or a minimally conscious state;

(b) cases involving organ or bone marrow donation by a person who lacks capacity to consent; and

(c) cases involving non-therapeutic sterilisation of a person who lacks capacity to consent.

6. Examples of serious medical treatment may include:

[76] Para 8.39.   [77] Para 8.18.

(a) certain terminations of pregnancy in relation to a person who lacks capacity to consent to such a procedure;

(b) a medical procedure performed on a person who lacks capacity to consent to it, where the procedure is for the purpose of a donation to another person;

(c) a medical procedure or treatment to be carried out on a person who lacks capacity to consent to it, where that procedure or treatment must be carried out using a degree of force to restrain the person concerned;

(d) an experimental or innovative treatment for the benefit of a person who lacks capacity to consent to such treatment; and

(e) a case involving an ethical dilemma in an untested area.

7. There may be other procedures or treatments not contained in the list in paragraphs 5 and 6 above which can be regarded as serious medical treatment. Whether or not a procedure is regarded as serious medical treatment will depend on the circumstances and the consequences for the patient.

Where there is a dispute or uncertainty over medical treatment, the application to the Court of Protection should normally be made by the NHS trust, or other body responsible for the patient's care. Where there is a dispute between family members, one of them may wish to apply to the court. Any person who is alleged to lack capacity will also be able to make an application, though more usually he will be made a party to the proceedings, and the Official Solicitor will be appointed to protect his interests.

(10) The Mental Capacity Act in Practice

The Mental Capacity Act 2005 is framed in strikingly patient-friendly terms, especially when contrasted with the mental health legislation that we consider in Chapter 6. Through various measures, such as the principle of assisted decision-making and the priority given to the patient's wishes, the MCA expands the group of people able to make decisions for themselves, or have a meaningful say over decisions involving their care. The Act was, to quote the House of Lords Select Committee on the Mental Capacity Act, 'visionary',[78] and it continues to be held in high regard. Whether it has made the difference in practice that many hoped is less certain.

The House of Lords Select Committee's post-legislative scrutiny of the Mental Capacity Act was published in 2014, and it found that the Act was not well understood, and that implementation was patchy.

House of Lords Select Committee on the Mental Capacity Act 2005[79]

The empowering ethos of the Act has not been widely implemented. Our evidence suggests that capacity is not always assumed when it should be. Capacity assessments are not often carried out; when they are, the quality is often poor. Supported decision-making, and the adjustments required to enable it, are not well embedded. The concept of unwise decision-making faces institutional obstruction due to prevailing cultures of risk-aversion and

---

[78] House of Lords Select Committee on the Mental Capacity Act 2005, Report of Session 2013–14, *Mental Capacity Act 2005: Post-Legislative Scrutiny.*

[79] Ibid.

paternalism. Best interests decision-making is often not undertaken in the way set out in the Act: the wishes, thoughts and feelings of P are not routinely prioritised. Instead, clinical judgments or resource-led decisionmaking predominate. The least restrictive option is not routinely or adequately considered. . . .

The presumption of capacity, in particular, is widely misunderstood by those involved in care. . . . The general lack of awareness of the provisions of the Act has allowed prevailing professional practices to continue unchallenged, and allowed decision-making to be dominated by professionals, without the required input from families and carers about P's wishes and feelings.

A fundamental change of attitudes among professionals is needed in order to move from protection and paternalism to enablement and empowerment. Professionals need to be aware of their responsibilities under the Act, just as families need to be aware of their rights under it.

In addition to raising awareness of the Act, the Committee recommended that there should be a single oversight body whose role would be to ensure that the Act's empowering ethos is, in practice, translated into more empowering care for those who lack capacity.

House of Lords Select Committee on the Mental Capacity Act 2005[80]

Despite the many organisations involved in implementing the Act, it appears that no single body has overall responsibility for it. This may help to explain the patchy implementation of the Act. Without central ownership and coordination of implementation, the very positive benefits of the legislation will not be realised. A permanent, proactive, dedicated and independent resource with responsibility for promoting awareness, understanding and good practice across affected sectors is needed to ensure a step change.

We recommend that overall responsibility for implementation of the Mental Capacity Act be given to a single independent body.

In its response, the government said that it would 'take a comprehensive approach to promoting implementation'.

HM Government[81]

We welcome the Committee's conclusion that the Act is a positive piece of legislation which has the potential to transform lives. We recognise that there is still some way to go to fully realise that potential, and share the Committee's concern at the low levels of awareness and understanding of the Act. Too many people who may lack capacity may be missing out on the legal rights that the MCA gives them. This is not tolerable and we are determined to put this right. This is a big challenge. It is about changing attitudes in society as a whole towards those who may lack capacity. Meeting this challenge will require the widespread support of everyone; those responsible for running services, professionals and the public at large . . .

[80] Ibid.
[81] HM Government, *Valuing Every Voice, Respecting Every Right: Making the Case for the Mental Capacity Act* (TSO: London, 2014).

> We intend to ensure that implementation is strengthened and co-ordinated and will consider the case for establishing a new independently chaired Mental Capacity Advisory Board. . . .
>
> We share the House of Lords' concern at the lack of awareness of the MCA. Everyone has responsibility for raising awareness and every professional who works with individuals who may lack capacity should regard the responsibility to familiarise themselves with the provisions of the MCA as a basic professional duty.

In 2015, the government established a National Mental Capacity Forum, chaired by Baroness Ilora Finlay, to bring together stakeholders in order to better promote effective understanding and implementation of the Act. It has also set up an online MCA Directory, in order to provide convenient access to a range of MCA tools and guidance.[82]

(b) CHILDREN

Although childhood lasts from birth until the age of 18, in practice, children acquire some rights and responsibilities before they reach the age of majority: at the age of 16, for example, it is lawful to join the army, give consent to sexual intercourse, and marry. At what age can a child consent to medical treatment? As we will see in the following sections, this will depend upon the child's age and the nature of the medical treatment, as well as the individual child's decision-making capacity.

(1) Parental Consent

Anyone with parental responsibility for a child can give consent to her medical treatment. Provided that both parents have parental responsibility, each would normally be able to give a valid consent to their child's treatment without consulting the other. As Dame Elizabeth Butler-Sloss P explains in *Re J (Specific Issue Orders: Child's Religious Upbringing and Circumcision)*, the consent of both parents is only necessary for certain treatments, such as non-therapeutic circumcision.

Re J (Specific Issue Orders: Child's Religious Upbringing and Circumcision)[83]

Dame Elizabeth Butler-Sloss P

There is, in my view, a small group of important decisions made on behalf of a child which, in the absence of agreement of those with parental responsibility, ought not to be carried out or arranged by one parent carer although she has parental responsibility under s 2(7) of the Children Act 1989. Such a decision ought not to be made without the specific approval of the court.... The issue of circumcision has not, to my knowledge, previously been considered by this court, but in my view it comes within that group. The decision to circumcise a child on grounds other than medical necessity is a very important one; the operation is

---

[82] See further www.scie.org.uk/mca-directory/keygovernmentdocuments.asp.
[83] [2000] 1 FLR 571.

> irreversible, and should only be carried out where the parents together approve of it or, in the absence of parental agreement, where a court decides that the operation is in the best interests of the child.

In *Re C (Welfare of Child: Immunisation)*,[84] a case in which the mother and the father disagreed over whether their child should receive the MMR vaccine, Thorpe LJ said that: 'In my opinion this appeal demonstrates that hotly contested issues of immunization are to be added to that "small group of important decisions".'

Hence, where the parents agree with each other, consent to circumcision and vaccination lies within a zone of parental discretion, and the court will not impose its own view of whether the procedure is in the child's best interests. Where the parents cannot agree, the court will make the decision according to its assessment of the child's best interests. In the case of routine childhood vaccinations, because they are supported by responsible medical opinion, vaccination is overwhelmingly likely to be found to be in a child's best interests.[85]

Vaccination decisions are usually made on behalf of very young children who are not capable of expressing a view, but what if the children are older and do not want to be vaccinated? This was the case in *F v F (MMR Vaccine)*. Following media coverage of Andrew Wakefield's now discredited finding of a link between autism and the MMR (measles, mumps, and rubella) vaccine, the parents had agreed that their elder daughter should not receive her second MMR booster, and their younger daughter should not be vaccinated at all. The father subsequently changed his mind and had become concerned for the health of his children, L and M, who were now aged 15 and 11. The mother was still against vaccination, as were the children. Theis J found that neither child was *Gillick*-competent (see Section 4(b)), and that vaccination was in both children's best interests.

F v F (MMR Vaccine)[86]

Theis J

Whilst I am acutely aware of both L and M's wishes and feelings in relation to this issue, … I consider their views have inevitably been influenced by a number of factors which affects the weight that should be attached to those wishes and feelings. First, from their perspective the parents were initially united in their decision for them not to be vaccinated and they can't understand why their father has changed his mind…. This perhaps displays a lack of maturity and an appreciation that views can change for a variety of reasons. Second, they have become focussed on the issue of the ingredients of the vaccine without being able to consider and balance the wider picture, and the consequences or actions of them not having it, including medication (and its contents) that would be required in the event of them becoming ill from one of the vaccine preventing diseases. Third, it is not surprising that they are likely to have become influenced by their mother's views. Those views are clearly strongly held and will inevitably have influenced both children….

---

[84] [2003] EWCA Civ 1148.   [85] See also *LCC v A, B, C & D* [2011] EWHC 4033 (Fam).
[86] [2013] EWHC 2683 (Fam).

> It is unfortunate the parents were not able to reach a consensus on this issue; that would have been best for both the children. In the absence of that the responsibility falls on the court to exercise that parental responsibility for the parents having regard to the welfare interests of each child.

If they are married, both parents automatically have parental responsibility. If they are unmarried, the father will have parental responsibility if he is registered on the child's birth certificate. Non-parents may also have parental responsibility (perhaps because the child is living with them, and they have a residence order), in which case they too would be able to give a valid consent to medical treatment. Non-parents who have temporary care of the child—such as teachers and childminders—are entitled to do what is reasonable in all the circumstances to safeguard or promote the child's welfare.[87]

In an emergency, if no one with parental responsibility is available to give consent, the doctors would be entitled to treat the child in her best interests. See, for example, the comments of Lord Templeman and Lord Scarman in *Gillick v West Norfolk and Wisbech AHA*, a case we consider in detail later in the chapter.

Gillick v West Norfolk and Wisbech AHA[88]

Lord Templeman

I accept that if there is no time to obtain a decision from the court, a doctor may safely carry out treatment in an emergency if the doctor believes the treatment to be vital to the survival or health of an infant and notwithstanding the opposition of a parent or the impossibility of alerting the parent before the treatment is carried out.

Lord Scarman

Emergency, parental neglect, abandonment of the child, or inability to find the parent are examples of exceptional situations justifying the doctor proceeding to treat the child without parental knowledge and consent.

If treatment could reasonably be delayed until the parents can be found or a court order obtained, doctors should not proceed with treatment.

Parents can consent to their child's medical treatment, but do they also have the right to refuse? Parental authority exists for the benefit of children, so parents do not have the right to make decisions that would harm their child. Hence, if one or both of the parents withhold consent to treatment that the doctors believe would be in the child's best interests, approval can be sought from another source, namely the courts.

(2) Court Involvement

The court's power to authorize the medical treatment of children derives from wardship, its inherent jurisdiction, and more recently from statute. Wardship differs slightly from the inherent jurisdiction—if a child is a ward of court, the court must make all important

---

[87] Children Act 1989, s 3(5)(b).   [88] [1984] QB 581.

decisions about her upbringing, whereas the inherent jurisdiction can apply to a one-off decision. In practice, however, the two processes are largely indistinguishable. Both derive from the Crown's prerogative power as *parens patriae*, exercised by judges of the High Court, and both give the courts more sweeping powers than are possessed by parents and mature minors.

If a child's parents refuse to consent to treatment that the doctors believe to be in her best interests, the NHS Trust where the child is being treated can apply to the court for a declaration that treatment would be lawful. It is also possible that another concerned individual might apply if, for example, the doctors and the parents were intending to do something that was not in the child's best interests. This happened in the 1970s in *Re D (A Minor) (Wardship: Sterilisation)*,[89] in which an educational psychologist applied to have an 11-year-old girl made a ward of court in order to challenge her doctors' and parents' decision to sterilize her.

In addition, under the Children Act 1989, the court can issue a specific issue order or a prohibited steps order to determine what treatment a child should receive.[90] In *Re C (Welfare of Child: Immunisation)*,[91] the fathers of two children who were living with their mothers sought specific issue orders to enable their children, who had received none of the recommended childhood vaccines, to be immunized. The judge ordered each mother to have her child immunized, and the Court of Appeal upheld his decision.

Under section 1 of the Children Act, in any question affecting a child's upbringing, her welfare must be the 'paramount consideration'.[92] What does this mean in practice? It is clear from the guidance of the General Medical Council (GMC) on the treatment of under-18s, that, as with adults, best interests is not confined to the child's clinical best interests. If the child is able to express her own wishes, these are relevant, regardless of whether she is *Gillick*-competent (discussed later). The GMC guidance also embodies the 'least restrictive alternative' principle.

General Medical Council[93]

12. An assessment of best interests will include what is clinically indicated in a particular case. You should also consider:

a. the views of the child or young person, so far as they can express them, including any previously expressed preferences

b. the views of parents

c. the views of others close to the child or young person

d. the cultural, religious or other beliefs and values of the child or parents

e. the views of other healthcare professionals involved in providing care to the child or young person, and of any other professionals who have an interest in their welfare

f. which choice, if there is more than one, will least restrict the child or young person's future options.

(a) Controversial medical treatments

There are times when it may not be obvious whether a particular medical procedure is in a child's best interests. Blood tests for the purposes of establishing paternity have been held to

---

[89] [1976] 2 WLR 279.　　[90] Section 8(1).　　[91] [2003] EWCA Civ 1148.　　[92] Section 1(1).
[93] *0–18 Years: Guidance for all Doctors* (GMC, 2007).

be in the child's best interests: taking a sample causes only mild discomfort, and the child is likely to benefit from knowing the truth about her origins.[94] Bone marrow, blood, or organ donation (see further Chapter 11) are not in a child's best clinical interests, although just like in *Re Y*, discussed earlier in this chapter, it might be possible to argue that saving a sibling's life by donating bone marrow is overwhelmingly in a child's emotional best interests. As yet, there have been no cases in the UK where the court has considered an application for a child to become a solid organ donor, although it might be predicted that it would be more difficult to establish that this would be in her best interests.

There have also been no cases in which the courts have had to determine whether aesthetic as opposed to reconstructive cosmetic surgery would be in a child's best interests. Could it be ever be in a child's best interests to undergo rhinoplasty (commonly called a 'nose job')? What if the parents want their child with Down's syndrome to have facial reconstructive surgery in order to look more 'normal', so that she will be less likely to be teased and/or discriminated against?[95]

Sterilization carried out in order to avoid pregnancy, rather than as treatment for a medical disorder, has also been treated as a special case—a 'drastic step'[96]—and it would require court approval. Improvements in contraceptive techniques mean that requests to perform sterilization operations on girls in order to avoid the risk of pregnancy should now be rare. Because long-acting contraceptives, such as injections or implants, can achieve the same effect, an irreversible operation under general anaesthetic would seldom be the 'least restrictive alternative'.

In the past few years, a new question has arisen, namely whether surgical and other interventions could ever be appropriate where the purpose is not to avoid pregnancy, but instead to stop a disabled child 'growing up'. The issue first arose in the US. In January 2007, the parents of a nine-year-old girl called Ashley published a blog explaining their decision to stunt her growth through chemical and surgical means. Unsurprisingly, there was an explosion of media interest in what her parents described as 'the Ashley treatment'.

Ashley X was nine years old, and very severely brain damaged. She suffered from static encephalopathy, which meant that she was unable to move around, or sit up unaided. Her parents' fear was that, as Ashley got bigger, they would cease to be able to care for her on their own. They believed that Ashley's quality of life would be better if she remained small enough to be cuddled and carried easily by her parents.

When Ashley began to display the early signs of puberty, her parents asked doctors to remove her uterus, appendix, and breast buds, and to give her oestrogen. Before going ahead, the doctors had obtained approval from the hospital's clinical ethics committee, which had agreed that this treatment was in Ashley's best interests.

A year later, there were reports that a British mother was seeking a hysterectomy for her daughter, Katie Thorpe, in order to avoid what she called the 'pain, discomfort and indignity of menstruation'. The hospital refused to agree to the operation, and so the case did not come before a court.

If a doctor in the UK had agreed to perform a hysterectomy on a girl like Katie Thorpe, or to carry out the full 'Ashley treatment', there is no doubt that, before proceeding, the

---

[94] *Re F (A Minor) (Blood Tests: Parental Rights)* [1993] 3 All ER 596; *Re H (A Minor) (Blood Tests: Parental Rights)* [1996] 4 All ER 28.

[95] See further RB Jones, 'Parental consent to cosmetic facial surgery in Down's syndrome' (2000) 26 Journal of Medical Ethics 101–2.

[96] *Re B (A Minor)* [1988] AC 199, per Lord Templeman.

case would have to come before the court for a declaration as to whether or not it would be lawful, and the basis for the court's decision would be the best interests test.

As we have seen, a child's best interests is not confined to their clinical best interests, and also encompasses their emotional and psychological wellbeing. If radical surgery would dramatically improve the child's quality of life, it might be said to be in her interests. On the other hand, the 'least restrictive alternative' principle would mean that long-acting contraceptives should be preferred to a hysterectomy, and, perhaps more importantly, better equipment and access to professional carers and other resources might be a less invasive way than surgery and growth restriction to ensure that Ashley could continue to be cared for at home.

On the one hand, it could be argued that it would be in Ashley's best interests to be carried by her parents, rather than by the sort of hoist used to transport industrial pallets, but on the other, Tan and Brassington suggest that this was a drastic medical solution to problems that either might not arise, or might be more appropriately dealt with through practical adjustments to the home.

N Tan and Iain Brassington[97]

[W]e would do well to remind ourselves that the direct benefits to Ashley of this invasive treatment were minimal. The treatment was not palliative: it did not address any existing symptoms. Nor did it purport to modify the prognosis of the underlying condition in any way . . . Strikingly, Ashley's doctors' reason for their intervention was that

> . . . [T]he primary benefit offered by growth attenuation is the *potential to make caring for the child less burdensome and therefore more accessible*. A smaller person is not as difficult to move and transfer from place to place.

What is notable about the statement is the manner in which it seems to shift the moral focus from Ashley and her needs towards her carers and theirs. It is not clear, though, whether this reason suffices to justify intervention. There are, after all, any number of situations in which medical intervention might well make caring for a patient more easy and accessible, and in most cases we would want to say that there is something odd (at best) about imposing an intervention—especially one as radical as the Ashley treatment—on Smith so that Jones' job might be easier. . . .

Increased movement and stimulation could feasibly be achieved, for example, by non-invasive environmental adjustments such as harnesses, hoists and the provision of carers. In a sense, the wider Ashley treatment—taking into account that it also involved a hysterectomy, appendicectomy and breast bud removal to protect against problems of as yet unknown severity that might not appear anyway—might represent less of an attempt to meet the challenges of Ashley's condition than an attempt not to *have* to meet them.

(b) Disagreements between parents and doctors

Most of the cases in which the courts have had to make decisions about a child's medical treatment have involved parents (or, as we see later, the child herself) disagreeing with doctors about what treatment should, or should not, be provided. The difficult question that arises is whether parents can ever legitimately take a different view from doctors about what is in their child's best interests. The answer to this question has usually been 'no': the courts

---

[97] 'Agency, duties and the "Ashley treatment"' (2009) 35 Journal of Medical Ethics 658–61.

have been willing to override parental refusals, and as we see later, refusals by the child too in order to protect the child's best interests.

In *Re C (A Child) (HIV Test)*, the mother, who was HIV-positive, rejected conventional medical thinking on the causes and treatment of HIV/AIDS, and refused to allow her child to be tested. At first instance, Wilson J overruled her objections on the grounds that it was overwhelmingly in the child's best interests to be tested for HIV, and the Court of Appeal refused permission to appeal.

Re C (A Child) (HIV Test)[98]

Butler-Sloss LJ

I have no doubt at all, for my part, that it is right that this child should have the test done . . . In my view, the child is clearly at risk if there is ignorance of the child's medical condition. The degree of intrusion into the child of a medical test is slight . . . It does not matter whether the parents are responsible or irresponsible. It matters whether the welfare of the child demands that such a course should be taken . . . This child has the right to have sensible and responsible people find out whether she is or is not HIV positive . . . What seems to me to be crucial is that someone should find out so that one knows how she should be looked after . . . Either way this child has her own rights. Those rights seem to me to be met at this stage by her being tested to see what her state of health is for the question of knowledge.

More recently, in *An NHS Trust v SR*, the court overruled his mother's refusal to consent and ordered that a seven-year-old boy should receive radiotherapy to treat his brain tumour. N's mother was concerned that radiotherapy might leave her son infertile, or damage his IQ. Given that, without it, N's life was in danger, the court's conclusion that her judgement had 'gone awry' was unsurprising: as Bodey J put it, 'one cannot enjoy even a diminished quality of life if one is not alive'. Bodey J also specified that the court would only prefer a complementary alternative to conventional medical treatment where an experienced clinician advocated that treatment, and was willing to carry it out.

An NHS Trust v SR[99]

Bodey J

I have to keep firmly in mind what is required for there to be any realistic prospect of the court's preferring some complementary alternative to the standard mainstream treatment for N's condition. It is not just a question of demonstrating that there is research and experimentation going on out there; nor that there are ideas and possibilities being floated, nor even that there are reported success stories of cures occurring without the use of radiotherapy and/or chemotherapy. What is required is the identification of a clinician experienced in treating children aged about 7 having this kind of brain cancer; a clinician with the access to the necessary equipment and infrastructure to put the suggested treatment into effect and able and willing to take over the medical care of and responsibility for N.

---

[98] [2000] Fam 48. [99] *An NHS Trust v SR* [2012] EWHC 3842 (Fam).

Similarly, in *Re JM (A Child)*,[100] in which the parents of a ten-year-old child with a rare and aggressive form of cancer wished to treat it with Chinese medicine, Mostyn J's conclusion that the operation to remove it would be in his best interests was unsurprising:

> It is a strong thing for me, a stranger, to disagree with and override the wishes of J and his parents. But I have absolutely no doubt that J must be given the chance, a very good chance, of a long and fulfilling life rather than suffering, quite soon, a ghastly, agonising, death.

There has been one exceptional, and now rather old, case in which the court refused to authorize a liver transplant against the parents' wishes, despite the likelihood that the child would not live beyond the age of two-and-a-half without a transplant. In *Re T (A Minor) (Wardship: Medical Treatment)*,[101] the Court of Appeal found that the parents' refusal to consent to their son's transplant was not prompted by 'scruple or dogma', and that there was 'genuine scope for a difference of view between parent and judge'. *Re T* is, however, probably best regarded as an idiosyncratic and anomalous judgment. Commenting upon it in *Re C (Welfare of Child: Immunisation)*,[102] for example, Thorpe LJ said 'the outcome of that appeal, denying a child life-prolonging surgery, is unique in our jurisprudence and is explained by the trial judge's erroneous focus on the reasonableness of the mother's rejection of medical opinion'.

In *The NHS Trust v A (A child)*, Holman J was impressed by the reasonableness of A's parents and the decision that they had made. They had refused to consent to a bone marrow transplant (BMT), in part because of the suffering it would cause A, and because it was not guaranteed to succeed. But since the BMT would give A, who would otherwise die, a 50 per cent chance of a normal life, Holman J decided that it would be in her best interests.

The NHS Trust v A (A child)[103]

Holman J

I have already described the qualities of the parents and their informed, reasoned and balanced approach to the issues in this case. I make clear that in my view the decision they have reached is an eminently reasonable as well as well-reasoned decision. This is not at all a case where, in the words of Waite LJ quoted above, they are 'prompted by scruple or dogma ...'; rather, this case is at the other end of Waite LJ's scale, and there is 'genuine scope for a difference of view.' The consideration does weigh heavily upon me that the best interests of this child include an expectation that difficult decisions will be taken for her by the excellent and reasonable parents to whom her care has been entrusted by nature. But ultimately the issue is not whether the parents or their decision are reasonable ...

My mind has wavered during the course of the hearing. I have been deeply impressed by the parents.... They are in intimate and constant contact with A. They witnessed her suffering during the ordeal. They know her happiness and contentment at home now. But by the end of the hearing, and in agreement with the guardian, I have become convinced that it is in the overall best interests of A to undergo a BMT ...

If a BMT could only prolong by a relatively short period her life; or if it would leave her alive but probably seriously impaired (e.g. significantly brain damaged) then I would or might take

[100] [2015] EWHC 2832 (Fam).   [101] [1997] 1 WLR 242.   [102] [2003] EWCA Civ 1148.
[103] [2007] EWHC 1696 (Fam).

> a different view. But in my view a 50 per cent prospect of a full, normal life (even though infertile) when set against the certainty of death before the age of one or one and a half, does in this case outweigh all other considerations and disadvantages.

Re King (A Child) was an unusual case, which had been played out dramatically in the media. Ashya King was five years old and suffering from brain cancer. Dissatisfied with the treatment available in the UK, his parents had taken him abroad. At first, it looked as though a desperately sick child's health was in danger as a result, and European arrest warrants were issued. Ashya was made a ward of court, but by the time the case reached the court, the picture had changed and his 'parents had put forward a treatment plan that was coherent and reasonable'. Baker J therefore authorized his removal to Prague for innovative proton treatment.

Re King (A Child)[104]

Baker J

> Having considered the evidence, I concluded that there was no reason to stand in the way of the parents' proposal. In some cases, this court is faced with a dispute between medical authorities and parents who are insisting on a wholly unreasonable course of treatment, or withholding consent to an essential therapy for their child—for example, a blood transfusion. This is manifestly not such a case. The course of treatment proposed by Mr and Mrs King is entirely reasonable. Ashya has a serious medical condition. Any parents in the position of Mr and Mrs King would do whatever they could to explore all options. Some parents would follow the advice of the local doctors to use conventional radiotherapy, others would prefer the relatively untested option of proton therapy (assuming the funds can be made available to meet the cost of transport and treatment) in the hope that the toxic effects of radiation will be reduced. Both courses are reasonable and it is the parents who bear the heavy responsibility of making the decision. It is no business of this court, or any other public authority, to interfere with their decision.

In the next extract, Jo Bridgeman is critical of Baker J's reliance upon the reasonableness of Mr and Mrs King's decision to take their son to Prague for unproven therapy.

Jo Bridgeman[105]

> His Lordship approved the 'reasonable' course of action proposed by Ashya's parents but neglected to provide a reasoned and principled analysis of the best interests of a child whose parents were refusing consent to conventional post-operative treatment because of a preference for innovative and as yet unproven therapy only available, privately funded, abroad . . .
>
> However, Baker J, approving the agreed treatment plan to secure the post-operative treatment Ashya urgently required, gave no further consideration to either his welfare or his rights. Baker J expressed the view that the 'course of treatment proposed by Mr and Mrs King is

---

[104] [2014] EWHC 2964 (Fam).
[105] 'Misunderstandings, Threats and Fear of the Law in Conflicts over Children's Healthcare' (2015) 23 Medical Law Review 477–89.

entirely reasonable'. . . . This view, that is, the reasonable choice of parents cannot be challenged by public authorities or re-considered by the court, does not reflect established law and thus creates potential for uncertainty about respective responsibilities in future disputes.

As with adults, the courts can declare that treatment would be lawful, in a child's best interests, but they will not force doctors to act contrary to their clinical judgement. As Lord Donaldson MR explained in *Re J (A Minor) (Wardship: Medical Treatment)*:[106]

I have to say that I cannot at present conceive of any circumstances in which this would be other than an abuse of power as directly or indirectly requiring the practitioner to act contrary to the fundamental duty which he owes to his patient. This, subject to obtaining any necessary consent, is to treat the patient in accordance with his own best clinical judgment.

Hence, when the court becomes involved in disputes over a child's medical treatment, it can declare that a particular treatment would be lawful, and it can overrule both a parent's and a child's refusal, but it cannot compel doctors to do something which is contrary to their clinical judgement.

(3) The Use of Force

The inherent jurisdiction gives courts the power to authorize the use of reasonable force in order to ensure that the child receives the treatment in question. As with adults, force should be used only when it is a 'therapeutic necessity', otherwise it might amount to inhuman and degrading treatment, and hence be outlawed by Article 3.

The use of force might also be challenged under Article 5 (the right to liberty and security). The detention of persons of 'unsound mind' can be justified under Article 5(1)(e), but Fortin suggests that some of the adolescents whose refusals of life-saving treatment have been overridden, such as the boy in *Re E* (discussed later), were certainly not of 'unsound mind'. Fortin therefore argues that the use of force could only be justified if Article 2 (the right to life) is allowed to trump Article 5.

Jane Fortin[107]

The courts might now find it difficult to justify employing the wardship jurisdiction to force an intelligent 16-year-old to undergo treatment against his will, as the High Court did in *Re E (A Minor) (Wardship: Medical Treatment)*. According to Ward J, the boy in that case was not *Gillick*-competent because he was unable to grasp the implications of a range of decisions. In particular, he did not have a full understanding of the implication of refusing treatment and choosing to die. But that, surely, is a very far cry from describing him as of 'unsound mind' within Article 5(1)(e) of the Convention. How then is the court to gain its authority to force such a patient to undergo medical treatment without itself infringing Article 5? In such circumstances, it might survive an Article 5 challenge by turning to Article 2 for a solution, when confronted by a teenager refusing life-saving treatment. It might argue that since a minor's rights under the Convention sometimes inevitably conflict, notably his rights under Articles

---

[106] [1991] 2 WLR 140.
[107] 'Children's Rights and the Use of Physical Force' (2001) 13 Child and Family Law Quarterly 243.

2 and 5, it must find an appropriate balance between those rights. Although a minor patient is entitled to freedom from restraint under Article 5, this right may be outweighed by the patient's right to life itself, particularly if he lacks the capacity to comprehend the implications of refusing life-saving treatment. Furthermore, Article 2 imposes a positive obligation on all public authorities, including the courts, to take all reasonable steps to preserve life. A court, when exercising its inherent jurisdiction, might therefore argue that it cannot ignore its duty to save the life of a desperately ill adolescent.

4 CHILDREN'S RIGHT TO MAKE THEIR OWN MEDICAL DECISIONS

(a) A RIGHT TO PARTICIPATE?

Even if parents have the legal right, subject to oversight by the courts, to consent to the medical treatment of children who are not yet *Gillick*-competent (see the following section), such children should still be consulted about their treatment. Depending upon the treatment in question, the views of a minor who lacks capacity might nevertheless carry very considerable weight. For example, in *Re X (A Child) (Capacity to Consent to Termination)*, X was 13 years old and lacked capacity in relation to the decision to terminate her pregnancy. Sir James Munby P was nevertheless clear that such an operation should go ahead only if she was 'accepting'.

Re X (A Child) (Capacity to Consent to Termination)[108]

Sir James Munby P

Only the most compelling arguments could possibly justify compelling a mother [sic] who wished to carry her child to term to submit to an unwanted termination. It would be unwise to be too prescriptive, for every case must be judged on its own unique facts, but I find it hard to conceive of any case where such a drastic form of order—such an immensely invasive procedure—could be appropriate in the case of a mother who does not want a termination, unless there was powerful evidence that allowing the pregnancy to continue would put the mother's life or long-term health at very grave risk. Conversely, it would be a very strong thing indeed, if the mother wants a termination, to require her to continue with an unwanted pregnancy ...

A child or incapacitated adult may, in strict law, lack autonomy. But the court must surely attach very considerable weight indeed to the albeit qualified autonomy of a mother who in relation to a matter as personal, intimate and sensitive as pregnancy is expressing clear wishes and feelings, whichever way, as to whether or not she wants a termination....

[T]he Consultant in Obstetrics and Gynaecology captured the point, as it seemed to me, very compellingly. He said, and I agree, that it would not be right to subject X to a termination unless she was both 'compliant' and 'accepting'....

'Consent', of course, is not the appropriate word, for by definition a child of X's age who, like X, lacks Gillick capacity, cannot in law give a valid consent. But something of the nature of consent or agreement, using those words in the colloquial sense, is required. The

---

[108] [2014] EWHC 1871 (Fam).

Consultant's word 'accepting' in my judgment captures the nuance very well.... Given that X's expressed wishes at the end of the hearing thus accorded with my assessment of her best interests, it was clearly appropriate for me to supply the necessary consent to enable the termination to proceed.

(b) *GILLICK*-COMPETENCE

Until the case of *Gillick v West Norfolk and Wisbech AHA* in 1986, it was not clear whether doctors could lawfully treat a minor in the absence of her parent's consent. Mrs Victoria Gillick had challenged a Memorandum of Guidance, from the Department of Health and Social Security (DHSS), as it then was, which stated that in exceptional cases, a doctor could decide whether contraceptive advice or treatment should be provided to under-16s without parental consent. Mrs Gillick, who was the mother of five girls, wrote to her local health authority seeking an assurance from them that no contraceptive advice or treatment would be given to any of her children while they were under the age of 16, without her knowledge and consent. The health authority refused, and Mrs Gillick sought a declaration that the Memorandum was unlawful. In the Court of Appeal, she succeeded, but by a 3:2 majority, the House of Lords allowed the DHSS's appeal.

Gillick v West Norfolk and Wisbech AHA[109]

Lord Fraser

Nobody doubts, certainly I do not doubt, that in the overwhelming majority of cases the best judges of a child's welfare are his or her parents. Nor do I doubt that any important medical treatment of a child under 16 would normally only be carried out with the parents' approval. That is why it would and should be 'most unusual' for a doctor to advise a child without the knowledge and consent of the parents on contraceptive matters....

There may well be other cases where the doctor feels that because the girl is under the influence of her sexual partner or for some other reason there is no realistic prospect of her abstaining from intercourse. If that is right it points strongly to the desirability of the doctor being entitled in some cases, in the girl's best interest, to give her contraceptive advice and treatment if necessary without the consent or even the knowledge of her parents. The only practicable course is to entrust the doctor with a discretion to act in accordance with his view of what is best in the interests of the girl who is his patient.... But there may well be cases, and I think there will be some cases, where the girl refuses either to tell the parents herself or to permit the doctor to do so and in such cases, the doctor will, in my opinion, be justified in proceeding without the parents' consent or even knowledge provided he is satisfied on the following matters: (1) that the girl (although under 16 years of age) will understand his advice; (2) that he cannot persuade her to inform her parents or to allow him to inform the parents that she is seeking contraceptive advice; (3) that she is very likely to begin or to continue having sexual intercourse with or without contraceptive treatment; (4) that unless she receives contraceptive advice or treatment her physical or mental health or both are likely to suffer; (5) that her best interests require him to give her contraceptive advice, treatment or both without the parental consent.

---

[109] [1984] QB 581.

Lord Scarman

I would hold that as a matter of law the parental right to determine whether or not their minor child below the age of 16 will have medical treatment terminates if and when the child achieves a sufficient understanding and intelligence to enable him or her to understand fully what is proposed. It will be a question of fact whether a child seeking advice has sufficient understanding of what is involved to give a consent valid in law....

When applying these conclusions to contraceptive advice and treatment it has to be borne in mind that there is much that has to be understood by a girl under the age of 16 if she is to have legal capacity to consent to such treatment. It is not enough that she should understand the nature of the advice which is being given: she must also have a sufficient maturity to understand what is involved. There are moral and family questions, especially her relationship with her parents; long-term problems associated with the emotional impact of pregnancy and its termination; and there are the risks to health of sexual intercourse at her age, risks which contraception may diminish but cannot eliminate. It follows that a doctor will have to satisfy himself that she is able to appraise these factors before he can safely proceed upon the basis that she has at law capacity to consent to contraceptive treatment.

Lord Fraser laid out several conditions that should be satisfied before a doctor should judge that it is in a child's best interests to be given contraceptive advice without her parents' knowledge. In effect, the parents' right to consent to their child's treatment cedes to the doctor's judgement about whether advice about contraception is in the child's best interests. This is not especially radical.

In contrast, Lord Scarman's judgment is potentially much more far-reaching. He suggests that when the child achieves sufficient maturity and understanding, her parents' right to consent to any medical treatment terminates, and is replaced by the minor's right to make her own decisions. Lord Scarman did not go so far as to spell out that this meant that the *Gillick*-competent child had the right to take decisions against her own best interests, instead suggesting, more modestly, that the *Gillick*-competent child would be able 'to exercise a *wise* choice in his or her own interests' (my emphasis).

Twenty years later, in *R (on the application of Axon) v Secretary of State for Health*, in deciding that a *Gillick*-competent child under the age of 16 could also give a valid consent to abortion, Silber J held that the parental right to make decisions terminated once the child acquired *Gillick*-competence. Like Lord Fraser, however, he framed this in terms of doctors being enabled to treat under-16s without parental knowledge or consent when they considered this to be appropriate. Silber J rejected Mrs Axon's application for judicial review of Department of Health guidance which had made it clear that people under the age of 16 could expect confidentiality when seeking advice about contraception and abortion.

R (on the application of Axon) v Secretary of State for Health[110]

Silber J

[T]he reasoning of the majority [in *Gillick*] was that the parental right to determine whether a young person will have medical treatment terminates if and when the young person achieves a sufficient understanding and intelligence to understand fully what is proposed,

---

[110] [2006] EWHC 37 (Admin).

with the result that the doctor was entitled in cases in which it was appropriate to do so, to provide advice and treatment to a young person on sexual matters without parental knowledge.

Silber J was 'fortified' in coming to this conclusion by the fact that young women would be deterred from seeking advice and treatment on sexual matters without the assurance of confidentiality, and that this would have 'very undesirable and far-reaching consequences'.

More recently, in *An NHS Trust v A*, a case involving a girl who was pregnant and only just over the age of 13, Mostyn J did appear to spell out the potentially radical implications of a finding of *Gillick*-competence. Mostyn J was clear that, if A was *Gillick*-competent, that would be the end of the matter. Having determined that A did have sufficient understanding of the options, including termination of pregnancy, the decision was for her alone.

An NHS Trust v A[111]

Mostyn J

[I]f I am to determine that A does have sufficient understanding and intelligence to know what a termination would involve, then that is the end of the matter....

It is implicit in that decision [*Gillick*] that provided the child, under the age of 16, has sufficient understanding and intelligence, she can then be lawfully prescribed with contraception even if the result of that would lead her to take steps which are wholly contrary to her best interests. So, the question of best interests does not really inform the primary decision I have to make which is whether she has the necessary capacity....

I am completely satisfied that A has sufficient understanding and intelligence within Lord Fraser's definition and I accordingly make a declaration to that effect. It will now be for A to decide what she wishes to do.

In the next extract, Kirsty Moreton suggests that it may have been easier for Mostyn J to take an apparently radical stance on childhood autonomy, given that A's wishes, in fact, coincided with the professionals' view as to what would be in her best interests. She also suggests that it is revealing that A was thought to need help with coping with her decision, although she was apparently able to make that decision entirely autonomously.

Kirsty L Moreton[112]

[A] more cynical interpretation is that *ABC* is really a best interests decision, dressed up in autonomy language. . . .

[T]here is an irony within *ABC* summed up in Mostyn J's statement that if *A* continued with the pregnancy, then 'her family and, indeed, Social Services will need to give her considerable support and assistance' while in the event of a termination 'her family will need to be at her side and to assist her and support her'. It is inconsistent that the law rejects collaboration in the decision-making process only to call upon it to deal with the consequences of that decision. . . .

---

[111] [2014] EWHC 1445 (Fam).
[112] 'Gillick Reinstated: Judging Mid-Childhood Competence in Healthcare Law (2015) 23 Medical Law Review 303–14.

Furthermore, reaching the outcome that it did may have been simpler for the court as the case involved the question of consent rather than refusal.

But it has to be queried whether the fact that A's wishes appeared to have concurred with the opinions of the doctors and the Court that a termination was in her best interests, may have fostered a situation of 'dependent compliance', and thereby facilitated a finding of competence.

(c) LIFE-THREATENING DECISIONS

In the cases that followed *Gillick*, the courts' respect for mature minors' autonomy did not extend to giving them the same right as competent adults to make foolish or irrational decisions, especially when those choices might be life-threatening. This has happened in two ways.

First, it has proved relatively easy to establish that children who are gravely ill are not *Gillick*-competent. In part, this is because capacity has to be judged in the context of the particular decision: the more complicated the decision, the greater the capacity needed to make it. So a child might be able to consent to having her broken leg X-rayed and put in plaster, but might not be capable of refusing life-saving surgery.

In *Re S (A Minor) (Consent to Medical Treatment)*,[113] Johnson J found that a 15-year-old girl suffering from thalassaemia who no longer wanted to undergo monthly blood transfusions, was not competent to make this decision:

It does not seem to me that her capacity is commensurate with the gravity of the decision which she has made. It seems to me that an understanding that she will die is not enough. For her decision to carry weight she should have a greater understanding of the manner of the death and pain and the distress.

Indeed, it sometimes seems that the test for capacity when the child wishes to make a life-or-death decision has been set so high that no child could ever be judged *Gillick*-competent, and this is especially true if the minor's decision is religiously inspired, rather than a response to the physical burdens of treatment.

In *Re E (A Minor) (Wardship: Medical Treatment)*, a 15-year-old boy, A, who was suffering from leukaemia, wished to refuse a blood transfusion because of his Jehovah's Witness beliefs. Ward J found that to be *Gillick*-competent it was not enough that A, who was 'obviously intelligent', knew that he would die, but also that he would have to understand the manner of his death and the extent of his and his family's suffering.

Re E (A Minor) (Wardship: Medical Treatment)[114]

Ward J

I find that A is a boy of sufficient intelligence to be able to take decisions about his own well-being, but I also find that there is a range of decisions of which some are outside his ability fully to grasp their implications. Impressed though I was by his obvious intelligence, by his

---

[113] [1994] 2 FLR 1065.   [114] [1993] 1 FLR 386.

> calm discussion of the implications, by his assertion even that he would refuse well knowing that he may die as a result, in my judgment A does not have a full understanding of the whole implication of what the refusal of that treatment involves …
>
> I am quite satisfied that A does not have any sufficient comprehension of the pain he has yet to suffer, of the fear that he will be undergoing, of the distress not only occasioned by that fear but also—and importantly—the distress he will inevitably suffer as he, a loving son, helplessly watches his parents' and his family's distress. They are a close family, and they are a brave family, but I find that he has no realisation of the full implications which lie before him as to the process of dying. He may have some concept of the fact that he will die, but as to the manner of his death and to the extent of his and his family's suffering I find he has not the ability to turn his mind to it nor the will to do so …
>
> One has to admire—indeed one is almost baffled by—the courage of the conviction that he expresses. He is, he says, prepared to die for his faith. That makes him a martyr by itself. But I regret that I find it essential for his well-being to protect him from himself and his parents, and so I override his and his parents' decision.

Of course, most adults do not fully understand what it is like to die, and it could therefore be argued that children like A are being held to an excessively demanding test for capacity. The durability of A's beliefs was confirmed when he continued to refuse blood after his 18th birthday, and died as a result. This was not because he had suddenly acquired an understanding of what it would be like to die, rather he had simply achieved the status of adulthood.

In *Re L (Medical Treatment: Gillick Competency)*,[115] Sir Stephen Brown P found that a 14-year-old girl who wanted to refuse a life-saving blood transfusion on religious grounds was not *Gillick*-competent. In part this was because she lacked vital information about the likely nature of her death because it had been deliberately withheld from her. This seems, with respect, to be a misreading of the *Gillick* test for competence, which is supposed to judge whether the child is capable of understanding information, not whether she has been given sufficient information to enable her to make an informed choice. Since the patient's doctors will largely control her access to information, as Andrew Grubb points out, it would be regrettable if an absence of information automatically led to a finding of incompetence:

> The fact that L was ignorant of the detail that the court required her to understand was hardly her fault. Of itself, this did not render her incompetent; rather, it left her uninformed. It cannot be right that a doctor may manipulate a patient's capacity to make a decision by failing to provide relevant information.[116]

In *Re S*, *Re L*, and *Re E*, the standard of competence demanded of children who wanted to refuse treatment was extremely high, and perhaps even unattainable. It is interesting to consider whether these cases would have been brought before the courts, and findings of incompetence made, if these children had instead given their *consent* to blood transfusions.

The judgment of Johnson J in *Re P (A Minor)*, another case involving a teenager (referred to as 'John') who wished to refuse blood products on religious grounds, is rather curious. On the one hand, Johnson J approached the case with a strong predilection to respect John's decision. Johnson J said that there may be cases in which a mature child's refusal 'would be determinative', and that John's wishes had to be at the forefront of his consideration. Indeed,

---

115 [1998] 2 FLR 810.
116 'Commentary on *Re L (Medical Treatment: Gillick-Competency)*' (1999) 7 Medical Law Review 58–61, 60.

he said that there were 'weighty and compelling reasons' to respect John's refusal and reject the doctors' application for a declaration that it would be lawful to give him blood products without consent.

Yet despite his reluctance to grant the order, and without a finding that John lacked capacity (he was 16 years and 10 months old, and so benefitted from the Family Law Reform Act's presumption of competence, considered later), Johnson J found that it would be in John's best interests to receive treatment with blood without consent.

Re P (A Minor)[117]

Johnson J

I put at the forefront of my consideration his wishes. He is nearly seventeen. He is a young man with established convictions. He is undoubtedly a young man whose religious faith must surely demand the respect of all about him. In a world in which religious or indeed any other convictions are not commonly held, John is a young man to be respected ...

So I find there to be weighty and compelling reasons why this order should not be made. In the words of Mr Stevens, a solicitor who has come to act for John ..., John said to him: 'I am my own person. I have a separate mind. It makes no difference what my parents think. I make my own decision.' John's instructions to Mr. Stevens are that he does not consent to receiving a blood transfusion in any circumstances. To overrule the wishes of John seems to me to be an order that I should be (as indeed I am) reluctant to make for the reasons which I have stated.

Nonetheless, looking at the interests of John in the widest possible sense—medical, religious, social, whatever they be—my decision is that John's best interests in those widest senses will be met if I make an order in the terms sought by the NHS Trust with the addition of those extra words, 'unless no other form of treatment is available'.

Cases in which minors have sought to refuse a relatively straightforward life-saving procedure, such as a blood transfusion, for religious reasons, can perhaps be distinguished from cases in which a terminally ill child wishes to refuse burdensome treatment. A few years ago, Herefordshire Primary Care Trust (PCT) sought a court declaration that a heart transplant could be performed on a 13-year-old girl against her wishes, but they dropped the case after a child protection officer found that she was adamant that she did not want the operation.[118] She changed her mind the following year, and a heart transplant was performed.

No cases involving a child's refusal of chemotherapy have reached the courts, but this does not mean that it never happens, and it can be assumed that there have been cases in which refusals of extremely burdensome treatment, like chemotherapy, where a dying child might reasonably conclude that they have had enough, have been respected by health care professionals.

As we saw earlier, the MCA Code of Practice is clear that someone might be competent to make a decision at one time of the day, and lack capacity at another. In contrast, in *Re R (A Minor) (Wardship: Consent to Treatment)*, a case we consider later, Lord Donaldson appeared to hold that *Gillick*-competence is a 'developmental stage'.

---

[117] [2003] EWHC 2327 (Fam).
[118] BBC News, 'Girl wins right to refuse heart', 11 November 2008.

Re R (A Minor) (Wardship: Consent to Treatment)[119]

Lord Donaldson MR

[E]ven if [R] was capable on a good day of a sufficient degree of understanding to meet the Gillick criteria, her mental disability, to the cure or amelioration of which the proposed treatment was directed, was such that on other days she was not only 'Gillick incompetent', but actually sectionable. No child in that situation can be regarded as 'Gillick competent' . . . 'Gillick competence' is a developmental concept and will not be lost or acquired on a day to day or week to week basis.

More recently, in *Re JA (A Minor) (Medical Treatment: Child Diagnosed with HIV)*, a 14-year-old boy, J, was found to be *Gillick*-competent in relation to some decisions, but not others. J had been diagnosed as HIV positive. His parents were both HIV positive, but they disputed their diagnoses and rejected conventional antiretroviral treatment (ART). J also did not want to take ART, and the question for the court was whether he was *Gillick*-competent in relation to that decision.

Re JA (A Minor) (Medical Treatment: Child Diagnosed with HIV)[120]

Baker J

It is plain that J is an intelligent, thoughtful and articulate teenager. He has received a very considerable amount of information about HIV and AIDS from a variety of sources....

On the other hand, in what I regard as the key exchange with the court during his informal oral evidence, J stated that he did not think the diagnosis of HIV given to him was true because he did not have the proof. He did not feel a piece of paper was enough. If he does not accept the diagnosis, it must follow, in my judgment, that he does not fully understand the implication of not receiving the treatment. He therefore lacks the understanding necessary to weigh up the information and arrive at a decision. Applying the test laid down by the House of Lords, this points to a conclusion that he is not Gillick competent.

To an extent, however, there is an element of unreality about this analysis. It could be argued, that if J were to give his consent, his parents having indicated that they would not oppose the treatment, the Trust would in reality provide the treatment without delay. In those circumstances, it could be argued that J falls into the category of patients identified in *Re W* [discussed in the next section], namely someone capable of giving consent but whose refusal to give consent is capable of being overridden by the court....

I conclude that, as J does not accept his diagnosis, he does lack the understanding of the consequences of not taking ART medication and therefore the understanding needed to weigh up the pros and cons before making a decision as to whether to take the medication. On balance, at this precise point in time, he is therefore not Gillick competent to make a decision as to whether or not to take ART.

As set out above, the test for Gillick competence is decision-specific. A person who is not Gillick competent in respect of some treatments may be Gillick competent in respect of others. The decision to take ART is a complex decision which turns in part on J's acceptance of the diagnosis. The decision to undergo monitoring, blood tests and chest x-rays is

---

[119] [1992] Fam 11 (CA).   [120] [2014] EWHC 1135 (Fam).

> less complex, and in any event in this case J has agreed to these measures. Equally, the decision to accept psychotherapy and peer support is less complex. These decisions are not specifically dependent on J's acceptance of his diagnosis but rather on the fact that the diagnosis has been given. He needs psychotherapy and peer support whether or not he accepts the diagnosis. Importantly, J accepts that he should have both psychotherapy and peer support. In all the circumstances, I conclude that he is Gillick competent in respect of decisions whether to undergo monitoring, and receive psychotherapy and peer support.

In the extract above, Baker J mentions the second and more controversial way in which the courts have ignored teenagers' decisions, namely by drawing a distinction between consent to treatment and refusal. *Gillick*, on this view, endows mature minors with the right to consent, but does not give them a corresponding right to refuse. Baker J admits that there is an 'element of unreality' in an analysis that decides that J lacks *Gillick*-competence to refuse ART, when, if he had agreed to start treatment, it is likely that his consent would have been regarded as effective.

It was Lord Donaldson MR in his judgments in *Re R* and *Re W* (discussed in the following section), who first proposed this distinction between consent and refusal. In *Re R (A Minor) (Wardship: Consent to Treatment)*, R, who was 15, had been admitted to an adolescent psychiatric unit. In a lucid interval, R indicated that she would refuse compulsory administration of anti-psychotic medication. The local authority began wardship proceedings, requesting court approval for the administration of the proposed medication without R's consent.

Re R (A Minor) (Wardship: Consent to Treatment)[121]

Lord Donaldson MR

In a case in which the 'Gillick competent' child refuses treatment, but the parents consent, that consent enables treatment to be undertaken lawfully, but in no way determines that the child shall be so treated. In a case in which the positions are reversed, it is the child's consent which is the enabling factor and again the parents' refusal of consent is not determinative. If Lord Scarman intended to go further than this and to say that in the case of a 'Gillick competent' child, a parent has no right either to consent or to refuse consent, his remarks were obiter, because the only question in issue was Mrs. Gillick's alleged right of veto. Furthermore I consider that they would have been wrong

The . . . refusal of the 'Gillick competent' child is a very important factor in the doctor's decision whether or not to treat, but does not prevent the necessary consent being obtained from another competent source.

Because of the similarities between the decision in *Re R* and that in *Re W* (where the Family Law Reform Act 1969 applied), we examine the implications of Lord Donaldson's distinction between consent and refusal after mention has been made of the statute which applies to children aged 16 and 17.

---

[121] [1992] Fam 11 (CA).

(d) THE FAMILY LAW REFORM ACT 1969

Children aged 16 or 17 may lack capacity within the terms of the MCA, considered previously, and hence treatment could be carried out in their best interests under the MCA. More usually, teenagers of 16 and 17 are likely to be *Gillick*-competent but, in addition, the Family Law Reform Act 1969 provides that their consent to medical treatment shall be as effective as it would be if they were an adult.

Family Law Reform Act 1969 section 8

8(1) The consent of a minor who has attained the age of sixteen years to any surgical, medical or dental treatment which, in the absence of consent, would constitute a trespass to his person, shall be as effective as it would be if he were of full age; and where a minor has by virtue of this section given an effective consent to any treatment it shall not be necessary to obtain any consent for it from his parent or guardian . . .

(6) In this section 'surgical, medical or dental treatment' includes any procedure undertaken for the purposes of diagnosis, and this section applies to any procedure (including, in particular, the administration of an anaesthetic) which is ancillary to any treatment as it applies to that treatment.

(7) Nothing in this section shall be construed as making ineffective any consent which would have been effective if this section had not been enacted.

It is worth noting that section 8 only applies to diagnosis and treatment. Bone marrow or organ donation, and non-therapeutic research, are not covered, and the validity of a 16- or 17-year-old's consent to such procedures would be governed by the common law: that is, by whether the child is *Gillick*-competent.

It is also important to remember that section 8 only creates a presumption in favour of capacity, which can be rebutted in the same way as the presumption of capacity in adulthood, namely by evidence that the child is not, in fact, able to believe, retain, and weigh information in the balance in order to arrive at a choice, and if this is the case, the MCA applies.

The most controversial question raised by section 8 is whether it applies only to consent, or whether it also gives 16- and 17-year-old children the right to refuse medical treatment. On the one hand, it might be argued that the right to refuse must complement the right to consent, otherwise this becomes the rather thin 'right' to agree with the doctor. A right to agree, unless accompanied by a parallel right to disagree, could hardly be said to protect patient autonomy.

On the other hand, the section itself refers only to the minor's 'consent' being effective, and states that it displaces the 'need' to obtain parental consent. Not only is it silent as to refusal, but also section 8(3) specifically states that although the 16- or 17-year-old has become capable of giving an effective consent, this does not render ineffective any consent (such as that of the parents), which existed before the statute was passed. It might then be argued that this section's principal purpose was simply to protect doctors, by enabling them to act lawfully when a 16- or 17-year-old gives consent, rather than to remove the parental right to consent.

Certainly this was the preferred interpretation of the Court of Appeal in *Re W (A Minor) (Medical Treatment: Court's Jurisdiction)*. W, a 16-year-old girl suffering from anorexia, wanted to refuse treatment for her anorexia, and claimed, unsuccessfully, that section 8 conferred on her the same right as an adult to refuse medical treatment.

Re W (A Minor) (Medical Treatment: Court's Jurisdiction)[122]

Lord Donaldson MR

On reflection I regret my use in *In Re R (A Minor) (Wardship: Consent to Treatment)* of the keyholder analogy because keys can lock as well as unlock. I now prefer the analogy of the legal 'flak jacket' which protects the doctor from claims by the litigious whether he acquires it from his patient who may be a minor over the age of 16, or a 'Gillick competent' child under that age or from another person having parental responsibilities which include a right to consent to treatment of the minor. Anyone who gives him a flak jacket (that is, consent) may take it back, but the doctor only needs one and so long as he continues to have one he has the legal right to proceed....

There is ample authority for the proposition that the inherent powers of the court under its parens patriae jurisdiction are theoretically limitless and that they certainly extend beyond the powers of a natural parent. There can therefore be no doubt that it has power to override the refusal of a minor, whether over the age of 16 or under that age but 'Gillick competent'. It does not do so by ordering the doctors to treat which, even if within the court's powers, would be an abuse of them or by ordering the minor to accept treatment, but by authorising the doctors to treat the minor in accordance with their clinical judgment, subject to any restrictions which the court may impose.

(e) A CHILD'S 'RIGHT' TO REFUSE TREATMENT?

The reasoning adopted by Lord Donaldson in both *Re R* and *Re W* can be simply stated. Doctors must have an effective consent before they can lawfully provide medical treatment. *Gillick* and the Family Law Reform Act 1969 endow older children with the right to give a valid consent to medical treatment, and hence allow doctors to proceed without seeking additional consent from a parent. But the parental right to consent is not thereby extinguished: rather, it coexists both with the child's right to consent, and with the court's even broader right to authorize medical treatment.

Because a doctor needs only one effective consent, once a child is *Gillick*-competent (or 16 or 17 years old), there are three possible sources of this consent: the parents, the courts, and the mature minor. Consent from any one of these three sources will protect the doctor from prosecution or liability in tort. That means that the parents' or the court's consent will be effective, even if the mature minor refuses to give her consent. The mature minor therefore has no right to have her refusal respected.

This distinction has subsequently been applied in a number of cases. According to Thorpe J in *Re K, W and H (Minors) (Medical Treatment):*[123]

The decision of the Court of Appeal in *Re R* made it plain that a child with *Gillick* competence can consent to treatment, but that if he or she declines to do so, consent can be given by someone else who has parental rights or responsibilities.

In *Re W*, Lord Donaldson MR did not qualify the courts' right to overrule the mature minor, but both Balcombe and Nolan LJJ attempted to confine the courts' and parents' power to

---

[122] [1993] Fam 64 (CA).   [123] [1993] 1 FLR 854.

overrule the mature minor's refusal to cases in which the treatment is necessary to prevent death or severe permanent injury.

This was also the approach adopted in the more recent case of *Re P (A Child)*, in which Baker J declared that, despite his finding that she did not lack capacity under the Mental Capacity Act, it would be lawful to give antidote treatment to a 17-year-old who had taken an overdose of paracetamol and was refusing to agree to antidote treatment.

Re P (A Child)[124]

Baker J

In exercising its inherent jurisdiction, the court must have the child's welfare as its paramount consideration. The wishes and feelings of the child, in particular those of a 17-year-old young person who is almost an adult, are an important component of the analysis of her welfare. They are not, however, decisive. In addition, the court must consider other factors and in particular in this situation any harm she has suffered or is at risk of suffering. In this case, the risk of harm is clearly at a high level. If she does not receive treatment to counteract the effects of the overdose of paracetamol, she will undoubtedly suffer serious damage to her liver and in probability will die....

In this case, balancing the competing factors, I have no hesitation in concluding that the balance comes down firmly in favour of overriding P's wishes. I recognise that this is not to be taken lightly. The wishes of a young person aged seventeen and a half are important. They are, of course, entitled to be taken into account as part of her Article 8 rights under ECHR. On the other hand, those rights are not absolute. Here, they are outweighed by her rights under Article 2—everyone's right to life shall be protected by law. The court is under a positive or operational duty arising from Article 2 to take preventative measures to protect an individual whose life is at risk ...

In those circumstances, this court is under a heavy duty to take what steps it can to protect P's life which is manifestly in danger tonight. Accordingly, I have made an order including a declaration that it is lawful and in P's best interests for the medical practitioners having responsibility for her care and treatment to treat her for the effects of her overdose notwithstanding the fact that she is refusing treatment.

Furthermore, it is conceivable that in the course of this life-sustaining treatment it may be necessary to sedate or restrain P. I very much hope that this will not be necessary. But if it is, I declare that such steps be lawful, notwithstanding the fact that they amount to a deprivation of liberty.

Until a child reaches the age of 18, her wishes are therefore important, but can be trumped by the need to do whatever is necessary to save her life. As Ward J has put it in *Re E (A Minor) (Wardship: Medical Treatment)*,[125] the court 'should be very slow to allow an infant to martyr himself'.

Certainly for religiously inspired refusals of blood products, the right to make life-ending decisions appears to be governed by a *status-based* test for competence. Caroline Bridge and Andrew Grubb argue that it would be better if the courts were explicit about this.

---

[124] [2014] EWHC 1650 (Fam).   [125] [1993] 1 FLR 386.

Caroline Bridge[126]

[J]udges should not go through the pretence of applying a functional test of capacity when the outcome of the young person's decision is not one that they, or probably society, would countenance. The law should openly declare that welfare reigns when grave decisions with momentous outcomes are considered and recognise that adolescent autonomy is, inevitably, circumscribed.

Andrew Grubb[127]

Clearly, the court is striving to act on its 'hunch' that society should not let children make a decision to die. In truth, it comes down to no more than the court (as society's instrument) acknowledging that at some point citizens must be allowed to make their own decisions, even ones which others might perceive as harmful to them. That point is the age of majority, which for us is 18 . . . Once that point is reached, the state does not have a compelling interest to prevent rational citizens from reaching (most) decisions. Until that point, however, the protective duty of society permits intervention. If this is the public policy of this country, it would be far better for the courts . . . simply to say so rather than to obfuscate matters by distorting the legal concept of competence.

Re E (A Minor) (Wardship: Medical Treatment)[128] offers a particularly compelling illustration of the status test for capacity to make life-threatening decisions. The day before his 18th birthday, A lacked capacity, but he gained it the following day, at which point he became entitled to, and subsequently did, refuse a blood transfusion. It is very unlikely that A's reasoning abilities underwent a dramatic change on the morning of his 18th birthday, so that he was unable to grasp what it was like to die when he was 17 years and 364 days old, but miraculously achieved this higher level of understanding within the next 24 hours.

This paternalistic approach to children's decision-making capacity is justified, according to Lowe and Juss, where a child's decision would cause irreparable harm.

Nigel Lowe and Satvinder Juss[129]

We must start with the assumption that a doctor will act in the best interests of his patient. Hence, if the doctor believes that a particular treatment is necessary for his patient, it is perfectly rational for the law to facilitate this as easily as possible and hence allow a '*Gillick* competent' child to give a valid consent, and also to protect the child against parents opposed to what is professionally considered to be in his best interests. In contrast, it is surely right for the law to be reluctant to allow a *child* of whatever age to be able to veto treatment designed for his or her benefit, particularly if a refusal would lead to the child's death or permanent damage. In other words, the clear and consistent policy of the law is to protect the child against wrong-headed parents and against itself.

---

[126] 'Religious Beliefs and Teenage Refusal of Medical Treatment' (1999) 62 Modern Law Review 585–94, 594.

[127] 'Commentary on *Re L (Medical Treatment: Gillick Competency)*' (1999) 7 Medical Law Review 58–61.

[128] [1993] 1 FLR 386.

[129] 'Medical Treatment—Pragmatism and the Search for Principle' (1993) 56 Modern Law Review 865–72.

In their support for Donaldson's approach, Lowe and Juss are in a minority. Recall that at the beginning of this chapter, we noted that consent is widely believed to be necessary both to provide the doctor with a defence to a charge of assault or to liability in damages for trespass, and to protect the patient's autonomy. In relation to children, as John Eekelaar points out, on Lord Donaldson's view, it appears that the former purpose of consent is the more important one: doctors need only one effective consent in order to treat a child lawfully; in contrast, respect for autonomy would mean offering equal protection to the child's right to refuse treatment.

John Eekelaar[130]

Lord Donaldson said that there were two reasons for requiring that a patient consents to medical treatment. The 'clinical' reason was that it made treatment easier. The 'legal' reason was 'to provide those concerned in the treatment with a defence to a criminal charge of assault or battery or a civil claim for damages for trespass to the person'. This is an astonishingly narrow view of the requirement, which . . . is surely rooted in the fundamental civil rights of all citizens that their personal integrity should not be infringed without their consent or lawful justification. Lord Donaldson is not unaware of this, for in a later case involving an adult, he relates it to the right 'to choose whether to consent to medical treatment, to refuse it or to choose one rather than another of the treatments being offered . . . notwithstanding that the reasons for making the choice are rational, irrational, unknown or even non-existent' . . .

Lord Donaldson seems to be reluctant to accept that the law should protect minors, even if competent, in the same manner. Rather, his primary concern is to fashion the law so as to minimise the risk of legal action against doctors.

Ian Kennedy further argues that Lord Donaldson's 'gloss' on the House of Lords' judgment in *Gillick* was illegitimate.[131]

Ian Kennedy[132]

But enter now Lord Donaldson. He had clearly taken against *Gillick* and decided that he was going to provide a gloss to it. The gloss he provided is such that if it were accepted as law, the House of Lords would have been overruled by a lower court—a rare legal phenomenon indeed . . .

In my respectful view, Lord Donaldson is wrong. His interpretation of *Gillick* is unique, which is an achievement given the buckets of ink spilt in analyzing that case. His failure to accept that the power to refuse is no more than the obverse of the power to consent and that they are simply twin aspects of the single right to self-determination borders on the perverse.

It is true that none of the judgments in *Gillick* distinguished between consent and refusal. The distinction between consent and refusal is also inconsistent with sections 38(6) and 44(7) of

130 'White Coats or Flak Jackets? Children and the Courts Again' (1993) 109 Law Quarterly Review 182–7.
131 See also Gillian Douglas, 'The Retreat from *Gillick*' (1992) 55 Modern Law Review 569–76.
132 'Consent to Treatment: The Capable Person' in Clare Dyer (ed), *Doctors, Patients and the Law* (Blackwell: Oxford, 1992) 44–71.

the Children Act 1989, which provide children with 'sufficient understanding' with a right to refuse to be examined or assessed: 'if the child is of sufficient understanding to make an informed decision he may refuse to submit to the examination or other assessment'.

In the next extract, John Harris argues that if a child understands enough to give consent to a particular treatment, then she also understands enough to refuse it.

John Harris[133]

The idea that a child (or anyone) might competently consent to a treatment but not be competent to refuse it is a palpable nonsense, the reasons for which are revealed by a moment's reflection on what a competent consent involves. To give an informed consent you need to understand the nature of the course of action to which you are consenting, which, in medical contexts, will include its probable and possible consequences and side effects and the nature of any alternative measures which might be taken and the consequences of doing nothing.

So, to understand a proposed treatment well enough to consent to it is to understand the consequences of a refusal. And if the consequences of a refusal are understood well enough to consent to the alternative then the refusal must also be competent.

Similarly, Sarah Elliston suggests that Lord Donaldson's 'gloss' means that children's medical decisions will be respected only if 'they know what is good for them'.

Sarah Elliston[134]

The situation we are faced with now is that the most that a competent child can expect is that their consent to medical intervention will be determinative. Therefore it may be seriously doubted whether any real question of autonomous decision making by them arises. Their consent is a mere acceptance or endorsement of a procedure that may be authorised to be carried out anyway. . . .

At present, the law in England permits those under 18 to have their medical decisions respected if, but only if, they know what is good for them and accept the treatment that is proposed. Such a situation is both illogical and unjust and may have wider implications for the way in which children are viewed in our society, in that it suggests that children are in some way less entitled to full respect as members of our society by virtue of their status.

It could even be argued that a right to refuse unwanted medical treatment might be of more importance than the right to consent to it. Jane Fortin draws attention to the practical consequences of ordering a fully grown adolescent to have treatment that he does not want:

the case-law is surprisingly reticent over the practical details. Indeed, the courts have barely mentioned that the implication of authorizing treatment against the wishes of a fully grown adolescent is that he may have to be held down physically to undergo it.[135]

---

[133] 'Consent and end of life decisions' (2003) 29 Journal of Medical Ethics 10–15, 12.

[134] 'If You Know What's Good for You: Refusal of Consent to Medical Treatment by Children' in Sheila McLean (ed), *Contemporary Issues in Law, Medicine and Ethics* (Ashgate: Dartmouth, 1996) 29–55.

[135] 'Children's Rights and the Use of Physical Force' (2001) 13 Child and Family Law Quarterly 243.

Indeed, the logical consequence of Lord Donaldson's consent/refusal distinction would be that, even if a pregnant 16-year-old girl is *Gillick*-competent, both her parents and the courts would retain the right to consent to a termination of pregnancy, which could be performed lawfully despite her competent refusal. Of course, this would not happen in practice. As Lord Balcombe explained in *Re W (A Minor) (Medical Treatment: Court's Jurisdiction)* itself:[136]

> In the course of the arguments before us it was suggested that a construction of section 8 of the Act of 1969 which denies a 16- or 17-year-old girl an absolute right to refuse medical treatment, but leaves it open to her parents to consent to such treatment, could in theory lead to a case where a pregnant 16-year-old refuses an abortion, but her parents' consent to her pregnancy being terminated. So it could in theory, but I cannot conceive of a case where a doctor, faced with the refusal of a mentally competent 16-year-old to having an abortion, would terminate the pregnancy merely upon the consent of the girl's parents. Leaving aside all questions of medical ethics, it seems to me inevitable that in such highly unlikely circumstances the matter would have to come before the court. I find it equally difficult to conceive of a case where the court, faced with this problem and applying the approach I have indicated above, would authorise an abortion against the wishes of a mentally competent 16-year-old. The dilemma is therefore more apparent than real.

In the next extract, Charles Foster and José Miola are critical of Lord Donaldson's willingness to leave a lacuna in the law to be filled by 'medical ethics', suggesting that the solution instead lies in the courts treating abortion as a special case.

Charles Foster and José Miola[137]

> This is quite a bold course of action to take. Lord Donaldson is recognising that the law does not fulfil what he implies is its desired function, but at the same time he expresses such confidence in medical ethics as a regulatory tool that he is happy to delegate the issue to it . . .
>
> Thus his Lordship assumed that 'medical ethics' would effectively police the medical profession's conduct. However, . . . not only do the GMC and BMA guidelines relating to this issue contain no specific prohibition of such a procedure, but doctors are repeatedly encouraged to seek legal advice in order to decide what they should do. . . .
>
> The result is that the law delegates responsibility to decision-making to professional medical ethics, while professional medical ethics in turn abrogates responsibility back to the law. . . .
>
> There was no need for Lord Donaldson's unhappy formulation in *Re W*. Should the unwilling 17 year old be forced by her parents to have an abortion? No. But that is really because abortion is a rather special type of 'treatment'. It cannot simply be lumped together with appendectomies.

[136] [1993] Fam 64 (CA).

[137] 'Who's in Charge? The Relationship between Medical Law, Medical Ethics and Medical Morality?' (2015) 23 Medical Law Review 505–30.

In *Re X (A Child) (Capacity to Consent to Termination)*,[138] as we saw earlier, Sir James Munby P was clear that an abortion should not be carried out against the wishes of a 13-year-old girl who was not *Gillick*-competent. In practice, then, children do retain the right to refuse some treatments, but the consent/refusal distinction essentially gives the courts a wide discretion to protect children against themselves.

5 VOLUNTARINESS

To be valid, consent to medical treatment must also have been given voluntarily. Patients will seldom be coerced by direct threats into consenting to medical treatment, but more subtle forms of pressure are possible. The important question is whether the external pressure was such as to overbear the patient's will, and vitiate her consent.

To begin with, it is important to note that the experience of serious and debilitating illness will often leave a patient feeling that she has no option but to agree to whatever is proposed. Yet the pressurized context in which medical decisions may have to be made does not mean that patients are incapable of consenting to treatment. As PDG Skegg has explained: 'Consent is no less effective when it is unwillingly or reluctantly given; few patients would consent to major surgery if it were not for the force of surrounding circumstances, and the knowledge that health or even life may be in jeopardy if they do not consent.'[139]

But where there has been what amounts to coercion, undue influence, or a fundamental mistake as to the nature of the procedure, it may be possible to argue that the patient's consent is not real.

(a) COERCION

Coercion may vitiate consent to treatment. If a patient was coerced into consenting to treatment, then her apparent consent will be invalid, and any medical treatment which was carried out may be both an assault and a battery. So what do we mean by coercion?

Ruth R Faden, Tom L Beauchamp, with Nancy MP King[140]

Coercion occurs if one party intentionally and successfully influences another by presenting a credible threat of unwanted and avoidable harm so severe that the person is unable to resist acting to avoid it. The three critical features in this definition . . . are that

1. the agent of influence must *intend* to influence the other person by presenting a severe threat,

2. there must be a credible *threat*, and

3. the threat must be *irresistible*.

On this definition, coercion will hardly ever vitiate a patient's consent to medical treatment. In fact, when people talk about coercion in the context of consent to medical treatment, they are usually referring to persuasion, manipulation, or exploitation, rather than coercion.

---

[138] [2014] EWHC 1871 (Fam).
[139] *Law, Ethics and Medicine: Studies in Medical Law* (Clarendon Press: Oxford, 1984) 97.
[140] *A History and Theory of Informed Consent* (OUP: Oxford, 1986) 339.

It is often said that offering someone money to become a research subject, or to sell their kidney, would be coercive. However, as Bonnie Steinbock explains in the next extract, an offer might be exploitative, in that it takes advantage of someone's straitened circumstances, but this is not necessarily the same thing as coercion.

Bonnie Steinbock[141]

The mere existence of external pressure or influence does not establish coercion. The influence or pressure must be of a kind and an amount that diminishes free choice. The central question for understanding the concept of coercion, then, is *how much, and what kind of influence or pressure deprives actions and decisions of their autonomous character.* As we will see, the question does not have a simple or straightforward answer. Moreover, pressure or influence that does not qualify as coercive may also be morally objectionable if, for example, it exploits a person's desperate situation . . .

Incentives, like threats, are ways of trying to get people to do things. Unlike threats, incentives are typically welcome offers that seem morally unobjectionable. Yet sometimes inducements and incentives are alleged to be coercive . . . Offering a poor person money for a body part exploits him or takes advantage of his poverty, but it is not clear that it forces or coerces him.

Incentives to do things that people ordinarily would not consider doing appear to be in the same category as exploitative offers. Whether they are coercive is unclear. However, even if they are not coercive, they may be morally impermissible.

While crude threats are unusual in health care settings, mentally ill patients, as Bean explains, may be particularly susceptible to coercive treatment.

Philip Bean[142]

In an obvious sense there can be no consent if coercion is used: X cannot be said to be consenting if agreement is extracted with Y's gun . . . The problem with coercion, as it affects mental patients . . . , is that it is never as naked as that but may involve more subtle threats of punishments, loss of privileges, threats of further detention etc. Where psychiatric staff say 'we shall do this or that to you unless you consent to this treatment', they are involved in coercion. Similarly, when they say 'we shall keep you in hospital unless you consent to this treatment' they are also involved in coercion . . .

So where consent is extracted with threats of punishment, loss of privileges and threats of further detention this is coercion for it takes unfair advantage of the patient's vulnerability.

In *Freeman v Home Office (No 2)*, a prisoner serving a life sentence claimed that he had received medical treatment that had been administered against his will. He argued that where the doctor is also a prison officer, a patient's consent could never be truly voluntary. The Court of Appeal rejected this argument. Whether or not consent had been given voluntarily was a question of fact, and that although the patient's imprisonment might alert the

141 'The Concept of Coercion and Long-Term Contraceptives' in Ellen Moskowitz and Bruce Jennings (eds), *Coerced Contraception? Moral and Policy Challenges of Long-Acting Birth Control* (Georgetown UP: Washington DC, 1996) 53–78.
142 *Mental Disorder and Legal Control* (CUP: Cambridge, 1986) 138–9.

court to a risk that the patient's apparent consent was not real, voluntariness could only be judged on a case-by-case basis.

Freeman v Home Office (No 2)[143]

> **Stephen Brown LJ**
>
> I find myself in complete agreement with the trial judge that the sole issue raised at the trial, that is to say whether the plaintiff had consented to the administration of the drugs injected into his body, was essentially one of fact: . . . 'The right approach, in my judgment, is to say that where, in a prison setting, a doctor has the power to influence a prisoner's situation and prospects a court must be alive to the risk that what may appear, on the face of it, to be real consent is not in fact so.'

(b) UNDUE INFLUENCE

In *Re T (Adult: Refusal of Treatment)*,[144] the court recognized that pressure to consent to medical treatment is unlikely to come from physical force or duress, and more likely to take the form of persuasion. Of course, many forms of persuasion are wholly legitimate. Doctors and relatives will often try to persuade patients of the merits of treatment. In *Re T*, Staughton LJ recognized that 'every decision is made as a result of some influence: a patient's decision to consent to an operation will normally be influenced by the surgeon's advice as to what will happen if the operation does not take place'.

Indeed, as Ruth Faden et al explain, trying to persuade someone to undergo beneficial treatment may be a good thing:

> Frequently in clinical situations, professionals would be morally blameworthy if they did not attempt to persuade their patients to consent to interventions that are medically necessitated. Reasoned argument in defense of an option is itself information, and as such is no less important in ensuring understanding that disclosure of facts . . . Paradigmatically, persuasion succeeds by *improving*, and not by undermining, a person's understanding of his or her situation.[145]

Whether or not the persuasion amounts to undue influence would have to be established on the facts of each case. One obviously relevant factor, as pointed out in *Re T (Adult: Refusal of Treatment)*, is the relationship between the persuader and the patient: the closer the relationship, the harder it may be for a patient weakened by illness to withstand pressure which is exerted upon them.

T had refused a blood transfusion, following discussions with her mother, a Jehovah's Witness. Since that refusal, T's condition had deteriorated, and her baby had been stillborn. Her father, supported by her boyfriend, applied successfully for a declaration that it would be lawful to give her a blood transfusion.

---

[143] [1993] Fam 64 (CA).   [144] [1993] Fam 95 (CA).
[145] Ruth Faden and Tom Beauchamp, with Nancy King, *A History and Theory of Informed Consent* (OUP: Oxford, 1986).

Re T (Adult: Refusal of Treatment)[146]

Lord Donaldson MR

When considering the effect of outside influences, two aspects can be of crucial importance. First, the strength of the will of the patient. One who is very tired, in pain or depressed
will be much less able to resist having his will overborne than one who is rested, free from
pain and cheerful. Second, the relationship of the 'persuader' to the patient may be of crucial
importance. The influence of parents on their children or of one spouse on the other can
be, but is by no means necessarily, much stronger than would be the case in other relationships. Persuasion based upon religious belief can also be much more compelling and the
fact that arguments based upon religious beliefs are being deployed by someone in a very
close relationship with the patient will give them added force and should alert the doctors to
the possibility—no more—that the patient's capacity or will to decide has been overborne.
In other words the patient may not mean what he says.

It is worth noting that in *Re T* the decision that the court decided had been undermined
by undue influence was a refusal of treatment. It might be predicted that if T's mother had
instead persuaded her to consent to a life-saving blood transfusion, it is unlikely that the
doctors would have sought a court declaration that T's apparent consent had been vitiated
by her mother's undue influence.

(c) MISTAKE

A decision may not reflect the patient's wishes if it is based upon a mistake, such as a misunderstanding of the seriousness of her condition. This was again an issue in *Re T (Adult:
Refusal of Treatment)*[147] where the patient had been reassured that a blood transfusion might
not be necessary, and that equally effective alternatives existed. Her condition had deteriorated since those assurances had been given, thus casting doubt upon whether her continuing refusal genuinely reflected her wishes.

The most likely scenario in which a patient might claim that her apparent consent was
vitiated by a mistake is through the claim that she was inadequately informed about the
treatment she underwent, and in particular about its risks or side effects. We considered this
sort of claim in more detail in the previous chapter.

6 CONCLUSION

In this chapter we have been concerned with the medical treatment of children and adults
who lack capacity, and it is clear that a great deal turns on whether a patient has capacity.
For patients with capacity, the principle of autonomy dominates, and the patient is entitled
to refuse treatment, including life-saving treatment, for irrational reasons or even for no
reason at all. If, on the other hand, the patient lacks capacity, doctors are entitled to act
paternalistically and treat the patient in her best interests. Since the consequences of lacking
capacity are that one's wishes can be overridden, it is important both that a clear definition
of incapacity exists, and that it is applied objectively and consistently.

---

[146] [1993] Fam 95 (CA).   [147] Ibid.

For some patients, such as very young children and permanently comatose adults, it will be self-evident that they lack the capacity to make decisions about their medical treatment. However, while the law insists upon a binary either/or categorization of patients as either competent or incompetent, the reality is that decision-making capacity exists on a spectrum. Towards either end of this spectrum, it will be completely obvious that the patient either has or does not have capacity. Towards the middle, decisions are more difficult.

Since the capacity/incapacity line is so critical, it is also important to consider who should be charged with making this assessment. While independent review by the courts is possible, usually the decision is made by the patient's doctors. Two important points follow from this. First, doctors are undoubtedly much less likely to question a patient's decision-making capacity when she has agreed to their proposed treatment. This means that uncooperative patients are more likely to be judged to lack capacity, and to therefore be treated against their wishes.

Secondly, once the doctor has determined that a patient lacks capacity, then, in the absence of a binding AD, she is entitled to treat the patient according to her assessment of the patient's best interests, as structured by the section 4(6) checklist. In most cases, then, doctors are responsible for applying both the test for incapacity and the best interests test, and therefore exercise considerable control over the treatment of patients who lack capacity.

Of course, cases can and are brought before the courts, and in the case of especially controversial treatments such as sterilization, court involvement is routine. But in the ordinary run of things, it is important to acknowledge that it is not judges, but rather doctors, who must interpret and apply both the test for capacity and the best interests test. In the light of this, the House of Lords Select Committee's finding that the Mental Capacity Act is poorly understood by health care professionals is particularly concerning.

House of Lords Select Committee on the Mental Capacity Act 2005[148]

The general lack of awareness of the provisions of the Act has allowed prevailing professional practices to continue unchallenged, and allowed decision-making to be dominated by professionals, without the required input from families and carers about P's wishes and feelings.

A fundamental change of attitudes among professionals is needed in order to move from protection and paternalism to enablement and empowerment. Professionals need to be aware of their responsibilities under the Act, just as families need to be aware of their rights under it.

FURTHER READING

Donnelly, Mary, 'Best Interests, Patient Participation and the Mental Capacity Act 2005' (2009) 17 Medical Law Review 1–29.

Donnelly, Mary and Kilkelly, Ursula, 'Child-Friendly Healthcare: Delivering on the Right to be Heard' (2011) 19 Medical Law Review 27–54.

Draper, Heather, 'Anorexia nervosa and respecting a refusal of life-prolonging therapy: a limited justification' (2000) 14 Bioethics 120–33.

---

[148] House of Lords Select Committee on the Mental Capacity Act 2005, Report of Session 2013–14, *Mental Capacity Act 2005: Post-Legislative Scrutiny*.

Herring, Jonathan and Foster, Charles, 'Welfare means Relationality, Virtue and Altruism' (2012) 32 Legal Studies 480.

Heywood, Rob, 'Revisiting Advance Decision Making Under the Mental Capacity Act 2005: A Tale of Mixed Messages' (2015) 23 Medical Law Review 81–102.

House of Lords Select Committee on the Mental Capacity Act 2005, Report of Session 2013–14, *Mental Capacity Act 2005: Post-Legislative Scrutiny.*

Jones, RB, 'Parental consent to cosmetic facial surgery in Down's syndrome' (2000) 26 Journal of Medical Ethics 101–2.

Maclean, Alasdair, 'Advance Directives and the Rocky Waters of Anticipatory Decision-Making' (2008) 16 Medical Law Review 1–22.

Michalowski, Sabine, 'Advance Refusals of Life Sustaining Treatment' (2005) 68 Modern Law Review 958.

Wrigley, Anthony, 'Proxy consent: moral authority misconceived' (2007) 33 Journal of Medical Ethics 527–31.

6

MENTAL HEALTH LAW

CENTRAL ISSUES

1. In a significant exception to the principle of patient autonomy, it can be lawful to detain and treat a mentally disordered patient even if she has capacity and is refusing treatment. To be lawful, compulsory treatment must be treatment for her mental disorder, and must not amount to 'inhuman and degrading treatment'.

2. Most mentally ill patients are not, however, subject to compulsory powers. Among hospital inpatients, a minority has been 'sectioned'. Most are admitted informally.

3. The 'Deprivation of Liberty Safeguards' are supposed to offer safeguards to patients who have not been subject to compulsory powers, but who are not,

in practice, free to leave. They are overly complex, and the Supreme Court judgment in *Cheshire West* has increased dramatically the number of cases reaching the Court of Protection.

4. The Mental Health Act 2007 made a number of significant changes to the Mental Health Act 1983. During the reform process, critics were concerned about the emphasis placed upon the risk mentally ill people pose to others.

5. Detaining people on the grounds of their mental illness, or interfering with their bodily integrity, both of which are permissible under the Mental Health Act, would appear to be contrary to the UN Convention on the Rights of Persons with Disabilities.

---

1 INTRODUCTION

In this chapter we attempt a broad overview of mental health law in the UK. There are arguments for and against including a chapter on mental health law in a medical law textbook. On the one hand, mental health law is a subject in its own right, and a single chapter is incapable of doing justice to its breadth and complexity. Yet, on the other hand, for a medical law textbook to exclude the special legal framework which applies to mentally ill patients might appear to mirror the misguided belief, described by Campbell and Heginbotham, that the mentally ill are not really like other patients.

Tom Campbell and Chris Heginbotham[1]

Persons with mental illnesses are made to suffer a range of unnecessary deprivations which result from crude and erroneous assumptions about mental illnesses which lead us to lump their victims together in a pariah class of sub-humans. People with a history of mental illness repeatedly experience the frustration and insult caused by a lack of respect for them as individuals and the absence of humane consideration for their situation.

While a mental illness can happen to any member of society, its natural effects are such that its victims rarely achieve or sustain economic security or social influence. Social attitudes accelerate and reinforce this downward spiral through social and economic exclusion. Mental illness thus routinely brings with it membership of a wronged, insulted and excessively deprived class of persons. . . .

[U]nreasonable hostile reactions to people with mental illnesses bring deprivations and disadvantages that would not be tolerated if they were inflicted on other citizens. The result is that mental illness discrimination exacerbates the often already unfortunate plight of those with mental illnesses.

We begin with a short history of mental health policy. Next we consider the various stages involved in the treatment of mental illness, starting with a definition of mental disorder and a description of how patients are admitted to the mental health system.

The previous chapter dealt with the concept of mental incapacity, and at the outset it is important to remember that mentally ill people are not necessarily incapable of making medical decisions. Recall the patient in *Re C*,[2] who suffered from paranoid schizophrenia, and yet was found to have the capacity to decide that he did not want his gangrenous leg amputated. If they have capacity, mentally ill patients have the same right to refuse medical treatment as other competent adults, but the Mental Health Act creates important exceptions to this. Finally, we explore discharge from the mental health system, and we look at how ex-patients can be kept on a 'long leash', through the use of community treatment orders.

The fundamental legal difference between mental health law and other areas of medical law is that it authorizes the detention and compulsory treatment of people suffering from mental illness. Detention and treatment without consent are radically out of line with the principle of patient autonomy which now dominates medical law. What justification could there be for treating people with mental health problems differently?

(a) It might enable a patient to access medical treatment. If a mentally ill patient is incapable of giving consent to treatment, the only way for her to receive treatment is for her to be treated without consent. This obviously only applies to mentally ill patients who *also* lack capacity. For competent patients, further justification is required.

(b) It could be argued that detention and treatment without consent are sometimes necessary to protect the patient from herself. Someone who is depressed and suicidal, for example, might subsequently be glad that she was prevented from taking her own life.

(c) Finally, it has been argued that detention and compulsory treatment may be necessary to protect the public from dangerous mentally ill patients.

As we shall see, this latter idea, that the public needs protection from people with mental health problems, was the driver behind the 2007 reforms to the Mental Health Act 1983.

---

[1] *Mental Illness: Prejudice, Discrimination and the Law* (Dartmouth: Aldershot, 1991).
[2] [1994] 1 WLR 290.

It is, however, extremely controversial because it has been invoked to justify what is essentially *preventative detention*: that is, detaining someone not because they have been found guilty of a criminal offence, but because there is perceived to be a *risk* that they *might* cause harm to others. Not only does this create an exception to some basic principles of criminal justice, but it also rests upon the mistaken assumption that a diagnosis of mental illness is an accurate predictor of future violent behaviour. We do not detain men who regularly binge drink on the grounds that there is a chance that they might, in the future, get involved in a pub brawl or hit their partner. Rather, detention is possible only after they have, in fact, broken the law.

There is considerable media interest whenever mentally ill people commit serious offences, perhaps the most infamous of which is the Michael Stone case. Stone—who had mental health as well as substance abuse problems—was convicted of the horrific murders of Lin and Megan Russell, who were beaten to death in 1996 while on a country walk with Megan's surviving sister Josie. In its coverage of dreadful crimes committed by a person who has previously had contact with mental health services, the press often takes the view that there must have been a failure on the part of those services. Of course, it is not necessarily possible to predict in advance that someone is going to break the law. Nevertheless, there seems to be a common assumption that mental health services should always be able to prevent mentally ill people from harming other people.

Interestingly, despite the received wisdom that Michael Stone was 'free to kill', the inquiry into the circumstances leading up to the Russell murders found that at no point was Stone refused help by mental health care services. He had been refused a place in an inpatient detoxification unit, but this finding received little publicity.[3]

In addition to the tendency to blame mental health services, this sort of press coverage may influence public attitudes towards the mentally ill. Most people who are mentally ill are harmless, and, if anything, pose a risk to themselves rather than to others. As Nancy Wolff explains in the next extract, the erroneous public perception that all mentally ill people pose a risk of harm to others bolsters public support for their detention.

Nancy Wolff[4]

Implicit in the public's perception of severe mental illness is the notion that not only are persons with these disorders more likely to engage in violent acts, but also that the higher relative risk is evenly distributed across the entire group of disordered individuals. Evidence suggests, however, that the distribution of risk within this population is bimodal forming two subgroups: low risk and high risk. . . . Evidence on homicides in England and Wales suggests that 0.05 per cent of persons with severe mental illness pose the greatest risk of homicidal violence. The low risk group is the larger of the two, comprising roughly 90 per cent of persons with severe mental illness. While individuals in the low-risk group have violence profiles that are more like the general population, they may still engage in non-violent criminal or social deviance that arouses the concern of the public and brings them to the attention of law enforcement agencies. Behaviours that deviate from social norms, such as dishevelled and unkempt appearance, talking to oneself, sleeping on public sidewalks, may be interpreted by the public as evidence of menace potential. Guided by fear, the public may misinterpret and overreact to the behaviour or appearance of persons with mental illness. . . .

[3] Robert Francis, 'The Michael Stone Inquiry: a reflection' (2007) Journal of Mental Health Law 85–96.

[4] 'Risk, response and mental health policy: learning from the experience of the United Kingdom' (2002) 27 Journal of Health Politics, Policy and Law 801–32.

> If the public remains committed to the perfectability expectation, each violent act committed by a person with a mental illness will be interpreted as potentially avoidable, which could motivate the public to rightfully (a) demand that the government allocate more money to reduce future events through more secure care and supervision of high-risk individuals or (b) support legal reforms that constrain the civil liberties of persons with mental illness.

An emphasis upon the risk mentally ill people might pose to others dominated the Labour government's approach to the process of reforming the Mental Health Act 1983. An Expert Committee, chaired by Genevra Richardson, was set up in 1998, and its review of the Mental Health Act was submitted to the Department of Health the following year.[5] There then followed two Green Papers, one White Paper, and two substantial draft Bills, in 2002 and 2004, both of which were subjected to overwhelming and near-universal criticism. Eventually, and after some passionately argued parliamentary debates, a shorter amending statute—the Mental Health Act 2007—came into force in 2008.

It is worth noting that the passage of the Mental Capacity Act 2005, at around the same time, proceeded almost entirely separately from these troubled mental health law reforms. As we saw in the last chapter, the Mental Capacity Act 2005 is patient-centred and autonomy-enhancing, in stark opposition to the more draconian reforms effected by the Mental Health Act 2007.

This difference in approach is especially important given that a significant proportion of the patients who are covered by the Mental Health Act will also lack capacity, and hence also be subject to the Mental Capacity Act (MCA). Owen et al's 2008 study found that 60 per cent of all patients who were admitted to psychiatric hospitals lacked capacity, and the percentage was even higher for compulsorily detained patients (86 per cent).[6] For these patients, the MCA's patient-centred 'best interests checklist', which we considered in the previous chapter, applies unless they are receiving treatment for their mental disorder, when the Mental Health Act takes priority.

One principal difference between the MCA and the Mental Health Act is that the former contains a set of statutory principles—such as the presumption of capacity and the 'least restrictive alternative' principle. In Scotland, the Mental Health (Care and Treatment) (Scotland) Act 2003 also includes a set of guiding principles, such as respect for the past and present wishes of the patient, and encouragement of equal opportunities. In contrast, and contrary to the recommendations of the Richardson Committee, the Mental Health Act 2007 does not contain any statutory principles.

Principles are included in the Mental Health Act Code of Practice, and it is worth noting that there has been a marked change of tone in the 2015 Code of Practice (CoP), as compared with the 2008 one. In 2008, the CoP referred to 'protecting others from harm' as a justification for the use of compulsory powers. This is absent in the 2015 version, which instead emphasizes listening to patients and promoting recovery.

---

[5] *Review of the Mental Health Act: Report of the Expert Committee* (DH: London, 1999).
[6] Gareth S Owen, Genevra Richardson, Anthony S David, George Szmukler, Peter Hayward, and Matthew Hotopf, 'Mental capacity to make decisions on treatment in people admitted to psychiatric hospitals: cross sectional study' (2008) 337 British Medical Journal 448.

Mental Health Act Code of Practice 2015

1.1 . . . It is essential that all those undertaking functions under the Act understand the five sets of overarching principles which should always be considered when making decisions in relation to care, support or treatment provided under the Act . . .

The five overarching principles are:

Least restrictive option and maximising independence Where it is possible to treat a patient safely and lawfully without detaining them under the Act, the patient should not be detained. Wherever possible a patient's independence should be encouraged and supported with a focus on promoting recovery wherever possible.

Empowerment and involvement Patients should be fully involved in decisions about care, support and treatment. The views of families, carers and others, if appropriate, should be fully considered when taking decisions. Where decisions are taken which are contradictory to views expressed, professionals should explain the reasons for this.

Respect and dignity Patients, their families and carers should be treated with respect and dignity and listened to by professionals.

Purpose and effectiveness Decisions about care and treatment should be appropriate to the patient, with clear therapeutic aims, promote recovery and should be performed to current national guidelines and/or current, available best practice guidelines.

Efficiency and equity Providers, commissioners and other relevant organisations should work together to ensure that the quality of commissioning and provision of mental health-care services are of high quality and are given equal priority to physical health and social care services. All relevant services should work together to facilitate timely, safe and supportive discharge from detention.

At the outset, it should be noted that the very existence of 'mental illness' is doubted by what is referred to as the 'anti-psychiatry' movement. These critics, including Thomas Szasz and Erving Goffman, have argued that psychiatry is not concerned with treating the sick, but instead with controlling strange or inconvenient behaviour. And, of course, as Szasz explains in the next extract, if there is no such thing as mental illness, a special set of laws governing the treatment of the mentally ill would also be unnecessary.

Thomas Szasz[7]

If 'mental illness' is a bona fide illness—as official medical, psychiatric, and mental health organizations, such as the World Health Organization, the American and British Medical Associations, and the American Psychiatric Association, maintain—then it follows, logically and linguistically, that it must be treated like any other illness. Hence, mental hygiene laws must be repealed. There are no special laws for patients with a peptic ulcer or pneumonia; why, then, should there be special laws for patients with depression or schizophrenia?

If, on the other hand, 'mental illness' is, as I contend, a myth, then, also, it follows that mental hygiene laws should be repealed . . . When I assert that mental illness is a myth, I am

---

[7] *Law, Liberty and Psychiatry: An Inquiry into the Social Uses of Mental Health Practices* (Routledge & Kegan Paul: London, 1974).

not saying that personal unhappiness and socially deviant behaviour do not exist; but I am saying that we categorize them as diseases at our peril.

The expression 'mental illness' is a metaphor which we have come to mistake for a fact. We call people physically ill when their body-functioning violates certain anatomical and physiological norms; similarly, we call people mentally ill when their personal conduct violates certain ethical, political, and social norms. . . .

We should guard against . . . the discomfort that the mental patient's behaviour may cause us. Labeling conduct as sick merely because it differs from our own may be nothing more than discrimination disguised as medical judgment.

2 A SHORT HISTORY OF MENTAL HEALTH LAW AND POLICY

There is a long history of subjecting people who have been classified as 'mad' to special treatment. Compulsory detention has been possible for hundreds of years, although it used to be the preserve of poor law officers and Justices of the Peace, rather than doctors. The Vagrancy Act 1744, for example, enabled two or more Justices of the Peace to direct a constable, church-warden, or overseer of the poor to apprehend and detain 'persons of little or no estates, who, by lunacy, or otherwise, are furiously mad, and dangerous to be permitted to go abroad'.

While private asylums existed, most 'lunatics' were paupers, and kept in poorhouses. Conditions were appalling. Beatings, whippings, and rape were common, and prolonged restraint was the norm. A select committee established in 1877 proposed a number of reforms, such as the provision of a system of asylums at public expense; a requirement that two medical certificates accompany an application to detain an individual; and a system of independent inspection of asylums. From the Lunacy Act 1890 onwards, a series of statutes brought such a system into being.

The Mental Treatment Act 1930 was intended to reduce the stigma associated with mental illness, a move that had its origins in the changing attitudes to people with mental health problems prompted by the return of 'shell-shocked' soldiers from the First World War. It also represented a shift towards 'medicalism'; that is, the idea that the mentally ill are patients who need treatment, rather than disruptive individuals who need to be removed from society.

The Percy Commission was set up to consider further reform in the 1950s, and its report culminated in the passage of the Mental Health Act 1959. This emphasized voluntary rather than compulsory admission to hospital, and short-term rather than permanent detention. Although based upon the 1959 Act, the Mental Health Act 1983 attempted to offer more legal safeguards, in order to protect the rights of mentally ill patients. The 2007 Act made a number of significant changes, but the 1983 Act's basic structure remains intact.

Many commentators have analysed mental health law as if it were a pendulum swinging between legalism—with an emphasis upon legal protection—and medicalism—where the medical profession is left to determine how individual patients should be treated. This distinction is described by Fennell in the following extract.

Phil Fennell[8]

On the one hand has been legalism, which has emphasized the need to put limits on the power of mental health professionals and the rights of patients to respect for their autonomously expressed wishes. On the other has been that of medicalism which stresses that the safeguards for the individual rights of patients are not so cumbersome as to impede medical interventions aimed at serving those same patients' best interests.

As Nicola Glover-Thomas explains, legal constraints not only protect patients' rights, but also help to legitimate psychiatric practice.

Nicola Glover-Thomas[9]

Clearly, the law acts as a mechanism of control because it establishes a framework in which care decisions are made and incorporates legal safeguards surrounding detention, treatment and other coercive aspects of the legislation. The formation of these safeguards protects both the patient and those working within the psychiatric field. They legitimate psychiatric practices because they ensure the decisions are made in a procedurally sound way. . . . The existence of a formal legal framework allows the public to accept decisions which overtly remove rights from individuals. The need for psychiatrists to seek second medical opinions and to obtain opinions from other professionals allows psychiatric practice to be seen as accountable and legitimate.

Before we look at the law in detail, it is worth highlighting two particularly significant trends in mental health policy.

(a) DECARCERATION

The twentieth century saw two dramatic shifts in attitudes towards institutionalizing people with mental illnesses. In 1850, there were 7,140 inpatients; by 1954 there were 148,000. Asylums were believed to offer humane and decent surroundings for some of the most marginal members of society. They also undoubtedly facilitated greater social control and surveillance of the insane.[10]

Then, in the second half of the twentieth century, the asylums were closed down. Now around 20,000 patients will be receiving inpatient treatment at any one time,[11] usually in psychiatric wards in general hospitals or in care homes.

Several reasons are commonly given for the move to decarceration. First, community care was (misguidedly) perceived to be cheaper than keeping a patient in an institution. Secondly, the discovery of widespread abuse of mentally ill people within institutions meant that asylums were no longer seen as places of safety. Thirdly, the development of drugs, such

---

8 'Inscribing paternalism in the law: consent to treatment and mental disorder' (1990) 17 Journal of Law and Society 29–51.

9 *Reconstructing Mental Health Law and Policy* (Butterworths: London, 2002).

10 See further, Michel Foucault, *The Birth of the Clinic: An Archaeology of Clinical Perception* (Penguin: London, 1973).

11 Health and Social Care Information Centre, *Inpatients Formally Detained in Hospitals 2014–15* (HSCIC, 2015).

as anti-psychotics, contributed to a medical model of mental disorders: that is, that they are illnesses that can be effectively managed, if not cured, so that sufferers can lead relatively normal lives. Finally, the discovery that mental illness is in fact much more common than had been previously realized contributed to the view that a diagnosis of mental disorder did not necessarily justify locking someone up.

A growing emphasis on community care is evident in mental health policy from the 1960s onwards, but while the number of hospital beds declined, other services were not put in place to replace inpatient care. It had been assumed that mentally ill people would be cared for at home, and readily reintegrated into the community. This assumption proved to be hopelessly over-optimistic. It has not been easy for people with mental illnesses to find jobs and accommodation, and their families are not always able or willing to provide the care that they need.

High-quality community care is expensive, perhaps even more so than treatment provided in a hospital setting, where patients can be guaranteed to stay put. The principal failing of community care is not that decarceration is a bad idea. No one would want to see a return to the days when people with mental disorders were kept in vast asylums, effectively 'out of sight and out of mind'. Rather, the mistake has been to underestimate the cost of providing high-quality care and other services—such as housing and help with finding employment—which people with mental disorders may need in order to live functioning lives in the community.

Jill Stavert suggests that we have tended to think about mental health patients' rights as the right to be free from unwarranted detention. In the community, socioeconomic rights to services and resources may be of much greater importance.

Jill Stavert[12]

Over the last two decades we have come some way in Europe towards recognising that those suffering from mental illness require enforceable rights so that they are not subjected to abuse and neglect. These rights are, however, mainly civil rights which are applicable to the patient–institution relationship. If care takes place outside institutions, a far greater emphasis on socio-economic rights is required. This will enable those with mental illness to access and receive those services and that support which is necessary for them to function as effectively as possible within the communities in which they live.

(b) DETENTION FOR DANGEROUSNESS

In reforming the 1983 Act, the then Labour government focused on a small number of patients suffering from what it described as dangerous and severe personality disorders (DSPD). The government was concerned that the 1983 legislation placed obstacles in the way of the detention of DSPD patients, in part because it is not clear that their conditions are treatable. In the next extract, Eric Matthews argues that this is because personality disorders are not really illnesses at all, and that it is a mistake to deal with personality-disordered individuals as if they were ill.

---

[12] 'Mental health, community care and human rights in Europe: still an incomplete picture?' (2007) Journal of Mental Health Law 182.

Eric Matthews[13]

[T]here are some conditions classified as mental disorders . . . in which the harm caused by the disorder is not, or at least not primarily, to the disordered person, but to others. The various sorts of sexual deviation called 'paraphilias', such as paedophilia, represent good examples. These disorders seem to have no parallel among physical illnesses: someone who is physically ill suffers him- or herself, and any harm caused to others (eg through infection) is contingent. But a paedophile does not himself suffer from his paedophilia (except indirectly, in that he suffers social disapproval): those who suffer are the children he abuses . . .

Paedophiles are often said to be 'untreatable': but that is rather misleading. They do not *require* treatment in the medical sense, since their condition is not an illness, not something which causes them suffering contrary to their own wishes. It is their personality itself, and the wishes which emanate from it, which are said to be disordered. The treatment which they require is that which would prevent this disordered personality causing harm to others . . .

This suggests that what is legally required to deal with such cases is, again, not a 'Mental Health Act', which among other things has the unfortunate effect of reinforcing popular prejudices about the allegedly violent and dangerous character of all mentally ill people . . . Rather we need to address the difficult issues involved in the containment of people who behave in anti-social ways.

So is 'personality disorder' a disease? The World Health Organization's *International Statistical Classification of Diseases and Related Health Problems*, tenth revision (known as ICD-10), contains definitions of 'dissocial personality disorder',[14] and the Diagnostic and Statistical Manual (known as DSM-V) which is published by the American Psychiatric Association, sets out diagnostic criteria for all recognized mental disorders, including a wide range of personality disorders, including antisocial personality disorder and narcissistic personality disorder. While their inclusion in the DSM might appear to be evidence that personality disorders are mental illnesses, it is worth bearing in mind that these diagnostic manuals are themselves controversial: for example, it is often pointed out that homosexuality was only deleted from the DSM's list of mental disorders in 1974.[15]

Regardless of whether personality disorders are mental illnesses or not, the shift in emphasis towards detaining dangerous people was heavily criticized. Psychiatrists, for example, feared that they would be forced to detain people where there is no clinical reason for keeping them in hospital, thus undermining their status as doctors, whose first priority is the care of their patients. The Joint Scrutiny Committee was critical of the then government's approach to reform of the Mental Health Act. In the next extract, its Chair, Lord Carlile, argues that psychiatrists should not be put in the position of 'least worst jailers'.

Alex Carlile[16]

Naturally there is a desire at large to anticipate and limit the damage DSPD cases may cause. The stories make good news copy, lend themselves to exaggeration in terms of the mental health treatment potential available, and worst of all excite all too easily demands by elected

---

[13] 'Mental and Physical Illness—An Unsustainable Separation?' in Nigel Eastman and Jill Peay (eds), *Law Without Enforcement: Integrating Mental Health and Justice* (Hart Publishing: Oxford, 1999) 47–58.

[14] ICD-10 Version for 2016 (WHO, 2016) F60.2.

[15] See further Roy Porter, 'Is Mental Illness Inevitably Stigmatizing?' in A Crisp (ed), *Every Family in the Land: Understanding Prejudice and Discrimination against People with Mental Illness* (Royal Society of Medicine Press: London, 2004) 3–13.

[16] 'Legislation to law: Rubicon or Styx?' (2005) Journal of Mental Health Law 107.

politicians that 'something should be done', usually equated with the assumption that something can be done.

The Committee was firmly of the view that where there is treatment available and a degree of therapeutic benefit, compulsory powers may well have a part to play in DSPD. . . . However, the Committee was always clear that the Bill was fundamentally flawed and too focused on addressing public misconception about violence and mental illness, in effect creating mental health ASBOs. We had no doubt that hospitals and their clinical staff should not be placed in the position of least worst jailers without any realistic medical intervention taking place.

There are two further practical problems with the assumption that mental health law can reduce the risk posed by dangerous individuals. First, it presupposes that it is, in fact, possible accurately to predict which patients pose a risk to others, whereas the evidence points in the opposite direction: in practice, it is extremely difficult accurately to predict dangerousness.

The MacArthur project in the US involved 939 people, who were divided into five categories of risk and whose behaviour was monitored for the next 12 months.[17] Sixty-three individuals were categorized as high risk, and of these, 48 were violent in the subsequent year. That means that almost one-quarter of these 'high risk' individuals were not violent, and if they had been detained because of their perceived dangerousness, the deprivation of their liberty would not have prevented any violence at all. In total, 176 individuals in the study committed violent acts in the year following assessment, only 48 of whom would have been captured by a dangerousness standard which detained those in risk category five.[18] To prevent the other 128 violent individuals from harming other people, individuals who fell into the lower risk categories would have to be detained, and in these the predictions of violence were extremely unreliable. In risk category three, for example, 74 per cent of individuals were not violent in the year following assessment. If people in this risk category had been compulsorily detained in order to prevent harm to others, in the majority of cases, the detention would have been unwarranted.

Secondly, this 'public safety' approach to mental disorder presupposes that there is, in fact, a correlation between mental illness and dangerousness. Again, the evidence does not bear this out. It is also perhaps interesting that other factors that are implicated in the homicide statistics, such as alcohol use, do not lead to the same levels of public anxiety and desire for surveillance and control. In commenting on a previous draft Bill, the Royal College of Psychiatrists pointed out that not only was the emphasis on risk misguided, but that, by deterring potentially violent individuals from seeking help, this approach might actually increase the danger they pose to the public.

Royal College of Psychiatrists[19]

Every death is a tragedy, for the victim, perpetrator, their family and friends and any professionals involved. The percentage of homicides committed each year by the mentally ill, as a percentage of the total is falling. The following figures are not intended to minimize the importance of each death but may help to put the matter into perspective.

---

[17] John Monahan et al, *Rethinking Risk Assessment: The MacArthur Study of Mental Disorder and Violence* (OUP: Oxford, 2001).

[18] Ibid.

[19] *Evidence Submitted to the Joint Committee on the Draft Mental Health Bill* (RCP: London, 2004) 31–4.

For each citizen killed by a mentally ill person:

- 10 are killed by corporate manslaughter
- 20 by people who are not mentally ill
- 25 by passive smoking
- 125 by NHS hospital acquired infection.

The proposed legislation is extremely unlikely to have any impact on suicide or homicide rates. With reference to suicide, recent research demonstrated that even within the high-risk group of in-patients there would need to be 100 patients detained unnecessarily in order to prevent one suicide. With regard to homicide, [Crawford] has shown that with a predictive test with a sensitivity and specificity of 0.8 (far better than anything available currently) 5000 people would need to be detained to prevent one homicide. Szmukler has shown that if the predictive test became even better (0.9) this would still require the detention of 2000 people to prevent each homicide. This emphasises that prevention of homicide and suicide can only ever arise as a secondary benefit from improved mental health care for a population and never via prediction per se of such events.

The starting point in risk reduction is encouraging patients to seek help and talk about their thoughts and feelings . . . It is hard to believe that potential patients will not be deterred from the services if they know that psychiatrists will have a duty to enforce treatment on them, not only in hospital but also in the community, even when they are perfectly able to make decisions for themselves. Patient avoidance will certainly limit effective intervention.

In the next extract, Sweeney et al describe how the emphasis on risk can itself have a negative effect on service users' mental wellbeing.

Angela Sweeney, Steve Gillard, Til Wykes, and Diana Rose[20]

In the context of the community, public fear of service users has consistently been described as a key cause of discrimination, and evidence suggests that it is a barrier to seeking support from mental health services. Our participants sometimes feared community rejection: many had lost friends, and described loneliness as their biggest problem. Similarly, an international literature review concluded, 'rejection and avoidance of people with mental illness appear to be a universal phenomena'. This can be so severe that it causes mental distress, and in our study occasionally resulted in people needing additional support from services . . .

Mental health policy has responded to perceptions of dangerousness by facing in two directions at once. There is a focus on risk management and public order, leading to policies of control and compulsion such as the Mental Health Act 2007. Yet policy is also shaped by the human rights agenda and social inclusion, leading to a focus on choice and anti-discrimination. This has meant that service users are encouraged to enact choices whilst fearing compulsion if they do not make the choices that are sanctioned by powerful mental health professionals. Those who choose not to engage with mental health services can be labelled resistant.

[20] 'The role of fear in mental health service users' experiences: a qualitative exploration' (2015) 50 Social Psychiatry and Psychiatric Epidemiology 1079–87.

It is noteworthy that the tone of more recent government discussion of mental health services has been less focused on risk-avoidance, and apparently more concerned with reducing stigma and achieving 'parity of esteem' between physical and mental health services.

In 2013, NHS England launched a parity of esteem campaign, in order to ensure that mental illness is diagnosed and treated 'on a par with physical illness'. While this is to be welcomed, funding for mental health services has not necessarily kept pace with these good intentions. As we see later, more patients are detained each year, while the number of inpatient beds has decreased. A 2015 briefing from the King's Fund set out the problem.

The King's Fund[21]

What is clear is that it is a sector under huge pressure. While increased political support and a stronger policy focus is welcome, parity of esteem for mental health remains a long way off.

Funding for mental health services has been cut in recent years. Our analysis shows that around 40 per cent of mental health trusts experienced reductions in income in 2013/14 and 2014/15. There is widespread evidence of poor-quality care. Only 14 per cent of patients say that they received appropriate care in a crisis, and there has been an increase in the number of patients who report a poor experience of community mental health care.

Bed occupancy in inpatient facilities is frequently well above recommended levels, with community services, in particular crisis resolution and home treatment teams, often unable to provide sufficient levels of support to compensate for reductions in beds. This is having a negative impact on safety and quality of care. . . .

A Royal College of Psychiatry report described wards as overcrowded and understaffed, with 15 per cent of wards lacking segregated sleeping accommodation and fewer than 60 per cent having separate lounges for men and women. Patients and carers report that many acute wards are not always safe, therapeutic or conducive to recovery and in some cases could have a negative effect on an inpatient's wellbeing and mental health.

In 2015, a cross-party campaign—Equality for Mental Health—was launched to exert pressure on ministers to increase funding and support for mental health services.

Equality for Mental Health[22]

We ask for the same right to timely access to evidence based treatment as those with physical health problems.

We accept, and urge ministers to accept, that this will require additional investment in mental health services. But we are strongly persuaded that sustained investment in mental health services will lead to significant returns for the Exchequer, both by reducing the burden on the NHS through the improved wellbeing of our citizens, and by helping people to stay in, or get back into work.

We note the many comments from ministers and opinion formers acknowledging the huge cost of mental ill health not just to individuals and their families, including veterans of our armed forces, but to the economy as a whole. Some estimates put this cost as high as £100bn a year, spent on visits to A&E, lost jobs, unemployment benefits, homelessness support, police time and even prison places.

---

21 *Mental Health Under Pressure* (King's Fund, 2015).
22 See further equality4mentalhealth.uk.

So the economic argument for a new approach is clear. And so is the human and moral argument. Because ministers have also accepted that whatever improvements in attitude may have been made in British society, with a greater understanding and awareness of mental ill health, those who experience it still do not get a fair deal from our health services. In effect, they suffer discrimination in our publicly funded NHS. This must be addressed.

3 WHAT IS MENTAL ILLNESS?

Mental health problems are common: it is estimated than one in six adults in the UK suffers from a mental disorder each year. Some mental disorders are relatively easy to live with; others can be fatal. Mental illness is often more difficult to diagnose than physical illness. Unlike the X-rays, blood tests, and scans which are used to diagnose broken bones, HIV, and cancer, for example, it can be much harder to establish precisely what is wrong with a person's mental health. Some people believe that brain-imaging techniques will lead to more accurate and objective diagnoses, but at present, psychiatrists continue to diagnose mental disorders by listening to the patient's description of her symptoms and observing her behaviour.

In order to define mental illness it might first be necessary to have some idea of what we consider to be normal mental functioning. But, for obvious reasons, this is incredibly difficult to pin down. Feeling sad from time to time is normal, and is certainly not evidence of mental illness. On the other hand, major depression is an extremely debilitating condition which is capable of interfering with a person's ability to lead a normal life as much as any physical illness.

Because mental health law can sanction involuntary detention and compulsory treatment, accurate diagnosis of conditions that might justify detention in hospital is essential.

(a) DEFINING MENTAL DISORDER

Under the 1983 Act, as amended, the statutory definition of mental disorder is contained in section 1(2):

Mental Health Act 1983 section 1

1(2) In this Act—

'mental disorder' means any disorder or disability of the mind;

(2A) But a person with learning disability shall not be considered by reason of that disability to be—

(a) suffering from mental disorder . . .

(b) requiring treatment in hospital for mental disorder . . .

unless that disability is associated with abnormally aggressive or seriously irresponsible conduct on his part.

(3) Dependence on alcohol or drugs is not considered to be a disorder or disability of the mind for the purposes of subsection (2) above.

(4) In subsection (2A) above, 'learning disability' means a state of arrested or incomplete development of the mind which includes significant impairment of intelligence and social functioning.

Before it was amended in 2007, the Act specifically stated that no one should be treated as mentally disordered by reason only of 'promiscuity or other immoral conduct' or 'sexual deviancy'. The reason for this was that, in the past, people who did not conform to accepted moral standards were routinely confined to asylums. At the start of the twentieth century, becoming pregnant outside marriage was believed to be evidence of moral depravity and mental defectiveness. Towards the end of the twentieth century, when the large asylums were closed down, it was clear that they contained many elderly women who had been perfectly sane when they were committed as unmarried pregnant women, but who had since become institutionalized and incapable of living independently.

This provision was removed by the 2007 reforms because the government believed it placed an obstacle in the way of detaining sex offenders with personality disorders, since the implication was that someone should not be treated as mentally disordered where the principal manifestation of their personality disorder was their sexual deviancy. In short, it was thought that mental health legislation should facilitate, rather than obstruct, the detention of people, like paedophiles, whose personality disorder manifests itself in sexually deviant behaviour.

It is important to remember that simply being defined as mentally disordered does not necessarily mean that someone will be subject to formal powers: it is a necessary but certainly not a sufficient condition. The other necessary conditions are described in the next section.

4 ADMISSION TO THE MENTAL HEALTH SYSTEM

In 2014–15, there were 58,399 detentions under the Mental Health Act, an increase of 9.8 per cent compared to 2013–14 (53,176).[23] Over the same time period, 1,835,996 people were in contact with mental health and learning disability services and 103,840 people spent time in hospital.[24] While the proportion of those who have been compulsorily detained or 'sectioned' has increased in recent years, it continues to be a tiny minority of those suffering from mental illness. Interestingly, then, 'mental health law' has little application to the vast majority of people living with mental disorders.

There are three routes to admission to the mental health system: informal admission; detention under the Mental Capacity Act's 'deprivation of liberty' procedure; and formal detention.

(a) VOLUNTARY ADMISSION UNDER THE 1983 ACT

Under section 131 of the 1983 Act, anyone who 'requires treatment for mental disorder' may be admitted informally.

---

[23] Health and Social Care Information Centre, *Inpatients Formally Detained in Hospitals 2014–15* (HSCIC, 2015).

[24] Health and Social Care Information Centre, *Mental Health Bulletin, Annual Report—2014–15* (HSCIC, 2015).

Mental Health Act 1983 section 131

131(1) Nothing in this Act shall be construed as preventing a patient who requires treatment for mental disorder from being admitted to any hospital or [registered establishment] in pursuance of arrangements made in that behalf and without any application, order or direction rendering him liable to be detained under this Act, or from remaining in any hospital or [registered establishment] in pursuance of such arrangements after he has ceased to be so liable to be detained.

Informal admission may take place because the patient is willingly seeking treatment, and, where this is the case, there are clear advantages in avoiding the use of compulsory powers. Restricting a patient's liberty may reduce patient trust, and if a patient has chosen to admit herself to hospital, she may be more likely to cooperate with treatment, and find the experience less distressing.

Of course, it is possible that the patient will come under pressure, perhaps from her family, to agree to informal admission, and, in practice, she may not have anywhere else to go. It is also possible for an informally admitted patient to subsequently be formally detained under section 5 of the 1983 Act. Once in hospital, as Phil Fennell explains in the next extract, informally admitted patients are not necessarily free to leave.

Phil Fennell[25]

Even if there were an unlimited right for informal patients to leave hospital, to speak of mentally incapacitated patients having it makes little sense. There may be nowhere else capable of providing the care which the patient needs, he may have no home to go to and be too dependent to survive in sheltered accommodation. Any hospital or nursing home accepting responsibility for looking after mentally incapacitated informal patients thereby assumes a duty of care towards them. That duty of care extends to preventing them from leaving when to do so would put them at risk. Not being detained does not make an informal patient 'freer'.

In the next extract, Michael Cavadino draws upon his interviews with patients at an unidentified NHS psychiatric hospital, which he refers to as Fardale, in order to examine whether informal patients' stays in hospital are genuinely voluntary.

Michael Cavadino[26]

It is possible for patients to enter hospital voluntarily or acquiescently but at some later stage to be prevented from leaving, or be subjected to some other forcible control, which would normally be incompatible with informal admission. This can happen if patients are restrained from leaving hospital by force or threat of force; or led to believe that they are not free to leave; or locked in a side-room; or denied access to their clothes; or given medical treatment such as drugs by force or threat of force; or if the patient demands discharge and is not allowed to take it. Such occurrences were by no means uncommon in Fardale . . .

[25] 'Doctor Knows Best? Therapeutic Detention under Common Law, the Mental Health Act and the European Convention' (1998) 6 Medical Law Review 322–53.

[26] *Mental Health Law in Context* (Dartmouth: Aldershot, 1989).

> On the question of whether they would like to leave hospital, a substantial minority of the informal patients (38 per cent) said that they would . . . So why were so many patients still in hospital informally who would rather leave? . . . Of the informal patients who expressed a desire to leave, 14 per cent did indeed believe that they were not free to leave hospital . . . But in most cases, patients perceived other constraints as being more important. Foremost among these other constraints was lack of accommodation, or suitable accommodation, outside the hospital . . .
>
> It seems, then, that although there are indeed *some* informal patients who stay in hospital because they feel coerced to do so, factors such as lack of accommodation are of much greater importance than the fear of legal or extra-legal force—certainly in the eyes of the patients themselves.

There are also times when patients are informally admitted because they are too incapacitated to express a preference. Notice that section 131 states that nothing in the Act prevents a patient from '*being* admitted' to hospital, implying that there is no need for informal patients to admit themselves voluntarily.

Informal admission in such circumstances potentially leaves the patient without the formal protections which are in place to protect compulsorily detained patients. This was the issue that arose in the *Bournewood* case, which led to the introduction of the Deprivation of Liberty Safeguards.

In *R v Bournewood Community and Mental Health NHS Trust, ex parte L,*[27] HL was a 48-year-old man, who was autistic and profoundly mentally retarded. He had been living with paid carers for a number of years, but on a visit to a day centre he had become agitated and was admitted to Bournewood hospital informally. His carers were denied access to him, on the grounds that if he saw them, he might want to leave. If HL had tried to leave, the trust admitted that he would have been compulsorily detained, but it also argued that, so long as HL was not trying to leave, he could continue to be kept in hospital informally under section 131. A majority in the House of Lords agreed.

But in *HL v United Kingdom* the European Court of Human Rights (ECtHR) took a different view and found that HL had been detained, and that the lack of protections in place for people in his position did not satisfy the requirements of Article 5(4), the right to liberty and security: 'Everyone who is deprived of his liberty by arrest or detention shall be entitled to take proceedings by which the lawfulness of his detention shall be decided speedily by a court and his release ordered if the detention is not lawful'.

HL v United Kingdom[28]

Judgment of the ECtHR

[T]he concrete situation was that the applicant was under continuous supervision and control and was not free to leave. Any suggestion to the contrary was, in the Court's view, fairly described by Lord Steyn [dissenting] as 'stretching credulity to breaking point' and as a 'fairy tale'. . . . The Court therefore concludes that the applicant was 'deprived of his liberty' within the meaning of Article 5 § 1 of the Convention. . . .

---

[27] *R v Bournewood Community and Mental Health NHS Trust, ex parte L* [1998] 3 WLR 107.
[28] Application no 45508/99 (5 October 2004).

[T]he Court finds striking the lack of any fixed procedural rules by which the admission and detention of compliant incapacitated persons is conducted. The contrast between this dearth of regulation and the extensive network of safeguards applicable to psychiatric committals covered by the 1983 Act is, in the Court's view, significant . . ..

The Court therefore finds that this absence of procedural safeguards fails to protect against arbitrary deprivations of liberty on grounds of necessity and, consequently, to comply with the essential purpose of Article 5 § 1 of the Convention. On this basis, the Court finds that there has been a violation of Article 5 § 1 of the Convention.

As a result of this decision, the government had to put in place measures to plug what had become known as the '*Bournewood* gap': namely, the lack of any mechanism to authorize and challenge the de facto detention of patients like HL who are compliant and incapacitated. It did not do so especially speedily, however, and the Deprivation of Liberty Safeguards (DoLS)—which are contained in the Mental Capacity Act—came into force in 2008.

(b) MCA 'DEPRIVATION OF LIBERTY' SAFEGUARDS

(1) What is a 'Deprivation of Liberty'?

The Mental Capacity Act Deprivation of Liberty Safeguards (DoLS) only apply when someone is actually deprived of their liberty, as opposed to having their freedom restricted. The distinction between restriction and deprivation of liberty is therefore important, but it may be a fine one and a question of degree.

In *HL* itself, and in subsequent cases, the central question has been whether the person who lacks capacity is free to leave. If he is, then he has not been deprived of his liberty. If, however, he would be stopped from leaving were he to attempt to do so, then he is being deprived of his liberty, and a DoLS authorization is necessary. Whether or not the incapacitated person wishes to leave, or is able to do so, is irrelevant. Instead the focus is on how those caring for him would react were he to try to leave.

Is a patient deprived of his liberty when caring for him inevitably involves a degree of restraint? This was the question that arose in the landmark Supreme Court decision in *Cheshire West and Chester Council v P.*[29] In the first case two sisters, P and Q, had learning disabilities and did not have the capacity to give a valid consent to any arrangements for their care. The Court of Appeal had held that although neither sister was free to leave their accommodation, the 'relative normality' of their living arrangements, which were no more intrusive than was necessary for their own protection, meant that neither P nor Q was deprived of her liberty so as to engage Article 5.

In the second case, P was a 39-year-old man, suffering from cerebral palsy and Down's syndrome, who lacked the mental capacity to make decisions about his care. His occasionally aggressive behaviour, and his habit of putting his incontinence pads in his mouth, necessitated some physical restraint. Once again, the Court of Appeal had held that the restraints to which P was subject were 'normal' for someone with his capabilities, and therefore did not amount to a deprivation of liberty.

---

[29] [2014] UKSC 19.

By a majority, in *Cheshire West and Chester Council v P*, the Supreme Court decided that even where the restraints to which individuals were subject were a necessary consequence of their learning disabilities, that nevertheless amounted to a deprivation of liberty, for which a DoLS authorization was required.

Cheshire West and Chester Council v P[30]

Baroness Hale

In my view, it is axiomatic that people with disabilities, both mental and physical, have the same human rights as the rest of the human race. It may be that those rights have sometimes to be limited or restricted because of their disabilities, but the starting point should be the same as that for everyone else. . . .

Those rights include the right to physical liberty, which is guaranteed by article 5 of the European Convention. This is not a right to do or to go where one pleases. It is a more focused right, not to be deprived of that physical liberty. But, as it seems to me, what it means to be deprived of liberty must be the same for everyone, whether or not they have physical or mental disabilities. If it would be a deprivation of my liberty to be obliged to live in a particular place, subject to constant monitoring and control, only allowed out with close supervision, and unable to move away without permission even if such an opportunity became available, then it must also be a deprivation of the liberty of a disabled person. The fact that my living arrangements are comfortable, and indeed make my life as enjoyable as it could possibly be, should make no difference. A gilded cage is still a cage.

For that reason, I would reject the 'relative normality' approach of the Court of Appeal . . . , where the life which P was leading was compared with the life which another person with his disabilities might be leading. . . .

So is there an acid test for the deprivation of liberty in these cases? . . . The answer, as it seems to me, lies in those features which have consistently been regarded as 'key' in the jurisprudence which started with *HL v United Kingdom*: that the person concerned 'was under continuous supervision and control and was not free to leave'. I would not go so far as Mr Gordon, who argues that the supervision and control is relevant only insofar as it demonstrates that the person is not free to leave. A person might be under constant supervision and control but still be free to leave should he express the desire so to do. Conversely, it is possible to imagine situations in which a person is not free to leave but is not under such continuous supervision and control as to lead to the conclusion that he was deprived of his liberty.

It is very easy to focus on the positive features of these placements for all three of the appellants. The local authorities who are responsible for them have no doubt done the best they could to make their lives as happy and fulfilled, as well as safe, as they possibly could be. But the purpose of article 5 is to ensure that people are not deprived of their liberty without proper safeguards, safeguards which will secure that the legal justifications for the constraints which they are under are made out: in these cases, the law requires that they do indeed lack the capacity to decide for themselves where they should live and that the arrangements made for them are in their best interests. It is to set the cart before the horse to decide that because they do indeed lack capacity and the best possible arrangements have been made, they are not in need of those safeguards. . . .

---

[30] [2014] UKSC 19.

Lord Carnwath and Lord Hodge (dissenting on *P* and *Q*)

We are concerned that nobody using ordinary language would describe people living happily in a domestic setting as being deprived of their liberty. . . . No doubt P and Q can be said to have had their liberty restricted, by comparison with a person with unimpaired health and capacity. But that is not the same as a deprivation of liberty. Parker J summarised their position in this way:

' . . . The "concrete situation" is that each lives exactly the kind of life that she would be capable of living in the home of her own family or a relative: their respective lives being dictated by their own cognitive limitations.'

Essentially, then, there is a two-pronged 'acid test' to determine whether someone is being deprived of their liberty: are they under continuous supervision and control, and are they free to leave? In a post-*Cheshire West* case, *Re BS*, Mostyn J found that the two-pronged test was not made out, even though it had been admitted that if the patient, Ben, did leave, and attempts to persuade him to return were unsuccessful, the police might be asked 'to exercise the powers under section 136 of the Mental Health Act 1983 to remove Ben to a place of safety'.

Re BS[31]

Mostyn J

The continuing legal controversy shows how difficult it is to pin down a definition of what is a deprivation of liberty (i.e. detention by the state) as opposed to a restriction on movement or nothing beyond humane and empathetic care. . . .

I cannot say that I know that Ben is being detained by the state when I look at his position. Far from it. I agree with Mr Mullins that he is not. First, he is not under continuous supervision. He is afforded appreciable privacy. Second, he is free to leave. Were he to do so his carers would seek to persuade him to return but such persuasion would not cross the line into coercion. The deprivation of liberty line would only be crossed if and when the police exercised powers under the Mental Health Act. Were that to happen then a range of reviews and safeguards would become operative. But up to that point Ben is a free man. In my judgment, on the specific facts in play here, the acid test is not met. Ben is not living in a cage, gilded or otherwise.

(2) What are the 'Deprivation of Liberty Safeguards'?

Schedule 1A to the Mental Capacity Act 2005, as amended, fleshes out six requirements, all of which must be met before a deprivation of liberty may be authorized:

Mental Capacity Act 2005 Schedule 1A Part 3

(a) the age requirement: the patient must be at least 18 years old.

(b) the mental health requirement: the patient must be suffering from a mental disorder within the meaning of the MHA.

---

[31] [2015] EWCOP 39.

(c) the mental capacity requirement: the patient must lack capacity.

(d) the best interests requirement;

- it is in the best interests of the relevant person to be deprived of liberty
- it is necessary for them to be deprived of liberty in order to prevent harm to themselves, and
- deprivation of liberty is a proportionate response to the likelihood of the relevant person suffering harm and the seriousness of that harm.

(e) the eligibility requirement: they must not be detained under the Act or subject to restrictions on their freedom in the community.

(f) the no refusals requirement: there must not be a valid and applicable advance refusal of the treatment for which the deprivation of liberty authorization of liberty is sought.

Deprivation of liberty thus has to be (a) necessary to protect P from harm, (b) proportionate, and (c) in P's best interests. Consistent with the MCA's section 4 checklist (see Chapter 5), best interests is not confined to the patient's *clinical* best interests. In *A London Local Authority v JH*,[32] Eldergill J was presented with evidence that there were some health risks in JH continuing to be cared for by her husband at home. Because this was her preferred option, she could only be taken to and kept in a nursing home—which would have been clinically preferable—if she was deprived of her liberty. Taking account of the strength of JH's preference to continue to live with her husband, the deprivation of her liberty was not in her best interests and no order was made.

As part of the DoLS procedure, a representative, who must be someone that the P knows and trusts, must be appointed. If there is no one available to act as their representative, an Independent Mental Capacity Advocate (IMCA, see Chapter 5) must be appointed 'to represent and support the relevant person in all matters relating to the deprivation of liberty safeguards, including, if appropriate, triggering a review, using an organization's complaints procedure on the person's behalf or making an application to the Court of Protection'.[33]

A deprivation of liberty can be authorized by 'the supervisory' body, which will be the local authority. Applications for authorizations are made by the person responsible for running the hospital or care home in which the patient is being treated or cared for and, if granted, the authorization will last for 12 months. Under section 21A of the Mental Capacity Act, the authorization can be subject to review by the Court of Protection, which may vary or terminate it. It is also possible for applications to be made to the Court of Protection by the patient or someone acting on her behalf.

Indeed, there may be circumstances when the local authority is under a duty to facilitate the authorization's review by the court. This was the case in *Hillingdon v Neary*,[34] in which Peter Jackson J found that the local authority had to do more than simply point out that the patient had the right to challenge the authorization himself. The London Borough of Hillingdon had taken Steven Neary, who suffered from autism and a severe learning disability, into respite care for a few days, at his father's request, in December 2009. Steven stayed there until December 2010, against both his own and his father's wishes. The local authority maintained that it had Steven's father's consent for the first four months, and thereafter was entitled to rely upon DoLS authorizations that it had effectively granted to itself. Peter Jackson J found that Steven had been deprived of his liberty throughout. Because the local

---

[32] [2011] EWHC 2420 (COP).   [33] Ibid.   [34] [2011] EWHC 1377 (COP).

authority had granted authorizations 'on the basis of perfunctory scrutiny of superficial best interests assessments', the DoLS authorizations had been unlawful.

(3) The Relationship Between DoLS and Compulsory Admission Under the Mental Health Act 1983

In addition to DoLS, incapacitated patients can also be detained under the Mental Health Act powers of detention, described in the next section. Under Schedule 1A, para 5, if the incapacitated person meets the criteria for detention and objects to being detained in the hospital, or to some or all of the proposed treatment, he is ineligible for detention under DoLS, and the Mental Health Act must be used.[35]

The existence of this provision was one factor behind Charles J's decision in *GJ v Foundation Trust*, that the Mental Health Act should have primacy over the Mental Capacity Act, and that practitioners are not free to 'pick and choose' between the two procedures when depriving someone of their liberty.

GJ v Foundation Trust[36]

Charles J

In my judgment, the MHA 1983 has primacy in the sense that the relevant decision makers under both the MHA 1983 and the MCA should approach the questions they have to answer relating to the application of the MHA 1983 on the basis of an assumption that an alternative solution is not available under the MCA . . .

[I]n my view this does not mean that the two regimes are necessarily always mutually exclusive. But it does mean . . . that it is not lawful for the medical practitioners referred to in ss. 2 and 3 of the MHA 1983, decision makers under the MCA, treating doctors, social workers or anyone else to proceed on the basis that they can pick and choose between the two statutory regimes as they think fit having regard to general considerations (e.g. the preservation or promotion of a therapeutic relationship with P) that they consider render one regime preferable to the other in the circumstances of the given case.

My reasons for this conclusion are:

(a) It is in line with the underlying purpose of the amendments to the MCA 2005, to fill a gap namely the '*Bournewood Gap*'. This shows that the purpose was not to provide alternative regimes but to leave the existing regime under the MHA 1983 in place with primacy and to fill a gap left by it and the common law.

(b) The regime under the MHA 1983 has been in place for some time and includes a number of checks and balances suitable to its subject matter that are not replicated under the MCA.

Because DoLS apply only to patients who lack capacity, to rule out the use of DoLS, the patient's objection to detention or treatment necessarily will not be a competent one. It need not even be verbal; rather, as McKillop et al explain, objection can be inferred from a person's behaviour.

---

[35] See also, Code of Practice, para 4.45.   [36] [2009] EWHC 2972 (Fam).

Matthew McKillop, John Dawson, and George Szmukler[37]

Capacity to object is irrelevant. . . . It is clear too than an effective objection need not be a verbal one. In determining whether a person has objected, eligibility assessors are required to take into account the person's behaviour, as well as their wishes, feelings, beliefs and values. These latter views will normally require communication through language, either verbally or otherwise, but the concept of behaviour clearly encompasses all the responses of a person to their deprivation of liberty, including physical responses . . .

An inability to communicate feelings verbally, combined with an inability to make controlled movements indicative of a desire to leave a place, would make objection very difficult. Some individuals may be so profoundly disabled that there is no feasible way for them to object to a deprivation of liberty.

(4) What is Wrong with DoLS?

The short answer is 'a great deal'. They have been criticized by the judiciary, by the House of Lords Select Committee on the Mental Capacity Act 2005, and by the Law Commission, not to mention the weight of academic criticism they have attracted. First, as Brenda Hale, writing extra-judicially, points out, they are unnecessarily complicated.

Brenda Hale[38]

The Schedules [to the Mental Capacity Act 2005] consist of a total of 205 paragraphs, and there are then a further 40 regulations, and all this to define a single, simple power. It is not just the length of the Schedules which makes them so impenetrable, but their obscure language, their relentless over-specification of detail, and their convoluted structure which makes it impossible to find the answer to any question in any one place.

In his evidence to the House of Lords Select Committee, Charles J, Vice-President of the Court of Protection, described the experience of writing a judgment on the safeguards 'as if you have been in a washing machine and spin dryer',[39] and in *Cheshire West*, Baroness Hale said that 'the safeguards have the appearance of bewildering complexity'.

There have also been criticisms of the way in which DoLS have been drafted. The language is at odds with the rest of the Mental Capacity Act, with its emphasis on promoting patients' freedom rather than removing it, and as the Law Commission has pointed out, carers find it baffling and upsetting.

Law Commission[40]

Terms such as 'standard authorisations', 'managing authority' and 'supervisory body' have been described variously as cumbersome, Orwellian, and failing to reflect modern health

---

[37] 'The concept of objection under the DOLS regime' (2011) Journal of Mental Health Law 61.
[38] 'Taking stock' (2009) Journal of Mental Health Law 111–27.
[39] House of Lords Select Committee on the Mental Capacity Act 2005, Report of Session 2013–14, *Mental Capacity Act 2005: Post-Legislative Scrutiny* (TSO: London, 2014) para 271.
[40] *Mental Capacity and Deprivation of Liberty: A Consultation Paper* (Law Commission, 2015) para 2.37.

and social care functions. Particular criticism has been directed at the label 'Deprivation of Liberty Safeguards'. It is suggested that care providers are put off by the label, and do not want to acknowledge that they are depriving people of their liberty because they see themselves as helping and protecting people. Carers have described to us the distress caused when informed that their loved one needs to be made subject to the 'Deprivation of Liberty Safeguards'—especially where nobody is dissatisfied with the care and support arrangements.

In the next extract, Cairns et al agree that the term 'deprivation of liberty' is counter-intuitive where a care relationship is working well, and they also highlight the sheer numbers of patients likely to be affected by *Cheshire West*.

Ruth Cairns, Matthew Hotopf, and Gareth S Owen[41]

Around 200 000 people with dementia live in care homes, and some 40 000 people with learning disabilities live in residential and nursing homes. If the acid test is applied, many will require deprivation of liberty safeguards. On general medical wards, 40% of patients lack capacity to make decisions about care, with higher proportions on elderly care wards and intensive treatment units. Are these patients free to leave? In a large number of cases the answer is no. Are they under the complete supervision and control of those caring for them? The answer, for many inpatients, is probably yes.

If care homes and acute hospitals are looked at through this legal lens, deprivations of liberty are widespread. Yet a healthcare worker's lens is different. The understanding of individual patients' disabilities and their acceptance of offers of care are regarded as important indications of whether a care relationship is working. If it is thought to be working, then identifying a deprivation of liberty is likely to be a foreign instinct.

Secondly, most compliant, incapacitated patients are not in hospital, but instead live in care homes and supported living facilities. There are 20,000 care homes in the UK, many of them small and privately run, where knowledge and understanding of DoLS is likely to be poor or non-existent. The responsibility for applying for a DoLS authorization rests with the care home's proprietor, but comparatively few owners of care homes understand the need to do this. It is therefore by no means clear that DoLS have plugged the *Bournewood* gap for most patients to whom they should apply. In addition, because DoLS only apply to hospitals and care homes, they do not offer any safeguards for incapacitated people living in supported living facilities, who may be especially vulnerable because such places are not subject to inspection by the Care Quality Commission.

Thirdly, some of the protections that exist for patients under the Mental Health Act—the need for second opinions in relation to some controversial medical treatments, for example—are not replicated for patients deprived of their liberty under the DoLS process. Instead medical treatment must simply be appropriate and in their best interests. The requirement that continued detention be subject to review by the tribunal is also absent, and there is no requirement to fund aftercare, once someone ceases to be deprived of their liberty. It is therefore at least arguable that the new regime continues to leave compliant, non-objecting patients with fewer protections and rights than their objecting, detained counterparts.

---

[41] 'Deprivation of liberty in healthcare' (2014) 348 British Medical Journal g3390.

Fourthly, it could be argued that there could be conflicts of interest for local authorities, which commission and pay for social care services, while also authorizing deprivations of liberty within those services. How likely is it that a local authority will decline to authorize living arrangements for which it is also ultimately responsible?

Fifthly, DoLS is directed towards ensuring that hospitals and care homes do not inadvertently breach incapacitated persons' Article 5 rights. Although important legally, whether or not their living arrangements have been authorized via DoLS may make little practical difference to compliant, incapacitated patients. Of more practical importance, but irrelevant under DoLS, are such individuals' Article 8 rights: for HL himself, being prevented from seeing his carers may have made much more difference to his quality of life than whether he was, in fact, free to leave.

Finally, the decision in *Cheshire West* has revealed the scale of the problems inherent in DoLS. From July to September 2015, 40,182 applications were made under DoLS,[42] compared with 7,157 in the whole of the first year of their operation. One of the consequences of the dramatic increase in the number of affected patients after *Cheshire West*, is a dramatic increase in the number of people who become entitled, as a result of Article 5, to have the lawfulness of their detention reviewed speedily by a court. As a result, the Court of Protection was immediately faced with a huge increase in its caseload.

In *A Hospital NHS Trust v CD*, for example, Mostyn J found it counter-intuitive to have to authorize a Deprivation of Liberty in order that a woman who fervently wanted to undergo an operation to remove large ovarian masses could undergo that operation.

A Hospital NHS Trust v CD[43]

Mostyn J

But for we hoplites who have to administer it at first instance the scope and ramifications of the test are, with respect, extremely confusing . . . . I do not accept the criticism that my approach to these cases is 'distorted' by my 'passionate' and 'tenacious' belief that *Cheshire West* is wrong. Rather, it is a loyal approach which tries to apply literally and purposively the Supreme Court's test while at the same time pointing out how confusing and curious it is, to say nothing of the cost it causes to the public purse . . .

[CD] actively and fervently wishes to undergo the operation to remove the surgical masses. How can it be said that in taking her to the hospital and having the operation performed there under general anaesthetic amounts to her being deprived of her liberty? . . .

She says she will go freely to the hospital but, as explained above, that is not a decision she can make. The decision I make on her behalf is intrinsically coercive even if she is enthusiastically compliant. If she changes her mind she will be taken to the hospital and operated on nonetheless. Although counterintuitive this state of affairs is to my mind clearly within the Supreme Court's test and it is therefore necessary to authorise her deprivation of liberty under Article 5.

A few months after the Supreme Court handed down its judgment, in *Re X and others (Deprivation of Liberty) Nos 1 and 2*,[44] Sir James Munby, the President of the Family Division, attempted to devise a more streamlined system to provide speedy review of the

---

[42] Department of Health, *Deprivation of Liberty Safeguards (DoLS): July to September 2015* (DH: London, 2015).

[43] [2015] EWCOP 74.   [44] [2014] EWCOP 25 and [2014] EWCOP 37.

lawfulness of detention via DoLS. Sir James Munby P held that it was not necessary for the patient (P) to be joined as a party, and nor was an oral hearing necessary, and a practice note was issued to that effect. In *Re X (Court of Protection Practice)*, the Court of Appeal found that it did not have jurisdiction to entertain an appeal against the President's decision in the abstract, when the questions remained hypothetical. It was nevertheless critical of the President's ruling, and especially so of his conclusion that P need not be joined as a party.

Re X (Court of Protection Practice)[45]

Black LJ

Counsel were unable to identify any situation where the issue before a court or tribunal was an adult's liberty, in which the person would not, themselves, be a necessary party to the proceedings. . . . [I]t is generally considered indispensable in this country for the person whose liberty is at stake automatically to be a party to the proceedings in which the issue is to be decided. The President's conclusion that it was unnecessary for this to be so in relation to an adult without capacity appears therefore to run counter to normal domestic practice. It might, therefore, be thought to require very firm foundations if it is to be regarded as acceptable. . . . I stress that I am only concerned, at present, with whether P must be a party to the deprivation of liberty proceedings. Given the tools presently available in our domestic procedural law, I see no alternative to that being so in every case.

Given the Court of Appeal's view about P's participation, it was unsurprising that further litigation followed. If P is to be a party, then the Official Solicitor might need to be appointed to represent him, but the Official Solicitor has been clear that he does not have the resources to do this in all the cases now coming before the Court of Protection. In *Re MOD (Deprivation of Liberty)*,[46] District Judge Marin described the situation that had arisen as follows:

What results therefore is a complete impasse. The Court of Appeal strongly suggests that P should be a party. If so, he must have a litigation friend before he can become a party. If family members cannot take on this role either because it is legally or procedurally wrong or simply because none exist, then all eyes turn to the Official Solicitor. But he says that he cannot act as he has no resources to do so. The result therefore is that the cases all stand still and cannot proceed as will hundreds and potentially thousands of other cases. The ramifications of this are huge. In fact, I cannot think of a more serious situation to have faced a court in recent legal history.

The matter is yet to be resolved. In *Re P*, for example, Charles J disagreed with the Court of Appeal; maintaining that it was unnecessary for the P to be a party to every DoLS application, provided other safeguards were in place.

---

[45] [2015] EWCA Civ 599.   [46] [2015] EWCOP 47.

Re P[47]

Charles J

The essential issue is therefore whether P must be a party to such applications based on a care package that is presented as being non-contentious and so in all such cases, until accredited legal representatives are available, a litigation friend must be appointed.

In my view, the answer is 'No' and so I disagree with the reasoning and obiter conclusion of the Court of Appeal on this point and prefer that of the President . . ..

In my view, in deciding what the minimum is in the circumstances of a given case the determinative issue is whether in practice the procedure adopted enables P's position in respect of the essence of P's Article 5 right to be properly protected and promoted by his case and his wishes and feelings on the determinative test (having regard to the consequence that the implementation of the care package will deprive him of his liberty) being fairly and appropriately put before the court when it is considering the making of the first welfare order and on its review.

(5) Reform of DoLS

In 2014, the House of Lords Select Committee on the Mental Capacity Act declared that DoLS were not fit for purpose and recommended their replacement 'with provisions that are compatible in style and ethos with the Mental Capacity Act'.[48] To this end, the government asked the Law Commission to undertake a review.

In its 2015 consultation paper, the Law Commission proposed replacing DoLS with a new scheme called 'Protective Care'. The proposed protective care system will have a wider scope than DoLS; it will apply not only to hospitals and care homes but extend to supported living arrangements and treatment provided in a domestic setting.

The Law Commission's proposed overarching system of protective care would be made up of three different schemes. First, the supportive care scheme would involve local authorities keeping people's care plans under review. This would apply to people who lack capacity to consent to their living arrangements, who are living in care homes, supported living, and 'shared lives accommodation', and who might require more restrictive care in the future.

Secondly, restrictive care would directly replace DoLS, but it would focus not upon the deprivation of liberty, but on the care required. If such care might involve restrictions, such as not being free to leave, the person will be allocated an 'Approved Mental Capacity Professional' (AMCP), who will undertake or arrange for a best interests assessment to be carried out in relation to the proposed care.

Thirdly, the hospital care system would provide protection to people who lack capacity who are receiving treatment in hospital which does, or may in the next 28 days, amount to a deprivation of liberty. Where this is the case, a doctor would have to certify that the proposed treatment is in the patient's best interests and is proportionate to the risk of harm. After 28 days, the AMCP would carry out an assessment and could authorize the deprivation of liberty for another 12 months.

At the time of writing, the Law Commission has said that it expects to publish its final recommendations and a draft Bill in 2016.

---

[47] [2015] EWCOP 59.

[48] House of Lords Select Committee on the Mental Capacity Act 2005, Report of Session 2013–14, *Mental Capacity Act 2005: Post-Legislative Scrutiny* (TSO: London, 2014) para 33.

(c) INVOLUNTARY ADMISSION UNDER THE 1983 ACT

Before we flesh out the most common routes through which patients are compulsorily detained under the Mental Health Act, it is worth noting that there are other routes into the mental health system. In an emergency, a patient can be admitted under section 4 on the basis of one medical recommendation that 'it is of urgent necessity for the patient to be admitted and detained under section 2'.

Under section 136, if a police officer finds 'a person who appears to him to be suffering from mental disorder and to be in immediate need of care or control' in a public place, he can be removed to a place of safety for 72 hours 'for the purpose of enabling him to be examined by a registered medical practitioner and to be interviewed by an Approved Mental Health Professional (AMHP) and of making any necessary arrangements for his treatment or care'.

If the person's behaviour poses 'an unmanageably high risk to other patients, staff or users of a healthcare setting', a police station may be used as a place of safety,[49] but, as Bynoe, an Independent Police Complaints Commissioner explains, this should be exceptional.

Ian Bynoe[50]

Police custody is an unsuitable environment for someone with mental illness and may make their condition worse, particularly if they are not dealt with quickly and appropriately and don't receive the care they need. The . . . use of cells not only diverts police resources from fighting crime but criminalises behaviour that is not a crime. A police cell should only be used when absolutely necessary, for example, when someone is violent and not as a convenience.

The Crisis Care Concordat was launched in 2014 in order to try to reduce the use of police custody for those in need of mental health crisis care. It has resulted in a 55 per cent reduction in England in the use of police cells as a place of safety for people detained under the Mental Health Act since 2011–12, and a 34 per cent reduction since 2013–14.

Finally, under section 5 a voluntarily admitted patient can be compulsorily detained for up to 72 hours in order to prevent him from leaving hospital, after which continued detention is possible only if the formal powers in section 3 are invoked.

(1) The Process of Applying for Formal Powers

The 1983 Act provides for the compulsory admission of patients for assessment under section 2, and for treatment under section 3. At any one time, approximately 20,000 patients are detained in hospital.

---

[49] Mental Health Act Code of Practice 2015, para 16.38.

[50] Quoted in Andrew Cole, 'Overuse of police cells for detaining people with mental health problems "intolerable"' (2008) 337 British Medical Journal 1635.

Mental Health Act 1983 sections 2 and 3

2(2) An application for admission for assessment may be made in respect of a patient on the grounds that—

(a) he is suffering from mental disorder of a nature or degree which warrants the detention of the patient in a hospital for assessment (or for assessment followed by medical treatment) for at least a limited period; and

(b) he ought to be so detained in the interests of his own health or safety or with a view to the protection of other persons.

(3) An application for admission for assessment shall be founded on the written recommendations in the prescribed form of two registered medical practitioners, including in each case a statement that in the opinion of the practitioner the conditions set out in subsection (2) above are complied with.

(4) ... [A] patient admitted to hospital in pursuance of an application for admission for assessment may be detained for a period not exceeding 28 days beginning with the day on which he is admitted, but shall not be detained after the expiration of that period unless before it has expired he has become liable to be detained by virtue of a subsequent application, order or direction under the following provisions of this Act. ...

3(2) An application for admission for treatment may be made in respect of a patient on the grounds that—

(a) he is suffering from mental disorder of a nature or degree which makes it appropriate for him to receive medical treatment in a hospital; and

(b) it is necessary for the health or safety of the patient or for the protection of other persons that he should receive such treatment and it cannot be provided unless he is detained under this section [and]

(c) appropriate medical treatment is available for him.

(3) An application for admission for treatment shall be founded on the written recommendations in the prescribed form of two registered medical practitioners, including in each case a statement that in the opinion of the practitioner the conditions set out in subsection (2) above are complied with ...

(4) In this Act, references to appropriate medical treatment, in relation to a person suffering from mental disorder, are references to medical treatment which is appropriate in his case, taking into account the nature and degree of the mental disorder and all other circumstances of his case.

Applications for section 2 and 3 orders can be made by the patient's nearest relative, but most are made by an Approved Mental Health Professional (AMHP), usually a social worker, and the application must be supported by two medical practitioners, one of whom must be approved under section 12(2) of the Act, 'as having special experience in the diagnosis or treatment of mental disorder', and one of whom must have 'previous acquaintance with the patient'.

Under section 2, an individual can be detained for assessment for up to 28 days, after which the patient must either be: (a) discharged; (b) admitted as an informal patient; or (c) detained under section 3. Under section 3, individuals can be admitted for treatment, initially for up to six months, and this can be renewed for a further six months. Thereafter, the individual can be detained for a year, with annual renewal for long-term inpatients.

The justifications for compulsory detention under the Act are a combination of preventing the individual from harming herself and/or others, and enabling her to receive treatment. For example, under sections 2 and 3, the person must be suffering from a mental disorder of, 'a nature or degree which warrants admission to hospital' (section 2), or, 'which makes it appropriate for him to receive medical treatment in a hospital' (section 3), both of which have a therapeutic intent. But under section 2, detention is permissible if the patient 'ought to be detained' to protect the health or safety of the patient, or to protect other persons, or under section 3, detention must be 'necessary for the health or safety of the patient or for the protection of other persons'.

The need to be in hospital means that these powers should be used only where the intention is that the patient will actually become an inpatient. It would not be possible to use section 3 where the intention is immediately to discharge the patient under a Community Treatment Order (discussed later). It is also necessary to prove that the treatment cannot be provided unless the patient is detained, so where it would be possible to provide treatment in the community, section 3 is not satisfied. This is sometimes referred to as the 'least restrictive alternative' principle: treatment in hospital must be necessary, not just convenient.

It should, however, be noted that the use of the word 'or' may run counter to the 'least restrictive alternative' principle. This is because, in theory at least, a patient might be detained because she is suffering from a disorder whose *nature* warrants detention in hospital, but to a *degree* which does not. We return to this point again later in the context of discharge from hospital.

In the next extract, Jill Peay further suggests that the patient's 'need' to be in hospital may arise not because of the nature of her illness, but as a result of her attitude towards treatment.

Jill Peay[51]

Curiously, in clinical terms, 'the need to be in hospital' may not arise. This is not because the illness *can only* be treated in hospital, but because the patient will not *accept* treatment where he is (in the community). Since the only route by which *compulsory* treatment can be legally achieved is via the Act, and since the Act only allows compulsory treatment *in hospital*, such treatment can only be achieved via admission to hospital. Hence, the person is perceived as needing to be in hospital because of his/her attitude to treatment, which may or may not be determined by the illness itself.

The statute takes for granted that it will be possible to tell when a patient poses a risk sufficient to justify detention. In practice, as Nicola Glover-Thomas's empirical research suggests, those charged with making decisions under the Act take a range of different factors into account, most importantly the person's past history, but that 'gut feelings' and intuitions also play a role when judging risk. Interestingly, too, Glover-Thomas's research suggested that, in practice, people living in deprived areas may be more likely to satisfy the risk threshold.

Nicola Glover-Thomas[52]

It is perhaps telling that without a clear definitional guide under the 2007 Act, there was a significant variation in the meanings attributed to risk by decision-makers in the research sample. . . . It appears that decision-makers apply self-authored 'working definitions', which appear somewhat esoteric and abstruse . . .

[51] *Decisions and Dilemmas: Working with Mental Health Law* (Hart Publishing: Oxford, 2003).
[52] 'The Age of Risk: Risk Perception and Determination Following the Mental Health Act 2007' (2011) 19 Medical Law Review 581–605.

The overwhelming view of the research sample was that 'past behaviour' is regarded as the 'main predictor' of a patient's current risk profile. In addition, decision-makers must be aware of contextual factors, such as the effects of illicit substances and alcohol, particularly in relation to how these affect the patient's mental state. These factors, which feature in a patient's psychiatric background, are then fed into the overall risk assessment process . . .

[T]he suggestion that a patient's socio-economic background could become a dominant feature in a Mental Health Act risk assessment was categorically refuted by the interviewees: 'it's not about socio-economic status, it's about support networks, it's about alternatives to admission'. In spite of this, it was acknowledged that where an individual is living in a deprived area where there are limited support services, the risk of harm to self or others is deemed higher than for someone living in an affluent area with family and friends rallying round . . .

Gut instinct has a significant role to play and this stems largely from professional experience and the context of decision-making—whether decision-makers are working in an in-patient or community environment. Decision-makers certainly do identify relevant factors, as discussed above, but they then filter these by using 'personal intuition' in order to generate an outcome.

(2) The 'Treatability' Requirement

The, at first sight, innocuous condition for detention in section 3(d), namely that 'appropriate medical treatment is available' in fact represents one of the most contested aspects of the 2007 reforms. Under the original Act, detention was only possible if treatment was 'likely to alleviate or prevent a deterioration of his condition'. This was known as the 'treatability' requirement, and it was considered problematic because it is not clear that personality disorders are, in fact, treatable. If untreatable patients cannot be detained, it might be difficult to justify the detention of personality-disordered individuals. Since making it easier to detain people with 'dangerous and severe personality disorders' (DSPD) was a primary goal of the reform agenda, this meant abandoning or modifying the treatability requirement. The reason this is so important is that detaining people who cannot be treated, just in order to protect others, amounts to preventative detention. Psychiatrists were adamant that their role must be to treat patients who are unwell, rather than to lock up antisocial individuals.

In the next extract, Robert Francis QC, who chaired the inquiry into the circumstances leading to the murders of Lin and Megan Russell, suggests that powers of indefinite detention under the Criminal Justice Act, which can be used if the person has previously been convicted of a serious offence, would be a better response to fears about an individual's dangerousness than detention under the Mental Health Act.

Robert Francis[53]

It is difficult to believe that there are many persons who are known to the statutory agencies to be so dangerous that they would warrant detention to protect the public, but who have not been convicted of at least one serious offence. Mr Stone was certainly not such a person: he had more than one conviction for a serious offence and was regarded within the criminal justice system as being dangerous. In regard to such cases the sentencing powers

---

[53] 'The Michael Stone Inquiry—a reflection' (2007) Journal of Mental Health Law 41.

> and obligations under the Criminal Justice Act 2003 provide a more fruitful means of reassuring the public . . .
>
> A risk of using the mental health legislation for non-clinical purposes is that the hospitals will become as full as the prisons are now, with the consequent adverse effect on the care and supervision of those already within that system, to the detriment not only of the patients themselves, but to the public who deserve properly focussed and informed protection.

After protracted debates in the House of Lords, the compromise in the Act is that appropriate medical treatment has to be available; it no longer needs to be likely to work. Medical treatment receives a further definition in section 145(4).

Mental Health Act 1983 section 145

> 145(4) Any reference in this Act to medical treatment, in relation to mental disorder, shall be construed as a reference to medical treatment the purpose of which is to alleviate, or prevent a worsening of, the disorder or one or more of its symptoms or manifestations.

The Code of Practice gives more detailed guidance on what appropriate treatment means. It specifically spells out that locking someone up is not appropriate medical treatment, but it also indicates that the test will be satisfied if treatment is available, even if the patient in fact refuses to engage with it. 'Talking cures', almost by definition, will not work without the patient's cooperation, and so the 'availability of treatment' criterion for detention may be satisfied, even if the patient is not actually receiving any treatment at all.

Mental Health Act Code of Practice 2015

> 23.18 Simply detaining someone, even in a hospital, does not constitute medical treatment.
>
> 23.19 A patient's attitude towards the proposed treatment may be relevant in determining whether the appropriate medical treatment test is met. An indication of unwillingness to co-operate with treatment generally, or with a specific aspect of treatment, does not make such treatment inappropriate.
>
> 23.20 In particular, psychological therapies and other forms of medical treatments which, to be effective, require the patient's co-operation are not automatically inappropriate simply because a patient does not currently wish to engage with them. Such treatments can potentially remain appropriate and available as long as it continues to be clinically suitable to offer them and they would be provided if the patient agreed to engage.

(3) The Use of Compulsory Powers in Practice

The proportion of patients who are admitted compulsorily is increasing. It is also increasingly common for NHS patients to be admitted to private care facilities. The Care Quality Commission monitors patients who are deprived of their liberty and issues an annual report on its findings.[54]

---

[54] A role previously carried out by the Mental Health Act Commission.

Care Quality Commission[55]

> The MHA was used 53,176 times to detain patients in hospital for longer than 72 hours, 5% (2,768) more than 2012/13 and 30% more than 2003/04.
>
> Since 2010, the number of people in hospital subject to the MHA has increased by 9% (1,544). In that time, the population in England has increased by 3% (1.67 million), so the number of people being detained cannot be linked to an increase in the number of people in the general population.
>
> The number of people detained in care from non-NHS providers is increasing. This year independent hospital providers have reported an increase of 21% in detained patients. This is 10% of all longer-term detentions and more than double the proportion of 10 years ago.

A further and consistent trend in admissions under the Mental Health Act has been the over-representation of people from black, asian and minority ethnic (BAME) groups, both in terms of all admissions, and in the use of compulsory powers.[56] In 2014–15, for example, people who identified as Black or Black British were twice as likely as white people who had been in contact with mental health services to spend time in hospital.[57] They were also more likely to be detained: for every 100 Black or Black British patients who spent time in hospital, 56.9 had been detained, compared with 37.5 detentions per 100 hospital admissions among white patients.[58]

There is considerable debate over whether the reasons for the persistent over-representation of some BAME groups are patient-related or service-related. Patient-related explanations suggest that there may be a higher incidence of mental health problems within these groups, perhaps as a result of the pressures faced by people who are discriminated against and who may be more likely to experience poverty and deprivation. Service-related explanations suggest these statistics represent institutional racism, perhaps because unwarranted assumptions about people from minority ethnic groups are made within the mental health system.

In 2002, the Sainsbury Centre conducted a review of the relationship between mental health services and African and Caribbean communities, and concluded that there was a vicious circle at play, as a result of what they described as 'circles of fear'. Partly as a result of poor and discriminatory service provision, and partly due to the particular stigma attached to mental illness in some communities, black people were less likely to access treatment services in the early stages of mental illness, and were therefore more likely to reach a crisis point, when detention might be needed. This would then reinforce the perception of mental health services as coercive, thus further deterring early access to treatment.

The Sainsbury Centre for Mental Health[59]

> There is a profound paradox at the centre of black people's experience of mental health services in England. Young black men, in particular, are heavily over-represented in the most restrictive parts of the service, including secure services. And black people generally have an

---

55 *Monitoring the Mental Health Act in 2013–14* (CQC, 2015).

56 Bernard Audini and Paul Lelliott, 'Age, gender and ethnicity of those detained under Part II of the Mental Health Act 1983' (2002) 180 British Journal of Psychiatry 222.

57 Health and Social Care Information Centre, *Mental Health Bulletin, Annual Report—2014–15* (HSCIC, 2015).

58 Health and Social Care Information Centre, *Inpatients Formally Detained in Hospitals 2014–15* (HSCIC, 2015).

59 'Breaking the Circles of Fear: A Review of the Relationship Between Mental Health Services and African and Caribbean Communities' (SCMH, 2002).

overwhelmingly negative experience of mental health services. Yet these same communities are not accessing the primary care, mental health promotion and specialist community services which might prevent or lessen their mental health problems. They are getting the mental health services they don't want but not the ones they do or might want. . . .

Black people with potential mental health problems are not engaging with services at an early point in the cycle when they could receive less coercive and more appropriate services. Instead they tend only to come to services in crisis when they face a range of risks including over- and mis-diagnosis, police intervention and use of the Mental Health Act. In order to break this cycle, it is necessary to address the issue both from the perspective of services—by making primary care and other services more welcoming, accessible and relevant—and from the perspective of the black community—by increasing understanding and knowledge and reducing the stigma associated with mental illness.

(d) RESTRICTED PATIENTS AND THE CRIMINAL JUSTICE SYSTEM

It is possible for people who are convicted in the criminal courts to be diverted to the mental health system if they suffer from a mental disorder. Under section 37 of the Mental Health Act, a court can make a hospital order where someone has been found guilty of an offence punishable by imprisonment. Before making such an order, the court has to be satisfied that the section 3 grounds for admission are satisfied, and, under section 27(2)(b), the court must be 'of the opinion, having regard to all the circumstances including the nature of the offence and the character and antecedents of the offender, and to the other available methods of dealing with him, that the most suitable method of disposing of the case is by means of an order under this section'. The effect of a hospital order is that the person will be detained in one of the three high security special hospitals (Ashworth, Broadmoor, and Rampton) or, where appropriate, in a medium secure ward.

It should, however, be remembered that a significant proportion of the ordinary prison population suffers from mental health problems. It has been estimated that over half of all female and three-quarters of all male prisoners suffer from personality disorders, and rates of other conditions, such as schizophrenia, are much higher than in the population as a whole.[60]

In *Jean-Luc Rivière v France*,[61] the ECtHR found that containing mentally disordered offenders in prison could constitute a breach of Article 3. Detaining a seriously mentally disordered person, without medical supervision appropriate to his condition, 'entailed particularly acute hardship and caused him distress or adversity of an intensity exceeding the unavoidable level of suffering inherent in detention'. It would clearly not be feasible to empty UK prisons of all prisoners with mental health problems, but in order not to breach their human rights, appropriate medical services should nevertheless be available to them.

In addition to being detained at the outset in a special hospital, there is also some movement between the prison system and the mental health system. This is especially marked when prisoners are nearing the end of their sentences, but are perceived to pose a continuing risk to the public. Detention under section 3 of the Mental Health Act has been used to prevent the release of people who can no longer be detained within the criminal justice system, because they have completed their sentences.

[60] Phil Fennell, *Mental Health: The New Law* (Jordan: Bristol, 2007) 162.
[61] Application no 33834/03 (2006).

5 TREATMENT OF THE MENTALLY ILL

At the outset, it is important to remember that the normal rules which cover consent to medical treatment apply to people with mental disorders. Adults with capacity have the right to refuse medical treatment, regardless of whether they are suffering from a mental disorder, and those who lack capacity may be treated in their best interests. There are, however, some important exceptions that apply only to those who have been formally admitted to the mental health system. Some of these create special protections for compulsorily detained individuals, while others permit treatment without consent, regardless of the patient's competence.

(a) TREATMENT UNDER SECTION 57 OF THE MENTAL HEALTH ACT 1983

Under section 57 of the Act, certain types of treatment cannot be given without both the patient's consent *and* the agreement of a doctor appointed to give a second opinion (known as a SOAD). The SOAD must consult two other people who have been involved in the patient's medical treatment, at least one of whom must be a nurse.

The treatments to which section 57 applies are psychosurgery ('any surgical operation for destroying brain tissue or for destroying the functioning of brain tissue') and 'the surgical implantation of hormones for the purpose of reducing male sex drive', otherwise known as chemical castration. Under section 57, these treatments cannot be given without the patient's consent, so it would not be lawful to carry out psychosurgery or chemical castration on patients who lack capacity unless such treatment could fit within the emergency exception in section 62 (discussed in Section 5(c)).

Section 57 is seldom used. The surgical implantation of hormones would be unusual: most treatments to suppress a male patient's sex drive take the form of pills or injections, neither of which are covered by this section. Such drugs can therefore be given under section 63 (discussed in Section 5(d)) for up to three months, after which they would fall within section 58, and require consent or a second opinion.

(b) TREATMENT UNDER SECTION 58 OF THE MENTAL HEALTH ACT 1983

Under section 58, the administration of psychiatric medicines for periods longer than three months requires the informed consent of a competent patient *or* a second opinion from an independent doctor that *either* the patient is not capable of consenting *or* the patient is capable and has not consented, but it is nevertheless appropriate for them to receive the treatment.

Mental Health Act 1983 section 58

> 58(3) Subject to section 62 below, a patient shall not be given any form of treatment to which this section applies unless—
>
> (a) he has consented to that treatment and either the approved clinician in charge of it or a registered medical practitioner appointed for the purposes of this Part of this Act by the Secretary of State has certified in writing that the patient is capable of understanding its nature, purpose and likely effects and has consented to it; or

> (b) a registered medical practitioner appointed as aforesaid (not being the responsible clinician or the approved clinician in charge of the treatment in question) has certified in writing that the patient is not capable of understanding the nature, purpose and likely effects of that treatment or being so capable has not consented to it but that it is appropriate for the treatment to be given.

There is no need for a second opinion if medication is given for less than three months (this will fall within section 63, discussed in Section 5(d)). There have been calls for this three-month period to be shortened, since three months is quite a long time for someone to be subject to unwanted, compulsory medication. Under section 58(2), the Secretary of State has the power to reduce this period, but he has not chosen to exercise it. Of course, some patients will be discharged within this three-month period, and hence will never have their medication regime reviewed.

Electro-convulsive therapy (ECT) used to be subject to the same provision, and hence could be given without consent to a competent, refusing patient provided that it was authorized by a SOAD. Following pressure from service users, among others, it is now dealt with separately in section 58A, and cannot be given without consent, unless section 62 applies in an emergency (see the following section). Under section 58A, ECT can be given only if the patient has consented or, if the patient lacks capacity, it is appropriate for it to be given and the patient did not refuse it in an advance directive.

It is important to note that there is a difference between sections 58 and 58A of the Mental Health Act and the Mental Capacity Act 2005. If the patient is detained under the Mental Health Act, then even if they lack capacity, the Mental Capacity Act does not apply in relation to treatments which are covered by sections 57, 58, and 58A. This has two principal consequences. First, the 'best interests' checklist, which we considered in the previous chapter, with its emphasis upon the wishes and feelings of the incapacitated adult, does not apply and the much lower threshold, namely that the doctor believes that treatment is 'appropriate', governs whether long-term medication for mental disorder or ECT is given to patients who lack capacity. Secondly, the bar on giving the 'special treatments' covered by section 57 to patients who lack capacity is an absolute one, and cannot be avoided by relying on the best interests test in the MCA.

The need for a second opinion under sections 57 and 58 was intended to protect the interests of detained patients. It is, however, interesting to note that the presence of a second opinion may, in practice, deprive psychiatric patients of the opportunity to challenge treatment through tort law.

Peter Bartlett[62]

> As for medication, the very protections provided by section 58 make a negligence action effectively impossible. How can a claim be made that the psychiatrist is negligent under Bolam when an SOAD, an officially selected and trained expert in the field, has signed off the treatment?

In the past, there was undoubtedly a tendency for the SOAD to rubber stamp the first clinician's judgement. In the 1990s, Phil Fennell found that the SOAD approved the treatment plan in 96 per cent of cases.[63] In *R (Wilkinson) v Broadmoor Special Hospital Authority*, the

---

[62] 'Psychiatric Treatment in the Absence of Law?' (2006) 14 Medical Law Review 124–31.
[63] Phil Fennell, *Treatment without Consent* (Routledge: London, 1996) 211.

Court of Appeal was critical of the tendency to regard the SOAD's role as one of review, rather than independent assessment, and held that a less deferential approach was needed.

R (Wilkinson) v Broadmoor Special Hospital Authority[64]

Simon Brown LJ

Whilst, of course, it is proper for the SOAD to pay regard to the views of the RMO [responsible medical officer] who has, after all, the most intimate knowledge of the patient's case, that does not relieve him of the responsibility of forming his own independent judgment as to whether or not 'the treatment should be given'. And certainly, if the SOAD's certificate and evidence is to carry any real weight in cases where, as here, the treatment plan is challenged, it will be necessary to demonstrate a less deferential approach than appears to be the norm.

SOADs are now under a duty to provide reasons for their decisions. In *R (Wooder) v Feggetter*, the claimant's clinician decided that he should receive anti-psychotic medication, despite his refusal to consent. The SOAD had provided the necessary certificate under section 58(3)(b), but the claimant, who wanted his delusional condition to be treated without drugs, argued that the SOAD should provide reasons. The Court of Appeal agreed.

R (Wooder) v Feggetter[65]

Brooke LJ

With the coming into force of the Human Rights Act 1998 the time has come, in my judgment, for this court to declare that fairness requires that a decision by a SOAD which sanctions the violation of the autonomy of a competent adult patient should also be accompanied by reasons . . . I would be disposed to grant a declaration that fairness demands that a SOAD should give in writing the reasons for his opinion when certifying under section 58 of the Mental Health Act 1983 that a detained patient should be given medication against his will, and that these reasons should be disclosed to the patient unless the SOAD or the RMO considers that such disclosure would be likely to cause serious harm to the physical or mental health of the patient or any other person.

(c) TREATMENT UNDER SECTION 62 OF THE MENTAL HEALTH ACT 1983

An exception to sections 57 and 58 is created by section 62:

Mental Health Act 1983 section 62

62(1) Sections 57 and 58 above shall not apply to any treatment—

(a) which is immediately necessary to save the patient's life; or

(b) which (not being irreversible) is immediately necessary to prevent a serious deterioration of his condition; or

---

[64] [2001] EWCA Civ 1545.   [65] [2002] EWCA Civ 554.

(c) which (not being irreversible or hazardous) is immediately necessary to alleviate serious suffering by the patient; or

(d) which (not being irreversible or hazardous) is immediately necessary and represents the minimum interference necessary to prevent the patient from behaving violently or being a danger to himself or to others. . . .

(3) For the purposes of this section treatment is irreversible if it has unfavourable irreversible physical or psychological consequences and hazardous if it entails significant physical hazard.

This means that, in an emergency, all treatments covered by sections 57 and 58 can be given without a second opinion or the patient's consent. Given that the treatments covered by section 57 are rarely used, and will be even more unlikely to be 'immediately necessary', section 62's suspension of the protection contained in section 57 is of little practical importance. Instead, section 62 is mainly used to suspend the second opinion requirements in sections 58 and 58A, in relation to medication and ECT.[66] Although used comparatively infrequently, the principal effect of section 62's suspension of section 58 is that emergency ECT can be administered to a competent, refusing patient without her consent.

(d) TREATMENT UNDER SECTION 63 OF THE MENTAL HEALTH ACT 1983

Of more practical importance is section 63, which permits medical treatment for mental disorder to be provided without consent:

Mental Health Act 1983 section 63

The consent of a patient shall not be required for any medical treatment given to him for the mental disorder from which he is suffering, not being a form of treatment to which section 57, 58 or 58A above applies, if the treatment is given by or under the direction of the approved clinician in charge of the treatment.

Mental Health Act 1983 section 145(4)

Any reference in this Act to medical treatment, in relation to mental disorder, shall be construed as a reference to medical treatment the purpose of which is to alleviate, or prevent a worsening of, the disorder or one or more of its symptoms or manifestations.

---

[66] Phil Fennell, *Treatment Without Consent: Law, Psychiatry and the Treatment of Mentally Disordered People since 1845* (Routledge: London, 1996) 199; Andy Bickle et al, 'Audit of statutory urgent treatment at a high security hospital' (2007) Journal of Mental Health Law 66.

It is important to remember that section 63 applies to competent adults. If a competent adult patient consents to treatment, there would be no need to resort to the power contained in section 63. In practice, then, this section enables treatment for mental disorder to be given to a competent adult, against her wishes, without the need for a second opinion.

Although the statute does not specify this, it has been taken for granted that it is also permissible to use force to administer treatment authorized under section 63. In *R v Broadmoor Special Hospital Authority, ex parte S, H and D*, Auld LJ suggested that the power to detain and treat without consent was, by implication, accompanied by 'the necessary incidents of control'.

R v Broadmoor Special Hospital Authority, ex parte S, H and D[67]

Auld LJ

Sections 3 and 37 of the 1983 Act provide for detention, not just for its own sake, but for treatment. Detention for treatment necessarily implies control for that purpose. . . . Both statutes leave unspoken many of the necessary incidents of control flowing from a power of detention for treatment, including: the power to restrain patients, to keep them in seclusion . . . , to deprive them of their personal possessions for their own safety and to regulate the frequency and manner of visits to them.

As Genevra Richardson explains in the next extract, section 63 is radically out of step with the increasingly dominant principle of patient autonomy.

Genevra Richardson[68]

At present the law in England and Wales is unusually inconsistent and discriminatory in the way it deals with questions of competence and patient autonomy with regard to mental disorder. The Mental Health Act 1983 permits a person suffering from a mental disorder of the necessary degree to be detained in hospital and treated for that disorder against her competent wishes. . . . Thus, while the common law grants patient autonomy a central role in relation to both physical and mental disorder, in relation to treatment of mental disorder of sufficient severity statute requires patient autonomy to cede to the values of paternalism and social protection. It was suggested above that the paternalist justification for this statutory approach originated in the now contested belief that mental disorder equates to loss of judgment. It is therefore interesting to note that the statutory powers of compulsion are limited to treatment for mental disorder; compulsory patients can still refuse treatment for physical disorder: judgment, it seems, is lost in relation to treatment for *mental* disorder only . . .

Much, therefore, turns on the meaning given to mental disorder and if it is interpreted too generously there is a danger that a competent patient could be forced to accept treatment for a condition which has little or no bearing on his or her mental state.

Obviously the scope of section 63 depends upon the breadth or narrowness of the interpretation of the words 'treatment for the mental disorder from which he is suffering'.

---

[67] The Times, 17 February 1998.

[68] 'Autonomy, Guardianship and Mental Disorder: One Problem, Two Solutions' (2002) 65 Modern Law Review 702–23.

In *Re KB (Adult) (Mental Patient: Medical Treatment)*, Ewbank J held that force-feeding an anorexic patient was treatment for her mental disorder.

Re KB (Adult) (Mental Patient: Medical Treatment)[69]

Ewbank J

[A]norexia nervosa . . . is an eating disorder and relieving symptoms is just as much a part of treatment as relieving the underlying cause. If the symptoms are exacerbated by the patient's refusal to eat and drink, the mental disorder becomes progressively more and more difficult to treat and so the treatment by nasogastric tube is an integral part of the treatment of the mental disorder itself. It is also said that the treatment is necessary in order to make psychiatric treatment of the underlying cause possible at all . . . feeding by nasogastric tube in the circumstances of this type of case is treatment envisaged under s 63 and does not require the consent of the patient.

It is, of course, clear that force-feeding does not cure anorexia, and, as Lewis explains in the next extract, repeated episodes of force-feeding can make recovery less likely.

Penney Lewis[70]

The anorexic's holy grail is control . . . Force-feeding crushes the patient's will, destroying who the patient is. This is the antithesis of what a successful, therapeutic treatment must be . . . The patient may be force-fed up to a more healthy weight and then discharged from hospital, free to return to her previous eating pattern and to lose the weight she has been forced to gain. As her trust has been violated, she may be less likely to seek medical help for her anorexia or for any other medical problem. The gain has been short-term, rather than long-term. The immediate crisis has been averted, but long-term damage has been done. Forcing treatment upon a young sufferer of anorexia merely reinforces her lack of self-confidence by taking this decision out of her control, and denies her the capacity for self-directed action which must be developed if she is to recover from this illness. Anorexics who have been force-fed may turn to the more life-threatening behaviour associated with bulimia, including vomiting and laxative abuse. They may be more likely to commit suicide, or to become entrenched in their refusal to eat and thereby become chronic sufferers.

Kirsty Keywood points out that the courts have also been surprisingly disinterested in whether clinicians would characterize force-feeding as 'treatment' for anorexia.

Kirsty Keywood[71]

A number of clinicians perceive involuntary treatment as being necessary in a small number of cases in order to preserve life, restore weight, and restore patients' cognitive abilities to a sufficient degree that they may engage meaningfully in psychotherapy, without necessarily

---

[69] [1994] 2 FCR 1051.
[70] 'Feeding Anorexic Patients Who Refuse Food' (1999) 7 Medical Law Review 21–37.
[71] 'Rethinking the anorexic body: how English law and psychiatry "think"' (2003) 26 International Journal of Law and Psychiatry 599–616.

damaging the therapeutic alliance between doctor and patient. Others observe that compulsory treatment, with its higher mortality rate at follow up, may well compromise the relationship between doctor and patient and erode further the patient's self-esteem. Indeed, the courts' assessment of the appropriateness of involuntary treatment pays little regard to the consequences of overriding the expressed wishes of the patient diagnosed with anorexia nervosa. Notwithstanding the paucity of evidence that involuntary treatment of anorexia nervosa yields significant benefits to the patient in the long term, it is perhaps surprising that the courts have not given greater consideration to the appropriateness of interventions such as non-consensual nasogastric feeding . . . The courts have traditionally premised their judgments on a set of assumptions about the appropriateness of involuntary intervention in the treatment of anorexia nervosa which find (as yet) no firm empirical support within the domains of evidence-based medicine.

In *B v Croydon Health Authority*[72] the patient's compulsion to self-harm was said to be a symptom of her mental disorder, and hence the Court of Appeal again authorized force-feeding under section 63. In *R v Collins, ex parte Brady*,[73] Ian Brady, one of the Moors murderers who was detained under the Mental Health Act 1983, had gone on hunger strike in order to protest against his perceived ill-treatment. Maurice Kay J held that force-feeding was justified under section 63 as treatment for the mental disorder from which he was suffering, because 'the hunger strike is a manifestation or symptom of the personality disorder'.

Using section 63 to compel refusing patients to undergo treatments such as force-feeding sits rather oddly with the special protections given to other sorts of treatment in sections 58 and 58A of the Act. Neither ECT nor long-term medication can be given to a refusing patient without the approval of a SOAD. Forcibly inserting a nasogastric tube, against a patient's wishes, is arguably as intrusive as ECT or the long-term use of medication, and yet it is not subject to the same restrictions.

Nevertheless, if categorizing force-feeding as treatment for mental disorder is controversial, in *Tameside and Glossop v CH*, Wall J gave section 63 an extraordinarily expansive interpretation, holding that a caesarean section could be authorized as treatment for CH's schizophrenia.

Tameside and Glossop v CH[74]

Wall J

There are several strands in the evidence which, in my judgment, bring the proposed treatment within s 63 of the Act. Firstly, there is the proposition that an ancillary reason for the induction and, if necessary the birth by Caesarian [sic] section is to prevent a deterioration in the Defendant's mental state. Secondly, there is the clear evidence of Dr M that in order for the treatment of her schizophrenia to be effective, it is necessary for her to give birth to a live baby. Thirdly, the overall structure of her treatment requires her to receive strong anti-psychotic medication. The administration of that treatment has been necessarily interrupted by her pregnancy and cannot be resumed until her child is born. It is not, therefore, I think stretching language unduly to say that achievement of a successful outcome of her pregnancy is a necessary part of the overall treatment of her mental disorder.

---

[72] [1995] Fam 133.   [73] [2000] Lloyd's Rep Med 355.   [74] [1996] 1 FCR 753.

The judgment in *Tameside* has been criticized for what Andrew Grubb describes as its 'sheer breadth'.[75] Although it has not been overruled, a few years later, in *St George's Hospital v S*—another case involving a woman with mental health problems who was refusing to consent to a caesarean section—the Court of Appeal took a more restrictive approach to section 63.

St George's Hospital v S[76]

Judge LJ

Section 63 of the Act may apply to the treatment of any condition which is integral to the mental disorder provided the treatment is given by or under the direction of the responsible medical officer. The treatment administered to MS was not so ordered: she was neither offered nor did she refuse treatment for mental disorder.

More recently, in *R (on the application of SP) v Secretary of State for Justice*, it was acknowledged that section 63 could be invoked to carry out a blood transfusion upon a man whose personality disorder resulted in serious self-harming behaviour, but that it would be 'an abuse of power' to impose a blood transfusion on him.

R (on the application of SP) v Secretary of State for Justice[77]

Mostyn J

It cannot be disputed that the act of self harming, the slashing open of the brachial artery, is a symptom or manifestation of the underlying personality disorder. Therefore to treat the wound in any way is to treat the manifestation or symptom of the underlying disorder. So, indisputably, to suture the wound would be squarely within section 63 . As would be the administration of a course of antibiotics to prevent infection. A consequence of bleeding from the wound is that haemoglobin levels are lowered. While it is strictly true, as Dr Latham says, that 'low haemoglobin is not wholly a manifestation or symptom of personality disorder', it is my view that to treat the low haemoglobin by a blood transfusion is just as much a treatment of a symptom or manifestation of the disorder as is to stitch up the wound or to administer antibiotics . . ..

In my judgment it would be an abuse of power in such circumstances even to think about imposing a blood transfusion on RC having regard to my findings that he presently has capacity to refuse blood products and, were such capacity to disappear for any reason, the advance decision would be operative. To impose a blood transfusion would be a denial of a most basic freedom. I therefore declare that the decision of Dr S is lawful and that it is lawful for those responsible for the medical care of RC to withhold all and any treatment which is transfusion into him of blood or primary blood components (red cells, white cells, plasma or platelets) notwithstanding the existence of powers under section 63 MHA.

This trend towards a more restrictive interpretation of section 63 was continued in *A NHS Trust v A*, a case involving an Iranian doctor who was, like Ian Brady, on hunger strike,

[75] 'Commentary: Treatment without Consent (Pregnancy) Adult' (1996) 4 Medical Law Review 193–8.
[76] [1996] 1 FCR 753.   [77] [2010] EWCA Civ 159.

but where his physical need for nutrition was not said to be a manifestation of his mental disorder.

A NHS Trust v A[78]

Baker J

I have found the views articulated by the treating clinicians, and in particular Dr WJ, persuasive. She does not consider that the administration of artificial nutrition and hydration to Dr A in the circumstances of this case to be a medical treatment for his mental disorder, but rather for a physical disorder that arises from his decision to refuse food. That decision is, of course, flawed in part because his mental disorder deprives him of the capacity to use and weigh information relevant to the decision. The physical disorder is thus in part a consequence of his mental disorder, but, in my judgment, it is not obviously either a manifestation or a symptom of the mental disorder. This case is thus distinguishable from both the *Croydon Health Authority* case and *Ex p Brady*.

In *R (on the application of B) v Ashworth Hospital Authority*, a slightly different question arose. The House of Lords had to consider whether section 63 only applied to treatment for the particular type of mental disorder that initially justified the patient's detention. B had been detained on the grounds that he was suffering from schizophrenia, but while he was in hospital he was diagnosed with a psychopathic disorder. B argued that the decision to place him on a ward for patients with psychopathic disorders was unlawful because this was not the type of mental disorder that had justified his detention. The House of Lords rejected this argument.

R (on the application of B) v Ashworth Hospital Authority[79]

Baroness Hale

I conclude that the words of section 63 mean what they say. They authorise a patient to be treated for any mental disorder from which he is suffering, irrespective of whether this falls within the form of disorder from which he is classified as suffering in the application, order or direction justifying his detention.

As I said earlier, compulsory patients are a vulnerable group who deserve protection from being forced to accept inappropriate treatment. But restricting their treatment to that which is designed for their 'classified' disorder is so haphazard as to be scarcely any protection at all. . . . [P]sychiatry is not an exact science. Diagnosis is not easy or clear cut. As this and many other cases show, a number of different diagnoses may be reached by the same or different clinicians over the years. As this case also shows, co-morbidity is very common . . .

Once the state has taken away a person's liberty and detained him in a hospital with a view to medical treatment, the state should be able (some would say obliged) to provide him with the treatment which he needs. It would be absurd if a patient could be detained in hospital but had to be denied the treatment which his doctor thought he needed for an indefinite period while some largely irrelevant classification was rectified.

---

[78] [2013] EWHC 2442 (Fam).   [79] [2005] UKHL 20.

Peter Bartlett disagrees, arguing that Baroness Hale's conflation of detention and forcible treatment is not necessarily appropriate, given that forcibly introducing drugs into a person may be more intrusive than the deprivation of liberty, and hence should require further justification.

Peter Bartlett[80]

Forced physical confinement is quite a different intervention into liberty from the introduction of drugs into an individual's body. While many certainly find the beneficial effects of the drug treatments outweigh the adverse effects, this does not change the fact that they act within the body, and are as such extraordinarily intrusive.

Kris Gledhill further comments that the consequence of the Lords' decision in *B* is 'that a person can be detained for treatment in relation to one form of disorder but also treated for a form of disorder, which would not have justified his or her detention in the first place'.[81]

(e) THE IMPACT OF THE HUMAN RIGHTS ACT ON TREATMENT OF PEOPLE WITH MENTAL DISORDERS

Since the Human Rights Act 1998, the courts have had to consider whether treatment without consent might violate a patient's Convention rights.

(1) Article 3

According to Article 3 'no one shall be subjected to torture or to inhuman or degrading treatment or punishment'. This is supposed to be an absolute right, with no qualification, and yet it could be argued that the test which the courts use when applying Article 3 to treatment of the mentally ill introduces, by the back door, a qualification which applies only to the mentally disordered. The source of this is the ECtHR's judgment in *Herczegfalvy v Austria*.

Herczegfalvy v Austria[82]

Judgment of the ECtHR

While it is for the medical authorities to decide, on the basis of recognised rules of medical science, on the therapeutic methods to be used, if necessary by force, to preserve the physical and mental health of patients who are entirely incapable of deciding for themselves and for whom they are therefore responsible, such patients nevertheless remain under the protection of art 3, the requirements of which permit of no derogation.

The established principles of medicine are admittedly in principle decisive in such cases; as a general rule, a measure which is a therapeutic necessity cannot be regarded as inhuman or degrading. The court must nevertheless satisfy itself that the medical necessity has been convincingly shown to exist.

---

[80] 'A Matter of Necessity? Enforced Treatment under the Mental Health Act' (2007) 15 Medical Law Review 86–98.

[81] Kris Gledhill, 'The House of Lords and the unimportance of classification: a retrograde step' (2005) Journal of Mental Health Law 174.

[82] (1992) 15 EHRR 437.

Herczegfalvy concerned a detained patient who was handcuffed and strapped to his bed, and these measures were said to be a therapeutic necessity:

> In this case, according to the psychiatric principles generally accepted at that time, medical necessity justified the treatment in issue, including forcibly administered food and neuroleptics, isolation, and attaching handcuffs to a security bed. Thus, there was no violation of Article 3.

It is also worth noting that *Herczegfalvy* involved a patient who lacked capacity, where a 'therapeutic necessity' test may not be very different from a judgement about whether treatment is in their best interests. Its 'therapeutic necessity' test has, nevertheless, been invoked in order to justify treatment without consent of patients who have capacity and are refusing treatment. This approach appears to create an exception to the absolute prohibition in Article 3, provided that the inhuman treatment is medically necessary treatment for the patient's mental disorder.

In *R (on the application of Munjaz) v Ashworth Hospital Authority*,[83] by a majority, the House of Lords held that a hospital authority's policy on seclusion, which provided for more infrequent review than that set out in the Mental Health Act Code of Practice, did not amount to inhuman or degrading treatment. The Lords took the view that the risk of ill-treatment was, in practice, very low and it would be disproportionate to require the hospital to change its policy. Stephanie Palmer has argued that this reasoning is problematic insofar as it introduces a proportionality balancing exercise into an unqualified Convention right: 'The unconditional wording of Article 3 renders the motivation for the alleged treatment irrelevant: the ends can never justify the means.'[84]

The introduction of qualifications to the Article 3 prohibition is contrary to the absolute approach advocated by the Committee for the Prevention of Torture, Inhuman or Degrading Treatment or Punishment.

Committee for the Prevention of Torture, Inhuman or Degrading Treatment or Punishment[85]

> The admission of a person to a psychiatric establishment on an involuntary basis should not be construed as authorising treatment without his consent. It follows that every competent patient, whether voluntary or involuntary, should be given the opportunity to refuse treatment or other medical intervention. Any derogation from this fundamental principle should be based upon law and only relate to clearly and strictly defined exceptional circumstances.

Peter Bartlett suggests that the courts' interpretation of section 63 does not meet this standard:

> The interpretation afforded to the section . . . allows unfettered treatment of any mental disorder with which the confined patient is affected without the patient's consent, no matter how small or great and whether or not the patient has capacity to consent to it. This throws to the wind any concept of autonomy for the civilly or criminally confined psychiatric patient.[86]

[83] [2005] UKHL 58.

[84] Stephanie Palmer, 'A Wrong Turning: Article 3 ECHR and Proportionality' (2006) 65 Cambridge Law Journal 438–52.

[85] Council of Europe, *Report of the Committee for the Prevention of Torture, Inhuman or Degrading Treatment or Punishment* (Council of Europe, 2000) para 41.

[86] 'Psychiatric Treatment in the Absence of Law?' (2006) 14 Medical Law Review 124–31.

Non-consensual treatment, and any associated use of force or restraint, can only avoid being categorized as inhuman or degrading treatment if 'convincingly shown' to be a medical or therapeutic necessity. What does this mean in practice, and how high is the standard of proof? These questions arose in *R (on the application of N) v M and Others*, a case in which a patient wanted to refuse anti-psychotic medication. Because she had obtained an independent opinion that she should not be given anti-psychotic medication, she argued, unsuccessfully, that it could not have been convincingly shown that a medical necessity existed.

R (on the application of N) v M and Others[87]

Dyson LJ

In the light of [*Herczegfalvy v Austria*], it is common ground that the standard of proof required is that the court should be satisfied that medical necessity has been 'convincingly' shown. . . .

Mr Kelly [for the claimant] submitted that this test is, in effect, the same as the criminal standard of proof. We disagree. It seems to us that no useful purpose is served by importing the language of the criminal law. The phrase 'convincingly shown' is easily understood. The standard is a high one. But it does not need elaboration or further explanation. . . .

Mr Kelly's submission on analysis involves the proposition that, in a case where there is a responsible body of opinion that a patient is not suffering from a treatable condition, then it cannot be convincingly shown that the treatment proposed is medically necessary. We reject this submission. . . . In our judgment, the fact that there is a responsible body of opinion against the proposed treatment is relevant to the question whether it is in the patient's best interests or medically necessary, but it is no more than that.

In *R (on the application of JB) v Haddock (Responsible Medical Officer)*, the Court of Appeal decided that it was not necessary to show that the treatment, which was found to be a medical necessity, would actually work. While the Court of Appeal resisted expressing the burden of proof in forensic terms, they suggested that it probably amounted to no more than that it was more likely than not that the treatment was a 'necessity'.

R (on the application of JB) v Haddock (Responsible Medical Officer)[88]

Auld LJ

The s.58(3) power to treat a patient capable of consent against his will or a patient incapable of consent is potentially a violation of his Art.3 right not to be subjected to degrading treatment and/or his Art.8 right to respect for his private life. However, it is common ground that, while the risk of infringement of those rights may be greater when the patient is capable of giving or refusing consent, it is not necessarily an infringement to treat him against his will where such treatment can be convincingly shown to be medically or therapeutically necessary. . . .

To require of psychiatrists a state of mind of precision and sureness in matters of diagnosis akin to that required of a jury in a criminal case, even in this fraught context of forcible

---

[87] [2002] EWCA Civ 1789.   [88] [2006] EWCA Civ 961.

treatment potentially violating detained patients' human rights, is not sensible or feasible. . . . And, as to whether the treatment will do any good, it is unreal to require psychiatrists, under the umbrella of a requirement of medical or therapeutic necessity, to demonstrate sureness or near sureness of success, especially when the Act itself, in s.58(3)(b) hinges the SOAD's certificate on his conclusion as to 'the likelihood' of it benefiting him.

Accordingly I do not consider that the requirement on a court to be convinced, in this context, of medical necessity in the light of the medical evidence and other evidence, is capable of being expressed in terms of a standard of evidential proof. It is rather a value judgement as to the future—a forecast—to be made by a court in reliance on medical evidence according to a standard of persuasion. If it is to be expressed in forensic terms at all, it is doubtful whether it amounts to more than satisfaction of medical necessity on a balance of probabilities, or as a 'likelihood' of therapeutic benefit.

Peter Bartlett is critical of the decision in *Haddock*, suggesting that it invokes professional uncertainty as grounds for weakening, rather than strengthening, the protection of patients' human rights.

Peter Bartlett[89]

This is an odd argument from a human rights standpoint, as it suggests that the fact that an area is fraught with uncertainty is a justification for restricting human rights protection within that area. If we are serious that treatment without consent constitutes an 'invasion', to use Auld LJ's word, it would instead seem that enforced interventions in such uncertain circumstances ought to be approached with particular caution . . .

B's expert witness had called into question the appropriateness of treatment with antipsychotic medication for personality disorder. He acknowledged that such treatment was used by some clinicians, but stated that the evidence base for its efficacy was weak. Evidence-based practice is not a new concept in medicine; it seems not unreasonable to insist that practitioners wishing to treat persons without consent should at the very least be able to demonstrate a solid and objective foundation for their belief that the treatment would be beneficial to the patient. . . .

The outcome of the *Haddock* case would appear to be that any rights under Articles 3 or 8 of the ECHR to be free from involuntary treatment are to be subject to the professional practice of the psychiatric profession: that is not to be subject to significant scrutiny.

While section 63 can be used to justify the compulsory treatment of competent patients, the protection that is superimposed upon it by the Human Rights Act applies equally to patients who lack capacity. Hence, if a patient who lacks capacity nevertheless manifests a desire not to be treated, treating her against her wishes could amount to inhuman or degrading treatment, and thus would be acceptable only if it could be convincingly shown to be a therapeutic necessity. In *Keenan v United Kingdom*, the solitary confinement of an incapacitated patient, who hanged himself shortly after he was placed in solitary confinement, was held to have been a violation of Article 3.

---

[89] 'A Matter of Necessity? Enforced Treatment under the Mental Health Act' (2007) 15 Medical Law Review 86–98.

Keenan v United Kingdom[90]

Judgment of the ECtHR

The lack of effective monitoring of Mark Keenan's condition and the lack of informed psychiatric input into his assessment and treatment disclose significant defects in the medical care provided to a mentally ill person known to be a suicide risk. The belated imposition on him in those circumstances of a serious disciplinary punishment—seven days' segregation in the punishment block and an additional twenty-eight days to his sentence imposed two weeks after the event and only nine days before his expected date of release—which may well have threatened his physical and moral resistance, is not compatible with the standard of treatment required in respect of a mentally ill person. It must be regarded as constituting inhuman and degrading treatment and punishment within the meaning of Article 3 of the Convention.

Accordingly, the Court finds a violation of this provision.

(2) Article 2

In *Keenan* the ECtHR also considered whether the failure to protect Mark Keenan might additionally amount to a breach of the state's positive obligations under Article 2, to protect his right to life. The Court asked itself 'whether the authorities knew or ought to have known that Mark Keenan posed a real and immediate risk of suicide and, if so, whether they did all that reasonably could have been expected of them to prevent that risk?' It held that while the risk was real, the authorities' response to the risk of suicide was sufficient to discharge their duties under Article 2.

More recently, in *Savage v South Essex Partnership NHS Foundation Trust*, the House of Lords found that hospital authorities are under a general obligation to try to prevent suicides in detained patients, but that also—where there is a real and immediate risk of a particular patient committing suicide—there is a more specific 'operational' obligation under Article 2 to do all that can reasonably be expected to prevent her from committing suicide.

Savage v South Essex Partnership NHS Foundation Trust[91]

Lord Rodger

The hospital authorities are . . . responsible for the health and wellbeing of their detained patients. Their obligations under article 2 include an obligation to protect those patients from self-harm and suicide. Indeed . . . the very fact that patients are detained carries with it a risk of suicide against which the hospital authorities must take general precautions.

I am accordingly satisfied that, as a public authority, the trust was under a general obligation, by virtue of article 2, to take precautions to prevent suicides among detained patients in Runwell Hospital. . . . The hospital's systems of work—and, doubtless, also its plant and equipment—had to take account of the risk that detained patients might try to commit suicide. When deciding on the most appropriate treatment and therapeutic environment for detained patients, medical staff would have to take proper account of the risk of suicide. But the risk would not be the same for all patients. Those who presented a comparatively low risk could be treated in a more open environment, without the need for a high degree of

[90] Application no 27229/95 (2001) 10 BHRC 319.   [91] [2008] UKHL 74.

supervision. Those who presented a greater risk would need to be supervised to an appropriate extent, while those presenting the highest risk would have to be supervised in a locked ward. The level of risk for any particular patient could be expected to vary with fluctuations in his or her medical condition. In deciding what precautions were appropriate for any given patient at any given moment, the doctors would take account of both the potentially adverse effect of too much supervision on the patient's condition and the possible positive benefits to be expected from a more open environment. Such decisions involve clinical judgment. . . .

[A]rticle 2 imposes a further 'operational' obligation on health authorities and their hospital staff. This obligation is distinct from, and additional to, the authorities' more general obligations. The operational obligation arises only if members of staff know or ought to know that a particular patient presents a 'real and immediate' risk of suicide. In these circumstances article 2 requires them to do all that can reasonably be expected to prevent the patient from committing suicide. If they fail to do this, not only will they and the health authorities be liable in negligence, but there will also be a violation of the operational obligation under article 2 to protect the patient's life.

The House of Lords decided that the question of whether there had, in this case, been a breach of Carol Savage's rights, should be allowed to go to trial. Two years later, in *Savage v South Essex Partnership NHS Foundation Trust*, Mackay J held that the trust had not done all that could reasonably have been expected of them to prevent Carol Savage's suicide. He awarded her daughter £10,000 in damages, not to compensate for her mother's death but as 'a symbolic acknowledgement' of her loss.

Savage v South Essex Partnership NHS Foundation Trust[92]

Mackay J

As to whether the defendant did all it could reasonably have been expected to do the answer to that must be that it did not. At the least there was a real prospect or substantial chance that had she been made subject to level two observations at 15 or even 30-minute intervals she would not have slipped away unnoticed in the way she did . . . [I]n my judgment all that was required to give her a real prospect or substantial chance of survival was the imposition of a raised level of observations, which would not have been an unreasonable or unduly onerous step to require of the defendant in the light of the evidence in this case.

Four years after the House of Lords' decision in *Savage*, the Supreme Court extended the operational duty to prevent a patient from committing suicide to a patient who had not been formally detained. Following a number of suicide attempts, Melanie Rabone had been admitted to hospital as an informal patient in April 2005. The risk of further attempts at suicide was judged to be moderate to high. At the time of her admission, it was noted that, if she tried to leave, she should be assessed for detention under the Mental Health Act. On 19 April, Melanie requested home leave, which was granted; the following day she committed suicide. Her parents brought both a civil negligence claim and a claim for damages for breach of a positive duty to protect Melanie's right to life under Article 2 against the Pennine Care NHS Foundation Trust.

92 [2010] EWHC 865 (QB).

The trust admitted that the decision to allow home leave was negligent and settled that claim on behalf of Melanie's estate for £7,500. The Rabones' own Article 2 claim for damages was unsuccessful in the High Court and in the Court of Appeal, but in *Rabone v Pennine Care NHS Foundation Trust*, the Supreme Court allowed their appeal. It held that informally admitted patients might nevertheless be just as vulnerable and just as much under the control of the state as detained patients. In reality, Melanie should not have been free to leave. In these circumstances, the operational duty under Article 2 could be owed if there was a 'real and immediate risk' to life. Because preventing Melanie from attempting suicide was the reason why she was admitted to hospital, it was clear that the risk in this case was real and immediate.

Rabone v Pennine Care NHS Foundation Trust[93]

Lord Dyson

When finding that the article 2 operational duty has been breached, the ECtHR has repeatedly emphasised the vulnerability of the victim as a relevant consideration. In circumstances of sufficient vulnerability, the ECtHR has been prepared to find a breach of the operational duty even where there has been no assumption of control by the state . . .

The jurisprudence of the operational duty is young. Its boundaries are still being explored by the ECtHR as new circumstances are presented to it for consideration. But it seems to me that the court has been tending to expand the categories of circumstances in which the operational duty will be found to exist. . . .

As regards the differences between an informal psychiatric patient and one who is detained under the MHA, these are in many ways more apparent than real. . . . She had been admitted to hospital because she was a real suicide risk. By reason of her mental state, she was extremely vulnerable. The trust assumed responsibility for her. She was under its control. Although she was not a detained patient, it is clear that, if she had insisted on leaving the hospital, the authorities could and should have exercised their powers under the MHA to prevent her from doing so. . . . In reality, the difference between her position and that of a hypothetical detained psychiatric patient, who (apart from the fact of being detained) was in circumstances similar to those of Melanie, would have been one of form, not substance.

Baroness Hale

There is a difficult balance to be struck between the right of the individual patient to freedom and self-determination and her right to be prevented from taking her own life. She wanted to go home and her doctor thought that it would be good for her to begin to take responsibility for herself. He was obviously wrong about that, but was he so wrong that the hospital is to be held in breach of her human rights for failing to protect her?

[I]in this case it also appears that there was no proper assessment of the risks before she was given leave and no proper planning for her care during the leave. . . . There is every indication that had she remained in hospital she would not have succeeded in killing herself. The question was whether she should have been allowed to go home for a whole weekend. Having regard to the nature and degree of the risk to her life, and the comparative ease of protecting her from it, I agree that her right to life was violated.

---

[93] [2012] UKSC 2.

(3) Article 8

The right to be free from non-consensual medical treatment might also be protected by Article 8, the right to respect for private and family life. In *X v Austria*,[94] for example, the European Commission explicitly stated that 'compulsory medical intervention, even if it is of minor importance, must be considered an interference with this right'. In practice, however, the protection offered by Article 8 is qualified if the interference can be shown to be 'necessary in a democratic society' for, among other things, 'the protection of health'. This, as the Court of Appeal explained in *R (on the application of N) v M and Others*,[95] means that if the treatment has been convincingly shown to be medically necessary, neither Article 3 nor Article 8 will have been violated, since the interference with the right to respect for private life would be proportionate, and justified within the terms of Article 8(2).

Article 8 has also been invoked in order to challenge other sorts of restrictions on mental health patients' freedom. In *R (on the application of G) v Nottinghamshire Healthcare NHS Trust*, patients who were detained at Rampton high security hospital challenged the smoking ban on the grounds that Rampton was their home, and, like others, they should be permitted to smoke inside their home (for security reasons, smoking outside was not possible). The Administrative Court rejected the claim that Article 8 created a 'right to smoke'.

R (on the application of G) v Nottinghamshire Healthcare NHS Trust[96]

Pill LJ

Preventing a person smoking does not, at any rate in the culture of the United Kingdom, generally involve such adverse effect upon the person's 'physical or moral integrity' . . . as would amount to an interference with the right to respect for private or home life within the meaning of Art.8 . . .

We are not persuaded that the requirement to respect private life and home in Art.8 imposes a general obligation on those responsible for the care of detained people to make arrangements enabling them to smoke. Whether it is put in terms of moral integrity, identity or personal autonomy, no general right for mental patients to smoke, or general obligation to permit smoking, arises . . .

The legislative intention of reg.10 and the Trust policy was not merely to reduce smoking but also to increase the number of smoke-free enclosed public places and work places, thereby reducing levels of exposure to second hand smoke. . . .

We . . . are satisfied that the legislative objectives are sufficiently important to justify limiting any rights the claimants have under Art.8.

(f) THE UNITED NATIONS CONVENTION ON THE RIGHTS OF PERSONS WITH DISABILITIES

The UK has signed and ratified the United Nations Convention on the Rights of Persons with Disabilities. This does not mean that it is incorporated into UK law, but it is at least

---

[94] (1980) 18 DR 154 at 156. [95] [2002] EWCA Civ 1789. [96] [2008] EWHC 1096 (Admin).

arguable that the provisions in the Mental Health Act that permit compulsory treatment and detention are non-compliant.

Article 1 of the Convention sets out its purpose, and Articles 14 and 17 specifically address the liberty and bodily integrity of people with mental disabilities:

UN Convention on the Rights of Persons with Disabilities

Article 1

The purpose of the present Convention is to promote, protect and ensure the full and equal enjoyment of all human rights and fundamental freedoms by all persons with disabilities, and to promote respect for their inherent dignity.

Persons with disabilities include those who have long-term physical, mental, intellectual or sensory impairments which in interaction with various barriers may hinder their full and effective participation in society on an equal basis with others . . .

Article 14

1. States Parties shall ensure that persons with disabilities, on an equal basis with others:

   a. Enjoy the right to liberty and security of person;

   b. Are not deprived of their liberty unlawfully or arbitrarily, and that any deprivation of liberty is in conformity with the law, and that the existence of a disability shall in no case justify a deprivation of liberty . . .

Article 17

Every person with disabilities has a right to respect for his or her physical and mental integrity on an equal basis with others.

Unlike the European Convention, with its 'unsound mind' exception to the right to liberty, the UN Convention states explicitly that mental disability does not justify the deprivation of liberty or interference with someone's physical or mental integrity. As Peter Bartlett explains, this is extraordinarily significant.

Peter Bartlett[97]

For people with mental disabilities, the CRPD [Convention on the Rights of Persons with Disabilities] represents an additional and highly significant change. Previously, international regulation had assumed that control of this group was in some circumstances justified; the issue was determining the bounds of permitted compulsion. The CRPD takes no such starting point. Indeed, as will be discussed below, the CRPD appears to proceed on the basis that disability cannot be used as a factor in determining whether compulsion may be imposed. For people with mental disabilities, this would be an extraordinary change. . . . The UN High Commissioner for Human Rights has stated that the CRPD requires the abolition

---

[97] 'The United Nations Convention on the Rights of Persons with Disabilities and Mental Health Law' (2012) 75 Modern Law Review 752–78.

of laws that allow for detention, for the removal of legal capacity, or for criminal defences, when those laws rely in whole or in part on mental disability. Insofar as this is correct, it is difficult to see that UK mental health legislation is remotely compliant. The terms of the CRPD also raise profound questions about the compliance of UK legislation governing mental capacity. The government would appear to be in denial about this, taking the view that UK legislation is in fact in compliance with the CRPD.

Of course, as John Dawson points out, it could plausibly be argued that there are problems with expunging any reference to mental impairment from the law.

John Dawson[98]

It is not discrimination to say that a blind person can be denied the right to drive, under the relevant legislation, when they cannot see. Nor is it discrimination to say that a person's firearms license can be suspended when acute paranoid delusions about their neighbours affect their ability to use a weapon responsibly—even when that decision does involve treating that person differently to others, and does rely on aspects of their mental functioning, that may be associated with a disability, when applying the legal test. . . [O]nly an impoverished legal system would consider it wholly irrelevant to a person's ability to make a will, or take full responsibility for hitting someone, or serve on a jury or as a judge, or continue as a company director, that they currently suffer significant cognitive impairment as a consequence of Alzheimer's disease.

Dawson advocates a 'conservative' interpretation of the Convention, which would not completely rule out substitute decision-making. But this would appear to be at odds with the General Comment, issued by the UN's Committee on the Rights of Persons with Disabilities in 2014,[99] which appeared to give the words in the Convention a literal interpretation, thus outlawing compulsory treatment, involuntary admission, and substituted decision-making.

In the next extract, Freeman et al are critical of this General Comment, suggesting that, in practice, it might interfere with individuals' right to health and increase stigma.

Melvyn Freeman et al[100]

[I]f a person having a severe exacerbation of affective or psychotic illness is not provided proven, effective treatment, can he or she be said to be receiving the highest attainable standard of health? Best evidence so far on psychiatric disorders tells us that some severe psychotic illnesses can impair decision-making capacity. . . . That is, decision-making might be by definition impaired and hence merely supporting decisions when a person is in a state of severe psychosis, including treatment decisions, could seriously undermine that person's right to health care . . .

[98] 'A realistic approach to assessing mental health laws' compliance with the UNCRPD' (2015) 40 International Journal of Law and Psychiatry 70–9.

[99] Committee on the Rights of Persons with Disabilities, General Comment No. 1, *Article 12: Equal Recognition Before the Law*, 11th session, 31 March–11 April 2014.

[100] 'Reversing hard won victories in the name of human rights: a critique of the General Comment on Article 12 of the UN Convention on the Rights of Persons with Disabilities' (2015) 2 The Lancet Psychiatry 844–50.

Importantly, the likelihood of a person making a recovery to the point of regaining capacity and therefore being able to give informed consent is often diminished without treatment. In the example of psychosis, we might be undermining the right to health to allow a person to stay in a psychotic state and never allow them to get to a point of refusing or accepting treatment in an informed manner.

One might imagine that a consequence of the General Comment's interpretation is that there might end up being more persons with severe mental illness untreated in the community, which might exacerbate ignorance, fear, and stigma surrounding mental disorders. An unintended consequence of the General Comment might be more public calls for the locking up of people with mental disabilities or human rights violations of untreated persons with severe mental illness in the community.

More optimistically, Genevra Richardson wonders whether the Convention might help to ensure that service users are routinely involved in decisions about their care.

Genevra Richardson[101]

There are, however, grounds for optimism. At the heart of supported decision-making lies the need to encourage and enhance the participation of service users at all stages of their care. This can only improve services and, even in the absence of large-scale legislative reform, it can be emphasized and encouraged across the sector in relation to both intellectual impairments and psychosocial disorders. . . .

The importance of participative decision-making is certainly now recognized officially, but a major culture shift may be required if we are to achieve a fundamental move away from the imposition of substitute decisions, in favour of finding ways of encouraging the participation of service users in practice, and of supporting them to make their own decisions. Perhaps the UN Convention can provide the necessary spur. . . .

There is now a small but growing literature discussing the possible measures of support that might be developed, such as the Swedish system of mentors and personal assistants . . . 'Social connectedness' interventions have also been trialled in the simple form of sending a series of reassuring postcards to patients who had been admitted after self-harm . . .

If we are to achieve a significant cultural shift from substitute, to participative and supported decision-making, across the entire sector much, much more work is needed. That, in my view, would be a significant paradigm shift to aim for right now while we await the political will to tinker once again with the law.

6 DISCHARGE

Once a patient has been detained, her detention must continue to be justified by her condition. The exception to the right to liberty in Article 5(1)(e), which permits the lawful detention of persons of unsound mind, exists only when detention is in accordance with procedure prescribed by law, and where it is possible to challenge the lawfulness of detention speedily in a court.

---

[101] 'Mental Disabilities and the Law: From Substitute to Supported Decision-Making?' (2012) 65 Current Legal Problems 333–54.

In *Winterwerp v The Netherlands*,[102] the ECtHR fleshed out three conditions that apply to the 'unsound mind' exception in Article 5(1)(e):

> In the court's opinion, except in emergency cases, the individual concerned should not be deprived of his liberty unless he has been reliably shown to be of 'unsound mind'. The very nature of what has to be established before the competent national authority— that is, a true mental disorder—calls for objective medical expertise. Further, the mental disorder must be of a kind or degree warranting compulsory confinement. What is more, the validity of continued confinement depends upon the persistence of such a disorder.

The lawfulness of continued detention therefore depends upon the mental disorder's persistence. The responsible clinician (RC) has an ongoing duty to consider whether the conditions that justified the patient's original detention continue to exist. Because the extent to which a patient is affected by their mental disorder may fluctuate, Article 5(4) requires that there is a formal mechanism to review or challenge the lawfulness of continued detention at reasonable intervals.

(a) REVIEW OF DETENTION

Detentions under section 2 will automatically lapse after 28 days, and unless the patient is formally detained under section 3, the patient must be discharged. For patients detained under section 3, section 68 provides that hospital managers have a duty to refer their case to the First-Tier Tribunal (Mental Health) after six months, and thereafter every three years.

Under section 66 of the 1983 Act, a patient who has been admitted to hospital compulsorily under section 2 or 3 of the 1983 Act has a right to request that the Tribunal considers whether they should be discharged. In practice, orders for the discharge of patients are comparatively rare. In 2013–14, there were 27,380 applications to the Tribunal against detention, 68 per cent of which resulted in a hearing, and only 9 per cent of hearings resulted in discharge.[103]

Of course, not all patients will have the capacity to exercise their right to challenge their detention, and in the case of *MH v United Kingdom*, the question arose whether, for such patients, automatic referral to a court was necessary in order that the lawfulness of their detention could be reviewed speedily by a court, as required by Article 5. MH was a woman in her thirties with Down's syndrome, who had been admitted under section 2. She lacked the capacity to appeal to the Tribunal herself, but the House of Lords unanimously held that the failure to refer her case for judicial review of her detention did not amount to a breach of Article 5(4).[104] MH then appealed to the European Court of Human Rights, which eight years later held that the UK must have 'special safeguards' in place to protect the rights of those who lack the capacity to challenge the lawfulness of their detention.

---

[102] Application no 6301/73, ECHR series A, vol 33 (1979).
[103] Care Quality Commission, *Monitoring the Mental Health Act in 2013–14* (CQC, 2015).
[104] *R (on the application of H) v Secretary of State for Health [2005] UKHL 60.*

MH v United Kingdom[105]

Judgment of the ECtHR

As the right set forth in Article 5 § 4 of the Convention is guaranteed to everyone, it is clear that special safeguards are called for in the case of detained mental patients who lack legal capacity to institute proceedings before judicial bodies. However, it is not for this Court to dictate what form those special safeguards should take, provided that they make the right guaranteed by Article 5 § 4 as nearly as possible as practical and effective for this particular category of detainees as it is for other detainees. While automatic judicial review might be one means of providing the requisite safeguard, it is not necessarily the only means . . .

Neither the applicant nor her mother acting as her nearest relative was able in practice to avail themselves of the normal remedy granted by the 1983 Act to patients detained under section 2 for assessment. That being so, in relation to the initial measure taken by social services depriving her of her liberty, the applicant did not, at the relevant time, before the elucidation of the legal framework by the House of Lords in her case, have the benefit of effective access to a mechanism enabling her to 'take proceedings' of the kind guaranteed to her by Article 5 § 4 of the Convention. The special safeguards required under Article 5 § 4 for incompetent mental patients in a position such as hers were lacking in relation to the means available to her to challenge the lawfulness of her 'assessment detention' in hospital for a period of up to twenty-eight days.

Therefore, in the particular circumstances of the present case there was a violation of Article 5 § 4 of the Convention in relation to the applicant's initial detention by administrative order for the purposes of medical assessment in hospital.

(b) CRITERIA FOR REVIEW

In its original form, the Mental Health Act 1983 required the patient applying to the Tribunal to prove that their continued detention was no longer justified. In effect, this amounted to a presumption against discharge, and was found to be incompatible with Article 5 of the Convention. Now it is for those who do not wish to see the patient discharged to establish that she continues to meet the criteria for detention, and not for the patient to prove that she does not.

Mental Health Act 1983 section 72

72(1) . . .

(a) the tribunal shall direct the discharge of a patient liable to be detained under section 2 above if [it is] not satisfied—

  (i) that he is then suffering from mental disorder of a nature or degree which warrants his detention in a hospital for assessment (or for assessment followed by medical treatment) for at least a limited period; or

  (ii) that his detention as aforesaid is justified in the interests of his own health or safety or with a view to the protection of other persons;

---

[105] Application no 11577/06 (22 October 2013).

(b) the tribunal shall direct the discharge of a patient liable to be detained otherwise than under section 2 above if [it is] not satisfied—

    (i) that he is then suffering from mental disorder of a nature or degree which makes it appropriate for him to be liable to be detained in a hospital for medical treatment; or

    (ii) that it is necessary for the health or safety of the patient or for the protection of other persons that he should receive such treatment; or

    (iia) that appropriate medical treatment is available for him; or

    (iii) in the case of an application by virtue of paragraph (g) of section 66(1) above, that the patient, if released, would be likely to act in a manner dangerous to other persons or to himself.

Notice that, as with detention under sections 2 and 3, for continued detention to be justified, the patient has to be suffering from a mental disorder of a nature *or* degree which warrants detention in hospital. In *R v Mental Health Review Tribunal for the South Thames Region, ex parte Smith*,[106] the court held that this means that someone might be detained on the grounds that the condition from which they are suffering generally justifies detention, even if at the time of the application, they are not affected to a 'degree' which warrants detention in hospital. Bartlett and Sandland are critical of this wording.

Peter Bartlett and Ralph Sandland[107]

[T]he requirement in *Winterwerp* is for unsound mind sufficient to 'justify' detention, and we would want to argue, as has not been done to date before the European Court, that a test which allows nature 'or' degree permits detention when a person's disorder is of a nature but *not* of a degree to justify compulsory hospitalisation, which is outside of the spirit of the Convention. In our, perhaps optimistic, view, the preferable and Convention-compliant wording must be that the mental disorder in question is of both a nature *and* a degree to warrant detention.

As Collins J explains in *R (on the application of Care Principles Ltd) v Mental Health Review Tribunal*, tribunals do not assess the lawfulness of the initial detention, but rather, on the balance of probabilities, whether grounds for detention exist at the time of the hearing.

R (on the application of Care Principles Ltd) v Mental Health Review Tribunal[108]

Collins J

[T]he Tribunal is concerned with the condition of the patient when the Tribunal considers the matter. Whether or not he was properly taken into hospital is not material for that consideration. When I say 'properly', I mean whether there was indeed material which justified the

---

106 The Times, 9 December 1998.
107 *Mental Health Law: Policy and Practice*, 3rd edn (OUP: Oxford, 2007) 403.
108 [2006] EWHC 3194 (Admin).

> admission, or indeed the other way round, whether at the time it was clearly justified. The question before the Tribunal is: is the detention proper now? The burden is upon the hospital, or those who seek his continued detention, to establish that that detention is necessary and within the terms of the Act.
>
> It is always necessary for any such detention to be justified. The standard required is the balance of probabilities. The Tribunal has to be persuaded that it is more probable than not that the detention is needed. It has been said in another context that there needs to be some cogent evidence before the Tribunal to establish that the detention is necessary.

If the Tribunal decides that the criteria for detention are not made out, it must order the patient's discharge. Discharge can, however, be deferred, if arrangements have to be made for the patient's accommodation and/or care.

The Tribunal must give reasons for its decision. Where there is conflicting evidence, the Tribunal must explain, in language that can be understood by the patient, why one witness's evidence was preferred. In *R v Ashworth Hospital Authority, ex parte H*,[109] the Tribunal ordered the immediate discharge of a patient, despite the fact that five out of six medical reports had been against discharge. The Court of Appeal found that this decision was *Wednesbury*[110] unreasonable, since no reasonable tribunal could have come to this decision in the light of the evidence before it, and furthermore that the Tribunal's reasons— namely that it simply preferred the evidence of the one doctor who believed discharge to be appropriate—were insufficient.

(c) THE NEED FOR SPEEDY REVIEW

The question of how 'speedy' the legal challenge must be to satisfy Article 5(4) arose in *R (on the application of C) v Mental Health Review Tribunal*. C had been detained in hospital under section 3 of the Mental Health Act 1983 and immediately applied to the Tribunal for discharge. At the time, it was the practice of the Tribunal to list hearings of applications for discharge eight weeks after the application had been made. C submitted that the practice was arbitrary and insufficiently 'speedy'. The Court of Appeal agreed.

R (on the application of C) v Mental Health Review Tribunal[111]

Lord Phillips MR

> I do not consider lawful a practice which makes no effort to see that the individual application is heard as soon as reasonably practicable, having regard to the relevant circumstances of the case. Such a practice will inevitably result in some applications not leading to the speedy decision required by article 5(4). The present case is an instance of this result.

Similarly, in *R v Mental Health Review Tribunal, ex parte KB*, a conjoined application was brought by a number of patients who had waited between four and 27 weeks for a hearing. The reasons for the delays included difficulties in preparing reports and in timetabling

---

[109] [2003] 1 WLR 127.
[110] *Associated Provincial Picture Houses v Wednesbury Corporation* [1948] 1 KB 223.
[111] [2002] 1 WLR 176.

tribunal hearings. Stanley Burton J found that lack of resources did not offer a defence to the breach of Article 5(4).

R v Mental Health Review Tribunal, ex parte KB[112]

Stanley Burton J

Under Article 5(4), it is for the state to ensure speedy hearings of detained patients' applications. The state must establish such Tribunals or courts and provide such resources, as will provide speedy hearings. It is therefore irrelevant to the question whether there has been an infringement of Article 5(4) which government department or other public authority was at fault.

(d) STATUS OF THE TRIBUNAL DECISION

If the responsible clinician (RC) disagrees with the Tribunal's decision to order a patient's discharge, is there anything to stop her simply readmitting the patient under section 3? Of course, if circumstances have changed significantly between the time of the hearing and the time of readmission, then this might be legitimate. But where there has not been a substantial change of circumstances, RCs should not attempt to override the Tribunal's decision through a new admission.

In *R v East London and the City Mental Health NHS Trust, ex parte Von Brandenburg*, the patient's discharge had been ordered by the Tribunal, but had been deferred for seven days so that suitable accommodation could be found. Six days later, the patient's clinician (then referred to as a responsible medical officer, or RMO) arranged for his readmission under section 3 of the Mental Health Act 1983. The patient sought judicial review of the decision to readmit him.

The House of Lords found that there might be circumstances when it would be lawful to readmit a patient despite the Tribunal's decision to discharge her, but that these would depend upon the Approved Mental Health Practitioner (AMHP) (which used to be known as an approved social worker, or ASW) forming the reasonable and bona fide belief that she had information not known by the tribunal which put a 'significantly different complexion' on the case. Re-sectioning is therefore only appropriate where new material facts have come to light, and must not be used to override Tribunal decisions with which the RC disagrees.

R v East London and the City Mental Health NHS Trust, ex parte Von Brandenburg[113]

Lord Bingham

[A]n ASW may not lawfully apply for the admission of a patient whose discharge has been ordered by the decision of a Mental Health Review Tribunal of which the ASW is aware unless the ASW has formed the reasonable and bona fide opinion that he has information not known to the Tribunal which puts a significantly different complexion on the case as compared with that which was before the Tribunal. It is impossible and undesirable to

---

[112] [2002] EWHC 639 (Admin).   [113] [2003] UKHL 58.

attempt to describe in advance the information which might justify such an opinion. I give three hypothetical examples by way of illustration only:

- The issue at the Tribunal is whether the patient, if discharged, might cause harm to himself. The Tribunal, on the evidence presented, discounts that possibility and directs the discharge of the patient. After the hearing, the ASW learns of a fact previously unknown to him, the doctors attending the patient and the Tribunal: that the patient had at an earlier date made a determined attempt on his life. Having taken medical advice, the ASW judges that this information significantly alters the risk as assessed by the Tribunal.

- At the Tribunal hearing the patient's mental condition is said to have been stabilised by the taking of appropriate medication. The continuing stability of the patient's mental condition is said to depend on his continuing to take that medication. The patient assures the Tribunal of his willingness to continue to take medication and, on the basis of that assurance, the Tribunal directs the discharge of the patient. Before or after discharge the patient refuses to take the medication or communicates his intention to refuse. Having taken medical advice, the ASW perceives a real risk to the patient or others if the medication is not taken.

- After the Tribunal hearing, and whether before or after discharge, the patient's mental condition significantly deteriorates so as to present a degree of risk or require treatment or supervision not evident at the hearing.

In cases such as these the ASW may properly apply for the admission of a patient, subject of course to obtaining the required medical support, notwithstanding a Tribunal decision directing discharge.

7 COMMUNITY CARE

As we have seen, there has been a move away from inpatient care towards what is euphemistically known as 'care in the community'. There are two types of community care: first, primary care services are supposed to ensure that mentally disordered individuals living in the community have access to appropriate treatment. Secondly, in recent years there has been interest in how a degree of control and supervision might be exercised over people who are not ill enough to be detained in hospital.

In *R (on the application of H) v Mental Health Review Tribunal*, a patient who had been discharged from hospital was subject to a condition that he should receive fortnightly injections. Holman J reiterated that the special exceptions to the need for the consent of a competent person contained in the Mental Health Act 1983 could not be used to force the patient to submit to treatment in the community.

R (on the application of H) v Mental Health Review Tribunal[114]

Holman J

The law with regard to consent to treatment is clear . . . An adult of full capacity has an absolute right to choose whether to consent to medical treatment. . . . Thus in this case, on each occasion that SH attends, or should attend, for his fortnightly depot injection he has an

---

[114] [2007] EWHC 884 (Admin).

absolute right to choose whether to consent to it or not. The treating doctor or nurse must, on each occasion, satisfy himself that the apparent consent is a real consent and that the independence of the patient's decision or his will has not been overborne.

(a) AFTERCARE SERVICES

Section 117 of the Mental Health Act 1983 requires clinical commissioning groups and local social services, in cooperation with voluntary agencies, to provide aftercare services to those who have been discharged from detention under the Act. Usually, aftercare services involve medical treatment, help with accommodation, and assistance with education and training. Although initially there was some confusion over whether local authorities could charge patients for services provided under section 117, the House of Lords in *R v Manchester City Council, ex parte Stennett*[115] agreed with the Court of Appeal that the exceptional vulnerability of compulsorily detained patients meant that aftercare services must be provided free of charge.

It is also clear that there is a duty to provide aftercare services. In *R v Ealing District Health Authority, ex parte Fox*, Otton J held that once the Tribunal has ordered a conditional discharge, the health authority must ensure that the appropriate arrangements are in place.

R v Ealing District Health Authority, ex parte Fox[116]

Otton J

[A] district health authority is under a duty under s 117 of the Mental Health Act 1983 to provide after-care services when a patient leaves hospital, and acts unlawfully in failing to seek to make practical arrangements for after-care prior to that patient's discharge from hospital where such arrangements are required by a mental health review Tribunal in order to enable the patient to be conditionally discharged from hospital.

But what if a health authority cannot find health care professionals who are prepared to take responsibility for a patient's treatment after discharge? This issue arose in *Camden and Islington Health Authority, ex parte K*, where it proved impossible to find a psychiatrist willing to supervise the applicant's care in the community. The House of Lords held that section 117 should not be taken to impose an absolute and unworkable obligation on health authorities.

Camden and Islington Health Authority, ex parte K[117]

Lord Phillips

[S]ection 117 imposes on health authorities a duty to provide aftercare facilities for the benefit of patients who are discharged from mental hospitals. The nature and extent of those facilities must, to a degree, fall within the discretion of the health authority, which must have regard to other demands on its budget. . . .

---

[115] [2002] UKHL 34.   [116] [1993] 1 WLR 373.   [117] [2001] EWCA Civ 240.

> I can see no justification for interpreting section 117 so as to impose on health authorities an absolute obligation to satisfy any conditions that a Tribunal may specify as prerequisites to the discharge of a patient. . . . An interpretation of section 117 which imposed on health authorities absolute duties which they would not necessarily be able to perform would be manifestly unreasonable.

Of course, if a patient is no longer sufficiently mentally disordered to justify detention in hospital, then the failure to facilitate her release might amount to a breach of Article 5(4). However, where a patient's release is conditional upon the provision of services, Lord Phillips suggests that, if it proves impossible to arrange those services, she may continue to be sufficiently mentally disordered to justify detention under Article 5:

Lord Phillips

If a health authority is unable, despite the exercise of all reasonable endeavours, to procure for a patient the level of care and treatment in the community that a Tribunal considers to be a prerequisite to the discharge of the patient from hospital, I do not consider that the continued detention of the patient in hospital will violate the right to liberty conferred by article 5.

K then appealed to the ECtHR, which, in *Kolanis v United Kingdom*,[118] confirmed that there had been no violation of Article 5(1)(e).

Judgment of the ECtHR

As events in the present case showed, the treatment considered necessary for such conditional discharge may not prove available, in which circumstances there can be no question of interpreting Article 5 § 1(e) as requiring the applicant's discharge without the conditions necessary for protecting herself and the public or as imposing an absolute obligation on the authorities to ensure that the conditions are fulfilled.

A similar result was reached in *R v Secretary of State for the Home Department, ex parte IH*.[119] Because it was impossible to find a psychiatrist willing to supervise IH in the community, the conditions attached to his discharge could not be met. In these circumstances, the House of Lords found that there had been no violation of Article 5(1)(e) and continued detention remained lawful, despite the tribunal's order.

(b) COMMUNITY TREATMENT ORDERS

One of the most significant changes introduced by the 2007 Act is the community treatment order (CTO). CTOs are intended to ensure that patients receive treatment in the least restrictive environment. They are also supposed to address what is known as the 'revolving door' problem: a patient is admitted to hospital, their condition is stabilized, and they are

---

[118] Application no 517/02 [2005] All ER (D) 227 (Jun).   [119] [2003] UKHL 59.

discharged into the community, only to stop taking their medication, resulting in deterioration and readmission to hospital, where the pattern then repeats itself.

Under section 17A, a responsible clinician (RC) can only make a community treatment order with the written agreement of an Approved Mental Health Professional (AMHP), and if the criteria in section 17A(5) are satisfied.

Mental Health Act 1983 section 17A

17A(5) . . .

(a) the patient is suffering from mental disorder of a nature or degree which makes it appropriate for him to receive medical treatment;

(b) it is necessary for his health or safety or for the protection of other persons that he should receive such treatment;

(c) subject to his being liable to be recalled as mentioned in paragraph (d) below, such treatment can be provided without his continuing to be detained in a hospital;

(d) it is necessary that the responsible clinician should be able to exercise the power under section 17E(1) below to recall the patient to hospital; and

(e) appropriate medical treatment is available for him.

Essentially, CTOs do not allow treatment with compulsion in the community, but they provide for immediate recall, under section 17E, if the patient becomes in need of compulsory treatment.

Mental Health Act 1983 section 17E

17E(1) The responsible clinician may recall a community patient to hospital if in his opinion—

(a) the patient requires medical treatment in hospital for his mental disorder; and

(b) there would be a risk of harm to the health or safety of the patient or to other persons if the patient were not recalled to hospital for that purpose.

If a patient is recalled, she can be detained for up to 72 hours, after which time she may be discharged, and continue to be subject to the CTO, or if she refuses to comply with a condition in the CTO or continues to refuse treatment, the CTO can be revoked and she will become a detained patient once again.

Treatment without consent can be given as soon as the patient is recalled, so it is clearly possible that the power of recall could be used temporarily in order to force treatment upon the patient, who is then released until their need for compulsory medication arises again. It is therefore possible that a patient could 'yo-yo' between recall (and compulsory depot injections) and living in the community with a CTO. In the House of Lords debates over the Bill, Lord Patel drew attention to the fact that it might be possible to use CTOs routinely when discharging patients in order to retain control over them.

Lord Patel[120]

They could even become part of the normal discharge process for detained patients generally, as a kind of safety net for risk-averse mental health service staff and managers. If this happens, Parliament will not have produced a measure that enables a less restrictive alternative for the effective management of this small group of patients, but instead will have increased massively the legal coercion of psychiatric patients generally.

In addition to giving the power of recall to hospital, a CTO can be used to impose conditions—such as that the patient make himself available for treatment or desist from certain behaviour—if those conditions are necessary *or* appropriate for one of three purposes, set out in section 17B(2):

(a) ensuring that the patient receives medical treatment;

(b) preventing risk of harm to the patient's health or safety;

(c) protecting other persons.

The statute does not specify what sort of conditions might be imposed: rather, the RC has a wide discretion, subject only to the need for the condition to be 'necessary or appropriate' for one of these three rather broad purposes. Once again, the use of the word 'or' makes this criterion especially loose—or 'lax indeed', according to Phil Fennell.[121] Necessary *and* appropriate would have forced the RC to consider whether the condition was necessary to fulfil a purpose *and* appropriate in these particular circumstances. 'Necessary *or* appropriate' instead suggests that a condition could be attached because it was thought appropriate, even if it is not, in fact, necessary.

While the Code of Practice does state that the conditions should be kept to a minimum and restrict freedom as little as possible, CTOs undoubtedly have the potential to interfere with a person's private life. An RC might decide that a patient should not be allowed to associate with certain individuals, for example, if seeing them might make it more likely that the patient will resume their drug habit.

Mental Health Act Code of Practice 2015

29.31 The conditions must not deprive the patient of their liberty and should:

• be kept to a minimum number consistent with achieving their purpose

• restrict the patient's liberty as little as possible while being consistent with their care plan and recovery goal

• have a clear rationale, linked to one or more of the [statutory] purposes

• be clearly and precisely expressed, so that the patient can readily understand what is expected.

---

[120] Hansard HL 2 July 2007, col 844.
[121] Phil Fennell, *Mental Health: The New Law* (Jordan: Bristol, 2007) 212.

29.32 The nature of the conditions will depend on the patient's individual circumstances. They should be stated clearly having regard to the least restriction principle. Subject to paragraph 29.31, they might cover matters such as:

- where and when the patient is to receive treatment in the community
- where the patient is to live, and
- avoidance of known risk factors or high-risk situations relevant to the patient's mental disorder.

In addition to the conditions that may be attached to CTOs, sections 64A to 64K authorize the giving of 'relevant treatment' to community patients. 'Relevant treatment' is defined as medicines for mental disorder and ECT, and can be provided to competent patients in the community only if they consent and there is, within a month of the CTO being issued, a certificate from a SOAD authorizing treatment. For patients who lack capacity, treatment in the community without consent is possible under section 64D. Patients with capacity cannot be subject to compulsory treatment within the community; this is possibly only by exercising the power to recall them to hospital.

Patients have the right to apply to the Tribunal if one of more of the conditions for making a CTO are not satisfied, and the Tribunal must order discharge if, for example, the power of recall to hospital is no longer necessary.

CTOs have been subject to several criticisms. First, it has been suggested that patient trust, and in particular a patient's willingness to seek out psychiatric services, might be compromised by the prospect of having restrictive conditions imposed upon one's lifestyle. In the next extract, Caldicott et al point out that compulsion in the community is rejected for physical illnesses on the grounds that patients might avoid contact with health services, and they question why similar arguments are not accepted in the context of mental illness.

Fiona Caldicott, Edna Conlan, and Anthony Zigmund[122]

Patients ask why it is that any prospective deterioration in their condition through failure to follow medical advice should be subject to compulsion? If the answer seeks justification in the risk that such failure poses a danger to the well-being of others, why is it that diabetics or epileptics who fail adequately to follow a prescribed medical regime should nonetheless still be able, for example, to drive their cars (until such time as their licence is removed based on a report from their doctor), without them being removed to hospital for forcible administration of a sticky bun or insulin (as appropriate) or of an anti-convulsant? Were this the case, is it not likely that even more patients suffering from disorders that might bring them within the ambit of state control would find ways to avoid contact with the medical profession in order never to risk being subject to such coercive care? In summary, such a response runs a high risk of being anti-therapeutic. If the argument is so readily understood in respect of HIV and sexually transmitted diseases (ie that we need confidentiality if patients are to volunteer themselves for treatment and thereby reduce the aggregate risk and extent of suffering) why

[122] 'Client and Clinician—Law as an Intrusion' in Nigel Eastman and Jill Peay (eds), *Law Without Enforcement: Integrating Mental Health and Justice* (Hart Publishing: Oxford, 1999) 75–88.

> is it seemingly so hard to understand that marking out those with mental disorders as suitable for subjection to a coercive regime is likely, in the short term in respect of that patient and in the long term in respect of the body of patients, to reduce overall patient compliance?

Secondly, Judith Laing queries whether community treatment orders will genuinely represent the least restrictive alternative.

Judith Laing[123]

> The government's assertion that the community treatment order is justified on the basis of providing a less restrictive alternative is also debatable and somewhat 'illusory'. Opponents of compulsory community treatment allege that it is a controlling mechanism and will not be the least restrictive alternative due to the fact that it actually increases the potential for monitoring and controlling people's lives . . . Indeed, compulsory community orders may well exacerbate the problems faced by the mentally ill by increasing the stigma directed towards them as well as the discrimination and social exclusion experienced by them.

Thirdly, in the next extract, Patricia Walton, writing from the perspective of an Approved Social Worker (ASW), suggests that, in any event, a patient's refusal to take psychotropic drugs may not be a decision that needs to be treated by compulsion: rather, it may be a rational response to the unpleasant side effects of these drugs.

Patricia Walton[124]

> ASWs are strongly opposed to compulsion in the community on social and human rights grounds: some people find the drug effects intolerable; some people find relentless awareness of their circumstances intolerable; the risks of suicide and other effects of unwanted long term drug treatment have not been considered; psychiatric treatments can be harmful; the impact of forcible treatment on the family and within the community have not been considered; a person's home should be a safe haven; people ultimately have the right to choose ill health . . . In the experience of ASWs, when people stop taking medication there is often complex interplay of reasons and the thinking around compulsory community treatment takes a simplistic view of this . . . In their experience many, possibly most, people on long-term medication choose to come off it from time to time, to be free of side-effects or to achieve a feeling of autonomy.

Finally, it could be argued that CTOs disproportionately emphasize the administration of medication, at the expense of other services, such as psychotherapy, and help with housing and employment, which may be equally or perhaps more important in helping patients to function in the community.

In the years since this new measure was introduced, how have CTOs worked in practice? In 2014–15, 4,564 CTOs were issued, there were 2,369 recalls to hospital, and 3,918 CTOs were revoked or discharged. More CTOs were issued in 2014–15 than in 2013–14 (an increase of 130, or 2.9 per cent), though the rate of increase was lower than in the previous five years.

---

[123] 'Rights Versus Risk? Reform of the Mental Health Act 1983' (2000) 8 Medical Law Review 210–50, 240.
[124] 'Reforming the Mental Health Act 1983: an approved social worker perspective' (2000) 22 Journal of Social Welfare and Family Law 410–14.

Since their introduction, each year more CTOs have been issued than have been discharged, resulting in an increasing number of people being subject to CTOs. Once again, there is evidence of the over-representation of patients from minority ethnic groups amongst those subject to CTO powers.

Despite their increasing use, there is little evidence for the effectiveness of CTOs. Indeed, Rugkåsa et al go so far as to suggest that there is no evidence of patient benefit.

Jorun Rugkåsa, John Dawson, and Tom Burns[125]

It is hard to dismiss the consistent conclusions from three RCTs [randomized controlled trials] and three reviews. It is not our intention to sweep aside the methodological limitations with the existing RCTs; no study is perfect. We believe, however, that the lack of evidence for patient benefit, particularly when combined with restrictions to personal liberty, is striking and needs to be taken seriously. Clinicians have a duty to provide their patients with treatment in the least restrictive environment. The paucity of rigorous experimental research evidence for such an invasive intervention that has been in use for over three decades is quite remarkable. It raises a question of whether this would have been accepted in other branches of medicine. Surely major, intrusive interventions in community psychiatry should be expected to conform to the highest standards of evidence.

The rationales for introducing CTOs are usually to reduce repeated relapses and to provide a less restrictive alternative to hospital. . . . The weight of empirical evidence, however, is against them. CTOs do neither appear to reduce relapse and readmission nor, overall, to reduce coercion.

8 CONCLUSION

If the 2007 reforms were not the best way forward, what alternative approaches might there be? In the next extract, Nigel Eastman and Jill Peay argue that detention and treatment without consent should only be possible (a) if the patient lacks capacity, or (b) under some dangerousness criterion, and that the two routes to admission should be clearly separated in order to avoid stigmatizing those who suffer from mental illness.

Nigel Eastman and Jill Peay[126]

We are not alone in suggesting that thought ought to be given to replacing our current structure of mental health law, possibly with generic legislation separately covering incapacity and dangerousness, and certainly by legislation which puts on an equal footing the treatment of mental and physical disorders.

Generic dangerousness legislation with tightly drawn criteria based on established behaviour and a clear and present threat is attractive if only because it is likely to make us think seriously about the need for protection of the rights of offenders, rather than confusing the

---

[125] 'CTOs: what is the state of the evidence?' (2014) 49 Social Psychiatry and Psychiatric Epidemiology 1861–71.

[126] 'Afterword: Integrating Mental Health and Justice' in Nigel Eastman and Jill Peay (eds), *Law Without Enforcement: Integrating Mental Health and Justice* (Hart Publishing: Oxford, 1999) 197–218.

advantages of dangerousness legislation with a therapeutic justification. Moreover, since most dangerous people are not mentally ill the balance of any generic legislation would immediately shift the focus of attention away from those suffering from mental disorder . . . Where the evidence is that mentally disordered people are in the aggregate little more dangerous . . . than other citizens and that it is substance abuse that most significantly raises the rate of violence in both patient and comparison groups, it is wrong that the mentally disordered in general should be tainted with an association with these high risk offenders.

A generic dangerousness criterion for detention is not without risks, however. As we saw earlier, the United Nation Convention on the Rights of Persons with Disabilities appears to prohibit civil detention solely on the ground of mental disorder. The UN High Commissioner for Human Rights has suggested that this does not rule out detention of people with mental disorders on the grounds of dangerousness, as long as this applies equally to non-disordered individuals. In the next extract, Peter Bartlett cautions that this could be open to abuse.

Peter Bartlett[127]

While the High Commissioner states that detention cannot be based on disability, as is the form in virtually all domestic mental health legislation including that of the United Kingdom, she was at pains to say that this did not necessarily preclude persons with disabilities from being subject to preventive detention. . . . Presumably, this would mean passage of a general law for preventive detention. If it is dangerousness that is of concern, for example, a disability-neutral law could be introduced to detain people who are perceived as dangerous, irrespective of disability. While this might satisfy the problems of interpretation of Article 14, it is difficult to see that it is a good idea. It is difficult to see that it would be wise in human rights terms to encourage autocratic regimes to introduce laws allowing detention of people perceived as dangerous (whether mentally disabled or not), as such a law invites political abuse.

Szmukler et al have proposed what they describe as a 'Fusion Law' which would give procedural protections to all patients who are treated without consent. Under their proposal, incapacity would be the only justification for treatment without consent with one exception: treatment without consent could be given to convicted criminals where a serious mental impairment, that could be effectively treated, had contributed to the commission of a serious offence.

George Szmukler, Rowena Daw, and John Dawson[128]

A major strength of non-consensual treatment schemes that are based on incapacity principles is the respect shown for the autonomy of those patients who retain their capacity; but these schemes are, nevertheless, often weak on the regulation of emergency treatment powers, detention in hospital, and forced treatment. These are the areas, in contrast, in which civil commitment schemes are strong. The use of force, and the detention and involuntary treatment of objecting patients, is clearly authorised and regulated by mental health legislation. We therefore advocate a legal regime that retains the strengths of both, but still

---

[127] 'The United Nations Convention on the Rights of Persons with Disabilities and Mental Health Law' (2012) 75 Modern Law Review 752–78.

[128] 'A model law fusing incapacity and mental health legislation' (2010) Journal of Mental Health Law 11–24.

relies squarely on the incapacity of the person to make necessary care or treatment decisions as the primary justification for intervention in their life. . . .

Some modification of pure capacity principles may be required in the forensic field . . . [A]ny criminal defendant found unfit to plead or not guilty due to insanity might still be treated without their consent, even if they retain or regain their capacity, if certain conditions apply:

- the person has committed acts or omissions constituting a serious offence; and

- a serious mental impairment or disturbance has contributed significantly to that conduct; and

- an effective treatment can be offered that could be expected to reduce the risk of that disorder's reoccurrence.

This compromises pure incapacity principles, in narrowly defined circumstances, in order to prevent harm to others. However, we believe that the number of persons likely to fall into this category who retain capacity is extremely small.

In Scotland, under the Mental Health (Care and Treatment) (Scotland) Act 2003 compulsory powers can be used only where the patient is suffering from 'significantly impaired ability to make decisions' about treatment. The Scottish Code of Practice spells out that 'impaired decision-making is not simply disagreeing with the doctors'.

In Northern Ireland, the Bamford Review recommended that a single statute should deal with the treatment of patients who lack capacity and those who are mentally ill.[129] The new framework will have overarching principles, applicable to all, the most important of which is respect for the patient's autonomy. It is noteworthy, then, that within the UK there is considerable divergence between the legal regimes which apply to patients suffering from mental disorders.

For patients who lack capacity, treatment without consent, and a degree of paternalism, is clearly justifiable. But for the subgroup of mentally ill patients who have capacity, paternalism needs some further justification than that they need treatment, or pose a risk to themselves. As we saw in the previous chapter, competent patients who refuse life-saving treatment undoubtedly pose a risk to themselves, but this does not justify treating them without consent. The 'risk to others' exception is problematic because it applies differentially to the mentally ill. In extreme cases, a person suffering from a highly contagious disease—plague or smallpox, perhaps—might be quarantined, but there is no legal provision that would justify treating them without consent. On this point, it is worth returning to the question of whether the Mental Health Act is compliant with the UN Convention on the Rights of Persons with Disabilities. Article 17 states simply: 'Every person with disabilities has a right to respect for his or her physical and mental integrity on an equal basis with others.' Could section 63 possibly be compliant with this, given that it permits the forced treatment of people who are mentally disordered? The answer is clearly 'no'.

Of course, it is true that some mental disorders create self-destructive desires, such as the desire to end one's life, which can be effectively treated by medication or therapy. On the other hand, the pain and dependency which result from physical illness can also lead to the desire to end one's life, and yet provided the patient retains capacity, forcing her to undergo life-saving treatment against her wishes would be unlawful. Permitting competent mentally ill people to be treated without consent for their mental disorders discriminates between identically situated patients on the grounds of mental illness, and on that basis

---

[129] Maura McCallion and Ursula O'Hare, 'A new legislative framework for mental capacity and mental health legislation in Northern Ireland: an analysis of the current proposals' (2010) Journal of Mental Health Law 84–90.

alone, is seriously problematic. Also, as Earl Howe explained in the House of Lords, it may be counterproductive by acting as a powerful disincentive to seeking help.

Earl Howe[130]

The Government say that every limitation on the ability of doctors to detain patients against their will has the effect of preventing those patients receiving the treatment that they need. To put the matter in those terms, however, presupposes that compulsion is the only means by which effective treatment can be delivered. Of course, it is not: good treatment is available without compulsion, and the fear of some of us is that the wider the gateway to compulsion and the easier the law makes it to get people through it, the less likely it is that those who need help will come forward to ask for it. Never let us forget the anguish, trauma and humiliation involved in subjecting a patient to compulsion—and never let us forget . . . that compulsion should never be seen as a substitute for good healthcare.

Finally, it is undoubtedly true that there is a very small subset of mentally disordered people who are likely to be violent, but this is, of course, equally true of the population as a whole. A tiny minority of people, whether they are mentally ill or not, are more likely to commit violent offences than the rest of us. But our capacity to predict in advance who these people are is not sufficiently accurate to justify the deprivation of their liberty. In any event, the propensity to violence appears to correlate at least as much with substance abuse and drunkenness as it does with mental illness.

FURTHER READING

Bartlett, Peter, 'A Matter of Necessity? Enforced Treatment Under the Mental Health Act' (2007) 15 Medical Law Review 86–98.

Bartlett, Peter, 'The United Nations Convention on the Rights of Persons with Disabilities and Mental Health Law (2012) 75 Modern Law Review 752–78.

Bartlett, Peter and Sandland, Ralph, *Mental Health Law: Policy and Practice*, 3rd edn (OUP: Oxford, 2007).

Eastman, Nigel and Peay, Jill (eds), *Law Without Enforcement: Integrating Mental Health and Justice* (Hart Publishing: Oxford, 1999).

Fennell, Phil, *Treatment Without Consent: Law, Psychiatry and the Treatment of Mentally Disordered People since 1845* (Routledge: London, 1996).

Fennell, Phil, *Mental Health: The New Law* (Jordan: Bristol, 2007).

Palmer, Stephanie, 'A Wrong Turning: Article 3 ECHR and Proportionality' (2006) 65 Cambridge Law Journal 438–52.

Peay, Jill, *Decisions and Dilemmas: Working with Mental Health Law* (Hart Publishing: Oxford, 2003).

Richardson, Genevra, 'Autonomy, Guardianship and Mental Disorder: One Problem, Two Solutions' (2002) 65 Modern Law Review 702–23.

Richardson, Genevra, 'Mental Disabilities and the Law: From Substitute to Supported Decision-Making?' (2012) 65 Current Legal Problems 333–54.

---

[130] Hansard HL 2 July 2007, col 826.

7

CONFIDENTIALITY

CENTRAL ISSUES

1. There are two reasons why it is important for doctors to respect patients' confidentiality. First, information about a person's health is private, and she should have the right to control who has access to it. Secondly, without an assurance of confidentiality, a patient might withhold information that is necessary in order to diagnose and treat her properly.

2. The Data Protection Act 1998, which implemented a European Directive, provides that sensitive personal data must be processed fairly and lawfully. Normally the patient's consent is necessary, but there are a number of exceptions, such as the need to protect a person's 'vital interests' and the use of

data for research and audit. A new EU General Data Protection Regulation will replace the Data Protection Act by 2017.

3. The legal duty of confidentiality is not absolute. The reality of modern medical treatment is that patient information will be shared among a team of health care professionals. Information can also be disclosed where the public interest in disclosure outweighs the public interest in respecting confidentiality, perhaps because there is a risk of serious harm to others.

4. Genetic information raises a number of complex issues in relation to confidentiality; these are dealt with in Chapter 8.

1 INTRODUCTION

Unlike patient autonomy, which is a relatively recent preoccupation of medical law and ethics, a doctor's duty to respect her patients' confidentiality has its origins in the first codes of medical ethics. The Hippocratic oath, for example, states that:

> whatsoever things I see or hear concerning the life of men, in my attendance on the sick or even apart therefrom, which ought not to be noised abroad, I will keep silence thereon, counting such things to be as sacred secrets.

Patient confidentiality receives unqualified protection in the modern version of the Oath, the Declaration of Geneva:

I will respect the secrets which are confided in me, even after the patient has died.

In this chapter, we begin by considering the ethical justifications for protecting patient confidentiality. We then examine the legal sources of the duty of confidence. Next, we flesh out exceptions to the duty of confidence, and the remedies available for its breach. Finally, we look briefly at patients' rights to gain access to their medical records.

2 WHY RESPECT CONFIDENTIALITY?

Both deontological (duty-based) and teleological (consequentialist) reasoning (see Chapter 1) can be used to justify the existence of a duty of confidence between a doctor and her patients. Deontological arguments would emphasize the patient's right to privacy, and her interest in controlling access to what will often be sensitive and personal information. For example, the Medical Research Council's guidance on confidentiality states:

Respect for private life is a human right, and the ability to discuss information in confidence with others is rightly valued. Keeping control over facts about one's self can have an important role in a person's sense of security, freedom of action, and self-respect.[1]

The consequentialist argument for respecting patient confidentiality is, as Gillon explains, that good medical care depends upon patients being honest with their doctors.

Raanan Gillon[2]

[I]n order to do a good job for their patients doctors often need to have information of a sort that people generally regard as private, even secret. . . . Doctors routinely ask a series of questions about bodily functions that people would not dream of discussing with anyone else. When a patient's medical problems may relate to genitourinary functions a doctor may need to know about that patient's sexual activities, sometimes in detail. When a patient's problems are psychological a doctor may need to know in great detail about the patient's experiences, ideas and feelings, relationships past and present, even in some contexts about the person's imaginings and fantasies . . .

Such intrusive medical inquiries are based not on prurience or mere inquisitiveness but on the pursuit of information that is of potential assistance to the doctor in treating and helping the patient. Nonetheless many patients are unlikely to pass on this information unless they have some assurances of confidentiality. . . .

---

[1] *Personal Information in Medical Research* (MRC: London, 2003).
[2] 'Confidentiality' in Helga Kuhse and Peter Singer (eds), *A Companion to Bioethics* (Blackwell: Oxford, 1998) 425–31.

In the context of transmissible diseases, especially sexually transmissible diseases, so long as the patient continues to trust his or her doctor the doctor is left in a position of being able to educate and influence the patient in ways that can reduce the likelihood of the disease being passed on. As soon as confidentiality is broken the trusting relationship is likely to be undermined and the opportunity to help reduce the spread of disease is lost.

And there is evidence that patients would be reluctant to be candid with their doctors if their confidentiality was not protected. Chris Jones's study confirmed that patients might be deterred from seeking treatment if their confidentiality was not respected. At the same time, some patients also thought this might sometimes be a price worth paying in order to protect others from harm.

Chris Jones[3]

The utilitarian justification for maintaining medical confidentiality rests ultimately on a calculation of the effects of confidentiality or disclosure on the behaviour of current and potential future patients. This calculation is often based upon theoretical views of how patients are likely to behave, but in principle it is also open to empirical study: how does the behaviour of patients alter when presented with different standards of confidentiality? . . .

The utilitarian position receives considerable support from the views expressed in this study by patients. They clearly value confidentiality, see it as important in a medical consultation, and recognise that disclosure without consent would be likely to deter some patients from seeking treatment. To this extent it seems that the generally accepted view of the benefits of confidentiality can be justified. However for many people the utility of confidentiality appears to be outweighed by the benefits of disclosure in order to protect third parties. They were prepared to endorse disclosure of information at the same time as recognising that treatment might be impaired as a result.

Although important, confidentiality is not an absolute obligation. The Hippocratic oath only instructs doctors to keep secret that 'which ought not to be noised abroad', the implication being that there are circumstances in which information should be 'noised abroad'.

Most obviously, an absolute duty of confidentiality would be incompatible with the reality of medical treatment, where information has to be shared with other health care professionals. In hospitals, for example, treatment is provided by teams of doctors and nurses. Patients may be referred to specialist consultants, or for diagnostic procedures, such as blood tests, X-rays, and scans. If information about the patient's condition could never be shared with anyone else, the provision of health care would grind to a halt.

While the belief that what one tells one's doctor 'will go no further' has probably always been an illusion, in the next extract, Gostin points out that, as a result of new technologies, patients' notes now contain a great deal of information that can very easily be shared and transferred.

[3] 'The utilitarian argument for medical confidentiality: a pilot study of patients' views' (2003) 29 Journal of Medical Ethics 348–52.

Lawrence Gostin[4]

Only a few generations ago, physicians kept minimal written records about their patients. Physicians usually knew their patients and did not see a need to maintain extensive written reminders of patients' clinical histories. Today, the quantity of health records and the nature of the data they contain have increased substantially. The health records of patients, therefore, contain significant amounts of sensitive information that are available for inspection by many others. . . .

The combination of emerging computer and genetic technologies poses particularly compelling privacy concerns. Science has the capacity to store a million fragments of DNA on a silicon microchip . . . This technology can markedly facilitate research, screening, and treatment of genetic conditions. But it may also permit a significant reduction in privacy through its capacity to inexpensively store and decipher unimaginable quantities of highly sensitive data.

Aside from sharing information within the health service, other exceptions to the duty of confidentiality exist, usually justified by the 'public interest'. Because the principal justification for respecting patient confidentiality is also the public interest, working out whether disclosure is justified in a particular case will often involve a complex balancing exercise between competing interests.

If a patient confides in his doctor that he has committed a very serious crime, such as child abuse, should the doctor inform the police? What if the offence is recreational drug use? On the one hand, there is a clear public interest in the prevention and detection of crime but, on the other, it is also in the public interest for paedophiles and drug users to come forward to seek help and treatment.

Given the number of variables, it is difficult to draw hard and fast rules about the circumstances that would justify disclosure of confidential information. The lack of clarity that results from this sort of case-by-case balancing exercise undoubtedly makes it difficult for doctors to know exactly when their primary duty of confidentiality will be trumped by competing considerations. To make an already confusing situation worse, the law in this area is especially difficult to understand. This is largely because there are several possible sources of the legal duty of confidentiality.

A legal duty of confidence exists in vastly different situations, from duties under the Official Secrets Act to the protection of commercially sensitive information. Some statutes, most notably the Data Protection Act 1998, clearly have an impact upon medical records, and yet because this was never their principal focus, their application to the doctor–patient relationship can be ambiguous and confusing.

At the outset, it should be remembered that not all patient information is equally sensitive. A patient might be very anxious to keep her HIV status private, but be much less concerned about whether a consultant has used an X-ray of her broken foot in a lecture to junior doctors.

Furthermore, it could be argued that the priority given to patient confidentiality rests upon an unrealistically individualistic model of medical decision-making. In practice, most patients do not want to keep information about their health secret from the whole world. Rather, while people might not want their employers or insurers, or the media, to have access to their medical records, they often do want to discuss their health with people who are

---

[4] 'Health Informational Privacy' (1995) 80 Cornell Law Review 451.

close to them. Patients facing difficult medical choices, or the diagnosis of serious illness, often want a partner, family member, or friend to be present during discussions with their doctors. In the next extract, Roy Gilbar argues that, in the context of familial relationships, the strict rule of confidentiality should be reconsidered.

Roy Gilbar[5]

While the relationship between patients and employers or insurers is primarily confrontational, with patients anxious to protect their rights and not be discriminated against, the relationship with family members is generally based on care, commitment and mutual responsibility. . . .

[P]atients often consider the interests of their relatives and the implications of their decision on their familial relationship, while doctors are willing to involve family members more than the law currently permits to help the patient cope with the bad news. In other words, doctors and patients value the patient's familial relationship as a separate and significant component in this area. Thus, the strict legal rule of medical confidentiality, which is adopted by many lawyers and policy-makers, should be reconsidered. . . .

Doctors in various areas of medicine have learned to accept that the support and comfort that family members provide to the patient during all the stages of his/her illness is important, and that the family rather than the individual patient, should be considered as the unit of medical care. This, in many cases, leads to the conclusion that adhering to a strict rule of confidentiality may compromise the interests of the patient instead of promoting them.

It may be true that most people do not want to keep information about their health secret from close friends and relatives, but disclosure should still lie within the patient's control. Not all intimate and familial relationships are harmonious and supportive, and there will be times when a patient might have good reasons for wanting to keep information from her partner or her relatives.

3 A DUTY OF CONFIDENTIALITY

In the following sections we examine a number of different sources of the legal duty of confidence.

(a) AT COMMON LAW

The origins of the legal duty of confidence lie in the equitable jurisdiction of the Chancery Division to grant injunctions in order to prevent the infringement of legal and equitable rights. So what gives rise to an enforceable duty of confidentiality? In *Attorney General v Guardian Newspapers (No 2)*, known as the *Spycatcher* case, Lord Goff explained when a duty of confidence arises.

---

[5] 'Medical Confidentiality Within the Family: The Doctor's Duty Reconsidered' (2004) 18 International Journal of Law, Policy and the Family 195.

Attorney General v Guardian Newspapers (No 2)[6]

Lord Goff

[A] duty of confidence arises when confidential information comes to the knowledge of a person (the confidant) in circumstances where he has notice, or is held to have agreed, that the information is confidential, with the effect that it would be just in all the circumstances that he should be precluded from disclosing the information to others.

Lord Goff went on to suggest three limiting principles: first, that the information must itself be confidential, and not already in the public domain; secondly, there is no duty of confidentiality in relation to useless information or trivia; and, thirdly, the duty to respect confidentiality is not an absolute one, and can sometimes be trumped where there is a weightier public interest in disclosure.

The factors that give rise to a duty of confidentiality are thus vague and question-begging: effectively a duty of confidence arises when someone knows, or ought to know, that the information she has acquired is confidential. It is both the nature of the information and the circumstances in which it was disclosed that create a duty of confidentiality.

For our purposes, however, the position is relatively clear. Medical information is exactly the sort of information which is treated as confidential, and the doctor–patient relationship is plainly one in which a duty of confidence arises. As Boreham J stated in *Hunter v Mann*:[7] 'in common with other professional men, for instance a priest and there are of course others, the doctor is under a duty not to disclose, without the consent of his patient, information which he, the doctor, has gained in his professional capacity, save . . . in very exceptional circumstances'.

In *W v Egdell*, a case which we consider in more detail later, the existence of a duty of confidence between Dr Egdell and W was not in doubt.

W v Egdell[8]

Bingham LJ

It has never been doubted that the circumstances here were such as to impose on Dr Egdell a duty of confidence owed to W. He could not lawfully sell the contents of his report to a newspaper, as the judge held. Nor could he, without a breach of the law as well as professional etiquette, discuss the case in a learned article or in his memoirs or in gossiping with friends, unless he took appropriate steps to conceal the identity of W. It is not in issue here that a duty of confidence existed.

An alternative basis for the existence of a duty of confidentiality at common law would be that it is an aspect of the doctor's duty of care. A doctor who discloses information that should have been kept private will generally not have acted as a reasonable doctor, and the patient might therefore be able to bring an action in negligence. This will only be possible, however, if the patient has suffered some sort of damage as a result of the negligent disclosure: an example might be being turned down for insurance coverage. More commonly, the

---

[6] [1990] AC 109.   [7] [1974] QB 767.   [8] [1990] Ch 359.

'harm' that results from a breach of confidentiality will be less tangible, and an action in tort less promising.

It is usually assumed that the duty of confidentiality is owed to the patient, rather than to those treating her. However, health providers might also have an interest in ensuring the confidentiality of their patient records. In *Ashworth Hospital Authority v Mirror Group Newspapers (MGN)*, the *Mirror* newspaper had published information about the medical treatment of Ian Brady, one of the Moors murderers. Ian Brady had been keen to publicize what he perceived to be his ill treatment, and he had attempted to put information about his treatment into the public domain. The hospital obtained an order requiring the newspaper to identify the employee who had leaked Brady's medical notes. On appeal, the House of Lords decided that the security of medical records was of such overriding importance that it was essential that the person who had disclosed them to the newspaper was identified and punished, even if the patient himself did not object to the disclosure.

Ashworth Hospital Authority v Mirror Group Newspapers (MGN)[9]

Lord Woolf

[W]hile Ian Brady's conduct in putting similar information into the public domain could well mean that he would not be in a position to complain about the publication, this did not destroy the authority's independent interest in retaining the confidentiality of the medical records contained in Ashworth's files. . . . The care of patients at Ashworth is fraught with difficulty and danger. The disclosure of the patients' records increases that difficulty and danger and to deter the same or similar wrongdoing in the future it was essential that the source should be identified and punished. This was what made the orders to disclose necessary and proportionate and justified. The fact that Ian Brady had himself disclosed his medical history did not detract from the need to prevent staff from revealing medical records of patients . . . The source's disclosure was wholly inconsistent with the security of the records and the disclosure was made worse because it was purchased by a cash payment.

The decision in *Ashworth* was not the end of the story, however. Instead of disclosing the name of the staff member who had leaked Brady's records, MGN only disclosed the name of the investigative journalist, Ackroyd. Ashworth Hospital had by this time been subsumed within the Mersey Care NHS Trust, which then brought an action against Ackroyd, requiring him to reveal his sources (he had admitted there was more than one).

When the case reached the Court of Appeal, it had to engage in a fresh balancing act between the public interest in disclosure and the public interest in protecting the confidentiality of medical records. By this time, more facts had emerged about the circumstances of the leak: first, the motivation had not, in fact, been financial greed, as had previously been assumed; secondly, only part of Brady's notes had been disclosed; and, thirdly, it was not clear that the source had been a member of the hospital's staff. In *Mersey Care NHS Trust v Ackroyd (No 2)*[10] the Court of Appeal decided that the journalist did not have to disclose his sources.

This case is a good illustration of the fact that the confidentiality of medical records must be balanced with other important interests, such as press freedom, which as Sandland explains, will sometimes take priority.

---

[9] [2002] 1 WLR 2033. [10] [2007] EWCA Civ 101.

Ralph Sandland[11]

From the perspective of Mersey NHS Trust and Ashworth Hospital, *Ackroyd* is bad news. The hospital's victory in *Ashworth* has been rendered pyrrhic; all that effort, over seven years of litigation, including three visits to the Court of Appeal and one to the House of Lords, has been for nothing. The hospital still does not know—but does now know that it will probably never know—the identities of the sources of the leak. From the perspective of journalists, the effective legal protection of sources, seen as having been damaged by *Ashworth*, has been largely restored.

(b) THE HUMAN RIGHTS ACT 1998

A patient's interest in confidentiality also receives protection from Article 8 of the European Convention on Human Rights: the 'right to respect for private and family life'. Article 8 is not an absolute right, however, and is qualified by Article 8(2):

(1) Everyone has the right to respect for his private and family life, his home and his correspondence.

(2) There shall be no interference by a public authority with the exercise of this right except such as is in accordance with the law and is necessary in a democratic society in the interests of national security, public safety or the economic well-being of the country, for the prevention of disorder or crime, for the protection of health or morals, or for the protection of the rights and freedoms of others.

In relation to medical information, it will generally be straightforward to establish that the disclosure of medical information constitutes a prima facie violation of Article 8.

An unusual case in which Article 8 was held not to have even been engaged was *Department of Health v Information Commissioner*, in which Cranston J found that where the likelihood of identifying individuals was 'remote', there could be no interference with Article 8(1). The Department of Health had sought to resist a Freedom of Information Act request from a pro-life pressure group to publish statistical data about the conditions that had justified late terminations of pregnancy on the grounds of fetal abnormality. Cranston J held that the chance of identifying individual women was 'remote'—but note, not non-existent—and that Article 8 therefore did not apply. Given the potentially devastating consequences of identifying women who had undergone late abortions, it is interesting that a remote risk of identification was not thought to engage their human rights.

Department of Health v Information Commissioner[12]

Cranston J

The Department of Health had never suggested that identification was probable. Rather its case had been that if there was some meaningful possibility of identification the disputed

---

[11] 'Freedom of the Press and the Confidentiality of Medical Records' (2007) 15 Medical Law Review 400–9.
[12] [2011] EWHC 1430 (Admin).

> information should not be released, given that the circumstances were of an unparalleled sensitivity and the consequences ghastly . . . the Tribunal accepted the devastating consequences of identification. While it placed great weight on them, it concluded that these consequences were all dependent upon a patient being identified. The Tribunal was satisfied that this was extremely remote . . .
>
> In my view, the Tribunal was not flawed in concluding that the risk of individual identification is so remote that the right under Article 8.1 was not engaged.

In relation to medical information, more usually Article 8 will be engaged, and the principal obstacle to a successful claim will be the possibility that disclosure was justifiable under Article 8(2).

In *Z v Finland*, for example, Z was married to a man who had been charged with a number of sexual offences. He was HIV-positive, and in order to find out when he became aware of his HIV status, the police sought and gained access to Z's medical records. The European Court of Human Rights (ECtHR) held that seizing Z's medical records and ordering her doctors to give evidence was justifiable under Article 8(2): a legitimate aim was being pursued and the measures taken were not disproportionate.

Z v Finland[13]

Judgment of the ECtHR

In view of the highly intimate and sensitive nature of information concerning a person's HIV status, any state measures compelling communication or disclosure of such information without the consent of the patient call for the most careful scrutiny on the part of the court, as do the safeguards designed to secure an effective protection . . .

At the same time, the court accepts that the interests of a patient and the community as a whole in protecting the confidentiality of medical data may be outweighed by the interest in investigation and prosecution of crime and in the publicity of court proceedings, where such interests are shown to be of even greater importance.

Disclosure without consent was also justified under Article 8(2) in *Stone v South East Coast Strategic Health Authority*, the convicted murderer Michael Stone sought to suppress publication of a homicide inquiry, which contained considerable detail about his medical treatment. While Davis J acknowledged his right to privacy, and the argument that publication might deter patients from being frank with their doctors and with homicide inquiry panels, this was outweighed by the public interest in knowing more about the treatment that Mr Stone had, and perhaps more importantly had not received. Also relevant was the fact that the need for this inquiry arose from Mr Stone's own criminal acts, and that a great deal of information about his treatment was already in the public domain. Davis J further decided that a redacted (where personal information is blacked-out) or summarized version of the report would be useless and 'might be viewed with scepticism by the public, who might even suspect a cover-up'.

---

[13] (1997) 25 EHRR 371.

Stone v South East Coast Strategic Health Authority[14]

Davis J

So far as Mr Stone is concerned, much the most weighty point in his favour, as it seems to me, is his very entitlement to claim a right of privacy: in respect moreover of an aspect of private information (medical information) which—as the jurisprudence from Europe shows—is regarded as a vital and central element of that which should be protected under Article 8. Further, that is reinforced by other and wider considerations of the public interest: first, that persons may talk freely with their doctors, probation officers and other such persons without being deterred by risk of subsequent disclosure . . . ; second, that such persons may give access to such information for the purposes of an inquiry without being deterred from doing so through fear of such matters later being released into the public domain.

But it seems to me that the force of those points is significantly outweighed by a number of other considerations . . .

[T]here is a true public interest in the public at large knowing of the actual care and treatment supplied (or, as the case may be, not supplied) to Mr Stone: and knowing, and being able to reach an informed assessment of, the failures identified and steps that may be recommended to be taken to address identified deficiencies. . . .

[I]t is, I think, of importance as a justification for restricting Mr Stone's right to privacy in this context that this inquiry, and all this publicity, have arisen out of Mr Stone's own acts—acts found to have been criminal. He has, as it were, put himself in the public domain by reason of those criminal acts, which inevitably created great publicity. Of course that is not to say that a convicted murderer forfeits all his rights under Article 8; of course he does not. But here the information sought to be disclosed relates—and relates solely—to the investigation foreseeably arising out of the very murders which he himself committed.

I also think it a point of considerable importance as a justification for restricting Mr Stone's right to privacy in this context that a great deal of information relating to the background, treatment and mental health of Mr Stone has already been put in the public domain, and at a significant level of detail . . . [P]revious publication of private information in the public domain does not mean that an individual necessarily loses his right to privacy in respect of a proposal to put yet more such material in the public domain. But, as it seems to me, it must be relevant to the balancing exercise and to the issue of proportionality: and here the previous disclosure in the public domain has already been very extensive indeed. That must tell against the asserted detrimental impact of publication of further, albeit more detailed, information.

In addition to Article 8(2)'s qualification of the right to privacy, Article 8 has to be put into the balance with Article 10, the right to freedom of expression, and section 12 of the Human Rights Act, which specifies that, 'The court must have particular regard to the importance of the Convention right to freedom of expression.'

There is no presumptive priority for either right; rather, the competing interests have to be balanced according to the facts of the individual case. In *W v M (An Adult Patient)*, the Court of Protection was about to hear an application in which it would decide on the legality of withholding nutrition from a woman in a minimally conscious state (considered in Chapter 17). It was an issue of public importance, which militated in favour of a public hearing, but this had to be balanced with the Article 8 rights of the woman herself, and those of

14 [2006] EWHC 1668 (Admin).

her mother, sister, and her partner. Also relevant were their Article 6 rights (the right to a fair trial), since the three of them had stated that press intrusion would be likely to lead them to drop the case.

W v M (An Adult Patient)[15]

Baker J

It is axiomatic that the freedom to report proceedings in open court is in the public interest. The court has determined that the issues in this case are sufficiently important to justify public hearing, and the press must be allowed to report the proceedings as far as possible. Furthermore, . . . it seems likely that the court will be asked to make an order that has not been made before in this country, namely to approve the withholding of nutrition from a patient whose consciousness is above that of the vegetative state. This potentially raises issues of the utmost importance which the media must be fully free to report.

In addition, the court recognises that the reporting of such cases is difficult if the restrictions imposed on the media are too onerous. The issues raised are invariably given sharper focus if the media are free to report the human stories behind the legal issues . . .

The evidence manifestly demonstrates that M's right to respect for family and private life would be infringed by any publication that identified her, or any attempt by the media to communicate with or photograph her.

In my judgment, the article 8 rights engaged in this case are not only those of M, but also those of W, B and S. On the evidence filed in this case, any publication of the identity of W, B and S, or any attempt by the media to communicate with, or take a photograph of, those three individuals would not only infringe their own article 8 rights, but also the article 8 rights of M, since, on the evidence of B and S, it would be likely to reduce the frequency of their visits to the care home.

I also take into account the statements by B and S that the risk of press intrusion might lead them to abandon these proceedings altogether. It is therefore arguable that, if it failed to restrain the press from identifying, communicating with or photographing the family members, the court would be infringing the article 6 rights of B, S and M. Given the importance of the issues at stake in these proceedings, such an infringement would be extremely serious . . .

In my judgment, the balance manifestly falls in this case in favour of granting the orders sought by the applicant and the Official Solicitor. The terms of the order will ensure that the article 8 rights of family members are properly protected. The freedom of expression enjoyed by the press will be restricted, but the extent of that restriction will, in my judgment, not prevent the press from reporting the issues, evidence (including expert evidence) and arguments at the hearing.

The need to balance the interests protected by Articles 8 and 10 in the context of patient information arose in *Campbell v Mirror Group Newspapers*. The House of Lords had to determine whether the press's freedom to publish information about the model Naomi Campbell's treatment for drug addiction should take priority over her right to privacy. Ms Campbell accepted that the newspaper had been entitled, in the public interest, to disclose the information that she was a drug addict and that she was receiving treatment for her addiction, because she had previously falsely and publicly stated that she was not a drug addict. But

---

[15] [2011] EWHC 1197 (Fam).

she claimed that the details of her attendance at Narcotics Anonymous, and accompanying photographs, amounted to a breach of her privacy. The House of Lords agreed.

Campbell v Mirror Group Newspapers[16]

Baroness Hale

I start, therefore, from the fact—indeed, it is common ground—that all of the information about Miss Campbell's addiction and attendance at NA [Narcotics Anonymous] which was revealed in the *Mirror* article was both private and confidential, because it related to an important aspect of Miss Campbell's physical and mental health and the treatment she was receiving for it. It had also been received from an insider in breach of confidence. . . .

What was the nature of the freedom of expression which was being asserted on the other side? There are undoubtedly different types of speech, just as there are different types of private information, some of which are more deserving of protection in a democratic society than others. Top of the list is political speech. The free exchange of information and ideas on matters relevant to the organisation of the economic, social and political life of the country is crucial to any democracy. . . . Artistic speech and expression is important for similar reasons . . .

But it is difficult to make such claims on behalf of the publication with which we are concerned here. The political and social life of the community, and the intellectual, artistic or personal development of individuals, are not obviously assisted by poring over the intimate details of a fashion model's private life. . . .

The weight to be attached to these various considerations is a matter of fact and degree. Not every statement about a person's health will carry the badge of confidentiality or risk doing harm to that person's physical or moral integrity. The privacy interest in the fact that a public figure has a cold or a broken leg is unlikely to be strong enough to justify restricting the press's freedom to report it. What harm could it possibly do? Sometimes there will be other justifications for publishing, especially where the information is relevant to the capacity of a public figure to do the job. But that is not this case and in this case there was, as the judge found, a risk that publication would do harm. The risk of harm is what matters at this stage, rather than the proof that actual harm has occurred. People trying to recover from drug addiction need considerable dedication and commitment, along with constant reinforcement from those around them. That is why organisations like NA were set up and why they can do so much good. Blundering in when matters are acknowledged to be at a 'fragile' stage may do great harm.

Notice that the House of Lords found that an obligation of confidence existed because of the nature of the information about Ms Campbell's treatment for drug addiction, rather than because of any pre-existing relationship between her and the *Mirror* newspaper. Unlike actions for breach of confidence, considered in the previous section, the right to privacy attaches to any private information, regardless of the circumstances in which that information is acquired.

In *R (on the application of B) v Stafford Combined Court*, there was a conflict between two different competing interests: the need for a fair trial and a patient's right to confidentiality. B was a 14-year-old girl who was the main prosecution witness in the trial of a defendant, W, who was accused and subsequently convicted of sexually abusing her. His legal team had

---

[16] [2004] UKHL 22.

sought access to her psychiatric records, on the grounds that they were relevant to her credibility as a witness. At first instance, the judge had held that the interest in a fair trial was more important than the patient's interests in the confidentiality of her medical records, and ordered disclosure. The judge had then invited B to attend court. There was no arrangement or opportunity for her to be represented, and in court she agreed reluctantly to disclosure, because she could not face the prospect of the trial being delayed.

B applied successfully for judicial review of the Crown Court decision ordering disclosure of her medical records. In *R (on the application of B) v Stafford Combined Court*, May LJ was sharply critical of the judge's conduct, and found that the court itself had breached B's Article 8 rights.

R (on the application of B) v Stafford Combined Court[17]

May LJ

I strongly deprecate what happened on 6 December 2005. It seems to me to be quite unacceptable for a vulnerable 14-year-old school girl known to have attempted suicide, the victim of alleged sexual abuse and a prosecution witness in the impending trial, to be brought to court at short notice, without representation or support, to be faced personally with an apparent choice between agreeing to the disclosure of her psychiatric records or delaying a trial which was bound to cause her concern and stress.

In my judgment, procedural fairness in the light of article 8 undoubtedly required in the present case that B should have been given notice of the application for the witness summons, and given the opportunity to make representations before the order was made. Since the rules did not require this of the person applying for the summons, the requirement was on the court as a public authority, not on W, the defendant. B was not given due notice or that opportunity, so the interference with her rights was not capable of being necessary within article 8(2). Her rights were infringed and the court acted unlawfully in a way which was incompatible with her Convention rights.

(c) THE DATA PROTECTION ACT 1998

The Data Protection Act 1998 implemented a 1995 European Directive. Readers should note that it is due to be replaced by a new EU General Data Protection Regulation in 2017. We therefore briefly consider the Data Protection Act's provisions, before looking at the new data protection regime.

Schedule 1 to the Data Protection Act 1998 contains eight Data Protection Principles, the first of which states that all personal data must be processed 'fairly and lawfully'. 'Processing' essentially means doing anything at all with information, so obtaining, storing, disclosing, and using information will all be covered.

(1) What is Personal Data?

Usually, of course, information about a person's health, such as their medical records, will be paradigmatically personal data. But there are times when it may be less clear whether information qualifies as 'personal'. This issue arose in *Department of Health v Information*

Commissioner, in which, as we saw earlier, the Department of Health sought unsuccessfully to defend its refusal to publish a breakdown of the conditions that had justified late terminations of pregnancy on grounds of fetal abnormality. The Department of Health maintained that this was personal data, which—because of the tiny number of abortions carried out post-24 weeks—might be used to identify potentially vulnerable women and the clinicians who had carried out these terminations. Cranston J decided that this was not personal data.

With respect, information that creates even a remote risk of identification of the grounds on which an individual woman had had a late termination of pregnancy is at least potentially personal information. It is, of course, true, as Cranston J pointed out, that the statistic that 100,000 women had a termination of pregnancy is not personal data; but it is arguable that the statistic that in 2015 one woman had a termination of pregnancy for a genetic condition that affects one family in the UK is potentially personal information about her medical treatment.

Department of Health v Information Commissioner[18]

Cranston J

The Department of Health's interpretation is that any statistical information derived from reporting forms or patient records constitutes personal data. If that were the case, any publication would amount to the processing of sensitive personal data. . . . Thus, the statistic that 100,000 women had an abortion in a particular year would constitute personal data about each of those women, provided that the body that publishes this statistic has access to information which would enable it to identify each of them. That is not a sensible result and would seriously inhibit the ability of healthcare organisations and other bodies to publish medical statistics.

More recently, in *R (on the application of W, X, Y and Z) v The Secretary of State for Health v The Secretary of State for the Home Department*, information about the date and cost of a person's treatment was held to be confidential. In 2011, the Immigration Rules had been amended so that anyone not resident in the UK could be refused entry or leave to remain if they had unpaid NHS debts of more than £1,000, incurred for treatment other than A&E services, family planning, or treatment with public health implications. In order to enforce this new rule, information identifying NHS debtors, and the amount of their debt, would be passed to the Secretary of State for Health, and then to the Home Office.

W, X, Y, and Z were likely to be affected by this change in the Immigration Rules and they challenged it on the grounds that the relevant bodies had no power to disclose confidential information about the date and cost of their medical treatment without their consent. At first instance, it had been held that the information was not confidential. On appeal, in *R (on the application of W, X, Y and Z) v The Secretary of State for Health v The Secretary of State for the Home Department*, the Court of Appeal decided that the information was private, but that there could be no expectation of privacy with respect to the Secretary of State and the Home Office.

---

[18] [2011] EWHC 1430 (Admin).

R (on the application of W, X, Y and Z) v The Secretary of State for Health v The Secretary of State for the Home Department[19]

Lord Dyson MR

The fact that the disclosure may be 'less intrusive' than disclosure of detailed information about an individual's medical condition and treatment does not mean that it is not intrusive at all or that the information is not inherently private. Instead, it means that it is likely to be easier to justify disclosure.

We accept the submission of [counsel] that the Information is inherently private information, particularly because it reveals information of substance about the health of the data subjects, namely that they were unwell to the extent that they had to seek medical care at a particular point in time from one or more NHS bodies . . .. The fact that the data also includes charging information, which in itself reveals whether the treatment was relatively fleeting or extensive, only reinforces the conclusion that the Information is inherently private in nature. As we have said, the identity of the NHS body will in some cases be sufficient to indicate the nature of the patient's illness. Indeed, given that the information tells you something of substance about an identified patient's health, it must be treated as falling squarely within the definition of sensitive personal data as set out in section 2 of the Data Protection Act 1998 . . .

A patient liable to charges will reasonably expect that, in the event of default, steps will be taken to enforce payment, which may include informing others of the fact, duration and cost of his stay at the hospital concerned; and that to this extent their stay at the hospital will not necessarily be kept confidential.

We do not see how overseas visitors who, before they are treated in an NHS hospital, are made aware of the fact that, if they incur charges in excess of £1,000 and do not pay them within 3 months, the Information may be passed to the Secretary of State for onward transmission to the Home Office for the stated immigration purpose can have any, still less any reasonable, expectation that the Information will not be transmitted in precisely that way. They will, however, have a reasonable expectation of privacy in relation to the Information vis-à-vis anyone else . . .. It follows that, even if the claimants had a right to privacy and confidentiality in the Information, it was not infringed by the disclosure.

(2) What Does it Mean to Process Data Fairly and Lawfully?

Obviously, to be lawful, processing must comply with common law obligations of confidentiality, but the Act itself further defines 'fairness' and 'legality' in a way which is, to say the least, rather confusing. For sensitive personal data, which under section 2(e) includes information about a person's 'physical or mental health or condition', processing will have been fair and lawful provided that (in addition to meeting common law obligations of confidentiality) at least one condition from Schedule 2 to the Act and one from Schedule 3 are satisfied.

---

[19] [2015] EWCA Civ 1034.

Data Protection Act 1998 Schedules 1–3

Schedule 1

1. Personal data shall be processed fairly and lawfully and, in particular, shall not be processed unless—

   (a) at least one of the conditions in Schedule 2 is met, and

   (b) in the case of sensitive personal data, at least one of the conditions in Schedule 3 is also met.

Schedule 2

CONDITIONS RELEVANT FOR PURPOSES OF THE FIRST PRINCIPLE: PROCESSING OF ANY PERSONAL DATA

1. The data subject has given his consent to the processing . . .
4. The processing is necessary in order to protect the vital interests of the data subject.
5. The processing is necessary—

   (a) for the administration of justice,

   (b) for the exercise of any functions conferred on any person by or under any enactment,

   (c) for the exercise of any functions of the Crown, a Minister of the Crown or a government department, or

   (d) for the exercise of any other functions of a public nature exercised in the public interest by any person.

6. (1) The processing is necessary for the purposes of legitimate interests pursued by the data controller or by the third party or parties to whom the data are disclosed, except where the processing is unwarranted in any particular case by reason of prejudice to the rights and freedoms or legitimate interests of the data subject.

(2) The Secretary of State may by order specify particular circumstances in which this condition is, or is not, to be taken to be satisfied.

Schedule 3

CONDITIONS RELEVANT FOR PURPOSES OF THE FIRST PRINCIPLE: PROCESSING OF SENSITIVE PERSONAL DATA

1. The data subject has given his explicit consent to the processing of the personal data. . . .
3. The processing is necessary—

   (a) in order to protect the vital interests of the data subject or another person, in a case where—

      (i) consent cannot be given by or on behalf of the data subject, or

      (ii) the data controller cannot reasonably be expected to obtain the consent of the data subject, or

   (c) in order to protect the vital interests of another person, in a case where consent by or on behalf of the data subject has been unreasonably withheld. . . .

8. (1) The processing is necessary for medical purposes and is undertaken by—

   (a) a health professional, or

   (b) a person who in the circumstances owes a duty of confidentiality which is equivalent to that which would arise if that person were a health professional.

(2) In this paragraph 'medical purposes' includes the purposes of preventative medicine, medical diagnosis, medical research, the provision of care and treatment and the management of healthcare services.

Under Schedule 2, either the data subject must consent to the 'processing' of personal data, or disclosure must fit within one of the six exceptions to the need to obtain consent contained in Schedule 2, three of which are worth highlighting here. First, data may be processed without consent if it is necessary to protect the vital interests of the data subject. This exception is not confined to situations where the patient's life is in danger: rather, it could simply mean that sharing the information is necessary in order to protect her health. It is, however, only justifiable if the processing is necessary, as opposed to merely convenient.

Secondly, processing without consent might be justifiable under Schedule 2 if it is 'necessary' for functions of a public nature exercised in the public interest, or for the exercise of functions of government departments or a Secretary of State. Provided that the processing of patient information was necessary for the Secretary of State to meet his obligation to promote a comprehensive health service, for example, it would appear to be lawful to use patient records without consent. Here, of course, the problem is what is meant by 'necessary': is the maintenance of a nationwide cancer registry necessary for the promotion of a comprehensive health service, for example?

Thirdly, processing without consent is legitimate if it is necessary for the purposes of the data controller's legitimate interests. This might allow disclosure for the purposes of training or audit, and again the crucial question is whether the use of data is necessary for these purposes.

Once a condition from Schedule 2 has been satisfied, it is then necessary to turn to Schedule 3, which contains ten exceptions to the need to obtain the data subject's 'explicit consent' to the processing of sensitive personal data. Here things become slightly clearer because the eighth condition in Schedule 3 is that processing without consent is justifiable if it 'is necessary for medical purposes', and is undertaken by a health professional or a person who owes an equivalent duty of confidentiality. Medical purposes are not confined to treatment, but include 'preventative medicine, medical diagnosis, medical research, the provision of care and treatment and the management of health care services'. Given this expansive list, the only limiting criterion here is again that the processing should be necessary for one of these purposes.

A further exception to the explicit consent requirement is contained in paragraph 3 of Schedule 3, which provides that processing will be fair and lawful if it is in the vital interests of the data subject or another person. Hence, information can be disclosed without consent to protect the health of a third party.

The Data Protection (Processing of Sensitive Personal Data) Order 2000 added a further condition to Schedule 3. This allows for processing which is in the 'substantial public interest' where necessary for the discharge of certain public functions, such as protecting the public against malpractice, or other seriously improper conduct, unfitness, or incompetence. Disclosure to the General Medical Council (GMC) in relation to an allegation of professional misconduct therefore would be permissible without consent. The limiting factors are that the processing must be in the substantial public interest, and, again, that it must be necessary for discharging the particular public function.

The second Data Protection Principle specifies that information must be obtained only for one or more specified and lawful purposes, and must not be further processed in a way that is incompatible with those purposes. Section 33 contains an exception where the further processing is for the purposes of research. The final Data Protection Principle which is relevant for our purposes is the fifth one, which specifies that information must be kept no longer than necessary for the purposes for which it is processed. Again, there is an exception for information that is processed for research purposes, which can be kept indefinitely.

If any of these provisions are breached, the Data Protection Act provides for three different remedies. First, under section 10 a data subject can serve a notice requiring the data controller to cease or refrain from processing his personal data. The data subject must establish that the processing is causing, or would be likely to cause, substantial damage, either to her or to a third party. Secondly, it is possible to seek compensation under section 13 where the data subject or another has suffered damage and consequent distress as a result of the disclosure. The data controller will, however, have a defence if he can show that he took reasonable care to comply with the Act. Thirdly, under section 14 the court can order the data controller to rectify or destroy inaccurate data.

(3) The New General Data Protection Regulation

The new EU Data Protection Regulation is expected to come into force towards the end of 2017. Its principal purposes are to give individuals more control over their personal data and to simplify the regulatory environment for business. The main reason for reform was the need to keep pace with the 'new digital environment' in which Europe's 250 million internet users are uploading more and more personal data online. Mechanisms are also to be put in place to protect the 'right to be forgotten' in relation to online information. Individuals will have the right to obtain a portable electronic copy of all data held in relation to them. Data Protection Authorities are to be given greater investigative powers and the power to issue fines for breaches of up to €1 million.

Just as with the Data Protection Act, the new Regulation is not directed specifically at medical information, and so a set of rules which are intended to protect individual's interests in their data in the world of social media and online shopping may not necessarily be a good fit with health care data. For example, a right to be forgotten makes sense in the context of social networking sites, but it might be problematic within the NHS, when there are very good reasons to retain patient records.

Funders of medical research have been worried about the consequences of the new Regulation for research. Earlier versions of the Regulation had specified that health data could be used without consent for research purposes, but only where that research serves a 'high public interest', and the data are pseudonymized, and where the data subject has had the right to object to their use. The final text of the Regulation is more research-friendly, allowing for derogations from the protections in the Regulation for research purposes.

EU Data Protection Regulation 2016

Article 19(2aa)

Where personal data are processed for scientific and historical research purposes or statistical purposes pursuant to Article 83(1), the data subject, on grounds relating to his or her particular situation, shall have the right to object to processing of personal data concerning him or her, unless the processing is necessary for the performance of a task carried out for reasons of public interest.

Article 83

1. Processing of personal data for archiving purposes in the public interest, or scientific and historical research purposes or statistical purposes, shall be subject to in accordance with this Regulation appropriate safeguards for the rights and freedoms of the data subject. These safeguards shall ensure that technical and organisational measures are in place in particular in order to ensure the respect of the principle of data minimisation. These measures may include pseudonymisation, as long as these purposes can be fulfilled in this manner. Whenever these purposes can be fulfilled by further processing of data which does not permit or not any longer permit the identification of data subjects these purposes shall be fulfilled in this manner.

2. Where personal data are processed for scientific and historical research purposes or statistical purposes, Union or Member State law may provide for derogations from the rights referred to in Articles 15 [right of access], 16 [right of rectification], 17a [right to restriction on processing] and 19 [right to object to processing] subject to the conditions and safeguards referred to in paragraph 1 in so far as such rights are likely to render impossible or seriously impair the achievement of the specific purposes, and such derogations are necessary for the fulfilment of these purposes.

(d) OTHER STATUTORY PROVISIONS

In certain situations, additional obligations to respect confidentiality are created by statute. For example, section 33 of the Human Fertilisation and Embryology Act 1990 imposes restrictions upon the disclosure of information held in confidence by the Human Fertilisation and Embryology Authority and by people working in licensed centres. Under the Abortion Regulations 1991, there is a duty to report each termination of pregnancy to the Chief Medical Officer, but there are also restrictions upon any further disclosure of this information.

(e) GOOD MEDICAL PRACTICE

The GMC's good practice guidance *Confidentiality*,[20] is supplemented by more specific guidance on, for example, disclosing information for education and training purposes; reporting gunshot and knife wounds; and disclosing information about serious communicable diseases. Note that at the time of writing, the GMC has announced its intention to consult upon new guidance so readers should check the availability of more recent guidance on confidentiality on the GMC website.[21]

General Medical Council[22]

6. Confidentiality is central to trust between doctors and patients. Without assurances about confidentiality, patients may be reluctant to seek medical attention or to give doctors the information they need in order to provide good care. But appropriate information sharing is essential to the efficient provision of safe, effective care, both for the individual patient and for the wider community of patients. . . .

---

[20] *Confidentiality* (GMC, 2009).　　[21] www.gmc-uk.org.　　[22] *Confidentiality* (GMC, 2009).

8. Confidentiality is an important duty, but it is not absolute. You can disclose personal information if:

(a) it is required by law

(b) the patient consents—either implicitly for the sake of their own care or expressly for other purposes

(c) it is justified in the public interest.

9. When disclosing information about a patient, you must:

(a) use anonymised or coded information if practicable and if it will serve the purpose

(b) be satisfied that the patient:

(i) has ready access to information that explains that their personal information might be disclosed for the sake of their own care, or for local clinical audit, and that they can object, and

(ii) has not objected

(c) get the patient's express consent if identifiable information is to be disclosed for purposes other than their care or local clinical audit, unless the disclosure is required by law or can be justified in the public interest

(d) keep disclosures to the minimum necessary, and

(e) keep up to date with, and observe, all relevant legal requirements, including the common law and data protection legislation.

Although GMC guidance does not have the status of law, it is certainly not without teeth. As we have seen, the legal sources of the duty of confidentiality are complex and confusing, so in practice GMC guidance is more useful to doctors faced with a dilemma about breaching patient confidentiality. In addition, breach of GMC guidance may lead to disciplinary proceedings, and if found guilty of serious professional misconduct, the doctor can be struck off the medical register. The Nursing and Midwifery Council's *Code of Professional Conduct* sets out similar duties and penalties for nurses, midwives, and health visitors.

In addition, any failure to follow GMC guidance might offer evidence that a doctor had not acted as a reasonable medical practitioner and was therefore in breach of his duty of care. Proving that a doctor has been negligent might be relatively straightforward where there has been a clear breach of GMC guidance. As noted earlier, however, the patient will only be able to bring an action in negligence if damage was caused by the breach of confidence.

In 1997, a review of the use of patient-identifiable information in the NHS, chaired by Fiona Caldicott, was published by the Department of Health. It set out six guiding principles, which were updated by a second report by Fiona Caldicott in 2013.

The Caldicott Principles[23]

1. Justify the purpose(s)

Every proposed use or transfer of personal confidential data within or from an organisation should be clearly defined, scrutinised and documented, with continuing uses regularly reviewed, by an appropriate guardian.

---

[23] *Information: to share or not to share? The Information Governance Review* (DH: London, 2013).

2. Don't use personal confidential data unless it is absolutely necessary

Personal confidential data items should not be included unless it is essential for the specified purpose(s) of that flow. The need for patients to be identified should be considered at each stage of satisfying the purpose(s).

3. Use the minimum necessary personal confidential data

Where use of personal confidential data is considered to be essential, the inclusion of each individual item of data should be considered and justified so that the minimum amount of personal confidential data is transferred or accessible as is necessary for a given function to be carried out.

4. Access to personal confidential data should be on a strict need-to-know basis

Only those individuals who need access to personal confidential data should have access to it, and they should only have access to the data items that they need to see. This may mean introducing access controls or splitting data flows where one data flow is used for several purposes.

5. Everyone with access to personal confidential data should be aware of their responsibilities

Action should be taken to ensure that those handling personal confidential data—both clinical and non-clinical staff—are made fully aware of their responsibilities and obligations to respect patient confidentiality.

6. Comply with the law

Every use of personal confidential data must be lawful. Someone in each organisation handling personal confidential data should be responsible for ensuring that the organisation complies with legal requirements.

7. The duty to share information can be as important as the duty to protect patient confidentiality

Health and social care professionals should have the confidence to share information in the best interests of their patients within the framework set out by these principles. They should be supported by the policies of their employers, regulators and professional bodies.

The Department of Health's *Confidentiality: NHS Code of Practice* lays out detailed guidance on the use of identifiable patient information,[24] supplemented in 2010 by more specific guidance on public interest disclosures. In 2014, NHS England published its *Confidentiality Policy*, which sets out 'the requirements placed on all staff when sharing information within the NHS and between NHS and non-NHS organisations', one of which is compliance with the *NHS Code of Practice*.

[24] (DH: London, 2003).

4 PATIENTS WHO LACK CAPACITY

If the legal basis for the general duty of confidence is unclear, its application to children and adults who lack capacity is even more obscure. On the one hand, it seems clear that this fundamental aspect of a doctor's duty towards her patients should be universal. Medical records self-evidently contain confidential information, and if the duty of confidentiality arises from the nature of the information itself, then it must apply equally to the records of those who lack capacity. In *Venables v News Group Newspapers*,[25] Dame Elizabeth Butler-Sloss P stated that 'Children, like adults, are entitled to confidentiality in respect of certain areas of information. Medical records are the obvious example.'

On the other hand, it will sometimes be necessary to involve others in decisions about the treatment of young children and adults who lack capacity. Obviously, a baby or young child's right to confidentiality does not involve keeping treatment information from her parents. On the contrary, a baby's parents are under a duty to take decisions about her medical treatment, and they can only do this if they are properly informed. The doctor's duty of confidentiality is therefore owed to the parent(s) and the child, rather than just to the child herself.

The House of Lords decision in the *Gillick* case (considered in detail in Chapter 5) established that children who have reached an age of sufficient maturity will in certain circumstances have the right to keep information about their medical treatment from their parents. Following *Gillick*, in *R (on the application of Axon) v Secretary of State for Health*, Silber J confirmed that 2004 Department of Health guidance, which stated that children had a right to confidentiality in relation to treatment for abortion, was lawful.

R (on the application of Axon) v Secretary of State for Health[26]

Silber J

This application raises a tension between two important principles of which the first is that a competent young person under sixteen years of age (who is able to understand all aspects of any advice, including its consequences) is an autonomous person, who first should be allowed to make decisions about his or her own health and second is entitled to confidentiality about such decisions even vis-à-vis his or her parents. The second principle is that a parent of a young person has a responsibility for that young person's health and moral welfare with the consequence that he or she should be informed if a medical professional is considering providing advice and treatment on sexual matters to that young person so that the parent could then advise and assist the young person. There is also a significant public policy dimension because there is evidence that without the guarantee of confidentiality, some of these young people might not seek advice or treatment from medical professionals on sexual matters with potentially disturbing consequences . . .

[I]n the period between the decision of the Court of Appeal in *Gillick* and that of the House of Lords during which medical professionals were required to pass on information to children's parents, the number of young women aged under 16 who sought advice on contraception fell from 1.7 per resident thousand to 1.2 per resident thousand, which was a striking and disturbing reduction of just under one-third. In addition, the rates of attendance at places

---

[25] [2001] 2 WLR 1038.   [26] [2006] EWHC 37 (Admin).

where contraception advice and treatment were given did not return until 1988–89 to their previous levels prior to the Court of Appeal decision in December 1984. These statistics provide clear and powerful evidence of what happens when young people are not assured of confidentiality when they are considering obtaining advice and treatment on sexual matters.

Interestingly, the 2004 guidance which was challenged in *Axon* did not confine a child's right of confidentiality to children who are *Gillick*-competent:

The duty of confidentiality owed to a person under 16, in any setting, is the same as that owed to any other person. This is enshrined in professional codes.

All services providing advice and treatment on contraception, sexual and reproductive health should produce an explicit confidentiality policy which reflects this guidance and makes clear that young people under 16 have the same right to confidentiality as adults.[27]

If only *Gillick*-competent children can consent to treatment without parental knowledge, then the right to have information about that treatment kept from their parents, in practice, only arises for children who are competent to give consent. Under-16s who are not *Gillick*-competent are therefore in a rather curious position. They are owed a duty of confidentiality, which may not arise in practice because their inability to give consent means that their parents will usually have to be involved in decisions about their medical treatment.

Adults who lack capacity are undoubtedly also owed a duty of confidentiality but, as we saw in Chapter 5, under section 4(7) of the Mental Capacity Act 2005 people who are involved in their care should be consulted about their wishes and beliefs. The Mental Capacity Act Code of Practice insists that the duty of confidence still applies, and that discussions with carers must be necessary and proportionate.

Mental Capacity Act 2005 Code of Practice[28]

5.56 Decision-makers must balance the duty to consult other people with the right to confidentiality of the person who lacks capacity. So if confidential information is to be discussed, they should only seek the views of people who it is appropriate to consult, where their views are relevant to the decision to be made and the particular circumstances.

5.57 There may be occasions where it is in the person's best interests for personal information (for example, about their medical condition, if the decision concerns the provision of medical treatment) to be revealed to the people consulted as part of the process of working out their best interests. Healthcare and social care staff who are trying to determine a person's best interests must follow their professional guidance, as well as other relevant guidance, about confidentiality.

The GMC guidance further suggests that doctors should seek the agreement of the adult who lacks capacity to sharing information with others, and should disclose information against their wishes only where disclosure is 'essential in their medical interests'.

---

[27] Department of Health, *Best Practice Guidance for Doctors and other Health Professionals on the Provision of Advice and Treatment to Young People under 16 on Contraception, Sexual and Reproductive Health* (DH: London, 2004).

[28] (DCA, 2014).

General Medical Council[29]

> 59. When making decisions about whether to disclose information about a patient who lacks capacity, you must:
>
> (a) make the care of the patient your first concern
>
> (b) respect the patient's dignity and privacy, and
>
> (c) support and encourage the patient to be involved, as far as they want and are able, in decisions about disclosure of their personal information. . . .
>
> 61. If a patient who lacks capacity asks you not to disclose personal information about their condition or treatment, you should try to persuade them to allow an appropriate person to be involved in the consultation. If they refuse, and you are convinced that it is essential in their best interests, you may disclose relevant information to an appropriate person or authority. In such a case you should tell the patient before disclosing the information and, if appropriate, seek and carefully consider the views of an advocate or carer. You should document in the patient's record your discussions and the reasons for deciding to disclose the information.
>
> 62. You may need to share personal information with a patient's relatives, friends or carers to enable you to assess the patient's best interests. But that does not mean they have a general right of access to the patient's records or to have irrelevant information about, for example, the patient's past healthcare. You should also share relevant personal information with anyone who is authorised to make decisions on behalf of, or who is appointed to support and represent, a mentally incapacitated patient.

In a pre-Mental Capacity Act case, *R (on the application of S) v Plymouth City Council*, Hale LJ explained that while C, a 27-year-old man with serious learning and behavioural difficulties, did have an interest, albeit 'purely theoretical', in the confidentiality of his medical records, disclosure to his mother who wished to challenge a local social services authority's recommendation, was both necessary and proportionate.

R (on the application of S) v Plymouth City Council[30]

Hale LJ

> C's interest in protecting the confidentiality of personal information about himself must not be underestimated. It is all too easy for professionals and parents to regard children and incapacitated adults as having no independent interests of their own: as objects rather than subjects. But we are not concerned here with the publication of information to the whole wide world. There is a clear distinction between disclosure to the media with a view to publication to all and sundry and disclosure in confidence to those with a proper interest in having the information in question. . . .
>
> There is no suggestion that C has any objection to his mother and her advisers being properly informed about his health and welfare. There is no suggestion of any risk to his health and welfare arising from this. The mother and her advisers have sought access to the information which her own psychiatric and social work experts need in order properly to advise her. That limits both the context and the content of disclosure in a way which strikes a proper balance between the competing interests.

---

[29] *Confidentiality* (GMC, 2009).   [30] [2002] EWCA Civ 388.

Degenerative brain diseases, such as Alzheimer's and other types of dementia, raise particularly difficult questions in relation to patient confidentiality. Depending on the stage the patient has reached when her dementia is diagnosed, her partner or relatives may have to be involved in the diagnostic process, and in decisions about her care. Indeed, Pucci et al's research indicated that most relatives of patients suffering from Alzheimer's disease believed that the patient should not be told about the diagnosis, for fear of provoking or aggravating depressive symptoms.[31]

As the Nuffield Council on Bioethics has pointed out, carers of people with dementia need both support and information in order to fulfil their caring role.

Nuffield Council on Bioethics[32]

3.22 Whilst the principle of patient confidentiality is an important one in the doctor–patient relationship, a diagnosis of dementia has implications not only for the person with dementia, but also for close family members who are likely to take on a significant caring role and need appropriate information and support to do so. . . .

7.26 When a person with dementia lacks capacity to make a particular decision about their health or welfare, it is clearly in their best interests that those involved in making the decision on their behalf have access to the necessary information and are appropriately supported. Professionals should be made aware of the legitimate reasons why carers may ask for medical or other confidential information, and ordinarily start from the assumption that if a carer is involved in making a decision on behalf of the person with dementia, then they will need the same level of information as any other member of the care team. In short, carers should be provided with any information that it is necessary for them to know in order to carry out their caring role.

5 DECEASED PATIENTS

Does the duty of confidentiality survive a patient's death? The Department of Health's Code of Practice[33] and GMC Guidance are both clear that the *ethical* duty to respect patient confidentiality continues to exist after the patient has died.

General Medical Council[34]

70. Your duty of confidentiality continues after a patient has died. Whether and what personal information may be disclosed after a patient's death will depend on the circumstances. If the patient had asked for information to remain confidential, you should usually respect their wishes. If you are unaware of any instructions from the patient, when you are considering requests for information you should take into account:

(a) whether the disclosure of information is likely to cause distress to, or be of benefit to, the patient's partner or family

---

[31] E Pucci et al, 'Relatives' attitudes towards informing patients about the diagnosis of Alzheimer's disease' (2003) 29 Journal of Medical Ethics 51–4.

[32] *Dementia: Ethical Issues* (NCOB, 2009).

[33] *Confidentiality: NHS Code of Practice* (DH: London, 2003) para 12.

[34] *Confidentiality* (GMC, 2009)

(b) whether the disclosure will also disclose information about the patient's family or anyone else

(c) whether the information is already public knowledge or can be anonymised or coded, and

(d) the purpose of the disclosure . . .

Until relatively recently, it was unclear whether the legal duty of confidence survived death, and the assumption had been that it did not.

Reporting restrictions which were intended to protect a patient's family or medical team could continue after the patient's death, however. For example, in *Re C (Adult Patient: Restriction of Publicity After Death)*, an order restricting the identification of a patient in a permanent vegetative state had been made at the same time as an order authorizing the withdrawal of treatment from him. After his death, the court was asked for confirmation that the order remained effective, and Sir Stephen Brown P held that it did.

Re C (Adult Patient: Restriction of Publicity After Death)[35]

Sir Stephen Brown P

I have already referred to the potential effect on medical and other staff, knowing that on the death of the patient their anonymity would be lost and that that might well have some detrimental effect upon the way in which they might care for the patient. I believe that that consideration also applies to the parents and members of the family of the patient, and to such people in future cases. I am also satisfied that there is a principle of medical confidentiality which is relevant in the context of the facts of this case and similar cases. It is a further matter of public interest that those who may be faced with considering the making of an application of the kind which was made in this case should be untrammelled by the fear of publicity in coming to the very sensitive and fundamental decision which it involves.

Notice that while Sir Stephen Brown P refers to medical confidentiality, his principal concern is with the interests of those caring for the patient, rather than with whether the patient himself has a right to confidentiality after death.

That question arose in *Lewis v Secretary of State for Health*, a case in which a doctor had been reluctant to disclose patient records, after the patients' deaths, to the Redfern Inquiry, which was investigating the removal and retention of tissue samples from individuals who had worked at the Sellafield nuclear plant. The first question for Foskett J was whether it was at least arguable that the duty of confidentiality applied after these patients' deaths. Having concluded that it was, he decided that disclosure could nevertheless be justified in the public interest.

---

[35] [1996] 1 FCR 605.

Lewis v Secretary of State for Health[36]

Foskett J

There is no doubt that it is the view of those who administer the medical profession, both in the United Kingdom and worldwide, that the professional obligation of the doctor is to maintain the medical confidences of the patient after the patient's death. The Hippocratic oath, the Declaration of Geneva and guidance given by the General Medical Council all point to this professional obligation. The content of an obligation imposed upon a professional by his profession is not, of course, necessarily coterminous with the obligation imposed by law in similar circumstances although it may be a useful indicator of the perceived values by which the relationship of the professional to his client (in this case, patient) are to be judged.

In the course of argument, I ventured the proposition that if anyone is asked whether they thought that something said in confidence to their doctor would remain confidential after their death, the answer would almost certainly be 'yes'. That seems to me to accord with contemporary notions of what is accepted practice and indeed it might even reflect notions of what the law, not merely professional ethics, may require . . .

[T]he period for which the obligation can be expected to continue will depend on many circumstances . . .. The more intimate and sensitive the type of examination, and the more sensitive the kind of results obtained, the more onerous and prolonged would be the obligation to maintain confidence . . .

I have not the slightest doubt that this is an appropriate case in which to hold that the public interest in disclosure of the material sought outweighs the other public interest, namely, that of maintaining the confidentiality of medical records and information, provided, of course, proper safeguards are put in place to ensure that no inappropriate information becomes public.

In support of this conclusion I would merely say that there is plainly a public interest (and by that I mean not just 'the interest of the public') in determining what happened and why in connection with the very difficult and sensitive issues that arise from these matters. Those families that know broadly what happened are entitled to fuller answers to the questions raised if they wish to have them and there is a wider public interest in maintaining confidence in the NHS and the nuclear industry.

This was followed by *Press Association v Newcastle Hospitals Foundation Trust*, in which the Press Association sought to discharge a reporting restriction order which had prevented them from naming a woman who had since died. Peter Jackson J had declared that it would be lawful for LM's doctors to withhold the blood transfusion to which she had refused to consent. LM was a Jehovah's Witness with no relatives or close friends. The Press Association had submitted that anonymity was no longer necessary because LM had died. Peter Jackson J held that the court did have the power to preserve anonymity after death, but that, in the present case, that power should not be exercised and LM's identity could be disclosed.

---

[36] [2008] EWHC 2196 (QB).

Press Association v Newcastle Hospitals Foundation Trust[37]

Peter Jackson J

It is not in dispute between the parties that the court has the power to make an order preventing the reporting of the deceased's name in order to uphold the rights of others, such as medical or care staff or family members . . .. What is in dispute is the existence of any independent right to protection for the deceased person herself. This comes into sharp focus in LM's case, because she had no known family or friends. In consequence, she cannot be kept anonymous for the sake of others . . .

None of the information given in the judgment or referred to during the hearing is of particular sensitivity or confidentiality, nor does it reflect any discredit on LM. The physical, mental and spiritual challenges that she faced could confront anyone. Also, her way of life, whether better described as independent or isolated, makes it unlikely that any wider harm will come from linking her name with her story.

There is a proper interest in the name of a person who dies being a matter of public record, whether or not there is to be an inquest. The right to privacy is only likely to outweigh this consideration in very special circumstances . . ..

I take account of the fact that LM was a private person who would not have wanted her private information to be made public. I also have regard to her medical confidentiality. In this instance, that has not been extensively breached. The fact that she suffered from mental illness would have been apparent to those who knew her and little detail is given of her physical illness. Nor can it be said that to reveal her name would deter applications in similar situations when the degree of scrutiny given to this case is considered.

All things considered, I find that the balance in this case falls in favour of discharging that part of the order that confers anonymity on LM. But there is a balance to be struck, and in other cases the conclusion might be different.

Towards the end of 2015, there was considerable press interest in the Court of Protection's decision, in *Kings College NHS Foundation Trust v C*,[38] that a 50-year-old woman who was said to have lost her 'sparkle' had capacity, and was therefore entitled to refuse dialysis. After her death, a reporting restriction order remained in place, pending a full hearing. In granting a time-limited extension, Theis J weighed in the balance that much of the evidence 'reflects discredit on C', inevitably causing distress to her family, especially her 15-year-old daughter and grandson, while there was 'no public interest in C or her family being identified'.[39] A week later, that order was continued by Charles J, pending the submission of further evidence by the media.[40] At the time of writing, that evidence has not been received and the reporting restriction remains in place.

It therefore appears that the right to confidentiality can survive a person's death, but also that it may be easier to establish that this is outweighed by other considerations after the person is dead. In the next extract, Mary Donnelly and Maeve McDonagh explain why the living have an interest in the maintenance of confidentiality after a patient's death.

---

[37] [2014] EWCOP 6.   [38] [2015] EWCOP 80.

[39] *Re V (Out of Hours Reporting Restriction Order)* [2015] EWCOP 83.

[40] *V v Associated Newspapers* [2015] EWCOP 88.

Mary Donnelly and Maeve McDonagh[41]

> In light of the conceptual challenges faced by accounts of posthumous harm, it may be more helpful to focus on a less ambitious case in favour of protecting the 'interests' of the dead. This argument is not that the dead are harmed by posthumous events but that the living may be harmed by the prospect of posthumous events. . . . Thus, the interests of the living person may be harmed, not by the attribution of posthumous harm . . . , but by the prospect that post-humous harm will occur. If a living person cannot be confident that, for example, a degree of respect will be shown to his or her dead body or that his or her wishes will be respected after death, then he or she may experience harm in the sense of considerable anxiety and unhappiness while alive. The same might be said in respect of a person's broader reputation or place in his or her family's affections. The thought that this would be threatened after his or her death would no doubt be a source of considerable concern to a (living) person. Thus, one might reasonably argue that failure to accord a certain degree of protection to the dead could significantly harm the interests of the living.

Insofar as one of the reasons to respect confidentiality after death is the distress disclosure could cause to surviving relatives, the duty of confidentiality owed to the dead will, as GMC guidance points out, weaken with the passage of time.

General Medical Council[42]

> 72. Archived records relating to deceased patients remain subject to a duty of confidentiality, although the potential for disclosing information about, or causing distress to, surviving relatives or damaging the public's trust will diminish over time.

We can see a particularly clear example of the duty of confidentiality to the dead dwindling in the case of *Éditions Plon v France*. Ten days after the death of François Mitterrand, who had been the French President, his doctor sought to publish a book which revealed that Mitterrand had been suffering from cancer for the whole of his presidency. Mitterrand's widow and children sought, and were granted, a temporary injunction to prevent publication. According to the judge who granted the injunction:

> By their very nature, they constitute a particularly serious intrusion into the intimate sphere of President François Mitterrand's private family life and that of his wife and children. The resulting interference is especially intolerable in that it has occurred within a few days of President Mitterrand's death and burial.

Ten months later, a court had continued these injunctions and that decision was subsequently challenged before the ECtHR. Interestingly, in *Éditions Plon v France*, the ECtHR found that ten months after Mitterrand's death, the balance had shifted and the public interest in free expression now outweighed the duty to respect the medical secrets of the dead.

---

[41] 'Keeping the Secrets of the Dead? An Evaluation of the Statutory Framework for Access to Information About Deceased Persons' (2011) 31 Legal Studies 42–70.

[42] *Confidentiality* (GMC, 2009).

Éditions Plon v France[43]

Judgment of the ECtHR

[B]y October 23, 1996, when the Paris *tribunal de grande instance* gave judgment, François Mitterrand had been dead for nine-and-a-half months. Clearly, the context was no longer the same as on January 18, 1996, when the urgent-applications judge issued the interim injunction prohibiting the distribution of *Le Grand Secret*. The judge issued the injunction the day after the book's publication, which itself had taken place barely 10 days after President Mitterrand's death; as the Court has already held, distribution of the book so soon after the President's death could only have intensified the legitimate emotions of the deceased's relatives, who inherited the rights vested in him. In the Court's opinion, as the President's death became more distant in time, this factor became less important. Likewise, the more time that elapsed, the more the public interest in discussion of the history of President Mitterrand's two terms of office prevailed over the requirements of protecting the President's rights with regard to medical confidentiality.

6 EXCEPTIONS TO THE DUTY OF CONFIDENTIALITY

As was noted earlier, the duty of confidentiality is not absolute, and a number of exceptions exist which we flesh out in the following sections. Before we consider them, it is worth noting that breaches of confidentiality do not always involve deliberate decisions to share information. Rather, inadvertent breaches of confidentiality are probably more common. NHS inpatients spend most of their time on wards, which may mean that their conversations with doctors and nurses may be overheard by others. Patients' physical privacy can be protected by curtains, but it is harder to ensure the confidentiality of discussions at the patient's bedside. Where there is particularly sensitive information to impart, it might therefore be important to ensure that the patient is given the opportunity to receive it in private.

Patient data might also be inadvertently shared through breaches of IT security. Sophisticated encryption systems can be used to protect electronic patient records, but they cannot eliminate simple human errors, like leaving information on a computer screen visible to other people. NHS England's *Confidentiality Policy* reminds staff of the importance of avoiding carelessness.

NHS England[44]

4.4 Carelessness

4.4.1 All staff have a legal duty of confidence to keep person-identifiable or confidential information private and not to divulge information accidentally. Staff may be held personally liable for a breach of confidence and must not:

- Talk about person-identifiable or confidential information in public places or where they can be overheard.

---

[43] (2006) 42 EHRR 36.
[44] *Confidentiality Policy* (NHS England, 2014).

- Leave any person-identifiable or confidential information lying around unattended, this includes telephone messages, computer printouts, faxes and other documents, and

- Leave a computer terminal logged on to a system where person-identifiable or confidential information can be accessed, unattended.

(a) CONSENT

If the patient explicitly consents to the disclosure of information, the doctor is clearly no longer under a duty keep it secret. This is not strictly speaking an exception to the duty of confidence: rather, the patient's agreement to disclosure means that no duty of confidence exists.

More complicated is the question of whether a patient could ever be said to have given their implied consent to disclosure. The British Medical Association's *Confidentiality Toolkit* suggests that:

In the absence of evidence to the contrary, patients are normally considered to have given implied consent for the use of their information by health professionals for the purpose of the care they receive. Information sharing in this context is acceptable to the extent that health professionals share what is necessary and relevant for patient care on a 'need to know' basis.[45]

In order to establish that there was implied consent to disclosure, as the GMC's guidance to doctors and the Department of Health's Code of Practice make clear,[46] the patient must be aware of the practice of disclosure and given an opportunity to object to it.

General Medical Council[47]

7. You should make sure that information is readily available to patients explaining that, unless they object, their personal information may be disclosed for the sake of their own care and for local clinical audit. Patients usually understand that information about them has to be shared within the healthcare team to provide their care. But it is not always clear to patients that others who support the provision of care might also need to have access to their personal information. And patients may not be aware of disclosures to others for purposes other than their care, such as service planning or medical research. You must inform patients about disclosures for purposes they would not reasonably expect, or check that they have already received information about such disclosures.

If a patient undergoes a medical examination requested by a third party, such as an employer, could it be said that she has impliedly consented to the disclosure of the medical report to that third party? In the Court of Appeal decision in *Kapadia v London Borough of Lambeth*, *obiter dicta* suggested that the patient's consent to disclosure could be implied from her agreement to undergo the examination. In this case an employee, who claimed that he had been discriminated against on the grounds of disability, had refused to consent to the disclosure of a medical report to his employer, unless he was given the opportunity to see it first.

---

[45] *Confidentiality and Disclosure of Health Information Tool Kit* (BMA, 2008).
[46] *Confidentiality: NHS Code of Practice* (DH: London, 2003) para 14.
[47] *Confidentiality* (GMC, 2009).

According to Pill LJ, having agreed to the examination, the employee's further consent to the report's disclosure was not required.

Kapadia v London Borough of Lambeth[48]

> **Pill LJ**
>
> On the facts the court knows, the report should, in my judgment, have been disclosed by the doctor to the employers. No further consent was required from the claimant. By consenting to being examined on behalf of the employers the claimant was consenting to the disclosure to the employers of a report resulting from that examination. A practice under which a person who has agreed to be examined in circumstances such as these, but then claims a veto upon disclosure of the report to those who obtained it is not, in my view, a good practice. Indeed it is an impediment to the fair and expeditious conduct of litigation.

(b) PUBLIC INTEREST

Probably the most important exception to the duty of confidentiality is where the public interest in disclosure of information outweighs the public interest in protecting patient confidentiality. In *Attorney General v Guardian Newspapers*,[49] Lord Goff explained that:

> although the basis of the law's protection of confidence is that there is a public interest that confidences should be preserved and protected by the law, nevertheless that public interest may be outweighed by some other countervailing public interest which favours disclosure.

Because there is a strong public interest in protecting confidentiality, only weighty countervailing public interest factors will override the doctor's prima facie duty of confidence, and disclosures should always be justified and kept to a minimum. In the following sections we consider several overlapping public interest justifications for the disclosure of confidential information.

(1) Preventing Harm to Others

Where the possibility of harm to others is used to justify disclosure, there should be a real risk of serious harm.

General Medical Council[50]

> 36. There is a clear public good in having a confidential medical service. . . . However, there can also be a public interest in disclosing information: to protect individuals or society from risks of serious harm, such as serious communicable diseases or serious crime . . .
>
> 37. Personal information may therefore be disclosed in the public interest, without patients' consent, and in exceptional cases where patients have withheld consent, if the benefits to an individual or to society of the disclosure outweigh both the public and the patient's interest in

---

[48] (2000) 57 BMLR 170.
[49] [1988] 3 WLR 776.   [50] *Confidentiality* (GMC, 2009).

> keeping the information confidential. You must weigh the harms that are likely to arise from non-disclosure of information against the possible harm both to the patient, and to the overall trust between doctors and patients, arising from the release of that information.

W v Egdell is a relatively straightforward example of the public interest in disclosure trumping the public interest in protecting confidentiality. W had killed five people and wounded two others, and had been detained in a secure hospital. His application for release was turned down. His solicitors commissioned an independent psychiatrist's report from Dr Egdell, which indicated that W continued to pose a risk to the public. Dr Egdell disclosed this information both to the hospital and to the Secretary of State. W applied unsuccessfully for an injunction to stop them from using the report and damages for breach of confidence.

W v Egdell[51]

Bingham LJ

There is one consideration which in my judgment, as in that of the judge, weighs the balance of public interest decisively in favour of disclosure. It may be shortly put. Where a man has committed multiple killings under the disability of serious mental illness, decisions which may lead directly or indirectly to his release from hospital should not be made unless a responsible authority is properly able to make an informed judgment that the risk of repetition is so small as to be acceptable. A consultant psychiatrist who becomes aware, even in the course of a confidential relationship, of information which leads him, in the exercise of what the court considers a sound professional judgment, to fear that such decisions may be made on the basis of inadequate information and with a real risk of consequent danger to the public is entitled to take such steps as are reasonable in all the circumstances to communicate the grounds of his concern to the responsible authorities.

While the balancing exercise in *W v Egdell* was relatively straightforward, other situations may be less clear-cut. What if the patient has never actually harmed anyone, but has violent thoughts or fantasies?

In the well-known US case *Tarasoff v Regents of the University of California*, the patient, Poddar, had confided in a university psychotherapist, Dr Moore, that he intended to harm T, a fellow student who had rejected his advances. The therapist informed the university police, but did not inform T herself, whom the patient subsequently murdered. The California Supreme Court held that the university's employee was under a duty to protect T by disclosing these threats to her.

Tarasoff v Regents of the University of California[52]

Justice Trobriner

When a therapist determines, or pursuant to the standards of his profession should determine, that his patient presents a serious danger of violence to another, he incurs an obligation to use reasonable care to protect the intended victim against such danger . . . We

---

[51] [1990] Ch 359.   [52] 551 P 2d 334 (Cal 1976).

> conclude that the public policy favoring protection of the confidential character of patient–psychotherapist communications must yield to the extent to which disclosure is essential to avert danger to others. The protective privilege ends where the public peril begins.

Commenting on the likely response to a *Tarasoff*-type case in the UK, McLean and Mason have suggested that 'the probability is that there would be no legal obligation to warn the person at risk but that, should the doctor do so, the breach of confidentiality would be regarded as justified'.[53] In short, both warning and not warning would be within the bounds of acceptable conduct. Doctors are therefore in the difficult position of having to make a judgement about whether the circumstances justify the disclosure of information acquired in confidence.

While there is plainly a public interest in preventing a patient from harming someone else, routine disclosure in such circumstances might make patients reluctant to share information about their fantasies with their psychotherapists, which in turn might make it more likely that their underlying problems will remain untreated. Paradoxically, then, routinely breaching the confidentiality of potentially dangerous patients might increase the risks such patients pose to others. This point was made forcefully by Clark J in his dissenting judgment in *Tarasoff*.

Justice Clark

Assurance of confidentiality is important for three reasons. First, without substantial assurance of confidentiality, those requiring treatment will be deterred from seeking assistance. . . . Second, the guarantee of confidentiality is essential in eliciting the full disclosure necessary for effective treatment . . . Third, even if the patient fully discloses his thoughts, assurance that the confidential relationship will not be breached is necessary to maintain his trust in his psychiatrist—the very means by which treatment is effected . . .

By imposing a duty to warn, the majority contributes to the danger to society of violence by the mentally ill and greatly increases the risk of civil commitment—the total deprivation of liberty—of those who should not be confined. Although . . . only a relatively few receiving treatment will ever present a risk of violence, the number making threats is huge, and it is the latter group—not just the former—whose treatment will be impaired and whose risk of commitment will be increased.

Here there is an overlap with an issue we considered in the previous chapter, namely that if mentally ill people fear that coercive measures will be taken against them, they may avoid contact with health care professionals and this could, in fact, increase the risk they pose to others.

Similar difficulties arise in relation to communicable diseases. If a doctor knows that an HIV-positive individual has not informed his sexual partner of his HIV status, does the public interest in disclosure trump the public interest in protecting confidentiality? Although it might at first sight seem that alerting his sexual partner may enable that person to take steps to avoid infection, there are two reasons why confidentiality should prevail. First, there has always been a strong public interest in encouraging people to come forward for HIV testing and treatment, by promising them confidentiality in relation to their test results. Secondly, now that it is clear that someone whose viral load is being effectively controlled

---

[53] *Legal and Ethical Aspects of Healthcare* (Greenwich Medical Media: London, 2003) 42.

by antiretroviral medication is considerably less likely to pass on the disease, treating the patient may be a more effective way to prevent onward transmission than breaching his confidentiality.

What if the HIV-positive person is also a health care worker? The risk of HIV transmission by health care workers is negligible: there have only ever been three reported cases worldwide.[54] Guidance from Public Health England is clear that only HIV-positive health care workers whose viral load is below a certain level should be cleared to perform exposure-prone procedures.[55] Regular retesting is required. If a health care worker refuses to be tested, he or she will not be cleared to perform exposure-prone procedures. Where there has been a risk that a patient has been exposed to a health care worker's blood, the patient should be informed and post-exposure prophylaxis offered only where a fresh blood test reveals that the health care worker's viral load is now above the specified level.

Before it became possible to judge through testing the likelihood of an HIV-positive health care worker passing on the virus, and before regular HIV testing became mandatory for workers carrying out exposure-prone procedures, there were cases in which the courts had to balance the confidentiality of HIV-positive health care workers with other considerations, such as press freedom. In *H (A Healthcare Worker) v Associated Newspapers Ltd*, for example, H was a health care worker, who had been diagnosed as HIV-positive. He notified his employers, N Health Authority, which proposed to carry out a 'lookback' exercise, that is, to notify H's patients and offer them advice and an HIV test. Citing evidence that no infected patient had ever been identified by one of these lookback exercises, H claimed that it would be unlawful. Meanwhile, the *Mail on Sunday* wanted to publish a story about H's action against N.

H obtained an injunction restraining the soliciting or publication of any information which might directly or indirectly lead to the disclosure of his identity, or his whereabouts, or his speciality. The Court of Appeal stressed the importance of maintaining patient confidentiality, and granted orders restraining the publication of information of H's and N's identity. It refused to order that his speciality too should be kept secret. The risk that this would reveal H's identity was too small to justify inhibiting debate 'on what is a matter of public interest'.

H (A Healthcare Worker) v Associated Newspapers Ltd[56]

Lord Phillips MR

The consequences to H if his identity were to be disclosed would be likely to be distressing on a personal level. More than this, there is an obvious public interest in preserving the confidentiality of victims of the AIDS epidemic and, in particular, of healthcare workers who report the fact that they are HIV positive. Where a lookback exercise follows, it may prove impossible to preserve the identification of the worker but, if healthcare workers are not to be discouraged from reporting that they are HIV positive, it is essential that all possible steps are taken to preserve the confidentiality of such reports.

There is clearly a difference between disclosing information about a health care professional's health status to the press and disclosing it to an employer or to the GMC. Where a health care worker might be putting patients or colleagues at risk because of her failure to disclose

---

[54] Public Health England, *The management of HIV infected healthcare workers who perform exposure prone procedures: updated guidance* (PHE, 2014).
[55] Ibid.   [56] [2002] EWCA Civ 195.

relevant information about her health, disclosing this to an appropriate person will not be a breach of confidentiality, whereas publicly broadcasting the same information might be. This was the issue in *Saha v General Medical Council*, in which Stephen Morris QC, sitting as a High Court Judge, explained that informing the GMC about a doctor's Hepatitis B status did not amount to a breach of his confidentiality.

Saha v General Medical Council[57]

Stephen Morris QC

Medical confidentiality is not an absolute right, but necessarily involves a balancing of competing public interests. The public interest in patient safety and welfare is an extremely important consideration. A further highly relevant consideration is the persons to whom the disclosure has taken place or is envisaged; disclosure to a person who is aware of the confidentiality and who has a role in its consideration or evaluation (such as a health care worker) is to be distinguished from general disclosure or publication . . .

In my judgment, the disclosure by the three doctors of the Appellant's records, ultimately, to the GMC was justified by reference to the concerns that each of them had at the relevant time, and indeed each was under a duty to do so.

(2) Preventing or Detecting Crime

Both GMC guidance and the Department of Health Code of Practice specifically mention that disclosure of confidential information may be justified where it would assist in the prevention or detection of a serious crime.

Department of Health[58]

30. Under common law, staff are permitted to disclose personal information in order to prevent and support detection, investigation and punishment of serious crime and/or to prevent abuse or serious harm to others where they judge, on a case by case basis, that the public good that would be achieved by disclosure outweighs both the obligation of confidentiality to the individual patient concerned and the broader public interest in the provision of a confidential service.

31. Whoever authorizes disclosure must make a record of any such circumstances, so that there is clear evidence of the reasoning used and the circumstances prevailing. Disclosures in the public interest should also be proportionate and be limited to relevant details . . .

32. Wherever possible the issue of disclosure should be discussed with the individual concerned and consent sought. Where this is not forthcoming, the individual should be told of any decision to disclose against his/her wishes. This will not be possible in certain circumstances, e.g. where the likelihood of a violent response is significant or where informing a potential suspect in a criminal investigation might allow them to evade custody, destroy evidence or disrupt an investigation.

---

[57] [2009] EWHC 1907 (Admin).
[58] *Confidentiality: NHS Code of Practice* (DH: London, 2003).

Section 11 of the Police and Criminal Evidence Act 1984 classifies medical records as 'excluded material' to which the police will not usually be allowed access. An exception exists if the police are investigating a 'serious arrestable offence'.[59] In such cases, the police may obtain a special procedure warrant that will require the disclosure of medical records. During a trial, the judge has discretion to excuse a witness from answering a question when it would involve a breach of confidence, but equally he can order that confidential information is disclosed if it is necessary in the interests of justice.

Under section 172 of the Road Traffic Act 1988, a person can be required to give information which may lead to the identification of a driver who is alleged to have committed certain offences. In *Hunter v Mann*, a doctor had treated two people who had been involved in a car crash on the same day as a hit-and-run accident had occurred. A police officer asked the doctor to disclose the names and addresses of the two people he had treated, but he refused on the grounds that he would be breaching his duty of confidentiality. He was convicted under the Road Traffic Act 1972 (which preceded the 1988 Act), and this was upheld on appeal.

Hunter v Mann[60]

Boreham J

May I say, before leaving this case, that I appreciate the concern of a responsible medical practitioner who feels that he is faced with a conflict of duty. That the appellant in this case was conscious of a conflict and realised his duty both to society and to his patient is clear from the finding of the justices, but he may find comfort, although the decision goes against him, from the following. First that he has only to disclose information which may lead to identification and not other confidential matters; secondly that the result, in my judgment, is entirely consistent with the rules that the British Medical Association have laid down.

Often, of course, disclosure justified by the need to prevent serious crime could also be justified by the 'harm to others' exception we have just considered. But the two are not necessarily synonymous. There is a public interest in the detection of crime even when there is no immediate risk of reoffending, and even when the crime itself did not involve physical injury, though obviously, the less serious the criminal offence, the less likely that the public interest in protecting confidentiality will be trumped by the public interest in facilitating the prevention and detection of crime.

In 2010, the Department of Health issued supplementary guidance on public interest disclosures which explains that although some crimes are clearly 'serious', and would justify breaching confidentiality, there are also grey areas where judgements have to be made.

Department of Health[61]

12. . . . 'Serious crime' is not clearly defined in law but will include crimes that cause serious physical or psychological harm to individuals. This will certainly include murder, manslaughter, rape, treason, kidnapping, and child abuse or neglect causing significant harm and

---

[59] Schedule 1.   [60] [1974] QB 767.
[61] *Confidentiality: NHS Code of Practice Supplementary Guidance: Public Interest Disclosures* (DH: London, 2010).

will likely include other crimes which carry a five-year minimum prison sentence but may also include other acts that have a high impact on the victim.

13. On the other hand, theft, fraud or damage to property where loss or damage is not substantial are less likely to constitute a serious crime and as such may not warrant breach of confidential information, though proportionality is important here. It may, for example, be possible to disclose some information about an individual's involvement in crime without disclosing any clinical information.

14. In the grey area between these two extremes a judgement is required to assess whether the crime is sufficiently serious to warrant disclosure. The wider context is particularly important here. Sometimes crime may be considered as serious where there is a prolonged period of incidents even though none of them might be serious on its own (e.g. as sometimes occurs with child neglect). Serious fraud or theft involving significant NHS resources would be likely to harm individuals waiting for treatment. A comparatively minor prescription fraud might be serious if prescriptions for controlled drugs are being forged.

The GMC has issued specific guidance on what doctors should do where they suspect that a patient has been a victim of gun or knife crime. The police should be informed quickly whenever a person arrives at hospital with a gunshot wound or an injury from an attack with a knife, blade, or other sharp instrument. At this initial stage, personal information should not be disclosed, but, if the police seek further information, doctors may disclose this without the patient's consent if they believe that someone else may be at risk, or in order to assist in the detection of serious crime, such as gun and knife crime. Of course, the potential downside to routine disclosure in such cases is that if an injured person fears either retribution or their own arrest, it might act as a disincentive to seeking medical attention for what might be very serious injuries.

General Medical Council[62]

5. The police should be informed whenever a person arrives at hospital with a gunshot wound. Even accidental shootings involving lawfully held guns raise serious issues for the police about, for example, gun licensing.

6. The police should also be informed when a person arrives at a hospital with a wound from an attack with a knife, blade or other sharp instrument.

7. The police should not usually be informed if a knife or blade injury is accidental, or a result of self-harm. . . .

9. Personal information, such as the patient's name and address, should not usually be disclosed in the initial contact with the police . . .

12. If it is probable that a crime has been committed, the police will ask for more information. If the patient cannot give consent because, for example, they are unconscious, or refuses to disclose information or to allow you or your colleagues to do so, you can still disclose information if it is required by law or if you believe it is justified in the public interest.

13. Disclosures in the public interest may be justified when:

   (a) failure to disclose information may put the patient, or someone else, at risk of death or serious harm, or

   (b) disclosure is likely to help in the prevention, detection or prosecution of a serious crime.

---

[62] *GMC supplementary guidance: reporting gunshot and knife wounds* (GMC, 2009).

It is worth noting that disclosure has also been justified in non-criminal proceedings. In *A Health Authority v X*,[63] a complex case involving disciplinary procedures for medical malpractice, the Court of Appeal held that disclosure, subject to conditions, would be justified on the grounds that the administration of disciplinary proceedings was analogous to the administration of criminal justice. According to Thorpe LJ: 'There is obviously a high public interest, analogous to the public interest in the due administration of criminal justice, in the proper administration of professional disciplinary hearings, particularly in the field of medicine.'

Similarly, in *Woolgar v Chief Constable of the Sussex Police*, the Court of Appeal held that the police were entitled to disclose information to a professional regulatory body on public interest grounds. Following the death of a patient in her care, and allegations of the over-administration of diamorphine, W, a registered nurse, had been arrested and interviewed by the police. No criminal charges were brought. The regulatory body for nursing and midwifery sought access to those interviews and W, and the Royal College of Nursing on her behalf, resisted this on the grounds that a person who is interviewed by the police has a reasonable expectation that what they say will go no further. The Court of Appeal accepted that there was an expectation of confidentiality, but that this was outweighed by a stronger public interest in disclosure.

Woolgar v Chief Constable of the Sussex Police[64]

Kennedy LJ

Even if there is no request from the regulatory body, it seems to me that if the police come into possession of confidential information which, in their reasonable view, in the interests of public health or safety, should be considered by a professional or regulatory body, then the police are free to pass that information to the relevant regulatory body for its consideration.

(3) Teaching, Research, and Audit

Without access to patient information, it would be impossible to train medical staff, conduct clinical research, and carry out audits of patient care. Usually, of course, the patient's consent to the use of her medical notes should be sought. But in certain circumstances, disclosure without consent may be legitimate. Initially, fitting this within the 'harm to others' exception that we considered earlier might seem unpromising, since the benefits to patients from well-trained staff, properly tested treatments, and regulated services, although substantial, are not sufficiently direct or immediate to establish that any particular instance of disclosure will avert an immediate risk of death or serious injury.

Remember, however, that the balancing exercise does not just involve looking at the harm that might be prevented by disclosure, but also involves taking into account the importance of respecting patient confidentiality in the particular case. Where the disclosure involves the use of medical records in an epidemiological study, with no intention to disclose the patient's identity, or to feed any information back to her, the public interest in protecting secrecy may be more easily outweighed by the public interest in improved health care provision.

---

[63] [2001] EWCA Civ 2014.   [64] [1999] 3 All ER 604.

For research purposes, it may be possible to anonymize data, and in *R v Department of Health, ex parte Source Informatics*, the Court of Appeal decided that disclosing anonymized information cannot amount to a breach of confidence. The applicants had paid GPs and pharmacists for anonymized information from prescription forms, which they then sold to pharmaceutical companies. The Department of Health had issued advice that anonymization did not remove the duty of confidence, and that general practitioners and pharmacists should not participate in the scheme. The applicants applied for judicial review, seeking a declaration that the Department of Health's policy guidance was wrong. Latham J dismissed their application, and they appealed successfully to the Court of Appeal.

R v Department of Health, ex parte Source Informatics[65]

Simon Brown LJ

To my mind the one clear and consistent theme emerging from all these authorities is this: the confidant is placed under a duty of good faith to the confider and the touchstone by which to judge the scope of his duty and whether or not it has been fulfilled or breached is his own conscience, no more and no less. One asks, therefore, on the facts of this case: would a reasonable pharmacist's conscience be troubled by the proposed use to be made of patients' prescriptions? Would he think that by entering Source's scheme he was breaking his customers' confidence, making unconscientious use of the information they provide? . . .

In my judgment the answer is plain. The concern of the law here is to protect the confider's personal privacy. That and that alone is the right at issue in this case. The patient has no proprietorial claim to the prescription form or to the information it contains. . . .

If, as I conclude, his only legitimate interest is in the protection of his privacy and, if that is safeguarded, I fail to see how his will could be thought thwarted or his personal integrity undermined. . . . [I]n a case involving personal confidences I would hold . . . that the confidence is not breached where the confider's identity is protected . . .

I would . . . hold simply that pharmacists' consciences ought not reasonably to be troubled by co-operation with Source's proposed scheme. The patient's privacy will have been safeguarded, not invaded. The pharmacist's duty of confidence will not have been breached.

The Data Protection Act 1998 raises another question in relation to the anonymization of records. While completely anonymized data is not covered by the Act, it will often be difficult to ensure that there is no possibility of linking the individual and their information. If linkage is possible, then the Data Protection Act applies to the processing of that information.

Even if the law is clear that the disclosure of anonymized records is not a breach of confidence, the process of anonymization itself undoubtedly involves the 'processing' of sensitive personal data, and will therefore be subject to the Data Protection Act. Under the First Data Protection Principle, this must be done fairly and lawfully. If the patient has not specifically consented to the anonymization, it would have to be established that it was 'necessary' under Schedule 2, and done for 'medical purposes' under Schedule 3.

With respect, it is not clear that either requirement is easily satisfied in the *Source Informatics* case. Certainly, it would be hard to argue that anonymizing data so that it could be sold to pharmaceutical companies, and used for marketing purposes, is 'necessary' for the exercise of public functions under Schedule 2. While it might be possible to argue that it

---

[65] [2001] QB 424.

was done for 'medical purposes' under Schedule 3, it could equally plausibly be argued that the marketing of medicines is not a medical purpose. In any event, it was not the pharmaceutical companies which were anonymizing the data. Rather, Source Informatics did this purely for financial gain, and it would be difficult to argue that increasing a private company's profits was a medical purpose.

There is a further problem with the application of the Data Protection Act's Principles to the *Source Informatics* case. The Second Principle is that data should be obtained for specific purposes, and not used for others. In this case, patient information was obtained for the purposes of treatment, and then used for commercial purposes by Source Informatics. The Second Data Protection Principle is qualified by section 33, which provides that it will not be breached where the further processing is done for 'research purposes'. Again, it might be possible to argue that Source Informatics were anonymizing the prescription forms for research purposes, but it is also at least arguable that Source Informatics's principal interest in the anonymized data was in fact commercial, and not a 'research purpose'.

In order to trace the progression of disease, it is sometimes necessary to use coded (or pseudonymized) data, where the patient is not identified, but where it would be possible to trace the information back to the patient. If information had to be completely anonymized (and hence usable without consent), it would be impossible to validate and update data, and eliminate duplication.

If patient consent to the use of records is necessary when data has been pseudonymized rather than anonymized, this would be a significant obstacle to the generation of useful data. Cancer registries, for example, hold an enormous amount of information about past patients, and if these historical records could not be used without tracing every patient and retrospectively asking for consent, invaluable epidemiological research into the causes of cancer would grind to a halt.

Moreover, as Michael Ferriter and Martin Butwell explain in the next extract, there would also be a danger of 'consent bias' since some people (perhaps those suffering from diseases which attract stigma) might be less likely than others to give consent, and the data would therefore no longer be representative of the population as a whole. Patients who have died or lost capacity would also be excluded, once again skewing results. Seeking consent could also cause unnecessary alarm to patients who might fear that a request to re-examine their medical records has been prompted by concern for their health.

Michael Ferriter and Martin Butwell[66]

There are whole areas of observational research—epidemiological research using case notes, case registers and disease registers—which do not require direct contact with the patient and where gaining consent may be impractical, impossible or undesirable: impractical because of dealing with such large numbers; impossible because of tracing all the participants; undesirable because in seeking consent the sample may be biased; or in gaining consent, needless anxiety may be caused to participants. . . .

[C]onsent can fundamentally damage research by introducing bias. On a technical level, one of the strengths of carrying out research where hitherto consent has not been needed is its freedom from many such biases. It is acknowledged that certain groups of people are more likely to consent to take part in research than others. For whatever reasons, younger

---

[66] 'Confidentiality and Research in Mental Health' in Christopher Cordess (ed), *Confidentiality and Mental Health* (Jessica Kingsley Publishers: London, 2001) 159–69.

patients, men and members of ethnic minorities are all less likely to consent to participate in health research. This leads to a consequent bias in research carried out, problems in generalisation to the wider population as a whole and, ultimately, to the disadvantage of people in less compliant groups. . . .

The crucial question that needs to be asked is: Has anyone ever been harmed by the use of their healthcare data in a case or disease register?

Of course, it is possible that identifiable data could be used without consent if it meets one of the criteria in Schedule 2 and one in Schedule 3 to the Data Protection Act 1998. For example, epidemiological research could be said to be 'necessary for medical purposes', under Schedule 3 para 8. Nevertheless, when the Data Protection Act 1998 came into force in 2000, there were fears that meeting the burden of establishing the 'necessity' of a particular project might prove to be a significant obstacle to valuable epidemiological research. These fears led to the passage of section 60 of the Health and Social Care Act 2001, which has now been replaced by section 251 of the National Health Service Act 2006.

National Health Service Act 2006 section 251

251 Control of patient information

(1) The Secretary of State may by regulations make such provision for and in connection with requiring or regulating the processing of prescribed patient information for medical purposes as he considers necessary or expedient—

(a) in the interests of improving patient care, or

(b) in the public interest . . .

(4) Regulations under subsection (1) may not make provision requiring the processing of confidential patient information for any purpose if it would be reasonably practicable to achieve that purpose otherwise than pursuant to such regulations, having regard to the cost of and the technology available for achieving that purpose.

Section 251 allows the Secretary of State to make regulations which authorize the disclosure of confidential patient information without consent where it is needed to support essential NHS activity. Under regulation 5 of the Health Service (Control of Patient Information) Regulations 2002, this does not mean that regulations must be laid before parliament on each occasion, rather the Secretary of State can essentially give what is known as 'section 251' support to applications to use patient-identifiable data for a number of specified purposes, such as contacting patients with a view to inviting them to participate in medical research.

Section 251 can only be used to support medical purposes that are, first, in the interests of patients or the wider public; secondly, where consent is not a practicable alternative; and, thirdly, where anonymized information will not suffice. It was originally intended to be a transitional arrangement, while the NHS developed mechanisms to seek and record consent and put more sophisticated anonymization techniques into place, but it is now acknowledged that section 251 powers will be necessary in the longer term.

Responsibility for advising on section 251 applications lies with the Confidentiality Advisory Group within the Health Research Authority (HRA). The HRA itself can approve research applications and, for non-research applications, it advises the Secretary of State for Health on whether to give approval.

Detailed information about all the projects which have received section 251 support is publicly available. For each project, there is a summary explaining why the use of identifiable information would be necessary. For example, the research project summarized below needed section 251 approval in order to access GP records to assess the frequency of prescribing errors:

> This research application from the University of Nottingham set out the purpose of a research study to assess error rates in prescribing by GP registrars. . . . A recommendation . . . was requested to cover access by a CCG-employed pharmacist to notes of 1,000 GP patients in the East Midlands, in order to assess the appropriateness of the most recent 100 prescriptions issued by each of 10 GP registrars recruited to the study. Access was requested to patient records on GP practice sites in order to extract anonymised data.[67]

In the next extract, Ian Brown et al maintain that it has become too easy to use identifiable data without consent. Instead they argue that this should only be possible where the research is necessary to protect the public against very serious diseases.

Ian Brown, Lindsey Brown, and Douwe Korff[68]

> Medical research using patient records is rarely required to meet a serious and immediate threat of harm to particular people, although it can of course result in longer-term benefits to the general public, such as improved health. . . .
>
> In our opinion, this means that the law . . . should not just allow the use of patient data without the latter's consent for certain generally-defined types of research. Rather, such use of such data can only ever be allowed on a case-by-case basis, and only if the particular research that is proposed serves a particularly important public interest. This allows, for instance, the compulsory reporting of certain very serious infectious diseases in order to protect the general public, and use of this reporting data for statistical purposes and for research into measures to counter such a disease. It will not allow the use of patient data without consent for research into less serious diseases.
>
> Any authorisation for use of patient data for secondary research purposes (without consent) must also be strictly 'necessary' for such a purpose—that is, there must really not be any other measures available that impinge less on the patients' privacy and autonomy. This has two implications. Under the law, it should only be possible to authorise disclosure without consent for very important research (as defined above), but even then only if it is really impossible or prohibitively difficult to obtain the consent of the data subject.

But do patients in fact mind if their records are used in research and audit? In the next extract, Richards et al explain that patients in a breast cancer study seemed unconcerned about the use of their medical notes for the purposes of research.

---

[67] 'April 2013 onward Approved Research Applications', available at www.hra.nhs.uk.
[68] 'Using NHS patient data for research without consent' (2010) 2 Law, Innovation and Technology 219–58.

MPM Richards et al[69]

None of those we interviewed had any concerns about confidentiality in relation to the ABC study. We asked if they knew how they had been selected for the study. None did; most simply assumed the researchers would have been told by their GPs or the cancer clinic of their breast cancer. Such possible passing on of information did not cause any concerns. In fact, the sample had been identified through the regional cancer registry but this was not stated in the information given at recruitment. The existence of such a registry was unknown to all but one of the interviewees, who included two nurses and a GP's secretary. The woman who knew of the registry had a close relative who worked in cancer research.

Women were asked how they would feel if their blood sample was passed to other medical researchers for work on other diseases 'such as heart disease or mental illness'. All said they would be quite happy for this to be done. They were further asked what they would feel about their samples going to a commercial company or a drug company for research. Most were also content with this though a couple were a little hesitant. One had concerns over patenting and said she would only agree if it was for a drug that would be available to everyone. She said she thought that cancer research should be done by the government, not private companies. . . .

Our interviews suggest that those who have had breast cancer are pleased to take part in genetic epidemiological research and do not perceive any particular issues related to confidentiality. Furthermore, participants said they were content for their blood samples to be used for other medical research. Most, but not all women, included commercial or drug company research in this.

On the other hand, in their study of patient perspectives, the Wellcome Trust found that while people generally did not mind their NHS records being used for research purposes, they appreciated being asked first. The view was consistently expressed that 'grounded in social conventions of courtesy: it is polite to ask. Not being asked is impolite and signals disrespect and being taken for granted. Implicit consent is no consent at all.'[70]

We can see a stark illustration of this finding in the response to the care.data programme. Led by NHS England and the Health and Social Care Information Centre, the intention behind care.data is to use the data held by the NHS in order to improve patient care, by, for example, understanding trends in public health and being able to plan the provision of NHS services more effectively. Powers to do this had been created under the Health and Social Care Act 2012, which had established the Health and Social Care Information Centre and empowered it to obtain identifiable patient information from GP practices, unless patients had specifically opted out. The NHS Constitution had also been amended to include an expectation that patients would be willing to share their information for planning and research purposes.

A public information campaign was launched, but not very successfully—the leaflet that was supposed to be sent to all households often failed to arrive or was discarded as junk mail—and the programme had to be paused. At the time of writing, it is being piloted in four areas in order to learn further lessons before the next attempt to roll it out nationally.

---

[69] 'Issues of consent and feedback in a genetic epidemiological study of women with breast cancer' (2003) 29 Journal of Medical Ethics 93–6.

[70] Wellcome Trust, *Public Perspectives on the Governance of Biomedical Research: A Qualitative Study in a Deliberative Context* (Wellcome Trust: London, 2007) 87.

In the next extract, Carter et al warn of the dangers of assuming that public support for the use of their data in specific research projects will translate into support for unspecified future uses.

Pam Carter, Graeme T Laurie, and Mary Dixon-Woods[71]

[M]ost of what is known about patients' support for research is based on quite particular examples of research participation—often those where patients already have an interest in a medical condition and where they are asked for quite specific consent to a project or programme. . . . The extent to which the findings of this body of research about participation in specific, relatively well-bounded studies or cohorts by defined, consenting patients can be generalised to the broader conception of NHS citizenship implicit in the new policy direction is not clear.

There are many reasons to doubt that *care.data* could *reasonably* assume that the public would automatically confer upon it the same legitimacy and endorsement as that enjoyed by research where individual informed consent is sought and clear information about study aims is provided. For instance, the mobility of electronic data and the practical difficulties of specifying in advance the research questions for which data might be used or the populations to be studied mean that *care.data* was in many ways quite distinct from conventional research projects. . . .

If *care.data* is to succeed, patients need to have the confidence that their medical records will be held securely, anonymised appropriately, and that secondary use of this personal data is in the public interest: the conditions of the social licence need to be respected in ways that go beyond compliance laid down in a legal framework.

(4) Statutory Exceptions

Under the Health Protection (Notification) Regulations 2010, registered medical practitioners (RMPs) are under a duty to notify a proper officer at their local authority Health Protection Team (HPT) if they have 'reasonable grounds for suspecting' that the patient:

- has a notifiable disease as listed in Schedule 1 to the Notification Regulations; or
- has an infection not included in Schedule 1 which in the view of the RMP presents, or could present, significant harm to human health (eg emerging or new infections); or
- is contaminated (eg with chemicals or radiation) in a manner which, in the view of the doctor presents, or could present, significant harm to human health; or
- has died with, but not necessarily because of, a notifiable disease, or other infectious disease or contamination that presents or could present, or that presented or could have presented, significant harm to human health.

Schedule 1 contains a long list of notifiable diseases, including measles, mumps, rubella, food poisoning, TB, and whooping cough. Notification must include a set of prescribed information about the patient, including, but not limited to, her name and address, occupation (this might be important if the patient could have infected others at work, for example if her job involves handling food), overseas travel history, and information about the onset

---

[71] 'The social licence for research: why care.data ran into trouble' (2015) 41 Journal of Medical Ethics 404–9.

of her symptoms. The proper officer is then under a duty to pass this information to Public Health England within strict time limits.

The Health Protection (Local Authority Powers) Regulations 2010 and the Health Protection (Part 2A Orders) Regulations 2010 permit various powers to be exercised over people who are unwilling to cooperate with voluntary measures. For example, a child can be required to stay away from school. Local authorities can also apply to a Justice of the Peace for a Part 2A Order, and these can be more draconian. If necessary to protect public health, a Part 2A Order can require a person to undergo medical examination (but crucially, it cannot require them to receive treatment or vaccination); be taken to hospital; be kept in isolation or quarantine; answer questions about their health or other circumstances or have their health monitored and the results reported. Such powers should be used only if it is not possible to secure voluntary cooperation in order to avert a health risk, and their use must be proportionate in order not to represent a breach of Articles 5 and 8 of the European Convention on Human Rights.

The Health Service (Control of Patient Information) Regulations 2002 further allow for the common law duty of confidence to be set aside in certain circumstances in order to protect public health. Under regulation 3, confidential information may be processed in order to diagnose, control, and monitor communicable diseases, and, as we saw earlier, regulation 5 allows confidential information to be processed, with the approval of the Health Research Authority or the Secretary of State for Health, for other medical purposes, including research.

7 REMEDIES

If a patient discovers an impending breach of confidence, she can apply for an injunction to prevent disclosure. But what if the disclosure has already taken place? If an action in negligence was possible because the breach of confidence also amounted to a breach of the doctor's ordinary duty of care, then it might be possible to recover damages for harm caused as a result. But what if the patient has not suffered injury or economic loss, and the only 'harm' is the patient's distress?

Usually, it is not possible to recover damages for injury to feelings or reputation, but there are exceptions, such as damages for defamation. It is not entirely clear whether the courts would be willing to award damages for the injured feelings caused by a breach of confidentiality. At first instance in *W v Egdell*, Scott J stated that he thought this was 'open to question' (the point was not considered when the case reached the Court of Appeal):

> I think [it] open to question whether shock and distress caused by the unauthorised disclosure of confidential information can . . . properly be reflected in an award of damages . . . In my judgment, W would not, even if I had found Dr Egdell to be liable, have been entitled to damages. He would have had to be content with a declaration and an injunction.[72]

In *Cornelius v De Taranto*, a psychiatric report, which contained certain potentially defamatory statements, had been circulated without the subject's consent. At first instance, Morland J awarded the claimant £3,750 damages, which included £3,000 'for the injury to the claimants feelings caused by the unauthorized disclosure of the confidential information'.

---

[72] *W v Egdell* [1989] 2 WLR 689.

Cornelius v De Taranto[73]

Morland J

Under art 8 of the Convention for the Protection of Human Rights and Fundamental Freedoms 1950 'everyone has the right to respect for his private and family life' . . . In my judgment, it would be a hollow protection of that right if in a particular case in breach of confidence without consent details of the confider's private and family life were disclosed by the confidant to others and the only remedy that the law of England allowed was nominal damages. In this case an injunction or order for delivery up of all copies of the medico-legal report against the defendant will be of little use to the claimant. The damage has been done. . . .

In the present case, in my judgment, recovery of damages for mental distress caused by breach of confidence, when no other substantial remedy is available, would not be inimical to 'considerations of policy' but indeed to refuse such recovery would illustrate that something was wrong with the law . . .

My conclusion is that I am entitled to award damages for injury to feelings caused by breach of confidence. Although it is a novel instance of such a remedy, it is in accord with the movement of current legal thinking.

On appeal, the Court of Appeal did not specifically address the question of compensation for breach of confidence, but it left the damages award intact.

As we saw earlier, there is a right to compensation for distress under section 13 of the Data Protection Act 1998, although the scope of this right is limited. The claimant must prove that she has suffered physical, financial, or psychiatric damage, and the data controller has a defence if she took all reasonable care to comply with the Act.

8 ACCESS TO MEDICAL RECORDS

Patients have a right of access to personal data, which includes their health records, under section 7 of the Data Protection Act 1998. In order to claim access to information, the data subject must make a request in writing; pay the specified fee (in the case of medical records held on computer, this is £10); and supply information which confirms his identity and helps to locate the particular information. Information must then be supplied promptly, within 40 days or less. If the data controller fails to supply the relevant information, a court can order him to do so.

So what information can 'data subjects' request under the Act? First, they can ask whether their personal data is being processed by the data controller; secondly, they can ask for a description of the data and the purposes for which it is being processed and the identity of its recipients; and, thirdly, where possible, for a copy of any information held.

The right of access to health records under the Data Protection Act is not absolute, however. Under the Data Protection (Subject Access Modification) (Health) Order 2000,[74] data which might otherwise have to be disclosed can be withheld if it would be likely to cause serious harm to the physical or mental health of the data subject or any other person, or would lead to the identification of another person (other than a health professional who has been involved in the care of the data subject) who has not consented to the disclosure of his or her identity.

---

[73] (2001) 68 BMLR 62. [74] SI 2000/413.

The Data Protection Act 1998 must now be read in the light of the Freedom of Information Act 2000 which provides another route for access to information held by public bodies. Personal information is, however, exempt from the Freedom of Information Act's provisions both in relation to the patient's own access to her health records and to third parties seeking access to them. It is only non-personal health information, such as health policy decisions, which might be subject to requests under the Freedom of Information Act.

Clearly, a patient might want access to her medical records is if she is contemplating an action in negligence. Under section 33 of the Senior Courts Act 1981, she can apply for a court order which will require the relevant doctor or hospital to disclose her records or notes. There must be a real prospect of litigation before disclosure will be ordered, however. A patient cannot use section 33 in order to engage in a 'fishing expedition' in the hope that some evidence of negligence might emerge. In addition, limitations can be imposed upon disclosure, for example the court might decide to restrict disclosure to the patient's legal and/or medical advisers.

9 ELECTRONIC PATIENT RECORDS

The NHS is in the process of moving towards fully electronic patient records. Essentially each patient will—unless they object—have two electronic patient records. The summary care record will contain details about a patient's allergies and any medication they are taking. This will be available nationally, so that if a person is taken to hospital in an emergency, the doctors treating her can have ready access to important information, without having to track down and make contact with her GP's surgery. The detailed record will be available locally, and will make it easier to provide care without physically having to access a patient's paper notes.

The Secretary of State for Health has announced that he expects the NHS to operate paperlessly by 2018. It has been estimated that this would save the NHS as much as £4.4 billion each year. There is, however, evidence from other countries that online access to services may significantly increase patient use of those services, thus reducing or cancelling out any anticipated savings. A paperless NHS would undoubtedly be more convenient for health care professionals and often for patients too, although there are clearly risks. Using text messages to communicate negative test results, for example, might be less time-consuming than speaking to a patient in person, but it is not secure and could be distressing.

In the next extracts, Ross Anderson is concerned about increased electronic sharing of information, while Mark Walport maintains that effective use of electronic patient records is the best way to improve patient care.

Ross Anderson[75]

The summary care record was marketed to the public as a way for accident and emergency staff to check up on unconscious patients. According to Tony Blair, if you ended up in hospital in Bradford, doctors could look up your records with your general practitioner in Guildford. But this is nonsense. Very few patients have conditions that must be made known to emergency staff; for those that do, the properly engineered solution is MedicAlert. Unconscious patients

---

[75] 'Do summary care records have the potential to do more harm than good? Yes' (2010) 340 British Medical Journal 3020.

often can't be reliably identified, so a database is less robust than a tag or card; the record doesn't have everything accident and emergency staff might want to see; and it is not even available in Scotland (let alone on a beach in Turkey) . . .

Furthermore, the summary care record's consent procedures are completely unsatisfactory; sharing medical data requires informed consent, yet large numbers of patients are unaware that the record even exists. Expecting patients to be aware of it, and to opt out every time they interact with health care, is ridiculous . . . [T]his is not just a matter of law but goes to the heart of the relationship between patients and doctors. The summary care record and the national information technology plan will make even highly sensitive information such as mental health records available by default to hundreds of thousands of people—and not just in the core NHS but in Whitehall, local authorities, and research laboratories. This is totally at odds with the expectations of patients, with safe systems engineering, and with prudent clinical practice, as well as with human rights law.

Mark Walport[76]

There is another huge potential benefit of a nationwide electronic patient record system, to improve treatment through research. Research provides the evidence that medical treatments work or, equally importantly, that they don't. It is an integral part of the best health systems. . . . I do not believe that Connecting for Health has been marketed well to either patients or the medical profession. There has been much too much about its use as a management tool and too little about its primary aim, which should be to improve care . . . But one thing is certain—the best care requires the best medical records. A world class NHS demands a world class infrastructure. The future for medical records is digital.

Perhaps they are both right. Information sharing for research purposes is undoubtedly the best way to understand the causes of disease and improve health outcomes. At the same time, the IT systems that facilitate the sharing of data as sensitive as a patient's medical records need to be exceptionally robust.

It should, however, be noted that the greatest threat to patient confidentiality is probably human error, rather than data sharing for health and research purposes. In 2015, for example, it was revealed that a London clinic had sent a newsletter to 780 HIV-positive patients without taking steps to hide the distribution list, thus revealing every other patient's name and email address. In response, the Secretary of State for Health has asked the Care Quality Commission to review data security measures within the NHS, and to incorporate checks on data security into its inspection regimes. While more robust data security measures may be able to minimize the risk of inadvertent disclosure, they probably cannot eliminate human frailty.

10 CONCLUSION

Doctors are unquestionably under a duty to respect their patients' confidentiality, but the duty is not an absolute one. On the contrary, in a wide range of situations, the duty to

---

[76] 'Do summary care records have the potential to do more harm than good? No' (2010) 340 British Medical Journal 3022.

respect confidentiality is suspended or modified. For example, patient notes will be shared among health care professionals; information can be disclosed where there is a serious risk of harm to others; and patient records can be used for epidemiological research and clinical audit. Most exceptions to the duty of confidentiality could be justified on 'public interest' grounds, but the 'public interest' exception to the duty of confidence does not offer very clear guidance to doctors about when the disclosure of patient information will be justifiable. Essentially, the public interest exception requires the merits of disclosure in a particular case to be weighed against the general public interest in the maintenance of patient confidentiality.

Finally, it is worth bearing in mind that recent discussion about the use of data without consent has taken place against the backdrop of the revelations, by Edward Snowden, of the extent of state surveillance of electronic communications. As Mark Taylor points out, this makes it even more important to be able to clearly explain and justify the use of data in the public interest.

Mark Taylor[77]

The care.data debate has been carried out in an atmosphere tainted by the Snowden revelations. . . . Individuals, uncertain of the model of public interest being applied, cannot be sure the extent to which their own interests are being respected. To put it simply, without a clearer determination of what is meant by 'the public interest', there is understandable concern that any given individual's interests might be sacrificed 'for the greater good' with that 'good' being defined and enjoyed by others. . . .

We need to do this better. There are classic examples of how gathering and linking data has enabled important insights—e.g. smoking and lung cancer—and of times when an inability to make the links quickly enough has had tragic consequences—e.g. thalidomide. The idea of the public interest needs to be developed to make clear that the reasons for such use must be accessible to members of the public. . . . The public interest should only be called upon to defend interferences that individual members of the public can be given reason to accept. If people have confidence that data will *only* be used in ways that they have reason to accept, even when any legal requirement for individual informed consent may be formally overridden by the demands of 'the public interest', then the social legitimacy of the systems will be promoted.

FURTHER READING

Carter, Pam, Laurie, Graeme T, and Dixon-Woods, Mary, 'The social licence for research: why *care.data* ran into trouble' (2015) 41 Journal of Medical Ethics 404–9.

Case, Paula, 'Confidence Matters: The Rise and Fall of Informational Autonomy in Medical Law' (2003) 11 Medical Law Review 208–36.

Department of Health, *The Power of Information, Putting All of Us in Control of the Health and Care Information We Need* (DH: London, 2012).

Gilbar, Roy, 'Medical Confidentiality Within the Family: The Doctor's Duty Reconsidered' (2004) 18 International Journal of Law, Policy and the Family 195.

---

[77] 'Information governance as a force for good? Lessons to be learnt from care.data' (2014) 11 SCRIPTed 1.

Jones, C, 'The utilitarian argument for medical confidentiality: a pilot study of patients' views' (2003) 29 Journal of Medical Ethics 348–52.

Sandland, Ralph, 'Freedom of the Press and the Confidentiality of Medical Records' (2007) 15 Medical Law Review 400–9.

Taylor, Mark, 'Information governance as a force for good? Lessons to be learnt from care.data' (2014) 11 SCRIPTed 1.

8

GENETIC INFORMATION

CENTRAL ISSUES

1. Genetic information raises several complex issues in relation to confidentiality:

   (a) First, the inherently shared nature of genetic information poses particular challenges for an individualistic model of confidentiality.

   (b) Secondly, genetic tests are often predictive rather than diagnostic. Results may provide information about a healthy person's risk of future ill health, which might be of interest to third parties, such as employers and insurers.

   (c) Thirdly, DNA databases might be useful for the police, for epidemiological research and NHS resource planning, and for the pharmaceutical industry.

2. In some other countries—but not in the UK—genetic discrimination is prohibited by law in the same way as discrimination on the grounds of sex, race, and disability.

3. Most genetic testing takes place within the NHS. Direct-to-consumer testing can enable the 'worried well' to discover whether they are at increased risk of a number of conditions.

4. In the future, pharmacogenetics may transform the way in which medicines are prescribed, by enabling doctors to know in advance whether a drug is likely to be safe and effective for a particular patient.

1 INTRODUCTION: WHAT IS GENETIC INFORMATION?

Progress in the field of genetics has been especially rapid in recent years. The mapping of the human genome—which was completed in 2003—informed us that we have fewer genes than had previously been assumed: only twice as many as the roundworm. The sequence of most of our 20–25,000 genes is identical (99.9 per cent), and indeed we share a surprising proportion of our DNA with chimpanzees (96 per cent), and, even more surprisingly, with fruit flies (60 per cent).

In this chapter, we are principally concerned with questions about the regulation of access to genetic information. One reason why this is especially important is that faulty genes, or mutations, can increase someone's chance of developing disease(s) in the future. Genetic test results may reveal predictive information about a person's future health prospects.

There are several different sorts of genetic disease. Single gene disorders are conditions that are caused by a particular genetic mutation, and they can be further divided into two groups. First, if the gene is dominant, a single gene inherited from either parent will cause the disease. An example is Huntington's disease, an incurable neurological degenerative disease, which people usually develop between the ages of 30 and 50, and which causes progressive deterioration of bodily functions and cognitive abilities. If someone who has inherited the Huntington's mutation has a child, there is a 50 per cent chance that he or she will inherit the disease. The penetrance of the mutation is also high: if a person has inherited it, then, provided they do not die first from another cause, they can be certain that they will develop Huntington's disease.

Single gene disorders can also be recessive. This means that a person will develop the disease only if they inherit the relevant gene from both parents. People who have one copy of the gene are carriers. They will not develop the disease themselves, but if they reproduce with another carrier, there is a one-in-four chance that any child they might have will receive a double dose of the relevant gene, and hence will suffer from the disease. As Figure 8.1 shows, there is also a one-in-four chance that their child will be completely unaffected and not carry the gene at all, and a one-in-two chance that their child will also be a carrier.

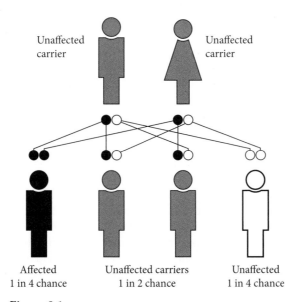

Figure 8.1

Examples of recessive genetic conditions are cystic fibrosis, a chronic lung disease, and sickle cell disease, a serious blood disorder. Within some population groups, being a carrier for one of these conditions is fairly common. Among people of European descent, one in 25 are carriers of the cystic fibrosis gene. Families are often completely unaware that they are passing on this gene until someone has a baby with another carrier. Sickle-cell trait (being a carrier of the sickle-cell gene) is more common among people of African, Eastern Mediterranean, Asian, and Middle-Eastern descent.

A third group of genetic diseases are X-linked disorders, which are triggered by a mutation on the X chromosome. Women have two X chromosomes, and so they will usually have a second normal X chromosome to compensate for the defective one. Women will usually therefore only be carriers of these diseases, and may pass the disease to their male offspring. Men have an X and a Y chromosome, and so if they inherit a mutation on their X chromosome from their mother, they will develop the disease. Examples of X-linked disorders are Duchenne Muscular Dystrophy and haemophilia.

Chromosomal disorders arise when a person has an abnormality in their chromosomes, perhaps because they have too many copies of a particular chromosome. Examples are Down's syndrome and Turner syndrome.

Single gene disorders are unusual. Most conditions are, instead, complex and multifactorial; that is, they result from the interaction of several genes, and from the interaction between a person's genes and their environment. Some people will have genes that predispose them to heart disease, for example, but whether or not they develop heart disease, and at what age, may also be determined by lifestyle factors, such as diet, exercise, alcohol consumption, and smoking.

In recent years, there has been particularly rapid progress in identifying susceptibility genes: that is, genes which increase a person's risk of developing a condition, but where there is no guarantee that they will do so. This means that their penetrance (unlike Huntington's) is less than 100 per cent. Certain types of cancer may be triggered by genetic mutations, for example. Approximately 5 per cent of breast cancers are the result of faulty BRCA1 and BRCA2 genes, which increase the lifetime risk of developing breast cancer to 60–80 per cent, and the lifetime risk of ovarian cancer to around 60 per cent.[1]

Finding out that someone has a genetic mutation associated with a genetic condition raises several specific issues. First, our capacity to identify genetic disorders outstrips our capacity to treat them. It has been possible to test for the Huntington's mutation for many years, but there is still no cure. This means that the decision to be tested is different from being tested for conditions like cancer or HIV/AIDS, where a positive test result will lead to discussions about the most appropriate treatment.

A positive test for Huntington's instead involves the discovery that one will develop an incurable and fatal condition. Suicide rates in people who receive positive Huntington's test results are higher than normal,[2] and it is not surprising that many people who know they are at risk have chosen not to be tested (we return to this point later).

The only way in which 'something can be done' when one knows that an untreatable genetic condition runs in one's family, is to undergo preimplantation (or prenatal) genetic diagnosis, or to reproduce with donor gametes (sperm or eggs), or not to reproduce at all in order to ensure that future generations are not born with the condition in question. Because the special regulatory regime covering assisted conception also covers preimplantation genetic diagnosis, we deal with this separately in Chapter 15. Prenatal diagnosis, unless carried out in order to help the parents prepare for the birth of an affected child, is generally done so that affected fetuses can be aborted. The law covering abortion for abnormality is dealt with in Chapter 13.

A second important difference is that genetic test results may be predictive, rather than diagnostic. If I discover that I have the BRCA1 mutation, I may be healthy now and for decades to come. Indeed, it is possible that I will never develop breast or ovarian cancer. But

[1] For more information on cancer genetics, see www.macmillan.org.uk.
[2] Thomas D Bird, 'Outrageous fortune: the risk of suicide in genetic testing for Huntington's disease' (1999) 64 American Journal of Human Genetics 1289.

I have found out that I am much more likely than most women to develop both cancers, and at a younger age than normal. This information might be useful to others, such as insurance companies, who base their calculations of premiums upon actuarial tables that predict a person's life expectancy.

Another important issue is that if I find out that I have the BRCA1 mutation, I must have inherited this from one of my parents. Discovering this information about myself means that I also know that other family members may be at risk. As Lori Andrews explains in the next extract, this means that genetic test results raise particularly interesting questions about confidentiality. The problem is obviously most acute for identical twins, who share the same DNA. If one twin is diagnosed with a genetic disorder, she cannot avoid knowing that her twin sister has the same genetic mutation. For other relatives, the implications of a relative's positive diagnosis are less certain, but nonetheless significant.

Lori B Andrews[3]

A parent and a child have half their genes in common, as do siblings. Cousins share one-quarter of their genes, as do grandparents and grandchildren. The acquisition and disclosure of genetic information raise new and profound questions of 'gen-etiquette', questions about the moral obligations owed to relatives. If a woman learns she has a genetic mutation predis-posing her to breast cancer, does she have a moral or even a legal duty to share that informa-tion with her sister? What about an estranged cousin? . . .

Genetic information influences people's relationships with third parties, such as insurers and employers. While individuals might want to know their own genetic makeup in order to make important life decisions, such information can also be used against them. . . . The chill-ing irony of genetic testing is that, even in rare cases where a treatment exists, people may be afraid to get tested for the disorder because their insurer might drop them entirely or an employer may refuse to hire them based on their test results.

In addition to providing information about future ill health, genetic tests might also be useful to the police by enabling them to maintain a DNA database that could be searched rapidly as soon as evidence is found at a crime scene. Of course, the public interest in the identification and prosecution of criminals is substantial, but difficult questions arise about whose DNA should be placed on a database, and how long it should be kept. DNA databases might also be useful for research purposes, and to assist the management and planning of health care provision.

One of the most important issues that arises in relation to genetic test information is therefore confidentiality, and we begin this chapter with a discussion of various third par-ties' interests in genetic test results and DNA profiles, and the extent to which genetic pri-vacy is protected by the law.

The second important issue raised by genetic information is the possibility of discrimi-nation against those found to have genetic disorders. Adam Moore recounts an extreme example of genetic discrimination in Orchemenos, Greece, where sickle-cell anaemia is common.[4] Researchers tested everyone in the village so that carriers could ensure they did

---

[3] 'A Conceptual Framework for Genetic Policy: Comparing the Medical, Public Health and Fundamental Rights Models' (2001) 79 Washington University Law Quarterly 221.

[4] 'Owning genetic information and gene enhancement techniques: why privacy and property rights may undermine social control of the human genome' (2000) 14 Bioethics 97–119.

not marry each other. It was assumed that carriers would choose to marry non-carriers, in order to avoid having children with sickle-cell disease. The problem was that the non-carriers refused to cooperate. Carriers became a stigmatized subclass, and were forced to marry among themselves, which of course meant that there were even more babies born with the condition than before.

The potential for genetic discrimination may be exacerbated by the fact that some genetic traits are particularly associated with particular ethnic groups. Ashkenazi Jews, for example, are disproportionately likely to inherit the BRCA1 or BRCA2 mutations and to carry the gene associated with Tay-Sachs disease.

In 2008, the US passed the Genetic Information Nondiscrimination Act, which prevents discrimination by employers and health insurers. In contrast in the UK, the government explicitly decided against including 'genetic discrimination' within the categories of unlawful discrimination, now brought together in the Equality Act 2010.

The third issue is the expansion of genetic testing, and in particular the growth of direct-to-consumer testing. For some years, there has been a market in paternity testing 'kits', which enable suspicious men to test their children's DNA in order to confirm or rebut paternity. Now companies are selling genetic screening kits to the 'worried well'. For £125 (shipping included), 23andMe will ship a kit direct to a consumer. After returning a tube containing her saliva, the customer will receive information about her inherited traits, risk factors, and ancestral origins.

Clearly a host of difficult practical and legal issues arise from direct-to-consumer testing. If I could send back a tube containing someone else's saliva, could I find out information about them that is none of my business? Is it a good idea to receive complicated and potentially alarming news by email, rather than in the course of a consultation with a trained professional?

Finally, we consider the implications of pharmacogenetics, and the possibility that a genetic test could reveal whether a medicine is likely to work for a patient, and whether that patient is likely to suffer adverse side effects. If our genetic make-up affects the way in which we metabolize medicines, pharmacogenetics could reduce the 'trial and error' approach to prescribing, and lead to more accurate, personalized medication regimes.

2 GENETIC PRIVACY

Let us first turn to consider in more detail the various third parties who might have an interest in acquiring a patient's genetic test results.

(a) INSURERS

In the UK, a minority of the population purchases health insurance, but other sorts of insurance—such as life insurance for the purposes of obtaining a mortgage or to ensure that one's dependants do not suffer financially as a result of one's death—are common. The Association of British Insurers estimates that private health insurance covers 5.1 million people in the UK, while 29.3 million people are covered by life insurance, or income protection, or critical illness insurance policies.

On the one hand, it instinctively seems unfair if a genetic test result, which is plainly not within her control, prevents someone from obtaining insurance, or means that she faces hugely increased premiums. On the other hand, insurance contracts rely on the duty of 'utmost good faith' (*uberrimae fides*) in the disclosure of risk. Insurance companies already take into account a person's health status, family history, and lifestyle risks, such as smoking, when setting premiums. Someone who has just been diagnosed with cancer, for example, would be under a duty to disclose that fact when seeking health insurance.

Preventing insurance companies from taking genetic information into account might also have adverse consequences. If individuals discover that they are very likely to suffer from a serious disease, they might purchase a great deal of insurance, whereas other people with no elevated risk of future ill health might not bother buying insurance at all. This phenomenon is known as adverse selection. Plainly, it would be very difficult to maintain a functioning market in insurance if only people who are 'bad' risks choose to insure themselves.

In 2001, insurance companies in the UK agreed to impose a voluntary ban on the use of positive genetic test results to set insurance premiums. This moratorium has been extended several times and will now run until 2019.[5] There are strictly limited exceptions to the ban on the use of genetic test results in setting premiums, which are intended to limit the problem of adverse selection. For income protection insurance of more than £30,000 per year, life insurance cover greater than £500,000, and health insurance (critical illness, income protection, or long-term care insurance) cover greater than £300,000, positive genetic test results may be used provided that the government has approved the test in question. Ninety-seven per cent of insurance policies are below these limits. For policies above these amounts, the only test approved so far is for Huntington's disease for life insurance of more than £500,000.

The moratorium on the use of genetic tests applies only to positive results. Negative test results can be taken into account. So a person with a family history of Huntington's disease, who has been tested and knows that she has not inherited the mutation, can ask an insurer to take this fact into account, rather than basing her premiums on her family history.

It is impossible to know the extent of adverse selection under the current moratorium. Zick et al studied the insurance-purchasing behaviour of people following testing for a variation on the ApoE gene, which appears to correlate with an increased risk of late onset Alzheimer's disease. They found that those who received a positive test result were nearly six times more likely to have altered their long-term care insurance arrangements than those whose results were negative.[6]

With the growth in direct-to-consumer genetic screening, more individuals may find out that they are at increased risk of developing a wide range of conditions, such as Parkinson's disease or dementia, and be prompted to take out critical illness cover that they might not otherwise have purchased.

(b) EMPLOYERS

For several reasons, as Alexander Capron explains, employers might find genetic test results useful when planning recruitment and promotion.

---

[5] HM Government and ABI, *Concordat and Moratorium on Genetics and Insurance* (2014).
[6] Cathleen D Zick et al, 'Genetic testing for Alzheimer's disease and its impact on insurance purchasing behavior' (2005) 24 Health Affairs 483.

Alexander Capron[7]

First, an employee who is prone to get sick will generate expenses: medical treatment costs, sick days, and potentially even disability benefits. Second, if the problem might be described as job-related, then the genetic condition could lead directly to workers compensation payments—for instance, a genetic predisposition to a bad back in an employee who has to do a lot of lifting. Finally, employers generally want to avoid hiring persons who are going to be sick a great deal because such persons cannot be relied upon to be present when needed and the expense of training them may thus be wasted if they become totally disabled.

Employers might also want to know about the risk an employer might pose to others: for example, an airline would want to know whether its pilots were at increased risk of epilepsy or narcolepsy.

Genetic test results might reveal that a person is particularly susceptible to a workplace hazard, such as chemicals used in industrial processes. Excluding potential employees with a genetic predisposition to work-related injuries may initially appear to be a sensible precautionary step, both in order to protect the employee's health and to avoid having to pay compensation. But it could be argued that this looks at the problem of workplace hazards from the wrong direction. Employing individuals who are more resistant to dangerous workplaces assumes that the environment could not be made any safer. Rather than excluding people who are particularly susceptible to toxic substances, it might be preferable to make the working environment safer for everyone.

It might also be argued that this apparently benevolent concern for employees' health is unduly paternalistic. An individual might rationally choose to engage in work that poses a small risk to her health in preference to unemployment, which itself may have an adverse effect on her physical and mental health, and that of her children. Few people now have jobs for life, and it seems disingenuous for employers to rely upon possible future ill health as a reason not to employ someone on a short-term contract.

In the US, employers' interest in their employees' health status is magnified by the fact that health insurance is commonly provided by employers, thus providing a double disincentive to employ anyone with a genetic predisposition to ill health. Not only might a high-risk employee have a shorter or less productive working life, but also their insurance premiums are likely to be higher, making them more costly to employ even while they are healthy.

In the next extract, Richard Epstein argues that full disclosure should be the norm where there are informational asymmetries between, for example, people who know that they will develop Huntington's disease and their employers or insurers. Epstein would extend this duty of disclosure to potential spouses who, he argues, have a right to know that the person they are marrying will develop a terminal degenerative disease in middle age.

Richard A Epstein[8]

I think that in the case of Huntington's disease it is immoral for a person to marry (or even take a job) and conceal the condition from the potential spouse or employer. This conclusion is valid in commercial settings as well as in marital ones so long as it results in selective

[7] 'Which Ills to Bear? Reevaluating the "Threat" of Modern Genetics' (1990) 39 Emory Law Journal 665, 692.

[8] 'The Legal Regulation of Genetic Discrimination: Old Responses to New Technology' (1994) 74 Boston University Law Review 1.

knowledge to one side that is denied to the other. When an individual has knowledge that he is at risk of incapacitation, perhaps from family history, then full disclosure should be the norm. . . .

At this point it is critical to note that the plea for privacy is often a plea for the right to misrepresent one's self to the rest of the world . . . No doubt the individual who engages in this type of deception has much to gain. But equally there can be no doubt that this gain exists in all garden variety cases of fraud as well. To show the advantage of the fraud to the party who commits it is hardly to excuse or to justify it, for the same can be said of all cases of successful wrongs. On the other side of the transaction, there is a pronounced loss from not knowing the information when key decisions have to be made. For example, a woman may choose the wrong husband; an employer may pass up a good employee with a strong medical record and a clear upward path in favor of a worker who will, in the end, be the source of enormous personal and financial costs.

(c) FAMILY MEMBERS

Genetic disease is transmitted through procreation, and so the results of genetic tests will often reveal information (albeit sometimes imprecise and uncertain) about other family members. If a person finds out that she has a particular genetic condition, she will inevitably also have found out that one or both of her parents passed on the relevant gene(s), and that her siblings may be at an increased risk of developing the same condition.

In addition, the process of genetic diagnoses may rely upon information from other family members. Indeed, the principal reason for undergoing genetic testing in the first place will usually be a shared family history of a particular condition. One of the first diagnostic tools is often to construct a family tree showing which other members of the family had, or might have had, the disease in question.

There is an inevitable tension between an individualistic model of confidentiality, in which a person's health information is regarded as paradigmatically private, and the inherently shared nature of genetic information. As a result, there are those who have argued that genetic information is, in some sense, 'communal'. As Alastair Kent points out, this tends to be the view of members of families who are at risk of genetic disease:

Among those living in families where there is a diagnosis of a substantial risk of genetic disease, there is a strongly held view that such information should not be seen as the private property of the individual. Rather it should be seen as family information held in common by all those to whom it applies.[9]

Although genetic counselling is non-directive, genetic counsellors will usually encourage disclosure.[10] In the next extract, Katherine O'Donovan and Roy Gilbar point out that while a legal duty to share genetic information may not exist, most people who are given genetic diagnoses feel obliged to inform relatives who might also be at risk.

---

[9] 'Consent and confidentiality in genetics: whose information is it anyway?' (2003) 29 Journal of Medical Ethics 16–18, 17.

[10] Laura E Forrest, Martin B Delatycki, Loane Skene, and MaryAnne Aitken, 'Communicating genetic information in families—a review of guidelines and position papers' (2007) 15 European Journal of Human Genetics 612–18.

Katherine O'Donovan and Roy Gilbar[11]

[W]hen individuals enter into close relationship and become members of family, they realise that their membership entails some responsibilities. This recognition emerges from the empirical data regarding patients' views about disclosure of genetic information to family members. These studies indicate that patients who receive genetic information from their doctors feel morally responsible for communicating the information to their family members . . .

The argument that intimate relationship implies responsibility is reflected in another study conducted by Lehmann et al. This study reports that 85% of the respondents believe that patients should disclose genetic information to relatives even when the disease is unavoidable and incurable. This suggests that the underlying reason for sharing information within the family does not derive solely from the desire to prevent harm to others, as lawyers argue, but from a strong sense of moral responsibility and from the recognition that medical information has implications in various aspects of family members' lives.

What if the person who has been tested refuses to tell her relatives? Could disclosure without her consent be justifiable? Alissa Brownrigg has suggests that five factors should be taken into account when deciding whether to disclose a person's positive genetic test result to other family members:

(1) the severity of the disease identified by testing;

(2) the availability of preventive or curative options for that disease;

(3) the accuracy and reliability of the test performed;

(4) the ability of the physician or health care provider to interpret and address issues relevant to the test performed; and lastly,

(5) the protections afforded to the tested individual against discrimination.[12]

First, the severity of the disease is important because breaching confidentiality should be a last resort, and justifiable only if a potential harm is imminent or serious. Secondly, if there are no available means of treating the disease or preventing its onset, knowing that one faces an increased risk of developing a serious disease may cause significant distress, without any possibility of averting the risk in question. Of course, there may be some steps that individuals can take to reduce the risk of serious adverse consequences, even if a complete cure does not exist. Women who discover that they have the BRCA1 gene will be offered routine mammograms, which might enable breast cancer to be diagnosed in its early stages. Some women have chosen to undergo prophylactic double mastectomies.

Genetic information might also be useful for people who are planning to have children. Preimplantation genetic diagnosis, discussed in Chapter 15, will enable couples to take steps to ensure that any child they have will not have the genetic condition which runs in their family.

Thirdly, the risk of false positives and false negatives should also be taken into account. Both can cause significant harm: a false negative result may mean that an individual does not receive the treatment that she needs. A false positive result will cause unnecessary anxiety, and may result in the person undergoing painful and unnecessary treatment.

Fourthly, genetic test results are complex and difficult to interpret. Disclosure without a proper explanation of the result's significance would be inappropriate. Finally, if a genetic

[11] 'The Loved Ones: Families, Intimates and Patient Autonomy' (2003) 23 Legal Studies 353.

[12] Alissa Brownrigg, 'Mother Still Knows Best: Cancer-Related Gene Mutations, Familial Privacy and a Physician's Duty to Warn' (1999) 26 Fordham Urban Law Journal 247, 273.

test reveals a person's susceptibility to debilitating illness, it may make it difficult to obtain insurance or employment, and again this may militate against disclosure.

In essence, these factors are relevant to whether disclosure to a family member fits within the 'public interest' exception to the duty of confidentiality which we considered in the previous chapter: that is, there must be a real risk of serious harm to others which could be averted by non-consensual disclosure. In the next extract, Dean Bell and Belinda Bennett argue that genetic information should not be treated as a special case, and that a doctor should divulge an individual's genetic test results only where it would 'prevent or lessen a serious or imminent threat to the life or health of a relative'.

Dean Bell and Belinda Bennett[13]

[W]here a patient poses a risk to another individual the courts have accepted that limited disclosures of confidential information may be justified in order to avert that harm. In other words, if the concern is that patients might not advise their relatives of their genetic risk, and that relatives may suffer as a result, the existing law of confidentiality arguably already provides a framework for disclosure to be permitted if the health of another is at risk.

Because one family member's genetic test results will usually just reveal that their relatives have an elevated risk of being predisposed to a condition, the 'public interest' exception will rarely be satisfied. Not only is the risk of suffering the particular disease uncertain, for many genetic conditions there is no known cure, and so disclosure would seldom enable someone to prevent the risk from materializing. As a result, Loane Skene disagrees with Bell and Bennett, arguing that genetic information is a special case and that disclosure of familial risk will sometimes be justifiable even where it would not fit within the normal 'public interest' exception.

Loane Skene[14]

Bell and Bennett suggest that the common law is adequate to protect a doctor who feels compelled to disclose a genetic risk to a relative of the patient without the patient's consent. They base this on the 'public interest' exception to the general confidentiality requirement, which will justify disclosure where there is a serious and imminent risk to the person or a third party . . .

I have some doubts about the adequacy of this little-tested principle in relation to genetic testing . . . The law requires the risk to be serious and imminent. It is difficult to imagine a situation in which a genetic risk would be of this type. Take FAP [Familial Adenematous Polyposis, a type of colorectal cancer], for example, where in my view disclosure is most arguably justified. The risk is serious; it is a potentially lethal condition. The diagnosis is certain. And there is an effective intervention (monitoring and surgery if needed). Yet the risk could not be described as imminent. For these reasons I do not believe the common law exception is sufficient.

In the next extract, Allen Buchanan cautions against treating all genetic tests in the same way. There are genetic conditions, such as hereditary hemochromatosis, which are serious,

[13] 'Genetic Secrets and the Family' (2001) 9 Medical Law Review 130–61, 132.
[14] 'Genetic Secrets and the Family: A Response to Bell and Bennett' (2001) 9 Medical Law Review 162–9.

but for which a safe, relatively non-invasive, cheap, and effective treatment exists. Here the potential to avert harm by disclosure is strong. In contrast, hereditary Alzheimer's disease is untreatable, and there is considerable stigma attached to its diagnosis. Buchanan argues that genetic conditions thus exist upon a spectrum, with conditions like hemochromatosis at one end and Alzheimer's at the other. Furthermore, where a condition lies on this spectrum is subject to change as more genetic diseases become treatable, thus steadily increasing the number of cases in which doctors will face difficult dilemmas about whether to breach patient confidentiality.

Allen Buchanan[15]

At present, with a few exceptions, diagnosis for genetic diseases outstrips treatment. This is especially true for the genetic tests that currently receive the most extensive media coverage and public discussion, including tests for the BRCA1 and BRCA2 genes, the APO E4 Alzheimer's gene test, and the test for the Huntington's gene. In each of these cases, the medical benefit of testing is very dubious at present because there is no effective treatment for the condition. . . .

The situation is quite different if there is an effective treatment for a potentially lethal disease that can be detected by a genetic test. In this case, the clinician will reasonably believe that there is a single right course of action, and that the ethical responsibilities of the patient are clear from the perspective of widely accepted and easily defended values.

At present there are few such conditions. Perhaps the clearest case of a lethal late-onset disease that meets this description is hereditary hemochromatosis. If detected early enough, hereditary hemochromatosis has a simple, inexpensive, virtually riskless, and fully effective treatment; yet this disease has devastating effects on the liver, heart, and endocrine system if left untreated . . . It is reasonable to expect that in the future there will be more cases where those who test positive for a serious genetic condition will have the option of a successful treatment.

In any event, it seems clear that family members do not have a right to be informed about a relative's genetic diagnosis. In *ABC v St George's Healthcare NHS Foundation Trust*, the claimant sought to argue that her father's doctors owed her a duty of care to inform her about her father's diagnosis with Huntington's disease. The claimant had been pregnant when her father was diagnosed. At the time, she was known to the medical team caring for her father, because he was in a secure hospital, having murdered her mother, and she had been engaging in family therapy at the hospital. Her father was asked to consent to disclosure to her at the time, but he had refused. She subsequently found out accidentally about her father's diagnosis, and tests revealed that she had inherited the condition from him. The claimant maintained that she would have terminated the pregnancy if she had been informed that she was at risk of the disease herself, and of passing it on to her children.

In the first legal claim of its kind, she claimed that her father's doctors had breached the duty of care they had owed to her by failing to inform her about her risk of inheriting Huntington's, claiming that she had suffered psychological harm as a result. She also claimed that the failure to inform her of her risk breached her Article 8 rights. In the event

[15] 'Ethical responsibilities of patients and clinical geneticists' (1998) 1 Journal of Health Care Law and Policy 391, 395–7.

that her daughter, who had not been tested, had inherited the disease, she also claimed for any extra expense this entailed. Nicol J struck out her claim; imposing a duty of care in these circumstances would be a radical departure from ordinary tort law principles, and the balancing exercise between confidentiality and her interest in knowing this information came down firmly in favour of confidentiality.

ABC v St George's Healthcare NHS Foundation Trust[16]

Nicol J

In my judgment, therefore, this is not a case where the Claimant can show that a novel duty of care would be but an incremental development from some well established duty. It would, on the contrary, be a radical departure to impose liability in circumstances such as these....

Yet still, on analysis, the complaint remains, as it is put in the PoC [particulars of claim] about what the Defendants did not do—they did not tell her about her father's condition. Whether that is actionable depends on whether they were under a duty to do so. There was no assumption of responsibility towards the Claimant in this regard and, even taking account of all the facts pleaded in the PoC, I do not accept [counsel's] submission that there was a special relationship between the Defendants and the Claimant....

It has to be the Claimant's case that the positive duty implicit in art.8 required the Defendants to disclose her father's condition to her.... Either way there is plainly a balance to be struck between the value to the Claimant of knowing that her father had this genetic condition (and so that she had a 50 per cent chance of also being afflicted) on the one hand and her father's right (also under art.8) to have the confidentiality of his medical information preserved.... [A]ll the reasons which I have set out in the context of the common law claim, mean that the balance comes down decisively against the Claimant.

It is also important to recognize that disclosure to relatives might jeopardize their right not to know about any predisposition they might have to genetic disease. Where a condition is incurable, a positive test result might lead to depression, and make it difficult for an individual to purchase insurance. There may then be good reasons for preferring to remain in ignorance. Although testing might reveal that an individual is unaffected, and hence remove a source of anxiety, it is equally likely that she will discover that she is destined for a short, painful, and distressing future. We should not perhaps be surprised that take-up of genetic tests within families who know that there is a risk that they may have inherited the Huntington's mutation has been low: studies have suggested that fewer than 15 per cent of at-risk individuals opt to take the test.[17]

There is also some evidence that both positive and negative test results may be difficult to come to terms with within families at risk of Huntington's. Gargiulo et al's study found that 58 per cent of asymptomatic carriers and 24 per cent of non-carriers were depressed in the months after being tested.[18] Tibben et al report that some of those who tested negative for

---

[16] [2015] EWHC 1394 (QB).

[17] PJ Morrison, S Harding-Lester, and A Bradley, 'Uptake of Huntington disease predictive testing in a complete population' (2011) 80 Clinical Genetics 281–6.

[18] Marcela Gargiulo et al, 'Long-term outcome of presymptomatic testing in Huntington disease' (2009) 17 European Journal of Human Genetics 165–71.

the gene found themselves rejected by their families, once it became apparent that they no longer shared a bond which had previously brought the family closer.[19]

It is also important to note that it is not only direct disclosure that might threaten the right 'not to know'. Simply alerting relatives to the existence of information, and asking them whether they wish to receive it, reveals to them that there is something to worry about.

The right 'not to know' is enshrined in a number of international documents, for example Article 5c of the UNESCO Declaration on the Human Genome provides that:

> The right of every individual to decide whether or not to be informed of the results of genetic examination and the resulting consequences should be respected.

Is a right to ignorance in tension with the duty of doctors to be honest and frank with their patients, which we considered in the previous chapter? Graeme Laurie thinks not, and argues instead that our right to control information about ourselves encompasses a right not to know that information.

Graeme Laurie[20]

> To disclose genetic information to someone who has not expressed a desire to know can be disrespectful in two ways.
>
> First, furnishing an individual with information that she has actually said she does not want to receive disrespects her wishes and is an affront to her as an autonomous person. The pivotal ethical principle of respect for autonomy surely requires that we respect her wishes.
>
> Second, even if no wish has been expressed, we cannot ignore the spatial privacy interests which are also compromised . . . Control of information about ourselves must be an essential part of any concept of ourselves as autonomous persons, but 'control' should not be limited merely to control of who has access to that information. It should also include the facility not to accept the information *ab initio* . . .
>
> The precise content of the 'right' not to know will be context specific. For example, in the familial milieu, it might include a right not to be given information about a relative's diagnosis or a right not to be required to take part in linkage studies in order to build up an overall family profile. In the context of insurers and employers, it would certainly include a right not to be required to undergo testing and would probably also include a right to resist disclosure of test results if these were required simply to further the interests of third parties. . . .
>
> Yet irrespective of context—and in each case—the kernel of the right not to know is the concept of respect for an individual privacy interest in not being subjected to unwarranted information about themselves.

The need to protect the right 'not to know' is one reason why parents can only consent to the genetic testing of their children if this will enable the child to receive treatment; that is, the testing must be done for therapeutic reasons rather than in order to find out information about future risk.

In addition to ensuring the child herself can exercise her right not to know, there has been concern over the motives of parents seeking to test their children. Wexler gives the extreme

---

[19] A Tibben et al, 'Testing for Huntington's disease with support for all parties' (1990) 335 The Lancet 553.
[20] 'In Defence of Ignorance: Genetic Information and the Right Not to Know' (1999) 6 European Journal of Health Law 119–32.

example of a woman in the US who requested genetic testing for Huntington's disease for her two children, on the grounds that she could only afford to send one of them to Harvard.[21]

On the other hand, in the next extract, PJ Malpas argues that parents are overwhelmingly likely to have their child's best interests at heart when making decisions about genetic testing.

PJ Malpas[22]

A parent may comment that they would not save for their affected child's college education, intending instead to use that money to ensure that the child had a very positive and memorable childhood. One can imagine the parents who, knowing the child may only live until his or her early adulthood, devote their energies and resources into supporting and enabling the child's self esteem and confidence, and providing the child with opportunities they may otherwise not have had. For instance, travelling the world, regularly spending more time with older extended family members, actively pursuing a child's passions and hobbies, deciding not to send the child to boarding school, doing more together as a family, or simply spending more time with the child by limiting work hours.

(d) THE POLICE

Unlike most other biobanks, as Patyn and Dierickx point out, the justification for storing a person's DNA in a forensic database cannot be that they have given their informed consent.

Annemie Patyn and Kris Dierickx[23]

While medical biobanks can rely on the principle of 'informed consent', forensic DNA databases cannot. After all, individuals do not benefit from having their own data stored in such a database: the inclusion of a DNA profile is favourable only for other persons, not for the tested persons themselves. Consequently, these databases are controlled by the government or police services, who can force someone's data to be included in the database.

Consent to store data in a forensic DNA database thus can hardly be given at the level of the individual, but, rather, is a societal choice. . . . While forensic DNA databases (probably) increase security, at the same time they restrict the liberty of citizens. A society thus has to determine what importance it attaches to these different values.

If the DNA of every citizen were recorded and stored on a central police database, the identification of criminals from biological traces left at a crime scene would be much more straightforward. But while the police might find a central record of every citizen's DNA extremely useful, it would be impractical and ethically dubious. Universal testing would be

---

[21] Nancy Wexler, 'Clairvoyance and Caution: Repercussions from the Human Genome Project' in Daniel J Kevles and Leroy Hood (eds), *The Code of Codes: Scientific and Social Issues in the Human Genome Project* (Harvard UP: Cambridge, MA, 1992) 211–43, 233.

[22] 'Predictive genetic testing of children for adult-onset diseases and psychological harm' (2008) 34 Journal of Medical Ethics 275–8.

[23] 'Forensic DNA databases: genetic testing as a societal choice' (2010) 36 Journal of Medical Ethics 319–20.

expensive, and the database would be useful only if non-volunteers could be compelled to give samples. But if there is no reason to suspect someone of committing a crime, what justification could there be for taking a sample without her consent?

More plausible are databases of DNA profiles extracted from biological samples taken from people who have been arrested and/or convicted of offences. Samples will have been taken anyway, and the costs of retaining DNA profiles and samples would be relatively low. But should a distinction be drawn between those who have been convicted, and those who have been acquitted or released without charge? Should we also distinguish between serious and trivial offences?

Until the end of 2008, under section 64(1A) of the Police and Criminal Evidence Act 1984, DNA samples could be retained from all suspects—that is, anyone who had ever been arrested—regardless of whether they were subsequently convicted of an offence, provided that the samples were used only for the prevention and detection of crime. Samples taken from volunteers, who supplied them in order to eliminate themselves from suspicion, were also routinely retained.

Unsurprisingly, given the wide range of people whose profiles could find their way onto the database, the UK's National DNA Database (NDNAD) became one of the largest in the world, containing the DNA profiles of approximately 6 per cent of the population. For certain minority ethnic groups, the proportion was much higher: over-representation of people from a minority ethnic group in police arrest practices automatically translated into their over-representation on the database. In London, for example, 55 per cent of the unconvicted people on the database were black or Asian.[24]

Whether or not retaining samples from people who have not been convicted is compatible with the Human Rights Act 1998 came before the House of Lords in *R (on the application of S) v Chief Constable of South Yorkshire*,[25] a case concerning two individuals who, in separate cases, had had their DNA samples retained, despite not being convicted of the crimes for which they had been arrested. By a 4:1 majority the House of Lords rejected their claim that this breached their Article 8 rights.

The applicants then took their case to the European Court of Human Rights (ECtHR). In *Marper v United Kingdom*, the ECtHR unanimously held that retaining samples and DNA profiles from people who had been acquitted or never charged was an interference with their private or family life, and that, while it served a legitimate aim, namely the detection of crime, it was disproportionate and could not be regarded as necessary in a democratic society.

Marper v United Kingdom[26]

Judgment of the ECtHR

Given the nature and the amount of personal information contained in cellular samples, their retention per se must be regarded as interfering with the right to respect for the private lives of the individuals concerned . . .

In the Court's view, the DNA profiles' capacity to provide a means of identifying genetic relationships between individuals is in itself sufficient to conclude that their retention interferes with the right to the private life of the individuals concerned. . . .

---

[24] Nuffield Council on Bioethics, *The Forensic Use of Bioinformation: Ethical Issues* (NCOB, 2008).
[25] [2004] UKHL 39.   [26] Application nos 30562/04 and 30566/04 (2008).

The Court further notes that it is not disputed by the Government that the processing of DNA profiles allows the authorities to assess the likely ethnic origin of the donor and that such techniques are in fact used in police investigations. The possibility the DNA profiles create for inferences to be drawn as to ethnic origin makes their retention all the more sensitive and susceptible of affecting the right to private life. . . .

In view of the foregoing, the Court concludes that the retention of both cellular samples and DNA profiles discloses an interference with the applicants' right to respect for their private lives, within the meaning of Article 8 § 1 of the Convention . . .

The question, however, remains whether such retention is proportionate and strikes a fair balance between the competing public and private interests.

In this respect, the Court is struck by the blanket and indiscriminate nature of the power of retention in England and Wales. The material may be retained irrespective of the nature or gravity of the offence with which the individual was originally suspected or of the age of the suspected offender; fingerprints and samples may be taken—and retained—from a person of any age, arrested in connection with a recordable offence, which includes minor or non-imprisonable offences. The retention is not time-limited; the material is retained indefinitely whatever the nature or seriousness of the offence of which the person was suspected.

In conclusion, the Court finds that the blanket and indiscriminate nature of the powers of retention of the fingerprints, cellular samples and DNA profiles of persons suspected but not convicted of offences, as applied in the case of the present applicants, fails to strike a fair balance between the competing public and private interests and that the respondent State has overstepped any acceptable margin of appreciation in this regard.

Four years after this judgment, the Protection of Freedoms Act 2012 amended the Police and Criminal Evidence Act 1984 in order to eliminate indefinite and indiscriminate retention of samples. Before the new sections 63 and 64 came into force in late 2013, the Home Office engaged in a systematic destruction of samples and profiles that no longer met these new requirements.

The retention of all DNA samples is now prohibited after six months. In this time, the sample can be analysed and a DNA profile produced for inclusion in the database. In exceptional circumstances, such as complex court cases, a court order can permit longer retention of the DNA sample.

DNA profiles, which are essentially just a string of 20 numbers, and two letters to indicate gender, can be retained according to the rather complicated scheme shown in the following table (NB qualifying offences are serious violent or sexual offences, terrorism offences, and burglary offences).

CATEGORY	RETENTION
CONVICTION Adult	Indefinite
CONVICTION Under-18 qualifying offence	Indefinite
CONVICTION Under-18 conviction minor offence	First conviction: five years (plus length of any custodial sentence), or indefinite if the custodial sentence is five years or more. Second conviction: indefinite
NON-CONVICTION Qualifying offence: charge	Three years plus possible two-year extension by court

(Continued)

(Continued)

CATEGORY	RETENTION
NON-CONVICTION Qualifying offence: arrested	Possible three years on application to Biometrics Commissioner (or indefinite retention if they hold a previous conviction for a recordable offence) plus two-year extension possible
NON-CONVICTION Minor offence: penalty notice	Two years
NON-CONVICTION Minor offence: arrested or charged	No retention-but speculatively searched to check if they match to any crime on the database
NATIONAL SECURITY	Indefinite

Would this new system withstand a second *Marper*-style challenge? While the new scheme does not adopt a one-size-fits-all approach to retention, it continues to be problematic. It permits the indefinite retention of the DNA profiles of every adult who has been convicted, and of every child who has been convicted of more than one offence.

More significantly, the scheme retains the dubious assumption that some suspicion continues to attach to people who have been arrested but not convicted of certain offences. During the Protection of Freedoms Bill's passage through parliament, the campaigning organization Liberty argued that the process of judicial oversight of extensions to retention is particularly hard to square with the presumption of innocence.

Liberty[27]

> 11. We are also concerned about the potential for retention to be extended by Court order. While initially the application procedure looks attractive, in as much as there is judicial oversight, we believe it is seriously flawed. The proposed model allows a Court to formally state that while a person has not been proven guilty of any offence, doubts remain about them which justify the retention of their biometric material after the blanket three year period. Those for whom such an application was successfully granted would be made to feel that there was greater suspicion over them than others against whom an application had been unsuccessful. To introduce an application procedure whereby a Court adjudicates on whether there is enough evidence against an accused to raise some doubt, but not enough evidence to prove guilt beyond a reasonable doubt, is a major, and we submit a dangerous, step. We believe that the mechanism for renewal introduced by the Bill easily lends itself to becoming a rubber-stamping exercise, creating a real risk that applications would become routine, as police seek to prevent blame being attributed if, in any given case, an application has not been made and an individual later goes on to commit a crime . . .
>
> 13. Another significant concern on the face of the Bill is provisions permitting the indefinite retention of any biometric information which a chief officer concludes should be retained in the interests of national security, subject only to the reviewing function of the newly appointed Commissioner. There is nothing in the Bill to prevent a high proportion of DNA and fingerprints being retained on undefined notions of national security.

[27] *Liberty's Second Reading Briefing on the Protection of Freedoms Bill in the House of Commons* (Liberty, 2011).

The Human Genetics Commission produced a report on the NDNAD in 2009. The Commission argued that the NDNAD had moved from being a database of offenders to being a database of suspects, and that retention of the unconvicted was being justified on the grounds of a population-wide, risk-based calculation that—as a group—the arrested but unconvicted are statistically more likely to commit crime than the section of the population which has never been arrested. But given that retention of the DNA profiles of people who have never been convicted of an offence undermines the presumption of innocence, this approach is problematic. The Commission was also critical of the assumption which underpins the Protection of Freedoms Act, namely that more suspicion attaches to someone who is not convicted of a serious offence, than to someone who is not convicted of a minor offence.

Human Genetics Commission[28]

Although these limitations are used in other Council of Europe Member States, those that relate to the seriousness of the offence, grounds for suspicion, previous arrests, etc. may, from one point of view, appear to threaten the presumption of innocence. The argument might be expressed something like this: suppose two people are arrested and brought to a police station to have a DNA sample taken; one is suspected of a serious crime (murder or rape, for example) the other of a minor crime (say, taxi touting). Criminal proceedings run their course and both are found not guilty (or perhaps proceedings are dropped or they are never charged). In the eyes of the law, both are presumed to be innocent. Given that the offences happened, this entails that people other than the arrestees (perhaps as yet unidentified) are presumed to have committed the offences of which they were suspected. If this is the case, it cannot therefore make sense to keep the DNA profile of one suspect longer than that of the other—to keep the profile of someone who is not guilty of a murder longer than that of someone who is not guilty of taxi touting. This is because the person who is not guilty of taxi touting is *also* not guilty of the murder *in the same way and to the same extent* as the person suspected—but acquitted—of the murder. And because being not guilty is the reciprocal of being guilty and neither admit of degree, it can make no sense to keep the profile of the suspected murderer or taxi tout and not that of any other member of the population *who is equally not guilty*.

In the next extract, Stephen Sedley, writing extra-judicially, advocates a different solution to the inequity of storing samples from people who have come into contact with the police but who have not actually been convicted.

Stephen Sedley[29]

My argument is that the case is growing for a national database holding the DNA profile of everyone living in or entering the country. The present system, sanctioned by legislation, is that the police may take and keep a DNA sample from everyone they arrest, whether or not the person is charged or convicted. This has the unfortunate effect of putting the innocent on

---

[28] *Nothing to Fear, Nothing to Hide* (HGC: London, 2009).
[29] An extract from a lecture, '"Rarely Pure and Never Simple": The Law and the Truth', delivered in 2004 at Leicester University and published under the title 'Short cuts' (2005) 27 London Review of Books.

a par with the guilty. It draws a not very logical line between innocent people who have and have not passed through the hands of the police. But it does not follow that the law should be moved back to what it once was, so as to require the police to destroy their DNA records of everyone not eventually convicted. What follows no less logically is that the taking and retention of an individual's DNA profile should not depend at all on whether he or she happens to have come into the hands of the police. . . . It can be, in fact, something rather worse than a fortuity. We know that there is an ethnic imbalance in arrests for certain types of offence, as well as in the use of stop and search powers. This . . . has the unacceptable consequence that members of some ethnic minorities face a disproportionately high chance of getting on to the police DNA database without being convicted of anything. A universal and uniform database will at least resolve this problem.

In 2007, an Ethics Group was set up to monitor the operation and uses of the NDNAD. It is perhaps noteworthy that this only happened after the NDNAD had been in operation for several years, rather than at the outset. The Group considered, and rejected, the possibility of a population-wide database.

NDNAD Ethics Group[30]

- A database containing the DNA profiles of all the supposed inhabitants of the United Kingdom at any one time would in fact never absolutely do so in practical terms. There would for example, be those who would avoid profiling (by illegal means or on the grounds of human rights), temporary visitors, migrant workers, and the deliberate submission of false identities;

- Despite the existing legislative controls, there are unknown and unpredictable social consequences of being potentially able to identify the parentage and sibling status of all individuals. The ramifications extend beyond the discovery of unexpected birth relationships to inheritance rights and the penetration of genetic traits.

- Consequently, it is inappropriate without public debate and fraught with ethical and social problems and questions of personal freedom, to allow a criminal intelligence database to convert into a national repository of the nation's DNA characteristics. Arguing that the database should be expanded to include all the population, (the majority of whom will never commit a crime), to prevent inequality and discrimination is, on balance, unsustainable when issues of proportionality and personal privacy are taken into account.

A further issue that arises in relation to the forensic use of genetic information is its use in the courtroom, where a match between the DNA profile of an individual and samples found at a crime scene is often assumed to offer irrefutable, objective evidence of guilt. This is misleading, however, for several reasons. First, the fact that DNA evidence proves that person X was in a location where a crime was committed does not establish that person X committed that crime; merely that person X has been at that location at some point in the past. Secondly, there is always the possibility of human error or contamination or degradation of samples: crime scenes, almost by definition, involve the antithesis of ideal laboratory conditions.

---

[30] *1st Annual Report* (Home Office: London, 2008).

Thirdly, let us imagine that there is a match between the DNA of an individual suspect and that of the person who committed the crime, and that the chance of this happening randomly is put at one in a million. While that sounds like fairly conclusive evidence of guilt, in a country with a population of 62 million, there are likely to be 61 other individuals with the same DNA profile who might also have been responsible for leaving their DNA at the crime scene. If one takes into account people from other countries who might also be a match, there may be many hundreds of people worldwide who could have left this DNA at this crime scene.

Even if we confine ourselves to the UK population, rather than establishing that there is a one in a million chance that the defendant is not guilty, this 'one in a million' match in fact establishes that there is a one in 62 chance that the defendant is the person whose DNA was left at the crime scene, which sounds rather different. Of course, there may be other evidence that points to the defendant being the perpetrator, rather than one of these other 61 people, but DNA evidence alone does not establish their guilt.

(e) OTHER DNA DATABASES

There are now a wide variety of collections of DNA samples and profiles, loosely described as biobanks. Most exist for the purposes of research, but they vary hugely in size and scope. Some collections are small disease-specific registries, whereas others are large-scale epidemiological resources. In the next extract, Susan Gibbons suggests that both small and large biobanks may result in different sorts of risks to the interests of participants whose samples or sensitive information is stored.

Susan MC Gibbons[31]

> Regulators may wish to expect more detailed and demanding standards, procedures, and protocols from 'bigger' biobanks (however defined).
>
> But 'size' can cut both ways. . . . A good example here is oversight and governance. Greater scrutiny may be thought necessary for 'bigger' databases—commensurate, say, with the potentially greater risks to participants' privacy, confidentiality, and consent (insofar as relevant) posed by widespread data set interlinking, having multiple collaborators or end-users, international transfers of materials (especially to jurisdictions lacking equivalent legal protections), or the amassing of much more detailed and revealing phenotypic and genotypic material. Yet, 'smaller' biobanks may well be less visible, and so less amenable to external scrutiny. Unlike 'bigger' biobanks, they are also highly unlikely to have their own bespoke, internal oversight committees, or governance systems. Following the REC [research ethics committee] approval stage, they may not be subject to any formal ongoing monitoring at all. Here too, then, arguably a greater potential danger to significant rights and interests arises.

In the UK, the Biobank is a research initiative which is tracking the health of a representative sample of the population from the time at which they sign up until their deaths.[32] Between 2006 and 2010, UK Biobank recruited half a million volunteers aged between 40 and 69.

---

[31] 'Regulating Biobanks: A Twelve-Point Typological Tool' (2009) 17 Medical Law Review 313–46.

[32] Jean V McHale, 'Regulating Genetic Databases: Some Legal and Ethical Issues' (2004) 12 Medical Law Review 70–96.

Recruits gave a blood sample, answered questions about their lifestyle and medical history, and perhaps most significantly, prospectively granted full access to their past and future medical records. Participants in the project give generic consent at the outset to their data's use in research, and to being contacted in the future by UK Biobank or other researchers. By 2014, UK Biobank had received 260 access applications from researchers.

People are free to withdraw from UK Biobank at any time. In order to try to ensure that as much information as possible remains on the database, if someone develops reservations about continued participation, there are three different levels of withdrawal: no further contact (UK Biobank would no longer contact the person but would be able to continue to use their information, including their future health records, and stored samples); no further access (UK Biobank would no longer contact the person or obtain additional information from their health records, but would still have permission to use the information and samples provided previously), and most drastic 'no further use' (there would be no use of any information and their samples would be destroyed).[33]

Unlike the NDNAD, from the outset UK Biobank has had to operate within an ethics and governance framework (EGF), a 'living document', currently in its third version.[34] It has an independent Ethics and Governance Council, which monitors compliance with the EGF, oversees the Biobank's activities, and advises on ethical and legal issues which arise during the different phases of the project. In 2011, it played an important role in the development of Biobank's Access Principles, which include a commitment to open access, confidentiality, and the public interest.

UK Biobank[35]

- [T]he resource is available to all bona fide researchers for all types of health-related research that is in the public interest, without preferential or exclusive access for any person. All researchers, whether in universities, charities, government agencies or commercial companies, and whether based in the UK or abroad, will be subject to the same application process and approval criteria;

- safeguards will be maintained to help ensure the anonymity and confidentiality of participants' data and samples. Researchers will enter a legal agreement with UK Biobank not to make any attempt to identify participants, and data and/or samples provided to researchers from the resource will not identify any particular participant (i.e. they will be 'anonymised');

- researchers granted access to the resource will be required to publish their findings and return their results to UK Biobank so that they are available for other researchers to use for health-related research that is in the public interest;

To maximize usefulness, the consent given by people whose samples or profiles are to be stored in a biobank should be as general or generic as possible. In the next extract, Margaret Otlowski argues that obtaining 'broad' consent is not only convenient for researchers, but may also be better for participants, and—as a result of the relative homogeneity of genetic database research—will still allow them to have the information they need, albeit in fairly general terms, before they give consent.

---

[33] UK Biobank, *Ethics and Governance Framework version 3.0* (UK Biobank, 2007).   [34] Ibid.
[35] 'Principles of Access', available at www.ukbiobank.ac.uk/principles-of-access/.

Margaret FA Otlowski[36]

[R]epeated consent may be seen not only as impracticable but also as intrusive from the research participant's perspective, and may in fact operate as a deterrent. From other research, there is some indication of consent 'fatigue' and of people not wanting extensive information. . . . There is also accumulating evidence that patients who consent to donate their tissue are keen to see that the maximum benefit will be obtained from its use, and just want researchers to get on with their work . . .

If we reflect on what subjects would normally be expected to be informed about when their specific consent is sought (aims/objectives, methods, demands, risks and harms, inconvenience and discomfort, possible outcomes including commercialisation potential, right to withdraw etc), much of this can be dealt with in advance in more generic terms. . . . Whilst the specifics of each research project may not be knowable, there is enough information available to prospective subjects for them to understand the general nature of what the research is about. . . .

Further, there are a number of strategies that can be taken to help promote ongoing active consent: after the initial collection of samples and information, it is essential that open lines of communication be maintained so that subjects can be kept informed of research directions and possible planned uses of samples and information in the future.

It is also important to acknowledge a particular feature of collections of DNA profiles and samples. The nature of this information means that, as Schmidt and Callier point out, it is vital that participants understand that complete anonymization of a DNA sample—which of its very nature identifies the person whose sample it is— is impossible.

Harald Schmidt and Shawneequa Callier[37]

Provided that the biological or genetic material is of suitable quality and quantity, samples that contain DNA always, by their very nature, retain a link to the person from whom they came: 'DNA is itself uniquely identifiable.' Reidentification may require a great deal of effort, time and expense, as illustrated by the processes employed to identify victims of a natural disaster or terrorism (such as the Tsunami in the Indian Ocean in 2004 or the attacks on the World Trade Center in 2001). But it is wrong to suggest that such reidentification is impossible. As a number of recent scientific developments have demonstrated, it is increasingly easier to establish such matches. This trend looks set to continue, and the growing interconnectivity of increasingly larger and numerous genetic and non-genetic databases are of particular relevance, as are different ways in which people engaging in consumer-driven genomics might themselves initiate matching . . .

It would help to recognise more fully that the various stages of anonymisation are merely incremental levels that make it increasingly difficult to identify samples, but never impossible.

---

[36] 'Tackling Legal Challenges Posed By Population Biobanks: Reconceptualising Consent Requirements' (2012) 20 Medical Law Review 191–226.

[37] 'How anonymous is "anonymous"? Some suggestions towards a coherent universal coding system for genetic samples' (2012) 38 Journal of Medical Ethics 304–9.

3 GENETIC DISCRIMINATION

Should genetic discrimination in the workplace or in the supply of goods and services be outlawed in the same way as other sorts of discrimination? It has been illegal to discriminate on the grounds of disability in the UK since 1995, and so where someone has a genetic condition 'which has a substantial and long-term adverse effect on his ability to carry out normal day-to-day activities',[38] unjustified discrimination is already unlawful. This will clearly not cover people with genetic conditions who are not yet symptomatic.

In the next extract, Lawrence Gostin advocates the specific prohibition of genetic discrimination.

Lawrence O Gostin[39]

Discrimination based upon actual or perceived genetic characteristics denies an individual equal opportunity because of a status over which she has no control. Discrimination based on genetic factors can be as unjust as that based on race, gender or disability. In each case, people are treated inequitably, not because of their inherent abilities, but solely because of pre-determined characteristics. The right to be treated equally and according to one's abilities in all the diverse aspects of human endeavor is a core social value.

Genetic discrimination is harmful not merely because it violates core social values, but also because it thwarts the creativity and productivity of human beings, perhaps more than the disability itself. By excluding qualified individuals from education, employment, government service or insurance, the marketplace is robbed of skills, energy and imagination. Such exclusion promotes physical and economic dependency, draining rather than enriching social institutions.

In the US, the Genetic Information Nondiscrimination Act 2008 (GINA) prohibits providers of health insurance and employers from discriminating against individuals on the basis of genetic test results, and forbids them from requesting or demanding that a person undergoes a genetic test. Certain sorts of insurance are not covered: an insurer is allowed to ask for genetic test results before providing life insurance, disability insurance, and long-term care insurance. This means that, despite the existence of GINA, people may continue to be deterred from undergoing genetic testing in case it increases their insurance premiums for these excluded types of insurance.

Furthermore, GINA does not protect people who are symptomatic, and hence once the genetic condition manifests itself, discrimination is not prohibited under the Act. As in the UK, discrimination on the grounds of disability is outlawed in the US. Nevertheless, people with genetic disorders may find themselves in a legal limbo in the period after first experiencing symptoms of the disorder, when GINA will cease to apply, but before they become sufficiently disabled to be covered by disability discrimination legislation.

In addition, the Harvard Law Review's commentary on GINA criticizes its 'genetic exceptionalism'. The consequence of GINA is that people with other sorts of knowledge about their likelihood of future ill health are treated less favourably than those whose predictive diagnoses happen to be genetic.

---

[38] Equality Act 2010, s 6(1)(b).

[39] 'Genetic Discrimination: The Use of Genetically Based Diagnostic and Prognostic Tests by Employers and Insurers' (1991) 17 American Journal of Law and Medicine 109.

Harvard Law Review[40]

Although superficially appealing, GINA suffers from significant flaws. It implies and promotes genetic exceptionalism—the idea that genetic information needs special treatment—despite lacking a sound basis for separating genetic conditions from nongenetic ones that people did not knowingly cause and cannot change ...

Though instinctively accepted by most people outside the bioethics community, genetic exceptionalism produces unsettling results. Consider three women who have the same increased probability of breast cancer: one who carries the BRCA1 gene, a second who has unknown environmental hazards in her neighborhood, and a third who was exposed to diethylstilbestrol as a fetus. None of these women deserves blame for her predisposition to cancer, but under GINA an insurer could deny coverage or raise premiums based on the exposure-based conditions but not the genetic one. Discomfort with this result probably stems from the intuition that wellbeing should depend not on pure luck but rather on what we think of as conscious choices. The blamelessness of all three women makes it difficult to support giving benefits to the first woman but denying them to the others. The apparent equivalence of this genetic and nongenetic information makes separate genetic antidiscrimination legislation questionable—why should we care less about those with nongenetic health risks? ... Passing antidiscrimination legislation for genes, but not for uncontrollable nongenetic factors, seems at best an unfinished job.

James Mittra agrees, and asks why genetic information that bears on a person's future health and life expectancy should receive special protection, when other sorts of diagnoses—a positive HIV test, for example—must be disclosed.

James Mittra[41]

The practice of fair discrimination, as an underlying commercial philosophy, dictates that individuals pay a premium for life assurance that is commensurate with the risks they bring to the insurance pool. If a genetic test with demonstrable predictive efficacy predisposes an individual to a particular disease that is actuarially relevant, fairness demands that they are charged a higher premium for commercial insurance or are denied coverage. Those who argue that we should privilege such individuals, and bestow on them a specific right of non-disclosure, appear to permit inequity within the market. The implicit logic of their argument is that those individuals whose risk status has been discovered through a specific genetic test are more deserving of protection, and therefore have a greater moral claim to access a particular insurance product, than those individuals denied cover because an uninsurable risk has been identified by a clinical test not deemed sufficiently novel or problematic to justify unique treatment.

Hoyweghen et al contrast faulty genes with lifestyle factors, such as smoking and being overweight, which, just like genetic tests, tell us something about a person's risk of future health. They argue that treating genetic risk factors differently from lifestyle risk factors reflects a normative judgement about whether a person deserves the solidarity of mutual insurance.

---

[40] (2009) 122 Harvard Law Review 1038.
[41] 'Predictive genetic information and access to life assurance: the poverty of "genetic exceptionalism"' (2007) 2 BioSocieties 349–73.

Ine Hoyweghen, Klasien Horstman, and Rita Schepers[42]

The legal prohibition of genetics in insurance then seems to introduce a kind of fault-based labelling in insurance. . . . [A] good lifestyle has become decisive in offering cover and at what cost. By using lifestyle risk factors, insurers focus on the applicants' self-control over their risk. . . .

Although both lifestyle and family history can be identified as asymptomatic risks and as predictors for an individual's future health status, lifestyle has gained ascendancy in the risk calculation process. Both sections of the group share the fact that the illness is not yet developed, and will possibly never do so, but the legal and moral evaluation of these risks in insurance is completely different. Implicitly insurers thus draw on the argument that our biological fate outweighs our social fate, and therefore deserves more solidarity. This underscores again how insurance is a normative technology. Risk selection is neither a purely technical procedure nor simply the application of insurance principles—but much more of a social and normative undertaking. In the selection of risks, insurance expresses normative claims . . . of who does or who does not deserve solidarity.

In bringing equality legislation together into the single Equality Act 2010, the government decided against specifically prohibiting genetic discrimination. Interestingly, in making this decision it chose not to follow the advice of its advisory body, the Human Genetics Commission (HGC). According to the government, there was no evidence that people are, in fact, discriminated against as a result of genetic test results.

Department for Communities and Local Government[43]

8.29 At present, there is little, if any, evidence of discrimination against those who have a genetic predisposition, or that genetic testing is being used in a way which would give rise to such discrimination in the UK. We therefore do not believe there is currently a need to legislate to prohibit discrimination on grounds of genetic predisposition.

8.30 However, we wholeheartedly endorse the Human Genetics Commission's view that no-one should be unfairly discriminated against on the basis of their genetic characteristics and we are committed to the continued monitoring of the use of genetic testing in the UK. There is a need to ensure that individuals are able to take medically recommended genetic tests secure in the knowledge that the results will not be used unfairly, while recognising the needs of employers to protect the public and their workforce and the need of insurers to be able to assess risk.

4 DIRECT-TO-CONSUMER GENETIC TESTING

Until relatively recently, genetic testing had little relevance for the majority of the population. Only 'at risk' individuals were plausible candidates for testing. But in the past few years there has been rapid progress in identifying markers associated with an increasingly wide

---

[42] 'Genetic "risk carriers" and lifestyle "risk takers": which risks deserve our legal protection in insurance?' (2007) 15 Health Care Analysis 179.

[43] *Discrimination Law Review: A Framework for Fairness: Proposals for a Single Equality Bill for Great Britain* (DCLG, 2007).

range of common diseases. This information does not have the predictive accuracy of the test for Huntington's disease: rather, it may show that a person is slightly more at risk than the rest of the population of developing one condition, and slightly less at risk of developing another.

As a result, it is now plausible to offer screening to healthy, asymptomatic individuals with no family history of genetic disease. This sort of 'personal genome analysis' is performed by looking at up to a million genetic variations known as single nucleotide polymorphisms (SNPs). As Peter Donnelly explains in the next extract, genome-wide analysis is likely to show that each of us is in a high-risk group for one or more conditions.

Peter Donnelly[44]

For a particular disease, most individuals will have inherited some sequence variants that confer risk and some variants that provide protection, and they will therefore have an overall risk around the average. . . . Across 50 diseases, making the simplifying assumption that susceptibility to each disease is independent of susceptibility to every other disease, almost everyone will be in the top 5% of risk for at least one disease, and nearly half of all people will be in the top 1% for at least one disease. So, for example, I will be at particularly high risk of developing some diseases because of common variants that I inherited. At present, it is unclear which diseases these are, but with the advent of personal genomics, I can find out.

Unsurprisingly, the value of results which show that there is a slight increase in risk compared with the population as a whole has been questioned.[45] For example, Gert van Ommen and Martina Cornel explain what predictive genetic tests in relation to type 2 diabetes might reveal.

Gert-Jan B van Ommen and Martina C Cornel[46]

Although the average inhabitant of the Netherlands now has a lifetime risk of developing type II diabetes of 13%, for some people this might be 10 or 17% after testing. Whether this makes any difference to people is not known. Effective interventions to reduce a risk of 17% to the population average of 13% are not yet available. Whether paying US$300 or even $1000 helps to motivate people to follow-up their individual lifestyle advice is not known either.

Indeed, it is possible that the results of genetic tests with a low predictive value might be positively harmful. Bertrand Jordan and Daniel Tsai give the example of autism. A genetic test which predicts that a child is at elevated risk of autism in fact establishes that, although the risk of being autistic is higher than in the population as a whole, there is a 90 per cent

---

[44] 'Progress and challenges in genome-wide association studies in humans' (2008) 456 Nature 728–31.

[45] A Cecile JW Janssens et al, 'A critical appraisal of the scientific basis of commercial genomic profiles used to assess health risks and personalize health interventions' (2008) 82 American Journal of Human Genetics 593–9.

[46] 'Recreational genomics? Dreams and fears on genetic susceptibility screening' (2008) 16 European Journal of Human Genetics 403–4.

chance that the child will never develop autism. But by labelling the child as 'at risk', the child may be stigmatized, or even treated as if they have a condition that they will almost certainly never develop.

Bertrand R Jordan and Daniel Fu Chang Tsai[47]

So far, whole-genome association studies for autism can predict only a higher risk of disease susceptibility: an increase of the incidence from 0.7% (1/150) to 10%. That is, only 1 in 10 children who test positive are expected to actually have an autistic syndrome. This is of low predictive value, and the high false positive rate will inevitably have strong psychosocial impact on the individual and family involved. . . .

Extra burden may be generated by the pressure of seeking for more psychiatric evaluations and diagnosis, methods for prevention, and various types of therapeutic intervention including alternative treatment. The children may be stigmatised by being regarded as sick, abnormal, or different from other siblings or classmates, and consequently subjected to different management or even discrimination. If the test result is in fact a false positive, all these hardships would be totally unnecessary and in effect counterproductive.

When evaluating the results of one's 'personal genome analysis', it is also important not to confuse absolute and relative risk. If the risk of developing stomach cancer in the population as a whole is 1 per cent, and a predictive test suggests that my risk is double that of the general population, that sounds serious, and as though it is something that I should be concerned about. In fact it means that I now have a 2 per cent chance of developing stomach cancer, and a 98 per cent chance of being free from stomach cancer. Without specialist genetic counselling to help people make sense of complex predictive information, people who in fact are at very low risk of developing conditions may become unnecessarily anxious.

Commercial companies' success in marketing personal genome testing direct to the public has been variable. Some years ago, 23andMe emerged as the market leader, but then in 2013, citing concerns about false positives, the US Food and Drug Administration (FDA) issued a 'cease and desist' order against it, preventing it from offering any health testing. Immediately afterwards, 23andMe also stopped offering health testing in the UK, but this service has since been restored. For £125, consumers can receive reports on their genetic risk factors, inherited conditions, traits, and drug responses, as well as ancestry information. In 2015, 23andMe was permitted to resume health testing in the US, but only for carrier status.

Part of the sales pitch for direct-to-consumer genetic testing has been that information about elevated risk can enable people to take steps to reduce their lifetime risk of developing the disease by making changes to their lifestyle. Of course, it could be argued that we all already know what lifestyle changes are likely to reduce our risk of developing common conditions, such as cancer. Someone who is at elevated risk of heart disease does not need a genetic test result in order to learn that he ought to exercise more, eat less sugar, drink less alcohol, and stop smoking.

It has been argued that one danger of these new tests is that people who receive results that suggest they are not at increased risk of, say, heart disease will wrongly believe that it is less important for them to give up smoking or do more exercise. If this sort of false reassurance makes people less likely to do anything about their unhealthy lifestyles, it may,

[47] 'Whole-genome association studies for multigenic diseases: ethical dilemmas arising from commercialization—the case of genetic testing for autism' (2010) 36 Journal of Medical Ethics 440–4.

paradoxically, increase the chance of them developing a range of conditions including coronary heart disease, diabetes, and cancer.

It is also possible that people's reactions to learning that they face an elevated risk of ill health—particularly where it suggests that addiction to smoking or alcoholism[48] may be 'in their genes'—could be fatalism rather than behavioural modification.

Theresa M Marteau and Caryn Lerman[49]

[G]iven a common perception that genetic risks are immutable, it might decrease motivation by weakening beliefs that changing behaviour will reduce risks. Genetic risk information may also weaken belief in the ability to change behaviour or example, among people who learn that they have a genetic vulnerability to nicotine addiction. . . .

The current evidence suggests that providing people with DNA derived information about risks to their health does not increase motivation to change behaviour beyond that achieved with non-genetic information. For some people, genetic information may even reduce motivation to change behaviour.

In relation to certain psychiatric conditions, there is also a danger, as Bortolotti and Widdows point out, that the communication of an elevated risk becomes a self-fulfilling prophesy: 'A general worry is that people may become more prone to depressions as a result of being told that they are at risk of developing depression.'[50] And, as Melzer et al explain, the risks from both false negatives and false positives may be considerable.

David Melzer et al[51]

Onlookers may view most of this activity as genetic astrology, producing entertaining horoscopes. Unfortunately, . . . misleading results could trigger erroneous treatment and involve major hazards. Recent reports that false negative . . . testing in breast cancer led to women being denied specific treatment indicates the high stakes involved. On the other hand, direct marketing of the BRCA1 and 2 familial breast cancer tests to women at low risk (for whom evidence of utility is lacking) was criticised for risking unfounded anxiety and unnecessary prophylactic surgery. False reassurance from tests for common diseases could result in effective prevention measures, such as controlling weight and exercising, being ignored.

One of the most important issues raised by direct-to-consumer genetic testing is the question of consent. There are two potential problems here. First, where a sample is taken at home, there is no guarantee that the person whose DNA is sent for analysis is, in fact, the person who purchased the test. If I could persuade you to let me have some of your saliva, could I then find out extremely personal information about you, without your knowledge? Could parents send in their children's saliva in order to obtain information about their child's risk of future ill health?

---

[48] Christian Hopfer, 'Alcoholism: study boosts evidence on linkage regions associated with alcoholism' (2006) 14 European Journal of Human Genetics 1231–2.

[49] 'Genetic risk and behavioural change' (2001) 322 British Medical Journal 1056–9.

[50] 'The right not to know: the case of psychiatric disorder' (2011) 37 Journal of Medical Ethics 673–6.

[51] 'Genetic tests for common diseases: new insights, old concerns' (2008) 336 British Medical Journal 590–3.

Section 45 of the Human Tissue Act 2004 attempts to address the possibility of 'DNA theft' by making it an offence to analyse someone's DNA without consent:

(1) A person commits an offence if—

(a) he has any bodily material intending—

   (i) that any human DNA in the material be analysed without qualifying consent, and

   (ii) that the results of the analysis be used otherwise than for an excepted purpose,

Qualifying consent means the person's own consent, or, in the case of a child who is not competent to give consent themselves, consent from someone with parental responsibility. Under Schedule 4, excepted purposes include 'the medical diagnosis or treatment of the person whose body manufactured the DNA'. That means that a parent could use a child's sample for diagnostic purposes, but predictive genetic testing would not be permissible. In practice, however, it would be difficult to prevent parents from sending their children's samples for testing.

The second concern is whether or not consent to this sort of testing could be said to be properly informed. The only information people receive about these tests is from the companies' websites, the principal purpose of which is to persuade potential customers to buy their kits, rather than to offer unbiased, objective information about the value or otherwise of predictive testing.

In 2010, the Human Genetics Commission laid out the principles which ought to apply to direct-to-consumer testing, and these stressed the importance of information provision.

Human Genetics Commission[52]

2.2 Promotional and technical claims for genetic tests should accurately describe both the characteristics and the limitations of the tests offered, and the test provider should not overstate the utility of a genetic test. . . .

5.1 Where the test is a genetic test in the context of inherited or heritable disorders, that test should only be provided to consumers who are given a suitable opportunity to receive pre- and post-test counselling. . . .

6.2 A genetic test should be carried out only after the person concerned has given free and informed consent. Informed consent can only be provided when a consumer has received sufficient relevant information about the genetic test to enable them to understand the risks, benefits, limitations and implications (including the implications for purchasing insurance) of the genetic test.

6.3 The test provider should take reasonable steps to assure themselves that a biological specimen provided for testing was obtained from the person identified as the sample provider . . .

6.9 . . . Genetic tests in respect of children when, according to applicable law, that child does not have capacity to consent should normally be deferred until the attainment of such capacity, unless other factors indicate that testing during childhood is clinically indicated.

[52] *A Common Framework of Principles for Direct-to-Consumer Genetic Testing Services* (HGC, 2010).

Inevitably the safeguards in place when someone purchases a genetic test on the internet are in sharp contrast with the non-directive counselling which the NHS provides in order to help individuals to decide whether or not to be tested. Genetics counsellors will talk through the possible benefits and disadvantages of being tested, and ask the person to consider how they would feel about the result if it was positive, negative, or inconclusive. Following genetic counselling, an individual may decide that they would rather not be tested. In contrast, it is less likely that someone will decide not to go ahead with testing once they have purchased a testing kit, for which they will have had to pay up front.

In addition to the range of practical problems raised by purchasing genetic test results from an internet-based company, rather than receiving expert advice from a clinical geneticist or specialist counsellor, Rose situates the growth of genome-wide association studies within broader social trends towards the individualization both of risk and of responsibility for ill health.

Nikolas Rose[53]

This growing empire of risk management tries to bring our medical future into the present, making it calculable and obliging us to act in the light of such calculations in the name of a new kind of biological prudence. Such risk assessments partake of the apparently unquestionable logic of preventive medicine. This is not so much 'discipline and punish' as 'screen and intervene'—to identify risks before they become apparent in frank illness, and intervene early and preventively by a combination of therapeutic measures and lifestyle changes. It is in this context that we can locate the growing use of screening tests—whether from genomics or neuroscience—and the belief that these novel medical technologies can make the invisible seeds of future health or illness visible. And the promise of these tests is to move from risks assessed epidemiologically to susceptibilities assessed individually—that is to say, to the individualization of risk.

5   PHARMACOGENETICS

Pharmacogenetics is another relatively recent development in the field of genetics, and has the potential to transform the way in which medicines are designed and used. Currently, drugs are developed and prescribed for the whole population, even though we know that patients respond to drugs in different ways. A medicine which is effective for some patients may not work for others. Treatments for conditions such as diabetes, depression, and asthma may be effective in only 60 per cent of patients, and for some treatments for cancer, the figure is as low as 25 per cent.[54]

In addition, some patients suffer adverse reactions to medicines, and others will need a higher or lower dose than normal. Doctors therefore often have to engage in a 'trial-and-error' process, until they find a medication programme which works effectively for the individual patient. The delays this causes are particularly significant in relation to antidepressants, which often have to be taken for up to six weeks before any therapeutic effect

---

[53] 'Race risk and medicine in the age of "your own personal genome"' (2008) 3 Biosocieties 423–39.
[54] *Pharmacogenetics: Ethical Issues* (Nuffield Council on Bioethics: London, 2003).

becomes noticeable. The 'trial-and-error' approach to the prescription of antidepressants may then mean that patients spend many months in a depressed state waiting to find a medicine that will relieve their symptoms.

Obviously, if it were possible for doctors to know in advance whether or not a medicine would be likely to suit a particular patient, it would be possible to ensure that patients receive effective medication immediately, and do not undergo useless or dangerous treatment.

Genetic differences between patients are responsible for some of these differences in the way in which drugs are absorbed and metabolized. Pharmacogenetics would involve carrying out a genetic test before a medicine is prescribed in order to find out whether it would be likely to work, what dose would be appropriate, and whether the patient would be likely to suffer any adverse reactions. In practice, pharmacogenetics would be likely to identify genotype groups for whom particular medicines would be effective, or for whom they pose unacceptable risks of adverse side effects.

A good example of how pharmacogenetics works comes from trastuzumab (brand name Herceptin). Trastuzumab is only effective for the 25–30 per cent of patients with breast cancer in whom the oncogene, HER2, is present at abnormally high levels. It is therefore only prescribed to this subset of breast cancer patients, and prescription is always preceded by a test to identify the patient's HER2-status.

A pharmacogenetic algorithm can also be used to predict the correct dose of Warfarin, an anticoagulant drug used in patients who are at risk of stroke or heart attack. Some patients need as much as ten times the standard dose, while others can only tolerate lower levels.[55]

The Nuffield Council on Bioethics has suggested that the body which licenses medicines (discussed in Chapter 10) might require the use of a pharmacogenetic test as a condition of issuing a licence for a medicine's use.[56] Drugs which have been withdrawn from circulation because of adverse reactions could be reinstated for use only in population subgroups in whom they do not pose a risk of unacceptable side effects.

As well as improving patient care, reducing prescribing errors has the potential to save NHS resources, through eliminating the prescription of drugs that do not work, and through reducing the number of GP appointments a patient has before she finds a drug that suits her. Clinical trials could also be designed so that the drug is only tested on subgroups in whom it is likely to be safe and effective.

Despite these obvious benefits, pharmacogenetics raises a number of important questions. First, if clinical trials were redesigned so that a drug was only tested on a genetically selected subgroup, there could be no guarantee that it would be safe for a patient with a different genotype, thus potentially increasing the risk of prescription errors.

Secondly, as Corrigan points out in the next extract, although genes undoubtedly affect the metabolism of medicines, other factors—such as the patient's age, sex, diet, or exposure to other drugs—will also have an impact. Genetic tests alone cannot establish exactly what medicine will work effectively, in what dose, and with what side effects, leading Corrigan to argue that effort should also be put into identifying non-genetic reasons for variable responses to medicines.

55 The International Warfarin Pharmacogenetics Consortium, 'Estimation of the Warfarin dose with clinical and pharmacogenetic data' (2009) 360 New England Journal of Medicine 753–64.
56 *Pharmacogenetics: Ethical Issues*, xvi.

O Corrigan[57]

> [T]he likelihood that pharmacogenetics can make a substantial impact on the reduction of the incidence of serious adverse drug reactions is also highly debatable. The [Nuffield] report accepts the premise that pharmacogenetics will be an effective mechanism for reducing the incidence of adverse drug reactions [ADRs], a claim about benefit that has underpinned much of the ethical impetus for pharmacogenetics research. Although the report acknowledges that ADRs can be caused by various factors other than genetic variation, it fails to mention the importance of other variables such as age or sex, to name only two. A recent study of ADRs in the elderly has shown that serious ADRs are predictable, and that more than two thirds of ADRs are therefore preventable. In other words, the problem of ADRs could be radically reduced if other non-genetic based prescribing interventions were adopted.

Thirdly, genetic test results will rarely come in the form of a 'yes/no' answer, but rather are more likely to suggest the probability of success and safety. This means it will be necessary to decide what probability of effectiveness justifies treatment. If a genetic test reveals that the only available treatment for a patient's condition has a 30 per cent chance of working, does this justify prescribing it? And should the choice lie with the patient or the doctor? From the point of view of those in charge of NHS resources, a 30 per cent chance of efficacy looks poor, but if this is the only available treatment, the patient nevertheless may be keen to try it.

Fourthly, pharmacogenetics will involve a massive expansion of genetic testing, which raises all the issues we considered earlier in this chapter, namely confidentiality, discrimination, and the patient's right 'not to know' information which may be inadvertently discovered during testing.

Fifthly, the ability to target drugs more effectively will not necessarily reduce NHS expenditure on drugs. Rather, if there is a dramatic reduction in the quantity of drugs prescribed, pharmaceutical companies will face a corresponding reduction in their profits, unless, as seems likely, they respond by increasing the price of drugs in order to cover both the reduction in demand, and the costs associated with developing new pharmacogenetic tests. Prescribing itself will also become more expensive, since it will no longer just take a couple of minutes for a doctor to write a prescription, but instead samples must be taken and sent for testing and the results interpreted. It is therefore by no means clear that there would be a reduction in costs as a result of pharmacogenetic testing; indeed, it is possible that costs may rise.

Sixthly, drug companies are likely to concentrate their research and development budgets on drugs which will work for the majority of patients, leaving others with unusual diseases or unusual genetic reactions with no effective treatment. It is also possible that population differences in metabolizing medicines may be drawn along racial lines. If this is the case— and there seems to be some evidence that it might be—it suggests that race might matter at the molecular level, while being an irrelevant difference at the level of social policy. The symbolic significance of this has led many US commentators to resist what they have described as a move towards 'race-based medicine'.[58]

---

[57] 'Pharmacogenetics, Ethical Issues: review of the Nuffield Council on Bioethics report' (2005) 31 Journal of Medical Ethics 144–8.

[58] Dorothy E Roberts, 'Is race-based medicine good for us? African American approaches to race, biomedicine and equality' (2008) 36 Journal of Law, Medicine and Ethics 537.

Finally, as Van Delden et al point out in the next extract, there is, of course, the danger that genetic tests will reveal that there is no effective treatment for a particular patient. As well as being extremely upsetting, being identified as hard, or even impossible, to treat might have negative practical consequences for an individual, such as difficulties in obtaining insurance. This in turn might prompt people to refuse genetic testing, with the result that the doctor cannot know whether the patient is in the subgroup for whom a medicine is unsuitable or dangerous.

Johannes Van Delden et al[59]

The first problem that might occur in genotyping is that by testing the patient it might be revealed that the patient is a non-responder for all available drug options. The patient turns out to be an 'orphan' for whom genotyping provided no advantage, but only the knowledge that he probably cannot be treated. . . . [S]omeone might turn out to be a non-responder for multiple drugs, which might give him the label 'hard to treat'. Therefore, some patients might not want to be tested for pharmacogenetic profiles, as they do not want to gain knowledge that might put them in a disadvantageous position.

This leads to the question of what a physician should do if a patient refuses to be genotyped. He could give the patient the 'bulk drug', but by doing so he in fact gives the patient a suboptimal treatment. Besides, he knowingly increases the risk of potentially dangerous side-effects by not testing the patient. If such side-effects emerge, who can then be considered to be responsible for them, the physician or the patient?

The Nuffield Council on Bioethics' report considered this problem, and argued that the way in which pharmacogenetics are presented to the public will inevitably affect people's willingness to undergo pre-treatment genetic testing.

Nuffield Council on Bioethics[60]

A question arises regarding whether patients will have the option to receive treatment without taking an associated test. It cannot be assumed that patients will be keen to take a pharmacogenetic test, even if it will improve the likelihood of their receiving a safe and effective treatment. Such an aversion may be irrational, but may be based on a legitimate fear that information produced by the test could make it difficult to obtain insurance, or that it might indirectly reveal information about a medical condition which cannot be effectively treated. . . .

The public perceptions of pharmacogenetics are important in part because resistance to pharmacogenetic testing could lead to patients not receiving the best care. Patients might not be given the most beneficial medicines if these may only be prescribed with a genetic test they refuse to take. Even more serious is the possibility that a medicine may be administered without an associated pharmacogenetic test, and result in a serious, predictable and avoidable adverse reaction. We think it likely that the acceptance of pharmacogenetics will depend not only on which tests are introduced and for which purposes they are used, but also on the way they are presented to the public at large and to individual patients.

[59] 'Tailor-made pharmacotherapy: future developments and ethical challenges in the field of pharmacogenomics' (2004) 18 Bioethics 303–21.
[60] *Pharmacogenetics: Ethical Issues*, xxii, 7.

6 CONCLUSION

This chapter has provided only a very brief snapshot of some issues raised by the rapid developments in human genetics. In conclusion, one thread that connects the various issues we have considered here is that we are currently witnessing a move from genetic testing being relevant only to the relatively small proportion of the population with a family history of a single gene disorder, towards it having much wider application, and potentially being relevant to all of us.

Each of us has a number of faulty genes, some of which might mean that we are at higher than average chance of developing a range of conditions in later life. If we can find this information out easily, questions of genetic privacy and discrimination become relevant to an increasing proportion of the population. If the prescription of a growing number of medicines must be preceded by a genetic test, again, issues of confidentiality and discrimination have much wider significance than has previously been the case.

While new developments in genetics are undeniably exciting and now incredibly fast moving, it is also important to bear in mind that there are other fairly accurate predictors of future ill health which we should not ignore just because they seem more prosaic. We know, for example, that child poverty has a dramatic impact upon a child's health prospects in later life. Having an unhealthy diet—which often correlates with relative poverty—increases one's chance of developing heart disease and cancer. It is easy to be seduced into imagining that my 'personal genome analysis' holds the key to my future life chances when, in fact, how much I exercise, and what I eat and drink will often be at least as important.

FURTHER READING

Bell, Dean and Bennett, Belinda, 'Genetic Secrets and the Family' (2001) 9 Medical Law Review 130–61.

Forrest, Laura et al, 'Communicating genetic information in families—a review of guidelines and position papers' (2007) 15 European Journal of Human Genetics 612–18.

Gibbons, Susan, 'Regulating Biobanks: A Twelve-Point Typological Tool' (2009) 17 Medical Law Review 313–46.

Laurie, Graeme, *Genetic Privacy: A Challenge to Medico-Legal Norms* (CUP: Cambridge, 2002).

Mittra, James, 'Predictive genetic information and access to life assurance: the poverty of genetic exceptionalism' (2007) 2 BioSocieties 349–73.

Nuffield Council on Bioethics, *The Forensic Use of Bioinformation: Ethical Issues* (NCOB, 2008).

Otlowski, Margaret, 'Tackling Legal Challenges Posed By Population Biobanks: Reconceptualising Consent Requirements' (2012) 20 Medical Law Review 191–226.

Rose, Nikolas, 'Race risk and medicine in the age of your own personal genome' (2008) 3 Biosocieties 423–39.

Skene, Loane, 'Genetic Secrets and the Family' (2001) 9 Medical Law Review 162–9.

Van Ommen, Gert-Jan B and Cornel, Martina C, 'Recreational genomics? Dreams and fears on genetic susceptibility screening' (2008) 16 European Journal of Human Genetics 403–4.

9

CLINICAL RESEARCH

CENTRAL ISSUES

1. Animal experiments usually precede trials involving human subjects. To obtain a licence from the Home Office, researchers have to establish that the use of animals is necessary, and animal suffering must be minimized.

2. International codes of research ethics, most importantly the Helsinki Declaration, have established universally applicable principles of good research practice.

3. A new EU Clinical Trials Regulation is intended to simplify the process of clinical trial approvals. It will replace the Medicines for Human Use (Clinical Trials) Regulations 2004 and will come into force during the lifetime of this book.

4. All clinical trials must first be approved by a research ethics committee.

5. Consent to participation in research must be both informed and voluntary.

It is sometimes difficult to ensure that when patients are enrolled in clinical trials, they understand that they are taking part in an experiment, rather than receiving treatment which is in their best interests.

6. For subjects who lack capacity, consent must be sought from their 'representative', and it must be impossible to carry out the research on competent adults.

7. It is increasingly recognized that questions of conflicts of interests, selective publication, and bias raise important ethical issues in the context of clinical trials.

8. While it is vitally important that medicines are developed to treat diseases that are prevalent in the poorest nations in the world, carrying out research in low and middle-income countries raises some distinctive and complex ethical issues.

1 INTRODUCTION

Without research, medical progress would be impossible. New treatments can be tested on animals, but animal experiments are an imperfect way to predict how a treatment will affect human beings. As we see later, the compound, known as TGN1412, which caused multiple organ failure in the six men who took part in its 'first in man' trial at Northwick Park

Hospital, had not caused adverse effects in animals, and was believed to be safe. Research on human subjects is the only way in which we can satisfactorily establish the effectiveness and safety of medical treatment. But while we all want the medical care that we receive to have been rigorously tested, serving as a research subject may pose risks to an individual's health.

One of the most basic questions raised by the regulation of clinical trials is how to balance the competing interests of society (which wants medical treatment to have been proved safe and effective), and the individual research subject (who does not want their health endangered). Although research on human subjects is not the only time when the interests of society have to be weighed against the welfare of individuals, this balancing exercise offers a good example of the conflict between deontological (duty-based) and teleological (consequentialist) reasoning that we considered in Chapter 1.

If we adopt a strict utilitarian perspective, conducting research on a small number of people—with or without their consent—in order to benefit the rest of society might be justifiable, even if it poses a considerable risk to their health. Take the example of Edward Jenner's discovery of the smallpox vaccine, described here by Brazier:

Margaret Brazier[1]

Edward Jenner, injected an eight year old boy, James Phipps, with cowpox. Months later, he injected the boy with smallpox. The vaccination 'took' and the boy survived. Jenner's experiment has saved millions of lives and led to the virtual eradication of smallpox. . . . [I]t has often been said no modern ethics committee would have sanctioned such an experiment. Consider the case—the experiment used a child subject, who was too young to consent for himself, in non-therapeutic research where there was a high risk of death or disfigurement. The 'exploitation' of James Phipps undoubtedly saved the lives of some of us reading this.

In contrast, a deontological approach would condemn any course of action that disregarded the wellbeing of individual research subjects, regardless of the benefits to the rest of society. According to the Kantian imperative, we should never treat people solely as a means, but always as an end in themselves (see further Chapter 1). Hans Jonas has gone so far as to say research on humans involves treating subjects as 'things', and he argues that we should rule this out, despite the adverse consequences this might have for people suffering from potentially curable diseases.

Hans Jonas[2]

Let me say only in conclusion that if some of the practical implications of my reasonings are felt to work out toward a slower rate of progress, this should not cause too great dismay. Let us not forget that progress is an optional goal, not an unconditional commitment, and that its tempo in particular, compulsive as it may become, has nothing sacred about it. Let us also remember that a slower progress in the conquest of disease would not threaten society, grievous as it is to those who have to deplore that their particular disease be not yet conquered, but that society would indeed be threatened by the erosion of those moral values

---

[1] 'Exploitation and enrichment: the paradox of medical experimentation' (2008) 34 Journal of Medical Ethics 180–3.

[2] 'Philosophical reflections on experimenting with human subjects' (1969) 98 Daedalus 219–47.

> whose loss, possibly caused by too ruthless a pursuit of scientific progress, would make its most dazzling triumphs not worth having.

Both extreme utilitarianism and its opposite are unattractive and caricatured moral positions. In practice, most people adopt a mixed approach, which takes into account both individual rights and the common good. We do not want to sacrifice some human beings' lives for the benefit of others, but at the same time we do not want to stifle medical progress by refusing to allow any experiments on human subjects.

We all benefit from living in a society in which drugs and other treatments have been properly tested. It might therefore be argued that we are under a moral obligation to incur some inconvenience or slightly increased risk to our health by participating in medical research. If we wish to benefit from experiments on humans, but are not actually willing to take part in them ourselves, could we be said to be 'free-riding' on the sacrifices of others?

When thinking about how research on humans should be regulated, it is also important to remember that there are more interests at stake than just the individual research subject's concern for her own health, and society's interest in innovation. Researchers will benefit personally from devising, carrying out, and publishing significant research, which may, as McNeill suggests, create a powerful incentive towards 'cutting corners'.

Paul M McNeill[3]

> While society, or at least some individuals within it, *may* benefit from research, there are very direct and tangible benefits for the researcher . . . The researcher's interest in his or her own advancement and standing may be an added pressure to cut corners and act in ways that are unsafe . . .
>
> Instances of blatant disregard for subjects' welfare have understandably gained the most attention. However, it is likely that more harm has been caused (in total) by researchers who mean no harm but are unaware of the extent of risk to their patients. Their bias towards achieving the goals of their research may lead them to minimise, in their own thinking, the risks inherent in their research and give a disproportionate value to the research enterprise . . . Scientists are as capable as any other group of pursuing their own interests to the exclusion of the interests of others.

Not only is the reputation of the researcher at stake, but, as Benatar points out, sponsors of research—most importantly pharmaceutical companies—have considerable financial interests in producing profitable medicines.

Solomon Benatar[4]

> Clinical research has become a burgeoning activity in recent years, largely stimulated by the pharmaceutical industry's interest in new drugs with high marketing profiles . . . The desire to make vast sums of money from medicinal drugs can be viewed as a modern version of

---

[3] *The Ethics and Politics of Human Experimentation* (CUP: Cambridge, 1993).
[4] 'Avoiding exploitation in clinical research' (2000) 9 Cambridge Quarterly of Healthcare Ethics 562–5.

the gold rush. Why make drugs for sick people who cannot afford them when one can make drugs for people with resources who seek marginal improvements or those who are well and will pay for the possibility of a healthier old age. Proliferation of clinical research, much of it promotional and of dubious scientific value, follows.

The World Trade Organization's TRIPS Agreement gives pharmaceutical companies a minimum 20-year period of patent protection.[5] If a new medicine with a potentially large market-share has been proved to be safe and effective, it can be phenomenally profitable. 'Big pharma' has become one of Britain's principal manufacturing industries, spending billions each year on research and development.[6]

Clinical trials involving human subjects have been subject to EU-wide regulation since the Clinical Trials Directive 2001/20/EC, which was transposed into English law through the Medicines for Human Use (Clinical Trials) Regulations 2004. In 2014, a new Clinical Trials Regulation was published in the Official Journal of the EU.[7] As a Regulation rather than a Directive, it will come into force directly in the UK, without the need for further regulations. It is due to come into force no sooner than May 2016, and only when the necessary IT infrastructure is fully functional. The Health Research Authority expects the new Regulation to be come into force some time in 2017. Although not yet in force at the time of writing, this chapter will include extracts from this new EU Regulation.

In this chapter, we begin with a brief summary of the rules governing experiments on animals, which will usually precede trials involving human subjects. Next we look at what is meant by 'research'. It is important to remember that not all medical research consists in the testing of new treatments or drugs. Epidemiological research, for example, may just involve tracking the incidence of a particular condition in the population, and thus raises different, and perhaps fewer, ethical issues.

We then turn to examine the various international ethical codes, and the UK's regulatory system, and we examine the role of ethics committees in authorizing and monitoring research. The subject's voluntary and informed consent to participation is widely believed to be what justifies exposing her to the risks inherent in a research trial, and we consider what qualifies as sufficiently 'voluntary' and 'informed' consent. If consent is a necessary precondition of ethical research, we also investigate whether, and in what circumstances, it would be legitimate to carry out research on individuals who cannot give consent.

We then examine whether the benefits and burdens of research participation are evenly distributed, drawing particular attention to the special issues raised when research is conducted in low and middle-income countries. Next, we review the question of conflicts of interests and publication ethics—should there be a legal duty to disseminate the results of research findings, and does a failure to do so amount to scientific misconduct? Finally, we look at the question of compensation for injuries sustained as a result of participation in research.

---

[5] WTO, Trade Related Aspects of Intellectual Property Rights (WTO, 1994).
[6] See further www.abpi.org.uk.   [7] Regulation (EU) No 536/2014.

2 ANIMAL EXPERIMENTS

(a) REGULATION OF EXPERIMENTS INVOLVING ANIMALS

In the UK, research involving laboratory animals is regulated by the Animals (Scientific Procedures) Act 1986, as amended. The Act defines 'protected animals' as all non-human vertebrates and cephalopods (such as squid). Insects such as fruit flies are also commonly used in research but are not protected by the Act.

Before any experiment can be carried out on a protected animal, a licence must first have been obtained from the Home Office. Under section 3 of the Act, the laboratory, the individual researcher, and the project itself must each be separately approved.

Animals (Scientific Procedures) Act 1986 section 3

3. Prohibition of unlicensed procedures

No person shall personally apply a regulated procedure to an animal unless—

  (a) he holds a personal licence qualifying him to apply a regulated procedure of that description to an animal of that description;

  (b) the procedure is applied as part of a programme of work specified in a project licence authorising the application, as part of that programme, of a regulated procedure of that description to an animal of that description; and

  (c) the place where the procedure is carried out is a place specified in the project licence.

To obtain a Personal Licence, the individual researcher must have been on an approved training course covering the law and ethics of animal research, the basics of caring for animals, and ways of recognizing symptoms of illness or distress. Laboratories must meet strict Home Office criteria on staffing, veterinary care, and the quality of housing, lighting, ventilation, and temperature control. Each laboratory must have a 'Named Veterinary Surgeon' and a 'Named Animal Care and Welfare Officer', responsible for protecting the health and welfare of animals within the laboratory.

Before applying for a Project Licence, the researchers must first have received the approval of an ethics committee. Applications are then made to the Home Office. In determining whether to grant a project licence, under section 5(B)(2), the Secretary of State must verify:

  (a) that carrying out the programme of work is justified from a scientific or educational point of view or is required by law;

  (b) that the purposes of the programme of work justify the use of protected animals; and

  (c) that the programme of work is designed so as to enable the regulated procedures applied as part of it to be applied in the most humane and environmentally sensitive manner possible.

Section 5B(3)(b) specifies that the Secretary of State must 'assess the compliance of the programme of work with the principles of replacement, reduction and refinement'. This is a reference to the 3Rs approach, first developed by Russell and Burch in 1959: Replacement (of conscious, living vertebrates by non-sentient alternatives); Reduction (in the number of animals used to obtain information); and Refinement (of procedures to reduce to suffering).[8]

A European Directive in 2010 required Member States to implement the 3Rs approach, and it has been transposed into UK law via section 2A of the Animals (Scientific Procedures) Act.

Animals (Scientific Procedures) Act 1986 section 2A

2A Principles of replacement, reduction and refinement

(1) The Secretary of State must exercise his or her functions under this Act with a view to ensuring compliance with the principles of replacement, reduction and refinement.

(2) For the purposes of this Act—

(a) the principle of replacement is the principle that, wherever possible, a scientifically satisfactory method or testing strategy not entailing the use of protected animals must be used instead of a regulated procedure;

(b) the principle of reduction is the principle that whenever a programme of work involving the use of protected animals is carried out the number of protected animals used must be reduced to a minimum without compromising the objectives of the programme;

(c) the principle of refinement is the principle that the breeding, accommodation and care of protected animals and the methods used in regulated procedures applied to such animals must be refined so as to eliminate or reduce to the minimum any possible pain, suffering, distress or lasting harm to those animals.

Section 5B(3)(d) further provides that the Secretary of State must:

carry out a harm-benefit analysis of the programme of work to assess whether the harm that would be caused to protected animals in terms of suffering, pain and distress is justified by the expected outcome, taking into account ethical considerations and the expected benefit to human beings, animals or the environment.

Almost all animals used in experiments are bred especially for the purposes of research in order to ensure that they are free from infection or disease. Increasingly, research on animals involves genetic modification: in 2014, 50 per cent of all animal procedures related to the creation or breeding of genetically altered animals that were not used in further experiments.[9]

For complex licence applications, such as those involving primates, the Home Office may refer the project to the Animals in Science Committee, which has replaced the Animals Procedures Committee. This is a committee of scientific, legal, and ethical experts which provides advice on controversial legal and ethical issues. As well as advising

---

[8] WMS Russell and RL Burch, *The Principles of Humane Experimental Technique* (Methuen & Co: London, 1959).

[9] *Statistics of Scientific Procedures on Living Animals Great Britain 2014* (Home Office: London, 2015).

on individual applications—such as those involving primates—the Animals in Science Committee offers guidance on more general ethical issues, such as appropriate methods for humane euthanasia.

The Home Office issues detailed statistics each year on the use of animals in experiments in the UK.[10] In 2014, 3.87 million procedures were started involving animals. Mice (60 per cent), fish (14 per cent), and rats (12 per cent) were used in the largest numbers of procedures, while dogs, cats, and non-human primates were used in 0.8 per cent of all procedures (16,000 in total).[11]

(b) THE ACCEPTABILITY OF RESEARCH ON ANIMALS

In what circumstances, if any, is it acceptable to use animals in research? Opinion on this question is, as Munro explains, deeply divided.

Lyle Munro[12]

Experimentalists claim that as there is no satisfactory alternative, the use of animals is essential to human health. The antivivisectionists maintain that the researcher's case is deeply flawed and that the availability of cruelty free alternatives renders animal experimentation morally reprehensible. Neither side is willing to compromise since each perceives the other's position as evil. That it is no exaggeration to use the term 'evil' is borne out by the language of vilification that continues to be used by some of the protagonists in the controversy.

The Nuffield Council on Bioethics report on *The Ethics of Research Involving Animals* suggests that instead of thinking in terms of two diametrically opposed positions on whether animal experiments are justifiable, it would be more accurate to divide opinion into four camps.

Nuffield Council on Bioethics[13]

The 'anything goes' view—if humans see value in research involving animals, then it requires no further ethical justification.

The 'on balance justification' view—although research involving animals has costs to animals, which must be taken seriously in moral reasoning, the benefits to human beings very often outweigh those costs in moral terms.

The 'moral dilemma' view—however one decides to act, one acts wrongly, either by neglecting human health or by harming animals.

The 'abolitionist' view—since any research that causes pain, suffering and distress is wrong, there is no moral justification for harmful research on sentient animals that is not to the benefit of the animal concerned.

---

[10] Ibid.   [11] Ibid.

[12] 'From vilification to accommodation: making a common cause movement' (1999) 8 Cambridge Quarterly of Healthcare Ethics 46–57.

[13] *The Ethics of Research Involving Animals* (NCOB, 2005).

In the next extract, Richard Ryder suggests that few scientists in fact hold the 'anything goes' view of animal research.

Richard D Ryder[14]

As scientists we acknowledge that the human species is but one of many species. We know that other animals often behave as we do when in pain and that their nervous systems and their biochemistry are similar to our own. We know that nonhumans are related to us through evolution and that, therefore, it is inconsistent to put our own species on a moral pedestal entirely separate from all the others. How can it be moral to cause pain or misery to monkeys, dogs, or rats, if it is immoral to do this to humans? There are no *rational* grounds for asserting this. If it is wrong to experiment painfully upon unconsenting humans, it must, logically speaking, be wrong to do likewise to nonhumans. We cannot, with consistency argue that nonhumans are so like us that they produce valid experimental results and then claim that they are morally different. We should remember simply this: pain is pain regardless of species.

The critical issue is whether humans are entitled to use animals for their own ends, and one obvious point of comparison is the food industry. If killing animals for food is morally acceptable (and obviously not everyone agrees that it is), then it would seem legitimate to use animals in potentially valuable scientific experiments. Of course, many opponents of animal experiments are also vegetarians or vegans, but there are also those who maintain that laboratory animals suffer more than those bred for food. This claim is hard to sustain, however, given the nature of intensive factory farming and the strict controls that govern the treatment of animals used in experiments. It is also no longer lawful to use animals for 'trivial' research, such as the testing of cosmetics or tobacco products.

In the next extract, David Thomas argues that, because animals can feel pain and cannot give consent, a better analogy would be research involving people who lack capacity.

David Thomas[15]

[W]hy should the fact (if this is what it is) that A has more value than B mean that A is at liberty to cause pain to B for A's benefit? This is the crucial gap in logic which pro-vivisectionists rarely address. Let us accept for the sake of argument that it was provable that the human species was more important than other species—whether because people generally (though not always) have greater capacity for rational thought, may have greater self awareness, are better able to empathise, or have more sophisticated culture. It is not explained why those attributes mean that we can cause pain to those we relegate further down the hierarchy of value. And, if cruel exploitation of *other* species is justified on a relative value basis, then, logically, so must cruel exploitation *within* our species. Some people, indisputably, have greater capacity for rational thought, have greater self awareness, are better able to

[14] 'Painism: some moral rules for the civilized experimenter' (1999) 8 Cambridge Quarterly of Healthcare Ethics 35–42.

[15] 'Laboratory animals and the art of empathy' (2005) 31 Journal of Medical Ethics 197–202.

empathise, or have a deeper cultural appreciation than other people. However, most people do not conclude that the more endowed are for that reason entitled to cause pain to the less endowed for their own benefit . . .

With non-consensual experiments on people, a *deontological* approach is taken. The prevailing view is that such experiments are *inherently* wrong, whatever the potential benefits to others . . . With animals, by contrast, the approach is a kind of *utilitarianism*. The law allows scientists to cause pain to animals if *others* might benefit.

In 2006, the Academy of Medical Sciences, the Medical Research Council, the Royal Society, and the Wellcome Trust commissioned a working group report into the use of non-human primates in research, chaired by Sir David Weatherall. It adopted an explicitly quantitative utilitarian approach to animal suffering in research.

Weatherall Working Group Report[16]

One issue often neglected here is the fact that the numbers of non-human primates used in any medical experiment are very small, and the number of humans whose suffering is ameliorated is often very large. So the equation to be made is not simply between suffering caused and benefits to humans: both sides must be multiplied by the number of individuals involved. In the case of AIDS research, for instance, the number of macaques used may be measured in dozens, the number of humans who stand to benefit could be measured in millions. Suffering or harm caused in animal experiments, both in terms of numbers and in terms of degree, is likely to be less than the benefits to humankind from properly licensed research carried out with meticulous care.

Muireann Quigley is critical of this approach, suggesting that non-human primates should instead be regarded as a particularly vulnerable group of potential research subjects.

Muireann Quigley[17]

It seems to me that most non-human primates are of a level of capacity that, if they were human, would fall into this category of vulnerable persons and would therefore be protected. If, as argued previously, we cannot differentiate between non-human primates and humans merely on the grounds of species membership, and if there is no difference in capacity between non-human primates and some humans, then surely these guidelines ought to protect both.

In the next extract, RG Frey goes further and suggests that it may be preferable to carry out experiments on non-sentient human subjects than on sentient rodents.

---

[16] 'The Use of Non-Human Primates in Research' (2006), available at www.acmedsci.ac.uk/.

[17] 'Non-human primates: the appropriate subjects of biomedical research?' (2007) 33 Journal of Medical Ethics 655–8.

RG Frey[18]

The truth is, I think, that some human lives have fallen so far in value, quality, richness, and scope for enrichment that some animal lives exceed in value those human lives. Anencephalic infants and people in permanently vegetative states are cases in point. It was comforting in the past to think that all human lives were more valuable than any animal life, but the quality of life of a perfectly healthy dog or cat must vastly exceed the quality of any human life that has ceased to have experiences of any sort, that has ceased to have in essence any sort of content . . .

If we have to experiment . . . , then which life do we use? We use that life of lower quality, and we have a non-speciesist way of determining which life that is . . . How can we justify an experiment on a perfectly healthy rodent with an experiential life as opposed to an anencephalic infant with, so far as we know, no experiential life at all?

In order to facilitate open discussion about the ethics of animal research, it is important that researchers are transparent about their use of animals. The ARRIVE guidelines are intended to promote openness about animal research. First set out in a 2010 article by Kilkenny et al, they have since been endorsed by all of the major funders of biomedical research in the UK.

Carol Kilkenny et al[19]

Most bioscience journals currently provide little or no guidance on what information to report when describing animal research. Our review found that 4% of the 271 journal articles assessed did not report the number of animals used anywhere in the methods or the results sections. Reporting animal numbers is essential so that the biological and statistical significance of the experimental results can be assessed or the data reanalysed, and is also necessary if the experimental methods are to be repeated. Improved reporting of these and other details will maximise the availability and utility of the information gained from every animal and every experiment, preventing unnecessary animal use in the future. . . .

The ARRIVE guidelines consist of a checklist of 20 items describing the minimum information that all scientific publications reporting research using animals should include, such as the number and specific characteristics of animals used (including species, strain, sex, and genetic background); details of housing and husbandry; and the experimental, statistical, and analytical methods (including details of methods used to reduce bias such as randomisation and blinding). All the items in the checklist have been included to promote high-quality, comprehensive reporting to allow an accurate critical review of what was done and what was found.

3 WHAT IS RESEARCH?

(a) USE OF ANONYMOUS DATA OR SAMPLES

A great deal of medical research is carried out without making contact with patients. Epidemiology, for example, is 'the study of the occurrence and distribution of diseases and

---

[18] 'Pain, vivisection, and the value of life' (2005) 31 Journal of Medical Ethics 202–4.

[19] 'Improving bioscience research reporting: the ARRIVE guidelines for reporting animal research' (2010) 8 PLoS Biology e1000412.

other health-related conditions in populations'. Originally the study of epidemics, it now involves analysis of the prevalence and distribution of medical conditions, in order to test hypotheses about causes of disease and risk factors.

Major difficulties would be posed if patients had to give informed consent to the use of information from their medical notes. The process of tracking down every patient and asking their permission would be incredibly time-consuming, and it also might cause unnecessary alarm. Ideally, the patient's agreement to the use of information gathered during treatment should be sought, but if it would be impossible to obtain consent, then there are times, as we saw in Chapter 7, when pseudonymized patient records can be used for research purposes.

(b) INNOVATIVE THERAPY

Ordinary medical treatment, as we saw in Chapter 3, must satisfy the *Bolam* test, as modified by *Bolitho*: that is, it must reach a standard of care which is both accepted as proper by a responsible body of medical opinion, and capable of withstanding logical analysis. In general, this means that doctors should only offer patients treatments that have been properly tested and are known to be effective. In certain circumstances, however, a doctor might act reasonably by offering a patient treatment that has not yet been tested on humans.

If all orthodox treatments have been exhausted and the patient's condition is extremely serious, it might be acceptable to try a treatment which has not yet been licensed for use in humans. Certainly, the Helsinki Declaration endorses the use of unproven treatment where no other options exist:

Helsinki Declaration[20]

37. In the treatment of an individual patient, where proven interventions do not exist or other known interventions have been ineffective, the physician, after seeking expert advice, with informed consent from the patient or a legally authorised representative, may use an unproven intervention if in the physician's judgement it offers hope of saving life, re-establishing health or alleviating suffering. This intervention should subsequently be made the object of research, designed to evaluate its safety and efficacy. In all cases, new information must be recorded and, where appropriate, made publicly available.

The desire of a desperately sick patient to 'try anything' is understandable, but at the same time patients may overestimate the likelihood of success and underestimate the risks of untested treatments. Darrow et al explain that 'expanded access' to as yet unapproved medicines may represent a clash between autonomy and informed consent.

Jonathan J Darrow, Ameet Sarpatwari, Jerry Avorn, and Aaron S Kesselheim[21]

The primary ethical argument for expanded access is that patients should have a right to mitigate extreme suffering and to enhance self-preservation. This logic holds that as

---

[20] World Medical Association, *Declaration of Helsinki: Ethical Principles for Medical Research Involving Human Subjects* (version adopted at the 64th WMA General Assembly, Fortaleza, Brazil, October 2013).
[21] 'Practical, legal, and ethical issues in expanded access to investigational drugs' (2015) 372 New England Journal of Medicine 279–86.

rational actors, patients are presumed to be capable of making well-informed treatment decisions in consultation with their physicians. According to this argument, not only can patients with serious or life-threatening conditions accurately identify promising experimental drugs, but they should also be entitled to utilize their own risk–benefit thresholds in deciding whether to consume such products. Advocates of expanded access argue that deference to the assumed capacity of patients to thereby make appropriate treatment decisions should be greatest when the stakes are highest (i.e., when death is likely or certain).

By contrast, those who seek to limit access to unapproved medications argue that the odds of an experimental therapy working in many expanded-access settings are extremely small—the probability of clinically meaningful benefit from early-stage experimental trials may be less than 10%—and informational asymmetries can lead to patient vulnerability. . . . Risk comprehension among the general public is low, is not strongly correlated with self-perceived ability to understand risk, and may be more impaired in sicker patients. Skeptics of expanded access caution that the risk of treatment-selection decisions that could exacerbate suffering or hasten death justifies greater—not reduced—paternalism for patients with serious or life-threatening conditions.

The fact that treatment is experimental is undoubtedly a material fact, non-disclosure of which might be likely to be negligent (see further, Chapter 4). If the patient lacks capacity, an additional safeguard—such as the court declaration, which was sought and granted in the following case—might be necessary.

Simms v Simms involved an 18-year-old boy and a 16-year-old girl, who were in the advanced stages of vCJD (variant Creutzfeldt-Jakob disease—a rare, fatal, and incurable neurodegenerative disorder). Researchers had identified a treatment (PPS) which appeared to inhibit the progress of a similar disease in mice, but this had not yet been tested on humans. The patients' parents wanted their children to receive PPS, and they applied for, and were granted, a declaration that the treatment would be in their best interests, and hence lawful.

Simms v Simms[22]

Dame Elizabeth Butler-Sloss P

Where there is no alternative treatment available and the disease is progressive and fatal, it seems to me to be reasonable to consider experimental treatment with unknown benefits and risks, but without significant risks of increased suffering to the patient, in cases where there is some chance of benefit to the patient. A patient who is not able to consent to pioneering treatment ought not to be deprived of the chance in circumstances where he would have been likely to consent if he had been competent . . .

The chance of improvement is slight but not non-existent . . . I think it is reasonable, at this stage of my judgment, to put into the balance that, if there is a possibility of continuation of a life which has value to the patient and the patient is bound to die sooner rather than later without the treatment, these two young people have very little to lose in the treatment going ahead. I am satisfied it is a reasonable risk to take on their behalf.

[22] [2002] EWHC 2734 (Fam).

(c) NON-THERAPEUTIC AND THERAPEUTIC RESEARCH: PHASES I, II, AND III

After satisfactory evidence from animal trials has been gathered, there are usually three phases of trials on humans. Phase I trials involve a small number of healthy volunteers, who are given the drug so that researchers can study its toxicity, and the way in which it is absorbed. Next, in a phase II trial, the drug is given to a group of people suffering from the condition it is intended to treat in order to evaluate its effectiveness, and discover if it has any side effects. Finally, phase III trials involve monitoring a larger group of subjects who take the medicine under supervision for a longer period of time.

After licensing, the drug will continue to be monitored before it can be categorized as an 'established' medicine. Although no longer strictly research, because the intention is now to treat patients rather than to generate knowledge, this is sometimes referred to as a phase IV trial. Phase IV trials involve looking at how drugs work 'in the real world', and will therefore include patients who are routinely excluded from clinical trials, such as pregnant women and people suffering from multiple comorbidities.

Normally, phase I trials are non-therapeutic, whereas the subjects recruited for phase II and III trials will often be patients who may hope to receive some health benefit from participation. For certain new drugs, it would plainly be unethical to begin trials in healthy volunteers. An obvious example would be the use of toxic substances, such as chemotherapeutic agents in the treatment of cancer. The benefits associated with these drugs may outweigh the risks for patients with cancer, but there could be no justification for imposing them upon healthy volunteers. Hence, some trials will involve patients from the outset.

The possible dangers of non-therapeutic phase I trials exploded into the public consciousness in 2006, when eight healthy male volunteers were enrolled in a phase I drugs trial of monoclonal antibody TGN1412 (thought to have potential uses in the treatment of arthritis, leukaemia, and multiple sclerosis) at Northwick Park Hospital. Primate toxicology studies had not shown any adverse effects, and it was anticipated that, at the proposed doses, TGN1412 would be well tolerated in humans. This expectation was wrong. Six of the men immediately suffered life-threatening multiple organ failure; the other two had been given a placebo. None of the six men died, but in August 2006, it was reported that the most seriously affected volunteer had been diagnosed with the early stages of an aggressive lymphoma, and all of them face an increased risk of ill health in the future.

An expert scientific group was appointed to investigate what had gone wrong, and its report made a number of recommendations about the proper conduct of 'first in man' studies.[23] When deciding on the dose to be given, investigators should always err on the side of caution. Careful consideration should also be given to the route and rate of administration: the Expert Group recommended slow infusion, which can be stopped immediately at the first sign of any adverse effects. The report was also critical of the decision in the TGN1412 trial to give all six men the active dose at the same time. Instead, it recommended that 'New agents in first-in-man trials should be administered sequentially to subjects with an appropriate period of observation between dosing of individual subjects.'[24]

The TGN1412 trial was self-evidently non-therapeutic, whereas phase II and III trials will normally be therapeutic, in the sense that there is a possibility that subjects might receive effective treatment for their condition. The therapeutic/non-therapeutic distinction may

---

[23] *The Expert Group on Phase One Clinical Trials: Final Report* (DH: London, 2006).   [24] Ibid.

seem straightforward, but as a way of classifying clinical trials, as Levine explains, it can be problematic.

Robert J Levine[25]

> Every clinical trial has some components that are non-therapeutic. When we evaluate entire protocols as either therapeutic or non-therapeutic . . . we end up with what I call the 'fallacy of the package deal'. Those who use this distinction typically classify as 'therapeutic research' any protocol that includes one or more components that are intended to be therapeutic; therefore, the non-therapeutic components of the protocol are justified improperly according to the more permissive standards developed for therapeutic research.

The fact that there is not, in fact, a sharp distinction between therapeutic and non-therapeutic trials is important given that, as Verdun-Jones and Weisstub explain, the principal consequence of labelling research 'therapeutic' is to weaken the protection available to vulnerable subjects. Patients who lack capacity can be enrolled in a research trial more easily if the trial can be described as 'therapeutic', even if it contains elements that are quite self-evidently non-therapeutic. There is then a danger that researchers might exaggerate the likelihood of a direct benefit to research subjects—what Lars Noah refers to as 'benefit creep'[26]—in order to make it easier to enrol people who lack capacity. It is therefore important that a researcher's claim that an experiment is 'therapeutic' should be rigorously scrutinized.

Simon Verdun-Jones and David Weisstub[27]

> Since the classification of an experiment as either therapeutic or non-therapeutic will profoundly affect the legal and ethical restrictions that apply, a high standard must be met before an experiment should be classified as *therapeutic* . . . [A]n element of uncertainty is, by definition, inherent in all experiments. However, 'possible', 'hypothetical', or 'speculative' benefits should not be sufficient in the present context. Rather, a therapeutic benefit must be 'likely', 'probable' or 'reasonably foreseeable'. If this standard cannot be achieved, then the experiment must be classified as *non-therapeutic*.

A further problem with the therapeutic/non-therapeutic distinction is that the whole point of doing the trial in the first place is that we do not yet know whether the treatment will be effective. To say that a trial is therapeutic implies that it is known in advance that subjects will benefit from participation.

Randomized controlled trials (RCTs), discussed in the next section, give rise to a further difficulty in categorizing research as either therapeutic or non-therapeutic. In a placebo-controlled RCT, there may be a 50 per cent chance that the patient will receive no treatment

---

[25] 'International Codes of Research Ethics: Current Controversies and the Future' (2002) 35 Indiana Law Review 557.

[26] 'Informed Consent and the Elusive Dichotomy between Standard and Experimental Therapy' (2002) 28 American Journal of Law and Medicine 361.

[27] 'Drawing the Distinction between Therapeutic Research and Non-Therapeutic Experimentation: Clearing a Way Through the Definitional Thicket' in David N Weisstub (ed), *Research on Human Subjects: Ethics, Law and Social Policy* (Elsevier Science: Oxford, 1998).

at all. Is such a trial 'therapeutic'? On the one hand, there is a chance that the patient will be in the active arm of the study, and will receive a treatment that has some chance of working; but it is equally likely that the patient will receive no treatment at all.

(d) RANDOMIZED CONTROLLED TRIALS?

Although it is true that some of the most important medical breakthroughs—such as the discovery of penicillin—were the result of luck, RCTs are generally regarded as the 'gold standard' in medical research.

The purpose of research is to discover whether a new treatment works, and while this might sound straightforward, researchers have to ensure that their results are not distorted by positive results caused by factors other than the treatment itself. Some patients would be likely to have got better anyway, for example, regardless of whether they received effective treatment.

In an RCT, the research participants are randomly allocated, usually by computer, to the control or the active arm of the study. Those in the active arm are given the new treatment, while those in the control group are given either an inert placebo or, as we see later, the best available treatment. In both groups, it can be anticipated that some patients' conditions will improve regardless of whether they have received any treatment, so researchers will be interested in whether the extent of improvement in the active arm is greater than in the control group.

An RCT is also intended to eliminate the distortions that result from the 'placebo effect'. Many people will report feeling better after receiving a new 'treatment', even if they have in fact been given a sugar pill. If, say, 1,000 patients are allocated to each arm of the study, and 600 in the active arm experience some improvement, while 300 in the control group also report feeling better, this suggests that the new treatment has actually worked in 300 subjects.

Two ethical dilemmas are posed by RCTs. First, while they offer the best way to establish whether a new treatment actually works, randomly allocating a patient to the active or control arm of the study is in conflict with the doctor's normal duty to decide what treatment would be best for her patient. If a doctor believes that drug X is the optimum treatment for a patient's condition, enrolling that patient in an RCT—in which she may be given a placebo instead—clearly breaches the doctor's duty to place the interests of the research subject above the interests of science. As a result, it has been said that RCTs are ethical only if there is 'equipoise': that is, as London explains, there must be genuine uncertainty about which treatment is best.

Alex John London[28]

In its most basic formulation equipoise represents a state of genuine and credible doubt about the relative therapeutic merits of some set of interventions that target a specific medical condition. The requirement that equipoise exist as a necessary condition for the moral acceptability of a clinical trial comparing these interventions is motivated by two interlocking ideas. First, when equipoise obtains it is morally permissible to allow an individual's medical treatment to be assigned by a random process because there is no sufficiently credible evidence to warrant a judgment that one intervention is superior to the other(s). Second, clinical trials that are designed to break or disturb equipoise provide information that will enable the medical community to improve its existing clinical practices.

---

[28] 'Equipoise and international human subjects research' (2001) 15 Bioethics 312–32.

The conflict between the duty to protect participants' wellbeing and the need to obtain sci-entifically valuable results is thrown into particularly sharp focus in decisions about when a trial should be stopped. Preliminary results may indicate that subjects receiving the new treatment are doing better than those in the control group. At this point, there are two good reasons for stopping the trial. First, it might be in the best interests of the individual subjects for the trial to be halted so that all patients can receive the new treatment. Secondly, the state of equipoise that justified carrying out the trial may have been lost, because the researcher now has some evidence that the new treatment works.

On the other hand, stopping the trial in the early stages will reduce the scientific valid-ity of the results. The patients' initial improvement might turn out to be short-lived, and treatment that has been inadequately tested may endanger the health of future patients. The interests of science and society are therefore served by continuing the research until statisti-cally significant results have been obtained.

The dilemma here, as Franklin G Miller and David Wendler explain, is that the point at which interim results become relevant to the individual's decision whether to continue to participate may be sooner than when they become sufficiently compelling to justify stop-ping the trial:

> The point of becoming relevant to individual treatment decisions is reached when findings provide evidence indicating the comparative superiority of one treatment; the point neces-sary for stopping a trial is not reached until this evidence becomes sufficiently compelling to support a change in treatment guidelines, including evidence that will convince clinicians to adopt the preferred treatment.[29]

The second ethical dilemma raised by RCTs is whether it is ever possible to give informed consent to participation. A patient cannot be told whether they have been allocated to the active or the control arm of the test, because an RCT is dependent upon the patients in the control group not knowing what treatment they will receive. As a result, it is impossible for their consent to be fully informed.

Against this, it could be argued that the patient gives informed consent to random alloca-tion, and to participating in a trial in which they will be told which treatment they received only after the trial has ended. As we see later, however, there is evidence that patients find the concept of randomization difficult to understand, perhaps because it is radically at odds with the way they expect their doctors to behave.

(e) THE USE OF PLACEBOS

Giving the control group a placebo is relatively uncontroversial where there is no known treatment for the condition that the new medicine is supposed to treat. In such cases, it is probably not strictly true to say that the researcher is in complete equipoise between the new treatment and doing nothing, since animal experiments are likely to have shown that there is a fairly good chance that this treatment might work. A better way to understand the justification for using a placebo control where no treatment exists is that the participant who receives a sugar pill is not left any worse off by taking part in the trial, because if they had not taken part they would have received no treatment at all.

---

[29] 'Is it ethical to keep interim findings of randomised controlled trials confidential?' (2008) 34 Journal of Medical Ethics 198–201.

Because a placebo-controlled trial may deprive research subjects of appropriate treatment, it would appear to offend one of the most basic principles of the Helsinki Declaration, incorporated into UK law by the Medicines for Human Use (Clinical Trials) Regulations 2004 and reproduced in the new EU Clinical Trials Regulation 2014: 'While the primary purpose of medical research is to generate new knowledge, this goal can never take precedence over the rights and interests of individual research subjects.'[30]

The Helsinki Declaration's solution to this problem is, in most cases, to ensure that patients in the control group are given the 'best proven intervention' for the particular condition. Not only does this protect the wellbeing of research subjects, but it has also been suggested that it may lead to more useful results: researchers will be able to establish whether or not the new treatment is better than existing treatments, rather than proving only that it is marginally better than nothing.

Helsinki Declaration[31]

33. The benefits, risks, burdens and effectiveness of a new intervention must be tested against those of the best proven intervention(s), except in the following circumstances:

- Where no proven intervention exists, the use of placebo, or no intervention, is acceptable; or

- Where for compelling and scientifically sound methodological reasons the use of any intervention less effective than the best proven one, the use of placebo, or no intervention is necessary to determine the efficacy or safety of an intervention

- and the patients who receive any intervention less effective than the best proven one, placebo, or no intervention will not be subject to additional risks of serious or irreversible harm as a result of not receiving the best proven intervention.

Extreme care must be taken to avoid abuse of this option.

This second bullet point captures the idea that a blanket prohibition on placebo-controlled trials where treatment already exists may be inappropriate. When testing new treatments for relatively minor conditions, such as headaches or hay fever, it might seem unduly paternalistic to insist that the control group should receive 'the best proven intervention'.

Particularly for conditions where the placebo effect is especially marked, statistically significant proof of efficacy can be obtained more quickly, using fewer research participants, when a placebo is used. Because approximately 75 per cent of participants in research into pain relief for headaches display a placebo response,[32] a trial that just compares the new treatment with an existing treatment will be difficult to interpret, since a large proportion of the apparent therapeutic effect in both groups will be due to the placebo effect. The Helsinki Declaration therefore suggests that placebo-controlled trials where effective treatment exists are acceptable if (a) there are compelling scientific reasons, and (b) the subjects would not be exposed to a risk of serious harm.

---

[30] Helsinki Declaration (WMA, 2013), Principle 8.
[31] Ibid.   [32] *RCP guidelines*, 4th edn (RCP: London, 2007) para 6.13.

(f) SHAM SURGERY

So far we have assumed that the most invasive experiments involving human subjects are trials of new medicines. In a placebo-controlled drugs trial, patients in the control arm may not receive any treatment, but they are subjected to no extra risk. Where a course of medical treatment, such as surgery, is more intrusive, conducting a randomized controlled trial would involve carrying out a sham procedure on patients in the control group that does expose them to additional risks. Could this ever be ethical?

The issue first arose in the context of trials of fetal tissue grafting for patients suffering from Parkinson's disease. Experiments in animals, and preliminary trials on humans, appeared to indicate that transplanting fetal tissue into patients' brains could be effective in the treatment of Parkinson's disease. Because these preliminary trials had not been RCTs, it was impossible to tell how much of this improvement was due to the placebo effect.

The placebo effect can be particularly striking in Parkinson's disease research, because it is thought that one of the sources of the placebo response is that the expectation of relief triggers the release of chemicals in the brain. It is also clear that surgery is associated with a strong placebo response, because invasive procedures and decisive treatment appear to result in a strong placebo effect. The only way to eliminate the distortions caused by the placebo effect would be to carry out sham surgery on a control group.

Patients receiving the sham surgery have a hole drilled in their skull, and would therefore be exposed to the risks inherent in undergoing any surgical procedure, with no possibility of any benefit at all. As a result, some commentators have condemned these trials for putting the interests of science above the welfare of individual research subjects.

On the other hand, it could be argued that unless surgical techniques are properly tested, future patients may be exposed to potentially ineffective and/or unsafe treatment. Carrying out sham surgery on a small number of patients might then benefit thousands of people in the future, and prevent the NHS from wasting resources on useless or dangerous procedures. While this argument makes sense from a utilitarian perspective, does it involve sacrificing the interests of a few individuals in order to benefit society as a whole?

The preferred solution to this problem has not been a blanket prohibition of sham surgery. Rather, as RL Albin explains in the next extract, their use has to be rigorously justified, and the risks to subjects must be minimized. In particular, extra care should be taken when obtaining informed consent to ensure that the research subjects understand what is meant by randomization, and are aware that they may be about to undergo a surgical procedure which carries some risks, but which may have no chance of improving their condition.

RL Albin[33]

[I]t is common for surgical techniques to be introduced into clinical practice without rigorous evaluation. The result can be exposure of substantial numbers of patients to procedures that incur significant risks and have no benefit. In addition to becoming a public health hazard, inadequately evaluated surgical methods can consume valuable societal resources . . . This is not a theoretical concern. There are abundant examples of widely adopted surgeries that were abandoned subsequently for lack of efficacy . . .

---

[33] 'Sham surgery controls: intercerebral grafting of fetal tissue for Parkinson's disease and proposed criteria for use of sham surgery controls' (2002) 28 Journal of Medical Ethics 322–5.

> Use of sham surgery is unattractive because the increased risk to control subjects is not accompanied by any possibility of benefit. In some cases, however, sham surgery controls are strongly preferred on scientific grounds and may be necessary to answer the key questions. Sham surgery controls cannot be prohibited absolutely but their use must be balanced carefully against the safety of research subjects.

In their systematic review of all 53 published trials involving placebo-controlled trials of surgery, Wartolowska et al found that such trials were an invaluable way of telling whether an intervention is worthwhile and cost-effective. They also found that it was generally possible to take steps to ensure that the placebo arm posed minimal risk to participants, for example by making the placebo surgery itself less invasive.

Karolina Wartolowska et al[34]

> Surgical randomised clinical trials incorporating a placebo arm are rare but this review shows that the results of many of the trials provide clear evidence against continued use of the investigated surgical procedures and in well designed studies the risks of adverse effects are small and the placebo arm is safer than surgery. . . . In the reviewed trials, the placebo arm was usually designed to pose as little risk to the participants as possible and to be significantly less risky than the active surgical procedure. . . .
>
> Placebo controlled trials in surgery are as important as they are in medicine, and they are justified in the same way. They are powerful, feasible way of showing the efficacy of surgical procedures. They are necessary to protect the welfare of present and future patients as well as to conduct proper cost effectiveness analyses. Only then may publicly funded surgical interventions be distributed fairly and justly. Without such studies ineffective treatment may continue unchallenged.

Remy L Brim and Franklin G Miller challenge the prevailing assumption that subjects who receive sham surgery are harmed without receiving any benefit. Instead they argue that for research into conditions where the placebo response is well understood, such as pain and Parkinson's disease, the placebo effect should be treated as a possible benefit of participation.

Remy L Brim and Franklin G Miller[35]

> Placebos can elicit strong physiological effects and produce meaningful symptomatic relief. Indeed, there is often more sound evidence on the benefits of placebos than there is for experimental treatments under investigation. . . .
>
> Despite growing scientific knowledge concerning placebo effects, investigators and RECs [Research Ethics Committees] have continued to characterise sham procedures as 'non-therapeutic' interventions that carry risks to subjects without providing any prospect of benefit. There has been little consideration of whether the potential benefits from the placebo effect should be included in risk–benefit assessments, and whether the

---

[34] 'Use of placebo controls in the evaluation of surgery: systematic review' (2014) 348 British Medical Journal g3253.

[35] 'The potential benefit of the placebo effect in sham-controlled trials: implications for risk–benefit assessments and informed consent' (2013) 39 Journal of Medical Ethics 703–7.

informed consent process should describe the positive aspects of the placebo effect to participants. . . .

The placebo effect should be regarded by RECs and IRBs [Institutional Review Boards] as a potential benefit to patients receiving sham invasive interventions in trials of treatments for conditions that have sound medical evidence demonstrating placebo benefit to patients. Currently, pain and PD fall into this category, and the list will likely grow. Finally, considering potential benefit from the placebo effect would ease ethical concerns about sham-controlled trials insofar as there is evidence to support a prospect of benefit from sham procedures, which can at least partially offset the risks of these procedures.

4 INTERNATIONAL ETHICAL CODES

The first national code of research ethics was promulgated in Germany in 1900, when the Prussian Minister of Religious, Educational and Medical Affairs issued a directive which provided that research should only be carried out on competent adults, who had given consent after a proper explanation of the possible adverse consequences. Ironically, it was the grotesque corruption of some German scientists and doctors under the Nazis that led to the first international code of research ethics.

(a) THE NUREMBERG TRIALS

The discovery of what had been done in the name of medical research during the Second World War resulted in the prosecution of 20 doctors and three scientists at Nuremberg.[36] Some of the defendants were eminent and internationally renowned physicians. Others, according to the prosecutor Telford Taylor, were 'the dregs of the German medical profession'.[37] The trials were conducted by the Allied Forces, and the judges were American lawyers appointed by the Military Governor of the American zone. Sixteen defendants were found guilty; seven, including Hitler's physician Karl Brandt, were hanged.

Many of the experiments carried out in the concentration camps were, as Taylor explains, directed towards the 'war effort'. In Dachau, victims were forced to remain outdoors without clothing for 9–14 hours, or were kept in tanks of iced water for three hours at a time, in order to find out the best way to re-warm German pilots who had parachuted into the North Sea. Also at Dachau, inmates were deliberately infected with malaria in order to test immunization and treatment options. At Ravensbrück, battle conditions were simulated by making incisions that were contaminated with glass, woodshavings, and bacteria. Vaccines for diseases such as typhus, smallpox, and cholera were tested by deliberately infecting a group of prisoners who had been given the vaccine, and members of a control group who had not been immunized, and who were obviously likely to develop life-threatening diseases as a result. Because mass surgical sterilization would be costly and time-consuming, the Nazis were keen to develop techniques which could sterilize large numbers of people, ideally without them noticing. Several thousand women were sterilized by injection, and men were castrated using X-rays.

---

[36] *Trials of War Criminals before the Nuremberg Military Tribunals, United States v Karl Brandt* (US Government Printing Office: Washington DC, 1949).

[37] Telford Taylor, *Opening Statement of the Prosecution*, 9 December 1946 (US Government Printing Office: Washington DC, 1949).

Telford Taylor[38]

Experiments concerning high altitude, the effect of cold, and potability of processed sea water have an obvious relation to aeronautical and naval combat and rescue problems. The mustard gas and phosphorus burn experiments, as well as those relating to the healing value of sulfanilamide for wounds, can be related to air-raid and battlefield medical problems. It is well known that malaria, epidemic jaundice and typhus were among the principal diseases which had to be combated by the German Armed Forces and by German authorities in occupied territories. To some degree, the therapeutic pattern outlined above is undoubtedly a valid one, and explains why the Wehrmacht, and especially the German Air Force, participated in these experiments. Fanatically bent upon conquest, utterly ruthless as to the means or instruments to be used in achieving victory, and callous to the sufferings of people whom they regarded as inferior, the German militarists were willing to gather whatever scientific fruit these experiments might yield.

But our proof will show that a quite different and even more sinister objective runs like a red thread through these hideous researches. We will show that in some instances, the true object of these experiments was not how to rescue or to cure, but how to destroy and kill. The sterilization experiments were, it is clear, purely destructive in purpose. The prisoners at Buchenwald who were shot with poisoned bullets were not guinea pigs to test an antidote for the poison; their murderers really wanted to know how quickly the poison would kill . . .

The thanatological knowledge, derived in part from these experiments, supplied the techniques for genocide, a policy of the Third Reich, exemplified in the 'euthanasia' program, and in the widespread slaughter of Jews, Gypsies, Poles, and Russians. This policy of mass extermination could not have been so effectively carried out without the active participation of German medical scientists.

While in no sense justifying these appalling crimes, Caplan points out an interesting comparison between the Nazis' willingness to sacrifice some lives in order to save others and the Allies' similar preparedness knowingly to sacrifice some conscripts' lives for the greater good.

Arthur L Caplan[39]

The most distinguished of the scientists who was put on trial, Gerhard Rose, the head of the Koch Institute of Tropical Medicine in Berlin, said that he initially opposed performing potentially lethal experiments to create a vaccine for typhus on camp inmates. But he came to believe that it made no sense not to risk the lives of 100 or 200 men in pursuit of a vaccine when 1000 men a day were dying of typhus on the Eastern front. What, he asked, were the deaths of 100 men compared to the possible benefit of getting a prophylactic vaccine capable of saving tens of thousands? Rose, because he admitted that he had anguished about his own moral duty when asked by the Wehrmacht to perform the typhus experiments in a concentration camp, raises the most difficult and most plausible moral argument in defense of lethal experimentation.

[38] Ibid.
[39] 'How did Medicine Go so Wrong?' in Arthur L Caplan (ed), *When Medicine Went Mad: Bioethics and the Holocaust* (Human Press: Totowa, NJ, 1992) 53–92.

> The prosecution encountered some difficulty with Rose's argument. The defense team for Rose noted that the Allies themselves justified the compulsory drafting of men for military service throughout the war, knowing many would certainly die, on the grounds that the sacrifice of the few to save the many was morally just.

It is also worth noting that the United States' interest in prosecuting German doctors and scientists who had carried out inhuman experiments on concentration camp inmates did not extend to abuses by Japanese researchers in the 1930s and 1940s. Between 1930 and 1945, at a site in China known as Unit 731, over 3,000 people died through deliberate exposure to germs such as anthrax, cholera, and typhoid, and as a result of experiments involving being dehydrated, frozen, or given transfusions of horse blood.[40] At the end of the war, the US gave Japanese experimenters immunity from prosecution in return for information about biological warfare.

In addition to judging the conduct of the defendants, the court at Nuremberg set out a Code to govern the future conduct of medical research in order to protect the subjects' interest.

Nuremberg Code[41]

1. The voluntary consent of the human subject is absolutely essential.

2. The experiment should be such as to yield fruitful results for the good of society, unprocurable by other methods or means of study, and not random and unnecessary in nature.

3. The experiment should be so designed and based on the results of animal experimentation and knowledge of the natural history of the disease or other problem under study that the anticipated results will justify the performance of the experiment.

4. The experiment should be so conducted as to avoid all unnecessary physical and mental suffering and injury.

5. No experiment should be conducted where there is an a priori reason to believe that death or disabling injury will occur; except, perhaps, in those experiments where the experimental physicians also serve as subjects.

6. The degree of risk to be taken should never exceed that determined by the humanitarian importance of the problem to be solved by the experiment.

7. Proper preparations should be made and adequate facilities provided to protect the experimental subject against even remote possibilities of injury, disability, or death.

8. The experiment should be conducted only by scientifically qualified persons. The highest degree of skill and care should be required through all stages of the experiment of those who conduct or engage in the experiment.

9. During the course of the experiment the human subject should be at liberty to bring the experiment to an end if he has reached the physical or mental state where continuation of the experiment seems to him to be impossible.

10. During the course of the experiment the scientist in charge must be prepared to terminate the experiment at any stage, if he has probable cause to believe, in the exercise of the good faith, superior skill and careful judgment required of him that a continuation of the experiment is likely to result in injury, disability, or death to the experimental subject.

---

[40] See further Sheldon H Harris, *Factories of Death: Japanese Biological Warfare 1932–45 and the American Cover-Up* (Routledge: London, 1994).

[41] *Trials of War Criminals before the Nuremberg Military Tribunals under Control Council Law No. 10*, vol 2 (US Government Printing Office: Washington DC, 1949) 181–2.

Although the publication of the Nuremberg Code had tremendous symbolic resonance, its impact upon medical practice was limited. In part, this is because many assumed that it was specifically addressing the abuses of Nazism, and that it therefore had limited relevance for the medical profession in general. Most of the defendants at Nuremberg were guilty of murder, and if the Code were simply directed towards ensuring that doctors did not kill their patients in the interests of science, its impact upon the conduct of ordinary clinical research would be minimal.

The Code's scope is, however, wider than this: the permissible limits of medical research were also on trial. The first principle in the Nuremberg Code—that the voluntary consent of the human subject is absolutely essential—would be redundant if the defendants' only crimes had been murder, where the consent of the victim is never a defence.

Although there have not been research abuses on the scale of those conducted in Nazi concentration camps since the Nuremberg trials, exploitative medical research did not start and stop with the Nazis. On the contrary, there were plenty of examples of unethical research prior to the Second World War: in the eighteenth and nineteenth centuries, for example, experiments would often be carried out on orphans, prostitutes, and other 'expendable' social groups.

There have also been incidences of exploitation since the end of the Second World War. In the 1960s, Henry Beecher's seminal article 'Ethics and Clinical Research',[42] and Maurice Pappworth's book *Human Guinea Pigs*,[43] gave details of extensive violations of the principles encapsulated in the Nuremberg Code. For example, in the US, between 1932 and 1972 the United States Public Health Services carried out the now infamous Tuskegee study, in which effective treatment for syphilis was withheld from 400 poor and uneducated black men without their knowledge or consent, so that the disease's progression could be observed.

In 2011, it was revealed that one of the doctors involved in the Tuskegee study also carried out syphilis research in Guatemala, in which prostitutes known to be infected with syphilis were sent into prisons to have sex with prisoners, who were then given prophylactic treatment in order to find out if it was capable of preventing infection.[44]

(b) THE HELSINKI DECLARATION

In 1954, the Eighth General Assembly of the World Medical Association drafted a set of principles to be followed in research involving human subjects. This document was redrafted in the early 1960s and adopted at the Eighteenth World Medical Association Assembly in Helsinki in 1964. The Helsinki Declaration has since been revised nine times, most recently in Brazil in 2013.

The Helsinki Declaration goes into much greater detail than the Nuremberg Code as to the circumstances in which research on human subjects is legitimate. It also now specifically states that its provisions must not be diluted by national legislation (para 10). Through regular updating, the Declaration has been able to respond to new concerns: for

---

[42] 'Ethics and clinical research' (1966) 274 New England Journal of Medicine 1354–60.
[43] *Human Guinea Pigs: Experimentation on Man* (Beacon Press: Boston, 1967).
[44] Susan M Reverby, '"Normal exposure" and inoculation syphilis: a PHS "Tuskegee" doctor in Guatemala 1946–48' (2011) 23 Journal of Policy History 6–28.

example, para 11 now specifies that 'Medical research should be conducted in a manner that minimises possible harm to the environment.'

Helsinki Declaration[45]

> 9. It is the duty of physicians who are involved in medical research to protect the life, health, dignity, integrity, right to self-determination, privacy, and confidentiality of personal information of research subjects. The responsibility for the protection of research subjects must always rest with the physician or other health care professionals and never with the research subjects, even though they have given consent.
>
> 10. Physicians must consider the ethical, legal and regulatory norms and standards for research involving human subjects in their own countries as well as applicable international norms and standards. No national or international ethical, legal or regulatory requirement should reduce or eliminate any of the protections for research subjects set forth in this Declaration.

(c) THE CIOMS GUIDELINES

In 1982, in response to the concern that research was being carried out in poorer countries in order to save money and to avoid restrictive regulations, the Council for International Organizations of Medical Sciences (CIOMS) published their *International Ethical Guidelines for Biomedical Research Involving Human Subjects*. Their purpose is to address the practical difficulties in implementing universally applicable ethical standards in countries with vastly different standards of health care provision. At the heart of the CIOMS Guidelines are three basic ethical principles: respect for persons, beneficence, and justice:

Council for International Organizations of Medical Sciences[46]

> In general, the research project should leave low-resource countries or communities better off than previously or, at least, no worse off. It should be responsive to their health needs and priorities in that any product developed is made reasonably available to them, and as far as possible leave the population in a better position to obtain effective health care and protect its own health.
>
> Justice requires also that the research be responsive to the health conditions or needs of vulnerable subjects. The subjects selected should be the least vulnerable necessary to accomplish the purposes of the research.

In 2015, CIOMS consulted on proposed revisions to these guidelines. The new draft guidelines have been substantially revised and expanded. Following a public consultation, the finalized guidelines are expected to be published in 2016.

---

[45] World Medical Association, *Declaration of Helsinki: Ethical Principles for Medical Research Involving Human Subjects* (WMA, 2013).

[46] *International Ethical Guidelines for Biomedical Research Involving Human Subjects* (CIOMS, 2002).

CIOMS Working Group on the Revision of CIOMS 2002 International Ethical Guidelines for Biomedical Research Involving Human Subjects[47]

Guideline 1: Social value

The ethical justification of health-related research involving humans is its social value: the prospect of generating the knowledge and/or the means necessary to protect and promote people's health. Clinicians, researchers, policy makers, public health officials, patients, pharmaceutical companies and others rely on the results of research for activities and decisions that impact individual and public health, welfare, and the use of limited resources. Therefore, researchers, regulators, research ethics committees, and sponsors must ensure that proposed studies are scientifically sound, build on an adequate prior knowledge-base, and are likely to generate valuable information. Such research must always be carried out in ways that uphold human rights, and respect, protect, and are fair to study participants and the communities in which the research is conducted.

Guideline 2: Research conducted in low-resource settings

Before instituting a plan to undertake research in a population or community with limited resources or infrastructure, the sponsor, researchers, and relevant public health authority must ensure that the research is responsive to the health needs or priorities of the communities or populations where the research will be conducted.

As part of their obligation, sponsors, researchers must also:

- Make every effort in cooperation with government and civil society to make available as soon as possible any intervention or product developed, and/or knowledge generated, for the population or community in which the research is carried out. This requirement does not preclude capacity building or the provision of additional benefits to the population or community;

- Consult with and inform communities about the plans for making any intervention or product developed intervention available, including the responsibilities of all relevant stakeholders.

(d) THE INTERNATIONAL CONFERENCE ON HARMONISATION OF TECHNICAL REQUIREMENTS FOR REGISTRATION OF PHARMACEUTICALS FOR HUMAN USE

The International Conference on Harmonisation of Technical Requirements for Registration of Pharmaceuticals for Human Use (ICH) brings together the regulatory authorities of Europe, Japan, and the US, as well as experts from the pharmaceutical industry. Its purpose is to make recommendations on ways to achieve greater harmonization of regulations, in order to reduce the need to duplicate trials of new medicines. To facilitate the mutual acceptance of data by regulatory authorities worldwide, the ICH has published a number of guidelines on the conduct of clinical trials, including the general ICH *Good Clinical Practices: Consolidated Practices Guideline* (GCP). Compliance with ICH Guidelines enables data generated by trials in low and middle-income countries to be used in applications for marketing authorizations in the lucrative US, European, and Japanese markets.

---

[47] (CIOMS, 2015).

The ICH GCP states that: 'Compliance with this standard provides public assurance that the rights, safety and well-being of trial subjects are protected; consistent with the principles that have their origin in the Declaration of Helsinki, and that the clinical trial data are credible.' It requires ethical review, but most of its guidance in fact relates to technical, administrative matters, such as record-keeping. As a result, Sharon Kaur and Choong Yeow Choy question how far ICH guidelines are able to protect individual research subjects.

Sharon Kaur and Choong Yeow Choy[48]

[The ICH process] is concerned with two things: first, ensuring that regardless of where drug development and manufacturing takes place, drugs are developed, tested, registered and monitored in a manner that ensures their quality and safety; and second, making the process of developing new drugs more efficient and less expensive. It does these things by prescribing harmonized standards for what are mostly scientific and quantitative processes, which mainly involve close observation and documentation. . . .

Admittedly, these administrative processes lend themselves well in the scientific arena as a manner of demonstrating compliance to standards. . . . To ensure that a drug is safe for use, information needs to be compiled regarding how many people have had bad reactions during the trial; the type of reactions; the severity of the events; the possible causal links between the reactions and the drugs; and so on. The accurate and careful compilation of relevant data is essential to any meaningful analysis. . . . The question is whether or not this same approach is appropriate in situations that involve non-science based activities such as the activity of ethics review?

(e) IMPACT OF INTERNATIONAL CODES

Certain principles are common to all of these international documents, and the practical requirements that emerge from them could, perhaps, be summarized as follows:

(a) Before the research starts:
- it must be established that the research is scientifically valid;
- the risks must be proportionate to the benefits;
- the research protocol should have been approved by an ethics committee;
- if the subject has capacity, she must give informed consent;
- if the subject lacks capacity, other protections must be in place.

(b) During the research:
- the experiment must be stopped if there is a risk of injury or death;
- the experiment must be stopped once equipoise has been lost;
- the subject must be free to withdraw from the trial at any time.

(c) After the research has finished:
- the subject should have access to information about the trial, and to treatment which has been proved to be effective as a result of the trial;
- research findings should be disseminated;
- subjects who have been injured as a result of the trial should be appropriately compensated.

---

[48] 'Ethical considerations in clinical trials: a critique of the ICH-GCP Guideline' (2014) 14 Developing World Bioethics 20–28.

To be ethical, research must satisfy the requirements of good scientific practice. Unless research will produce valid results, there could be no justification for imposing its risks upon research subjects.

Risks to participants must also be reasonable in relation to the trial's anticipated benefits. For several reasons, however, this principle is rather imprecise. First, it does not tell us how much risk it is reasonable to impose on subjects if the benefits might be very great indeed. Secondly, because the outcome of the research is necessarily unknown, the researcher will rarely be in a position to know exactly what risks and benefits might flow from the research. If she was already sure of the answer to this question, then carrying out experiments on humans would be scientifically pointless, and hence unethical. Judging whether the risks are proportionate to the anticipated benefits will inevitably involve informed guesswork.

Invoking a risk/benefit calculation in order to justify research on human subjects may also be dangerously misleading. If told that the risks of participation in a research trial are outweighed by its benefits, not only might subjects not realize that this assessment is speculative, but also they might assume that they will be the ones to benefit from the research. We know that most people volunteer to participate in research as a result of perceived self-interest, so unwittingly exaggerating the probability that the subject will benefit from participation may mean that her consent is based upon a misunderstanding, and hence is not fully informed. Even if participation in research might benefit the individual subject, it is important to remember that this will never be a trial's principal purpose. On the contrary, any anticipated benefit to individual research subjects will be incidental to its primary aim, which is to produce generalizable knowledge.

5 REGULATION OF RESEARCH IN THE UK

(a) THE CLINICAL TRIALS REGULATION 2014

The new EU Regulation on clinical trials on medicinal products for human use[49] comes into force on or after May 2016.

Clinical Trials Regulation 2014

> 3 A clinical trial may be conducted only if:
>
> (a) the rights, safety dignity and well-being of subjects are protected and prevail over all other interests; and
>
> (b) it is designed to generate reliable and robust data.

Clinical trials must have been subject to scientific and ethics approval, carried out by a properly constituted ethics committee. The EU Clinical Trials Regulation introduces a single, electronic EU portal for all applications to carry out clinical trials, with one set of paperwork for both the trial authorization and REC-approval stages. This will be maintained by the European Medicines Agency (see Chapter 10). Until the new EU electronic portal

---

[49] Regulation (EU) No 536/2014 on clinical trials on medicinal products for human use, and repealing Directive 2001/20/EC (16 April 2014).

is functional, clinical trial authorizations in the UK will be issued by the Medicines and Healthcare products Regulatory Agency (MHRA; we consider the work of the MHRA in the next chapter, when we look at the licensing of medicines).

One of the main reasons for replacing the 2001 Directive (transposed into English law as the Medicines for Human Use (Clinical Trials) Regulations 2004) was that the applications process was cumbersome and bureaucratic, and especially so in the case of multi-country trials. Where trials are carried out in several European countries at once, differences in the processes for ethical approval was leading to unnecessary duplication and delay, and offered a disincentive for carrying out trials within Europe.

The Clinical Trials Regulation provides for notification, within strict time limits, of actual and suspected serious adverse events. Sponsors are required to provide an annual list of all serious adverse events, and a report on the safety of the trial's subjects. The Clinical Trials Regulation also contains detailed provisions on obtaining informed consent from participants and the circumstances in which research on those who lack capacity is legitimate. We consider these later in the context of a more detailed discussion of the role of consent in research.

(b) GUIDELINES

In the UK, a variety of bodies—including the Department of Health, the Royal College of Physicians, the Royal College of Psychiatrists, the Royal College of Paediatrics and Child Health, and the Medical Research Council—have issued guidance on good practice in research. All reproduce the fundamental principle that the subject's health and wellbeing must take priority over other considerations. For example, the General Medical Council's (GMC) guidance, *Good Practice in Research and Consent to Research* states that:

> 8 You must make sure that the safety, dignity and wellbeing of participants take precedence over the development of treatments and the furthering of knowledge.
> 9 You must make sure that foreseeable risks to participants are kept as low as possible. In addition, you must be satisfied that:
> - the anticipated benefits to participants outweigh the foreseeable risks, or
> - the foreseeable risks to participants are minimal if the research only has the potential to benefit others more generally.[50]

(c) ETHICS COMMITTEES

The first research ethics committees (RECs) were set up in the 1960s, and a centralized system, now administered by the Health Research Authority, has been in place since the 1990s. The favourable opinion of an ethics committee is a necessary precondition of any clinical trial. All applications are submitted centrally. Applications which raise no material ethical issues can then be fast-tracked by a virtual sub-committee of two experienced research ethics advisers. This means that only applications which do raise material ethical issues will receive full REC review.

---

[50] *Good Practice in Research and Consent to Research* (GMC, 2013).

Of course, this system depends upon a clear and consistent definition of what counts as a 'material ethical issue'. Any invasive study will raise material ethical issues, and so it is only research which does not involve any physical intervention which is likely to be fast-tracked. An example might be research that just involves surveys or questionnaires. A blanket rule that survey-based research does not require full REC review would be inappropriate, however, because some surveys covering sensitive issues, such as exposure to sexually transmitted diseases, may pose risks for participants. Poorly designed questionnaires could cause distress, and if sensitive data is collected, breaches of confidentiality could have serious adverse consequences.

The Clinical Trials Regulation sets a time limit of 60 days between receipt of a valid application and the issuing of the REC's opinion, unless the trial involves gene therapy, somatic cell therapy, or a medicinal product containing a genetically modified organism, in which case longer time limits (of up to 180 days) apply.

RECs—of which there are about 80 in the UK—will commonly have between 12 and 18 members, about one-third of whom should be 'lay' members. The responsibility of RECs is to ensure that research involving human subjects is ethical. There has been some debate over whether they have any role in judging the scientific validity of research. On the one hand, RECs may not have sufficient expertise to evaluate a project's scientific merit, and the question of whether research is ethical may be different from whether it is good science. Yet, on the other hand, if research is scientifically invalid and, as a result, will not generate any useful data, then this is also an ethical issue, because the 'anticipated benefits' to society do not justify the risks to the research subjects.

Certainly there is evidence that a considerable proportion of REC letters to applicants, which raise issues which must be addressed before approval is given, are concerned with scientific matters: in one study of REC decisions in relation to proposed oncology trials, 71 per cent raised scientific design issues.[51]

Because of their access to the original protocol, RECs are particularly well placed to monitor adherence to the ethical standards upon which REC approval was based. In practice, however, RECs exercise little ongoing scrutiny of research after the protocol has been approved. While progress reports must be submitted, the committee's role is largely confined to collecting information volunteered by the researchers, rather than investigating compliance for itself.

Standard Operating Procedures for RECs make clear that monitoring compliance is the job of the trial sponsor (which may be the pharmaceutical company whose drugs are being tested), rather than the REC:

> In general, the REC is not responsible for proactive monitoring of research. However, it has a duty to keep the favourable ethical opinion under review in the light of progress reports and significant developments, and may review the opinion at any time... The primary responsibility for monitoring the safety of research participants lies with the trial sponsor.[52]

If deviations from the protocol are likely to go unnoticed, researchers may have little incentive to ensure compliance. As a result, it is probably unsurprising that deviations from the original protocol are not uncommon: in one US study of the reasons for

---

[51] Mary Dixon-Woods et al, 'What do research ethics committees say about applications to do cancer trials?' (2008) 9 Lancet Oncology 700–1.

[52] *Standard Operating Procedures for Research Ethics Committees* Version 6.1 (HRA, 2015).

'warning letters' issued by the FDA, 95 per cent had involved 'deviation from the investigational plan'.[53]

6 CONSENT TO PARTICIPATION IN RESEARCH

(a) THE COMPETENT SUBJECT

(1) Voluntariness

Because the research subject will commonly be exposing herself to some increased risk, without necessarily gaining any benefit in return, her consent must have been given voluntarily, and she must not have been pressurized into taking part.

We begin by looking at whether payments to research subjects might unduly influence their decisions. Next we consider the special vulnerability of patients. Finally, we look at other 'vulnerable' groups, such as prisoners and medical students.

(a) Payments

Paying people to participate in research has been criticized for several reasons. First, it has been argued that the offer of money may prove irresistible, especially for the poorest sections of society.

Paul McNeill[54]

The reason that inducement is particularly of concern is that those most susceptible to inducement may be the least able to assess the aims and technical information relating to the research and to decide on whether or not the risk is worth taking. It is already the poor and socially disadvantaged who volunteer for most research yet it is typically the better off members of society who benefit from research . . .

There is something repugnant about offering money to relatively poor people, impecunious students, travellers and others, to take part in research, which, by its nature, exposes them to risks of harm. The poor in our societies already have higher risks of poor health and other adverse life events. Inducement to take part in experimentation should not be allowed when it adds to those risks.

Not only could money persuade poor people to volunteer for research, but it might also offer an incentive to misrepresent characteristics—such as depression or drug use—which would otherwise disqualify someone from participation. This may increase the health risks to participants, as well as potentially invalidating the trial's results. In the next extract, JP Bentley and PG Thacker draw on empirical research which suggests that payments increase subjects' willingness both to participate in research, and to conceal information about 'restricted activities'.

---

[53] Yashashri C Shetty and Aafreen A Saiyed, 'Analysis of warning letters issued by the US Food and Drug Administration to clinical investigators, institutional review boards and sponsors: a retrospective study' (2015) 41 Journal of Medical Ethics 398–403.

[54] 'Paying people to participate in research: why not?' (1997) 11 Bioethics 391–6.

JP Bentley and PG Thacker[55]

This study suggests that monetary payment increases respondents' willingness to participate in research regardless of the level of risk; higher levels of payment make respondents more willing to participate, even if the study is relatively risky . . . .

Monetary payments appeared to influence respondents' propensity to neglect to tell researchers about restricted activities they have engaged in either before or during a study, with higher payment levels leading to a higher propensity to neglect to tell.

This study also showed that higher levels of monetary payment may influence subjects' behaviours regarding concealing information about restricted activities. If such activities were actually engaged in, the results of the hypothetical studies may have been distorted (that is, alcohol, caffeine, medications, herbal products may all affect the pharmacokinetics of a study drug).

Secondly, some commentators believe that the 'taint' of money contaminates the ethical virtue of altruism. Tod Chambers, for example, argues that 'the gift of one's own health should not be thought of as a commodity'.[56]

Thirdly, because payments may skew subject selection, they might also undermine the robustness of the trial's results. Testing medicines on students in their early twenties, for example, does not establish that they are safe for middle-aged or elderly patients. In an empirical study of phase I participants in Tayside, Pamela Ferguson found that they 'conform[ed] to the stereotype of the typical Phase I volunteer; . . . they were predominantly male (74 per cent), aged between 18 and 45 (73 per cent), with a minority (23 per cent) in full-time employment'; 25 per cent were students, and half of these were medical students.[57]

The advertisement for recruitment to the TGN1412 trial, described previously, was designed to appeal to young adults: 'You'll be paid for your time . . . Free food . . . digital TV, pool table, video games, DVD player and now FREE internet access!' Volunteers were paid around £2,000. Following media coverage of the terrible side effects experienced by the six men who had received TGN1412, agencies that recruit volunteers for trials reported an increase in inquiries from the public. As Pamela Ferguson explains: 'Paradoxically, the case helped to advertise the high fees that could be earned by taking part, and the rarity of adverse events.'[58]

In favour of payments, it could be argued, first, that since participation in medical research will often be time-consuming, inconvenient, and uncomfortable, without payments it might be difficult to recruit enough participants. Secondly, it is not clear why being paid to assume the burdens of research participation is necessarily more problematic than paying wages to people whose jobs pose a risk to their health, such as cycle couriers, firemen, and soldiers. In the next extract, Martin Wilkinson and Andrew Moore argue that inducements are not necessarily coercive.

---

[55] 'The influence of risk and monetary payment on the research participation decision making process' (2004) 30 Journal of Medical Ethics 293–8.

[56] 'Participation as commodity, participation as gift' (2001) 1 American Journal of Bioethics 48.

[57] Pamela R Ferguson, 'Clinical Trials and Healthy Volunteers' (2008) 16 Medical Law Review 23–51.

[58] Ibid.

Martin Wilkinson and Andrew Moore[59]

Consider the following argument for allowing inducements. Some researchers would find it worthwhile to pay inducements in order to attract enough subjects. Those who would accept this reward would not do so unless it were worthwhile to them. As a result of offering the reward, the researchers get the subjects they want. As a result of participating, the subjects get the reward they want. Both are better off. No one is worse off. Inducement is thus a good thing.

This seems to us to be a good argument, which at least makes a *prima facie* case for inducement. It has the same structure as an argument justifying wages for work, or any other market transactions. Many people would not work if they were not paid; in that sense wages are inducements. Few people think that, as a result, it is wrong to offer wages. Those that do have concerns about the existing wage system usually object that wages are too *low*, not that they are too high, or that they are offered at all . . .

If badly off people were in some way coerced into participating as subjects, then their autonomy would be infringed upon and their consent invalidated. Coercion is paradigmatically a case of the denial of autonomy, since it consists in the deliberate imposition of one person's will on another. However, coercion usually takes the form of threats, which restrict people's options. Inducements are offers, not threats, and they expand people's options.

Thirdly, the offer of experimental treatment to desperately ill patients, and the 'therapeutic misconception' (considered in the next section), will often offer a more powerful incentive than money for agreeing to participate in research, and for misrepresenting disqualifying characteristics. A research subject who has been paid is probably more likely to have given fully informed consent to participation in a trial than a patient who is mistakenly under the assumption that her doctor is treating her in her best interests.

The assumption behind the guidance that exists on payments is that payments are acceptable provided that they are not so large that they might prompt someone to act against her better judgement.

General Medical Council[60]

17 You should make sure that participants are not encouraged to volunteer more frequently than is advisable or against their best interests. You should make sure that nobody takes part repeatedly in research projects if it might lead to a risk of significant harm to them.

In the next extract, Christine Grady defends modest payments to research subjects.

Christine Grady[61]

Commentators and common wisdom have argued that limiting the amount of payment offered for research participation minimizes the possibility that money will distort judgment and push people towards deception. Payment as recognition of the research participant's

---

[59] 'Inducement in research' (1997) 11 Bioethics 373–89.

[60] *Good Practice in Research and Consent to Research* (GMC: London, 2009).

[61] 'Money for research participation: does it jeopardize informed consent?' (2001) 1 American Journal of Bioethics 40–4.

> contribution and calculated according to some regularly applied and locally acceptable stand-ard (per day, visit, or procedure) is likely to be more modest and less likely to distort judge-ment than amounts designed solely to attract subjects and outperform the competition in terms of recruitment.

In contrast, writing from a Canadian perspective, Trudo Lemmens and Carl Elliott suggest that the compromise position in which subjects are paid, but not much, is disingenuous. They argue that it would be better straightforwardly to admit that the researcher is employ-ing the research subject. This would enable these 'employees' to benefit from health and safety rules that would prevent them from being exposed to unreasonable risks.

Trudo Lemmens and Carl Elliott[62]

> In the world that regulatory bodies have created, healthy subjects take part in studies because of the money, yet researchers have to pretend that the subjects are motivated by something other than money. Research subjects cannot negotiate payment, since payment is not sup-posed to be the focus of the transaction . . .
>
> It is time to stop pretending that the relationship between for-profit, multibillion-dollar cor-porate entities and healthy volunteers is the same as the relationship between an academic physician-investigator and sick patients. We have argued that research studies on healthy subjects—unlike research on sick patients—are best characterized as a kind of labor relation. If regulatory bodies realized this, they would be in a far better position to protect these subjects from exploitation. Labor-type legislation could give research agencies the clout of occupational health and safety agencies by giving them the power to conduct inspections and ensure that 'working' conditions are safe. Collective negotiations and unionization could give research par-ticipants a stronger voice in arguing for good working conditions. Research participants could negotiate standards of payment based on the level of discomfort they are asked to undergo, the number and types of procedures, the duration of the studies and other factors . . .
>
> Ethical guidelines and regulations ought to protect healthy research subjects from exploita-tion. But instead, the current regulatory scheme prohibits subjects from receiving a fair wage and denies them the legal resources available to other high-risk workers.

There is certainly evidence that some people are effectively professional trial participants. Roberto Abadie carried out an ethnographic study of self-identified 'professional guinea pigs' in Philadelphia and found that some volunteers had taken part in more than 80 phase I trials.[63]

Roberto Abadie[64]

> Most clinical trial volunteers are in their twenties and thirties, single and childless, with flex-ible schedules and no permanent attachments. Trial income offers them the opportunity to have fun and travel . . . In their spending habits, guinea pigs show a clear understanding that their bodies are commodities, almost using their bodies as ATMs to fund their lifestyles.

---

[62] 'Justice for the professional guinea pig' (2001) 1 American Journal of Bioethics 51–3.
[63] Roberto Abadie, *The Professional Guinea Pig: Big Pharma and the Risky World of Human Subjects* (Duke UP: Durham, NC, 2010).
[64] Ibid, 39–40, 46.

> Volunteers understand their participation as trial subjects as a particular type of work not based on physical labor . . . Professional guinea pigs have the sense that while volunteering for a trial they do not do much except just lie there . . . Most guinea pigs would agree with Spam, who was quoted in the introduction as describing the trials as 'a weird type of work' in a 'mild torture economy' in which one is paid not to produce something, but to 'endure something'.

In the next extract, Rebecca Dresser points out that 'subversive subjects', who might lie about their compliance with a trial's requirements, are not limited to those who are paid. Patients too, as we see in the next extract, may have powerful self-interests which persuade them to act subversively. She also argues that the best way to ensure compliance is to treat subjects with respect.

Rebecca Dresser[65]

> Clinical trial subjects are not passive followers of researchers' orders, they are active agents living their own lives and promoting what they see as their own interests. In rejecting the constraints research imposes, however, subversive subjects diminish the value of research results. . . . Volunteers focused on earning money through research participation adopt a variety of deceptive practices to gain admission to studies. . . . Patients who see trial participation as a means to obtain better treatment commit a variety of subversive acts. Some enter trials with the specific intent to drop out early if their symptoms do not improve within a certain time. Subjects have also been known to share drugs to ensure that each person receives at least some of the preferred one. . . .
>
> Thus, the best way to proceed is to replace practices that devalue subjects' contributions with practices that demonstrate appreciation for what they do. . . . Simple quality-of-life upgrades could go a long way toward improving the situation. . . . The research staff also plays a major role in subjects' commitment to play by the rules. Subjects have high praise for studies conducted by personable and efficient teams. Subjects are grateful when staff members pay attention and respond to their concerns. Subjects appreciate sincere expressions of thanks for the pain, discomfort, and disruption they endure.

(b) Patients

There is a danger that patients who volunteer for clinical trials may not understand that they are taking part in research, where the purpose is generating generalizable knowledge, rather than improving their health. This is known as the 'therapeutic misconception', and for obvious reasons it only applies in phase II and III trials, when research subjects are patients who suffer from the condition the new drug is intended to treat.

Standard consent forms can exacerbate this problem by setting out what the study hopes to achieve for future patients. Confusion between the goals of the research and what patients hope for themselves is then inevitable. Nancy King advocates a much blunter approach: 'When benefit cannot reasonably be expected, the consent form should say, "You will not benefit".'[66]

---

[65] 'Subversive subjects: rule-breaking and deception in clinical trials' (2013) 41 Journal of Law, Medicine and Ethics 829–40.

[66] 'Defining and describing benefit appropriately in clinical trials' (2000) 28 Journal of Law, Medicine and Ethics 332, 334.

Terminally ill patients are an especially vulnerable group, particularly if none of the standard treatments have worked, and they have been told that no more can be done for them. In such circumstances, enrolling in a trial of an experimental new drug may offer the best hope of a cure. As Frances Miller has put it, 'these desperate souls want to believe in the omnipotence of medicine'.[67] Of course, someone's desperation to try anything does not vitiate their consent, but it does suggest that researchers should be careful not to overstate the likelihood that the patient will receive a direct health benefit.

The doctor–patient relationship is based upon trust, and, as Charuvastra and Marder explain, it is often difficult for patients to understand that their doctor might be suggesting a course of action which may not be in their best interests.

A Charuvastra and SR Marder[68]

[W]hen a patient is reading an informed consent document, he is also seeing a person in a white coat and appreciating that he is in a hospital or medical centre, and his evaluation of the intention of the researcher and the benefits and risks of his relationship with this researcher will reflect to some degree all his prior social encounters with similar people in similar white coats in similar settings. A therapeutic misconception is even more likely to take place if the person proposing the research is someone the patient already knows, and especially if it is someone the patient already receives care from.

Certainly, there is evidence that some subjects do not realize that they have taken part in research, even when they have apparently given informed consent. It also seems clear that patients find it especially difficult to understand the concept of randomization. In their study of cancer patients who had signed informed consent forms for RCTs, Sanchini et al found that nearly 40 per cent of subjects were unaware that they had taken part in a trial, and only 11 per cent of participants had understood that the trial had involved randomization.[69] In the next extract, Katie Featherstone and Jenny L Donovan describe interviews with trial participants who clearly found it very hard to believe that the treatment they received had really been randomly allocated.

Katie Featherstone and Jenny L Donovan[70]

Allocation according to randomisation appeared to some to be very haphazard. It was difficult for these men to believe that such a haphazard procedure was reasonable, particularly when they had completed so many questionnaires about their symptoms and undergone clinical tests, some of which were very invasive. The men reasoned that the data from the questionnaires and clinical tests must be useful, not just for research purposes, but

---

[67] FH Miller, 'Trusting Doctors: Tricky Business When it Comes to Clinical Trials' (2001) 81 Boston University Law Review 423.

[68] 'Unconscious emotional reasoning and the therapeutic misconception' (2008) 34 Journal of Medical Ethics 193–7.

[69] Virginia Sanchini et al, 'Informed consent as an ethical requirement in clinical trials: an old, but still unresolved issue. An observational study to evaluate patient's informed consent comprehension' (2014) 40 Journal of Medical Ethics 269–75.

[70] '"Why don't they just tell me straight, why allocate it?" The struggle to make sense of participating in a randomized controlled trial' (2002) 55 Social Science and Medicine 709–19.

also for clinicians to make individualised treatment decisions—hence the unacceptability of randomisation . . . .

[E]ven when trials adhere to strict informed consent procedures and ensure that 'simple language' is used, this does not guarantee that subjects will fully understand the implications of participation and that they may still have unrealistic treatment expectations.

It is common for patients to feel grateful to the medical team which is caring for them, and if asked to participate in research, refusal may not feel like a realistic option, especially if they have an ongoing relationship with the doctor who has invited them to take part.

In the next extract, Franz J Ingelfinger further draws attention to the fact that illness can increase patients' vulnerability and dependency, which may make it harder for them to object.

Franz J Ingelfinger[71]

Incapacitated and hospitalized because of the illness, frightened by strange and impersonal routines, and fearful for his health and perhaps life, he is far from exercising a free power of choice when the person to whom he anchors all his hopes asks, 'Say, you wouldn't mind, would you, if you joined some of the other patients on this floor and helped us to carry out some very important research we're doing?' When 'informed consent' is obtained, it is not the student, the destitute bum, or the prisoner to whom, by virtue of his condition, the thumb screws of coercion are most relentlessly applied; it is the most used and useful of all experimental subjects, the patient with disease.

(c) Other vulnerable groups

It is worth noting that the category of people who are considered vulnerable in the context of consent to research extends beyond those who lack capacity. Medical students or junior employees, for example, may feel pressure to agree to participate in their teachers' or employers' research projects. The Helsinki Declaration requires researchers to be particularly cautious if the subject is in a dependent relationship, and to ensure that consent is taken by an independent physician.

Helsinki Declaration[72]

27. When seeking informed consent for participation in a research study the physician must be particularly cautious if the potential subject is in a dependent relationship with the physician or may consent under duress. In such situations the informed consent must be sought by an appropriately qualified individual who is completely independent of this relationship.

In the eighteenth and nineteenth centuries, prisoners were often used as research subjects. Not only did their lowly social status make them expendable, but also using captive research subjects is particularly convenient: follow-up studies are much more straightforward when

---

[71] 'Informed (but uneducated) consent' (1972) 287 New England Journal of Medicine 466.
[72] (WMA, 2013).

research subjects can be guaranteed to stay in the same place for many years. Now, however, for several reasons prisoners are categorized as a vulnerable group for the purposes of consent to research.

Small financial rewards may be disproportionately attractive in prison, where the opportunities for earning money are limited. Boredom too might encourage prisoners to enrol in scientific studies. Of course, a prisoner who wants to take part in research in order to relieve the monotony of prison life, or to earn a small amount of money, has not been coerced. But more worryingly, prisoners may wrongly believe that agreeing to take part in research might lead to early parole or other privileges, and as a result may not feel that refusal is an option. It has been argued that, because of their special vulnerability, prisoners should only be recruited when their incarceration is directly relevant: an example might be a psychological study investigating whether imprisonment increases the incidence or severity of depression. For example, the Royal College of Physicians' guidelines state that:

> Research that can be conducted on patients or healthy volunteers who are not in prison should not be conducted on prisoners. Incarceration in prison creates a constraint which could affect the ability of prisoners to make truly voluntary decisions without coercion to participate in research.[73]

Others, like Charles et al, have argued that this paternalism is unjustified and that prisoners should have an equal right to participate in research.

Anna Charles, Annette Rid, Hugh Davies, and Heather Draper[74]

> Rigorous ethical oversight and the shift in the prevailing attitude towards the risks and benefits of participation suggest that it may be time for research to be more accessible to prisoners in line with the principle of equivalence in prison healthcare, particularly research offering potential health benefits, such as phase 3 clinical trials. Current UK guidance appears protectionist, and our study has shown that prisoners are rarely offered access to participation in research. While the practice of routinely exploiting prisoners as a captive research population must never be repeated, the current approach protects to the point of inequitable exclusion.

(2) Information

As we saw in Chapter 4, treating someone without her consent may constitute battery. For consent to be valid, the patient must have been informed 'in broad terms' about the nature of the treatment.[75] If someone has not been told that she is participating in a trial, her apparent consent may not be real and a charge of battery might be possible.

---

[73] Royal College of Physicians, *Guidelines on the Practice of Ethics Committees in Medical Research with Human Participants*, 4th edn (RCP: London, 2007) para 8.47.

[74] 'Prisoners as research participants: current practice and attitudes in the UK' (2014) Journal of Medical Ethics, first published online 23 June 2014.

[75] *Chatterton v Gerson* [1981] QB 432.

The rule that subjects must give fully informed consent to participation in research is common to all of the various guidelines and codes governing experiments on human subjects from Nuremberg onwards. The Clinical Trials Regulation 2014 spells out what 'informed consent' entails.

Clinical Trials Regulation 2014

Chapter V Article 29 …

2. Information given to the subject or, where the subject is not able to give informed consent, his or her legally designated representative for the purposes of obtaining his or her informed consent shall:

(a) enable the subject or his or her legally designated representative to understand:

   (i) the nature, objectives, benefits, implications, risks and inconveniences of the clinical trial;

   (ii) the subject's rights and guarantees regarding his or her protection, in particular his or her right to refuse to participate and the right to withdraw from the clinical trial at any time without any resulting detriment and without having to provide any justification;

   (iii) the conditions under which the clinical trial is to be conducted, including the expected duration of the subject's participation in the clinical trial; and

   (iv) the possible treatment alternatives, including the follow-up measures if the participation of the subject in the clinical trial is discontinued;

(b) be kept comprehensive, concise, clear, relevant, and understandable to a layperson;

(c) be provided in a prior interview with a member of the investigating team who is appropriately qualified …

(d) include information about the applicable damage compensation system …

(e) include the EU trial number and information about the availability of the clinical trial results.…

3. The information referred to in paragraph 2 shall be prepared in writing and be available to the subject or, where the subject is not able to give informed consent, his or her legally designated representative.

4. In the interview referred to in point (c) of paragraph 2, special attention shall be paid to the information needs of specific patient populations and of individual subjects, as well as to the methods used to give the information.

5. In the interview referred to in point (c) of paragraph 2, it shall be verified that the subject has understood the information.

6. The subject shall be informed that the summary of the results of the clinical trial and a summary presented in terms understandable to a layperson will be made available in the EU database.

Of course, the concept of 'informed consent' begs the question of how much information an individual has to be given before their consent can be considered 'informed'. GMC guidance fleshes out this requirement.

General Medical Council[76]

> 7. You must make sure that people are given information in a way that they can understand. You should check that people understand the terms that you use and any explanation given about the proposed research method. If necessary, you should support your discussions with simple and accurate written material or visual or other aids.

Of course, subjects must obviously be told about any risks involved in participation, but there are also grey areas, where it is less clear whether disclosure is essential. Do participants need to know about any personal or financial benefit that the researcher may receive as a result of the trial, for example? Should they be told if the researcher has been paid to recruit subjects?

Because gaining the subject's informed consent is a necessary precondition of participation in a research trial, there is a danger that the provision of information happens only once, when the consent form is signed before the trial begins. But to be valid, the subject's consent to participation must be fully informed throughout the trial, and researchers should be under a duty to ensure that subjects are provided with information that emerges after the trial has begun, so that their decision to continue to participate is also properly informed. As we saw earlier, however, this raises an obvious problem—if researchers must disclose their preliminary findings, participants may exercise their right to withdraw from the trial before statistically significant data has been gathered.

The subject's informed consent should normally be formally recorded on a signed, written consent form. It is, however, important to remember that a signed consent form is not the same thing as a binding contract between subject and researcher. The existence of a signature on a consent form does not mean that the subject is under any obligation to keep her side of the 'bargain': on the contrary, participants must be free to withdraw from the trial, at any time, and without being subject to any penalty at all.

It is also worth noting that there is an important difference between providing information and ensuring that patients actually understand the information that they have been given. Evidence that patients are sometimes unaware that they have taken part in research, despite having signed an unambiguous consent form, suggests that simply providing information will not always be sufficient to ensure that the subject's consent is informed.

As Jay Katz explains in the following extract, obtaining fully informed consent will take time, and will not be achieved by simply offering research subjects a printed sheet of information.

Jay Katz[77]

> Patients come to hospitals with the trusting expectation that their doctors will care for them. They will view an invitation to participate in research as a professional recommendation that is intended to serve their individual treatment interests. It is that belief, that trust, which physician-investigators must vigorously challenge so that patient-subjects appreciate that in research, unlike therapy, the research question comes first. This takes time and is difficult to convey. It can be conveyed to patient-subjects only if physician-investigators are willing to challenge the misperceptions that many patients bring to the invitation. Thus, recruitment of subjects will prove to be more time consuming.

---

[76] *Good Practice in Research and Consent to Research* (GMC: London, 2009).
[77] 'Human Experimentation and Human Rights' (1993) 38 Saint Louis University Law Journal 7.

It should be noted that there are those, like Miller and Wertheimer, who query the priority given to informed consent to research participation, especially when the research is low risk, and may even benefit the subject. Miller and Wertheimer also point out that protecting patients through their informed consent is at odds with the way in which we normally protect consumers from agreeing to contractual terms that they do not understand.

Franklin G Miller and Alan Wertheimer[78]

The [Autonomous Authorisation] model is unfair to investigators. They need to have fair notice about when they are permitted to enroll subjects in clinical trials based on consent transactions. The lengths to which investigators should be expected to go in assessing the quality of informed consent should be reasonable in view of the risk–benefit profiles of different studies. . . .[R]igorous testing of informed consent is costly in time and energy for both investigators and subjects, which seems neither reasonable nor fair in the case of many low-risk studies that offer subjects a personally favorable risk–benefit ratio. . . .

Consider, for example, ordinary consent in the case of employment or purchase of goods and services. . . . When people rent automobiles or take out mortgages, they are asked to sign lengthy boilerplate contracts, which few people bother to read. Consumers who sign such contracts should be adequately protected by regulatory guidelines . . . , despite their uncomprehending consent, and, therefore, we don't deem such consent to be invalid. As the recent crisis over subprime mortgages suggests, when those institutional protections are not in place, we do not think that the remedy is to assure that people adequately understand the terms of their agreements. Rather, the remedy is to institute regulations to protect consumers from predatory lenders.

In the case of research, prior review and approval and ongoing monitoring by research ethics committees in accordance with detailed regulations (should) provide comparable safeguards.

(b) SUBJECTS WHO LACK CAPACITY

If the consent of the subject is what makes research ethically acceptable, where does this leave individuals—children and adults who lack capacity—who are unable to give consent to treatment?

In Chapter 5 we saw that parents usually give consent to their children's treatment, subject to the courts' power to overrule parental decision-making in order to protect the child's best interests. The treatment of adults who lack capacity is governed by the Mental Capacity Act 2005, which specifies that, unless the patient has made a valid and applicable advance decision, patients who lack capacity should be treated in their best interests.

These rules would not appear to facilitate the participation of people who lack capacity in research. Since taking part in a trial involves being exposed to uncertain risks, it may not be in the patient's best interests. It is, however, important to remember that a blanket ban on research involving patients who lack capacity might also be inappropriate. If no trials can ever take place involving children and mentally incapacitated adults, members of these groups will have access only to inadequately tested treatments. Children absorb drugs differently, and so simply giving them a reduced dose of a medicine that has been tested on

---

[78] 'The fair transaction model of informed consent: an alternative to autonomous authorization' (2011) 21 Kennedy Institute of Ethics Journal 201–18.

adults is likely to be either ineffective or unsafe. In the next extract, Paul Miller and Nuala Kenny explain that shielding children from the dangers of research might itself cause children significant harm.

Paul B Miller and Nuala P Kenny[79]

Ironically, the protective impulse to shield children entirely from the harms of research participation has the potential to cause them significant harm. History tells of the dangerous consequences of presuming treatments tested on adults to be safe and efficacious for children . . . For scientific and ethical reasons, children should receive wherever possible only those treatments that have been adequately evaluated on children. . . . Reliance on the results of research involving adults as the knowledge base from which to develop the care of children may make the provision of such care unnecessarily dangerous.

Moreover, as Lainie Friedman Ross points out, we allow parents to subject their children to other sorts of risks, such as being a passenger in a car or taking part in sporting activities.

Lainie Friedman Ross[80]

Parental authorization of a child's participation in research of minimal risk and harm does not necessarily treat the child solely as a means. Rather, parents who value participation in social projects will try to inculcate similar values into their child . . .

Many activities in a typical child's life, in fact, will present greater risks and harms, including such routine activities as participation in contact sports and traveling as a passenger in the family car . . . Parents are morally and legally authorized to decide which risks their child can take and in what settings. Parental authorization or prohibition of a child's participation in this type of research, then, is not abusive or neglectful . . . .

Given the minimal amount of risk which the proposed research entails, the child's participation will not interfere with the child's developing personhood even if she is forced to participate against her will. Their decision to override their child's dissent is not abusive; parents legitimately override their child's decisions in many daily activities.

In recent years, the dangers of routinely excluding children from research have been recognized. The EU's Regulation on Medicinal Products for Paediatric Use[81] has created a system of incentives, including an additional six months of patent protection for carrying out high-quality paediatric trials. It has also set up a European database of paediatric trials, including a requirement to publish both favourable and unfavourable results, in order to ensure that trials in children are not unnecessarily duplicated.

Since some mental illnesses impede decision-making capacity, it would only be possible to test drugs that might improve the lives of people with these conditions if research is carried out on patients who cannot give consent. Emergency medicine may involve treating

---

[79] 'Walking the moral tightrope: respecting and protecting children in health-related research' (2002) 11 Cambridge Quarterly of Healthcare Ethics 217–29.

[80] 'Children as Research Subjects: A Proposal to Review the Current Federal Regulations Using a Moral Framework' (1997) 8 Stanford Law and Policy Review 159.

[81] Regulation (EC) No 1901/2006.

patients who have lost consciousness, and this can only improve if new treatments can be tested on unconscious subjects.

If a blanket ban on the participation in research of subjects who lack capacity is not justified, when might it be permissible to carry out research on individuals who cannot give consent? Although slightly different rules apply depending upon whether the person is a child or an adult, some common principles can be detected:

- It should be impossible to do the research on individuals who are able to consent to participation.
- The research should be likely to benefit either the individual subject, or other members of the group to which the subject belongs.
- Efforts should be made to gain the subject's assent to participation.

In the following extract, Penney Lewis argues that non-therapeutic research on patients who lack capacity can only be justified by engaging in a utilitarian calculation, in which the gains to society justify infringing the rights and dignity of the individual subject.

Penney Lewis[82]

In the context of non-therapeutic research, the existence of an international 'consensus', supporting the participation of incompetent persons, is used to avoid providing a justification for a utilitarian calculation that allows the use of vulnerable members of society in order to benefit others . . .

Judicial approval is generally considered desirable for organ and tissue donation from incompetents and for their non-therapeutic sterilization. It is not, however, encouraged for the approval of non-therapeutic research with incompetent subjects. To obtain judicial approval for all research projects would be overly burdensome on both the judiciary and the research community. A separate system has evolved of research ethics committees, which approve research projects. These committees may be more willing than judges to engage in utilitarian balancing of the interests of society against the interests of the incompetent prospective research subject.

(1) Seeking a Representative's Consent

Where a child or an adult cannot give consent to participation, consent must be obtained from their 'legally designated representative'. Usually, it is envisaged that someone will act as a potential research subject's legal representative by virtue of their relationship with her. For a child, the personal legal representative should be a person with parental responsibility. The personal legal representative of an adult should be a person who is capable of giving consent, and who has a close personal relationship with the potential subject.

There will, however, be times when it is impossible to find a suitable personal legal representative, either because there is no one who is sufficiently close to the patient willing to take on this role; or in an emergency, identifying and contacting a close relative may not be feasible. In such circumstances, the patient's doctor should fulfil the role of the 'professional legal representative', unless she is involved in the trial. This will disqualify

---

[82] 'Procedures that are Against the Medical Interests of Incompetent Adults' (2002) 22 Oxford Journal of Legal Studies 575–618.

not only the principal researcher and those on her team, but also anyone who provides health care under the direction or control of members of the investigating team. If the patient's doctor has any connection with the trial, the health care trust must nominate someone else.

Once a legal representative has been identified, her consent to the subject's participation in the clinical trial should be sought. She is expected to base her decision on the subject's 'presumed will', hence the desirability of finding a personal legal representative who knows the subject's values and preferences. The legal representative should be given an opportunity to understand the objectives, risks, and inconveniences of the trial, and the conditions under which it is to be conducted. She should be informed that her decision should be based on what the potential subject would have wanted, and that she can withdraw consent to the subject's participation at any time. Independent advice about the role should be made available. Where a professional legal representative has been appointed, subject to the duty to respect patient confidentiality, she may consult anyone who might be able to advise her on the potential subject's wishes.

The legal representative is also responsible for ensuring that the subject's continued participation remains appropriate. This will be comparatively straightforward where the personal legal representative is a close friend or relative. Where a professional legal representative has been appointed, specific arrangements should be in place to ensure that the legal representative regularly re-evaluates the subject's continued participation.

(2) Children

If a child is ill, and there is no standard treatment available for her condition, enrolling her in a research trial, in which she might receive an experimental new treatment, could be consistent with her doctor's ordinary duty of care. But where the research is purely non-therapeutic and, by definition, not in the child's best interests, should children ever be used as research subjects? The Clinical Trials Regulation permits non-therapeutic trials on minors, provided that the trial could not be carried out on adults and imposes no more than minimal risk on the child subject.

Clinical Trials Regulation 2014

Article 32 Clinical trials on minors

1. A clinical trial on minors may be conducted only where, in addition to the conditions set out in Article 28, all of the following conditions are met:

(a) the informed consent of their legally designated representative has been obtained;

(b) the minors have received the information referred to in Article 29(2) in a way adapted to their age and mental maturity and from investigators or members of the investigating team who are trained or experienced in working with children;

(c) the explicit wish of a minor who is capable of forming an opinion and assessing the information referred to in Article 29(2) to refuse participation in, or to withdraw from, the clinical trial at any time, is respected by the investigator;

(d) no incentives or financial inducements are given to the subject or his or her legally designated representative except for compensation for expenses and loss of earnings directly related to the participation in the clinical trial;

(e) the clinical trial is intended to investigate treatments for a medical condition that only occurs in minors or the clinical trial is essential with respect to minors to validate data obtained in clinical trials on persons able to give informed consent or by other research methods;

(f) the clinical trial either relates directly to a medical condition from which the minor concerned suffers or is of such a nature that it can only be carried out on minors;

(g) there are scientific grounds for expecting that participation in the clinical trial will produce:

    (i) a direct benefit for the minor concerned outweighing the risks and burdens involved; or

    (ii) some benefit for the population represented by the minor concerned and such a clinical trial will pose only minimal risk to, and will impose minimal burden on, the minor concerned in comparison with the standard treatment of the minor's condition.

2. The minor shall take part in the informed consent procedure in a way adapted to his or her age and mental maturity.

3. If during a clinical trial the minor reaches the age of legal competence to give informed consent as defined in the law of the Member State concerned, his or her express informed consent shall be obtained before that subject can continue to participate in the clinical trial.

The new Regulation has corrected an unsatisfactory aspect of the 2004 Regulations, which provided that the wishes of the minor simply had to be 'considered' by the investigator. Now, if the child is capable of forming an opinion, and assessing the information provided, their refusal to participate should be respected by the investigator. The Regulation also provides that researchers must adapt the informed consent process to accommodate the minor's age and maturity, so researchers will need to tailor their information to enable as many children as possible to express their own view about participation.

(3) Adults

Again, in addition to the consent of their representative, a number of additional conditions and principles are laid out in the Clinical Trials Regulation.

Clinical Trials Regulation 2014

Article 31 Clinical trials on incapacitated subjects

1. In the case of incapacitated subjects who have not given, or have not refused to give, informed consent before the onset of their incapacity, a clinical trial may be conducted only where, in addition to the conditions set out in Article 28, all of the following conditions are met:

(a) the informed consent of their legally designated representative has been obtained;

(b) the incapacitated subjects have received the information referred to in Article 29(2) in a way that is adequate in view of their capacity to understand it;

(c) the explicit wish of an incapacitated subject who is capable of forming an opinion and assessing the information referred to in Article 29(2) to refuse participation in, or to withdraw from, the clinical trial at any time, is respected by the investigator;

(d) no incentives or financial inducements are given to the subjects or their legally designated representatives, except for compensation for expenses and loss of earnings directly related to the participation in the clinical trial;

(e) the clinical trial is essential with respect to incapacitated subjects and data of comparable validity cannot be obtained in clinical trials on persons able to give informed consent, or by other research methods;

(f) the clinical trial relates directly to a medical condition from which the subject suffers;

(g) there are scientific grounds for expecting that participation in the clinical trial will produce:

(i) a direct benefit to the incapacitated subject outweighing the risks and burdens involved; or

(ii) some benefit for the population represented by the incapacitated subject concerned when the clinical trial relates directly to the life-threatening or debilitating medical condition from which the subject suffers and such trial will pose only minimal risk to, and will impose minimal burden on, the incapacitated subject concerned in comparison with the standard treatment of the incapacitated subject's condition.

2. Point (g)(ii) of paragraph 1 shall be without prejudice to more stringent national rules prohibiting the conduct of those clinical trials on incapacitated subjects, where there are no scientific grounds to expect that participation in the clinical trial will produce a direct benefit to the subject outweighing the risks and burdens involved.

3. The subject shall as far as possible take part in the informed consent procedure.

It is important to remember that adults who lack capacity exist on a spectrum from those who are permanently insensate (eg patients in a permanent vegetative state), to those whose cognitive impairments are only slightly greater than those of adults who fall on the other side of the legal 'cut-off' point for capacity. Individuals in this latter group, while unable to give a valid consent to medical treatment, may nevertheless be able to express their unwillingness to participate in research.

Just as with minors, the new Regulation gives incapacitated adults more right to participate in the decision than the 2004 Regulations. The explicit wish of an incapacitated adult who can express an opinion and understand the information should be respected, and, as far as is possible, the subject must take part in the informed consent procedure. This brings the law into line with GMC guidance, which has been clear for some time that if it is obvious that someone who lacks capacity does not want to participate, this should be the end of the matter.

General Medical Council[83]

30 You must make sure that a participant's right to withdraw from research is respected. You should consider any sign of objection, distress or indication of refusal, whether or not it is spoken, as implied refusal.

[83] *Good Practice in Research and Consent to Research* (GMC: London, 2009).

It is, however, important to remember that if a person is used to being treated without consent, she may have no reason to believe that her reluctance to take part in research would be respected. As we saw earlier, it is difficult for all patients to understand the difference between treatment and research, and this problem may be even more acute for mentally incapacitated individuals. Simply stating that research should not be carried out against the wishes of an adult who lacks capacity presupposes that such patients will understand that they have more robust rights to refuse to participate in research than they do for treatment, and that they will feel able to make their feelings known.

The Mental Capacity Act 2005 (MCA) applies to 'intrusive' research not covered by the Regulation; that is, it does not apply to clinical trials and non-intrusive research. Research is 'intrusive' if it would be unlawful if carried out on a competent adult without consent. Such research will be unlawful unless it has been approved by an appropriate body (ie a REC), and the conditions in sections 31 to 33 of the MCA are satisfied. These include that it must not be possible to carry out the research on people who could give consent, and that:

> 31(5) The research must—
>
> (a) have the potential to benefit P without imposing on P a burden that is disproportionate to the potential benefit to P, or
>
> (b) be intended to provide knowledge of the causes or treatment of, or of the care of persons affected by, the same or a similar condition.

If the research does not have the potential to benefit P, the risk to P must be likely to be negligible; it must not significantly interfere with P's freedom of action or be unduly invasive or restrictive. Under section 32 of the MCA, the researcher must identify someone who is caring for or interested in the welfare of P (other than in a professional capacity), in order to ask for advice on how P would feel about taking part in the project, if he had capacity. If this person advises that P would not want to take part, or would want to withdraw, he must not participate in the research project. Section 33 further bolsters the need to take account of the P's views.

Mental Capacity Act 2005 section 33

> 33(2) Nothing may be done to, or in relation to, him in the course of the research—
>
> (a) to which he appears to object (whether by showing signs of resistance or otherwise) except where what is being done is intended to protect him from harm or to reduce or prevent pain or discomfort, or
>
> (b) which would be contrary to—
>
> (i) an advance decision of his which has effect, or
>
> (ii) any other form of statement made by him and not subsequently withdrawn . . .
>
> (4) If he indicates (in any way) that he wishes to be withdrawn from the project he must be withdrawn without delay.

(4) Emergencies

In an emergency, it may not be possible to identify and appoint a representative before the trial starts. The Regulation therefore provides for a mechanism to enrol subjects in trials of emergency medicine, with safeguards in place to ensure that the view of their representative, and their own view, is sought as soon as practicable.

Clinical Trials Regulation 2014

Article 35 Clinical trials in emergency situations

1. By way of derogation from ... Article 28(1), ... Article 31(1) and ... Article 32(1), informed consent to participate in a clinical trial may be obtained, and information on the clinical trial may be given, after the decision to include the subject in the clinical trial, provided that this decision is taken at the time of the first intervention on the subject, in accordance with the protocol for that clinical trial and that all of the following conditions are fulfilled:

(a) due to the urgency of the situation, caused by a sudden life-threatening or other sudden serious medical condition, the subject is unable to provide prior informed consent and to receive prior information on the clinical trial;

(b) there are scientific grounds to expect that participation of the subject in the clinical trial will have the potential to produce a direct clinically relevant benefit for the subject resulting in a measurable health-related improvement alleviating the suffering and/or improving the health of the subject, or in the diagnosis of its condition;

(c) it is not possible within the therapeutic window to supply all prior information to and obtain prior informed consent from his or her legally designated representative;

(d) the investigator certifies that he or she is not aware of any objections to participate in the clinical trial previously expressed by the subject;

(e) the clinical trial relates directly to the subject's medical condition because of which it is not possible within the therapeutic window to obtain prior informed consent from the subject or from his or her legally designated representative and to supply prior information, and the clinical trial is of such a nature that it may be conducted exclusively in emergency situations;

(f) the clinical trial poses a minimal risk to, and imposes a minimal burden on, the subject in comparison with the standard treatment of the subject's condition.

The GMC guidance also accepts that, provided agreement has been sought from an independent doctor or ethics committee, it should be possible to start 'urgent' research without consent.

General Medical Council[84]

34 The Mental Capacity Act 2005 permits urgent research in emergencies to start when it is not practical to consult someone about involving a person who lacks capacity in research. In this situation you must either get agreement from a doctor not involved in the research, or

---

[84] Ibid.

follow a procedure approved by a research ethics committee. Similarly, you can start a clinical trial of investigational medicinal products when it needs to be undertaken urgently if you cannot get the consent of a legal representative, as long as a research ethics committee has given approval for such action.

Where a professional legal representative has been appointed in an emergency, review of the person's continued participation is especially important. It would also be appropriate for the role of legal representative to be transferred subsequently to an individual who is closely connected with the subject.

Of course, the basic provisions of the Mental Capacity Act continue to apply, so where a patient has been temporarily incapacitated in an emergency, and is likely to regain capacity, decisions should not be taken unless they cannot wait for her to make them herself. Hence, unless participation in a research trial might be in a patient's best interests, it would be difficult to justify enrolling her in a trial without her consent.

7 FACILITATING PARTICIPATION IN RESEARCH

(a) THE BENEFITS OF PARTICIPATION

So far, we have concentrated on the special vulnerability of research subjects. Because the outcome of research is, by definition, uncertain, our assumption has been that research participants are exposed to risks, without necessarily receiving any benefits in return. But this view of participation in clinical trials as a burden has been challenged in recent years as a result of the recognition that being a research subject might sometimes hold out the possibility of very great benefits.

The catalyst for this was the HIV/AIDS pandemic. Before the first antiretroviral drugs were licensed for use in humans, most people who were diagnosed as HIV-positive could expect to die from an AIDS-related illness within a comparatively short space of time. People living with HIV knew that research into drugs that might be capable of prolonging their lives was ongoing. Unsurprisingly, there was no shortage of volunteers for these studies. For some cancer patients too, the very latest treatments may only be available to participants in clinical trials. If the important issue becomes access to the benefits of taking part in research, rather than protection from its dangers, different ethical issues are raised. We might, for example, need to ensure that there is fair and equitable distribution of places in research trials.

In the next extract, Rebecca Dresser explains the role of patient advocacy groups in promoting research participation, and draws attention to the danger that they may overestimate the benefits of research participation.

Rebecca Dresser[85]

During the 1980s, HIV/AIDS activists became major figures in biomedical research . . . [Patient] advocates tend to stress the positive dimensions of biomedical research. In much advocacy communication, there is a failure to clearly distinguish between partially tested experimental

---

[85] 'Patient Advocates in Research: New Possibilities, New Problems' (2003) 11 Washington University Journal of Law and Policy 237.

interventions and proven medical care. Consistent with this approach, advocates often portray study participation as the way to obtain cutting-edge therapy . . .

Patient advocates may also promote the therapeutic misconception at a broader level. For example, patient advocates often suggest that research can end the suffering and deprivation inflicted by illness. The general message is that with more funding for research, cures are destined to emerge. Although this feel-good message may lift the spirits of people coping with disease and injury, and aid with fundraising, it may also promote public misunderstanding of the research process. There is no question that research can lead to health care improvements. Almost always, however, it takes many years and many false starts before effective practical applications become available.

(b) EXCLUSION FROM RESEARCH

Several different groups within society have traditionally been under-represented among research subjects. Most notable, perhaps, has been the exclusion of women, not only from research into conditions which affect only men, but also from trials of treatments for conditions that affect both sexes.

It used to be suggested that, because women's physiology is different, it might complicate results, and lead to less 'clean' data. Of course, women's monthly hormonal fluctuations are only a complicating factor if the male body is regarded as the norm. There is also a central paradox in this justification for women's exclusion. If the female body reacts differently, and hence might distort a study's results, then dosages of a treatment that have only been tested on men are likely to be either ineffective or unsafe for female patients. Despite having been historically under-tested in women, most drugs are prescribed to both sexes, and it is therefore unsurprising that women are more likely than men to report adverse drug reactions.

A second reason for excluding women is the possibility that they might become pregnant, thus exposing their fetus to the unknown toxicity of the new drug, and the researchers to potential liability for prenatal injury. Of course, there might be good reasons for not recruiting pregnant women, or women who are trying to conceive, onto trials of experimental drugs, but a blanket ban on all women's participation is unwarranted. Not all women of reproductive age are heterosexually active and fertile, and a more appropriate and less paternalistic approach would be to ask women whether there is a chance that they might become pregnant during the trial.

While it is understandable that few pregnant women would volunteer to take part in clinical trials, if drugs are never tested on pregnant women it will be impossible to know whether they can be taken safely during pregnancy. This is why so many medicinal products contain a warning that they should not be used by pregnant women. Most of these warnings are designed not to protect women and their fetuses from drugs that are known to be harmful: rather, they simply indicate that the product has not been proved to be safe, because no studies have been carried out.

For most women, abstaining from taking medicines during pregnancy is relatively unproblematic, but this is not true for all women. A woman who suffers from severe depression, and who might be likely to harm herself if she stops taking her medication, is faced with an invidious dilemma. She must either take a medicine that has not been proved safe during pregnancy, or risk the potentially serious consequences of stopping her medication.

In the next extract, Marie Fox criticizes the neglect of women's health needs which results from gender bias in research design.

Marie Fox[86]

> Although the justifications for explicit exclusions are generally couched in the rhetoric of protecting women and their unborn children, the issue which looms largest for those sponsoring or conducting trials is likely to be fear of liability for any teratogenic impact . . . Again feminist lawyers have challenged this rationale, arguing that there is potentially greater liability if unsafe products are marketed, since pharmaceutical companies do not bar women, including women of child-bearing capacity, from purchasing or being prescribed such drugs . . .
>
> The relative neglect of women's health needs raises issues of justice, as well as calling into question the scientifically dubious practice of marketing drugs and procedures which have been inadequately tested for their impact on women. Since the choice and definition of problems for research is influenced by the under-representation of women at all stages of the research process, research on conditions specific to females receives low priority, funding and prestige.

Other groups have also tended to be under-represented in research, with obvious implications for their access to safe and effective medical treatment. Elderly people, for example, have been excluded in part as a result of concerns that long-term follow-up might be impeded by the subjects' deaths, and in part because elderly subjects might suffer from multiple comorbidities that could distort the results. But not only is research on older subjects essential in order to improve the quality of care available to the elderly, it is also a mistake to assume that all elderly people are equally infirm or close to death. On the contrary, many old people are healthier and more independent than younger adults.

Exclusionary tendencies in research are increasingly regarded as illegitimate. And according to the UK's Governance Arrangements for Research Ethics Committees, researchers must now justify any recruitment restrictions in their protocols.

UK Health Departments[87]

> 3.2.3 The benefits and risks of taking part in research, and the benefits of research evidence for improved health and social care, should be distributed fairly among all social groups and classes. Selection criteria in research protocols should not unjustifiably exclude potential participants, for instance on the basis of economic status, culture, age, disability, gender reassignment, marriage and civil partnership, pregnancy and maternity, race, religion or belief, sex or sexual orientation. RECs should take these considerations into account in reviewing the ethics of research proposals, particularly those involving under-researched groups.

(c) A DUTY TO PARTICIPATE?

A further issue missed by the emphasis upon protecting research subjects from harm is the question of whether users of health care services should be under a duty to share the burdens of research participation. It is certainly true that these burdens are not distributed evenly

---

[86] 'Research Bodies: Feminist Perspectives on Clinical Research' in Sally Sheldon and Michael Thomson (eds), *Feminist Perspectives on Health Care Law* (Cavendish: London, 1998) 115–34.

[87] *Governance Arrangements for Research Ethics Committees: A Harmonised Edition* (DH: London, 2012).

across society. Most experiments are carried out on people who are ill. Among healthy volunteers, certain groups—in particular students and the unemployed—are over-represented, while wealthy individuals in full-time employment seldom participate.

Uneven recruitment of research subjects gives rise to two distinct problems. First, the de facto exclusion of certain groups means that we cannot be sure that treatment will be safe or effective when given to members of the excluded group. Secondly, it might be argued that the risks associated with participation in research should be distributed fairly across society, and that it is unjust for certain sections of society to bear a disproportionate burden. Since the sort of financial rewards that persuade students or the unemployed to volunteer are unlikely to act as an incentive to others, we might have to think in terms of a duty to enrol as a research subject. We could, for example, view serving as a research subject as one of the obligations we assume under the 'social contract', in which we accept some restrictions upon our freedom in return for the benefits of living in a safe and cohesive community.

In the UK, there is no legal duty to participate in research, but it could be argued that anyone who expects to have access to NHS services is under a moral duty to participate in research, if asked. Indeed, the NHS Constitution now contains a commitment on the part of NHS organizations to inform patients about research projects in which they could participate. Arthur Caplan would go further, arguing that, in certain circumstances, it might be appropriate for a hospital to refuse to treat those who are unwilling to take part in research.

Arthur L Caplan[88]

> Modern medicine is a vast social enterprise in which certain benefits are produced at the cost of various burdens, which include the need to conduct medical research. If individuals consciously, knowingly, and continuously accept the benefits of medical care by seeking out physicians and hospital personnel when they are ill, then they would seem to meet the conditions for being bound by the principle of fair play. If the only way the knowledge and skills utilized in modern medicine can be generated is through research involving human subjects, then those who accept the fruits of such research would appear to be under a duty to bear the burdens of research when called upon by the group to do so . . .
>
> Medical institutions which clearly and forthrightly identify themselves to patients as research institutions would be within their rights to exclude persons who refuse to participate in any form of research.

John Harris also believes that we have an obligation to participate in research. According to Harris, whether or not a research subject stands to benefit from participation should not be confined to the narrow question of whether her health will be directly improved. Instead, he argues that we all benefit from living in a society in which medical research takes place, and that participation should no longer be regarded as a supererogatory act, but, like jury service and taxation, as one of a number of mandatory contributions to the public good which we accept as the price of living in a civilized society.

---

[88] 'Is There an Obligation to Participate in Biomedical Research?' in Stuart F Spicker, Ilai Alon, Andre de Vries, and H Tristram Engelhardt (eds), *The Use of Human Beings in Research* (Kluwer: Dordrecht, 1988) 229–48.

John Harris[89]

We all benefit from the existence of the social practice of medical research. Many of us would not be here if infant mortality had not been brought under control, or antibiotics had not been invented. Most of us will continue to benefit from these and other medical advances . . . . Since we accept these benefits, we have an obligation in justice to contribute to the social practice which produces them . . . .

We all also benefit from the knowledge that research is ongoing into diseases or conditions from which we do not currently suffer but to which we may succumb. It makes us feel more secure and gives us hope for the future, for ourselves and our descendants, and for others for whom we care. If this is right, then I have a strong general interest that there be research, and in all well founded research; not excluding but not exclusively, research on me and on my condition or on conditions which are likely to affect me and mine. All such research is also of clear benefit to me. A narrow interpretation of the requirement that research be of benefit to the subject of the research is therefore perverse . . . .

If it is right to claim that there is a general obligation to act in the public interest, then there is less reason to challenge consent and little reason to regard participation as actually or potentially exploitative. We do not usually say: 'are you quite sure you want to' when people fulfil their moral and civic obligations.

Not only do we all benefit from living in a society in which medical research takes place, but Ozdemir et al found that patient mortality rates are lower in research-active hospitals. It is therefore in an individual patient's best interests to be treated by research-active health care professionals.

Baris A Ozdemir et al[90]

Furthermore it has been suggested that patients in research active hospitals may have better outcomes than patients in poorly research-active hospitals because greater research participation leads to accumulated knowledge, develops infrastructure and, brings in resources that can be used to improve clinical care. . . . The suggestion was that hospitals within research networks implement research findings more easily and more quickly, and that clinicians were more likely to adopt evidence-based practice and, follow up-to-date clinical guidelines.

8 CONFLICTS OF INTEREST AND RESEARCH MISCONDUCT

The legacy of the research abuses of the twentieth century was a system of ethical review which emphasizes the importance of voluntary and informed consent to participation. More recently, it has been acknowledged that unethical research practices are not confined to putting pressure on people to consent, or failing to tell them that they have been enrolled in research. In recent years, unethical practices that happen during and after the research has taken place—such as the failure to publish results—have received more attention.

---

[89] 'Scientific research is a moral duty' (2005) 31 Journal of Medical Ethics 242–8.
[90] 'Research Activity and the Association with Mortality' (2015) 10 PLoS ONE e0118253.

(a) SELECTIVE PUBLICATION

If information gathered during a trial is not published, research subjects will have been exposed to the trial's risks without any possible benefit to society. A failure to publish a trial's results also undermines the subjects' informed consent: if the subjects had known that the trial would serve no useful purpose, they might have been less likely to agree to take part.

It is important that both negative and positive results are published. While positive results (which prove that a new treatment works) may be more interesting and newsworthy than negative results (which show that the treatment is ineffective or harmful), unless negative results are also published, there is a danger that other researchers may instigate identical and futile trials, thus exposing more research subjects to wholly avoidable risks. Researchers should therefore be under a duty to ensure that a trial's results are properly disseminated, regardless of whether they are positive or negative, and indeed Principle 36 of the Helsinki Declaration is clear that 'negative and inconclusive as well as positive results should be published or otherwise made publicly available'.

In addition to the widespread under-reporting of negative results, positive results are sometimes published multiple times.[91] This means that the published data is not representative of the total body of evidence, rather it may overemphasize positive results (which are thereby double-counted) and underemphasize negative results (which may not be counted at all). Meta-analyses which consolidate all publicly available data will then magnify and exaggerate this publication bias.[92]

If both prescribing and funding decisions are made on the basis of distorted meta-analyses, the consequences of over-publication of positive results and under-publication of negative data will be poorer treatment of patients and wasteful use of health care resources.

As Richard Smith, former editor of the *British Medical Journal* explains, it is difficult for the editors of medical journals to know whether articles submitted to them duplicate data that is already in the public domain.

Richard Smith[93]

A large trial published in a major journal has the journal's stamp of approval . . . will be distributed around the world, and may well receive global media coverage, particularly if promoted simultaneously by press releases from both the journal and the expensive public-relations firm hired by the pharmaceutical company that sponsored the trial . . . Fortunately from the point of view of the companies funding these trials—but unfortunately for the credibility of the journals who publish them—these trials rarely produce results that are unfavourable to the companies' product . . .

Journal editors are becoming increasingly aware of how they are being manipulated . . . Editors work by considering the studies submitted to them. They ask the authors to send them any related studies, but editors have no other mechanism to know what other

---

[91] Martin R Tramèr et al, 'Impact of covert duplicate publication on meta-analysis: a case study' (1997) 315 British Medical Journal 635.

[92] Hans Melander et al, 'Evidence b(i)ased medicine—selective reporting from studies sponsored by pharmaceutical industry: review of studies in new drug applications' (2003) 326 British Medical Journal 1171–3.

[93] 'Medical journals are an extension of the marketing arm of pharmaceutical companies' (2005) 2 PLoS Medicine 138.

> unpublished studies exist. It's hard even to know about related studies that are published, and it may be impossible to tell that studies are describing results from some of the same patients. Editors may thus be peer reviewing one piece of a gigantic and clever marketing jigsaw—and the piece they have is likely to be of high technical quality. It will probably pass peer review, a process that research has anyway shown to be an ineffective lottery prone to bias and abuse.

There have been several attempts to solve this problem. One of the first was mandatory pre-trial registration of all clinical trials, so that unfortunate results cannot be buried. In 2004, the International Committee of Medical Journal Editors (ICMJE) published a statement which unequivocally required pre-trial registration as a condition of publication:

> The ICMJE member journals will require, as a condition of consideration for publication, registration in a public trials registry. Trials must register at or before the onset of patient enrolment.[94]

And Principle 35 of the Helsinki Declaration now states that 'Every research study involving human subjects must be registered in a publicly accessible database before recruitment of the first subject.'

Pre-trial registration is now the norm. Within the EU, the Clinical Trials Register is a searchable, publicly available registry of all clinical trials taking place in the EU.[95] At the time of writing, it contains detailed information about 26,778 trials.

Pre-trial registration may not be sufficient, however, if other information—most importantly the trial's outcomes—are not also registered. Ross et al analysed a random sample of trials that had been registered on the US trials registry, ClinicalTrials.gov, and found that only 40 per cent of industry-sponsored registered trials had published their results and, of those, only one-third had the citation recorded on ClinicalTrials.gov. So—despite mandatory registration—the results of the majority of trials were still not published.

It has therefore been recognized that mandatory reporting needs to go beyond the initial registration of a trial, and extend to the mandatory reporting of results in trial registries. This has happened in the US, where the 'basic results' of phase II and III trials must be submitted to ClinicalTrials.gov no later than one year after the primary completion date, defined as when 'the last subject was examined or received intervention for purposes of final collection of data for the primary outcome'.[96]

Within the EU, a similar requirement to publish results was introduced in 2012.[97] Results must now be posted in EudraCT within a year of the end of the trial (or six months in the case of paediatric trials). Result-related data should be posted earlier if it becomes available, for example if the results are published in a scientific journal. Since 2015, the European Medicines Agency has also proactively published the clinical reports submitted with applications for marketing authorizations (see Chapter 10).

---

[94] Catherine De Angelis et al, 'Clinical trial registration: a statement from the International Committee of Medical Journal Editors' (2004) 351 New England Journal of Medicine 1250–1.

[95] www.clinicaltrialsregister.eu/.

[96] FDA Amendments Act 2007. See further www.clinicaltrials.gov/.

[97] European Commission, Guidance on posting and publication of result-related information on clinical trials in relation to the implementation of Article 57(2) of Regulation (EC) No 726/2004 and Article 41 of Regulation (EC) No 1901/2006, Official Journal of the European Union 2012/C 302/03.

(b) OUTSOURCING

In relation to clinical trials, it is increasingly common for drug companies to pay commercial organizations to design trials, recruit subjects, and disseminate results.

(1) Contract Research Organizations (CROs)

Outsourcing the running of trials to CROs is now the norm: at least 70 per cent of clinical trials are now managed by these private companies.[98] CROs recruit healthy volunteers themselves, and they may pay doctors to help them find willing patients for phase II and III trials. While outsourcing to CROs is efficient, these organizations are employed by drugs manufacturers to speed up approval times; they are not employed to investigate, in a completely disinterested way, how best to treat a particular condition. Satisfying their commercial clients means ensuring that drugs are approved as speedily as possible. CROs therefore have a clear financial interest in the outcome of the trials that they run.

David Hunter draws attention to a new issue raised by the practices of CROs, namely the 'pre-recruitment' of potential volunteers, who only later are allocated to a particular research project. He points out that pre-recruitment is not constrained by the strict rules which govern direct recruitment to a particular trial, and that it is therefore not uncommon for CROs to make extravagant claims about how much money volunteers can make, and how much good they can do.

David Hunter[99]

These adverts appear to violate the three well-established general requirements of the recruitment of research participants . . . They emphasise in emotive language the likely benefits for others of participating, they focus on the financial recompense and portray the research as likely to succeed. . . . Since the advert was for *general* recruitment rather than to a specific trial, there is no formal regulation of this activity. You do not currently need research ethics committee approval to approach people to pre-recruit them, nor is there any formal guidance for this sort of recruitment either from the Health Research Authority (HRA) or from the ABPI. . . .

The present disparity in practices of the pre-recruitment and recruitment of research participants seems problematic—to put it starkly, if you are recruited onto a list of potential participants on the promise of riches and heroism via clinical trials and are then recruited from that list into a specific trial in a much more neutral fashion, your beliefs about the actual trial will be informed by what you were told during pre-recruitment—in other words, you will think you are being heroic and earning lots of money, precisely the views that the current regulations are trying to prevent participants from having. As such, unregulated pre-recruitment runs the risk of making a mockery of the careful standards which have evolved to try and protect people from exploitation and harm in clinical trials.

---

[98] Carl Elliott, 'The mild torture economy' (2010) 32 London Review of Books 26–7.

[99] 'We could be heroes: ethical issues with the pre-recruitment of research participants' (2015) 41 Journal of Medical Ethics 557–8.

The Health Research Authority (HRA) recognized this problem in 2013, when it set up the Phase 1 Generic Advert Review Group. Admitting that it is not a requirement that pre-recruitment materials have REC approval, the HRA has nevertheless said that its 'expectation [is] that ethical advice regarding any proposed generic advertising is sought from the HRA, prior to its being used, as a matter of best practice'. The Phase 1 Generic Advert Review Group is made up of three experienced members of Research Ethics Committees that review Phase 1 studies, and it has so far considered posters, website adverts, scripts for radio broadcasts, and television adverts.

(2) Medical Writing Agencies

A second type of outsourcing involves the writing up of results, both for publication and for submission to regulators. There are now several companies that write medical manuscripts, liaise with the formally identified 'authors', and submit these articles to prestigious medical journals.

In 2009, the *New York Times* published 'A case study in medical writing', using documents released in a personal injury action against Wyeth.[100] Wyeth paid DesignWrite $25,000 to draft an article about the treatment of vasomotor symptoms (hot flushes and sweating) in menopausal and pre-menopausal women. According to the documentation, the author was 'to be determined' later. An outline was sent to an eminent professor who agreed to be its author. She was then sent a first draft, this time with her name attached. She made one correction, and the article was then published in the *Journal of Reproductive Medicine* in her name.

Ghost authorship of articles is a serious ethical issue. Students who put their name to papers they have not written are guilty of plagiarism, for which the penalties are serious. Carl Elliott has suggested that similar penalties should apply to academics who agree to be ghost authors: 'Department heads could treat faculty who sign onto paid editorials the same way they treat students who sign their names to papers they buy on the Internet'.[101]

In 2012, the *British Medical Journal* and the Committee on Publication Ethics issued *A Consensus Statement on Research Misconduct in the UK* which specified that ghostwriting, and other practices, amount to research misconduct:

British Medical Journal and the Committee on Publication Ethics[102]

- This meeting believes that the UK's mechanisms for ensuring good research conduct and investigating research misconduct need to be strengthened
- Research misconduct is defined as behaviour by a researcher, intentional or not, that falls short of good ethical and scientific standards. Research misconduct includes fabrication, falsification, suppression, or inappropriate manipulation of data; inappropriate image manipulation; plagiarism; misleading reporting; redundant publication; authorship malpractice such as guest or ghost authorship; failure to disclose funding sources or competing interests; misreporting of funder involvement; and unethical research (for example, failure to obtain adequate patient consent). Research misconduct is important as it wastes resources, damages the credibility of science, and can cause harm (for example, to patients and the public).

---

[100] See further Natasha Singer, 'Medical papers by ghostwriters pushed therapy', *New York Times*, 4 August 2009.
[101] Carl Elliott, 'The mild torture economy' (2010) 32 London Review of Books 26–7.
[102] (2012) 344 British Medical Journal 1111.

9 RESEARCH IN LOW AND MIDDLE-INCOME COUNTRIES

People living in low and middle-income countries need access to affordable medical treatments. Clinical trials of low-cost interventions are desperately needed but, at the same time, the populations of low and middle-income countries should not be exposed to unacceptable risks. In the next extract, Benjamin Mason Meier explains how the governments of poor countries are themselves sometimes complicit in ensuring that researchers face comparatively few obstacles when planning clinical trials.

Benjamin Mason Meier[103]

National regulation of human experimentation differs dramatically between developed and developing, particularly African, nations. Many African nations lack any legislative protections for subjects of medical research. To a large degree, this legislative vacuum is intentional. While governments of these nations are desperate to bring medical research to their dying populations, their nations cannot afford such research without subsidies from multinational pharmaceutical corporations. To court these pharmaceutical corporations, African nations vie to minimize regulation on the conduct of medical research. They fear that legislation, and resulting lawsuits, could have a chilling effect on beneficial research efforts. As a result, African nations have shown great reluctance to impose any restrictions on human research, thereby creating a medical 'race to the bottom' at the expense of human rights and human life.

India has become a particularly attractive site for trials. Most Indian doctors speak English, and many have been trained in the UK or the US. What India lacks, however, is a robust ethical review system.[104] The principal task for regulation must therefore be to ensure that high-quality research capable of improving the lives of people in the world's poorest nations is encouraged, while also ensuring that these countries do not become the pharmaceutical industry's 'sweat shop'.

Most codes of ethics suggest that western companies should only carry out research in vulnerable populations where it is responsive to their health needs. Paragraph 20 of the Helsinki Declaration, for example, provides that:

20. Medical research with a vulnerable group is only justified if the research is responsive to the health needs or priorities of this group and the research cannot be carried out in a non-vulnerable group. In addition, this group should stand to benefit from the knowledge, practices or interventions that result from the research.[105]

Similarly, the Nuffield Council on Bioethics' report on *The Ethics of Research Related to Healthcare in Developing Countries* suggested that externally sponsored research should

---

[103] 'International Protection of Persons Undergoing Medical Experimentation: Protecting the Right of Informed Consent' (2001) 20 Berkeley Journal of International Law 513.

[104] Priya Satalkar and David Shaw, 'Not fit for ourpose: the ethical guidelines of the Indian Council of Medical Research' (2015) 15 Developing World Bioethics 40–7.

[105] (WMA, 2013).

'fall within the ambit of the national priorities for research related to health care in developing countries'.[106]

It is also important to recognize that incentives to participation in research may work differently in poorer countries. Not only might comparatively small sums of money be disproportionately attractive, but also simply taking part in a research trial may involve access to medical care that might not otherwise be available. Regular contact with a team of health care professionals may mean that an unrelated medical condition is diagnosed and treated more speedily than normal. The offer of any medical care at all can represent a considerable incentive to participation.

In addition, levels of trust in the medical profession may be particularly high in some low and middle-income countries. In northern India, DeCosta et al found that one of the most important reasons for people's willingness to take part in research 'was an implicit faith in doctors and the medical system'.[107] This confidence in the medical profession led a significant minority (17.5 per cent) of their interviewees to report that they would not want any information before deciding whether to participate. One subject explained that 'doctors are in a way godly. Who would know better than them?'[108]

In some low and middle-income countries, it may be usual practice for decisions—such as whether to participate in research—to be taken by the leader of the community, or a senior family member, rather than by the individual herself. Does respect for cultural difference demand that consent should be sought from this authority figure, or is the duty to obtain the individual subject's free and informed consent a universal moral requirement?

The CIOMS Guidelines (and the new draft guidelines) recommend that seeking consent from someone other than the research subject may sometimes be advisable in order to show appropriate respect for a community's cultural traditions, but that it could never replace the additional need to obtain the subject's own consent.

Council for International Organizations of Medical Sciences[109]

Commentary on Guideline 4: Individual informed consent

In some cultures an investigator may enter a community to conduct research or approach prospective subjects for their individual consent only after obtaining permission from a community leader, a council of elders, or another designated authority. Such customs must be respected. In no case, however, may the permission of a community leader or other authority substitute for individual informed consent.

The Nuffield Council on Bioethics further recommends that where an individual does not wish to participate in research, despite the community leader's agreement, researchers have a duty to facilitate their non-participation.

---

[106] Nuffield Council on Bioethics, *The Ethics of Research Related to Healthcare in Developing Countries* (NCOB, 2002).

[107] A DeCosta et al, 'Community based trials and informed consent in rural north India' (2004) 30 Journal of Medical Ethics 318–23.

[108] Ibid.

[109] International Ethical Guidelines for Biomedical Research Involving Human Subjects (CIOMS, 2002).

Nuffield Council on Bioethics[110]

6.22 . . . In some cultural contexts it may be appropriate to obtain agreement from the community or assent from a senior family member before a prospective participant is approached. If a prospective participant does not wish to take part in research this must be respected. Researchers must not enrol such individuals and have a duty to facilitate their non-participation.

Another ethical problem is the extent of the researchers' obligations towards the community after the trial is over. Should researchers be under a duty to make treatments that have been proved to be effective available to all of the participants in the trial, or to the wider community as well? If the research subjects have benefited from better general health care during the trial, is there an obligation to continue to provide this level of care once the trial has ended?

It would be difficult to compel drugs companies to assume responsibility for all of the future health needs of low-income countries, but providing post-trial access to the participants themselves is a different matter. Of course, not all trials result in beneficial medicines, and some participants will not need continuing access to drugs. However, where the trial has led to the development of a new intervention, which benefited the research participants, the Helsinki Declaration suggests that subjects should be entitled to access to interventions which have been proved beneficial.

Helsinki Declaration[111]

34. In advance of a clinical trial, sponsors, researchers and host country governments should make provisions for post-trial access for all participants who still need an intervention identified as beneficial in the trial. This information must also be disclosed to participants during the informed consent process.

Notice that the Helsinki Declaration highlights the obligations of host country governments, as well as trial sponsors. In the context of a study of HIV trials, Haire and Jordens point out that governments of low and middle-income countries have a vital role to play in facilitating post-trial access.

Bridget Haire and Christopher Jordens[112]

[T]his study shows on the one hand that HIV prevention researchers recognise the importance of post-trial access to ARV for seroconverters . . . It also shows the complexity of post-trial access to successful products . . . If communities that participate in research are to benefit from its results, governments must be prepared to support the implementation of those interventions within their policy framework. This is easier said than done . . .

---

[110] 'The Ethics of Research Related to Healthcare in Developing Countries' (April 2002), available at www.nuffieldbioethics.org.uk.
[111] (WMA, 2013).
[112] 'Mind the gap: an empirical study of post-trial access in HIV biomedical prevention trials' (2015) 15 Developing World Bioethics 85–97.

Securing the reasonable availability of a successful intervention post-trial is intended to ensure that research conducted in lower income countries is responsive to needs, and does not exploit vulnerable population to test interventions for the consumption of those in high income countries. A major problem with this requirement, however, is the determining who is responsible for this form of access. It is clearly beyond the control of principal investigators, and is a matter for governments and their regulatory bodies—though sponsors certainly have a responsibility to actually apply for regulatory approval. . . . Careful alignment of national HIV strategies with approval criteria for ethical review committees might be a mechanism for ensuring that the research that goes ahead tests interventions that the national government will be prepared, later down the line, to fund, should the intervention prove successful. Even with such safeguards, however, political expediency may hamper funding, promotion and uptake of proven interventions.

One of the most controversial issues raised by trials in low and middle-income countries is the use of placebo or no-intervention controls when their use would be impermissible in high-income countries. In 1997, Peter Lurie and Sidney Wolfe published an article in which they criticized 15 placebo-controlled clinical trials, involving 12,000 HIV-positive women in nine countries, which were designed to test whether low-cost treatments might be effective in reducing perinatal (mother-to-baby) transmission of the HIV virus.[113]

Standard treatment for HIV-positive pregnant women in high-income countries at that time was known as the 076 protocol, and it involved oral and intravenous doses of an antiretroviral drug (brand name AZT) to pregnant women throughout pregnancy, and during childbirth; abstaining from breastfeeding; and the provision of AZT to babies for six weeks after birth. On its own, the 076 protocol reduced transmission rates from 25 per cent to 8 per cent, and delivery by caesarean section could further reduce the risk to approximately 1 per cent.

The 076 protocol was unavailable in low-income countries, however. Not only was it prohibitively expensive, but it also required the provision of health services—such as early pregnancy testing and intravenous drug delivery during childbirth—that were unavailable in poorer countries. In addition, in countries without reliable clean water supplies, abstaining from breastfeeding may represent a greater threat to infant health than HIV transmission.

The trials that were the subject of the *New England Journal of Medicine* article involved a simpler and cheaper course of treatment. The studies were RCTs, in which one group of HIV-positive pregnant women received a short course of AZT during the last four weeks of pregnancy, and a control group received a placebo. Following positive preliminary results from a trial in Thailand, in which perinatal transmission rates were halved (19 per cent of babies in the control group were infected, compared with 9 per cent of the babies whose mothers had received the short course of AZT), the research was halted. Controversy continues, however, over whether these trials should ever have taken place.

In short, the problem was that the control group was given a placebo despite the existence of effective treatment (the 076 protocol). It has been estimated that before the trials were stopped, over 1,000 babies in the control group became infected with the HIV virus. This would appear to conflict with two basic ethical principles. First, using a placebo control in these HIV trials deprived the patients in the control group of the 'best proven' treatment to prevent the perinatal transmission of the HIV virus. Secondly, could it really be said that a

---

[113] 'Unethical trials of interventions to reduce perinatal transmission of the human immunodeficiency virus in developing countries' (1997) 337 New England Journal of Medicine 853–6.

state of equipoise existed over which treatment was best for the patients? Because the 076 protocol had been proved to be effective, the uncertainty which justifies imposing risks on research subjects was absent.

Lurie and Wolfe accused researchers of a double standard in research, whereby subjects in rich countries are guaranteed a higher level of care than those from poorer nations. Not only does this seem unfair, it also offers a compelling incentive for sponsors of trials to locate them in countries where subjects can legitimately be offered a lower standard of care.

Peter Lurie and Sidney M Wolfe[114]

What are the potential implications of accepting such a double standard? Researchers might inject live malaria parasites into HIV-positive subjects in China in order to study the effect on the progression of HIV infection, even though the study protocol had been rejected in the United States and Mexico. Or researchers might randomly assign malnourished San (bushmen) to receive vitamin-fortified or standard bread. One might also justify trials of HIV vaccines in which the subjects were not provided with condoms or state-of-the-art counseling about safe sex by arguing that they are not customarily provided in the developing countries in question. These are not simply hypothetical worst-case scenarios; the first two studies have already been performed, and the third has been proposed and criticized . . .

Residents of impoverished, postcolonial countries, the majority of whom are people of color, must be protected from potential exploitation in research. Otherwise, the abominable state of health care in these countries can be used to justify studies that could never pass ethical muster in the sponsoring country . . . It is time to develop standards of research that preclude the kinds of double standards evident in these trials . . . Tragically, for the hundreds of infants who have needlessly contracted HIV infection in the perinatal-transmission studies that have already been completed, any such protection will have come too late.

In contrast, supporters of the trials argued that local solutions to the burden of disease should be sought, and that research capable of having practical application in poor countries should not be stopped in order to ease western consciences. No woman in the control group was actually any worse off than she would have been if she had not enrolled in the trial, and using a placebo control meant that statistically significant results could be, and indeed were, obtained quickly.

In the debates over the ethical legitimacy of these trials, the prohibitive cost of treatment was often taken for granted. It is, however, important to remember that, while it may have cost a lot to develop, AZT was not, in fact, expensive to manufacture. The 076 protocol was unaffordable in part because the TRIPS Agreement allowed one company to hold the global patent on AZT for 20 years, during which time no generic equivalent could be produced. Permitting poor countries to manufacture generic versions of expensive patented drugs within this 20-year period might offer a more ethically defensible solution to the problem of unaffordable medicines than permitting a double standard in research ethics.

The TRIPS Agreement has always allowed for the compulsory licensing of medicines in an emergency. In the 2001 Doha Declaration, the World Trade Organization (WTO) reaffirmed that this could be used in response to public health crises, like the HIV/AIDS pandemic.

---

[114] Ibid.

World Trade Organization[115]

> 4. We agree that the TRIPS Agreement does not and should not prevent members from taking measures to protect public health. Accordingly, while reiterating our commitment to the TRIPS Agreement, we affirm that the Agreement can and should be interpreted and implemented in a manner supportive of WTO members' right to protect public health and, in particular, to promote access to medicines for all.
>
> In this connection, we reaffirm the right of WTO members to use, to the full, the provisions in the TRIPS Agreement, which provide flexibility for this purpose.
>
> 5. Accordingly and in the light of paragraph 4 above, while maintaining our commitments in the TRIPS Agreement, we recognize that these flexibilities include:
>
> . . .
>
> b. Each member has the right to grant compulsory licences and the freedom to determine the grounds upon which such licences are granted.
>
> c. Each member has the right to determine what constitutes a national emergency or other circumstances of extreme urgency, it being understood that public health crises, including those relating to HIV/AIDS, tuberculosis, malaria and other epidemics, can represent a national emergency or other circumstances of extreme urgency.

Consistent with TRIPS, public health concerns can therefore override intellectual property rights by allowing a country to compulsorily license generic drugs without the consent of the original manufacturer. This might look like a good solution to the problem of unaffordable medicines, so at first sight it might seem surprising that the Doha Declaration has not made that much difference.

In practice, however, governments in low and middle-income countries tend to be concerned about the impact of compulsory licensing upon their country's reputation as a trading partner.[116] This problem is exacerbated by the negotiation of regional and bilateral free trade agreements (FTAs)—described as TRIPS-plus measures—between richer and poorer countries. Most commonly, these involve the US or the EU negotiating an FTA with a low or middle-income country or countries, in which the poorer countries agree to waive some of their rights under TRIPS in return for import/export agreements.[117] TRIPS is, after all, a minimum standards agreement and countries which are concerned about finding markets for their goods are free to negotiate away the rights they would normally have under TRIPS.[118]

10 COMPENSATION FOR INJURIES

If a subject did not consent to her participation in a research trial, she could bring an action in battery (see further Chapter 4). In practice, this is unlikely because a person who takes part in a research project will invariably have signed a consent form, so it will be difficult for her to establish that she was not informed 'in broad terms' about the nature of the trial.

---

[115] *Declaration on the TRIPS Agreement and public health* (WTO, 2001).

[116] Vanessa Bradford Kerry and Kelley Lee, 'TRIPS, the Doha Declaration and paragraph 6 decision: what are the remaining steps for protecting access to medicines?' (2007) 3 Globalization and Health 1–12.

[117] Oxfam, *Trading Away Access to Medicines: How the European Union's Trade Agenda has Taken a Wrong Turn* (Oxfam: Brussels, 2009).

[118] Carlos Maria Correa, 'Implications of bilateral free trade agreements on access to medicines' (2006) 84 Bulletin of the World Health Organization 399–404.

If a subject suffers injury during a research trial, she might be able to claim that the researcher, who undoubtedly owes her a duty of care, was in breach of that duty. This could happen in two ways. First, a person might be injured as a result of negligence in the design or execution of the research project. Secondly, the information provided to the subject, although sufficient to avoid a charge of battery, may have been inadequate, and amount to a breach of the researcher's duty of care. In this latter situation, the research subject will have to establish that she would not have consented to take part in the research trial if she had been provided with proper information, and hence would not have suffered whatever injury has materialized as a result of her participation.

Where it is the design of the research project that caused the subject's injuries, could the members of the REC also be liable for failing to notice that the protocol itself was defective? It could be argued that it is foreseeable that negligent approval of a dangerous research project will cause injury, and that there is a relationship of proximity between the REC and the research subjects. But would it be fair, just, and reasonable to impose liability on the members of the REC? There have been no cases in which injured research subjects have sued REC members, and such actions are improbable, given the much deeper pockets of other potential defendants, such as the pharmaceutical company.

As we saw in Chapter 3, victims of medical mishaps face numerous obstacles when bringing actions in negligence, and this will be equally true for individuals who have been injured during research rather than treatment. It has, however, been argued that people injured during research trials should not have to overcome all of the hurdles the tort of negligence places in the path of those seeking compensation for their injuries. In 1978, the Pearson Commission advocated a 'no fault' compensation scheme for people injured during medical research, drawing an analogy with the statutory compensation offered to people injured by vaccination programmes. The community as a whole benefits from both vaccination and research, and should therefore be prepared to compensate the small proportion of the population who will suffer injuries as a result. This proposal was never implemented. Not having to prove fault might make it easier to obtain compensation, but it should be remembered that the subject still has to establish causation, which can be a significant obstacle, particularly where the subject was ill before they took part in the trial.

Principle 15 of the Helsinki Declaration provides that: 'Appropriate compensation and treatment for subjects who are harmed as a result of participating in research must be ensured', and the Clinical Trials Regulation requires Member States to have compensation mechanisms in place.

Clinical Trials Regulation 2014

Article 76

1. Member States shall ensure that systems for compensation for any damage suffered by a subject resulting from participation in a clinical trial conducted on their territory are in place in the form of insurance, a guarantee, or a similar arrangement that is equivalent as regards its purpose and which is appropriate to the nature and the extent of the risk.

It might also be thought that the adverse publicity, which would result from a court action in which a pharmaceutical company was sued for injuries inflicted on a research subject, represents a powerful incentive towards the making of ex gratia payments. Certainly, the

Association of the British Pharmaceutical Industry's guidelines recommend that compensation should be paid, even if the victim cannot establish negligence.

The assumption that the pharmaceutical industry would move quickly to compensate anyone injured in a drugs trial, in order to avoid any adverse publicity, was undermined in the UK in the immediate aftermath of the TGN1412 trials at Northwick Park Hospital. Although the case has now been settled, the injured men were initially offered an interim payment of only £5,000 in return for an agreement not to sue, and it was revealed that TGN1412's manufacturer, TeGenero, which was subsequently declared insolvent, only had insurance coverage of £2 million.

11 CONCLUSION

Throughout this chapter, we have seen that there is generally assumed to be a sharp distinction between research and ordinary medical treatment. In particular, in relation to research, there is undoubtedly a duty to obtain 'informed consent', whereas, as we saw in Chapter 4, the judiciary was slower to introduce the 'doctrine of informed consent' for routine medical treatment. People who volunteer to take part in research are regarded as more vulnerable, and in greater need of clear and frank information than patients. But is this special concern for research subjects justified?

On the one hand, the long history of the abuse of research subjects should undoubtedly alert us to the need to have protective mechanisms in place to ensure that vulnerable individuals do not end up taking part in research without knowing that this is what they are doing, or without being given the option of refusal. Yet, on the other hand, it is worth remembering that the decision to consent to treatment will also sometimes be a difficult decision, which requires an individual to balance risks and benefits, some of which may be uncertain and speculative. Rather than viewing research subjects as uniquely vulnerable and in need of sensitively provided information, perhaps we should acknowledge that patients too are often faced with complex decisions, and with information which may be difficult for them to understand and evaluate.

A final interesting distinction between patients and research subjects is the insistence, in the Helsinki Declaration, that any control group should be assured of the 'best proven treatment'. Again, this draws a distinction between participants in research and patients. Within the NHS at least, patients are clearly not assured of the best proven treatment. Rather, it is generally accepted that limited resources mean that sometimes less than optimal treatment may have to be provided in order to ensure that the NHS can continue to run a comprehensive health service. As we saw in Chapter 2, the reality of rationed health care is that patients are deprived of beneficial treatment. If it is absolutely clear that patients do not have the right to demand the 'best proven treatment', is it anomalous that participating in research, in theory at least, gives subjects precisely this right?

FURTHER READING

Brim, Remy L and Miller, Franklin G, 'The potential benefit of the placebo effect in sham-controlled trials: implications for risk–benefit assessments and informed consent' (2013) 39 Journal of Medical Ethics 703–7.

Dresser, Rebecca, 'Subversive subjects: rule-breaking and deception in clinical trials' (2013) 41 Journal of Law, Medicine and Ethics 829–40.

Elliott, Carl, 'The mild torture economy' (2010) 32 London Review of Books 26–7.

Ferguson, Pamela, 'Clinical Trials and Healthy Volunteers' (2008) 16 Medical Law Review 23–51.

Harris, John, 'Scientific research is a moral duty' (2005) 31 Journal of Medical Ethics 242–8.

Hunter, David, 'We could be heroes: ethical issues with the pre-recruitment of research participants' (2015) 41 Journal of Medical Ethics 557–8.

Miller, Franklin G and Wertheimer, Alan, 'The fair transaction model of informed consent: an alternative to autonomous authorization' (2011) 21 Kennedy Institute of Ethics Journal 201–18.

Smith, Richard, 'Medical journals are an extension of the marketing arm of pharmaceutical companies' (2005) 2 PLoS Medicine 138.

THE REGULATION OF
MEDICINES

CENTRAL ISSUES

1. Before any new medicine can be put into circulation, it must have a marketing authorization.

2. European harmonization of the rules covering the licensing and marketing of medicines has two main aims: consumer protection and facilitating trade through the free movement of goods.

3. All medicines must have a marketing authorization, from the European Medicines Agency or the UK's Medicines and Healthcare products Regulatory Agency. Safety and efficacy must be established before a medicine can be licensed for use, but it is also important that safety continues to be monitored after a drug is put into circulation.

4. The Consumer Protection Act 1987 implemented a European Directive and introduced strict liability for injuries caused by defective products. There has been less litigation than was initially anticipated, and hardly any cases involving medicines.

1 INTRODUCTION

In this chapter, we consider the regulation of medicines. Although the availability of safe and effective pharmaceutical drugs is not the only reason why average life expectancy nearly doubled over the course of the twentieth century—better sanitation and nutrition were at least as important—there is no doubt that the availability of effective medicines has significantly improved public health.[1] It is now comparatively rare for people living in the world's richest countries to die from infectious diseases, and it is the degenerative diseases of old age, such as cancer and heart disease, which have become the most common causes of death.

---

[1] Jasper Woodcock, 'Medicines—The Interested Parties' in R Blum et al (eds), *Pharmaceuticals and Health Policy: International Perspectives on Provision and Control of Medicines* (Croom Helm: London, 1981) 27–35.

In high-income countries, huge profits can be made from successful drugs. Blockbuster drugs are defined as medicines that generate over $1 billion per year, and some drugs are much more profitable than this. In the year before it came out of patent protection, Pfizer's statin Lipitor made $10.7 billion. For obvious reasons, an effective treatment for depression or obesity is likely to generate much higher profits than a cure for a 'neglected disease', like malaria or sleeping sickness. A *British Medical Journal* editorial spelled out the problem.

British Medical Journal[2]

When it comes to the world's most neglected diseases . . . these present absolutely no market opportunities. Without such opportunities, there is no incentive for the pharmaceutical industry to invest in drug research and development. The patients have no purchasing power, no vocal advocacy group is pleading for their needs, and no strategic interests—military or security—are driving concern about these conditions.

For example, sleeping sickness, which claims thousands of lives annually in Africa, can be considered as a most neglected disease. Current drug treatments are in scarce supply, difficult to administer, and often toxic. Melarsoprol, which was developed over 50 years ago, kills up to 10% of people who are given the drug, and in some regions drug resistance means it is ineffective in a third of patients. An effective, less toxic drug, has been developed—eflornithine—but the company that developed it stopped its production in 1995, citing commercial failure. African patients could not afford to buy the drug. Eflornithine became available again five years later in the United States, when it was found to reduce unwanted facial hair in women.

The drive to provide a pharmacological solution to an ever-increasing range of conditions is referred to as 'medicalization'. The menopause can be 'treated' with hormone replacement therapy; medication exists for behavioural difficulties in children; and drugs can be used to combat some of the normal consequences of ageing.

The research and development of new drugs involves enormous financial investment. On average it takes between ten and 12 years to develop a new medicine.[3] Of every 10,000 compounds that are synthesized and tested, only one or two will reach the market,[4] and 90 per cent of compounds which get as far as the preclinical development stage will fail before launch.[5] The money invested in these failures inevitably increases the price of successful drugs.

In order to recoup their investment, pharmaceutical companies can hold the patent on a new drug for 20 years, during which time they have the right to prevent others from making or selling an identical product.[6] Some of this patent term will expire while the drug is being tested, and so in reality there may be only ten years of 'on the market' patent protection. Once the patent expires, other companies can produce generic and much cheaper versions of the same drug. For example, in 2000, treatment for HIV/AIDS in low-income countries was

---

[2] 'The world's most neglected diseases' (2002) 325 British Medical Journal 176–7.

[3] Zosia Kmietowicz, 'Regulations are stifling development of new drugs' (2004) 328 British Medical Journal 600.

[4] Richard Sykes, *New Medicines, The Practice of Medicine, and Public Policy* (Nuffield Trust: London, 2000) 65.

[5] Ibid.

[6] Patent Act 1977, s 25(1). World Trade Organization (WTO) Agreement on Trade-Related Intellectual Property Rights (TRIPS), Art 33.

prohibitively expensive, costing an average of $10,000 per person per year; by 2010, when the patent on AZT had expired, the cost had dropped to $67.[7]

There is some evidence that pharmaceutical companies attempt to delay or block competition from generic manufacturers. One strategy, described by the House of Commons Health Select Committee, is to make a number of minor modifications to the patented drug.

House of Commons Health Select Committee[8]

Evergreening involves extending the patented life of a branded product, typically by reformulating the drug, for instance by using a different drug delivery system, changing a dosage form, or presentation (e.g. from tablet to capsule) . . .

The significance of evergreening is underlined by the increased range of drug attributes eligible for patent protection. . . . In the 1990s, the list extended protection in relation to range of use, methods of treatment, mechanism of action, packaging, delivery profiles, dosing route, regimen and range, drug combinations, screening and analytical methods, biological targets and field of use.

The British Generic Manufacturers Association (BGMA) listed five examples in which the originating company had employed evergreening methods, resulting in little or no therapeutic gain, but at a cost to the NHS estimated between £164 and £369 million.

A particularly audacious example of evergreening happened when Prozac, an antidepressant, was about to lose its patent protection. Its manufacturer, Eli Lilly, rebranded the active ingredient—fluoxetine—by producing pink and lavender pills (Prozac was green and white), naming it Sarafem, and marketing it for the treatment of premenstrual dysphoric disorder.

Although intellectual property rights undoubtedly raise the price of medicines, and hence might not appear to be in the interests of consumers, the counter-argument is that, without them, investing in research and development would be so risky that the development of innovative medicines would be stifled, and public health would suffer. This claim is disputed in the next extract by Graham Dukes, who argues that the pharmaceutical industry's commercial accountability to shareholders takes priority over its duty to the community.

MN Graham Dukes[9]

Two definitions of industry accountability predominate: commercial duty to shareholders; and duty to the community.

In the commercial sense, a pharmaceutical company is obliged to deliver a sound return on investment for shareholders. That return must be adequate to reward investors but also be sufficient to attract new capital when needed. From this point of view, the pharmaceutical industry has done very well. Throughout periods of economic stagnation and even recession over the past 30 years, it has remained highly and increasingly profitable. . . .

From the broad social point of view, the pharmaceutical industry has a duty to supply communities with good drugs at an affordable price, and to provide reliable information on them

---

[7] United Nations Development Programme, *Good Practice Guide: Improving Access to Treatment by Utilizing Public Health Flexibilities in the WTO TRIPS Agreement* (UNDP: New York, 2010).

[8] *The Influence of the Pharmaceutical Industry*, Fourth Report of Session 2004–05.

[9] 'Accountability of the pharmaceutical industry' (2002) 260 The Lancet 1682–4.

> . . . The much-repeated argument from pharmaceutical companies, that high drug prices are mainly attributable to research costs, merits cautious scrutiny. With publicly available data, we can ascertain that costs of advertising and promotion generally much exceed research expenditure. Furthermore, industrial research usually benefits from public support, either in the form of tax breaks or as direct scientific input.

A good example of this last point comes from so-called 'orphan' drugs, which are defined by the European Medicines Agency (EMA) as:

- intended for the diagnosis, prevention or treatment of a life-threatening or chronically debilitating condition affecting no more than five in 10,000 persons in the European Union, or

- intended for the diagnosis, prevention or treatment of a life-threatening, seriously debilitating or serious and chronic condition and without incentives it is unlikely that expected sales of the medicinal product would cover the investment in its development.[10]

Although each rare disease will, by definition, affect very few people (most affect fewer than one person in every 100,000), there are so many rare diseases that the total affected population is, in fact, substantial. It has been estimated that there are 8,000 diseases which qualify as 'rare', and that these affect 8 per cent of the population, which in Europe is 36 million people. Developing drugs to treat rare diseases is nevertheless unlikely to be profitable, and hence will be a low priority for companies whose duty is to maintain shareholder value. As a result, a system of tax breaks and incentives is in place to ensure that people with rare diseases are not abandoned by the pharmaceutical industry.

For several reasons, medicines are unlike other products. First, in the case of prescribed drugs, the decision to purchase a medicine is not taken by its consumer, but by her doctor. And neither the consumer nor the prescriber will actually pay the full costs of the medicine.

Secondly, any medicine that is powerful enough to cure disease or alleviate symptoms will also be strong enough to cause adverse side effects, in at least some users. If complete safety is unattainable, deciding when a medicine is safe *enough* involves a complex risk/benefit calculation. Chemotherapy, for example, has a long list of extremely unpleasant side effects, which would rule it out as a treatment for a comparatively trivial condition, like hay fever. Where the benefit might be the successful treatment of cancer, the risk/benefit calculation is different.

Thirdly, the cultural and symbolic significance of medicines is demonstrated by the placebo effect, which we considered in the previous chapter. The placebo effect is also at work, as Law explains, when the same active ingredient is marketed, often under different names, for a range of different purposes.

Jacky Law[11]

> The drugs work according to what the label says, what the doctor says, and what we believe. Our minds and bodies respond, in other words, to what the label says, to what we are told the drug will do. GlaxoSmithKline's Zyban for smoking cessation, for example, is a long-acting form of Wellbutin for depression, by another name. And Organon's antidepressant, Zispin is

---

[10] *Orphan Drugs and Rare Diseases at a Glance* (EMA: London, 2007).

[11] *Big Pharma: Exposing the Global Healthcare Agenda* (Carroll and Graf: New York, 2006) 63–4.

also marketed for sleeping disorders . . . Different studies are done to get different licensing data to get them known as different drugs so they can operate in different markets.

The active ingredient, however, remains the same. As such, the various effects the drugs have can be put down to the response elicited from expectation. What makes a smoker more likely to kick their habit on Zyban than on the identical drug posing as an antidepressant is the fact that this is what the doctor says, what the label says, and what the data from clinical studies corroborate. Such drugs are a triumph of branding.

Because the special licensing regime only applies to medicines, we begin this chapter by considering what counts as a medicine. Secondly, it is important to ensure that drugs are both safe and effective, and we examine the licensing process which is supposed to prevent unsafe and ineffective drugs reaching the market. Thirdly, we consider the increasing standardization of the regulation of medicines within the EU. Finally, we consider the law's response to defective medicines, examining in turn the role of contract, negligence, and statute.

At the outset it is worth noting that government policy in this area will be influenced by several competing factors, which may pull in different directions. On the one hand, the government has an interest in containing costs within the NHS, perhaps by restricting access to new and expensive drugs. On the other hand, in order to improve health outcomes, the government may want to increase access to new medicines. Because the pharmaceutical industry is phenomenally profitable, and a major employer—it invests over £4 billion each year on R&D in the UK[12]—the government has a further interest in ensuring that the UK is an attractive location for the industry, by, for example, making sure that its licensing processes are not overly cumbersome and that its product liability regime does not stifle innovation. At the same time, however, in order to promote patient safety, a government might wish to ensure that the licensing process is rigorous and that there is strict liability for drug-related injuries.

2 WHAT IS A MEDICINE?

(a) DEFINING MEDICINAL PRODUCTS

In practice, it will sometimes be difficult to determine whether a product, like a food supplement or a herbal remedy, is a medicine. Because the Human Medicines Regulations apply only to medicinal products, it is obviously important to be able to tell whether a particular product needs a marketing authorization. This is a job for the Medicines and Healthcare products Regulatory Agency (MHRA; previously the Medicines Control Agency (MCA)), and as we can see from *R v Medicines Control Agency, ex parte Pharma Nord*, the courts will be slow to interfere with the Agency's determination of whether or not something is a medicinal product. In this case, the applicants had marketed melatonin tablets in the UK. The MCA informed manufacturers, importers, distributors, and retailers of unlicensed melatonin that, in its view, melatonin was a medicinal product and should only be supplied on prescription. The applicants argued that melatonin was a dietary supplement rather than a medicine, and applied for judicial review of the MCA's classification of it as a medicinal product. Recognizing that they were unlikely to succeed in proving *Wednesbury*[13]

---

[12] See further www.abpi.org.uk.

[13] Ie that the decision was so unreasonable that no reasonable regulator could have taken it: *Associated Provincial Picture Houses v Wednesbury Corporation* [1948] 1 KB 223.

unreasonableness, they sought a full trial on the merits of whether melatonin should be considered a medicinal product. Collins J refused to exercise his discretion to transfer the case to the civil courts, and in *R v Medicines Control Agency, ex parte Pharma Nord*, the Court of Appeal dismissed the applicant's appeal.

R v Medicines Control Agency, ex parte Pharma Nord[14]

Lord Woolf MR

Under European and domestic law it is the MCA which has the initial heavy responsibility of protecting the public against the dangers to health which can result from the unlicensed marketing of medicinal products. It is also the MCA's equally important initial responsibility to decide what is or is not a medicinal product. Unless it determines that a substance is a medicinal product there is no action which it can lawfully take to control its use . . .

The determination of the facts and the application of the policy in a case such as this are not ideally suited to the adversarial processes of the courts . . . [T]he MCA is in a better position to evaluate the evidence than a judge. It has accumulated experience in relation to other products which a court lacks. It is an expert body. The MCA has to develop a consistent policy between similar products. The issues are . . . ones in relation to which the court should be wary of becoming involved.

So how does the Agency decide whether a product is a medicine? 'Medicinal products' are defined in the Human Medicines Regulations 2012, regulation 2(1) as follows:

(a) any substance or combination of substances presented as having properties of preventing or treating disease in human beings; or

(b) any substance or combination of substances that may be used by or administered to human beings with a view to—

   (i) restoring, correcting or modifying a physiological function by exerting a pharmacological, immunological or metabolic action, or

   (ii) making a medical diagnosis.

There are therefore two tests for whether something is a medicinal product: is it *presented* as a medicine, or does it *function* as one. If a product is either marketed for the treatment or prevention of disease, or used to modify physiological function, it is a medicinal product, and needs a marketing authorization.

When determining whether a product has been *presented* for the treatment of disease, the MHRA will consider any claims—both explicit and implicit—made for it, and will look at the presentation of the product as a whole, including its packaging and advertising.[15] Also relevant will be the form the product takes and the way it is to be used: in effect, does it look like a medicine? Claims that a product relieves symptoms, such as stress or anxiety, will be regarded as medicinal claims.[16] The reference to 'prevention' means that pills that claim to 'protect against' disease will be treated as medicinal products.[17] Just saying that a product

---

[14] (1998) 44 BMLR 41.

[15] MHRA, 'A Guide to What is a Medicinal Product' (MHRA Guidance Note 8, revised 2012).

[16] Ibid.   [17] Ibid.

'helps to maintain a healthy lifestyle', in contrast, has not been regarded by the MHRA as a medicinal claim.[18]

The second limb of the test refers to the medicinal *purpose* of the product. The MHRA must consider whether products are medicines on a case-by-case basis, rather than applying a general rule to all similar products, and a relevant consideration is the purpose for which a medicine is used. At the time of writing, an appeal is pending in the case of *R (on the application of Blue Bio Pharmaceuticals Ltd) v Secretary of State for Health*.[19] The claimants hold marketing authorizations permitting them to sell Dolenio, a glucosamine-containing product (GCP) as a medicine for the treatment of osteoarthritis of the knee. Other GCPs— usually supplied to 'maintain healthy joints'—are sold as food supplements. The claimants sought a declaration that all GCPs are medicinal; or a declaration that all GCPs with a daily recommended dose of 1500mg are medicines. Their claim failed in the Administrative Court. Supperstone J held that the MHRA was entitled to have regard to the purpose of use when deciding whether GCPs are medicines under the 'functional limb' of the Directive. Some GCPs were simply food supplements, but he also pointed out that the MHRA would take (and had taken) action against manufacturers of GCPs who made medicinal claims.

(b) LIFESTYLE DRUGS AND THE PROBLEM OF ENHANCEMENT

We generally assume that people take medicines when they are unwell, in order to cure them or alleviate their symptoms. In recent years, however, there has been increasing interest in the use of medicines not to restore normal functioning, but to improve upon it. It is by no means easy to draw a line between enhancements and ordinary medical treatment. Many modern medicines are intended to reverse some of the symptoms of ageing, such as forgetfulness, baldness, and sexual dysfunction. Are these treatments for age-related conditions, or enhancements?

Treatments for medical disorders may also be taken by people who have nothing wrong with them, but who want to feel 'better than well'.[20] Sildenafil citrate (brand name Viagra) is licensed for the treatment of erectile dysfunction, but it is also taken recreationally. An effective treatment for memory loss might be regarded as treatment for patients with Alzheimer's disease, but it could be used as an enhancement by students or professional chess players.[21] In the next extract, Peter Conrad and Deborah Potter consider whether there is anything wrong with using medicines as a 'quick fix'.

Peter Conrad and Deborah Potter[22]

In a sense, we can see biomedical enhancement as a double temptation: the object itself is tempting (eg several inches of height, younger features or improved performance) *and* the biomedical route to the enhancement is a temptation as well (eg a rapid road to improvement,

---

[18] Ibid.   [19] [2014] EWHC 1679 (Admin).

[20] Carl Elliott, *Better than Well: American Medicine meets the American Dream* (Norton: New York, 2003); Peter Kramer, *Listening to Prozac* (Penguin: New York, 1994).

[21] Peter Conrad and Deborah Potter, 'Human growth hormone and the temptations of biomedical enhancement' (2004) 26 Sociology of Health and Illness 184–215.

[22] Ibid.

a technological strategy, a medical solution). . . . The key to enhancement, however, is that only some are enhanced. There is no edge if it is universal . . .

Biomedical enhancements do not involve hard work, in fact they are something of a technological fix. It seems likely most people do not . . . consider runners who raise their aerobic ability and run marathons in under three hours unnatural. Indeed we admire such individuals for their fortitude. They have achieved their enhancement through diligence and hard work, exemplary characteristics in our culture. If women could enhance their breasts at the gym or children increase their height by working out, would unnaturalness be an issue at all? . . .

[W]e might note that our society has adopted a sort of 'pharmaceutical Calvinism' when it comes to taking medications. This entails a belief that it is better to achieve an objective naturally than with drugs or medications; this includes pleasure, sexual satisfaction, mental stability and bodily fitness. Using drugs is an inferior and even suspect way of reaching a goal.

What we consider to be 'normal functioning' may itself be socially constructed and cultur-ally variable. As Carl Elliott explains, the pharmaceutical industry has learned that to sell new drugs successfully, it is sometimes first necessary to 'sell' the existence of the disease that they are intended to treat.

Carl Elliott[23]

The pharmaceutical industry . . . has learned that the key to selling psychiatric drugs is to sell the illnesses they treat. Antidepressants are a case in point. Before the 1960s, clinical depression was thought to be an extremely rare problem. Drug companies stayed away from depression because there was no money to be made in antidepressants. So when Merck started to produce amytriptaline, a tricyclic antidepressant, in the early 1960s, it realised that in order to sell the antidepressant it needed to sell depression.

Forty years later, of course, it is now clear to everyone that the market for antidepressants was not a shallow one at all: that it was, in fact, a tremendously lucrative market, as the remarkable success of Prozac and its sister drugs have demonstrated. The notion of 'clinical depression' has expanded tremendously to include many people who might once have been called melancholic, anxious, or alienated. . . .

This does not mean that drug companies are simply making up diseases out of thin air, or that psychiatrists are being gulled into diagnosing well people as sick. No one doubts that some people genuinely suffer from, say, depression, or attention-deficit/hyperactivity disorder, or that the right medications make these disorders better. But surrounding the core of many of these disorders is a wide zone of ambiguity that can be chiseled out and expanded.

In the next extract, L McHenry goes so far as to suggest that the 'chemical imbalance' explanation of depression—upon which Selective Serotonin Reuptake Inhibitors (SSRIs) depend—is 'probably false'. If depression is 'caused by' serotonin deficiency, a pill to remedy this (which is what SSRIs are supposed to do) would work as a cure for depression. McHenry points out that the evidence that this is the case is weak, and perhaps even non-existent. In short, it may be that SSRIs 'work' largely because of the placebo effect.

---

[23] *Better than Well: American Medicine meets the American Dream* (Norton: New York, 2003) 123–4.

L McHenry[24]

Although there seems to be no question about the fact that SSRIs act on the serotonin system, what has not been established is an abnormality of serotonin metabolism in depression or that SSRIs correct a chemical imbalance. Instead of going back to the proverbial drawing board . . . , however, the pharmaceutical company marketing departments revived the serotonin theory in the late 1980s and channelled all their financial might into promoting the SSRIs. It was a triumph of marketing over science . . .

The clinical trials that form the basis of Food and Drug Administration (FDA) approval of SSRIs demonstrate repeatedly that these drugs show a clinically negligible advantage over inert placebo (sugar pills) in the treatment of depression. . . . According to the best data available, there is a less than 10% difference in the effect of FDA approved antidepressants versus placebo . . . The idea of selling us depression, whether we are truly ill or not, has become an immensely lucrative strategy for selling SSRIs, a large part of which succeeds on the basis of the idea of chemical imbalance. . . . The marketing strategy plays on the public's desire for a quick fix for all the vicissitudes of life and the power of the suggestion contained in the easy to understand model of chemical imbalance.

In the next extract, Moynihan et al use anti-baldness medication as another example of industry-sponsored medicalization.

Ray Moynihan et al[25]

There's a lot of money to be made from telling healthy people they're sick. Some forms of medicalising ordinary life may now be better described as disease mongering: widening the boundaries of treatable illness in order to expand markets for those who sell and deliver treatments. Pharmaceutical companies are actively involved in sponsoring the definition of diseases and promoting them to both prescribers and consumers. The social construction of illness is being replaced by the corporate construction of disease . . .

The medicalisation of baldness shows clearly the transformation of the ordinary processes of life into medical phenomena. Around the time that Merck's hair growth drug finasteride (Propecia) was first approved in Australia, leading newspapers featured new information about the emotional trauma associated with hair loss. The global public relations firm Edelman orchestrated some of the coverage but largely left its fingerprints off the resulting stories. An article . . . in the *Australian* newspaper featured a new 'study' suggesting that a third of all men experienced some degree of hair loss, along with comments by concerned experts and news that an International Hair Study Institute had been established. It suggested that losing hair could lead to panic and other emotional difficulties, and even have an impact on job prospects and mental wellbeing. The article did not reveal that the study and the institute were both funded by Merck and that the experts quoted had been supplied by Edelman.

So how should doctors respond to patients' requests for so-called 'lifestyle' drugs? Improving a person's quality of life can sometimes be a legitimate use of NHS resources: the contraceptive pill, for example, does not treat a disease, but rather enhances women's quality of

---

[24] 'Ethical issues in psychopharmacology' (2006) 32 Journal of Medical Ethics 405–10.

[25] 'Selling sickness: the pharmaceutical industry and disease mongering' (2002) 324 British Medical Journal 886–91.

life by enabling them to control their fertility.[26] It is nevertheless regarded as such a public health good that it has never been subject to the prescription charge. Other 'life enhancing' medications may be less deserving of NHS funding. In the next extract, the British Medical Association advises that patients do not have the right to be provided with any drug that they believe will improve their quality of life, especially since all medicines carry some risks, and these may be less acceptable where there is no clinical indication for prescribing the drug in question.

British Medical Association[27]

It is generally accepted that doctors should prescribe medication only if they consider it necessary for the patient, but views of what is 'necessary' differ. More frequent request from patients for what have been termed 'lifestyle drugs', such as anti-obesity drugs, antidepressants, and hair loss treatments, illustrate the way in which perceptions of 'clinical need' have changed. Although there are certainly those for whom antidepressants and appetite suppressants are clinically indicated and cannot be considered as lifestyle drugs, for many others they are seen as a quick and easy solution. . . .

There are inherent risks with virtually all medication and part of the doctor's role is to balance those risks against the anticipated benefits for the patient. When the drug is not clinically indicated, the benefits the patient will, or believes he or she will, derive need to be weighed against the risks. Doctors must be willing to justify their decisions to prescribe in these circumstances and should not prescribe based on patient demand or preference alone.

It is not always easy to tell whether a medicine is being used therapeutically or as an enhancement. A good example comes from Shakespeare et al's study of prescribing practices of Norethisterone, a drug which is prescribed for menorrhagia (abnormally heavy periods) and the menopause, but which can also be used to delay menstruation.[28] They discovered that there were peaks of prescribing during the summer holidays. Women, they concluded, were being prescribed Norethisterone because they did not want to get their periods when they were on holiday. Is this 'lifestyle or convenience prescribing'? In responding to Shakespeare et al's study, Bryant et al argue that it is not.[29] Women suffering from menorrhagia often decide to put up with their problem periods—thus saving the NHS £100 per year per woman. Using Norethisterone to delay menstruation once a year costs about £5. Bryant et al therefore conclude that 'women who tolerate their symptoms for most of the year but who take a period holiday make efficient use of NHS resources'.[30]

---

[26] See further, Silvia Pezzini, 'The effect of women's rights on women's welfare: evidence from a natural experiment' (2005) 115 The Economic Journal C208.

[27] *Medical Ethics Today: The BMA's Handbook of Ethics and Law*, 3rd edn (BMA: London, 2012) 547–8.

[28] Judy Shakespeare, Elizabeth Neve, and Karen Hodder, 'Is Norethisterone a lifestyle drug? Results of database analysis' (2000) 320 British Medical Journal 291.

[29] Gerry Bryant, Ian Scott, and Anne Worrall, 'Is Norethisterone a lifestyle drug? Health is not merely the absence of disease' (2000) 320 British Medical Journal 1605.

[30] Ibid.

3 LICENSING

Thalidomide was marketed in the late 1950s as a remedy for morning sickness in pregnancy. Clinical trials gave no indication of its propensity to cause birth defects, and its manufacturer claimed that it could 'be given with complete safety to pregnant women and nursing mothers without adverse effect on mother or child'.[31] This turned out to be untrue, and between 1956 and 1961 12,000 children were born in over 30 countries with very severe limb defects. A third of these 'thalidomide' babies died within a month.

Before the 1960s, there were remarkably few restrictions upon the marketing of medicines. Pharmaceutical companies were not under a legal obligation to prove the safety and efficacy of new medicines before putting them into circulation. Unsurprisingly, the thalidomide tragedy prompted interest in regulating the safety of medicines, and the result was the Medicines Act 1968. The 1968 Act set up the MCA which, in 2003, was merged with the Medical Devices Agency to form the MHRA. In 2012, the Medicines Act and the bewildering set of amendment regulations which had implemented a series of EU Directives were repealed and consolidated in the Human Medicines Regulations 2012.

(a) MARKETING AUTHORIZATION

Only when clinical trials (considered in the previous chapter) have indicated that a drug is reasonably safe and effective can a drug company apply for what used to be known as a product licence, and is now called a marketing authorization. Before any medicinal product (including generic equivalents of established drugs) can be sold or supplied, under regulation 46(2) of the Human Medicines Regulations, it must have a marketing authorization.

Human Medicines Regulations 2012 regulation 46

46.— ...

(2) A person may not sell or supply, or offer to sell or supply, a medicinal product otherwise than in accordance with the terms of—

(a) a marketing authorisation;

(b) a certificate of registration [this applies to homeopathic 'medicines'];

(c) a traditional herbal registration; or

(d) an Article 126a authorisation [this applies to vitamins that are known to be safe].

Although the Secretary of State for Health is formally responsible for the licensing of medicines, in practice this role is undertaken by the MHRA, with advice from the Commission on Human Medicines (formerly the Committee on the Safety of Medicines (CSM)). Regulation 58(4) specifies a number of factors that the MHRA should take into account when deciding whether to grant a marketing authorization.

---

[31] Pamela Ferguson, *Drug Injuries and the Pursuit of Compensation* (Sweet & Maxwell: London, 1996) 5.

Human Medicines Regulations 2012 regulation 58

58(4) The licensing authority may grant the application only if, having considered the application and the accompanying material, the authority thinks that—

(a) the applicant has established the therapeutic efficacy of the product to which the application relates;

(b) the positive therapeutic effects of the product outweigh the risks to the health of patients or of the public associated with the product;

(c) the application and the accompanying material complies with regulations 49 to 55; and

(d) the product's qualitative and quantitative composition is as described in the application and the accompanying material.

Notice that one factor which is not relevant is the price of the medicinal product. So the fact that a medicine is prohibitively expensive is not a good reason to deny it a marketing authorization. Of course, the National Institute for Health and Care Excellence (see Chapter 2) might subsequently decide that an expensive medicine should not be prescribed within the NHS, but provided that it meets the threshold levels of safety, effectiveness, and quality, it should be granted a marketing authorization.

Also irrelevant to the MHRA's assessment of a drug's efficacy is the comparative question of whether other medicines are equally or more effective than this new one. This is important because it facilitates the licensing of what are known as 'me too' drugs: that is, drugs that are new versions of medicines which are already on the market. The proliferation of 'me too' drugs is criticized here by Angell.

Marcia Angell[32]

[I]n the five years 1998 through 2002, 415 new drugs were approved by the Food and Drug Administration (FDA), of which only 14% were truly innovative. A further 9% were old drugs that had been changed in some way that made them, in the FDA's view, significant improvements. And the remaining 77%? Incredibly, they were all me-too drugs—classified by the agency as being no better than drugs already on the market to treat the same condition. Some of these had different chemical compositions from the originals; most did not. But none were considered improvements.

This travesty is made possible by one crucial weakness in the law—namely, drug companies have to show . . . only that new drugs are 'effective'. They do not have to show that they are *more effective than* (or even as effective as) what is already being used for the same condition. They just have to show that they are better than nothing. . . . If companies had to show their drugs were better than older treatments, there would be far fewer me-too drugs, because not many of them would pass that test. The companies would have no choice but to look for important new drugs, instead of taking the easier and cheaper route of spinning out old ones.

---

[32] *The Truth about the Drug Companies* (Random House: London, 2005) 75–6.

When applying for a marketing authorization, the pharmaceutical company must submit full details of the research that has been carried out and the results obtained, including any adverse reactions. The manufacturer must also provide information about the manufacturing process and quality control mechanisms. It must indicate how the drug will be marketed and must submit any leaflets to be supplied with the product. The Commission on Human Medicines will analyse all of the information submitted by the manufacturer and its recommendation that a medicine should or should not be licensed for use will be based solely upon this industry-submitted data.

Once granted, a marketing authorization lasts for five years, after which a manufacturer must apply for renewal. The House of Commons Health Select Committee criticized the renewal process for being, in practice, a formality rather than a fresh opportunity for rigorous review of the evidence: 'the 5-year renewal procedure has not been used to good effect, and appears to have become an automatic process focusing on safety issues rather than an opportunity to review both efficacy and safety data rigorously'.[33]

If a manufacturer is applying for a marketing authorization for a generic medicine, it is not necessary to supply the MHRA with such full information if it can be demonstrated that the product is 'essentially similar' to a product which has been in circulation for ten years.[34] In *In Re Smith Kline*[35] the applicant company, which had held the patent on Cimetidine for nearly 20 years, did not want the MCA to rely upon its research when considering other companies' applications to manufacture generic versions of its product, claiming that this was confidential information. The House of Lords held that the MCA was under a duty to protect the public, and that when considering applications for product licences for generic versions of a drug, it was necessary to compare the information supplied in the later application with that in the original application, in order to ensure that both products were similarly safe, effective, and reliable. The MCA therefore had a right and a duty to make use of all the information obtained by it under the Act.

A different issue arose in *R (on the application of Merck Sharp & Dohme Ltd) v Licensing Authority*. Merck Sharp and Dohme Limited (MSD) held marketing authorizations for Fosamax 5mg, 10mg (product A) and Fosamax Once Weekly, 70mg (product B), both of which were used to treat osteoporosis. A generics company wished to rely on its data in order to obtain a marketing authorization for a drug (product C) which was identical to product B. Product B (which was essentially seven times the dose of the daily version, to be taken weekly) had not yet been in circulation for the requisite ten years. MSD therefore claimed that the generics company was not entitled to rely on the data for product A, which had been in circulation for more than ten years, because product C's dosage was not 'essentially similar' to product A, only to product B.

Moses J gave this argument short shrift. There were no new safety or efficacy questions in relation to product C, and so requiring the generics company to submit new data would result in unnecessary additional testing, with no benefit to public health. The only purpose of this exercise would be to grant additional protection to innovators' ten-year right to keep their data confidential, and this was not within the spirit of the Directive.

[33] Para 301.　[34] Article 10 of Directive 2001/83/EC, as amended by Directive 2004/27/EC.
[35] [1990] 1 AC 64.

R (on the application of Merck Sharp & Dohme Ltd) v Licensing Authority[36]

Moses J

The right to cross-refer stems from the notion of one medicinal product being 'essentially similar' to another. Public health is safeguarded by ensuring that . . . a medicinal product is only authorised without reliance on further data if it is essentially similar to a product which has already been authorised. . . .

[T]he suggestion that the generic companies should be compelled to produce their own data, from their own tests, in relation to a product which is identical to Fosamax Once Weekly 70mg has nothing whatever to do with safety or efficacy . . . Since it is agreed that the product generic companies wish to develop is identical to Fosamax Once Weekly, any further data the generic companies were required to produce would involve unnecessary testing . . .

Product C is no less safe or efficacious because it is essentially similar to B rather than A. The only purpose to be achieved is to give a further period of protection to innovators.

In *Organon v Department of Health and Social Security*, the Court of Appeal had to consider whether it was appropriate to take into account not only a drug's safety when taken in the recommended dose for its intended purpose, but also its toxicity following overdose. Organon wanted to submit evidence that Mianserin was less toxic than other antidepressants, and hence less likely to be fatal if a patient took an overdose. The CSM considered that it was only entitled to take account of the drug's safety when taken for the purposes indicated in the licence, and hence evidence of toxicity following misuse was not relevant. The Divisional Court disagreed and held that the risks a drug posed if it was misused could be relevant to an assessment of its safety, and this decision was upheld by the Court of Appeal.

Organon v Department of Health and Social Security[37]

Mustill LJ

It strikes me as plain, and this much was virtually conceded, that however sympathetically paragraph (g) is read, administering the drug for the purposes of alleviating the symptoms of depression cannot be stretched to include the taking of the drug for the purpose of suicide . . .

I do not, however, believe that this is the right approach to the Medicines Act, the object of which is to promote public health and safety, and which should, if at all possible, be construed in a way favourable to the attainment of that object. To read paragraph (g) in the narrow sense for which the Authority contends, and which the words at first sight themselves seem to indicate, would work in the opposite direction. This would entail that if the Authority discovered, after the grant of a licence, that although in the intended dosage the drug remained acceptably safe, nevertheless if taken in even moderate excess it was potentially lethal, it would be beyond the Authority's jurisdiction even to consider whether the original risk/benefit analysis should be reconsidered, with a view to variation, suspension or cancellation of the licence. This result strikes me as so absurd that it cannot have

36 [2005] EWHC 710 (Admin).   37 The Times, 6 February 1990.

been within the contemplation of Parliament. It must therefore be taken that the references to 'administered' and 'purposes' extend beyond circumstances which involve strict compliance with the intended use of the drug, and that the risks attaching to misuse can properly be brought into account.

(b) COMPLEMENTARY AND ALTERNATIVE MEDICINE

A special exception from the need to obtain a marketing authorization exists for herbal remedies. Under section 12 of the Medicines Act 1968, herbal remedies which contain only plant materials are exempt from the requirement to obtain a marketing authorization if:

(a) the herbal remedy was made up on the premises from which it was supplied and prescribed after a one-to-one consultation (s 12(1)); or,

(b) if it is a pre-prepared over-the-counter remedy, it is not sold under any brand name, and does not make any written therapeutic claims (s 12(2)).

Over-the-counter herbal remedies which do make therapeutic claims must have a marketing authorization.

A registration scheme for authorizing manufactured over-the-counter traditional herbal medicines (known as the Traditional Herbal Medicines Registration Scheme) was set up in 2005.[38] The scheme applies to traditional herbal remedies, which do not meet the criteria for a marketing authorization under the Medicines Act. Under the terms of the scheme, manufacturers have to demonstrate safety and quality, but not efficacy.

Evidence of efficacy is often unavailable for herbal medicines because randomized-controlled trials, which as we saw in the previous chapter are the 'gold standard' in clinical research, are seldom carried out. Applicants must submit a review of safety data and an expert report on quality, in addition to evidence of at least 30 years of traditional use, 15 of which should have been in the EU. In exceptional circumstances, registration will be possible even if the product has not been in use in the EU for 15 years, but it will still be necessary to prove that it has been used elsewhere for at least 30 years. The product label must inform the consumer that the basis for registration is traditional use, rather than clinical trial data.

In order to avoid the submission of duplicate evidence, the Committee for Herbal Medicinal Products (CHMP), which is part of the European Medicines Agency (EMA), has developed a European 'positive list' of ingredients. Establishing that a product contains an ingredient that is on the indicative list does not necessarily mean that an application for registration will be successful, but it will mean that applicants do not need to submit detailed evidence of safety or traditional use. Evidence of quality will still be necessary.

The assumption behind the 'traditional use' requirement is that there must be some level of efficacy if the remedy has been used for this length of time. This is problematic, to say the least. People have been reading horoscopes and having their palms read for many years, but this does not amount to evidence that astrologers and palm readers can predict the future.

There is also a special scheme for homeopathic 'medicines'. Homeopathy involves taking highly diluted substances, usually in tablet form. It is, however, scientifically improbable. In his evidence to the House of Commons Science and Technology Committee, Professor

---

[38] The Traditional Herbal Medicinal Products Directive (2004/24/EC), Official Journal of the European Union L136/85.

David Colquhoun stated bluntly: 'If homeopathy worked the whole of chemistry and physics would have to be overturned'.[39]

There are two ways in which a new homeopathic product can be registered. First, it can receive a certificate of registration. For this, manufacturers must establish the safety and quality of products, and must make no therapeutic claims.[40] The scheme only applies to medicines for oral or external use, and products must be sufficiently dilute to guarantee safety. Secondly, what are known as national homeopathic medicinal products can be marketed for the relief or treatment of minor symptoms and conditions, defined as those that can be relieved or treated without the supervision or intervention of a doctor. Applications must establish quality, safety, *and efficacy*; that is, they must provide study reports in relation to the product or published scientific literature or what are referred to as 'homoeopathic provings'. The MHRA has suggested that, 'whatever data is provided, it should be sufficient to demonstrate that UK homeopathic practitioners would accept the efficacy of the product for the indications sought'.[41] This, once again, is problematic insofar as it amounts to the claim that a homeopathic medicine works if other people, who believe in homeopathy, believe that it works.

In addition to the questionable assumption that proof of traditional use, or proof that other homeopaths believe it works, amounts to proof of efficacy, two further problematic assumptions underpin the common view that complementary and alternative medicines—while not necessarily very effective—are essentially harmless. First, it is often assumed that anything that is herbal or natural is necessarily safe. This is simply wrong. Many plants—an example would be digoxin from foxgloves—can be highly toxic.

Secondly, it is also often assumed that complementary and alternative medicines are used by the worried well, who may be wasting their money on ineffective 'natural' remedies, but who are not likely to suffer any serious ill effects as a result. Again, this is mistaken. It is common for people with, or at risk of, extremely serious illnesses, like cancer and malaria, to consult alternative medical practitioners.[42] Choosing to rely on alternative medicine may mean that access to effective treatment is delayed or foregone altogether, which may have serious consequences for the person's health,[43] and perhaps for NHS resources as well.

In the next extract, Jonathan Waxman argues that all complementary and alternative medicines should be forced to meet the same standards as conventional medicines.

Jonathan Waxman[44]

So why do patients take alternative medicines? Why is it that science is disregarded? How can it be that treatments that don't work are regarded as life saving? In my view it is because the complementary therapists offer something that we doctors do not offer, they

---

[39] House of Commons Science and Technology Committee, *Evidence Check 2: Homeopathy*, Fourth Report of Session 2009–10, para 59.

[40] Council Directive of 22 September 1992 widening the scope of Directives 65/65/EEC and 75/319/EEC on the approximation of provisions laid down by Law, Regulation or Administrative Action relating to medicinal products and laying down additional provisions on homeopathic medicinal products (92/73/EEC), Official Journal of the European Union L297/8.

[41] 'The Homeopathic National Rules Scheme: Brief Guidance for Manufacturers and Suppliers' (MHRA, 2006).

[42] Eric H Liu et al, 'Use of alternative medicine by patients undergoing cardiac surgery' (2000) 120 Journal of Thoracic and Cardiovascular Surgery 335–41.

[43] Ben Goldacre, 'Benefits and risks of homoeopathy' (2007) 370 The Lancet 1672–3.

[44] 'Shark cartilage in the water' (2006) 333 British Medical Journal 1129.

offer hope, hope of cure. If you eat this, take that, rub with this, manipulate this bit of your cranium, avoid this, and really believe this then we can promise you sincerely that you will be cured . . .

Reclassify these agents as drugs—for this is after all how they are marketed—and protect our patients from vile and cynical exploitation whose intellectual basis, at best, might be viewed as delusional.

(c) CLASSIFICATION OF MEDICINES

In addition to deciding whether to grant a marketing authorization, the MHRA also classifies medicines into one of three categories:

(a) prescription-only medicines (POM);

(b) suppliable by a pharmacist without prescription (P);

(c) general sale list medicines, which can be sold over the counter and do not need to be dispensed by a pharmacist (GSL).

Regulation 62(3) of the Human Medicines Regulations specifies the factors relevant to this classification. When deciding whether a medicine should be prescription-only, the MHRA must consider whether it:

(a) is likely to present a direct or indirect danger to human health, even when used correctly, if used without the supervision of a doctor or dentist; or

(b) is frequently and to a very wide extent used incorrectly, and as a result is likely to present a direct or indirect danger to human health; or

(c) contains substances or preparations of substances of which the activity requires, or the side effects require, further investigation;

(d) is normally prescribed by a doctor or dentist for parenteral administration [ie intravenously or by injection].

Regulation 62(4)(c) also specifies that the Secretary of State should take into account whether a medicine is likely, if incorrectly used, to present a substantial risk of medicinal abuse, lead to addiction, or be used for illegal purposes.

Medicines can be reclassified and, in recent years, an increasing number of prescription-only medicines have been reclassified so that they can be bought in pharmacies. In 2000, for example, the MCA and the CSM agreed that the risks posed by post-coital contraception (the 'morning-after pill') did not justify its prescription-only status, so it was reclassified as a pharmacy-available medicine.

Where self-medication is safe, as is the case in relation to treatments for colds or hay fever, for example, there are obvious advantages in enabling individuals to buy medicines over the counter. This will often be more convenient, and it will save the NHS money; not only will the patient pay for the drug themselves, but also there will be no need for a GP appointment in order to obtain a prescription. Of course, one consequence of reclassification is that the leaflets supplied with medicines become more important, since they may represent the only information the patient receives about how to take the medicine safely. In the next extract, David Prayle and Margaret Brazier evaluate this trend towards the reclassification of medicines.

David Prayle and Margaret Brazier[45]

[T]he pharmaceutical industry has an obvious and powerful interest in reclassification. Increased sales of P and GSL medicines can be expected, particularly as such medicines, unlike POM medicines, can be advertised to the general public. As a number of previously profitable POM medicines reach the stage when patent protection expires, the manufacturer must seek means of combating competition from generic copies. Altering the medicine's status to P and enthusiastically advertising the product under its tried and tested brand name is a useful strategy to maintain, if not increase sales figures.

A brave new world of more open access to medicines beckons. Should it be applauded? A restrictive approach to access to medicines restricts individual autonomy. The longer the list of POM medicines, the less able individuals are to control their own health status via self-diagnosis and self-medication . . . Reducing the list of POM medicines might be seen as enhancing autonomy. The flaw in this approach derives from the anomalous P category of medicines. They can be purchased, but only from a pharmacy under the supervision and control of a pharmacist. Persons seeking a P medicine must in theory submit to an interrogation from the pharmacist (or his assistant) about their familiarity with the drug, their medical history and their potential use of the product. This 'consultation' may well take place before an audience of other customers.

(d) ONLINE PHARMACIES

The system for the classification of medicines rests upon the assumption that it is possible to exercise control over access to prescription-only medicines. The rise of online pharmacies poses a significant challenge to this classificatory system. Some websites offer virtual 'consultations', which may amount to no more than filling in a questionnaire. Doctors employed by the owners of these websites then prescribe and dispense medicines without a face-to-face encounter with the patient. It is hard to see how this is compatible with a doctor's duty of care. General Medical Council (GMC) good practice guidance instructs doctors that:

In providing clinical care you must . . . prescribe drugs or treatment, including repeat prescriptions, only when you have adequate knowledge of the patient's health, and are satisfied that the drugs or treatment serve the patient's needs.[46]

Even more worryingly, there are websites, based offshore, which proudly advertise that there is 'no need for a prescription', and in these cases control over access to prescription-only medicines, or counterfeit products, is non-existent.

For many reasons, it is unwise to buy medicines online. In the absence of a professional gatekeeper, there is no way to ensure that the purchaser's self-diagnosis is accurate. Online pharmacies are also willing to supply medicines to patients in whom they are clearly contraindicated. Gunther Eysenbach, for example, found it easy to obtain Viagra online, despite

---

[45] 'Supply of medicines: paternalism, autonomy and reality' (1998) 24 Journal of Medical Ethics 93–8.
[46] *Good Medical Practice* (GMC, 2013) para 16(a).

pretending to be an obese 69-year-old woman suffering from coronary artery disease and hypertension.[47]

If drugs are purchased from an unregistered online pharmacy, they are more likely than not to be counterfeit medicines.[48] Fake drugs pose a serious risk to consumers' health, both because the substance ingested may be dangerous, or in a dangerous dosage, and because access to effective treatment may be delayed.

Despite these risks, it is increasingly common for people to buy prescription drugs online. One survey found that 15 per cent of British adults had bought a prescription-only medicine online without a prescription. It can be predicted that the number of people buying medicines online is likely to increase significantly. Currently, the group of people most likely to be taking many different medicines, namely the very elderly, is also the section of society which is least likely to be familiar with the internet, and more specifically with using the internet to self-diagnose and manage health problems. As people who spend much of their life online grow older, and suffer from more health problems, use of online pharmacies is likely to become much more common.

The sanctions that exist in relation to online drug supply are focused on the supplier rather than the purchaser. Unless the medicine is a controlled substance—when importing into the UK is subject to particular restrictions—it is not an offence to buy prescription drugs online from an overseas website. It is, however, a criminal offence for someone who is not properly qualified and registered to prescribe and supply a prescription-only medicine. The MHRA monitors online pharmacies, and if websites are based in the UK, and not registered, their owners can be prosecuted. If the MHRA is concerned about a site that is registered abroad, it will inform the relevant regulatory authority in that country, but it is clearly impossible for the MHRA to control the activities of overseas internet pharmacies.

In the next extract, Nicola Glover-Thomas and John Fanning draw attention to a further consequence of the rise of e-pharmacies, namely a blurring of the line between illegal recreational drugs and prescription medicines.

Nicola Glover-Thomas and John Fanning[49]

In some countries, the scale of the abuse of pharmaceutical products is second only to that of cannabis, surpassing all other illicitly produced substances combined . . . e-Pharmacies are beginning to define a generation. The *Wall Street Journal* revealed in March 2008 that some teenagers and young people had begun throwing 'pharm parties', to which they 'bring whatever pharmaceuticals they can find, mix the drugs up in a big bowl and eat them like candy'. . . . Sandhill notes that the increased availability of prescription drugs illustrates 'how hazy the line is that separates the gear you buy from a dealer on the street and the stuff prescribed by the guy in a white coat'.

[47] Gunther Eysenbach, 'Online prescribing of sildanefil (Viagra) on the world wide web' (1999) 1(2) Journal of Medical Internet Research e10.

[48] Susan Mayor, 'More than half of drugs sold online are fake or substandard' (2008) 337 British Medical Journal 618.

[49] 'Medicalisation: The Role of E-Pharmacies in Iatrogenic Harm' (2010) 18 Medical Law Review 28–55.

(e) POST-LICENSING REGULATION

(1) Pharmacovigilance

Because clinical trials are, by necessity, carried out on a relatively small number of patients, compared with the number of eventual users, they will inevitably detect only common adverse reactions. It is therefore important to monitor adverse reactions that are likely to be identified only when the drug is taken by larger groups of patients, including people who are often excluded from clinical trials, such as pregnant women or people with multiple comorbidities. As a result, manufacturers are under a duty to keep a record of all reported adverse drug reactions (ADRs), and report them to the European Medicines Agency's Eudravigilance web-system for the management of safety reports.[50]

The 'yellow card scheme' enables GPs, nurses, midwives, health visitors, and patients to report ADRs electronically.[51] Drugs are divided into two groups for the purposes of the yellow card scheme: new drugs (denoted by a black triangle) are monitored closely for a minimum of two years, during which time all suspected ADRs should be reported. For established drugs, only serious suspected ADRs must be reported. Other areas of special interest have been identified, for which all suspected ADRs should be reported, such as reactions in children and the elderly. In 1996, following the identification of liver toxicity associated with a traditional Chinese medicine, the yellow card scheme was extended to include unlicensed herbal products. Monitoring ADRs from herbal remedies has proved particularly difficult, however, since patients appear to be less likely both to attribute symptoms to the herbal medicine and to consult their doctor about their adverse reaction.

In 2014, 31,544 ADRs were reported, 86 per cent of which were classified as 'serious'.[52] This number, while high, is a massive underestimate: most ADRs are not reported. The purpose of the yellow card scheme is not, however, to provide accurate data on the extent of ADRs, but rather to signal the existence of potential problems, so that they can be investigated further.

Very few products are withdrawn as a result of safety concerns. The existence of an adverse reaction does not necessarily mean that a medicine has become unacceptably unsafe. Aspirin is unsafe for use in children, for example, but that does not mean that it should not be available to other patients, who benefit enormously from it. It is necessary to balance the risks to a minority of patients against the benefits the drug may have for the majority, and so, rather than withdrawing a product which causes adverse reactions in some users, a more appropriate response might be to give a more specific warning about contraindications for its use.

As we see in the next section, there has been substantial criticism of the MHRA's post-licensing surveillance system. The House of Commons Health Select Committee found that it concentrated its efforts on scrutiny of pre-marketing data, and gave too little attention to post-marketing surveillance. Witnesses had suggested to the Committee that this might be because it is not in the MHRA's interests to discover that its initial findings on safety were mistaken.

---

[50] Directive 2010/84/EU amending, as regards pharmacovigilance, Directive 2001/83/EC on the Community code relating to medicinal products for human use.

[51] www.yellowcard.mhra.gov.uk.

[52] *Human Medicines Regulations 2012: Annual Report 2014* (MHRA, 2015).

House of Commons Health Select Committee[53]

Several witnesses expressed concerns not only about the relatively weak emphasis on post-marketing investigations, but also about possible conflicts of interest that might arise when the same Agency is responsible for both pre- and post-marketing drug evaluation: if problems arise once a drug is on the market, it might indicate flaws in the original assessment and require the regulators to examine their own earlier failings.

(2) Marketing

Schedule 27 of the Regulations specifies the information that must be provided with a medicine, such as instructions for use, contraindications, and warnings about side effects. Leaflets supplied with medicines must contain information about its active ingredients; indications for its use; warnings about the product's interaction with other substances, such as alcohol; and about any effect it might have on the user's capacity to drive or operate machinery. Dosage instructions, such as how the medicine should be taken, and how frequently, must also be included, and if appropriate, what should be done in the event of an overdose.

The advertising of medicines is also controlled. Prescription-only medicines cannot be marketed directly to the public (unlike in the US), but they can be advertised to health care professionals. As well as marketing their products to doctors, the pharmaceutical industry sponsors 'disease awareness' campaigns, which can involve briefing journalists or providing web-based resources. These can be effective ways of drawing the public's attention to the possibility that they might have a condition, and to the existence of effective drugs. The aim of these initiatives is to persuade people, who may not have realized that they have a medical condition, to visit their GP and ask for treatment. Where there is only one medicine to treat a condition, promoting that condition to the public comes very close to direct promotion of that product.

The House of Commons Health Select Committee found that the ban on direct advertising to consumers does not stop the pharmaceutical industry from thinking creatively about how to persuade more people to make an appointment to discuss their symptoms with their GP, in the hope that this will increase prescription rates.

House of Commons Health Select Committee[54]

There is clear evidence that the industry is concerned with identifying populations who are not currently presenting for diagnosis. In one document relating to the 'strategic planning process,' these patients, who, 'do not currently present to their GP or take prescription medications,' are referred to as 'the missing millions' and are estimated to comprise almost 2 million people in the UK. This population is viewed as providing a 'significant opportunity' for the company.

Research is then conducted on behalf of the company that aims to understand what barriers exist to prevent these people from presenting and to identify factors, both rational and emotional, that will overcome these barriers and encourage patients to seek professional advice.

---

[53] *The Influence of the Pharmaceutical Industry*, Fourth Report of Session 2004–05, para 302.
[54] Ibid, paras 253–4.

The pharmaceutical industry also attempts to influence prescribing practices by funding and supporting patient groups, as explained by Tim Kendall, a psychiatrist who gave evidence to the Health Select Committee:

> I am aware that there are some . . . like Depression Alliance, which have very substantial funding at times from drug companies. They do lobby for an increased accessibility to drugs which the drug companies are selling to these patient organisations. They are persuading them that these are the drugs they must have, with very little evidence to support it.[55]

The Health Select Committee was critical of this process.

House of Commons Health Select Committee[56]

> This leads to a situation in which, instead of representing the interests of patients, groups 'become marketing tools for the pharmaceutical companies'. Referral by the pharmaceutical industry to patient organisations as 'ground troops' for lobbying Government to increase access to new drugs is further evidence of this . . . The pharmaceutical industry's promotional efforts are relentless and pervasive. The evidence presented showed the lengths to which the industry goes to ensure that promotional messages reach their targets, and that these targets include not only prescribing groups, but patients and the general public.

(f) THE IMPACT OF REGULATION

Obviously, the stricter the licensing requirements, the more difficult it is to introduce new medicines to the market. A stringent regulatory framework might then increase patient safety, but at the cost of stifling innovation, which in turn may mean that patients are denied access to beneficial medicines. In the next extract, Harvey Teff claims that regulators are likely be risk-averse, since the damage to their reputation should they license another thalidomide would be catastrophic, whereas any risk to public health through not licensing a potentially beneficial medicine will be much less visible:

> [T]he regulator tends to be unduly risk averse. In the context of pharmaceuticals, he has little or nothing to lose by refusing, or at least delaying, the grant of a licence; everything to lose if he approves a thalidomide. Thus where guidelines are bound to be arbitrary to some extent—how many species of animals should be tested, over what period of time, for what risks—the regulator is prone to err on the side of caution, to indulge in a kind of 'defensive licensing'.[57]

---

[55] Ibid, para 265.   [56] Ibid, paras 267, 271.
[57] 'Regulation under the Medicines Act 1968: A Continuing Prescription for Health' (1984) 47 Modern Law Review 303–23.

This, however, is now an unusual view. In the next extract, John Abraham argues that the pharmaceutical industry has too much influence over the licensing authority, leading to what he describes as 'regulatory capture'.

John Abraham[58]

Pharmaceutical firms have well-oiled lobbying strategies to capture regulatory agencies: more subtly, industry can penetrate into the heart of regulatory political subculture via the so-called revolving door . . . In the UK, a large proportion of scientists in the British drug regulatory authority started their careers in industry, and many move back there . . .

Regulatory capture is especially important because the risk–benefit assessment of drugs has a high degree of technical uncertainty, which is inherent in toxicology, clinical trials, and epidemiology. Therefore, it is crucial to know how far regulators are willing to give the manufacturer the benefit of scientific doubt about safety and efficacy of their product. Indeed, regulators too often consistently award industry the benefit of scientific doubt when reviewing products.

For the past 50 years, industry has been quick to ward off regulation it perceives to be contrary to its interests by threatening that such regulation will have damaging results for the nation's export trade, balance of payments, or employment. Too often, regulatory agencies have accepted these threats uncritically.

Several criticisms are commonly made of the UK's licensing system. First, the MHRA is funded entirely by the pharmaceutical industry, through licensing and other fees. This undoubtedly leads to pressure on the MHRA to provide a speedy licensing service.

House of Commons Health Select Committee[59]

In return for the licensing and service fees paid by the industry, companies expect an efficient and rapid service . . . The speed at which the UK regulatory authority has historically processed licence applications has been one of the fastest in the world, which means that its services are much in demand from EU applications. In 2003, time from application to the granting of a licence of a new chemical entity, if no further information was needed, was approximately 70 working days, whereas a response may now usually be expected in approximately 30 working days.

Secondly, the MHRA relies on company data, presented as a series of detailed assessment reports, in its decision whether or not to license a drug. Raw data is rarely analysed, leading the House of Commons Health Select Committee to suggest that the MHRA may be too 'trusting'.

---

[58] 'The pharmaceutical industry as a political player' (2002) 360 The Lancet 1498–502.
[59] Paras 99, 100.

House of Commons Health Select Committee[60]

Trust is critical in the relationship between regulators and industry. However, at the heart of this inquiry are the concerns of those who believe that the MHRA is too trusting. Trust should be based on robust evidence; it should be earned rather than presupposed. The evidence indicated that the MHRA examined primary (raw) data on drug effects only if it suspected some misrepresentation in the summary data supplied. It was argued that such trust in regulated companies goes too far: reliance on company summaries is neither sufficient nor appropriate, in the absence of effective audit and verification of data that companies provide. The secrecy surrounding this information is also unacceptable.

The Health Select Committee's conclusions on the regulator's performance were damning.

House of Commons Health Select Committee[61]

The regulatory authority, which is responsible for controlling much of the behaviour of the industry has significant failings. Lack of transparency has played a major part in allowing failings to continue. The traditional secrecy in the drug regulatory process has insulated regulators from the feedback that would otherwise check, test and stimulate their policies and performance. Failure can be measured by the MHRA's poor history in recognising drug risks, poor communication and lack of public trust. Regulatory secrecy also underpins publication bias, and other unacceptable practices. The closeness that has developed between regulators and companies has deprived the industry of rigorous quality control and audit. . . .

Unfortunately, a number of drugs which have been licensed and widely prescribed, have produced severe adverse reactions, and in some cases death, in large numbers of people. In this report we have highlighted the problems with SSRIs antidepressants, notably Seroxat, and the COX-2 inhibitors, Vioxx and Celebrex [drugs for arthritis which were withdrawn in 2004 after it emerged that they had probably caused many thousands of heart attacks and strokes].

Problems with these and other drugs have revealed major failings not just in the pharmaceutical industry relating to the design and presentation of clinical trials and the supply of data to the regulator, but also in the regulatory system. The regulator's analysis of trial data and advice to prescribers and patients have been inadequate and its responses to indications of adverse reactions slow . . .

Such problems are compounded by an excessive reliance on results from premarketing clinical trials, together with a failing system of pharmacovigilance. The lack of pro-active and systematic monitoring of drug effects and health outcomes in normal clinical use is worrying. Improvements in post-marketing surveillance are clearly needed and would, no doubt, have led to the earlier detection of problems with SSRI antidepressants, COX-2 inhibitors and other drugs.

A particularly striking example of failures in the system of pharmacovigilance emerged in March 2008, when the MHRA announced that there would be no prosecution of GlaxoSmithKline (GSK), for withholding trial data and meta-analyses, which demonstrated conclusively that paroxetine should not be prescribed to under-18s.

GSK had carried out two trials, Studies 329 and 377, which tested the efficacy of paroxetine (known as Seroxat in the UK and Paxil in the US) in children and adolescents in

---

[60] Para 284.   [61] Paras 340, 342–3, 349.

the mid-1990s in 11 countries. The trials were concluded by October 1998. The data, and a meta-analysis carried out on the data in 2002, were not submitted to the MHRA until May 2003, as part of an application to extend Seroxat's licensed indications for use. As soon as it was received, this information was analysed by the Committee on the Safety of Medicines, which found that it provided clear evidence (a) that 'there is no good evidence of efficacy in major depressive disorder in the population studied';[62] and (b) that there was 'a clear increase in suicidal behaviour versus placebo'.[63] The MHRA immediately published a 'Dear Doctor' letter, informing doctors that Seroxat should not be prescribed to under-18s. A few months later, a criminal investigation into GSK's failure to submit this data was launched.

In early 2004, a leaked internal GSK document suggested that the decision to withhold Studies 329 and 377 had been intentional. The document, dated October 1998, stated that it would be 'commercially unacceptable to include a statement that efficacy had not been demonstrated, as this would undermine the profile of paroxetine'.[64]

Following a four-and-a-half year criminal investigation, the conclusion was reached that GSK could not be prosecuted for withholding this data, not because GSK had acted properly, but because the law was insufficiently clear to give a reasonable prospect of conviction. This was because the duty placed upon manufacturers to provide '*any* information relevant to the evaluation of benefits and risks' (my emphasis), could be read as applying only to information which emerged during 'normal conditions of use'.

Seroxat had not been specifically licensed for use in children, because at the time carrying out paediatric clinical trials was not encouraged, and so its widespread use by under-18s was effectively 'off label'. Perhaps ironically, GSK had carried out paediatric trials, but again because these adverse reactions had emerged during trials, and not during 'normal conditions of use', they were not captured by the relevant provisions. The duty to report adverse reactions in clinical trials, then in section 31 of the Medicines Act, at the relevant time only applied to UK trials, and so again did not bite on this withheld data.

Linsey McGoey and Emily Jackson[65]

The existence of so many qualifications to what initially looks like a clear and comprehensive duty to submit '*any* other information relevant to the evaluation of the benefits and risks afforded by a medicinal product' is perhaps surprising. Certainly, two ordinary rules of statutory interpretation would militate against this conclusion. First, the words used in legislation are normally assumed to have their 'ordinary language meaning', unless otherwise specified. Use of the word 'any', according to the Oxford English Dictionary, captures the idea of 'indifference as to the particular one or ones that may be selected', which would suggest that 'any relevant information' should not, without a clear indication to the contrary, be qualified to mean 'only information gathered in a particular setting'.

The second rule of statutory interpretation which is at odds with the existence of these legal loopholes is that, in the event of statutory ambiguity, it is legitimate to ask what the legislator's intention was in drafting the provision in question. Here the intention was evidently

---

[62] MHRA Assessment Report: Paroxetine (Seroxat) 4 June 2003.   [63] Ibid.

[64] 'GSK Seroxat/Paxil Adolescent Depression: Position Piece on the Phase III Clinical Studies', available at https://www.justice.gov/sites/default/files/opa/legacy/2012/07/02/complaint-ex1.pdf.

[65] 'Seroxat and the suppression of clinical trial data: regulatory failure and the uses of legal ambiguity' (2009) 35 Journal of Medical Ethics 107–12.

> to create a duty to report all relevant data, and in particular, to disclose suspected adverse reactions and other information relevant to the regulator's evaluation of risks and benefits.
>
> The interpretation of the law which has led to the decision not to prosecute would seem to subvert the intention of the creators of the regulatory regime, which was indubitably not to provide a series of 'get-out' clauses for drugs companies who withhold, deliberately, evidence of lack of efficacy and serious side effects for a group of patients who are routinely being prescribed the drug in question.

Following the collapse of this criminal investigation, the MHRA pressed for an immediate change in the law, in order to provide for a comprehensive duty of candour.

Human Medicines Regulations 2012 regulation 75

75.—(1) The holder of a UK marketing authorisation must provide the licensing authority with any new information that might entail the variation of the authorisation.

(2) The holder must, in particular, provide the licensing authority with the following information—

(a) information about any prohibition or restriction imposed in relation to the product to which the authorisation relates by the competent authority of any country in which the product is on the market;

(b) positive and negative results of clinical trials or other studies in all indications and populations, whether or not included in the marketing authorisation;

(c) data on the use of the medicinal product where such use is outside the terms of the marketing authorisation; and

(d) any other information that the holder considers might influence the evaluation of the benefits and risks of the product.

4 EUROPEAN REGULATION

European regulation of the pharmaceutical industry has become increasingly important. Its two principal aims are to protect consumer safety, and to harmonize the regulatory regimes throughout Europe in order to facilitate trade and the free movement of goods.

There has been progressive harmonization of rules on labelling and package leaflets,[66] advertising,[67] and the reporting of adverse side effects.[68] These Directives amended the UK's regulations and are now consolidated in the Human Medicines Regulations 2012. The European Medicines Agency (EMA) was established in 1993, and a European system for the authorization of medicinal products was set up in January 1995. It offers two routes for the licensing of medicinal products, both with strict timetables:

(a) A centralized procedure with applications made directly to EMA.[69] Assessments are carried out by a sub-committee, the Committee for Medicinal Products for Human Use (CHMP). Use of this procedure is compulsory for products derived from biotechnology and other high-technology processes, and for medicines intended for the

---

[66] Directive 92/27/EEC.   [67] Directive 92/28/EEC.   [68] Directive 75/319/EEC.
[69] Directive 93/41/EEC, Council Regulation (EEC) No 2309/93.

treatment of HIV/AIDS, cancer, diabetes, neurodegenerative diseases, autoimmune and other immune dysfunctions, and viral diseases, as well as so-called 'orphan medicines' for the treatment of rare diseases.

(b) In the mutual recognition procedure, the application for a medicine's marketing authorization is made to the Regulatory Authority in one EU Member State, which makes its decision in accordance with its national procedures. The manufacturer can then seek further marketing authorizations from other EU countries, which agree to recognize the validity of the original, national marketing authorization. Member States are entitled to object to the mutual recognition of another country's marketing authorization on the grounds that the product poses a risk to public health, although they do not have the final say, and following arbitration, the decision is taken centrally.

Under the mutual recognition procedure, European regulatory agencies are effectively in competition with each other for regulatory business, which is especially significant given that the drug's manufacturer must pay a fee to the regulator. A drug company seeking to market a new drug throughout Europe can obtain a marketing authorization in any EU country, and it will obviously select the one with the speediest and least demanding licensing regime. It is probably unsurprising that approval times for new medicines have been dropping throughout Europe. While this is good news for the pharmaceutical industry, it has been argued that it amounts to a 'race to the bottom' towards increasingly and perhaps dangerously light-touch regulation.[70]

Govin Permanand has argued that EU regulation is dominated by the interests of the pharmaceutical industry, rather than by patient safety considerations. There is, for example, no indication that patients have benefited from EMA's faster approval times.[71]

Govin Permanand[72]

Recent murmuring by several of the larger European multinationals about relocating their R&D elsewhere (specifically to the US where the research environment is said to be more conducive) has seen not just the member states, but so too the Commission, seek to placate the industry on a number of levels e.g. intellectual property rights and preferential tax arrangements. . . . The reason for the Commission's supportive approach to the industry in general is clear. The pharmaceutical industry is a major contributor to the European economy . . .

In the case of the EMA 'policy', . . . industry was heavily involved throughout the policy-process. The Commission's first point of contact was the industry—to ascertain its views and requirements . . . Consequently, industry's demands helped to ensure an agency remit which, in many respects, is limited to speeding market approval rather than quality of assessment.

Efforts to harmonize the regulation of medicines also exist outside the EU. Mutual recognition arrangements exist between the EU and Switzerland, Canada, Australia, and New Zealand, and are intended to facilitate trade by eliminating the need to undergo duplicate testing and scrutiny of new products.

---

[70] John Abraham and Graham Lewis, 'Harmonising and competing for medicines regulation: how healthy are the EU's systems of drug approval?' (1999) 48 Social Science and Medicine 1655–67.

[71] Peter Edmonds, Dermot Glynn, and Claudia Oglialoro, 'Access to important new medicines' (2000) 13 European Business Journal 146–58.

[72] *EU Pharmaceutical Regulation* (Manchester UP: Manchester, 2006).

The International Conference on Harmonisation (ICH), launched in 1990, attempts to harmonize regulatory requirements in the US, Europe, and Japan, so that a company can prepare the same data set in order to obtain approval worldwide.[73] The first ICH steering committee reaffirmed its:

> commitment to increased international harmonisation, aimed at ensuring that good quality, safe and effective medicines are developed and registered in the most efficient and cost-effective manner. These activities are pursued in the interest of the consumer and public health, to prevent unnecessary duplication of clinical trials in humans and to minimise the use of animal testing without compromising the regulatory obligations of safety and effectiveness.

Again, the question arises whether international harmonization can possibly achieve the twin goals of speeding up the licensing of medicines and improving safety standards, when these inevitably may be in tension with each other. Abraham and Reed's study suggests that industry interests have taken priority.

John Abraham and Tim Reed[74]

> [W]e conclude that, in the field of carcinogenicity testing, the ICH management of international harmonisation of medicines regulation is not achieving the simultaneous improvements in safety standards and acceleration of drug development . . . Rather, our research supports the more sceptical view that the latter is being achieved *at the expense of* the former. . . . Reductions in drug testing requirements and increased flexibility in interpretations of what counts as evidence of carcinogenic risk make it easier for regulators to approve drugs—and approve them more quickly.

5 PRODUCT LIABILITY

No drug is 100 per cent safe; most will produce ADRs in some users. A patient who suffers an ADR will only have a remedy if she can establish that the medicine was unacceptably unsafe, such that it should not have been marketed at all; or that it was unsafe for her, and so it either should not have been prescribed to her, or that it should have been marketed with an appropriate warning. In the following sections, we briefly consider the options open to a patient who wishes to seek compensation for injuries suffered as a result of taking a medicine.

(a) CONTRACT

Contractual remedies are of limited relevance to people who suffer drug-related injuries. Consumers of medicines do not buy them from their manufacturers. When a drug is prescribed under an NHS prescription, there will be no contract with either the pharmacist or

---

[73] See further www.ich.org.

[74] 'Reshaping the carcinogenic risk assessment of medicines: international harmonisation for drug safety, industry/regulator efficiency or both?' (2003) 57 Social Science & Medicine 195–204.

the doctor who wrote the prescription.[75] It is only when drugs are supplied privately, or when medicines are bought over the counter, that a contractual remedy for a defective medicine is possible.

If the consumer does have a contract, either with the pharmacist or with a doctor dispensing a private prescription, then the ordinary rules of contract law apply. If the product does not correspond with its description, or is not of satisfactory quality, there might be a breach of the Sale of Goods Act 1979.[76] Liability does not require proof of fault. It would be relatively straightforward to establish liability for what are known as manufacturing defects, such as the contamination of a particular batch of medicines. But since almost all drugs cause side effects, it will be difficult to establish that an adverse reaction to a medicine breaches the implied condition of satisfactory quality.

One complicated question raised by the application of contract law to the sale of medicines relates to sections 14(2B) and 14(3) of the Sale of Goods Act, under which goods must be fit for the purpose for which they are commonly supplied, or if the buyer makes known the particular purpose for which they are being bought, that they are reasonably fit for that purpose. How much information about the consumer's condition must the pharmacist obtain in order to assess whether the medicine is fit for the purpose for which it is being bought? If a consumer has a contraindication, such as high blood pressure or diabetes, for taking an over-the-counter medicine, then arguably that medicine is not fit for the purpose for which she has bought it. Pharmacists who fail to inquire whether a medicine is fit for the purpose for which the particular consumer has purchased it might then find themselves strictly liable for any consequent injuries.

(b) NEGLIGENCE

The manufacturer of a medicine could be liable in negligence if the consumer can prove that she was owed a duty of care, and that the manufacturer's breach of that duty caused her injury. Since *Donoghue v Stevenson*,[77] it is uncontroversial that manufacturers owe the ultimate consumers of their products a duty to take reasonable care to ensure that the product is safe, so establishing the existence of a duty of care will be straightforward.

In order to determine whether the manufacturer has breached its duty, it is necessary to work out what standard of care a pharmaceutical manufacturer owes to the consumers of its products. The duty is to exercise such care as is reasonable in all the circumstances. Factors relevant to this assessment include the magnitude of any risk; the probability of harm; the burden of taking precautions to prevent the risk materializing; and the utility of the defendant's conduct. Manufacturers are certainly not under a duty to ensure that every drug is completely safe for every consumer. All medicines present some risks: penicillin, for example, is generally considered safe and effective, even though it causes very serious allergic reactions in some people.

Three different types of product defect might be identified: manufacturing defects, design defects, and the failure to give adequate warnings. It will be relatively straightforward to prove that there has been a breach of duty when the patient's injury was caused by a manufacturing defect: an example might be where an error during the manufacturing process massively increased the quantity of the active ingredient in each pill. A manufacturer that

---

[75] *Pfizer Corporation v Minister of Health* [1965] 2 WLR 387.
[76] Sections 14(2) and 14(3), as amended.   [77] [1932] AC 562.

does not take reasonable care to ensure that medicines leave its premises in a fit state for human ingestion would clearly be in breach of its duty to consumers.

Design defects are more complicated. Plainly, manufacturers have a duty to design medicines safely, but particular difficulties arise if an unforeseen adverse side effect subsequently emerges, as happened with thalidomide. The claimants would have to prove that the risk of injury was foreseeable, and that supplying the product in the light of this risk was unreasonable. Not only will it be very difficult for claimants to gain access to the information necessary to prove this, but also clinical trials cannot be expected to discover every possible side effect in every possible consumer. The benefits of new medicines mean that it will generally be reasonable to put them into circulation once clinical trials indicate that they meet an acceptable level of safety.

It would not be reasonable to expect manufacturers to have identified all ADRs before marketing a new drug: this would stifle innovation, unreasonably delay the availability of potentially valuable new medicines, and require vastly increased rates of participation in clinical trials. If the company that manufactured thalidomide could not reasonably have been expected to have found out that it would cause devastating birth defects if taken at a particular time in pregnancy, it would not have been in breach of its duty of care.

Manufacturers might also be liable for defective warnings. No drug is completely safe for all users, and a manufacturer will generally have acted reasonably if it took steps to alert consumers to the risk of a side effect, or to contraindications for use. Prescription drugs are a rather special case in that it is not necessary for them to be made safe for everyone. Unlike products that can be bought over the counter, it should be possible to ensure that a drug is not prescribed to individuals in whom it would be unsafe. If, for example, the information supplied to doctors categorically states that medicine X should never be taken by anyone with high blood pressure, the manufacturer would be able to avoid liability if someone with high blood pressure subsequently suffers injuries after being wrongly prescribed medicine X.

In the US, this is known as the 'learned intermediary' rule: that is, it is for the doctor to determine whether to prescribe a particular drug to her patient, and to give appropriate warnings. Patients generally rely upon their doctors' advice, and a manufacturer's package insert is unlikely to override assurance from their GP that they can safely take the prescribed medicine. Of course, doctors might make prescribing errors or fail to explain how to take the medicine safely. If a patient then wanted to sue her GP, this would be a straightforward clinical negligence action (see Chapter 3).

If the patient's claim is that a manufacturer's failure to warn her of possible side effects caused her injury, then even if she succeeds in establishing that it breached its duty of care, she will come up against the vexed problem of proving causation in 'failure to warn' cases (considered in Chapter 4). In short, the problem is that she must prove that she would not have been injured if she had been properly informed and, in this context, this means that she must establish that she would not have taken the drug in question if she had been warned of the particular side effect. Let us imagine that a patient was not warned about a 0.1 per cent risk of hair loss associated with taking an antidepressant. Even if she had been warned, she might have judged that the benefits of alleviating her depression outweighed this very small risk of losing her hair. But after this risk has materialized, and with the benefit of hindsight, she now knows for certain that she is the one of the unfortunate minority who will suffer hair loss. How reliable is her evidence that, if she had known about this tiny risk, she would have chosen not to take the drug?

Pharmacists also owe the consumers of medicines a duty of care. If a pharmacist negligently dispenses the wrong drug, or the wrong dosage, she could be liable for the resulting injury. In *Prendergast v Sam and Dee Ltd*,[78] a doctor had written a prescription for Mr Prendergast, an asthmatic suffering from a chest infection, which included Amoxil tablets. The pharmacist misread the doctor's unclear handwriting, and dispensed Daonil instead, a drug used in the treatment of diabetes. As a result of taking an excessive dose of Daonil, Mr Prendergast suffered permanent brain damage. He sued both the doctor and the pharmacist, and both were found to have been negligent. Despite the unclear handwriting, the pharmacist should have realized that it was extremely unlikely that the doctor had meant to write Daonil on the prescription. The prescription was for a short course of Amoxil, to be taken three times a day. Diabetics would usually be on continuous courses of Daonil, which is taken only once a day. The dosage would also have been unusually high for Daonil. Since Mr Prendergast paid for his prescription, the pharmacist should have realized that he was not diabetic (people with diabetes do not pay the prescription charge). The Court of Appeal refused to overturn the judge's apportionment of liability: the pharmacist was liable to pay 75 per cent of Mr Prendergast's damages, and the doctor 25 per cent.

Might it also be possible for an injured patient to bring an action against the regulator for its failure to ensure that a drug was safe enough? Liability for breach of statutory duty is extremely unlikely, since it seems implausible that parliament intended to create a private law action for damages for breach of the Human Medicines Regulations, which were passed in order to protect public health, rather than to provide redress to individuals. In a negligence action, it would be necessary for the claimant to establish that there was a relationship of proximity between the regulatory agency and the injured patient, and that it would be fair, just, and reasonable to impose a duty in these circumstances.

In *Smith v Secretary of State for Health (on behalf of the Committee on Safety of Medicines)*, an aspirin tablet had been given on two consecutive days to Amanda Smith, a six-year-old, suffering from chickenpox. Her condition worsened, and she was diagnosed with Reye's syndrome. A month later, her parents discovered that the CSM had advised that aspirin should not be given to children under the age of 12, except on medical advice. The status of warnings on aspirin was due to be changed, and junior aspirin was about to be reclassified. Amanda became permanently disabled with spastic tetraplegia, frequent epileptic convulsions, and lack of speech. She brought an action for negligence, arguing that the Secretary of State for Health or the CSM was liable for failure to issue public warnings immediately after it had decided to change its advice on aspirin.

Smith v Secretary of State for Health (on behalf of the Committee on Safety of Medicines)[79]

Morland J

In my judgment, no common law duty was owed by the CSM or the Secretary of State in respect of the decisions allegedly negligent, even if there was fault in failing to stick to the original timetable. . . .

I wish to make it clear that I am not asserting that the Secretary of State or the CSM could never be liable at common law for breach of duty of care to an individual member of the public from a failure to exercise or a improper exercise of statutory powers and duties: for example, if the Secretary of State had delayed implementation of the CSM 29/30 May decision until

---

[78] The Times, 14 March 1989.   [79] [2002] EWHC 200 (QB).

> after a bye-election in a marginal constituency where there was a large aspirin factory; or if
> the CSM had postponed its May meeting until the end of June because it clashed with the
> Epsom Derby meeting.

Even if a claimant were to succeed in establishing that a regulatory authority owed her a duty of care, proving that it had breached its duty would not be straightforward. If the CSM's duty is to act in accordance with a responsible body of medical opinion, given that it is composed of medical experts, proving that their collective judgement represented a breach of their duty of care would be exceptionally difficult.

(c) CONSUMER PROTECTION ACT 1987

In 1985, the EU adopted a Directive which was intended to harmonize European product liability regimes,[80] both in order to remove the distorting impact differing standards of legal liability within the EU were having upon competition, and to ensure that consumers throughout Europe enjoyed equal protection against dangerous products through the introduction of a strict liability regime.

Strict liability promotes loss spreading: rather than the costs of injuries falling on individual consumers, they will be borne by manufacturers, who are better able to absorb and spread the costs by purchasing insurance and raising prices, so the costs are ultimately borne by all consumers. The Directive included a number of defences which were intended to lighten the insurance burden on industry. Jane Stapleton argues that by trying to protect both consumers and businesses, the Directive was a classic example of 'Euro-fudge'.

Jane Stapleton[81]

> The Directive did not result from some perceived bottom-up forensic pressure from claims.
> Rather, the engine of this reform was social and political. In particular, the concern of the
> public in these countries had been galvanized by the disaster caused by the unforeseen side
> effects of the thalidomide pregnancy drug. Meanwhile, by the late 1970s, the European
> Commission was keen to promote consumer protection measures to show Europeans that
> the 'common market' was not there simply to serve big business. It proposed very pro-
> consumer draft Directives in 1976 and 1979. Yet there remained intense concern within the
> European Parliament and the Council that substantial exculpatory provisions be included in
> any future Directive.
>
> As a result, the Directive is one of the high-water marks of Euro-fudge and textual
> vagueness. The point is that the Directive tries to square a circle: it uses the rhetoric of
> 'strict liability,' and yet, in Articles 6(2) and 7(e), it seems to provide solid protection for
> reasonable businesses, a compromise demanded by the UK Government of Margaret
> Thatcher.

The Directive was given effect in the UK by the Consumer Protection Act 1987 (CPA). There are some differences in wording between the Directive and the CPA, but in *Commission*

---

[80] Products Liability 85/374/EEC.
[81] 'Bugs in Anglo-American Products Liability' (2002) 53 South Carolina Law Review 1225.

v United Kingdom,[82] the European Court of Justice (ECJ) found that there was no evidence that the UK courts were interpreting the Act in a way that was inconsistent with the Directive, though this may have been because there had been virtually no cases. In any case, section 1 of the CPA specifically states that the provisions in the relevant part of the Act were passed in order to comply with the Directive, and should be construed accordingly.

In *A v National Blood Authority*,[83] Burton J relied upon the judgment in *Commission v United Kingdom*[84] and section 1 of the CPA as evidence that the Act must be interpreted consistently with the Directive. In the spirit of consistency, he decided to go straight to the Directive and apply it directly.

The Act imposes strict liability on manufacturers and, in certain circumstances, suppliers for defective products which cause physical injury, or property damage greater than €500. Pure economic loss is not covered. Any claim must be brought within three years of the discovery of the damage or injury, with a longstop of ten years from when the product was first put into circulation. This ten-year time limit is intended to make it easier for manufacturers to insure against liability, because no claims are possible more than ten years after a product reaches the marketplace. Some adverse reactions take many years to manifest themselves, and if this happens more than ten years after the product was first marketed, the consumer's only option will be an action in negligence

Because the Act only applies to products put into circulation after it came into force in 1988, it could have been anticipated that there would be relatively little litigation immediately following its introduction. The paucity of cases in the past decades has, however, been surprising—certainly the evidence does not bear out Lord Griffiths (writing extra-judicially) et al's prediction in 1988: 'We have little doubt that, once it is no longer necessary to prove negligence, there will be a significant increase in product liability litigation in England.'[85]

There have been hardly any reported cases involving medicines. *XYZ and Others v Schering Health Care Ltd* involved a group action by claimants who had taken different brands of the Combined Oral Contraceptive pill (COC), and who claimed to have suffered various cardio-vascular injuries (which come under the collective description of venous-thromboembolism (VTE)). The women argued that the pills they had taken were defective under the CPA and/or the Product Liability Directive. Their claims followed a 'pill scare' in 1995, when the CSM had written to doctors stating that three unpublished studies into the safety of COCs had indicated 'around a twofold increase in the risk' of VTE. The defendants claimed that there is, in fact, no increased risk and that the CSM's warning was misjudged.

Both the defendants and the claimants agreed that the action under the CPA could proceed only if there was a twofold increase in the risk of VTE associated with oral contraceptive pills. After an extraordinarily lengthy analysis of the evidence, Mackay J concluded that:

> [T]here is not as a matter of probability any increased relative risk of VTE carried by any of the third generation oral contraceptives supplied to these Claimants by the Defendants as compared with second generation products containing Levonorgesterel.[86]

Because the claimants' case had failed on this preliminary issue, it was not necessary for Mackay J to consider the application of the CPA.

---

[82] [1997] All ER (EC) 481.   [83] [2001] 3 All ER 289.   [84] [1997] All ER (EC) 481.
[85] Lord Griffiths, Peter De Val, and RJ Dormer, 'Developments in English Product Liability Law: A Comparison with the American System' (1988) 62 Tulane Law Review 353, 375.
[86] *XYZ and Others v Schering Health Care Ltd* [2002] EWHC 1420 (QB).

In a more recent medicines case, and another one involving a class action, *Multiple Claimants v Sanifo-Synthelabo*,[87] Andrew Smith J was asked to resolve a number of questions, including whether Epilim, an anti-epileptic drug, was defective within the meaning of the Act. The claimants in this case were children whose mothers had taken Epilim during pregnancy. Their claim was that Epilim is a known teratogen (ie that it damages the fetus *in utero*), but for some women it is the only effective treatment for epilepsy. This clearly places pregnant women with epilepsy in an impossible dilemma, but does it mean that the product is 'defective' under the CPA? Andrew Smith J declined to make preliminary findings on this point. Following a number of preliminary hearings and having already provided around £3 million in legal aid, the Legal Services Commission (LSC) withdrew any further funding 'at the door of the courtroom' and the case had to be dropped.

The problem for claimants is that, in the absence of legal aid, this sort of litigation is prohibitively expensive. Because the factual issues are complex, trials involving injuries caused by medicinal products are likely to be lengthy, and so the decision not to grant legal aid, or to withdraw it, will almost inevitably mean that the action cannot continue. This happened in relation to a class action against the manufacturer of the MMR vaccine after the LSC decided that there was insufficient chance of success to justify continued funding. Andrew Wakefield's claim, in 1998, that there was a link between the MMR vaccine and autism has subsequently been completely discredited, and so there would almost certainly be no chance of succeeding on the question of causation.

Legal aid was also refused, more surprisingly, to claimants who wished to sue Merck, the manufacturer of Vioxx, which was withdrawn after evidence emerged that it caused strokes and heart attacks. In the US, actions against Merck, the manufacturer of Vioxx, have been successful, and Merck had set aside $4.85 billion with which to settle further legal claims. After legal aid was refused in the UK, the UK victims attempted to bring actions in the US courts, but these were rejected on the grounds that US juries could not be expected to understand another country's system of drug regulation.[88] Following this decision, one of the lawyers responsible for bringing the claims, Martyn Day, commented: 'We are in a total quandary. I am totally stumped as to how we can get these cases into the courts anywhere . . . [The Vioxx case was] the strongest drug-related case we've seen in the UK for a long time.'[89]

(1) Who Can be Liable?

Under section 2, a number of actors may be jointly and severally liable under the Act. This means that an injured consumer can choose to sue any of the various possible defendants, each of whom may be liable for the total loss. It would then be up to the losing defendant to recoup its losses from the other defendants. Those who can be strictly liable for defective products include producers, importers into the EU, and 'own-brand' suppliers (in relation to medicines, this might mean *Boots* could be liable for defects in their own-brand cold remedies). Under section 2(3) suppliers will be liable if they are unable to identify the producer.

It is clear that a pharmacist is a supplier. Doctors might also be suppliers if they actually provided the medicine, as opposed to simply writing a prescription. To absolve themselves of responsibility, both supplying doctors and pharmacists should therefore keep detailed records of the manufacturers of the drugs which they supply for at least ten years.

---

[87] [2007] EWHC 1860 (QB).

[88] Clare Dyer and Sarah Boseley, 'US court ruling shuts door on drug claimants' compensation hopes', *The Guardian*, 7 October 2006.

[89] Ibid.

(2) What is a Product?

Medicines and medical devices are unquestionably 'products', for the purposes of the Act but, until fairly recently, it was unclear whether human tissues or fluids were covered. In *A v National Blood Authority*,[90] it was accepted by both parties that blood was a product under the Act. While calling them 'products' seems counter-intuitive, it is possible that gametes (ie sperm and eggs) might also be subject to the Act's provisions.

(3) What is a Defect?

In order to have a remedy, the consumer must establish that the product was 'defective'. The definition of defect under section 3 of the Act is, to say the least, rather confusing.

Consumer Protection Act 1987 section 3

> 3(1) Subject to the following provisions of this subsection, there is a defect in a product for the purposes of this Part if the safety of the product is not such as persons generally are entitled to expect; and for those purposes 'safety', in relation to a product, shall include safety with respect to products comprised in that product and safety in the context of risks of damage to property, as well as in the context of risks of death or personal injury.
>
> (2) In determining for the purposes of subsection (1) above what persons generally are entitled to expect in relation to a product all the circumstances shall be taken into account, including—
>
> (a) the manner in which, and purposes for which, the product has been marketed, its get-up, the use of any mark in relation to the product and any instructions for, or warnings with respect to, doing or refraining from doing anything with or in relation to the product;
>
> (b) what might reasonably be expected to be done with or in relation to the product; and
>
> (c) the time when the product was supplied by its producer to another; and nothing in this section shall require a defect to be inferred from the fact alone that the safety of a product which is supplied after that time is greater than the safety of the product in question.

The Act does not distinguish between manufacturing, design, or failure to warn defects. It simply states that a product is defective if its safety is not such as persons generally are entitled to expect. This definition of defect will apply easily and straightforwardly to manufacturing defects, where the product is less safe than it should have been because of a mistake in the production process.

Because manufacturers must have rigorous quality management systems in place, manufacturing defects in medicines are unusual. Instead, patients who have been injured by a medicine will generally want to allege either that its design was defective, or that they were inadequately warned about a particular risk, and in both cases, working out what level of safety 'persons generally' are entitled to expect is more difficult. Indeed, Jane Stapleton has argued that a consumer expectation test is inherently unhelpful: 'The core theoretical problem with the definition, however, is that it is circular. This is because

---

[90] [2001] 3 All ER 289.

what a person is entitled to expect is the very question a definition of defect should be answering.'[91]

In relation to new or complex products, such as medicines, consumers may have no clear expectations about the level of safety they are entitled to expect. Of course, it could be argued that consumers never actually expect to be injured by a medicine,[92] so that any drug which causes injury is defective. The test is an objective one, however: it is what consumers are entitled to expect, and people are not entitled to expect that medicines will never cause unwanted side effects. On the contrary, it is to be expected that medicines which are powerful enough to alter physiological function will sometimes cause adverse reactions.

Section 3(2) sets out a number of factors which are relevant to what consumers generally are entitled to expect, such as, under section 3(2)(a), any warnings provided with the product. Of course, the existence of a warning does not necessarily mean that a product is not defective. If it did, then given the relatively low cost of warnings, manufacturers would simply warn of every conceivable risk in order to avoid liability. This would be undesirable, however, because the danger signal imparted by warnings would be diluted if they became ubiquitous and over-inclusive. Moreover, it should not be possible for manufacturers of manifestly unsafe products, which could have been made safer, to avoid liability by warning of the risk. Rather, warnings should only absolve a manufacturer of liability if avoiding the risk altogether was not feasible.

Also relevant under section 3(2)(b) is what might reasonably be expected to be done with the product. Plainly, this means that injuries caused by taking an overdose are not covered by the Act. A more difficult question is the extent to which it is reasonable to expect consumers to take medicines exactly according to the manufacturer's instructions. Studies suggest that as many as 60 per cent of patients fail to comply with directions for the use of medicines.[93] Because it can reasonably be expected that a patient might take two pills instead of one, or leave too short a time between doses, a medicine should be safe enough even if there is a minor deviation from the product's instructions.

Section 3(2)(c) specifies that a product is not to be considered defective simply because a better product is subsequently put into circulation. A product's defectiveness must be judged according to prevailing safety standards at the time when it was supplied, rather than at the time when the claim is brought.

A different sort of approach to the question of whether a product is defective would be to adopt a straightforward risk/benefit calculation: are the risks which the product presents justified by its benefits? So, for example, aspirin and penicillin cause adverse side effects in a minority of users, but given their overwhelming benefits for other patients, persons generally are not entitled to expect that aspirin or penicillin can safely be taken by everyone.

In contrast, thalidomide might have alleviated morning sickness, but the risks of premature death and severe disability are far too grave to justify its use in relieving nausea in early pregnancy, and adopting a risk/benefit approach, it would therefore be categorized as a defective product. Interestingly, there has been some interest in using thalidomide in the treatment of leprosy and to slow the growth of brain tumours. Gravely ill patients, suffering from advanced brain cancer, are very unlikely to object to the condition that they do not become pregnant while taking thalidomide, and hence for them the benefits may outweigh its risks.

A risk/benefit safety assessment would also enable us to take account of the availability of alternative products. Let us imagine that a new contraceptive pill will cause a very undesirable side effect, such as blindness, in 0.01 per cent of consumers. Not only might we want

[91] *Product Liability* (Butterworths: London, 1994) 234.   [92] Ibid, 235.
[93] Richard Sykes, *New Medicines, The Practice of Medicine, and Public Policy* (Nuffield Trust: London, 2000).

to weigh the risk of blindness against the benefit of effective contraceptive protection, but it would also be relevant that other contraceptive pills exist which do not have this undesirable side effect. If, however, a drug with this risk profile was capable of curing people with stage 4 liver cancer, a 0.01 per cent risk of blindness might be judged acceptable.

So how has the consumer expectation test worked in practice? Before Burton J's judgment in *A v National Blood Authority*, in a handful of cases the courts appeared to suggest that what consumers were entitled to expect depended upon the reasonableness of the defendant's conduct. This looked very like an assessment of whether the defendant had been negligent.

In *Richardson v LRC*,[94] for example, a condom had failed inexplicably. Ian Kennedy J held that although users did not expect condoms to fail, persons generally were not entitled to expect any contraceptive to be 100 per cent effective. He reached this conclusion after extensive discussion of the reasonableness of the testing procedures adopted by the defendants. But if what the defendant could have done differently is relevant to what consumers generally are entitled to expect, 'strict liability' may be indistinguishable from negligence.[95]

This trend towards a negligence-based interpretation of 'defectiveness' was interrupted by the decision of Burton J in *A v National Blood Authority*. The claimants had become infected with Hepatitis C from blood transfusions at a time when it was known that there was a strain of Hepatitis known only as non-A non-B Hepatitis, with which a small percentage of blood was infected. At the time, while the risk was known, reliable tests to identify this new strain of Hepatitis had not yet been devised. In deciding whether the infected blood was defective, Burton J asked himself what consumers were entitled to expect, and explicitly declined to take into account whether the defendants had acted reasonably.

A v National Blood Authority[96]

Burton J

It is quite plain to me that the directive was intended to eliminate proof of fault or negligence. I am satisfied that this was not simply a legal consequence, but that it was also intended to make it easier for claimants to prove their case, such that not only would a consumer not have to prove that the producer did not take reasonable steps, or all reasonable steps, to comply with his duty of care, but also that the producer did not take all legitimately expectable steps either. . . .

I conclude therefore that avoidability is not one of the circumstances to be taken into account within article 6. I am satisfied that it is not a relevant circumstance, because it is outwith the purpose of the directive, and indeed that, had it been intended that it would be included as a derogation from, or at any rate a palliation of, its purpose, then it would certainly have been mentioned; for it would have been an important circumstance.

Crucially, then, Burton J found that whether or not the risk of harm could be avoided was not relevant to what consumers might reasonably expect. Also irrelevant were the costs, difficulty, or impracticability of taking precautionary measures, and the benefit to society or

---

[94] [2000] PIQR P164.
[95] See also *Worsley v Tambrands* [2000] PIQR P95 and *Foster v Biosil* (2000) 59 BMLR 178.
[96] [2001] 3 All ER 289.

the utility of the product. The public, Burton J found, expected blood to be free from infection: 'I am satisfied that the public at large was entitled to expect that the blood transfused to them would be free from infection'.

Whether or not it was possible to ensure that all blood was infection-free did not affect the consumer's expectation that all blood products are safe. As a result, consumers are entitled to expect 100 per cent safety, even if this is an unreasonable and wholly impractical expectation. In the context of HIV-infected blood, Andrew Grubb and David Pearl have, however, argued that consumers do take into account what might reasonably be done to avoid the risk of infection: 'If a reasonable person has any expectation about the safety of blood, it will be that the blood has been tested to the usual extent currently employed.'[97]

The central problem is that a consumer expectation test which excludes considerations of what the defendant could reasonably have done to avoid the risk has an air of artificiality about it, particularly when the test is what people generally are entitled to expect. Are consumers really entitled to expect an unattainable level of safety? Yet once we start to take into account the reasonableness of the defendant's actions, the inquiry begins to look indistinguishable from a negligence action.

One way out of this apparent impasse would be to categorize blood as an unavoidably unsafe product. In *A v National Blood Authority* Burton J accepted that unavoidably unsafe products, such as knives or alcohol, would not be defective under the Act:

> There are some products, which have harmful characteristics in whole or in part, about which no complaint can be made. The examples that were used of products which have obviously dangerous characteristics by virtue of their very nature or intended use, were, on the one hand knives, guns and poisons and on the other hand alcohol, tobacco, perhaps foie gras. . . . Drugs with advertised side effects may fall within this category.

Where a product is unavoidably unsafe, and the danger is generally known, consumers are not entitled to expect 100 per cent safety. Burton J rejected this solution to the problem of infected blood, in part because consumers had not been warned about the risk of infection, and so the danger was not generally known.

In the next extract, Richard Goldberg argues that adopting a risk/benefit approach to the question of whether a product is defective would have made more sense in *A v National Blood Authority*, because it would have allowed the utility of blood to be weighed against the unavoidable risk of infection.

Richard Goldberg[98]

> It is arguable that all medicinal products carry a risk of adverse reactions, even in a minority of consumers, and that these consumers are not necessarily entitled to expect that the products will be risk free. Despite the emphasis on consumer expectation in Burton J's judgment, there is an inherent logic in addressing the problems of defective medicinal products by weighing the risks against the anticipated benefits and against the 'costs' of not using the product, such as the risk of disease.

---

[97] *Blood Testing, AIDS and DNA Profiling* (Jordan: Bristol, 1990) 144.
[98] 'Paying for Bad Blood: Strict Product Liability after the Hepatitis C Litigation' (2002) 10 Medical Law Review 165–200, 174.

In the US, what are known as 'blood shield statutes' have been adopted to exempt blood products from strict liability regimes. In part, this is because a risk/benefit analysis suggests that where the utility of a product is great, and is not achievable by a substitute product, and where the risk of infection is known and unavoidable, strict liability would be unreasonable.

(4) Causation

Even if a claimant does succeed in establishing that a product is defective, the problem of establishing causation remains. The 'but for' test applies, which means that the claimant must prove that 'but for' the defendant's negligence, she would not have suffered her injuries.

There are several reasons why causation causes particular difficulties in product liability cases. People who take medicines are generally ill, which means that their symptoms might be caused by their underlying condition, rather than by a reaction to a medicine. Many adverse drug reactions are indistinguishable from conditions that occur spontaneously, and so may be difficult to prove that the patient's symptoms were caused by a particular medicine.

In addition, patients will often take many different medicines, either simultaneously or over a period of time. Pinpointing which drug was responsible for the adverse reaction is therefore difficult, and exacerbated by the fact that the reaction might have been triggered by a combination of drugs. If each taken singly would be safe, could any manufacturer be said to be responsible for a reaction caused by several drugs' interaction with each other?

In the next extract, Pamela Ferguson discusses some of the practical difficulties which a claimant faces in trying to prove causation.

Pamela Ferguson[99]

Studies have shown that many people who are neither ill nor taking any medication perceive that they are suffering from 'symptoms'. Had such people been receiving drug therapy, they might have attributed their symptoms to the treatment.

A person who is injured by a car which has faulty brakes or by an exploding kettle is at least aware that the car or the kettle was 'involved' in causing the injury . . . This is in contrast to the position with pharmaceutical drugs which may leave little or no trace once consumed . . . [W]hile some people do suffer from immediate allergic reactions to drugs, in the majority of cases . . . , the injuries which are alleged to have been caused by these drugs took several months, or in some cases years, to become manifest.

Even if it is clear that the patient's injuries were caused by taking a particular drug, a further problem is that it might be difficult to prove which manufacturer produced the drug in question. Once a drug can be produced generically, many different manufacturers will be producing an identical product, and by the time the patient's injury materializes, it may be impossible to establish which company manufactured the drug that was taken by this patient. Additionally, patients may have taken the same drug, manufactured by a number of different companies, for several years, in which case it will be virtually impossible to identify which manufacturer's medicine actually caused the patient's injury.

---

[99] *Drug Injuries and the Pursuit of Compensation* (Sweet & Maxwell: London, 1996).

In the US, the courts have adopted a variety of strategies in order to assist claimants who cannot identify the correct defendant. Probably the most well known, derived from the case of *Sindell v Abbott Laboratories*,[100] is 'market share liability' explained by Ferguson in the following extract:

Pamela Ferguson[101]

The market share theory requires a plaintiff to demonstrate that the defendants were responsible for a substantial share of the drug market. Each defendant must then show that it did not produce the particular drug which was responsible for the plaintiff's injury . . . Each manufacturer which fails to demonstrate this is liable to pay a percentage of the compensation awarded to the plaintiff, and this percentage is dependent on the share of the market for which the company was responsible at the relevant time (that is, at the time when the plaintiff's injury or loss occurred). A defendant may bring other producers of the drug into the action as co-defendants.

In essence, market share liability means that the defendants are held liable for creating a risk of harm. Would the English courts be likely to adopt such an approach?

In *Fairchild v Glenhaven Funeral Services*,[102] there was some evidence of a flexible approach to causation. The claimants had suffered mesothelioma as a result of exposure to asbestos in the workplace, but they had worked for a number of companies during their lifetimes, and none could prove which employer had caused their illness. The House of Lords found that each of the employers had increased the risk to the workers, and causation was established against all of them. It is, however, unclear whether *Fairchild* would help people who suffer injuries after taking a drug, which is manufactured by several companies. In *Fairchild* itself, Lord Hoffmann distinguished the market share approach adopted in *Sindell*:

The case bears some resemblance to the present but the problem is not the same. For one thing, the existence of the additional manufacturers did not materially increase the risk of injury. The risk from consuming a drug bought in one shop is not increased by the fact that it can also be bought in another shop.

Nevertheless, he described the market share approach adopted in *Sindell* as 'imaginative', and suggested that such cases should 'be left for consideration when they arise'.

Although holding defendants liable in the absence of proof that their product actually caused the claimant's injuries might initially appear to be a measure which protects consumers' interests, it is important to remember that pharmaceutical companies would have to insure against the possibility of market share liability. Inevitably, premiums would rise and the costs of medicines would increase.

---

[100] 607 P 2d 924 (1980).
[101] *Drug Injuries and the Pursuit of Compensation* (Sweet & Maxwell: London, 1996) 140–1.
[102] [2002] UKHL 22.

(5) Defences

If an injured consumer is able to establish that the product was defective and that it caused her injury, the manufacturer might nevertheless be able to take advantage of one of the defences in section 4 of the Consumer Protection Act. First, it is a defence if the defect is attributable to compliance with a statutory obligation. This does not amount to a 'regulatory compliance' defence, which would offer a defence simply because the defective product had obtained a marketing authorization from the appropriate regulator: rather, it offers a defence only if the defect itself could be attributed to compliance with a regulatory requirement. This will be unusual.

Secondly, a defence exists if the defendant can prove that the product was never supplied to another, or was not supplied in the course of a business. Thirdly, there is a defence if the defect was not present when the product was supplied, as was held to be the case in *Piper v JRI Ltd*. The claimant, Terence Piper, had undergone a hip replacement operation, which involved the insertion of a prosthetic hip, manufactured by the defendant company. Eighteen months later, the hip fractured. Mr Piper had to undergo a further operation, and was left with significantly impaired movement and mobility. He brought an action against the defendants, claiming that the hip had been defective within the meaning of section 3 of the Act.

By the time of the trial, expert examination had established that the prosthesis fractured as a result of a defect in the titanium alloy from which it was made. The question then was whether the defect was present at the time that the defendant supplied the hip to the hospital, in which case they would be liable, or whether it occurred subsequently, perhaps during implantation.

At first instance, the judge found that the defendant manufacturer had subjected this product to a 'vigorous and meticulous process of work and inspection of the highest quality'. Because the defect would have been visible, and hence easily detectable in the defendant's factory, given his finding as to the rigorousness of the defendant's processes, he said: 'I am simply not prepared to accept that such a mistake was made with the product.' In *Piper v JRI Ltd*, the Court of Appeal dismissed Mr Piper's appeal.

Piper v JRI Ltd[103]

Thomas LJ

As the system was capable of detecting the only type of surface point defect capable of initiating the fatigue failure, given the view taken of those operating the system, it could be inferred that any such defect would have been detected had it been present prior to delivery to the hospital and that in the case of the prosthesis implanted into the claimant that the inspection system had not failed.

It seems to me that on an analysis of the evidence before the judge and on the way the case was presented to him, the judge was therefore correct in making the finding of fact made by him that the prosthesis was not defective at the time it was supplied to the hospital.

---

[103] [2006] EWCA Civ 1344.

In essence, the Court of Appeal found for the manufacturer because the claimant had been unable to prove that it had made a mistake. This appears to re-introduce a negligence-type inquiry—did the manufacturer take reasonable care?—into the question of whether the product was defective when it left its premises.

Fourthly, contributory negligence applies, and so a patient who takes the wrong dose of a drug which subsequently causes injury may be responsible in whole or in part for her own injuries. The application of contributory negligence to a strict liability regime is rather complicated. If damages are apportioned according to the parties' degree of fault, how might this work when the defendant was not necessarily at fault at all? In practice, the application of contributory negligence just means that the claimant's damages will be reduced according to the extent to which their injury was caused by their blameworthy conduct.

The most important and controversial defence is known as the development risks defence and is contained in section 4(1)(e).

Consumer Protection Act 1987 section 4

> 4(1)(e) [I]t shall be a defence . . . that the state of scientific and technical knowledge at the relevant time was not such that a producer of products of the same description as the product in question might be expected to have discovered the defect if it had existed in his products while they were under his control.

The UK Act's version of the development risks defence is slightly different from that in Article 7(e) of the Directive:

> The producer shall not be liable as a result of this Directive if he proves: . . . that the state of scientific and technical knowledge at the time when he put the product into circulation was not such as to enable the existence of the defect to be discovered.

The UK's defence appears to be broader in scope than that of the Directive since the relevant state of knowledge is that of 'producer[s] of products of the same description', rather than the state of scientific knowledge. Hence, a manufacturer could have a defence if other producers were equally ignorant, even if the defect was in fact discoverable. In contrast, under the Directive, there would only be a defence if the defect was, in the light of contemporary scientific knowledge, actually undiscoverable. This inconsistency prompted the European Commission to bring unsuccessful infringement proceedings against the UK. In *European Commission v United Kingdom*,[104] the ECJ found that, despite the difference in wording, section 4(1)(e) was capable of being interpreted in accordance with Article 7(e).

This defence was included because it was feared that liability for undiscoverable defects would impede innovation. In particular, it was thought that strict liability for undiscoverable risks would make it impossible to obtain liability insurance. The defence is optional, and although most countries have chosen to include it, some have not, while others specify that it does not apply to medicines. This uneven take-up of the defence means that manufacturers which wish to market drugs throughout the EU will, in any event, have to insure against liability for undiscoverable risks in countries where the defence is unavailable.

Clearly, the development risks defence will only apply in relation to design defects, and failures to warn, when a manufacturer might seek to rely upon evidence that the risk in

---

[104] [1997] All ER (EC) 481.

question was not discoverable when the product was put into circulation. The question of discoverability is, as Pugh and Pilgerstorfer point out, of critical importance.

Charles Pugh and Marcus Pilgerstorfer[105]

There is an additional limit on what knowledge is relevant for the purposes of Article 7(e). Knowledge must be accessible in what has become known as the 'Manchurian' sense. [In *Commission v United Kingdom*] the ECJ held that it was 'implicit in the wording of article 7(e) that the relevant scientific and technical knowledge must have been accessible at the time when the product in question was put into circulation'. The much debated example given by the Advocate General is of an academic in Manchuria publishing in a local scientific journal in Chinese which does not go outside the boundaries of the region. In such cases the defence will remain available notwithstanding that the total world body of scientific and technical knowledge might have enabled the defect to be discovered. The relevant body of knowledge on which to focus is 'accessible knowledge'. . . .

Once the relevant knowledge has been ascertained, the next stage in the Court's enquiry into the availability of the Article 7(e) defence is to consider the discoverability of the defect. The presence of this second criterion puts it beyond doubt that it is insufficient for the producer to show simply that the defect was not 'known' at the time the product was put into circulation. A producer must go further and show that the relevant knowledge was not such as to 'enable the existence of the defect to be discovered'.

As we can see from the next two extracts, the development risks defence has been controversial. Christopher Newdick explains that unforeseen risks are precisely the sort of defects that are most likely to occur in medicines. If manufacturers have a defence for such risks, the impact of strict liability on the pharmaceutical industry will be minimal. Jane Stapleton further questions why we should treat unforeseeable design errors more leniently than equally blameless manufacturing errors.

Christopher Newdick[106]

It will be recalled that it was the tragedy of thalidomide that gave rise to the debate concerning strict liability in this country. Ironically, however, it is the future victims of an accident of precisely this form that would most seriously be prejudiced by a state of the art defence. The pharmaceutical industry in this country has not generally been accused of irresponsible or unreasonable behaviour. By its very nature it works in an area in which unforeseeable accidents are inevitable, where fault is usually absent and known risks frequently judged acceptable as regards the few, in the interests of the many. In addition, their actions have the approval of an official licensing body. These factors would effectively be sufficient to guarantee that, unless a special exception were made to such a defence, the pharmaceutical industry would be its principal beneficiary.

---

[105] 'The Development Risk Defence: Knowledge, Discoverability and Creative Leaps' (2004) 4 Journal of Personal Injury Law 258–69.

[106] 'Strict Liability for Defective Drugs in the Pharmaceutical Industry' (1985) 101 Law Quarterly Review 405–31.

Jane Stapleton[107]

> We still have no principled explanation of why, for example, it is fair to hold a manufacturer strictly liable for some product flaws he could not discover (for example, some manufacturing errors), but not fair to do so in relation to a different set of product flaws he could not discover (namely, unforeseeable design dangers).

The development risks defence does have its supporters, however. Christopher Hodges, for example, points out that the defence's positive impact upon innovative practices is, in the long run, likely to serve the interests of patients as well as manufacturers.

Christopher Hodges[108]

> It is the essence of innovation that the risks which may be encountered in the use of a product cannot reasonably be identified or quantified at the time at which it is marketed—either fully or, in some cases, at all. Of course, one approach might be to require producers to test products fully before marketing them. But that would be unrealistic. First, testing usually includes testing in use by real humans in real life situations . . . there must be a limit to the duration and cost of such an exercise. With medicines, the limit is effectively prescribed by regulation, taking into account ethical constraints on repetitive or excessive testing. If testing were required to continue until all possible risks which might occur with use of a product had now been identified, few producers could afford to innovate and consumers would not benefit from advances in science and technology. Research would stagnate if denied practical application and commercial advantage . . .
>
> The basic problem with the defence is that a literal concept of *undiscoverability* is an unworkable test. The truth is that *any* defect can be discovered prior to marketing given sufficient testing. Such testing simply requires time and money. . . . The issue, however, is how much testing it is reasonable to expect the producer of an innovative product to undertake pre-marketing.

Burton J's judgment in *A v National Blood Authority* may have come as a surprise to academic commentators. Most people had assumed that the development risks defence meant that liability under the Act would in practice be indistinguishable from negligence, in that manufacturers which had acted reasonably in attempting to discover possible risks would be able to avoid liability for defective products. In *A v National Blood Authority*, the defendants knew about the risk of infection from non-A non-B Hepatitis, but they did not yet know how to detect it in individual bags of blood. The only way in which it would have been possible to ensure that no recipients of blood transfusions became infected with what became known as the Hepatitis C virus would have been to stop carrying out blood transfusions altogether, which would have breached the National Blood Authority's obligation to supply blood. A moratorium on all blood transfusions would also have posed a much greater risk to public health than the comparatively small risk of Hepatitis C infection. In short, the National Blood Authority almost certainly had exercised reasonable care.

---

[107] 'Bugs in Anglo-American Products Liability' (2002) 53 South Carolina Law Review 1225, 1241.
[108] 'Development Risks: Unanswered Questions' (1998) 61 Modern Law Review 560–70.

Nevertheless, in *A v National Blood Authority*, Burton J held that once the manufacturer knew of the existence of a defect, it was a known risk and the development risks defence could not apply, even if there was no way of avoiding the risk in question.

A v National Blood Authority[109]

Burton J

[T]he risk ceases to be a development risk and becomes a known risk not if and when the producer in question . . . had the requisite knowledge, but if and when such knowledge were accessible anywhere in the world outside Manchuria. Hence it protects the producer in respect of the unknown. . . .

In the light of my construction of art 7(e), and the conclusion that the risk of Hepatitis C infection was known, the art 7(e) defence does not arise.

Geraint Howells and Mark Mildred point out that Burton J:

certainly did not fit the stereotype of a judge intoxicated by a negligence-based world view. Rather, he displayed a reformist zeal to show that he appreciated that the Directive was intended to make a break with the past and introduce a new form of civil liability.[110]

In the next extract, Jane Stapleton argues that this 'reformist zeal' was misplaced.

Jane Stapleton[111]

In short, the court in the Hepatitis C case was determined to give the Directive 'work to do' in the United Kingdom; that is to give it a wider ambit of entitlement than existed elsewhere in the English law of obligations. It was eager to avoid a construction that would 'not only be toothless but pointless'. The trial judge seems to have thought this required an adoption of the construction urged by the claimants. In my view, this was mistaken. . . . In my view, the 'reformist zeal' of the trial judge in the Hepatitis C case simply preferred the heroic rhetoric of the claimants' cause.

A v National Blood Authority is a difficult case. On the one hand, it is hard not to feel sympathy for the claimants, who had already had the misfortune to be in need of blood transfusions, from which they were then unlucky enough to contract a potentially life-threatening illness. On the other hand, the National Blood Authority was also in a difficult position. In two important respects, the National Blood Authority is unlike a manufacturer of a defective product, and so an Act which was designed to apply to manufacturers which have

---

[109] [2001] 3 All ER 289.

[110] 'Infected Blood: Defect and Discoverability. A First Exposition of the EC Product Liability Directive' (2002) 65 Modern Law Review 95–106.

[111] 'Bugs in Anglo-American Products Liability' (2002) 53 South Carolina Law Review 1225.

deliberately chosen to put defective products into circulation may apply somewhat awkwardly to this sort of public body.

First, the manufacturer of a product, such as a medicine, is not under a legal duty to supply that medicine. If the manufacturer has any doubts about a product's safety, on the contrary, its duty would be to ensure that it is not put into circulation. The National Blood Authority, in contrast, is under a duty to supply blood. It was not open to them to stop all blood transfusions in the UK while they worked out how to identify this new strain of Hepatitis.

Secondly, as we saw earlier, a principal purpose of the CPA was to facilitate loss spreading. Rather than the loss falling on the unlucky victim, it would be transferred to the manufacturer, and the assumption was that the manufacturer would be able to spread the loss among all consumers by raising the price of its products. This is not an option for the National Blood Authority, which does not charge recipients for blood and so cannot spread its losses in the same way as a drug manufacturer.

Even if, on balance, it is thought fair for the National Blood Authority to bear the costs of the claimant's injuries, it is perhaps ironic that, in the field of medical law, the only successful action under the CPA has not been against the deep pockets of the pharmaceutical industry, but rather against a part of the financially overstretched NHS.

(6) Vaccine Damage

Special state compensation exists for patients who are disabled as a result of population-wide vaccination programmes. Vaccines are different from ordinary medicines in that the intention is not just to benefit the individual child who is immunized, but also to contribute towards the public health goal of eliminating certain diseases through population-wide immunization. Indeed, it has been argued that vaccination programmes are ethically problematic because the intervention is performed on an asymptomatic individual, who bears the risk associated with the vaccine, but who may not actually benefit from it.[112] Peter Cane explains the problem.

Peter Cane[113]

[V]accination is a classic case of the 'free-rider' problem much discussed by economists. The benefit to each individual child of being vaccinated may not be very great in view of the fact that most other children are likely to be vaccinated, and that the risk of infection has been thus greatly reduced; yet if the parents of all children reasoned in this way, vaccination would decline and the diseases in question would spread more widely again, with greater risk to all. Further, the main beneficiary from vaccination is often not the vaccinated child but other younger children with whom he or she comes into contact: whooping cough is most dangerous for very young babies, prior to the normal age for vaccination; by the time a child is vaccinated it is normally past the age at which the disease could prove fatal. There is thus a case for arguing that young children who are vaccinated before they are old enough to understand the issues are being used for the benefit of others.

[112] P Skrabanek, 'Why is preventive medicine exempted from ethical constraints?' (1990) 16 Journal of Medical Ethics 187–90.

[113] *Atiyah's Accidents, Compensation and the Law*, 6th edn (Butterworths: London, 1999) 89–90.

Because vaccination involves the injection of small quantities of active, infectious agents in order to trigger the body's immune response, the existence of rare but serious adverse reactions is unsurprising. There is evidence of a causal link between some vaccinations and adverse reactions, but not others. Most notably, there is no evidence for the discredited connection that Andrew Wakefield drew between the MMR vaccine and autism.

It would be difficult for an individual who suffers an adverse reaction following routine vaccination to establish negligence on the part of either the health care professional who performed the vaccination or the vaccine's manufacturer. Since responsible medical opinion strongly supports all of the recommended vaccinations, it will be impossible to establish that vaccinating a child was negligent, unless the child has some special characteristics which make vaccination unwise. Similar difficulties would be present in an action against the vaccine's manufacturer, which will be able to argue that it is impossible to ensure absolute safety from a vaccination programme.

Yet if vaccination programmes pose a risk of injury to a small number of people, which is believed to be outweighed by the enormous public health benefits of universal immunization, it would seem fair to offer some compensation to the small group of individuals whose health is compromised for the greater good. Of course, the cost–benefit calculation will not always favour vaccination. The chance of being exposed to smallpox, for example, is now so small that the risk of harm from vaccination is no longer justified.

In the 1970s, the Pearson Commission recommended that a strict liability scheme should be set up to compensate those who suffer injuries following vaccination. This proposal was never implemented, and instead an 'interim' scheme was introduced by the Vaccine Damage Payments Act 1979. As amended, the Act continues to apply today.

Under section 1, a person who has been severely disabled as a result of vaccination against a number of specified diseases, including diphtheria, tetanus, whooping cough, poliomyelitis, measles, rubella, tuberculosis, mumps, Haemophilus type b infection (hib), and meningitis C, is entitled to a sum of £120,000 for claims made since July 2007 (reduced amounts are payable for claims made before this date).[114]

Applicants must have been vaccinated in the UK since 1948. Under section 3(1), claims must usually be made before the claimant's 21st birthday (this was increased from a six-year time limit in 2000), unless the vaccine is one given to adults, such as those for pandemic flu and meningitis C. 'Severe disability' is defined in section 1(4) as 60 per cent disablement (this was reduced in 2000 from 80 per cent). And under section 3(5), the causal link between the vaccine and the disability has to be proved, on the balance of probabilities.

The scheme is funded from the welfare budget, and claims are made initially to the Department for Work and Pensions. If the claim is rejected, under section 4 the claimant can appeal to an independent tribunal. There is no further appeal to a court, although the Secretary of State is empowered to reverse the tribunal's decision.[115]

There have been comparatively few successful claims. As might have been expected, the majority of claims were made in the first few years after the scheme was set up. Rates of success vary between different vaccines: a high proportion of claims resulting from the single measles vaccine are successful, compared with low rates of success for the MMR vaccine.[116]

The reduction in the disability threshold in 2000 might have marginally increased the number of eligible claimants, but it could plausibly be argued that setting any threshold

---

[114] Written Ministerial Statement, 3 May 2007. Details at www.dwp.gov.uk.   [115] SI 1999/2677.
[116] Stephanie Pywell, 'The Vaccine Damage Payment Scheme: A Proposal for Radical Reform' (2002) 9 Journal of Social Security Law 73–93, 83.

level of disablement is unfair, regardless of the level at which it is set. Leaving aside the question of whether it is, in fact, possible to evaluate the extent of a child's disablement with this sort of precision, why should a child who suffers 59 per cent disablement receive nothing, while a child with 60 per cent disablement might be entitled to £120,000? A sliding scale that compensated a child according to the extent of her disabilities might be fairer.

Moreover, the sum of £120,000, while undoubtedly substantial, will not necessarily be sufficient to meet all of the child's needs throughout his life, especially if the vaccine caused severe brain damage. It is certainly much less than an award in tort, where full compensatory damages are the norm, and brain-damaged children can receive many millions of pounds. On the other hand, as is pointed out in the following extract, children who receive lump sum payments under the Act are still treated more generously than most disabled children.

Peter Cane[117]

> Why should children disabled in this particular way be treated so generously in a financial sense, as compared with other disabled children? The OPCS [Office of Population Censuses and Surveys] Disability Survey estimated that there were some 136,000 children under 16 in the four most serious disability categories; and the Pearson Commission estimated that 90% of severely disabled children were suffering from congenital defects. Why does a very small number of vaccine-disabled children have a better claim to financial support than other disabled children? It appears that in this case, as in some others, preferential treatment for a small group was the result of a well conducted political campaign which played on public sympathy for particularly heart-rending cases.

6 CONCLUSION

The regulation of medicines, once they are ready to be marketed, cannot be viewed in isolation from the rules that govern the stages before medicines can be licensed for general use. It is worth noting that when we considered the regulation of clinical trials in the previous chapter, it was also apparent that European law has played an increasingly dominant role. This is interesting, because in many of the other areas of medical law that we consider in this book, European law is of comparatively little importance. In relation to issues such as abortion, euthanasia, organ transplantation, and stem cell research, for example, there are significant differences between the laws in different European countries. The European Convention on Human Rights has Europe-wide application, but Member States often have a wide margin of appreciation in its interpretation.

When regulating the pharmaceutical industry and access to medicines, however, there is increasing European harmonization. Why is this? One obvious answer is that it involves the regulation of a market, rather than sensitive ethical issues. Protecting consumers and promoting economic growth are familiar aims for European regulation, whereas balancing the rights and wrongs of complex ethical dilemmas has usually been left to individual nation states.

---

[117] *Atiyah's Accidents, Compensation and the Law*, 6th edn (Butterworths: London, 1999) 89–90.

There is a connection between the challenges of regulating the pharmaceutical industry and the inadequacies of the tort system discussed in the second half of this chapter. In a country like the US, where litigation against drug companies is much more likely to be successful, the information gathered during court proceedings can be fed back to the regulator, and may prompt it to take action, such as insisting on a new warning, in order to protect patient safety. Where the chances of a successful claim against a drug company are almost non-existent, this 'feedback loop' is absent.

In this chapter, one of the recurring themes has been the existence of a tension between the pharmaceutical industry's profit motive—where increasing shareholder value is a primary goal—and the needs of patients and the NHS, not to mention people in low-income countries, who want access to effective and affordable medicines. Regulating the pharmaceutical industry is difficult, not least because a series of takeovers means that there are now a handful of hugely profitable companies supplying medicines within a global market. The economic and political power these companies wield is considerable, and time-limited patent protection means that they are under continual pressure to bring new and profitable medicines to the marketplace. The consequences of this pressure are, as we have seen, not necessarily always in the best interests of patients.

FURTHER READING

Elliott, Carl, *Better than Well: American Medicine meets the American Dream* (Norton: New York, 2003).

Ferguson, Pamela, *Drug Injuries and the Pursuit of Compensation* (Sweet & Maxwell: London, 1996).

Goldberg, Richard, 'Paying for Bad Blood: Strict Product Liability after the Hepatitis C Litigation' (2002) 10 Medical Law Review 165–200.

House of Commons Health Select Committee, *The Influence of the Pharmaceutical Industry*, Fourth Report of Session 2004–05, available at www.publications. parliament.uk.

Howells, Geraint and Mildred, Mark, 'Infected Blood: Defect and Discoverability. A First Exposition of the EC Product Liability Directive' (2002) 65 Modern Law Review 95–106.

Jackson, Emily, *Law and the Regulation of Medicines* (Hart Publishing: Oxford, 2012).

McGoey, Lindsey and Jackson, Emily, 'Seroxat and the suppression of clinical trial data: regulatory failure and the uses of legal ambiguity' (2009) 35 Journal of Medical Ethics 107–12.

Mildred, Mark, 'Pharmaceutical Products: The Relationship between Regulatory Approval and the Existence of a Defect' (2007) European Business Law Review 1276–82.

Sykes, Richard, *New Medicines, The Practice of Medicine, and Public Policy* (Nuffield Trust: London, 2000).

ORGAN TRANSPLANTATION

CENTRAL ISSUES

1. Organ transplantation is usually successful and cost-effective, but there is an acute shortage of organs available for transplant in the UK.

2. Under the Human Tissue Act 2004, consent to cadaveric donation is necessary, either from the deceased person, her nominee, or from the highest-ranking qualified relative.

3. Steps have been taken to improve the coordination and effectiveness of organ procurement. But more significant legal reform might include moving to an 'opt-out' system; requiring people to make a decision about organ donation; offering financial or non-financial incentives; and, most drastically, treating the organs of the dead as a public resource.

4. In recent years, the number of living organ donors has increased. Regulation of living organ donation is directed towards ensuring that the donor has given informed consent, and that no money has changed hands.

5. Most organ transplantation is of solid organs, like kidneys and lungs. Other types of transplant—for example, of hands, faces, and wombs—are now possible.

6. Xenotransplantation (animal-to-human transplantation) could potentially solve the organ shortage, but it raises several ethical and practical issues. Currently, the most compelling objection to xenotransplantation is the unknown and possibly unknowable risk of cross-species infection, not only for individual recipients, but also for society as a whole.

---

1 INTRODUCTION

For two reasons, the first attempts to transplant organs from one person's body into another were inevitably unsuccessful. First, before it became possible to suppress the recipient's immune system, foreign tissue would automatically be rejected. Secondly, because organs deteriorate rapidly as soon as a person's cardio-respiratory system stops working, it was also difficult to ensure that organs taken from cadavers 'survived' the transplant process. The first recipients of transplanted organs tended to be selected because they were in the final stages of acute organ failure, and they generally died within a matter of days or weeks.

The first successful organ transplant was a live kidney transplant, between identical twins, which took place in Boston in 1954. Six years later, a similar operation was performed successfully in the UK. Since the 1960s, techniques for maintaining the quality of organs before and during transplantation have improved, and immunosuppressant therapy can minimize the problem of rejection. The prognosis for transplant patients is now extremely good.

After one year, 82 per cent of heart transplants, 93 per cent of liver transplants, 99 per cent of living donor kidney transplants, and 96 per cent of cadaveric kidney transplants will still be functioning well (after five years, the percentages are 60, 82, 95, and 89 respectively).[1] Of course, transplant surgery sometimes fails, and there are risks—an increase in the lifetime risk of developing certain cancers, for example—associated with taking immunosuppressant drugs. But transplantation will often be the optimum treatment for organ failure. Heart and liver transplants are life saving. Kidney failure is not necessarily fatal, but a transplant will enable someone who would otherwise be dependent upon dialysis to lead a relatively normal life.

A successful transplant will also often save the NHS money. Kidney transplantation is much cheaper than providing dialysis to a patient with renal failure. The National Institute for Health and Care Excellence has estimated that a 25 per cent increase in the number of kidney donors would save the NHS £9.2 million per year.[2]

In short, transplantation surgery is a successful and cost-effective medical procedure. The chief difficulty, as is well known, is that there are insufficient organs to meet demand. This problem is exacerbated by improvements in transplant technology which expand the pool of potential recipients to include older patients and those who might have previously been judged too ill to undergo such a major operation. Ironically, artificial organs have increased the gap between supply and demand because, while not yet effective enough to offer permanent replacements, they allow transplant teams temporarily to 'bridge' patients who would otherwise die, enabling them to be put on the organ donor waiting list until a human organ becomes available. The pool of possible recipients therefore continues to grow steadily, while the number of cadaveric organs available for transplant has fallen, in part because of a reduction in deaths from road traffic accidents.

Given waiting times of well over a year, it is not surprising that mortality rates on the organ donor waiting list are high: in 2014–15, 1,300 people on the waiting list either died or became too sick to receive a transplant. This understates the scale of the problem, however, because many potential recipients are never put on the waiting list because their doctors recognize that it is unlikely that they would become eligible for a transplant in time.

The most important issue raised by organ transplantation is therefore how to increase the number of available organs. An Organ Donation Taskforce was appointed in 2006 to investigate how this might best be achieved. In 2008, it issued two separate reports: the first looked at ways to increase donation rates without the need for legislative change, and the second considered whether law reform—specifically introducing an opt-out system—would be desirable. The Taskforce's decision that no change in the law was necessary was controversial, and while there have been some improvements since their proposals were implemented, many would still advocate more significant legal change.

[1] NHS Blood and Transplant, *Annual Activity Report 2014–15: Survival Rates Following Transplantation* (NHSBT, 2015).

[2] NICE, *Organ Donation for Transplantation Costing Report: Implementing NICE Guidance* (NICE, 2011).

There is, it seems, widespread public support for organ transplantation. Opinion polls consistently indicate that 70–90 per cent of the population would want their organs to be used to save others in the event of their death, while only 33 per cent of the population is registered on the organ donor register. The paradox of this situation is pointed out by Sheila McLean:

> We have the doctors ready, willing and able to undertake the surgery, we have people dying with usable organs and we apparently have a compliant public. Why then is the programme so strapped?[3]

Some people believe that organ donation is incompatible with their religious beliefs, but scholars from all the major religions have endorsed transplantation, on the grounds that the imperatives of healing and saving life trump other considerations, such as a proscription of the mutilation of corpses. A 1995 Fatwa, for example, stated that giving and receiving organs is compatible with Islam.[4] Nevertheless, the Organ Donation Taskforce drew attention to a study that suggested that attempts to publicize broad religious acceptance of donation, via leaflets, have been unsuccessful.

Organ Donation Taskforce[5]

> There was little prior awareness among the interviewees of the leaflets published some years ago setting out the views of some prominent faiths on organ donation. This was under-lined by a recent study carried out in Birmingham, in which 60% of Muslims, from a wide variety of ethnic backgrounds, said that organ donation was contrary to their faith, when it is not. This suggests that written leaflets alone may be ineffective and that other methods of engagement need to be found.

It is important to recognize that approval of organ transplantation is not necessarily the same thing as endorsing a brain stem definition of death (see further below). So the state-ment that organ donation is compatible with Judaism and Islam misses the point that some Jewish and Islamic scholars are not convinced that the soul leaves the body when the brain stem is dead,[6] but rather may consider that that happens only after the heart stops beat-ing. This does not rule out donation, but it does suggest that donation following cardio-respiratory diagnosis of death (as opposed to brain death) may be more acceptable for some religious groups.

In the UK, relatives from minority ethnic groups are more likely to refuse to agree to trans-plantation: for potential donors after brain-stem death, the consent rates were 70 per cent

---

[3] 'Transplantation and the "Nearly Dead"; The Case of Elective Ventilation' in Sheila McLean (ed), *Contemporary Issues in Law, Medicine and Ethics* (Dartmouth: Aldershot, 1996) 143–61.

[4] For discussion of Muslim attitudes towards organ donation, see Clare Hayward and Anna Madill, 'The meaning of organ donation: Muslims of Pakistani origin and white English nationals living in north England' (2003) 57 Social Science and Medicine 389–401; and Şahin Aksoy, 'A critical approach to the cur-rent understanding of Islamic scholars on using cadaver organs without permission' (2001) 15 Bioethics 461–72.

[5] *The Potential Impact of an Opt Out System for Organ Donation in the UK: An Independent Report from the Organ Donation Taskforce* (DH: London, 2008).

[6] Ahmet Bedir and Şahin Aksoy, 'Brain death revisited: it is not "complete death" according to Islamic sources' (2011) 37 Journal of Medical Ethics 290–4.

for white patients and 39 per cent for patients from minority ethnic groups (for donors after cardiac death, the rates were 55 and 33 per cent). This discrepancy is particularly significant because renal failure is more common in non-white populations, in part as a result of increased rates of type 2 diabetes. Given a greater need for organs, and fewer tissue-matched donors, the organ shortage has a disproportionate impact upon minority ethnic groups. According to UK Transplant, 31 per cent of the people on the kidney waiting list people are from Black, Asian, and minority ethnic (BAME) groups, while only 5.6 per cent of donors are from these groups. The median time on the waiting list for a white patient is 2 years and 362 days; for a black patient it is 3 years and 324 days. Inevitably, these BAME patients are more likely than white patients to die before a suitable organ becomes available.

The law relating to organ donation in England, Wales, and Northern Ireland is contained in the Human Tissue Act 2004, which came into force in 2006. Wales has amended this through the Human Transplantation (Wales) Act 2013, which introduced an 'opt out' system in 2015. In Scotland, although some provisions of the 2004 Act have UK-wide application, most of the law is contained in the Human Tissue (Scotland) Act 2006.

It is important to bear in mind that the Human Tissue Act 2004 was not passed in order to improve the law relating to organ transplantation. The catalyst for reform was instead the retained organs scandals at Bristol Royal Infirmary and Alder Hey Children's Hospital. In the late 1990s, it became apparent that, at both institutions, children's organs had been retained without parental knowledge, let alone consent.[7] The Human Tissue Act covers the storage and use of almost all human tissue (sperm and eggs are not included), and the Act's central organizing principle is the need for specific consent to the storage and use of tissue and organs. Its remit is much broader than transplantation—it covers research, postmortems, anatomy, and public display—but in this chapter we concentrate upon the Act's application to organ transplantation.

The Human Tissue Authority (HTA), set up by the 2004 Act, issues licences for the storage and use of tissues. Most organs that are used in transplantation cannot be stored for any length of time, and so licensing is only relevant to the transplantation of tissue, such as bone marrow, which is routinely banked for future use. Because our focus in this chapter is on solid organ donation, the licensing process will not be discussed in any detail. Of more importance are the HTA's Codes of Practices. At the time of writing, these are being revised. Reference will be made to the draft Codes in this chapter, but readers should bear in mind that the finalized versions (expected in 2016) may differ. Draft Code A deals with principles and consent, and Draft Code F with organ donation.

In this chapter, we begin with cadaveric donation, looking first at who may become a donor, and which organs can be taken. The system of organ retrieval in the UK is then summarized, and we look at the consent-based model adopted in the Human Tissue Act 2004. Because of the shortage of organs from cadavers, several strategies to increase the number of cadaveric donors have been canvassed, including the opt-out model which was rejected by the Organ Donation Taskforce, but which has been introduced in Wales.

Next we look at living organ donation. We consider the legitimacy of performing such a serious operation in order to benefit a third party. Could a person give valid consent to the harm involved, and could it ever be appropriate to take an organ from a child or an adult who lacks capacity? We look at the restrictions placed on living organ donation in the

---

[7] See further, M Brazier, 'Organ retention and return: problems of consent' (2003) 29 Journal of Medical Ethics 30–3; M Brazier, 'Human tissue retention' (2004) 72 Medico-Legal Journal 39; John Harris, 'Law and Regulation of Retained Organs: The Ethical Issues' (2002) 22 Legal Studies 527–49; M Brazier, 'Retained Organs: Ethics and Humanity' (2002) 22 Legal Studies 550–69.

Human Tissue Act, and the controversial question of whether it would be acceptable to pay people to 'donate' their organs. Finally, we consider the ethical, practical, and legal obstacles to transplanting organs taken from animals into human recipients.

2 DEAD DONORS

(a) THE 'DEAD DONOR' RULE AND BRAIN DEATH

If organs can only be removed once someone has died, and if they must be removed as soon as possible after death, accurately pinpointing the moment of death is vitally important. The problem, however, is that death is a process: a person's organs do not all stop functioning at the same moment, rather they fail progressively once the brain has irreversibly died.

Brain death itself involves two distinct changes, which do not always happen simultaneously. One is the permanent loss of consciousness (caused by death of the upper brain), and the other is the loss of the brain's ability to regulate other bodily functions, such as breathing (caused by death of the lower brain).

Throughout history, it has been important to designate a point at which a person's loss of bodily functions becomes irreversible. Centuries ago, a body could not conclusively be considered dead until putrefaction had begun. In the nineteenth century, death started to be diagnosed after a person had stopped breathing and their heart had stopped beating. During the twentieth century, it became apparent that it is sometimes possible to resuscitate a person whose heart has stopped beating. Obviously, if someone is successfully resuscitated, then she was not dead, despite her temporary loss of heart function.

The invention of the artificial ventilator made it necessary to decide whether a diagnosis of death could ever be made while a person's heartbeat was being maintained artificially. If such patients are alive, removing them from a ventilator would kill them. It is much less problematic to remove someone from a ventilator if they have previously been diagnosed as dead.

Pressure to rethink the definition of death also came from developments in transplant surgery. Loss of cardio-respiratory function rapidly causes damage to a person's organs. In recent years, there has been considerable success in perfusing organs taken from people whose hearts have stopped beating, but it is still preferable to obtain organs following a diagnosis of irreversible brain death. Continuing to ventilate a person who has been diagnosed as brain dead enables doctors to remove their organs while their heart function is being maintained artificially. It is, of course, essential that these 'heart beating donors' must have been satisfactorily diagnosed as dead before their organs are taken: in Hans Jonas's words, 'the patient must be absolutely sure that his doctor does not become his executioner'.[8]

The first attempt to define death as the cessation of brain function took place in France in 1959, when a group of neurosurgeons described a condition in which there was no detectable brain activity. They called this 'death of the central nervous system', and concluded that removing a patient whose central nervous system had died from a ventilator would be justified, despite their artificially maintained heartbeat.

Debate over the need for a new definition of death continued during the 1960s, and brain death was formally defined in 1968 by an Ad Hoc Committee of the Harvard Medical School in its report, *A Definition of Irreversible Coma*.[9] The concept of brain death has now been adopted

---

[8] *Philosophical Essays: From Ancient Creed to Technological Man* (Prentice Hall: Englewood Cliffs, NJ, 1974) 131.

[9] 'Ad Hoc Committee of the Harvard Medical School to examine the definition of death' (1968) 205 Journal of the American Medical Association 85–8, 85.

by most countries, including, since 2010, Japan. As a result of cultural attitudes towards death and traditional Japanese death rituals, opposition to the concept of brain death had been particularly strong in Japan, and indeed the Japanese surgeon who performed the first heart transplant in 1968 was charged with murder. Even now, in Japan the dead person's family is entitled to refuse to accept brain death, in addition to being able to veto organ donation.

In the UK there is no statutory definition of death. Rather, the diagnosis of death is regarded as a matter of clinical judgement. Since the late 1970s, brain-stem death, or the irreversible loss of brain-stem function, has been treated as the definitive criterion for diagnosing death. The Department of Health's *Code of Practice for the Diagnosis of Brain Stem Death* was superseded in 2008 by a Code of Practice issued by the Academy of Medical Royal Colleges.

Academy of Medical Royal Colleges[10]

Death entails the irreversible loss of those essential characteristics which are necessary to the existence of a living human person and, thus, the definition of death should be regarded as the irreversible loss of the capacity for consciousness, combined with irreversible loss of the capacity to breathe. This may be secondary to a wide range of underlying problems in the body, for example, cardiac arrest.

The irreversible cessation of brain-stem function whether induced by intracranial events or the result of extracranial phenomena, such as hypoxia, will produce this clinical state and therefore irreversible cessation of the integrative function of the brain-stem equates with the death of the individual and allows the medical practitioner to diagnose death . . .

[T]here are some ways in which parts of the body may continue to show signs of biological activity after a diagnosis of irreversible cessation of brain-stem function; these have no moral relevance to the declaration of death for the purpose of the immediate withdrawal of all forms of supportive therapy.

The diagnosis of brain-stem death must be made by at least two senior registered medical practitioners, and to avoid conflict of interests, neither of these should be a member of the transplant team.[11] Although death is pronounced following two sets of brain-stem tests, the legal time of death will be when the first test indicates brain-stem death.[12]

Because organ transplantation depends so heavily upon public goodwill, it is important that the public accepts that brain-stem death is not an especially 'early' diagnosis of death. In 1980, a *Panorama* TV programme questioned the validity of brain-death criteria, leading to an immediate and sharp reduction in the number of organs becoming available for transplant. It took 15 months for organ donation rates to recover.

It has been difficult for the public to accept that a person whose heart is still beating, and who appears to be breathing, albeit with mechanical assistance, is really dead. A warm, breathing body certainly does not look dead, and relatives often find it difficult to contemplate organ retrieval before the cessation of heart and lung function. Shah et al found that it was not uncommon for people to believe that, following a diagnosis of brain death, doctors would, in fact, wait until the person's heart stopped beating before removing their organs.[13]

---

[10] Academy of Medical Royal Colleges, *A Code of Practice for the Diagnosis and Confirmation of Death* (AoMRC, 2008).

[11] Ibid, para 3.3.   [12] Ibid. See also *Re A* [1992] 3 Med LR 303.

[13] Seema K Shah, Kenneth Kasper, and Franklin G Miller, 'A narrative review of the empirical evidence on public attitudes on brain death and vital organ transplantation: the need for better data to inform policy' (2015) 41 Journal of Medical Ethics 291–6.

In the next extract, Robert Truog points to a further possible reason for confusion. If brain-dead patients are anaesthetized before organ retrieval, does this imply that we are not sure whether such patients are really dead?

Robert D Truog[14]

Most interesting is a debate that has occurred in the European anesthesia literature regarding the question of whether brain dead patients should receive an anesthetic during organ procurement. Some argue that the brain death criterion is insufficient to be absolutely sure that patients are incapable of experiencing pain, even if only at a rudimentary level, and so should receive 'the benefit of the doubt' and be given an anesthetic. Others respond, not by defending the criterion itself, but by arguing that administration of anesthesia to these patients will send a message to society that we are uncertain whether brain death is truly a state of permanent unconsciousness. As such, they argue, administration of an anesthetic to these patients will undermine the trust of the public and jeopardize the organ transplantation enterprise.

Peter Singer argues that the concept of brain death is a 'convenient fiction' and, in the next extract, explains why it has nevertheless proved to be relatively uncontroversial.

Peter Singer[15]

Human beings are not the only living things in the world. All living things eventually die, and we can generally tell when they are alive and when they are dead. Isn't the distinction between life and death so basic that what counts as dead for a human being also counts as dead for a dog, a parrot, a prawn, an oyster, an oak, or a cabbage? . . . 'Brain death' is only for humans. Isn't it odd that for a human being to die requires a different concept of death from that which we apply to other living beings? . . .

When warm, breathing, pulsating human beings are declared to be dead, they lose their basic human rights. They are not given life support. If their relatives consent . . . , their hearts and other organs can be cut out of their bodies and given to strangers. The change in our conception of death that excluded these human beings from the moral community was one of the first in a series of dramatic changes in our view of life and death. Yet, in sharp contrast to other changes in this area, it met with virtually no opposition? How did this happen? . . .

In summary, the redefinition of death in terms of brain death went through so smoothly because it did not harm the brain-dead patients and it benefited everyone else: the families of brain-dead patients, the hospitals, the transplant surgeons, people needing transplants, people who worried that they might one day need a transplant, people who feared that they might one day be kept on a respirator after their brain had died, taxpayers and the government.

Further evidence that we cannot disassociate brain death from the needs of transplantation services comes from Robert Truog's prediction that if xenotransplantation were perfected,

---

[14] 'Brain death—too flawed to endure, too ingrained to abandon' (2007) Journal of Law, Medicine and Ethics 273–81.

[15] *Rethinking Life and Death: The Collapse of our Traditional Ethics* (OUP: Oxford, 1994).

and the need for cadaveric donors disappeared, we would revert to pre-transplantation definitions of death:

> Without the need to obtain organs from other humans, the raison d'être of brain death will disappear. The concept, and the philosophical debate that has surrounded it, will become historical footnotes, and the term will no longer be found in the indices of medical textbooks. The concept will have died a natural death of its own.[16]

It has also been suggested that new medical techniques, which might enable brain-stem function to be maintained artificially, cast doubt upon the continued validity of brain-stem death. As Kerridge et al suggest in the following extract, people who have been diagnosed as brain dead can have some bodily functions maintained artificially for increasingly long periods of time. If brain-dead patients can 'survive' on a ventilator for several months, are they really dead?

Ian H Kerridge et al[17]

> When the concept of brain death was first introduced it was argued that death of the brain stem inevitably implied the imminent death of the whole body . . . This argument is no longer tenable as medical therapy and intensive care have become increasingly sophisticated at replacing brain stem function, and we now know that bodies with a dead brain stem may be kept alive for prolonged periods of time. Brain dead pregnant women have been maintained for months and later given birth to healthy infants and brain dead children have been reported to survive for up to 14 years with ventilatory and nutritional support . . .
>
> Suggestions that the brain stem is the supreme regulator of the body seem both biologically and philosophically simplistic . . . Furthermore the heart, the liver, the kidneys, and other organs are all required to maintain bodily integrity, and loss of the functions of any of these organs will result in eventual disintegration of the organism without artificial support. Many individuals who are clearly alive depend upon technology such as pacemakers, dialysis machines or even ventilators to live. Whether there is a 'supreme regulator' therefore seems open to question. This argument may also be confused by the fact that the functions of the kidneys, heart, and lungs can be replaced by technological means, whereas that of the brain stem cannot. This is, however, very dependent upon technology; indeed aspects of brain stem function can now be replaced and it seems likely that more progress might be made in this area.

Perhaps it should be admitted that it is impossible to define the moment of death with complete certainty and precision, and that the important task therefore is to determine at what point *in the process of dying* organ retrieval becomes legitimate. The rule that organs may only be taken once a person is dead, fosters public trust in the transplantation system. It is, however, at least arguable that the certainty implied by this 'dead donor' rule misrepresents the ambiguity of death.[18]

---

[16] 'Brain death—too flawed to endure, too ingrained to abandon' (2007) Journal of Law, Medicine and Ethics 273–81.

[17] 'Death, dying and donation: organ transplantation and the diagnosis of death' (2002) 28 Journal of Medical Ethics 89–94.

[18] Elyssa R Koppelman, 'The dead donor rule and the concept of death: severing the ties that bind them' (2003) 3 American Journal of Bioethics 1–9.

Robert Truog and Franklin Miller argue that there is a difference between being legally dead, when the person can no longer be harmed and organ donation can take place, and being biologically dead, when the biological organism has died. Acknowledging this might enable organs to be extracted slightly earlier, thus increasing their potential usefulness.

Robert D Truog and Franklin G Miller[19]

In sum, we fully support the current retrieval of organs from patients declared dead by neurological or circulatory criteria—not because they are biologically dead (they are not), but because they are not harmed or wronged by the donation . . .

By changing the conversation around brain death, and honestly acknowledging that patients diagnosed as brain dead are not biologically dead but are considered to be legally dead for reasons of public policy, we open up the discussion to whether modifications of this legal fiction may actually better serve public needs. Consider, for example, the fact that for most DCD [donors after circulatory death] donations only the kidneys are procured for transplant, since the other organs typically have suffered too much ischemic injury during the time from stopping life support to cardiac arrest and after the 2–5 minutes of pulselessness required by most DCD protocols. Given that these patients or their surrogates have expressed a desire to donate organs, . . . what would be unethical about allowing patients to choose to have their organs removed under anesthesia before stopping life support and thus obviating ischemic damage to the organs? . . . Not only would this approach yield more and better organs for transplantation, but it would permit the desires of the donor to be more completely fulfilled.

Julian Savulescu suggests that we should straightforwardly admit that it is legitimate to retrieve organs from the 'imminently dying', with their consent.

Julian Savulescu[20]

Since I believe we die when our meaningful mental life ceases, organs should be available from that point, which may significantly predate brain death. At the very least, people should be allowed to complete advance directives that direct that their organs be removed when their brain is severely damaged or they are permanently unconscious.

In the next extract, Potts and Evans criticize these sorts of argument on the grounds that taking organs from living patients, even if they have given consent and are close to death, would involve doctors killing their patients.

M Potts and DW Evans[21]

One difficulty with this is that once utilitarian considerations are used to justify killing ventilator/dependent patients who are dying, those same considerations could also be used to justify killing non-ventilator/dependent patients or patients who are not dying . . . Currently,

---

[19] 'Changing the conversation about brain death' (2014) 14 American Journal of Bioethics 9–14.
[20] 'Death, us and our bodies: personal reflections' (2003) 29 Journal of Medical Ethics 127–30.
[21] 'Does it matter that organ donors are not dead? Ethical and policy implications' (2005) 31 Journal of Medical Ethics 406–9.

the statement on organ donor cards asserts that organs may be taken 'after my death'. We believe that such wording should be changed to reflect the fact that 'brain dead' individuals are not dead in the usual understanding of what death is. Explanatory literature accompanying organ donor cards should be frank that a 'brain dead' donor's heart is beating during part of the organ removal surgery.

In an attempt to sidestep debates over whether brain-stem death is really death, Tännsjö suggests that the search for one definition of death is futile. The circulatory and respiratory criteria make sense in some circumstances: we would only bury or cremate someone after their heart has stopped beating. In contrast, the brain-stem criterion makes practical sense in relation to organ donation.

Torbjörn Tännsjö[22]

We can now define death of a person as the point at which the person in question ceases to exist. This happens when there is too little psychological continuity and connectedness left over. If there is no consciousness at all, then there is no person at all. And we can define the death of the body as the point at which the body ceases to function as a unified organism. This means that bodies, in contradistinction to persons, often continue to exist after their death . . .

But could it not be objected that to have a beating heart is to be a person? I do not think that this is a plausible move. First of all, it could simply be rejected on linguistic grounds. Most of us would not call someone without a working brain, someone whose brain had irreversibly ceased to exist, a 'person'.

Secondly, and more importantly, even if some would do so, they would still have to admit that something of importance was gone once someone's brain had ceased to exist.

Patients in a permanent vegetative state, or anencephalic infants, have permanently lost the capacity for consciousness: that is, their upper brain is dead, but their lower brain continues to function. Because a person can be categorized as brain dead only after the whole brain has stopped functioning, such patients are undoubtedly still alive. There are, however, those who would argue that the current definition of death is too restrictive, and that categories of patients whom we now treat as alive—such as patients in a permanent vegetative state, or anencephalic infants—should instead be regarded as dead, and hence as potential organ donors.

Anencephalic babies are born without a cerebral cortex. Most will be stillborn, and those that are born alive will die shortly after birth. Anencephalic babies will never achieve consciousness, but they do have a functioning brain stem. Because there is no chance that an anencephalic baby will recover, it will not be in her best interests to be connected to an artificial ventilator. Since ventilation would be started to benefit a third party, does it involve using the baby as a means to an end? There may be some emotional value to the parents from the knowledge that their inevitably doomed child was able to save another baby's life, but again, the benefit here is to a third party, and not to the anencephalic infant herself.

The solution advocated by John Robertson is to suggest that when the capacity for sentience is irrevocably absent, an anencephalic baby or a patient in an irreversible coma cannot be harmed by organ retrieval.

---

[22] 'Two concepts of death reconciled' (1999) 2 Medicine, Health Care and Philosophy 41–6.

John Robertson[23]

A major reason for the requirement that the organ donor be dead is to protect the donor from being harmed by organ removal. If the donor is dead, taking his organs will not harm him. In contrast, if he or she is alive, it is assumed that removing organs will kill or otherwise injure the donor.

This view of the dead donor rule, however, assumes that the live donor has interests in continued living and in not being physically injured. Whereas this assumption is true in most instances and thus should be strictly followed, it may not apply to situations of irreversible coma, near-dead pediatric patients and anencephalics . . . Such patients, though legally still alive, may no longer have interests in living or in avoiding physical harm that should be respected.

Treating the destruction or absence of the cerebral cortex as evidence of death would increase the pool of potential organ donors, but not everyone would agree that this means we should further redefine death. William May, for example, warns of the dangers of the slippery slope (see further Chapter 1).

William F May[24]

To invoke the need for organs as a reason for declaring a specific class of people dead creates a runaway, imperial argument, difficult to limit. Under the press of one kind of exigency or another, one could redefine death to include anencephalics, and then perhaps the next time, hydrocephalics, microcephalics, and so on, denying any independent and firm boundaries to mark off the dead from the dying or the vegetative . . .

An opportunistic redefinition of death would eventually produce other unfortunate results. It would lead patients to distrust doctors and hospitals, and would weaken the readiness of families to donate the organs of truly dead patients. Convenience and utility should not justify enlarging the kingdom of the dead. While, historically the need for organs and the development of the technology for perfusing and successfully transplanting them supplied the *occasion* for reflection on the criteria for determining death, the need for healthy organs should not influence the standards for determining that a patient or a class of patient is dead. That decision should rest solely on the patient's condition.

(b) CIRCULATORY DEATH

Until relatively recently, deceased donors were almost exclusively people who had been diagnosed as brain dead while their heart-lung function was being artificially maintained on a mechanical ventilator. Now, however, there are two sorts of deceased donors: donors after brain death (DBD) and donors after circulatory death (DCD). DBDs are patients in whom death has been confirmed using neurological criteria; most DCDs are patients for whom imminent death was anticipated and treatment was withdrawn. This is known as 'controlled DCD'. 'Uncontrolled DCD' would involve donation after sudden and unexpected death. It is possible but rare.

---

[23] 'Relaxing the Death Standard for Organ Donation in Pediatric Situations' in Deborah Mathieu (ed), *Organ Substitution Technology: Ethical, Legal and Public Policy Issues* (Westview Press: Boulder, CO, 1988) 69–76.

[24] *The Patient's Ordeal* (Indiana UP: Bloomington, IN, 1991).

Fewer organs can be taken from DCD donors: kidneys, livers, and lungs have been successfully transplanted from DCD donors, but hearts have not. This may change in the near future. In 2015, Australian doctors reported performing three cardiac transplants from DCD donors.[25] At first, success rates using organs taken from DCD donors were much lower than when organs were retrieved from deceased heart-beating donors. This is still the case in relation to livers, but kidney success rates are now about the same.

James Bernat notes an interesting difference between families' and doctors' concerns about the definition of death in DBD and DCD donors. Families may worry that DBD donors are not really dead, while being untroubled about the diagnosis of death in someone whose heart has stopped beating. Conversely, doctors may worry that someone whose heart has stopped beating could still be resuscitated, while being confident in the diagnosis of brain-stem death.

James L Bernat[26]

Family members of DCDD donors usually consider the patient to be dead immediately once breathing and heartbeat cease. Physicians, by contrast, do not consider the donor dead at that moment because they worry that breathing or heartbeat might restart spontaneously within a few minutes and that if cardiopulmonary resuscitation (CPR), extracorporeal membrane oxygenation (ECMO), or other resuscitative technologies were employed, they might be able to restore circulation, even though these interventions will not be initiated because of a DNR order. They therefore mandate a 5-minute 'hands off' period after circulation and respiration cease before declaring death . . . I have observed the opposite pattern of attitudes in organ donation after brain determination of death (DBDD). Physicians generally accept brain death as equivalent to human death but families often question its validity because they are unfamiliar with the concept of brain death, they erroneously equate brain death with coma, which they know may be reversible, or they intuit that the patient does not appear dead. The discordance of family versus physician attitudes toward death determination between DCDD and DBDD usually follows this recurring theme: Physicians seem more concerned about DCDD while family members seem more concerned about DBDD.

When death is diagnosed using cardiac criteria, rather than brain-stem tests, in order to preserve their viability, organs are cooled by in situ perfusion. The Human Tissue Act 2004 confirms the legality of cold perfusion techniques: under section 43, if part of a body is or may be suitable for use for transplantation, it is lawful to take the minimum necessary steps for the purpose of preserving the part for use in transplantation, until it has been established that consent for transplantation has not been, and will not be, given.

More complex is the question of whether steps to ensure that the organs will be suitable for transplantation may be taken before the patient has died, such as giving the dying patient anti-coagulant drugs. On the one hand, treatment which is not intended to benefit the dying patient would not appear to be in her best interests. On the other hand, if donation is the clear wish of the dying patient, then facilitating this might nevertheless be compatible with the Mental Capacity Act 2005. This was the view of the UK Donation Ethics Committee.

---

[25] Kumud K Dhital et al, 'Adult heart transplantation with distant procurement and ex-vivo preservation of donor hearts after circulatory death: a case series' (2015) 385 The Lancet 2585–91.

[26] 'Harmonizing standards for death determination in DCDD' (2015) 15 American Journal of Bioethics 10–12.

UK Donation Ethics Committee[27]

> 1.6.2 [I]f the patient is known to have wanted to be a donor, or to have values and beliefs compatible with being a donor, the possibility of facilitating donation provides a reason to continue treatments which may have no direct medical benefit to the patient; rather the benefit accrues to the potentially donatable organs and thereby ultimately to the recipients. This concept can leave some clinicians feeling conflicted, concerned that they are no longer acting for the overall benefit of the patient, but rather for the overall benefit of the potential recipients.
>
> 1.6.3 This is a narrow interpretation of 'overall benefit' . . . The Mental Capacity Act Code of Practice emphasises the importance of considering a person's social, emotional, cultural and religious interests in determining what course of action may be in their best interests, and the clinician is legally obliged to take this wider view. When planning end of life care for a patient for whom life-sustaining treatment is no longer appropriate, if the patient wished to become an organ donor, then care that facilitates successful donation is likely to be highly compatible with their best interests (or to be of overall benefit to them).

(c) TYPES OF TRANSPLANT

Donor cards allow people to specify which organs they are prepared to donate for use: it is preferable to allow people to opt out of donating certain parts of their body (commonly hearts and corneas) if this will increase the chance that they will donate their kidneys, lungs, and pancreas.

In recent years, it has become possible to transplant other body parts, such as limbs, faces, tongues, and wombs, and these transplants raise some new ethical and practical issues. First, while the side effects and health risks of immunosuppressant drugs will often be worth taking when the alternative is death, or very severely impaired existence, the risk/benefit calculation may be less clear when the alternative is an otherwise normal and healthy life without the use of a hand, or with a disfigured face. Indeed, it has been argued that hand or face transplants convert a healthy person with an amputated hand or facial disfigurement 'into a morbidly ill individual who must endure a toxic regime of drugs for the remainder of their life'.[28]

On the other hand, there are disadvantages in having only one functioning hand. Living with facial disfigurement can be difficult: the recipient of one of the first full face transplants had lived as a recluse for 15 years.[29] Without a functioning tongue, it is impossible to speak, swallow, and eat normally, leading one commentator to claim that while 'the tongue is not a vital organ in sustaining life, it may be a vital organ in sustaining the will to live in many people'.[30] There is even some evidence that people might be willing to incur more risk in order to have a new face than a new kidney.[31]

Secondly, the long-term impact, both physiological and psychological, of receiving another person's hand, limb, or face remain unknown. People may feel less comfortable about the transplant of a visible part of another person's body than they do about an unseen

---

[27] *An Ethical Framework for Controlled Donation after Circulatory Death* (AoMRC, 2011).

[28] Richard Huxtable and Julie Woodley, 'Gaining face or losing face? Framing the debate on face transplants' (2005) 19 Bioethics 505–22.

[29] See further www.umm.edu/programs/face-transplant.

[30] TA Day, quoted in Martin Birchall, 'Tongue transplantation' (2004) 363 The Lancet 1663.

[31] Michael Cunningham et al, 'Risk acceptance in composite tissue allotransplantation reconstructive procedures—instrument design and validation' (2004) 30 European Journal of Trauma 12–16.

internal organ. For the same reason, it is also likely that fewer people would be willing to donate their face or their limbs after death, and there is the further concern that people might be less likely to agree to donate their internal organs because of some vague, albeit unfounded, fear that their face might be used as well.

Womb transplants are a rather special case because, unlike any other sort of transplant, they are deliberately temporary.

(1) Limbs and Hands

The first human hand transplant took place in 1998. The recipient regretted the operation and could not cope with his new hand. He failed to comply with the drug regime, and, following chronic rejection, the transplanted hand had to be amputated. Other hand and limb transplants have been successful and have dramatically improved the quality of life of amputees or those who are born without functioning hands or limbs. The first successful hand transplant in the UK took place in 2012, and was the first operation to involve the removal of a non-functioning hand before the donor hand was attached. Although it can take up to three years for full sensation to be restored, after a relatively short period of time, the recipient was able to wash and dress himself, and pick up his grandchildren.

Despite the obvious benefits of restoring hand function, Dickenson and Widdershoven argue that our intimate relationships with our hands, and those of others, makes hand transplants more complex than transplants of 'invisible' internal organs.

Donna Dickenson and Guy Widdershoven[32]

It might be argued that hand allografts entail the transposition of an organ with personal qualities from one person to another. This goes beyond the issue of the hand's visibility, though that too is an issue . . . Likewise, it may be conceivable that the intimacy which the hand can express is transformed as a result of transplantation, necessarily having an emotional impact on those who are intimately related to both donor and recipient . . .

The hand, as an expression of both agency and intimacy, occupies a different place in our moral sensibility than internal organs. Again, this is not a reason for absolutely prohibiting hand transplants, if those intimate with both donor and recipient consent, but it is a reason for thinking that the decision is not down to the individual donor or recipient alone.

(2) Faces

The first face transplant took place in France in 2005. The recipient, Isabelle Dinoire, had been attacked by her dog and had suffered very severe facial injuries. The operation was a success, and improved both appearance and function. Since then, in addition to further face transplants in France, face transplants have taken place in China, the US, Spain, Turkey, Belgium, and Poland.

Face transplants raise a particularly difficult issue in the event of transplant failure. Removal of a face is not as straightforward as the amputation of a failed hand transplant. On the contrary, the failure of a face transplant might leave the recipient in a worse position than they were before the operation. In their review of all of the 28 face transplants performed in the nine years since Isabelle Dinoire's transplant, Khalifian et al reported

---

[32] 'Ethical issues in limb transplants' (2001) 15 Bioethics 110–24.

that none had failed spontaneously.[33] There was only one case in which the graft did not succeed, and this was because the patient had stopped taking their immune-suppressant medication.

Because the loss of a hand or a limb is disabling, the transplant would be done in order to improve function, rather than purely for aesthetic reasons. While some facial disfigurement can have an effect on function, as Clarke explains, disfigured people suffer principally as a result of others' reactions to them, which can include 'visual and verbal assaults, and a level of familiarity from strangers, naked stares, startled reactions, double takes, whispering, remarks, furtive looks, curiosity, personal questions, advice, manifestations of pity or aversion, laughter, ridicule and outright avoidance'.[34]

Richard Huxtable and Julie Woodley have therefore argued that face transplant surgery is done because of society's intolerance of disfigured people.

Richard Huxtable and Julie Woodley[35]

In an important sense, one must query whether the 'patient' is actually society, and in particular image-conscious Western society . . . This apparent obsession with beauty is probably one of the strongest reasons for permitting this procedure and also ironically one of the main reasons why it gives cause for concern. Ideally, of course, society would celebrate, rather than alienate, such diversity. There nevertheless lingers the suspicion that the influence of societal norms amounts to a form of coercion, which might again threaten the validity of any consent. Furthermore, we wonder whether alternative responses to disfigurement, such as counselling, would suffer once the transplantation doors are opened. As Strauss has pointed out, 'when something is correctable, our willingness to accept it as untouched is reduced'.

Of course, it is true that disfigured people should not have to endure discriminatory attitudes and hostility, but if a person finds her disfigurement disabling and distressing, and gives voluntary and informed consent to facial transplantation, it is not clear why her choice should not be respected just because we might wish that society was a more tolerant place.

In the UK, the Royal College of Surgeons has adopted a permissive but cautious approach to facial transplantation. Its Working Party's report lays out the special considerations which apply and the questions which must have been answered satisfactorily before a research ethics committee (REC) should give approval.[36] With proper safeguards in place, the Royal College of Surgeons concluded that 'there is no a priori reason why prospective patients who have been shown to be sufficiently autonomous cannot be accurately informed about both known and unknown risks of transplantation—assuming that the REC has agreed the risk benefit ratio to be acceptable'.[37]

The Working Party emphasized the psychological challenges facing not only recipients, but also their families and the families of donors.

[33] Saami Khalifian et al, 'Facial transplantation: the first 9 years' (2014) 384 The Lancet 2153–63.
[34] A Clarke, 'Psychosocial aspects of facial disfigurement' (1999) 4 Psychology, Health and Medicine 127–42.
[35] 'Gaining face or losing face? Framing the debate on face transplants' (2005) 19 Bioethics 505–22.
[36] Royal College of Surgeons of England, *Facial Transplantation. Working Party Report* (2003; 2nd edn 2006).
[37] Ibid.

Royal College of Surgeons[38]

All stages of the face transplantation process will present psychological challenges for recipients, their families and donor families . . .

The prospective patient should be sufficiently resilient to cope with the considerable stress associated with the transplant, including the 'unknowns' associated with a new procedure of this nature, the complex immunological and behavioural post-operative regimen, the risks of rejection and intrusive media interest . . .

Teams should be vigilant for signs of psychological rejection of the donor face, for example, lack of interest in looking at the face in a mirror, or indications that the patient feels the new face is 'not the real me' . . . The recipient may need assistance to resolve complex feelings about the donor (for example, curiosity about the sort of person, guilt about the donor's death, gratitude to the family) . . .

Post-operatively, family members should be monitored for signs of excessive stress and anxiety . . . Strategies may be needed to encourage acceptance of the new face.

Khalifian et al's review of the first 28 face transplants bears out these concerns, reporting that the most important predictor of success was rigorous pre-transplant screening of recipients.

Saami Khalifian et al[39]

Initial concerns about feelings of depersonalisation towards the new face and donor identity transfer or split have not been substantiated, and recipients do not resemble donors according to donor families, recipients, and transplant teams. A review of psychological outcomes after face transplantation showed a decreased prevalence of depression and verbal abuse and significantly improved body image, sense of self, and social reintegration. Patients have accepted their new face and describe improved quality of life, with several patients returning to work.

The overwhelmingly positive psychological outcome is probably a result of rigorous preoperative psychiatric and psychological selection of patients deemed to be stable, motivated, and compliant by a multidisciplinary team. The most notable exception is the patient who—displeased with the side-effects of immunosuppressive treatment—came to rely instead on traditional remedies on several occasions, leading to multiple rejection episodes and death. This outcome might have been prevented by more careful preoperative assessment and education, and postoperative psychiatric follow-up. . . .

The best candidate is one who: fully understands the implications of potentially lifelong immunosuppression and its serious morbidities, including infections, cancer, graft loss, and death; is motivated, committed, and compliant with intense post-operative rehabilitation, psychological treatment, and immunosuppression protocols; and has a strong social support system that will help them to address the many challenges, including media exposure, body image adaptation, and societal reintegration.

(3) Wombs

At the time of writing, wombs have been successfully transplanted to several women in Sweden, and the first child was born to a woman who had received a transplanted womb in 2014. Doctors from Imperial College NHS Trust in London have received ethics committee

---

[38] Ibid. [39] 'Facial transplantation: the first 9 years' (2014) 384 The Lancet 2153–63.

approval to carry out a trial of womb transplantation in the UK, with the first births expected in 2017.

Wombs could be transplanted from living or dead donors. A more complete transplant might be possible if a deceased donor is used, because it would be possible to extract more arteries and veins.[40] Using a deceased donor may also be preferable in order not to impose the risks of such a serious operation on living donors. On the other hand, if a relative donates their womb, there is a better chance that they will be a good tissue match. In the first Swedish cases, all the transplanted wombs came from living donors; in two cases, the women's mothers donated their uteruses to their daughters. The UK doctors are intending to use cadaveric donors. Following the transplant, the woman will be monitored for a year before embryos created by *in vitro* fertilization are implanted into the transplanted womb.

Some of the same considerations apply to womb transplants as to other novel transplants, but there are also differences. Like face or limb transplants, uterine transplantation is not life-saving. But, as Catsanos et al point out, the lack of a functioning uterus is not as disabling as the lack of a hand or face; nor does it prevent women from becoming mothers through surrogacy or adoption. The point of a womb transplant is simply to enable a woman without a uterus to experience pregnancy and childbirth.

Ruby Catsanos, Wendy Rogers, and Mianna Lotz[41]

Women who lack a functioning uterus do not have compromised health in terms of impaired day-to-day physiological function; nor is their lack of a uterus visible or socially inhibiting in the way that prosthetic upper limbs or facial deformities typically are. Furthermore, access to adoption and surrogacy would allow such women to become mothers; their children may even be genetically related to them. However, it would seem that a key motivating factor for UTx [uterine transplantation] is the desire to actually *bear* genetically-related children.

The strength of this desire may stem from a number of factors. For many women, experiencing pregnancy is a central aspect of their identity as women. The uterus represents a symbol of femininity, of women's biological difference from men. Pregnancy and childbirth is a unique physical and emotional experience shared only by women. Many women facing the removal of their uterus through hysterectomy undergo feelings of loss and damage to their gender identity; like the heart, the uterus is an organ with symbolic significance. The psychological and emotional aspects of pregnancy, the contribution of gender roles to personal identity, and societal expectations regarding procreation are difficult things to measure and weigh in relation to its risks, thereby raising questions about the ethical justification for UTx.

Three further special issues are raised by womb transplants. First, the woman will have to take immunosuppressant drugs while she is trying to conceive and during her pregnancy. Taking this sort of medication during pregnancy is not ideal, although pregnancy is not uncommon in women who have received other organs, and who are therefore taking immunosuppressive drugs. Evidence from these women indicates that immunosuppressive drugs are associated with an increased risk of miscarriage, prematurity, growth retardation, and low birthweight, although not with any increased risk of fetal anomaly.[42] These are

---

[40] Giuseppe Del Priore et al, 'Uterine transplantation—a real possibility? The Indianapolis consensus' (2013) 28 Human Reproduction 288–91.

[41] 'The ethics of uterus transplantation' (2013) 27 Bioethics 65–73.

[42] Giuseppe Del Priore et al, 'Uterine transplantation—a real possibility? The Indianapolis consensus' (2013) 28 Human Reproduction 288–91.

risks which are judged to be worth taking in women who wish to have children after having undergone organ transplantation, and so it might be argued that there is no difference between these women and women who need a transplanted uterus in order to experience pregnancy.

Secondly, if the transplant were to fail after pregnancy had been achieved, the removal of the uterus would, unless the pregnancy had reached the third trimester, inevitably cause the death of the fetus. This risk is minimized by the requirement that a year should elapse between the transplant and the first embryo transfer, but it cannot be eliminated.

Thirdly, the woman only needs the transplanted womb for the purposes of pregnancy. The risks associated with immunosuppressant drugs are such that the transplanted womb will be removed once the woman no longer needs it. A full hysterectomy would then be carried out soon after the birth of the woman's first or second child.

(d) AUTHORIZATION OF REMOVAL

(1) The Human Tissue Act 2004

According to section 1 of the Human Tissue Act 2004, no organ can be taken without 'appropriate consent'.

(a) Adults

For adults appropriate consent can, under section 3, be obtained in three different ways.

Human Tissue Act 2004 section 3

3(6) Where the person concerned has died . . . 'appropriate consent' means—

(a) if a decision of his to consent to the activity, or a decision of his not to consent to it, was in force immediately before he died, his consent;

(b) if—

    (i) paragraph (a) does not apply, and

    (ii) he has appointed a person or persons under section 4 to deal after his death with the issue of consent in relation to the activity,

(c) consent given under the appointment;

(d) if neither paragraph (a) nor paragraph (b) applies, the consent of a person who stood in a qualifying relationship to him immediately before he died.

If the deceased has consented to organ transplantation by being registered on the organ donor register, the doctors would act lawfully in retrieving her organs. Of course, some would argue that the process of signing up to the register is very far removed from normal informed consent processes, which we considered in Chapter 4. People can fill in a brief registration form online, or they can sign up by ticking the relevant box on an application form for a driving licence. Registration rates have also been boosted by the inclusion of a tick box on applications for a Boots Advantage Card.[43] But just ticking a box online gives

---

[43] A loyalty card from the UK's largest chain of pharmacists.

no opportunity to assess the person's capacity to make the decision, and there is no formal information-giving process.

Organ Donation Taskforce[44]

> Amongst clinicians there is a certain amount of concern that the carrying of a donor card, or even registration with the donor register, falls short of what would usually be defined as consent in a medical setting. Furthermore, in the absence of independent evidence of a persisting wish, the passage of time between registration and death is seen by some to weaken the ethical force of the action.

Of course, agreeing to become a donor after death is different from giving informed consent to medical treatment. But because 'consent' has such a specific meaning in medical law, it might be worth thinking about using a different term. The Human Tissue (Scotland) Act 2004, for example, refers to 'authorization', rather than consent.

The deceased's consent (or authorization) does not have to be in writing, and if there is no donor card, or the deceased is not on the organ donor register, other efforts should be made to find out whether the deceased wished to donate her organs after death.

HTA Draft Code of Practice[45]

> 122. If no records are held, an approach should be made to the deceased person's spouse or partner, relatives or close friends by a SN-OD [specialist nurse for organ donation]. Best practice recommends that the approach to the deceased person's relatives should be made together by the SN-OD and a member of the team who is caring for the person to establish any known decision of the potential donor.

If the deceased's wishes are not known, but she has appointed someone under section 4 of the Act to deal with consent, then the appointed person's consent will be sufficient. A person might want to nominate a representative, or more than one, to give consent in order to ensure that the decision is taken by someone who knows her wishes, rather than leaving it to whoever turns out to be the highest ranking qualified relative at the time of her death. This might be particularly important for someone who knows that members of her family disagree about transplantation, in order to ensure that the decision is taken by someone who shares her views. An appointment can be made orally, if witnessed by two people, or in writing, with one witness.

Where the deceased person had not given consent and had either not nominated someone to give proxy consent, or under section 3(7) and (8) their nominee is unable to consent, or 'it is not reasonably practicable to communicate with [him or her] within the time available', then consent can be sought from someone in a qualifying relationship.

Qualifying relationships are defined in section 27(4) and are ranked, so that the consent of a spouse or partner should be sought first, and that of a parent or child only if no spouse

---

[44] *Organs for Transplants: A Report from the Organ Donation Taskforce* (DH: London, 2008).
[45] Draft Code F Organ Donation (HTA, 2015).

or partner is available to consent, and that of a brother or sister only if no spouse, partner, parent, or child can give consent, and so on. The full hierarchy is as follows:

(a) spouse or partner;[46]

(b) parent or child;

(c) brother or sister;

(d) grandparent or grandchild;

(e) child of a brother or sister;

(f) stepfather or stepmother;

(g) half-brother or half-sister;

(h) friend of long standing.

Because organs must be retrieved as quickly as possible after death, it may not always be feasible to contact the person highest in the hierarchy of qualifying relatives, or they may not wish to make the decision, or may lack the capacity to do so. In such circumstances, the HTA's draft Code of Practice provides that 'a person's relationship can be left out of account', and 'the next person in the hierarchy would become the appropriate person to give consent'.[47]

Section 27(5) states that 'Relationships in the same paragraph of subsection (4) should be accorded equal ranking', so where there is both a parent and a child, either is able to give consent. And under section 27(7): 'If the relationship of each of two or more persons to the person concerned is accorded equal highest ranking . . . it is sufficient to obtain the consent of any of them.' This means that if the deceased has both an estranged spouse and a new partner, the consent of the estranged spouse would be sufficient, even if their current partner objects. Similarly, where the deceased has no spouse or partner, but several children, any one of them can give consent, even if all of the other children are opposed to organ retrieval.

It is important to remember that under the Human Tissue Act 2004, it is lawful to take organs where an appropriate consent exists, but not obligatory. In practice, relatives' views will be taken into account even if the deceased has made her wishes known. Although the deceased's family do not have a legal right of veto, doctors may be reluctant to retrieve organs where relatives object, both for compassionate reasons and from the more pragmatic desire to avoid the bad publicity that might result from ignoring the wishes of distraught, recently bereaved relatives. The draft Code of Practice suggests that health professionals should try to encourage the family to respect the deceased's wishes.

HTA Draft Code of Practice[48]

114. Where valid consent has been given by the donor, but relatives object to organ donation proceeding, then they should be sensitively supported to respect the prospective donor's consent to ensure his or her wishes are fulfilled. A relative's objection does not nullify appropriate, valid consent from the prospective donor.

---

[46] Partner is defined in s 54(9): 'For the purposes of this Act, . . . a person is another's partner if the two of them (whether of different sexes or the same sex) live as partners in an enduring family relationship.'

[47] Draft Code A Principles and Consent (HTA, 2015) para 35.

[48] Draft Code F Organ Donation (HTA, 2015).

> 115. The existence of appropriate, valid consent permits an activity to proceed, but does not mandate that it must. The final decision about whether to proceed with the activity rests with the medical practitioner.

It could be argued that giving relatives any say over what happens to a person's body after death is inconsistent with the dominant principle of patient autonomy: why should one of my relatives who has absolutely no say over my medical treatment during my life be permitted, in practice, to overrule my decision to donate my organs after my death?

On the other hand, Margaret Lock suggests that it is families, rather than donors, who make the greatest sacrifice when organs are taken from a dead body.

Margaret Lock[49]

> [W]e encourage the idea that donation is a selfless act, but it can also be thought of as the giving away of something no longer of any use: it takes virtually no effort to sign a donor card. But donor families make a much greater emotional sacrifice. They must usually come to terms with the fact that someone dear to them has been transformed, in the space of a few hours, and often through a violent encounter, from a healthy individual into an irrevocably damaged entity, suspended between life and death. To give selflessly under these circumstances requires courage, as well as faith in the ICU staff and in the truth of their assessments.

Each year NHS Blood and Transplant carries out an audit of all potential donors. In 2014–15, there were 1,733 people on mechanical ventilation where all of the criteria for neurological testing of death were satisfied.[50] Neurological tests to confirm death were performed on 1,444 potential donors, and in 1,422 cases, death was confirmed using neurological criteria. Fifty potential DBD donors were ruled out because of medical contraindications for donation, and the families were then approached in 1,283 cases. Of these, 858 families agreed to donation, and solid organ donation took place in 779 cases.

A similar audit for DCD patients revealed that there were 17,798 deceased people on mechanical ventilation in whom death was not confirmed using neurological criteria. Imminent death was anticipated in 6,725 cases, and treatment was withdrawn in 6,028 cases. In 1,764 cases there were contraindications to donation, but of the 4,262 in whom there were no contraindications, the family was asked about donation in 2,012 cases. Of these, 1,045 families agreed to donation, and donation occurred in 494 cases.

It is clear that although it is now normal practice to ask the family about donation in the cases of DBD donors, practice is more variable in relation to DCD donors. In both cases, however, there is considerable scope to increase the number of donors at almost every stage. Given that an average of 3.9 organs can be taken from each DBD donor and 2.5 from each DCD donor, obtaining organs from all of the unused but suitable potential donors undoubtedly has the potential massively to increase the number of transplants.

---

[49] *Twice Dead: Organ Transplants and the Reinvention of Death* (University of California Press: Berkeley, 2002) 373.

[50] NHS Blood and Transplant, *Annual Activity Report 2014–15: National Potential Donor Audit* (NHSBT, 2015).

In practice, when a patient is known to have expressed a wish to donate, the consent rate for potential DBDs is 93 per cent. This means that 7 per cent of families refuse to agree to donation despite the individual having consented to donation during his or her lifetime. For potential DCD donors, the consent rate when the person's wish to donate is known is 85 per cent, which means that 15 per cent of families override the deceased's known wishes. When the person's wishes are not known, 53 per cent of families consent to DBD donation, and 38 per cent consent to DCD donation.[51]

NHS Blood and Transplant also records the reasons for relatives' refusal. Other than either knowing that the person did not want to be a donor (17 per cent), or not knowing their wishes (15 per cent), common reasons given were not wanting surgery to the body (8 per cent), a feeling that the deceased has suffered enough (7 per cent), and religious beliefs (5 per cent).[52]

In 2011, the National Institution for Health and Clinical Excellence (NICE; now the National Institute for Health and Care Excellence) issued a clinical guideline on improving donor identification and consent rates which stressed the importance of presenting the option of donation in a positive light.

National Institute for Health and Clinical Excellence[53]

1.1.17 Approach those close to the patient in a setting suitable for private and compassionate discussion . . .

1.1.20 Discussions about organ donation with those close to the patient should only take place when it has been clearly established that they understand that death is inevitable or has occurred.

1.1.21 When approaching those close to the patient:

- discuss with them that donation is a usual part of the end-of-life care

- use open-ended questions—for example 'how do you think your relative would feel about organ donation?'

- use positive ways to describe organ donation, especially when patients are on the NHS organ donor register or they have expressed a wish to donate during their lifetime—for example 'by becoming a donor your relative has a chance to save and transform the lives of many others'

- avoid the use of apologetic or negative language (for example 'I am asking you because it is policy' or 'I am sorry to have to ask you').

(b) Children

Where the deceased is a child, organ retrieval will be lawful if there is appropriate consent under section 2(7):

---

[51] Ibid.

[52] NHS Transplant, *Delivering a Revolution in Public Behaviour in Relation to Organ Donation: A Summary of the Evidence* (NHSBT, 2014).

[53] *Organ Donation for Transplantation: Improving Donor Identification and Consent Rates for Deceased Organ Donation* (NICE: London, 2011).

Human Tissue Act 2004 section 2

2(7) Where the child concerned has died . . . 'appropriate consent' means—

(a) if a decision of his to consent to the activity, or a decision of his not to consent to it, was in force immediately before he died, his consent;

(b) if paragraph (a) does not apply—

(i) the consent of a person who had parental responsibility for him immediately before he died, or

(ii) where no person had parental responsibility for him immediately before he died, the consent of a person who stood in a qualifying relationship to him at that time.

Hence a *Gillick*-competent minor's consent will be sufficient for organ retrieval to be lawful.[54] The problem here is that the child is now dead, and so establishing that they were, in fact, *Gillick*-competent will be difficult. As the draft Code of Practice makes clear, even where the child's wishes are known, retrieval should not go ahead without discussion with someone with parental responsibility.

HTA Draft Code of Practice[55]

87. In some cases it may be advisable to establish with the person who had parental responsibility for the deceased child whether the child was competent to make the decision. . . . In any case where a child has consented to the use of their body or tissue, it is essential to discuss this with the child's relatives.

(2) Liability for Unlawful Removal

Section 5 of the Human Tissue Act 2004 provides that anyone who takes organs without appropriate consent commits an offence, unless he reasonably believes that he did in fact have appropriate consent. The maximum penalty is three years' imprisonment.

(e) SYSTEM FOR REMOVAL AND ALLOCATION

NHS Blood and Transplant oversees transplantation arrangements in the UK. Its responsibilities include maintaining the national transplant waiting list; matching and allocating organs; transporting organs to recipient centres; and maintaining the organ donor register. It also promotes organ donation and transplantation, and maintains transplant coordination services.

Once a patient is identified as a potential organ donor, the local specialist nurse for organ donation (SN-OD) should be contacted. SN-ODs are responsible for ascertaining the views of the potential donor's family, and they will also contact NHS Blood and Transplant in order to find out whether the donor is on the organ donor register. Once agreement to organ donation has been obtained, the SN-OD will notify NHS Blood and Transplant, which maintains a national database of all potential organ recipients. When the appropriate recipient has been identified, the SN-OD liaises between the surgical teams responsible for both the donor and the recipient's care.

---

[54] See Chapter 5 for a description of *Gillick*-competence.
[55] Draft Code F Organ Donation (HTA, 2015).

Cadaveric organ donation is usually anonymous. It is, however, possible for the donor's family to be given some information, such as the age and sex of the people who have benefited from the donation. Patients who receive organs can obtain similar information about their donors.

Obviously, efforts must be made to ensure that the potential donor does not have a serious condition that could jeopardize the recipient's health. Contraindications for donation include severe or untreated infections, cancers that have spread within the last 12 months, and Creutzfeldt–Jakob disease (CJD). Organs from donors known to be HIV-positive would not ordinarily be used, but there have been a few cases in which they have been transplanted to HIV-positive recipients.

Given advances in treatments for people who are HIV-positive, it is interesting to consider whether there might be circumstances in which it would be in the best interests of an HIV-negative individual to receive an organ from an HIV-positive donor. Clearly this is not ideal, especially in the light of the immunosuppressant drugs which must be taken post-transplantation, but if the potential recipient is likely to die before an HIV-negative organ becomes available, the risk of HIV infection and the need to take more medication after transplantation might be risks an individual would consider worth taking. As yet, no such operations have taken place in the UK, but there are those who would argue that this sort of transplantation should not be completely ruled out.

Bram P Wispelwey, Ari Z Zivotofsky, and Alan B Jotkowitz[56]

If the potential recipient demonstrates full awareness of the risks of receiving an organ from an HIV-positive donor, he or she has the right via the principle of autonomy to accept those risks along with the potential life-saving benefits. . . . It is true that informed consent . . . may be more difficult to achieve given the complexities of living with HIV, and significant patient counselling and education over multiple sessions would likely be necessary. But there is no reason to believe that a robust informed consent could never be given. . . .

When the consequence of doing nothing is uniformly fatal, as in the case of liver transplantation, the ethical obligation of beneficence—offering the possibility of survival—in the absence of non-infected donation surely outweighs the potential harm of risking transmission of a controllable if lifelong viral infection.

(f) THE SHORTAGE OF ORGANS

NHS Transplant issues detailed statistics on transplant activity in the UK each year.[57]

Year	Cadaveric donors	Cadaveric transplants	Waiting list	Living donors
2013/14	780 DBD 540 DCD	4,655	7,026	1,146
2014/15	772 DBD 510 DCD	4,431	6,943	1,092

[56] 'The transplantation of solid organs from HIV-positive donors to HIV-negative recipients: ethical implications' (2015) 41 Journal of Medical Ethics 367–70.

[57] NHS Blood and Transplant, *Annual Activity Report 2014–15: Summary of Transplant Activity* (NHSBT, 2015).

As is clear from the table, there are many more people on the waiting list for transplants than there are available organs. When it reformed the law on transplantation in 2004, the government opted to stick to a consent model for transplantation. The Organ Donation Taskforce did not recommend a change to this system, arguing instead that it should be possible to increase donation rates without changing the law.

(1) Improved Coordination

In Spain, following the introduction of a new transplant coordinator network in 1990, every hospital with an intensive care unit, not just those that also have a transplant unit, has a transplant team. This means that organ procurement and intensive care are effectively integrated, and health care professionals working in intensive care units are well informed about the procedures involved in obtaining organs for transplant. The effect on procurement rates has been positive. In Spain, there are, on average, 35.3 donors per million population, in the UK the equivalent figure is 21 per million.[58]

The first report from the Organ Donation Taskforce recommended improving the donation system in the UK by making the preparatory steps for donation routine, removing bureaucratic obstacles to donation, and facilitating greater recognition of donors. All of their recommendations have been implemented. Each hospital now has a clinical lead for transplantation, who is responsible for ensuring that processes are in place to optimize potential donor identification and management. There has also been success in establishing regional multi-organ retrieval teams, which are available 24 hours a day, seven days a week, in order to advise on donor management prior to donation, and increase the quality and effectiveness of organ retrievals. Throughout the UK, steps have also been taken to recognize and thank organ donors. An online book of remembrance has been set up,[59] and many hospitals now have public commemorative plaques to organ donors.

A UK Donation Ethics Committee was set up in 2010 to provide advice on the ethical aspects of organ donation and transplantation. It has considered a number of issues, such as the care of donors after circulatory death, and it has recommended that consent to organ donation should be routinely accompanied by consent to research as well, so that if a donated organ is unsuitable for transplantation, it might nevertheless be used in medical research.

In the final report on the implementation of the Taskforce's proposals, a 25 per cent increase in the number of deceased donors was recorded. It should, however, be noted that most of this increase was attributable to an 87 per cent increase in the numbers of DCD donors. The increase in the rates of donation among DBD donors was only 4 per cent. This is important because fewer organs can be taken from DCD donors: they can provide kidneys, but are less suitable as liver donors, and currently they do not provide hearts and lungs. It is also important to note that the steady increase in donors between 2008 and 2013 was not sustained in 2014–15, when there was a drop in the number of deceased donors.

In 2013, NHS Blood and Transplant published a new strategy to take organ transplantation to 2020.[60] Its aims are to increase consent rates for organ donation, and make sure as many organs as possible are transplanted from each donor. One step that has already been taken is to ensure that people can register their wishes, both positive or negative, on the organ donor register in order to increase the chances both of registration and of adherence to the donor's wishes.

---

[58] European Commission, *Organ Donation: Recent Facts and Figures* (EC, 2014).
[59] www.donorfamilynetwork.co.uk/book-of-remembrance/.
[60] NHSBT, *Taking Organ Transplantation to 2020: A detailed strategy* (NHSBT, 2013).

Clearly it is sensible to make organ donation more routine, and to ensure that the transplantation system is fit for purpose. There are, however, those who would advocate more radical reforms in order to address the gap between supply and demand.

(2) Elective Ventilation

In May 1988, the Royal Devon and Exeter Hospital introduced a new protocol designed to enable organs to be taken from potential donors who were dying outside intensive care units (ICUs). Once identified, and with the agreement of the relatives, such patients would be transferred to an ICU and 'electively ventilated' to ensure that their organs would be suitable for transplant. The relatives were told that the patient was not going to recover, and were asked to agree both to organ donation and to the patient's transfer to an ICU to enable organ donation to proceed after the patient's death. During the next 19 months, the number of organs available for transplant increased by more than 50 per cent. The scheme had to be stopped, however, when the Department of Health declared it to be unlawful.

Unconscious patients lack capacity, which means that—in the absence of a binding advance decision—doctors must treat them in their best interests. Placing a patient who is not expected to recover on a ventilator in order to ensure that her organs are suitable for transplant is not done to benefit her, but rather to benefit third parties on the organ transplant waiting list. But, as John Coggon has pointed out, when the Exeter protocol was halted in the early 1990s, 'best interests' assessments were narrowly confined to the patient's best clinical interests. Under section 4 of the Mental Capacity Act 2005, best interests receives a more holistic interpretation and so it might be possible to establish that the patient was so strongly committed to being an organ donor that elective ventilation would allow her wishes to be fulfilled.

John Coggon[61]

> The courts have been clear that they will not allow best interests to be reduced just to 'medical' or 'clinical' interests. Instead, a more 'holistic' appraisal is required, that looks to a much richer concept of welfare. This finds clarity particularly in statements made by the courts around the turn of the century, saying, for example, that best interests must 'incorporate broader ethical, social, moral and welfare considerations.' Of course this change does not allow patients who lack capacity to become simple means to others' ends, but it does allow for non-therapeutic benefits, including non-physical and non-experiential benefits, to feature in decision-making. . . .
>
> Of particular note, section 4(6) of the Act demands that decision-makers, when assessing best interests, account for the patient's past and present wishes, and the beliefs and values that would influence his decision if he were making it. It is therefore very hard to say, in the abstract, that a given measure such as [elective ventilation] would *never* be in any patient's best interests as judged at law.

On the other hand, as JK Mason points out, insofar as there is a small risk that once placed on a ventilator, the patient might lapse into a coma or a permanent vegetative state, it would be hard to argue that it is in her best interests.

---

[61] 'Elective ventilation for organ donation: law, policy and public ethics' (2013) 39 Journal of Medical Ethics 130–4.

J Kenyon Mason[62]

[There are] three possible untoward outcomes: the patient may develop some other condition while under intensive care, such as sepsis, which invalidates him as a donor; the patient may recover sufficiently to be discharged from hospital; or the patient may stabilise in the persistent vegetative state. It is this last possibility which raises the greatest fears and it is, probably, the least unlikely of the three scenarios to develop. The production of a persistent vegetative state in a person who was close to a peaceful natural death could only be described as a clinical disaster which, if publicised, could be catastrophically detrimental to the whole transplantation programme.

A further consideration is that beds in ICUs are scarce and expensive. Is it legitimate to transfer a dying patient to a high-dependency unit when this is done not for her own good, but in order to ensure that her organs will be capable of benefiting others? There are often not enough beds in an ICU for every patient who might need one, and it would seem unreasonable to deprive a patient who might recover from treatment in order to ventilate someone who is going to die. Of course, there might be circumstances in which a dying patient could be placed in a bed that would otherwise be unused in order to ensure that her organs would be available to others after her death. Could it then be unethical to leave a bed empty when its use might save several lives? Moreover, because transplantation is more cost-effective than dialysis, a substantial increase in the number of organs available for transplant might save the NHS money, thus offsetting the costs of elective ventilation.

Nevertheless, the Academy of Medical Royal Colleges' Code of Practice is clear that ventilation should only be initiated and maintained if it is in the patient's best interests, and not to ensure that her organs can be used in transplantation.

Academy of Medical Royal Colleges[63]

7.3 If further intensive care is not considered appropriate because it can be of no benefit, nor in the patient's best interests, then neither is a continuation of the respiratory support being provided.

Endotracheal intubation and artificial ventilation of the patient should only be initiated and maintained to further the patient's benefit and not as a means of preserving organ function.

(3) Allowing Conditional Donation

In July 1998, a man who was unconscious and in a critical condition was admitted to an ICU in the north of England. His relatives agreed to organ donation in the event of his death, but only on condition that the organs went to white recipients. In this instance, the person on the waiting list who was most urgently in need of a liver transplant was white, and without the organ he would have died within 24 hours. The two people who came top in the kidney transplant points system also happened to be white. Because the condition would have made

---

[62] 'Contemporary Issues in Organ Transplantation' in Sheila McLean (ed), *Contemporary Issues in Law, Medicine and Ethics* (Dartmouth: Aldershot, 1996) 117–41.

[63] Academy of Medical Royal Colleges, *A Code of Practice for the Diagnosis and Confirmation of Death* (AoMRC, 2008).

no difference, the organs were accepted and two kidneys and a liver were successfully transplanted into three different individuals.

Unsurprisingly, the case received a great deal of publicity, and the Department of Health set up an investigation.[64] It was established that the three organs went to the same people who would have received them if no condition had been attached, so no one was in fact disadvantaged. But the panel also concluded that it had been wrong for the organs to have been accepted in the first place, and recommended that organs must not be accepted if the donor or the family wishes to attach conditions. This was accepted by the Department of Health, and the prohibition on conditional donation applies to all conditions, not just to racist and discriminatory ones.

Although conditional donation like this is plainly objectionable, the issue is made more complicated by the existence of identifiable individuals on the waiting list who will die if a suitable organ is turned down on moral grounds. The liver recipient in this case would have died within 24 hours if this organ was not accepted, making it extremely unlikely that an alternative non-conditional organ would have become available in time to save his life.

It might also be argued that there is an inconsistency between living organ donation, where donation is almost always to a specified individual, and cadaveric donation, which must be unconditional. As TM Wilkinson points out in the next extract, it is hard to see what would be wrong with allowing directed donation to a close friend or relative after death.

TM Wilkinson[65]

Is it really so bad to attach a condition to an organ donation? Of course it was bad in the case of the racist. The motive there was some mix of hatred and contempt and there is nothing to be said for it. But what about the condition that an organ go to a relative? There seems nothing morally wrong about agreeing to donate a kidney, say, on condition that it go to a sibling, whether the donation is to be from a living person or a dead one . . .

Setting aside a special concern for one's nearest and dearest, let us consider the panel's explanation of what is wrong with attaching a condition to a donation. The panel claims that conditional donation 'offends against the fundamental principle that organs are donated altruistically and should go to patients in the greatest need'. Altruism in its normal sense refers roughly to a non-self-interested concern for the interests of others. Importantly, a wide variety of other-regarding motives can be regarded as altruistic, such as a special concern for children, or the deaf, or the poor. 'Altruism' . . . does not require, for example, that actions be motivated out of adherence to a greatest happiness principle or, saliently here, a greatest needs principle. Consequently, there need be nothing non-altruistic about conditional donation. Wanting organs to go to a child—although also apparently opposed by the panel—is not a violation of altruism any more than donating to a children's charity is.

Of course, it is seldom possible for cadaveric donation to be directed to a specific individual because organ donors will often be unaware of their impending and often sudden death. But in rare cases, a person might die after expressing a preference that one of her organs should be used to treat a close relative.

Indeed this happened in 2008, when the HTA was criticized for not permitting conditional donation in the case of Laura Ashworth, who had expressed an interest in becoming

---

[64] *An Investigation into Conditional Organ Donation: The Report* (DH: London, 2000).
[65] 'What's not wrong with conditional organ donation?' (2003) 29 Journal of Medical Ethics 163–4.

a living kidney donor for her mother, Rachel Leake. Laura then died from an acute attack of asthma, before having taken any formal steps towards becoming a living donor. Because she was registered on the organ donor register, her organs were retrieved for transplantation, and her kidneys went to the two strangers on the waiting list with the most 'points'. Of course, if Laura Ashworth had been a living, rather than a deceased donor, there would have been no question of her donated kidney being given to a stranger in preference to her mother.

This case led the Department of Health to issue new guidance which reiterates that donation must always be unconditional, but which also allows for 'requested allocation' in exceptional circumstances, where there is no one on the waiting list in desperately urgent clinical need for the organ.

Department of Health[66]

3. The fundamental principle of all deceased organ donation, is that it must be unconditional. Having first established that the consent or authorisation to organ donation is unconditional, a request for the allocation of a donor organ can be considered in exceptional cases, where all the following principles apply:

- that there is appropriate consent, or authorisation in Scotland, to organ donation;
- that the consent or authorisation for organ donation is not conditional on the request for the allocation of a donor organ to the specified relative or friend of long standing going ahead;
- that there are not others in desperately urgent clinical need of the organ who may be harmed by a request for the organ to be allocated to a named individual going ahead;
- that in life the deceased had indicated a wish to donate to a specific named relative or friend of long standing in need of an organ; or, in the absence of that indication, the deceased's family expresses such a wish; . . .
- that the need for a transplant is clinically indicated for the intended recipient.

4. Priority must be given to a patient in desperately urgent clinical need over any requested allocation.

Antonia Cronin and James Douglas have argued that the Department of Health's interpretation of the Human Tissue Act is wrong. The Act requires 'appropriate consent' for donation of a cadaveric organ, and makes transplantation without such consent an offence.

Antonia J Cronin and James F Douglas[67]

If a donor's consent has been limited to specific situations, it follows that any allocation of organs contrary to such limitations vitiates that consent and amounts to dealing with the organs *without* consent [and] would be an offence under section 5 of the Act.

---

[66] *Requested Allocation of a Deceased Donor Organ* (DH: London, 2010).
[67] Antonia J Cronin and James F Douglas, 'Directed and Conditional Deceased Donor Organ Donations: Laws and Misconceptions' (2010) 18 Medical Law Review 275–301.

In the HTA's draft new Code of Practice A, Principles and Consent, this anomaly has been corrected.

HTA Draft Code of Practice[68]

Where any conditions attached to consent cannot be acted upon, the person who has attached the condition should be made aware of this and asked whether they are willing to put these conditions aside in order to allow the activity to proceed. It would be an offence to proceed with an activity for a scheduled purpose in the knowledge that a persisting condition on consent could or would not be fulfilled, as valid consent would not be in place. **Only the person who has attached the condition to the consent can put the condition aside.**

(4) Required Request

If doctors do not mention the possibility of donation, potentially life-saving organs may be lost. A 'required request' system would remove clinical discretion and place medical practitioners under a duty to raise the question of organ donation whenever a suitable donor is dying.

In practice, however, it is not clear that required request would make much difference. Certainly, NHS Transplant's Potential Donor Audit has found that there are comparatively few cases in which solid organ donation is possible, but not mentioned to relatives.

(5) An 'Opt-Out' System

Organ donation in England is an 'opt-in' system, where individuals are able to volunteer to become organ donors, and if they have not done so, under the Human Tissue Act 2004, their nominated representative or a qualifying relative may give appropriate consent. In contrast, in an 'opt-out' system, sometimes also referred to as 'presumed consent', it is assumed that every potential donor is willing to donate their organs, but people can opt out by formally registering their unwillingness to donate.

Certainly, on the basis of the evidence, this assumption seems warranted: most people say that they would be willing to donate their organs after death. There are those who argue that we should be cautious about accepting the results of public opinion surveys, on the grounds that people commonly respond to questions by giving the answer that they think will show themselves in a good light. Nevertheless, even if opinion polls overstate the percentage of those who wish to donate organs after death, it seems clear that donation is supported by a majority of the population.

While not insurmountable, several practical and ethical issues would have to be addressed before moving towards an opt-out system. First, an opt-out system rests upon the assumption that the public is sufficiently well informed that any failure to register an objection reflects a person's willingness to donate, rather than their lethargy or ignorance. It has been predicted that fewer people would register an objection than actually have reservations about donation, and that less educated or minority groups will be less likely to consent to donation and less likely to understand how to opt out.

---

[68] Draft Code A Principles and Consent (HTA, 2015).

Secondly, it has been argued that the term 'presumed consent' is misleading. As we saw in Chapters 4 and 5, consent in medical law is generally assumed to be active and positive, rather than something which can be assumed from inaction. The reality, in an opt-out system, is that organs could be taken without consent.[69] Thirdly, it would be necessary to maintain a large, centralized database on which objections could be recorded, and amended if people changed their minds. It would further be necessary to ensure that this database could be rapidly and accurately accessed as soon as a potential donor is identified.

A number of countries have adopted opt-out systems, but in most of these relatives continue to be consulted about organ transplantation. Taking organs in the face of a relative's vigorous objection would generally be counterproductive because of the adverse publicity it would be likely to generate. In France, for example, doctors always ask for familial consent to organ donation.[70] Nevertheless, as English and Sommerville suggest in the following extract, changing the default position may reduce the burden on relatives.

V English and A Sommerville[71]

Arguably, simply changing the default position could have huge benefits. Not least for relatives themselves who, at a time of emotional upheaval and bereavement, may not relish being asked to decide in the absence of any indication of the wishes of the deceased. One of the advantages of a presumed consent system is that the main burden of making this decision is lessened for the relatives although they would still be involved . . .

The possibility of relatives refusing donation when the deceased person actually wished to donate has already been mentioned. The opposite can also happen. Currently, individuals who strongly object to donation lack any formal mechanism for registering that objection and the decision to donate may ultimately be made by distant relatives. Under the opt in system, there are no guarantees that relatives will not act contrary to the strongly held views of a deceased person, either through lack of knowledge or lack of agreement with them. In this way, an opt out system where objections can be registered and must be respected, would enhance individual autonomy for those who do not want to be donors.

In contrast, the Organ Donation Taskforce concluded that an opt-out system might instead erode trust.

Organ Donation Taskforce[72]

8.2 The clinical Working group heard from a number of clinicians from intensive care (where the majority of deaths leading to donation occur) who were persuasive in articulating the view that a presumption of consent might make families feel that they were being pressured and erode the relationship of trust between clinician and family . . .

---

[69] Charles A Erin and John Harris, 'Presumed consent or contracting out' (1999) 25 Journal of Medical Ethics 365–6.

[70] Bernard Teo, 'Is the adoption of more efficient strategies of organ procurement the answer to persistent organ shortage in transplantation?' (1992) 6 Bioethics 113–29, 127.

[71] 'Presumed consent for transplantation: a dead issue after Alder Hey?' (2003) 29 Journal of Medical Ethics 147–52.

[72] *The Potential Impact of an Opt Out System for Organ Donation in the UK: An Independent Report from the Organ Donation Taskforce* (DH: London, 2008).

8.6 . . . An opt out system has the potential to erode the trust between clinicians and families at a distressing time. The concept of a gift freely given is an important one to both donor families and transplant recipients. The Taskforce feels that an opt out system of consent has the potential to undermine this concept.

The main reason for moving towards an opt-out system is the possibility of increasing the supply of organs for transplantation. In the next extract, Kennedy et al discuss the increase in the number of kidneys available for transplant which followed the introduction of a presumed consent system in Belgium.[73]

Ian Kennedy et al and the International Forum for Transplant Ethics[74]

In the whole country organ donation rose by 55% within 5 years despite a concurrent decrease in the number of organs available from road traffic accidents. Citizens who wish to opt out of the scheme may register their objection at any Town Hall; since 1986 less than 2% of the population have done so. Use of a computerised register has simplified ascertaining the existence of any objection. In Belgium, despite the existence of this law, doctors are encouraged to approach the relatives in all cases and practitioners may decide against removing the organs if in their opinion this would cause undue distress or for any other valid reason. Less than 10% of families do object compared with 20–30% elsewhere in Europe . . . It would seem from the Belgian experience that relatives may be reluctant to take a personal decision about the removal of organs, but they find it easier to agree if they are simply confirming the intention of the dead person. If this is so, a contracting out system has a moral benefit of relieving grieving relatives of the burden of deciding about donation at a time of great psychological stress. A change in the law thus achieves the dual effect of increasing the supply of organs and lessening the distress of relatives.

Interestingly, the Taskforce was not persuaded that an opt-out system would increase donations.

Organ Donation Taskforce[75]

11.4 It is worth noting that presumed consent legislation was passed in Spain in 1979 but it was only a decade later, in 1989, when their national transplant organisation was founded, putting a new infrastructure in place, that donor rates began to rise.

11.5 . . . The Taskforce is not confident that the introduction of opt out legislation would increase organ donor numbers, and there is evidence that donor numbers may go down.

Despite the Taskforce's opposition, in its consultation on post-2013 Organ Donation Strategy, NHS Blood and Transplant once again invited comments on moving to an opt-out system. In answer to a question about the best way to 'make organ donation a normal part

---

[73] See also Kenneth Gundle, 'Presumed consent: an international comparison and possibilities for change in the United States' (2005) 14 Cambridge Quarterly of Healthcare Ethics 113–18.

[74] 'The case for "presumed consent" in organ donation' (1998) 351 The Lancet 1650–2.

[75] *The Potential Impact of an Opt Out System for Organ Donation in the UK: An Independent Report from the Organ Donation Taskforce* (DH: London, 2008).

of UK culture', approximately half of all respondents were in favour of changing the consent system.[76]

The British Medical Association (BMA) has been one of the most consistent supporters of a soft opt-out system, which would allow organs to be removed after the individual's death if there is no evidence from the non-donor register, or volunteered by the family, that the individual objected to his or her body, or any specific part of the body, being used for transplantation after death. If, however, the individual has not expressed any views about donation while alive but it is apparent that to proceed with the donation would cause major distress to a first-degree relative or long-term partner, the donation should not proceed.

In a soft opt-out system, close relatives would retain a right of veto, but the difference would be the nature of the approach to the relatives. Family members would not be asked to give permission for organ donation. Rather, they would be told that the individual had not registered an objection to donation while alive and that unless they object—either because they are aware of an unregistered objection by the individual or because it would cause a close relative or long-term partner major distress—the donation will proceed.

British Medical Association[77]

The main reasons for the BMA's support [for an opt-out system] can be summarised as follows.

- We believe that, as one part of a broader strategy, a shift to an opt-out system will have a positive effect on donation rates.
- Studies show that a large majority of people would be willing to donate but only 29% of the population are on the NHS Organ Donor Register or carry a donor card. While this level of apathy exists despite people's good intentions, people will continue to die while waiting for donor organs.
- The BMA supports the principle behind an opt-out system—that if people do not object to their organs being used after death, they should be used to save lives.
- Under an opt-out system individuals have exactly the same choice as in an opt-in system—to donate or not to donate.
- The decision not to opt out of donation is as much of a gift as a decision to opt in.
- An opt-out system gives added protection to those who do not wish to donate and makes it more likely that those who are willing to donate will be able to do so.
- Organ donation becomes the default position which, with public support, changes cultural expectations in society. This represents a more positive view of organ donation which is to be encouraged.
- Overall an opt-out system is better for recipients (because more organs will be available) better for donors (because it is more likely their wishes will be respected) and better for relatives (because it is more likely that the individual's own wishes will be known).

In Wales, the Human Transplantation (Wales) Act 2013 introduced a soft opt-out system which came into force in 2015. It was preceded by a major public awareness campaign so that those who wish to opt out understand how to do so. The Welsh opt-out system applies only to adults who have lived in Wales for at least six months (so that it can be assumed that they had had a chance

---

[76] NHS Blood and Transplant, *Post 2013 Organ Donation Strategy Written Engagement Exercise Summary of Responses* (NHSBT, 2012).

[77] *Building on Progress: Where Next for Organ Donation Policy in the UK?* (BMA, 2012).

to find out about the opt-out system), who also die in Wales. The Welsh system gives people four options: to opt in to donation; to opt out of donation; to nominate someone to make the decision; or to do nothing and be 'deemed' to consent. When the new system came into force on 1 December 2015, 3 per cent of the population had opted out, while 34 per cent had opted in. Organs donated in Wales will be available in the normal way throughout the UK. It is therefore likely that people living in other parts of the UK may benefit from the Welsh opt-out system.

If a Welsh resident has not opted out, clinicians will nevertheless approach family members in order to find out if they had an unregistered objection. According to the Welsh government, involvement of the family is necessary in order to recognize 'the doctor's duty of care towards relatives to relieve and not add to their distress and bereavement'.[78] At the time of writing, private members' bills containing similar proposals are under consideration in the Scottish Parliament and the Northern Ireland Assembly.

Most countries which have introduced opt-out systems have 'soft' versions, in which relatives' wishes continue to be relevant. It would be possible to have a 'hard' version, where the failure to register an opt-out would be decisive, and organs would be taken even if relatives object. This happens in Austria, where donation rates rose from 4.6 donors per million population to 27.2 within five years,[79] and the total number of kidney donations each year now almost equals the number of people on the waiting list.[80]

(6) Mandated Choice

A mandated choice system would allow people to opt in or opt out; what it would not allow them to do is not to make a decision. This could then avoid the problems faced by both opt-in and opt-out systems, namely that they each allow organs to be either taken, or not taken, against the wishes of the donor. In an opt-out system, organs might be taken from people who do not wish to donate but have not got around to opting out, and the reverse problem exists with opt-in systems: as we have seen, more people wish to donate than have registered on the organ donor register.

Mandated choice would be analogous to other non-optional public duties, such as filling in the electoral register or paying taxes. Like an opt-out system, it would require the maintenance and updating of an easily accessible database. As Chouhan and Draper explain in the next extract, it would also require extensive public education.

P Chouhan and H Draper[81]

A move to mandated choice would also have to be accompanied by extensive public education so that when making their choices, people are sufficiently informed about both the need for choice and the implications of their decision. Finally, choices, though binding would also be revocable: indeed, people could change their minds as often as they wish, and the most recent choice would prevail . . . To avoid coercion, registered choices would be confidential and no privileges would accrue from the particular choice made.

---

[78] Welsh Government, *Proposals for Legislation on Organ and Tissue Donation: A Welsh Government White Paper* (Welsh Government, 2011).

[79] Organ Donation Taskforce, Annex E.

[80] Kenneth Gundle, 'Presumed consent: an international comparison and possibilities for change in the United States' (2005) 14 Cambridge Quarterly of Healthcare Ethics 113–18.

[81] 'Modified mandated choice for organ procurement' (2003) 29 Journal of Medical Ethics 157–62, 158.

A number of other practical difficulties would have to be resolved. What penalty would there be for failing to make a decision, for example? There would also be questions about what to do in the case of children or adults who lack the capacity to make a choice. While acknowledging that it was a popular option among their focus groups, the Organ Donation Taskforce decided against mandated choice, citing enforcement difficulties.

Organ Donation Taskforce[82]

> 6.7 In general in the UK, we do not require people to make choices. For example, we do not make voting mandatory as it is in Australia. We encourage UK citizens to make choices but also allow them the right not to make choices. A system of mandated choice on organ donation would be a significant departure from established UK norms.
>
> 6.8 It is debatable whether such a system would be effective in practice, since it would be difficult to force people to make a decision if they do not want to. The Taskforce was uncomfortable with the idea of a legal sanction if people did not make a choice. If sanctions were imposed, enforcement would raise difficult issues, especially for clinical staff. Moreover, the Taskforce was concerned that if people were forced to choose, this might cause resentment and have a negative impact on organ donation rates.

While it certainly did not go as far as mandating choice, it is interesting to note that when the government produced the first NHS Constitution in 2009, setting out patients' rights and responsibilities within the NHS, the need to discuss wishes about organ donation with others is listed as one of the responsibilities patients should have in return for the rights they have to NHS care. According to the Constitution: 'You should ensure that those closest to you are aware of your wishes about organ donation.'[83]

(7) Incentives

(a) Financial incentives

Financial incentives to cadaveric donation could not operate as a straightforward sale, in the same way as payments to living donors (considered later). When the organs are retrieved, the donor is dead and is therefore unable to receive money in return for donating their organs. Instead, there are several other ways in which payments might be used to incentivize cadaveric donation.

First, people could receive a payment in return for their agreement to donate their organs after death. However, since few of us are likely to be suitable organ donors after death, money would generally be paid to non-donors. Moreover, in order to protect patient autonomy it would have to be possible for people to change their minds about donation after they had been paid, leaving the system open to abuse. More plausibly, money could be paid to a third party after death; an example might be meeting the funeral expenses of someone who has registered on the organ donor register, and whose organs are suitable for donation.

The Nuffield Council on Bioethics has recommended that there should be a pilot study in order to determine whether a system of payment of funeral expenses would increase donation rates. Importantly, under the Nuffield proposal, the payment of funeral expenses would

---

[82] *The Potential Impact of an Opt Out System for Organ Donation in the UK: An Independent Report from the Organ Donation Taskforce* (DH: London, 2008).
[83] (DH, 2009).

not be offered to families in return for their agreement to donation. Rather, it would be triggered only if someone had agreed in advance to donate their organs; families would be free to decline the payment if they found it offensive. It would therefore operate as a 'spur' or 'nudge' to someone who was already inclined to donate, rather than acting as an incentive to donation for families who are worried about being able to afford to pay for their loved one's funeral.

Nuffield Council on Bioethics[84]

6.44 . . . [I]t might be argued that any decision by their family to consent to donation solely for financial reasons would constitute a very clear example of that person's body being used as a means for others' ends and not as an end in itself. Given these concerns, coupled with a lack of evidence as to the likely effectiveness of such an intervention, we do not think it should be pursued.

6.45 The situation would seem rather different if the payment were triggered by the future donor signing up to the ODR, rather than being offered to the bereaved relatives at the time of death . . . : acting as a final spur for a person already inclined to donate, with the added altruistic feature that others, and not the donor themselves, would benefit. Alternatively, the incentive might seem sufficiently strong for someone to decide to register as a donor simply to spare their relatives the financial burden of a funeral . . . Moreover, while those who are neutral about donation after death might be swayed by such an incentive, it seems unlikely that a person actively opposed to the use of their bodily material after death (for example because of concerns about the integrity of the body) would be tempted to act against those beliefs.

6.46 . . . [P]ayment of funeral expenses in these circumstances could be ethically justified. Donors cannot be physically harmed—and are highly unlikely to have signified their willingness to donate in these circumstances if they had strong objections. Those close to the donor may benefit directly, and also would clearly have the option of declining the offer of burial costs being met by the NHS. While there is no direct evidence as to how effective or popular such a system would be, the fact that a very similar system exists for covering cremation costs of those who donate their bodies to medical science (which appears to be regarded by both professionals and families as an appropriate acknowledgment of the person's gift), suggests that the extension of such a scheme to organ donors would not be detrimental either to professional values or the common good. We recommend that NHS Blood and Transplant should consider establishing a pilot scheme to test the public response to the idea of offering to meet funeral expenses for those who sign the Organ Donation Register and subsequently die in circumstances where they could become organ donors. The precise way in which such a scheme might operate—factors such as what, if any, role family members should have in authorising the use of organs in such circumstances, and whether expenses should be covered if in fact the person's organs prove to be unsuitable for transplant—would be key questions for such a pilot scheme to determine.

Of course, one of the other practical issues which would have to be addressed is ensuring that people are not under the mistaken impression that signing up for the organ donor register means that their funeral expenses will be covered. Most of us do not die in circumstances in which it is possible for us to donate our organs. The vast majority of people on the register would still have to pay for their own funerals.

---

[84] *Human Bodies: Donation for Medicine and Research* (NCOB, 2011).

It is unclear whether financial incentives would persuade potential donors to agree to organ donation. Haddow found that the reaction to financial incentives among potential donors was 'tepid', but for donor families, it was overwhelmingly negative.

G Haddow[85]

Offering a payment of £20 to register proved to be the least popular of all options. Approximately 40% of respondents reacted positively to the grants after death of a £2000 payment per organ to the family, to a favourite charity, or toward funeral costs. (We found certain groups to be more favourable toward incentives, especially the 16–24 age cohort and men.) . . . Importantly, there is a prominent level of 'would make no difference' response to all options—even the favoured 'cash to relatives' option. Therefore, the overall reaction to any of the financial options was decidedly tepid.

[Among donor families] the reaction to the general issue of financial incentives was unambiguous: sixteen of seventeen donor relatives asked were opposed. Others suggested that the introduction of financial incentives would produce the effect of non-donation . . . The response to financial incentives was it was 'immoral'.

Of course, any financial incentives to organ donation will come up against the arguments against commodification of the human body, which we consider in more detail in relation to living donors. In the next extract, Arthur Caplan explains why he finds the offer of cash for body parts offensive.

Arthur L Caplan[86]

There is no empirical evidence that families raise the issue of money or compensation at the time when they are faced with requests or decisions about making organs and tissues available for transplantation. What factual evidence there is lends support to the opposite conclusion—that significant numbers of Americans would be angered, offended and insulted by offers of money or financial rewards for the organs and tissues of their deceased loved ones . . .

If the only way US society, or any other, can find to pay for the uncompensated costs of medical care or funerals for the indigent is to offer cash for their body parts, such a society has no right to call itself humane, decent, or fair . . . Calls for markets, compensation, bounties, or rewards should be rejected because they convert human beings into products, a metaphysical transformation that cheapens the respect for life and corrodes our ability to maintain the stance that human beings are special, unique, and valuable for their own sake, not for what others can mine, extract, or manufacture from them. Nor will markets do what their proponents hope. The inevitable opposition such proposals will encounter from many religious leaders means any increase in lives saved attributable to cash prizes will be swamped by the number of lives lost when those who refuse to see the human body as available for sale decline to participate in anything having to do with transplants.

---

[85] '"Because you're worth it?" The taking and selling of transplantable organs' (2006) 32 Journal of Medical Ethics 324–8.

[86] *Am I my Brother's Keeper? The Ethical Frontiers of Biomedicine* (Indiana UP: Bloomington, IN, 1997) 96–8.

(b) Non-financial incentives

A different sort of incentive would be to give those who have indicated their willingness to donate priority if they ever need an organ themselves. If signing up to the organ donor register might have future health benefits for the potential donor, people might be more likely to opt in. Alternatively, in an opt-out system, people might be less likely to opt out if this might adversely affect their chance of receiving an organ. Insofar as apathy rather than disapproval of transplantation is the principal reason why people do not register their agreement to donation, and given that registering is not difficult, Jarvis argues that an appeal to the reciprocity of organ donation might be a cheap and effective way to increase donation rates.

Rupert Jarvis[87]

I suggest that legislation governing organ donation be amended such that all and only those who identify themselves as potential donors (perhaps by a card similar to the one currently in use, or by registration on a central computer) are eligible themselves to receive transplant organs . . .

This contract . . . trades a—if not *the*—central interest in remaining alive, against one's *post mortem* interest in not having one's organs removed. This latter is at best *de minimis*: my interests in my organs after death can hardly be said to be enormous. We are presented, then, with what appears to be a thoroughly attractive option: by sacrificing our minimal *post mortem* interests we guarantee our inclusion on the waiting list for the donor organ which might save or vastly improve the quality of our own life . . .

It hardly seems fanciful to suggest that the vast majority of people would elect to join the scheme, since it is so clearly in their interests to do so, with the potential gain (life) being infinite and the potential loss (*post mortem* dissection which, depending on the manner of their death, they might well have to undergo anyway) being zero.

It is also worth noting that we are more likely to need an organ than we are to die in circumstances in which our organs would be suitable for transplantation, so most people who sign up to this sort of scheme will not, in fact, ever become organ donors, but they would benefit from knowing that they would be able to receive an organ if they suffer organ failure in the future.

Of course, as Raanan Gillon explains, it would almost certainly be unethical and impracticable to make willingness to donate the only relevant factor when allocating organs to potential transplant recipients.

Raanan Gillon[88]

Here seems to be the Achilles heel of Mr Jarvis's proposal. For even if such non-volunteers can properly be said to have only themselves to blame for their predicament; even if they can properly be said to have deliberately and autonomously made their choice and rejected the opportunity to give themselves priority for receipt of transplanted organs; even if they can

---

[87] 'Join the club: a modest proposal to increase availability of donor organs' (1995) 21 Journal of Medical Ethics 199–204.

[88] 'On giving preference to prior volunteers when allocating organs for transplantation' (1995) 21 Journal of Medical Ethics 195–6.

properly be said to have been selfish, and/or inconsiderate and/or foolish, even immoral, in refusing to pre-volunteer their own organs, nonetheless there is an important countervailing moral tradition in medicine. It is that patients should be given treatment in relation to their medical need, and that scarce medical resources should not be prioritised on the basis of a patient's blameworthiness . . .

If the fault and/or inconsiderateness of not previously volunteering his or her organs for transplantation were to justify withholding scarce life-saving resources from a patient, then all other prior faults and inconsiderateness of equal or greater weight could, logically, also be regarded as morally relevant and potentially justificatory for withholding scarce life-saving medical resources from patients. Such a prospect hardly bears contemplation.

It would be more plausible for the points system for allocation, which takes into account a range of factors such as immediacy of clinical need and time spent on the waiting list, to be weighted so that willing donors receive a higher ranking than similarly situated individuals who would not be prepared to donate their own organs.

This sort of system has been introduced in Israel, in response to concerns that some groups in society were willing to receive organs, but were never willing to donate. The new law gives priority to organ donors and their first-degree relatives and to people who have been registered on the organ donor register for at least three years (this is to stop someone who finds that they need an organ from signing up solely in order to jump the queue):

- Consent given by a person during his life to donate an organ following his death, accords both the person and his first degree relatives priority in organ allocation.
- An organ donated by a person following his death accords his first degree relatives priority in organ allocation.
- An organ donated by a person during his life not for a designated recipient accords him or his first degree relatives priority in organ allocation.[89]

Priority under the Israeli system is also weighted, so that a transplant candidate with a first-degree relative who has signed a donor card is given half the allocation priority of a candidate who has signed his or her own donor card. A transplant candidate with a first-degree relative who has actually donated organs after death is given allocation priority 1.5 times greater than that of candidates who have just signed an organ donor card.

The United Network for Organ Sharing (UNOS) guidelines in the US specify that living donors should have priority for organs in the future. However, this may be better described not as an incentive, but as a removal of a disincentive to donation. Insofar as someone might be reluctant to donate a kidney out of fear that her remaining kidney might fail in the future, this provision offers reassurance that, in such circumstances, she would be given priority for a new organ.

It would also be possible to incorporate priority for donors as part of a move to an opt-out system. As Stephanie Eaton argues in the following extract, the presumption would be (a) that the deceased person had consented to donation; and (b) that she was not a free-rider. It would be for those who did not want their organs to be used after their death to register their objection, and as part of that process, they could be warned that opting out might reduce their likelihood of being allocated an organ if they ever need one.

---

[89] Jacob Lavee, Tamar Ashkenazi, Gabriel Gurman, and David Steinberg, 'A new law for allocation of donor organs in Israel' (2010) 375 The Lancet 1131–3.

Stephanie Eaton[90]

> If it is agreed that most people would consent to benefiting from transplant technology and that free riding is a morally precarious position to hold, it is possible to arouse people's awareness to the moral consequences of the stance which they are taking when they choose to opt out. Where people still choose to opt out knowing that this constitutes free riding, they should be made aware that they may be disadvantaged in the future if they should ever become potential recipients of organs . . .
>
> Publicity that promotes the idea that an opted out person may be less likely to receive a transplant if he or she ever needs one, forces opters-out to reconsider their own moral standards. It is hoped that the unease that will be felt when opting-out is acknowledged as being a form of free riding will have the consequence that few people will choose to opt out.

One of the most controversial questions on NHS Blood and Transplant's 2012 consultation on its post-2013 Organ Donation Strategy was a question about whether donors should be given priority for transplantation. Interestingly, among members of the public, there was a fairly even split, with 49 per cent in favour and 51 per cent against. Amongst NHS employees with experience of transplantation, this option was less popular, with 40 per cent in favour and 60 per cent against.[91] This option has not been taken forward in the strategy for 2020.[92]

(8) A Duty to Donate? Organs as a Public Resource?

If it were possible to take organs from dead bodies without the need for anyone's agreement, many lives could be saved. In the next extract, HE Emson argues that, once dead, a person's organs should be treated as a public resource, to be distributed to those in need of them.

HE Emson[93]

> The body should be regarded morally as on loan to the individual from the biomass, to which the cadaver will inevitably return . . .
>
> I am deeply concerned with the right of the person to govern disposal of their body after death, when separation of body and soul is irrevocably complete and the individual is incapable of reconstitution. The person no longer exists, the soul has departed, and the individual who was but is no longer has no further use for the body which has been part of him or her during life. The concept of the right of a person to determine before death, the disposal of their body after death, made sense only when there was no continuing use for that body. It makes neither practical nor moral sense now, when the body for which the dead person no longer has any use, is quite literally a vital resource, a potential source of life for others . . .
>
> If this argument is correct, then it is even more morally unacceptable for the relatives of the deceased to deny utilisation of the cadaver as a source of transplantable organs. Their only claim upon it is as a temporary memorial of a loved one, inevitably destined to decay or be burned in a very short time. To me, any such claim cannot morally be sustained in the face of what I regard as the overwhelming and pre-emptive need of the potential recipient.

---

[90] 'The subtle politics of organ donation: a proposal' (1998) 24 Journal of Medical Ethics 166–70.

[91] NHS Blood and Transplant, *Post 2013 Organ Donation Strategy Written Engagement Exercise Summary of Responses* (DH: London, 2012).

[92] NHSBT, *Taking Organ Transplantation to 2020: A detailed strategy* (NHSBT, 2013).

[93] 'It is immoral to require consent for cadaver organ donation' (2003) 29 Journal of Medical Ethics 125–7.

Alternatively, it could be argued that we are under a moral duty to donate our organs after death, equivalent to the duty of easy rescue, explained by Lindemann Nelson in the next extract.

James Lindemann Nelson[94]

[T]here is a strong presumption that refusing to save another person's life when doing so is virtually costless to the person in a position to act, is seriously wrong . . .

I think that people typically have duties to provide organs to others, should the opportunity arise, and indeed, duties to reconsider and possibly refigure their attitudes about themselves and others insofar as those attitudes threaten their inclinations to be organ providers. Or, to put it a bit more carefully, since it seems a bit strained to think of dead people having duties, I think that removing organs from the dead typically neither harms nor wrongs them, and that therefore we the living have a prima facie duty to support the retrieval of useful organs, both from our own dead bodies, and from those of others. If we find ourselves repulsed or otherwise distressed by this prospect, we have a derivative duty: to seek to revamp our attitudes.

John Harris further points out that since the human body never remains intact for very long after death, objections to organ donation are intrinsically irrational, and, in any event, must be of less importance than the interest of potential recipients who might otherwise die.

John Harris[95]

All the moral concern of our society has so far been focused on the dead and their friends and relatives. But there are two separate sets of individuals who have moral claims upon us, not just one. There is the deceased individual and her friends and relatives on the one hand, and the potential organ or tissue recipient and her friends and relatives on the other. Both have claims upon us, the claims of neither have obvious priority. . . .

My point is that it is surely implausible to think that having one's body remain whole after their death is an objective anyone is entitled to pursue at the cost of other people's lives! It is implausible to the point of wickedness, not least because the objective is irrational and impossible of achievement . . . No dead body remains intact; the worms . . . or the fire and eventually dust claim it . . . The alternatives are not burial intact or disintegration. There is no alternative which does not involve disintegration. Given the irrationality of the aim, it is difficult to defend a right to pursue such an aim when it is clear that doing so costs lives.

In the next extract, Sheelagh McGuinness and Margaret Brazier are critical of Harris's brisk dismissal of the views of those who find organ donation difficult.

[94] *Hippocrates' Maze: Ethical Explorations of the Medical Labyrinth* (Rowman & Littlefield: New York, 2003) 119.

[95] 'Organ procurement: dead interests, living needs' (2003) 29 Journal of Medical Ethics 130–4, 130, 133.

Sheelagh McGuinness and Margaret Brazier[96]

Death is not akin to a switch that once 'off' means that the dead person ceases to matter at all. Death is described by some as, and can traditionally be seen to be, a socially constructed event. Death rituals have formed an important part of the grieving process. Throughout history there has been an expectation that in death the body will be respected as a symbol of the living person. Death of someone close to you is difficult to accept. We struggle to adjust to an understanding that the person is gone. Identifying with the dead is so hard that we think of the dead body as a symbol of the pre-mortem person.

The dead infant, the wife succumbing to breast cancer at 35, the elderly father dying suddenly of a heart attack, do not change their nature for their mother, husband or daughter. They remain Susannah, Lucy and Dad. They are not simply things.

Walter Glannon goes further and contends that our interest in what is done to our bodies after our death outweighs the interests of those in need of organs.

Walter Glannon[97]

Because the body is so closely associated with who we are, we can have an interest in what is done to it even after we cease to exist. The fact that my body is mine and is essential to my life plan means that I have a deep interest in what is done to it. If it is treated in a way that does not accord with my wishes or interests, then in an important respect this can be bad for me and I can be harmed. The special relation between humans and their bodies can make it wrong for others to ignore the expressed wish that one's organs not be harvested at death, despite their viability for transplantation . . .

Given the special relation between humans and their bodies, the moral importance of individual autonomy in having a life plan, and that what happens to one's body after death is part of such a plan, the negative right to bodily integrity after death outweighs any presumed positive right of the sick to receive organs from those who did not consent to cadaver donation.

It is, however, worth noting that we do not allow relatives to object to forensic post-mortems. This is not because they are less invasive than transplantation. Rather, the public interest in the detection of serious crime trumps concern about the family's feelings about what happens during a post-mortem. It is perhaps interesting that the death of identifiable people on the transplant waiting list is not regarded as of comparable public importance.

3 LIVE DONORS

(a) THE ETHICAL ACCEPTABILITY OF LIVING ORGAN DONATION

Non-vital organs can be taken from living donors. It has been estimated that the increased risk of mortality from living with only one kidney is 0.03 per cent, which is 'equivalent to

---

[96] 'Respecting the Living Means Respecting the Dead Too' (2008) 28 Oxford Journal of Legal Studies 297–316.

[97] 'Do the sick have a right to cadaveric organs?' (2003) 29 Journal of Medical Ethics 153–6, 154.

driving back and forth to work 16 miles a day'.[98] Kidney donors are at increased risk of suffering from renal failure in the future, but the absolute risk remains small.[99] Approximately 2 per cent of kidney donors experience major morbidity, and 10–20 per cent experience minor morbidity. Risks from living liver donation are higher, with mortality rates of 0.5–0.1 per cent, and morbidity rates of 40–60 per cent.[100]

As we saw at the beginning of this chapter, survival rates for recipients of kidneys from living donors are slightly higher than those for recipients of cadaveric organs. In part, this may be because the organ is taken from a healthy, living person, rather than from someone who has died. But perhaps more importantly, the timing of the transplant can be controlled. When a cadaveric organ becomes available, the operation has to take place as soon as possible after the donor's (usually sudden) death. From the recipient's point of view, this may be less than ideal: she will have no opportunity to prepare for the operation, and it may take place when she is unwell. In contrast, when an organ is taken from a living donor, the transplant team can ensure the operation is carried out when the recipient is in the best possible health.

Despite the obvious advantages in increasing the pool of potential organ donors to include living people, the practice remains controversial. Unlike cadaveric donation, living organ donation does pose real, albeit small, health risks to the donor. One study found that 15 per cent of live donors believed that donation had had a negative impact upon their health.[101] Another study found that approximately 4 per cent of live donors regretted their decision to donate.[102] Of course, this means that the vast majority of donors did not regret their decision, and that most did not believe that there had been any negative impact upon their health. Most studies appear to show that donors more commonly experience increased self-esteem and feelings of wellbeing.[103] Watching someone one loves suffer is itself a miserable experience, and being able to alleviate their suffering, or save their life, is likely to have substantial non-clinical benefits for the donor herself.

Interestingly, there appears to be a gender imbalance both among living organ donors, who are more likely to be female, and among recipients, more of whom are male.[104] A German study found that mothers were the most frequent donors (27 per cent), followed by wives (19 per cent), fathers (13 per cent), sisters (12 per cent), and husbands (11 per cent).[105] It is not clear why this difference exists, although possible explanations have included men's greater capacity to resist family pressure, and their higher wage-earning capacity, which may mean

---

[98] James F Blumstein, 'The Use of Financial Incentives in Medical Care: The Case of Commerce in Transplantable Organs' in Andrew Grubb and Maxwell J Mehlman (eds), *Justice and Health Care: Comparative Perspectives* (John Wiley & Sons: Chichester, 1995) 9–39.

[99] Abimereki D Muzaale et al, 'Risk of end-stage renal disease following live kidney donation' (2014) 311 Journal of the American Medical Association 579–86.

[100] James Neuberger and David Price, 'Role of living liver donation in the United Kingdom' (2003) 327 British Medical Journal 676–9.

[101] Leslie R Schover et al, 'The psychosocial impact of donating a kidney: long term follow-up from a urology based center' (1997) 157 Journal of Urology 1596–601. See also the study by M Walter et al, 'Quality of life of living donors before and after living donor liver transplantation' (2003) 35 Transplantation Proceedings 2961–3, which indicated that 10 per cent of living liver donors were having difficulty coping with psychological symptoms.

[102] Eric M Johnson, Michael J Remucal, and Arthur J Matas, 'Living kidney donation: donor risks and quality of life' (1997) Clinical Transplantation 231–40.

[103] Roberta G Simmons, Susan D Klein, and Richard L Simmons, *Gift of Life: the Social and Psychological Impact of Organ Transplantation* (Wiley: New York, 1977).

[104] Nikola Biller-Andorno, 'Gender imbalance in living organ donation' (2002) 5 Medicine, Health Care and Philosophy 199–204, 201.

[105] Ibid, 201.

that sparing time for donation and recuperation is perceived to be easier for female family members.

While the altruistic act of the donor might be laudable, in the next extract Elliott argues that both recipients of live organs and doctors who perform living organ retrieval are encouraging the donor's self-sacrifice, and that this is more problematic.

Carl Elliott[106]

[W]hile it is admirable to risk harm to oneself, it is not admirable to encourage another person to risk harm to himself for one's own benefit . . .

Accepting a sacrifice of great magnitude is not mere passive acquiescence, devoid of any moral import. If I allow someone else to risk his life or health for my sake, I am endorsing his self-sacrifice and agreeing to profit by it . . . If an ailing patient were to take advantage of a healthy donor's self-sacrifice, it might well be understandable, but it would not be morally admirable. It would not be the sort of behaviour that we would aspire to and want to encourage.

[T]he doctor is also a moral agent who should be held accountable for his actions . . . This shifts the moral balance of the problem in an important way, because while we admire the person who *undergoes* harm to himself for the sake of another, we do not necessarily admire the person who *inflicts* harm on one person for the sake of another. And the latter is what the doctor must do.

It has been argued that concern about the possibility of harm to living donors should lead us to be reluctant to encourage living donation until we have exhausted all possible means of increasing the number of cadaveric organs available for transplant. In addition to avoiding unnecessary health risks to living donors, there may also be concerns, as Arthur Caplan explains, about the genuineness of a live donor's consent to donation.

Arthur L Caplan[107]

[M]any critics of live donation worry that the environment in which live donation takes place makes it impossible for anyone to give free and voluntary consent. Family members will ordinarily feel extraordinary pressures to 'volunteer'. The realization that one could be blamed for the failure to help a spouse, a sibling, or a child may be so frightening that potential donors see themselves as having no choice.

It may be preferable to use cadaveric organs, but as we have seen, demand outstrips supply, and will probably continue to do so. Two conclusions follow from this. First, we should recognize that any mechanisms—such as an opt-out system, which might increase the pool of potential cadaveric donors—might also reduce our need to resort to living organ donation. Increased rates of cadaveric donation would have health benefits not only for the recipients of those organs, but also for potential live donors, whose services might no longer be needed.

---

[106] 'Doing harm: living organ donors, clinical research and the tenth man' (1995) 21 Journal of Medical Ethics 91–6.

[107] 'Am I My Brother's Keeper?' (1993) 27 Suffolk University Law Review 1195.

Secondly, if it is inevitable that we will continue to pursue alternatives to cadaveric donation, we need to think about the circumstances in which live organ donation should be permitted.

(b) TYPE OF TRANSPLANT

Obviously, it is only possible for living organ donors to donate non-vital organs, such as kidneys and lobes of the lung or liver. Most living organ donation involves kidneys: in 2014–15, there were 1,052 living donor kidney transplants, 40 living donor liver lobe transplants, and no living lung transplants.[108]

A difficult ethical question about the limits of autonomous decision-making arose in the US in 1998 when a man sought to donate his second kidney to his daughter after the first transplant failed.[109] The operation would not have killed Mr Patterson, but it would have left him dependent upon dialysis for the rest of his life, unless, of course, he himself received a kidney transplant. Unlike ordinary living kidney transplants, someone who donated both kidneys would face a dramatic and substantial deterioration in his own health. It might therefore be argued that carrying out this operation conflicts with the doctor's duty to do no harm, and it is unlikely that a doctor would be prepared to carry out this sort of operation in order to benefit a third party, particularly given the chance that this second transplant would also fail.

(c) LIVE TRANSPLANTATION IN THE UK

In the UK, there has been a steady increase in the use of living donors, particularly for kidney transplants. The Human Tissue Act covers consent to the use and storage of tissue taken from the living, but its removal continues to be dealt with at common law and under the Mental Capacity Act 2005.

(1) Consent to the Removal of Tissue

The criminal law places limits upon the extent to which an adult can consent to the infliction of harm. Although the increased risk of morbidity from living with only one kidney is low, nephrectomy (kidney removal) is a serious operation done under general anaesthetic, and as a result, carries with it a small risk of death or permanent injury. It would undoubtedly qualify as grievous bodily harm, for which consent is no defence. As we saw in Chapter 5, 'proper medical treatment' has been said to stand outside the criminal law, and, according to the Law Commission: 'there is no doubt that once a valid consent has been forthcoming, English law now treats as lawful donation of … non-regenerative tissue that is not essential to life'.[110] This assumption of legality has been questioned, however. Govert den Hartogh, for example, has suggested that in other contexts, we would not allow someone to incur this level of risk in order to help others:

---

[108] NHS Blood and Transplant, *Annual Activity Report 2014–15: Summary of Transplant Activity* (NHSBT, 2015).

[109] Ryan Sauder and Lisa S Parker, 'Autonomy's limits: living donation and health-related harm' (2001) 10 Cambridge Quarterly of Healthcare Ethics 399–401.

[110] Law Commission Consultation Paper No 139, *Consent in the Criminal Law* (HMSO: London, 1995) para 8.32.

Imagine yourself a member of a medical ethics committee that has to assess a medical experiment that involves a similar set of invasive procedures, risks, and burdens for its participants. Even if the therapy to be tested could save people's lives, would you approve the experiment? I have put that question to some members of such committees, and their answer is that their committee would almost certainly reject it.[111]

Because the living organ donor is undergoing non-therapeutic surgery, it is especially important that their consent is fully informed and voluntary. In practice, however, as Ryan Sauder and Lisa Parker point out, many living donors feel that donating an organ to a desperately sick relative is effectively 'non-optional'.

Ryan Sauder and Lisa S Parker[112]

Frequently, a prospective donor, particularly a parent or sibling of the prospective recipient, will experience the decision to donate as automatic. They frequently report feeling that they had no choice but to donate, and proceed to offer their organs willingly and without hesitation, sometimes even before hearing of the risks involved in such a donation. Disclosure of risks frequently has no effect on the decision to donate. These decisions hardly seem to meet the traditional requirements of informed consent. Failing to take risks of an intervention into account when deciding whether to consent to it, and feeling compelled to consent, are typically hallmarks of a failure of the informed consent process. Yet we are reluctant to suggest that these prospective donors are not making autonomous decisions to donate and, consequently, that their decisions (and organs) should not be accepted.

Most of us can put ourselves in the shoes of someone who has the chance to donate an organ to someone we love, and we would not consider that our eagerness to donate made us unable to make an autonomous choice. Indeed, in their interviews with parents who had donated organs to their children, Burnell et al found not only that they were making a choice to donate, but also that they felt lucky to have the option.

Philippa Burnell, Sally-Anne Hulton, and Heather Draper[113]

The majority of participants made reference to choice: they felt that they were making a decision where not donating was a genuine alternative, just not one they personally could countenance. . . .

When they described the first discussion with health professionals about live donation, this was not reported as a situation where they felt pressure to donate. Instead, parents *wanted* to donate . . . Parents were typically pleased that live donation was a possibility: 'I never resented being put in that position' . . .

Commonly, participants felt 'lucky' when they discovered they *could* donate and the only circumstance in which they envisaged themselves not donating was if they were tissue incompatible. Some parents described the upset this would have caused for them.

---

[111] 'Is consent of the donor enough to justify the removal of living organs?' (2013) 22 Cambridge Quarterly of Healthcare Ethics 45–54.

[112] 'Autonomy's limits: living donation and health-related harm' (2001) 10 Cambridge Quarterly of Healthcare Ethics 399–401.

[113] 'Coercion and choice in parent–child live kidney donation' (2015) 41 Journal of Medical Ethics 304–9.

> Indeed, it was being *incompatible* that one participant described as being a situation of 'no choice': . . .
>
> They reported donating because improving the well-being of their child was important for that child *and* therefore for themselves. For our participants, donation also served their own interests because they tended not to separate their child's interests from their own.

Of course, not all potential donors will want to donate to relatives or friends, and in practice, clinicians will commonly provide a 'medical alibi' if someone does not want to donate, but is fearful of their family's reaction.[114] This does not necessarily involve deception: after all, if a potential donor does not give her consent to donation, it would be true to say that she is not a suitable donor.

In addition to full disclosure of the risks to their own health, potential living organ donors should also be given frank information about the possibility that the transplant might not work, and the emotional impact of an unsuccessful donation. If the recipient's need for a transplant results from a genetic condition, more than one family member may require the same transplant, and donors need to understand that they may be able to act as a donor only once.

Given this emphasis on informed consent, could organs ever be taken from those who lack the capacity to consent?

(a) Children

In the case of children, although parents normally consent to their minor children's medical treatment, sibling-to-sibling organ donation would present parents with a particularly difficult conflict of interest. How could they separate their responsibility for the interests of the potential donor from their equally compelling concern for the potential recipient, and for their own interests? As with other especially controversial procedures, court approval should be sought. While bone marrow donation between child siblings could be said to be in the donor's best interests, given that it is a relatively minor and risk-free procedure, which could save a loved sibling's life, whether a court would ever be prepared to authorize the removal of a non-regenerative organ, such as a kidney, is another matter.

There have, as yet, been no cases but there were *obiter* comments about organ donation in *Re W (A Minor)*.[115] The Court of Appeal suggested that the Family Law Reform Act 1969, which gives minors of 16 and 17 years of age the right to consent to medical treatment, would not apply to organ donation because, 'so far as the donor is concerned, these do not constitute either treatment or diagnosis'.[116] Instead, until the age of 18, 'the jurisdiction of the court should always be invoked'.[117] Until such a case arises, it is not clear whether the courts would ever be prepared to authorize such an operation.

There have been instances of child organ donation in the US. In *Hart v Brown*,[118] for example, the court was satisfied that the psychological benefit to the donor from her identical twin sister's survival and continued companionship, justified the risks of donation.

---

[114] Mary Simmerling et al, 'When duties collide: beneficence and veracity in the evaluation of living organ donors' (2007) 12 Current Opinions in Organ Transplantation 188–92.

[115] [1993] Fam 64.   [116] Per Lord Donaldson.   [117] Per Nolan LJ.

[118] 289 A 2d 386 (Conn Sup Ct 1972).

(b) Adults who lack capacity

Under the Mental Capacity Act 2005, the position of adults who lack capacity is similar to that of children. Paragraph 8.20 of the Mental Capacity Act Code of Practice makes it clear that court approval would be required for organ donation:

> 8.20 Cases involving organ or bone marrow donation by a person who lacks capacity to consent should also be referred to the Court of Protection.

The court would then have to decide whether organ donation was in the person's best interests, and it would be guided by the checklist of factors in section 4 which, as we saw in Chapter 5, places particular emphasis upon the values and previously expressed wishes of the incompetent person.

In *Re Y (Mental Patient: Bone Marrow Donation)*[119]—a pre-Mental Capacity Act case—bone marrow donation from a woman who lacked capacity was authorized, on the grounds that it would be in her social or emotional interests. However, Connell J doubted whether similar reasoning could justify organ donation:

> It is doubtful that this case would act as a useful precedent in cases where the surgery involved is more intrusive than in this case, where the evidence shows that the bone marrow harvested is speedily regenerated and that a healthy individual can donate as much as two pints with no long term consequences at all.

As yet, no cases have arisen and so, as with children, it is unclear whether a court would ever be satisfied that solid organ donation was in the best interests of an adult who lacked capacity. Again, this has happened in the US. In *Strunk v Strunk*,[120] the court approved kidney donation on the grounds that the death of his brother would have caused the potential donor psychological and emotional injury greater than the risks associated with the removal of one of his kidneys.

(2) The Human Tissue Act 2004

Under section 33(1) and (2), taking an organ from a living person for the purposes of transplantation (regardless of whether they are related to each other or not) is an offence, unless the requirements in section 33(3) and (5) are satisfied. These are, under section 33(3), that no payment or reward has been given in contravention of section 32, and that such other conditions and requirements as may be specified in regulations are satisfied. Section 33(5) offers a defence if the person who takes an organ reasonably believes that the transplant satisfies the section 33(3) requirements.

(a) Consent

Under section 1 of the Act, there must be 'appropriate consent' to the use of human tissue for transplantation. For competent adults, under section 3(2) 'appropriate consent' means 'his

---

[119] [1997] Fam 110.   [120] 445 SW 2d 145 (1969).

consent'. The HTA Draft Code of Practice contains detailed guidance on the information that should be provided as part of the consent process:

HTA Draft Code of Practice[121]

65. To ensure that the informed consent of the donor is secured, the transplant team must make sure the following areas are discussed with the donor:

a) the nature of the surgical/medical procedure and medical treatments involved for the donor, and any material short and long term risks (this should be explained by a medical practitioner with appropriate qualifications to give this information). A material risk is where, in the circumstances, a reasonable person in the donor's position would be likely to attach significance to the risk, or the transplant team is or should be reasonably aware that the donor would be likely to attach significance to it. This information should include the risk of death to the donor;

b) the chances of the transplant being successful, and any significant side effects or complications for the recipient, and in particular the donor should be made aware of the possibility of graft failure in the recipient;

c) the right to withdraw consent at any time before the removal of the transplantable material;

d) that the decision to donate must be free of duress or coercion;

e) that it is an offence to give or receive a reward for the supply of, or for an offer to supply, any organ. It is also an offence to seek to find a person willing to supply any organ for reward. If found guilty of this offence a person may face up to three years in prison, a fine, or both.

66. The donor must have a clear understanding of the benefits and disadvantages of living donor transplantation in their particular case, as well as the general risks and benefits.

As with the common law on organ retrieval, the Act does not rule out the possibility of using organs taken from adults who lack capacity, but any such transplants would have to be approved by a panel of at least three members of the HTA and comply with regulations. These effectively duplicate the assessment that the court would carry out in deciding whether retrieval would be lawful, namely that the donation must be in the best interests of the child or adult who lacks capacity.

Human Tissue Act 2004 (Persons who Lack Capacity to Consent and Transplants) Regulations 2006 regulation 3(2)

(2) An adult ('P') who lacks capacity to consent . . . is deemed to have consented to the activity where—

(a) the activity is done for a purpose specified in paragraph 4 or 7 [7 is transplantation] by a person who is acting in what he reasonably believes to be P's best interests.

---

[121] Draft Code F Organ Donation (HTA, 2015).

Under section 2(3) of the Human Tissue Act, children who have sufficient maturity to consent to such a serious operation (see Chapter 5) might be able to make their own decision to donate an organ.

Human Tissue Act 2004 section 2

> 2(3) Where—
>
> (a) the child concerned is alive,
>
> (b) neither a decision of his to consent to the activity, nor a decision of his not to consent to it, is in force, and
>
> (c) either he is not competent to deal with the issue of consent in relation to the activity or, though he is competent to deal with that issue, he fails to do so,
>
> 'appropriate consent' means the consent of a person who has parental responsibility for him.

Where the child lacks capacity or does not wish to make a decision, anyone with parental responsibility could give consent, but this alone would not be sufficient for the transplant to go ahead, and court approval should be sought.

HTA Draft Code of Practice[122]

> 43. Children can be considered as living organ donors only in extremely rare circumstances. The HT Act defines a child as being under 18 years old. If a clinician intends to consider a child as a living organ donor, they are advised to discuss the case with the HTA at the earliest opportunity.
>
> 44. In accordance with common law and the Children Act 1989, court approval should be obtained before the removal of a solid organ or part organ from a child for donation. Transplant Units should obtain their own legal advice regarding seeking court approval.
>
> 45. Living donation by a child under the HT Act can only go ahead with the approval of an HTA panel. Such cases must only be referred to the HTA for decision after court approval for the removal has been obtained.

(b) Restrictions on live donation

Independent Assessors (IAs) must assess all living solid organ donor-recipient pairs and make a recommendation to the HTA. The HTA will then decide whether the donation can go ahead. IAs should be NHS consultants, or of equivalent standing, should not be working in the field of organ transplantation, and should have been trained and accredited by the HTA. These IAs consider all living organ donations for transplantation that fall into the following categories:

Directed:

- genetically related;
- emotionally related;
- paired and pooled.

---

[122] Ibid.

Non-directed:

- domino;
- altruistic (the decision in these cases should be made by the HTA until practice is established as routine).

Directed donation means that the donor's organs are to be donated to a specified individual, usually a partner or family member. In non-directed donation, the recipient's identity is not known to the donor. Paired donation takes place when a person volunteers to donate to someone she knows, but she turns out to be a poor tissue match. In such circumstances, the would-be donor and donee might be paired with a similar couple so that each recipient can receive a well-matched organ. Pooled donation is similar, but involves a larger pool of willing but unmatched related donors.

Non-directed donations include 'domino' transplants, where the primary purpose of the donation is the medical treatment of the donor. Because it is more straightforward to carry out a heart and lung transplant than to transplant lungs alone, someone who is in need of a lung transplant might receive the heart and lungs from a cadaveric donor. The recipient's heart might then become available for transplant into another person. This would, of course, be a living unrelated transplant, but, unlike most living donation, the donor is undergoing the operation for her own benefit.

The IA must interview donor and recipient and certify that all statutory and other requirements are satisfied. This report will be valid for six months, after which a further report will become necessary, in case the circumstances have changed.

In 2014–15, there were 107 non-directed altruistic living kidney transplants. These are cases where the living donor does not know the recipient. The HTA takes extra care to ensure that consent has been given voluntarily, and requires there to have been a psychiatric assessment of the would-be donor. Walter Glannon and Lainie Friedman Ross argue that suspicion of the motives of non-directed altruistic donation is not necessarily justified, since a potential organ donor who has no emotional ties to the recipient may in fact be better able to make a free and unpressurized decision to donate.

Walter Glannon and Lainie Friedman Ross[123]

An altruistic donor has no obligation to donate. The decision to donate goes beyond the obligatory and permissible to the supererogatory, and a decision not to donate does not invite or warrant moral criticism because there is no moral basis on which to criticize not performing an act that would have been beyond the call of duty. In contrast, the family member who is a potential donor has a prima facie obligation to donate because of the nature of relationships within the family.

In contrast, in their interviews with health care professionals involved in living liver donation, Thomas et al found that many believed it was too risky in the case of strangers, but that the benefits that would accrue to donors where they were very close to the recipient (especially if the donor was a parent) tipped the risk–benefit calculation in favour of allowing donation.

---

[123] 'Do genetic relationships create moral obligations in organ transplantation?' (2002) 11 Cambridge Quarterly of Healthcare Ethics 153–9.

Elin H Thomas et al[124]

[A]lthough HCPs [health care professionals] claim that their assessments are more objective (less clouded by emotion) than those of the donor and recipient, their assessment of risk often reflects their own values regarding the nature of familial relationships. For example, a greater level of risk was judged to be acceptable in the case of an LLD [living liver donation] from a parent to his or her adult child than an LLD from an adult child to his or her parent (despite the similar medical risk associated with both cases). Here, the participants seemed to be factoring into their judgement, a view that it is more acceptable for parents to take risks for their children than vice versa. Likewise . . . altruistic (stranger) donation was regarded as too risky, even though the risks are similar to those between relatives or family friends.

(c) Payment

In 2015, the Council of Europe adopted a Convention against Trafficking in Human Organs, Article 4 of which requires each of the following acts to be a criminal offence:

(a) where the removal is performed without the free, informed and specific consent of the living or deceased donor, or, in the case of the deceased donor, without the removal being authorised under its domestic law;

(b) where, in exchange for the removal of organs, the living donor, or a third party, has been offered or has received a financial gain or comparable advantage;

(c) where in exchange for the removal of organs from a deceased donor, a third party has been offered or has received a financial gain or comparable advantage.

And under section 32 of the Human Tissue Act, payment for human organs is a criminal offence.

Human Tissue Act 2004 section 32

32 Prohibition of commercial dealings in human material for transplantation

(1) A person commits an offence if he—

(a) gives or receives a reward for the supply of, or for an offer to supply, any controlled material;

(b) seeks to find a person willing to supply any controlled material for reward;

(c) offers to supply any controlled material for reward;

(d) initiates or negotiates any arrangement involving the giving of a reward for the supply of, or for an offer to supply, any controlled material;

(e) takes part in the management or control of a body of persons corporate or unincorporate whose activities consist of or include the initiation or negotiation of such arrangements.

---

[124] 'Live liver donation, ethics and practitioners: "I am between the two and if I do not feel comfortable about this situation, I cannot proceed"' (2014) 40 Journal of Medical Ethics 157–62.

Under section 32(8) and (10), the prohibition covers both cadaveric and living organ dona-tion. Notice that it is not just organ traffickers who would commit an offence under section 32(1). Recipients of organs too could face prosecution, as could anyone involved in arrang-ing an organ sale. The maximum penalty for offences under section 32(1) is three years' imprisonment. Under section 32(2), it is also an offence to publish or distribute an advertise-ment for the sale of an organ, with a maximum penalty of 51 weeks' imprisonment.

Under section 32(6)(a) payment to the holder of a licence (ie the hospital) in money or money's worth is not to be considered a reward if it 'is in consideration for transporting, removing, preparing, preserving, or storing controlled material'. This means that covering the costs associated with the transplantation process is not to be treated in the same way as a payment for an organ. Similarly, under section 32(7)(a), 'any expenses incurred in, or in connection with, transporting, removing, preparing, preserving or storing the material' are not to be treated as a reward.

Section 32(7)(c) permits payments to living organ donors to cover 'any expenses or loss of earnings incurred by the person from whose body the material comes so far as reason-ably and directly attributable to his supplying the material from his body'. A living organ donor could therefore expect to receive compensation for time that she has to take off work during the organ donation process, and for associated expenses, such as travel costs. The reference to expenses or loss of earnings makes it clear that any such payments are not to be seen as payment for the organ itself, or even compensation for the inconvenience of donation, but rather must simply cover financial costs that are directly attributable to the donation.

(d) WHAT, IF ANYTHING, WOULD BE WRONG WITH A MARKET IN ORGANS?

Several reasons are commonly put forward for prohibiting the sale of organs. First, it is argued that there is something intrinsically wrong with commodifying the human body, and that it would be either impossible or degrading to put a value on human body parts. Secondly, commercialization of organ transplantation is believed to undermine the prin-ciple that donation should be altruistic. In the next extract, for example, Barbro Bjorkman adopts a virtue ethics approach (see Chapter 1), and suggests that selling an organ is not something a virtuous person would do.

Barbro Bjorkman[125]

Virtue ethics rejects commodification of organs because it fails to make us flourish, not because it has bad consequences or breaks some rule . . . Virtuous persons would not sell their organs but rather donate them because they wish to help their less fortunate fellow man, they 'see' that this is fine, noble, and worthwhile. The fact that this is not the current practice in society today only shows that people in general are not virtuous. The way to redeem the problems of organ shortage in a given society is not to create a market but rather to increase the sense of virtue.

---

[125] 'Why we are not allowed to sell that which we are encouraged to donate' (2006) 15 Cambridge Quarterly of Healthcare Ethics 60–70.

Thirdly, a black market in organs already exists in some parts of the world. Wealthy patients have travelled to countries such as India, Estonia, Moldova, Turkey, and Ukraine for transplant surgery, which depends upon the payment of relatively modest sums to 'donors'. It is, as Simon Rippon has pointed out, 'a matter of empirical fact' that 'people who are not financially desperate generally do not want to become living organ vendors. Few of us would consider selling a kidney to obtain frivolous luxuries'.[126] In the next extracts, Berlinguer and Goyal et al highlight the consequences of markets in organs for the poorest and most vulnerable.

Giovanni Berlinguer[127]

The truth of the matter is that, as far as human organs are concerned, the traffic always takes place between the South and the North of the world, or between the poor who sell and the rich who buy . . . [I]n the twenty-first century, the North could attempt to treat its more seriously ill by importing and using organs from members of the poorer classes, in particular from the underdeveloped countries. Supplies would be more than sufficient, as bodies are the only goods that these countries produce in abundance.

M Goyal, RL Mehta, LJ Schneiderman, and AR Seghal[128]

[S]elling a kidney did not help poor donors overcome poverty. Family income actually declined by one third, and most participants were still in debt and living below the poverty line at the time of the survey. . . . [M]ost participants would not recommend that others sell a kidney, which suggests that potential donors would be unlikely to sell a kidney if they were better informed of the likely outcomes . . . [N]ephrectomy was associated with a decline in health status. Previous qualitative reports suggest that a diminished ability to perform physical labor may explain the observed worsening of economic status. . . . A majority of donors were women. Given the often weak position of women in Indian society, the voluntary nature of some donations is questionable. In fact, two participants said that their husbands forced them to donate.

Fourthly, it has been argued that financial incentives may overbear a person's will, and thus cast doubt upon the voluntariness of their consent.

Eugene B Brody[129]

In countries without legal prohibition of organ selling, recruitment campaigns have used selling techniques which effectively negate informed consent among the poorest citizens for whom the possibility of a one-time financial gain of previously unimaginable proportions is so irresistible as to obviate rational judgement. Financial incentives in these circumstances are tantamount to coercion.

---

[126] Simon Rippon, 'Organ markets and harms: a reply to Dworkin, Radcliffe Richards and Walsh' (2014) 40 Journal of Medical Ethics 155–6.

[127] *Everyday Bioethics: Reflections on Bioethical Choices in Daily Life* (Baywood Publishing: New York, 2003) 101.

[128] 'Economic and health consequences of selling a kidney in India' (2002) 288 Journal of the American Medical Association 1589–93.

[129] *Biomedical Technology and Human Rights* (UNESCO: Paris, 1993) 100.

Kate Greasley objects to organ markets not because vendors cannot consent, but because we know that their consent will have been prompted by poverty.

Kate Greasley[130]

[T]he real concern does not turn on consent as such, but rather, on the claim that consensual or not, the kind of trading entailed by a living donor market in organs will almost always play on the natural disadvantages of the poor. The situation of the kidney-seller in the imaginary example continues to be deeply disconcerting, not because we are unsure of whether he consented, but because we are certain that he never *would* have consented but for his poverty.

Fifthly, donation involves pain, discomfort, and risk, and there are those who are troubled by the prospect of people assuming some risk to health in return for financial reward. Indeed, as Julian Koplin points out, the evidence appears to indicate that the outcomes for organ vendors are, on average, worse than for organ donors, perhaps because of their pre-existing poverty.

Julian Koplin[131]

Almost every study that has asked the question has found that the majority of vendors regret selling a kidney and/or would not recommend doing so to others. Moreover, a study of 100 Iranian donors (97 of whom were vendors) found that 76% were in favor of banning kidney sales. According to vendors' own accounts, selling a kidney left them worse off physically, psychologically, socially, and financially. In the face of this body of research, and in the absence of compelling reasons to believe that such outcomes are entirely attributable to black-market abuses, the ubiquitous claim that regulated systems of kidney selling would improve vendors' well-being lacks evidential warrant. The available research, despite its limitations, suggests the opposite: that vendors will usually experience a range of significant harms that ultimately leave them worse off than before the sale.

And it is not just the risks of donation that worry some commentators. Simon Rippon has argued that, if organ sale were permitted, a poor person facing debts or bankruptcy might be harmed by their refusal to sell their kidney.

Simon Rippon[132]

Selling your organs would become something that is simply expected of you as and when financial need arises. Our new 'option' can thus easily be transformed into a social or legal demand, and it can drastically change the attitudes that others adopt towards you. . . . My contention, then, is that because people in poverty often find themselves either indebted

---

[130] 'A legal market in organs: the problem of exploitation' (2014) 40 Journal of Medical Ethics 51–6.

[131] 'Assessing the likely harms to kidney vendors in regulated organ markets' (2014) 14 American Journal of Bioethics 7–18.

[132] 'Imposing options on people in poverty: the harm of a live donor organ market' (2014) 40 Journal of Medical Ethics 145–50.

or in need of cash to meet their own basic needs and those of their families, they would predictably find themselves faced with social or legal pressure to pay the bills by selling their organs, if selling organs were permitted. . . . Once we have come to conceptualise our 'excess' organs and organ parts as pieces of unnecessary property by commodifying them, there would naturally follow genuine social and legal costs to pay for failing to sell them when economically necessary, just as there are social and legal costs to pay for failing to take employment when you are able to do so. We should ask questions such as the following: Would those in poverty be eligible for bankruptcy protection, or for public assistance, if they have an organ that they choose not to sell? Could they be legally forced to sell an organ to pay taxes, paternity bills or rent?

Finally, a free market in organs would mean that only rich people would be able to afford to buy them, thus disrupting the principle that scarce health care resources should be distributed according to need rather than ability to pay.

There are those who would dispute some of these claims. For example, it is not strictly true that it is impossible to put a value on a human organ, nor that doing so is inevitably degrading. Tort law routinely quantifies the loss of various body parts. Victims of criminal injuries are paid damages, without any assumption that such damages undermine the intrinsic value of the human body.

Secondly, even if poor people do find the offer of money in return for a kidney especially attractive, this must also be true of other sources of income that may pose some risk to a person's health (often much greater than the small risk of living with one kidney). Yet few people would argue that we should pay soldiers modest wages in order to ensure that they have not signed up for a career in the army because of the lure of the salary. Against this, Kate Greasley argues that the exploitation involved in organ selling is more 'extreme' than in most potentially dangerous jobs.

Kate Greasley[133]

[O]rgan selling is quite simply one of the more extreme cases, so that it falls more clearly within the bracket of exploitative behaviour which is serious enough to invoke the coercive power of the law (slavery and child labour being clear examples of other practices in that category). The permanency of losing one's organ, the invasiveness of surgery, the particular health repercussions and psychological impact on the vendor may lead one to the conclusion *this* form of exploitation is especially objectionable. . . .

It might be argued that there is yet a morally significant difference, in that although there may be a risk involved, there is every chance that the risk will not materialise. In contrast, poor people who sell their organs do not just take a risk—they incur a *certain* loss, a loss which they only deem justified on the pretext that it will do something that in reality it does not: help alleviate their poverty.

Thirdly, it is clear that a black market in human organs already exists, and Radcliffe-Richards et al argue that it is this, rather than a regulated market, which poses the greatest risk to organ donors.

---

[133] 'A legal market in organs: the problem of exploitation' (2014) 40 Journal of Medical Ethics 51–6.

J Radcliffe-Richards et al[134]

> If our ground for concern is that the range of choices is too small, we cannot improve matters by removing the best option that poverty has left, and making the range smaller still . . . The only way to improve matters is to lessen the poverty until organ selling no longer seems the best option; and if that could be achieved, prohibition would be irrelevant because nobody would want to sell. . . .
>
> [A]ll the evidence we have shows that there is much more scope for exploitation and abuse when a supply of desperately wanted goods is made illegal. It is, furthermore, not clear why it should be thought harder to police a legal trade than the present complete ban.

Only one country has a legal market in organs. The Iranian government provides each kidney vendor approximately US$1,200 plus a year's health insurance.[135] The recipient or, if the recipient is poor, a charitable organization will give the vendor an additional sum of between US$2,300 and US$4,500. Recipients must be Iranian, so Iran is not a destination for transplant tourism. Vendors must be aged between 20 and 35 years of age and their next of kin must have given consent. The shortage of kidneys has largely disappeared, but vendors are, perhaps unsurprisingly, disproportionately from the poorest sections of society.

Fourthly, as we saw in Chapter 5, the principle of patient autonomy means that we let people assume considerable risks to their own health by refusing life-sustaining treatment, and that they are entitled to exercise this choice for irrational reasons or even for no reason at all. Is it then unduly paternalistic to prevent someone from incurring a less serious risk to her health in order to save another person's life?

Fifthly, it is not clear that paid organ donation is necessarily incompatible with altruism. We would permit a mother to donate a kidney to her son if he had kidney failure, but what if the son's condition is instead a rare form of cancer, and optimum treatment is expensive and only available abroad? We would forbid this mother from selling a kidney in order to pay for her son's life-saving treatment, even though her motivation could be said to be as altruistic as the mother whose son happens to have renal failure.

Sixthly, as Stephen Wilkinson points out, there is something wrong with the argument that we should not allow paid organ donation because it is risky. If this is true, then unpaid organ donation is equally risky, and presumably should also be prohibited.

Stephen Wilkinson[136]

> No matter how dangerous paid donation is, it needn't . . . be any more risky than unpaid donation, since the mere fact of payment doesn't *add* any danger. So if paid donation is wrong because of the danger to which the donor is subjected, then free donation must also be wrong on the very same grounds. Free donation, though, is not wrong; on the contrary, we tend to regard it as commendable, heroic even. Therefore paid donation isn't wrong either— or, if it is wrong, it's wrong because of something other than the danger to which the donor is subjected.

---

134 'The case for allowing kidney sales' (1998) 351 The Lancet 1950–2.

135 Benjamin E Hippen, 'Organ sales and moral travails: lessons from the living kidney vendor program in Iran' (2008) Cato Institute Policy Analysis No 614.

136 *Bodies for Sale: Ethics and Exploitation in the Human Body Trade* (Routledge: London, 2003) 108.

Seventhly, allowing payments for organs does not necessarily mean embracing a completely free market. Instead, it would be possible for payments to be made by the NHS rather than individual recipients, and for the organs to then be distributed according to need. Because the cost savings of transplantation are so great, NHS-funded payments to donors could be cost-effective. In the next extract, Charles Erin and John Harris suggest that it is possible to contemplate an 'ethical market' in organs.

Charles A Erin and John Harris[137]

There is a lot of hypocrisy about the ethics of buying and selling organs and indeed other body products and services . . . What it usually means is that everyone is paid but the donor. The surgeons and medical team are paid, the transplant coordinator does not go unremunerated, and the recipient receives an important benefit in kind. Only the unfortunate and heroic donor is supposed to put up with the insult of no reward, to add to the insult of the operation . . .

The bare bones of an ethical market would look like this: the market would be confined to a self-governing geopolitical area such as a nation state or indeed the European Union. Only citizens resident within the union or state could sell into the system and they and their families would be equally eligible to receive organs. Thus organ vendors would know they were contributing to a system which would benefit them and their families and friends since their chances of receiving an organ in case of need would be increased by the existence of the market . . . There would be only one purchaser, an agency like the National Health Service (NHS), which would buy all organs and distribute according to some fair conception of medical priority. There would be no direct sales or purchases, no exploitation of low income countries and their populations (no buying in Turkey or India to sell in Harley Street). The organs would be tested for HIV etc, their provenance known, and there would be strict controls and penalties to prevent abuse.

Sellers of organs would know they had saved a life and would be reasonably compensated for their risk, time, and altruism, which would be undiminished by sale. We do not after all regard medicine as any the less a caring profession because doctors are paid.

Of course, while Erin and Harris's ethical market would eliminate one unsatisfactory aspect of a completely free market in organs—in that organs would not be distributed according to ability to pay—it would not, as Kate Greasley points out, eliminate the other:

the organ vendors themselves would still be self-selecting, and quite naturally, will self select on the basis of poverty and desperation. Hence, it will remain the case, whoever benefits from the organs, that it will be largely (if not wholly) poor people selling them.[138]

Finally, insofar as the offer of money might persuade someone to volunteer to be a live organ donor, should we, as Harvey suggests, perhaps be equally or even more concerned about non-financial pressure, such as that exerted within families?

---

[137] 'An ethical market in human organs' (2003) 29 Journal of Medical Ethics 137–8.
[138] 'A legal market in organs: the problem of exploitation' (2014) 40 Journal of Medical Ethics 51–6.

J Harvey[139]

> Now I think there is financial pressure when the potential donor is in poverty. And perhaps it may be argued that this alone is sufficient for banning all paid-for donations. But then, in consistency, the same reasoning should be applied to related donors: since *some* of them are open to heavy psychological and emotional pressure (for example, perhaps by being the submissive and 'guilt'-ridden offspring of an extremely domineering and now ailing parent), then all donations from relatives should be forbidden.

4 XENOTRANSPLANTATION

Although whole organ transplants from animals to humans are still at the experimental stage, other sorts of animal tissues have been used in human medicine for many years. Pig heart valves, for example, can be processed so that they act like inert material rather than living tissue, and their safe and effective use in human patients is well established.

There have been examples of animal-to-human whole organ transplants, but none has been successful, with maximum survival times of a few months. In the most infamous case, a baboon heart was transplanted into a 14-day-old baby, known as 'Baby Fae', and she died within three weeks. Her parents were poor and uneducated, and the consent form they signed appeared to overstate the likely benefits from the transplant. It suggested that: 'Long-term survival with appropriate growth and development may be possible following heart transplantation . . . this research is an effort to provide your baby with some hope of immediate and long term survival.'[140]

In the next extract, Jeffrey Barker and Lauren Polcrack explain that the history of experimentation in xenotransplantation is not 'ethically promising'.

Jeffrey H Barker and Lauren Polcrack[141]

> Many early xenotransplant recipients were unconscious and therefore never consented to the procedure; many were poor and uneducated. Some were prisoners, some were children. The first cardiac xenotransplantation subject (in 1964) was a deaf-mute who never consented to the procedure, and the consent form signed by his step-sister did not mention a non-human organ. Throughout the history of xenotransplantation, the medically, ethically and socially vulnerable have been used as experimental subjects.
>
> The first documented xenotransplantation involving a human host occurred in 1902, when a pig kidney was used in the case of a young woman suffering from end-stage renal failure. Early in the twentieth century, kidneys were transplanted into humans from rabbits, pigs, lambs, goats, macaques, chimpanzees, marmosets and baboons. In each case, however, the transplant failed, and in most cases the patient died as a result.

The principal reason for pursuing research into xenotransplantation is that it would enable many more patients to receive potentially life-saving organ transplants. If we could breed

---

[139] 'Paying organ donors' (1990) 16 Journal of Medical Ethics 117–19.

[140] Jeffrey H Barker and Lauren Polcrack, 'Respect for persons, informed consent and the assessment of infectious disease risks in xenotransplantation' (2001) 4 Medicine, Health Care and Philosophy 53–70, 59.

[141] Ibid.

animals for their organs, in the same way as we breed them for food, the organ shortage might disappear. Not only would this benefit the thousands of patients currently on the organ waiting list, but it could also potentially eliminate the risks to health incurred by living organ donors.

For several reasons, pigs, rather than primates, are regarded as the most promising source animal. First, chimpanzees and other primates, such as orangutans, are endangered species. Secondly, primates are much 'closer' to humans: they look like us and we do not eat them. Although note that Fox suggests such reasoning is morally arbitrary.

Marie Fox[142]

Certainly, given that pigs and primates are alike in the morally relevant respects, since both species are sentient, intelligent and sociable, the real reason to distinguish them seems not to rest on mental ability or capacity for suffering but on practical or emotional grounds . . . [B]y permitting use of certain animals, but not others, as research tools and potential organ donors, law reflects the moral arbitrariness in our response to them.

Thirdly, the chance of zoonosis, that is cross-species disease transmission, seems to be more likely between more closely related species. Fourthly, pigs breed much more quickly than primates, and the organ supply could therefore be replenished more quickly. Finally, pig organs are about the same size as human organs.

Despite the obvious advantages in locating a potentially unlimited supply of transplantable organs, there are several reasons why xenotransplantation is controversial. These are either practical problems, such as the risk of rejection and disease transmission, or ethical concerns, such as animal welfare considerations. We consider these in turn, before looking at the regulation of xenotransplantation in the UK.

(a) PRACTICAL PROBLEMS

(1) Rejection

The first major obstacle to successful xenotransplantation is the likelihood of a hyper-acute rejection reaction within minutes or hours of the transplant. Although immunosuppressant therapy can largely eliminate the risk of rejection in human-to-human transplants, much larger doses might be necessary in animal-to-human transplants, and if given in sufficient quantities these drugs will destroy a person's immune system, and themselves cause death.

A more promising solution is to introduce human genes into the animal's genome. There has been some success in creating transgenic pigs, and experiments involving primates appear to indicate that the rejection of organs from transgenic pigs can be controlled using drugs.[143]

More promising still are recent successes involving the creation of hybrid animals, known as chimaeras. Scientists have bred mice embryos with genetic mutations that would mean that they would develop without a specific organ, such as a pancreas. They have found that if they inject rat stem cells into these embryos, the rat cells effectively take over, and a rat

---

[142] 'Re-Thinking Kinship: Law's Construction of the Animal Body' (2004) 57 Current Legal Problems 469–93.

[143] Christopher GA McGregor et al, 'Cardiac xenotransplantation: early success in the orthotopic position' (2005) 24 Journal of Heart and Lung Transplantation S95.

pancreas will develop inside the rat/mouse chimaera. If this technique could be applied to humans and pigs, it might therefore be possible to grow human organs inside the bodies of pigs. As Shaw et al explain:

> Anyone in need of a new organ could provide iPSCs [induced pluripotent stem cells] which would be inserted in a pig embryo prior to implantation and gestation. After around 6 months, the resulting pig would be sacrificed and the human organ removed and implanted in the original donor.[144]

(2) Risk of Infection

Progress in techniques to minimize rejection means that the most pressing danger currently presented by xenotransplantation is the possibility of cross-species infection. Variant Creutzfeldt-Jakob disease (vCJD), the human form of bovine spongiform encephalitis (BSE) or 'mad cow' disease, is a dramatic example of cross-species disease transmission. The risk of infection from transplantation would be particularly acute since placing an animal organ inside a human body provides a perfect 'platform' for cross-species infection.

It is thought that some viruses, such as the porcine endogenous retrovirus (PERV), which is harmless to pigs, and incorporated into the pig genome, would be impossible to eliminate from transgenic pigs, and might be able to cross the species barrier and cause cancer, or irreversible damage to the human immune system. Any risk of cross-species infection would, of course, be exacerbated if the recipient is taking immunosuppressive drugs which reduce her ability to fight a new virus.

It is important to remember that if a disease crosses the species barrier, the risk of infection is faced not only by the recipient herself, but also by her close contacts and the rest of society, which as we can see in the next sections, raises some complicated ethical issues.

(a) Impact upon the recipient and her close contacts

Could someone give a valid consent to receiving an animal's organ in the light of the risk of cross-species infection? The first problem is whether their consent could ever be adequately informed. Insofar as the risks of cross-species infection cannot be known with any certainty before trials in humans have begun, and perhaps for some time afterwards, it would be impossible to give a potential recipient full disclosure of the risks associated with xenotransplantation.

Nuffield Council on Bioethics[145]

> It is not possible to predict or quantify the risk that xenotransplantation will result in the emergence of new human diseases. But in the worst case, the consequences could be far-reaching and difficult to control . . . Put bluntly, it may be possible to identify any infectious organism transmitted by xenografting only if it causes disease in human beings, and after it has started to do so.

---

[144] 'Creating human organs in chimaera pigs: an ethical source of immunocompatible organs?' (2015) 41 Journal of Medical Ethics 970–4.

[145] Nuffield Council on Bioethics, *Animal-to-Human Transplants: The Ethics of Xenotransplantation* (NCOB, 1996) paras 10.25, 6.14.

If there is an unknown and unquantifiable risk to recipients' health, it is arguable that they could never give sufficiently informed consent to xenotransplantation.

A second problem comes from the fact that allografts (human-to-human transplants) will continue to be the best treatment for individuals with acute organ failure. It might be argued that xenotransplantation should therefore only be tried in patients who would not be eligible for a human organ transplant. Patients who are not on the organ donor waiting list might be offered a xenograft on the grounds that this could have a greater chance of success than the treatment—that is, nothing—that would otherwise be available to them.

Related to this, if the first recipients are asked to choose between immediate death or the unknown risks associated with xenotransplantation, it is of course understandable that they might opt to receive an animal organ. But being faced with such an invidious choice leads McLean and Williamson to suggest that 'there must be questions about whether or not the vulnerability of the patients likely to be involved in early trials would cast doubt upon their competence or capacity to consent'.[146]

A further issue is the restrictions that would have to be placed on xenograft recipients. It would be necessary to monitor their health for the rest of their lives. If infection occurred, very serious restrictions might have to be placed upon recipients' liberty. It is also possible that their present and future sexual partners would have to be monitored, and that, at least at first, their freedom to have children might be restricted, and they would have to use barrier methods of contraception. Recipients could be asked to consent in advance to these limitations, and if the alternative is death, it is understandable that a person would agree in order to obtain a potentially life-saving transplant. In the next extract, however, Jeffrey Barker and Lauren Polcrack question whether it would, in fact, be possible to give fully informed consent to such serious curtailment of one's future liberty.

Jeffrey H Barker and Lauren Polcrack[147]

> [T]here are significant concerns with regard to the individual informed consent of the potential xenograft recipient. The recipient must understand as completely as possible the risks to him or herself, to his or [her] contacts, and the risks to society at large, and must be willing to move forward despite those risks. The immediate contacts of the potential recipient must also consent to the probable risks. Any clinical trials of xenotransplantation would require long-term—and probably lifetime—monitoring and surveillance of recipients and their contacts, with the possibility of lifetime quarantine should serious xenosis occur. All recipients would need to be registered and monitored in order to protect public health. Truly informed consent to these types of radical changes in personal freedom would be difficult to obtain.

If third parties, such as recipients' sexual partners, might be subject to surveillance and restrictions upon their liberty, should their consent also be necessary? Informing them about the recipient's medical treatment would not only represent a breach of confidentiality, but also, as Sheila McLean and Laura Williamson point out in the next extract, it would be most unusual to give a third party a right of veto over another's medical treatment. McLean and Williamson further highlight the difficulties in enforcing the sort of surveillance regime that many people think would be necessary following the first xenografts.

---

[146] 'Xenotransplantation: A Pig in a Poke?' (2004) 57 Current Legal Problems 443–68, 464.

[147] 'Respect for persons, informed consent and the assessment of infectious disease risks in xenotransplantation' (2001) 4 Medicine, Health Care and Philosophy 53–70, 66.

Sheila McLean and Laura Williamson[148]

If the consent of third parties is an essential prerequisite to a xenograft, then they are placed in the unusual position of being able, by refusal, to prevent the potential recipient from accepting a therapy which may be of benefit. Secondly, it is unclear just how such agreements [to restrict liberty] could be policed; agreement pre-transplant does not guarantee compliance post-transplant, yet compliance is presumably of the highest order of significance otherwise it would not be required in the first place. What, for example, would be done if a recipient decided not to use barrier contraception? It must be doubted whether or not the state could effectively enter the bedroom and prevent this from happening . . .

To continue with this example, it must be asked what would be the state's authority should an individual xenotransplant recipient or the partner of one become pregnant. Could the state compel a pregnancy termination, and if so on what grounds—ethical or legal? In other words, if the surveillance regime is necessary—as seems to be generally agreed—then there are serious concerns about its enforceability. Indeed the . . . working party which drafted the surveillance document noted that any attempt to require rather than invite patients to agree to the limitations to be imposed on their future life would be likely to run contrary to the terms of the Human Rights legislation, in particular Article 8.

(b) Impact upon society

Although it is clearly the recipient of an animal organ who is most immediately at risk from cross-species infection, transmission of disease to others may be possible, and hence xenotransplantation also poses as yet unquantifiable risks to public health. Since it will be impossible to prove that no such risk exists, we instead have to determine whether the degree of risk is acceptable.

Interestingly, xenotransplantation reverses the usual risk/benefit calculation in clinical trials. Generally, as we saw in Chapter 9, the research subject assumes some risk to her own health and wellbeing for the benefit of medical progress. Although the subject may hope to obtain a health benefit from participation, this is not its principal purpose, which is instead to benefit society through the furthering of scientific knowledge and the development of new treatments. In xenotransplantation, the benefit may be to the individual recipient, since it is likely that she would die soon without a transplant. The risk instead may be to society as a whole through the introduction of animal viruses into the human population. It would, however, be impossible to obtain the public's informed consent before a clinical trial began. Instead, Jeffrey Barker and Lauren Polcrack advocate greater public participation in the decision to go ahead with clinical trials.

Jeffrey H Barker and Lauren Polcrack[149]

Xenografts put at risk not only the recipient but those directly associated with the recipient, including caregivers and family members. They also put at risk the public at large by creating the distinct possibility of introducing new or modified pathogens into the human species, pathogens whose virulence, infectivity and mode of retransmission, and potential for treatment are all highly uncertain . . .

---

[148] 'Xenotransplantation: A Pig in a Poke?' (2004) 57 Current Legal Problems 443–68.

[149] 'Respect for persons, informed consent and the assessment of infectious disease risks in xenotransplantation' (2001) 4 Medicine, Health Care and Philosophy 53–70, 65.

Where there is a significant risk to the public, as we believe there is in xenotransplantation, there must be a public process for informing and educating the public, and for ascertaining the willingness of the public to encounter, to consent to these risks. This process of 'collective informed consent' requires not merely public education but active public participation in the decision-making process.

Sara Fovargue and Suzanne Ost reject the idea that public consultation is a sufficient response to the unknown risks xenotransplantation might pose to society. They claim that the risks are so great that, even if it could solve the organ shortage, xenotransplantation must be banned.

Sara Fovargue and Suzanne Ost[150]

Even if xenotransplantation could solve the organ shortage, the potential public health benefits would need to outweigh the risks to justify going ahead with it—the condition of proportionality. This is hard to satisfy. Societal public health is likely to suffer more of a detriment from the severity of the potential risk of an infectious disease pandemic than the benefit potentially achieved through increased organs available for transplantation. Everyone in society is placed at risk of a pandemic by allowing xenotransplantation to proceed. As a consequence, society's infrastructure might collapse . . .

In the light of the limited pre-clinical survival times, uncertainty as to the ability of genetically engineered pig organs to support human life, the potentially catastrophic risks, and the difficulties in identifying, managing, and controlling those risks, it is unclear why some still view xenotransplantation as a viable solution to the shortage of organs. In this environment, the public interest in health and state obligations to protect public health *require* the state to prohibit clinical xenotransplantation.

Of course, even if we were to ban xenotransplantation in the UK, then, in the absence of an enforceable global prohibition, as Sykes et al explain, 'xenotourism' is likely to make it difficult for a country to eliminate the risks posed by xenotransplantation.

Megan Sykes, Anthony d'Apice, and Mauro Sandrin[151]

The potential risks of xenotransplantation will not be confined to the country in which the transplant is performed. Even the most assiduous safety efforts of any nation or group of nations may be ineffective in the absence of internationally agreed regulations and monitoring procedures for xenotransplantation. This problem arises because patients are mobile and could receive a xenograft in one country, which may or may not have appropriate regulatory and monitoring processes, and later leave that country and enter another without ever having to state that they are the recipient of a xenograft . . .

The scale of such 'casual' xenotourism is likely to be small. However, there is a risk that entrepreneurial xenotransplanters may deliberately set up business in countries with minimal

---

[150] 'When Should Precaution Prevail? Interests in (Public) Health, the Risk of Harm and Xenotransplantation' (2010) 18 Medical Law Review 203–329.

[151] 'Position paper of the Ethics Committee of the International Xenotransplantation Association' (2003) 10 Xenotransplantation 194–203.

or no regulation and set about attracting foreigners with organ failure to come to be transplanted and then return home. The absence of questioning about xenotransplantation upon re-entry, and the absence of a mechanism for bringing such patients into surveillance programs in their home countries almost guarantee that such patients will avoid surveillance when they return home.

(b) ETHICAL CONCERNS

(1) Revulsion

Many people are repelled by the idea of transplanting animal organs into human beings. For some, this will be prompted by their religious beliefs. If a person's faith stops them from eating pork, it is possible that they might also object to receiving a pig's organ. In any future regulation of xenotransplantation there would undoubtedly have to be a conscientious objection clause, similar to that in the Abortion Act, so that doctors did not have to participate in xenotransplantation; and patients too would be reassured that their refusal to accept an animal organ would not mean that they would be removed from the transplant waiting list. Provided that no one is compelled to take part in xenotransplantation against their wishes, it would seem inappropriate for some people's instinctive revulsion to be allowed to determine whether xenotransplantation goes ahead, especially since potential recipients' lives may be at stake.

There have also been suggestions that introducing human genes into pigs, and animal organs into humans, threatens to blur the barriers between the species.

Jason Scott Robert and Françoise Baylis[152]

[S]cientifically, there might be no such thing as fixed species identities or boundaries. Morally, however, we rely on the notion of fixed species identities and boundaries in the way we live our lives and treat other creatures . . .

All things considered, the engineering of creatures that are part human and part nonhuman animal is objectionable because the existence of such beings would introduce inexorable moral confusion in our existing relationships with nonhuman animals and in our future relationships with part-human hybrids.

Of course, barriers between the species are constantly evolving, albeit slowly. We share about 96 per cent of our DNA with chimpanzees, and so basing moral status upon biology is fraught with difficulty. Moreover, there would seem to be no doubt that patients who have received pig heart valves continue to be members of the human species. Perhaps, as Henry Greely suggests, it is a question of degree.

---

[152] 'Crossing species boundaries' (2003) 3 American Journal of Bioethics 1–13.

Henry T Greely[153]

> [A]fter a few early reports of patient qualms, the use of pig heart valves for medical proce-
> dures now raises little concern. Apart from pragmatic fear of the passage of disease and
> some animal rights concerns that are quite distinct from issues of chimerism . . . other plausi-
> ble single organ xenotransplants into human beings seem unlikely to be heavily controversial.
> On the other hand, if it were feasible to transplant a chimpanzee brain into a human, or if a
> human were given a large number of organs from nonhuman sources, people might worry
> whether the resulting organism was really human . . .
>
> Chimeras made by moving human parts into nonhuman beings would raise concerns when
> they are significant enough to raise the question of the possible humanity of the recipient. In
> both cases the 'importance' of the parts—brains and gametes are more important than heart
> valves or skin—and the number of parts moved—transplanting five visceral organs would be
> more troubling than transplanting one—seems significant.

(2) Animal Rights

It is often said that if we are prepared to breed and kill animals for food, we should logically
also accept xenotransplantation, especially since the purpose of breeding animals for their
organs—ie saving lives—would seem to be more valuable and of more immediate benefit
than the production of meat. This simple analogy between eating meat and xenotransplantation has, however, been challenged.

Robin Downie[154]

> [W]hereas the eating of animal flesh may or may not be ethically right, it is 'natural' in the
> sense that many other animal species in fact do it and (as has been claimed by some) human
> beings are biologically carnivorous or at least omnivorous. On the other hand, the transplant
> of animal tissue into human beings is 'unnatural'.

Of course, as Downie himself admits, all medical interventions, including human-to-human
transplants, are also 'unnatural'. Downie therefore goes on to suggest that the insertion of
human genes into animals and then transplanting their organs into humans is 'profoundly
different from previous medical interventions'. This is, of course, a subjective judgement,
and it is not clear why xenotransplantation is necessarily any more 'profoundly unnatural'
than, say, *in vitro* fertilization.

Secondly, donor animals would have to be bred and raised in isolation in completely barren and sterile surroundings, and genetic modification might further impair their quality
of life. Would this represent a more substantial interference with their welfare than happens
when they are bred for meat? Possibly, although it should be remembered that the conditions
in battery farms, and the techniques used to produce veal and foie gras can be gruesome.
Of course, inhumane treatment of animals by the food industry does not justify inhumane
treatment in pursuit of organ transplantation. But insofar as the goal of xenotransplantation

---

153 'Defining chimeras . . . and chimeric concerns' (2003) 3 American Journal of Bioethics 17–20, 19.
154 'Xenotransplantation' (1997) 23 Journal of Medical Ethics 205–6, 206.

would be to save the lives of people who would otherwise die, there would seem to be no reason to be more squeamish about animal welfare where the goal is transplant retrieval than if the intention is to produce cheap chicken or foie gras.

A better analogy might be with the use of animals in research, when it is common for animals to be specially bred to take part in experiments, and to subsequently be killed. In animal experiments, we are using animals in order to further scientific knowledge and to improve the treatments that are available to humans. The benefits to individuals may be less direct and immediate than they would be if xenotransplantation were to be successful, but the ethical issues are similar.

Just like experiments on animals and eating meat, xenotransplantation rests upon the assumption that it is ethically acceptable to kill other species in order to benefit human lives. According to commentators such as Peter Singer, this is an example of speciesism (ie favouring one's own species and devaluing other species), which he argues is as morally objectionable as racism or sexism.

Peter Singer[155]

What kind of ethic can tell us that it is all right to rear sentient animals in barren cages that give them no decent life at all, and then kill them to take their organs, while refusing to permit us to take the organ of a human being who is not, and never can be, even minimally conscious? Obviously a speciesist ethic . . .

In a world that needlessly rears several billion animals in factory farms each year and then kills them to satisfy a mere preference of taste, it is difficult to argue persuasively against the rearing and slaughter of a few thousand animals so that their organs can be used to save people's lives. That, however, is not a reason for using animals: it is, rather, a reason for changing our views about animals. In a better world, a world that cared properly for the interests of animals, we would do our utmost to avoid choices that pit the essential interests of animals against our own . . . This might involve more effective ways of obtaining organs from humans who are brain dead, or cortically dead. It might involve the development of artificial organs. Or it might involve using our limited medical resources to educate people in looking after the organs with which they were born.

Why do we think that human beings' lives are more valuable and important than animals' lives? Often some appeal is made to distinctively human qualities, such as sentience, consciousness, and the capacity for reason. But, as Singer explains, the problem here is that not all human beings possess these characteristics—patients in a permanent vegetative state or anencephalic infants, for example, do not—whereas they are possessed to some degree by animals such as chimpanzees and dolphins. If it is these qualities, and not species membership per se, that count morally, then as Jonathan Hughes points out, two possible consequences follow. Either we should refuse to contemplate using animals that possess the relevant characteristics as xenograft sources. Or we should also be prepared to take organs from human beings who have irrevocably lost the capacities in question.[156]

---

[155] 'Xenotransplantation and speciesism' (1992) 24 Transplantation Proceedings 728–32.

[156] See also, RG Frey, 'Medicine, animal experimentation, and the moral problem of unfortunate humans' (1996) 12 Social Philosophy and Policy 181–211.

Jonathan Hughes[157]

Imposing harms on animals in order to benefit humans is acceptable, it is argued, because the harms and benefits that humans are capable of experiencing are greater than those that can be experienced by other animals. . . .

[T]his kind of argument is vulnerable to a well-known objection. The problem is that capacities for pleasure and pain, fulfilment and suffering vary not only between but within species, including humans. So while it is true that the capacities of a normal adult exceed those of a pig, the same cannot be said for all humans. There are many whose mental capacities are severely and tragically impaired, and it follows that if we are prepared to take organs from animals on the grounds of their limited capacities we should also be prepared to take the organs of those humans whose capacities are similarly restricted. Or conversely, if we insist that we should *not* take organs from such humans, then consistency demands that we refrain also from taking the organs of animals with similar or greater capacities.

Against this, Arthur Caplan argues that humans matter more morally because of their relationships with others.

Arthur L Caplan[158]

Severely retarded children and those born with devastating conditions such as anencephaly have never had the capacities and abilities that confer a greater moral standing on humans as compared with animals. Should they be used as the first donors and recipients in xenografting research instead of primates?

The reason they should not has nothing to do with the properties, capacities and abilities of children or infants who lack and have always lacked significant degrees of intellectual and cognitive function. The reason they should not be used is because of the impact using them would have upon other human beings, especially their parents and relatives. A severely retarded child can still be the object of much love, attention, and devotion from his or her parents. These feelings and the abilities and capacities that generate them are deserving of moral respect. Animals do not appear to be capable of such feelings.

If a human mother were to learn that her severely retarded son had been used in lethal xenografting research, she would mourn this fact for the rest of her days. A baboon, monkey, dog or pig would not.

Of course, this argument might lead to the unedifying conclusion that where a profoundly incapacitated individual has no family or friends, then she could legitimately be used for research purposes or organ retrieval, since no one will be harmed by learning that she was used as a means to an end. If we want to argue that friendless people's membership of our species determines that we should treat them differently from animals, is this differential treatment an example of speciesism?

It might also be argued that we should not address the question of xenotransplantation's ethical legitimacy in isolation from other possible solutions to the shortage of organs, especially since human organs are, at least for the foreseeable future, likely to be better for

---

[157] 'Xenografting: ethical issues' (1998) 24 Journal of Medical Ethics 18–24, 23.

[158] *Am I my Brother's Keeper? The Ethical Frontiers of Biomedicine* (Indiana UP: Bloomington, IN 1997) 111.

recipients than animal organs. We could increase the availability of organs if we moved away from a consent model for cadaveric donation, and instead treated the organs of the recently dead as a public resource. This would, admittedly, offend some people's desire to control what happens to their bodies after death, and it could cause distress to their relatives. But animal rights advocates might argue that these harms are relatively trivial when compared with the harm endured by a sentient animal, bred in an entirely sterile environment and then killed for its organs.

(c) XENOTRANSPLANTATION IN THE UK

In 1997, the UK Xenotransplantation Interim Regulatory Authority (UKXIRA) was set up, in order to add an additional layer of review to applications to carry out clinical trials involving xenotransplantation. UKXIRA was disbanded nine years later, partly because no trials were taking place, and partly because the system of research ethics governance, considered in Chapter 9, was assumed to offer sufficient safeguards. In announcing the abolition of UKXIRA, the Department of Health issued guidance on the research governance arrangements for xenograft trials.

Department of Health[159]

> The Government believes that it is right to explore the potential of xenotransplantation in a cautious, stepwise fashion. It is extremely important to carry out a xenotransplant procedure in a controlled research context. Clearly, the wellbeing of the individuals concerned, and the safety of the public in general, must be foremost in the consideration of any proposal to undertake a xenotransplantation procedure. No xenotransplantation procedures involving humans will be allowed to take place unless the approving body is fully satisfied that the evidence put forward is sufficient to justify the particular procedure proposed.
>
> Any proposal for a *clinical trial* of a xenogenic medicinal product requires approval from MHRA, who will assess safety, quality and efficacy. Such proposals must also go for ethical review.

Research involving animals will, as we saw in Chapter 9, also require Home Office authorization.

Williamson et al are critical of the decision to disband UKXIRA. In addition to the concerns expressed in the next extract, they note that, unless the organs are modified in some way after removal from the animal's body, they are very unlikely to amount to 'medicinal products', and hence are unlikely to be subject to the Clinical Trials Regulations and to regulation by the MHRA. They are also concerned that the first uses of xenografts may not come through organized trials, with REC approval, but through clinicians' freedom to use innovative therapies, which have not been properly tested, when the person's condition is extremely grave and there are no other available treatments.

---

[159] *Xenotransplantation Guidance* (DH: London, 2006).

Laura Williamson, Marie Fox, and Sheila McLean[160]

While, as we have stressed, updating governance arrangements is to be welcomed in the face of developments in medicine and science, it is important that the drive for modernization does not result in a relaxation of safeguards necessary to protect the individual and the public. Elsewhere in healthcare law the normalization of certain biotechnologies, such as embryo research and IVF, has prompted calls for less state intervention, and a drive toward liberalization may well be a factor in the current review of the law in this area. However, the history of xenotransplantation to date, particularly difficulties in calculating the safety risks that it poses and its potential to transcend regulatory and national borders, should make us wary of acceding to attempts to normalize this technology as simply another form of research. The recent emphasis on promoting the United Kingdom as a centre for biotech research, coupled with what Woods has called the 'xenotransplantation imperative' lend weight to the argument that we should hesitate before abolishing an oversight body which, for all its flaws, had positioned the United Kingdom as a leader in this regulatory field.

At the time of writing, solid organ xenotransplantation still looks some way off. In contrast, trials involving non-human primates suggest that other tissues and cells from pigs might be likely to reach the clinical trial stage within the next few years.

Burcin Ekser et al[161]

Experimental results obtained with pig-islet, neuronal-cell, and corneal xenotransplantation have been encouraging. With new genetically modified pigs becoming available that are likely to improve the outcome of cellular and corneal xenotransplantation further, we believe that clinical trials will be justified within the next 2–3 years. No safety concerns that would prohibit such clinical trials have been reported . . . With regard to pig tissues and cells, as opposed to organs, it would seem that clinical xenotransplantation could soon become a reality.

5 CONCLUSION

As life expectancy increases, the number of people experiencing organ failure will rise, and the shortage of organs available for transplantation looks set to continue. Persuading more people to register their agreement to the use of their organs after death, and increasing the number of living donors, will save some lives, but it will not eliminate the ever-widening gap between supply and demand.

How could this problem be solved? It is not yet clear whether the ethical and clinical difficulties raised by xenotransplantation can be satisfactorily addressed. In the next chapter, we will encounter another possible 'solution' to the organ shortage, namely the possibilities opened up by stem cell research. Routine derivation of whole organs from stem cells is still some way off, however. In the short to medium term, then, it is inevitable that people will die while waiting for organs that could save their lives.

---

[160] 'The regulation of xenotransplantation in the United Kingdom after UKXIRA: legal and ethical issues' (2007) 34 Journal of Law and Society 441–64.

[161] Burcin Ekser et al, 'Clinical xenotransplantation: the next medical revolution?' (2012) 379 The Lancet 672–83.

It could plausibly be argued that it is extraordinary that we routinely burn or bury organs that could save lives. Of course, taking organs without the consent of the deceased person, or in the face of their relatives' objections, might cause offence and distress, but it is worth remembering that the cost of avoiding this offence and distress is the certain death of identifiable individuals with acute organ failure.

Perhaps regrettably, the emphasis upon patient autonomy and the need for consent has spilled over into the treatment of our bodies after death. I do not mean to suggest that there is no value in respecting an individual's wishes after her death. For many people, exercising some control over what happens to their resources and their bodies after they have died is of critical importance. But, in relation to testamentary freedom, the deceased's wishes are not always decisive. If I choose to leave all of my assets to a donkey sanctuary, when this will leave my family destitute, my choice can be overridden. In relation to organ donation, could it be argued that the decision to have one's organs burned or buried, when they could be used to save lives, should be similarly open to challenge?

Here we may have another interesting example of the difference between legal and moral duties. It would be difficult (though perhaps not impossible) to argue that I have a legal duty to donate my organs after death, but the moral duty of easy rescue—that is, the duty to save a life when to do so would be virtually costless—might be said to be unarguable. Julian Savulescu is more forceful, arguing that the organ 'shortage' represents a failure of practical ethics.

Julian Savulescu[162]

Organ transplantation is another example of the lethal effects of bad ethics. Organ transplantation is a lifesaving intervention. Millions of people die around the world because of a shortage of organs. But there is no shortage in reality—we just don't use all the organs that could be used because of bad ethical reasons. . . .

[T]his is not just an easy rescue, it is a *zero cost* rescue. Organs are of no use to us when we are dead, but they are literally lifesaving to others. Nonetheless, most people choose to bury or burn these lifesaving resources, and are allowed to. Yet the state extracts death duties and inheritance taxes, but not the most important of their previous assets—their organs. The failure to meet even our most minimal moral obligations is damning. It represents the failure of modern practical ethics.

FURTHER READING

BMA, Building on Progress: Where Next for Organ Donation Policy in the UK?' (BMA, 2012).

Burnell, Philippa, Hulton, Sally-Anne, and Draper, Heather, 'Coercion and choice in parent–child live kidney donation' (2015) 41 Journal of Medical Ethics 304–9.

Coggon, John, 'Elective ventilation for organ donation: law, policy and public ethics' (2013) 39 Journal of Medical Ethics 130–4.

Emson, HE, 'It is immoral to require consent for cadaver organ donation' (2003) 29 Journal of Medical Ethics 125–7.

---

[162] 'Bioethics: why philosophy is essential for progress' (2015) 41 Journal of Medical Ethics 28–33.

Erin, Charles A and Harris, John, 'An ethical market in human organs' (2003) 29 Journal of Medical Ethics 137–8.

Greasley, Kate, 'A legal market in organs: the problem of exploitation' (2014) 40 Journal of Medical Ethics 51–6.

Harris, John, 'Organ procurement: dead interests, living needs' (2003) 29 Journal of Medical Ethics 130–4.

Human Tissue Authority, www.hta.gov.uk.

McGuinness, Sheelagh and Brazier, Margaret, 'Respecting the Living Means Respecting the Dead Too' (2008) 28 Oxford Journal of Legal Studies 297–316.

NHS Blood and Transplant, www.nhsbt.nhs.uk.

Nuffield Council on Bioethics, *Animal-to-Human Transplants: The Ethics of Xenotransplantation* (Nuffield Council on Bioethics: London, 1996).

Thomas, Elin H et al, 'Live liver donation, ethics and practitioners: "I am between the two and if I do not feel comfortable about this situation, I cannot proceed"' (2014) 40 Journal of Medical Ethics 157–62.

Williamson, Laura, Fox, Marie, and McLean, Sheila, 'Regulation of xenotransplantation in the United Kingdom after UKXIRA: legal and ethical issues' (2007) 34 Journal of Law and Society 441–64.

EMBRYO AND STEM CELL RESEARCH

CENTRAL ISSUES

1. Some people believe that an embryo is a person from the moment of conception. A more common view is that an embryo does not have the same status as a person, but that it is nevertheless special and should be treated with respect.

2. In the UK, embryo research is regulated by the Human Fertilisation and Embryology Act 1990, as amended, and by the Human Fertilisation and Embryology Authority.

3. The original Act stood the test of time well, but between 1990 and 2008, there were a few new scientific advances, including the birth of Dolly the sheep and the isolation of the first human embryonic stem cell line, which put pressure on the original wording of the statute. A substantial amending statute came into force in 2009.

4. The Act lays down a number of restrictions on the use of embryos for research: no research can be carried out on an embryo after 14 days; the research must be necessary or desirable for one of the statutory purposes; and the use of embryos must be necessary. This latter restriction means it would not be possible to obtain a licence if the research could be carried out on animals, or using tissue taken from adults, such as induced pluripotent stem cells.

1 INTRODUCTION

Until relatively recently, it was not possible to create human embryos outside a woman's body, and so the question of what protection, if any, should be afforded to the early stages of new human life was inextricably bound up with the issue of abortion. Now that eggs can be fertilized *in vitro*, new questions arise about how embryos created and stored outside a woman's body should be treated.

In this chapter our focus is upon whether, and in what circumstances, research on human embryos might be acceptable. Some people believe that the respect due to a human embryo will always be incompatible with carrying out experiments upon it, regardless of the potential health benefits, while others would say that, provided it is properly regulated, embryo research can be legitimate.

To begin with, some of the terminology in this chapter may be unfamiliar to law students: when an egg (*oocyte*) is fertilized by a sperm, a single cell *zygote* is formed. This then begins the process of cell division. After approximately four to five days, a *blastocyst* is formed, which will contain 50 to 150 cells. At the blastocyst stage it is possible to distinguish between the outer shell or *trophoblast* and the *inner cell mass*. The trophoblast will become the placenta. The inner cell mass will contain *stem cells*. These are undifferentiated cells that will subsequently differentiate in order to become skin, bones, blood, solid organs, etc. As we see later, the goal of stem cell research is to extract stem cells and then control the process of *differentiation* in order to reprogramme them to become specialized tissue. In the future, this sort of *regenerative medicine* might be able to offer cures for a wide range of degenerative conditions.

In this chapter, we begin with a brief survey of philosophical debates over the embryo's moral status. Next, we cover regulation in the UK, through the statutory provisions in the Human Fertilisation and Embryology Act 1990, as amended, and the Human Fertilisation and Embryology Authority's licensing regime.

2   WHAT IS THE MORAL STATUS OF THE EMBRYO?

Deciding upon the embryo's moral status is not just an abstract question of philosophy, theology, or morality. As Maureen Junker-Kenny explains, because the embryo's status determines how we should treat it, this is also a question of enormous practical importance.

Maureen Junker-Kenny[1]

Any definition of the beginning and end of human personhood is caught up in a hermeneutical circle. We define its starting point because we want to act in a certain way, and we act according to how we have defined it. If we consider the moment of implantation in the uterus, or the presence of brain activity, or the ability to communicate, as the starting-point for ascribing personhood, we are free to use the embryo prior to this stage in any way we consider useful.

Each definition has a practical intent. Once we ascribe human life and personhood to an entity, we want to protect it. If one wants to give maximum protection, one has to use a minimal definition, such as the new genetic unity created by egg and sperm. A maximal definition of human life, such as the ability to communicate, or to act independently, offers minimal protection to the stages prior to these competencies and after they have been lost.

(a)   IS THE EMBRYO A PERSON?

Any embryo that is used in research will be destroyed or allowed to perish, so if an embryo is a person, research would obviously be unacceptable. While the law is clear that a legal

---

[1] 'The Moral Status of the Embryo' in Neil Messer (ed), *Theological Issues in Bioethics: An Introduction with Readings* (Darton, Longman and Todd: London, 2002) 8–75.

person only exists after a child has been born, according to some religions, most notably Roman Catholicism, a person exists from the moment of conception.

Catechism of the Catholic Church

2270 Human life must be respected and protected absolutely from the moment of conception.

2274 Since it must be treated from conception as a person, the embryo must be defended in its integrity, cared for, and healed, as far as possible, like any other human being.

2275 It is immoral to produce human embryos intended for exploitation as disposable biological material.

Interestingly, this Catholic position is relatively new. Until the nineteenth century, ensoulment was believed to be the point at which the developing fetus achieved humanity, and this took place some time after fertilization. Male fetuses were ensouled at 40 days, and female fetuses at 80 days.

It is also worth noting that fertilization does not happen instantly. In normal sexual reproduction, fertilization may not begin until some time after sexual intercourse, and it can take up to 30 hours for a sperm to fertilize an egg. Implantation—which is when the fertilized egg attaches itself to the woman's body—will not start until about six or seven days later, and may also take several days.

Moreover, an embryo will not autonomously become a baby. This is only possible if it is successfully implanted in a woman's uterus and carried for at least five months. These are substantial prerequisites: most fertilized eggs fail to implant or to complete their development, and the vast majority of this natural wastage goes unnoticed. Even if a fertilized egg does implant, some of its cells will divide to form the placenta and umbilical cord. These are tissues that are discarded at birth, and are obviously not a 'person'. Up to about 14 days after fertilization begins, an embryo may split and become two embryos (which will, if born, be identical twins), so the early human embryo is not necessarily one human being, but may become two different ones.

In 2008, an updated Papal *Encyclical on Bioethics* was issued, which restated the Catholic Church's opposition to all research on embryos.

Congregation for the Doctrine of the Faith[2]

The obtaining of stem cells from a living human embryo . . . invariably causes the death of the embryo and is consequently gravely illicit: 'research, in such cases, irrespective of efficacious therapeutic results, is not truly at the service of humanity. In fact, this research advances through the suppression of human lives that are equal in dignity to the lives of other human individuals and to the lives of the researchers themselves. History itself has condemned such a science in the past and will condemn it in the future, not only because it lacks the light of God but also because it lacks humanity' (Benedict XVI).

Not all Catholics disapprove of all research on embryos, however. In the next extract, Margaret Foley offers a different Catholic perspective.

---

[2] 'Instruction *Dignitas Personae* on Certain Bioethical Questions' (Vatican, 2008).

Margaret Foley[3]

[A] case for human embryo stem cell research can be made on the basis of positions developed within the Roman Catholic tradition. Growing numbers of Catholic moral theologians, for example, do not consider the human embryo in its earliest stages (before development of the primitive streak or implantation) to constitute an individualized human entity with the settled inherent potential to become a human being. In this view the moral status of the embryo is therefore not that of a person, and its use for certain kinds of research can be justified. Since it is, however, a form of life, some respect is due to it; for example, it should not be bought and sold. Those who make this case prefer a return to the centuries-old Catholic position that a certain amount of development is necessary in order for a conceptus to warrant personal status. Embryologic studies now show that fertilization (conception) is itself a process (not a moment), and provide warrant for the opinion that in its earliest stages (including the blastocyst stage, when the inner cell mass is isolated to derive stem cells for purposes of research) the embryo is not sufficiently individualized to bear the moral weight of personhood.

Some adherents to other religions—perhaps most notably Anglicanism and Judaism—share the belief that, while it is important to treat the human embryo with respect, this does not necessarily rule out embryo research. According to the then Chief Rabbi's evidence to the House of Lords Select Committee on Stem Cell Research, in certain circumstances Judaism would allow the respect due to the early human embryo to be 'trumped' by the benefits that might flow from research:

In Jewish law neither the foetus nor the pre-implanted embryo is a person; it is, however, human life and must be accorded the respect due to human life. Personhood, with its attendant rights and responsibilities begins at birth. Prior to birth, we have duties to both the embryo and the foetus, but these may, in certain circumstances, be overridden by other duties, namely those we owe to persons.[4]

In particular, given Judaism's emphasis upon healing, research into stem cell therapies, which could offer cures for serious diseases, may be permitted.

Laurie Zoloth[5]

The task of healing in Judaism is not only permitted, it is mandated; if stem cells can save a life, then not only can they be used, they must be used . . . Furthermore, it is mandated to use the best methods available as soon as they are proved efficacious and not dangerous to the patient. Paradoxically, it might violate rabbinic premises to *stop* research if such research is life saving.

---

[3] 'Roman Catholic Views on hES Cell Research' in Suzanne Holland, Karen Lebacqz, and Laurie Zoloth (eds), *The Human Embryonic Stem Cell Debate: Science, Ethics and Public Policy* (MIT Press: Cambridge, MA, 2001) 113–18.

[4] *Stem Cell Research Report* (February 2002) para 4.19.

[5] 'The Ethics of the Eighth Day: Jewish Bioethics and Research on Human Embryonic Stem Cells' in Suzanne Holland, Karen Lebacqz, and Laurie Zoloth (eds), *The Human Embryonic Stem Cell Debate: Science, Ethics and Public Policy* (MIT Press: Cambridge, MA, 2001) 95–111.

In the next extract, however, Søren Holm suggests that the standard liberal claim that embryos lack the criteria we associate with personhood, and that research is therefore justified, may 'prove too much'. In particular, it could also be used to defend research on young babies or adults suffering from dementia, on the grounds that they too lack qualities such as consciousness or the capacity to reason.

Søren Holm[6]

By far the most common pro-stem cell argument is that derivation of human embryonic stem cells is morally innocuous because human embryos have no moral status. By analyzing their characteristics, we can see that they are not persons and that it is not wrong to kill them . . .

One main problem with this argument is that it proves far too much . . . First, and perhaps most important, it justifies the (nonpainful) killing and use of any prepersonal human entity from the fertilized egg to the prepersonal infant. Such a killing can be justified by any kind of net benefit to others. In the current context, it can therefore just as easily justify the killing of infants for their stem cells as it can the destruction of embryos for the same purpose. There is no in principle difference between the two killings.

Second, it places no restrictions on the use of biological material from prepersonal human entities that can justify the destruction of these entities, as long as those uses are beneficial. The derivation of a new and effective antiwrinkle cream can therefore be a perfectly acceptable justification for the production and destruction of embryos.

(b) THE ARGUMENT FROM POTENTIAL

Even if we accept that an early human embryo is not a person, does its potential to become a person give it a special moral status?

John Marshall[7]

Why then do I oppose experimentation of the kind that I have defined, namely experiments which lead to the destruction of the entity? It is because I regard the potential to become a human person as of tremendous importance, particularly in our society where there is a certain ambivalence about, and paradoxical attitude towards, life. In opposing experimentation I recognize and do not hide the fact that some advances in knowledge will be lost, but I do assert that those advances are not so great as the scientists would have us believe. I do not therefore hold that the gain is commensurate with the loss . . .

On this argument, because the entity has the potential to become a person, one affirms that it should *not* be interfered with, that *nothing* should be done that prevents it realizing that potential, and things *can* be done which will help it to attain that potential. Therefore one opposes experimentation.

In contrast, Dan Brock argues that while an entity's potential is relevant to how it should be treated when it realizes that potential, it does not confer a right to be treated as if the potential were already realized.

---

[6] 'The ethical case against stem cell research' (2003) 12 Cambridge Quarterly of Healthcare Ethics 372–83.
[7] 'The Case Against Experimentation' in Anthony Dyson and John Harris (eds), *Experiments on Embryos* (Routledge: London, 1990) 55–64.

Dan W Brock[8]

> Sam has the potential to run faster than all the other competitors in the race, then he has the potential to claim the prize, but he has no actual claim or right to the prize until this potential becomes actuality and he has in fact run faster than all the other competitors. Moral rights in general have this character—they are grounded in the actual, not just potential, properties of a being. So the embryo's potential to become a person is relevant to the moral status it will have if and when it does become a person, but it does not confer the moral status on it when still an embryo that it will have later when it has become a person.

Not all embryos have the potential to become persons. In IVF, as with natural conception, it is not uncommon for embryos to be chromosomally or morphologically so abnormal that they have no chance of implanting in a woman's womb and developing to term. Does the potentiality argument then mean that a particular embryo's moral status will depend upon whether it is viable or not?

In the next extract, John Harris explains another difficulty with the argument from potential. If the embryo is special because it has the potential to become a human being, then since gametes (eggs and sperm) have the potential to become an embryo, logically they must also have the potential to become a human being.

John Harris[9]

> There are two sorts of objections to the 'potentiality argument' for the moral significance of the embryo. The first is simply that the fact that an entity can undergo changes that will make it significantly different does not constitute a reason for treating it as though it had already undergone those changes. We are all potentially dead, but no-one supposes that this fact constitutes a reason for treating us as if we were already dead.
>
> The second objection is simply that if the potentiality argument suggests that we have to regard as morally significant anything which has the potential to become a fully fledged human being and hence have some moral duty to protect and actualize all human potential, then we are in for a very exhausting time of it. For it is not only the fertilized egg, the embryo that is potentially a fully fledged adult. The egg and the sperm taken together but as yet ununited have the same potential as the fertilized egg. For something, or some things, have the potential to become a fertilized egg and whatever has the potential to become an embryo has whatever potential the embryo has.

Of course, the embryo is clearly a significant step further on in the process of becoming a person than a spermatozoa or an unfertilized egg. The mixing of the DNA from the sperm and the egg give it an entirely new genome. It is also true that most human gametes have the potential to be a person only in a rather remote sense. But for the sperm and eggs in a petri dish immediately before fertilization occurs, there is, according to Peter Singer and Karen Dawson, little difference between their potential and that of the newly fertilized egg.

---

[8] 'Is a consensus possible on stem cell research? Moral and political obstacles' (2006) 32 Journal of Medical Ethics 36–42.

[9] 'On the Moral Status of the Embryo' in Anthony Dyson and John Harris (eds), *Experiments on Embryos* (Routledge: London, 1990) 65–81.

Peter Singer and Karen Dawson[10]

IVF has reduced the difference between what can be said about the embryo and what can be said about the egg and sperm, considered jointly. Before IVF, any normal human embryo known to us had a far greater chance of becoming a child than any egg plus sperm prior to fertilization taking place. But with IVF, there is a much more modest difference in the probability of a child resulting from a two-cell embryo in a glass dish, and the probability of a child resulting from an egg and some sperm in a glass dish . . .

[L]urking in the background of discussions of the embryo's potential is the idea that there is a 'natural' course of events, governed by the 'inherent' potential of the embryo. We have seen, however, that this notion of 'natural' development, not requiring the assistance of a deliberate human act, has no application to the IVF embryo. Hence those who wish to use the potential of the IVF embryo as a ground for protecting it cannot appeal to this notion of natural development; and for this reason, they find themselves in difficulty in explaining why the embryo in the laboratory has a potential so different from that of the egg alone, or the egg and sperm considered jointly. Unless a woman agrees to have an embryo transferred to her uterus, and someone else agrees to perform this transfer, that embryo has no future.

A different sort of problem with the argument from potential is that if the early human embryo's potential to become a human being rules out its destruction, this would cast doubt on the legitimacy of certain types of contraception, such as the intrauterine device (IUD) and the morning-after pill, both of which may prevent the implantation of a newly fertilized egg. Indeed, the ordinary oral contraceptive pill also sometimes works by preventing implantation. If interfering with a fertilized egg's progress towards personhood is always illegitimate, the only acceptable form of contraception would be the condom.

In vitro fertilization (IVF) treatment almost always involves the creation of embryos that are unsuitable for implantation. It is also common for more embryos to be created than are actually used in treatment and, if not frozen for future use or donated, these leftover embryos may be allowed to perish. IVF treatment therefore routinely results in the destruction of embryos. If we accept post-coital contraception and IVF treatment—on the grounds that the benefits of enabling women to control their fertility or have babies are legitimate aims, which may justify the destruction of embryos—does this give us a good reason also to accept research on embryos?

In the next extract, John Harris goes further and argues that anyone who believes that normal sexual reproduction, which inevitably involves the creation and destruction of embryos, is acceptable should, as a matter of consistency, also accept research on human embryos.

John Harris[11]

We now know that for every successful pregnancy that results in a live birth many, perhaps as many as five, early embryos will be lost or will 'miscarry' (although these are not perhaps 'miscarriages' as the term is normally used because this sort of very early embryo loss is almost always entirely unnoticed). . . .

---

[10] 'IVF Technology and the Argument from Potential' in Peter Singer et al (eds), *Embryo Experimentation* (CUP: Cambridge, 1990) 76–89.

[11] 'Stem cells, sex, and procreation' (2003) 12 Cambridge Quarterly of Healthcare Ethics 353–71.

How are we to think of the decision to attempt to have a child in the light of these facts? One obvious and inescapable conclusion is that God and/or nature has ordained that 'spare' embryos be produced for almost every pregnancy and that most of these will have to die in order that a sibling embryo can come to birth. Thus, the sacrifice of embryos seems to be an inescapable and inevitable part of the process of procreation. It may not be intentional sacrifice, and it may not attend every pregnancy, but the loss of many embryos is the inevitable consequence of the vast majority (perhaps all) pregnancies.

Given that decisions to attempt to have children using sexual reproduction as the method (or even decisions to have unprotected intercourse) inevitably create embryos that must die, those who believe having children or even running the risk of conception is legitimate cannot consistently object to the creation of embryos for comparably important moral reasons . . .

[A]lthough we might rather not have to sacrifice embryos to achieve a live healthy birth, we judge it to be defensible to continue natural reproduction in the light of the balance between the moral costs and the benefits. And if we make this calculation in the case of normal sexual reproduction we should, for the same reasons, make a similar judgment in the case of the sacrifice of embryos in stem cell research.

Finally, the possibility of human cloning adds some interesting twists to the potentiality argument. We do not yet know whether it will be possible to create cloned human beings using cell nuclear replacement (the technique which was used to create Dolly the sheep). If reproductive cloning is possible, in theory at least, any cell could become a new human being. Would my skin cell's potential to become a new person weaken the argument that potentiality confers special moral status?

If, on the other hand, human reproductive cloning is not scientifically possible, then embryos created in this way would not have the potential to become human beings, and hence would not receive special protection, if that protection is grounded in an entity's potentiality.

(c) THE COMPROMISE POSITION

Most people believe that embryos are in an important sense 'special', but would fall short of according them the same status as people. An embryo is clearly a member of our species, but this does not necessarily require us to treat a four-cell embryo, which cannot be seen with the naked eye, as if it had the same rights as a person. The 1984 Warnock Report embodied this compromise position. It admitted that the instrumental use of the early human embryo will offend those who believe that a person comes into being at fertilization, but that that offence has to be put into the balance with the benefits which may flow from embryo research. The Warnock Committee recommended that embryo research should be permitted, provided that the embryo is not simply treated as a resource for scientists but is instead accorded proper 'respect'. The Warnock Report's recommendations form the basis of the Human Fertilisation and Embryology Act 1990, an Act which is intended to safeguard scientific progress within restrictions, which are designed to indicate that the early human embryo has some intrinsic moral importance, and should not be used frivolously or unnecessarily.

Interestingly, Baroness Warnock has since suggested that the report's use of the word 'respect' to describe the treatment of embryos used in research was 'foolish'.

Baroness Warnock[12]

I regret that in the original report that led up to the 1990 legislation we used words such as 'respect for the embryo'. That seems to me to lead to certain absurdities. You cannot respectfully pour something down the sink—which is the fate of the embryo after it has been used for research, or if it is not going to be used for research or for anything else.

I think that what we meant by the rather foolish expression 'respect' was that the early embryo should never be used frivolously for research purposes. That is perfectly exemplified by the regulations that are brought in and the licensing provisions that are looked after by the HFEA. It is the non-frivolity of the research which is conveyed by such expressions as 'respect for' or 'protection for' the embryo.

In contrast, Karen Lebacqz argues that it is possible to treat an embryo that will be used in research with respect.

Karen Lebacqz[13]

I believe that one can indeed speak meaningfully of respecting embryos or embryonic tissue, and that criteria for such respect can be established. Specifically, the tissue must not be treated cavalierly, but as an entity with value . . . To approach something with awe or reverence means that we never become hardened to its intrinsic value, its value apart from us . . .

An entity is treated cavalierly if it is demolished without any sense of violation or loss; if it is treated as only one of many and easily replaceable; if its existence is made the butt of jokes or disrespectful stereotyping. Thus, to require that a blastocyst not be treated cavalierly is to require that it be treated as an entity with incredible value; as something precious which cannot be replaced by any other blastocyst, whose existence is to be celebrated and whose loss is to be grieved.

Regardless of whether the word 'respect' is useful in the context of embryo research, it is clear—as Robertson explains—that the compromise position is not concerned to protect individual human embryos, since these will ultimately be destroyed, but is instead directing towards protecting the symbolic value of early human life.

John A Robertson[14]

Many people, for example, reject the view that the embryo is a person but believe that the embryo is different from ordinary human tissue because of the unique potential it has to develop into a new human being. Sometimes described as 'special respect', this attitude towards human embryos shows or symbolizes our respect for human life generally . . .

In the context of *in vitro* fertilization (IVF) treatment, for example, the generation of more embryos than can be safely transferred to the uterus is widely accepted as not being unduly disrespectful of human life, because it enables children to be born to infertile

---

[12] Hansard 5 December 2002, col 1327.

[13] 'On the Elusive Nature of Respect' in Suzanne Holland, Karen Lebacqz, and Laurie Zoloth (eds), *The Human Embryonic Stem Cell Debate: Science, Ethics and Public Policy* (MIT Press: Cambridge, MA, 2001) 149–62.

[14] 'Human embryonic stem cell research: ethical and legal issues' (2001) 2 Nature Reviews Genetics 74–8.

couples. Similarly, destroying embryos that are left over from IVF procedures to develop cell-replacement therapies should also be ethically acceptable, for the goal of treating disease and saving life justifies the symbolic loss that arises from destroying embryos in the process. By contrast, selling human embryos or using them in cosmetic-toxicology testing seems to be disrespectful of the symbolic meaning that many people attach to embryos because those uses fulfil no life-affirming or other important purpose.

An analogy might be drawn with research on non-human primates. Aside from great apes, it is possible to use non-human primates in medical research, provided that the research serves an important scientific purpose and could not be done on creatures with lower neurophysiological sensitivity. Dan Brock has suggested that primates, like embryos, have an intermediate moral status: they need not be treated in the same way as human persons, but at the same time it would be unacceptable to use and destroy them for trivial purposes.[15]

One important dimension of the compromise position is that alternatives should always be pursued in preference to embryo research. The destruction of human embryos is therefore permissible only if there are no other ways of carrying out the research. As we see later, this limiting criterion has become especially significant given recent progress in inducing pluripotency in adult cells.[16]

(d) MORE ROBUST ARGUMENTS IN FAVOUR OF EMBRYO RESEARCH

The compromise position involves a utilitarian calculation: do the good consequences from permitting research outweigh the symbolic harm of disposing of early human life? There are, however, those who believe that reverence for early human embryos makes little sense. In the next extract, Helga Kuhse and Peter Singer argue that embryos do not possess the qualities which ground our respect for persons—such as consciousness and sentience—and that it would therefore be legitimate to use them as a resource for experimentation up to the point at which they can feel pain, which would be several months later than the current 14-day limit.

Helga Kuhse and Peter Singer[17]

We believe the minimal characteristic needed to give the embryo a claim to consideration is sentience, or the capacity to feel pleasure or pain. Until that point is reached, the embryo does not have any interests and, like other non-sentient organisms (a human egg, for example), cannot be harmed—in a morally relevant way—by anything we do. We can, of course,

[15] 'Is a consensus possible on stem cell research? Moral and political obstacles' (2006) 32 Journal of Medical Ethics 36–42.

[16] Kazutoshi Takahashi et al, 'Induction of pluripotent stem cells from adult human fibroblasts by defined factors' (2007) 31 Cell 861–72; Gretchen Vogel and Constance Holden, 'Developmental biology: Field leaps forward with new stem cell advances' (2007) 318 Science 1224–5; Junying Yu et al, 'Induced pluripotent stem cell lines derived from human somatic cells' (2007) 318 Science 1917–20; In-Hyun Park et al, 'Reprogramming of human somatic cells to pluripotency with defined factors' (2008) 451 Nature 141.

[17] 'Individuals, Humans and Persons: The Issue of Moral Status' in Peter Singer et al (eds), Embryo Experimentation (CUP: Cambridge, 1990) 65–75.

damage the embryo in such a way as to cause harm to the sentient being it will become, if it lives, but if it never becomes a sentient being, the embryo has not been harmed, because its total lack of awareness means that it never has had any interests at all . . .

Finally, we point to a curious consequence of restrictive legislation on embryo research. In sharp contrast to the human embryo at this early stage of its existence, non-human animals such as primates, dogs, rabbits, guinea pigs, rats and mice clearly can feel pain, and thus often are harmed by what is done to them in the course of scientific research . . . Why, then, is it considered acceptable to poison conscious rabbits in order to test the safety of drugs and household chemicals, but not considered acceptable to carry out tests on totally non-sentient human embryos?

In the next extract, Julian Savulescu defends embryonic stem (ES) cell research from an explicitly utilitarian perspective, arguing that it is likely to be of such overwhelming benefit that it is justified, even if embryos are considered persons.

Julian Savulescu[18]

To employ the Rawlsian veil of ignorance again, I would prefer a world in which I have some chance of being snuffed out as an embryo but a much higher chance of having my fatal diseases successfully treated as an embryo, foetus, child or adult . . .

We are all at risk of death and serious disability. ES cell technology stands to benefit everyone: embryos, children and adults. It is this property which makes it reasonable to kill some embryos to conduct ES cell research even if the embryo is a person . . . Opponents of ES cell research will likely remain unconvinced. They will argue that whatever the benefits, intentionally killing embryos is failing to 'respect human dignity' . . .

Is it respecting of human dignity to allow people to wither in nursing homes, unable to swallow, speak or move while all the time embryos are destroyed? What more twisted version of respect for human dignity could there be? It is ES cell research, like organ transplantation, that is respectful of human dignity in its reverence for the lives of the living.

3 REGULATION IN THE UK

(a) THE BACKGROUND TO THE HUMAN FERTILISATION AND EMBRYOLOGY ACT 1990

Research into the possibility of *in vitro* fertilization started in the first half of the twentieth century. In 1969, Bob Edwards, Barry Bavister, and Patrick Steptoe published a groundbreaking paper in *Nature*, in which they reported that they had successfully fertilized human oocytes *in vitro*.[19] With the benefit of hindsight, the tentativeness of the paper's conclusion is striking: 'There may be certain clinical and scientific uses for human eggs fertilized by this procedure'.

Nine years later, in July 1978, the first IVF baby, Louise Brown, was born in Oldham. Her birth prompted the government to assemble a committee, chaired by Mary Warnock, to consider how both embryo research and fertility treatment should be regulated. The

---

[18] 'The embryonic stem cell lottery and the cannibalization of human beings' (2002) 16 Bioethics 508–29.
[19] 'Early stages of fertilization in vitro in human oocytes matured in vitro' (1969) 221 Nature 632–5.

Committee started its deliberations in 1982, and published its final report in 1984. On the question of embryo research, the Committee was divided, and the minority issued a formal expression of dissent.

A year after the publication of the Warnock Report, a private member's Bill, the Unborn Children (Protection) Bill, which would have banned all embryo research, attracted considerable parliamentary support. On its second reading, 238 MPs voted in favour, and 66 against. Only lack of parliamentary time prevented it from becoming law. The following year, the Unborn Children (Protection) Bill was re-introduced, and again commanded a significant parliamentary majority, but it too failed for lack of parliamentary time.

By the end of the 1980s, public and parliamentary attitudes to embryo research had changed. In part, this was as a result of greater understanding of exactly what embryo research involves. A six-cell embryo is invisible to the naked eye, and even by the 200-cell stage, it is still no bigger than a pinhead. The Act itself embodied the Warnock Report's compromise position, and permitted embryo research within strict limits. In 2004, when the government announced its intention to introduce new legislation to update the 1990 Act, it made it clear that it did not intend to reopen the question of whether embryo research is legitimate. The existing regulatory regime would simply be updated in order to accommodate scientific developments since 1990.

(b) THE DEFINITION OF AN EMBRYO

Section 1(1)(a) of the original version of the Human Fertilisation and Embryology Act 1990 appeared to contain a statutory definition of the word 'embryo'. It stated: 'in this Act, except where otherwise stated, embryo means a live human embryo where fertilisation is complete'. This wording became problematic in relation to two new ways of creating embryos: cloning and animal/human hybrids.

(1) Cloned Embryos

Dolly the sheep, whose birth was announced in 1997, had been created through a technique called cell nuclear replacement (CNR). This involves removing the nucleus from an egg, and inserting a cell taken from an adult into the denucleated egg. An electric current is used to trick it into beginning the process of cell division. This process undoubtedly leads to the creation of embryos, but it does not involve fertilization, and so would not appear to fall within section 1(1)(a)'s statutory 'definition'.

This apparent gap between the statutory wording and the procedure involved in Dolly's creation was the subject of a judicial review action brought by Bruno Quintavalle, on behalf of the ProLife Alliance. He claimed that the definition of 'embryo' in the 1990 Act did not cover embryos created by CNR. If he was right about this, then creating embryos in this way would fall outside the statutory regime, and be entirely unregulated. Deregulation was not, of course, Bruno Quintavalle's preferred outcome. Rather, he wanted parliament to revisit the regulation of embryo research, with the hope that this would result in more restrictive legislation.

At first instance, Bruno Quintavalle succeeded. The government had argued that the subsection should be interpreted as if it read: 'a live human embryo where [if it is produced by fertilisation] fertilisation is complete', but Crane J held that the words were not sufficiently ambiguous to allow him to ignore their clear meaning. Following his judgment, emergency legislation was passed to ban human reproductive cloning, but the question of whether the HFEA was entitled to regulate cloning for research purposes remained in doubt. The government appealed successfully to the Court of Appeal, and, in *R (on the application of Quintavalle) v Secretary of State for Health*, the House of Lords dismissed Bruno Quintavalle's appeal.

R (on the application of Quintavalle) v Secretary of State for Health[20]

Lord Bingham

Does the creation of live human embryos by CNR fall within the same genus of facts as those to which the expressed policy of Parliament has been formulated? In my opinion, it plainly does. An embryo created by in vitro fertilisation and one created by CNR are very similar organisms. The difference between them as organisms is that the CNR embryo, if allowed to develop, will grow into a clone of the donor of the replacement nucleus which the embryo produced by fertilisation will not. But this is a difference which plainly points towards the need for regulation, not against it . . .

While it is impermissible to ask what Parliament would have done if the facts had been before it, there is one important question which may permissibly be asked: it is whether Parliament, faced with the taxing task of enacting a legislative solution to the difficult religious, moral and scientific issues mentioned above, could rationally have intended to leave live human embryos created by CNR outside the scope of regulation had it known of them as a scientific possibility. There is only one possible answer to this question and it is negative.

Lord Steyn

The long title of the 1990 Act makes clear, and it is in any event self-evident, that Parliament intended the protective regulatory system in connection with human embryos to be comprehensive. This protective purpose was plainly not intended to be tied to the particular way in which an embryo might be created. The overriding ethical case for protection was general . . . For my part I am fully satisfied that cell nuclear replacement falls within the scope of the carefully balanced and crafted 1990 Act.

Lord Millett

The definition in para (a) is in part circular, since it contains the very term to be defined. It assumes that the reader knows what an embryo is. The purpose of the opening words of the paragraph is not to define the word 'embryo' but rather to limit it to an embryo which is (i) live and (ii) human. These are the essential characteristics which an embryo must possess if it is to be given statutory protection. The important point is that these characteristics are concerned with what an embryo is, not how it is produced . . .

This construction does not require words to be written into the section. There is no gap to be filled by implication. Nor is it a matter of updating the meaning of the word embryo by reference to subsequent developments. It is simply a matter of giving the opening words of para (a) their natural meaning . . . Once it is accepted that the embryo is defined by reference to what it is and not by reference to the process by which it is created, all need for updating falls away.

The House of Lords avoided having to strain the language in the statute. It was only necessary to insert words into section 1(1)(a) if it contained a special statutory definition of the

[20] [2003] UKHL 13.

word 'embryo', which the House of Lords held it did not. Instead it was clear that the 'ordinary language' meaning of the word embryo (which would undoubtedly include embryos created through CNR) must have been taken for granted by the statutory draftsman because the definition is 'a live human *embryo* where fertilisation is complete', which itself contains the word it is supposed to define, with no further elaboration. The important words in this phrase, according to Lord Millett, are 'live' and 'human'—this is the sort of embryo that is regulated by the statute—so dead and/or animal embryos are not covered.

Unsurprisingly, the 2008 amendments to the 1990 Act remove the reference to fertilization. Section 1(1) now reads: 'In this Act . . . embryo means a live human embryo and does not include a human admixed embryo.' As with the previous legislation, embryos that are in the process of creation, whether by fertilization or otherwise, are brought within regulation as well by section 1(1)(b).

(2) Hybrid Embryos

Notice the reference in the amended Act to 'human admixed embryos'. These are not covered by section 1(1)(a), but can be created for research purposes under section 4A. 'Admixed' means animal/human hybrid embryos. The only sort of admixed embryos that scientists have expressed any interest in creating are ones created through CNR, using denucleated animal eggs and human nuclear DNA. These embryos contain only mitochondrial animal DNA (this is the DNA in the outer 'shell' of the denucleated egg). The embryos themselves will be 99.9 per cent human, and any stem cell lines extracted from them would be 100 per cent human.

The reason for wanting to use animal eggs in this way is that human eggs are in short supply. The process of egg donation is uncomfortable and time-consuming and, unsurprisingly, few women have offered to donate their eggs for research. In addition, the process of deriving stem cell lines from embryos is inefficient—it has been estimated that there is a success rate of around 0.7 per cent in primates.[21] Some scientists have therefore argued that we should not use scarce human eggs to perfect these techniques, and that it would be sensible to carry out this sort of basic research on animal eggs, retrieved from abattoirs, which can be easily obtained in large numbers.

In September 2007, following a public consultation exercise, the HFEA determined that licensing the creation of this sort of hybrid embryo lay within its statutory powers under the original legislation. Drawing upon the House of Lords judgment in *Quintavalle*, the HFEA decided that these embryos are within the same 'genus of fact' as other embryos covered by the 1990 Act, in particular that embryos created in this way have a full human nuclear genome and are live.

The HFEA also took into account that parliament's intention was for the regulatory scheme to be comprehensive. As Lord Bingham had put it: 'there was to be no free for all'. If human admixed embryos were not covered by the 1990 Act, then since they would also not be subject to Home Office regulation (this would not be research on live animals), their creation and use would be unregulated, and there would indeed be a 'free for all'.

The HFEA's research Licence Committee issued the first two licences for research projects which intended to use animal eggs to create admixed embryos in January 2008, and a third one was licensed a few months later. Scientists announced in April 2008 that they had

---

[21] Stephen Minger, 'Interspecies SCNT-derived human embryos—a new way forward for regenerative medicine' (2007) 2 Regenerative Medicine 103–6.

successfully created the first animal/human hybrid embryo, but since then, it proved hard to secure funding and research involving hybrid embryos has ceased in the UK.[22]

The decision to grant these first licences was challenged in the courts. Comment on Reproductive Ethics (CORE) and the Christian Legal Centre (CLC) sought judicial review of the research Licence Committee's decision on the grounds that the HFEA had acted outside its powers. Their claim was that these sorts of embryos cannot be described as 'human' and therefore the 1990 Act did not apply.

Before the case came to court, parliament had enacted the 2008 amendments to the 1990 Act, although these were not yet in force at the time of the hearing. The creation of admixed embryos was one of the most controversial provisions in the amending legislation, and MPs had been given a free vote on the issue. A majority voted in favour, and the amended Act specifically permits the creation of human admixed embryos for research purposes, subject to the restrictions discussed later, such as not keeping embryos for longer than 14 days.

The fact that parliament had expressed its intention to permit the creation of human admixed embryos made it difficult for the applicants to argue that granting these licences was contrary to parliament's intention. In December 2008, in *R (on the application of Quintavalle and CLC) v HFEA*, Dobbs J refused to grant permission for leave to apply for judicial review of the decision to grant the first two licences, describing the application as 'entirely without merit'.

The 1990 Act did not define 'human', and Dobbs J agreed that the HFEA's legal advice—namely, that it should take a cautious approach and treat such embryos as human to ensure that they are regulated—was in accordance with the spirit and purpose of the 1990 Act. She also noted that parliament had made its intention in relation to hybrid embryos clear, and that the scientists who had received the first two licences to carry out this research would, even if the original Licence Committee decision was struck down, be able to re-apply for their licences when the new Act came into force in October 2009.

R (on the application of Quintavalle and CLC) v HFEA[23]

Dobbs J

The Act did not seek to define 'human embryo'. What is 'human' will be dependent on the particular facts of any case and informed by scientific knowledge at the time. I do not accept the claimants' submission, that the fact that this technique is in a separate category under the new Act, means that Parliament did not intend it to fall within the definition of 'human embryo' under section 1 of the 1990 Act. The technique was unknown and not envisaged at the time. What is clear, as I have already found, is that regulation of these activities was important. The approach advocated by the defendant's lawyers in the advice of November 2007—namely to take a cautious approach by treating the technique as coming within regulation—is, in my judgment, in accordance with the spirit and purpose of the 1990 Act . . .

It would be futile to suggest that the licence be revoked for what might be a matter of months, with the attendant disruption to the third parties, whilst knowing full well that Parliament intends such work to be subject to regulation by the defendant, who has

---

[22] Susan Mayor, 'Lack of funding prevents human-animal stem cell research in UK' (2009) 338 British Medical Journal 207.

[23] [2008] EWHC 3395 (Admin).

the power to grant licences in appropriate cases. To be expending the court's time and resources, as well as those of the defendants and the interested parties, bodies relying to some degree on public funding, in debating what Parliament intended, is not in the interests of good administration, in my judgment; the more so, when it is now known what Parliament intends in this regard.

(c) THE UK'S RESTRICTIONS ON EMBRYO RESEARCH

The restrictions placed upon embryo research, discussed in the following sections, embody the compromise position discussed earlier. That is, they are intended to ensure that valuable scientific research can take place within limits that are designed to show some 'respect' for the early human embryo, or to ensure its non-frivolous treatment.

Responsibility for ensuring that research on embryos only takes place within these limits lies with the HFEA's Licence Committee. The committee receives legal advice, reports from peer reviewers, and information gathered by the HFEA's inspectors. Licences are normally granted for three years, although for novel projects, 12-month licences can be issued in order to facilitate closer monitoring.

(1) The 14-Day Limit

Under the Act, no research can be carried out on an embryo after 14 days. Fourteen days was chosen in part because this is when what is known as the 'primitive streak' first appears. The primitive streak is a heaping up of cells that will eventually become the spinal column. Fourteen days is also the last point at which twinning can occur, so before this time it is not clear whether the embryo will become one individual or two.

Mary Warnock[24]

Fourteen days was decided on as the limit because of the great change in the development of the embryo heralded by the development of the primitive streak. It is only after that that an individual exists with its own now quickly developing central nervous system, its own limbs, its own brain. Even though before that an embryo has a genetic individuality, it has no pattern of human identity, any more than human tissue has. The history of each person who is born can be traced back to the development of the primitive streak and not before. Before that there could have been two or three people formed of the same material. It is because of the enormous change that comes at this stage of development that scientists generally prefer to think of the embryos as actually beginning to exist at this stage. Before that there is the egg and the sperm, and the *conceptus*, that which comes from their conjunction. All these, egg sperm and *conceptus* are human (that is, they differ from the eggs, sperm and *conceptus* of other animals) and are of course alive, but are not yet distinct embryos.

Others would contest the idea that something special happens to the embryo at 14 days. Bernard Williams, for example, suggests that the 14-day limit does not reflect a relevant

---

[24] 'Experimentation on Human Embryos and Fetuses' in Helga Kuhse and Peter Singer (eds), *A Companion to Bioethics* (Blackwell: Oxford, 1998) 390–6.

characteristic in the embryo itself, but is instead simply a reasonable regulatory response to fears of a slippery slope. The limit could equally well, Williams implies, have been drawn a bit earlier or later, but that does not undermine the value of choosing to draw a line somewhere.

Bernard Williams[25]

Is drawing a line in this way reasonable? Can it be effective? The answer to both these questions seems to me to be 'yes, sometimes', and, as that unexciting reply suggests, there is not a great deal to be brought to deciding them beyond good sense and relevant information. It may be said that a line of this kind cannot possibly be reasonable since it has to be drawn between two adjacent cases in the range, that is to say, between two cases that are not different enough to distinguish. The answer is that they are indeed not different enough to distinguish if that means that their characteristics, unsupported by anything else, would have led one to draw a line there. But though the line is not, in this sense, uniquely reasonable, it is nevertheless reasonable to draw a line there. This follows from the conjunction of three things. First, it is reasonable to distinguish in some way unacceptable cases from acceptable cases; second, the only way of doing that in these circumstances is to draw a sharp line; third, it cannot be an objection to drawing the line just here that it would have been no worse to draw it somewhere else—if that were an objection, then one could conclude that one had no reason to draw it anywhere.

Dan Brock makes a similar point, drawing an analogy between the 14-day limit and setting the voting age at 18.[26] Both lines are inherently arbitrary. There is no essential moral difference in the status of the embryo at 13 days and at 15. Likewise, a person does not miraculously acquire the capacity to exercise sound political judgement on her 18th birthday. However, in both cases it is desirable to draw a line somewhere, and, in the context of embryo research, 14 days is judged a reasonable time limit.

Many other countries, such as Australia, Japan, and Singapore, have also adopted a 14-day limit. Currently, there is little pressure from scientists to extend this limit because it has proved impossible to keep an embryo alive *in vitro* for as long as 14 days. If, or perhaps when, this becomes feasible, scientists might be likely to argue that the 14-day limit is an arbitrary cut-off point, which could stifle valuable research.

(2) The Sources of Embryos

There are two possible sources of embryos for use in research. First, research might be carried out on embryos that are left over after a couple has had fertility treatment. This happens in one of two ways. During an ordinary IVF cycle, it is common for couples to produce more embryos than the one or two which will be transferred in one treatment cycle. Spare embryos that are suitable for use in future cycles will usually be frozen. Embryos that are of poor quality will be unsuitable for immediate use or freezing. Unless they are donated to research, these will have to be discarded.

Secondly, after their family is complete, or perhaps after they have separated, a couple may decide that they do not wish to use their frozen embryos. At that point, the stored embryos

[25] 'Types of Moral Argument Against Embryo Research' in The Ciba Foundation, *Human Embryo Research: Yes or No?* (Tavistock: London, 1986) 184–94.

[26] 'Is a consensus possible on stem cell research? Moral and political obstacles' (2006) 32 Journal of Medical Ethics 36–42.

can be destroyed, donated for the treatment of others, or donated for research. Most embryo research in the UK is carried out on these two sorts of 'spare' IVF embryos, donated by people who have undergone fertility treatment.

In the next extract, Sarah Franklin explains that embryos donated to research often have what she describes as a dual reproductive identity. They were created in order to become children, but once they become 'spare' or 'leftover' they have a different sort of potential. Because IVF treatment would have been impossible without embryo research, many couples feel that donating their leftover embryos to research is a way of 'giving something back'.

Sarah Franklin[27]

[T]he embryos that form the basis for hES [human embryonic stem cell] derivation and banking have a *dual reproductive identity*: their reproductive past, or pedigree, is determined by their production in the context of the highly emotive and labour-intensive process of IVF—a procedure that usually fails. Their reproductive future, or potential, lies in the capacity of science to transform the vital power of individual cells into colonies of regenerative cells . . .

The factors that influence couples' decisions to donate embryos to stem cell research, or not to, vary and are not well understood. Some couples may be particularly keen to donate their embryos to stem cell research as a result of the publicity and excitement surrounding this field, whereas for others such publicity may arouse suspicion . . .

Embryo donation rates in the UK are high, and this is often correlated in studies of donor motivations to a sense of obligation to 'give something back'. A research project undertaken at the Guy's and St Thomas' Centre for PGD [Preimplantation Genetic Diagnosis] to find out more about factors affecting patient perceptions of embryo donation to stem cell research which ran from 2002 to 2005 identified a 67% rate of willingness to donate, of whom more than 80% expressed a desire to 'give something back'.

It is clear that many patients object to use of the word 'spare' to describe embryos that they will not use in treatment. These are embryos that could have become a member of their family, and it can be difficult for a couple to come to terms with their stored embryos' transition from being potential future children to being classified as 'spare', and hence available for research. Bobbie Farsides and Rosamund Scott's interviews with embryologists suggest that they too found the use of the word 'spare' challenging, and that they had a preference for using embryos that could never have been used in treatment, perhaps because they were known to be affected by serious genetic conditions.

Bobbie Farsides and Rosamund Scott[28]

We were greatly struck by the fact that participants were typically very cautious about describing any embryo created for treatment purposes as *spare*, and thus potentially available for research. For instance, Embryologist 2 emphasised that the embryos that are given to research by a couple are only 'spare' for them 'after the patient's use, yes they're spare at that point technically. So when you've got enough heads on pillows or you've

---

[27] 'Embryonic economies: the double reproductive value of stem cells' (2006) 1 BioSocieties 71–90.

[28] 'No Small Matter For Some: Practitioners' Views on the Moral Status and Treatment of Human Embryos' (2012) 20 Medical Law Review 90–107.

decided you don't want any more out of your treatment, then they're spare embryos.' In this way, s/he might be thought to be concerned to protect the reproductive interests of parents so that, only if such parents decide not to have further treatment, should remaining embryos be seen as ones which can legitimately pass from the treatment to the research context. At the same time, caution around the definition of an embryo as 'spare' could be seen to reflect the importance of the origins of the embryo within a treatment context aimed at the creation of a child. . . .

We were also struck by what one might call an 'ethical hierarchy' of the ethical suitability of embryos for research. A number of participants commented that fresh affected PGD embryos were those in relation to which they felt most comfortable seeking consent for research. . . . An ethical hierarchy of embryos, in which the first choice for research embryos is affected PGD ones and the next are frozen embryos that will never be used in treatment, could be seen as protecting the embryo's chance of life as a born person as much as possible.

Secondly, embryos could be specifically created for use in research. This might be necessary if scientists wish to create embryos with particular characteristics, such as a specific genetic disease. It is not generally possible to control the characteristics of embryos which are left over from IVF treatment, but by creating embryos using tissue from people with particular genetic conditions, it is possible to carry out disease-specific research, most commonly on stem cell lines extracted from these embryos. In addition, if scientists wish to create embryos using cell nuclear replacement, or cloning, there will obviously not be any embryos left over after fertility treatment, since reproductive cloning is a criminal offence. CNR research then requires embryos to be created specifically for research.

Is there a moral difference between conducting research on spare IVF embryos and creating embryos with the express purpose of carrying out experiments upon them? Many people believe so, but why? The House of Lords Stem Cell Research Committee suggested that where the initial intention is to create a baby, the embryo is less instrumentalized than where the intention is to create an embryo for use in research.

House of Lords Stem Cell Research Committee[29]

4.27 The creation of embryos (whether by IVF or CNR) for research purposes raises difficult issues. Some argue that, if an embryo is destined for destruction, it is more honest to create it specifically for the purpose of research than to use one created for reproductive purposes. But most of those who commented on this issue regarded it as preferable to use surplus embryos than to create them specifically for research. They took the view that an embryo created for research was quite clearly being used as a means to an end, with no prospect of implantation, whereas at the time of creation the surplus embryo had a prospect of implantation, even if, once not selected for implantation (or freezing), it would have to be destroyed. We agree that for this reason it is preferable to use surplus embryos for research purposes if the same results can be achieved with them. It is currently unavoidable that there should be some surplus embryos from IVF treatment, although desirable that the numbers should be reduced as more effective techniques are developed.

[29] *Stem Cell Research Report* (February 2002).

In contrast, Erik Parens argues that it is unusual to base an entity's moral status upon the intention of its creator.

Erik Parens[30]

One ethical intuition that seems to motivate the discarded-created distinction is that whereas the act of creating an embryo for reproduction is respectful in a way that is commensurate with the moral status of embryos, the act of creating an embryo for research is not . . . In this view, the moral status of the embryo (and thus the moral status of research on it) is a function of the intention of its maker. The problem with this intuition is that it is difficult to see what the intention of the maker of something has to do with the moral status of that thing once it has come into being. We do not think, for example, that the moral status of children is a function of their parents' intentions at the time of conception. If what something is obliges us to treat it some ways and not others, how it came to being is usually thought to be morally irrelevant.

Unlike many other countries, in the UK it is permissible to create embryos for research purposes. Under Schedule 2 para (3)(1)(a) to the 1990 Act, as amended, a research licence may authorize 'bringing about the creation of embryos in vitro . . . for the purposes of a project of research'. But this does not mean that scientists in the UK are free to create as many research embryos as they like. There is no statutory limit upon the number of embryos which can be created for research purposes in the Act, but in deciding whether to grant a licence, the HFEA's Licence Committee must be satisfied that the creation of embryos is *necessary*.

So what proportion of embryos used in research come from these various different sources? Although now slightly out of date, the figures in the following table provide a useful snapshot of the proportion of different types of eggs and embryos used in research, demonstrating that the vast majority are donated, rather than created.

Human Fertilisation and Embryology Authority[31]

2005–7	Number used
Fresh eggs	368
Frozen eggs	64
Failed to fertilise eggs	2,432
Fresh embryos (not suitable for use in treatment or for freezing)	5,994
Frozen embryos (which a couple decide not to use themselves)	2,146
Created embryos	429

[30] 'On the Ethics and Politics of Embryonic Stem Cell Research' in Suzanne Holland, Karen Lebacqz, and Laurie Zoloth (eds), *The Human Embryonic Stem Cell Debate: Science, Ethics and Public Policy* (MIT Press: Cambridge, MA, 2001) 37–50.

[31] *Human Embryo Research in the UK 2006–7* (HFEA, 2007).

(3) The Purposes of Research: Stem Cell Research and Therapeutic Cloning

(a) The statutory purposes

A further restriction on the use of embryos in research is that they can only be used for certain purposes. The restrictions are contained in Schedule 2 to the Act, as amended:

The Human Fertilisation and Embryology Act 1990 Schedule 2

2(3A)(1) A licence under paragraph 3 cannot authorise any activity unless the activity appears to the Authority—

(a) to be necessary or desirable for any of the purposes specified in sub-paragraph (2) ('the principal purposes')

(b) to be necessary or desirable for the purpose of providing knowledge that, in the view of the Authority, may be capable of being applied for the purposes specified in sub-paragraph (2)(a) or (b), or

(c) to be necessary or desirable for such other purposes as may be specified in regulations.

(2) The principal purposes are—

(a) increasing knowledge about serious disease or other serious medical conditions,

(b) developing treatments for serious disease or other serious medical conditions,

(c) increasing knowledge about the causes of any congenital disease or congenital medical condition that does not fall within paragraph (a),

(d) promoting advances in the treatment of infertility,

(e) increasing knowledge about the causes of miscarriage,

(f) developing more effective techniques of contraception,

(g) developing methods for detecting the presence of gene, chromosome or mitochondrion abnormalities in embryos before implantation, or

(h) increasing knowledge about the development of embryos.

Notice that the Schedule builds in the possibility of the statute's revision by Regulations that can extend the purposes for which embryo research may be carried out. This is an attempt to 'future-proof' the legislation, in case unanticipated research purposes subsequently emerge. The original legislation contained a similar provision, which was used in 2001 to extend the statutory research purposes to include human embryonic stem cell (hES) research.

Embryonic stem cells are undifferentiated cells that are capable of becoming all of the specialized cells in the body. The inner cell mass of the early human embryo contains stem cells of remarkable plasticity. The first embryonic stem cells are totipotent, which means that they can become every cell in the human body, and even a whole new human organism. Later on, embryonic stem cells are pluripotent, which means they are capable of differentiating into different types of tissue. Stem cells are also immortal: they can continue to divide indefinitely without losing their genetic structure.

In 1998, researchers at the University of Wisconsin published a paper explaining how they had, for the first time, derived and cultured a human embryonic stem cell line.[32] If these

---

[32] James A Thomson et al, 'Embryonic stem cell lines derived from human blastocysts' (1998) 282 Science 1145–7.

pluripotent embryonic stem cell lines can be directed into differentiating into different types of tissue, this could be used to repair damaged tissues or organs.

CNR—that is, cloning—and the development of induced pluripotent stem (iPS) cells add a further dimension to stem cell research. Therapeutic cloning would involve the extraction of embryonic stem cells from cloned embryos, as illustrated in Figure 12.1 below.

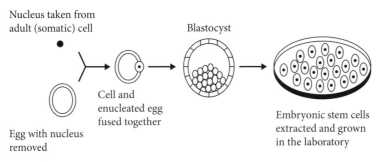

Figure 12.1

If the embryo from which embryonic stem cells are removed had been cloned from the person with a damaged organ, the replacement tissue would be a perfect genetic match, and there would be no possibility of rejection. Similarly, iPS cells would be created from the patient's own cells and again if they could be used to create replacement tissue, it would be a perfect match.

For example, imagine that I need some replacement tissue—perhaps because I have a degenerative neurological condition such as Parkinson's disease. If stem cells could be created from my cells (either through cloning or via iPS cells), and they could be differentiated into becoming new brain tissue, it will be genetically identical to me. This removes the problem of rejection, and the need to suppress the recipient's immune systems with immunosuppressant drugs. If this process were to become relatively straightforward, it potentially offers a solution to the organ shortage we considered in the previous chapter: anyone whose organs had failed could simply generate genetically compatible replacement tissue.

In practice, however, it did not prove easy to extract stem cells from embryos created using CNR and scientists were unsure why. Then, in 2011, it appeared that the process of complete denucleation might in fact be part of the problem. After having left some of the maternal DNA inside the egg, scientists in New York successfully extracted stem cell lines from embryos created using CNR.[33] Of course, the resulting embryos were genetically abnormal: they had a triploid genome, with the double genome of the inserted adult cell in addition to the single genome of the egg. Such cells are unstable, potentially cancerous, and could never be used in treatment. But insofar as this research suggests that some of the difficulties encountered thus far may be soluble, it represented a significant breakthrough.

(b) The 'necessity principle'

It is important to remember that scientists are not entitled to a licence just because they want to do research that is desirable for one of the specified purposes. Licences can be granted only if the Licence Committee is also satisfied that the proposed use of embryos is necessary (sometimes referred to as the 'necessity principle'). The Licence Committee must

---

[33] Scott Noggle et al, 'Human oocytes reprogram somatic cells to a pluripotent state' (2011) 478 Nature 70–5.

be satisfied that the research could not be done without using human embryos, and peer reviewers are specifically asked to comment upon whether this is the case. This means that if it were possible to conduct the research on animals or on tissue taken from adults, the Licence Committee could not be satisfied that the use of embryos was necessary, and no licence could be granted.

The 'necessity principle' is fairly easily satisfied where the research is directed towards improving IVF techniques. Research into new embryo freezing methods or new techniques for preimplantation genetic diagnosis can only discover their impact upon the human embryo if human embryos are actually used in the research.

Until relatively recently, research scientists who wanted to carry out hES research could also satisfy the necessity principle comparatively easily. In the past ten years, however, scientists have had remarkable success in inducing adult cells to act in the same way as embryonic stem cells. If a proposed stem cell research project could be carried out on these induced pluripotent stem (iPS) cells, rather than embryonic stem cells, then it would not be possible to establish that the use of embryos is necessary. So far, pluripotency can only be induced in adult cells with the help of viral factors. Because it has been estimated that around 20 per cent of such cells are carcinogenic, cells derived in this way would not be suitable for clinical use.

Most scientists believe that hES research and research on iPS cells should continue in parallel. Opponents of embryo research, on the other hand, have seized upon iPS cell research to argue that using embryos in research is not only unethical, but that it is also now unnecessary. This, as Mark Brown explains in the next extract, misses the point that it will only be possible to do the research necessary to understand how far iPS cells can be reprogrammed to behave in the same way as hES cells if hES are used as controls. Indeed, Brown argues that 'embryo protection advocates who endorse or collaborate in iPS research nonetheless are morally complicit in embryo sacrifice'.

Mark Brown[34]

In order to know the degree to which iPS cells can function as substitutes for ES cells in science and in medicine it will be necessary to understand in much greater detail the differences and similarities between reprogramming induced in the laboratory and the natural processes of reprogramming in fertilization and embryological development. Human embryonic stem cell research will be needed to characterize the natural developmental pathways through the epigenetic landscape . . . At some point iPS derived tissues may enable mainstream medicine to avoid institutionalized production of human embryonic stem cells for drug development, disease modeling and cell replacement therapy, but that day has not yet come. . . . Embryo protection advocates who hail iPS as an ethically uncompromised source of pluripotent cell should recognize that as a matter of fact they are promoting a research program that depends upon embryo sacrifice. The science that might make iPS substitutes available almost certainly will require comparative pluripotency studies in which embryonic stem cells function as models for the molecular mechanisms of reprogramming.

An interesting twist to the triumphant claims made for iPS cells by opponents of embryo research is described in the next extract. With appropriate reprogramming, iPS cells might

---

[34] 'No ethical bypass of moral status in stem cell research (2013) 27 Bioethics 12–19.

themselves be able to become embryos. Far from resolving debates over the instrumental use of human embryos, this might create a new dilemma.

RM Green[35]

Nor is it clear that this technology really solves the ethical problem of embryo destruction that has generated the opposition to hES cell research. iPS cell technology brings an adult cell back to its pluripotent embryonic state. As the work of Nagy and others has shown, with appropriate technical manipulations and sufficient support, such a cell might have the potential to develop into a human being. Since opponents of stem cell research and therapeutic cloning research usually base their arguments for the sanctity of fertilised or nuclear transfer embryos on precisely this kind of developmental capacity, it is not clear why they have not voiced similar concerns about iPS cell technology . . .

The opponents of hES cell research—now enthusiasts for iPS cell research—appear less concerned about the lives of the entities that could become people than with declaring victory in a cultural war.

(c) In-vitro *derived gametes*

Of course, if it is possible to create any human cell type from a stem cell line, it will also be possible to create reproductive cells, or gametes.[36] In 2011, researchers in Japan created fully functioning sperm from mouse embryonic stem cells. These sperm cells were used to fertilize mouse eggs *in vitro*. The resulting embryos were implanted in female mice, leading to the birth of healthy and normal offspring.[37]

It is possible, and perhaps even likely, that human eggs and sperm will be generated from stem cell lines during the lifetime of the amended 1990 Act. The 2008 amendments specifically allow stem-cell derived gametes to be created for research purposes, but forbid their use in treatment. This is achieved by allowing only 'permitted embryos' and 'permitted eggs and sperm' to be used in treatment services.

Human Fertilisation and Embryology Act 1990 sections 3 and 3ZA

3(2) No person shall place in a woman—

(a) an embryo other than a permitted embryo (as defined by section 3ZA), or

(b) any gametes other than permitted eggs or permitted sperm (as so defined) . . .

3ZA(2) A permitted egg is one—

(a) which has been produced by or extracted from the ovaries of a woman, and

(b) whose nuclear or mitochondrial DNA has not been altered.

(3) Permitted sperm are sperm—

(a) which have been produced by or extracted from the testes of a man, and

(b) whose nuclear or mitochondrial DNA has not been altered.

---

[35] 'Embryo as epiphenomenon: some cultural, social and economic forces driving the stem cell debate' (2008) 34 Journal of Medical Ethics 840–4.

[36] See further Giuseppe Testa and John Harris, 'Ethics and synthetic gametes' (2005) 19 Bioethics 146.

[37] Katsuhiko Hayashi et al, 'Reconstitution of the mouse germ cell specification pathway in culture by pluripotent stem cells' (2011) 146 Cell 519–32.

> (4) An embryo is a permitted embryo if—
>
> (a) it has been created by the fertilisation of a permitted egg by permitted sperm.
>
> (b) no nuclear or mitochondrial DNA of any cell of the embryo has been altered, and
>
> (c) no cell has been added to it other than by division of the embryo's own cells.

Stem-cell derived gametes will be very useful for research purposes. It would, for example, be possible to create a ready supply of eggs for use in stem cell research. Equally clearly, stem-cell derived gametes might be exceptionally useful for treatment purposes. The shortage of donated gametes would no longer be an issue, since people who could not use their own gametes could make them, and would no longer need to resort to gamete donation. Stem-cell derived gametes would enable a man with no sperm to nevertheless produce sperm from his stem cells and therefore have a child who is genetically 'his'. The child's right to know the identity of the donor would disappear, since the sperm would have come from her own father, and donors would not have to be concerned about being contacted by 20 children a couple of decades into the future.

Given the benefits of eliminating the need for gamete donation, it is interesting that the government chose not to 'future-proof' this aspect of the legislation by including regulation-making powers, which could enable the law to be changed fairly quickly to permit the use of stem-cell derived gametes in treatment services, if research establishes that this would be safe. Instead, new primary legislation will be necessary in order to overturn the ban on the use of stem-cell derived gametes in treatment.

The reason for the government's caution was the fact that stem-cell derived gametes might fundamentally change the way in which people have children. If, as looks likely, it is possible to create sperm from stem cells derived from a woman, and eggs from stem cells derived from a man, it would be possible for a same-sex couple to produce a child that is genetically related to both of them. While this would indeed be novel, Timothy Murphy does not see any reason to be suspicious about facilitating genetic parenthood in a same-sex couple.

Timothy F Murphy[38]

> [T]he idea that two men or two women conceive and raise a child together is represented as self-evidently controversial, requiring no supporting explanation at all.
>
> Interpretations like these treat same-sex couples as a novelty act in bioethics, primarily by suggesting that their moral standing as parents requires levels of moral scrutiny not required of other parents. At the very least, discussions like these still suppose that someone—moral and social authorities—have to function as gatekeepers for homosexual men and women wanting to be parents, as against assuming in advance that any safe and effective treatment for infertility should be presumptively available to any adult.

In theory, it would also be possible for someone to reproduce with herself; the child would not be a clone of the DNA source, because of the shuffling of genes that takes place at fertilization. It would, however, be inadvisable to try this, given that we know that

---

[38] 'The meaning of synthetic gametes for gay and lesbian people and bioethics too' (2014) 40 Journal of Medical Ethics 762–5.

reproducing with close (but not identical) genetic relatives increases the chance of genetic abnormalities.

A further mind-boggling possibility is what Palacios-González et al refer to as 'multiplex parenting'.

César Palacios-González, John Harris, and Giuseppe Testa[39]

IVG [*in vitro* derived gametes] could permit instead a much more substantive sharing of genetic kinship, through what is in essence a generational shortcut. Imagine that four people in a relationship want to parent a child while being all genetically related to her. IVG would enable the following scenario: first, two embryos would be generated from either couple through IVF with either naturally or in vitro generated gametes. hESC lines would be then established from both embryos and differentiated into IVG to be used in a second round of IVF. The resulting embryo would be genetically related to all four prospective parents, who would technically be the child's genetic grandparents.

And, of course, it would be possible to go further than just skipping one generation. Instead of implanting the new embryo, it could be used to derive more embryonic stem cells, from which new egg or sperm could be created and used to fertilize other *in vitro*-derived gametes. This process could continue indefinitely, or it could be interrupted at any stage so that an embryo could be implanted into a woman. In this scenario, all of the child's immediate ancestors would have been embryos that had been allowed to perish *in vitro*. At first sight, it is hard to see why anyone would want to do this, but, as Sparrow explains, it could be used to study hereditary diseases or to engage in the sort of selective breeding that would otherwise be impracticable in humans:

Robert Sparrow[40]

Repeated iterations of this process would allow scientists to proceed through multiple human generations 'in the lab'. *In vitro* eugenics might be used to study the heredity of genetic disorders and to produce cell lines of a desired character for medical applications. More controversially, it might also function as a powerful technology of 'human enhancement' by allowing researchers to use all the techniques of selective breeding to produce human individuals with a desired genotype.

If a child is born as a result of skipping one or more generations, would the child's genetic 'parents' be embryos that had never 'lived' outside the petri dish in which she was created? Robert Sparrow has argued that embryos cannot be parents within any normal understanding of what it means to be a parent. Instead such children would have no genetic parents, although when only one generation is skipped, it might make sense to say that they had genetic grandparents.

---

[39] 'Multiplex parenting: IVG and the generations to come' (2014) 40 Journal of Medical Ethics 752–8.
[40] '*In vitro* eugenics' (2014) 40 Journal of Medical Ethics 725–31.

Robert Sparrow[41]

Individuals cannot interpret their lives and experiences in the light of 'biographies' of embryos. Institutions cannot assign responsibility for the care of children to embryos or consult embryos about the fate of embryos created with their gametes. More fundamentally, it is internal to the concept of parenthood that parents are *persons*, living or dead, who stand in the appropriate (social, gestational, causal, genetic, etc.) relationship to the child. Thus, I would suggest that to have embryos as genetic 'parents' is to have no genetic parents at all. Instead, the children born of such matings might be said to be 'orphaned at conception'.

It is also true that, while such children would not have genetic parents, they would have genetic *grandparents*. The couple who conceived the embryos from which the stem cell lines were derived would be the genetic grandparents of children conceived using gametes derived from these stem cells. However, once it becomes possible to create gametes from stem cell lines it will also be possible to create new embryos via the fusion of these gametes and then to derive gametes from these embryos. Repeated iterations of this process would lead to the creation of embryos that had no meaningful genetic relation to any living individual.

(d) The need for eggs

As we have seen, CNR is impossible without a supply of eggs, from which the nucleus can be removed in order to insert a cell, commonly a skin cell, taken from an adult. For research purposes, adult cells taken from people suffering from particular conditions, such as motor neurone disease, might be used in order to extract disease-specific stem cells. If therapeutic cloning becomes possible, a skin cell would be taken from a patient in need of replacement tissue and stem cells extracted from the resulting embryo in order to grow new patient-specific tissue.

Some feminists have drawn attention to the emphasis placed upon the scientific and therapeutic potential of stem cell lines extracted from CNR embryos, and the corresponding lack of attention paid to the need for a plentiful supply of eggs. Renate Klein, for example, is concerned about 'the biotech industry's voracious appetite for eggs', and argues that 'women's lives and bodies should not be invaded for the so-called public good'.[42] Beeson and Lippman have suggested that women may come under pressure to consent to egg donation, arguing that 'the apparently purposeful use of misleading language to describe this research has the potential to be coercive'.[43] Their proposed solution, however, is not to insist that women are given clear and frank information: instead they propose 'a moratorium on egg harvesting for cloning purposes'.

It is, of course, true that there are risks associated with ovarian stimulation, but proper monitoring should be able to minimize the chance of a woman suffering from ovarian hyper-stimulation syndrome (OHSS). In clinical trials, subjects not uncommonly expose themselves to unknowable risks.[44] In relation to egg donation, the risks are at least well known, usually controllable, and the donor can be properly informed in advance.

There is also the possibility that women may volunteer to donate eggs because they are under the mistaken impression that the research project will lead to a cure for someone they love. This is a variation of the 'therapeutic misconception' that we considered in relation to

---

[41] 'Orphaned at conception: the uncanny offspring of embryos' (2012) 26 Bioethics 173–81.

[42] 'Rhetoric of Choice Clouds Dangers of Harvesting Women's Eggs for Cloning', available at www.onlineopinion.com.au/view.asp?article=5229.

[43] 'Egg harvesting for stem cell research: medical risks and ethical problems' (2006) 13 Reproductive Biomedicine Online 573–9.

[44] See, eg, the TGN1412 trial discussed in Chapter 9.

clinical trials in Chapter 9, whereby patients misunderstand the benefits that are likely to flow from their participation in research. The solution normally adopted to this problem is not, however, to prevent patients from participating in research at all, but rather to ensure that information sheets and consent forms are as frank and comprehensive as possible.

In 2005, it was revealed that Professor Woo Suk Hwang—a Korean scientist who claimed to have cloned the first human embryo and extracted the first patient-specific stem cell line[45]—had falsified research results and obtained eggs, in very large quantities, by paying donors and recruiting them from his junior technicians and PhD students. Because Hwang himself was deeply involved in the consent process, this almost certainly amounted to a breach of the Helsinki Declaration:

> 27. When seeking informed consent for participation in a research study the physician must be particularly cautious if the potential subject is in a dependent relationship with the physician or may consent under duress. In such situations the informed consent must be sought by an appropriately qualified individual who is completely independent of this relationship.[46]

In the UK, women might donate eggs to research, either as a one-off donation or through an egg-sharing scheme. Egg-sharing involves women who themselves need IVF being offered cheaper or free IVF in return for donating some of their eggs. The HFEA's Code of Practice sets out that where women donate via an egg-sharing arrangement, the eggs must be divided by someone independent of the research project, and that there should be no difference in the benefits provided to women sharing their eggs for research compared with those sharing their eggs for the treatment of others.

HFEA Code of Practice paras 12.31 and 12.32

> 12.31 If gametes are being donated to research through a benefits in kind agreement, the centre must ensure that the eggs are divided between the donor and the recipient (the research project) by someone not directly involved in the research project.
> 12.32 If a centre offers benefits in kind in exchange for donating gametes both to other patients and to research, equal benefits in kind should be available. This ensures there is no advantage in donating to one recipient rather than the other.

In 2011, the HFEA changed its rules on compensation for egg donors for both treatment and research. Women can now receive up to £750 per cycle of donation, to cover all of their out-of-pocket expenses, such as taking time off work, travel costs, and childcare expenses.

(e) The move from bench to bedside: animal experiments and clinical trials of stem cell therapies

Stem cell therapies are now being tested in large animal models and some clinical trials are underway. For example, it appears that embryonic stem cells can regenerate heart tissue in non-human primates.[47] Stomach tissue has been derived from both hESCs and

---

[45] See further Emily Jackson, 'Fraudulent stem cell research and respect for the embryo' (2006) 1 BioSocieties 349–56.

[46] (WMA, 2013).

[47] James JH Chong et al, 'Human embryonic-stem-cell-derived cardiomyocytes regenerate non-human primate' (2014) 510 Nature 273–7.

iPS cells, suggesting that it might be possible to derive solid organs from stem cells.[48] And clinical trials involving human participants are already taking place. A trial in the US involved injecting replacement retinal pigment epithelial cells, derived from hESCs, into the eyes of patients suffering from macular degeneration and Stargardt's macular dystrophy. Most of the patients reported improvements in their sight.[49] In 2015, it was announced that a similar operation had taken place at Moorfield's Eye Hospital in the UK. Trials involving injecting stem cells into patients with spinal cord injuries are also taking place.[50]

Kalina Kamenova and Timothy Caulfield studied media reports of stem cell therapies and found that they were overwhelmingly optimistic, both about the promise of stem cell therapies and about how soon they might be available to patients.

Kalina Kamenova and Timothy Caulfield[51]

Overall, the news reporting on the clinical translation of SC therapies between 2009 and 2013 has remained optimistic and very much in tune with the predominantly optimistic slant in media reporting of emerging technologies in biomedicine and heightened public expectations established by previous studies. Remarkably, 69% of all news reports that indicated timelines predicted that SC therapies will be available within 5 to 10 years or sooner, just around the corner, or in the near future. . . .

Another key finding was the shift from ethical, legal, and social issues, which were central to media framing and public debates in the past, to stories about clinical translation (37.1%) and new discoveries (22.8%). Previous research on the evolution of the SC controversy has established that questions concerning the moral status of the human embryo and reproductive cloning no longer dominate public, policy, or scholarly debates; rather, clinical translation and new ethical issues arising from it have become increasingly important.

(f) Regenerative medicine

It is possible that stem cell therapies could lead to a new sort of regenerative medicine. Most people in the west now die as a result of degenerative diseases, such as heart disease and cancer. If it is possible to generate new replacement tissue when it is required, these techniques might be able to reverse some aspects of the human body's natural degeneration. This prompts John Harris to consider a world in which ageing, and even death, might no longer be inevitable. If stem cells, appropriately reprogrammed, could be used for the constant regeneration of organs and tissue, might we significantly extend the lifespan?

---

[48] Kyle W McCracken et al, 'Modelling human development and disease in pluripotent stem-cell-derived gastric organoids' (2014) 516 Nature 400–4.

[49] Joseph Maguire et al, 'Human embryonic stem cell-derived retinal pigment epithelium in patients with age-related macular degeneration and Stargardt's macular dystrophy: follow-up of two open-label phase 1/2 studies' (2015) 385 The Lancet 509–16.

[50] Nirupama Shevde, 'Stem cells: flexible friends' (2012) 483 Nature 22–6.

[51] 'Stem cell hype: Media portrayal of therapy translation' (2015) 7 Science Translational Medicine 278ps4.

John Harris[52]

This brings us to the central issue: would substantially increased life expectancy or even immortality be in fact a benefit or a good? There are people who regard the prospect of immortality with distaste or even horror; there are others who desire it above all else. In that most people fear death and want to postpone it as long as possible, there is some reason to suppose that the prospect of personal immortality would be widely welcomed. But it is one thing to contemplate our own personal immortality, quite another to contemplate a world in which increasing numbers of people were immortal, and in which we and all or any future children would have to compete indefinitely with previous generations for jobs, space and everything else . . .

To come down to earth, there is no doubt that immortality would be a mixed blessing, but we should be slow to reject cures for terrible diseases even if the price we have to pay for those cures is increasing life expectancy and even creating immortals. Better surely to accompany the scientific race to achieve immortality with commensurate work in ethics and social policy to ensure that we know how to cope with the transition to parallel populations of mortals and immortals.

On the one hand, an endless supply of replacement tissue for people whose bodies are degenerating might appear to give rise to some complex ethical issues. For example, these techniques are likely to be expensive, and so significantly increased life expectancy initially might be available only to a small minority of very rich people, raising important questions of distributive justice. In addition, if, in time, regenerative medicine became more widely available, would significantly increased lifespans put pressure on the world's resources?

On the other hand, it could be argued that finding cures for diseases such as cancer and heart disease is self-evidently desirable. Just as the discovery of cures for infectious diseases increased lifespans dramatically during the twentieth century, we should not be surprised if average lifespans continue to increase during the twenty-first century. It could also be argued that there is already a difference between the average lifespans of rich and poor people. In the UK, average life expectancy may be around 80 years, but for homeless women it is 43 years. In some African countries, the average lifespan has been dropping as a result of the HIV/AIDS pandemic, and in some countries is now as low as 35. Regenerative medicine would not then pose uniquely difficult questions about distributive justice.

(g) Patenting stem cells

As stem cell research moves slowly from the laboratory to the clinic, one of the most significant issues that arises is whether it should be possible to patent a stem cell line. Stem cell therapies—like new medicines—are extremely costly to develop, and without patent protection to enable researchers to recoup their investment, research might grind to a halt. Against this, would patenting a stem cell line amount to taking out a patent on life itself?

Article 6(1) of the EU Biotechnology Directive[53] provides that inventions must be considered unpatentable where their commercial exploitation would be contrary to *ordre public* or morality. In order to provide national courts and patent offices with guidance on what this means, there is, in Article 6(2), an illustrative list of examples, which includes, in Article 6(2) (c), 'uses of human embryos for industrial or commercial purposes'.

---

[52] 'The Ethics and Justice of Life-Extending Therapies' (2002) 55 Current Legal Problems 65–95.
[53] Directive on the Legal Protection of Biotechnological Inventions (98/44/EC).

In *Brüstle v Greenpeace*,[54] the Grand Chamber of the European Court of Justice (ECJ) held that 'human embryo' should be uniformly interpreted to include any entity that is 'capable of commencing the process of development of a human being'. As soon as a human egg is fertilized, it is therefore a human embryo. If the embryo is destroyed in the process of extracting stem cells, then even if the destruction of the embryo took place a long time before the invention, as is the case when banked hESC lines are used, the invention involves the destruction of embryos and is hence unpatentable.

The ECJ also gave a wide definition to use 'for industrial or commercial purposes', deciding that this includes the use of human embryos in scientific research, because a patent will entitle the holder 'to prohibit third parties from exploiting it for industrial and commercial purposes'.

The *Brüstle* decision was followed three years later by another decision of the Grand Chamber in *International Stem Cell Corp v Comptroller General of Patents, Designs and Trade Marks*.[55] The question for the court was whether 'unfertilised human ova whose division and further development have been stimulated by parthenogenesis and which, in contrast to fertilised ova, contain only pluripotent cells and are incapable of developing into human beings' are human embryos within the meaning of Article 6(2) of the Directive. Parthenogenesis involves asexual reproduction, in which the egg is not fertilized. It happens in some other species, but in humans, while eggs have been 'tricked' into starting the process of cell division, they cannot develop beyond the blastocyst state.

In *Brüstle v Greenpeace*,[56] the ECJ had appeared to include embryos created by parthenogenesis in the definition of 'human embryo':

> Therefore, any human ovum was to be regarded as a 'human embryo' for the purposes of art.6(2)(c) from the moment of fertilisation, that point being the commencement of the process of development of a human being. That classification also applied to a non-fertilised human ovum into which the cell nucleus from a mature human cell has been transplanted and a non-fertilised human ovum whose division and further development have been stimulated by parthenogenesis. Although those organisms have not, strictly speaking, been the object of fertilisation, due to the effect of the technique used to obtain them they are, as is apparent from the written observations presented to the Court, capable of commencing the process of development of a human being just as an embryo created by fertilisation of an ovum can do so.

In *International Stem Cell Corp*, however, applying the definition of a human embryo to a parthenote, the court found that an oocyte in which cell division had been activated through chemical and electrical means only had the capacity to develop to the blastocyst stage. It did not have the inherent capacity to develop into a human being, and hence was not a human embryo. Patent protection could therefore apply. *International Stem Cell Corp* therefore refines and slightly narrows the *Brüstle* interpretation of what is meant by 'human embryo': a parthenote might be able to 'commence' development, but it does not have the capacity to develop into a human being. It nevertheless confirms the ECJ's position that inventions that involve the destruction of human embryos are not patentable. Parthenotes, and stem cells derived from them, could therefore be subject to patient protection, while stem cells derived from human embryos could not be.

---

[54] [2012] 1 CMLR 41.   [55] Case C-364/13, 18 December 2014.   [56] [2012] 1 CMLR 41.

It has been argued that the ECJ was too interventionist in both these judgments, insisting on an EU-wide definition of human embryo, rather than leaving individual Member States to decide for themselves when commercial exploitation would be contrary to morality.[57] In the next extract, Julian Hitchcock and Clara Sattler de Sousa e Brito go further and suggests that given the steps taken by the EU to regulate and license stem cell research and stem cell therapies, a claim that a ban on patients is necessary on grounds of morality is 'ludicrous'.

Julian Hitchcock and Clara Sattler de Sousa e Brito[58]

Any claim that it is 'necessary' to ban hESC patents in order to uphold *ordre public* or morality is immediately punctured by the EU Directives on Human Tissue and Cells (EUTCD), which since 2004 have provided a clear legislative framework for the clinical use of human embryo derived products in the EU. The claim that a clinical use sanctioned by Europe's highest legislature is immoral is, therefore, ludicrous. In principle, such clinical use could be wholly non-commercial, in which case a patent ban would be prohibited even if such use *did* happen to be immoral. . . .

Given that the Council of Ministers and European Parliament have passed laws to facilitate and encourage the development and commercial exploitation of human embryo-derived inventions in Europe, it is plainly impossible to maintain that it is 'necessary' for the European Union and its Member States to *prevent* it, whether the supposed purpose is that of protecting *ordre public*, morality or satisfying religious or environmental pressure groups.

If stem cell therapies which involve the destruction of embryos are unpatentable throughout the EU, some commentators, like Faeh, have been concerned that Europe may be left behind once the work of stem cell scientists moves from 'bench to bedside'.

Andrea Faeh[59]

[I]n the current economic climate it was not wise to deprive a whole innovative sector of future investment by denying the patentability of their inventions. Investments in such a promising area are now more important than ever, since they not only promise growth for the economy and employment of highly skilled workers but also contribute to the advancement of health treatment and care. These aims should equally have been taken into account in the Court's judgments instead of allowing extreme moral and religious views to decide the future of human embryonic stem cell research and the economic value it could have given the Union. Now the US will lead developments and the Union will lose out economically, scientifically and at the health and ethical levels by the Court not foreseeing the consequences of its judgments.

It is, however, worth noting that it may be possible to patent other aspects of a proposed new therapy, such as a diagnostic tool, so that the unpatentability of the stem cell line itself may not have the chilling effect on research that some have feared.

---

[57] Andrea Faeh, 'Judicial activism, the Biotech Directive and its institutional implications: is the court acting as a legislator or a court when defining the "human embryo"?' (2015) 40 European Law Review 613–27.

[58] 'Should patents determine when life begins?' (2014) 36 European Intellectual Property Review 390–8.

[59] 'Judicial activism, the Biotech Directive and its institutional implications: is the court acting as a legislator or a court when defining the "human embryo"?' (2015) 40 European Law Review 613–27.

(4) Consent

One important prerequisite to the use of embryos in research is that, with three strictly limited exceptions, gamete or tissue providers must have specifically donated them to research. Under Schedule 3 para (2) to the 1990 Act, consent to an embryo's use in any project of research must be in writing. Consent can be withdrawn under Schedule 3 para (4) at any time until the embryo has been used in the project of research. Schedule 3 para (3) specifies that the person giving consent must have been given a suitable opportunity to receive counselling, and must be provided 'with such relevant information as is proper'. Guidance on the information which should be provided is contained in the HFEA's Code of Practice.

HFEA Code of Practice para 22.7

22.7 For any research project, the centre should ensure that before donors give their consent to their gametes or embryos, or cells used to create embryos, being used in research, they are given oral information (supported by relevant written material) that confirms:

a) the specific research project and its aims

b) details of the research project, including likely outcomes and how any individual donation will impact on the overall project

c) whether the embryos will be reversibly or irreversibly anonymised, and the implications of this

d) whether donors will be given any information that is obtained during the research and is relevant to their health and welfare

e) that donors are expected to have an opportunity to ask questions and discuss the research project

f) that donating gametes or embryos to research in the course of treatment services will not affect the patient's treatment in any way

g) that patients are under no obligation to donate gametes and embryos for research and that their decision whether to do so will have no repercussions for any treatment they may receive

h) that only fresh or frozen gametes and embryos not required for treatment can be used for research

i) that research is experimental, and so any gametes and embryos used and created for any research project must not be used in treatment

j) that donors may specify conditions for the use of the gametes or embryos

k) that after the research has been completed, all donated gametes and embryos will be allowed to perish, and

l) that, for any individual who donates cells for creating embryos for research, consent to use these cells includes consent to do so after the individual's death, unless stated otherwise.

New consent issues are raised by the possibility of extracting stem cell lines from embryos, since these lines are potentially immortal and might be useful to scientists (and in the future, pharmaceutical companies) for many years to come. Again, the HFEA's Code of Practice specifies that it must be made clear to potential donors 'that any stem cell lines created may continue indefinitely and be used in many different research projects'.[60]

---

[60] Para 22.8.

The HFEA and the Medical Research Council have jointly contributed towards a standard consent form for the use of embryos for stem cell research. This stresses, among other things, that the couple will not benefit, medically or financially, from any discoveries made during research on their cells. The HFEA will not grant licences for stem cell research unless the researchers have made a commitment to deposit each stem cell line with the UK stem cell bank. People donating embryos for stem cell research must be informed of the intention to bank any stem cell lines derived from their embryos.

Centralized banking of stem cell lines is important because their immortality means that they can continue to be made freely available to scientists throughout the world. At the time of writing, the UK stem cell bank contains more than 20 stem cell lines, which are available to other researchers, with many more waiting to be approved for release.

It is possible that there will come a time when the worldwide stem cell banks contain sufficient high-quality embryonic stem cell lines to meet researchers' needs, and it will no longer be necessary to create more. Two issues arise from this. First, the open sharing of stem cell lines with researchers throughout the world means that it would be highly desirable, albeit perhaps impractical, to have greater regulatory harmonization. If scientists in California, say, are only permitted to carry out research on stem cell lines where the gamete/embryo donors received no direct or indirect compensation, a high-quality stem cell line deposited in the UK bank, derived from eggs provided by a woman who received £750 in return, may be unavailable to them. While cross-national regulation of embryonic stem cell research would have many practical advantages, it is unlikely to ever become a reality. There is certainly no global consensus on the moral status of the embryo, and, in the future, countries may effectively be in competition with each other as attractive locations for pharmaceutical companies producing lucrative stem cell therapies.

Secondly, in an application to carry out human embryonic stem cell research, the Licence Committee must now ask itself a further question, namely whether it would be possible to carry out the research project using already existing stem cell lines which have been deposited in a stem cell bank and are available for use by others. Only if the answer to this question is 'no'—perhaps because the researchers wish to create a disease-specific cell line for a disease which is not among those represented in the bank—could a licence be issued. This issue arose in a case in which the Licence Committee had refused an application for a licence on the grounds that it could not be satisfied that it would be impossible to use existing stem cell lines in the particular drug toxicology research project. A preference to create a new line, free from third party entanglements, did not amount to a necessity to do so, and the application was refused.[61]

(5) Creating Embryos without Consent

The 2008 reforms to the 1990 Act create three exceptions to the need to obtain consent to the use of an embryo in a research project. Scientists and clinicians had argued that there might be certain diseases, for which stem cell research might offer the possibility of a cure, where it would be impossible to obtain a person's consent to the use of their tissue to create an embryo. An obvious example would be a disease like Tay-Sachs disease, which leads to a child's death, normally by the age of four, but in any event, always long before a child would have the capacity to consent to tissue donation. As a result, Schedule 3 now provides that, provided the 'parental consent conditions' are met, someone with parental responsibility can give consent to the use of their child's cells to create an embryo for research purposes.

---

[61] Minutes available at www.hfea.gov.uk.

Human Fertilisation and Embryology Act 1990 Schedule 3

PARENTAL CONSENT CONDITIONS

15(2) Condition A is that C [the child] suffers from, or is likely to develop, a serious disease, a serious physical or mental disability or any other serious medical condition.

(3) Condition B is that either—

(a) C is not competent to deal with the issue of consent to the use of C's human cells to bring about the creation in vitro of an embryo or human admixed embryo for use for the purposes of a project of research, or

(b) C has attained the age of 16 years but lacks capacity to consent to such use of C's human cells.

(4) Condition C is that any embryo or human admixed embryo to be created in vitro is to be used for the purposes of a project of research which is intended to increase knowledge about—

(a) the disease, disability or medical condition mentioned in sub-paragraph (2) or any similar disease, disability or medical condition, or

(b) the treatment of, or care of persons affected by, that disease, disability or medical condition or any similar disease, disability or medical condition.

(5) Condition D is that there are reasonable grounds for believing that research of comparable effectiveness cannot be carried out if the only human cells that can be used to bring about the creation in vitro of embryos or human admixed embryos for use for the purposes of the project are the human cells of persons who—

(a) have attained the age of 18 years and have capacity to consent to the use of their human cells to bring about the creation in vitro of an embryo or human admixed embryo for use for the purposes of the project, or

(b) have not attained that age but are competent to deal with the issue of consent to such use of their human cells.

In short, parents can consent to the child's cells being used for stem cell research if it would not be possible to do research into the child's condition using cells taken from someone else who can give consent.

A similar provision applies to adults who lack capacity. Again, provided it would not be possible to carry out the research on cells taken from people who can give consent, it may be possible to use cells from an adult who lacks capacity in stem cell research involving the creation of embryos.

Human Fertilisation and Embryology Act 1990 Schedule 3

CONSENT TO USE OF HUMAN CELLS ETC. NOT REQUIRED: ADULT LACKING CAPACITY

17(7) Condition F is that there are reasonable grounds for believing that research of comparable effectiveness cannot be carried out if the only human cells that can be used to bring about the creation in vitro of embryos or human admixed embryos for use for the purposes of the project are the human cells of persons who—

> (a) have attained the age of 18 years and have capacity to consent to the use of their human cells to bring about the creation in vitro of an embryo or human admixed embryo for use for the purposes of the project, or
>
> (b) have not attained that age but are competent to deal with the issue of consent to such use of their human cells.

Paragraph 18 goes on to provide that the person responsible under the licence (here referred to as R) must identify someone (F) who is able and willing to be consulted as to whether, if they had capacity, P would have agreed to letting their cells be used in this sort of research.

Human Fertilisation and Embryology Act 1990 Schedule 3

> 18(4) R must provide the person identified F . . . with information about the proposed use of human cells to bring about the creation in vitro of embryos or human admixed embryos for use for the purposes of the project and ask F what, in F's opinion, P's wishes and feelings about the use of P's human cells for that purpose would be likely to be if P had capacity in relation to the matter.

The final way in which the need for consent can be dispensed with is if the person's cells were stored before the Act came into force, and they have since died. This is so that cells stored in an existing tissue bank could be used for stem cell research, where it is not possible to obtain similar cells from someone who could give consent. For these stored cells to be used to create an embryo, there must be no evidence that the person would have objected to the use of their cells in this sort of research, and there must be agreement from someone who stands in a qualifying relationship with them (this is from the Human Tissue Act 2004, and refers to a list of relatives, described in the previous chapter).

It will be difficult to establish that it is necessary to use cells from deceased people who have not given consent because para 21 provides that there must be 'reasonable grounds for believing that scientific research will be adversely affected to a significant extent' if the only human cells that can be used are ones for which there is effective consent (or ones covered by the first two exceptions).

4 CONCLUSION

In conclusion, it is worth thinking about the existence of tensions between abortion law, considered in the next chapter, and the rules governing embryo research. For example, anti-abortion campaigners might argue that if embryos are protected when they are 14 days old, it is illogical to permit the destruction of fetuses at 23 weeks for 'social' reasons. Others might say that if a woman can abort a fetus during the first 24 weeks of pregnancy in order to promote her wellbeing, it makes little sense to prohibit potentially life-saving research on 16-day-old embryos.

Certainly the House of Lords Science and Technology Committee suggested that given the legality of abortion, a ban on embryo research would be rather odd: 'It would be difficult to justify an absolute prohibition on the destruction of early embryos while permitting abortion in a relatively wide range of circumstances post-implantation—indeed well after the emergence of the primitive streak and into the foetal stage of development.'

It is worth noting that when the original 1990 Act was passed, fertility treatment and embryo research were equally novel and controversial, and there were good reasons to subject both to a special licensing regime. Now the reality is rather different. IVF treatment has become a routine medical procedure, whereas public confidence in embryo research continues to depend upon the drawing of strict lines, a rigorous licensing procedure, and the ongoing monitoring of individual research projects.

At first sight, this might seem a good reason to support the previous government's now abandoned plan to abolish the HFEA and divide its functions between the Care Quality Commission (which would license treatment services) and the Health Research Authority (HRA) that would take over the regulation of embryo research.

On the other hand, there are reasons why this was not a good idea. First, a combination of diminished funding opportunities and the existence of the functioning UK stem cell bank mean that there is less embryo research to be licensed than there was in the past. Transferring the HFEA's functions to the HRA would have meant that the HRA would have to have set up a new inspectorate and licensing system in order to deal with a comparatively small number of research projects. It is much more efficient for the existing regulator to continue to inspect and license those centres which are carrying out embryo research.

In addition, there are also substantive reasons for keeping together the regulation of embryo research and the regulation of the treatment that creates the embryos used in that research. Separating them would miss the crucial point that embryo research and IVF treatment usually involve the same embryos: almost all of the embryos used in research were created with the intention that they should be used in fertility treatment. The people who consent to donate their embryos to research do so when they are patients, during the consent process in which they give their consent to IVF treatment. With two regulators, that consent process would have to be regulated by two different bodies, which might impose different standards or have different requirements.

More importantly still, there are issues which arise at the intersection of treatment and research. Hypothetically, if a centre were to adopt a policy that it will only freeze embryos for patients if they have a minimum of four spare grade A embryos, then a couple which has three spare grade A embryos would be unable to freeze those embryos for their future use, and if they are asked whether they would be willing to donate those embryos to research, they might be likely to say yes. This is unfair on the patients, however, whose desire to have a baby should always take priority over the researchers' interest in obtaining embryos to use in research. The freezing policy in the treating centre is then of critical importance to the ethical acceptability of the process through which people consent to donate their embryos for research, but this might be likely to be missed by a treatment inspectorate, which is not concerned with research, and by a research inspectorate, which is not concerned with treatment.

In January 2013, the government announced that it was no longer intending to abolish the HFEA as part of its 'bonfire of the quangos'. While this change of heart was to be welcomed, it is regrettable that the government did not consult widely before it made its initial announcement, at which point it surely would have been obvious that there was little to be gained by shifting statutory responsibilities from one well established expert body to two new ones.

FURTHER READING

Brock, DW, 'Is a consensus possible on stem cell research? Moral and political obstacles' (2006) 32 Journal of Medical Ethics 36–42.

Brown, Mark, 'No ethical bypass of moral status in stem cell research' (2013) 27 Bioethics 12–19.

Green, RM, 'Embryo as epiphenomenon: some cultural, social and economic forces driving the stem cell debate' (2008) 34 Journal of Medical Ethics 840–44.

Halliday, Samantha, 'A Comparative Approach to the Regulation of Human Embryonic Stem Cell Research in Europe' (2004) 12 Medical Law Review 40–69.

Harris, John, 'Stem cells, sex, and procreation' (2003) 12 Cambridge Quarterly of Healthcare 353–71.

Jackson, Emily, 'Fraudulent stem cell research and respect for the embryo' (2006) 1 BioSocieties 349–56.

Palacios-González, César, Harris, John, and Testa, Giuseppe, 'Multiplex parenting: IVG and the generations to come' (2014) 40 Journal of Medical Ethics 752–8.

Savulescu, Julian, 'The embryonic stem cell lottery and the cannibalization of human beings' (2002) 16 Bioethics 508–29.

Sparrow, Robert, 'Orphaned at conception: the uncanny offspring of embryos' (2012) 26 Bioethics 173–81.

13

ABORTION

CENTRAL ISSUES

1. Underlying the issue of abortion's legitimacy are two questions. First, what is the fetus's moral status, and, secondly, should a pregnant woman's right to autonomy include the right to terminate an unwanted pregnancy?

2. When the Abortion Act was passed in 1967, its principal purpose was to enable doctors to carry out safe, lawful abortions, rather than to give women rights. Access to abortion therefore depends upon whether two doctors believe that the woman's circumstances fit within one of the statutory grounds.

3. The most commonly used ground for abortion is that continuing the pregnancy poses a greater risk to the woman's physical or mental health than termination. Abortions carried out for this reason are subject to a 24-week time limit. Improvements both in fetal imaging techniques and in neonatal survival rates have led some to argue that the 24-week time limit should be lowered.

4. Abortion on the grounds of serious fetal abnormality is lawful until birth. Doctors have considerable discretion in determining what counts as a sufficiently serious handicap.

1 INTRODUCTION

In this chapter we consider a contentious but common medical procedure: the termination of pregnancy. In 1969—the first full year in which the Abortion Act was in operation—49,829 abortions were notified to the Department of Health. In 2014, 184,571 abortions were performed on women resident in England and Wales, and 5,521 on non-residents.[1] Twenty years ago, access to abortion within the NHS was patchy, and approximately half of all abortions took place in the private sector.[2] In 2014, 98 per cent of abortions were funded by the NHS, 67 per cent of which took place in the independent sector under NHS contract.

We begin this chapter with a necessarily brief survey of the ongoing debate over abortion's moral legitimacy. Should pregnant women have the right to terminate their unwanted

---

[1] *Abortion Statistics 2014* (DH: London, 2015).
[2] Emily Jackson, *Regulating Reproduction* (Hart Publishing: Oxford, 2001).

pregnancies, or do fetuses have a right to life that 'trumps' women's reproductive freedom? As will be obvious, there is never likely to be agreement on the morality of abortion. Nevertheless, despite the absence of anything remotely resembling consensus, abortion has been legal in England, Scotland, and Wales for nearly 50 years. We then examine the current legal position, and consider how the Abortion Act 1967, as amended, works in practice. The conflict between the interests of the fetus and those of the pregnant woman could also be framed in terms of 'rights', and so we briefly consider the impact of the Human Rights Act 1998.

In certain circumstances, the legality of abortion has proved to be especially controversial, and we investigate these cases separately. In particular, in recent years there has been considerable interest first, in whether abortion on the grounds of fetal abnormality amounts to eugenic selection, and, secondly, whether technological developments that enable very premature babies to survive mean that we should rethink the time limits within which abortion is legal. Finally, we highlight some differences between the regulation of abortion in England, Scotland, and Wales and in other jurisdictions.

2 THE ETHICS OF ABORTION

In what circumstances, if any, is it legitimate for a woman to terminate an unwanted pregnancy? Instinctive responses to this question will lie somewhere upon a spectrum which has 'never' at one end, and 'whenever she likes' at the other, with most people falling somewhere in between, believing that abortion is sometimes, but not always justifiable. Towards the restrictive end of the spectrum, it might be argued that abortion is legitimate where the woman's life is in danger, or when she is pregnant as a result of rape. At the more permissive end, it might be contended that abortion should be available upon request, at least during the first few months of pregnancy.

But while an instinctive response to the legitimacy of abortion may be a useful starting point, as we saw in Chapter 1, the requirement to give reasons, or to justify one's moral views is an important feature of ethical reasoning. Fortunately, in relation to abortion, there is a rich philosophical literature from which to draw. At the risk of drastic oversimplification, three different perspectives are worth identifying:

- an emphasis on the moral status of the fetus, and in particular upon its personhood, or potential personhood;
- an emphasis upon the physical invasiveness of pregnancy, and upon the degree of self-sacrifice which would be forced upon a woman who is compelled to continue an unwanted pregnancy;
- a compromise position in which abortion is permitted, but only in certain restricted circumstances which are designed to offer the fetus some protection.

(a) THE MORAL STATUS OF THE FETUS

A central concern of opponents of abortion is the moral status of the fetus. In the next extract, John Finnis argues that conception is the moment at which a new individual comes into being, and that this should be the point at which it should acquire all the rights of personhood.

John Finnis[3]

I have been assuming that the unborn child is, from conception, a person and hence is not to be discriminated against on account of age, appearance or other such factors insofar as such factors are reasonably considered irrelevant where respect for basic human values is in question . . .

[At conception] two sex cells, each with only twenty-three chromosomes, unite and more or less immediately fuse to become a new cell with forty-six chromosomes providing a unique genetic constitution . . . which thenceforth throughout its life, however long, will substantially determine the new individual's makeup. This new cell is the first stage in a dynamic integrated system that has nothing much in common with the individual male and female sex cells, save that it sprang from a pair of them and will in time produce new sets of them. To say that *this* is when a person's life began is not to work backwards from maturity, sophistically asking at each point 'How can one draw the line *here*?' Rather it is to point to a perfectly clear-cut beginning to which each one of us can look back.

This sort of argument has been disputed by others, such as Warren, who contend that while the fetus may be human, it is not yet a person, and so its interests cannot take priority over the rights of an actual person, namely the pregnant woman.

Mary Ann Warren[4]

What characteristics entitle an entity to be considered a person? . . . I suggest that the traits which are most central to the concept of personhood . . . , are, very roughly, the following:

(1) Consciousness . . . , and in particular the capacity to feel pain.

(2) Reasoning (the *developed* capacity to solve new and relatively complex problems);

(3) Self-motivated activity . . .

(4) The capacity to communicate . . .

(5) The presence of self-concepts, and self-awareness . . .

We needn't suppose that an entity must have *all* these attributes to be properly considered a person . . . Neither do we need to insist that any one of these criteria is necessary for personhood . . .

All we need to claim, to demonstrate that a fetus is not a person, is that any being which satisfies *none* of (1)–(5) is certainly not a person. I consider this claim to be so obvious that I think anyone who denied it, and claimed that a being which satisfied none of (1)–(5) was a person all the same, would thereby demonstrate that he had no notion at all of what a person is—perhaps because he had confused the concept of personhood with that of genetic humanity. . . .

[A] fetus is a human being which is not yet a person, and which therefore cannot coherently be said to have full moral rights . . . But even if a potential person does have some prima facie right to life, such a right could not possibly outweigh the right of a woman to obtain an abortion, since the rights of any actual person invariably outweigh those of any potential person, whenever the two conflict.

---

[3] 'The rights and wrongs of abortion: a reply to Judith Thomson' (1973) 2 Philosophy and Public Affairs 117–45.

[4] 'On the moral and legal status of abortion' (1973) 1 The Monist 43–61.

Warren's criteria for personhood are themselves controversial. Philip Abbott, for example, points out that this test for personhood would exclude not only fetuses, but also some seriously disabled children and adults.

Philip Abbott[5]

What makes one a person (or human in the moral sense)? Warren suggests five 'traits' . . . Note how deftly Warren plies her trade. A fetus *might* be able to feel pain, but surely he or she is unable to reason, especially with *developed* capacity. What is shocking about this criterion (2) is that a two-year old may fail to meet it. What this means . . . , and let us be direct about this, is that we must restrain our emotions and come to regard an infant as not a person at all but a mere clump of genetic humanity. Are not then the comatose patient, the schizophrenic, the catatonic, the unaided mute, the paraplegic in danger of slipping into that awful category 'genetic human'.

While, in legal terms at least, it is clear that a person with rights exists after birth but not before, in the next extract, Gillon argues that it is not evident that a newborn baby is a morally different entity to a fetus immediately prior to birth.

Raanan Gillon[6]

While in practical terms the simple criterion of birth is generally easy to apply and corresponds to a stage when what was previously hidden and private inside another human being is now a revealed, public, and clearly separate social entity, as a criterion for moral differentiation of a human being's intrinsic moral status it seems highly implausible. Essentially it is a criterion of what might be dubbed biological geography, asserting that a human being does not have a right to life if it lies north of a vaginal introitus but has a right to life once it has passed south and has (entirely) emerged from the vagina. What morally relevant changes can there have been in the fetus in its passage from inside to outside its mother's body to underpin such a momentous change in its intrinsic moral status?

Don Marquis avoids the person/not a person question, and instead claims that abortion is wrong because it is relevantly similar to killing an adult human being. According to Marquis, what makes killing adult human beings wrong is that it deprives them of everything they might value in the future. Since the killing of a fetus will also deprive it of everything it might value in the future, by analogy, he argues that abortion is just as wrong as killing an adult human being.

Don Marquis[7]

When I am killed, I am deprived both of what I now value which would have been part of my future personal life, but also what I would come to value. Therefore, when I die, I am deprived of all of the value of my future. Inflicting this loss on me is ultimately what makes killing me

5 'Philosophers and the abortion question' (1978) 6 Political Theory 313–35.
6 'Is there a "new ethics of abortion"?' (2001) 26 suppl II Journal of Medical Ethics ii5–ii9, ii8.
7 'Why abortion is immoral' (1989) 86 Journal of Philosophy 183–202, 192.

> wrong. This being the case, it would seem that what makes killing *any* adult human being prima facie seriously wrong is the loss of his or her future . . .
>
> The claim that the primary wrong-making feature of a killing is the loss to the victim of the value of its future has obvious consequences for the ethics of abortion. The future of a standard fetus includes a set of experiences, projects, activities, and such which are identical with the futures of adult human beings and are identical with the futures of young children. Since the reason that is sufficient to explain why it is wrong to kill human beings after the time of birth is a reason that also applies to fetuses, it follows that abortion is prima facie seriously morally wrong.

Of course, using contraception or even deciding not to have sexual intercourse on a particular day may also deprive a potential person of a future that they would value, but that does not necessarily mean that either is the wrong thing to do.[8]

A different criticism of Marquis comes from Mark T Brown, who argues that people are deprived of futures they might value whenever they die prematurely. Someone who needs a heart transplant, but does not get one in time, has been deprived of a future of value, but that does not mean that they had a right to that future, nor that they had any rights over someone else's heart. To give fetuses the right not to be killed would, according to Brown, be to give them:

> [A] right to satisfy their needs at the expense of the autonomy, bodily integrity and wellbeing of another person. If I need a bone marrow transplant in order to realise my potential future of value, I do not thereby gain a right to your bone marrow.[9]

This line of argument is further developed in the following section.

(b) THE PREGNANT WOMAN'S RIGHT TO SELF-DETERMINATION

This approach to abortion emphasizes the physical invasiveness of carrying a pregnancy to term, and argues that restrictions on women's access to abortion effectively compel them to exercise a wholly unprecedented degree of self-sacrifice. As Margaret Olivia Little explains:

> To be pregnant is to be *inhabited*. It is to be *occupied*. It is to be in a state of physical intimacy of a particularly thorough-going nature. The fetus intrudes on the body massively; whatever medical risks one faces or avoids, the brute fact remains that the fetus shifts and alters the very physical boundaries of the woman's self.[10]

Of course, the fetus is not a malicious intruder; it is occupying the woman's body through no fault of its own. However, the claim being made is that the state does not have the right to force the woman to continue in this relationship of unparalleled intimacy without her consent.

---

[8] Julian Savulescu, 'Abortion, embryo destruction and the future of value argument' (2002) 28 Journal of Medical Ethics 133–5.

[9] 'The morality of abortion and the deprivation of futures' (2000) 26 Journal of Medical Ethics 103–7.

[10] 'Abortion, intimacy, and the duty to gestate' (1999) 2 Ethical Theory and Moral Practice 295–312.

Eileen L McDonagh[11]

Pregnancy is a condition constituting massive transformations of a woman's body and liberty, and, thus, constitutes serious harm without her consent.

The massive effects of a fetus on a woman's body correspond to the level of injury justifying the use of deadly force, if a woman does not consent to those effects. If a born person were to affect another born person's body in even a fraction of the ways a fetus affects a woman's body, the magnitude of the injury would be easy to recognize. Imagine a born person who injected into another's body, without consent, hormones 400 times their normal level, or someone who, without consent, took over the blood system of another to meet her own personal use, or someone who, without consent, grew a new organ in that person's body. . . .

Some may object that if a woman consents to sexual intercourse (action X), then by extension she has consented to pregnancy (condition Y) as a foreseeable consequence of sexual intercourse. . . .

Generally, when a person creates a risk, it does not follow that the person consents to injuries occurring subsequent to the risk. Thus, if a person consensually creates a risk that she will be mugged by walking down an alley alone, late at night, responsibility for causing the risk does not constitute consent to the injury of mugging that may be subsequent to that risk . . . In addition, even if a woman is contributorily negligent in creating the risk that a fetus will harm her, she nevertheless retains the right to self-defense to stop the fetus from harming her.

The woman's right to an abortion is not, on this view, necessarily dependent upon proving that the fetus is not a person. Rather, as Judith Jarvis Thomson argues in the next extract, even if the fetus is a person, pregnant women might have the right to defend themselves from the physical invasion of an unwanted pregnancy.

Judith Jarvis Thomson[12]

[S]urely a person's right to life is stronger and more stringent than the mother's right to decide what happens in and to her body, and so outweighs it. . . . It sounds plausible. But now let me ask you to imagine this. You wake up in the morning and find yourself back to back in bed with an unconscious violinist. A famous unconscious violinist. He has been found to have a fatal kidney ailment, and the Society of Music Lovers has canvassed all the available medical records and found that you alone have the right blood type to help. They have therefore kidnapped you, and last night the violinist's circulatory system was plugged into yours, so that your kidneys can be used to extract poisons from his blood as well as your own. The director of the hospital now tells you, 'Look, we're sorry the Society of Music Lovers did this to you—we would never have permitted it if we had known. But still, they did it, and the violinist is now plugged into you. To unplug you would be to kill him. But never mind, it's only for nine months. By then he will have recovered from his ailment, and can safely be unplugged from you.' Is it morally incumbent on you to accede to this situation? No doubt it would be very nice of you if you did, a great kindness. But do you *have* to accede to it? . . . What if the director of the hospital says, 'Tough luck, I agree, but you've now got to stay in bed, with the violinist plugged into you, for the rest of your life. Because remember this. All persons have a right to life, and violinists are persons. Granted you have a right to decide what happens in and

[11] 'My Body, My Consent: Securing the Constitutional Right to Abortion Funding' (1999) 62 Albany Law Review 1057.

[12] 'A defence of abortion' (1971) 1 Philosophy and Public Affairs 47.

> to your body, but a person's right to life outweighs your right to decide what happens in and to your body. So you cannot ever be unplugged from him.' I imagine you would regard this as outrageous, which suggests that something really is wrong with that plausible-sounding argument I mentioned a moment ago.

It is often assumed that deciding to have an abortion is a more difficult and serious moral choice than deciding to carry a pregnancy to term, even though motherhood involves an extraordinarily demanding and long-lasting commitment. Through the presumptions that women seeking abortion need counselling, and conversely, that women who are about to become mothers do not, motherhood is assumed to be an easy and natural choice for women, whereas, as Siegel explains, rejecting motherhood is perceived to be unnatural and selfish.

Reva Siegel[13]

> Legislators may condemn abortion because they assume that any pregnant woman who does not wish to be pregnant has committed some sexual indiscretion properly punishable by compelling pregnancy itself. Popular support for excusing women who are victims of rape or incest from the proscriptions of criminal abortion laws demonstrates that attitudes about abortion do indeed rest on normative judgments about women's sexual conduct. . . .
>
> If legislators assume that women are 'child-rearers', they will take for granted the work women give to motherhood and ignore what it takes from them, and so will view women's efforts to avoid some two decades of life-consuming work as an act of casual expedience or unseemly egoism. Thus, they will condemn women for seeking abortion 'on demand', or as a mere 'convenience', judging women to be unnaturally egocentric because they do not give their lives over to the work of bearing and nurturing children—that is, because they fail to act like mothers, like normal women should.

The idea that women should have the right to decide for themselves whether they want to become mothers is disputed by Rosalind Hursthouse, who analyses abortion from the perspective of virtue ethics (considered in Chapter 1). According to Hursthouse, because motherhood is intrinsically good, a woman who rejects it without a compelling or 'virtuous' reason, is acting wrongly.

Rosalind Hursthouse[14]

> The familiar facts support the view that parenthood in general, and motherhood and childbearing in particular, are intrinsically worthwhile, are among the things that can be correctly thought to be partially constitutive of a flourishing human life. If this is right, then a woman who opts for not being a mother (at all, or again, or now) by opting for abortion may thereby be manifesting a flawed grasp of what her life should be, and be about—a grasp that is childish, or grossly materialistic, or shortsighted, or shallow.

---

[13] 'Reasoning from the Body: A Historical Perspective on Abortion Regulation and Questions of Equal Protection' (1992) Stanford Law Review 261.

[14] 'Virtue Theory and Abortion' in Daniel Statman (ed), *Virtue Ethics* (Edinburgh UP: Edinburgh, 1997) 227–44.

I say 'may thereby': this *need* not be so. Consider, for instance, a woman who has already had several children and fears that to have another will seriously affect her capacity to be a good mother to the ones she has—she does not show a lack of appreciation of the intrinsic value of being a parent by opting for abortion. Nor does a woman who has been a good mother and is approaching the age at which she may be looking forward to being a good grandmother. Nor does a woman who discovers that her pregnancy may well kill her, and opts for abortion and adoption. Nor, necessarily, does a woman who has decided to lead a life centred around some other worthwhile activity or activities with which motherhood would compete . . .

But some women who choose abortion rather than have their first child, and some men who encourage their partners to choose abortion, are not avoiding parenthood for the sake of other worthwhile pursuits, but for the worthless one of 'having a good time', or for the pursuit of some false vision of the ideals of freedom or self-realisation.

(c) A COMPROMISE POSITION?

Thirdly, as with the question of embryo research we considered in the previous chapter, a middle ground exists that acknowledges both that the fetus's potential personhood is a good reason to afford it some protection, and that the pregnant woman has a legitimate interest in self-determination. This 'third way' would protect the woman's right to terminate her pregnancy, but only in certain circumstances. This is consistent with most countries' regulation of abortion: abortion is permitted within parameters—such as time limits—which are supposed to indicate the seriousness of fetal destruction.

Ronald Dworkin argues that people share a deep belief in the sanctity of human life, and therefore regard abortion as a morally serious matter, but that they also do not believe that the fetus has exactly the same status as a person, otherwise it would be impossible to justify abortion if the pregnant woman's life is in danger, or if she is pregnant as a result of rape.

Ronald Dworkin[15]

[D]iscussions of abortion almost all presume that people disagree about abortion because they disagree about whether a fetus is a person with a right to life from the moment of its conception, or becomes a person at some point in pregnancy, or does not become one until birth. And about whether, if a fetus is a person, its right to life must yield in the face of some stronger right held by pregnant women. . . .

[T]his account of the abortion debate, in spite of its great popularity, is fatally misleading. . . . [E]ven those conservatives who believe that the law should prohibit abortion recognize exceptions. It is a very common view, for example, that abortion should be permitted when necessary to save the mother's life. Yet this exception is . . . inconsistent with any belief that a fetus is a person with a right to live. Some people say that in this case a mother is justified in aborting a fetus as a matter of self-defense; but any safe abortion is carried out by someone else—a doctor—and very few people believe that it is morally justifiable for a third party, even a doctor, to kill one innocent person to save another.

Abortion conservatives often allow further exceptions. Some of them believe that abortion is morally permissible . . . when pregnancy is the result of rape or incest. The more such

---

[15] *Life's Dominion* (HarperCollins: London, 1993).

exceptions are allowed, the clearer it becomes that conservative opposition to abortion does not presume that the fetus is a person with a right to life. It would be contradictory to insist that a fetus has a right to life . . . that ceases to exist when the pregnancy is the result of a sexual crime of which the fetus is, of course, wholly innocent.

3 THE LAW

(a) THE CRIMINAL LAW

Until 1803, abortion was governed by the common law, which drew a distinction between fetal destruction before and after 'quickening' (the moment when the woman can first feel the fetus moving inside her), which is normally about 16–18 weeks into the pregnancy.

William Blackstone[16]

Life . . . begins in contemplation of law as soon as an infant is able to stir in the mother's womb. For if a woman is quick with child, and by a potion, or otherwise, killeth it in her womb; or if any one beat her, whereby the child dieth in her body, and she is delivered of a dead child; this, though not murder, was by the ancient law homicide or manslaughter. But at present it is not looked upon in quite so atrocious a light, though it remains a very heinous misdemeanor.

Since Lord Ellenborough's Act of 1803, abortion has been regulated by statute. Under the 1803 Act abortion became a felony throughout pregnancy, and the death penalty was introduced for abortion after quickening, though this was abolished 34 years later, as was the distinction between abortions before and after quickening.

A nineteenth-century statute continues to apply to abortion today. Statutory defences do now exist, but under sections 58 and 59 of the Offences Against the Person Act 1861, the maximum sentence for a woman who intentionally procures her own miscarriage is life imprisonment, and anyone who assists her could be imprisoned for up to five years.

Offences Against the Person Act 1861 sections 58 and 59

58 Every woman, being with child, who, with intent to procure her own miscarriage, shall unlawfully administer to herself any poison or other noxious thing, or shall unlawfully use any instrument or other means whatsoever with the like intent, and whosoever, with intent to procure the miscarriage of any woman, whether she be or not with child, shall unlawfully administer to her or cause to be taken by her any poison or other noxious thing, or shall unlawfully use any instrument or other means whatsoever with the like intent, shall be guilty of felony.

59 Whosoever shall unlawfully supply or procure any poison or other noxious thing, or any instrument or thing whatsoever knowing that the same is intended to be unlawfully used or employed with intent to procure the miscarriage of any woman, whether she be or not be with child, shall be guilty of a misdemeanor.

[16] *Commentaries on the Laws of England*, vol 1 (1765).

The critical ingredients of the offences under sections 58 and 59 are, first, that someone must *do* something with a poison or instrument or other noxious thing, and, secondly, that they must *intend* to procure a miscarriage. Notice also that the first limb of section 58 applies only to women who are in fact 'with child'. A woman could not be convicted of the full offence under section 58 unless she was actually pregnant. A woman who mistakenly believed that she was pregnant could instead be guilty of conspiring to procure an abortion, as was the case in *R v Whitchurch*.[17] Other people can be guilty 'whether she be or not with child', provided that they believe her to be pregnant, and intend to cause her to miscarry.

It is also important to note that sections 58 and 59 refer to poison or instruments being used *unlawfully*. On one interpretation, the word 'unlawfully' is redundant here: the purpose of these sections is to create a criminal offence, so it goes without saying that the act described is unlawful. A more plausible explanation is that the offence is only committed where the abortion is carried out unlawfully, meaning that it might be possible to procure an abortion lawfully. Because it has never been doubted that doctors are entitled to carry out life-saving surgery, even if its consequence would be to end the woman's pregnancy, the word 'unlawfully' creates an exception—akin to the one contained in the Infant Life Preservation Act 1929 (considered later)—for terminations performed to preserve the pregnant woman's life.

This was certainly the interpretation preferred by Macnaghten J in his summing up to the jury in *R v Bourne*, a case in which a distinguished obstetric surgeon, Aleck Bourne, had carried out an abortion on a 14-year-old girl, who was pregnant following a violent rape. His defence was that the operation was not unlawful, because, in his opinion, the continuance of the pregnancy posed a serious risk to the girl's mental health. In his direction to the jury, Macnaghten J agreed that it would be possible for an abortion to be carried out lawfully not only where the pregnant woman was in imminent danger of death, but also where the effect of carrying the pregnancy to term might be to 'make the woman a physical or mental wreck'.

R v Bourne[18]

Macnaghten J

A man of the highest skill, openly, in one of our great hospitals, performs the operation. Whether it was legal or illegal you will have to determine, but he performs the operation as an act of charity, without fee or reward, and unquestionably believing that he was doing the right thing, and that he ought, in the performance of his duty as a member of a profession devoted to the alleviation of human suffering, to do it. . . .

[T]he words of that section [section 58 of the Offences Against the Person Act 1861] are that any person who 'unlawfully' uses an instrument with intent to procure miscarriage shall be guilty of felony. In my opinion the word 'unlawfully' is not, in that section, a meaningless word. I think it imports the meaning expressed by the proviso in s. 1, sub-s. 1, of the Infant Life (Preservation) Act, 1929 [that 'no person shall be found guilty of an offence under this section unless it is proved that the act which caused the death of the child was not done in good faith for the purpose only of preserving the life of the mother'] and that s. 58 of the Offences Against the Person Act, 1861, must be read as if the words making

[17] (1890) LR 24 QBD 420.   [18] [1939] 1 KB 697.

it an offence to use an instrument with intent to procure a miscarriage were qualified by a similar proviso.

What then is the meaning to be given to the words 'for the purpose of preserving the life of the mother' . . . I think those words ought to be construed in a reasonable sense, and, if the doctor is of opinion, on reasonable grounds and with adequate knowledge, that the probable consequence of the continuance of the pregnancy will be to make the woman a physical or mental wreck, the jury are quite entitled to take the view that the doctor who, under those circumstances and in that honest belief, operates, is operating for the purpose of preserving the life of the mother. . . .

You are the judges of the facts and it is for you to say what weight should be given to the testimony of the witnesses; but no doubt you will think it is only common sense that a girl who for nine months has to carry in her body the reminder of the dreadful scene and then go through the pangs of childbirth must suffer great mental anguish, unless indeed she be feeble-minded or belongs to the class described as 'the prostitute class' . . . But in the case of a normal, decent girl brought up in a normal, decent way you may well think that Dr. Rees [a clinical psychologist] was not overstating the effect of the continuance of the pregnancy when he said that it would be likely to make her a mental wreck, with all the disastrous consequences that would follow from that.

Following Aleck Bourne's acquittal, it was apparent that an abortion could lawfully be performed if the pregnant woman's mental health was endangered by her unwanted pregnancy. Some doctors were prepared to interpret this 'mental wreck' exception quite broadly, and terminate the pregnancies of women who were distressed, rather than mentally ill. Because such doctors were risking prosecution, their fees tended to be high, and these safe 'legal' abortions were therefore inaccessible to the majority of women, who relied instead on the services of illegal abortionists. Although exact figures are not available, it is thought that there were probably at least 100,000 illegal abortions each year prior to abortion's partial decriminalization in 1967. Some of these 'backstreet' abortionists' practices were extremely dangerous, and mortality rates were high.

Although it is now of minimal practical relevance, brief mention should be made of the Infant Life (Preservation) Act 1929, under which it is an offence to destroy the life of a child capable of being born alive, unless the act is done in good faith for the purpose only of preserving the life of the mother. The purpose of this Act was to close a legal loophole. In 1929, it was unlawful to kill a fetus *in utero*, and it was murder to kill a child after birth. However, no protection was afforded to the child during the process of birth, before it had been completely separated from its mother. In order to fill this gap, the Infant Life (Preservation) Act provided that killing the child during childbirth would also be an offence.

Although not intended to apply to abortion, which was, of course, unlawful in 1929, once the Abortion Act 1967 came into force, the 1929 Act had the effect of setting a time limit for lawful abortion, since it provided that it is an offence to destroy the life of a fetus which is 'capable of being born alive'. In 1929, this was the case at around 28 weeks. By the time a statutory time limit was added to the Abortion Act in 1990, the age at which a fetus was capable of being born alive had dropped to 24 weeks.

The 1929 Act is no longer relevant in determining whether a proposed abortion is lawful. The Abortion Act 1967 was amended in 1990 to provide that no offence under the Infant Life (Preservation) Act is committed provided that the pregnancy is terminated in accordance with the provisions in the 1967 Act. The 1990 amendments also set a 24-week time limit for the most common ground for abortion.

(b) THE ABORTION ACT 1967

(1) The Background to Legalization

In order to understand the form that abortion's legalization took in 1967, it is important to realize that the Abortion Act 1967 was not enacted in order to provide women with the *right* to terminate their unwanted pregnancies. Rather, the principal factor behind public and parliamentary support for legalization was concern about high mortality rates resulting from illegal abortions, especially among the poor. Inadequate contraception—the pill only became widely available during the 1960s—meant that unwanted pregnancies were common. Many women were therefore faced with an invidious choice between giving birth to a child for whom they would be unable to provide adequate care, or resorting to an illegal and often hazardous abortion. In *R v Scrimaglia*,[19] a case in which a 'backstreet' abortion took place after legalization, the then Lord Chief Justice commented that 'one of the objects, as everyone knows, of the new Act was to try to get rid of the back-street insanitary operations'.

By the mid-1960s, it was clear that the law was not preventing women from terminating their unwanted pregnancies; instead it was ensuring that abortions were performed by amateurs, often in unhygienic surroundings, using dangerous techniques. Successful prosecutions were rare: women who had had abortions would seldom be prepared to give evidence and the police were reluctant to prosecute. The law was, in short, completely ineffective.

A few doctors were prepared to perform abortions, but they were risking prosecution and so access to their services was patchy. It was, however, common for doctors to encounter the consequences of botched illegal abortions, which included large numbers of avoidable deaths. Unsurprisingly, the medical profession resented the criminal law's interference with their freedom to act in the best interests of their patients. Abortion, then, was not legalized in order to enhance women's reproductive autonomy: rather, the Abortion Act's principal purpose was to enable doctors to act lawfully in assisting desperate women to end their pregnancies.

In the next extract, Sally Sheldon argues that supporters of David Steel's Abortion Bill in fact shared their opponents' belief that women were incapable of making rational decisions about their unwanted pregnancies.

Sally Sheldon[20]

[In] the parliamentary debates preceding the introduction of the Abortion Act . . . [t]he doctor is talked of as a 'highly skilled and dedicated', 'sensitive, sympathetic' member of a 'high and proud profession' which acts 'with its own ethical and medical standards' displaying 'skill, judgement and knowledge'. The woman who experiences an unwanted pregnancy, on the other hand, is portrayed as someone who is fundamentally incapable of taking such an important decision for herself—either because she is downtrodden and driven to desperation (in the language of the reformers) or, for the opponents of reform, because she is selfish and morally immature. The first of these two images is summed up in the following quotation taken from the parliamentary debates:

There is the woman who already has a large family, perhaps six or seven children . . . There is the question of the woman who loses her husband during pregnancy and has to go out to

---

[19] (1971) 55 Cr App R 280.

[20] 'The Abortion Act 1967: A Critical Perspective' in Ellie Lee (ed), *Abortion Law and Politics Today* (Macmillan: London, 1998) 43–58.

work, and obviously cannot bear the strain of doing a full day's work, and looking after a child. There is the woman whose husband is a drunkard or a ne'er-do-well, or is in prison serving a long term, and she has to go to work.

On the other side of the debate, the opponents of reform portrayed the woman as selfish, feckless and irresponsible. Jill Knight, a Conservative MP, was one of the leading opponents of reform . . . She reveals an image of women seeking abortion as selfish, treating babies 'like bad teeth to be jerked out just because they cause suffering . . . simply because it may be inconvenient for a year or so to its mother'. She later adds that a 'mother might want an abortion so that a planned holiday is not postponed or other arrangements interfered with'. The ability and willingness of the woman to make a serious decision regarding abortion, considering all factors and all parties, is dismissed. Rather, she will make a snap decision for her own convenience. The task of the law is thus perceived essentially as one of responsibilization: if the woman seeks to evade the consequences of her carelessness, the law should stand as a barrier.

Given this background, the form that legalization took is not surprising. Abortion is not available upon request. Rather, abortion continues to be proscribed by the Offences Against the Person Act 1861 (and in Scotland by the common law), but the Abortion Act 1967 provides that abortion will be lawful (in England, Scotland, and Wales—the Act does not apply in Northern Ireland), and no offence will have been committed, if the criteria laid out in the Act are met. We consider these in more detail later, but they are, in short, that two doctors agree that the woman's circumstances satisfy one of the four statutory 'grounds' for abortion; that the abortion is carried out by a registered medical practitioner in an approved place; and that it is notified within seven days to the relevant Chief Medical Officer. Although the basic substance of the legislation remains unaltered since 1967, the Abortion Act was amended in 1990 by the Human Fertilisation and Embryology Act. Several further attempts have been made to amend the statute since 1990, but none has so far been successful. In 2016, as a result of the Scotland Act 2016, abortion became a devolved matter in Scotland, although the Scottish government has said that it has no plans to change the law on abortion.

It is important to stress that if a termination of pregnancy does not satisfy the criteria in the Abortion Act, it would be a criminal offence. In 2012, Sarah Catt bought abortion pills from an internet site which she took in order to terminate her own pregnancy, shortly before she was due to give birth. She was convicted under section 58 of the Offences Against the Person Act and initially sentenced to eight years in prison.[21] In *R v Sarah Catt*, the Court of Appeal reduced her sentence to three and a half years.

R v Sarah Catt[22]

Rafferty LJ

There are the following aggravating features: the termination was at full term; the body has never been recovered; there was careful planning and acquisition of the abortifacient; the criminal acts were done despite considerable experience of pregnancy and its range of consequences. There are these mitigating features: the plea of guilty, the views of Dr Frazer, a man of significant experience, that Mrs Catt appeared very remorseful, and of Ms Lowe

---

[21] *R v Sarah Louise Catt*, 17 September 2012. Sentencing remarks available at www.judiciary.gov.uk/.
[22] [2013] EWCA Crim 1187.

that her emotional attachment to a child in utero is difficult; Mrs Catt has two young children to whom it is accepted she is a good mother and whose development will be adversely affected by her absence from the family home …

[T]his woman from, at the latest, her undergraduate years had a history of struggle. Her obstetric history we suggest would, without more, prompt attention to her emotional state.... Of one thing we are confident: a wise disposition of this case should remember two young children and a notably forbearing husband....

In our view, however, a starting point of 12 years was manifestly excessive and, after reduction for plea, eight years similarly so. The appropriate starting point was in the region of five years and, loyal to the judge's assessment of credit for the plea, the end result should be a term of imprisonment of three-and-a-half years. To that limited extent, this appeal succeeds.

(2) The Grounds for Abortion

The statutory defences to the criminal offences in the Offences Against the Person Act are contained in section 1 of the Abortion Act 1967, as amended:

Abortion Act 1967 section 1

1(1) Subject to the provisions of this section a person shall not be guilty of an offence under the law relating to abortion when a pregnancy is terminated by a registered medical practitioner if two registered medical practitioners are of the opinion, formed in good faith:

(a) that the pregnancy has not exceeded its twenty fourth week and that the continuation of the pregnancy would involve risk, greater than if the pregnancy were terminated, of injury to the physical or mental health of the pregnant woman or any existing children of her family; or

(b) that the termination is necessary to prevent grave permanent injury to the physical or mental health of the pregnant woman; or

(c) that the continuance of the pregnancy would involve risk to the life of the pregnant woman, greater than if the pregnancy were terminated; or

(d) that there is a substantial risk that if the child were born it would suffer from physical or mental abnormalities as to be seriously handicapped.

(2) In determining whether the continuance of a pregnancy would involve such risk of injury to health as is mentioned in paragraph (a) or (b) of subsection (1) of this section, account may be taken of the woman's actual or reasonably foreseeable environment.

In what follows, we investigate the meaning of this section, and how it works in practice.

(a) Unsuccessful terminations

There is an unfortunate ambiguity in the first sentence of section 1. It appears to suggest that the defence only exists 'when a pregnancy is terminated'. Does this mean that the defence does not exist where the pregnancy is *not* terminated? Because the 1861 Act criminalizes anything done with the intention to procure a miscarriage, a literal interpretation of section 1 might leave unsuccessful terminations in an awkward lacuna: a person can be guilty of an offence under the 1861 Act even if the woman's pregnancy is not terminated, but the defence only exists if the pregnancy *is* terminated.

A similar problem arises if the woman having the abortion turns out not to have been pregnant. The doctor could still be charged under the 1861 Act for attempting to procure a miscarriage, but no defence would exist if there had not in fact been a pregnancy to terminate.

The issue was considered by the House of Lords in *Royal College of Nursing v Department of Health and Social Security* (discussed in more detail later). A majority held that it would be 'absurd' and 'cannot have been the intention of Parliament' that anyone taking part in an unsuccessful termination would be unable to rely upon the defences contained in the Abortion Act and would therefore be guilty of an offence under the Offences Against the Person Act 1861. As Lord Edmund-Davies explained:

> Were it otherwise the unavoidable conclusion is that doctors and nurses could in such cases be convicted of what in essence would be the extraordinary crime of attempting to do a lawful act.[23]

He then quoted with approval from Smith and Hogan's *Criminal Law*:

> [T]he legalisation of an abortion must include the steps which are taken towards it. Are we really to say that these are criminal until the operation is complete, when they are retrospectively authorised, or alternatively that they are lawful until the operation is discontinued or the woman is discovered not to be pregnant when, retrospectively, they become unlawful? When the conditions of the Act are otherwise satisfied, it is submitted that [the doctor] is not unlawfully administering, etc, and that this is so whether the pregnancy be actually terminated or not.

Hence, it seems likely that a doctor who unsuccessfully attempted to terminate a pregnancy within the terms of the Abortion Act 1967 would nevertheless have a defence to the criminal offence contained in section 59 of the Offences Against the Person Act.

(b) The need for medical approval

Notice that the Act does not entitle a woman to decide to terminate an unwanted pregnancy, even if her circumstances fit within the statutory grounds. Instead, what matters are two doctors' opinions that one or more of the grounds is satisfied. It is also worth noting that the statute does not specify that the section 1(1) criteria have to actually be satisfied. The legality of an abortion rests wholly upon whether two doctors have formed the opinion, in good faith, that the woman's case fits within the statutory grounds, not upon whether those grounds in fact exist. An abortion would be legal even if the woman's circumstances did not satisfy the statutory grounds, provided that the two doctors who authorized her termination had acted in good faith. Doctors performing abortions will therefore only fail to be protected by the defence in section 1(1) if there is evidence that they did not act in good faith.

There has been one successful prosecution of a doctor since the Act came into force. In *R v Smith*, the evidence indicated that the doctor had failed to carry out an internal examination, had made no inquiries into the pregnant woman's personal situation, and had not sought a second doctor's opinion. He was convicted on the grounds that he had not, in good faith, attempted to balance the risks of pregnancy and termination. The Court of Appeal appeared to indicate that a doctor will have acted in good faith if he complies with accepted

---

[23] [1981] AC 800.

medical practice: 'good faith' thus seems to be synonymous with the *Bolam* test (discussed in Chapter 3).

R v Smith[24]

Scarman LJ

The [Abortion] Act (though it renders lawful abortions that before its enactment would have been unlawful), does not depart from the basic principle of the common law as declared in *R v Bourne*, namely, that the legality of an abortion depends upon the opinion of the doctor. It has introduced the safeguard of two opinions: but, if they are formed in good faith by the time when the operation is undertaken, the abortion is lawful. Thus a great social responsibility is firmly placed by the law upon the shoulders of the medical profession. . . .

The sequence of events was such as to call for very careful consideration as to whether it was possible to believe that Dr Smith had formed in good faith, or at all, the opinion necessary to give him the protection of the Abortion Act. Had he, or had he not, abused the trust reposed in him by the Act of Parliament? The burden was on the prosecution to prove beyond reasonable doubt that he had. . . . We quote only one passage towards the end of the summing up:

> . . . If two doctors genuinely form an opinion in each case that they deal with that the risk of continuance is more than the risk of termination, it does not matter whether they are right or wrong in that view. If they form that opinion genuinely and in good faith, that in fact comes within the Act, and there is no guilt attached to it. You have to wonder in the case of Dr Smith whether such a view could genuinely be held by a medical man. . . . The only indication on the case notes about any danger to her mental or physical health was the word 'depressed', 'not willing to marry and depressed'. Those are the only words about it on the case notes. You have to ask yourselves, was there any balancing of the risks involved in allowing the pregnancy to continue and allowing the pregnancy to be terminated, or was this a mere routine abortion for cash?

Further evidence that the statute's purpose is to protect medical discretion rather than women's autonomy comes from the inherent vagueness of the statutory grounds. The Act does not, for example, specify that abortion is legal where the pregnancy has resulted from an act of rape or incest. This ambiguity was deliberate. David Steel's Abortion Bill did initially contain more specific clauses, such as one which permitted abortion where the woman was pregnant as a result of rape, but these were opposed by both the British Medical Association (BMA) and the Royal College of Obstetricians and Gynaecologists (RCOG). While doctors will invariably allow rape victims to terminate their pregnancies, a definitive list of situations in which abortion is lawful was rejected, in part because it would erode medical discretion, and might give women the impression that in certain circumstances they would have the right to an abortion. In *Paton v British Pregnancy Advisory Service Trustees*, a case in which a man wanted to stop his wife from terminating her pregnancy, the President of the Family Division explained that, under the 1967 Act, it is doctors rather than pregnant women who bear principal responsibility for deciding whether a pregnancy should be terminated.

---

[24] [1974] 1 All ER 376.

Paton v British Pregnancy Advisory Service Trustees[25]

Sir George Baker P

My own view is that it would be quite impossible for the courts in any event to supervise the operation of the Abortion Act 1967. The great social responsibility is firmly placed by the law upon the shoulders of the medical profession . . . The two doctors have given a certificate. It is not and cannot be suggested that the certificate was given in other than good faith and it seems to me that there is the end of the matter in English law. . . .

This certificate is clear, and not only would it be a bold and brave judge . . . who would seek to interfere with the discretion of doctors acting under the Abortion Act 1967, but I think he would really be a foolish judge who would try to do any such thing, unless, possibly, where there is clear bad faith and an obvious attempt to perpetrate a criminal offence.

In the next extract, Sally Sheldon criticizes the Abortion Act's delegation of abortion decision-making to doctors, arguing that the decision to terminate a pregnancy is not necessarily one that requires clinical expertise.

Sally Sheldon[26]

The granting of such power to doctors in the field of abortion is often justified by the argument that abortion is essentially a medical matter. However, the actual decision whether or not a given pregnancy should be terminated is not normally one that requires expert medical advice, or the balancing of medical criteria. Further, the doctors' decision-making power is not, according to the terms of the Abortion Act, contained within a narrow, limited medical field. In judging whether or not abortion could be detrimental to the mental or physical health of the pregnant woman, under s. 1(2) of the Act, 'account may be taken of the pregnant woman's actual or reasonably foreseeable environment'. The woman's whole lifestyle, her home, finances and relationships are opened up to the doctor's scrutiny, so that he may judge whether or not the patient is a deserving case for relief. The power given to doctors here far exceeds that which would accrue merely on the basis of a technical expertise.

In their 2007 Report, *Scientific Issues Relating to Abortion*, the House of Commons Science and Technology Committee was critical of the 'two doctors' requirement, suggesting that it served no useful purpose and delayed women's access to early abortions (it should be noted that the final Report represents a majority view, and a minority of the Committee publicly distanced themselves from its conclusions).

House of Commons Science and Technology Select Committee[27]

The Department of Health has ruled that both doctors are able to sign the HSA forms without seeing the patient, so long as they believe, in good faith, that the woman meets the legal grounds for abortion on the basis of the clinical notes. We have heard that the process of

---

[25] [1979] QB 276.
[26] *Beyond Control: Medical Power and Abortion Law* (Pluto: London, 1997).
[27] *Scientific Developments Relating to the Abortion Act 1967*, Twelfth Report of Session 2006–07.

certifying abortions has become, in the words of the Christian Medical Fellowship, a 'sham'. Dr Vincent Argent . . . claims to have witnessed HSA1 signing practices that include:

- Signing batches of forms before patients are even seen for consultation;
- Signing the forms with no knowledge of the particular patient and without reading the notes;
- Signing forms without seeing or examining the patients;
- Signing forms after the abortion has been performed;
- Faxing the forms to other locations for signature;
- Use of signature stamps without consultation with the doctor.

If requests for abortions are being 'rubber stamped' by doctors, either the requirement for two signatures does not play a meaningful role in abortion practice or the law is not being properly applied . . .

We were not presented with any good evidence that, at least in the first trimester, the requirement for two doctors' signatures serves to safeguard women or doctors in any meaningful way, or serves any other useful purpose. We are concerned that the requirement for two signatures may be causing delays in access to abortion services. If a goal of public policy is to encourage early as opposed to later abortion, we believe there is a strong case for removing the requirement for two doctors' signatures. We would like to see the requirement for two doctors' signatures removed.

In 2012, as we see later, concern about doctors' signing practices resurfaced, but instead of arguing that the two-doctors requirement should be removed, the then Secretary of State for Health, Andrew Lansley, ordered the Care Quality Commission to carry out inspections of all abortion providers and called for disciplinary action, and even criminal proceedings against doctors willing to sign forms without seeing the patient.

In the following sections we look at the four different grounds for abortion contained in section 1(1) in more detail.

(c) The 'social' ground

Abortion Act 1967 section 1

1(1)(a) that the pregnancy has not exceeded its twenty fourth week and that the continuation of the pregnancy would involve risk, greater than if the pregnancy were terminated, of injury to the physical or mental health of the pregnant woman or any existing children of her family;

(i) The time limit

Section 1(1)(a), often referred to as the 'social ground', is the only one with a time limit. As we saw earlier, following the 1990 amendments to the Abortion Act 1967 the Infant Life (Preservation) Act no longer applies, and so the other three grounds for abortion are—in theory at least—available until birth.

Obviously, the existence of a time limit means that it is important to know the moment at which a pregnancy begins. When calculating the length of a pregnancy that is being carried to term, the convention is to treat the first day of the pregnant woman's previous period as the relevant start date, even though conception would usually have occurred about two weeks later. The reason for this is that fertilization and implantation are processes that take place imperceptibly over several days. Fertilization may not begin until a few days after sexual intercourse, and will usually take several hours; implantation again takes several days and does not start until six or seven days after fertilization began. It is therefore impossible to detect the moment at which the fertilized egg attaches itself to the wall of the uterus, and the woman can be considered pregnant. Dating the pregnancy from the woman's previous period allows doctors to calculate the length of gestation with greater precision.

For the purposes of the Abortion Act, however, using this convenient fictional start date is more problematic. Insofar as section 1(1)(a) contains a defence to a criminal offence, any ambiguity must be construed in favour of the defendants: that is, the pregnant woman and her doctor. It would seem unfair to deny a woman an abortion when she was, as a matter of fact, 22 weeks pregnant, but the date of her previous period fell outside the 24-week limit. Rather, the better interpretation is that the pregnancy began when, according to medical judgement, implantation is likely to have occurred. This undoubtedly introduces a margin of uncertainty, but again, if a borderline case were to arise, the ambiguity would have to be construed in favour of the pregnant woman and her doctors.

In practice, 80 per cent of abortions take place during the first ten weeks of pregnancy, and 92 per cent take place within the first 12 weeks.[28] Only a tiny minority (2 per cent) take place after the nineteenth week of pregnancy, most of which are carried out as a result of the late detection of a serious fetal abnormality.[29] The introduction of a 24-week time limit for what is known as the 'social' ground has had almost no practical impact, especially since the Infant Life Preservation Act had already been interpreted as imposing a 24-week time limit upon abortion. It is, however, important to remember that women do not have the right to an abortion up to 24 weeks: rather, doctors are permitted to carry out terminations if they believe the grounds in the Act are satisfied. Not all obstetricians are, in practice, prepared to carry out abortions for 'social' reasons late into the second trimester. Medical discretion, therefore, may lead to an earlier time limit than that specified in the statute.

Advances in neonatal medicine, which have lowered the age at which premature babies are capable of survival, coupled with developments in visualization techniques, such as 4D ultrasound, which can now show fetal movements in extraordinary detail, have given rise to renewed interest in the time limits for abortion. In the next extract, D Kirklin discusses the role of medical imaging in the abortion debate.

D Kirklin[30]

The latest developments in fetal ultrasound technology, made public by a group called *Create*, and first introduced to the wider UK public by the *Evening Standard* . . . , have evoked a flood of responses from the public, pro-life and pro-choice campaigners, and politicians, re-igniting the debate about abortion in the UK and elsewhere. The focus of the *Evening Standard* articles, on the smiling, walking, and waving babies that the images purport to show, was echoed throughout the worldwide media coverage that followed. In July 2004, Sir David Steel, sponsor of the 1967 Abortion Act, publicly stated that the *Create* images led him to believe it was time to review the legal time limit for abortions. . . .

What interests me here is the powerful role that biomedical imaging, and the human artifice it involves, can play in influencing the nature, timing, and tone of this debate. The

---

[28] *Abortion Statistics 2014* (DH: London, 2015).   [29] Ibid.

[30] 'The role of medical imaging in the abortion debate' (2004) 30 Journal of Medical Ethics 426.

ultrasound technology involved is without doubt impressive. A computer is used to simulate the 3D appearance of the fetus in the womb by combining a series of 2D images and then filling in any gaps; the 4D images are generated by using the simulated 3D images to produce a rapidly changing sequence of images, an illusion of fetal movement is thereby created. . . . What is not immediately apparent when viewing the video clips is that these video clips are in fact video loops, with the same movement shown again and again. Thus the waving fetus is an illusion created by showing the movement of the fetus' arm, from left to right across its body, over and over again. The smiling fetus, who appears to coyly smile then relax its mouth before coyly smiling again, is also an illusion. We do indeed see the fetus draw back its lips but instead of seeing what happens next, the illusion of smiling is created by the loop presentation of the images.

John Wyatt argues that developments in neonatal medicine since 1967 have also affected attitudes towards late abortion.

John Wyatt[31]

Medical practice in modern perinatal centres can have a paradoxical element. In one part of the hospital a huge concentration of resources, human expertise, parental concern and professional dedication is devoted to ensuring the survival of babies born as early as twenty-three to twenty-four weeks. In an adjacent part of the hospital agonised discussions about the possibility of feticide in a much more mature fetus are taking place. Hospital staff may feel deeply uneasy about raising the option of feticide when a major abnormality is detected in the third trimester . . . Although late feticide is performed relatively rarely, the juxtaposition of this practice with neonatal intensive care units inevitably poses ethical conflicts for health professionals.

The development of neonatal intensive care is predicated on the belief that even tiny, immature and uniquely vulnerable babies deserve the very best care and that professionals have an ethical duty to act in each baby's own interests even at considerable cost to society. If there is no responsibility to consider fetal interests until delivery, then it must be explained why the moment of birth in itself leads to a transformation of our ethical responsibilities.

The 24-week time limit is generally assumed to be based upon when a fetus might be viable, but it is not necessarily self-evident that viability should determine the time limit for abortion. Viability is an inherently unstable boundary. It will, for example, depend upon the availability of sophisticated medical equipment. A baby born next door to a neonatal intensive care unit will be 'viable' at a much earlier stage than a baby delivered without medical assistance in a croft in the Outer Hebrides.

Furthermore, deciding that 23 or 24 weeks marks the point at which a baby is 'viable', and abortion thereby impermissible, assumes that we can accurately date the duration of a pregnancy, whereas most doctors would say that there is a margin of error of a week or more in their capacity to diagnose gestational age.

It is also important to be clear about what we mean by viability. Is a fetus viable if it is born alive but dies in the delivery room, or in the neonatal intensive care unit? Or should we only consider a fetus to be viable, as the BMA have suggested, at the point 'at which the

31 'Medical paternalism and the fetus' (2001) 27 Journal of Medical Ethics ii15–ii20.

premature infant has a reasonable chance of surviving, without a very serious or life-threatening abnormality'?[32]

Some countries, such as France, have chosen a lower cut-off point for the legality of abortion, and we should acknowledge that setting the limit at 12 weeks, 14 weeks, 20 weeks, or 24 weeks is essentially a political decision, rather than a biologically determined fact. Indeed, in the UK it is possible to terminate a fetus until birth where the pregnant woman's life is at risk, or where abortion would prevent grave permanent injury, or where the fetus is likely to be seriously disabled. In these cases, the fact that the fetus might be viable is outweighed by other factors, such as the need to protect the woman's life.

In the next extract, Sally Sheldon argues that reliance on viability as the cut-off point for lawful abortion might have negative consequences for women's access to abortion services.

Sally Sheldon[33]

The adoption of viability as the cut-off point for abortions was heralded as a victory for pro-choice campaigners, as it currently ensures an upper limit which is high in comparison to other Western abortion laws. However, the effect of the 1990 debates has been to entrench in the public—and parliamentary—consciousness that abortion is permissible prior to viability, but should be forbidden after this point. This is a notion which future campaigns may find hard to dislodge. . . . While the present state of medical science makes it impossible to sustain neo-natal life at much less than twenty-four weeks of gestational development for reasons of lung development, it is surely not inconceivable that this limit will be gradually pushed downwards. If this happens, pro-choice groups will face a particularly bitter struggle to try and separate out the legitimacy of abortion from the notion of viability . . .

The other worrying trend, highlighted during the [1990] debates . . . is the use of medical knowledges to support the construction of the fetus as a separate individual . . . During the 1990 parliamentary debates, the Society for the Protection of Unborn Children (SPUC) sent each MP a plastic replica of a foetus at twenty weeks of gestation. Although various MPs expressed their distaste at this strategy . . ., not one commented on what I would see as the most worrying aspect of this tactic: that the foetus is represented in total abstraction from the body of the woman that carried it . . . [T]he foetus is not and cannot exist without the body of the pregnant woman which actively nourishes and supports it. Its representation as a free-floating and separate entity embodies a fundamental deceit.

Of course, it is true that the UK's adoption of a viability-related cut-off point means that abortion for social reasons is lawful until later in pregnancy than in many other European countries. Some, including the BMA, have argued that the law should be changed to permit abortion 'on request' during the first 13 weeks, but that abortions after that date should continue to be subject to the 'two doctors' requirement. Others have argued that the time limit in section 1(1)(a) should simply be reduced. The current prime minister, David Cameron has said that he favours a modest reduction, to 22 weeks, while the Secretary of State for Health at the time of writing, Jeremy Hunt, favours 12 weeks. There are, however, no plans to introduce legislation to reduce the time limit and, as we see later, amendments to that effect failed in 2008.

Pro-choice campaigners have argued that it is important that abortion continues to be available in the second trimester. Once a woman has decided to terminate an unwanted

---

[32] *Abortion Time Limit: Briefing Paper* (BMA: London, 2008).
[33] 'The Law of Abortion and the Politics of Medicalisation' in Jo Bridgeman and Susan Millns (eds), *Law and Body Politics: Regulating the Female Body* (Dartmouth: Aldershot, 1995) 105–24.

pregnancy, she will want to do so as quickly as possible, but there may be good reasons why some women are not able to access abortion until after the first trimester. In Ingham et al's study into the reasons why women have abortions in the second trimester, they found a combination of 'women-related' reasons—such as not realizing one is pregnant or finding the decision difficult—and 'service-related' reasons, such as encountering delays in referral for termination.

Roger Ingham, Ellie Lee, Steve Clements, and Nicole Stone[34]

A lack of early awareness of pregnancy is a significant factor in second-trimester abortions. Half of the respondents were more than seven and a half weeks' gestation when they first suspected they were pregnant, while one quarter were over 11 weeks 2 days' gestation. For women who were more than seven and a half week's gestation, the key factors for a delay in suspecting pregnancy included:

- irregular periods (49 percent)
- continuing periods (42 percent)
- they were using contraception (29 percent). . . .

Around half of the respondents took one week or less between taking their test and then making the decision to have an abortion. For those who took more than one week to make the decision, the most commonly cited reason (by 65 percent of respondents) was: 'I was not sure about having the abortion, and it took a while to make up my mind and ask for one.' Reasons for this indecision included:

- concerns about what was involved in having an abortion
- difficulties in agreeing a decision with their partner.

A relatively large proportion of the sample (60 percent) reported a delay between requesting an abortion and having the procedure. Forty-two percent of the respondents waited more than two weeks between requesting and having an abortion, and 23 percent waited more than three weeks—beyond the minimum standard recommended by the Royal College of Obstetricians and Gynaecologists (RCOG). Some of the reasons for delay at this stage were clearly service related, and included:

- the person I first asked for an abortion took a long time to sort out further appointments for me (30 percent)
- there were confusions about where I should go to have the abortion (24 percent).

Ironically, it is common for those campaigners who wish to lower the time limit for abortion also to argue that the abortion decision is a difficult one, for which women need counselling and time for reflection. If the time limit were to be lowered, those women who need time to reflect upon a difficult choice might feel pressured into making a decision quickly.

(ii) The risk to health

For an abortion to be lawful under section 1(1)(a), continuing the pregnancy must pose a risk, greater than if the pregnancy were terminated, of injury to the physical or mental health of the pregnant woman or her children. Under section 1(2) the doctor is specifically directed to take account of the woman's actual or reasonably foreseeable environment. In

---

[34] Centre for Sexual Health Research University of Southampton, *Second Trimester Abortions in England and Wales* (University of Southampton, 2007).

2014, 98 per cent of all abortions were authorized on the grounds that the pregnancy posed a risk to the pregnant woman's own health, and 99.93 per cent of these were authorized solely because of the risk to her mental health. One per cent were authorized because of a risk to her children's health.[35] Usually, of course, having another brother or sister does not pose a direct risk to a child's health. Rather, by overstretching the family's resources and diverting the mother's attention away from her existing children, the arrival of a new baby may have an adverse effect upon their health.

For two reasons, section 1(1)(a) is very easily satisfied. First, if the World Health Organization's definition of 'health', as 'a state of physical and mental wellbeing, not merely an absence of disease or infirmity' is used, the abortion only needs to be necessary in order to promote the woman's mental wellbeing, rather than to prevent her from suffering physical or psychiatric harm. The mental wellbeing of a woman who does not want to be pregnant is, almost by definition, promoted by allowing her to end her pregnancy. Secondly, given that pregnancy and childbirth are almost always more risky than termination, an abortion will usually also pose less risk to the woman's physical wellbeing than carrying the pregnancy to term.

(d) Prevent grave permanent injury

Abortion Act 1967 section 1

> 1(1)(b) that the termination is necessary to prevent grave permanent injury to the physical or mental health of the pregnant woman.

An abortion may be lawful under section 1(1)(b) if it is necessary to prevent grave permanent injury to the pregnant woman's physical or mental health, or to prevent a risk to her life. 'Grave permanent injury' is not defined in the statute, but there seems to be no doubt that this ground will only be satisfied if the woman's condition is extremely serious. It is very seldom used: in 2014, 146 abortions took place under this ground (0.07 per cent). In the House of Lords debates in 1990, Lord Mackay described this as 'a stiff legal test to cover special situations'. It is also worth noting that abortion is not necessarily lawful under this ground just because the pregnancy is exposing the pregnant woman to the risk of grave permanent injury. Instead, the abortion must be 'necessary' to prevent this injury materializing. If the injury could be prevented without aborting the fetus, then an abortion would not be justifiable under this section.

(e) Risk to the pregnant woman's life

Abortion Act 1967 section 1

> 1(1)(c) that the continuance of the pregnancy would involve risk to the life of the pregnant woman, greater than if the pregnancy were terminated.

Under section 1(1)(c), doctors must judge that continuing the pregnancy poses a greater risk to the pregnant woman's life than abortion. It is not necessary that abortion should remove the risk to the pregnant woman's life: rather, abortion merely has to reduce the risk. An

---

[35] *Abortion Statistics 2014* (DH: London, 2015).

abortion may not save a terminally ill woman's life, but it might nevertheless pose less risk to her than carrying a pregnancy to term and going through childbirth. Recall that in *R v Bourne* 'risk to life' was broadly interpreted to encompass situations in which the pregnancy would 'make the woman a physical or mental wreck'. For the purposes of section 1(1)(c), however, an elastic interpretation of 'risk to life' would not be appropriate because it would render this section synonymous with section 1(1)(a), and therefore redundant as a separate ground. In 2014, 118 abortions took place under this ground.[36]

(f) The fetal abnormality ground

Abortion Act 1967 section 1

> 1(1)(d) that there is a substantial risk that if the child were born it would suffer from physical or mental abnormalities as to be seriously handicapped.

Approximately 2 per cent of all abortions in England and Wales are carried out under section 1(1)(d), which permits abortion until birth where there is a substantial risk that the resulting child would be born seriously handicapped.[37] Access to abortion under this ground depends upon two doctors agreeing that a particular handicap is 'serious', and that the risk of it materializing is 'substantial'. Again, notice the doctors' wide discretion to decide whether a particular abnormality meets the threshold level of seriousness, and whether the risk of it materializing is substantial. This flexibility means that doctors might, for example, refuse to perform very late abortions unless the disability is so grave that the fetus would be likely to die shortly after birth.

In deciding whether a fetus's abnormality is sufficiently serious, the RCOG has recommended that doctors take into account the probability that effective treatment will be available; the probable degree of self-awareness and ability to communicate with others; the suffering that would be experienced; and the extent to which the person might be dependent upon others. There is no definitive list of conditions which justify abortion, or of conditions which do not, rather the test is whether the two doctors consider, in good faith, that the child would be seriously handicapped.

The question of what might count as a serious handicap was raised in an application for judicial review by Joanna Jepson in 2003, following her discovery that an abortion had been carried out on a fetus with a cleft palate after 24 weeks.[38] Her argument was that when parliament debated the 1990 amendments to the Abortion Act, which enabled abortion until birth for serious abnormalities, its intention had been that third-trimester abortions would be justifiable only for extremely serious conditions, and not for fairly minor abnormalities like cleft palate. West Mercia police launched an investigation following her complaint, but no prosecution was instigated. It was this failure to prosecute which prompted Joanna Jepson's legal action. In *Jepson v Chief Constable of West Mercia Police Constabulary*,[39] Jackson J initially granted her leave to apply for judicial review, on the grounds that the case raised an issue of public importance, but he admitted that she would face substantial evidential and legal hurdles at the full hearing. It is obviously difficult to establish some years later that the doctor had not acted in good faith, and nor is it clear that an

---

[36] Ibid.   [37] Ibid.
[38] *Jepson v Chief Constable of West Mercia Police Constabulary* [2003] EWHC 3318 (Admin).
[39] Ibid.

'interested bystander' would have standing to challenge a decision about a stranger's medical treatment.

West Mercia police then conceded that their initial investigation may not have been sufficiently thorough, and the case was reopened under a different team of officers, who referred it to the Crown Prosecution Service (CPS). In 2005, the CPS determined that the doctors who authorized the abortion had acted in good faith.

Chief Crown Prosecutor[40]

This complaint has been investigated most thoroughly by the police and the CPS has considered a great deal of evidence before reaching its decision. . . . I consider that both doctors concluded that there was a substantial risk of abnormalities that would amount to the child being seriously handicapped. The evidence shows that these two doctors did form this opinion and formed it in good faith. In these circumstances I decided there was insufficient evidence for a realistic prospect of conviction and that there should be no charges against either of the doctors.

Under section 1(1)(d) there only needs to be a substantial *risk* of handicap, so an abortion could be justified under this section even if the fetus turns out not to suffer from any disability, provided that the doctor is of the opinion that there was a substantial risk that it might have done.

How might section 1(1)(d) apply to genetic tests which are increasingly able to predict future susceptibility to disease? Is a fetus, which has the gene that causes Huntington's disease (a degenerative adult-onset condition), at substantial risk of suffering from such abnormalities as to be seriously handicapped? If the child must be seriously handicapped from birth, many genetic diagnoses will not satisfy section 1(1)(d), and abortion would instead only be lawful within the first 24 weeks of pregnancy under section 1(1)(a). Where, as with Huntington's, possessing the abnormal gene will mean that, in adulthood, the child will develop an incurable degenerative disease, resulting in premature death, arguing that the child is at risk of 'serious handicap' would seem fairly straightforward. More difficult questions arise in relation to tests for genes that increase the susceptibility to adult-onset diseases, and we consider these questions in more detail in the context of preimplantation genetic diagnosis in Chapter 15.

For some commentators, the fetal abnormality ground is especially problematic. In the next extract, Simo Vehmas argues that once a woman has decided to have a baby, it is not legitimate for her to reject a particular fetus because it does not have the characteristics she requires.

Simo Vehmas[41]

When considering the parenting of a child with a cognitive impairment, people seem to forget the fact that *every* child is more or less a burden to her parents. Children without impairments may cause stress to their parents due to problems (e.g., drug and alcohol abuse and eating

---

[40] CPS Press Release, 'CPS decides not to prosecute doctors following complaint by Rev Joanna Jepson' (16 March 2005).

[41] 'Parental responsibility and the morality of selective abortion' (2002) 5 Ethical Theory and Moral Practice 463–84.

disorders) which children with cognitive impairments usually do not get involved in. Families of children with cognitive impairments do not necessarily experience any more difficulties than families with so-called normal children—their problems are just different . . .

Often . . . social and cultural factors contribute more to the well-being or ill-being of families than the child's impairment in itself. Families which receive support from their societies and communities are, despite a child's impairment, likely to cope better than families which are emotionally and financially on their own . . .

It is true that parents generally wish their future child to conform more or less to some culturally formed ideal. This means that parents characteristically prefer having a good-looking, healthy and intellectually average (or, preferably, above average) child instead of an ugly, sickly and intellectually subaverage child. But to perform parental tasks well, the parents' commitment to care for their child has to be unconditional, which means that the commitment holds even if the child turns out to be ugly, sickly and intellectually subaverage.

Sally Sheldon and Stephen Wilkinson criticize the fetal abnormality ground from a different perspective, arguing that it is difficult to find a defensible reason for treating abortion on the grounds of fetal abnormality differently from other sorts of abortion. They consider three possible justifications for maintaining section (1)(1)(d) as a separate ground: first, the interests of the child-to-be; secondly, allowing the pregnant woman to conceive a non-disabled child instead; and, thirdly, protecting the pregnant woman's interests. The only logical justification for allowing women to terminate pregnancies where the fetus is disabled is—they suggest—to protect the woman's own interests, in which case this ground for abortion is functionally indistinguishable from section (1)(1)(a).

Sally Sheldon and Stephen Wilkinson[42]

The 'Foetal Interests Argument' attempts to justify s.(1)(1)(d) by claiming that termination actually benefits the disabled foetus, by saving it from a life of suffering. It claims that termination in these circumstances can thus be thought of as a kind of foetal euthanasia. . . . The first [objection] is that it only applies to a very narrow range of cases. These are cases where the likely alternative to termination is a resultant child whose quality of life is not merely low, but negative: that is, she would, quite literally, be better off dead, or better off never having been born. Whilst we are happy to grant, for the sake of argument, that there are cases where any resultant child will have a negative quality of life (for example, a child suffering from Tay-Sachs disease) many actual foetal impairments are indisputably not like this. For in most cases, the resultant child will have a quality of life which, although arguably less good than it would have been without impairment, is still positive overall and therefore a 'life worth living'. . . .

The second argument for s.(1)(1)(d) is the 'Replacement Argument' . . . On this view, it is acceptable to 'trade off' the life of one foetus against that of another in a utilitarian way, their status being such that killing one solely in order to generate an increase in the general good is permissible. . . .

The first [objection] . . . is that it assumes something which cannot simply be assumed: that the woman in question will at least try to become pregnant again . . . A second . . . more serious objection [is that] if the fetuses in question really do have very low status,

[42] 'Termination of Pregnancy for Reason of Foetal Disability: Are There Grounds for a Special Exception in Law?' (2001) 9 Medical Law Review 85–109.

> such that they can be killed for purely utilitarian reasons, then it is not clear why *special* provisions covering disability are required. . . . We have a justification not for having a special exception for disabled fetuses but rather for a much more permissive policy across the board.

Even if section (1)(1)(a) more accurately describes the reason for aborting an abnormal fetus, a time limit is attached to it. Maintaining fetal abnormality as a separate ground might therefore be necessary in order to accommodate the tiny number of abortions carried out in the third trimester of pregnancy following the discovery of a grave fetal abnormality. For example, a condition such as anencephaly, in which the fetus is born without much of its brain and skull, is incompatible with life. A woman whose fetus is discovered to be anencephalic at, say, 24 weeks, might prefer to undergo a termination, rather than endure another three months of pregnancy and childbirth, in the knowledge that her baby will die during childbirth or very shortly afterwards.

If, however, the reason for retaining section 1(1)(d) as a separate ground is to permit post-24-week terminations for conditions which are either incompatible with life, or so grave that they would justify withholding or withdrawing life-prolonging treatment from a neonate, McGuinness suggests that it should be worded differently.

Sheelagh McGuinness[43]

> It would be illogical to refuse a termination for a condition that, if realised at birth, would justify a 'best interests' decision of non-treatment of a neonate . . . Where the best interests standard allows medical decisions that will end the life of neonate to be informed by parental values, the baby's condition must be severe. So, even if the law were applied using this standard of foetal interests, it would rule out as impermissible all abortions after 24 weeks, save in those few instances where the analogous threshold for non-treatment of a neonate is reached . . .
>
> If a foetus-centred approach is the justification for some abortions, it may be better to frame the wording of s.1(1)(d) as permitting abortion when the presence of a 'severe abnormality incompatible with any significant period of survival' or any quality of life is identified.

(3) Other Restrictions upon Access to Abortion

(a) Personnel

Section 1 of the Abortion Act specifies that abortion will only be lawful if it is carried out by a doctor. Terminations carried out by nurses or by the woman herself would therefore be unlawful. This restriction has particular significance for medical (as opposed to surgical) abortions. In an early medical abortion, the woman first takes a drug (mifepristone) that blocks the hormones that help a pregnancy to continue. Two days later, she returns to the clinic when misoprostol is given to dislodge the embryo from the lining of the uterus and trigger a miscarriage, which usually happens between four and six hours later. Medical abortions are increasingly common: in 2014, 51 per cent of all abortions were carried out in this way.[44]

---

[43] 'Law, Reproduction and Disability: Fatally "Handicapped"' (2013) 21 Medical Law Review 213–42.
[44] *Abortion Statistics 2014* (DH: London, 2015).

If the woman takes medication which causes her to miscarry, has she terminated her own pregnancy, and hence committed an offence under the Offences Against the Person Act 1861, to which the Abortion Act could not offer a defence? The question of whether a woman who takes an abortion pill, given to her by a doctor, might nevertheless be terminating her own pregnancy has never been considered by a court. Nurses' involvement in medical abortions has, however, been approved by a majority of the House of Lords in *Royal College of Nursing v Department of Health and Social Security*. Nurses, according to the majority, could actively participate in terminating pregnancies, provided that a registered medical practitioner is supervising the procedure.

Royal College of Nursing v Department of Health and Social Security[45]

Lord Diplock

What limitation . . . is imposed by the qualifying phrase: 'when a pregnancy is terminated by a registered medical practitioner'? In my opinion in the context of the Act, what it requires is that a registered medical practitioner, whom I will refer to as a doctor, should accept responsibility for all stages of the treatment for the termination of the pregnancy. The particular method to be used should be decided by the doctor in charge of the treatment for termination of the pregnancy, he should carry out any physical acts, forming part of the treatment, that in accordance with accepted medical practice are done only by qualified medical practitioners, and should give specific instructions as to the carrying out of such parts of the treatment as in accordance with accepted medical practice are carried out by nurses or other members of the hospital staff without medical qualifications. To each of them, the doctor, or his substitute, should be available to be consulted or called on for assistance from beginning to end of the treatment. In other words, the doctor need not do everything with his own hands; the requirements of the subsection are satisfied when the treatment for termination of a pregnancy is one prescribed by a registered medical practitioner carried out in accordance with his directions and of which a registered medical practitioner remains in charge throughout.

Women's own involvement in their medical terminations might be justified on similar grounds, provided that they are supervised by a medical practitioner, who retains responsibility for their care. As we saw earlier when we considered the case of Sarah Catt, a woman who takes an abortion pill which she has obtained herself from an online pharmacy is likely to be found to have terminated her own pregnancy, and might expect to receive a prison sentence.

(b) Conscientious objection

Under section 4 of the Act, medical staff have a right of conscientious objection to participation in the provision of abortion services, unless the abortion is necessary to prevent grave permanent injury to the physical or mental health of a pregnant woman, or to save her life.

---

[45] [1981] AC 800.

Abortion Act section 4

> 4(1) [N]o person shall be under any duty, whether by contract or by any statutory or other legal requirement, to participate in any treatment authorised by this Act to which he has a conscientious objection.

Section 4 not only protects doctors who believe abortion is always wrong, but could also be used by doctors who are willing to perform abortions in the early stages of pregnancy, but who 'conscientiously object' to later abortions.

While the right is not limited to doctors, it is limited to a right not to 'participate'. What does 'participation' mean? In *Janaway v Salford Health Authority*[46] the House of Lords rejected a medical receptionist's claim that she had been unlawfully dismissed for refusing to type a letter of referral for an abortion. Lord Keith held that participation 'in its ordinary and natural meaning referred to actually taking part in treatment administered in a hospital or other approved place in accordance with section 1(3), for the purpose of terminating a pregnancy'.

More recently in the Scottish case of *Doogan v Greater Glasgow and Clyde Health Board*, two Catholic midwives had initially failed to persuade the Court of Session that section 4(1) entitled them to refuse to supervise and support staff who were directly involved with the provision of abortion services.[47] The midwives appealed successfully to an Extra Division of the Inner House,[48] which gave the right to conscientious objection a surprisingly broad interpretation, on the grounds that a 'wide interpretation' was 'in keeping with the reason for the exemption'. In 2014, in *Doogan v Greater Glasgow and Clyde Health Board*, that decision was overturned unanimously by the Supreme Court.

Section 4, Lady Hale (with whom the other Lords Justices agreed) explained, is concerned with a conscientious objection to those acts which were made lawful by section 1, that is, to the termination of pregnancy itself, rather than to various administrative, managerial, and ancillary tasks associated with the provision of an abortion service.

Doogan v Greater Glasgow and Clyde Health Board[49]

Lady Hale

The more difficult question is what is meant by 'to participate in' the course of treatment in question. The employers accept that it could have a broad or a narrow meaning. On any view, it would not cover things done before the course of treatment began, such as making the booking before the first drug is administered. But a broad meaning might cover things done in connection with that treatment after it had begun, such as assigning staff to work with the patient, supervising and supporting such staff, and keeping a managerial eye on all the patients in the ward, including any undergoing a termination. A narrow meaning would restrict it to 'actually taking part', that is actually performing the tasks involved in the course of treatment.

In my view, the narrow meaning is more likely to have been in the contemplation of Parliament when the Act was passed. The focus of section 4 is on the acts made lawful by section 1. It is unlikely that, in enacting the conscience clause, Parliament had in mind the host of ancillary, administrative and managerial tasks that might be associated with those

---

[46] [1989] AC 537.   [47] [2012] CSOH 32.   [48] [2013] CSIH 36.   [49] [2014] UKSC 68.

acts. Parliament will not have had in mind the hospital managers who decide to offer an abortion service, the administrators who decide how best that service can be organised within the hospital (for example, by assigning some terminations to the Labour Ward, some to the Fetal Medicine Unit and some to the Gynaecology Ward), the caterers who provide the patients with food, and the cleaners who provide them with a safe and hygienic environment. Yet all may be said in some way to be facilitating the carrying out of the treatment involved. The managerial and supervisory tasks carried out by the Labour Ward Co-ordinators are closer to these roles than they are to the role of providing the treatment which brings about the termination of the pregnancy. 'Participate' in my view means taking part in a 'hands-on' capacity.

It seems clear that a doctor cannot claim that referring a pregnant woman to another doctor is 'participating' in her treatment. Certainly, in *Barr v Matthews* Alliott J suggested that 'once a termination of pregnancy is recognized as an option the doctor invoking the conscientious objection clause should refer the patient to a colleague at once'. The RCOG guidelines advise doctors with a conscientious objection to abortion that they should at the very least inform women of their right to see another doctor, but more usually should refer a woman themselves:[50]

Doctors who have a conscientious objection to abortion must tell women of their right to see another doctor. NHS GPs who have contracted to provide contraceptive services and who have a conscientious objection to the abortion must, where appropriate, refer women promptly to another doctor.[51]

Doctors are not legally obliged to publicize their conscientious objections to abortion, so a woman may not know that her GP is a conscientious objector. However, the General Medical Council's latest guidance on doctors' personal beliefs instructs doctors that they must tell women that they have a right to see another doctor, and that they should also take steps prospectively to inform their patients about their unwillingness to refer for abortion. If the woman cannot easily make her own arrangements to see another doctor, the doctor is under a duty to assist her.

General Medical Council[52]

21. Patients may ask you to perform, advise on, or refer them for a treatment or procedure which is not prohibited by law or statutory code of practice in the country where you work, but to which you have a conscientious objection. In such cases you must tell patients of their right to see another doctor with whom they can discuss their situation and ensure that they have sufficient information to exercise that right. In deciding whether the patient has sufficient information, you must explore with the patient what information they might already have, or need.

22. In the circumstances described in paragraph 21, if the patient cannot readily make their own arrangements to see another doctor you must ensure that arrangements are made,

---

[50] (2000) 52 BMLR 217.

[51] *The Care of Women Requesting Induced Abortion: Evidence-Based Clinical Guideline Number 7* (RCOG, 2011).

[52] *Personal Beliefs and Medical Practice* (GMC, 2008).

without delay, for another doctor to take over their care. You must not obstruct patients from accessing services or leave them with nowhere to turn. Whatever your personal beliefs may be about the procedure in question, you must be respectful of the patient's dignity and views.

23. You must be open with patients—both in person and in printed materials such as practice leaflets—about any treatments or procedures which you choose not to provide or arrange because of a conscientious objection, but which are not otherwise prohibited.

While a woman whose GP has a conscientious objection to abortion clearly has the right to seek another doctor's assistance, if she lives in a rural or remote part of the country, her need to find another doctor may delay her abortion.

Because conscientious objections to abortion are not formally recorded, it is impossible to tell exactly how many doctors do conscientiously object, though it has been estimated to be between 18 and 24 per cent.[53] Significantly, there seems to be some evidence—highlighted in the next two extracts—that conscientious objection is becoming more common among medical students, who are also less likely to specialize in obstetrics and gynaecology. This may have implications for abortion provision in the future.

R Gleeson et al[54]

One of the most striking results was that only half of all students thought they would sign paperwork and only 36% would perform an abortion in cases where the child was unwanted. . . . If there were a risk to the mother's health or life, 80% and 84% of students, respectively, would sign paperwork, and even most pro-life students would sign in these circumstances. Therefore, even though the students in our study would be willing to provide abortion services in these more extreme situations, their views might well prevent them from providing services in the vast majority of cases where abortion is requested.

Sophie LM Strickland[55]

The survey revealed that almost a third of students would not perform an abortion for a congenitally malformed fetus after 24 weeks, a quarter would not perform abortion for failed contraception before 24 weeks, and a fifth would not perform abortion on a minor who was the victim of rape. . . .

In light of increasing demand for abortions, these results may have implications for women's access to abortion services in the future. The Department of Health has issued statistics showing that, although there are an increasing number of abortions taking place in the UK, fewer doctors are willing to perform them. The Royal College of Obstetricians and Gynaecologists has issued a statement recognising the growing problem of its doctors refusing to train in abortion. . . . Furthermore, there are fewer students opting for a career in obstetrics and gynaecology, which could further complicate the problem. In 1995, it was the main career choice of 26 out of 545 UK graduates, in 1998 this was 16 out of 509, and by 2002 only six out of 487.

---

[53] *General Practitioners: Attitudes to Abortion* (Marie Stopes International, 1999).
[54] 'Medical students' attitudes towards abortion: a UK study' (2008) 34 Journal of Medical Ethics 783–7.
[55] 'Conscientious objection in medical students: a questionnaire survey' (2012) 38 Journal of Medical Ethics 22–5.

(c) Places

Under section 1(3) of the 1967 Act, except in an emergency, 'any treatment for the termination of pregnancy' must be carried out in an NHS hospital, or in a place approved for the purposes of the Act by the Secretary of State. As we saw earlier, two-thirds of NHS-funded terminations now take place in independent clinics, such as those run by charities like Marie Stopes and the British Pregnancy Advisory Service (BPAS). Regulations provide that special approval is necessary to perform an abortion after 20 weeks in an abortion clinic, and that pregnancies of 24 weeks or more can only be terminated in NHS hospitals.

Early medical abortions raise some obvious difficulties here. First, if taking both pills is 'treatment for the termination of pregnancy', then both must be taken in an NHS hospital or an approved place. There is no clinical reason why either drug should have to be taken in a hospital or specialist clinic. Could women therefore be prescribed mifepristone in their GPs' surgeries? Section 1(3A) of the 1967 Act was added in 1990 to allow the Secretary of State for Health to approve classes of places where the treatment consists 'primarily in the use of such medicines as may be specified'. In theory, then, it would be possible for all GPs' surgeries and family planning clinics to be approved for the purposes of medical abortion. This has not happened, however, and both drugs must be dispensed and taken in an NHS hospital or other approved place.

It would also, of course, be possible for women to take either drug at home. This would have particular advantages in the case of the second drug misoprostol, which is taken a few days after the first pill in order to ensure that the pregnancy has been terminated. Currently women must attend the specialist clinic or NHS hospital on two separate occasions. This will be especially inconvenient for women with young children or women who live a long way from their nearest clinic. Because in most cases it is the misoprostol which actually triggers the abortion, there is also the possibility that the woman might miscarry on her way home from the clinic.

In 2012, BPAS sought a declaration that it would be lawful to prescribe misoprostol when the woman attended the clinic to take the mifepristone, so that she could take the misoprostol home with her. This, they argued, would be more convenient for women, who could take the second pill at home, safe in the knowledge that they will be in the comfort of their own homes when the abortion actually occurs. According to BPAS, the pregnancy would still be 'terminated by a registered medical practitioner' where the registered medical practitioner prescribed an abortifacient drug with the intention of terminating a pregnancy. If prescribing the drug, rather than taking it, is the 'treatment for the termination of pregnancy', it would be possible for the drug to be prescribed in an approved place, and then taken at home. In *British Pregnancy Advisory Service (BPAS) v Secretary of State for Health*, their action failed. According to Supperstone J, the 'treatment', which had to take place in an approved place, was the taking of the drug, not its prescription.

British Pregnancy Advisory Service (BPAS) v Secretary of State for Health[56]

Supperstone J

The critical phrase in section 1(3) is 'any treatment for the termination of pregnancy'. 'Treatment' is not, in my view, properly restricted to the act of diagnosis and the prescription of drugs or medicine. If the drugs or tablets were prescribed by the registered medical

---

56 [2012] 1 WLR 580.

> practitioner and not taken by the woman, the opportunity for treatment would have been available but it would not have been taken . . .
>
> The interpretation put by the claimant on the words 'any treatment for the termination of pregnancy' requires it to submit that the pregnancy is terminated by a registered medical practitioner in section 1(1) when that person merely prescribes an abortifacient drug. However termination may or may not be the consequence of the prescription. A woman may decide not to proceed to take the drug.

The irony of Supperstone J's judgment is that a provision in the statute which was supposed to protect women's safety—by ensuring that surgical abortions could only be carried out in properly equipped and staffed premises—in fact, in the case of early medical abortions, could make them *less* safe. In 1967, it was eminently sensible to require a surgical procedure to take place in a specialized hospital or clinic. But requiring women to attend the clinic twice, and sending them home after the second drug is taken, increases the likelihood that they will experience a miscarriage while travelling or in a public place.

Indeed, it is noteworthy that in its latest evidence-based guideline on the treatment of women requesting abortion, the RCOG suggests that taking misoprostol at home is safe, and that it would be desirable for women to be given the choice about how and where to undergo abortion.

Royal College of Obstetricians and Gynaecologists[57]

> Several studies have confirmed that home use of misoprostol is safe, acceptable and effective up to 63 days of gestation and in many other countries it is the standard of care. In a Swedish study of women undergoing early medical abortion at home at up to 49 days of gestation, the home regimen was safe and 98% of women said they would use this method if they had a further abortion.
>
> . . . In a recent publication, 249 women who [had recently had abortions] in England and Wales were surveyed. One hundred and sixty-two women responded and, of these, 85% preferred being able to complete their abortion in a home rather than in a clinical setting. Ninety-six percent found the experience acceptable and 96% felt that they would have been able to obtain clinical help if required. . . . It is clear that women who are able to choose their method of abortion are more satisfied with the outcome than women denied a choice. Neither early medical abortion nor home administration of misoprostol suits all women. However, published data do not suggest any clinical reason why women should remain in hospital during their abortion, and demonstrate that it is safe for women to administer misoprostol at home.

A further difficulty presented by medical abortions is that, after the woman takes the mifepristone, she must wait between 36 and 48 hours (during which time she may miscarry) before returning to the clinic to take the misoprostol. For up to two days, then, the drug is acting to terminate her pregnancy and may in fact do so. If 'treatment for the termination of pregnancy' is occurring throughout this period, the woman would have to remain in hospital, which would make medical abortions much more inconvenient and expensive than they need to be. In practice, women are routinely sent home after

---

[57] *The Care of Women Requesting Induced Abortion: Evidence-Based Clinical Guideline Number 7* (RCOG, 2011).

being observed for a few hours, suggesting that, in law, the treatment is simply the taking of the pill.

(d) Emergencies

Abortion Act 1967 section 1

> 1(4) Subsection (3) of this section, and so much of subsection (1) as relates to the opinion of two registered medical practitioners, shall not apply to the termination of pregnancy by a registered medical practitioner in a case where he is of this opinion formed in good faith that the termination is immediately necessary to save the life or to prevent grave permanent injury to the physical or mental health of the pregnant woman.

Under this provision, emergency abortions do not have to be performed in an NHS hospital or other approved place, and may be carried out without a second doctor's opinion. A similarly worded provision in section 4 means that doctors cannot invoke the conscientious objection clause where the abortion is necessary to save the woman's life or prevent grave permanent injury.

(e) Reporting

All terminations must be notified to the Chief Medical Officer (CMO) of the relevant devolved nation within 14 days. In addition to notifying the CMO of the grounds on which the abortion has been authorized, and the length of gestation, the notification form also records information such as the woman's age and marital status, her place of usual residence, and the outcome of any previous pregnancies. This data allows detailed abortion statistics to be produced each year.

(4) Third Parties' Rights (Or Lack of Them)

(a) Men

As we have seen, authority over whether a pregnancy may lawfully be terminated rests with the two medical practitioners who, in good faith, must decide whether the woman's circumstances fit within one of the statutory grounds. Given that the Act treats the decision as a medical one, to be taken by two doctors, it is unsurprising that the pregnant woman's sexual partner has no right to obstruct medical discretion and prevent her from obtaining an abortion. In *Paton v Trustees of the British Pregnancy Advisory Service*, a husband sought an injunction to restrain the defendants from terminating his estranged wife's pregnancy. Sir George Baker P rejected his application.

Paton v Trustees of the British Pregnancy Advisory Service[58]

Sir George Baker P

[T]here can be no doubt, in my view, that in England and Wales the foetus has no right of action, no right at all, until birth. . . .

---

[58] [1979] QB 276.

The father's case must therefore depend upon a right which he has himself. . . . [T]his plaintiff must, in my opinion, bring his case, if he can, squarely within the framework of the fact that he is a husband . . . The two doctors have given a certificate. It is not and cannot be suggested that the certificate was given in other than good faith and it seems to me that there is the end of the matter in English law. The Abortion Act 1967 gives no right to a father to be consulted in respect of a termination of a pregnancy. True, it gives no right to the mother either, but obviously the mother is going to be right at the heart of the matter consulting with the doctors if they are to arrive at a decision in good faith . . . The husband, therefore, in my view, has no legal right enforceable in law or in equity to stop his wife having this abortion or to stop the doctors from carrying out the abortion. . . .

Today the only way [counsel for Mr Paton] can put the case is that the husband has a right to have a say in the destiny of the child he has conceived. The law of England gives him no such right; the Abortion Act 1967 contains no such provision. It follows, therefore, that in my opinion this claim for an injunction is completely misconceived and must be dismissed.

Mr Paton then took his case to the European Commission of Human Rights,[59] where his submission that he had standing to protect his 'unborn child's right to life' was again dismissed. The Commission also rejected his claim that his right to respect for his private and family life, guaranteed by Article 8 of the European Convention on Human Rights, had been violated. Instead, the Commission found that the pregnant woman's right to respect for her private life prevailed.

In *C v S (Foetus: Unmarried Father)*,[60] Robert Carver had applied for an injunction to restrain Oxfordshire Health Authority and his former girlfriend, who was between 18 and 21 weeks pregnant, from terminating her pregnancy, on the ground that the fetus was a 'child capable of being born alive' for the purposes of section 1(1) of the Infant Life (Preservation) Act 1929. His claim was rejected on the basis of evidence that this fetus was not capable of being born alive, so his right to be heard did not arise. If it had, Lord Donaldson MR said that the court would have had to give 'very considerable thought to the words of Sir George Baker P in *Paton v British Pregnancy Advisory Service Trustees*', when he said 'not only would it be a brave and bold judge … who would seek to interfere with the discretion of doctors acting under the Abortion Act 1967, but I think he would really be a foolish judge who would try to do any such thing'.

It would be possible for the woman's sexual partner to notify the police if he believed that there had not been compliance with the Abortion Act 1967. However, because the statute gives doctors very broad discretion to determine the legality of abortion, this strategy would be unlikely to succeed.

(b) Other interested parties

Aside from the putative father, other third parties might be interested in trying to prevent a woman from having an abortion, an obvious example being anti-abortion campaigners. Usually, such groups attempt to dissuade women from seeking terminations by distributing anti-abortion literature; providing 'counselling' services and—increasingly in recent years—protesting outside abortion clinics. On one occasion, however, an anti-abortion pressure group sought a court injunction in order to try to prevent an abortion from taking place. The case arose after an obstetrician, Professor Philip Bennett, had revealed in a press interview that a woman who was expecting twins had asked him to

[59] *Paton v United Kingdom* (1980) 3 EHRR 408.   [60] [1988] QB 135.

terminate one twin. On the assumption that the woman's request had been prompted by her straitened financial circumstances, the Society for the Protection of the Unborn Child (SPUC) approached the hospital, wishing to offer the pregnant woman a substantial sum of money to enable her to continue the pregnancy. The hospital refused to pass on their offer, and SPUC applied to the High Court, where they were initially granted an interlocutory injunction preventing the hospital from carrying out an abortion until after the full hearing, which was due to take place the following morning. Later that day, it was revealed that the abortion had already taken place, and SPUC's application for judicial review was withdrawn.

SPUC's claim had been that the hospital was under a duty to inform the pregnant woman about their offer of financial assistance, since this could be relevant when considering the woman's 'actual or reasonably foreseeable circumstances' under section 1(2) of the Abortion Act. This would be unlikely to have succeeded given the breadth of discretion doctors have in deciding whether the grounds are satisfied. As Sally Sheldon points out in the next extract, the Abortion Act's reliance on medical discretion has at times worked to protect the freedom of women seeking abortions.

Sally Sheldon[61]

If SPUC had succeeded in restraining this termination pending the giving of certain information to [the pregnant woman], it would have set a very dangerous precedent. The idea that it is the anti-choice groups who should dictate what information should be given to women considering abortion cannot fail to alarm. The spectre is raised of the kinds of measures deployed in the United States where, in some states, women have been subjected to dissuasive counselling or forced to watch anti-choice material before deciding on termination in the name of the right to make an informed choice. However, this spectre seems unlikely to haunt British women. In this country, the approach taken by the courts has been one of protecting a broad space for medical discretion and refusing to second-guess the decisions made within it.

(5) The Human Rights Act 1998

It would, of course, be possible to frame the abortion issue in terms of rights, and in the context of the Human Rights Act, to pit the woman's right to respect for her private and family life under Article 8 against any right to life which the fetus might have under Article 2. In *Vo v France*,[62] a case that did not involve abortion, but negligence which led to a fetus's death, the European Court of Human Rights (ECtHR) decided that, at the European level, there was no consensus on the moral status of the fetus. The only common ground was that the fetus was a member of the human race. Its capacity to become a person meant that it should be protected as a matter of human dignity, but did not make it a person with a right to life.

More recently, the Council of Europe has suggested that Member States' 'margin of appreciation' on the moral status of the fetus should not be sufficiently wide to permit some states to make abortion unlawful. Rather, while Member States have the right to restrict access to abortion beyond a 'reasonable gestational limit', they should ensure that all women have

---

[61] 'Multiple pregnancy and re(pro)ductive choice' (1997) 5 Feminist Legal Studies 99–106.
[62] (2005) 40 EHRR 12.

access to safe and legal abortion. A number of countries, including Northern Ireland, do not satisfy this requirement.

Council of Europe[63]

> 7. The Assembly invites the member states of the Council of Europe to:
> 7.1. decriminalise abortion within reasonable gestational limits, if they have not already done so;
> 7.2. guarantee women's effective exercise of their right of access to a safe and legal abortion;
> 7.3. allow women freedom of choice and offer the conditions for a free and enlightened choice without specifically promoting abortion;
> 7.4. lift restrictions which hinder, *de jure* or de facto, access to safe abortion, and, in particular, take the necessary steps to create the appropriate conditions for health, medical and psychological care and offer suitable financial cover.

A further human rights dimension to the abortion issue is the freedom of expression of those who are opposed to abortion. This was an issue in *Connolly v Director of Public Prosecutions*, in which the defendant, Mrs Connolly, had sent photographs of dead 21-week-old fetuses to pharmacists who stocked the morning-after pill. Dyson J held that Article 10 was engaged, but that interference was justifiable under Article 10(2), in order to protect the rights of others, namely the pharmacists' employees' right to be protected from offensive material.

Connolly v Director of Public Prosecutions[64]

Dyson J

The sending of the photographs was an exercise of the right to freedom of expression. It was not the mere sending of an offensive article: the article contained a message, namely that abortion involves the destruction of life and should be prohibited. Since it related to political issues, it was an expression of the kind that is regarded as particularly entitled to protection by art 10 . . .

In my judgment, the persons who worked in the three pharmacies which were targeted by Mrs Connolly had the right not to have sent to them material of the kind that she sent when it was her purpose, or one of her purposes, to cause distress or anxiety to the recipient. Just as members of the public have the right to be protected from such material (sent for such a purpose) in the privacy of their homes, so too, in general terms, do people in the workplace. But it must depend on the circumstances. The more offensive the material, the greater the likelihood that such persons have the right to be protected from receiving it. But the recipient may not be a person who needs such protection. Thus, for example, the position of a doctor who routinely performs abortions who receives photographs similar to those that were sent by Mrs Connolly in this case may well be materially different from that of employees in a pharmacy which happens to sell the 'morning after pill'. It seems to me that such a doctor would be less likely to find the photographs grossly offensive than the pharmacist's employees.

---

[63] Resolution 1607 (2008) on access to safe and legal abortion in Europe.
[64] [2007] EWHC 237 (Admin).

4 SPECIAL SITUATIONS

(a) PATIENTS WHO LACK CAPACITY

As we saw in Chapter 4, patients who lack capacity to consent to medical treatment can be given treatment that is in their best interests. It is therefore possible for minors or women who are mentally incapacitated to have their pregnancies terminated, if this is judged to be in their best interests.

(1) Adults

Unlike sterilization or organ donation, abortion is not a 'special case' for which court approval is always necessary.[65] In *D v An NHS Trust (Medical Treatment: Consent: Termination)*[66]—a pre-Mental Capacity Act case—Coleridge J explained why:

> I have no doubt that the carrying out of a termination in accordance with requirements of the Abortion Act 1967, in circumstances where an incapacitated patient's best interests require it, is a legitimate and proportionate interference with Article 8(1) rights carried out for the protection of health under Article 8(2). I also accept that proposed terminations of pregnancies in mentally incapacitated women are not uncommon. And I agree that it would be both impractical and unnecessary to require that in each case an application to the court be made for a declaration of lawfulness. In my view, where the issues of capacity and best interests are clear and beyond doubt, an application to the court is not necessary.

Coleridge J went on to consider some cases when court approval should be sought, and these are reproduced in the Social Care Institute for Excellence's *Good Practice Guidance on Accessing the Court of Protection*, which sets out when cases involving termination of pregnancy should be taken to the Court of Protection:

> This includes situations where:
>
> - there is a dispute about capacity
> - the patient may regain capacity during or shortly after pregnancy
> - the decision of the medical team is not unanimous
> - the patient, the potential father or the patient's close family disagree with the decision
> - the procedures under section 1 of the Abortion Act have not been followed or
> - there are other exceptional circumstances, for example the pregnancy is the patient's last chance to conceive.[67]

For cases that do not need to be taken to the Court of Protection, it will generally be up to the woman's doctor to determine that she lacks capacity and to decide whether abortion is in her best interests, bearing in mind the emphasis the Mental Capacity Act 2005

---

[65] Mental Capacity Act 2005 Code of Practice. This was also the case at common law, *Re SG (Adult Mental Patient: Abortion)* [1991] 2 FLR 329.

[66] [2004] 1 FLR 1110.

[67] *Good Practice Guidance on Accessing the Court of Protection* (SCIE, 2011).

places on the woman's own values, beliefs, and feelings. Of course, that is not the end of the matter and before the abortion can take place, two doctors must additionally certify that the woman's circumstances fit within one of the grounds in section 1(1) of the Abortion Act 1967.

(2) Children

As we saw in Chapter 5, 16- and 17-year-old girls' consent to medical treatment, which would clearly include abortion, is as valid as it would be if they were adults. Where a girl is under 16, but *Gillick*-competent (see Chapter 5), as in *R (on the application of Axon) v Secretary of State for Health*,[68] it is clear that she can give a valid consent to abortion, and that the termination can take place without her parents' consent or knowledge.

What about girls who are not yet *Gillick*-competent? Decisions about their medical treatment would normally be taken by their parents, subject to the possibility of being overridden by the courts if their decision is judged not to be in the child's best interests. It is, however, hard to imagine circumstances in which it could be in the best interests of a girl (or woman) who lacks capacity to terminate her pregnancy, or carry it to term against her wishes. Certainly this was the view of Sir James Munby P in *Re X (A Child) (Capacity to Consent to Termination)*, a case we considered in Chapter 5, involving a pregnant 13-year-old girl.

Re X (A Child) (Capacity to Consent to Termination)[69]

Sir James Munby P

I find it hard to conceive of any case where such a drastic form of order—such an immensely invasive procedure—could be appropriate in the case of a mother who does not want a termination, unless there was powerful evidence that allowing the pregnancy to continue would put the mother's life or long-term health at very grave risk. Conversely, it would be a very strong thing indeed, if the mother wants a termination, to require her to continue with an unwanted pregnancy...

A child or incapacitated adult may, in strict law, lack autonomy. But the court must surely attach very considerable weight indeed to the albeit qualified autonomy of a mother who in relation to a matter as personal, intimate and sensitive as pregnancy is expressing clear wishes and feelings, whichever way, as to whether or not she wants a termination.

(b) THE BOUNDARY BETWEEN CONTRACEPTION AND ABORTION

Post-coital contraception, such as the morning-after pill, works by preventing the implantation of a fertilized egg. If a woman is considered to be pregnant as soon as fertilization occurs, then preventing a fertilized egg from implanting would trigger an extremely early abortion, and this could be lawful only if the conditions set out in the Abortion Act were satisfied. Two doctors would have to certify that, in their opinion, one of the statutory grounds exists; the pill would have to be administered by a doctor,

---

[68] [2006] EWHC 37 (Admin).   [69] [2014] EWHC 1871 (Fam).

in an approved place, and the procedure would have to be reported to the CMO. Plainly this would make the use of post-coital contraception time-consuming, expensive, and inconvenient.

As we saw earlier, the Offences Against the Person Act 1861 defines abortion as 'procuring a miscarriage', so an offence would only be committed if the morning-after pill causes a woman to 'miscarry'. Miscarriage is the antonym of 'carriage', a word that seems to imply that the fertilized egg must have attached itself to the pregnant woman's body. The legislation itself is silent on the meaning of miscarriage, leading Glanville Williams to suggest that 'there is, therefore, nothing to prevent the courts interpreting the word "miscarriage" in a way that takes account of customary and approved birth control practices'.[70] In a written answer to parliament when the morning-after pill was first licensed for use in 1983, the Attorney General explained that the words in the 1861 statute should be presumed to have been used 'in their popular, ordinary or natural sense':

[I]t is clear that, used in its ordinary sense, the word 'miscarriage' is not apt to describe a failure to implant . . . Likewise, the phrase 'procure a miscarriage' cannot be construed to include the prevention of implantation.[71]

It seems to be settled medical opinion that pregnancy occurs when the fertilized egg implants in the woman's uterus (which will normally be around six or seven days after fertilization began), rather than when the sperm starts to fertilize the egg. Pregnancy tests reveal the presence of the hormone human chorionic gonadotropin (hCG), which is released only once implantation has begun. It is therefore impossible to tell whether or not an egg has been fertilized unless and until it implants itself. Approximately 75 per cent of all naturally fertilized eggs will be lost before the woman's next period, and it would be counterintuitive to describe these losses as miscarriages. Rather, until a pregnancy test reveals that a fertilized egg has attached itself to her uterus, we would not consider a woman to be pregnant.

Despite the widespread belief that post-coital contraception does not involve the termination of pregnancy, Regulations (mentioned in Chapter 10) which allowed the morning-after pill to be dispensed by pharmacists were challenged by SPUC on the grounds that the morning-after pill is an abortifacient. If they were right about this, these Regulations would involve women and pharmacists committing offences under the Offences Against the Person Act.

In *R (on the application of Smeaton) v Secretary of State for Health*, Munby J held that there were multiple reasons for dismissing SPUC's claim. First, because miscarriage is not defined in the 1861 Act, it should be used in its ordinary sense, which is the termination of an established pregnancy. Before implantation, there is no pregnancy, and there can therefore be no miscarriage. Secondly, because other contraceptives, such as the pill and intra-uterine devices (IUDs) may also work by inhibiting the implantation of a fertilized egg, if SPUC's arguments were to be accepted, every method of contraception, except the condom, could involve the commission of a criminal offence. This would mean that 34 per cent of all women between the ages of 16 and 49 (approximately 4.5 million women) might be guilty of criminal offences. Thirdly, complying with the conditions set out in the Abortion Act would be likely to delay the use of the morning-after pill. Because this would

---

[70] *Textbook on Criminal Law* (Stevens and Son: London, 1983) 294.
[71] Hansard Written Answers for 10 May 1983.

make it less effective, it would be likely to lead to an increase in the number of unwanted pregnancies and abortions.

R (on the application of Smeaton) v Secretary of State for Health[72]

Munby J

On the logic of its own case SPUC's challenge, and the allegations of serious criminality *inter alia* by the woman concerned, are not simply to the morning-after pill. They extend to *any* chemical or device which operates, or may operate, by impeding, discouraging or preventing the natural process at any time after fertilisation has started, alternatively has completed. They extend to *any* drug or device which may operate in that way, even if it may also operate in a way which impedes, discourages or prevents the process of fertilisation. The medical profession and female members of the public have for years been operating on the basis that the use, prescription and supply of such chemicals and devices is legal and involves no potential criminality. The pill has been available since the 1960s and the morning-after pill since the early 1980s....

If SPUC were to succeed in this challenge, the result would be, as I have said, that Levonelle could be prescribed only by doctors who had complied with the requirements of the Abortion Act 1967. This in turn would mean that:

- Levonelle would tend to be administered either not at all or at a later stage, when the expert evidence is that it is less effective and more likely to operate post-fertilisation.

- There would inevitably be an increase in the number of abortions as conventionally understood, a result which . . . SPUC would presumably not welcome.

[T]he correct approach can be set out in the form of four propositions:

  (i) the 1861 Act is an 'always speaking' Act;

  (ii) the word 'miscarriage' is an ordinary English word of flexible meaning which Parliament in 1861 chose to leave undefined;

  (iii) it should accordingly be interpreted as it would be *currently* understood;

  (iv) it should be interpreted in the light of the best current scientific and medical knowledge that is available to the court . . .

[T]here is in truth no substantial dispute as to the current meaning of the word 'miscarriage' . . . miscarriage is the termination of . . . a post-implantation pregnancy. Current medical— and, indeed, I would add, current lay and popular—understanding of what is meant by 'miscarriage' plainly excludes results brought about by IUDs, the pill, the mini-pill and the morning-after pill. . . .

Finally, it is not irrelevant to note that my decision accords with social realities. I am declaring licit—not criminal—that which has in fact been the daily practice of countless people in this country for many, many years.

There would in my judgment be something very seriously wrong, indeed grievously wrong with our system—by which I mean not just our legal system but the entire system by which our polity is governed—if a judge in 2002 were to be compelled by a statute 141 years old to hold that what thousands, hundreds of thousands, indeed millions, of ordinary honest, decent, law abiding citizens have been doing day in day out for so many years is and always has been criminal. I am glad to be spared so unattractive a duty . . .

---

[72] [2002] Crim LR 664.

Government's responsibility is to ensure the medical and pharmaceutical safety of products offered in the market place and the appropriate provision of suitable guidance and advice. Beyond that, as it seems to me, in this as in other areas of medical ethics, respect for the personal autonomy which our law has now come to recognise demands that the choice be left to the individual.

In the next extract, John Keown criticizes the *Smeaton* decision on two grounds. First, he disputes whether there is in fact a medical consensus as to when pregnancy begins, and when a 'miscarriage' could therefore be procured, and, secondly, he suggests that Munby J placed too much emphasis upon the social consequences of a finding that the morning-after pill is an abortifacient.

John Keown[73]

Tunkel advanced inter alia the telling argument that to hold that s 58 did not bite until implantation: 'would, in effect, give a sort of free-for-all moratorium of a week or more after intercourse during which every sort of abortionist could ply his craft with impunity . . .'

[T]o assert that 'carriage' requires implantation seems the merest invention. The judge cited not a single dictionary of English to ground his assertions about the popular meaning of the word or that there cannot be 'carriage' without 'attachment'. The dictionary meaning of 'carry' is simply 'To transport . . .' There is no requirement here of physical attachment . . .

There can surely be little doubt that . . . the 'great object' of s 58 was the protection of the unborn child from fertilisation. . . . Any suggestion that the legislature which enacted s 58 intended its prohibition on attempted abortion to apply only after implantation is unsustainable.

Early in his judgment Munby J correctly observed that the issue for his decision was whether the use of the MAP [morning-after pill] may constitute an offence under the 1861 Act. It was not whether the MAP was either morally right or socially desirable . . . In view of this it may be thought surprising that significant portions of the judgment in *Smeaton* were devoted to the social implications of the case and disclosed the judge's opinion that the social consequences of finding for the claimant would have been highly undesirable.

Even if it is clear that the morning-after pill does not engage the Offences Against the Person Act, newer types of contragestive contraceptives might do so. For example, there are new medicinal products which work during a wider window than the morning-after pill (which must be taken within 72 hours after sexual intercourse). A woman might take one of these drugs once during each menstrual cycle, or only if her period is late. Products like these might be more convenient for women, and could have considerable public health benefits, if they reduced unwanted pregnancy rates. They would, however, almost certainly be unlawful in the UK; if they were to act after implantation, they would amount to 'procuring a miscarriage' and both the person prescribing the medicine and the woman taking it would commit a criminal offence, unless the terms of the Abortion Act 1967 were satisfied.

In the next extract, Sally Sheldon is critical of the fact that the wording of a Victorian statute could prevent women in the twenty-first century from benefiting from new contragestive methods of birth control.

---

[73] '"Morning after" pills, "miscarriage" and muddle' (2005) 25 Legal Studies 296–319.

Sally Sheldon[74]

The regulatory cliff edge between 'contraception' and 'abortion' in English law results not from careful consideration but from historical accident. . . . That archaic legislation, which has remained largely unconsidered for one and a half centuries, is drafted so as to block the development and use of safe, effective forms of fertility control that operate so soon after intercourse provides a compelling argument for a fundamental review of, at least, this aspect of its operation. . . . The fact that life exists as a seamless continuum means that the attempt to identify markers that allow us to make moral and legal distinctions between different stages of biological development is a fraught enterprise, with any purported bright lines liable to be criticised as misplaced or arbitrary. . . . While such lines will be inevitably (and appropriately) subject to contestation, it is important to ensure that the process by which they are drawn is capable of robust defence: that they are grounded in careful consideration, informed by clear moral reasoning and a solid medical evidence base. The modest claim defended in this paper is that the current basis for distinguishing between contraception and abortion falls woefully short of meeting this test. Rather, it is determined by a statutory phrase that is a product of a world, which 'in matters sexual was almost unimaginably different from ours' having been passed by a Victorian Parliament within which women had no voice. This is an indefensible basis for the regulation of health services that matter so intimately to modern women.

(c) SELECTIVE REDUCTION

Fetal reduction, or the selective termination of one or more fetuses, is a more complex procedure than complete termination, made possible by advances in ultrasonography. Initially it was unclear how the Offences Against the Person Act 1861 and the Abortion Act 1967 would apply to a procedure in which one or more fetuses are destroyed, but the woman continues to be pregnant. This confusion was addressed by a further amendment to the Abortion Act, effected by the Human Fertilisation and Embryology Act 1990.

Abortion Act 1967 section 5

5(2) For the purposes of the law relating to abortion, anything done with intent to procure a woman's miscarriage (or, in the case of a woman carrying more than one foetus, her miscarriage of any foetus) is unlawfully done unless authorised by section 1 of this Act and, in the case of a woman carrying more than one foetus, anything done with intent to procure her miscarriage of any foetus is authorised by that section if—

(a) the ground for termination of the pregnancy specified in subsection (1)(d) of that section applies in relation to any foetus and the thing is done for the purpose of procuring the miscarriage of that foetus, or

(b) any of the other grounds for termination of the pregnancy specified in that section applies.

Section 5(2) specifies that the ordinary Abortion Act grounds apply equally to selective reduction. In 2014, there were 132 abortions which involved selective terminations: in 80

---

[74] 'The regulatory cliff edge between contraception and abortion: the legal and moral significance of implantation' (2015) Journal of Medical Ethics 762–5.

cases, two fetuses were reduced to one fetus; in 35 cases, three fetuses were reduced to two; and in 14 cases three fetuses were reduced to one. Eighty-three per cent of all selective terminations were justified under section (1)(d); that is, there was a substantial risk that if the child were born it would suffer from such physical or mental abnormalities as to be seriously handicapped.

(d) THE LIVING ABORTUS

The vast majority of abortions are performed when the fetus is not capable of surviving outside the pregnant woman's body. Hence, removing the fetus from the woman's uterus inevitably leads to its death. Although abortion and fetal destruction are normally indistinguishable, they are not necessarily so. If the fetus happens to be born alive after an abortion, it will have an existence separate from its mother, and she could not insist upon its destruction. Where the fetus might be viable, abortion normally involves killing the fetus first, while it is still inside the woman's body. In practice, a tiny number of abortions involve feticide, and in most of these, the fetus has an abnormality—like anencephaly—so serious that it would be likely to die shortly after birth. Performing feticide in such circumstances has not been especially controversial because the baby will in any event die during or very soon after birth.

More complicated ethical dilemmas will be raised if 'artificial wombs' are developed which enable babies to live outside their mothers' bodies much earlier in pregnancy. During the second half of the twentieth century, progress in neonatal medicine has reduced the age at which a fetus became viable. Babies have survived after as little as 22 weeks' gestation, but this is very unusual,[75] and the risk that the baby will die soon after birth or be seriously disabled is very high. One of the largest studies of extremely premature babies, EPICure 2, found that most of the 152 babies born alive at 22 weeks' gestation died in the delivery room. Only 19 babies born at 22 weeks were admitted to the neonatal intensive care unit, and most of them (16) died there.[76] Of the three children who survived long enough to leave hospital, only one survived without disability.[77] Importantly, EPICure 2 compared results from 1995 and 2006 and found that although there had been improvements in survival rates for babies born at 25 and 26 weeks, the prognosis for pre-24-week births remained extremely poor.

It is not clear whether there is some absolute limit to the age at which a premature baby is capable of surviving independently. Before about 21 weeks, the fetus's lungs are solid and breathing would be impossible. A fetus that could not breathe could only survive outside the pregnant woman's body if scientists were able to develop some sort of 'artificial womb' that could simulate the uterine environment until the baby became capable of independent life.

If this becomes possible, it will clearly raise some very complicated questions for abortion law. If a fetus at 12 weeks' gestation could be transferred to an artificial womb to continue its development, could we say that a woman has the right to the fetus's removal from her body, but not the right to its death? Artificial wombs might enable the partners of pregnant women both to respect their partner's decision not to continue with the pregnancy and to bring up the child, which will be gestated artificially.

---

[75] EPICure, available at www.epicure.ac.uk.

[76] Kate L Costeloe et al, 'Short term outcomes after extreme preterm birth in England: comparison of two birth cohorts in 1995 and 2006 (the EPICure studies)' (2012) 345 British Medical Journal 7976.

[77] Ibid.

Given that the conflict between fetal life and women's self-determination has proved so intractable, the prospect of artificial wombs might seem to offer an attractive solution. Because a woman could end her unwanted pregnancy without also ending the fetus's life, it might be possible simultaneously to protect both the woman's reproductive autonomy *and* fetal life.[78] By extending her famous 'violinist analogy', Judith Jarvis Thomson argues that there is no right to 'secure the death of the unborn child':

> I have argued that you are not morally required to spend nine months in bed, sustaining the life of that violinist; but to say this is by no means to say that if, when you unplug yourself, there is a miracle and he survives, you then have a right to turn round and slit his throat. You may detach yourself even if this costs him his life; you have no right to be guaranteed his death, by some other means, if unplugging yourself does not kill him.[79]

In practice, however, it is unlikely that ectogenesis (gestation outside the woman's body) would satisfy either pro-choice or anti-abortion advocates. According to Leslie Cannold's empirical research, those who are against abortion would also reject ectogenesis on the grounds that it represents an abdication of the woman's duty to gestate and raise every fetus she conceives.[80] Cannold also encountered opposition among women who are pro-choice, who pointed out that women want abortions not just to avoid pregnancy and childbirth, but because they do not want to be responsible for bringing an unwanted child into the world.[81] It is unwanted motherhood and its responsibilities which lie behind the overwhelming majority of abortion decisions.

In addition, carrying out a fetal extraction rather than a termination would impose an additional physical burden on the woman. Medical abortions would not be possible, and a woman would have to undergo a type of caesarean section in order to remove the living fetus from her body. This would be a more serious, risky, and expensive operation. In the next extract, I explore the implications ectogenesis might have for the meaning of viability.

Emily Jackson[82]

> Ectogenesis would reveal a degree of ambiguity in the meaning of viability. Does this represent the time at which a fetus is capable of having an existence separate from its mother, or a stage in fetal development? If it is the former, and a fetus could be removed to an artificial uterine environment at, say, twelve weeks, some might argue that this becomes the gestational period before which abortions are legitimate and after which they are not. More significantly, if a fetus can live independently of its 'mother' from the moment of fertilisation, viability in this sense ceases to represent a feasible cut-off point for abortions, unless they are unlawful throughout pregnancy. . . .
>
> If instead we define viability as a stage in fetal development when it can survive with minimal assistance, we would have to acknowledge that hardly any babies born very prematurely can survive with minimal assistance. Neonatal intensive care units, where premature babies will spend the first weeks of life, are full of extremely high-tech equipment. While viability as

---

[78] Peter Singer and Deane Wells, *The Reproduction Revolution: New Ways of Making Babies* (OUP: Oxford, 1984) 135.

[79] 'A defence of abortion' (1971) 1 Philosophy and Public Affairs 47.

[80] 'Women, ectogenesis and ethical theory' (1995) 12 Journal of Applied Philosophy 55–64.

[81] Ibid.   [82] 'Degendering Reproduction' (2008) 16 Medical Law Review 346–68.

independent existence would, with the advent of ectogenesis, mean that all fetuses were potentially viable, viability as unassisted survival would push the point of viability back to well over thirty weeks.[83]

5 ABORTION IN OTHER JURISDICTIONS

There is insufficient space to provide a detailed survey of abortion laws throughout the world. Instead, we briefly consider the law in Northern Ireland, Ireland, and the US. It is, however, worth noting that there is enormous cross-national variation in the regulation of abortion. Despite European harmonization across many legal issues, there is no consistency in the regulation of abortion in Europe. Moreover, within different countries, abortion laws have changed dramatically in order to reflect shifts in political and religious affiliations. For example, the liberal abortion regime that existed in Poland prior to the break-up of the Soviet bloc was replaced by a much more restrictive system, in part as a result of the power the Catholic Church acquired through its role in the anti-Soviet Solidarity movement.

In countries that prohibit or severely restrict access to abortion, women who can afford it travel abroad to terminate their unwanted pregnancies. Irish and Northern Irish women commonly travel to Scotland, England, and Wales, for example. If travelling for abortion is not possible, women resort to illegal and often unsafe abortions. All of the evidence suggests that the illegality of abortion poses a serious risk to women's health. In Brazil, for example, there is a ban on abortion in most circumstances, but between 500,000 and a million illegal and unsafe abortions take place each year, and approximately 200,000 women are hospitalized following complications after illegal abortion.

In their global review of abortion provision, Sedgh et al found that the abortion rate was, in fact, higher in countries with restrictive abortion laws than it was where the law was more liberal. Alarmingly, they also found that while the global abortion rate was dropping, it was increasing in low-income countries where abortion is more likely to be illegal. Worldwide, the proportion of all abortions that are unsafe is increasing, and according to Sedgh et al's survey, represented very nearly half of all terminations.

Gilda Sedgh et al[84]

An estimated 43.8 million abortions occurred in 2008, compared with 41.6 million in 2003. Since 2003, the number of abortions fell by 0.6 million in the developed world, but increased by 2.8 million in developing countries . . . Worldwide, 49% of abortions were unsafe in 2008, up from 44% in 1995. Nearly all (97%) abortions were unsafe in Africa in 2008 . . . Some 91% of abortions in Europe are safe. Practically all the unsafe abortions in Europe take place in eastern Europe, where 13% of abortions were unsafe in 2008. . . . In 2008, the abortion rate was lower in subregions where larger proportions of the female population lived under liberal laws than in subregions where restrictive abortion laws prevailed.

The UN Special Rapporteur for the right to health has argued that a failure to make safe abortion services available represents an interference with women's right to health, and has

---

[83] Hyun Jee Son, 'Artificial Wombs, Frozen Embryos and Abortion: Reconciling Viability's Doctrinal Ambiguity' (2005) 14 UCLA Women's Law Journal 213.

[84] 'Induced abortion: incidence and trends worldwide from 1995 to 2008' (2012) 379 The Lancet 625–32.

jeopardized the world's ability to meet the Millennium Development Goal of a reduction in maternal mortality.[85] Of course, it is also vitally important to facilitate access to contraception in order to reduce the number of women who currently risk their lives in order to terminate their unwanted pregnancies.

(a) NORTHERN IRELAND

The Abortion Act 1967 does not apply in Northern Ireland, and so there are no statutory defences to sections 58 and 59 of the Offences Against the Person Act 1861. *R v Bourne* applies, so a defence would exist if the pregnancy is endangering the pregnant woman's life. Thus individual doctors must decide, on a case-by-case basis, and with the potential threat of criminal prosecution, whether a woman's circumstances are such that continuing with the pregnancy would leave her a 'physical or mental wreck'.

Court rulings in Northern Ireland have confirmed that there are circumstances in which abortion will not be a criminal offence, but because there is no statutory defence, the parameters within which abortion could be lawful remain unclear.[86] The first case to consider the lawfulness of abortion in the abstract was *Re Family Planning Association of Northern Ireland*.[87] The Family Planning Association of Northern Ireland sought a declaration that the Minister for Health had acted unlawfully in failing to provide guidance on when abortion could be lawfully performed. Initially, Kerr J rejected their claim on the grounds that the medical profession was not unclear about the law, which was governed by the *Bourne* exception—restrictively interpreted—to the Offences Against the Person Act 1861. This was, however, overturned on appeal. The Court of Appeal held that the Department of Health, Social Services and Public Safety could not be compelled to issue guidelines on abortion, but suggested it would be prudent to do so.

In 2009, guidance was eventually published, but it was immediately challenged by SPUC on the grounds that it misrepresented the law. In *Society for the Protection of the Unborn Child (SPUC) v NI*,[88] Girvan LJ found that the guidance was misleading in relation to counselling and conscientious objection and should be withdrawn 'with a view to the Guidance being reconsidered by the Department taking account of the contents of the judgment'. Girvan LJ also took the opportunity to set out what the *Bourne* judgment meant for women in Northern Ireland:

> In summary, it is lawful to perform an operation in Northern Ireland for the termination of a pregnancy, where:
>
> - it is necessary to preserve the life of a woman; or
> - there is a risk of real serious adverse effect on her physical or mental health, which is either long term or permanent.
>
> In other circumstance, it would be unlawful to perform such an operation.

New draft guidance was issued in 2013, but it was never finalized.[89] Given the inevitable uncertainty over whether any risk to the mother's mental health is sufficiently grave to

---

[85] Ingrid Torjesen, 'Banning abortion and contraception infringes women's right to health, UN assembly hears' (2011) 343 British Medical Journal 7046.

[86] *Northern Health and Social Services Board v F & G* [1993] NILR 268; *Northern Health and Social Services Board v A* [1994] NIJB 1; *Western Health and Social Services Board v CMB*, 29 September 1995, unreported; *Down Lisburn Health and Social Services Board v CH & LAH*, 18 October 1995, unreported.

[87] [2003] NIQB 48.   [88] [2009] NIQB 92.

[89] *The Limited Circumstances for a Lawful Termination of Pregnancy in Northern Ireland: A Guidance Document for Health and Social Care Professionals on Law and Clinical Practice* (DHSSPS, 2013)

justify abortion in Northern Ireland, and the serious consequences for doctors who break the law, it is not surprising that abortion is largely unavailable in Northern Ireland. There is one private abortion clinic in Belfast, which offers early medical abortions in the first nine weeks of pregnancy within the terms of the law, that is, only to women who fit within the *Bourne* exception.

It is not uncommon for Northern Irish women who wish to terminate unwanted pregnancies to travel to England, Scotland, or Wales. Officially, 837 women did so in 2014,[90] though because this figure only includes women who gave a Northern Irish address to the abortion clinic, it is undoubtedly an underestimate.

In addition to being inconvenient, having to travel to the mainland will inevitably delay Northern Irish women's abortions. Northern Irish women are also not entitled to NHS abortions, which means that they will have to pay for a private abortion, in addition to covering the costs of travel. In *R (on the application of A (A Child)) v Secretary of State for Health*,[91] X and Y, a 15-year-old girl and her mother, applied unsuccessfully for judicial review of the English Secretary of State for Health's failure to exercise his power to require free abortion services to be provided to women from Northern Ireland on the same basis as they are to women in England. X had had to pay for a private abortion in England. The Court of Appeal held that it was not unlawful or irrational for the Secretary of State to limit access to free NHS services according to residency. As Elias LJ put it: 'It is not irrational to take the view that English taxpayers should not have to bear the cost of providing abortion services to women from Northern Ireland.' At the time of writing, X and Y have been granted permission to appeal to the Supreme Court.

In 2015, a mother in Northern Ireland was prosecuted for two counts of unlawfully procuring a miscarriage, after she had obtained mifepristone and misoprostol for her pregnant underage daughter. The trial is due to take place after this book goes to press. If found guilty, she could face up to five years in prison. In protest, dozens of women appeared outside police stations, claiming that the police should arrest them as well for buying abortion pills online, or drop the case.[92]

In 2013, Sarah Ewart and her family decided to speak publicly about her experience of terminating her pregnancy following a diagnosis of anencephaly. Sarah described the trauma of having to take herself away from the care of the doctors and midwife who knew her in order to have an abortion in England, away from all of her support networks.

Following media coverage of Sarah Ewart's case, in 2014, the Department of Justice in Northern Ireland sought the public's views on the possibility of decriminalizing abortion in two strictly limited circumstances: where the fetus was suffering from a 'lethal abnormality', and if the woman was pregnant as a result of 'sexual crime'.[93] Most of the responses received were against any change in the law.

Nevertheless, in 2015 the Northern Ireland Human Rights Commission applied for judicial review of Northern Ireland's failure to provide for the option of termination in cases of lethal fetal abnormality and sexual crime. In *The Northern Ireland Human Rights Commission's Application*, Horner J held that the prohibition of abortion in Northern Ireland was incompatible with Article 8 in two limited circumstances: fatal fetal abnormality (FFA) at any time, and pregnancies that had resulted from sexual crime, but only until the fetus is viable. The prohibition of abortion in cases of serious

---

[90] *Abortion Statistics 2014* (DH: London, 2015).   [91] [2015] EWCA Civ 771.

[92] Henry McDonald, 'Pro-choice campaigners to picket police stations in Northern Ireland', *The Guardian*, 15 July 2015.

[93] Department of Justice, *The Criminal Law on Abortion: Lethal Foetal Abnormality and Sexual Crime* (DoJNI, 2014).

malformation of the fetus (SMF) interfered with women's Article 8 rights, but that interference was proportionate. Horner J's judgment does not change the law; rather, it is for the Northern Ireland Assembly to decide how to respond to the declaration of incompatibility. At the time of writing, pro-life campaigners are considering an appeal.

The Northern Ireland Human Rights Commission's Application[94]

Horner J

There is evidence that such a provision, forcing these young women to travel to England and Wales, can have the consequence of imposing a crushing burden on those least able to bear it if they cannot obtain charitable assistance. The Court can understand that for those women without support whether from their family or from a charity, such criminal provisions requiring them to travel abroad to have an abortion will impose a heavy financial burden upon them. That burden will weigh heavier on those of limited means. The protection of morals, as I have observed, should not contemplate a restriction that penalises the impoverished but can be ignored by the wealthy. It is surely not controversial that requiring women to travel to England and Wales in these exceptional categories, that is those carrying FFAs and those pregnant as a result of sexual crime, will place heavy demands on them both emotionally and financially. ...

The doctors know when a foetus has an FFA. This is primarily a medical diagnosis not a legal judgment. In those circumstances the doctor can be reasonably certain that the foetus will be unable to live independently outside the womb. That knowledge has to be communicated to the mother. Even worse, the mother will know that the foetus can die at any time inside her and if left in situ, will ultimately poison her. There can be no doubt that the mother's inability to access an abortion in those circumstances constitutes a gross interference with her personal autonomy. As discussed, a normal foetus does not have an Article 2 right to life, although it does have some statutory protections. But in the case of an FFA, there is no life to protect. When the foetus leaves the womb, it cannot survive independently. It is doomed. There is nothing to weigh in the balance. There is no human life to protect. Furthermore, no evidence has been put before the court that a substantial section of Northern Ireland's community, never mind a majority, requires a mother to carry such a foetus to full term. Therefore, even on a light touch review, it can be said with a considerable degree of confidence that it is not proportionate to refuse to provide an exception to the criminal sanctions imposed by the impugned provisions in this particular case.

Sexual crime is the grossest intrusion on a woman's autonomy in the vilest of circumstances.... Further, there can be no doubt as I have observed that the current law places a disproportionate burden on the victim of sexual crime. She has to face all the dangers and problems, emotional or otherwise, of carrying a foetus for which she bears no moral responsibility but is merely a receptacle to carry the child of a rapist and/or a person who has committed incest, or both.... By imposing a blanket ban on abortion, reinforced with criminal sanctions, it effectively prevents any consideration of the interests of any woman whose personal autonomy in those circumstances has been so vilely and heinously invaded. A law so framed, can never be said to be proportionate.... When a foetus becomes capable of existing independently of the mother both in respect of abortion and child destruction, there is a counter-balance to the rights of the mother. There is something to weigh in the balance that is expressly recognised by statute....

[94] [2015] NIQB 96.

The position with SMFs is different.... [I]t has to be recognised that the criminalisation of abortion in the case of an SMF does interfere with a woman's autonomy. But, to be weighed in the balance, is the fact that the foetus has the potential to develop into a child though it will have to cope with a mental and/or physical disability. But that child will be able to enjoy life. Further, it is not possible to define what an SMF is....

The incompatibility is simple to identify and straightforward to correct as is demonstrated by the legislation in other jurisdictions. In the case of an FFA, a requirement can be imposed before any termination takes place, that two qualified medical consultants must agree that the foetus is incapable of an independent existence outside the mother. In respect of rape and/or incest, the right to abortion can be made dependent on a certificate from the police officer in charge of the investigation and/or the prosecutor that the pregnancy is a consequence of a sexual crime. The right to an abortion must be restricted to the period immediately before the foetus becomes capable of living independently outside the womb.

(b) IRELAND

Until 2013, the law relating to abortion in the Republic of Ireland consisted in the Offences Against the Person Act 1861, supplemented by Article 40.3.3 of the Irish Constitution, which provides that the 'unborn' and the pregnant woman have an equal right to life. Hence, unless the pregnant woman's life is in danger, the fetus's right to life must take priority. As in Northern Ireland, women from the Republic of Ireland commonly travel to English (or Welsh or Scottish) clinics in order to terminate their unwanted pregnancies and, in 2014, 3,735 women did so.[95]

The legality of travelling to England to avoid Irish abortion law was called into question in the case of *Attorney General v X*,[96] in which a 14-year-old girl had become pregnant after being raped by a school friend's father. The Irish Attorney General sought, and was initially granted, an injunction to restrain X from travelling abroad to England to obtain an abortion. This was overturned on appeal, when the Irish Supreme Court held that the risk to X's life from suicide outweighed the destruction of the unborn life; hence the abortion would, in fact, have been lawful in Ireland.

In *A, B and C v Ireland*,[97] three adult women claimed that, for different reasons, being forced to travel to terminate their pregnancies was incompatible with their human rights. A was a recovering alcoholic, whose children were in care. She felt unable to cope with having another child. B had been warned that she was at risk of an ectopic pregnancy. C was recovering from cancer and was concerned about the risk pregnancy would pose to her life and health.

The ECtHR found that the Article 8 rights of all three women were engaged. By a majority, it drew a distinction between the cases of A and B, and that of C. Because A's and B's reasons for seeking an abortion were to promote their health and wellbeing, termination would have been unlawful in Ireland, and, according to the ECtHR, Ireland could legitimately prohibit abortion in such circumstances. C, on the other hand, may have needed a termination in order to protect her right to life. This meant she had the right to access abortion in Ireland, and the fact that she had had to travel violated this right. Effectively, then, the ECtHR suggested that the Convention only gives women an enforceable right to a termination in the

---

[95] *Abortion Statistics 2014* (DH: London, 2015).   [96] [1992] 2 CMLR 277.
[97] Application no 25579/05 [2010] ECHR 2032.

narrowest of circumstances, and that, except for abortions necessary to save a woman's life, states' margin of appreciation is extremely broad.

As the minority judgments pointed out, there is a contradiction between the majority's recognition that 'the process of travelling abroad for an abortion was psychologically and physically arduous for the first and second applicants, additionally so for the first applicant given her impoverished circumstances', and its suggestion that the interference with their rights was not disproportionate because they had the 'right to lawfully travel abroad'. In the next extract, Elizabeth Wicks points out a further contradiction: it is an odd sort of protection of fetal life that is in part justified by women's right to travel a short distance to destroy it.

Elizabeth Wicks[98]

If the views of the Irish people, and the Irish state, are so profound and fundamental to the continuation of its democratic society, how can the right to travel abroad for an abortion be tolerated? If a foetal life is to be regarded as one worthy of the full protection of the right to life, why are Irish women entitled, by a constitutional provision, to take a short journey across the Irish sea to terminate their pregnancies? . . . Having already recognised the 'significant psychological burden' faced by the applicants in being required to leave their home country to seek medical treatment prohibited there, the Court should have been more reluctant to present that psychological burden as the very guarantee of respect for the women's private life.

Sheelagh McGuinness is also critical of the majority's decision, suggesting that, for women who cannot travel, Ireland's wide 'margin of appreciation' is especially problematic.

Sheelagh McGuinness[99]

The Court, through its questionable use of the margin of appreciation and by focusing on narrow examples of the views of the Irish population, has endorsed a system where those like A and B are forced to continue to travel in their thousands each year, under shrouds of secrecy and shame, to Britain and elsewhere to access safe and legal abortion. And of course such a system relies on the mobility of those women and presumes a cosmopolitanism that is undermined by the existence of ash clouds and national borders. In 2009 customs in Ireland 'seized 1,216 packs of illegal abortion drugs'. Concern has also been expressed about illegal abortions taking place within the State. These abortions are a necessity for those women for whom travel is not just difficult but impossible. If one such woman were to bring a case would the ECtHR accept that current legislation falls within the margin of appreciation? Travel in these circumstances would not merely be 'psychologically and physically arduous': it would not be an option. Would the Irish Government's 'choice' to deal with abortion through allowing the provision of information and travel when travel is not possible still fail to breach Article 8 rights?

[98] 'A, B, C v Ireland: Abortion Law under the European Convention on Human Rights' (2011) 11 Human Rights Law Review 556–66.

[99] 'A, B, and C leads to D (For Delegation!): A, B and C v Ireland [2010] ECHR 2032' (2011) 19 Medical Law Review 476–91.

Despite the fact that it had always been lawful to terminate a pregnancy when the woman's life is at risk, in 2012 Savita Halappanavar died in a hospital in Galway after being denied a termination of pregnancy on the grounds that the doctors could still detect a fetal heartbeat. Mrs Halappanavar was 17 weeks pregnant when she started to miscarry. She was admitted to hospital and was told that her baby would not survive. In extreme pain, Mrs Halappanavar begged for a termination of pregnancy, but was told that this was not allowed because Ireland was a Catholic country, and the fetus could not be removed until its heartbeat had stopped. This was done several days later and Mrs Halappanavar died from blood poisoning.

Public outcry following Mrs Halappanavar's death resulted in the Protection of Life During Pregnancy Act (PLDPA) 2013, which repealed sections 58 and 59 of the Offences Against the Person Act. Under sections 7, 8, and 9 of the PLDPA, termination will be lawful where there is a real and substantial risk of loss of the woman's life and where the specified number of doctors (which varies according to the nature of the risk) certify that 'in their reasonable opinion (being an opinion formed in good faith which has regard to the need to preserve unborn human life as far as practicable) that risk can only be averted by carrying out a termination'.

Three different types of risk to life are covered by the Act. If there is a risk of loss of life from physical illness in an emergency, a single physician's certification is sufficient, and he or she may also carry out the abortion. Where the risk to the pregnant woman's life is the result of her physical illness, two physicians, one an obstetrician and the other a specialist in her condition, must provide this certification. If the termination is necessary to prevent a risk of loss of life from suicide, three physicians must provide the certification: an obstetrician and two psychiatrists, one of whom with specialist expertise in treating women. At least one of them should consult the woman's GP with her consent.

Although the Act may have clarified the law, it is not without difficulties. Shortly after it came into force, Miss Y, a pregnant and suicidal teenage asylum seeker, reported to be pregnant as a result of rape, sought a termination under section 9 when she was about nine weeks pregnant. By the time the panel of three physicians considered her case, however, although they agreed that there was a risk to her life which could be averted only by terminating her pregnancy, the fetus had become viable and abortion was therefore judged to be impermissible. Visa issues meant that she could not travel to the UK. Having gone on hunger strike, she was given artificial nutrition and hydration and her baby was delivered by caesarean section at 25 or 26 weeks.

In the next extract, Mairead Enright and Fiona de Londras point out that the requirement that the risk to life must be substantial and real may itself result in delays in accessing abortion, and if the request is made relatively late, steps may then have to be taken to try to preserve the life of a potentially viable fetus.

Mairead Enright and Fiona de Londras[100]

The danger is that a woman whose condition is likely to worsen might be required to deteriorate to the point where her life is definitely at risk before anything can be done to end her pregnancy. When would Miss Y, in William Wall's words, be 'suicidal enough

---

[100] '"Empty without and empty within": the unworkability of the Eighth Amendment after Savita Halappanavar and Miss Y' (2014) Medico-Legal Journal of Ireland 85.

> to spare her'? . . . When is a risk of death sufficiently real and substantial to allow for an abortion? The vagueness of the legal test enunciated in *X* and then enshrined in the PLDPA fails to offer sufficient guidance to doctors in this context and, given the severe penalties for providing an abortion outside of these legal parameters, it is reasonable to suggest that doctors may take a risk-averse approach and delay terminations until it is, effectively, too late.
>
> [Another] issue is that of viability and the extent to which the doctor's obligation to preserve unborn human life as far as practicable means that measures may be taken to ensure a viable foetus has the opportunity to be born alive. In the Miss Y case, a baby was delivered after 25 weeks by Caesarean section, in circumstances in which it appears medics agreed Miss Y was entitled to a termination at 22 weeks under s.9 of the PLDPA. . . .
>
> All . . . of these problems are products of the constitutional balancing test that gives equal constitutional status to the foetus and the pregnant women regardless of how advanced a pregnancy might be, and regardless of the health of the foetus and the health of the woman, unless her life is in real and substantial danger.

(c) THE UNITED STATES

In *Roe v Wade*,[101] the US Supreme Court recognized for the first time that a woman's freedom to choose whether to bear a child was a constitutionally protected liberty, which the state could restrict only in order to promote a compelling state interest. The right to privacy, the Supreme Court held, 'is broad enough to encompass a woman's decision whether or not to terminate her pregnancy'. Prior to viability, the state did not have a compelling interest in fetal life, and hence restrictions on a woman's right to decide to terminate her pregnancy would be unconstitutional.

The decision in *Roe v Wade* has never been explicitly overturned, but its scope has been significantly narrowed over the years, both by subsequent decisions of the Supreme Court and by the passing of restrictive state legislation. In *Webster v Reproductive Health Services*,[102] the Supreme Court weakened the notion of a constitutionally protected right to abortion, holding that restrictions on this right would be unconstitutional only if they imposed an 'undue burden', and even then, they might be justified by important state interests.

Three years later, in *Planned Parenthood v Casey*,[103] the Supreme Court upheld all but one of the restrictions that a Pennsylvania statute had imposed upon women's access to abortion. A mandatory 24-hour waiting period and a parental consent requirement for minors were held to be constitutional; only the spousal notification requirement was rejected on the grounds that, given the proportion of women who may fear assault at the hands of their sexual partner, it did represent an 'undue burden' on women's right to choose abortion. The state, it was argued in *Casey*, had a 'profound interest in potential life', and was therefore entitled, throughout pregnancy, to:

> take measures to ensure that the woman's choice is informed, and measures designed to advance this interest will not be invalidated as long as their purpose is to persuade the woman to choose childbirth over abortion, provided that they do not impose an 'undue burden on the right'.

---

[101] 410 US 113 (1973).   [102] 492 US 490 (1989).   [103] 112 S Ct 2791 (1992).

More recently, in 25 US states women seeking abortion must be offered an ultrasound scan, so that they have an opportunity to 'see' the fetus they wish to abort,[104] the assumption being that this will prompt some women to change their minds. In three states—Louisiana, Texas, and Wisconsin—abortion providers must perform an ultrasound on every woman seeking an abortion and must show or describe the image to her.

In the following extract, Sylvia Law argues that by permitting states to place obstacles in the path of women choosing abortion, the Supreme Court in *Casey* effectively overturned *Roe v Wade*.

Sylvia A Law[105]

Many times over the past few months I have been puzzled when sophisticated people . . . ask me whether the Supreme Court will overrule *Roe v Wade*. This surprises me because, like Justices Blackmun and Scalia, I believe that the Supreme Court effectively overruled *Roe* in 1989. . . .

From a pro-choice point of view, one plausible assessment of the *Casey* decision is that it represents the worst of all possible worlds. The joint opinion affirmed a woman's 'fundamental constitutional right' to abortion, but simultaneously allowed the state to adopt measures that effectively curtail many women's exercise of the abortion right. This curtailment hits hardest those women who are most vulnerable, i.e. the poor, the unsophisticated, the young, and women who live in rural areas.

The twenty-four-hour waiting requirement sends a powerful message that is degrading, condescending, and paternalistic to all women. It assumes that women make rash decisions, and reinforces negative stereotypes about women. It imputes women's competence as moral and practical decision-makers. Just as seriously, the impact of the twenty-four-hour waiting requirement will be sharply differentiated on lines of class, age, sophistication, and geography. . . .

A compromise that says the rich and sophisticated can have abortions but the poor and naïve cannot should be rejected as hostile to our most fundamental commitments to equal treatment.

States have further sought to restrict access to abortion by banning certain abortion procedures, such as those used in abortions carried out later in pregnancy. While not a medical term, late abortions have been emotively described as 'partial birth' abortions.

In *Gonzales v Carhart*,[106] by a 5:4 majority, the Supreme Court decided that a state law which banned a certain type of abortion procedure, used late in pregnancy, called intact D&X, did not impose an 'undue burden' on women's access to abortion, and hence was constitutional. The majority opinion, written by Justice Kennedy, claimed that women would be protected by a rule which prevents them from consenting to a particular sort of abortion. The majority assumed that women who have abortions later regret their decisions, and that this regret was bound to be exacerbated when they realized how the abortion had been carried out:

While we find no reliable data to measure the phenomenon, it seems unexceptionable to conclude some women come to regret their choice to abort the infant life they once created and sustained. Severe depression and loss of esteem can follow.

---

[104] Guttmacher Institute, *State Policies in Brief: Requirements for Ultrasound* (Guttmacher Institute, 2015).
[105] 'Abortion Compromise: Inevitable and Impossible' (1992) 25 University of Illinois Law Review 921.
[106] 550 US 124 (2007).

Because intact D&X is, in Kennedy's words, 'gruesome', the majority thought it likely that many doctors would not tell their patients precisely what it involves. This would therefore compromise the woman's ability to give informed consent and, as a result, the state was justified in banning the procedure. In the next extract, Graham Gee explains why this reasoning is problematic.

Graham Gee[107]

What the Court seems to be suggesting is that the pregnant woman—if only she knew what D&X entailed—would refuse to consent, and would instead carry the pregnancy to term. There is, however, a poor fit between the problem that the Court identifies (ensuring informed choice) and the solution the Court approves (banning D&X). The solution to the problem of informed consent—*if* such a problem exists—would be to require physicians to inform women, accurately and adequately, about what is involved in the different abortion procedures and their attendant risks. Yet this is not the solution the Court approves. Instead, the Court approves a ban on a specific abortion procedure, D&X. It seems, then, that the Court purports to protect a woman from (what it takes to be) the problem of ensuring that her consent to D&X is informed by depriving her of the right to elect to undergo that procedure in the first place . . .

In short, the woman is cast as too weak to decide for herself whether to have an abortion, and so the State must decide for her. Under the Act, the State does so by deciding that D&X is a procedure that no (well-informed) woman would decide to undergo. The State reduces the woman's reproductive choice under the pretext of protecting her.

One of the most interesting features of the decision in *Gonzales* is the Supreme Court's endorsement of the anti-abortion movement's claims, considered in the next section, that abortion hurts women, both psychologically and physically.

Since 1973, there has been an exceptionally acrimonious battle in the US over the legitimacy of abortion. Unlike in Britain, a candidate's views on abortion are often a crucial electoral issue, and nominations to the Supreme Court have been decided on the basis of a judge's track record on abortion. A hard-core minority of anti-abortion campaigners has murdered doctors and set fire to clinics. Fear of reprisals for carrying out abortions has resulted in few doctors being willing to provide abortion services. In the next extract, Marlene Gerber Fried describes how abortion in the US may be legal but also substantially unavailable, particularly to poorer women, teenagers, and women living in rural areas.

Marlene Gerber Fried[108]

Public funding, an absolute necessity if all women are to have access to abortion rights, was lost in 1976, just three years after *Roe v Wade* . . .

Publicity surrounding the murders of doctors and clinic workers has made the public at large sharply aware of the extreme vulnerability of abortion providers. In fact, clinics and providers have been targets of violence since the early 1980s . . . These acts included death threats, stalking, attacks with chemicals, arson, bomb threats, invasions and blockades. While federal legislation such as the Freedom of Access to Clinic Entrances Act will certainly

[107] 'Regulating Abortion in the United States after *Gonzales v Carhart*' (2007) 70 Modern Law Review 979–92.
[108] 'Abortion in the United States—Legal but Inaccessible' in Rickie Solinger (ed), *Abortion Wars: A Half Century of Struggle, 1950–2000* (University of California Press: Berkeley, 1998) 208–26.

help, anti-abortionists are increasingly turning to harassment of individual doctors and their families, picketing their homes, following them, circulating 'Wanted' posters.

The provider shortage has only recently come to public attention, although it represents a major threat to abortion rights . . . While the overall numbers are themselves very disturbing, of even greater concern is the very uneven distribution of services. Nine out of ten abortion providers are now located in metropolitan areas . . . Ninety-four per cent of nonmetropolitan counties have no services. . . .

Anti-abortion activists aim also to cut off the supply of potential future providers. They have targeted medical students, generating understandable concerns about taking up practice in such a dangerous and marginalized field . . . Few medical students are being trained in abortion techniques, despite the fact that abortion is the most common obstetrics surgical procedure. Almost half of graduating obstetrics and gynecology residents have never performed a first-trimester abortion.

There have also been direct legislative interventions which are intended to close the majority of abortion clinics. In Texas, a law known as House Bill 2 (HB2), first required abortion providers to have admitting privileges with a local hospital and, secondly, required providers to 'comply with hospital-like "ambulatory surgical center" standards'. Given that most abortions do not involve any incisions, and can be safely provided in an office, these standards are clinically unnecessary. The first restriction more than halved the number of abortion providers, from 41 to 18, and the second restriction would leave only ten providers in Texas. Similar laws have been passed in Alabama, Kansas, Louisiana, Mississippi, Oklahoma, Tennessee, and Wisconsin.

Before it came into effect, the second restriction in HB2 was struck down by a federal judge who described it as a 'a brutally effective system of abortion regulation', which was intended 'to reduce the number of providers licensed to perform abortions, thus creating a substantial obstacle for a woman seeking to access an abortion'. His decision was overturned by the US Court of Appeals for the 5th Circuit, but the Supreme Court later blocked the law from coming into force, pending its decision on whether to hear a full challenge to HB2. Towards the end of 2015, it announced that it would hear *Whole Woman's Health v Cole* in 2016.

6 ABORTION AND WOMEN'S HEALTH

At the end of 2011, the Academy of Medical Royal Colleges published a systematic review of the evidence of the impact of abortion upon women's mental health, which had been carried out by the National Collaborating Centre for Mental Health at the Royal College of Psychiatrists.

Academy of Medical Royal Colleges[109]

Taking into account the broad range of studies and their limitations, the steering group concluded that, on the best evidence available:

- The rates of mental health problems for women with an unwanted pregnancy were the same whether they had an abortion or gave birth.

[109] *Induced Abortion and Mental Health: A Systematic Review of the Evidence* (AoMRC, 2011).

- An unwanted pregnancy was associated with an increased risk of mental health problems.

- The most reliable predictor of post-abortion mental health problems was having a history of mental health problems before the abortion.

- The factors associated with increased rates of mental health problems for women in the general population following birth and following abortion were similar.

- There were some additional factors associated with an increased risk of mental health problems specifically related to abortion, such as pressure from a partner to have an abortion and negative attitudes towards abortions in general and towards a woman's personal experience of the abortion.

The evidence therefore suggests that the most important predictor of emotional and mental wellbeing in women who have terminated unwanted pregnancies is their wellbeing before the abortion took place.[110] According to the latest RCOG evidence-based guideline, women who have previous mental health problems may experience further problems as a result of an unwanted pregnancy, whether they terminate it or continue it to term.

Royal College of Obstetricians and Gynaecologists[111]

5.13 Women with an unintended pregnancy should be informed that the evidence suggests that they are no more or less likely to suffer adverse psychological sequelae whether they have an abortion or continue with the pregnancy and have the baby.

5.14 Women with an unintended pregnancy and a past history of mental health problems should be advised that they may experience further problems whether they choose to have an abortion or to continue with the pregnancy.

Regardless of the evidence, the anti-abortion movement has vigorously maintained that abortion is bad for women's health. As Reva Siegel explains, this tactic is regarded as more likely to persuade a larger section of the population that access to abortion should be restricted.

Reva B Siegel[112]

Growing numbers of movement leaders came to appreciate that woman-focused antiabortion discourse might have strategic utility in persuading segments of the electorate the movement had heretofore been unable to reach: it might reassure those who hesitated to prohibit abortion because they were concerned about women's welfare that legal restrictions on abortion might instead be in women's interest. And so in the early 1990s, leaders of the antiabortion movement began to use PAS [post-abortion syndrome] for new purposes and for a new audience . . .

---

[110] NF Russo and KL Zierk, 'Abortion, childbearing, and women's well-being' (1992) 23 Professional Psychology 269–80.

[111] *The Care of Women Requesting Induced Abortion: Evidence-Based Clinical Guideline Number 7* (RCOG, 2011).

[112] 'Dignity and the Politics of Protection: Abortion Restrictions under *Casey/Carhart*' (2008) 117 Yale Law Journal 1694.

In Making Abortion Rare, [David] Reardon is quite clear that empirical research on the psychological consequences of abortion is a useful way of talking about the moral evil of abortion in terms that have authority for audiences not moved by direct appeals to divine authority . . . [O]f course to make this claim about women's interest persuasive, Reardon needed some explanation for the large numbers of women seeking abortions. . . . Reardon's response was to insist that women who have abortions do not in fact want them; they are coerced into the procedure or do not grasp its implications . . .

In Making Abortion Rare, Reardon urged antiabortion politicians to 'take back the terms "freedom of choice" and "reproductive freedom"' and 'emphasize the fact that we are the ones who are really defending the right of women to make an informed choice; we are the ones who are defending the freedom of women to reproduce without fear of being coerced into unwanted abortions'.

7 ABORTION LAW REFORM IN THE UK

It is often claimed that the medicalization of abortion in England, Wales, and Scotland has effectively depoliticized the issue. If the decision to terminate a pregnancy is taken by a woman's doctor, on the grounds that pregnancy poses a risk to health, it becomes very difficult to challenge both individual abortion decisions, and the rules governing access to abortion. Partly, this is because of the confidentiality that attaches to the doctor–patient relationship and partly because of the trust and confidence that most people have in the medical profession. In recent years, however, there has been increasing political and media interest in the question of access to abortion.

One of the first areas of concern has been the time limit in section 1(1)(d) of the Abortion Act. If babies can survive at 22 weeks, it has been suggested that permitting abortion for 'social' reasons up until 24 weeks is anomalous. The reality is that fewer than 1 per cent of all abortions take place between 20 and 24 weeks, and most of these would fit within the fetal abnormality ground, and so be unaffected by any reduction of the time limit in section 1(1)(a). Reducing the time limit would, in practice, have virtually no impact upon the number of abortions carried out each year in the UK.

It is also important to think about the reasons why women have late abortions. First, the results from prenatal tests, such as the 18–20 week anomaly scan, may not be available until around the twentieth week of pregnancy. Secondly, a woman's circumstances may have changed drastically since she became pregnant. Her partner may have left her, or died, and she may feel unable to bring his child into the world. Thirdly, a woman may not realize she is pregnant until relatively late in pregnancy. This may be because she is close to the menopause, very young, or leads a chaotic life, perhaps because of drug use, and does not recognize the symptoms of pregnancy; or it may be because she is using a form of contraceptive, such as the progesterone-only pill, which can result in her periods stopping altogether.

In 2008, several amendments to the Human Fertilisation and Embryology Act were tabled, both from those seeking to restrict access and those seeking to liberalize it. First, the House of Commons voted on a series of amendments designed to reduce the 24-week time limit. None succeeded, although the vote on changing the time limit to 22 weeks was much closer (304 against, 233 in favour) than the vote to reduce the time limit to 12 weeks (393 against, 71 in favour).

Secondly, a set of what might be described as pro-choice amendments were tabled. The need for two doctors' signatures; the prohibition of nurse-led treatment, and abortion's continued illegality in Northern Ireland were the subject of liberalizing amendments supported by, among others, the RCOG. For reasons which it is hard to understand, the government ensured that these amendments were effectively 'guillotined', and lack of parliamentary time meant that there was no chance of them being voted upon, let alone becoming law. Suspicions were raised that this was part of a 'deal' with Northern Irish MPs from the Democratic Unionist Party in return for their support on a narrowly won vote on the length of time terrorist suspects can be detained without charge. This suspicion was bolstered by the fact that, as Sheldon points out, these amendments were guillotined shortly before MPs took the longest Christmas break since records began, making the 'lack of time' explanation rather dubious.

Sally Sheldon[113]

[T]he fact that abortion decisions are serious, with potentially far-reaching implications is all the more reason for believing that it is pregnant women themselves who must make them. The women concerned are more likely to agonise over abortion decisions and they are better placed than doctors to be able to understand the implications of the decision for their own lives and the lives of those closest to them. . . .

Further, any perception of a need to convince the doctor of the merits of one's case is hardly conducive to the medical encounter functioning as an occasion where one can discuss frankly one's concerns, doubts and options. Finally, it should be noted that the majority of doctors agree that the legal right to make these decisions would best be taken from them and given to the women concerned . . .

Ann Furedi, Chief Executive of the UK's largest abortion service provider, reports that:

Ministers and officials at the Department of Health have repeatedly said to us that they see no need to change the law because it is possible to 'work around' its deficiencies. This is not good enough. The law as it stands undermines the delivery of safe, evidence-based abortion services.

If this is the real explanation . . . the Government is not concerned by the point of principle: that the regulatory framework established in the Abortion Act is grounded in tired, inaccurate and sexist stereotypes of female irrationality, selfishness and moral immaturity.

More recently, political interest in abortion has crystallized around two issues: sex selection and the pre-signing of forms. In 2012, undercover reporters from the *Daily Telegraph* had filmed abortion providers allegedly agreeing to carry out terminations on the grounds of fetal sex. The reaction from the then Secretary of State for Health, Andrew Lansley, and the Chief Medical Officer, Sally Davies, was to declare that such abortions are unlawful.

The Act does not specify that abortion on the grounds of fetal sex is unlawful, however. Under section 1(1)(a) a termination's legality depends solely upon two doctors, in good faith, deciding that the woman's health would be more at risk if she continued the pregnancy than it would if her pregnancy was terminated. If a woman's mental health would be at risk if she feared rejection by her family on the grounds of the sex of her new baby, termination would not necessarily be unlawful.

Nevertheless, it has frequently been restated by politicians and by the Department of Health that abortion on the grounds of fetal sex is unlawful. In 2014, for example, the Department of Health issued *Guidance in Relation to Requirements of the Abortion Act*,

---

[113] 'A missed opportunity to reform an outdated law' (2009) 4 Clinical Ethics 3–5.

in order 'to provide support for doctors by setting out how the law is interpreted by the Department of Health'. According to this guidance: 'Abortion on the grounds of gender alone is illegal. Gender is not itself a lawful ground under the Abortion Act.'[114]

In support of this conclusion, it is commonly said that because 'fetal sex' does not appear as one of the grounds for abortion in section 1(1) of the Abortion Act, abortion for this reason is therefore unlawful. But this is to misunderstand how the Abortion Act works. It does not contain a list of the legitimate reasons for abortion: rape, for example, does not appear as a ground for abortion in section 1(1), but this certainly does not mean that abortion on the grounds of rape is unlawful. Instead, the Act simply gives two doctors considerable discretion to determine whether a woman's health would be better served by termination or by carrying the pregnancy to term.

An attempt was made in 2015 to put the supposed illegality of sex-selective abortions beyond doubt through a backbench amendment to the Serious Crime Bill, which read: 'Nothing in section 1 of the Abortion Act 1967 is to be interpreted as allowing a pregnancy to be terminated on the grounds of the sex of the unborn child.' This was defeated following concerns that it might prevent women from terminating pregnancies where the fetus was suffering from a sex-linked disorder. Anxieties were also expressed about the use of the term 'unborn child' in legislation. Instead, an alternative amendment was passed which required research to be carried out into the incidence of sex-selective abortion in the UK.

The Department of Health published its report into abortion on the grounds of fetal sex in August 2015.[115] It investigated sex ratios at birth in the UK, according to the mothers' country of birth and her ethnic group. Out of 171 different countries of birth, and 13 ethnic groups, there was only one case—that of women born in Nepal, giving birth to their third child— where the sex ratio at birth was not within the normal range. Given how small this group is, the most likely explanation for this abnormal result was random variation. When a further statistical test was carried out, comparing the birth ratios for third born (or more) across all countries of birth, including Nepal, the result was instead normal. Although the Department of Health said that it would continue to monitor the issue, its conclusion was: 'we have found no substantiated concerns of gender abortions occurring in England, Wales and Scotland'.

Immediately following the *Daily Telegraph*'s allegations about sex-selective abortions, the Care Quality Commission (CQC) was ordered to cancel 600 planned inspections of hospitals and care homes, and instead carry out unannounced inspections at 300 abortion providers. The CQC apparently found evidence that abortion forms had been pre-signed, which once again the Secretary of State for Health declared was unlawful.

Of course, it is true that a pre-signed form may raise a suspicion that the doctor does not plan to evaluate the woman's case in order to judge whether her circumstances fit within the statutory grounds, but it does not prove that he will not do so. The Department of Health's own advice has been that the second doctor does not actually have to see the pregnant woman himself, so a doctor might plan to have a telephone consultation with her, before authorizing a pre-signed form to be used.

In 2014, the Department of Health issued new guidance which sets out Required Standard Operating Procedures for independent providers of abortion services,[116] according to which: 'DH considers pre-signing of forms (without subsequent consideration of any information relating to the woman) to be incompatible with the requirements of the Abortion Act.'

---

[114] (DH: London, 2014).

[115] DH, *Assessment of termination of pregnancy on grounds of the sex of the foetus: Response to Serious Crime Act 2015* (DH: London, 2015).

[116] *Procedures for the Approval of Independent Sector Places for the Termination of Pregnancy* (DH: London, 2014).

Taken together, a common theme in recent media and political interest in abortion provision seems to be to build suspicion about the legitimacy of abortion providers and their practices. In the next extract, Sheelagh McGuinness and Michael Thomson point out that the tendency for abortion services to be provided in the independent sector enables abortion providers to be kept at arm's length from the mainstream medical profession, thus making it easier to impugn their professional integrity.

Sheelagh McGuinness and Michael Thomson[117]

The independent sector has clear benefits; in particular, the women-focused ethos that organisations such as BPAS advocate. However, there are also some negative effects, specifically a reduction in the perceived legitimacy of abortion care when compared with general health services. Noting the situation in the US, Joffe states that 'heavy reliance on clinics has further isolated abortion from the dominant medical institutions'. Both the service and its providers are corralled on the periphery of proper medical practice. This allows medicine to provide abortion but to not fully engage with it . . . This corralling of abortion provision on the periphery of proper medical practice has also meant that abortion providers often lack the support of the medical establishment and the full support of the RCOG. This was graphically evidenced in 2012 with the RCOG silence in the face of the *Telegraph* stings on abortion clinics and providers. The RCOG was silent even as the integrity of providers (their members) was impugned, notwithstanding the central place that professional integrity has to the professional project. Their response can be contrasted with the vociferous response of BPAS when the practice of their clinicians was called into question.

8 CONCLUSION

Students studying abortion law for the first time are often surprised to learn both that women do not have the right to terminate their unwanted pregnancies, and that abortion is still, prima facie, a criminal offence. This surprise is understandable, given that, in practice, abortion is available upon request in England, Scotland, and Wales within at least the first 13 weeks of pregnancy, and perhaps up to about 16 weeks. Regardless of the letter of the law, the reality is that women do make their own abortion decisions, and that the medical profession will seldom interfere with their 'right' to do so.

Nevertheless, it is still peculiar for the regulation of what is now a straightforward and common medical procedure to consist in a set of defences to the criminal offence of terminating pregnancy. For women seeking abortion to have to persuade two doctors that their health is at risk if they continue their pregnancies is radically out of step with the principle of patient autonomy, which, as we have seen, now dominates medical law. Rather than making a decision that she is uniquely well placed to make for herself, about whether she wants to become a mother (again) at this time, or with this partner, the law suggests that abortion-seeking women should instead adopt the role of a supplicant, portraying themselves as mentally fragile and unable to cope. One-third of all women in the UK will have at least one abortion during their lives, and the vast majority regard the question of whether this is the right thing to do as a decision for them, generally in consultation

---

[117] 'Medicine and Abortion Law: Complicating the Reforming Profession' (2015) 23 Medical Law Review 177–99.

with their partners, rather than a choice which is best made by two registered medical practitioners.

In the next extract, Sally Sheldon suggests that a more modern approach to abortion law might, in fact, be no specific law at all.

Sally Sheldon[118]

If the same broad purposes that had guided the Abortion Act—permitting socially acceptable abortions to take place in conditions of safety—were today allowed to guide the drafting of modern legislation, there is little doubt that this would result in a very different regulatory framework. Indeed, given substantial popular support for the view that, at least before viability, abortion decisions should be left to the women who must live with their consequences, there is a strong argument that a new 'abortion law' might be no specific law at all. Rather, abortion services might simply be regulated by the same mass of general criminal, civil, administrative and disciplinary regulations that govern all medical practice.

FURTHER READING

BMA, *Abortion Time Limits: A Briefing Paper from the BMA* (BMA: London, 2005).

Enright, Mairead and de Londras, Fiona '"Empty without and empty within": the unworkability of the Eighth Amendment after Savita Halappanavar and Miss Y' (2014) Medico-Legal Journal of Ireland 85.

Gee, Graham, 'Regulating Abortion in the United States after *Gonzales v Carhart*' (2007) 70 Modern Law Review 979–99.

Kirklin, D, 'The role of medical imaging in the abortion debate' (2004) 30 Journal of Medical Ethics 426.

Lee, Ellie, *Abortion, Motherhood and Mental Health* (Aldine: New York, 2004).

McGuinness, Sheelagh, 'Law, Reproduction and Disability: Fatally "Handicapped"' (2013) 21 Medical Law Review 213–42.

McGuinness, Sheelagh and Thomson, Michael, 'Medicine and Abortion Law: Complicating the Reforming Profession' (2015) 23 Medical Law Review 177–99.

Sheldon, Sally, *Beyond Control: Medical Power and Abortion Law* (Pluto: London, 1997).

Sheldon, Sally, 'The regulatory cliff edge between contraception and abortion: the legal and moral significance of implantation' (2015) Journal of Medical Ethics 762–5.

Sheldon, Sally, 'British Abortion Law: Speaking from the Past to Govern the Future' (2016) 79 Modern Law Review 283–316.

Wicks, Elizabeth, '*A, B, C v Ireland*: Abortion Law under the European Convention on Human Rights' (2011) 11 Human Rights Law Review 556–66.

---

[118] 'British Abortion Law: Speaking from the Past to Govern the Future' (2016) 79 Modern Law Review 283–316.

LIABILITY FOR OCCURRENCES BEFORE BIRTH

CENTRAL ISSUES

1. Under English law, it is generally assumed that children cannot have an action for 'wrongful life', where their claim is that, but for the defendant's negligence, they would not have been born.

2. At common law, the fetus cannot be owed a duty of care, but a child's action for prenatal injuries was said to crystallize at birth when she 'inherited' her damaged body. The Congenital Disabilities (Civil Liability) Act 1976 adopts a similar approach. With the exception of injuries sustained in road traffic accidents, a mother cannot be held liable for injuring her child *in utero*.

3. Parents can bring an action for 'wrongful pregnancy', usually following negligent sterilization or negligent post-sterilization advice. Recovery of the costs directly associated with pregnancy is straightforward, but the question of whether parents should be entitled to damages to cover the child's maintenance costs is much more controversial.

4. The courts have held that the maintenance costs of a healthy child are unrecoverable, but that parents are entitled to recover for the additional costs associated with caring for a disabled child. In *Rees v Darlington Memorial Hospital NHS Trust*, a disabled mother of a healthy child was awarded a 'conventional sum' of £15,000, which was intended to acknowledge that there had been a wrongful interference with her reproductive autonomy.

1 INTRODUCTION

In this chapter, we consider the possibility of liability, either to the child herself or to her parents, for events that occur before birth.

If a child is born suffering from an abnormality, because her mother was deprived of the option of termination, the claim is referred to as a 'wrongful life' action, because the disabled child is claiming that if the defendant had not been negligent, her disabled life would have been avoided.

More straightforward are cases in which the child is injured because of something that happens before she is born. Before a child is conceived, it is possible that her parents' capacity to conceive a healthy baby might be impaired: exposure to toxic substances, for example, might damage sperm or egg cells. Negligence during IVF treatment might also result in the birth of a disabled child. And, of course, the child might have sustained injuries while *in utero*. In all these cases, the Congenital Disabilities (Civil Liability) Act 1976 creates a remedy for the child.

Turning to the parents, in an action for 'wrongful pregnancy', the claim is that the defendant's negligence during, or following sterilization, led the female partner to become pregnant with an unwanted child. In such cases, the mother might want to claim for the pain and discomfort of pregnancy and childbirth, and expenses such as maternity clothes. More difficult and controversial is the question of whether the parents should also be able to claim for the costs of the child's upbringing. A 'wrongful birth' action involves the claim that the child's birth (as opposed to her conception) was the result of the defendant's negligence, perhaps because negligent prenatal testing deprived the pregnant woman of the option of termination.

In the next extract, Harvey Teff explains why the terms 'wrongful birth' and 'wrongful life' are problematic.

Harvey Teff[1]

These labels are unfortunate not least in their bizarre, even macabre, overtones. One is not instinctively attracted to the cause of someone who appears to be impugning life itself. This aside, the terms are neither immediately intelligible nor readily distinguishable from each other. Though both signify claims for damages when negligent conduct has resulted in a child being born, they conceal a host of different legal and social implications, depending both on the circumstances leading up to the birth and on its consequences. Thus 'wrongful life', 'wrongful birth' and other expressions canvassed by courts and commentators are potentially a source of considerable confusion.

It might be preferable to refer to these actions as reproductive or prenatal torts. But these generic terms do not capture the differences between negligently causing the child's *injuries*, or her *conception*, or her *birth*.

2 ACTIONS BY THE CHILD

(a) 'WRONGFUL LIFE'

The essence of a wrongful life claim is that, but for the defendant's negligence, the child would not have been born and the damage she has suffered—that is, her wrongful life— would have been avoided. It is not claimed that the defendant's action caused the child's disability, but rather that her parents were negligently deprived of the choice not to give birth to this particular child.

---

[1] 'The Action for "Wrongful Life" in England and the United States' (1985) 34 International & Comparative Law Quarterly 423–41.

A wrongful life action might arise in several different ways. First, before conception, the child's parents might be negligently advised that they are not at risk of passing on a genetic disorder. Secondly, negligence in preimplantation genetic diagnosis (see Chapter 15) might result in an embryo, which is likely to be born disabled, being transferred to the woman's uterus. Thirdly, negligent prenatal testing could mean that the fetus's abnormality is not detected, and the pregnant woman is not given the option of termination.

The issue has arisen in only one English case—*McKay v Essex AHA*—in which the Court of Appeal rejected the possibility that life itself could be compensatable damage. Mrs McKay had come into contact with rubella when she was less than two months pregnant. She sought medical advice, but her blood samples were mislaid, and she was wrongly informed that she had not been affected by rubella, and that she need not consider a termination. Mary McKay was born seriously disabled as a result of rubella infection during pregnancy.

McKay v Essex AHA[2]

Ackner LJ

What then are her injuries, which the doctor's negligence has caused? The answer must be that there are none in any accepted sense. Her complaint is that she was allowed to be born at all, given the existence of her pre-natal injuries. How then are her damages to be assessed? Not by awarding compensation for her pain, suffering and loss of amenities attributable to the disabilities, since these were already in existence before the doctor was consulted. She cannot say that, but for his negligence, she would have been born without her disabilities. What the doctor is blamed for is causing or permitting her to be born at all. Thus, the compensation must be based on a comparison between the value of non-existence (the doctor's alleged negligence having deprived her of this) and the value of her existence in a disabled state.

But how can a court begin to evaluate non-existence, 'the undiscovered country from whose bourn no traveller returns?' No comparison is possible and therefore no damage can be established which a court could recognise.

The Court of Appeal gave several reasons for their 'firm conclusion that our law cannot recognize a claim for "wrongful life"'.[3] First, it would be contrary to public policy for a doctor to owe a child a duty of care to ensure that she does not exist, since this would undermine the sanctity of human life. Secondly, if such actions succeeded, doctors might be under a duty to try to persuade pregnant women to terminate their pregnancies. Thirdly, the law did not recognize being born as damage: life, however disabled, had to be better than the alternative. Fourthly, assessing the quantum of damages in such a case would be impossible. Tort damages are intended to put the claimant in the position she would have been in if the tort had not been committed. This could not be done because it would require the court to judge the relative value of existence and non-existence.

There are some tensions in this reasoning. On the one hand, the Court of Appeal was anxious to stress that being born could not constitute damage because the law always treats life as beneficial. But, on the other hand, all three judges claimed that it is impossible to compare existence and non-existence. Surely we can only reach the first conclusion if we

---

[2] [1982] QB 1166.   [3] Per Griffiths LJ.

have compared the two outcomes, and decided that life is generally better than 'non-life'?[4] It is also perhaps a little misleading to suggest, first, that the law is incapable of comparing existence and non-existence, and, secondly, that if such a comparison is made, existence must always be preferred. When decisions are taken about withholding and withdrawing life-prolonging treatment (see further Chapter 17), the courts have sometimes decided that prolonging life is not in the patient's best interests. For example, according to Taylor LJ in *Re J (A Minor) (Wardship: Medical Treatment)*:

> Despite the court's inability to compare a life afflicted by the most severe disability with death, the unknown, I am of the view that there must be extreme cases in which the court is entitled to say: The life which this treatment would prolong would be so cruel as to be intolerable.[5]

The Court of Appeal thought that assessing damages in *McKay* would not just be difficult, it would be impossible: if the tort had not occurred, the claimant would not have existed, and so to put her in this position, we would have to be able to put a value on non-existence.

It is, however, worth bearing in mind that on exactly the same facts, the courts would find themselves able to assess the damages payable to Mary McKay's mother for negligent antenatal care. In wrongful birth actions the courts are less troubled by the prospect of compensating a parent for the costs associated with bringing up a disabled child, who would not have been born 'but for' the defendant's negligence. Given that the costs associated with Mary McKay's disabilities would be compensatable if her mother was the claimant, is it a little artificial to say that it is impossible to assess exactly the same costs where the claimant is Mary herself? This point has been made forcefully by Tony Weir:

> To assert that one cannot owe a duty to a foetus to kill it is plausible enough, but the plausibility fades a bit when one has to admit that a duty to kill the foetus may well be owed to the mother: if a duty is owed to one of the affected parties, why not to the other?[6]

Usually, of course, the existence of the mother's claim makes this distinction irrelevant, since the child will benefit from damages paid to her mother. If the mother is dead, however, or the child has been adopted or taken into care, the child is unable to bring a claim in her own right.

In *Whitehead v Searle*,[7] the mother had committed suicide before her wrongful birth claim—for a negligent failure to diagnose prenatally her son's spina bifida—reached the courts. It was accepted by all parties that *McKay* meant it was impossible for the son to have an action in his own right for his 'wrongful life'. Because the claim was against the mother's lawyers for their delay, the Court of Appeal did not have to decide whether the father might be able to bring a wrongful birth claim. Laws LJ considered that such a claim would be 'beset by difficulties', while Rix LJ was rather more sympathetic:

> I do not think that the fact that the law does not, wholly understandably, give a child a claim for his own wrongful birth leads to the conclusion that it is not fair, just and reasonable to give

[4] Harvey Teff, 'The Action for "Wrongful Life" in England and the United States' (1985) 34 International & Comparative Law Quarterly 423–41.

[5] [1991] Fam 33.

[6] 'Wrongful Life—Nipped in the Bud' (1982) 41 Cambridge Law Journal 225, 227.

[7] [2007] EWHC 1060 (QB).

> proper consideration to whether a father's undertaking of the care of the child, in the absence of a deceased mother, should not, in part out of concern for the child himself, be made the occasion for a claim.

In the following extract, JK Mason argues that the phrase 'wrongful life' may have been partly to blame for judicial hostility to Mary McKay's action.

JK Mason[8]

> [I]t is difficult to decide where and when the phrase 'wrongful life' originated—if it ever did as such. . . . Whoever is responsible, he or she certainly did the later plaintiffs no service as the implication that 'life' can, of itself, be wrongful, or a type of harm, has always been something that the courts—and perhaps even the general public—have found hard to accept. What the infant plaintiff finds 'wrong' is not that he or she is alive, but, rather, that he or she is *alive and suffering* as a result of another's negligence.

Harvey Teff makes a similar point about the judges' use of language, arguing that framing the issue as one of 'wrongful life' may explain the court's brisk dismissal of a claim that might have been dealt with more sympathetically if it had been described differently.

Harvey Teff[9]

> It is scarcely surprising that the characterization of 'birth' and 'life' as 'wrongful' has often prompted judicial hostility, if not sheer incredulity. . . . The widespread condemnation of 'wrongful life' actions thus affords a striking example of symbolic affirmation. Yet in such actions the child is manifestly not decrying birth or life *as such*. Rather he is making an undeniably powerful appeal to our sense of justice. He is asserting that he has been subjected to some particular disabling condition, typically because of the negligent conduct of a professionally qualified defendant, whose potential liability for inflicting comparable injuries on a live person would be beyond dispute.

There are other countries where wrongful life actions have had more success, perhaps because the courts have concentrated on the fact that the claimant's disabled existence is attributable to the defendant's negligence, and have downplayed the existential problem that dominated the judgments in *McKay*, namely that the child's claim is that they should not have been born. In 2005, the Dutch Supreme Court awarded damages to both the parents and the child, after a midwife decided no further investigation was necessary when told that two members of the father's family suffered from a serious chromosomal abnormality.[10] Kelly Molenaar was born suffering from severe mental and physical disabilities. The Hoge Raad considered whether awarding damages would violate the principle of 'the dignity of human life', but decided that it would, in fact, support that dignity by enabling Kelly to lead a more bearable life.

---

8 *The Troubled Pregnancy: Legal Rights and Wrongs in Reproduction* (CUP: Cambridge, 2007) 189.
9 'The Action for "Wrongful Life" in England and the United States' (1985) 34 International & Comparative Law Quarterly 423–41.
10 *Leids Universitair Medisch Centrum v Kelly Molenaar*, no C03/206, RvdW 2005, 42 (18 March 2005).

A wrongful life action, brought following the failure to diagnose rubella during pregnancy, succeeded in France in 2000 in the controversial *Perruche* case,[11] discussed in the next extract, but legislation passed shortly afterwards (known as the *loi anti Perruche*) means that the case is now only of historical interest. In the *Perruche* decision, as Anne Morris and Severine Saintier explain, the Cour de Cassation was adamant that it was compensating Nicolas for his disabilities, and not for his birth.

Anne Morris and Severine Saintier[12]

To condemn the Court for compensating Nicolas [Perruche] for being born is, however, to misconstrue the basis of the decision. Sargos, adviser to the court, . . . insisted that it is *not* for being born that the child seeks compensation, but for his disabilities and their consequences. The *Cour de Cassation* accepted that argument: since the child exists, the issue is not his birth but his disabilities. Some have argued that to accept that disabilities constitute 'harm' places a negative value on the life of a disabled child and is contrary to the principle of human dignity. For Sargos, refusing to compensate the child is equally contrary to human dignity. Compensation gives him the means to protect his dignity, and enhances that dignity by giving him, personally, the right to claim. It would be worse to allow only the parents to claim because that defines the child purely as a loss (or burden) to them and denies him the right, as any other legal person, to claim compensation for his injury . . .

Leaving aside the metaphysical considerations, the problems in wrongful life claims are not that different from other cases. In many cases of physical injury compensation cannot put the victim in the position he was in prior to the damage, rather it aims to give the victim, as far as money can, a 'normal' life or at least to ameliorate the effects of the tort. Similarly, compensation in a wrongful life claim could be aimed at ameliorating the consequences of the tort (living an impaired life) and providing the child with an improved quality of life.

The child in a wrongful life action is not necessarily claiming that she would have been better off if she had never existed. Even if life itself is deemed to be a benefit, it is perfectly possible for that benefit to coexist with the costs that flow from being born disabled. As the California Supreme Court observed in *Curlender v Bio-Science Laboratories*[13]—a US case in which a child recovered damages after negligent prenatal testing failed to detect that she had Tay-Sachs disease—someone can be both benefited and harmed at the same time: 'The reality of the "wrongful life" concept is that such a plaintiff both *exists* and *suffers* due to the negligence of others.'

The English courts' rejection of wrongful life actions can also be contrasted with the acceptance of a child's action for prenatal injury, discussed in the next section. Although there is clearly an important factual difference between the two claims, it does not necessarily seem fair that children whose injuries result from negligent prenatal testing should have to bear all of the financial costs associated with their disabilities, whereas children who are injured *in utero* receive full compensation.

So far, we have assumed that the defendant in a wrongful life action will be a doctor who gave negligent advice about the likelihood that this child would be born disabled. But if it were to be accepted that a disabled child might be able to claim that her birth ought to have

---

[11] Cass Ass Plen 17.11.00 JCP G2000, II-10438, 2309.

[12] 'To Be or Not to Be: Is That the Question? Wrongful Life and Misconceptions' (2003) 11 Medical Law Review 167–93.

[13] 106 Cal App 3d 811 (1980).

been avoided, should children also be able to sue their parents for bringing them into the world in an impaired or less than ideal state? Could a child sue her mother for choosing not to undergo prenatal tests, for example, or for not having an abortion if an abnormality is detected?

Certainly, in *McKay* Stephenson LJ appeared to assume that actions against mothers for not aborting disabled fetuses would be the logical corollary of permitting children to bring 'wrongful life' actions against doctors. And the point was conceded by counsel for the plaintiffs who had 'accepted that if the duty of care to the foetus involved a duty on the doctor, albeit indirectly, to prevent its birth, the child would have a cause of action against its mother, who had unreasonably refused to have an abortion'.

With respect, this seems doubtful. As we see later, the Congenital Disabilities (Civil Liability) Act 1976, with one exception that is not relevant here, prevents children from suing their mothers for prenatal injuries. It therefore seems improbable that the courts would allow an action at common law against a mother who elected to bring up a disabled child, especially since the reality would usually be that she would be paying damages to herself.

(b) PRENATAL INJURY

At common law, a fetus is not a legal person, which means that it cannot be owed a duty of care. On the other hand, applying the 'neighbour' principle,[14] it is plainly foreseeable that negligent conduct might cause injuries to a fetus, and result in a child being born disabled. At common law, the courts' solution was to say that the child only suffers damage when she is born, and acquires legal personality. In *Burton v Islington Health Authority*[15] the duty of care was said to 'crystallize' at birth when the child acquires legal personhood, and inherits her damaged body.

Since 1976, recovery for injuries sustained before birth has been covered by statute. The Congenital Disabilities (Civil Liability) Act 1976 replaced any common law action for pre-natal injuries for all births from 22 July 1976. It was amended by the Consumer Protection Act 1987 so that it also applies to children whose injuries are caused by defective products (see further Chapter 10).

Congenital Disabilities (Civil Liability) Act 1976 sections 1 and 4

1(1) If a child is born disabled as the result of such an occurrence before its birth as is mentioned in subsection (2) below, and a person (other than the child's own mother) is under this section answerable to the child in respect of the occurrence, the child's disabilities are to be regarded as damage resulting from the wrongful act of that person and actionable accordingly at the suit of the child.

(2) An occurrence to which this section applies is one which—

(a) affected either parent of the child in his or her ability to have a normal, healthy child; or

(b) affected the mother during her pregnancy, or affected her or the child in the course of its birth, so that the child is born with disabilities which would not otherwise have been present.

---

[14] *Donoghue v Stevenson* [1932] AC 562.   [15] [1993] QB 204.

(3) Subject to the following subsections, a person (here referred to as 'the defendant') is answerable to the child if he was liable in tort to the parent or would, if sued in due time, have been so; and it is no answer that there could not have been such liability because the parent suffered no actionable injury, if there was a breach of legal duty which, accompanied by injury, would have given rise to the liability.

(4) In the case of an occurrence preceding the time of conception, the defendant is not answerable to the child if at that time either or both of the parents knew the risk of their child being born disabled (that is to say, the particular risk created by the occurrence); but should it be the child's father who is the defendant, this subsection does not apply if he knew of the risk and the mother did not . . .

(7) If in the child's action under this section it is shown that the parent affected shared the responsibility for the child being born disabled, the damages are to be reduced to such extent as the court thinks just and equitable having regard to the extent of the parent's responsibility.

4(3) Liability to a child under section 1 [1A] or 2 of this Act is to be regarded . . . as liability for personal injuries sustained by the child immediately after its birth.

Under section 4(3) the Act adopts the common law 'fiction' that the injuries are sustained immediately after birth, when the child becomes a legal person, and the duty of care 'crystallizes'. The Act also confirms the common law position that there can be no liability when a child is stillborn. Under section 1(1), the action only arises if the child is born, and 'born' is defined in section 4(2) as being 'born alive (the moment of a child's birth being when it first has a life separate from its mother)'.

Under section 1(2)(a) and (b) the Act applies both to pre-conception occurrences which affect either parent's ability to have a healthy child, and to injuries sustained during pregnancy and childbirth. Section 1(4) provides that there is no liability for pre-conception risks if the parent knew of the risk of the child being born disabled, although this does not apply if the father is the defendant and he knew of the risk but the mother did not. This scenario might arise if the child's father had a disease, such as syphilis, which might cause his child to be born disabled. If, in such circumstances, he knew of the risk of infection but did not inform the child's mother, the child could have an action against her father.

Under section 1(3) the duty owed to a child under the Act is a derivative one, and exists only when a duty is owed to one of the child's parents. The parent does not actually have to have suffered actionable damage him or herself, but the defendant must have been in breach of a duty of care owed to one of the child's parents. This has a number of consequences. First, where the child suffers injuries because of a decision taken by the pregnant woman, for example to refuse caesarean delivery, the child could have no claim under the Congenital Disabilities (Civil Liability) Act 1976. Any claim is contingent upon establishing that there was a breach of a duty owed to the mother, and a doctor who respects a patient's refusal of medical intervention is not in breach of her duty of care.

Secondly, the defences of *volenti non fit injuria* and contributory negligence apply.[16] If the parent's claim would have been defeated by the defence of *volenti*, then the child can have no action for her injuries. And if the child's injuries are partly attributable to the defendant's fault, and partly attributable to her parent's behaviour, then under section 1(7) any damages must be reduced according to the extent to which the parent is responsible for the child being born disabled.

[16] See further Chapter 3.

Thirdly, because the child's action arises through the duty owed to her parents, the problem of liability to second- or third-generation claimants is resolved. It is only possible to recover for prenatal injuries if the defendant owed a duty of care to the claimant's parent, and this would not be the case when the claimant's parent was *in utero* when the injuries that led to the claimant's disabilities occurred. (This was the case with the drug diethylstilbestrol, which damaged female fetuses' reproductive organs.)

Fourthly, it is worth noting that under section 1(2)(b), liability for prenatal injuries will exist only when the occurrence affected the mother during her pregnancy. Adrian Whitfield has suggested that 'affected' should be broadly defined, and that, provided the defendant owed a duty of care to the pregnant woman in relation to the act which injured the fetus, regardless of whether it actually 'affects' her, the child will have a cause of action.[17]

Finally, the Act confines liability to cases where the child is disabled as a result of an 'occurrence'. In *Multiple Claimants v Sanifo-Synthelabo*[18] the claimants had suffered injuries as a result of the epilepsy medication their mothers had taken during pregnancy. The court was asked to determine certain preliminary issues, one of which was whether there could have been an 'occurrence' for the purposes of the 1976 Act. The problem was, as Andrew Smith J pointed out, that the wording of the Act 'does not allow for the possibility that the occurrence was by way of an accumulation of the drug within the mother'. Expert evidence would be needed, he concluded, to determine whether the alleged 'transplacental spread' could properly be described as an 'occurrence'. Legal aid was withdrawn in this case before it reached the courtroom, and so this issue remains unresolved.

The 1976 Act was amended in 1990 by the Human Fertilisation and Embryology Act, which added section 1A and section 4(4)(A):

Congenital Disabilities (Civil Liability) Act 1976 sections 1A and 4

1A(1) In any case where—

(a) a child carried by a woman as the result of the placing in her of an embryo or of sperm and eggs or her artificial insemination is born disabled,

(b) the disability results from an act or omission in the course of the selection, or the keeping or use outside the body, of the embryo carried by her or of the gametes used to bring about the creation of the embryo, and

(c) a person is under this section answerable to the child in respect of the act or omission, the child's disabilities are to be regarded as damage resulting from the wrongful act of that person and actionable accordingly at the suit of the child. . . .

(3) The defendant is not under this section answerable to the child if at the time the embryo, or the sperm and eggs, are placed in the woman or the time of her insemination (as the case may be) either or both of the parents knew the risk of their child being born disabled (that is to say, the particular risk created by the act or omission).

4(4A) In any case where a child carried by a woman as the result of the placing in her of an embryo or of sperm and eggs or her artificial insemination is born disabled, any reference in section 1 of this Act to a parent includes a reference to a person who would be a parent but

[17] 'Actions Arising from Birth' in Andrew Grubb with Judith Laing (eds), *Principles of Medical Law*, 2nd edn (OUP: Oxford, 2004) 789–851.
[18] [2007] EWHC 1860 (QB).

for sections 27 to 29 of the Human Fertilisation and Embryology Act 1990 [this is so that a child will still have an action where it is the sperm or egg donor (who will not be the child's legal parent) whose capacity to conceive a healthy child was affected].

Section 1A extends liability under the Act to injuries suffered as a result of assisted conception treatments. If the parents knew of the risk that their child would be born disabled, there is no liability. An example might be if the parents are informed of an incident that may have damaged their stored embryos, but, perhaps because those embryos represent their last chance of having a genetically related child, they nevertheless chose to have potentially damaged embryos implanted.

The application of the 1976 Act to cases where the child is born disabled as a result of the negligent selection of embryos raises the question of whether this might amount to a 'wrongful life' claim. In these cases, the negligent selection did not cause the child's disabilities. Rather, the negligent selection caused this child to exist. The child's claim must therefore be that if the doctors had exercised proper care and skill, she would never have existed. It is not clear that parliament intended to create a statutory wrongful life action for children born following negligent embryo selection, and yet it appears to have done so. As yet, no cases have come before the courts.

(1) The Need for 'Harm'

In *A and B v A Health and Social Services Trust*, the white parents of A and B had undergone IVF treatment with donor sperm. They had requested sperm from a white donor, and they were reassured that only sperm from 'Caucasian' or white donors would be used. Imported sperm which was described as 'Caucasian (Cape-coloured)' was used. A and B were born with darker skin than their parents, and it was claimed that this had resulted in them being subject to hurtful comments and abuse. According to Gillen J, being born with a different skin colour to their parents could not amount to harm: the birth of a healthy baby is a blessing and their skin colour could not amount to damage.

A and B v A Health and Social Services Trust[19]

Gillen J

In a modern, civilised society the colour of their skin—no more than the colour of their eyes or their hair or their intelligence or their height—cannot and should not count as connoting some damage to them. To hold otherwise would not only be adverse to the self-esteem of the children themselves but anathema to the contemporary views of right thinking people . . . The presence of persons sufficiently misguided and cruel as to issue racist comments directed to these children is no basis for a conclusion that they are somehow damaged.

In the next extract, Sally Sheldon draws on an interview with the father of a child conceived with the same batch of donor sperm, to suggest that there is some tension between the widespread acceptance of racial matching when people are treated using donated gametes and Gillen J's view that there can be no liability for negligent matching.

[19] [2010] NIQB 108.

Sally Sheldon[20]

> He 'couldn't love his children more' and gives no indication that he cares about any difference in race/ethnicity or, indeed, that he attaches any personal significance to their appearance. What he cares about is the fact that his son looks different from him and that this calls into question his wife's fidelity and his own paternity. In sum, the clinic's mistake has undermined their ability to 'pass' as a family in the small, overwhelmingly white village in which they live. . . . [R]acial matching is so routinely practiced and readily accepted as supporting a legitimate parental expectation, it seems far from obvious that no harm is suffered when this expectation is negligently undermined.

(2) 'Maternal' Liability/Immunity

Under section 1(1) of the Congenital Disabilities (Civil Liability) Act 1976, liability is confined to people 'other than the child's own mother', so a child cannot bring an action against her mother for injuries sustained *in utero*. Allowing a child to sue her mother would, the Law Commission had argued, create additional stress within the family.[21] Mothers of disabled children are unlikely to have sufficient funds to pay compensation to their children. More significantly, since a mother is normally already responsible for her child's care, any damages she might be ordered to pay would in practice usually be paid to herself.

An exception is, however, created in section 2 if the child's injuries were caused by her mother's negligent driving.

Congenital Disabilities (Civil Liability) Act 1976 section 2

> 2 A woman driving a motor vehicle when she knows (or ought reasonably to know) herself to be pregnant is to be regarded as being under the same duty to take care for the safety of her unborn child as the law imposes on her with respect to the safety of other people; and if in consequence of her breach of that duty her child is born with disabilities which would not otherwise have been present, those disabilities are to be regarded as damage resulting from her wrongful act and actionable accordingly at the suit of the child.

The reason for this exception is compulsory road traffic insurance. Damages will be paid by the mother's insurance company, so both she and her child will benefit from her own liability.

Fathers are not exempt. The most common scenario in which a father might injure a developing fetus would be an assault on the mother, and the Law Commission concluded that there were no good policy reasons to exclude liability in such circumstances. A child will only be able to bring an action against her father under the 1976 Act if he had been in breach of a duty of care to her mother, and so it would be difficult to sue a father if the child's injury was caused by his exposure to toxic substances, like drugs.

In the next extract, Sally Sheldon comments on the historically specific and now rather outdated gender assumptions which underlie the distinction the Act draws

---

[20] 'Only Skin Deep? The Harm of Being Born a Different Colour to One's Parents' (2011) 19 Medical Law Review 657–68.

[21] *Report on Injuries to Unborn Children* (Law Com Report No 60, Cmnd 5709, 1974).

between mothers and fathers. Sheldon also notes an interesting difference between the UK, where, aside from road traffic accidents, mothers are exempt from liability for pre-natal harm, and the US, where women have been imprisoned for taking drugs during pregnancy.

Sally Sheldon[22]

In this conceptualization of risks, the dangers posed by male bodies tend to be seen as occupational and this serves to generalize responsibility. Where female occupational risks are envisaged, these are those which result from housework, such as the use of air freshener and wood polish. However, more often, the dangers posed by female bodies result from the frivolous recreational behaviour of individual women who amuse themselves by drinking gin, smoking, going on rides at fun fairs, or by doing those other unspecified 'extraordinary things that women do to themselves'. . . .

In the United States criminal cases, the defendant is typically a black 'welfare mom' on crack cocaine. The woman who seems to have informed the deliberations of the Law Commission seems to be a middle class housewife who, if she is to be criticized is guilty primarily of frivolity.

3 ACTIONS BY THE PARENTS

First, we consider actions when negligence led to the child's conception, usually because one of the parents had undergone a sterilization operation that, for some reason, failed to achieve sterility. While it is the child's conception which is caused by the defendant's negligence, as Mason has pointed out, there will only be a plausible cause of action if the conception results in a pregnancy, and so we refer to these as 'wrongful pregnancy' cases.[23] Secondly, we consider claims for wrongful birth.

(a) 'WRONGFUL PREGNANCY'

If a woman becomes pregnant following a negligently performed sterilization operation, or is given negligent advice about her or her partner's sterility, there are three possible outcomes. First, she might miscarry or the baby might be stillborn, in which case an action for her pain and suffering would be uncontroversial. Secondly, she could decide to terminate the pregnancy. Again, a claim for the costs of an abortion, and any associated pain and suffering or loss of income, would be straightforward.

The third possibility is that the woman carries the pregnancy to term and gives birth to a live baby. In this third scenario, if the patient can establish that the sterilization operation was negligently performed, or that she or her partner was given negligent pre- or post-operative advice, the claim will be for damages to compensate them for costs associated with giving birth to a child that they did not want.

---

[22] 'ReConceiving masculinity: imagining men's reproductive bodies in law' (1999) 26 Journal of Law and Society 129–49.

[23] *The Troubled Pregnancy: Legal Wrongs and Rights in Reproduction* (CUP: Cambridge, 2007).

(1) Can there be Recovery for Wrongful Pregnancy?

(a) Contract

If a sterilization operation is carried out privately, the patient will have a contract with the clinic or hospital in which he or she is treated. If the sterilization is unsuccessful, and the patient (or in the case of a vasectomy, his partner) subsequently becomes pregnant, an action in contract is possible. In practice, however, as we saw in Chapter 3, the courts will only imply into the contract a duty to exercise reasonable care in carrying out the sterilization, and in giving advice about sterility. There will certainly not be an implied warranty that sterility will be achieved. As a result, cases brought in contract law will generally be indistinguishable from the negligence actions we consider in the next section.

(b) Tort

As we saw in Chapter 3, there are several stages to an action in tort. The defendant must owe the claimant a duty of care; the duty must be breached; and the breach must cause foreseeable damage.

(i) The existence of a duty of care

A person who is sterilized is unquestionably owed a duty of care by the surgeon. Whether a duty is owed to the patient's partner is slightly more complicated. If a woman's sterilization goes wrong, her partner's loss will be purely economic. In such cases, it would be necessary to establish that there was a proximate relationship between him and the doctor who carried out his partner's sterilization. This will generally only be possible if he was within the doctor's contemplation at the time of the operation.

If it is the man's vasectomy that fails, his female partner might be said to suffer physical injury as well as financial losses. It is clear that the courts will not find that a doctor owes a duty to all future sexual partners of a man who has a vasectomy, but only to women who are within the doctor's contemplation when the operation is carried out.

In *Goodwill v British Pregnancy Advisory Service*, Mr MacKinlay had had a vasectomy, arranged by the defendants, four years before he began having a sexual relationship with Mrs Goodwill. Although initially successful, the vasectomy had spontaneously reversed itself. Mrs Goodwill became pregnant, and sued the defendants for loss of income, and for the costs of bringing up her daughter. She argued that the defendants had owed her a duty of care to give Mr MacKinlay proper advice about the permanency of sterility. The Court of Appeal struck out her claim.

Goodwill v British Pregnancy Advisory Service[24]

Peter Gibson LJ

I cannot see that it can properly be said of the defendants that they voluntarily assumed responsibility to the plaintiff when giving advice to Mr MacKinlay. At that time they had no knowledge of her, she was not an existing sexual partner of Mr MacKinlay but was merely, like any other woman in the world, a potential future sexual partner of his, that is to say a member of an indeterminately large class of females who might have sexual relations with

[24] [1996] 1 WLR 1397.

Mr MacKinlay during his lifetime. I find it impossible to believe that the policy of the law is or should be to treat so tenuous a relationship between the adviser and the advisee as giving rise to a duty of care.

(ii) Breach of duty

Once a duty of care has been established, it is necessary to work out whether the duty has been breached. This might be the case where the operation was performed negligently, or where a doctor offered negligent advice about the operation's success, perhaps because post-vasectomy sperm samples were not properly tested.

It is, however, extremely unlikely that a case would be brought in which a doctor failed to warn either a male or a female patient of the risk that the operation may not succeed. Since the 1980s, it has been known that there is a small chance that a vasectomy might spontaneously reverse itself several years later, even when initial sperm samples indicate that the operation has been successful. In *Newell v Goldenberg*,[25] the court held that in 1985 no competent body of medical opinion would have failed to inform a patient of the small risk of vasectomy reversal. Similarly, there is a small risk that the most common type of female sterilization (tubal occlusion) will fail to achieve sterility. The Royal College of Obstetricians and Gynaecologists' evidence-based clinical guideline on male and female sterilization recommends full and frank disclosure of both these risks.[26]

Given that it would be unreasonable not to warn patients undergoing sterilization of the risk that the operation will not work, any future cases are overwhelmingly likely to be settled out of court.

(iii) Causation

While it is sexual intercourse, rather than the failed sterilization operation, that causes a pregnancy, having unprotected sex will not amount to a *novus actus interveniens* (an act which breaks the chain of causation), unless the patient knows that the sterilization has failed. This was the case in *Sabri-Tabrizi v Lothian Health Board*.[27] The court found that S's decision nevertheless to expose herself to the risk of pregnancy was unreasonable, and constituted a *novus actus interveniens*.

It is also clear, as Lord Steyn explained in *McFarlane v Tayside Health Board*, that the pregnant woman has no duty to mitigate her loss by having an abortion, or by putting the child up for adoption, and that her decision to continue the pregnancy and bring up the child herself will not break the chain of causation.

McFarlane v Tayside Health Board[28]

Lord Steyn

I cannot conceive of any circumstances in which the autonomous decision of the parents not to resort to even a lawful abortion could be questioned. For similar reasons the parents' decision not to have the child adopted was plainly natural and commendable. It is difficult to envisage any circumstances in which it would be right to challenge such a decision of the parents.

---

[25] [1995] 6 Med LR 371.   [26] *Male and Female Sterilisation* (RCOG, 2004).
[27] [1998] BMLR 190.   [28] [2000] 2 AC 59.

A further reason not to treat the decision not to abort as a *novus actus* is that this would imply that the pregnant woman has a right to an abortion, which she would be free to exercise simply because an unwanted child has been conceived. While this may, in practice, be the case in the early stages of pregnancy, it is contrary to the letter of the Abortion Act 1967 (see further Chapter 13).

(iv) What losses can be compensated?

It is undoubtedly foreseeable that negligent sterilization might lead to pregnancy, and the birth of a child. Could this amount to compensatable damage? Pregnancy and childbirth are natural processes, but because they involve pain and risk, the courts have held that they can nevertheless be considered personal injuries.[29] For example, as Lord Steyn explained in *McFarlane v Tayside Health Board*:[30]

> Counsel for the health authority argued as his primary submission that the whole claim should fail because the natural processes of conception and childbirth cannot in law amount to personal injury . . . [E]very pregnancy involves substantial discomfort and pain. I would therefore reject the argument of the health authority on this point.

There are also costs associated with pregnancy, such as maternity clothes, and these too have been recoverable on the grounds that they are consequential economic losses. The cost of the child's upbringing is also, of course, foreseeable, but its recovery in tort has proved to be more controversial.

The issue was first raised in *Udale v Bloomsbury AHA*[31] and it was decided that the maintenance costs of a healthy child were not recoverable for public policy reasons. Children, according to Jupp J, were a 'blessing', and their birth should be an occasion for joy not litigation.

The Court of Appeal took a different view in *Emeh v Kensington and Chelsea AHA*.[32] This was a case involving the birth of a disabled child, and it was held that public policy did not justify a blanket prohibition on the recovery of maintenance costs. The Court of Appeal did not specify whether its judgment applied only to disabled children, and so from the mid-1980s, it was assumed that the costs of a child's upbringing were, in principle, recoverable. And, of course, awards could be very high indeed. In *Benarr v Kettering*,[33] for example, following a negligently performed vasectomy, damages were awarded to cover the child's future private education. Several judges expressed some disquiet about these awards, but, until 1999, that appeared to be the law.[34]

In 1999, in *McFarlane v Tayside Health Board*, the House of Lords considered the issue for the first time, and decided that the maintenance costs of a healthy child were not recoverable. It is a complicated case, and it has been followed by several other cases that have tested its application to slightly different sets of facts, one of which also reached the House of Lords.

Six months after Mr McFarlane had undergone a vasectomy operation, the surgeon negligently informed him that his sperm counts were negative and that he and Mrs McFarlane no longer needed to use contraception. Eighteen months later, Mrs McFarlane became pregnant and gave birth to their fifth child, Catherine. A majority of the House of Lords (Lord Millett dissenting) found that Mrs McFarlane was entitled to general damages for the

[29] See, eg, *Walkin v South Manchester Health Authority* [1995] 1 WLR 1543. [30] [2000] 2 AC 59.
[31] [1983] 1 WLR 1098. [32] [1985] 2 WLR 233. [33] (1988) 138 NLJ 179.
[34] See, eg, *Allen v Bloomsbury Health Authority* [1993] 1 All ER 651, per Brooke J; *Jones v Berkshire Health Authority*, unreported, 2 July 1986, per Ognall J.

pain, suffering, and inconvenience of pregnancy and childbirth, but the Lords were unanimous that the McFarlanes were not entitled to be compensated for the costs associated with Catherine's upbringing.

McFarlane v Tayside Health Board[35]

Lord Steyn

It is possible to view the case simply from the perspective of corrective justice. It requires somebody who has harmed another without justification to indemnify the other. On this approach the parents' claim for the cost of bringing up Catherine must succeed. But one may also approach the case from the vantage point of distributive justice. It requires a focus on the just distribution of burdens and losses among members of a society. If the matter is approached in this way, it may become relevant to ask commuters on the Underground the following question: Should the parents of an unwanted but healthy child be able to sue the doctor or hospital for compensation equivalent to the cost of bringing up the child for the years of his or her minority, i.e. until about 18 years? My Lords, I am firmly of the view that an overwhelming number of ordinary men and women would answer the question with an emphatic 'No'. And the reason for such a response would be an inarticulate premise as to what is morally acceptable and what is not. . . . Instinctively, the traveller on the Underground would consider that the law of tort has no business to provide legal remedies consequent upon the birth of a healthy child, which all of us regard as a valuable and good thing.

My Lords, to explain decisions denying a remedy for the cost of bringing up an unwanted child by saying that there is no loss, no foreseeable loss, no causative link or no ground for reasonable restitution is to resort to unrealistic and formalistic propositions which mask the real reasons for the decisions. And judges ought to strive to give the real reasons for their decision. It is my firm conviction that where courts of law have denied a remedy for the cost of bringing up an unwanted child the real reasons have been grounds of distributive justice. That is, of course, a moral theory. It may be objected that the House must act like a court of law and not like a court of morals. That would only be partly right. The court must apply positive law. But judges' sense of the moral answer to a question, or the justice of the case, has been one of the great shaping forces of the common law. What may count in a situation of difficulty and uncertainty is not the subjective view of the judge but what he reasonably believes that the ordinary citizen would regard as right . . .

Relying on principles of distributive justice I am persuaded that our tort law does not permit parents of a healthy unwanted child to claim the costs of bringing up the child from a health authority or a doctor. If it were necessary to do so, I would say that the claim does not satisfy the requirement of being fair, just and reasonable.

Lord Hope

It is not difficult to see that in such cases a very substantial award of damages might have to be made for the child's upbringing. Awards on that scale would be bound to raise questions as to whether it was right for the negligent performance of a voluntary and comparatively minor operation, undertaken for the perfectly proper and understandable purpose of enabling couples to dispense with contraceptive measures and to have unprotected intercourse without having children, to expose the doctors, and on their behalf the relevant health

[35] [2000] 2 AC 59.

authority, to a liability on that scale in damages. It might well be thought that the extent of the liability was disproportionate to the duties which were undertaken and, consequently, to the extent of the negligence . . .

There are benefits in this arrangement as well as costs. In the short term there is the pleasure which a child gives in return for the love and care which she receives during infancy. In the longer term there is the mutual relationship of support and affection which will continue well beyond the ending of the period of her childhood.

In my opinion it would not be fair, just or reasonable, in any assessment of the loss caused by the birth of the child, to leave these benefits out of account. Otherwise the pursuers would be paid far too much. They would be relieved of the cost of rearing the child. They would not be giving anything back to the wrongdoer for the benefits. But the value which is to be attached to these benefits is incalculable. The costs can be calculated but the benefits, which in fairness must be set against them, cannot. The logical conclusion, as a matter of law, is that the costs to the pursuers of meeting their obligations to the child during her childhood are not recoverable as damages.

Lord Clyde

But in attempting to offset the benefit of parenthood against the costs of parenthood one is attempting to set off factors of quite a different character against themselves and that does not seem to me to accord with principle. At least in the context of the compensation of one debt against another, like requires to be offset against like. . . . A parent's claim for the death of a child is not offset by the saving in maintenance costs which the parent will enjoy. . . . Furthermore, in order to pursue such a claim against the risk of such a set-off, a parent is called upon in effect to prove that the child is more trouble than he or she is worth in order to claim. That seems to me an undesirable requirement to impose upon a parent and further militates against such an approach. Indeed, the very uncertainty of the extent of the benefit which the child may constitute makes the idea of a set-off difficult or even impracticable. . . .

But that the pursuers end up with an addition to their family, originally unintended but now, although unexpected, welcome, and are enabled to have the child maintained while in their custody free of any cost does not seem to accord with the idea of restitution or with an award of damages which does justice between both parties. . . .

Furthermore, reasonableness includes a consideration of the proportionality between the wrongdoing and the loss suffered thereby. . . . Counsel for the respondents sought to stress the modesty of the likely level of award in the present case. But once it is accepted that the cost of private education may be included in appropriate cases, a relatively much more substantial award could be justified.

Lord Millett

I do not consider that the present question should depend on whether the economic loss is characterised as pure or consequential. The distinction is technical and artificial if not actually suspect in the circumstances of the present case, and is to my mind made irrelevant by the act that Catherine's conception and birth are the very things that the defenders' professional services were called upon to prevent. . . .

I am also not persuaded by the argument that the remedy is disproportionate to the wrong. True, a vasectomy is a minor operation, while the costs of bringing up a child may be very large indeed, especially if they extend to the costs of a private education. But it is a commonplace that the harm caused by a botched operation may be out of all proportion to the seriousness of the operation or the condition of the patient which it was designed to alleviate . . .

> There is something distasteful, if not morally offensive, in treating the birth of a normal, healthy child as a matter for compensation . . . In my opinion the law must take the birth of a normal, healthy baby to be a blessing, not a detriment. In truth it is a mixed blessing. It brings joy and sorrow, blessing and responsibility. The advantages and the disadvantages are inseparable. Individuals may choose to regard the balance as unfavourable and take steps to forgo the pleasures as well as the responsibilities of parenthood. They are entitled to decide for themselves where their own interests lie. But society itself must regard the balance as beneficial. It would be repugnant to its own sense of values to do otherwise. It is morally offensive to regard a normal, healthy baby as more trouble and expense than it is worth . . .
>
> It does not, however, follow that Mr and Mrs McFarlane should be sent away empty handed. . . . They have suffered both injury and loss. They have lost the freedom to limit the size of their family. They have been denied an important aspect of their personal autonomy. Their decision to have no more children is one the law should respect and protect. They are entitled to general damages to reflect the true nature of the wrong done to them. This should be a conventional sum which should be left to the trial judge to assess, but which I would not expect to exceed £5000 in a straightforward case like the present.

Although their conclusion on the non-recovery of maintenance costs was unanimous, as Brooke LJ pointed out in the Court of Appeal judgment in *Parkinson*, the Law Lords certainly did not speak with one voice: 'Our task has been made more difficult because the five members of the House of Lords spoke with five different voices.'

The costs of Catherine McFarlane's upbringing were, according to the majority, pure economic loss. (Lord Millett dissented on this point, arguing that the distinction between consequential and pure economic losses was 'technical and artificial'.) Readers who are familiar with tort law may remember that special rules cover the recovery of pure economic loss. In short, the three-stage *Caparo v Dickman*[36] test applies:

(a) The loss should be foreseeable.

(b) There must be a relationship of sufficient proximity between the doctor and their patient.

(c) It should be fair, just, and reasonable to impose a duty of care in these circumstances.

The House of Lords accepted that the birth of a child, and the costs of her upbringing, were foreseeable consequences of negligently advising Mr and Mrs McFarlane that sterility had been achieved. There was also a relationship of sufficient proximity between the doctor who gave this advice and Mr McFarlane. Although Mrs McFarlane was not herself being treated, she was undoubtedly identifiable as someone who would be likely to suffer loss if she was negligently informed that her husband's vasectomy had been successful. The House of Lords rejected the McFarlanes' claim on the grounds that imposing liability on the health authority for the costs of their healthy child's upbringing would not be fair, just, and reasonable. Several different reasons were given for this conclusion:

(a) The 'offset' calculation

First, some of the Law Lords suggested that it would be unfair to compensate the parents for the costs of rearing a child, unless these could be reduced in order to take into account the pleasure that the child would bring to her parents. However, they refused to embark upon this sort of balancing exercise on the grounds that it would be impossible and/or unseemly. Lord Hope, for example, argued that while the costs of a child's upbringing can be calculated,

---

[36] [1990] 2 AC 651.

'the benefits, which in fairness must be set against them, cannot'. For Lord Millett, the crucial point was not that it was impossible to weigh the advantages of raising children against the costs, but that society must always regard the balance as beneficial because it would be 'morally offensive' to do otherwise.

The Lords thus appeared to assume that this sort of offset calculation was necessary, but either impossible or offensive. But is it really true that damages would have to be reduced in order to reflect the benefits the child brings to her parents? Two analogies, while imperfect, are instructive. First, and this point was specifically acknowledged by Lord Clyde, when parents bring an action for the death of their child, their damages are not reduced in order to reflect the money that they will save by not having to pay for the child's upkeep. Secondly, in family law cases, the child support that an absent parent must pay to the child's principal carer is not reduced in order to reflect the benefits the principal carer gains from the child's company. Again, an offset calculation would be unthinkable. Why, then, given that in other contexts the law will not engage in a cost–benefit calculation in order to reduce sums payable to a child's parents, is such an exercise essential, but impossible, following negligent sterilization?

Further, as Lord Clyde again points out, an offset rule is normally dependent upon comparing like with like. But, in relation to wrongful pregnancy, the House of Lords assumed that damages for the *economic costs* of bringing up a child would have to be reduced in order to take account of the *emotional benefits* of the child's companionship. A trade-off between incommensurate goods is unusual. We would not normally say that an injured employee's damages for being unable to work should be reduced in order to reflect the benefits he enjoys from being able to spend more time with his family. Lord Clyde gave the example of a mine-worker rendered unfit for work underground: if he claims damages for loss of earnings, the defendant is not entitled to offset 'the pleasure and benefit which he may enjoy in the air of a public park'.

Even if it were accepted that an offset calculation is necessary, it might also be argued that the question of whether an unplanned child's existence represents a net gain for a family is a question of fact. It may be true that most people, most of the time, consider that the advantages of having a child, even if she was initially unwanted, outweigh the disadvantages. But this will not always be the case. For some families, the birth of another child might be a disaster.

In his dissenting judgment in the Court of Appeal in *Rees v Darlington Memorial Hospital NHS Trust*,[37] Waller LJ gave the example of an impoverished single mother with four children, who believes that having a fifth child will lead to her mental breakdown, and who has no support from her family. If the birth of an unwanted child provokes the mother's physical or mental collapse, and results in all of her children being taken into care, she may be able to prove that the advantages of having another child have not, in fact, outweighed the disadvantages. Yet the law will not allow her to bring forward such evidence, because it has already decided that, in Lord Millett's words, 'society itself must regard the balance as beneficial'.

Given that the claimants in wrongful pregnancy cases have undergone invasive surgery in order permanently to prevent the possibility of conception, it is plain that, at the time of the operation at least, they believed that the disadvantages of having another baby outweighed any joy that an additional child might bring. People are sterilized precisely in order to avoid the 'benefits' of conceiving a child. It is perhaps odd that the law insists that such people should regard the failure of their surgery as a 'blessing' and an occasion for joy. If the benefits

---

[37] [2002] EWCA Civ 88.

of parenthood always outweigh its disadvantages, it is unclear why anyone would want to be sterilized in the first place.

(b) Proportionality

Secondly, both Lord Hope and Lord Clyde were concerned that the size of any claim in damages for a child's upbringing would be disproportionate to the degree of fault. As was clear from *Benarr v Kettering*, a child's maintenance costs will sometimes be very high indeed and, if recoverable, an NHS trust might have to pay vast damages for what might have been a relatively minor lapse of judgement. Moreover, not only would compensating parents for the costs of private education for the whole of a child's life lead to some extremely high awards, but it would also result in invidious distinctions between claimants, since wealthy parents would receive more money for their unwanted children than poor parents.

Lord Millett objected to this argument on the grounds that damages in tort are not intended to correspond to the gravity of fault, but rather to put the claimant in the position they would have been if the negligent act had not occurred. A minor and common lapse of judgement while driving—such as momentarily taking one's eyes off the road in order to admire the view—might have catastrophic consequences, and it would not be open to the driver to argue that the level of damages would be disproportionate to the degree of fault.

(c) Distributive justice

Thirdly, Lord Steyn based his judgment upon considerations of distributive justice. If children cannot claim for 'wrongful life', he reasoned that it would be unfair to allow parents to claim for 'wrongful pregnancy'. Lord Steyn was reluctant to squeeze his rejection of the McFarlanes' claim into existing principles of tort law, although, if forced to do so, he would say that 'the claim does not satisfy the requirement of being fair, just and reasonable'. Instead, Lord Steyn admitted that his was a moral judgement, and he specifically appealed to public opinion, or more precisely to commuters on the London Underground.

A final underlying reason for the Lords' rejection of the McFarlane's claim may have been the concern that scarce NHS resources should not be diverted to the parents of healthy children. The House of Lords might have been alarmed at the prospect that the NHS might have to pay very large sums of money for the private education and maintenance costs of a healthy child. This was certainly Tony Weir's principal objection to the post-*Emeh* case law: 'For the fourteen years since *Emeh* the National Health Service, short of resources for curing the sick, has been disbursing large sums of money for the maintenance of children who have nothing wrong with them.'[38]

In its later judgment in *Rees v Darlington Memorial Hospital NHS Trust*,[39] the House of Lords explicitly discussed the question of whether compensating parents for the birth of a healthy child is an appropriate use of NHS resources. But while it is undoubtedly true that Tayside Health Board has more pressing demands upon its budget than Catherine McFarlane's upkeep, it is not normally open to a court to deny a claimant damages because the defendant could deploy the money more usefully elsewhere.

In *McFarlane* Lord Millett made an interesting suggestion, which was not taken up by any of the other judges, namely that the McFarlanes should be entitled to a 'conventional sum' of £5,000 to compensate them for the wrongful interference with their freedom to limit the size of their family. In part, this proposal may have been prompted by the concern that full damages in a case such as this would not be a sensible use of scarce NHS resources. As we

---

[38] 'The Unwanted Child' (2000) 59 Cambridge Law Journal 238–41. [39] [2003] UKHL 52.

see later, Lord Millett's novel compensatory award was taken up subsequently by a majority of the House of Lords in *Rees*.

Of course, it was inevitable that issues that were not directly dealt with by the judgments in *McFarlane* would rear their heads in subsequent litigation. On a comparatively minor point, in *Greenfield v Irwin*,[40] the mother had been in full-time employment and sought to recover loss of earnings not just around the time of the birth, but during the first years of the child's life, when she would be caring for the baby at home. While *McFarlane* had not directly addressed future loss of earnings, the Court of Appeal decided that these costs were in fact part of the costs of raising the child, and, since *McFarlane* applied, they were not recoverable.

Greenfield v Irwin[41]

Laws LJ

It is to be noted that if this lady were to obtain the damages she seeks, she would happily be in a position whereby she would look after her much loved child at home, yet at the same time in effect would receive the income she would have earned had she stayed at work. In my judgment that is not just compensation; it is the conferment of a financial privilege, which has nothing to do with just compensation.

The second issue that was not addressed in *McFarlane* was whether the judgment would have been the same if Catherine McFarlane had been born disabled. Lord Steyn had suggested that 'in the case of an unwanted child, who was born seriously disabled the rule may have to be different', and Lord Clyde pointed out that 'it has to be noted in the present case we are dealing with a normal birth and a healthy child'.

Unsurprisingly, it was not long before the question of whether *McFarlane* applied to disabled children came before the courts in *Parkinson v St James and Seacroft University Hospital NHS Trust*. Angela Parkinson already had four children and did not think she could cope with a fifth. She was sterilized, but the operation was performed negligently, and she subsequently became pregnant. During the pregnancy, Mrs Parkinson was advised that the child might be born disabled, and Scott was born suffering from a serious behavioural disorder.

At first instance Longmore J held that Mrs Parkinson could recover the costs of providing for Scott's special needs, and his judgment was upheld by the Court of Appeal.

Parkinson v St James and Seacroft University Hospital NHS Trust[42]

Brooke LJ

(i) the birth of a child with congenital abnormalities was a foreseeable consequence of the surgeon's careless failure to clip a fallopian tube effectively;

(ii) there was a very limited group of people who might be affected by this negligence, viz Mrs Parkinson and her husband (and, in theory, any other man with whom she had sexual intercourse before she realised that she had not been effectively sterilised);

---

[40] [2001] EWCA Civ 113.   [41] [2001] EWCA Civ 113.   [42] [2001] EWCA Civ 530.

(iii) there is no difficulty in principle in accepting the proposition that the surgeon should be deemed to have assumed responsibility for the foreseeable and disastrous economic consequences of performing his services negligently;

(iv) the purpose of the operation was to prevent Mrs Parkinson from conceiving any more children, including children with congenital abnormalities, and the surgeon's duty of care is strictly related to the proper fulfilment of that purpose;

(v) parents in Mrs Parkinson's position were entitled to recover damages in these circumstances for 15 years between the decisions in Emeh's case and McFarlane's case, so that this is not a radical step forward into the unknown;

(vi) for the reasons set out in (i) and (ii) above, Lord Bridge of Harwich's tests of foreseeability and proximity are satisfied, and . . . an award of compensation which is limited to the special upbringing costs associated with rearing a child with a serious disability would be fair, just and reasonable;

(vii) if principles of distributive justice are called in aid, I believe that ordinary people would consider that it would be fair for the law to make an award in such a case, provided that it is limited to the extra expenses associated with the child's disability.

Hale LJ

Not surprisingly, their Lordships [in *McFarlane*] did not go into detail about what is entailed in the invasion of bodily integrity caused by conception, pregnancy and childbirth. But it is worthwhile spelling out the more obvious features. Some will sound in damages and some may not, but they are all the consequence of that fundamental invasion. They are none the less an invasion because they are the result of natural processes. They stem from something which should never have happened. And they last for a great deal longer than the pregnancy itself. Whatever the outcome, happy or sad, a woman never gets over it . . .

From the moment a woman conceives, profound physical changes take place in her body and continue to take place not only for the duration of the pregnancy but for some time thereafter. Those physical changes bring with them a risk to life and health greater than in her non-pregnant state . . . Along with those physical changes go psychological changes. Again these vary from woman to woman. Some may amount to a recognised psychiatric disorder, while others may be regarded as beneficial, and many are somewhere in between. . . .

Along with these physical and psychological consequences goes a severe curtailment of personal autonomy. Literally, one's life is no longer just one's own but also someone else's. One cannot simply rid oneself of that responsibility. The availability of legal abortion depends upon the opinions of others. . . .

Continuing the pregnancy brings a host of lesser infringements of autonomy related to the physical changes in the body or responsibility towards the growing child. The responsible pregnant woman forgoes or moderates the pleasures of alcohol and tobacco. She changes her diet. She submits to regular and intrusive medical examinations and tests. She takes certain sorts of exercise and forgoes others. She can no longer wear her favourite clothes. She is unlikely to be able to continue in paid employment throughout the pregnancy or to return to it immediately thereafter.

The process of giving birth is rightly termed 'labour'. It is hard work, often painful and sometimes dangerous. It brings the pregnancy to an end but it does not bring to an end the changes brought about by the pregnancy. It takes some time for the body to return to its pre-pregnancy state, if it ever does, especially if the child is breast-fed. There are well known psychiatric illnesses associated with childbirth and the baby blues are very common . . .

Quite clearly, however, the invasion of the mother's personal autonomy does not stop once her body and mind have returned to their pre-pregnancy state. . . . Parental responsibility is not simply or even primarily a financial responsibility . . . The primary responsibility is to care for the child. The labour does not stop when the child is born. Bringing up children is hard work. . . . The obligation to provide or make acceptable and safe arrangements for the child's care and supervision lasts for 24 hours a day, seven days a week, all year round, until the child becomes old enough to take care of himself. . . .

Of course, most pregnancies are not caused wrongfully. But this case proceeds on the basis that this one was. The whole object of the service offered to the claimant by the defendants was to prevent her becoming pregnant again. They had a duty to perform that service with reasonable care. They did not do so. She became pregnant as a result. On normal principles of tortious liability, once it was established that the pregnancy had been wrongfully caused, compensation would be payable for all those consequences, whether physical or financial, which are capable of sounding in damages. . . .

A disabled child needs extra care and extra expenditure. He is deemed, on this analysis, to bring as much pleasure and as many advantages as does a normal healthy child. Frankly, in many cases, of which this may be one, this is much less likely. The additional stresses and strains can have seriously adverse effects upon the whole family, and not infrequently lead, as here, to the break-up of the parents' relationship and detriment to the other children. But we all know of cases where the whole family has been enriched by the presence of a disabled member and would not have things any other way. This analysis treats a disabled child as having exactly the same worth as a non-disabled child. It affords him the same dignity and status. It simply acknowledges that he costs more.

It is important to remember that *Parkinson* is not a case in which the child's disability was caused by the defendant's negligence. If a botched sterilization operation not only failed to achieve sterility, but also damaged the patient's reproductive organs and impaired her ability to give birth to a healthy child, then the child would have a straightforward action under the Congenital Disabilities (Civil Liability) Act 1976.

In *Parkinson*, the defendant's negligence did not cause Scott's behavioural disorder; rather, it caused Scott, who just happened to be disabled, to be conceived. Because there is always a small risk—in *Parkinson* it was put at between one in 200 and one in 400—that a child might be born suffering from a congenital abnormality, the birth of a disabled child is a foreseeable consequence of any negligent sterilization operation.

It should, however, be noted that the maintenance costs of a healthy child are more foreseeable than the statistically less likely possibility that a child will be born disabled.[43] It is also true that the maintenance costs of a disabled child are likely to be higher than those of a normal healthy baby, and since we are not concerned with cases in which the defendant caused the disability, the concern expressed by Lords Clyde and Hope in *McFarlane* about the level of damages being disproportionate to the degree of fault would be more compelling on the facts in *Parkinson*.

Furthermore, recall that several of the judgments in *McFarlane* argued that the benefits of the child's existence had to be put into the balance with the costs, but that such a calculation

---

[43] Laura CH Hoyano, 'Misconceptions about Wrongful Conception' (2002) 65 Modern Law Review 883–906.

was either unseemly or impossible. Surely, as Alasdair Maclean points out, the same must be true when the child is born disabled.

Alasdair Maclean[44]

Unless one is prepared to argue that having a disabled child is not—as a matter of policy—a blessing, which might be interpreted as devaluing the disabled, then the [offset] calculation is no more possible for the birth of a disabled child than it is for the birth of a healthy child. The costs arising from the disability are simply additional maintenance costs and, if the detriments cannot be weighed against the benefits then simply increasing the detriments cannot change that: if x cannot be balanced against y then nor can x be balanced against y + z.

In *Parkinson*, the Court of Appeal appeared less than enthusiastic about the implications of *McFarlane*. In particular, Hale LJ's impassioned description of the physical and psychological invasions of pregnancy and motherhood was not specifically directed to the burdens of being a mother of a disabled child, but applies to motherhood in general. Nevertheless, *McFarlane* was binding upon them, and so the important question was whether Scott's disabilities meant that Angela Parkinson's case could be distinguished. The Court of Appeal decided that the cases were different, and the extra costs incurred as a result of the child's disability were recoverable. This was not, the Court of Appeal insisted, because the birth of a disabled child is not a 'blessing': rather, it simply acknowledges that disabled children cost more.

Three problems of interpretation remained after the Court of Appeal's decision in *Parkinson*. First, what counts as a disability for these purposes? The Court of Appeal suggested that the disability must be 'significant', and Hale LJ argued that the test should be the same as that in the Children Act 1989.

Parkinson v St James and Seacroft University Hospital NHS Trust[45]

Hale LJ

[H]ow disabled does the child have to be for the parents to be able to make a claim? The answer is that the law has for some time distinguished between the ordinary needs of ordinary children and the special needs of a disabled child. Thus, for the purposes of the services to be provided under Part III of the Children Act 1989, . . . 'a child is disabled if he is blind, deaf or dumb or suffers from mental disorder of any kind or is substantially and permanently handicapped by illness, injury or congenital deformity or such other disability as may be prescribed' . . . I see no difficulty in using the same definition here.

The child's disability must therefore meet some threshold level of seriousness before the extra costs associated with it are recoverable. But while we can be certain that parents are not entitled to recover the additional costs incurred as a result of a relatively minor anomaly, such as short-sightedness, future courts may have to address precisely what counts as a significant disability for these purposes.

---

[44] 'An Alexandrian Approach to the Knotty Problem of Wrongful Pregnancy: *Rees v Darlington Memorial Hospital NHS Trust* in the House of Lords' [2004] 3 Web JCLI.
[45] [2001] EWCA Civ 530.

Secondly, for there to be recovery, the Court of Appeal stressed that the child's disability must be a foreseeable consequence of the defendant's negligence. The Court of Appeal did not confine recovery to disabilities that were present from conception onwards.

> **Hale LJ**
>
> I conclude that any disability arising from genetic causes or foreseeable events during pregnancy (such as rubella, spina bifida, or oxygen deprivation during pregnancy or childbirth) up until the child is born alive, and which are not novus actus interveniens, will suffice to found a claim.

But what if the child subsequently becomes disabled: are her extra needs also a foreseeable consequence of the defendant's negligence? This question arose in *Groom v Selby*.[46] Ms Groom had undergone a sterilization operation when she was in fact in the very early stages of pregnancy. When she visited her doctor complaining of abdominal pains, and having missed a period, the doctor failed to test for pregnancy. Pregnancy was eventually diagnosed when Ms Groom was 12 weeks pregnant, by which time she did not feel able to have an abortion. It was admitted that the doctor's failure to carry out a pregnancy test was negligent, and that this had deprived Ms Groom of the opportunity to terminate the pregnancy. Ms Groom's daughter Megan was born prematurely, and subsequently developed meningitis complicated by brain abscesses.

The doctor contended that Megan was a healthy child at birth, and hence *McFarlane* and not *Parkinson* applied, thus ruling out recovery for the additional costs associated with Megan's disabilities. However, the Court of Appeal held that Megan could not properly be described as a 'healthy child' at birth because the bacteria, which was responsible for her meningitis, was already present on her skin.

> **Hale LJ**
>
> There will always be borderline cases in the application of any principle. In *Parkinson*, Brooke LJ and I were also agreed on the source of the disability: it must be genetic or arise from the processes of intra-uterine development and birth. That was what the doctor negligently failed to prevent. Megan's meningitis was 'bad luck', in the sense that many newborn babies do not succumb to such infections. But it arose from the process of her birth during which she was exposed to the bacterium in question.

Interestingly, when setting out which disabilities fit within the *Parkinson* exception, Hale LJ specifically gave the example of 'oxygen deprivation during childbirth'. It is therefore possible that a doctor who carried out a sterilization operation negligently might be liable to pay vast damages to a severely brain-damaged child, on the grounds that it is foreseeable that they will be deprived of oxygen during childbirth, and suffer catastrophic brain damage as a result. If the oxygen deprivation was due to negligent obstetric care, this would amount to a *novus actus*, but if negligence on the part of the obstetric team could not be proved, liability might be traced back to the surgeon who carried out the sterilization. Given that awards for brain damage caused by oxygen deprivation during birth are often very high indeed— awards of over £1 million are not unusual—it is again worth noting a tension with Lords Hope and Clyde's concerns about proportionality.

---

[46] [2001] EWCA Civ 1522.

Thirdly, what if it is not the child but the parent who is disabled? The issue has arisen twice since *Parkinson*. In *AD v East Kent Community NHS Trust*,[47] A was a mentally disabled woman who had become pregnant while being cared for on the defendant's mixed psychiatric ward. A gave birth to a healthy daughter, C, and A's mother, Mrs A, agreed to look after C. The Court of Appeal dismissed A's claim for the costs associated with C's upbringing. She herself had suffered no loss. Mrs A was providing her services voluntarily, which meant that she too could not have an action in her own right,[48] but even if Mrs A could have brought a claim, Judge LJ assumed that an offset calculation would be necessary, and argued that: 'it would be invidious to attempt to put a money value on the benefit that she will derive from the joy of having her healthy granddaughter living with her and growing up in her home'.

In the second case, *Rees v Darlington Memorial Hospital NHS Trust*, Karina Rees was severely visually handicapped. She was sterilized because she was concerned that her blindness meant that would be unable to look after a child. The operation was carried out negligently and, two years later, she gave birth to a healthy child. She claimed damages not only for the pain and discomfort of pregnancy and childbirth, but also for the additional costs incurred as a result of her disability.

By a majority, the Court of Appeal allowed recovery on the grounds that the claimant's case could be distinguished from *McFarlane* because *McFarlane* only applied to healthy parents.[49] Before we come to the House of Lords' decision, it is worth noting Waller LJ's powerful dissenting judgment in which he argued that whether the birth of an unwanted child is a 'disaster' will often depend more upon the resources and support available to the mother than on whether she happens to be disabled.

Rees v Darlington Memorial Hospital NHS Trust[50]

Waller LJ (dissenting)

If one takes the facts to be that a woman already has four children and wishes not to have a fifth; and if one assumes that having the fifth will create a crisis in health terms, unless help in caring for the child was available, she cannot recover the costs of caring for the child which might alleviate the crisis, as I understand McFarlane's case. I would have thought that her need to avoid a breakdown in her health was no different from the need of someone already with a disability, and indeed her need might be greater depending on the degree of disability. . . .

  If one were to add that the lady with four children was poor, but the lady with a disability was rich—what then? It would simply emphasise the perception that the rule was not operating fairly. One can add to the example by making comparisons between possible family circumstances of the different mothers. Assume the mother with four children had no support from husband, mother or siblings, and then compare her with the person who is disabled, but who has a husband, siblings and a mother all willing to help. I think ordinary people would feel uncomfortable about the thought that it was simply the disability which made a difference.

On appeal, the House of Lords was specifically invited to reconsider its judgment in *McFarlane*. In the intervening years, the High Court of Australia had been faced with a

---

[47] [2002] EWCA Civ 1872. [48] *Hunt v Severs* [1994] 2 All ER 385.
[49] *Rees v Darlington Memorial Hospital NHS Trust* [2002] EWCA Civ 88. [50] [2003] UKHL 52.

case with very similar facts to *McFarlane*, *Cattanach v Melchior*, in which it had accused the British courts of drifting too far from ordinary tort law principles.

McFarlane, *Cattanach v Melchior*[51]

Kirby J

Least of all may [judges] do so, in our secular society, on the footing of their personal religious beliefs, or 'moral' assessments concealed in an inarticulate premise dressed up, and described, as legal principle or legal policy . . . Neither the invocation of scripture nor the invention of a fictitious oracle on the Underground . . . authorises a court of law to depart from the ordinary principles governing the recovery of damages for the tort of negligence.

Despite this trenchant criticism, the seven Law Lords who were assembled to hear *Rees v Darlington Memorial Hospital NHS Trust*[52] unanimously declined to revisit the judgment in *McFarlane*. Only four years had elapsed and it would, in Lord Bingham's words, 'reflect no credit on the administration of the law if a line of English authority were to be disapproved in 1999 and reinstated in 2003 with no reason for the change beyond a change in the balance of legal opinion'. Lord Millett was also clear that, 'it requires much more than doubts as to the correctness of the previous decision to justify departing from it'. While JK Mason acknowledges that 'see-saw lawmaking' would be undesirable, he argues that 'the man in the street might well think that, if something is wrong, the sooner it is put right, the better'.[53]

Having upheld the decision in *McFarlane*, the Lords next had to consider whether an exception should be made where the mother was disabled. On this question, the House of Lords was divided. By a 4:3 majority it held that *Rees* could not be distinguished: the child was healthy so *McFarlane* applied. There could therefore be no recovery for any of the costs associated with the child's upbringing. In contrast, the dissenting judges would have allowed Karina Rees to recover for the extra costs associated with her disability. It should, however, be noted that the majority added a very significant 'gloss'.

Rees v Darlington Memorial Hospital NHS Trust[54]

Lord Bingham

The policy considerations underpinning the judgments of the House [in *McFarlane*] were, as I read them, an unwillingness to regard a child (even if unwanted) as a financial liability and nothing else, a recognition that the rewards which parenthood (even if involuntary) may or may not bring cannot be quantified and a sense that to award potentially very large sums of damages to the parents of a normal and healthy child against a National Health Service always in need of funds to meet pressing demands would rightly offend the community's sense of how public resources should be allocated. . . .

    Subject to one gloss, therefore, which I regard as important, I would affirm and adhere to the decision in *McFarlane*.

---

[51] [2003] HCA 38.   [52] [2003] UKHL 52.
[53] *The Troubled Pregnancy: Legal Rights and Wrongs in Reproduction* (CUP: Cambridge, 2007).
[54] [2003] UKHL 52.

My concern is this. Even accepting that an unwanted child cannot be regarded as a financial liability and nothing else and that any attempt to weigh the costs of bringing up a child against the intangible rewards of parenthood is unacceptably speculative, the fact remains that the parent of a child born following a negligently performed vasectomy or sterilisation, or negligent advice on the effect of such a procedure, is the victim of a legal wrong. . . .

I can accept and support a rule of legal policy which precludes recovery of the full cost of bringing up a child in the situation postulated, but I question the fairness of a rule which denies the victim of a legal wrong any recompense at all beyond an award immediately related to the unwanted pregnancy and birth. . . .

To speak of losing the freedom to limit the size of one's family is to mask the real loss suffered in a situation of this kind. This is that a parent, particularly (even today) the mother, has been denied, through the negligence of another, the opportunity to live her life in the way that she wished and planned. I do not think that an award immediately relating to the unwanted pregnancy and birth gives adequate recognition of or does justice to that loss. I would accordingly support the suggestion favoured by Lord Millett in *McFarlane* that in all cases such as these there be a conventional award to mark the injury and loss, although I would favour a greater figure than the £5,000 he suggested (I have in mind a conventional figure of £15,000) and I would add this to the award for the pregnancy and birth. This solution is in my opinion consistent with the ruling and rationale of *McFarlane*. The conventional award would not be, and would not be intended to be, compensatory. It would not be the product of calculation. But it would not be a nominal, let alone a derisory, award. It would afford some measure of recognition of the wrong done. And it would afford a more ample measure of justice than the pure *McFarlane* rule.

Lord Nicholls

I have heard nothing in the submissions advanced on the present appeal to persuade me that this decision by the House [in *McFarlane*] was wrong and ought to be revisited. On the contrary, that the negligent doctor or, in most cases, the National Health Service should pay all the costs of bringing up the child seems to me a disproportionate response to the doctor's wrong. It would accord ill with the values society attaches to human life and to parenthood . . .

But this is not to say it is fair and reasonable there should be no award at all except in respect of stress and trauma and costs associated with the pregnancy and the birth itself. An award of some amount should be made to recognise that in respect of birth of the child the parent has suffered a legal wrong, a legal wrong having a far-reaching effect on the lives of the parent and any family she may already have. The amount of such an award will inevitably have an arbitrary character. I do not dissent from the sum of £15,000 suggested by my noble and learned friend Lord Bingham of Cornhill in this regard.

Lord Millett

I still regard the proper outcome in all these cases is to award the parents a modest conventional sum by way of general damages, not for the birth of the child, but for the denial of an important aspect of their personal autonomy, viz the right to limit the size of their family. This is an important aspect of human dignity, which is increasingly being regarded as an important human right which should be protected by law. . . .

The award of a modest sum would not, of course, go far towards the costs of bringing up a child. It would not reflect the financial consequences of the birth of a normal, healthy child; but it would not be meant to. They are not the proper subject of compensation for the reasons stated in McFarlane. A modest award would, however, adequately compensate for the very different injury to the parents' autonomy.

Lord Steyn (dissenting)

In the present case the idea of a conventional award was not raised at first instance or in the Court of Appeal. For my part it is a great disadvantage for the House to consider such a point without the benefit of the views of the Court of Appeal. And the disadvantage cannot be removed by calling the new rule a 'gloss'. It is a radical and most important development which should only be embarked on after rigorous examination of competing arguments . . .

No United Kingdom authority is cited for the proposition that judges have the power to create a remedy of awarding a conventional sum in cases such as the present. There is none. It is also noteworthy that in none of the decisions from many foreign jurisdictions, with varying results, is there any support for such a solution. This underlines the heterodox nature of the solution adopted.

Like Lord Hope I regard the idea of a conventional award in the present case as contrary to principle. It is a novel procedure for judges to create such a remedy. There are limits to permissible creativity for judges. In my view the majority have strayed into forbidden territory. It is also a backdoor evasion of the legal policy enunciated in McFarlane. If such a rule is to be created it must be done by Parliament. The fact is, however, that it would be a hugely controversial legislative measure. It may well be that the Law Commissions and Parliament ought in any event, to consider the impact of the creation of a power to make a conventional award in the cases under consideration for the coherence of the tort system.

The gloss added by the majority in *Rees* is grounded in the recognition that, while full compensation for the birth of a healthy baby might be inappropriate and unaffordable, the parents in these cases have undoubtedly been wronged: they have been deprived of their freedom to control the size of their family. As a result, the majority of the House of Lords advocated what they described as a modest 'conventional award', which would not be intended to compensate for the actual loss suffered by the claimants, but rather to offer some recognition of the wrong done to them. In short, the majority in *Rees* decided that it did not want to compensate Karina Rees according to ordinary negligence principles because this would give her too much money. Instead, it preferred to compensate her according to its own novel scheme, which would acknowledge that she had been wronged, without giving her exorbitant damages.

As JK Mason puts it, 'it is hard to find a commentator who does not, at this point, start to scratch his or her head'.[55] One generous explanation is that the majority in *Rees* was attempting to find a judicial solution to some of the problems clinical negligence poses for the NHS. Patients who are treated negligently deserve some recognition that they received inadequate care, which may have caused them harm, inconvenience, discomfort, or financial loss. But, at the same time, giving them full compensation for all of their losses has an opportunity cost, insofar as it reduces the resources the NHS has to spend on providing treatment to the rest of the population. In these circumstances, it could be argued that it would be more sensible for patients who are the victims of inadequate treatment to receive a standard notional award, which recognizes that a wrong has been done to them, but does not attempt to provide full compensation.

But while moving towards a standardized compensation scheme within the NHS might have many merits, it is not clear that a decision of a narrow majority in the House of Lords is the right way to bring about such a system. The introduction of a radical departure from the existing tort system would, as the caustic dissenting judgments suggest, normally be a matter for parliament.

---

[55] *The Troubled Pregnancy: Legal Rights and Wrongs in Reproduction* (CUP: Cambridge, 2007) 176.

The purpose of the 'conventional award' is also opaque. It is there to compensate for 'a wrong comprised of an affront to autonomy',[56] which is a novel head of damages. However, in a case in which the baby was stillborn, *Less v Hussain*,[57] and the parents' claim in any event failed on the question of causation, His Honour Judge Cotter QC found that the conventional award could apply only where there were actual losses:

> [O]n any careful analysis of the judgments of either Lord Bingham or Lord Millett they were recognising that ordinarily the parents of a child born as a result of a legal wrong will, within the 'mixed blessings' of parenthood suffer real as opposed to theoretical losses. This I see as a driver behind their approaches to the issue and support of the award given. In the present case there are no such losses. Absent such losses I do not believe that an award should be made.

The conventional award is not meant to be derisory, and yet, while better than nothing, it comes nowhere near the amount that would be payable according to normal tort law principles. In the end, JK Mason may be right that it looks rather like 'a form of conscience money or as a charity designed to offset the sense of injustice left by the original *McFarlane* decision'.[58]

Following *Rees*, the status of the Court of Appeal judgment in *Parkinson* is uncertain. Three of the Law Lords specifically approved of the Court of Appeal's decision in *Parkinson*. Lord Hutton, for example, said: 'In my opinion the decision of the Court of Appeal in *Parkinson* was right . . . in my opinion it is fair, just and reasonable to award damages for the extra costs of bringing up a disabled child.' Similarly, according to one of the dissenting judges, Lord Hope: 'A disabled child is likely to need extra care and the provision of this care is likely to mean extra expenditure . . . I consider that, as a matter of legal policy, the Court of Appeal were right to hold that in principle these extra costs are recoverable.' And finally another dissenting judge, Lord Steyn, expressly confined *McFarlane* to the birth of a healthy child: 'The legal policy on which *McFarlane* was based is critically dependent on the birth of a healthy and normal child. That policy does not apply where the child is seriously disabled physically and/or mentally.'

In contrast, three of the Law Lords were critical of the *Parkinson* decision, and would have also applied the conventional award in cases where the child was born disabled. Lord Bingham, with whom Lord Nicholls agreed, offered a number of criticisms of the Court of Appeal's judgment in *Parkinson*:

Lord Bingham

I would for my part apply this rule also, without differentiation, to cases in which either the child or the parent is (or claims to be) disabled:

(1) While I have every sympathy with the Court of Appeal's view that Mrs Parkinson should be compensated, it is arguably anomalous that the defendant's liability should be related to a disability which the doctor's negligence did not cause and not to the birth which it did.

(2) The rule favoured by the Court of Appeal majority in the present case inevitably gives rise to anomalies such as those highlighted by Waller LJ in his dissenting judgment.

---

[56] Ibid, 179.   [57] [2012] EWHC 3513 (QB).
[58] *The Troubled Pregnancy: Legal Rights and Wrongs in Reproduction* (CUP: Cambridge, 2007) 178.

> (3) It is undesirable that parents, in order to recover compensation, should be encouraged to portray either their children or themselves as disabled . . .
>
> (4) In a state such as ours, which seeks to make public provision for the consequences of disability, the quantification of additional costs attributable to disability, whether of the parent or the child, is a task of acute difficulty.

Similarly, Lord Scott said that he had 'some doubts' about the Court of Appeal's conclusion on foreseeability in *Parkinson*.

Lord Scott

The possibility that a child may be born with a congenital abnormality is plainly present to some degree in the case of every pregnancy. But is that a sufficient reason for holding the negligent doctor liable for the extra costs, attributable to the abnormality, of rearing the child? In my opinion it is not. Foreseeability of a one in 200 to 400 chance does not seem to me, by itself, enough to make it reasonable to impose on the negligent doctor liability for these costs. It might be otherwise in a case where there had been particular reason to fear that if a child were conceived and born it might suffer from some inherited disability. And, particularly, it might be otherwise in a case where the very purpose of the sterilisation operation had been to protect against that fear. But on the facts of *Parkinson* I do not think the Court of Appeal's conclusion was consistent with *McFarlane*.

The seventh Law Lord, Lord Millett, did not express an opinion either way, on the grounds that 'it is not necessary for the disposal of the present appeal to reach any conclusion whether *Parkinson* was rightly decided, and I would wish to keep the point open'. Given this lack of consensus, it remains unclear whether the parents of disabled children should now receive the conventional award, or, following *Parkinson*, damages to compensate for the additional costs associated with the child's disability.

A factual variation, which has yet to be considered post-*McFarlane*, is where the sterilization operation was carried out privately, and an action might therefore be brought in contract. It is not clear what difference, if any, this would make. Certainly, it has been assumed that the choice of action is in practice immaterial, since the courts will simply imply into a contract a duty to take reasonable care in carrying out the operation and in providing accurate information.[59] Lord Slynn in *McFarlane* did suggest that 'If a client wants to be able to recover such costs he or she must do so by an appropriate contract', but it would seem highly improbable that any clinician would enter into a contract which provided for the full recovery of maintenance costs if the operation did not succeed.

Finally, it is important to note that although most 'wrongful pregnancy' cases have involved negligent sterilizations, or the giving of negligent advice about a sterilization operation's success or permanency, it is also possible that the negligent provision of other sorts of contraceptive treatment might lead to an unwanted conception. This happened in *Richardson v LRC*, in which the claimant had become pregnant after a condom burst inexplicably. She brought an action under the Consumer Protection Act 1987, including a claim for the costs of maintaining her child. Her claim was rejected, in part because *McFarlane* had excluded the possibility of recovering the costs of a healthy child's upbringing.

---

[59] CR Symmons, 'Policy Factors in Actions for Wrongful Birth' (1987) 50 Modern Law Review 269–306.

Richardson v LRC[60]

Ian Kennedy J

It is the policy of the law, albeit subject to the precise terms of any contract, to exclude from a claimant's claim the costs of the upbringing of an uncovenanted child. That is equally applicable whether the claim is laid in negligence or a breach of a statutory duty.

In *Richardson*, Ian Kennedy J suggested that Mrs Richardson would, in any event, have been barred from claiming damages because she could have taken the morning-after pill in order to avoid pregnancy. This sits slightly uneasily with the established principle that a woman's claim for damages for wrongful pregnancy is unaffected by her decision not to have an abortion. Of course, there are differences between taking a pill and terminating a pregnancy, but JK Mason argues that: 'It is possible to argue that, in terms of a woman exercising her reproductive choice, the difference is merely one of degree—and particularly so when one remembers that at least some women would regard the destruction of an embryo as being morally equivalent to the destruction of a fetus.'[61]

(2) Should there be Recovery for Wrongful Pregnancy?

If the ordinary principles of tort law are applied to these cases, the costs of the child's upbringing would be recoverable. The type of loss is foreseeable, and full recovery of maintenance costs would put the claimant in the position they would have been in if the tort had not been performed. Moreover, in the next extract Alasdair Mullis argues that considerations which commonly inform the courts' decisions in negligence actions—such as the availability of insurance or concerns about opening the floodgates—would also point in favour of recovery.

Alastair Mullis[62]

Secondly, there is the 'floodgates question'. Traditionally, the courts have been concerned to avoid imposing liability where to do so would involve making the defendant liable to an indeterminate number of people, in an indeterminate amount, for an indeterminate period of time. It is argued that generally, at least, there is no such risk here. First, the number of potential plaintiffs is in the usual case limited to two and they can recover once only. Secondly, in most of these cases the woman will become pregnant fairly soon, usually within a year, after the operation. Finally, the amounts awarded have not usually been excessive and will of course be limited to the first child.

Thirdly, the courts have in a number of cases considered the insurance position. In wrongful conception cases, as in other cases of medical negligence, the loss will not be borne by the doctor himself . . . The parents, however, will not only be unlikely to insure against the risk of pregnancy but they may well be unable to do so. It is surely better, given this background, that the loss should fall on the health authority.

---

[60] [2000] PIQR P164.
[61] *The Troubled Pregnancy: Legal Rights and Wrongs in Reproduction* (CUP: Cambridge, 2007) 142.
[62] 'Wrongful Conception Unravelled' (1993) 1 Medical Law Review 320–35.

Nevertheless, an exception to ordinary tort rules has been carved out in *McFarlane*. *Parkinson* offers a limited exception to that exception. *Rees* complicates matters further by permitting a novel non-compensatory award, and it is not clear whether this applies in all 'wrongful pregnancy' cases.

Is this satisfactory? As we can see from the following extracts, the consensus among academic commentators would appear to be 'no'. Even a commentator like Tony Weir who supported the result in *McFarlane*, questioned the coherence of its reasoning:

Tony Weir[63]

For the fourteen years since *Emeh* the National Health Service, short of resources for curing the sick, has been disbursing large sums of money for the maintenance of children who have nothing wrong with them. To give but a single example out of very many: in 1993 the Lambeth Health Authority had to pay Mrs Cort no less than £140,679 ('James might not have been planned, but I wouldn't give him up for the world'). The House of Lords has now put an end to that . . .

The result in *McFarlane* is quite right, and we should not be surprised if the reasoning is uneasy: whenever it enters the family home the law of obligations—not just tort, but contract and restitution as well—has a marked tendency to go pear-shaped.

We saw earlier that the Australian judiciary has been critical of Lord Steyn's appeal to the 'inarticulate premises' of London commuters, and they are not alone. First, some have wondered whether the appeal to public morality is a way of lending objectivity to a judge's reliance upon his own instincts. This was the view of Lord Morison in the Scottish case of *McLelland v Greater Glasgow Health Board*:[64]

I must confess that my perception of what 'the traveller on the Underground' would think fair does not differ from that which I myself think and that therefore the test appears to me to be no less subjective if expressed in this way.

Secondly, Robin Oppenheim questions whether Lord Steyn's commuters would, in fact, come up with a single view on the fairness or otherwise of recovery.

Robin Oppenheim[65]

The law's primary concern should be corrective justice. The courts are ill-equipped to start making judgments, at very least without evidence, as to what the hypothetical person would regard as an ideal solution of distributive justice. It assumes a hypothetical person who is, in truth a judicial cipher, in order to create a uniformity of view where perhaps none exists (as perhaps signified by the continuing legal debate as to the rights and wrongs of . . . McFarlane).

Thirdly, Laura Hoyano argues that appeals to commuters represent an abdication of judicial responsibility for producing coherent principled decisions.

---

[63] 'The Unwanted Child' (2000) 59 Cambridge Law Journal 238–41.   [64] 2001 SLT 446.
[65] 'The "Mosaic" of Tort Law: The Duty of Care Question' (2003) Journal of Personal Injury Law 151–71.

Laura Hoyano[66]

> The transmogrification of the man on the Clapham omnibus is not limited to a change of public transport, as he is no longer just a convenient measure for the standard of care expected on non-experts, but also the gatekeeper for negligence law itself . . . How much time is there between stops on the London Underground, to allow those passengers to assimilate the evidence, weigh up all the factors, and look down the track to future implications of their decision—as is the duty of the judiciary? Not only might London commuters not represent public opinion in the country as a whole, but they might not produce a clear majority, particularly in a complex case. With the utmost respect to Lord Steyn, it is not satisfactory for tort law to be based upon an 'inarticulate premise as to what is morally acceptable and what is not' . . .
>
> Distributive justice . . . permits the judiciary to abdicate its responsibility to identify and explain intellectually rigorous and coherent principles as the basis for decisions, in favour of an empirically untested appeal to public opinion, yielding unpredictable results which invite reversal at every level of appeal, depending on each judge's subjective and avowedly instinctive notions of what justice requires. Thus distributive justice is no more illuminating—and arguably less—than the public policy which the Law Lords were anxious to eschew.

Fourthly, Samantha Singer suggests that, in *Rees*, considerations of distributive justice would in fact point in favour of recovery.

Samantha Singer[67]

> The House of Lords' decision that the entire financial costs of raising children like Ms Rees' son should lie with the individual, disabled parent is wholly shortsighted . . . By denying disabled parents damages for negligence—whether for the full expenses of bringing up the child or the additional costs—the risks that children in Ms Rees' son's situation will face being placed in care must increase. In turn, the fear of having their children removed often breeds reluctance in disabled parents to seek help in caring for their children. If this devastating end is avoided, the children of disabled parents often find themselves acting as carers for their parents. Indeed, Lord Millett used this fact as a reason for Ms Rees to be grateful for her surgeon's negligence:
>
>> Once the child is able to go to school alone and be of some help around the house, his or her presence will to a greater or lesser extent help to alleviate the disadvantages of the parent's disability. And once the child has grown to adulthood, he or she can provide immeasurable help to an ageing and disabled parent.
>
> It is surprising that such a naïve and unhelpful passage found its way into a speech in the House of Lords. What parent would wish this existence upon their child? Certainly not Karina Rees—this was part of her reason for being sterilised.

The gloss in *Rees* has also been subject to criticism. In the next extract, Nicky Priaulx suggests that it undermines the decision in *McFarlane*, and is derisory.

---

[66] 'Misconceptions about Wrongful Conception' (2002) 65 Modern Law Review 883–906.
[67] 'Casenote: *Rees v Darlington*' (2004) 26 Journal of Social Welfare and Family Law 403–15.

Nicky Priaulx[68]

Quite simply, *McFarlane* no longer stands as good law in the light of *Rees*. If healthy children constitute a benefit serving to outweigh all of the detriments of parenthood, then surely a conventional award overcompensates parents? . . .

But, one might ask, what of this conventional award? . . . While some might welcome this type of development and regard it as curative of the *McFarlane* legacy, it is argued that this scheme of 'compensation' pays nothing more than lip service to the principle of reproductive autonomy. On reflection, the award *is* best described as a gloss on *McFarlane*. Not only is the award derisory in a financial sense, certain to leave women for the greater part reliant upon their own resources in caring for the products of negligence, but so too must their Lordships' 'respect for autonomy' be seen in a similar light. How does the assumption that *all* parents are identically situated, with the same impact on their lives through the birth of an unplanned child illustrate respect for the notion *of individual* autonomy?

While Alasdair Maclean supports the 'gloss' in *Rees*, he admits that it may 'end up pleasing no one'.

Alasdair Maclean[69]

The beauty of [the conventional] award is that it makes no unjustly arbitrary distinction between the claimants, all of whom will receive the same award. It will also make it considerably easier to come to an out of court settlement since there will be no need to haggle over the projected expenses of raising a child or the impact of a disability on those costs. It is, however, a bold but risky strategy. It is bold because, with one stroke, it destroys the knotty tangle weaved by the courts' ill-considered use of distributive justice. It is risky because it may end up pleasing no one, except perhaps the NHS. Given the potential costs involved in raising a child, the parents of a healthy child may still feel hard done by. Disabled parents may feel aggrieved because the comparatively small award is unlikely to meet the additional costs incurred because of their disability. Those in favour of a full award in line with corrective justice principles may feel that the solution fails to do justice and those who believe *McFarlane* was a wholly just decision may feel that the judgment has been undermined.

Peter Cane suggests that the triad of cases—*McFarlane, Parkinson*, and *Rees*—illustrate the dangers of dealing with individual cases in isolation. It was, he argues, inevitable that *McFarlane* left the way open for an action in relation to a disabled child, and that in turn the question of whether the mother's disability makes a difference would also arise.

Peter Cane[70]

The real problem here is not the majority's solution [in *Rees*]—about the wisdom and fairness of which people might disagree—but the fact that the court in *McFarlane* apparently did not see *Parkinson* or *Rees* coming. What this sequence of cases shows is that if the

---

[68] 'That's one heck of an "unruly horse"! Riding roughshod over autonomy in wrongful conception' (2004) 12 Feminist Legal Studies 317–31.

[69] 'An Alexandrian Approach to the Knotty Problem of Wrongful Pregnancy: *Rees v Darlington Memorial Hospital NHS Trust* in the House of Lords' [2004] 3 Web JCLI.

[70] 'Another Failed Sterilisation' (2004) 120 Law Quarterly Review 189–93.

Law Lords (and their successors on the UK Supreme Court) are to take their law-making function seriously—as they seem (to their credit) inclined to do—they must, at least, be prepared to contemplate the possibility that it may be dangerous to consider individual cases too much in isolation and on their precise facts. If the increasingly popular notion of 'distributive justice' is to earn its keep, it must force judges beyond the mantra of treating like cases alike to thinking hard about the criteria of likeness—which involves, at least, comparing and contrasting the case before the court with cases not before the court. Stumbling from one set of facts to the next is, as *Rees* shows, a formula for confusion and instability in the law.

Finally, Robin Oppenheim suggests an alternative route for deciding these cases under the Human Rights Act 1998. If the 'limited recovery rule' in *McFarlane* interferes with a person's legitimate family planning decision, and therefore violates Article 8 (respect for private and family life), it could be justified only if it was proved to be both proportionate and necessary under Article 8(2).

Robin Oppenheim[71]

The point of departure should be as Hale LJ suggests in *Parkinson*, that a wrongful conception or birth claim involves an invasion of bodily integrity. This raises issues that can be addressed under Article 8 of the Convention, which provide respectively for the right to respect for a person's private and family life and home. . . .

It is eminently arguable that the ability to regulate one's own fertility and plan the size of one's family, in the context of loss of autonomy and bodily integrity that unwanted pregnancy entails, falls within the ambit of this bundle of rights and where negligent advice has the consequence of disrupting that ability when conception takes place there is an infringement of Article 8(1). . . .

If the limited recovery rule laid down by *McFarlane* is treated on the facts of a given case as an infringement of Article 8(1), the court must then go on to consider whether it fits within any of the restrictions under Article 8(2) that are necessary in a democratic society, namely whether it is a legitimate aim answering a pressing social need and applied proportionately. The only relevant exception is probably Article 8(2) on the basis that it was necessary 'for the protection of health or morals'. . . . It is difficult to see how non-recognition of a claim for economic loss could be said to be necessary for the protection of health or morals, as required by Article 8(2). There is no pressing social need for the restriction.

(b) 'WRONGFUL BIRTH'

In a wrongful birth action, the parents' claim is that the defendant's negligence led to their child's birth. When the claim is that, as a result of the defendant's negligence, the pregnant woman was not given the option of termination, an action will only be possible if termination would, in fact, have been lawful.[72] If tests only revealed the existence of the disability

---

[71] 'The "Mosaic" of Tort Law: The Duty of Care Question' (2003) Journal of Personal Injury Law 151–71.

[72] *Rance v Mid-Downs Health Authority* [1991] 1 QB 587.

after 24 weeks, for example, abortion would be lawful only if the disability met the threshold level of seriousness (see Chapter 13).

The facts which give rise to a wrongful birth action on the part of the parents will often be indistinguishable from those that might prompt the child to bring a 'wrongful life' action. It is, however, worth noting Lord Steyn's *obiter* comments on this point in *McFarlane v Tayside Health Board.*

McFarlane v Tayside Health Board [73]

Lord Steyn

There is no support in Scotland and England for a claim by a disadvantaged child for damage to him arising from his birth: see *McKay v Essex AHA*. Given this position, which also pre-vails in Australia, Trindade and Cane, *The Law of Torts in Australia*, 3rd ed. (1999) observe:

'it might seem inconsistent to allow a claim by the parents while that of the child, whether healthy or disabled, is rejected. Surely the parents' claim is equally repugnant to ideas of the sanctity and value of human life and rests, like that of the child, on a com-parison between a situation where a human being exists and one where it does not.'

In my view this reasoning is sound. Coherence and rationality demand that the claim by the parents should also be rejected.

As with all negligence actions, the claimant must establish the existence of a duty of care, its breach, and the causation of damage. Usually, establishing a duty of care will be unprob-lematic: a person who carries out prenatal screening unquestionably owes a duty of care to her patient.

Of course, in the modern NHS, prenatal testing services may be outsourced, in which case the health care professional who advises the pregnant woman will not have carried out the test herself. The question of whether she might nevertheless be responsible for negligence on the part of a subcontractor arose in *Farraj v King's Healthcare NHS Trust and Cytogenetic DNA Services*. Mr and Mrs Farraj were both healthy carriers of the Beta Thalassaemia Major (BTM) gene, and Mrs Farraj underwent prenatal testing at King's College Hospital (KCH) in order to establish whether her fetus had BTM. KCH sent the tissue sample to the second defendants, CSL, to be cultured. On appeal, the Court of Appeal were of the view that KCH was not responsible for CSL's negligence, and the only option for Mr and Mrs Farraj was to sue the laboratory directly.

Farraj v King's Healthcare NHS Trust and Cytogenetic DNA Services [74]

Smith LJ

The duty on KCH was to take reasonable care in all the circumstances to provide the claimants with reliable information as to the BTM status of the child Mrs Farraj was car-rying. That would include the duty to advise the claimants whether it was going to be possible to provide reliable information about the child's BTM status from the sample

[73] [2000] 2 AC 59.   [74] [2009] EWCA Civ 1203.

which had been submitted. It was not argued . . . that KCH's decision to subcontract the cleaning, sorting and culturing of the sample to CSL was unreasonable or amounted to a breach of duty, given that it had no in-house cytogenetics facility. It was accepted that CSL was a suitable laboratory to carry out those aspects of the work. . . . [T]he only finding of fact open to the judge was that there was indeed a clearly understood arrangement as between KCH and CSL. . . . Under that arrangement, KCH was entitled to assume, unless it heard from CSL to the contrary, that the sample had provided some foetal material suitable for culture.

Once a duty of care has been established, the next question is whether that duty has been breached. This was an issue in *Lillywhite v University College London Hospitals NHS Trust*.[75] Mrs Lillywhite had had an abnormal routine ultrasound scan and was referred to an eminent expert in fetal medicine, Professor Rodeck. He had been asked to look for brain structures, which the first sonographer had been unable to find. The relevant brain structures were not in fact there, but Professor Rodeck wrongly concluded that they were. By a majority, the Court of Appeal found that 'there was no plausible explanation for how he could have done so in the exercise of reasonable care and skill'. Professor Rodeck was therefore found to have fallen below the standard of care that could be expected of a consultant sonologist.

Having established a breach of duty, the next step is to prove that the breach caused the damage. The damage which is caused when the mother is not given the option of termination is the birth of a disabled child, and, according to ordinary tort law principles, damages should attempt to put the mother in the position she would have been if the tort had not been committed. Two important issues arise. First, the mother must establish that, if she had known that her child was likely to be born disabled, she would have taken steps to avoid its birth; that is, that she would have had an abortion. This will be difficult because the woman is necessarily speculating about how she would have reacted to the diagnosis, with the benefit of hindsight, and with a claim for damages depending upon her assertion that she would have requested a termination.

In *Lillywhite*, it was relatively straightforward for the mother to prove, on the balance of probabilities, that she would have terminated the pregnancy if Professor Rodeck had alerted her to the fetus's abnormalities. Following the original abnormal scan, Mrs Lillywhite had sought two further second opinions: she was evidently concerned about the prospect that her child would be born disabled, and the judge was satisfied that she would have requested a termination if Professor Rodeck had identified the fetus's abnormal brain structure.

In contrast, in *Deriche v Ealing Hospital NHS Trust*[76] Mrs Deriche had contracted chicken pox during pregnancy. Because her reaction to having been told of the possibility of a 'congenital malformation' was not to investigate the possibility of a termination, Buckley J was not persuaded by her assertion that she would have terminated the pregnancy if the fetal anomaly scan had identified her son's disabilities: 'her assertion that any problem would have caused her to have a termination is, I am afraid, a product of the tragedy that subsequently occurred and I cannot accept it as an accurate statement of her state of mind in 1996'.

In addition to the factual difficulty of proving that, if she had known about her fetus's disability, she would have terminated the pregnancy, it might also be argued that this

[75] [2005] EWCA Civ 1466.   [76] [2003] EWHC 3104 (QB).

requirement puts the mother in an invidious position. By the time the case reaches court, the child is likely to be a much loved member of the family. The only way a mother can seek damages to help to cope with her child's special needs is to prove that, if she had known about her disabilities, she would have prevented her birth by having an abortion.

In the next extract, Wendy Hensel takes this point further and argues that 'wrongful birth' actions send a 'regrettable message' to disabled people in general.

Wendy F Hensel[77]

No matter how compelling the need, or how gross the negligence involved, no assistance will be extended to the family who would have chosen to embrace or simply accept the impaired child prior to his birth. Although the lost choice identified as the injury in wrongful birth claims is identical between the mother who would have aborted and the mother who would have decided to carry the impaired child to term, recovery is all or nothing. Against this background, the desperate parent is placed in an untenable position—either she must deny needing medical care for her child or disavow his very existence in open court in order to secure financial assistance. . . .

Because wrongful birth . . . actions extend compensation only to those parents who would have chosen to abort an impaired child, these torts strengthen and reinforce the message that abortion is the preferred means of 'curing' disability in society.

Secondly, what would it mean to put the mother in the position she would have been in if the tort had not been committed? Should damages cover all of the costs of the child's upbringing, or only those associated with the disability? On the one hand, the defendant's negligence caused this child to be born, and if the child had not been born, then none of the costs associated with their upbringing would have been incurred. On the other hand, if the child had been healthy, the pregnancy would not have been terminated, and the parents would, in any event, have incurred the costs of caring for a healthy child. It might therefore be argued that it is only the additional costs associated with the disability that were caused by the defendant's negligence. This was the approach taken by Toulson J in *Lee v Taunton and Somerset NHS Trust*:[78] 'If, following a termination of her pregnancy with George, she had continued with her attempts and had been successful, she would have incurred the costs of bringing up a healthy child in any event.'

Although wrongful birth cases differ from wrongful pregnancy claims, in the wrongful birth cases which followed *McFarlane*, we can see the lower courts grappling with what relevance, if any, *McFarlane* might have. For example, in *Hardman v Amin*, Henriques J held that *McFarlane* did not affect recovery for the wrongful birth of a disabled child. This was a case in which a GP had negligently failed to diagnose his pregnant patient's rubella infection, leading to the birth of her severely handicapped son. Henriques J was reassured that commuters on the Underground would accept that the defendant should be responsible for the costs of a child's disability, where it was his fault that the child was born disabled.

---

[77] 'The Disabling Impact of Wrongful Birth and Wrongful Life Actions' (2005) 40 Harvard Civil Rights–Civil Liberties Law Review 141.
[78] [2001] 1 FLR 419.

Hardman v Amin[79]

Henriques J

If the commuters on the underground were asked whether the costs of bringing up Daniel (which are attributable to his disability) should fall on the claimant or the rest of the family, or the state, or the defendant, I am satisfied that the very substantial majority, having regard to the particular circumstances of this case, would say that the expense should fall on the wrongdoer.

A similar approach was adopted in *Lee v Taunton and Somerset NHS Trust*. The couple believed themselves to be at risk of having a disabled child as a result of their epilepsy medication. A high-resolution ultrasound was performed during pregnancy, but it failed to detect the fetus's spina bifida. Toulson J suggested that commuters on the Underground would not necessarily regard the birth of a disabled child as a blessing, and nor would they regard it as unjust that a negligent doctor should be required to compensate the parents for failing to give them the option of preventing the child's birth.

Lee v Taunton and Somerset NHS Trust[80]

Toulson J

I do not believe that it would be right for the law to deem the birth of a disabled child to be a blessing, in all circumstances and regardless of the extent of the child's disabilities; or to regard the responsibility for the care of such a child as so enriching in the ordinary nature of things that it would be unjust for a parent to recover the cost from a negligent doctor on whose skill that parent had properly relied to prevent the situation.

If the matter were put to an opinion poll among passengers on the Underground, I would be surprised if a majority would support such a view.

4 CONCLUSION

The uncertainties that remained after the House of Lords' judgment in *McFarlane* made it inevitable that cases such as *Parkinson* and *Rees* would follow, in order to test whether slight variations to the facts would enable claimants to recover the maintenance costs of children conceived as a result of another's negligence. Neither *Parkinson* nor *Rees* has in fact clarified the scope of *McFarlane*. Following the decision in *Rees*, two questions remain unanswered. First, the status of the exception to *McFarlane* in *Parkinson* is uncertain. The House of Lords was split over whether *Parkinson* had been rightly decided, and so a question mark hangs over that decision.

Secondly, what is the scope of the conventional award in *Rees*? The justifications given for it are certainly not confined to disabled parents: in Lord Millett's words there had been a 'denial of an important aspect of . . . personal autonomy, viz the right to limit the size of their family'. Similarly, Lord Bingham held that 'the real loss suffered in a situation of this kind . . . is that a parent, particularly (even today) the mother, has been denied through the negligence of another, the opportunity to live her life in the way that she wished and planned'.

---

[79] *Hardman v Amin* (2000) 59 BMLR 58. [80] [2001] 1 FLR 419.

Should a future wrongful conception case reach the Supreme Court, it would be especially interesting if Baroness Hale were on the panel. In her judgments in the Court of Appeal in both *Parkinson* and *Rees*, her dissatisfaction with the decision in *McFarlane* is evident. Recall her extraordinarily detailed description of the physical and emotional invasiveness of pregnancy, childbirth, and motherhood. In *Rees*, a number of their Lordships admitted that the principal loss in these cases is an interference with the woman's reproductive autonomy, but none went quite so far as Hale LJ, as she then was, did in *Parkinson*.

Importantly, however, the modest conventional award, and the possibility that it might have universal application provides a substantial disincentive towards further litigation. The costs of bringing a claim will exceed the modest conventional award, and so both prospective claimants and their legal advisers are likely to decide that it is not worth engaging in expensive and time-consuming litigation if the best that one might hope for would be an award of £15,000.

In relation to 'wrongful life' actions, it is often assumed that the door closed on them many years ago in *McKay*. Yet, for two reasons, this assumption may be premature. First, the judgments placed considerable emphasis upon the sanctity of human life, and while this would undoubtedly still be a relevant factor, it may exert less force over the judiciary now than it did in 1982. As we see in Chapter 17, many cases have explored the question of when life-prolonging treatment might become futile, or not in the patient's best interests, and it is evident that the 'sanctity principle', while still important, does not always trump other considerations.

Secondly, there has not been very much litigation under the Congenital Disabilities (Civil Liability) Act 1976, but if or when a claimant brings an action under section 1A(2)(b), the court may be forced to address an inconsistency between the 1976 Act and the Court of Appeal's judgment in *McKay*. In such a case the claimant would be claiming that negligence in the process of embryo selection resulted in a genetically abnormal embryo being transferred to the woman's body. The disabled child would be arguing that non-negligent selection would have prevented her birth, and the courts would have to grapple with what would appear to be a statutory action for wrongful life.

FURTHER READING

Cane, Peter, 'Another Failed Sterilisation' (2004) 120 Law Quarterly Review 189–93.

Hoyano, Laura, 'Misconceptions about Wrongful Conception' (2002) 65 Modern Law Review 883–906.

Maclean, Alasdair, 'An Alexandrian Approach to the Knotty Problem of Wrongful Pregnancy: *Rees v Darlington Memorial Hospital NHS Trust* in the House of Lords' [2004] 3 Web JCLI.

Mason, JK, *The Troubled Pregnancy: Legal Wrongs and Rights in Reproduction* (CUP: Cambridge, 2007) chs 3–6.

Morris, Anne and Saintier, Severine, 'To Be or Not to Be: Is That the Question? Wrongful Life and Misconceptions' (2003) 11 Medical Law Review 167–93.

Priaulx, Nicolette, *The Harm Paradox: Tort Law and the Unwanted Child in an Era of Choice* (UCL Press: London, 2006).

Sheldon, Sally, 'Only Skin Deep? The Harm of Being Born a Different Colour to One's Parents' (2011) 19 Medical Law Review 657–68.

Singer, Samantha, 'Casenote: *Rees v Darlington*' (2004) 26 Journal of Social Welfare and Family Law 403–15.

15

ASSISTED CONCEPTION

CENTRAL ISSUES

1. Assisted conception services are regulated by the Human Fertilisation and Embryology Act 1990, as amended, and clinics must be licensed by the Human Fertilisation and Embryology Authority (HFEA). The HFEA inspects against more detailed guidance in its Code of Practice and in the Directions that it issues to clinics.

2. In theory, there are few restrictions upon access to fertility treatment in the UK. In practice, treatment is expensive and NHS funding is patchy.

3. It is increasingly common for people to travel to receive fertility treatment overseas, where regulation may be different or absent.

4. Anonymity used to be the norm when donated gametes (sperm and eggs) were used in treatment, but since 2005, donors must be identifiable. Donors receive a fixed sum to compensate them for their expenses and inconvenience. Egg-sharing schemes involve women receiving free or cheaper treatment in return for donating half of their eggs.

5. Preimplantation genetic diagnosis (PGD) is used to screen embryos for genetic conditions, so that only unaffected embryos are transferred to the woman's uterus. PGD can also be used to find out if the child would be a compatible tissue donor for a sick older sibling. Mitochondrial replacement is a new technique used to prevent children inheriting mitochondrial disease from their mothers. In the future, genome editing might also be used to promote the health of future children.

1 INTRODUCTION

The birth of Louise Brown, the first baby created by *in vitro* fertilization (IVF) in Oldham on 25 July 1978 undoubtedly represented one of the most important scientific breakthroughs of the twentieth century. Of course, assisted conception did not 'begin' in 1978. The first reported case of donor insemination dates back to the end of the nineteenth century. Nevertheless, the ability to fertilize eggs *in vitro* has been particularly significant, not least because it has facilitated the subsequent development of other techniques, such as preimplantation genetic diagnosis and mitochondrial replacement (discussed later).

Initially, the creation of 'test-tube' babies, as they were then described, was greeted with scepticism, and even hostility. But because infertility is a common problem—about one in seven couples experience difficulty in conceiving[1]—it was not long before there was widespread, although not universal, acceptance of techniques that can offer hope to people who are not able to have children naturally. Approximately 2 per cent of children born in the UK are now conceived *in vitro*,[2] and most people know of at least one family created with medical assistance.

It should, however, be remembered that fertility treatment is not always successful, and so IVF has by no means ended involuntary childlessness. In particular, and contrary to popular belief, IVF does not provide a solution to the problem of women's age-related fertility loss. Women may think that if they 'leave it too late', IVF will be able to help, but the figures tell a different story: the live birth rate per cycle of IVF treatment in women under the age of 35 is 32.8 per cent, falling to 20.7 per cent for women aged 38–39, 13.1 per cent for women aged 40–42, and 4.4 per cent for women aged over 43. As Daly and Bewley point out, changes in society are responsible for a widening gap between the age when women feel ready to become mothers and the age at which they are most likely to get pregnant, and IVF is not the solution.

Irenee Daly and Susan Bewley[3]

There is a public perception that fertility can be restored via IVF. For example, a participant in [a] study of childless women over thirty said: 'Women are having babies later because of technology. Fertility technology that allows us to kind of extend our fertility period, where before we couldn't you know?' . . .

Although IVF has brought joy to millions of people, it was not developed with the intention to encourage older motherhood. Assisted reproduction treatment may be able to assist a man with a low sperm count or overcome the problem of a woman with blocked Fallopian tubes, but unfortunately it is not designed to overcome egg degeneration. . . .

It takes the current younger generation longer to reach adult milestones which were more easily attainable for previous generations. These include moving away from home, financial independence, getting married and starting a family. . . . Passing through adult milestones at a later age has itself now become normalized. Given this, it is no wonder that many women no longer think in terms of a normative age to have children. Instead they focus on feeling psychologically ready to have children, a status attained by moving through these milestones.

While no longer a common view, there are still those who oppose assisted conception on principle. In 2008, a Papal Encyclical reaffirmed the Catholic Church's opposition to IVF, on the grounds that the only licit way to reproduce is through the 'conjugal act'.[4] Perhaps paradoxically, as Laura Purdy explains, opposition to the use of reproductive technologies has also come from feminists.

---

[1] *Fertility Treatment in 2013* (HFEA, 2014).   [2] Ibid.

[3] 'Reproductive ageing and conflicting clocks: King Midas' touch' (2013) 27 Reproductive BioMedicine Online 722–32.

[4] *Instruction Dignitas Personae on Certain Bioethical Questions* (Vatican, 2008).

Laura Purdy[5]

Feminist objections can be traced to the fear that assisted reproduction will help men to subjugate women. Feminists emphasize that social pronatalism leads many women to undertake costly and potentially risky procedures to remedy infertility that would not otherwise trouble them. Furthermore, since men still run society, and are especially prominent in science and medicine, women's quest for help with reproduction adds to men's power over them . . .

Women's consent might also be questioned on feminist grounds. Pronatalism is pervasive in human society, as is the attitude that women who do not have children are necessarily unfulfilled, or even worthless. . . . The onus of barrenness is so great that some women will even undertake IVF when it is their husbands who suffer from a reproductive problem. Although these points suggest that women considering IVF should have lengthy counselling, they do not support a ban on the practice. Doing so 'to protect women against themselves' would treat women as legal incompetents, damaging women more than unwise reproductive treatments.

In this chapter, we begin by looking at the regulation of assisted conception in the UK, which involves a detailed look at the legislation—the Human Fertilisation and Embryology Act 1990, which was substantially amended in 2008—and at the work of the Human Fertilisation and Embryology Authority (HFEA). We break this down into analysis of the licensing procedures, through which clinics are inspected and authorized to perform certain procedures; access to treatment; consent to the use of gametes (sperm and eggs); gamete donation; rules governing the parentage of children; preimplantation genetic diagnosis; and mitochondrial replacement. We also look briefly at genome editing and the as yet unrealized possibility of human reproductive cloning. In the next chapter we consider the regulation of surrogacy.

2 REGULATION OF ASSISTED CONCEPTION

In 1982, four years after the birth of Louise Brown, the Committee of Inquiry into Human Fertilisation and Embryology, chaired by Mary Warnock, an academic philosopher, was commissioned to make recommendations on the regulation of fertility treatment and embryo research.[6] Its report was published in 1984, and although it was debated in the House of Commons shortly afterwards, the Human Fertilisation and Embryology Bill, which was based upon the Warnock Committee's recommendations, was not introduced to parliament until 1989.

In the meantime, a number of private members' bills were introduced which would have prohibited embryo disposal, and, as a result, would have outlawed IVF treatment and research. In the mid-1980s, for example, the Unborn Children (Protection) Bill initially commanded a parliamentary majority of 172, and only failed to become law because of effective delaying tactics deployed by its opponents.

By the time the Human Fertilisation and Embryology Bill finally came before parliament, hostility towards embryo destruction appeared to have softened, and there was greater acceptance of both fertility treatment and embryo research. This was assisted by the announcement, towards the end of the 1980s, of the first successful cycles of preimplantation

---

[5] 'Assisted Reproduction' in Helga Kuhse and Peter Singer (eds), *A Companion to Bioethics* (Blackwell: Oxford, 1998) 163–72.

[6] *Report of the Committee of Enquiry into Human Fertilisation and Embryology* (HMSO: London, 1984).

genetic diagnosis, used to enable people at risk of having children with serious genetic diseases to give birth to healthy children. The Human Fertilisation and Embryology Act was passed in 1990, and came into force the following year.

There were a number of factors behind the decision substantially to reform the 1990 Act in 2008. As we saw in Chapter 12 when we considered embryo research, new scientific developments had put pressure upon the statutory language and resulted in legal challenges. This was also true in relation to some treatment services, such as tissue typing. The 2008 Act was an amending statute, and although much of the original regulatory framework was left intact, it did introduce some significant changes.

(a) THE HUMAN FERTILISATION AND EMBRYOLOGY AUTHORITY

Section 5 of the Human Fertilisation and Embryology Act set up the Human Fertilisation and Embryology Authority (HFEA). At the time of writing, the HFEA has 12 members, of which a majority must be 'lay', that is, they must not be clinicians or scientists.[7]

The HFEA has a number of different functions. It regulates fertility treatment and embryo research (see further Chapter 12) by inspecting clinics and issuing licences, and by maintaining a register of information about the provision of treatment and its outcomes. Under section 25, it must maintain a Code of Practice which gives guidance to clinics about the proper conduct of licensable activities. Section 8(cb) provides that the HFEA is under a duty to promote compliance with the Code. In addition to the Code, the HFEA also has the power to issue Directions on specific issues, with which clinics must comply.

There are obvious advantages in using a Code of Practice and Directions, rather than primary legislation, to regulate such a fast-moving area of clinical practice and scientific research. A good example of the flexibility offered by this model is the changes in the rules governing the number of embryos that may be transferred in one cycle of IVF.

The health risks associated with multiple pregnancies are serious for babies and for women. Twins and triplets are much more likely to be born prematurely, and the risk of death around the time of birth is 3–6 times higher for twins and nine times higher for triplets. As a result of these risks, HFEA policy—set out in the Code and via Directions—has been directed towards ensuring that those women who are most likely to have a multiple pregnancy have only one embryo put back per cycle. All clinics must now have a 'multiple birth reduction strategy', and should not exceed the HFEA's maximum multiple birth rate (this has come down from 24 to 10 per cent).

HFEA 8th Code of Practice

The strategy must set out:

(a) how the centre aims to reduce the multiple birth rate following treatment at that centre in any calendar year, and to ensure the rate does not exceed the maximum specified by the Authority as set out in Directions.

(b) the circumstances in which the person responsible would consider it appropriate to recommend Single Embryo Transfer (SET) to a patient.

[7] See further www.hfea.gov.uk.

The Code thus has the advantage of being able to respond to a shifting evidence base. The legal status of the Code of Practice is, however, a little unclear. A breach of the Code is not a criminal offence, unlike many breaches of the Act itself. Nevertheless, breaches of the Code can be taken into account by a licence committee when deciding whether to vary or revoke a licence.

The HFEA is also responsible for advising the Secretary of State for Health on, among other things, the need for new primary legislation. Under section 7 of the Act, it must produce an Annual Report to the Secretary of State for Health, describing the activities it has undertaken in the previous 12 months, and setting out its work programme for the following year. These Reports are laid before parliament by the minister.

(b) LICENSING

One of the HFEA's most important purposes is to control the activities of licensed clinics and research centres. Sections 3 and 4 of the Human Fertilisation and Embryology Act 1990 provide that the creation, use, and storage of embryos, and the storage and use of gametes, can only be carried out under a licence granted by the HFEA. Carrying out any of these activities without a licence is a criminal offence.[8] It is also a criminal offence to procure, test, process, or distribute gametes without a licence.

It is worth asking why fertility treatment is subject to this special regulatory regime. Several reasons might be put forward, not all of which are convincing. First, although there are health risks associated with treatments like IVF, such as the risk of ovarian hyperstimulation syndrome (OHSS), other potentially risky medical treatments are not subjected to this sort of special regulatory framework. In any event, some of the risks associated with IVF—such as OHSS or multiple pregnancy—also exist for unlicensed treatments, such as the prescription of fertility drugs.

A second possible explanation is the special moral concern for embryos created outside the female body. But, of course, this justification does not apply to other licensed treatments, such as donor insemination. Thirdly, it might be argued that the creation of children through artificial means raises ethical dilemmas, such as who should be permitted to have access to treatment; this explanation is, however, undermined by the comparatively lax regulation of surrogacy, discussed in the next chapter.

The most persuasive explanation is that the form regulation takes in the UK reflects the historical context in 1989, when the original Bill was drafted. Professional bodies, such as the Royal College of Obstetricians and Gynaecologists, had not yet produced their own good practice guidance. Given the novelty and ethical controversy of IVF in 1989, it seemed sensible to consolidate the rules on best practice within a licensing regime. Now, of course, there is extensive professional guidance available to clinicians. Indeed, the HFEA increasingly relies upon professional bodies to develop guidance: an example would be the British Andrology Society's involvement in setting appropriate age limits for sperm donors.

Under section 11 of the Act, the HFEA can grant four different types of licence: for treatment services; non-medical fertility services;[9] storage of gametes and embryos; and research on embryos (see Chapter 12). Once an application for a licence has been received by the HFEA, an inspection team will visit the premises and prepare a report. Licences are issued and renewed by the Executive Licensing Panel of HFEA staff, or in more controversial cases, by the Licence Committee of HFEA members. Licences for treatment and storage can be

---

[8] Section 41.

[9] Defined in s 2 as any services that are provided, in the course of a business, for the purpose of assisting women to carry children, but are not medical, surgical, or obstetric services.

granted for a maximum of five years,[10] and shorter licences can be used to ensure more regular oversight. In addition to its planned programme of renewal and interim inspections, the HFEA also carries out unannounced inspections.

Centres are under a duty to report incidents and 'near misses' to the HFEA. If there is a risk of reoccurrence, an anonymized 'Alert' will be issued to all licensed centres notifying them of the newly identified risk. Centres are not penalized for reporting incidents. On the contrary, the HFEA encourages them to do so as part of the trend towards learning from mistakes, which we explored in Chapter 3. In the light of the HFEA's well-established system of recording and learning from mistakes, it is interesting to note that the rate of incidents, or adverse events (less than 1 per cent)[11] is lower in the assisted conception sector than in other areas of the health service, where it has been estimated that approximately 10 per cent of treatments result in some sort of adverse event.

Sections 12–15 of the Act specify a number of standard licensing conditions, which are automatically attached to each licence. We look at some of these in detail later, but they include that the consent provisions contained in Schedule 3 are complied with; that account has been taken of the welfare of any child that might be born; and that the statutory storage periods for gametes and embryos are not exceeded. In addition, the Licence Committee may attach specific conditions to an individual centre's licence (perhaps in response to past breaches of the Act).

Under section 16(2) each licence application must designate a Person Responsible (PR), whom the licence committee must consider a suitable person to supervise the activities authorized by the licence, and in particular, under section 17, to ensure that suitable practices are used, and the conditions of the licence complied with. Until the *Attorney General's Reference (No 2 of 2003)*,[12] it was not clear whether the PR might be vicariously criminally liable for offences committed by his staff. In this case, a rogue embryologist had been guilty of extremely serious misconduct, but the Court of Appeal decided that the PR had not vicariously committed an offence.

Section 18 deals with the revocation and variation of licences. A licence can be revoked or varied for a number of reasons, including if misleading information was provided for the purpose of the licence application; or if the premises are no longer suitable; or if the PR has failed to discharge his responsibilities or comply with Directions; or if there has been any other material change in circumstances. Revocation and variation are also possible if the licence committee is not satisfied that the PR is a suitable person to discharge their duties, or if the PR dies or is convicted of an offence under the Act. Section 19 sets out the procedure for refusing, varying, or revoking a licence. Notice must be given to the PR, who then has an opportunity to make representations to the Licence Committee within 28 days, with a further appeal possible to the Authority's separate Appeal Committee, made up of non-members.

As a public body, decisions of the Authority and its licence committees must comply with the Human Rights Act and are judicially reviewable. Licensing decisions must therefore be proportionate, lawful (ie licence committees must act within their statutory powers), and rational (ie decisions must not be *Wednesbury*[13] unreasonable). Committees must take into account relevant factors, and disregard irrelevant considerations.

As we see in this chapter and Chapter 12, there have been several applications for judicial review of decisions of the HFEA. In one of the first, *R (on the application of Assisted*

---

[10] Schedule 2, paras 1(5) and 2(3).

[11] *Adverse incidents in fertility clinics: lessons to learn January–December 2014* (HFEA, 2015).

[12] [2004] EWCA Crim 785.

[13] The test is whether no reasonable body could have come to the same decision: *Associated Provincial Picture Houses v Wednesbury Corporation* [1948] 1 KB 223.

Reproduction and Gynaecology Centre) v Human Fertilisation and Embryology Authority, the Court of Appeal spelled out that, provided the Authority's decision was rational and that it had not exceeded its powers, the courts should have no role.

R (on the application of Assisted Reproduction and Gynaecology Centre) v Human Fertilisation and Embryology Authority[14]

Wall J

Disagreements between doctors and scientific bodies in this pioneering field are inevitable. The United Kingdom, through the Act, has opted for a system of licensing and regulation. The Authority is the body which is empowered by parliament to regulate. Like any public authority, it is open to challenge by way of judicial review, if it exceeds or abuses the powers and responsibilities given to it by parliament; but where, as is manifest here from an examination of the facts, it considers requests for advice carefully and thoroughly, and produces opinions which are plainly rational, the court, in our judgment, has no part to play in the debate, and certainly no power to intervene to strike down any such decision. The fact that the appellants may disagree with the Authority's advice is neither here nor there.

Rather than challenging the substance of an HFEA decision, applications for judicial review might be more likely to succeed on procedural grounds. For example, in *R (on the application of Assisted Reproduction and Gynaecology Centre) v HFEA*, the same clinic challenged successfully the Authority's power to place a condition (setting the maximum multiple birth rate) on all clinics' licences before it had had the chance to contest that decision through representations and an appeal.

R (on the application of Assisted Reproduction and Gynaecology Centre) v HFEA[15]

Patterson J

A consequence of [the HFEA's] interpretation would be that the centres would operate for a period of time in compliance with an imposed condition which may eventually be overturned by the appeals committee.... When, as here, a considerable time will have elapsed before the appeals committee can convene that could lead to an absurd and unfair position over a protracted period so far as any challenging claimant is concerned. The claimant may have to amend their clinical process to accommodate the condition only to have to revert to what is now their current practice if successful on appeal some time later. In that eventuality there would have been an unwarranted and unnecessary interference in clinical practice. Further, the person responsible would have to ensure that the conditions of the licence were complied with at the very time when those conditions were disputed and under appeal.

(c) LIMITS ON THE HFEA'S POWERS

It is worth noting that the HFEA's ability to regulate fertility services is not comprehensive. As Margaret Brazier points out in the following extract, the HFEA exercises

[14] [2002] EWCA Civ 20.   [15] [2013] EWHC 3087 (Admin).

little control over the market in fertility services. Most fertility treatment in the UK is provided in the private sector, but the HFEA cannot control the prices clinics charge. It is also increasingly common for people to travel abroad for treatment, where the HFEA has no power at all.

Margaret Brazier[16]

The most profound change in regulating reproductive medicine since Warnock is, I would argue, the dramatically increased role of commerce. Warnock based its recommendations in relation both to fertility treatment and research on the supposition that fertility services would be integrated into the NHS . . . The enormous commercial potential of developments in reproductive medicine was hardly foreseen . . .

The reproduction business, even in the United Kingdom, is set to spawn two rather different sorts of market. The first, which effectively exists today, is the market in fertility services. The private sector, involving both private licensed fertility clinics and the companies who will seek to develop both new fertility treatments and therapeutic cloning, necessarily operates on a profit-making basis. They have a vested interest in the expansion of their business. The more treatment cycles a woman undergoes, the more people who seek treatment, the greater the profit to a clinic. . . .

Another nightmare awaits the HFEA and its counterparts in continental Europe. Each national jurisdiction has sought to fashion a scheme of regulation acceptable to its own culture and community. However those wealthy enough to participate in reproduction markets can readily evade their domestic constraints. If I can order sperm on the internet, or hire a surrogate mother from Bolivia, are British regulators wasting their time? The international ramifications of the reproductive business may prove to be a more stringent test of the strength of British law than all of the difficult ethical dilemmas that have gone before.

Although it is impossible to give exact numbers, Shenfield et al have calculated that there are about 24–30,000 cycles of cross-border treatment in Europe each year, involving 11–14,000 patients.[17] There are several reasons why people might seek assisted conception services abroad: cost (IVF is cheaper in India); avoiding long waiting lists (there are more egg donors available in Spain); avoiding legal restrictions (in the UK this might mean avoiding the bans on sex selection and anonymous sperm donation); and a perception that care abroad will be better or more likely to succeed. In their interviews with UK couples who had travelled abroad for fertility treatment, Lorraine Culley et al found that many had done so after many years of unsuccessful treatment in the UK.

Lorraine Culley et al[18]

We found that 78% of cases had received some form of treatment in the UK before going overseas. In our sample, a substantial proportion of those needing donor oocytes were seeking treatment abroad at the end of a long history of other forms of treatment.

---

[16] 'Regulating the Reproduction Business?' (1999) 7 Medical Law Review 166–93.
[17] F Shenfield et al, 'Cross border reproductive care in six European countries' (2010) 25 Human Reproduction 1361–8.
[18] L Culley, 'Crossing borders for fertility treatment: motivations, destinations and outcomes of UK fertility travellers' (2011) 26 Human Reproduction 2373–81.

In some cases they had been unsuccessful in treatment with their own gametes, and had now reached an age where donor oocytes were the only realistic option. In other cases, patients using their own gametes had experienced repeated treatment failures in the UK, but reported that they were not being offered any alternative treatments by UK clinics and felt that they needed to 'try something different'. In a small number of cases (17%), patients were motivated to go overseas by a dissatisfaction with the level of care they received in their UK clinic and several mentioned better success rates abroad (29%).

Cross-border reproductive treatment has been called 'reproductive tourism', but many patients object to this label, with its implication that travelling for treatment is fun and pleasurable. In their interviews, Culley et al found that

All our participants . . . actively resisted the 'fertility tourist' label and felt that the connotations of pleasure and leisure in no way represented the process of organizing and undertaking fertility treatment. They felt strongly that this was an unfair and inaccurate representation of their experiences.[19]

It has therefore been suggested that 'reproductive exile' is a better, though equally loaded, term.[20]

In some countries there are no restrictions upon the number of embryos transferred in any one cycle. In 2009, for example, it was reported that a woman in the US had given birth to octuplets after a doctor put six embryos back into her womb. While this is an extreme example, British women have returned from having IVF treatment in India pregnant with triplets and quads. In addition to the health risks for pregnant women and their children, higher order multiple births impose significant additional costs on NHS neonatal services: a triplet pregnancy costs the NHS ten times as much as a singleton. In McKelvey et al's study of UCLH's specialist multiple pregnancy unit, a quarter of patients had had fertility treatment overseas.[21]

In the next extract, Debora Spar suggests that part of the problem of cross-border reproductive treatment is that it is only available to the wealthy.

Debora Spar[22]

One might argue that this market for reproductive services is not so remarkable. We trade all kinds of services internationally—why not babies, or the components thereof? One might also argue that the current regulatory patchwork makes political and commercial sense: if Germany wants to ban egg transfer, it should. And if German couples want to avoid this regulation, they should procure their eggs abroad. The problem with this approach, however, is that it turns assisted reproduction into a for-profit business, a lucrative marketplace in which rich couples scour the world in pursuit of high-tech offspring,

[19] Ibid.

[20] Guido Pennings, 'Reproductive exile versus reproductive tourism' (2005) 20 Human Reproduction 3571–2.

[21] A McKelvey et al, 'The impact of cross-border reproductive care or "fertility tourism" on NHS maternity services' (2009) 116 British Journal of Obstetrics & Gynaecology 1520–3.

[22] 'Reproductive tourism and the regulatory map' (2005) 352 New England Journal of Medicine 531–3.

> while poorer would-be parents are consigned to fate. A cross-border market for reproduction also means that societies that oppose assisted reproduction may nevertheless pay its costs. For who can prove that premature quintuplets born in Bremen were conceived in Istanbul?

RF Storrow further suggests that the availability of what might be described as the 'safety valve' of citizens' freedom to travel abroad has 'emboldened' some countries—such as Germany, Austria, and Italy—to enact more restrictive provisions.

RF Storrow[23]

> [T]he availability of cross-border reproductive travel emboldens legislatures to enact stricter and more symbolic prohibitions than they might otherwise have the political wherewithal to do. The result is the export of claimed harms into other jurisdictions that are inadequately equipped to address the complications and burdens that arise when foreigners enter their borders in search of solutions to reproductive problems. The exploitation of young gamete providers and the distortion in the delivery of medical care to the local population are the likely results of the cross-border reproductive phenomenon.

In *SH v Austria*, a judgment I criticize in the next extract, the Grand Chamber of the European Court of Human Rights (ECtHR) relied in part upon the availability of cross-border reproductive treatment in order to uphold Austria's restrictive rules on gamete donation.

Emily Jackson[24]

> What was especially striking about the majority's decision in *SH and Others v Austria* was that, while defending Austria's restrictive rules, the Grand Chamber also observed 'that there is no prohibition under Austrian law on going abroad to seek treatment of infertility that uses artificial procreation techniques not allowed in Austria and that in the event of a successful treatment the Civil Code contains clear rules on paternity and maternity that respect the wishes of the parents'. It therefore appeared to be a little easier to justify Austria's wide margin of appreciation because it was also simple for Austrian citizens to avoid its effects by travelling to another country with a more relaxed regulatory regime.
>
> In many ways, this is peculiar: it appears to suggest that the harshness of a prohibition can be defended, at least in part, because it is fairly easy to avoid it. If the margin of appreciation is so important to member states, isn't it a little odd that their citizens are simultaneously given a simple route through which they can access the banned treatment? . . .
>
> In short, the oddity of the majority judgment in *SH and Others v. Austria* is that the restrictions on treatment in Austria were slightly easier to justify because rich Austrian citizens might be able to avail themselves of the Wild West of assisted conception services elsewhere in the world.

---

[23] 'The pluralism problem in cross-border reproductive care' (2010) 25 Human Reproduction 2939–43.
[24] '*SH and Others v Austria*' (2012) 25 Reproductive BioMedicine Online 663–4.

(d) RECORDING AND DISCLOSING INFORMATION

Section 31 of the Human Fertilisation and Embryology Act requires the HFEA to keep a register of information collected from licensed centres. Through Directions, the HFEA requires licence holders to collect information about donors, recipients, treatment services, and the children born as a result, and, under section 33A, to maintain its confidentiality.

Until the 2008 reforms, the confidentiality provisions under the Act were so strict that it was impossible to use the information in the HFEA's register for research purposes. This meant that it was not possible to carry out epidemiological research into the risks of IVF and other techniques by linking the HFEA's register with other health databases, such as cancer registries. Now section 33D(1) provides that regulations can require 'the processing of protected information for the purposes of medical research' where this is 'necessary or expedient in the public interest or in the interests of improving patient care'.

Provided they have the approval of a research ethics committee, researchers from recognized research institutions can apply to access HFEA Register Data. The HFEA's Research Register Panel decides whether or not to grant researchers access to identifying data. Information about approved projects is available on the HFEA website: two of the first projects to receive approval were 'Are children born after assisted reproduction at increased risk of cancer? A population based linkage study' and 'Do hormonal treatments for assisted reproduction increase risks of cancer or mortality in women? A national cohort study'.[25]

(e) THE CONSCIENCE CLAUSE

As with the Abortion Act 1967, section 38(1) of the Human Fertilisation and Embryology Act 1990 gives health care workers the right to refuse to participate in activities to which they have a conscientious objection: 'No person who has a conscientious objection to participating in any activity governed by this Act shall be under any duty, however arising, to do so.'

The burden of proof of conscientious objection lies with the person claiming to rely upon it.[26] A person can invoke section 38 to exclude themselves from any activity governed by the Act. A clinician could not rely upon section 38 to 'conscientiously object' to treating particular sorts of patients, such as single women or lesbians, however. Not only is this not an 'activity governed by the Act', but also such a refusal would be incompatible with equality legislation and unlawful on human rights grounds. Certainly, the HFEA's Code of Practice stresses that Persons Responsible are under a duty to familiarize themselves with relevant equality legislation and to ensure that their staff members do not discriminate against patients.

HFEA 8th Code of Practice paras 29.9 and 29.11

> 29.9 A staff member's views about the lifestyle, beliefs, race, gender, age, sexuality, disability or other perceived status of a patient, patient's partner or donor should not affect that individual's treatment or care . . . .

---

[25] Available at www.hfea.gov.uk.   [26] Section 38(2).

29.11 The person responsible should satisfy themselves that the staff member has a conscientious objection to providing a particular activity, and is not unlawfully discriminating against a patient on the basis of their race, disability, gender, religion or belief, sexual orientation or age.

(f) REGULATING ACCESS TO TREATMENT

In the UK there are two ways in which access to fertility treatment is restricted. First, the Act provides that treatment services must not be provided unless account has been taken of the welfare of any child who may be born as a result. Secondly, there are restrictions on NHS funding for fertility treatment, and private treatment is expensive. As a result, access to treatment may depend upon a would-be patient's ability to pay for it.

(1) Section 13(5)

The Human Fertilisation and Embryology Act contains no formal restrictions upon access to treatment, so any individual, regardless of their age, sexual orientation, or marital status, can legally receive fertility treatment in the UK. When the Bill was debated in 1990, an amendment that would have allowed only married couples to be treated was defeated by one vote. As a result, in order to shore up support for the Bill, an amendment was introduced which instructed clinicians to take account of the welfare of any child to be born 'including the need of that child for a father'.

In 2008, the then government had assumed that deleting the 'need for a father' clause would straightforwardly bring the 1990 Act into line with post-1990 family law reforms and with equality legislation. Single women and lesbian couples can adopt children,[27] and by 2008, same-sex couples could enter into civil partnerships and thereby acquire the same legal rights as married couples.[28] In the light of these changes, it seemed anomalous for the statute governing fertility treatment to contain a statutory clause that, on the face of it, looks like an invitation to discriminate against women without male partners.

In addition, the existence of a potential father figure when assisted conception services are sought, offers no guarantee of his presence when the child is born, or throughout her childhood. Nor is a presumption against treating women without male partners, on child welfare grounds, supported by the evidence. It is true that there are studies that show some correlation between single motherhood and poor outcomes for children, but these generally reflect the poverty and greater mobility that may accompany divorce, separation, or unplanned single motherhood. Women who seek treatment without men in licensed clinics are a very different cohort from those who have single motherhood thrust upon them. This is reflected in the evidence, which in fact suggests that children conceived using donor insemination by women without male partners are, if anything, doing better than similarly conceived children who are being brought up by married couples.[29]

Most single or lesbian women who want to have children will be fertile, so if they are not able to access treatment services in a licensed clinic, they could instead engage in casual, unprotected sex. Not only would this be less safe, but it might also mean that the child would have no information about her genetic father. For reasons of safety and to ensure that

---

[27] Adoption and Children Act 2002.   [28] Civil Partnership Act 2004.
[29] C Murray and S Golombok, 'Solo mothers and their donor insemination infants: follow-up at age 2 years' (2005) 20 Human Reproduction 1655–60.

offspring have access to information from the register, it could be argued that it would be more sensible to encourage women without male partners to make use of licensed services.

The removal of the 'need for a father' clause nevertheless proved to be hugely controversial, with peers and MPs from all parties arguing that removing it was tantamount to impugning the role of men in family life. This led to a concession by the government, in which the 'need for a father' was replaced by 'the need for supportive parenting'. Section 13(5) now provides that:

> A woman shall not be provided with treatment services unless account has been taken of the welfare of any child who may be born as a result of the treatment (including the need of that child for supportive parenting), and of any other child who may be affected by the birth.

(a) Theoretical difficulties with section 13(5)

Section 13(5) has been the subject of considerable academic debate. Certainly a literal interpretation would be puzzling because it appears to instruct a clinician to base his decision as to whether to attempt to bring a child into the world upon a consideration of that child's welfare. It is difficult to see how a clinician could decide that a child would be benefited by not being born, unless its life would be likely to be so terrible that non-existence would be preferable. In practice, the section has not been interpreted literally, and is instead used to check whether prospective patients would be likely to be inadequate parents. But, for several reasons, this interpretation too is not without difficulty.

First, clinicians will not have access to all of the information which might be necessary in order to judge prospective patients' parenting abilities. Unlike adoption agencies, infertility clinicians will not make home visits, and nor do they undergo any specialist training in evaluating the capacity to be a good parent.

Secondly, policing section 13(5) is difficult. It is a standard licensing condition that account must be taken of the welfare of any child that might be born, and in practice clinics must have a protocol in place that sets out how this is done. It would, however, be very difficult to prove that the clinic had erred in its assessment. If account was not properly taken of the welfare of any child, and a future child's welfare suffered as a result, it is not clear that anyone would be able to sue the clinic for non-compliance with section 13(5). If the child were to bring an action, this would amount to a 'wrongful life' claim: the child would have to argue that the clinic failed to prevent her from being born into a life which is full of hardship. As we saw in Chapter 14, the courts have given very short shrift to the idea that life itself, however difficult, could amount to compensatable damage.

Thirdly, section 13(5) has also been criticized for placing an unfair burden upon infertile individuals, who are no more likely to pose a risk to their children than fertile people, who can reproduce without anyone scrutinizing their parenting ability.[30] Indeed, the evidence suggests that outcomes for children born following fertility treatment are at least as good or better than for children conceived naturally.[31] This should not be surprising since the pool of individuals who use assisted conception services are committed to having children and, due to restrictions on NHS treatment, will often also be fairly well off. In contrast, the pool of

---

[30] See, eg, Emily Jackson, 'Conception and the Irrelevance of the Welfare Principle' (2002) 65 Modern Law Review 176–203.

[31] See, eg, S Golombok, R Cook, A Bish, and C Murray, 'Families created by the new reproductive technologies: quality of parenting and social and emotional development of the children' (1995) 66 Child Development 285–98; S Golombok, A Brewaeys, MT Giavazzi, D Guerra, F MacCallum, and J Rust, 'The European study of assisted reproduction families: the transition to adolescence' (2002) 17 Human Reproduction 830–40; C Murray and S Golombok, 'Solo mothers and their donor insemination infants: follow-up at age 2 years' (2005) 20 Human Reproduction 1655–60.

people who conceive naturally will include individuals who may find parenting challenging, such as children and drug addicts.

Of course, there is a difference between refraining from interfering with a fertile couple's right to conceive a child naturally and an infertile couple's need for assistance. But if we think that pre-conception assessment of parenting ability is necessary whenever positive steps are taken to help a couple to conceive, we may need to draw a line between procedures that do require pre-conception parental assessment and procedures that do not. Surely we would not want to suggest that a doctor should not carry out investigations into the causes of infertility, or even try to repair a woman's fallopian tubes, without first assessing the couple's fitness to parent? Nor would it seem sensible to refuse to sell ovulation testing kits, which might help couples to conceive, unless consideration has first been given to the welfare of any child who might be born. If we think we need to judge parental fitness when doctors do some things that help women to become pregnant, but not others, we need to be able to explain why. For example, we could say that assessment is necessary only when doctors create a new life *in vitro*, but, of course, this would rule out the application of section 13(5) prior to donor insemination, when the creation of any new life will happen naturally *in vivo*.

The House of Commons Science and Technology Committee's 2005 report criticized section 13(5) and recommended its abolition in future legislation, but the government did not take up this suggestion.

House of Commons Science and Technology Committee[32]

> The welfare of the child provision discriminates against the infertile and some sections of society, is impossible to implement and is of questionable practical value in protecting the interests of children born as a result of assisted reproduction. We recognise that there will be difficult cases but these should be resolved by recourse to local clinical ethics committees. The welfare of the child provision has enabled the HFEA and clinics to make judgements that are more properly made by patients in consultation with their doctor.

(b) Section 13(5) in practice

Since 2005, the welfare of the child assessment has been regarded as a welfare of the child *risk* assessment. Rather than trying to ensure that prospective patients would be good or ideal parents, clinicians are instead instructed to consider whether there are any specific risk factors which might give cause for concern about a future child's wellbeing. The Code of Practice fleshes out the relevant considerations.

HFEA 8th Code of Practice paras 8.3, 8.7, and 8.10

> 8.3 The centre should assess each patient and their partner (if they have one) before providing any treatment, and should use this assessment to decide whether there is a risk of significant harm or neglect to any child . . .
>
> 8.7 Those seeking treatment are entitled to a fair assessment. The centre is expected to consider the wishes of all those involved, and the assessment must be done in a

---

[32] *Human Reproductive Technologies and the Law*, Fifth Report of Session 2004–05, paras 101, 107.

non-discriminatory way. In particular, patients should not be discriminated against on grounds of gender, race, disability, sexual orientation, religious belief or age.

8.10 The centre should consider factors that are likely to cause a risk of significant harm or neglect to any child who may be born or to any existing child of the family. These factors include any aspects of the patient's or (if they have one) their partner's:

(a) past or current circumstances that may lead to any child mentioned above experiencing serious physical or psychological harm or neglect, for example:

   (i) previous convictions relating to harming children

   (ii) child protection measures taken regarding existing children, or

   (iii) violence or serious discord in the family environment

(b) past or current circumstances that are likely to lead to an inability to care throughout childhood for any child who may be born, or that are already seriously impairing the care of any existing child of the family, for example:

   (i) mental or physical conditions

   (ii) drug or alcohol abuse

   (iii) medical history, where the medical history indicates that any child who may be born is likely to suffer from a serious medical condition, or

   (iv) circumstances that the centre considers likely to cause serious harm to any child mentioned above.

The Code of Practice also specifies that, in the absence of specific risk factors, all parents should be assumed to be supportive.

HFEA 8th Code of Practice para 8.11

8.11 When considering a child's need for supportive parenting, centres should consider the following definition: Supportive parenting is a commitment to the health, well being and development of the child. It is presumed that all prospective parents will be supportive parents, in the absence of any reasonable cause for concern that either the child to be born, or any other child, may be at risk of significant harm or neglect.

In their empirical study of how welfare of the child assessments work in practice, Lee et al found that refusals of treatment were rare, but that the 'spectre' of the child abuser meant that staff continued to believe that it was important to be vigilant. They also found an interesting distinction between would-be lesbian parents, often portrayed by clinic staff as 'ideal', and single women, whose motives for seeking treatment alone were sometimes regarded with suspicion.

Ellie Lee, Jan Macvarish, and Sally Sheldon[33]

In all cases, set against the size of the clinics, numbers of cases of concern are low. The clinics reported that the cases that would trigger further investigation typically related to mental illness (including depression), transmissible or inherited illness, physical illness or disability

---

[33] 'Assessing child welfare under the Human Fertilisation and Embryology Act 2008: a case study in medicalisation?' (2014) 36 Sociology of Health & Illness 500–15.

and drugs and alcohol. Only 10 clinics reported dealing with cases involving violence in the family environment and 11 had encountered convictions for harming children . . .

The study detected, in particular, a view that vigilance was necessary because 'you can never really know': the spectre of the child abuser as a person hardly ever encountered but whose threat nevertheless creates a powerful rationale for pre-emptive action influenced staff perceptions. As one nurse put it:

> '. . . you wouldn't want to bring a child into a relationship where the child was at any danger of child abuse or sexual abuse . . . [A]nything . . . that sets those alarm bells going would be something that we wouldn't want to risk'.

In general, treating lesbians was seen as straightforward, with some respondents keen to point out how good lesbian patients could be as parents because they were seen as well-prepared for parenthood: fully aware of the facts and consequences, equipped with strong support networks and open and honest in discussions with clinic staff. . . .

The discussion of single women patients had a rather different tone. . . . A minority of interviewees worried about other issues: the costs of childcare, the level of support needed from family or friends, or the demands a child might place on the mother, sometimes also expressing vaguer concerns that a particular single woman was rather odd and her personal circumstances were not conducive to raising a child.

It would be possible for a disgruntled would-be patient to apply for judicial review of a decision to refuse treatment in an NHS hospital. Rejected would-be patients could turn to the Human Rights Act 1998, and in particular Article 8 (right to respect for private and family life), Article 12 (the right to found a family), and Article 14 (the right not to be discriminated against in exercising one's Convention rights). Although there have been reports of people threatening litigation,[34] since 1990 there have been no reported cases involving people turned away from fertility clinics. There have, however, been two cases involving male prisoners seeking access to artificial insemination facilities while still in prison.

In the first case, *R v Secretary of State for the Home Department, ex parte Mellor*,[35] the Court of Appeal found that the restrictions on prisoners' right to found a family and their right to family life were justifiable and proportionate under Article 8(2). The Secretary of State's policy was that the grant of facilities for artificial insemination to prisoners was made only in exceptional circumstances. Mrs Mellor would be 31 years old at the time of Mr Mellor's release, so depriving the Mellors of access to artificial insemination (AI) facilities would be likely to delay rather than prevent parenthood. The Court of Appeal agreed that the Mellors case was not exceptional.

The second case had slightly different facts. In *Dickson v United Kingdom*, Mrs Dickson would be 51 years old at her husband's earliest possible release date. There was therefore no realistic chance that the couple would be able to conceive naturally. Without access to AI, their capacity to have a child together would not just be delayed, but eliminated. The Court of Appeal decided that, despite this, the Secretary of State had acted lawfully by deciding that their need for AI was trumped by other factors, such as legitimate public concern that the punitive and deterrent elements of Kirk Dickson's sentence would be circumvented.

At first, this decision was upheld by the ECtHR, but the Dicksons appealed successfully to the Grand Chamber of the ECtHR. By a majority, in *Dickson v United Kingdom*, the Grand

---

[34] Laura Donnelly, 'Couple sue for IVF in landmark "age discrimination" case', *The Telegraph*, 1 December 2012.

[35] [2001] EWCA Civ 472.

Chamber held that prisoners retained their human rights on incarceration, and so any interference with the prisoner's Article 8 rights had to be justified. It was not sufficient justification that providing AI facilities to prisoners would offend public opinion. Because the Secretary of State's policy set an 'inordinately high exceptionality burden', it amounted to a disproportionate interference with the Dicksons' Article 8 rights.

Dickson v United Kingdom[36]

Decision of the Grand Chamber

[T]he court considers that the policy as structured effectively excluded any real weighing of the competing individual and public interests, and prevented the required assessment of the proportionality of a restriction, in any individual case.

In particular, . . . the policy placed an inordinately high 'exceptionality' burden on the applicants when requesting artificial insemination facilities. They had to demonstrate, in the first place, as a condition precedent to the application of the policy, that the deprivation of artificial insemination facilities might prevent conception altogether (the starting point). Secondly, and of even greater significance, they had to go on to demonstrate that the circumstances of their case were 'exceptional' within the meaning of the remaining criteria of the policy (the finishing point).

The *Daily Mail*'s headlines were unsurprising—'Murderers and drug dealer to get IVF in prison and you'll be paying! Criminals using European Human Rights laws to start families at taxpayers' expense'.[37] And the *Dickson* case has been one of those invoked by Conservative MPs in order to argue that the Human Rights Act should be repealed. As one put it: 'It's another step towards an insane world where criminals have more rights than the rest of us.'[38]

(2) Financial Restrictions on Access

Infertility treatment is expensive—one cycle of IVF can cost over £5,000—and its availability within the NHS is patchy. In its 2013 clinical guideline, the National Institute for Health and Care Excellent (NICE) recommended that the NHS should fund three full cycles of IVF (ie a fresh cycle followed by further cycles using the frozen embryos) for women under 40 years old and one full cycle for women aged 40–42, who must additionally not have received IVF treatment before and not have low ovarian reserve.

National Institute for Health and Care Excellence[39]

1.11.1 Criteria for referral for IVF

1.11.1.3 In women aged under 40 years who have not conceived after 2 years of regular unprotected intercourse or 12 cycles of artificial insemination (where 6 or more are by intrauterine insemination), offer 3 full cycles of IVF, with or without ICSI [intracytoplasmic sperm

---

[36] Application no 44362/04 (2007).   [37] Jack Doyle, *Daily Mail*, 27 December 2012.
[38] Douglas Carswell MP, quoted in Jack Doyle, 'Prisoner allowed to father a child from jail because of "human right to a family life"', *Daily Mail*, 1 June 2011.
[39] *Fertility: Assessment and treatment for people with fertility problems* (NICE, 2013).

injection]. If the woman reaches the age of 40 during treatment, complete the current full cycle but do not offer further full cycles.

1.11.1.4 In women aged 40–42 years who have not conceived after 2 years of regular unprotected intercourse or 12 cycles of artificial insemination (where 6 or more are by intrauterine insemination), offer 1 full cycle of IVF, with or without ICSI, provided the following 3 criteria are fulfilled:

- they have never previously had IVF treatment
- there is no evidence of low ovarian reserve
- there has been a discussion of the additional implications of IVF and pregnancy at this age.

In 2014, NICE published a Quality Standard for Fertility Problems,[40] which reiterated that women who meet the criteria for IVF should be offered three full cycles of IVF, if they are under 40, or one full cycle if they are aged 40–42. Implementation of the NICE guideline and quality standard is not mandatory, in the same way as their technology appraisals (considered in Chapter 2). In 2015 it was reported that only 18 per cent of Clinical Commissioning Groups (CCGs) provide three full cycles of IVF to eligible women;[41] 24 per cent offer two cycles; 57 per cent fund one cycle only, and 1 per cent fund no treatment at all. Access to NHS-funded fertility treatment is therefore subject to a postcode lottery and, in some parts of the country, IVF is available only to the wealthy.

In the next extract, Emily McTernan argues, controversially, that there should be no privileged state funding for fertility treatment, as compared with other 'goods', like education or foreign holidays, that might make our lives go well.

Emily McTernan[42]

[F]ertility treatment is one among many goods that states could provide to enable citizens to pursue their diverse valuable life projects or have access to activities that make their life go well or seem meaningful. . . .

Yet, at present, many countries are disproportionately generous in their funding of fertility treatment, as compared to the other goods that might make one's life go well or enable valuable life projects. To illustrate, consider the following UK-based examples. IVF is not means-tested in its distribution as are other similar goods, like grants for higher education. So too, is it justifiable that a 40-year-old woman is funded to have a chance at having a child, but housing benefit is limited such that those under 35 cannot live in a flat of their own and unemployment benefit restricted so those on it are not permitted to holiday abroad? Alternatively, why is fertility treatment funded but not undergraduate or master's degrees that might provide a better choice of careers? Indeed, the cost of a master's degree is fairly similar to the cost of a couple of IVF cycles. Or, why fund a chance at having a child of one's own, but not the goods that might enable the formation of other kinds of valuable intimate relationships, such as dating websites?

---

[40] *Fertility Problems Quality Standard* (QS73) (NICE, 2014).

[41] Kate Brian, 'If you need IVF, you shouldn't have to check your postcode first', *The Guardian*, 3 November 2015. See further www.fertilityfairness.co.uk.

[42] 'Should fertility treatment be state funded?' (2015) 32 Journal of Applied Philosophy 227–40.

(3) Counselling

A further standard licensing condition, under section 13(6) of the Act, is that all patients, and where relevant their partners, should not be provided with certain treatments—involving the use of donated gametes or of embryos created outside the body—unless they have been given 'a suitable opportunity to receive proper counselling'. Counselling is not mandatory, however, and nor is there any duty upon clinics to make it available free of charge.

The Code of Practice specifies that counselling must be clearly separated from other forms of 'information giving', and from the welfare of the child assessment, and it must be confidential.

HFEA 8th Code of Practice para 3.7

3.7 The provision of counselling should be clearly distinguished from (a) the clinical assessment of a person's suitability to receive treatment, or to store or donate their gametes or embryos; (b) the provision of information before obtaining consent or providing treatment; and (c) the normal relationship between clinical staff and patients or donors.

(g) REGULATING THE USE OF GAMETES AND EMBRYOS

(1) Consent to the Use of Gametes

Consent to the storage and use of one's gametes must be voluntary and informed. Under Schedule 3 to the 1990 Act, unlike other more invasive medical procedures, consent to the creation of an embryo, or to the use of one's gametes in the treatment of others, *must* be in writing.

Consent must state what is to be done with the stored gametes in the event of the donor's death or incapacity, and must specify the maximum period of storage, if this is to be less than the statutory storage period of ten years. This ten-year limit can be extended for individuals if their fertility has been, or is likely to become, significantly impaired, perhaps because they are about to undergo treatment for cancer which will leave them infertile.

(a) Consent to the posthumous use of gametes

In the UK, gametes and embryos can be used posthumously, but only where the gamete provider(s) explicitly consented to posthumous use. If the man has died suddenly, he may not have had the chance to give consent and, in those circumstances, his sperm cannot be used posthumously in the UK. The HFEA has a wide discretion to permit the export of sperm samples, however, and so women unable to use their deceased partner's sperm in the UK have sought permission to export it to countries where treatment would be lawful.

This issue arose for the first time in *R v Human Fertilisation and Embryology Authority, ex parte Blood*. Sperm samples had been extracted at Mrs Blood's request, while her husband was in a coma. After his death, Mrs Blood wanted to be inseminated with the stored sperm. The problem was that although Mrs Blood said that she and her husband had discussed the posthumous use of his sperm, Mr Blood had not given written consent. In addition to the lack of consent, it is possible that the doctors who extracted the sperm acted unlawfully. Adults who lack capacity must be treated in their best interests. Since Mr Blood was not going to recover, it is hard to see how the surgical retrieval of sperm was in his best interests.

Without an effective consent, it would have been unlawful for Mrs Blood to use the sperm samples for treatment in the UK. The Court of Appeal admitted that their continued storage was also 'technically' an offence, although Lord Woolf MR said that there could be 'no question of any prosecution being brought in the circumstances'. Mrs Blood applied for permission to export the sperm to Belgium, where treatment without the gamete provider's consent would be lawful. When the HFEA refused, she applied for judicial review of this decision.

At first instance, despite expressing considerable sympathy for Mrs Blood, Sir Stephen Brown P decided that the HFEA had acted within its discretion. On appeal, Mrs Blood succeeded. In *R v Human Fertilisation and Embryology Authority, ex parte Blood*, the Court of Appeal took the view that despite the unlawfulness of the sperm retrieval, in exercising its discretion the HFEA had not taken adequate account of Mrs Blood's right under European law to receive treatment in another Member State.[43]

R v Human Fertilisation and Embryology Authority, ex parte Blood[44]

Lord Woolf MR

Parliament has delegated to the authority the responsibility for making decisions in this difficult and delicate area, and the court should be slow to interfere with its decisions. However, the reasons given by the authority, while not deeply flawed, confirm that the authority did not take into account two important considerations. The first being the effect of article 59 of the [EC] Treaty. The second being that there should be, after this judgment has been given, no further cases where sperm is preserved without consent.

Following the Court of Appeal's judgment, the HFEA allowed Mrs Blood to export her deceased husband's sperm. She has subsequently had two children.

In 2008, the Court of Appeal's prediction that there would be no further cases in which sperm was stored without consent was proved wrong. L's husband, H, had died suddenly following routine surgery. L and H already had one child and were keen to have a second. An out-of-hours application was made to the court, and Macur J declared that it would be lawful to remove and store sperm from H's body. This declaration was made on the basis of misinformation provided to Macur J about the scope of the Human Tissue Act 2004. She had been told that the Human Tissue Act permitted posthumous sperm retrieval, with the consent of a qualifying relative. In fact, the Human Tissue Act does not apply to gametes.

Because there was no written consent, H's sperm could not be used in the UK. An application to the HFEA for the sperm to be exported to a country where use without H's consent would be lawful was postponed pending L's application to the court to determine the lawfulness of the storage, use, and export of the sperm.

In *L v Human Fertilisation and Embryology Authority*,[45] Charles J found that the evidence that H would have wanted his sperm used posthumously by L was 'at least as compelling as that advanced by Mrs Blood': L and H already had a child together and six days before H's death they had made inquiries about access to IVF, as a result of L's age. Charles J also found that the law was clear, and that both the storage and use of H's sperm in the UK would be unlawful, but that the HFEA had a wide discretion to permit export. Following this judgment, and taking into account the decision in the *Blood* case, and the fact that L

---

[43] EC Treaty, Art 59.   [44] [1997] 2 WLR 806 (CA).   [45] [2008] EWHC 2149 (Fam).

could rely not only on European Treaty rights but also on Articles 8 and 12 of the European Convention on Human Rights, the HFEA permitted export to a clinic in the US, where the sperm could lawfully be used.

R (on the application of IM) v Human Fertilisation and Embryology Authority was the first case involving a lack of consent to the posthumous use of eggs rather than sperm. AM, who had been being treated for cancer, had had her eggs frozen in 2008, and had signed a form permitting their posthumous storage. Her parents believed that, before she died, AM had expressed the strong wish that one or more of her eggs should be fertilized and implanted in her mother, who would bring up the baby along with AM's father. Without AM's written consent to the use of her eggs in her mother's treatment, this would be unlawful. The HFEA's Statutory Approvals Committee refused to permit the eggs' export to the US, and AM's parents applied, unsuccessfully, for judicial review of that decision. Ouseley J found that AM had had the time before her death in 2011 to give clear instructions about what she wanted to happen to her eggs after her death, but that she had not done so. Permission to appeal this decision has been granted.

R (on the application of IM) v Human Fertilisation and Embryology Authority[46]

Ouseley J

The Committee, as I read the decision, concluded that, although AM had wanted her mother to be her surrogate in her lifetime, there was no sufficiently clear evidence that she had intended her mother to be her surrogate after her death in the particular circumstances which the application entailed. This is closely allied to and largely overlaps with its conclusion that AM's wishes were not a sufficiently clear and informed expression of her wishes about what was proposed to happen. Those were conclusions which it was entitled to reach ...

There was no evidence that AM had ever contemplated or consented to the export of her eggs, or to a sperm donor or overseas sperm donor or one selected by her parents, or had thought through and consented to the implications of foreign law governing the ability of the child to establish the identity of the father and to make contact. There was no evidence that AM had ever discussed the question of donor sperm with anyone. There was no evidence that she understood the implications for her mother's health or the legal implications of her mother acting as surrogate, namely that her mother would be the legal mother of her daughter's child....

Of course, she was battling cancer, but the Committee was entitled to find, indeed it is hard to see that it could reach any other conclusion, that her wishes lacked a definitive and settled expression, she had not focussed on the practical and legal issues, and that she had had time to discuss them with her mother and doctors but did not do so.

Under section 39 of the Human Fertilisation and Embryology Act 2008,[47] it is also now possible, provided a man has given consent, for him to be treated as the father of a child conceived after his death with his frozen sperm, but only for the purposes of birth registration. It is also possible for a man who was married or a woman who was in a civil partnership or married to a woman at the time of an embryo's creation with donated gametes to be treated as the father

---

46 [2015] EWHC 1706 (Admin).

47 Most of the 2008 Act simply amended the 1990 Act, but the provisions on parenthood in the 2008 Act are free-standing.

or the second legal parent if that embryo is subsequently used after his or her death. Again, this is only for the purposes of birth registration and is possible only if they have specifically consented both to the embryo's posthumous use and to the posthumous attribution of parenthood.

(b) Consent to extended storage

There are circumstances in which sperm might be removed from a child who is not yet *Gillick*-competent, and who cannot give a valid consent to retrieval or storage. Some treatments for cancer will leave a patient permanently sterile, and it would be straightforward to justify the retrieval of sperm for storage on the grounds that the preservation of fertility will almost always be in a child's best interests. Until the 2008 reforms, storage without consent was not possible. This has now been remedied, and the consent of someone with parental responsibility is treated as the child's own 'effective consent',[48] until he is old enough to make his own decision about continued storage.

A further difficulty with the original rules was that there was a ten-year limit on the storage of gametes. Where a boy or a man's sperm is stored in order to preserve his fertility before he undergoes cancer treatment, ten years may be insufficient to ensure that the frozen sperm are available for his use when he wants to start a family. This was changed in 2009 by Regulations which permit sperm to be stored for up to 55 years, with the man's consent and where a medical practitioner certifies that he is, or is likely to become, prematurely infertile.[49]

In *Warren v Care Fertility*, the clinic had failed to inform a man who had had sperm stored before treatment for a brain tumour of this change in the law. Mr Brewer had signed forms specifying that his wife, Mrs Warren, should be able to use his sperm after his death and Hogg J found that, if he had known about the possibility of an extension, he would have obtained the necessary medical certificate and signed the form.

Warren v Care Fertility[50]

Hogg J

I am in no doubt that had he had the relevant information and the opportunity he would have consented to a period beyond ten years.

I am also in no doubt that had he been informed by the clinic in clear terms that by regulations 4(3)(b) or 7(3)(b) of the 2009 Regulations a medical practitioner's written opinion as to his infertility or likely infertility was required he would have obtained such opinion. As it was he was not given that clear information by the clinic.

I have already indicated that the clinic failed to fulfil its obligations to Mr Brewer. As a consequence he was deprived of relevant information and the opportunity to meet the requirements of regulations 4(3) or 7(3) of the 2009 Regulations.... The failure of the clinic produced a great and conspicuous unfairness to Mr Brewer, and by extension, to Mrs Warren.

---

[48] Schedule 3, para 8(2ZA).

[49] Human Fertilisation and Embryology (Statutory Storage Period for Embryos and Gametes) Regulations 2009.

[50] [2014] EWHC 602 (Fam).

Taking into account Mrs Warren's Article 8 rights, and the fact that there were unlikely to be many other cases like this, Hogg J declared that it would be lawful for Mr Brewer's sperm to be stored and used beyond the period of time to which Mr Brewer had given his written consent, up to a maximum of 55 years if necessary.

(2) Consent to the Use of Embryos

When embryos are created *in vitro* they are graded by an embryologist in order to determine which embryos are suitable for use in treatment. Unsuitable embryos can be disposed of, or donated to research. Of the remaining embryos, one or two fresh embryos may be transferred to the woman's uterus, and the rest will be frozen for future use. These embryos can be stored for up to ten years. Once again, this limit can be extended in exceptional cases, such as when a young woman is about to undergo treatment for ovarian cancer, which will leave her without any more eggs.

Of course, it is possible that the gamete contributors will subsequently disagree about the use of their frozen embryos. As we saw in Chapter 13, when an embryo or fetus is *in utero*, men have no say over whether the pregnancy can be terminated. But if an embryo has been frozen and is being stored *in vitro*, the situation is rather different. To some extent, cryopreservation reduces the asymmetry that normally exists between men's and women's interests in their fertilized gametes.

Some differences remain, however. First, it is possible for the embryos to be transferred to the woman's body and carried to term without involving a third party. In contrast, if the male partner wishes to use the embryos in treatment without the egg provider's agreement, he must find another woman willing to be implanted with them.

Secondly, the use of frozen sperm is now well established, in contrast egg freezing is a newer option, and success rates have, until recently, been much lower. This means that it used to be common to advise women about to lose their eggs as a result of treatment for cancer to freeze embryos created with their partners' sperm, rather than eggs. If the couple subsequently split up, and the male partner withdraws his consent to their continued storage and use, the woman will be in a much worse position than a man in a similar situation, whose frozen sperm will be available for use with any future partner.

In the UK the law is clear: the Human Fertilisation and Embryology Act 1990 allows for the variation or withdrawal of consent to the use or storage of an embryo.[51] In practice, this gives whichever partner does not want their embryos to be used in treatment a right of veto over their use.

This provision was challenged in *Evans v United Kingdom*. Following the discovery that Natallie Evans had ovarian cancer, she and her then partner, Howard Johnston, underwent a cycle of IVF treatment resulting in the storage of six embryos. Ms Evans was then successfully treated for cancer. She could carry a child, but had no more eggs, and so the stored embryos represented her last opportunity to have a baby that was genetically related to her. The couple then separated, and Mr Johnston wrote to the clinic to notify it of their separation, and to state that the embryos could be destroyed. Ms Evans sought a declaration that the relevant provisions of the 1990 Act were incompatible with her rights under Article 8 of the European Convention on Human Rights. She failed at first instance, and before the Court of Appeal, and her appeals to the ECtHR and, in *Evans v United Kingdom*, to the Grand Chamber were also unsuccessful.

---

[51] Schedule 3, para 4.

Evans v United Kingdom[52]

Decision of the Grand Chamber

The dilemma central to the present case is that it involves a conflict between the art 8 rights of two private individuals: the applicant and J. Moreover, each person's interest is entirely irreconcilable with the other's, since if the applicant is permitted to use the embryos, J will be forced to become a father, whereas if J's refusal or withdrawal of consent is upheld, the applicant will be denied the opportunity of becoming a genetic parent. In the difficult circumstances of this case, whatever solution the national authorities might adopt would result in the interests of one or the other parties to the IVF treatment being wholly frustrated . . .

While the applicant contends that her greater physical and emotional expenditure during the IVF process, and her subsequent infertility, entail that her art 8 rights should take precedence over J's, it does not appear to the court that there is any clear consensus on this point either.

As regards the balance struck between the conflicting art 8 rights of the parties to the IVF treatment, the Grand Chamber, in common with every other court which has examined this case, has great sympathy for the applicant, who clearly desires a genetically related child above all else. However, given the above considerations, including the lack of any European consensus on this point, it does not consider that the applicant's right to respect for the decision to become a parent in the genetic sense should be accorded greater weight than J's right to respect for his decision not to have a genetically-related child with her.

The ECtHR thus affirmed that there were strong public policy justifications—namely the promotion of certainty and the avoidance of arbitrariness and inconsistency—for the inflexibility of the 'bright line' rule in the 1990 Act that requires both partners' consent to an embryo's use and storage.

The dissenting judges in both courts took a different view, and argued that this 'bright line' rule had a disproportionate impact upon Natallie Evans's Article 8 rights. Rosy Thornton agrees, and argues that the Courts were wrong to treat Ms Evans and Mr Johnston as though they were similarly situated.

Rosy Thornton[53]

To treat as like two such unlike situations does not produce true equality in terms of the law's effects . . . A blanket rule, insensitive to the realities of profoundly unequal situations, must amount to a disproportionate infringement of the female partner's right to respect for her private life . . .

The bright-line rule itself, though rooted in formal equality, in fact operates inconsistently and arbitrarily in terms of its real, differential impact on the female and male gamete providers in cases such as *Evans*. Second, if a bright-line rule is desirable at all, then why should it be fixed, as it is under the 1990 Act, at the time of implantation rather than allowing male consent to be withdrawn only up to the point of fertilization (as, for instance, in Austria and Estonia)? The latter threshold would both recognize the greater impact of the decision on the female partner and mirror more closely the situation of natural conception.

---

[52] Application no 6339/05 (2007).
[53] 'European Court of Human Rights: Consent to IVF Treatment' (2008) 6 International Journal of Constitutional Law 317–30.

Craig Lind draws attention to the sharp contrast between the law's unsympathetic attitude to men who are 'careless' with their sperm, in the context of sexual intercourse, and the overriding priority given in the *Evans* case to Mr Johnston's desire not to become a father.

Craig Lind[54]

It is, therefore, deeply ironic that, in the context of assisted reproduction, men are given such complete control over their procreative capacity. Mr Johnson is said to have had a fundamental objection to there being a child of his in the world which he was not actively raising with the child's mother. Yet, if he had fathered a child accidentally during sexual intercourse, he would have been denied the level of control over his procreation that the statute gives him. He would have had to support any child born as a result of that activity (even if it were of the briefest, most meaningless kind). His involvement in a clinical infertility venture is, however, a much more deliberate move to procreate than a casual sexual encounter is. However, only the latter can lead to substantial support obligations.

Sally Sheldon has criticized the *Evans* case from a different perspective. If Natallie Evans had instead created embryos with donated sperm, and these had been frozen, they would almost certainly have been available for her use in the future. Of course, given her cancer diagnosis, the need to make rapid decisions about IVF was thrust upon Ms Evans and Mr Johnston, with much less time for discussion than would normally be the case. Nevertheless, given the potentially devastating implications for a woman in Ms Evans's situation, it would be sensible to give a couple time to talk through the implications together, and for each of them to discuss their options separately with a member of the clinic's staff.

Sally Sheldon[55]

On the facts of this case, the robustness of the consent obtained from each party is surely open to question. The lack of space for confidential, private discussions between each party and clinic staff on the one hand, and between the two parties themselves, on the other, makes for rather less than the quality of consent which might be thought desirable. While the courts seem cognisant of the necessity of a 'bright line rule' to offer certainty to clinics, the consenting procedures in this case were such as potentially to leave Ms Evans and Mr Johnston in a position of considerable uncertainty about the implications of their treatment.

When reforming the 1990 Act, the government chose to retain the consent provisions, so under the amended Act, both partners continue to have the right to veto the use of embryos. There is, however, one small change that applies to this sort of dispute. Under Schedule 3 para 4A, if one party withdraws his or her consent to the use of embryos, the Act now provides for a 12-month 'cooling off period', during which the embryos cannot be used or disposed of without both parties' consent. The hope is that this will enable couples in a

---

54 '*Evans v United Kingdom*—Judgments of Solomon: Power, Gender and Procreation' (2006) 18 Child and Family Law Quarterly 576.

55 'Case Commentary: Revealing Cracks in the "Twin Pillars"?' (2004) 16 Child and Family Law Quarterly 437.

similar situation to Natallie Evans and Howard Johnston to come to an agreement about the embryos' use or disposal.

(3) Status of Gametes

In *Yearworth v North Bristol NHS Trust*, the court was faced with the question of whether or not stored gametes, in this case sperm, were property for the purposes of a claim in negligence. The containers that are used to store 'straws' of sperm are filled with liquid nitrogen. They must now have alarms fitted in order to alert staff to drops in the level of nitrogen, so that it can be topped up before the samples are compromised.

In *Yearworth*, following a reduction in nitrogen levels, the sperm samples had been thawed, and were no longer suitable for use in treatment. The claimants were men who had undergone treatment for cancer, and they brought an action in negligence, seeking damages for the loss of their samples, and for psychiatric disorders that they had suffered as a result. There were some factual complications: for some of the men, natural fertility had, in fact, been restored, and for one man, the stored sample did not contain sufficient sperm to give a reasonable chance of pregnancy. For our purposes, the important point is that the Court of Appeal, in *Yearworth v North Bristol NHS Trust*, invoked the 1990 Act's consent provisions in order to justify its conclusion that the sperm samples were property. Given the emphasis put upon consent, and the freedom people have under the Act to determine what should happen to their gametes, the Court of Appeal found that the rights the men had had in relation to their stored sperm samples were equivalent to property rights.

Yearworth v North Bristol NHS Trust[56]

Lord Judge CJ

In our judgment, for the purposes of their claims in negligence, the men had ownership of the sperm which they ejaculated: . . .

- The sole object of their ejaculation of the sperm was that, in certain events, it might later be used for their benefit. . . . It is true that, by confining all storage of sperm and all use of stored sperm to licence-holders, the Act has effected a compulsory interposition of professional judgment between the wishes of the men and the use of the sperm. . . . For two reasons, however, the absence of their ability to 'direct' its use does not in our view derogate from their ownership. First, there are numerous statutes which limit a person's ability to use his property—for example a land-owner's ability to build on his land or to evict his tenant at the end of the tenancy or a pharmacist's ability to sell his medicines—without eliminating his ownership of it. Second, by its provisions for consent, the Act assiduously preserves the ability of the men to direct that the sperm be *not* used in a certain way: their negative control over its use remains absolute.

- . . . Thus the Act recognises in the men a fundamental feature of ownership, namely that at any time they can require the destruction of the sperm.

- . . . [W]hile the licence-holder has *duties* which may conflict with the wishes of the men, for example in relation to destruction of the sperm upon expiry of the maximum storage period, no person, whether human or corporate, other than each man has any *rights* in relation to the sperm which he has produced.

[56] [2009] EWCA Civ 37.

(4) Egg Freezing

Vitrification (literally, turning to glass) is a new technique for preserving eggs. It is a rapid process, as opposed to slow freezing, and it has dramatically increased success rates.[57] Women's age-related fertility decline means that the possibility of storing eggs raises new issues that do not arise in relation to sperm. Men facing a loss of fertility (eg as a result of cancer treatment) might store their sperm for use in the future, but most experts agree that the routine storage of young men's sperm for use in their future treatment would be a pointless waste of money. In 2015, Kevin Smith controversially argued that because the risk of genetic mutations in sperm increases with age, sperm banking and artificial insemination should be the norm, and indeed should be publicly funded.

Kevin R Smith[58]

> Ideally, therefore, sperm could be taken (on a voluntary basis) from all young men, with AI becoming the norm for procreation. To be successful this would require state-funded infrastructure support, along with educational/publicity approaches to encourage young men to participate. If this form of society-wide sperm banking were to be widely adopted, and repeated throughout successive generations, it would have marked benefits for the human gene pool over the long term.

This suggestion was immediately rejected by fertility experts. According to Allan Pacey, a Professor of Andrology, the risks from fathering children later in life are 'really quite small':

> This is one of the most ridiculous suggestions I have heard in a long time . . . We know that the sperm from the majority of men won't freeze very well, which is one of the reasons why sperm donors are in short supply. Therefore, men who froze their sperm at 18, and returned to use it later in life, would essentially be asking their wives to undergo one or more IVF procedures in order to start a family.[59]

For a woman who thinks that she might postpone starting a family until her late thirties or forties, the situation is different. A woman's chance of conceiving using her own eggs declines sharply with age. Indeed, it has been suggested that egg freezing might be a popular option for a significant proportion of young women: in one study, nearly one-third of respondents said that they would consider what is sometimes called 'social egg freezing' for themselves.[60]

In practice, however, it seems that women are more likely to freeze their eggs when their fertility is already in decline. In Baldwin et al's small empirical study of women who had decided to freeze their eggs in order to try to preserve their fertility, all were over the age of 32, and some were in their forties.

---

[57] Ana Cobo et al, 'Use of cryo-banked oocytes in an ovum donation programme: a prospective, randomized, controlled, clinical trial' (2010) 25 Human Reproduction 2239–46.

[58] 'Paternal age bioethics' (2015) 41 Journal of Medical Ethics 775–9.

[59] Quoted in James Gallagher, 'Freeze sperm at 18, bioethicist urges men', BBC News website, 25 June 2015.

[60] D Stoop et al, 'A survey on the intentions and attitudes towards oocyte cryopreservation for non-medical reasons among women of reproductive age' (2011) 26 Human Reproduction 655–61.

Kylie Baldwin et al[61]

> At the time of undergoing the process of oocyte cryopreservation, participants were on average 36.7 years of age, with 61% of participants cryopreserving their oocytes between the ages of 36 and 39 years. Just over one-quarter (26%) were 35 years or under and 13% were between 40 and 44 years at the time of undergoing the procedure. All participants were heterosexual, 87% were single . . . All were educated to degree level . . .
>
> Although the participants sought to become mothers as part of a committed relationship with a male partner, this study found that some women were open to the option of family building through the use of donor sperm but regarded this as a 'last case scenario' that they would only pursue if they were unable to find a partner.

There is nothing in the 1990 Act to prevent clinics from offering egg freezing to women willing to pay for the egg retrieval and the long-term storage of the frozen (or more accurately, vitrified) eggs. It is extremely unlikely that the NHS would fund egg freezing for women who are not facing premature infertility: many, perhaps most, of the women who do this as an insurance policy against hypothetical future infertility will never use the stored eggs. A woman who froze her eggs in her twenties is likely to conceive naturally in her thirties and may well be able to do so well into her forties. Given that the NHS does not pay for most of the fertility treatment needed by people who cannot conceive, it is unthinkable that it would fund a clinically unnecessary and expensive procedure for fertile women.

So what issues are raised by 'social egg freezing'? Is it an example of the 'medicalization' of a social problem: that is, if women are delaying having children until an age where having children is biologically difficult, some commentators would suggest that we should make it easier for women to combine having babies with career progression, rather than encouraging women to undergo expensive and invasive egg retrieval. On the other hand, it could be argued that the decision about when to have children is a deeply personal one, and that for many women, the biologically optimum time is not the right time in terms of their personal circumstances and life plans.

Given that social egg freezing and storage is likely to be expensive, it is important that clinics do not misrepresent it as a guaranteed means to preserve fertility. Some eggs will not survive the freeze–thaw processes, and so a woman may have more chance of conceiving naturally than she does using her thawed eggs. When obtaining informed consent to the process of egg retrieval, clinics need to make sure that women understand the risks and the burdens of the process, in addition to being given clear and frank information about how unlikely it is that they will actually use the stored eggs, and should be clearly told that, even if they do, their treatment may fail.

Obtaining properly informed consent is also important as clinics develop what are known as 'freeze and share' programmes, in which women receive free or reduced price social egg freezing in return for donating half of their eggs for use in the treatment of others. These are like egg-sharing schemes, discussed later, but the benefits to the woman freezing her eggs are much more speculative and uncertain.

(5) Gamete Donation

Most people undergoing fertility treatment in the UK use their own gametes, but some people may need to use donated sperm or eggs. A number of distinctive questions are raised by

---

[61] 'Oocyte cryopreservation for social reasons: demographic profile and disposal intentions of UK users' (2015) 31 Reproductive BioMedicine Online 239–45.

gamete donation, such as whether donors should be anonymous, and whether they should be paid. It is also worth considering whether compensation should be the same for sperm and egg donors, given that sperm donation is much less intrusive and risky than egg donation.

In this chapter, our focus is on gamete donation that takes place in licensed clinics, and is regulated by the HFEA. In the case of sperm, however, informal and unregulated donation is possible. Until recently, informal sperm donation tended to happen between friends—a not uncommon scenario might be a man donating his sperm to a lesbian friend, who uses it for self-insemination at home.

Informal donation arrangements between strangers are becoming increasingly common as a result of introduction websites—akin to dating websites—through which potential donors and recipients make contact with each other. These websites are subject to regulation only if they involve the 'procurement' of sperm, for which a licence from the HFEA is necessary. If sperm is 'procured' without a licence, a criminal offence is committed: in 2010, two men who had run a website which arranged couriers to deliver sperm were convicted of procuring sperm without a licence, and given suspended jail sentences. Introduction websites, in which would-be donors and would-be recipients get in touch with each other by email and make their own arrangements, are unlikely to fall foul of the prohibition on procurement.

There are risks associated with entering into these arrangements, however. There is no vetting of would-be donors, some of whom advertise themselves as offering 'NI [natural intercourse] only'. The sperm will not be tested for HIV infection or common genetic disorders. There is no limit on how many families can be produced from one donor, and there is no register of information for donor-conceived individuals. And, as we can see from the case of *M v F (Legal Paternity)*, a case discussed later in relation to the attribution of legal fatherhood, these arrangements can be fraught with danger for all concerned. According to the judge, Peter Jackson J, F was a man with 'an unmistakable track record of inveigling or encouraging recipients into engaging in sexual activity with him from the very first meeting', who had once 'advertised himself in graphic terms as willing to participate in a "breeding party", i.e. a male-dominated orgy designed to get a woman pregnant'. In the next extract, Peter Jackson highlights some of the perils of unregulated sperm donation.

M v F (Legal Paternity)[62]

Peter Jackson J

[R]egulation is broadly successful in protecting participants from exploitation and from health risks, while providing some certainty about legal relationships. Codes of Practice limit the number of times a person can donate sperm: in this country a donor can normally donate to a maximum of 10 families. In comparison, participants in informal arrangements have to judge all risks for themselves. They may not be in a good position to do so. Those seeking to conceive may be in a vulnerable state and not all donors are motivated by altruism.

This informal trade is not unlawful, but it is not regulated in any meaningful way. The website in this case ... is a case in point. It charges not inconsiderable fees to those looking for donors while projecting a rose-tinted account of successful, problem-free conception. It supplies a document entitled 'Donor Agreement' that purports to record agreement that the donor will have no rights in relation to the child and that the mother *and the child* will have

---

62 [2013] EWHC 1901 (Fam).

no rights against the donor in any circumstances. The concern is that documents of this kind create the false impression that these informal arrangements are somehow regulated....

In reality, on the evidence I have heard, there is no effective control whatever of the activities resulting from websites of this kind: for example, although it is said to be a cardinal rule of the website that it is 'AI only', Mr F's own public profile on the site openly advertised him as offering 'AI and NI'.

The present case amply demonstrates the risks involved for all participants in this process. It has taken a high toll on the well-being of each of the adults and has threatened Mr F's career. The costs are enormous. The parties have spent almost £300,000 in legal fees.

On the other hand, there may also be some perceived advantages from informal sperm donation, and not only because privately arranged sperm donation might be cheaper. It is evident from the profiles posted on 'introduction' sites in the UK that many would-be donors and would-be recipients are interested in facilitating contact and involvement between donor and child throughout childhood. This was also the finding of Jadva et al's survey of members of an introduction website, most of whom envisaged ongoing, and perhaps romanticized, relationships. Given how hard co-parenting can be, it was noteworthy that Jadva et al found that most of the site's members intended to attempt conception after a relatively brief 'getting to know each other' phase.

Vasanti Jadva et al[63]

Overall, the motivations for seeking a co-parenting arrangement that were ranked as most important were 'Wanting the child to know both biological parents' and 'Wanting to know the person who provides the sperm/egg to create the child'. . . .

A particular concern arising from these findings is the length of time prospective co-parents planned to be in contact with each other prior to attempting conception. Most expected to be in contact for a few months which raises the question of whether this allows sufficient time to establish a sustainable co-parenting relationship. . . . The open-ended responses revealed that participants' expectations of co-parenting were idealised in that they wanted a friendship with the co-parent and a happy loving family in which all parents were accepted and the child was loved.

In *JB v KS (Contact: Parental Responsibility)*, a case in which the agreement between the mother and father had broken down, Hayden J explained why the mother had deliberately chosen to find a sperm donor via an 'introduction' website, rather than seeking treatment in a licensed centre.

JB v KS (Contact: Parental Responsibility)[64]

Hayden J

In her evidence she told me that she was very aware that there were less personal options for acquiring semen donation in organisations regulated by the HFEA in which she would

---

[63] '"Friendly allies in raising a child": a survey of men and women seeking elective co-parenting arrangements via an online connection website' (2015) 30 Human Reproduction 1896–906.
[64] [2015] EWHC 180 (Fam).

not have to run the gauntlet of potential future disagreements. She told me that she wanted to identify a father who would be a 'real' and 'physical presence' at stages throughout the child's life rather than 'just a name' that her son would be entitled to know when he reached his majority.

Hayden J granted the father a parental responsibility order in order to reflect the fact that he was registered on the child's birth certificate, was paying child support, and was unlikely to use the order to undermine the mother's decision-making. Hayden J also noted that, in this context, the word 'donor' was an inappropriate way to describe the child's father.

Hayden J

At no point in this hearing or in the judgment has the word 'donor' been used to describe the father, though it did appear in some of the papers. I would express the hope that the word becomes extinct, in this context, in the lexicon of the family law reports. I cannot easily contemplate any factual circumstance where its use is anything other than belittling and disrespectful to all concerned, most importantly the child.

In contrast, in *Re X (No 2: Application for Contact by the Biological Father)*, the child's parents, HS and KS, and the sperm donor JK, subsequently disagreed about the terms upon which they had entered into a sperm-donation arrangement, after meeting each other via an introduction website. HS and KS, who were civil partners and X's legal parents, claimed that they had been looking for a known donor. JK claimed that they had been looking for a co-parent. Relations between the parents and JK had broken down catastrophically, and the Children's Guardian told the court: 'it is unfortunate that the parties did not fully discuss matters before conception. It appears that the differing expectations caused great difficulty during the early weeks in X's life.' Theis J described the impact the dispute had had upon HS and KS, and ordered indirect contact once a year (not to include photographs for at least three years, after JK had posted pictures of X on Facebook immediately after being warned in court not to do so).

Re X (No 2: Application for Contact by the Biological Father)[65]

Theis J

HS said she had lost her job, had two county judgments registered because of legal fees and they have been forced to sell their home. She said she is medicated for anxiety, she is scared to go out of the front door and described how they go to events far away to avoid the risk of meeting JK. She and KS have undergone counseling and intensive therapy as they each blamed the other for the situation they have found themselves in. As she described, what had happened will impact their lives for years …

Having considered the matters set out above and keeping X's welfare needs as the court's paramount consideration I have reached the conclusion that there should be no direct contact between X and JK. To order it would place X at an unacceptable level of risk of emotional harm by putting the security of her placement with HS and KS at risk. Indirect contact once a year meets her current welfare needs to have information about her biological father.

---

[65] [2015] EWFC 84.

(a) Anonymity

Until 2005, most gamete donation was anonymous. Children born following anonymous donation can be given access to non-identifying information, such as the donor's ethnicity and occupation, and, once they reach the age of 16, they can ask the HFEA whether they were born following fertility treatment, and if they are related to a prospective spouse, civil partner, or 'person with whom the applicant is in an intimate physical relationship or with whom the applicant proposes to enter into an intimate physical relationship'.[66] The 1990 Act did not specify that donors had to be anonymous, and some people chose to use a known donor: for example, a person might offer to donate their gametes to an infertile friend or sibling.

In the past, anonymity was believed to be in the interests of donors, recipients, and children. It shielded donors from unwanted contact with their offspring, and protected the privacy and security of the recipient family. It also undoubtedly helped to persuade young men, often medical students, to donate sperm safe in the knowledge that the consequences of their donations would not come back to haunt them in middle age.

These justifications have been challenged in recent years. In particular, it has been argued that the interests of donor-conceived people in knowing about their genetic origins should take priority over the interests of parents and donors. In *R (on the application of Rose) v Secretary of State for Health*,[67] the court was faced with the question of whether a child's right to information about her genetic parentage might be protected by Article 8 of the Human Rights Act 1998. Scott Baker J accepted that Article 8 was engaged, but the full hearing to determine whether the failure to supply such information amounted to a breach of Article 8 was superseded by the government's decision to abolish anonymity.

Regulations passed in 2004, which came into force in April 2005, removed anonymity for donations after that date. Stocks of anonymously donated sperm could continue to be used until April 2006, but since then, gametes cannot be used in treatment unless the donor is prepared to be identifiable. Many predicted that the abolition of anonymity would lead to a drop in the number of donors, and although it probably has led to fewer students being willing to donate, clinics have been able to recruit older donors, often with children of their own. In 2004, 237 new sperm donors were registered with the HFEA; in 2013, there were 586 new donor registrations (almost a third of which are for imported sperm).[68]

Children born following non-anonymous donation will have access to identifying information about their donor once they reach the age of 18 (see the following section). Anonymity was not removed retrospectively, although it is possible for pre-2005 donors to register their willingness to be identified. This means that some children may be able to access identifying information before 2023, when the first children conceived after anonymity was abolished reach the age of 18. In 2014, it was reported that 126 pre-2005 donors have re-registered with the HFEA as identifiable donors.

Of course, a child will only be able to apply to the HFEA for identifying information if she knows, or suspects, that she was conceived using donated gametes. Unless a child born to heterosexual parents is told about the circumstances of her conception, she will ordinarily assume that she was conceived naturally, and will not have any reason to make an application to receive identifying information about her genetic parent.

---

[66] Section 31ZB(2).   [67] [2002] EWHC 1593 (Admin).

[68] Eric Blyth, 'From need "for a father" to need "for supportive parenting": changing conceptualisation of the welfare of the child following assisted reproductive technology in the United Kingdom' in Kirsty Horsey (ed), *Revisiting the Regulation of Human Fertilisation and Embryology* (Routledge: Abingdon, 2015) 12–30.

Although there has undoubtedly been a trend towards openness, parents of children conceived using donated gametes do not always tell their children. A European study of families where the children were conceived using donated sperm found that, by the time children reached the age of 12, only 5 per cent of British parents had told their children about their origins. Some were yet to tell them or yet to decide, but 78 per cent of parents had decided never to tell their children, usually because they thought that the information would be difficult for them, or that it might complicate the child's relationship with their non-genetic parent.[69] In a more recent study, over half of a cohort of 51 parents intended to tell the child about the circumstances of their conception; at follow up, 19 parents had dropped out, and of the remaining 32 families, 40 per cent had told their child.

Given widespread non-disclosure, the right to identifying information may make little difference to a significant proportion of children conceived using donated gametes. All possible solutions to this problem are problematic. The use of donated gametes could be recorded on the child's birth certificate, or the child could be informed by letter when she reaches the age of 18. While there was some support in parliament for the first option during the 2008 debates, it is hard to see how this could be in a child's best interests. All the evidence suggests that donor-conceived children who are told about the circumstances of their conception from an early age cope well, but that it is harder for children who find out later in life, or inadvertently. Not only would endorsing birth certificates unnecessarily stigmatize children, it might lead to them finding out about their donor-conceived status in a shocking and unhelpful way. Many people only see their birth certificate when they need it to obtain a passport, to get married, or because a new employer asks to see it. Sometimes people find their birth certificates only when going through their parents' personal effects after their deaths.

Instead, it is hoped that the removal of anonymity will promote a culture of openness, and that parents will be persuaded of the benefits of openness. Section 13(6C) of 1990 Act now specifies that counselling given to couples having treatment with donated gametes 'must include such information as is proper about the importance of informing any resulting child at an early age that the child results from the gametes of a person who is not a parent of the child, and suitable methods of informing such a child of that fact'. And the Code of Practice makes it clear that patients should be strongly advised of the merits of being frank with their offspring from early childhood.

HFEA 8th Code of Practice paras 20.7 and 20.8

20.7 The centre should tell people who seek treatment with donated gametes or embryos that it is best for any resulting child to be told about their origin early in childhood. There is evidence that finding out suddenly, later in life, about donor origins can be emotionally damaging to children and to forming relations.

20.8 The centre should encourage and prepare patients to be open with their children from an early age about how they were conceived. The centre should give patients information about how counselling may allow them to explore the implications of treatment, in particular how information may be shared with any resultant children.

---

[69] S Golombok, A Brewaeys, MT Giavazzi, D Guerra, F MacCallum, and J Rust, 'The European study of assisted reproduction families: the transition to adolescence' (2002) 17 Human Reproduction 830–50.

Evidence from Sweden, where anonymity was abolished in 1985, suggests that it may take time for attitudes to telling children to change. In 2000, Gottlieb et al found that 89 per cent of Swedish parents of children created using donated gametes had not told their children about the circumstances of their conception.[70] Most parents had, however, told someone else about their use of donated gametes, increasing the chance that the child might find out inadvertently from someone other than their parents. In a follow up study in 2007, 61 per cent of parents had told the child, though once again, almost all the parents had told someone other than the child.[71]

Ironically, as Andrew Bainham points out, children born to lesbian couples or to single women, will be 'put on notice' that a third party played a role in their conception. For them, access to identifying information will therefore be a real right, which they will be able to exercise once they reach adulthood. Bainham suggests that permitting children born to heterosexual couples to remain in ignorance means that they are effectively discriminated against in their access to information:

Andrew Bainham[72]

Given that the children of same-sex legal parents will be aware that the biological and legal positions diverge and can effectively exercise their rights in due course to obtain information about the donor, the question needs to be asked whether the much larger group of children of opposite-sex legal parents should not be given the legal right to be told of their conception so that they too may meaningfully exercise their rights to information when the time comes.

In the following extract, Lucy Frith describes a different solution, namely a two-track system in which both anonymous and non-anonymous donation is possible. This option was rejected in the UK, in part because it would lead to unfair differences between donor-conceived individuals' access to information. As Frith points out, however, such a difference will exist de facto between parents who tell their children about their donor conception and parents who do not.

Lucy Frith[73]

[Guido] Pennings has suggested a policy that would allow participants to choose between an anonymous or a non-anonymous donation programme. Donors would be able to choose whether they want to be identified and couples would be able to choose between an anonymous or a non-anonymous donor. In Iceland, where such a system already operates, donors can choose to give anonymously or non-anonymously and couples can choose what type of donor to use. This policy also operates at the Sperm Bank

---

[70] Claes Gottlieb, Othon Lalos, and Frank Lindblak, 'Disclosure of donor insemination to the child: the impact of Swedish legislation on couples' attitudes' (2000) 15 Human Reproduction 2052–6.

[71] Ann Lalos, Claes Gottlieb and Othon Lalos, 'Legislated right for donor-insemination children to know their genetic origin: a study of parental thinking' (2007) 22 Human Reproduction 1759–68.

[72] 'Arguments about Parentage' (2008) 67 Cambridge Law Journal 322–51.

[73] 'Gamete donation and anonymity: the legal and ethical debate' (2001) 16 Human Reproduction 818–24, 823.

of California, for example, where donors can choose whether they want to be 'an identity release donor'.

This type of donation programme would have the advantage of giving parents a greater choice over what they told their children and also of maintaining donor numbers. Such a programme would, though, while widening parental choice, still leave the provision of information at the discretion of the parents. However, as we have seen, unless a non-anonymous programme incorporates a formal mechanism to inform the children this too leaves the decision to the discretion of the parents.

It is noteworthy that in debates over the removal of anonymity of donors, it is often assumed that donor-conceived individuals' interest is principally in learning the identity of their donor. In practice, however, it seems clear that donor-conceived individuals are at least as interested—and perhaps even more interested—in identifying their half-siblings.[74] Indeed, donor-conceived people have used the internet in order to trace their half-siblings, and have set up their own voluntary contact registries.

(b) Opening the register

The HFEA register of information is particularly significant in the case of treatment involving donated gametes, because it is in these cases that the register will be 'opened' in order to provide information to donor-conceived people and to donors. The first requests for information under the 1990 Act became possible in 2007 when the first children born since the Act came into force in 1991 reached the age of 16, and could ask if they were related to a potential spouse. In 2009, the first children became 18, and could ask for further non-identifying information.

Since 2007, there has been a steady and increasing stream of applications for information from donor-conceived people. In 2014, there were 260 requests for information from the register.[75] It is thought that donor-conceived individuals may be more likely to seek information about the circumstances of their conception when they are contemplating marriage or starting a family themselves, rather than when they turn 18.

More requests for information are also likely in the future when children conceived using an identifiable donor become old enough to access information. When this happens, offspring will be told of the donor's:

(a) full name (and any previous name);

(b) date of birth and town or district where born;

(c) last known postal address.

Section 31ZA(3) of the Act provides that before information about donor conception is given, the recipient of the information must have had an opportunity to receive counselling.

The 2008 reforms mean that it is now possible for donor-conceived offspring to find out non-identifying information about the number, age, and sex of any half-siblings, and, if they and the other siblings consent, to find out identifying information about each other. Despite having exactly the same genetic connection as the genetic half-siblings born

---

[74] Vasanti Jadva et al, 'Experiences of offspring searching for and contacting their donor siblings and donor' (2010) 20 Reproductive BioMedicine Online 523–32.

[75] *HFEA Business Plan 2015–16* (HFEA, 2015).

following his donation, the donor's own children have no rights to information about their half-siblings. In Daniels et al's study, where donors had told their children about having been a sperm donor, 70 per cent of their children wanted to meet their genetic half-siblings.[76]

Donors can be told the number, age, and sex of children born following their donation, but not the children's identity. Donors can also be forewarned that a person conceived using their gametes has made a request for identifying information, though, of course, it will only be possible to inform the donor if the clinic or the HFEA has up-to-date contact information.

(c) Payment

Since 2011, sperm donors have been entitled to a fixed sum of £35 per clinic visit to cover all of their expenses, and egg donors to a fixed sum of £750 per cycle of donation, again including all expenses. This 'one size fits all' payment reduces the paperwork associated with processing expense claims, but it inevitably means that women who have few or no expenses will receive more 'compensation' than women who have to pay for expensive train journeys, childcare, or who face substantial loss of earnings from taking several days off work. There is, as Ahuja points out, some evidence that this new policy has led to an increase in the number of donors, which may reduce the number of British couples travelling to countries like Spain for treatment with donated eggs.

Kamal K Ahuja[77]

Our own figures from the London Women's Clinic in London (and its affiliated London Egg Bank) suggest that the revised policy introduced by the HFEA is now beginning to have a beneficial effect on egg donation trends and finally bringing some relief to the former chronic shortages. During the period January 2013 to July 2014, for example, eggs were collected from 220 registered non-patient donors, which was 10 times the number of non-patient egg donors we had recruited in any of the previous 2 years. This resulted in 222 completed recipient treatments. . . . The most recent UK analysis of the availability of gamete donors provides further support for this trend. The results published by the HFEA show over 50% growth over 5 years in the availability of non-patient gamete donors in the UK . . . [T]here are signs that the reasons for travelling are becoming fewer and that the tide of cross-border reproductive care is at last beginning to turn.

Modest compensation is believed to be fair to donors, who undergo intrusive medical tests and who have to make several visits to the clinic, and, in the case of egg donors, undergo an invasive surgical procedure, while not offering an incentive capable of 'overbearing their will'. Ravelingien et al's study of Belgian recipients of sperm found that most recipients believed that donors should be compensated, provided that they did not receive 'too much'.

---

[76] Ken R Daniels, Wendy Kramer, and Maria V Perez-y-Perez, 'Semen donors who are open to contact with their offspring: issues and implications for them and their families' (2012) 25 Reproductive BioMedicine Online 670–7.

[77] 'Patient pressure: is the tide of cross-border reproductive care beginning to turn?' (2015) 30 Reproductive BioMedicine Online 447–50.

An Ravelingien et al[78]

Although the participants claimed that the donor should receive some payment, at the same time, it seemed essential that donors are not paid too much. . . . [T]he amount must be modest enough to avoid attracting donors who were motivated only by the money. In the end, their donor should be driven by principles and intentions to help, 'an altruistic donor with a good heart'. . . .

Our results suggest that sperm donors . . . are considered legitimate only when they have a central desire to help families. The participants assumed that a mere focus on financial gain would attract the 'wrong kind of donor': lazy opportunists, people who are only interested in the money and don't realize what is important in life. Underlying these fears is apparently the wish to foster a favourable image of the 'genetic father' of their (future) child. They wanted to view their donor as someone with high moral standards, someone who is helpful and caring rather than egotistic and materialistic. It is possible that such a positive image is emotionally desirable when talking and thinking about one's family. It may also have to do with genetic deterministic assumptions about the heritability of certain traits . . . [I]t was clear the participants wanted to envisage their donor as a distant, albeit good person.

Egg-sharing schemes involve a woman who needs IVF treatment agreeing to donate half of the eggs retrieved during one cycle in return for free or much cheaper treatment for herself. Given inadequate NHS funding, these schemes are attractive to women who need treatment, but cannot afford the costs of around £5,000 per cycle. Nevertheless, it is clear that egg-sharing schemes involve substantial, albeit indirect, payment for egg donation. In the next extract, Stephen Wilkinson argues that it does not make sense to effectively pay egg-sharers £5,000 for their eggs, while limiting non-patient egg donors to £750.

Stephen Wilkinson[79]

The consistency problem is most simply expressed in a question. If £2,500 or £5,000 in money is an inducement for egg donors, then how can £2,500 or £5,000 in benefits-in-kind *not* be an inducement for egg sharers? Similarly, the Threshold Problem is perhaps best understood as a question: if £750 is not an inducement to donate eggs, then what makes £2,500 or £5,000 an inducement? What we need (or what the HFEA needs) is a threshold (and, what is more, a non-arbitrary and justified threshold) such that sums of money below it do not constitute an undue inducement to donate eggs, while sums above it do.

Egg-sharing schemes carry no extra clinical risk, since the donor would be having the egg retrieval in any event. It has, however, been suggested that there may be psychological issues for women who share their eggs, but whose own treatment fails. In practice, however, the common assumption that a woman would find it difficult to come to terms with another woman's successful treatment with her eggs is not supported by recent empirical evidence into the experience of egg-sharing.

---

[78] 'Recipients' views on payment of sperm donors' (2015) 31 Reproductive BioMedicine Online 225–31.
[79] 'Is the HFEA's Policy on Compensating Egg Donors and Egg Sharers Defensible?' (2013) 21 Medical Law Review 173–212.

Zeynep B Gürtin, Kamal K Ahuja, and Susan Golombok[80]

Contrary to expectations, however, none of these women [donors whose own treatment had failed while the recipient had conceived] expressed negative feelings regarding their recipient's conception, and three explicitly reported positive feelings (although one noted that she was 'upset at first'). Although the number of women in this category is very small, the data are nevertheless important. Considered in conjunction with the open-ended messages donors would write to their recipients if they could, which were 'well-wishing' in nature (as reported earlier), and findings from this study on egg-sharers' retrospective assessments and the very low levels of regret even among unsuccessful donors we can begin to paint a picture of participants in egg-sharing schemes as more robust, less fragile and much more positive about their experiences than some critics had feared.

In the US, egg donors are paid substantial sums of money, typically between $5,000 and $10,000 per donation. Much higher sums—well over $50,000—have reportedly been paid to models and Ivy League students and graduates. In the next extract, David Resnik defends paid egg donation.

David Resnik[81]

Some ethicists have pointed out that allowing the commodification of human tissues could destroy or threaten the gift relationship that currently exists between donors and recipients, which is an important moral value. If human tissues are assigned an economic value, they will no longer be considered gifts and people will sell tissues instead of giving them . . .

The mere fact that an object can be bought or sold need not destroy our ability to transfer that object as a gift. Many commodities that are routinely bought and sold are also given as gifts . . . People have reasons and motives for giving gifts, even when those gifts have commercial value. Of course, commodification may have some impact on the gift relationship: the ability to legally commodify something may encourage people to sell that thing instead of giving it as a gift. But once again, this is a speculative claim for which we have little evidence.

(d) Screening

There are limits upon who may donate their gametes. The HFEA imposes an upper age limit of 55 for male donors and 35 for female donors, and a lower age limit of 18 for both sexes. These restrictions are relaxed for the storage of an individual's gametes for their own treatment, so a 15-year-old who is about to undergo treatment for cancer could have his sperm stored for his own future use.

All donated sperm is frozen to enable the HIV status of the donor to be conclusively established by a further HIV test six months after the donation was made. Egg donors too are tested for HIV, but because eggs are used immediately, rather than being frozen for future use, there is a risk that the donor was in the seroconversion 'window'

---

[80] 'Emotional and relational aspects of egg-sharing: egg-share donors' and recipients' feelings about each other, each others' treatment outcome, and any resulting children' (2012) 27 Human Reproduction 1690–701.

[81] 'Regulating the market in human eggs' (2001) 15 Bioethics 1–25.

between infection and its detectability. Clinics are also expected to give careful consideration to the suitability of donors, taking into account their personal and family medical history, their potential fertility, including whether they have children of their own, and their attitude towards donation. It is, however, impossible to guarantee that the donor's medical history is accurate. Nor is it possible to screen gametes for all hereditary diseases.

As the number of identifiable genetic conditions increases, and the costs of screening decrease, there will inevitably be pressure upon clinics to carry out more tests on donated gametes. If a child is born suffering from a condition passed on by the gamete donor, it is possible that the parents and the child herself could argue that failure to screen for the particular disease was a breach of the clinic's duty of care. Such actions would be similar to the 'wrongful birth' and 'wrongful life' claims that we considered in the previous chapter. As we saw then, the courts have been hostile to a child's claim that the defendant should have prevented her birth, and so in practice the parents would have to argue that, had they been told of the risk of a particular genetic condition, they would have rejected the gametes that were used in their treatment, and the harm—that is the child's birth—would have been avoided.

It might also be possible to sue the gamete donor under the Congenital Disabilities (Civil Liability) Act 1976 (which we also considered in the previous chapter) for intentional or negligent failure to disclose an inherited condition, but as yet there have been no such claims.

(e) Number of offspring

There is a limit on the number of children that may be produced from the gametes of one donor, which is expressed as 'up to ten families'. Clearly, this is less specific than an upper limit of, say, ten children, but since under the previous 'ten live births' limit, it was always possible to extend this for sibling use, it was thought clearer to tell donors how many families could be created using their sperm. It is very unlikely that an egg donor would donate sufficient eggs to come anywhere near this upper limit.

Donors are entitled to choose to set a lower limit. Usually this is done where the donor is known to the recipient. A man might decide to donate sperm to his infertile brother's wife, but not be willing for it to be used by anyone else. He would therefore set a limit of one (named) family. It had been thought that the abolition of anonymity would lead more donors to set lower limits, in order to reduce the number of potential children who might make contact 18 years later, but there does not seem to be any evidence that this has happened.

The British Fertility Society has suggested—in the light of the shortage of donated sperm in the UK—that it would make sense to set a higher limit than ten families, drawing attention to the fact that in the Netherlands, which has a much smaller and less geographically dispersed population, the upper limit is 25.[82] Against this, others argue that it may be challenging for children to come to terms with the prospect of having a very large number of half-siblings.

In the next extract, Jenni Millbank suggests that the evidence does not support the claim that the limit should be based upon a 'manageable' number of future relationships between donor and children.

[82] British Fertility Society, 'Working party on sperm donation services in the UK' (2008) 11 Human Fertility 147–58.

Jenni Millbank[83]

[A] a new rationale for family limits has arisen in anticipation of future contact following donor identity disclosure, both between donor and offspring and between offspring. This new rationale posits containing the number of genetic relatives so that the number of available contacts is manageable, in particular to protect the psychological well-being of offspring. Some versions of this rationale have slipped over from anticipation of possible contact to embedded assumptions about the kinds of relationships that will ensue, with some proposing lower family numbers so that 'meaningful relationships' can be created and maintained or traditional families resembled. The limited available research on the experiences of donor conceived individuals and families in seeking contact through voluntary registers to date does not bear out these latter assumptions. Not all offspring desire contact with donors or other offspring. Of those who did pursue contact, and whose parents pursued it early on their behalf, in existing studies most contact was limited or periodic and made through email rather than face-to-face meetings. Seeking information and a sense of understanding the connection or link appears to be the dominant motivation for those initiating contact in previous studies, rather than the desire for an intimate or on-going relationship.

(h) PARENTAGE

A further special feature of treatment with donated gametes is the separation of genetic and social parenthood. In such circumstances, how do we determine the identity of a child's legal parents? While the rules covering the identity of the child's mother are clear and unambiguous, for fathers and 'second legal parents' (in the case of same-sex couples), the law is more complicated.

An added complexity is the way in which the 2008 Act's changes to the rules on parenthood have been brought into force. Sections 27 and 28 of the 1990 Act remain on the face of the statute, because these provisions describe the ascription of parenthood for children born before the new law came into force in 2009. For children whose mothers were treated using donated sperm before April 2009, fatherhood is governed by section 28 of the 1990 Act.

The new parenthood provisions apply only to children whose mothers were treated with donated sperm after April 2009, and they have not been incorporated into the 1990 Act like the other 2008 amendments. Instead, they are to be found in the free-standing Human Fertilisation and Embryology Act 2008.

(1) Maternity

At common law,[84] and under both the 1990 Act (s 27) and the 2008 Act, the woman who gives birth to a child is her mother.

Human Fertilisation and Embryology Act 2008 section 33

33(1) The woman who is carrying or has carried a child as a result of the placing in her of an embryo or of sperm and eggs, and no other woman, is to be treated as the mother of the child.

---

[83] 'Numerical Limits in Donor Conception Regimes: Genetic Links and "Extended Family" in the Era of Identity Disclosure' (2014) 22 Medical Law Review 325–36.

[84] *The Ampthill Peerage Case* [1977] AC 547.

The woman who gives birth is always the child's legal mother, regardless of whether she is the child's genetic mother. Indeed, section 47 of the 2008 Act spells out that a woman cannot be treated as a child's parent merely because of egg donation. In some ways, this is redundant. Given the clarity of the rule that the woman who gives birth is the child's mother, an egg donor could never be treated as the mother of any child born following egg donation. The reason for this provision is so that lesbian couples are clear that, for both of them to acquire parenthood, they will need to fulfil the agreed parenthood conditions or be spouses or civil partners. A lesbian couple might assume that if one woman gives birth to a child created using the other woman's egg, then they would both be the child's legal parents, but the non-gestational genetic mother could acquire parenthood only via marriage, civil partnership, or the agreed parenthood conditions.

It is also irrelevant that the egg donation took place in a country with different rules about parenthood. If a woman gives birth to a child in the UK, she is the child's mother.

(2) Paternity

The special rules governing paternity only apply where the mother has conceived through artificial insemination or IVF:

Human Fertilisation and Embryology Act 2008 section 34[85]

(1) Sections 35 to 47 apply, in the case of a child who is being or has been carried by a woman (referred to in those sections as 'W') as a result of the placing in her of an embryo or of sperm and eggs or her artificial insemination, to determine who is to be treated as the other parent of the child.

The artificial insemination does not need to have taken place in a licensed clinic: hence these special provisions could apply to children conceived as a result of informal sperm donation. But conception must not have been through sexual intercourse. In *M v F (Legal Paternity)*, a case we encountered earlier in the context of internet introduction websites, the legal fatherhood of the child depended upon whether he had been conceived through artificial insemination or sex. Although this was clearly a simple question of fact, it was one on which the accounts of the mother and the 'donor' differed.

Resolving this question was difficult not only because of the absence of witnesses, but also because both parties were wholly untrustworthy. Peter Jackson J's judgment starts with a remarkable timeline of events. The mother alleged that she had sex with the donor on multiple occasions and that, on some occasions, this had taken place without her consent. The 'father' claimed that the child's conception had been through artificial insemination, although he admitted to having had sexual intercourse with the mother while she was pregnant for the second time, her first pregnancy having been terminated after her husband reacted violently to the news of her pregnancy. In order to take revenge on the 'father', the mother was said to have adopted a number of aliases in order to publicize his activities to newspapers and to his professional body.

---

[85] For children conceived before April 2009, the Human Fertilisation and Embryology Act 1990, s 28 contains the same wording.

M v F (Legal Paternity)[86]

Peter Jackson J

On the strength of facts that they admit, [M and F] are both individuals that have over long periods of time been untruthful, devious and manipulative. In relation to contested issues, I regret that they both lied extensively throughout their evidence, and one of them was of course lying about the central issue of the child's conception.... I found Ms M to be an unimpressive witness in relation to the above matters and to show no sign of discomfort when caught in an obvious lie. She freely stated that she is motivated by her own need for Mr F to be punished.... Mr F's evidence was clearly given, but he had clearly taken the strategic decision to tell the truth where possible and to lie where necessary....

... I find that sexual intercourse took place between Ms M and Mr F on all occasions bar the first meeting. I accordingly declare that the child was conceived by ordinary sexual intercourse and that in consequence Mr F is not only his biological father but also his legal parent.

(a) Married couples

If the woman receiving treatment is married, both the 1990 Act (s 28(5)) and the 2008 Act (s 38(2)) provide for two routes that allow her husband to be recognized as the child's father. First, under section 28(5) of the 1990 Act and section 38(2) of the 2008 Act, the presumption of paternity within marriage remains intact. In sperm donor cases, this presumption of paternity could be rebutted by DNA tests that would establish that the husband is not the biological father of the child.

Secondly, the presumption in section 35 of the 2008 Act (s 28(2) of the 1990 Act) applies, and provides that the mother's husband will be the child's father unless he did not consent to her treatment.

Human Fertilisation and Embryology Act 2008 section 35

35(1) If—

(a) at the time of the placing in her of the embryo or of the sperm and eggs or of her artificial insemination, W was a party to a marriage, and

(b) the creation of the embryo carried by her was not brought about with the sperm of the other party to the marriage, then, subject to section 38(2) to (4), the other party to the marriage is to be treated as the father of the child unless it is shown that he did not consent to the placing in her of the embryo or the sperm and eggs or to her artificial insemination (as the case may be).

In *Re CH (Contact: Parentage)*,[87] a pre-2009 case, the husband had given written consent to his wife's treatment with donor insemination, and he had been registered as the child's father. The couple subsequently divorced, and the mother sought to prevent her former husband from obtaining a contact order on the grounds that he was not the child's biological father, and so could not benefit from a presumption in favour of contact. Callman J found that this father fitted squarely within the terms of the legislation, and that it would therefore be contrary to the intentions of parliament to deny that he was the child's legal father.

[86] [2013] EWHC 1901 (Fam).   [87] [1996] 1 FLR 569.

(b) Unmarried fathers before April 2009

Where a child's mother was treated with donated sperm before April 2009, and the mother is not married, under section 28(3) of the 1990 Act, her male partner will be the child's father if they were provided with treatment services 'together'. At first sight the wording of this section is puzzling because it is not clear in what sense the partner of a woman undergoing donor insemination is being provided with treatment. In practice, a man will acquire fatherhood under this section if he and his partner had jointly requested treatment 'as a couple'.[88]

(c) Agreed fatherhood conditions after April 2009

Where the woman having treatment is not married or in a civil partnership, and wishes a man to be the father of a child conceived using donated sperm, the agreed fatherhood conditions apply:

Human Fertilisation and Embryology Act 2008 section 37

37 The agreed fatherhood conditions

(1) The agreed fatherhood conditions referred to in section 36(b) are met in relation to a man ('M') in relation to treatment provided to W under a licence if, but only if,—

(a) M has given the person responsible a notice stating that he consents to being treated as the father of any child resulting from treatment provided to W under the licence,

(b) W has given the person responsible a notice stating that she consents to M being so treated,

(c) neither M nor W has, since giving notice under paragraph (a) or (b), given the person responsible notice of the withdrawal of M's or W's consent to M being so treated,

(d) W has not, since the giving of the notice under paragraph (b), given the person responsible—

(i) a further notice under that paragraph stating that she consents to another man being treated as the father of any resulting child, or

(ii) a notice under section 44(1)(b) stating that she consents to a woman being treated as a parent of any resulting child, and

(e) W and M are not within prohibited degrees of relationship in relation to each other.

Thus under the 2008 Act, fatherhood can be acquired through the consent of both mother and father. It is interesting that the government did not limit access to agreed fatherhood to the mother's unmarried partner. Other pieces of legislation, such as the Human Tissue Act, contain statutory definitions of cohabiting partners ('living together in an enduring family relationship'), but no such restriction applies here. The only limit upon who may become a father under these provisions is that he cannot be within the prohibited degrees of relationship (for the purposes of incest) with the mother. This means that, with his consent, a woman could agree to a male friend being her child's father, but she could not agree to her brother being the legal father of her child.

---

[88] *U v W (Attorney General Intervening)* [1997] 2 FLR 282.

(d) Same-sex couples

Under the 1990 Act, the female partner of a woman undergoing treatment with donated sperm could not acquire parenthood from birth, as was possible for male partners, both married and unmarried. The woman's female partner would be a legal stranger to the child at birth, even if she was the child's genetic mother. She could subsequently apply for a parental responsibility order or could become the child's second parent via adoption. The 2008 Act changes this, and, with the exception of a difference in terminology, equalizes the position of civil partners (and since 2014, same-sex married couples) and husbands, and treats unmarried same-sex and heterosexual partners in the same way.

The terminological difference is that while a mother's male partner can become the child's father from birth, the woman's same-sex partner cannot become the child's mother. If a child has two female parents, the one who gives birth will be the mother, and the other one is simply referred to as a 'parent'. In the next extract, Alan Brown draws upon a case involving lesbian parents and a known donor, referred to throughout as the biological father, to suggest that this terminological difference is in practice significant.

Alan Brown[89]

[I]t is suggested that 'parent' is not being conceptualised as an equivalent to either mother or father in judicial discourse and this is combined with the paucity of specific consideration of the role itself within the decisions. Consequently, the precise role of 'the parent' remains unclear and it is still the case that, in the courts, 'the parent' is not being constructed as a replacement for either the mother or the father, but rather is viewed as providing an additional, somewhat ill-defined, parenting presence. . . .

The constraints that ordinary language places on our ability fully to express the nature and extent of this parenting role, on its own terms, prevents the courts from being able to conceptualise this role as deserving to be on the same level as either 'mother' or 'father'. . . . [T]he 'parent' continues to be viewed as additional to rather than as a substitute for 'father' and therefore . . . the 'father' is still deemed to be serving a crucial parental role.

(i) Civil partners and married same-sex couples

Same-sex civil partners and married same-sex couples are in the same position as husbands in relation to the acquisition of parenthood.

Human Fertilisation and Embryology Act 2008 section 42

42 Woman in civil partnership or marriage to a woman at time of treatment

(1) If at the time of the placing in her of the embryo or the sperm and eggs or of her artificial insemination, W was a party to a civil partnership or a marriage with another woman, then subject to section 45(2) to (4), the other party to the civil partnership or marriage is to be treated as a parent of the child unless it is shown that she did not consent to the placing in W of the embryo or the sperm and eggs or to her artificial insemination (as the case may be).

---

[89] 'Re G; Re Z (Children: Sperm Donors: Leave to Apply for Children Act Orders): Essential Biological Fathers and Invisible Legal Parents' (2014) 26 Child and Family Law Quarterly 237–51.

(ii) Agreed female parenthood conditions

For same-sex couples who are neither married nor in a civil partnership, the agreed female parenthood conditions mirror the agreed fatherhood conditions for unmarried heterosexual couples. The only limit on who may become a second legal parent in this way is that she must not be within the prohibited degrees of relationship, so a woman could nominate a friend to be her child's second legal parent, but not her sister.

Human Fertilisation and Embryology Act 2008 section 44

44 The agreed female parenthood conditions

(1) The agreed female parenthood conditions referred to in section 43(b) are met in relation to another woman ('P') in relation to treatment provided to W under a licence if, but only if,—

(a) P has given the person responsible a notice stating that P consents to P being treated as a parent of any child resulting from treatment provided to W under the licence,

(b) W has given the person responsible a notice stating that W agrees to P being so treated,

(c) neither W nor P has, since giving notice under paragraph (a) or (b), given the person responsible notice of the withdrawal of P's or W's consent to P being so treated,

(d) W has not, since the giving of the notice under paragraph (b), given the person responsible—

(i) a further notice under that paragraph stating that W consents to a woman other than P being treated as a parent of any resulting child, or

(ii) a notice under section 37(1)(b) stating that W consents to a man being treated as the father of any resulting child, and

(e) W and P are not within prohibited degrees of relationship in relation to each other.

It is noteworthy that the outcry in parliament and in the press over the move to delete the largely symbolic reference to the child's 'need for a father' was not mirrored by similar outrage over these, in practice, much more radical changes to the parenthood provisions, which permit a child to have, in law and from birth, two female parents.

In the next extract, Andrew Bainham argues that recognizing the mother's partner (female or male), as the child's 'parent', rather than someone exercising parental responsibility, is regrettable. Parentage, according to Bainham, is a biological kinship relationship, not a social one.

Andrew Bainham[90]

The argument, therefore, is that while it may be appropriate to give to the lesbian partner and other social parents parental responsibility (depending on the extent to which the individual actually performs parenting functions), it is *inappropriate* to make that person the legal parent because this is to distort and misrepresent kinship. The lesbian partner's mother and father, for example, would become the child's grandparents and her brothers and sisters the child's uncles and aunts. . . .

[90] 'Arguments about Parentage' (2008) 67 Cambridge Law Journal 322–51.

> The concept of parentage should rather be confined, to reflect as far as possible the unique position of biological parents and, through the child's filiation with them, the wider kinship links to the extended maternal and paternal families.

Not everyone would agree that we should privilege the genetic tie as the hallmark of familial relationships in this way, however. Others might argue that we should recognize as a child's parents the individuals who do the exhausting and sometimes thankless work of parenting, rather than someone who simply shares some of her DNA.

(e) The importance of record-keeping

Because the agreed fatherhood and parenthood provisions depend upon a record of the parties' consents, it is obviously vitally important that clinics have robust record-keeping systems in place. Consent to being treated as the child's parent must be recorded in writing before the treatment takes place, in order that that consent has been properly informed, and that there has been the opportunity for counselling.

In *X v St Bartholomew's Hospital Centre for Reproductive Medicine*,[91] there was no record that the mother's partner, X, had signed the relevant consent form (known as the PP form), and he sought a declaration from the court that he was nevertheless the child's father. Theis J held that it was more likely than not that X had signed the PP form, and that it had subsequently been mislaid by the clinic. The clinic's mistake should not prevent X from being treated as the child's father. It would, Theis J found, 'be wholly inconsistent with that provision, and the underlying intention to provide certainty, if that status could then be removed from the father and the child in the event of the clinic mislaying the consent in PP form, possibly many years later'.

In *AB v CD and the Z Fertility Clinic*, CD had undergone donor insemination treatment, unsuccessfully and then successfully, with her female partner AB, both before and after the law changed in April 2009 (to enable the second parent to be the child's legal parent from birth). The clinic had not given either AB or CD adequate information about the change in the law, and the right forms had not been signed before their third treatment cycle, in May 2009, when CD finally conceived. CD had downloaded the forms from the internet and handed them to clinic staff after treatment had taken place, but Cobb J found that this was insufficient to attribute legal parenthood to AB.

AB v CD and the Z Fertility Clinic[92]

Cobb J

> There is a proper basis for requiring the WP and PP forms—in accordance with the principles of good practice—to be completed and submitted no less than one day before treatment; the treatment is almost always at some level a stressful one. It would be quite wrong to require the parties to consider for the first time important legal issues on the day of treatment.

This case brought the failings at Z Fertility Clinic to the attention of the HFEA. It immediately required all 109 licensed clinics to carry out an audit of their records. Alarmingly,

---

[91] [2015] EWFC 13.   [92] [2013] EWHC 1418 (Fam).

this revealed that there were anomalies in the records at 51 clinics, including forms being absent, incomplete, unsigned, or completed after treatment had begun. The HFEA required the clinics to contact affected patients, causing huge distress to parents who were concerned that they were not, in fact, the legal parents of their children.

In *Re A (Human Fertilisation and Embryology Act 2008)*, Sir James Munby P was asked to make declarations of parenthood in eight cases in which the forms had not been properly completed. He did so in all of them, finding in some cases that the court could rectify mistakes on the face of the forms. He was scathing about the evidence of incompetence that these cases had brought to light.

Re A (Human Fertilisation and Embryology Act 2008)[93]

Sir James Munby P

The picture thus revealed, and I am referring not just to Barts, is alarming and shocking. This is, for very good reason, a medical sector which is subject to detailed statutory regulation and the oversight of a statutory regulator—the HFEA. The lamentable shortcomings in one clinic identified by Cobb J, which now have to be considered in the light of the deeply troubling picture revealed by the HFEA audit and by the facts of the cases before me, are, or should be, matters of great public concern. The picture revealed is one of what I do not shrink from describing as widespread incompetence across the sector on a scale which must raise questions as to the adequacy if not of the HFEA's regulation then of the extent of its regulatory powers. That the incompetence to which I refer is, as I have already indicated, administrative rather than medical is only slight consolation, given the profound implications of the parenthood which in far too many cases has been thrown into doubt.

(f) Single women

The final category of patients envisaged by the Act is women who do not wish anyone to be their child's second parent. Women whose spouses (male or female) or civil partners do not consent to their treatment will also fall within this group. In these situations, the child has no legal father, and their mother is their only legal parent.

(g) What about transgender parents?

The statutory scheme does not specifically address the possibility of transgender parenthood. While normally couples who use their own gametes in treatment are self-evidently the child's parents, and not subject to any special rules, this may not be true for parents who have changed their gender. It is possible that people who store gametes, or embryos created using their gametes, before they undergo gender reassignment may find that their stored gametes or embryos have to be treated as those of a third party donor, rather than as their own.

If a male-to-female transsexual wants her female partner to be inseminated with sperm she stored before she became a woman, she could become the child's second legal parent, via the 'agreed parenthood conditions'. It would be irrelevant that her own gametes were used in treatment.

---

[93] [2015] EWHC 2602 (Fam).

Similarly, if a female-to-male transsexual had eggs, or embryos created with her eggs, stored before gender reassignment, these could be used in the treatment of his female partner, but the transsexual man could again only acquire fatherhood through the agreed parenthood conditions, rather than because he is the child's genetic 'mother'.

Not only are statutory provisions silent about the possibility of transsexual parenthood, but also, as McGuinness and Alghrani point out, it is interesting that the preservation of fertility is not a routine aspect of preparation for gender reassignment surgery, in the same way as it is for patients undergoing treatment for cancer.

Sheelagh McGuinness and Amel Alghrani[94]

There is some evidence which suggests that transsexuals are not being counselled about their reproductive options pre-operatively. This may be due to the fact that in the past, infertility was seen as a 'price to pay' for transitioning—being a transsexual and being a parent were seen as mutually exclusive. We reject the notion that transsexuals have in some way chosen to be infertile and that this negates their rights to access artificial reproductive technologies. It is, correctly we believe, no longer accepted that same sex couples have somehow waived any options to parent by the mere fact they have elected to be in a relationship where natural reproduction is not possible. Nor do patients who elect treatment that may affect their fertility waive their reproductive interests; it is recognised that patients undergoing cancer treatment should be counselled about fertility preservation techniques. Transsexuals should not be deemed to have chosen to be infertile by opting for a treatment that results in infertility.

In addition to preserving fertility through sperm or egg or embryo freezing, a more dramatic way to become a transsexual parent first arose in the US when a female-to-male transsexual, Thomas Beatie, became pregnant. He had not had his female reproductive organs removed, but had relied upon testosterone therapy and reconstructive surgery to change gender. Beatie was now married to a woman who had had a hysterectomy. In order to start a family, they decided that he would stop taking testosterone in order to become pregnant. He gave birth to a healthy girl in 2008, and became pregnant again soon afterwards.[95] This was followed by similar cases in Israel and Spain, and in 2012 a British transsexual man was reported to have given birth.

(i) PREIMPLANTATION GENETIC DIAGNOSIS (PGD)

(1) What is PGD?

When a newly fertilized egg has started the process of cell division, it is possible to remove one or two cells without compromising its capacity for normal development. The removed cell(s) can then be tested in order to detect genetic abnormalities. Affected embryos are discarded, or donated for research, and only unaffected embryos will be transferred to the woman's uterus or frozen for use in future treatment. It is also possible to discover the embryo's sex, and hence avoid the transmission of X-linked conditions,[96] that is, conditions which only affect boys, such as haemophilia.

---

[94] 'Gender and Parenthood: The Case for Realignment' (2008) 16 Medical Law Review 261–83.

[95] James Bone, 'Pregnant man, Thomas Beatie gives birth to baby girl', *The Times*, 4 July 2008.

[96] Because females have two X chromosomes, they will invariably have a 'normal' gene that can correct a defective gene on the other X chromosome. Males, on the other hand, have only one X chromosome, so if they inherit a defective gene on the X chromosome, they will develop the disease in question.

PGD is used by couples who are at risk of passing on a genetic disorder, and who will often have previously had affected children or pregnancies. If successful, it enables couples to start a pregnancy in the knowledge that the resulting child will not have a particular abnormality.

Removing one cell from a four-cell embryo, and testing it is an extremely complex and time-consuming process, requiring considerable technical expertise, and costing much more than regular IVF. Because it is used to prevent the birth of children who will suffer from serious diseases (which may be very expensive to treat), many couples receive NHS funding. It is by no means a common procedure: in 2013, of the 64,600 IVF cycles started, only 577 involved PGD. The live birth rate per cycle started is 25.7 per cent.

(2) How is PGD Regulated?

The original legislation did not mention PGD and instead guidance was developed by the HFEA and set out in its Code of Practice. Since 2008, however, the statute has contained detailed provisions which set out the circumstances in which it is lawful to carry out PGD.

Human Fertilisation and Embryology Act 1990 Schedule 2

ACTIVITIES FOR WHICH LICENCES MAY BE GRANTED

Licences for treatment: embryo testing

1ZA(1) A licence . . . cannot authorise the testing of an embryo, except for one or more of the following purposes—

(a) establishing whether the embryo has a gene, chromosome or mitochondrial abnormality that may affect its capacity to result in a live birth,

(b) in a case where there is a particular risk that the embryo may have any gene, chromosome or mitochondrion abnormality, establishing whether it has that abnormality or any other gene, chromosome or mitochondrion abnormality,

(c) in a case where there is a particular risk that any resulting child will have or develop—

(i) a gender-related serious physical or mental disability,

(ii) a gender-related serious illness, or

(iii) any other gender-related serious medical condition,

establishing the sex of the embryo,

(2) A licence . . . cannot authorise the testing of embryos for the purpose mentioned in sub-paragraph (1)(b) unless the Authority is satisfied—

(a) in relation to the abnormality of which there is a particular risk, and

(b) in relation to any other abnormality for which testing is to be authorised under sub-paragraph (1)(b),

that there is a significant risk that a person with the abnormality will have or develop a serious physical or mental disability, a serious illness or any other serious medical condition.

(3) For the purposes of sub-paragraph (1)(c), a physical or mental disability, illness or other medical condition is gender-related if the Authority is satisfied that—

(a) it affects only one sex, or

(b) it affects one sex significantly more than the other.

The detail in Schedule 2 essentially reproduces the rules that the HFEA had already developed. In short, embryo testing is acceptable where there is a significant risk that the child to be born will have or develop a serious illness, disability, or other condition.

It is possible to choose the sex of a child, but only where there is a risk that the child would have a serious gender-related condition. Jeanne Snelling and Colin Gavaghan are critical of the HFEA's 2014 decision to refuse an application to carry out sex selection in order to avoid the inheritance of autism spectrum disorder (ASD) in a family with two 'severely affected' male children. In turning down the application, the HFEA cited evidence from its peer reviewers that PGD could not guarantee that a female child would be free from ASD. Snelling and Gavaghan point out that the Act does not confine lawful sex selection to X-linked disorders, but instead refers to conditions that affect one sex 'significantly more' than another, which is the case for ASD.

Jeanne Snelling and Colin Gavaghan[97]

The reasoning underpinning the Committee's decision is not clear. It is possible that the HFEA were wary that sex selection for ASD was moving closer to 'social' sex selection or parental 'preference', and sought to avoid public criticism. Alternatively, it is possible that the Authority may not have wanted to be involved with facilitating the conception and birth of a child that might, because of the inherent uncertainty, nevertheless be born with ASD. Clearly a line was being drawn, but in the absence of further explanation, it is unclear on what basis. . . .

[T]he Licensing Committee's refusal to license sex selection in the case of a family with two sons affected by Autism Spectrum Disorder appears, at least *prima facie*, to be inconsistent with the statutory parameters governing permissible sex selection.

Sex selection for medical reasons is becoming less common as more sophisticated tests are developed so that it is possible to exclude only embryos that have, in fact, inherited the sex-linked condition, rather than the cruder technique of excluding all male embryos.

(a) What is a serious disease?

Many genetic conditions self-evidently meet the threshold level of seriousness. If a child is born with Tay-Sachs disease, for example, her nervous system will start to degenerate during her first year of life, and she will die within three or four years. In the next extract, Søren Holm suggests that it will, at other times, be difficult to draw a line between severe and non-severe conditions.

Søren Holm[98]

[I]t is very difficult to produce a non-arbitrary dividing line between severe and non-severe conditions . . . It is disabling to be blind and deaf at the same time, and no amount of re-description can change that . . .

There are, however, many conditions where the situation is not nearly as clear. Many conditions are not universally disabling but only disabling in specific circumstances. Severe myopia (near-sightedness) is only marginally disabling in our society, whereas it was a severe disability before the invention of glasses . . . A more serious problem is that severity varies not only historically but according to the precise social context of each affected person. Even if we assume that the physical and psychological manifestations of a given condition are constant,

[97] 'PGD past, present and future: I the HFE Act 1990 now "fit for purpose"?' in Kirsty Horsey (ed), *Revisiting the Regulation of Human Fertilisation and Embryology* (Routledge: Abingdon, 2015) 80–97.

[98] 'Ethical Issues in Preimplantation Diagnosis' in John Harris and Søren Holm (eds), *The Future of Human Reproduction* (Clarendon Press: Oxford, 1998).

there will be many conditions where the impact on the person with the condition will vary quite markedly. The degree to which for instance a severe case of club foot will affect a person will depend on the kind of family he or she is born into—whether physical or more sedate pursuits are the centre of family life—and the kind of other abilities which the person has. The severity in the global sense of a severe case of club foot is thus not determined by the medical severity of the condition. Two persons with the same medical severity might end up being widely separated on the global severity scale.

The statute appears to assume that an objective assessment of seriousness is possible, whereas many have argued that different people judge seriousness differently. The Code of Practice acknowledges this, and suggests that when deciding whether to offer PGD, the family's particular circumstances and their subjective views of the condition in question are relevant.

HFEA 8th Code of Practice paras 10.4, 10.5, and 10.6

10.4 When deciding if it is appropriate to provide PGD in particular cases, the centre should consider the circumstances of those seeking treatment, rather than the particular heritable condition.

10.5 . . . The perception of the level of risk for those seeking treatment will also be an important factor in the decision-making process.

10.6 The centre should consider the following factors when deciding if PGD is appropriate in particular cases:

(a) the views of the people seeking treatment in relation to the condition to be avoided, including their previous reproductive experience

(b) the likely degree of suffering associated with the condition

(c) the availability of effective therapy, now and in the future

(d) the speed of degeneration in progressive disorders

(e) the extent of any intellectual impairment

(f) the social support available, and

(g) the family circumstances of the people seeking treatment.

In Rosamund Scott et al's empirical research into the views of scientists and health care professionals, it was clear that the couple's previous experience—commonly of having an existing child with the condition—meant that their perception of the condition's seriousness carried considerable weight. In addition, they found that some couples with an existing child had a further reason to prefer PGD to termination of pregnancy.

Rosamund Scott, Clare Williams, Kathryn Ehrich, and Bobbie Farsides[99]

Doctor 20 recalls an interesting couple:

I saw a couple last week who came for Cystic Fibrosis, a fertile, intelligent couple, who have a Cystic Fibrosis child. And I said, 'What are you doing this for? Why don't you just

---

[99] 'The Appropriate Extent of Preimplantation Genetic Diagnosis: Health Professionals' and Scientists' View on the Requirement for a Significant Risk of a Serious Genetic Condition' (2007) 15 Medical Law Review 320–56.

haveanotherpregnancy?' Andtheycouldn'tconsiderterminatingaCysticchildbecause, firstly they said, 'we do not want to have another child that we have to watch die or be very ill. But on the other hand, if we kind of [terminate the] pregnancy it's like terminating [our existing child] . . . And we feel we can't do that. And we want some other way of approaching this.'

In this case, the testing seems very much in the interests of the parents: although PGD is not 100% accurate, these parents clearly saw the possibility of a pregnancy achieved through PGD as a way of avoiding the potentially very painful issues they might face if a foetus tested positive for Cystic Fibrosis. The question of trying to avoid the dilemmas around termination is extremely important in PGD . . .

[W]hen people approach a clinic about the possibility of PGD for something they have experienced in some way, they must think that it is important enough to try to 'do something about it'. As one member of staff put this, 'of course it must be serious for them to come here'.

More fundamental than the difficulty in drawing a line between serious and non-serious conditions is the idea that some disabilities are social rather than medical problems. It is increasingly recognized that some people whom we think of as disabled are disabled more by society's attitude towards them, and its failure to adapt to their needs, than they are by the condition from which they suffer. In the next extract, Jonathan Glover argues that only disabilities that limit functioning and human flourishing should properly be described as disabilities.

Jonathan Glover[100]

Belonging to a minority that suffers discrimination is not a disability. One consequence may be the need to reclassify some conditions now thought of as disabilities. For instance, achondroplasia, severely restricted height resulting from a genetic mutation, is normally classified as a disability. But the purely functional impairments are trivial, such as needing a stool to boost height when speaking in public. Provided that there are no associated medical complications, the only serious disadvantages result from the reactions of other people. This makes it the same as being Jewish in an anti-Semitic society or gay in a homophobic society. This could push us towards saying that sometimes ethnic or religious membership, or sexual orientation, can count as a disability. Or, with less offence to our linguistic and moral intuitions, we can say that achondroplasia is not a disability.

(b) Adult-onset conditions

It is possible to carry out PGD for adult-onset genetic conditions, such as Huntington's disease, and for an increased susceptibility to late-onset diseases, such as breast cancer. In such cases, the child would be born healthy, but would be at risk of developing a serious disease in adulthood. As we saw in Chapter 8, the genetic mutation responsible for Huntington's disease has a penetrance of 100 per cent, which means that if you inherit the mutation, then, unless you die first from an unrelated cause, you will develop Huntington's disease. Most cancers are not genetic, but there are some genes, like BRCA1 and 2, which are responsible for fewer than 5 per cent of all cases of breast cancer, but which greatly increase the risk

[100] *Choosing Children: Genes, Disability and Design* (Clarendon Press: Oxford, 2006) 10.

of developing the condition, usually at a much younger age than normal. Someone with a faulty BRCA1 or BRCA2 gene may have an 80 per cent chance of developing breast cancer and a 60 per cent chance of developing ovarian cancer. The HFEA has decided that, in principle, it is acceptable to use PGD to detect these lower penetrance late-onset conditions, and it has licensed PGD for a number of different cancer susceptibility genes, including the BRCA1 mutation.

Of course, unless PGD is permitted for all susceptibility genes, it may become necessary to draw a line between penetrance which does justify PGD and penetrance which does not. Locating the tipping point on the scale between an 85 per cent risk—which clearly is substantial—and a 0.01 per cent risk, which is not, is going to be difficult, not least because a range of other factors, such as the risk of mortality, age of onset, and availability of treatment options, may affect our judgement about whether PGD would be appropriate.

(c) Carrier embryos

It is possible to detect whether embryos are carriers of recessive disorders. These are diseases, like cystic fibrosis, where the defective gene must be inherited from both parents for the disease to manifest itself. Someone who has only one copy of the defective gene will be a carrier of the disease, but will not develop it herself. If she reproduces with another carrier, her offspring will have a 1 in 4 chance of receiving a double dose and inheriting the disease, and a 50/50 chance of inheriting one gene, and again being a carrier.

If a carrier embryo implants and is successfully carried to term, the resulting child will be free from the particular condition, but might go on to have a sick child or face difficult reproductive choices in the future. Testing for carrier status alone would not fit within the statutory criteria. In practice, however, carrier embryos may be identified during PGD cycles carried out where both parents are carriers, and are undergoing PGD in order to avoid the birth of a child with the recessive condition. In such circumstances, if there are viable embryos that are neither affected nor carriers, it may make sense to transfer those embryos to the woman's womb.

(d) PGD with non-disclosure

In recent years, the HFEA has been faced with the question of how clinics should respond to requests for PGD from people who know that they are at risk of inheriting Huntington's disease, but who do not wish to know whether they have, in fact, inherited the Huntington's mutation. As we saw in Chapter 8, most people who are at risk of inheriting the Huntington's mutation choose not to undergo pre-symptomatic genetic testing, preferring to exercise their 'right not to know' than to have to live with the certain knowledge that they will develop an incurable, degenerative disease in middle age. But it is also understandable that these people might wish to undergo PGD to ensure that their children do not have the Huntington's mutation.

The difficulty is that once the embryos are tested, it is likely that the clinicians will be able to tell whether the at-risk patient has the condition: if any of the embryos are affected, then the clinician knows that the parent has the genetic mutation and will develop the disease. Conversely, if the couple produces, say, ten embryos, and none are affected, it is also unlikely that the at-risk patient is affected. There may then be inevitable risk of inadvertent disclosure: we all know how hard it is to ensure that our expressions and body language do not unwittingly communicate whether news is good or bad.

Moreover, it has been argued that attempts to preserve parental ignorance might lead to unethical practices: if no embryos are suitable for transfer because all are affected, should the doctors try to fabricate an alternative reason why none are suitable (ie should they lie to the patients?), or should they carry out a sham transfer (which would be clinically inappropriate care)? Neither option would seem to be good medical practice. If the couple were to seek a second cycle of PGD, when the treating clinicians are sure that the at-risk patient is unaffected, and that there is no risk that the child would inherit a serious condition, would it be unethical and perhaps even unlawful to carry out PGD?

Some of these difficulties can be resolved by employing what is known as exclusion testing, which involves excluding embryos which have inherited the relevant chromosome from their affected grandparent. This means excluding embryos which are statistically at the same risk of inheriting the disease as the parent—that is, there is a 50/50 chance that an embryo which has inherited this chromosome from the affected parent will have the condition and a 50/50 chance that it will not. The advantage to exclusion testing is that the clinic staff will not find out the status of the parent, but it inevitably results in normal embryos being discarded. Exclusion testing is dependent upon being able to test the grandparent who has Huntington's disease, so it is only possible if he or she has not yet died from the disease.

As Asscher and Koops point out, even with exclusion testing, the ethical issue remains that potentially unnecessary PGD is carried out because the at-risk parent does not wish to know his or her status. This must be put in the balance with the 'harms' to parents forced to choose between finding out their status or having children who will themselves be at risk, or not having children at all.

E Asscher and B-J Koops[101]

The objections against honouring the right not to know in the Huntington PGD context all relate to the same issue: in half of the cases, PGD is strictly speaking unnecessary because the parents are unaffected. In these cases, we face the costs of the small but real IVF risks to the child ultimately to be born, the financial costs of the procedure, and the strain this puts on the solidarity of a publicly funded health system. The question is then whether these costs outweigh the costs of overriding the right not to know and disallowing the exclusion test. These costs consist, first, of psychological harm of those parents who want to have disease-free children and choose to undergo the procedure and thus have to relinquish their right not to know. Second, other parents will decide to forego genetic diagnosis at all and will conceive unselected children; these children will have to face exactly the same dilemmas as their parents. In addition, 50% of these children will carry the gene for Huntington's disease and thus become seriously ill and die in their third or fourth decade of life. Third, some of the prospective parents may decide against having genetically related children in order to preserve their right not to know.

(e) Testing for disability

The 2008 Act amendments prohibit a further possible use of PGD, namely if would-be patients want to positively select embryos affected by a particular condition, such as congenital deafness. No such cases had arisen under the previous law, but it had been anticipated that clinicians might be likely to invoke section 13(5)—the need to take the future child's

---

[101] 'Law, ethics and medicine: the right not to know and preimplantation genetic diagnosis for Huntington's disease' (2010) 36 Journal of Medical Ethics 30–3.

welfare into account—in order to refuse to provide PGD to someone who wanted to screen in a genetic condition. Now the positive selection of embryos or donors known to have a particular abnormality is specifically prohibited.

Human Fertilisation and Embryology Act 1990 section 13

13(9) Persons or embryos that are known to have a gene, chromosome or mitochondrion abnormality involving a significant risk that a person with the abnormality will have or develop—

(a) a serious physical or mental disability,

(b) a serious illness, or

(c) any other serious medical condition,

must not be preferred to those that are not known to have such an abnormality.

The Act does not ban the transfer of affected embryos: rather, it does not allow them to be 'preferred'. This means that it is not possible to select embryos known to suffer from congenital deafness, where unaffected embryos are available. If, however, the only embryos suitable for transfer happen to be affected, then they would not be being 'preferred' to unaffected embryos, and it would be acceptable to transfer them to the woman's womb.

Aside from the fact that it is not clear that anyone actually wishes to use PGD in order to select embryos affected by a disability, this scenario is very unlikely to arise because to be in a position to choose embryos known to be affected by a genetic abnormality, the couple must have first undergone PGD in order to avoid the birth of an affected child. If a couple did want to have affected children, they are unlikely to be in this position, and much more likely to reproduce naturally, when there is a one in four chance of having an affected child.

Section 13(9) also provides that a couple must not prefer a gamete donor because they suffer from a condition like congenital deafness. However, if a couple 'prefer' to use a relative—say, the infertile man's brother—as a donor, and he happens to be deaf, it could be argued that they would not be preferring him because of his deafness, but rather because of his genetic relatedness. Of course, it is almost impossible to legislate for people's preferences, and so a couple might prefer to use a deaf donor, but as long as they have other grounds for preferring the deaf man, it would be hard to prove that deafness was the principal reason for his selection.

During the legislative process, this provision was heavily criticized by disability groups, and most vociferously by the deaf community, which argued that it sent a negative message about living with disability. A deaf couple, who already had a deaf child but were contemplating using IVF in order to have a second child, became a focus of media attention. They did not want to positively select a deaf embryo, and would be equally happy to have a hearing child, but they did not want to be compelled to reject an embryo on the grounds of its deafness.[102] It is not clear that this would, in fact, have happened to them: there is no requirement for congenitally deaf IVF patients to undergo PGD. Nevertheless, they argued powerfully that it was offensive for legislation to insist that embryos that had inherited their deafness must be discarded in favour of embryos that had not.

---

[102] Robin McKie and Gaby Hinsliff, 'This couple want a deaf child. Should we try to stop them?', *The Observer*, 9 March 2008.

In the next extract, Julian Savulescu criticizes the prohibition on selecting for deafness from another direction, sometimes described as the non-identity problem. He argues that, unless the child's life would be so impaired as to be not worth living, it will always be better to be born rather than not born, and hence positively selecting for disability should be allowed.

Julian Savulescu[103]

What if a couple has in vitro fertilisation and preimplantation genetic diagnosis and they select a deaf embryo? Have they harmed that child? Is that child worse off than it would otherwise have been (that is, if they had selected a different embryo)? No—another (different) child would have existed. The deaf child is harmed by being selected to exist only if his or her life is so bad it is not worth living. Deafness is not that bad. Because reproductive choices to have a disabled child do not harm the child, couples who select disabled rather than non-disabled offspring should be allowed to make those choices, even though they may be having a child with worse life prospects.

(3) Is PGD Acceptable?

The use of PGD has been criticized by commentators such as King, who argue that it amounts to a new form of free-market eugenics.

David King[104]

In PGD, parents adopt a far more pro-active, directing role, choosing their children in a way which is not so far removed from their experience as consumers, choosing amongst different products.

There are a number of reasons why unrestricted free-market eugenics would be highly undesirable. Firstly, selecting the 'best' amongst multiple embryos sets up a new relationship between parents and offspring . . .They are no longer a gift from God, or the random forces of nature, but selected products, expressing, in part, their parents' aspirations, desires and whims . . .

Clearly, there is likely to be a tendency for parents to select offspring which conform best to social norms, with regard to health and physical ability, appearance and aptitudes. Disabled people have often expressed fears that an expanded free-market eugenics would correspondingly lessen society's tolerance for those with congenital and genetic disorders . . . It is also possible to imagine selection on grounds of IQ, skin colour, physical build and facial features, etc. It does not seem desirable to allow such forces to operate at the level of selection of who is permitted to be born. Rather, we should combat the social forces which lead us to disvalue some individuals and idealise others. . . .

[A] logical consequence of a system of free-market eugenics in societies where large disparities of wealth and social class continue to exist is a gradual polarisation of society into a genetically privileged ruling elite and an underclass.

[103] 'Deaf lesbians, "designer disability", and the future of medicine' (2002) 325 British Medical Journal 771–3.

[104] 'Preimplantation genetic diagnosis and the "new" eugenics' (1999) 25 Journal of Medical Ethics 176–81.

King is making a slippery slope claim about PGD: namely, that allowing people to test for serious and often fatal diseases makes it more likely that one day parents will select embryos on the basis of more trivial traits, like sporting ability or IQ. One problem with this argument is that complex characteristics like these are not purely genetic. Identical twin studies show that there may be some correlation between a person's genetic make-up and characteristics like intelligence. But if the sole cause were genetic, the correlation would be 100 per cent, which it is not. It is, in any event, far too simplistic to say that there is a single gene *for* these traits, and hence PGD—which is capable of testing for single gene mutations—could not be used to choose tall or sporty children.

A second problem with King's argument is that it presupposes that PGD is a relatively straightforward and generally successful technique, whereas nothing could be further from the truth. In their ethnographic study of couples who had undergone PGD, Franklin and Roberts describe how gruelling the process is, and how seldom it succeeds.

Sarah Franklin and Celia Roberts[105]

The question of how patients had 'arrived' at PGD was the first thing couples were asked during interviews—and was always met with lengthy and upsetting replies. These 'how we got to PGD' stories could begin far back in time, with an initial miscarriage, an affected birth, or a chance occurrence, such as reading a newspaper article about PGD. In discussing their 'route' to PGD, couples often provided epic tales of hardship and struggle, in which a characteristic determination featured prominently. 'Getting to PGD' had often involved going through numerous painful experiences—not only of tragic events such as the deaths of children or repeated miscarriages—but also of previous failed forms of treatment, complicated family situations, and challenges to the couple's relationship . . .

In casual conversations, and also formal interviews with clinicians, nurses, PGD coordinators and genetic counsellors, a constant and consistent theme is that although PGD is a valid and necessary choice, it is not for everyone, is very difficult and often fails.

Colin Gavaghan turns King's argument about the 'message' PGD sends to disabled people on its head. He argues that in order to avoid sending a message about the sort of lives that are and are not of value, it would be preferable for PGD to be made freely available, and for the state to play no role in deciding when it is, and is not, legitimate.

Colin Gavaghan[106]

When law and policy restrict the use of PGD to the avoidance of children with genetic defects, denying it to those with other values and priorities, it becomes at least arguable that our approach to this technology, far from being driven by an agenda of promoting individual choice and respecting diversity, is underpinned by judgments about the value of those lives that are avoided. It is scarcely surprising if those affected by genetic illnesses or disabilities, or those who care about or for such people, look with some offense and suspicion at those laws and policies.

---

[105] *Born and Made: An Ethnography of Preimplantation Genetic Diagnosis* (Princeton UP: Princeton, 2006).

[106] 'Right problem wrong solution: a pro-choice response to "expressivist" concerns about preimplantation genetic diagnosis' (2007) 16 Cambridge Quarterly of Healthcare Ethics 20–34.

> It is my contention, though, that their concerns could better be addressed by loosening the regulations applicable to PGD, thereby allowing . . .any other prospective parents to utilize this technology to implement their own values and preferences. In so doing, we might avoid the imposition by the state of a single, simplistic view of what constitutes 'normality' and 'disability,' a view that is clearly not universally shared. The appropriate response—from the state, from the public, and from the Authority itself—to the HFEA's question about the desirability of testing for cancer genes should be: 'We hold no view on this, other than that prospective parents should be permitted to make informed choices for themselves, free from coercion, and safe in the knowledge that whatever choice they make will be respected and supported.' Nothing, I submit, could be further removed from the pernicious taint of eugenics.

While fears of 'designer babies', selected for intelligence, beauty, and sporting ability, are grounded in a complete misunderstanding of genetics, there is no doubt that rapid progress in understanding the genetic basis of diseases is going to throw up new issues for the regulation of PGD. Gavaghan's proposal that we should abandon the attempt to draw lines between conditions which do and those which do not justify the use of PGD would remove the need to make difficult decisions in the future, but this is not the direction taken by the 2008 reforms. Instead, their much greater specificity about the legitimate uses of PGD means that there is likely to be more rather than less debate over whether conditions meet the threshold level of seriousness.

In the field of genetics there has been especially rapid progress in identifying genes that may play a part in increasing susceptibility to a range of common diseases. If a cell from an embryo could be tested for a wide range of susceptibility genes, it becomes plausible to offer PGD to people who do not already know that they have a particular genetic disease in their family. PGD is generally provided only to people who know that their family is at risk of a serious genetic condition, and this is comparatively rare. In contrast, all of us possess genes which increase our susceptibility to a range of conditions. When this sort of testing becomes available, anyone potentially becomes a possible candidate for PGD. While very few people are likely to be able to afford to pay thousands of pounds for this sort of testing, people who are already undergoing IVF might find paying for additional genome screening an attractive possibility.[107]

(4) Tissue Typing

A new use for PGD emerged at the start of the twentieth century. Tissue or HLA (Human Leukocyte Antigen) typing involves taking a cell from an early embryo, in the same way as for PGD, and testing it to see if the resulting child would be a good tissue match for a sick sibling in need of, say, a bone marrow transplant. If the selected embryo is a good tissue match, when the baby is born, blood taken from her umbilical cord can be used to treat her brother or sister.

When it first considered the issue in 2001, the HFEA decided that tissue typing could be licensed for use in treatment, but only if the child to be born was at risk of suffering from the same genetic disease as their sick older sibling. Following this decision, Josephine Quintavalle, on behalf of a pressure group called CORE (Comment on Reproductive Ethics),

---

[107] See also ZO Merhi and L Pal, 'Gender "tailored" conceptions: should the option of embryo gender selection be available to infertile couples undergoing assisted reproductive technology?' (2008) 34 Journal of Medical Ethics 590–3.

brought an application for judicial review. In *Quintavalle (Comment on Reproductive Ethics) v Human Fertilisation and Embryology Authority*, CORE argued that tissue typing was prohibited by the Act, which then defined 'treatment services' as services provided 'for the purpose of assisting women to carry children', including 'practices designed to secure that embryos are in a suitable condition to be placed in a woman or to determine whether embryos are suitable for that purpose'.

At first instance, Maurice Kay J interpreted the definition of 'treatment services' narrowly and literally. Since HLA typing was not *necessary* in order to help a woman to bear a child, it did not fall within this definition, and could not therefore be licensed by the HFEA. His decision would not just have prevented the HFEA from licensing HLA typing, however, but would also have made it impossible to license PGD. On appeal, the Court of Appeal unanimously reversed his decision, taking a much more purposive approach to the task of statutory interpretation. In *Quintavalle (Comment on Reproductive Ethics) v Human Fertilisation and Embryology Authority*, the House of Lords upheld the Court of Appeal's decision, again unanimously.

Quintavalle (Comment on Reproductive Ethics) v Human Fertilisation and Embryology Authority[108]

Lord Hoffmann

[T]he licensing power of the authority is defined in broad terms. Paragraph 1(1) of Sch 2 enables it to authorise a variety of activities (with the possibility of others being added by regulation) provided only that they are done 'in the course of' providing IVF services to the public and appear to the authority 'necessary or desirable' for the purpose of providing those services. Thus, if the concept of suitability in sub-paragraph (d) of 1(1) is broad enough to include suitability for the purposes of the particular mother, it seems to me clear enough that the activity of determining the genetic characteristics of the embryo by way of PGD or HLA typing would be 'in the course of' providing the mother with IVF services and that the authority would be entitled to take the view that it was necessary or desirable for the purpose of providing such services . . .

I would therefore . . . hold that both PGD and HLA typing could lawfully be authorised by the authority as activities to determine the suitability of the embryo for implantation within the meaning of para 1(1)(d).

Lord Brown

The fact is that once the concession is made (as necessarily it had to be) that PGD itself is licensable to produce not just a viable foetus but a genetically healthy child, there can be no logical basis for construing the authority's power to end at that point. PGD with a view to producing a healthy child assists a woman to carry a child only in the sense that it helps her decide whether the embryo is 'suitable' and whether she will bear the child.

Prior to the House of Lords' decision, in 2004 the HFEA reviewed the evidence and changed its policy. There was, the HFEA found, no evidence that embryo biopsy posed a risk to the future health of children. This was not because evidence had proved conclusively that the procedure was safe. Rather, there had been too few children born following embryo biopsy

---

[108] [2005] UKHL 28.

for any definitive conclusions to be drawn about the procedure's safety, although there was no evidence that it is not safe.

The 2004 guidance replaced the 2001 guidance with a new set of criteria to be taken into account by the Licence Committee when deciding an application to carry out PGD and HLA typing. Most importantly, it was no longer necessary for the recipient child's condition to be inherited, so HLA typing could be carried out even though the child to be born was not at risk of inheriting the same condition.

In 2004, the HFEA also removed the requirement that the intention should be to take cord blood only. Evidence from haematologists suggested both that there might be circumstances in which a bone marrow transplant might subsequently become necessary, and that extracting bone marrow from a very young child is less intrusive and painful than adult bone marrow donation. Obviously, the HFEA cannot control subsequent decisions about the medical treatment of children born following licensed treatment and so the previous criterion could not, in practice, prevent a bone marrow transplant from taking place if the cord blood transplant did not work.

The 2008 reforms put the criteria for tissue typing on a statutory footing, and essentially reproduce the HFEA's 2004 policy.

Human Fertilisation and Embryology Act 1990 Schedule 2

ACTIVITIES FOR WHICH LICENCES MAY BE GRANTED

Embryo testing

1ZA(1) A licence . . . cannot authorise the testing of an embryo, except for one or more of the following purposes— . . .

(d) in a case where a person ('the sibling') who is the child of the persons whose gametes are used to bring about the creation of the embryo (or of either of those persons) suffers from a serious medical condition which could be treated by umbilical cord blood stem cells, bone marrow or other tissue of any resulting child, establishing whether the tissue of any resulting child would be compatible with that of the sibling . . .

(4) In sub-paragraph (1)(d) the reference to 'other tissue' of the resulting child does not include a reference to any whole organ of the child.

Tissue typing can therefore only be carried out to select a tissue donor for an older sibling, and not for any other family member. It would therefore not be possible for a mother who herself needed a bone marrow transplant to undergo tissue typing to select a child who would be a good match. Why not? At first sight, it might seem that the mother in such a case would be seeking tissue typing for self-interested reasons, though, of course, a woman who does not want to leave her existing children without a mother would also be acting out of concern for their welfare. This restriction is not, however, directed at the intention behind the request for tissue typing: rather, it reflects the practical reality that while the chance of producing an embryo that is a good tissue match for an existing sibling is 1 in 4, for parents or more distant relatives, the chance of producing a tissue match is much more remote. For siblings, there is a realistic chance that one IVF cycle will produce at least one compatible embryo, but this is not the case for other relatives.

The Act also confirms that it could be legitimate to use tissue typing where the intention is to take bone marrow or other tissue, provided there is no intention to take a solid organ. This means that it would be possible for parents who have a child with leukaemia, which is currently in remission, to undergo tissue typing so that there would be a tissue-matched sibling, should her leukaemia return and a bone marrow transplant become immediately necessary.

The restriction upon taking a solid organ was inserted during the parliamentary debates in the House of Lords. While it undoubtedly means that a clinic could not carry out preimplantation tissue typing in order to select a child to be an organ donor in the future, it could not operate as a lifetime ban on the child who is born ever becoming an organ donor. As we saw in Chapter 11, the Human Tissue Act 2004 does not rule out childhood organ donation, although cases are expected to be rare, and would require court approval. It is more likely that a child born as a result of tissue typing might choose, when she reaches adulthood, to become a live organ donor for her sick sibling. The Human Fertilisation and Embryology Act could not prevent this happening.

When the 2008 reforms were debated, the creation of what have been called 'saviour siblings' was one of the issues that sparked the greatest controversy and debate. In addition to the arguments against PGD considered in the previous section, tissue typing raises some additional concerns, set out here by Wolf et al.

Susan M Wolf, Jeffrey P Kahn, and John E Wagner[109]

[W]e know almost nothing about the psychological impact of being conceived to serve as an HLA-matched donor and save a sibling's life. The effects on the donor child are potentially profound. Indeed, if the cord blood transplant fails or the donor child is otherwise repeatedly considered for harvest over a prolonged period of time, there may be a potential for serious effects. The potential may be all the greater if the donor child comes to resist or refuse further procedures . . .

Moreover, even if one debates whether using PGD solely to conceive an HLA-matched donor may be said to harm the donor child, this use of PGD exclusively to create an opportunity for later harvesting may be wrong on other grounds, such as violating the ethical injunction to respect each individual and avoid using persons as mere means . . .

The donor child is at lifelong risk of exploitation, of being told that he or she exists as an insurance policy and tissue source for the sibling, of being repeatedly subjected to testing and harvesting procedures, of being used this way no matter how severe the psychological and physical burden, and of being pressured, manipulated, or even forced over protest.

Wolf et al argue that the child conceived in order to save an older sibling's life is being used solely as a means, and not as an end in herself, thus offending the Kantian imperative (see Chapter 1). Of course, this would be equally true if a couple with a sick child decide to conceive another child naturally who might be a good tissue match; but few people would argue that couples should be prevented from having further children in the hope that they would be a good tissue match for a sick child. In any event, a child born following HLA typing is not used solely as a means, since she is not abandoned after the donation, but rather is overwhelmingly likely to be loved in her own right as a new and welcome member of the family.

People have children for a wide range of instrumental, and sometimes unedifying, reasons, such as trying to save a failing relationship or producing an heir to take over the family business. Having a second child in order to provide an only child with a companion is not

---

[109] 'Using preimplantation genetic diagnosis to create a stem cell donor: issues, guidelines and limits' (2003) 31 Journal of Law, Medicine and Ethics 327.

uncommon. Unless the parents planned to abandon the new child at birth, it is hard to see why having a child whose umbilical cord might be able to save their sibling's life should be singled out as an unacceptable parental motivation.

It could also plausibly be argued that although the psychological risks associated with being conceived in order to be a donor are speculative, we know that the impact of bereavement in childhood is overwhelmingly negative. Children conceived naturally in an attempt to find a good tissue match are likely to be born into families that either have or will soon experience the death of a child. As a result, Sally Sheldon and Stephen Wilkinson argue that child welfare arguments might be mobilized to support the use of HLA typing. The child born following tissue typing is benefited by being a good tissue match for an older sibling, since this enables her to be born into a family which is not wracked by bereavement, and to benefit from a relationship with her older sibling, which she would not otherwise have had.

Sally Sheldon and Stephen Wilkinson[110]

The first prohibitionist argument is that a saviour sibling would be 'a commodity rather than a person' and would be wrongfully treated as a means rather than an end in itself . . . [T]his argument fails to say what is wrong with creating a child as a saviour sibling, when creating a child for a number of other 'instrumental' purposes is widely accepted. . . .

We turn now to the idea that saviour siblings will be psychologically harmed . . . But even if we concede for the sake of argument that it would be hurtful or upsetting for a selected sibling (A) to discover that she had been conceived for the primary purpose of saving the life of an existing child (B), is it really plausible to suppose that A would be less happy than another, randomly selected sibling (C) who was unable to act as a tissue donor? For it could surely be argued that A would benefit from B's company and may well derive pleasure from knowing that she has saved B's life. In contrast, imagine the psychological impact on C, born into a bereaved family, later to discover that she was a huge disappointment to her parents because of her inability to save B's life. . . . [W]e can at least say that it is far from obvious that child welfare considerations should count against, rather than for, the practice of saviour sibling selection.

(5) Non-Medical Sex Selection

There are a variety of ways in which parents might try to control the sex of their offspring. First, there are ineffectual folk remedies, such as having sex at a particular time during the woman's menstrual cycle, or in a particular position. Secondly, sperm sorting involves separating X and Y sperm, and artificially inseminating the woman with the separated sperm. Until the European Tissues and Cells Directive came into force, this could be done without a licence in the UK. Now a licence would be necessary, but since success rates are too low to justify the use of sperm sorting for medical reasons, and sex selection for social reasons is prohibited, it would not be possible to obtain a licence.

Thirdly, and more successful, is preimplantation sex selection, using PGD. This needs a licence from the HFEA, and is permitted only for medical reasons.

[110] 'Hashmi and Whitaker, "An Unjustifiable and Misguided Distinction"' (2004) 12 Medical Law Review 137–63.

Fourthly, women can undergo prenatal sex diagnosis during pregnancy, and abort the fetus if it is the 'wrong' sex. This would be lawful only if it could be established that the pregnant woman's mental or physical health was endangered by carrying the pregnancy to term (see Chapter 13).

The legitimacy of sex selection for social reasons was considered by the HFEA following a public consultation in 2003. As is clear from the following extract, the HFEA was heavily influenced by the weight of public opinion against sex selection.

Human Fertilisation and Embryology Authority[111]

147. In reaching a decision we have been particularly influenced by the considerations set out above relating to the possible effects of sex selection for non-medical reasons on the welfare of children born as a result, and by the quantitative strength of views from the representative sample polled by MORI and the force of opinions expressed by respondents to our consultation. These show that there is very widespread hostility to the use of sex-selection for non-medical reasons. By itself this finding is not decisive; the fact that a proposed policy is widely held to be unacceptable does not show that it is wrong. But there would need to be substantial demonstrable benefits of such a policy if the state were to challenge the public consensus on this issue. In our view the likely benefits of permitting sex-selection for non-medical reasons in the UK are at best debatable and certainly not great enough to sustain a policy to which the great majority of the public are strongly opposed.

Again, the 2008 reforms simply place previous HFEA policy on sex selection on a statutory footing:

Human Fertilisation and Embryology Act 1990 Schedule 2 para 1ZB

(1) A licence . . . cannot authorise any practice designed to secure that any resulting child will be of one sex rather than the other . . .

(3) Sub-paragraph (1) does not prevent the authorisation of any other practices designed to secure that any resulting child will be of one sex rather than the other in a case where there is a particular risk that a woman will give birth to a child who will have or develop—

(a) a gender-related serious physical or mental disability,

(b) a gender-related serious illness, or

(c) any other gender-related serious medical condition.

So what are the arguments against allowing sex selection for social reasons? First, some people have argued that sex selection embodies a consumerist attitude towards children. Instead of welcoming a child regardless of its gender, would-be parents who want to choose their child's sex are accused of seeking to ensure that their new baby meets their specifications. Secondly, there are those who claim that sex selection for social reasons is inherently sexist and discriminatory. Thirdly, it is argued that allowing people to select the sex of their offspring might also have devastating demographic consequences.

---

[111] *Sex Selection: Options for Regulation* (HFEA, 2003).

Jodi Danis[112]

Some predict that a population in which males significantly predominate, known as a 'high sex ratio society', would have devastating results for women. A high sex ratio society might value women for their reproductive capacities, but would also be likely to force women to return to traditional roles centered around the home and family. Demographic imbalances would exacerbate existing sex discrimination because women would not have the political power or economic resources to change the status quo. The underrepresentation of women in positions of power would be even more significant. Oppression and violence against women might increase in male-dominated societies, especially if men felt the need to possess a limited resource and to ensure fidelity. . . .

Males, through their greater numbers, would also know that they were selected more often and were thus more desired, increasing their sense of self-worth and self-importance while diminishing the self-esteem of their younger sisters or other girls. . . .

[B]ecause only those in the middle or upper class can afford sex selection technology, and only those in the upper class can afford the more accurate in vitro technology, a higher proportion of boys would be born to the wealthy. This trend might result in the future masculinization of wealth.

Of course, a couple with three sons are not necessarily guilty of discriminating against boys when they hope their fourth child will be a girl. But it is further argued that even this sort of preference depends upon sexist preconceptions about a child's gender-specific nature. A couple with three boys only want a girl, some would argue, because they think that she will be different from their sons. In the next extract, Jonathan Berkowitz and Jack Snyder argue that this expectation of difference arises from sexist attitudes.

Jonathan Berkowitz and Jack Snyder[113]

[T]o choose a boy or a girl, parents must have preconceived notions, however vague, about the ramifications of having a certain sexed child: notions which are fundamentally sexist as they are predicated upon anticipated gender based behaviour. Preconceptive sex selection is disturbing because it can be used as a vehicle for parents to express spoken or unspoken sexual prejudice . . .

Furthermore, by making a choice, parents must essentially prefer one sex over another. This emphasis upon sex is in direct conflict with larger societal goals directed against sexism and which urge individuals to be sex-blind. Pre-conceptive sex-selection represents sexism in its purest most blatant form as prior to conception, before parents can possibly know anything about their child, a child's worth is based in large part upon its sex.

Even if we accept that inflicting gender stereotypes on one's children is undesirable, it is not PGD that causes this sort of behaviour. Rather, parents with sexist attitudes will also inflict them upon any child that they might have naturally.

The principal argument in favour of allowing sex selection for social reasons derives from John Stuart Mill's harm principle. Liberty, according to Mill, should be restricted only when its exercise might cause harm to others. If, and of course this is a contentious question, sex

---

[112] 'Sexism and "the superfluous female": arguments for regulating pre-implantation sex selection' (1995) 18 Harvard Women's Law Journal 219.

[113] 'Racism and sexism in medically assisted conception' (1998) 12 Bioethics 25–44.

selection does not harm anyone, then there is insufficient justification for restricting people's reproductive freedom. Of course, critics of sex selection would argue that it does harm others, such as the child herself (see Jonathan Berkowitz and Jack Snyder) and society in general (see Jodi Danis).

Others, such as David McCarthy and John Harris, disagree and contend that these harms are far too speculative to justify a restriction on freedom.

David McCarthy[114]

In a pluralistic democratic society built upon the ideals of free and equal citizenry, there is always a presumption in favour of liberty. The burden of proof is always on those who want to restrict the liberty of others. Defenders of the legality of sex selection are not seeking to restrict anyone's liberty, whereas opponents are. So the burden of proof is on the opponents to show that those whose liberties they propose to restrict cannot reasonably reject this restriction. It is never sufficient grounds for one group to restrict the liberty of others that it is clear, as they see it, that the behaviour they are trying to restrict is morally objectionable. What must be established is that the behaviour they are trying to restrict itself results in something like significant harm to others or infringement of their basic liberties or significant social costs. In the case of sex selection, I have argued that no such grounds have been established.

John Harris[115]

The suggestion that sons or daughters would be so unloved and treated so unacceptably badly that it would cause psychological damage is a piece of reckless speculation. Suffice it to say that for these highly speculative and fanciful dangers to count against the powerful formulation of the liberal imperative would be effectively to deny that imperative any weight or role at all . . .

The illiberalism of this conclusion and the poverty of the arguments produced to defend and sustain it make it imperative that [the HFEA's] report is not only rejected but that it be recognised for what it is, an attempt to formalise the tyranny of the majority and to institutionalise contempt for the principles of liberal democracy.

The so-called non-identity problem poses a difficulty for those who argue against sex selection for social reasons: any harm caused by choosing a child's sex is unlikely to be so grave that it would be better if the sex-selected child did not exist. If I found out that my parents had selected me from a range of embryos because I am female, I might think that they were a bit weird, but I cannot imagine thinking that it would have been preferable if I had never been born.

In the next extract, McDougall sidesteps this intractable debate between those who believe sex selection should be prevented because it harms the child to be born and those who believe that either it does not cause harm, or, even if it does, that harm is unlikely to be so great that it would be preferable for the child not to exist. Instead she advocates looking at sex selection from the point of view of virtue ethics (see Chapter 1). Because a virtuous

---

[114] 'Why sex selection should be legal' (2001) 27 Journal of Medical Ethics 302–7.
[115] 'Sex selection and regulated hatred' (2005) 31 Journal of Medical Ethics 291–4.

parent accepts their children, regardless of their characteristics, a sex-selecting parent does not act virtuously, even if the child herself is not, in fact, harmed.

R McDougall[116]

Because a child's characteristics are unpredictable, acceptance is a parental virtue. . . . Accepting one's child, regardless of his or her particular current characteristics, is already perceived as a necessary characteristic of the good parent . . .

In acting on a preference to parent only a child of a particular sex, the sex selecting agent fails to act in accordance with the parental virtue of acceptance. . . . The wrong is the sex selecting agent's failure to act in accordance with a parental character trait, acceptance, which is intrinsically linked on a general conceptual level to the flourishing of children. Sex selection is wrong because it is not in accordance with the parental virtue of acceptance, regardless of the outcome for a specific child.

Some people have argued in favour of limited access to sex selection in order to facilitate 'family balancing'. The American Society for Reproductive Medicine, for example, has argued that it is ethical to help couples to choose the sex of their babies for reasons of 'gender variety'. Similarly, the House of Commons Science and Technology Committee found that there was 'no adequate justification for prohibiting the use of sex selection for family balancing'.[117] In Israel, one of the only countries specifically to lay out criteria in which, exceptionally, sex selection for social reasons may be permitted, one of the criteria is that the couple must have at least four children of one sex and none of the other.[118]

Why do some people regard sex selection for 'family balancing' as more innocuous than other sorts of social selection? One possible argument is that, where there is an uneven number of children of each sex in a family, the would-be family balancer is not preferring one sex to another: rather, they value both sexes equally and would like to see both represented among their children. A second argument might be that family balancing would be unlikely to skew the sex ratio, because it might be predicted that the number of parents with daughters who would also like a son is likely to be roughly the same as the number with sons who would also like to have a daughter. In the next extract, however, Stephen Wilkinson disputes the suggestion that family balancing is necessarily less 'sexist' than 'regular' social sex selection.

Stephen Wilkinson[119]

[W]hile 'regular' sex selection is not *necessarily* supremacist, 'family balancing' *can* be supremacist. For example, a father who believes females to be second-rate might suffer (what he sees as) the misfortune of numerous daughters and want to even things up, not because he desires balance, but because he believes that boys are better. . . .

---

[116] 'Acting parentally: an argument against sex selection' (2005) 31 Journal of Medical Ethics 601–5.

[117] *Human Reproductive Technologies and the Law*, Fifth Report of Session 2004–05 (TSO: London, 2005) para 142.

[118] R Landau, 'Sex selection for social purposes in Israel: quest for the "perfect child" of a particular gender or centuries old prejudice against women?' (2008) 34 Journal of Medical Ethics e10.

[119] 'Sexism, Sex Selection and "Family Balancing"' (2008) 16 Medical Law Review 369–89.

As with 'regular' sex selection, whether 'family balancing' involves stereotyping depends on what exactly it is that the parents are aiming at. If what they want is a 'balance' of plainly biological features (if they want half their children to be capable of beard growth and other half to develop breasts, for example), then . . .while we may think that this is weird or objectionable in other ways, it does not seem to involve sex-stereotyping, for the desired sex-linked characteristics really are biologically determined. If, on the other hand, the sort of 'balance' that they are after is less clearly related to biology and more to do with character traits that may or may not be determined by physical sex, then there is a significant risk that the parents are guilty of stereotyping. It seems then that such stereotyping is as likely in the case of 'family balancing' sex selection as it is in 'regular' sex selection.

(6) Mitochondrial Replacement

Mitochondria have been described as the cell's battery: they produce energy to enable each cell in the human body to function normally. Mutations in the 13 genes contained in the mitochondria can cause serious disease. Because we inherit our mitochondrial genes from our mother's egg cell, replacing the defective mitochondria can prevent a woman from passing mitochondrial disease on to her offspring.

Replacing the mother's defective mitochondrial genes with mitochondria from a healthy donor means that the child will inherit genetic material from two women (about 25,000 genes from her mother and 13 genes from the mitochondria donor). Does this child then have three parents (as the predictable tabloid headlines claimed), or is this more akin to other kinds of transplant such as a blood transfusion or bone marrow transplant, when we would certainly not say that the blood or tissue donor was a third parent? One important difference between bone marrow transplantation and mitochondrial transfer is that by altering the embryo's genetic make-up, the germline of the resulting child will be altered—that is, it alters her DNA—and this will be passed on to her descendants.

In 2008, research into mitochondrial transfer had not yet established that it would be safe in treatment, and so the amending legislation did not include it as a licensable activity, but—sensibly—it enabled this to be changed by fast-track regulation-making powers. In 2011, the HFEA was asked by the Secretary of State to seek expert views on the effectiveness and safety of mitochondrial transfer, and a year later, it was invited to seek public views on techniques designed to prevent the transmission of mitochondrial disease, with a view to informing the government's decision as to whether to introduce regulations to amend the 1990 Act to permit the use of mitochondrial transfer in treatment.

Following a public consultation, in 2013 the HFEA advised the government that 'there is general support for permitting mitochondria replacement in the UK, so long as it is safe enough to offer in a treatment setting and is done so within a regulatory framework'.[120] Regulations permitting mitochondrial replacement came into force in October 2015.

Part 2 of the Human Fertilisation and Embryology (Mitochondrial Donation) Regulations 2015 enable eggs and embryos created using two different techniques known as maternal spindle transfer (MST) and pro-nuclear transfer (PNT) to be 'permitted' for use in treatment subject to certain conditions, such as that the HFEA has determined (a) that there is a particular risk that the eggs or embryos of the woman seeking treatment may have

---

[120] HFEA, 'Mitochondria Replacement Consultation: Advice to Government' (2013), available at www.hfea.gov.uk.

mitochondrial abnormalities caused by mitochondrial DNA, and (b) that there is a significant risk that a person with those abnormalities will have or develop serious mitochondrial disease (regulations 5 and 8).

The government had accepted the HFEA's recommendation that children born following mitochondrial donation should not have access to identifying information about the mitochondrial donor, on the grounds that donating a tiny number of cells was more akin to tissue donation. Also following the HFEA's recommendation, the Regulations modify sections 31ZA–31ZE of the 1990 Act to give children access to limited, non-identifying, information, and, likewise, the mitochondrial donor will be able to access limited, non-identifying, information about children born from their donation.

In the next extracts, Françoise Baylis argues that the risks of mitochondrial replacement are too great and the benefits insufficiently important to justify taking them. Martin Johnson disagrees, pointing out that similar arguments were used against IVF.

Françoise Baylis[121]

[T]he critical question is whether the risk to future children (subsequent generations) is worth taking. From one perspective, this approach to family making cannot be justified given the availability of less risky alternatives, which include not only adoption, embryo donation and egg donation, but also prenatal diagnosis followed by abortion and preimplantation genetic diagnosis followed by selective embryo transfer. . . . It is unclear why a 'wish' for a genetic link on the part of prospective parents should be taken to justify the imposition of health risks on future children and subsequent generations. . . .

Mitochondrial replacement technology will only become a safe and effective intervention with the continued investment of considerable research resources (time, talent and money). The opportunity costs associated with this investment give us reason to question the ethics of allocating resources to meet the needs of a very small minority for whom there are other reproductive options.

Martin H Johnson[122]

Had Edwards and Steptoe accepted these arguments, then would the infertile still have just adoption as the only route to 'parenthood'? . . .

It first appears to diminish the pain of those confronted with transmitting mitochondrial disease by their categorization as a 'very small minority', and then goes on to offer them 'other reproductive options' including prenatal diagnosis followed by abortion (unacceptable to many and distressing for most), adoption, embryo donation and egg donation—all perfectly acceptable to some, but lacking that genetic link that so many find desirable—or PGD which is not useful [it is not able to detect mitochondrial abnormalities]. It is a conclusion which I find unsympathetic to the plight of those faced with mitochondrial disease and disempowering of them in its paternalism. I am reminded of those referees that dismissed Edwards and Steptoe's bid for research funding on the grounds that infertility affected only a small group and that the real problem was overpopulation. . . . Even the economic argument

---

[121] 'The ethics of creating children with three genetic parents' (2013) 26 Reproductive BioMedicine Online 531–4.
[122] 'Tri-parenthood—a simply misleading term or an ethically misguided approach?' (2013) 26 Reproductive BioMedicine Online 516–19.

does not add up. Thus, whilst disease due to mutant mtDNA may be relatively rare, it costs a lot to treat the health problems of the affected children and the psycho-sociological impact on the parents.

(7) Genome Editing

Currently, the only way in which genetic knowledge can be used before implantation is by discarding embryos discovered to have some genetic abnormality or by replacing defective mitochondria. There has recently been considerable interest in a new technique known as genome editing. In 2014, researchers from the Broad Institute and Massachusetts Institute of Technology reported that they had created a new mouse model (known as CRISPR-Cas9) to simplify *in vivo* genome editing. Using this model, they had been able to edit multiple genes in a variety of cell types.

In the relatively near future it will be necessary to confront the question of whether genome editing should be attempted in humans. As with mitochondrial replacement, genetically modified embryos could not be used in treatment unless Regulations are passed to create an exception to the 1990 Act's ban on the use of anything other than a permitted embryo in treatment.

It is unlikely that it would ever be possible to modify multifactorial characteristics such as height, beauty, or intelligence. Rather, the only plausible possibility is simple gene insertion or deletion. At first sight, it might be thought that genome editing could help to prevent serious monogenic disorders, such as Huntington's disease or cystic fibrosis. But, of course, before attempting to 'edit' the genome of an affected embryo, it would first be necessary to have tested it, using PGD, in order to identify which embryos have inherited the disorder. At that point, it would be easier, cheaper, and less risky to simply discard the affected embryo, rather than attempt to modify its genome. There would be a potential use for genome editing of embryos only in extremely rare cases in which it is impossible for these parents to produce unaffected embryos.

A further possibility would be to insert a gene known to be protective against a common and debilitating disease, such as malaria. This is not straightforward, however, because genetic variants that decrease risk for some conditions may elevate the risk for others: for example, there are mutations that appear to protect against HIV, but which increase the risk of developing West Nile virus. In mice, the genetic modification of a gene that protected against cancer unexpectedly caused premature aging. It would be difficult to predict every possible interaction and hence many, such as Lander in the next extract, advocate taking a precautionary approach.

Eric S Lander[123]

Genetic modification of human embryos is not a new idea. At least among Western governments, there has been a long-standing consensus that manipulating the human germline is a line that should not be crossed. . . . The discussions that will begin in the fall may solidify a broad international consensus that germline editing should be banned—with the possible exception of correcting severe monogenic disease genes, in the few cases in which there is no alternative. . . . A ban could always be reversed if we become technically proficient,

---

[123] 'Brave new genome' (2015) 373 New England Journal of Medicine 5–8.

> scientifically knowledgeable, and morally wise enough and if we can make a compelling case. But authorizing scientists to make permanent changes to the DNA of our species is a decision that should require broad societal understanding and consent. It has been only about a decade since we first read the human genome. We should exercise great caution before we begin to rewrite it.

Within the UK, a joint statement was issued by the leading funders of medical research, calling not for a ban but for careful regulation and inclusive debate.

Wellcome Trust, Medical Research Council, the Academy of Medical Sciences, the Association of Medical Research Charities, and Bioscience for the Future[124]

> Research using genome editing tools holds the potential to significantly progress our understanding of many key processes in biology, health and disease and for this reason we believe that responsibly conducted research of this type, which is scientifically and ethically rigorous and in line with current legal and regulatory frameworks, should be allowed to proceed. We will continue to support the use of genome editing in preclinical biomedical research as well as studies that progress and refine these technologies. Within the UK, this research may involve the use of somatic (non-reproductive) or germ cells, including human embryos up to 14 days old—within the confines of the HFE Act 2008—where appropriately justified and supported by rigorous scientific and ethical review. . . .
>
> We also recognise, however, that there may be future potential to apply genome editing in a clinical context using human germ cells or embryos, though this is prohibited by law in the UK and unlikely to be permissible in other European jurisdictions at present. This raises important ethical and regulatory questions, which need to be anticipated and explored in a timely and inclusive manner as the basic research proceeds and prior to any decisions about clinical application. . . .
>
> Frameworks clearly demarcating research use of genome editing from potential clinical use, and carefully distinguishing use of somatic and germ cells, will ensure that the research community remains at the forefront of this novel area, while exploring the complex issues around different clinical applications in a robust and inclusive manner.

(8) Human Reproductive Cloning

The first cloned mammal was born in the UK in 1996. The birth of Dolly the sheep (named after Dolly Parton because she had been cloned from an adult mammary cell) was announced the following year, and was immediately followed by demands for the complete prohibition of human reproductive cloning.

In the UK, as we saw in Chapter 12 when we considered research on embryos, there was initially some confusion over whether cloning by cell nuclear replacement (CNR) was covered by the Human Fertilisation and Embryology Act 1990.[125] In response to Crane J's (subsequently reversed) decision in the *Quintavalle* case that we considered in Chapter 12, emergency legislation created a new criminal offence—of placing 'in a woman a human embryo which has been created otherwise than by fertilisation'. This was superseded by the 2008 reforms, which introduce the concept of the 'permitted embryo' (ie an embryo created

---

[124] *Initial joint statement on genome editing in human cells* (Wellcome Trust, 2015).
[125] See Chapter 12 for a description of what CNR involves.

using eggs produced or extracted from the ovaries of a woman and sperm from the testes of a man). Since section 3(2)(a) specifies that only a 'permitted embryo' may lawfully be transferred to a woman's body, reproductive cloning is against the law.

Currently human reproductive cloning would present an unacceptable risk to the health of the pregnant woman and any child that might be born. Dolly was the sole survivor following the successful transplantation of nuclei to 277 enucleated ewe's eggs.[126] Cloning in animals appears to cause high rates of spontaneous late abortion and early postnatal death.[127] There is also some evidence that successfully cloned animals suffer long-lasting deleterious effects—Dolly herself developed arthritis at an abnormally young age, and died prematurely of an unrelated condition. When an adult cell is cloned, it is possible that its advanced age will create an increased risk of cancer and other degenerative diseases. Given these risks, it would clearly be unethical to clone human beings for reproductive purposes.

If scientific progress means that at some point in the future the safety objection to cloning is removed, we will then have to decide whether human reproductive cloning is ethically acceptable. So what are the ethical arguments for and against human reproductive cloning?

First, it is sometimes argued that cloning would violate the individual's right to her own unique identity. This claim is, however undermined by the existence of identical twins, who have identical DNA, but undoubtedly have separate identities. A clone and her DNA source would be less alike than monozygotic twins because their uterine environments, childhood experiences, and upbringing will be completely different.

But even if we acknowledge the likelihood of significant differences between a clone and her DNA source, it has secondly been argued that clones would be burdened by the anticipation of uncanny similarity between the lives of the parent and her clone. Thirdly, because a cloned child would be produced by replicating one parent's DNA, some people are concerned about the impact this might have upon family relationships. Would it be disturbing to raise a child who shared the same DNA as one's spouse?

Not only is cloning unsafe, but very few people are interested in engaging in it. John Harris's defence of human reproductive cloning is essentially that we need a good reason to interfere with people's freedoms, and that the arguments against human reproductive cloning, which tend to be grounded in intuitive feelings of revulsion or uneasiness, offer insufficient justification for a ban.

John Harris[128]

In a long discussion entitled 'The Wisdom of Repugnance' [Leon] Kass tries hard and thoughtfully to make plausible the thesis that thoughtlessness is a virtue. 'We are repelled by the prospect of cloning human beings not because of the strangeness or novelty of the undertaking, but because we intuit and feel, immediately and without argument, the violation of things that we rightfully hold dear'. The difficulty is, of course, to know when one's sense of outrage is evidence of something morally disturbing and when it is simply an expression of bare prejudice or something even more shameful.

---

[126] I Wilmut et al, 'Viable offspring derived from fetal and adult mammalian cells' (1997) 385 Nature 810–13.

[127] Y Kato et al, 'Eight calves cloned from somatic cells of a single adult' (1998) 282 Science 2095–8.

[128] 'Clones, Genes and Human Rights' in Justine Burley (ed), *The Genetic Revolution and Human Rights* (OUP: Oxford, 1999) 61–94.

3 CONCLUSION

The 2008 reforms to the 1990 Act continue the UK's tradition of liberal but nonetheless rigorous regulation of assisted conception services. Access to parenthood has been widened by the reforms, so that lesbian second parents can be parents from birth. The statute now specifically sets out the criteria for PGD.

Within the next few years, pressure on the statutory scheme is likely to come from developments in genome editing and the creation of artificial gametes from stem cells (discussed in Chapter 12). New primary legislation would be needed to enable artificial gametes to be used in treatment. The government did not opt for regulation-making powers to allow their use more speedily (in the same way as it did for mitochondrial replacement), on the grounds that such a development would fundamentally change the way people have children.[129] While this is undoubtedly true, enabling people without their own sperm and eggs to reproduce without recourse to donor gametes would, at a single stroke, eliminate the shortage of donated gametes and resolve difficulties about anonymity and secrecy.

The UK's regulatory system was the first of its kind in the world, and it has been widely copied. It is not without its critics, however. Clearly many pro-life groups are concerned about the routine destruction of embryos in techniques like IVF and PGD. Disability rights groups have expressed anxiety about increasing recourse to embryo testing. Criticism has also come from a completely different direction, namely from those, like McLean, who believe that any regulation in this area unnecessarily restricts reproductive liberty.

Sheila McLean[130]

The state's interventionist role in assisted reproduction is based not in principle but on a general presumption of legitimacy: a presumption which can—and in my view should—be challenged. Most importantly it allows the imposition of the values of one group on others. Our relatively recent history—if nothing else—should teach us how potentially dangerous it is to cede authority over reproduction and reproductive practices to the state. Even if regulation is relatively benign, its very existence attacks freedom of choice; if it did not do so, it would have no reason to exist . . .

Certainly we will want to ensure that choices are taken in full knowledge of the risks, benefits and possible consequences of the decision, but this is a matter for the law on consent. It is not an argument against reproductive liberty . . .

De-regulating the provision of assisted reproductive services is the only option that adequately respects the liberties of citizens in this area, and the only one which reflects an appropriate role for the state in our intimate, private lives.

FURTHER READING

Baldwin, Kylie et al, 'Oocyte cryopreservation for social reasons: demographic profile and disposal intentions of UK users' (2015) 31 Reproductive BioMedicine Online 239–45.

---

[129] Dawn Primarolo MP, Hansard, 3 June 2008.
[130] *Modern Dilemmas: Choosing Children* (Capercaillie Books: Edinburgh, 2006).

Brazier, Margaret, 'Regulating the Reproduction Business?' (1999) 7 Medical Law Review 166–93.

Gavaghan, Colin, 'Right problem wrong solution: a pro-choice response to expressivist concerns about preimplantation genetic diagnosis' (2007) Cambridge Quarterly of Healthcare Ethics 20–34.

Gürtin, Zeynep et al, 'Emotional and relational aspects of egg-sharing: egg-share donors' and recipients' feelings about each other, each others' treatment outcome, and any resulting children' (2012) 27 Human Reproduction 1690–701.

Harris, John, 'Sex selection and regulated hatred' (2005) 31 Journal of Medical Ethics 291–4.

Horsey, Kirsty (ed), *Revisiting the Regulation of Human Fertilisation and Embryology* (Routledge: Abingdon, 2015).

Jackson, Emily, 'Conception and the Irrelevance of the Welfare Principle' (2002) 65 Modern Law Review 176–203.

Jadva, V et al, '"Friendly allies in raising a child": a survey of men and women seeking elective co-parenting arrangements via an online connection website' (2015) 30 Human Reproduction 1896–906.

Lander, Eric S, 'Brave new genome' (2015) 373 New England Journal of Medicine 5–8.

Lee, Ellie, Macvarish, Jan, and Sheldon, Sally, 'Assessing child welfare under the Human Fertilisation and Embryology Act 2008: a case study in medicalisation?' (2014) 36 Sociology of Health & Illness 500–15.

McDougall, R, 'Acting parentally: an argument against sex selection' (2005) 31 Journal of Medical Ethics 601–5.

Millbank, Jenni, 'Numerical Limits in Donor Conception Regimes: Genetic Links and "Extended Family" in the Era of Identity Disclosure' (2014) 22 Medical Law Review 325–36.

16

SURROGACY

CENTRAL ISSUES

1. Surrogacy agreements are not unlawful in the UK, but they are unenforceable.

2. In theory, surrogate mothers cannot be paid but, in practice, payments to surrogate mothers can be authorized retrospectively by the courts.

3. In the UK, the surrogate mother is always the legal mother of the child from birth. Identifying the legal father is more complicated.

4. There are two ways in which legal parenthood can be formally transferred to the commissioning couple: through a parental order or adoption. It is not uncommon for 'parents' of children born through surrogacy to fail to acquire legal parenthood.

5. An increasing number of UK citizens are travelling abroad for surrogacy and entering into complex and precarious arrangements without expert legal advice.

1 WHAT IS SURROGACY?

Surrogacy is the practice whereby one woman (the surrogate mother) becomes pregnant with the intention that the child should be handed over to the commissioning couple (or individual) after birth. A surrogate mother could simply inseminate herself with the commissioning father's sperm. This is known as 'partial' surrogacy, and because pregnancy can be achieved without professional assistance, it is difficult to exercise any control over these arrangements.

Alternatively, in 'full' surrogacy an embryo is created *in vitro*, usually using the commissioning couple's egg and sperm, and is transferred to the surrogate mother's uterus. Since *in vitro* fertilization (IVF) is involved, full surrogacy arrangements in the UK will involve treatment in a centre licensed under the Human Fertilisation and Embryology Act 1990, and regulated by the Human Fertilisation and Embryology Authority (HFEA). It is, however, increasingly common for people to enter into full surrogacy arrangements overseas, where this regulatory oversight is absent.

Although the numbers are increasing, in part as a result of the growth in cross-border surrogacy arrangements, surrogacy is still not a common way to have children. In 2007–8, there were 56 applications for parental orders; by 2013–14 this figure had risen to 241.[1] Not all surrogacy arrangements result in applications for parental orders. Although numbers are inevitably imprecise, it has been estimated that there are between 1,000 and 2,000 surrogate births in the UK each year.[2]

Until relatively recently, academic interest in surrogacy tended to be focused upon whether it is acceptable for one woman to bear a child for someone else in return for payment: does this sort of arrangement exploit the woman and commodify the child, for example? Since 2005, there has been a substantial increase in the number of surrogacy cases reaching the UK courts. Worldwide, there has been an explosion of media and academic interest in the cross-border surrogacy marketplace. What are the implications of the global surrogacy industry for women, and what can and should be done to protect the best interests of children born into the practical and legal minefield of cross-border surrogacy agreements?

In this chapter, we begin with a brief summary of debates first over the ethics of surrogacy in general and, secondly, over the particular issues raised by outsourcing surrogacy to India. We then turn to look at how surrogacy is, and is not, regulated and we focus on the increasingly important role of the family courts in resolving questions of parenthood and residence for children born through agreements 'in which the statutory requirements have not only not been met, but in some cases flagrantly breached'.[3]

2 IS SURROGACY ACCEPTABLE?

Some commentators have argued that surrogacy is more ethically problematic than other types of assisted conception. Elizabeth Anderson, for example, claims that it is not in the best interests of a child to discover that her gestational mother gave her away in return for money. Anderson further argues that surrogacy might undermine the surrogate mother's own children's sense of security.

Elizabeth Anderson[4]

Commercial surrogacy substitutes market norms for some of the norms of parental love . . . For in this practice the natural mother deliberately conceives a child with the intention of giving it up for material advantage. Her renunciation of parental responsibilities is not done for the child's sake, nor for the sake of fulfilling an interest she shares with the child, but typically for her own sake (and possibly, if 'altruism' is a motive, for the intended parents' sakes). She and the couple who pay her to give up her parental rights over her child thus treat her rights as a kind of property right. They thereby treat the child itself as a kind of commodity, which may be properly bought and sold . . .

---

[1] Cafcass, FOI CAF942.

[2] Jessica Lee MP, Hansard 14 October 2014, col 1WH.

[3] Claire Fenton-Glynn, 'The Difficulty of Enforcing Surrogacy Regulations' (2015) 74 Cambridge Law Journal 34.

[4] 'Is women's labor a commodity?' (1990) 19 Philosophy and Public Affairs 71–92.

> The unsold children of surrogate mothers are also harmed by commercial surrogacy. . . . Furthermore, the widespread acceptance of commercial surrogacy would psychologically threaten all children. For it would change the way children are valued by people (parents and surrogate brokers)—from being loved by their parents and respected by others, to being sometimes used as objects of commercial profit-making.

Janice Raymond also objects to surrogacy, arguing that altruistic surrogacy arrangements are just as demeaning for women as commercial exchanges.

Janice Raymond[5]

> Surrogacy, situated within the larger context of women's inequality, is not simply about the commercialization of women and children. On a political level, it reinforces the perception and use of women as a breeder class and the gender inequality of women as a group. The practice of surrogacy strikes at the core of what a society allows women to be and become. Taking the commerce out of surrogacy but leaving the practice intact on a non-commercial and contractual basis glosses over the essential violation—the social definition of women as breeders.

In contrast, Richard Arneson maintains that banning surrogacy in order to protect women from choosing to act as surrogate mothers would be both paternalistic and elitist.

Richard Arneson[6]

> My point is simply that a concern that some people are forced to choose their lives from an unfairly small menu of options is a reason to expand not restrict the range of options from which these people must choose . . . [T]he thought that commercial surrogacy should be banned because the poor working women who mostly choose it are too incompetent to be entrusted to make their own decisions in this sphere has an ugly, elitist sound.

Lori Andrews further points out that while money may influence a woman's decision to become a surrogate mother, it is seldom her only reason.

Lori Andrews[7]

> Studies have found that some surrogates have been affected by the plight of infertile family members and friends. Others enjoyed parenting and wanted to help infertile couples become parents. Many of the women I interviewed described the tremendous psychic benefits they received from the feeling that they were helping someone meet a joyous life goal. Many viewed themselves as feminists who were exercising reproductive choice and demonstrating

---

[5] *Women as Wombs: Reproductive Technologies and the Battle over Women's Freedom* (HarperCollins: New York, 1993).

[6] 'Commodification and commercial surrogacy' (1992) 21 Philosophy and Public Affairs 132–64.

[7] 'Beyond Doctrinal Boundaries: A Legal Framework for Surrogate Motherhood' (1995) 81 Virginia Law Review 2343–75.

an ethic of care. It seems crass not to try to understand the arrangement from the surrogate's vantage point, in which this type of employment is viewed as a higher calling, like being a health care professional or educator, and may consequently be preferable to working as a check-out clerk in a grocery store or at some other minimum wage job.

In recent years, concerns over whether surrogacy might be exploitative have crystallized around the cross-border surrogacy industry, in which couples and individuals from high-income countries seek out surrogate mothers in middle or low-income countries. As we see in the next section, the Indian surrogacy industry has been a particular focus of concern, and indeed India is about to implement a ban on foreign surrogacy.

3 SURROGACY IN INDIA

India is by no means the only country to which people have travelled for cross-border surrogacy arrangements: other common destinations include the US, Russia, Ukraine, Poland, and Mexico. But interest in cross-border surrogacy has tended to focus upon India, which has been the subject of countless newspaper and magazine articles, and several feature-length documentary films.[8] Why? Writing from a US perspective, Susan Markens suggests that one reason may be the difference in skin colour between the surrogate mothers and the babies they carry.

Susan Markens[9]

First, in many of the other countries where the surrogacy industry is growing, the (poor) women who become surrogates are 'white.' In contrast, the dark-skin of Indian surrogates, visually displayed in the pictures accompanying several of the stories, helps mark them as a racialized 'other' by which transnational surrogacy can be both exoticized and justified. The trans-racial aspect of such gestational and kinship relationships might also tap a certain U.S. cultural fascination. Another likely explanation is the general concern in the U.S. over outsourcing in general, and specifically of jobs to India.

India has been an attractive destination for westerners for several reasons. First, surrogacy is comparatively cheap: for example, in *Re A and B (No 2 Parental Order)*[10] the commissioning couple had travelled to India for surrogacy and paid a total of £16,500; in *Re G (Parental Orders)*,[11] the couple had employed a surrogate mother in the US, and had paid $59,700. Secondly, as the intended mothers who had travelled to India explained to Sheela Saravana, surrogacy in India was also simple and convenient, with virtually no risk that the surrogate mother might change her mind.

---

[8] See, eg, *Made in India* by Rebecca Haimowitz and Vaishali Sinha (2010); *Google Baby* by Zippi Brand Frank (2009).

[9] 'The global reproductive health market: US media framings and public discourses about transnational surrogacy' (2012) 74 Social Science and Medicine 1745–53.

[10] [2015] EWHC 2080 (Fam).   [11] [2014] EWHC 1561 (Fam).

Sheela Saravana[12]

One intended mother found the financial deal with this particular clinic convenient because it did not charge any upfront payment until the baby is handed over. In her words,

'One of the things that made me come to this clinic was the way the payment scheme works. Only a nominal payment is made to the surrogate mother, but you don't actually pay until the very end . . . it's a good incentive for her (the SM) to keep the baby and not do much work so she doesn't miscarry. She (the SM) doesn't really get compensated until she hands over the baby'.

The procedure in India was perceived as comparatively simple. One intended mother explained, 'Although it is legal in my country, the process is very complex and much more expensive than [in] India. The law expects surrogate mothers in India to sign over all rights to the baby even before the surrogacy begins, which is a big relief'.

Again drawing upon interviews with intended mothers, Pande points out that westerners choosing Indian surrogate mothers often resist the idea that they are exploiting them, instead emphasizing the transformative potential of the money that the surrogate mothers receive.

Amrita Pande[13]

The intended mother, Anne, underplayed the financial motivation for hiring a surrogate in India, and instead emphasized the desire to contribute towards a worthy cause. Judy, another intended mother from the USA, gave a similar justification: 'I have tried IVF five times in Florida and already spent a packet. Money is not an issue with us since we are both physicians. The biggest attraction was that for surrogates here the amount we pay would be a life-altering one. It would feel good to make such a change in someone's life. This seemed like a worthy cause.'

While most intended mothers accepted that the incentives for hiring surrogates in India range from easy laws to control over surrogates, they often reiterated that their primary motivation is to transform the life of a family living in desperate poverty. . . .

Intended mothers from the global north often construct their reproductive travel as a 'mission'. They emphasize the desire to contribute towards a worthy cause and save an Indian family from desperate poverty. The language of mission reifies the undeniably enormous inequities, based on race, class and nationality, between the buyers and sellers of this new form of reproductive travel.

So is there something inherently exploitative about rich westerners travelling to India for surrogacy? On the one hand, it is true that the money Indian women can make from acting as a surrogate—typically US$3,000–$6,000—far outstrips average earnings. It could therefore be argued that it is hypocritical for commentators in high-income countries to be squeamish about outsourcing surrogacy, while simultaneously buying cheap clothes or food products that may depend upon women in low and middle-income countries doing backbreaking work for very low wages.

---

[12] 'An ethnomethodological approach to examine exploitation in the context of capacity, trust and experience of commercial surrogacy in India' (2013) 8 Philosophy, Ethics, and Humanities in Medicine 10.

[13] 'Transnational commercial surrogacy in India: gifts for global sisters?' (2011) 23 Reproductive BioMedicine Online 618–25.

Two aspects of Indian surrogacy arrangements are perhaps especially troubling. The first is the contracts themselves, over which the surrogate mothers have little or no control and which are additionally usually in English. It is not uncommon for surrogacy contracts to contain terms that purport to override the surrogate mother's ability to make decisions about her pregnancy. In *AB v CT*, for example, a case in which a same-sex couple had had twins as a result of a surrogacy arrangement in India, Theis J shared the Australian judge's view (the couple had been living in Australia at the time), that the contractual terms, to which the surrogate mother had agreed with her thumbprint, were troubling.

AB v CT[14]

Theis J

The surrogacy agreement was 'signed' by CT by way of a thumb print. It is 29 pages long and contains numerous clauses, including some which limit CT's ability to manage her health during the pregnancy and make decisions about the delivery of the babies. I agree with the observations of Justice Ryan in her judgment in June 2013 in proceedings issued by the applicants in Australia that these provisions are '*troubling*'. There is some evidence that some documents were explained to CT although I share the concerns expressed by Justice Ryan in her judgment that '*there is nothing in the document which suggests that before the birth mother signed it that it was read and translated to her*' at the time she signed it.

As Daisy Deomampo and Amrita Pande found in their interviews with Indian surrogate mothers, their lack of bargaining power is exacerbated by the impression that they are commonly given that other women are queuing up for the chance to act as surrogate mothers.

Daisy Deomampo[15]

Nearly all of the surrogates with whom I spoke reported a lack of transparency and power in negotiating contracts. This process perhaps illustrated more than any other aspect of their experience the social and structural inequalities that both propel them into the surrogacy industry and circumscribe their experiences within it. For Nishi, like most surrogates, the experience of signing the contract was confusing and mysterious, and despite her assertive nature Nishi could not advocate on her own behalf:

DAISY: Can you tell me about the contract process?

NISHI: The contract was in two copies; one is original and other was Xerox.

DAISY: Did you ask for a copy for yourself?

NISHI: NO, actually I wanted one copy for myself, but I didn't dare to ask for one. In fact I don't prefer to sign any contract without knowing it in detail but . . . one page was also blank which I signed and also the amount was not filled in. And most importantly she didn't give us a chance to read the agreement. She was turning the pages very fast. If she had let me read the document, I would have read it quickly because I can read English and I can read fast.

---

[14] [2015] EWFC 12.
[15] 'Transnational surrogacy in India' (2013) 34 Frontiers: A Journal of Women Studies 167–88.

> While Nishi reported these objections to me, she said she could not speak up in front of the doctor and lawyer who were present when she signed. Indeed, this came up again and again in interviews: surrogates would not confront doctors and lawyers on crucial issues related to their payment for fear of losing their contract. They said that doctors often hinted at an ample supply of women ready and willing to take their place as surrogates.

Amrita Pande[16]

> The surrogacy contract, which lays out the rights of the surrogates, is in English, a language almost none of the surrogates can read. Some essential points of the contract, however, are translated for them. In the words of surrogate Gaud, 'The only thing they told me was that this thing is not immoral, I will not have to sleep with anyone, and that the seed will be transferred into me with an injection. They also said that I have to keep the child inside me, rest for the whole time, have medicines on time, and give up the child.'
>
> Although there are more couples waiting to hire a surrogate than there are women waiting to be surrogates at the clinic, the contract, the clinic rules, and the counseling reiterate the disposability of the surrogates.

Secondly, Indian surrogate mothers usually live away from their families in surrogacy hostels. These allow an extraordinary degree of control to be exercised over the women's diet and activities. Living in a surrogacy hostel is not necessarily compulsory, and as Karandikar et al point out, many women choose to stay there for the duration of the pregnancy in order to avoid the stigma they might otherwise face. Nevertheless, living in a hostel inevitably involves separation from the women's own families and children. It has also been argued that by keeping surrogacy out of view, surrogacy hostels enable communities to avoid having to acknowledge the surrogacy industry's widespread transgression of traditional reproductive norms.

Sharvari Karandikar, Lindsay B Gezinski, James R Carter, and Marissa Kaloga[17]

> More often than not, surrogates chose to live in the hostel to avoid stigma at home. Because the agency only allowed women who had previously successfully given birth to become surrogates, all the participants had biological children who were forced to remain at home while the surrogates lived in the surrogacy hostel. Typically, the surrogate's family home was located far from the surrogacy hostel, which resulted in limited contact with family members. . . .
>
> While family members' reactions to the surrogacy varied from negative to relatively supportive, community members' reactions were always negative. Surrogate mothers were typically stigmatized if community members became aware of the surrogacy . . .
>
> While the major incentive cited for the creation of the surrogate hostel was the maintenance of the surrogate's health, the information mentioned above points to an additional

---

[16] 'Commercial surrogacy in India: manufacturing a perfect mother-worker' (2010) 35 Signs: Journal of Women in Culture & Society 969–92.

[17] 'Economic necessity or noble cause? A qualitative study exploring motivations for gestational surrogacy in Gujarat, India' (2014) 29 Affilia 224–36.

reason: To maintain seclusion of the pregnant surrogate, thus shielding her from the eyes of a disapproving community. By providing a means of isolation, the surrogacy clinic is both meeting their own need for supervision of the pregnancy and meeting the need of the women to keep the surrogacy private. A third stakeholder in this arrangement is the community itself. By quarantining the practice of gestational surrogacy out of public view, it is a way to maintain the social norms of traditional reproduction, even as surrogacy becomes more and more common.

What, if anything, should be done about the outsourcing of reproductive labour to women in low and middle-income countries? Within host countries, there have been attempts to change the law. Thailand has banned foreign surrogacy and India is in the process of implementing a ban on all foreign surrogacy, unless the intended parents are of Indian descent.[18]

Given that it is estimated that the Indian surrogacy industry is worth around $2.3 billion per annum, the cross-border surrogacy trade is unlikely to disappear. If transnational surrogacy is inevitable, perhaps the most pressing concern should be to ensure that surrogate mothers give properly informed consent and are not subject to oppressive and exploitative contractual terms. Perhaps a future international convention on transnational surrogacy might introduce some minimum requirements, such as that women should never be expected to sign contracts that they cannot understand, and that they should never be required to sign away decision-making authority over their bodies during pregnancy.

4 REGULATION OF SURROGACY

In contrast to the regulation of assisted conception, considered in the previous chapter, surrogacy has never been the subject of a comprehensive regulatory regime. Such regulation as exists consists in piecemeal and often unsatisfactory amendments to the law and, increasingly importantly, the benevolent exercise of judicial discretion. Indeed, we can see from the extraordinarily weight of cases now reaching the courts, the judiciary has had to find ways to safeguard the interests of children *despite* the rules governing surrogacy.

(a) NON-ENFORCEABILITY

The Surrogacy Arrangements Act 1985 was passed hastily in response to the baby Cotton case (in which a British woman had been employed to act as a surrogate mother for a Swedish couple by a US agency). It was intended to discourage the practice of surrogacy. According to section 1B of the Act, it is not an offence to enter into a surrogacy arrangement, but the agreement itself is not enforceable: 'No surrogacy arrangement is enforceable by or against any of the persons making it.'

Hence, the commissioning couple cannot sue the surrogate mother if she refuses to hand over the baby, and nor can she sue them if she does not receive any of the agreed payments, or if they refuse to take the baby after birth. So while it is lawful to enter into a surrogacy contract, none of the parties are bound by any of the obligations it purports to contain. Given that surrogacy agreements are so precarious, it is perhaps surprising that most arrangements appear to go smoothly.

---

[18] 'India to ban foreign surrogate services', BBC News, 28 October 2015.

(b) COMMERCIALIZATION

Section 2 of the Surrogacy Arrangements Act 1985 prohibits commercial involvement in the initiation and negotiation of surrogacy arrangements. Under section 3, the commercial publication or distribution of advertisements indicating a willingness to take part in surrogacy arrangements is also a criminal offence. The Act was amended by the Human Fertilisation and Embryology Act 2008 to permit non-profit-making bodies to charge a reasonable fee in order to recoup their costs.

The ban on commercial involvement in surrogacy means that access to professional expertise, such as legal advice, has been limited. There are membership organizations, such as Childlessness Overcome Through Surrogacy (COTS) and Surrogacy UK, which offer advice and support, and which help to put potential surrogate mothers in touch with would-be commissioning couples. Nevertheless, as we see later, a lack of clear and accurate information on the legal consequences of surrogacy has resulted in some people entering into complicated and at times decidedly ill-advised arrangements.

(c) REGULATED AND UNREGULATED SURROGACY

When a surrogacy arrangement involves IVF treatment carried out in the UK, it must take place in a clinic which has a licence from the HFEA, and which is under a duty to comply with the Human Fertilisation and Embryology Act 1990, as amended. Under section 13(5) of the Act, before providing a woman with treatment services, the clinician must take account of the welfare of any child who may be born, and any other children who may be affected by the birth. Hence, before providing treatment, a clinician should not only evaluate the impact of the surrogacy arrangement upon the resulting child, but must also take into account the welfare of the surrogate's existing children.

Although people seeking surrogacy in licensed clinics must find their own surrogate mothers, the HFEA's Code of Practice requires all parties to be informed of the need for specialist legal advice, and to have the opportunity to receive counselling.

HFEA Code of Practice

14.2 The centre should ensure that those involved in surrogacy arrangements have received information about legal parenthood under the HFE Act 2008 and other relevant legislation. This information should cover who may be the legal parent(s) when the child is born. . . .

14.3 The centre should ensure that those involved in surrogacy arrangements have received information about the effect of the parenthood provisions in the HFE Act 2008 and in particular the Parental Orders provisions in the Act. These state that parental rights and obligations in respect of surrogacy arrangements may be transferred from the birth parent(s) to those who commissioned the surrogacy arrangement, as long as certain conditions are met.

14.4 The centre should advise patients that surrogacy arrangements are unenforceable and that they are encouraged to seek legal advice about this and any other legal aspect of surrogacy.

In contrast, if people enter into a partial surrogacy arrangement, involving home insemination, they may have no idea about the legal implications of what they are doing. There are no procedures for screening surrogate mothers and commissioning couples, and the use of fresh sperm means that there is a risk of HIV infection.

The HFEA's Code of Practice also requires centres to advise patients planning to travel abroad for surrogacy to obtain legal advice, but of course many people make contact directly with surrogacy agencies and clinics in other countries and may not discuss their plans with staff in a licensed clinic in the UK.

HFEA Code of Practice

14.6 The centre should advise patients intending to travel to another country for the purpose of entering into a surrogacy arrangement that they are encouraged not to do so until they have sought legal advice about:

a) legal parenthood of the prospective child

b) immigration status and passport arrangements

c) the adoption or parental orders procedures for that country, and

d) the degree to which those procedures would be recognised under the law of the part of the United Kingdom in which the patients live.

In practice, it is simply impossible for UK law to regulate prospectively the agreements that people enter into overseas. UK law becomes relevant only when the commissioning parent(s) try to bring the child back to the UK, and acquire legal parenthood.

(d) STATUS

When a child is born as a result of a surrogacy arrangement, who are her legal parents?

(1) Maternity

As we saw in the previous chapter, the legal definition of 'mother' in the UK is clear and unequivocal: the woman who gives birth to a baby is its mother.

Human Fertilisation and Embryology Act 2008 section 33

33 The woman who is carrying or has carried a child as a result of the placing in her of an embryo or of sperm and eggs, and no other woman, is to be treated as the mother of the child.

The law does not distinguish between different types of surrogacy and so the surrogate mother will always be the child's legal mother from birth, regardless of whether she is also the child's genetic mother. This means that, from birth, the surrogate mother has prima facie legal responsibility for a child that she did not want, while the commissioning couple has no legal responsibility for a child whose creation they brought about. Of course, it might be argued that it is important to preserve the surrogate mother's right to change her mind, by ensuring that her decision to relinquish her parental rights over the child is taken only after the child is born. But given that in the vast majority of cases the surrogate mother is happy to hand over the child after birth, UK law means that unless commissioning couples successfully apply for a parental order or adoption (and not all do so), the surrogate mother will continue to be the legal parent of a child who is being brought up in another family.

(2) Paternity

Because the provisions governing the ascription of legal fatherhood in the Human Fertilisation and Embryology Acts 1990 and 2008 were designed to apply to sperm donation, they lead to some rather odd results when applied to surrogacy (for a full description, see Chapter 15).

Section 28 of the 1990 Act and section 38 of the 2008 Act treat the surrogate mother's husband (if she has one) as the father of the child, unless it can be shown that he did not consent to her treatment. If the surrogate mother is married to another woman or in a civil partnership, there will be a presumption that her spouse or civil partner is the child's second legal parent. Where a married surrogate mother's husband (or spouse/civil partner) knows of her decision to become a surrogate mother and does not object, he (or she) may be assumed to consent, and will, as a result, be the child's father (or second legal parent).

If the surrogate mother is not married or in a civil partnership, the commissioning father may be registered as the father on the child's birth certificate, and he will thereby acquire parental responsibility. It will usually be impossible for a commissioning father to acquire legal paternity via the 'agreed fatherhood' provisions because these apply only to men whose sperm was not used in conception.

(e) TRANSFERRING LEGAL PARENTHOOD

At birth, then, the surrogate mother will be the child's legal mother from birth, and the commissioning father might or might not be the child's legal father. In order for both the commissioning couple to become the child's legal parents, they must either adopt the child or apply for a parental order under the Human Fertilisation and Embryology Act.

There are many reasons why parental orders are preferable to adoption. They are a better 'fit' for surrogacy in that they attribute legal parenthood to people with whom the child has usually lived from birth and who are also the child's genetic parent(s). The process is also less time-consuming and burdensome. Some people, such as single men, are ineligible for parental orders and hence adoption may be the only way to transfer parenthood. But if a parental order is an option, it is, as Sir James Munby P explained in *Re X (A Child) (Surrogacy: Time limit)*, very clearly preferable.

Re X (A Child) (Surrogacy: Time limit)[19]

Sir James Munby P

Adoption is not an attractive solution given the commissioning father's existing biological relationship with X. As X's guardian puts it, a parental order presents the optimum legal and psychological solution for X and is preferable to an adoption order because it confirms the important legal, practical and psychological reality of X's identity: the commissioning father is his biological father and all parties intended from the outset that the commissioning parents should be his legal parents.

[19] [2014] EWHC 3135 (Fam).

Similarly in *Re A (A Child)*, Russell J pointed out that while both parental orders and adoption would protect the children's lifelong welfare, parental orders were the only way to fully recognize the children's identity and protect their Article 8 rights.

Re A (A Child)[20]

Russell J

However in terms of their identity only parental orders will fully recognise the children's identity as the Applicants' natural children, rather than giving them the wholly artificial and, in their case, inappropriate status of adopted children....

To make adoption orders would effectively deny adequate recognition of the Applicants' and children's identity and their right to family life under Article 8 ECHR, particularly their established identity, their biological and social ties. There is no doubt in this case that as far as these children are concerned their identity has already been formed as the biological children of their father and the commissioning of their conception and birth involving their mother.

Furthermore this court is mindful of the fact that parental orders are the only orders which will enable the registration of A and B's births in the UK, as opposed to the issue of adoption certificates.

And in *AB v CT*, Theis J agreed that parental orders better reflected the reality of the children's relationship with their parents.

AB v CT[21]

Theis J

I agree a parental order and the consequences that flow from it are, from a welfare perspective, far more suited to surrogacy situations. They were specifically created to deal with these situations. Put simply, they are a more honest order which reflects the reality of what was intended, the lineage connection that already exists and more accurately reflects the child's identity. An adoption order in these situations leaves open the risk of a fiction regarding identity that may need to be resolved by the child later in life. The effect of an adoption order ... of treating the child '*as if*' the child is born as a child of the adopter or adopters is not the reality; the child is born with a biological connection to one of the applicants.

As we shall see, when deciding whether to make a parental order, the child's welfare throughout its life is now the court's paramount consideration.[22] The paramountcy principle has shaped the courts' interpretation of the statutory requirements for parental orders, but at the outset it is also worth nothing that it also operates to make adoption now very much a last resort in surrogacy cases.

---

[20] [2015] EWHC 911 (Fam).   [21] [2015] EWFC 12.

[22] The Human Fertilisation and Embryology (Parental Orders) Regulations 2010 applied s 1 of the Adoption and Children Act 2002 to applications for parental orders.

(1) Parental Orders

When a court makes a parental order, the Registrar General will re-register the child's birth. As with adoption, it will not be possible for the public to make a link between entries in the register of births and the parental order register, but once a child reaches adulthood, she will, after being offered counselling, have access to her original birth certificate. Section 54 of the 2008 Act contains the rules governing access to parental orders for children born after April 2010 (section 30 of the 1990 Act applied to children born before then).

Human Fertilisation and Embryology Act 2008 section 54

54 Parental orders

(1) On an application made by two people ('the applicants'), the court may make an order providing for a child to be treated in law as the child of the applicants if—

  (a) the child has been carried by a woman who is not one of the applicants, as a result of the placing in her of an embryo or sperm and eggs or her artificial insemination,

  (b) the gametes of at least one of the applicants were used to bring about the creation of the embryo, and

  (c) the conditions in subsections (2) to (8) are satisfied.

(2) The applicants must be—

  (a) husband and wife,

  (b) civil partners of each other, or

  (c) two persons who are living as partners in an enduring family relationship and are not within prohibited degrees of relationship in relation to each other.

  (3) Except in a case falling within subsection (11), the applicants must apply for the order during the period of 6 months beginning with the day on which the child is born.

  (4) At the time of the application and the making of the order—

  (a) the child's home must be with the applicants, and

  (b) either or both of the applicants must be domiciled in the United Kingdom or in the Channel Islands or the Isle of Man.

  (5) At the time of the making of the order both the applicants must have attained the age of 18.

  (6) The court must be satisfied that both—

  (a) the woman who carried the child, and

  (b) any other person who is a parent of the child but is not one of the applicants (including any man who is the father by virtue of section 35 or 36 or any woman who is a parent by virtue of section 42 or 43),

have freely, and with full understanding of what is involved, agreed unconditionally to the making of the order.

  (7) Subsection (6) does not require the agreement of a person who cannot be found or is incapable of giving agreement; and the agreement of the woman who carried the child is ineffective for the purpose of that subsection if given by her less than six weeks after the child's birth.

> (8) The court must be satisfied that no money or other benefit (other than for expenses reasonably incurred) has been given or received by either of the applicants for or in consideration of—
>
> (a) the making of the order,
>
> (b) any agreement required by subsection (6),
>
> (c) the handing over of the child to the applicants, or
>
> (d) the making of arrangements with a view to the making of the order,
>
> unless authorised by the court.

Section 54 therefore sets out several conditions that must be satisfied before a parental order can be made: for example, at least one of the applicants must be genetically related to the child (thus ruling out parental orders for couples who need to use a sperm and an egg donor, as well as a surrogate mother); the applicants must be domiciled in the UK; and conception must not have been by natural intercourse.

In the following sections, we consider five of the section 54 requirements which have caused particular difficulties in recent years: the need for the surrogate mother's free and unconditional agreement; the need for there to be two applicants; the requirement that the child must be living with the applicants at the time of the application; the requirement that no money or benefit, other than for expenses reasonably incurred, has been paid, unless authorized by the court; and the six-month time limit.

It should be noted that because the Human Fertilisation and Embryology (Parental Orders) Regulations 2010 require the child's welfare throughout its life to be the court's paramount consideration, it is almost impossible for the court to carry out any sort of balancing exercise between public policy considerations and the interests of the child. Instead, when making decisions about parental orders, the welfare of the child from birth to death must take priority over any other considerations.

(a) Consent (section 54(6))

Under section 54(6) a parental order can only be made if both the surrogate mother and any other person who is the child's parent (other than the commissioning father) have given their free and informed consent. Unlike adoption, it is not possible to dispense with their consent on the ground that it is being unreasonably withheld.

The only exception to the consent requirement is, under section 54(7), where a person cannot be found or is incapable of giving consent. This provision was invoked for the first time in *Re D (Minors) (Surrogacy)*, in which twins had been born to an Indian surrogate mother, as a result of an arrangement entered into by a British same-sex couple. They had taken specialist legal advice before entering into the agreement and were aware of the need for the surrogate to give consent six weeks after the children's birth. The clinic proved to be unhelpful, however, and the couple sought to rely upon this exception in section 54. Baker J accepted that, in this case, all reasonable steps had been taken to find the surrogate mother. There was evidence that the surrogate mother had agreed to give consent, shortly after the birth, and it was clearly in the twins' best interests that a parental order should be made.

Re D (Minors) (Surrogacy)[23]

Baker J

First, when it is said that the woman who gave birth to the child cannot be found, the court must carefully scrutinise the evidence as to the efforts which have been taken to find her. It is only when all reasonable steps have been taken to locate her without success that a court is likely to dispense with the need for valid consent. Half-hearted or token attempts to find the surrogate will not be enough. Furthermore, it will normally be prudent for the Applicants to lay the ground for satisfying these requirements at an early stage. Even where, as in this case, the Applicants do not meet the surrogate, they should establish clear lines of communication with her, preferably not simply through one person or agency, and should ensure that the surrogate is made aware during the pregnancy that she will be required to give consent six weeks after the birth.

Secondly, although a consent given before the expiry of six weeks after birth is not valid for the purposes of section 54, the court is entitled to take into account evidence that the woman did give consent at earlier times to giving up the baby. The weight attached to such earlier consent is, however, likely to be limited. The courts must be careful not to use such evidence to undermine the legal requirement that a consent is only valid if given after six weeks.

Thirdly, in the light of the changes affected by the 2010 regulations, the child's welfare is now the paramount consideration when the court is 'coming to a decision' in relation to the making of a parental order. [Counsel] submits, and I accept, that this includes decisions about whether to make an order without the consent of the woman who gave birth in circumstances in which she cannot be found or is incapable of giving consent. It would, however, be wrong to utilise this provision as a means of avoiding the need to take all reasonable steps to attain the woman's consent.

Applying these principles to this case, I accept that these Applicants have taken all reasonable steps to obtain the woman's consent.

In *R v T*, a different issue arose. It was impossible for the court to be satisfied that the surrogate mother had freely and with full understanding agreed unconditionally to the making of the order. Although the mother had signed consent documents more than six weeks after the child's birth, the court had limited information about what information she had received. The clinic was uncooperative and the political situation in Ukraine ruled out a media appeal to find the mother. As a result, the question for Theis J was whether the surrogate mother 'could not be found'.

R v T[24]

Theis J

On an issue as fundamental as consent, in the context of circumstances where what is being sought is to change the status of a child the court, in my judgment, should be very cautious about drawing inferences in circumstances such as this ... In my judgment, the court cannot be satisfied that the surrogate mother has 'freely, and with full understanding

---

[23] [2012] EWHC 2631 (Fam).   [24] [2015] EWFC 22.

of what is involved, agreed unconditionally to the making of a parental order' as required by s 54(6).

In those circumstances the court needs to consider whether the surrogate mother 'cannot be found' (s54(7)) and whether the applicants have taken all reasonable steps to find her. In my judgment they have. The only avenue not explored has been notification through the media. In circumstances such as this where the arrangement concerns a very sensitive subject, it is not known what country the surrogate mother is in and there is continued civil unrest in Ukraine this is not a step, in the circumstances of this case that is reasonable to take.

(b) Couples only (section 54(2))

Under section 30 of the 1990 Act, applicants for parental orders had to be married to each other. Now, under section 54, civil partners and cohabitees can apply, and in the six months after this came into force (in April 2010), this operated retrospectively so that people who were previously ineligible for parental orders could have their parental status recognized.

Although the 2008 Act broadened eligibility for parental orders, it continues to require the application to be made by a couple. Single people are ineligible, and if a single person enters into a surrogacy arrangement, the only option for the transfer of legal parenthood would be adoption.

In *A v P*, an unusual issue arose in that, although the application for a parental order for B, who had been born to a surrogate mother in India, had been made by Mr and Mrs A together, Mr A had died before the hearing. The question for the court was whether the word 'applicants' could be construed so as to require two people to make the application, but not to require there to be two living applicants at the time of the making of the order. Theis J held that it could, and in making this decision, she took into account that a failure to make an order in these circumstances would interfere with the family's Article 8 rights, and that that interference could not be justified.

A v P[25]

Theis J

Article 8 is engaged and any interference with those rights must be proportionate and justified. In the particular circumstances of this case the interference cannot be justified as no other order can give recognition to B's status with both Mr and Mrs A in the same transformative way a parental order can. To interpret [the Act] in the way submitted will not offend against the clear purpose or policy behind the requirements listed in section 54. It will not pave the way for single commissioning parents to apply for a parental order.

In *Re Z (A Child) (Human Fertilisation and Embryology Act: Parental Order)*,[26] Sir James Munby P was invited to 'read down' section 54, in the same way as he had in relation to the six-month time limit (see Section 4(e)(1)(d)), so that one person, rather than two, could apply for a parental order. He declined, quoting from the parliamentary debates in 2008. An amendment to extend parental orders to single applicants had been rejected by the

25 [2011] EWHC 1738 (Fam).   26 [2015] EWFC 73.

government, on the grounds, as the then health minister, Dawn Primarolo MP explained, that there is an important difference between surrogacy and adoption:

> The difference is this: adoption involves a child who already exists and whose parents are not able to keep the child, for whom new parents are sought. That is different, which is why there is no parallel. . . . Surrogacy, however, involves agreeing to hand over a child even before conception. The Government are still of the view that the magnitude of that means that it is best dealt with by a couple. That is why we have made the arrangements that we have.[27]

Sir James Munby P found that the law was clear, and that he did not have the discretion to grant a parental order to a single applicant, whose child, Z, had been born to a surrogate mother in the US.

Re Z (A Child) (Human Fertilisation and Embryology Act: Parental Order)[28]

Sir James Munby P

The principle that only two people—a couple—can apply for a parental order has been a clear and prominent feature of the legislation throughout. Although the concept of who are a couple for this purpose has changed down the years, section 54 of the 2008 Act, like section 30 of the 1990 Act, is clear that one person cannot apply. Section 54(1) could not be clearer, and the contrast in this respect—obvious to any knowledgeable critic—between adoption orders and parental orders, which is a fundamental difference of obvious significance, is both very striking and, in my judgment, very telling. Surely, it betokens a very clear difference of policy which Parliament, for whatever reasons, thought it appropriate to draw both in 1990 and again in 2008. And, as it happens, this is not a matter of mere speculation or surmise, because we know from what the Minister of State said in 2008 that this was seen as a necessary distinction based on what were thought to be important points of principle.

It is interesting to consider whether a single parents, like the father in this case, might be able to seek a declaration of incompatibility with Article 8 of the European Convention. It might be possible to argue that their ineligibility for a parental order is an interference with their right to respect for their family life. If a single commissioning parent's Article 8 rights are engaged, is such an interference 'necessary in a democratic society'? Might Article 14 of the European Convention offer additional protection to the right not to be discriminated against in the exercise of one's Convention rights?

If it is regarded as overwhelmingly in the best interests of a child born through a surrogacy arrangement to have her parentage resolved quickly and definitively, it is perhaps odd to rule out speedy resolution for single parents, especially since this makes it more likely in practice that parentage will not be formally transferred. As a result, restricting access to parental orders to couples might also appear to be in tension with the requirement that the child's welfare is the paramount concern when making decisions about parental orders.

---

[27] Hansard 12 June 2008, col 249.　　[28] [2015] EWFC 73.

(c) No payments, other than expenses reasonably incurred, unless authorized by the court (section 54(8))

The court has the power to authorize payments other than expenses reasonably incurred, and there has, as yet, been no case in which an application for a parental order has been refused on the grounds that an unacceptably large sum of money had changed hands.

Within the UK, the Surrogacy UK Working Group on Surrogacy Law Reform's survey of 111 UK surrogates found that payments to surrogates are generally under £15,000.

Surrogacy UK Working Group on Surrogacy Law Reform[29]

104 (95.4%) received compensation for being a surrogate. 29 (27.1%) of these received less than £10,000, while 73 (68.2%) received £10–15,000 and five (4.7%) received £15–20,000. No-one said they received any more than that. . . .

Data from our survey demonstrates that compensation paid to surrogates in the UK usually ranges between £0 and £15,000. There is not, therefore, any set 'price' for surrogacy in the UK and it is very much undertaken by women on an altruistic basis.

In one of the first foreign surrogacy cases to reach the courts, *Re X & Y (Foreign Surrogacy)*, a case in which a British couple had employed a Ukrainian surrogate mother, it had to be conceded that the payments of €235 per month to the surrogate mother during pregnancy and a lump sum of €25,000 on the live birth of the twins, to enable her to put down a deposit for the purchase of a flat, significantly exceeded 'expenses reasonably incurred'. Taking the twins' welfare into account, Hedley J agreed to authorize these payments in order to enable a parental order to be made, but he expressed considerable unease about doing so.

Re X & Y (Foreign Surrogacy)[30]

Hedley J

I feel bound to observe that I find this process of authorisation most uncomfortable. What the court is required to do is to balance two competing and potentially irreconcilably conflicting concepts. Parliament is clearly entitled to legislate against commercial surrogacy and is clearly entitled to expect that the courts should implement that policy consideration in its decisions. Yet it is also recognised that as the full rigour of that policy consideration will bear on one wholly unequipped to comprehend it let alone deal with its consequences (i.e. the child concerned) that rigour must be mitigated by the application of a consideration of that child's welfare. That approach is both humane and intellectually coherent. The difficulty is that it is almost impossible to imagine a set of circumstances in which by the time the case comes to court, the welfare of any child (particularly a foreign child) would not be gravely compromised (at the very least) by a refusal to make an order.

In *Re L (A Minor)*, a case involving a British couple who had made a commercial surrogacy arrangement in Illinois, Hedley J explained that the application of the paramountcy principle made it almost impossible to refuse a parental order.

---

[29] *Surrogacy in the UK: Myth Busting and Reform* (Surrogacy UK, 2015).
[30] [2008] EWHC 3030 (Fam).

Re L (A Minor)[31]

Hedley J

What has changed, however, is that welfare is no longer merely the court's first consideration but becomes its paramount consideration. The effect of that must be to weight the balance between public policy considerations and welfare decisively in favour of welfare. It must follow that it will only be in the clearest case of the abuse of public policy that the court will be able to withhold an order if otherwise welfare considerations supports its making. It underlines the court's earlier observation that, if it is desired to control commercial surrogacy arrangements, those controls need to operate before the court process is initiated i.e. at the border or even before.

There is effectively now a checklist for judges to consider when deciding whether to retrospectively authorize payments other than expenses reasonably incurred. Indeed, the judgments on payments are now almost formulaic. In *Re P-M*, for example, when deciding whether to exercise her discretion under section 54(8), Theis J turned once again to what she described as a 'well-trodden path'.

Re P-M[32]

Theis J

Turning now to the well-trodden path laid out by Hedley J as to the relevant considerations in considering whether the court can authorise any payments under section 54(8), the questions the court has to ask are as follows:

  i.   Was the sum paid disproportionate to reasonable expenses?

  ii. Were the applicants acting in good faith and without moral taint in their dealings with the surrogate mother?

  iii. Were the applicants' party to any attempt to de-fraud the authorities?

In addition to these questions, the incorporation of the paramountcy principle means that, as Theis J put it, 'where the welfare considerations demand that an order should be made, the court will only in the clearest case of abuse of public policy consider not making an order'.[33]

In practice, then, the prohibition on payments in the 2008 Act is a prohibition on grossly disproportionate payments, but with no payment ever having been found to be grossly disproportionate. Is there a sum of money so huge that the courts would be likely to refuse to make a parental order? Given the need to put the child's welfare first, it is impossible to imagine the circumstances in which a court would decide that a child's legal parentage should be left unresolved, with all of the potentially disastrous consequences this might have for the child, because the surrogate mother had been paid too much money. The UK's prohibition on commercial surrogacy is therefore completely ineffective.

---

[31] [2010] EWHC 3146 (Fam). [32] [2013] EWHC 2328 (Fam). [33] Ibid.

(d) The six-month time limit (section 54(3))

Until the judgment of the President of the Family Division, Sir James Munby P, in *Re X (A Child) (Surrogacy: Time limit)*,[34] it was thought, with good reason, that section 54(3)—which states that 'the applicants must apply for the order during the period of six months beginning with the day on which the child is born'—meant applications for parental orders had be made within six months of the child's birth.

For example, in *J v G (Parental Orders)*,[35] Theis J said 'It should be remembered parental order applications must be made within six months of the child's birth, there is no power vested in the court to extend that period.' And a few months later, in *JP v LP (Surrogacy Arrangement: Wardship)*,[36] Eleanor King J was again clear that her hands were tied in relation to a child who was 33 weeks old:

> There is no provision within the Act to provide for a discretionary extension to the statutory time limit and no one sought to argue that the court could, or should, whether by means of the use of its inherent jurisdiction or otherwise, seek to circumnavigate the mandatory provisions of the statute.

Then, in *Re X (A Child) (Surrogacy: Time limit)*, Sir James Munby P decided that this cannot have been parliament's intention.

Re X (A Child) (Surrogacy: Time limit)[37]

Sir James Munby P

Can Parliament really have intended that the gate should be barred forever if the application for a parental order is lodged even one day late? I cannot think so. Parliament has not explained its thinking, but given the transcendental importance of a parental order, with its consequences stretching many, many decades into the future, can it sensibly be thought that Parliament intended the difference between six months and six months and one day to be determinative and one day's delay to be fatal? I assume that Parliament intended a sensible result. Given the subject matter, given the consequences for the commissioning parents, never mind those for the child, to construe section 54(3) as barring forever an application made just one day late is not, in my judgment, sensible. It is the very antithesis of sensible; it is almost nonsensical ...

I have considered whether the result at which I have arrived is somehow precluded by the linguistic structure of section 54, which provides that 'the court may make an order ... if ... the [relevant] conditions are satisfied'. I do not think so. Slavish submission to such a narrow and pedantic reading would simply not give effect to any result that Parliament can sensibly be taken to have intended.

I conclude, therefore, that section 54(3) does not have the effect of preventing the court making an order merely because the application is made after the expiration of the six-month period.

---

[34] [2014] EWHC 3135 (Fam).   [35] [2014] 1 FLR 297.
[36] [2014] EWHC 595 (Fam).   [37] [2014] EWHC 3135 (Fam).

As Claire Fenton-Glynn points out, it would be hard to confine *Re X (A Child) (Surrogacy: Time limit)* to its facts, and, as a result, Sir James Munby P's judgment creates a potentially far-reaching precedent.

Claire Fenton-Glynn[38]

This decision will almost certainly have significant repercussions for the wider regulation of international surrogacy, and particularly for other surrogate mothers and commissioning parents who will know that the legal requirements carry little weight, despite being expressed in a mandatory manner. Although Munby P. emphasised that this judgment did not create a general rule, and instead relied on the particular facts of the case, there was nothing unique about this case that would make it distinguishable from the many hundreds of other surrogacy cases that go through the courts each year.

The decision strikes another blow to statutory regime in England, and throws into sharp relief the difficulty, indeed near impossibility, of trying to regulate surrogacy through reassigning parenthood after the fact. For this reason, there is an urgent need to review the regulation of surrogacy, both in this country, and internationally. Until this occurs, the courts will continue to have little choice but to stretch, manipulate, or even disregard the statutory wording in order to achieve justice for the child.

Unsurprisingly, *Re X* has been followed by more cases that would have otherwise been out of time. Although Sir James Munby P used the example of applications made a day late in order to illustrate his claim that this could not be what parliament had intended, parental orders have now been granted several years later. In *Re A (A Child)*, for example, Russell J made parental orders in respect of two children aged eight and five years old.

Re A (A Child)[39]

Russell J

The time that has elapsed before the applications were made very considerably exceeds the limit of 6 months provided for in s 54(3) of the Act. I have had regard to the statute, to the purpose for which it was enacted and the impact on the parties, the children in particular, if the application is not allowed despite the protracted delay. It would be manifestly unjust to give a delay that was innocently wrought, even a very long one such as this, greater weight than the welfare of these children.... I have decided to make parental orders as the orders which best meet the children's needs and meet the justice of this case.

(e) At the time of the application and the making of the order the child's home must be with the applicants (section 54(4))

What if the applicants are living apart at the time of the application and/or the making of the order? Could it nevertheless be argued that the child's home is 'with' both of them? In addition to being out of time, this was also an issue in *Re X (A Child) (Surrogacy: Time limit)*,

---

[38] 'The Difficulty of Enforcing Surrogacy Regulations' (2015) 74 Cambridge Law Journal 34.
[39] [2015] EWHC 911 (Fam).

where the applicants had separated at the time of the application, but were living together again when the case came before the court. Sir James Munby P found that X's home was with both of the commissioning parents at the time of the application, albeit that they were not living in the same place.

Re X (A Child) (Surrogacy: Time limit)[40]

Sir James Munby P

The real question arises in relation to section 54(4)(a) can it be said that X's 'home' was 'with' them at the time of the application (it plainly is now)? There are, in my judgment, two reasons why this question should be answered in the affirmative. In the circumstances as I have described them … , X had his 'home' with the commissioning parents, with both of them, albeit that they lived in separate houses. He plainly did not have his home with anyone else. His living arrangements were split between the commissioning father and the commissioning mother. It can fairly be said that he lived with them.

In the light of the reasoning Munby P invoked in relation to the time limit, his conclusion on section 54(4) seems inevitable. If parliament must have intended a sensible result, it could not have intended that children born through surrogacy arrangements should be disadvantaged if their parents separate. There is nothing to guarantee that parents who are together on the day of the making of the order will be together the day afterwards, so it would be odd to penalize children for something so arbitrary as the date of parental separation. And, of course, if parental orders can be granted beyond the six-month time limit, as appears now to be the case, the chance that the child's parents may have split up in the meantime becomes correspondingly greater.

Unsurprisingly, then, this issue has arisen again. In *Re A and B*, Theis J was faced with applications for parental orders in relation to three-year-old twin girls born as a result of a surrogacy arrangement in India. In addition to having to decide whether to make an order outside the six-month time limit, the parents had since separated from each other.

Re A and B (No 2 Parental Order)[41]

Theis J

It is submitted that Parliament could not have intended that a designation as important as legal parenthood should be denied because the commissioning parents occupied separate physical homes, notwithstanding that the children enjoyed family life with them….

Turning to the issue as to whether it can be said that the children's '*home*' was '*with*' the applicants at the time of the application and at the time when the court was making the order as required by s 54(4)(a) … It seems to me that I can, and should, purposively construe this provision in a way that results in this requirement being satisfied in the circumstances of this case….

> [A]lthough the parents have separated, they remain married. The evidence indicates that despite the differences between them they both remain committed to the children and ensuring their needs are met ... whilst the time B spends with the children is less than in *Re X* that is in part dictated by the limitations from his current accommodation and the fact that he works full time. It is not suggested that this is due to a lack of commitment by him to the children.
>
> As in *Re X* I am satisfied that if I am not correct in that analysis the Convention applies, Article 8 is undoubtedly engaged, and the statute should be 'read down' to achieve the same result.

(f) The role of social workers

An application for a parental order may be made in the Family Proceedings Court. In order to satisfy itself that the section 54 criteria are satisfied, the court is assisted by a report from an experienced social worker from the Child and Family Court Advisory and Support Service (Cafcass). Known as Parental Order Reporters (PORs), their duties are to investigate arrangements in order to establish whether the statutory criteria are satisfied; to find out how much money, if any, has changed hands; to assess the welfare of the child; and to advise the court as to whether an order is in the child's best interests. PORs are therefore charged with investigating the 'genetic link' and 'no payment' requirements, and with protecting the child's welfare.

Because the child must already be living with the commissioning parents before an application is made, her welfare will seldom be promoted by removing her from a settled home. Even if the POR discovers a blatant contravention of the 'no payment' rule, it is clear that the child's interests will generally be best served by making a parental order. In their interviews with PORs, Crawshaw et al found that some were frustrated by what they perceived to be a 'fait accompli'.[42] According to one:

> from the point of view of the child I felt it was in the best interests of the child, but it left me feeling quite uncomfortable . . . [W]hat an absolutely ridiculous situation that we are put in, that we are doing all of this work after the horse has bolted, and where it's almost too late to have a significant you know, impact on it, and my feeling was that this should have been done beforehand . . . [Y]ou wouldn't do an adoption assessment you know, on carers' ability to adopt a child, after you've just placed a baby with them for six months . . . [I]t just struck me as being completely bizarre and ridiculous.

(2) Adoption

There are several different reasons why a commissioning couple might not be able to apply for a parental order. If the surrogate mother has changed her mind and refuses consent to the making of an order, the only way in which the commissioning couple could acquire legal parenthood is through adoption, and an adoption order could be made only if the court is satisfied that the child's welfare requires that mother's consent should be

---

[42] Marilyn Crawshaw, Satvinder Purewal, and Olga van den Akker, 'Working at the margins: the views and experiences of court social workers on parental orders work in surrogacy arrangements' (2012) 42 British Journal of Social Work 1–19.

dispensed with. Single people are ineligible for parental orders, and so adoption is their only option.

This was the case in *B v C*, a case in which a single man (B)'s mother (C) acted as a surrogate mother for him. This meant that B and his child (A) had the same mother; legally they were brothers. While at first sight one might assume that this would complicate matters, in fact, it meant that when C and her husband placed the child for adoption with B, they had not committed a criminal offence because it was an intra-familial adoption. If C had not been related to B in this way, a criminal offence might have been committed. Once again, in making the adoption order, Theis J stressed the importance of seeking expert legal advice before embarking on surrogacy arrangements.

B v C[43]

Theis J

It is therefore imperative that single parents contemplating parenthood through surrogacy obtain comprehensive legal advice as to how to proceed as adoption is the only means to ensure that they are the only legal parents of their child. The process under which they can achieve this is a legal minefield, they need to ensure that all the appropriate steps are undertaken to secure lifelong legal security regarding their status with the child.

What is apparent from the reports is that the parties thought carefully about this arrangement, pausing, reflecting and seeking advice at each stage. In my judgment a critical feature of this case are the obviously close relationships within this family; it is an arrangement that was entered into not only with the support of the parties to this application, but, importantly, also the wider family. The strength of these familial relationships, and the consequent support they provide now and in the future, will ensure A's lifelong welfare needs are met. An adoption order will provide the legal security to A's relationship with B, which will undoubtedly meet A's long term welfare needs.

Adoption might also become necessary if neither the surrogate mother nor the commissioning couple are able to look after the child. *Re A (A Child)* was a tragic case in which the adults had met via an internet website and quickly embarked upon a partial surrogacy arrangement. Child protection measures had been taken in relation to some of the commissioning mother's existing children, and she had no contact with three of them. After A's birth, the relationship between the surrogate mother, Wendy, and the commissioning couple AC and JD had deteriorated badly and none were capable of providing for A's needs. The judge also found it hard to believe anything any of the adults involved said.

Re A (A Child)[44]

HHJ Matthews QC

This case represents a tragedy for all concerned but most particularly for the child at its centre. It is a cautionary tale as to what can go wrong in unregulated surrogacy. Such arrangements can no doubt work very well and there are likely to be many happy families in this

43 [2015] EWFC 17.   44 [2014] EWFC 55.

country where surrogacy has been a success. However, because of the special nature of surrogacy arrangements, they demand mature, balanced and sensitive handling. Surrogacy should not be approached without very considerable and careful reflection in respect of all of the ramifications for the child and the members of the families involved. A child is not a commodity to be bought and sold. This child is an individual for whom the consequences of the arrangements will have a lifelong impact....

Wendy, AC and JD have all presented to the court extremely badly. They have all lied at times, sometimes extensively, in relation to important events; credibility ratings in respect of all three of them are extremely low. Unless I have some tangible, concrete, independent evidence which I can rely upon to support what they say, I have to consider their evidence with suspicion.

A was taken into care and placed with prospective adopters, and the following year, Her Honour Judge Matthews QC made a closed adoption order.[45]

(3) Disputes over Residence

Not all surrogacy cases result in parental order or adoption applications. There have been times when cases have come to court as disputes over residence orders, now child arrangement orders. *Re N (A Child)*[46] is an unusual surrogacy case, in which despite the child, N, having lived with the surrogate mother, Mrs P, for his first 18 months, and despite evidence that Mr and Mrs P had given him a good standard of care, a residence order was nevertheless awarded to Mr J, the commissioning father, who was also N's biological father.

Although the courts are generally reluctant to remove a child from a settled home, here Coleridge J found that 'the P's had deliberately embarked on a path of deception, driven by Mrs P's compulsive desire to bear a child or further children, and that she had never had any other objective than to obtain insemination by surrogacy, with the single purpose of acquiring for herself, and her family, another child'. In such circumstances, the Court of Appeal agreed with Coleridge J that it would be better for N if he were to live instead with the Js and to have no contact with Mr and Mrs P.

Eight years later, in *Re M (A Child)*, Russell J once again removed a child (M) from her mother (S) and ordered that she should live instead with the same-sex couple (H and B) who thought that they had made a surrogacy arrangement with the mother. She claimed that the agreement had instead been that H would act as a sperm donor for her. The mother's behaviour had been disturbing: she had made homophobic and offensive allegations about H and B, and there were serious concerns about her parenting abilities, in relation to both M and her two older daughters. Russell J ordered that M should live with H and B, both of whom would have parental responsibility for her as a result, and that she should have only supervised contact with her mother.

Re M (A Child)[47]

Russell J

I find that S deliberately misled the Applicants in order to conceive a child for herself rather than changing her mind at a later date ...

---

[45] [2015] EWFC 63. [46] [2007] EWCA Civ 1053. [47] [2015] EWFC 36.

> Any decision that M lives with H and B and spends much less time with S is bound to affect her, likely to upset and distress her in the short term at least and necessarily amounts to a change in her circumstances. However familiar M is with her home with H and B she would miss her mother with whom she has spent most of her time. Against that I will weigh the harm that she is at risk of suffering if she remains with her mother.... [T]here are already grounds for concerns about her mother's over emotional and highly involved role in this infant's life. Ultimately the role of a parent is to help the child to become independent. This is a child who at 15 months old is still carried by her mother in a sling on her body.... There is a potential for enmeshment and stifling attachment rather than a healthy outward looking approach to the child's life ... The attachment which will develop in an infant who sleeps with her mother, spends all day being carried by her mother and is breastfed on demand through out the day and night raises questions about the long term effect on M.

Another troubling case which came before the court as an application for a residence order is *CW v NT*.[48] Mr and Mrs W had registered on several surrogacy websites and the mother had made contact with them and offered to act as a surrogate mother. An agreement was made that, if the mother became pregnant using Mr W's sperm, the Ws would pay her several sums by instalments during the pregnancy and the mother would hand the baby over at birth. £4,500 was handed over, but during the pregnancy the relationship between the mother and Mr and Mrs W deteriorated. They disagreed over whether the mother should undergo amniocentesis after a blood test revealed that she was at high risk of having a baby with Down's syndrome: the mother wished to undergo amniocentesis, and did so, but the Ws were concerned that the test might harm the baby.

Before T was born, the surrogate mother decided she wanted to keep the baby. When T was seven days old, Mr W applied for a residence order, which the mother opposed. There was some contact between the Ws and T, but T had lived with her mother since birth and, at the date of the hearing, she was five months old. Baker J's task was complicated by the fact that he had considerable concerns about the reliability of all three adults' evidence. The mother had falsified emails, and acted deceitfully. Baker J was also concerned about her use of the internet.

CW v NT[49]

Baker J

In one chatroom, she has chosen to use the soubriquet: 'Thongs, G-Strings, French Knickers, IT'S ALL GUD'. I am concerned that she is at risk of exposing herself to malign and possibly dangerous influences via the internet which could in turn affect the children. For the sake of her children, I advise her to adopt greater restraint in the use of the internet.

Baker J had similar concerns about the Ws: 'I am concerned about the dangerous and murky waters into which they, and particularly Mrs. W, have strayed via the internet.' They had invited a woman CL—a sex worker who claimed to have had 13 children—to stay at their home, claiming it was to protect her against domestic violence, although Baker J found that

---

[48] [2011] EWHC 33 (Fam).   [49] [2011] EWHC 33 (Fam).

they had met her through a surrogacy website, and there were unsubstantiated allegations that they were intending to buy CL's baby. More importantly still, Baker J found that the Ws had an alarming lack of insight into T's needs. In applying the best interests test, Baker J determined that a residence order should be made in favour of the mother, with an interim contact order to Mr W.

Baker J

The mother as a single carer will undoubtedly find it harder in some ways to meet T's needs, particularly as she also has to look after her sons who present challenges. She seemed in some ways to me to be a somewhat vulnerable young woman who may need help and guidance to assist her in caring for her children. But overall, despite my concerns about her deceitfulness, I conclude that she is better able to meet T's emotional needs, certainly at this stage and, on balance, in the long term as well. I accept that she has demonstrated that she has successfully established a close bond with T which, in all the circumstances, it would be wrong to break. I find that she is genuine when she says that she is committed to contact between T and the father. . . .

I am less confident that Mr and Mrs W would respect the relationship between T and her mother were they to be granted residence.

(4) Conflict of Laws and Immigration Issues

Particular difficulties arise in surrogacy arrangements made between citizens from different countries. For example, if a couple from overseas make an arrangement with a British surrogate, they would be ineligible for a parental order because they are not domiciled in the UK. Adoption would also be problematic because there are restrictions upon foreigners adopting British children. This issue arose in *Re G (Surrogacy: Foreign Domicile)*. McFarlane J found a way to enable Mr and Mrs G to take M back to Turkey with them, but his judgment is notable for the criticism he makes of the absence of any 'regulatory umbrella', which leaves these exceptionally complex arrangements in the hands of 'well meaning amateurs'.

Re G (Surrogacy: Foreign Domicile)[50]

McFarlane J

The procedural history of this case, to which I am about to turn, is a cautionary tale which highlights the legal, emotional, and not least the financial consequences of surrogacy arrangements which are undertaken in this jurisdiction involving commissioning parents who are not domiciled in the UK. . . .

It would be easy, but to a degree unjustified, to single COTS out as being responsible for bringing about this surrogacy in circumstances that it knew, or should have known, could not possibly result in a parental order and thereby creating the situation that has required substantial court intervention and the expenditure of some £35,000 of public money.

[50] [2007] EWHC 2814 (Fam).

Of more concern is the understanding that the court now has as to the scale of COTS involvement in cases where the commissioning couple are domiciled overseas…. It is therefore a matter of significant concern that COTS has, albeit naïvely, been involved in the activities that I have described which are, and have long been, outside the law. For an agency working in the surrogacy field not to be aware of one of the basic requirements needed to obtain a parental order is a matter of some real concern …

The court's understanding is that surrogacy agencies such as COTS are not covered by any statutory or regulatory umbrella and are therefore not required to perform to any recognised standard of competence. I am sufficiently concerned by the information uncovered in these two cases to question whether some form of inspection or authorisation should be required in order to improve the quality of advice that is given to individuals who seek to achieve the birth of a child through surrogacy. Given the importance of the issues involved when the life of a child is created in this manner, it is questionable whether the role of facilitating surrogacy arrangements should be left to groups of well-meaning amateurs.

As we have seen, more and more UK couples are travelling abroad for surrogacy. Because the surrogate mother is the child's mother, the child may not be a British citizen from birth, and hence bringing her back to the UK will not necessarily be straightforward. Regardless of what the local birth certificate says, UK law will always recognize the surrogate mother as the child's legal mother. In *Re X & Y (Foreign Surrogacy)*, the clash between UK and local law left the child parentless and stateless, leading Hedley J to warn of the 'many pitfalls' involved in foreign surrogacy arrangements.

Re X & Y (Foreign Surrogacy)[51]

Hedley J

It will be readily apparent that many pitfalls confront the couple who consider commissioning a foreign surrogacy. First, the quality of the information currently available is variable and may, in what it omits, actually be misleading. Secondly, potentially difficult conflict of law issues arise which may (as in this case) have wholly unintended and unforeseen consequences as for example in payments made. Thirdly, serious immigration problems may arise . . . Children born to foreign surrogate mothers, especially to married women, may have no rights of entry nor may the law confer complementary rights on the commissioning couple. . . .

Lastly, even if all other pitfalls are avoided, rights may depend both upon the unswerving commitment of the surrogate mother (and her husband if she has one) to supporting the surrogacy through to completion by Section 30 order and upon their honesty in not taking advantage of their absolute veto . . .

In any event part of the purpose of adjourning this case into open court was to illustrate the sort of difficulties that currently can and do appear. This relates to the obvious difficulties of nationality, control of the commercial element, the rules of consent and the question of legal parentage. Less obviously, but importantly, is the fact that the present law (at least as understood by this court) might encourage the less scrupulous to take advantage of the more vulnerable, unmarried surrogate mothers and to be less than frank in the arrangements that surround foreign surrogacy arrangements.

---

[51] [2008] EWHC 3030 (Fam).

Several years later, Hedley J was continuing to warn of the dangers of foreign surrogacy arrangements, and the need for expert legal advice. Once again, in *Re IJ (A Child)*, the problem was that Ukrainian law recognized the UK commissioning couple as IJ's legal parents, whereas UK law recognized the Ukrainian surrogate mother and her husband as the parents, creating 'real problems' in obtaining immigration clearance for IJ's entry to this country. The commissioning couple had 'been misled by some unduly simplistic advice from the Ukrainian surrogacy agency', and Hedley J again explained why he had decided to give his reasons for granting the parental order in open court.

Re IJ (A Child)[52]

Hedley J

One reason for adjourning these reasons into open court is to emphasise once again the legal difficulties that overseas surrogacy agreements can create. In the experience of the court to date, all overseas jurisdictions can confer parental status on the commissioning couple but that status is not recognised in our domestic law nor (at least where a commercial agreement has been in place) could it be. Those who travel abroad to make these arrangements really should take advice from those skilled in our domestic law to be sure as to the problems that will confront them (not the least of which is immigration) and how they can be addressed. Reliance on advice from overseas agencies is dangerous as the provisions of our domestic and immigration law are often not fully understood.

If one googles 'find surrogate mothers online', it is easy to find a range of internet sites making misleading claims about the ease of cross-border surrogacy arrangements. UK citizens may be lulled into a false sense of security if they are promised and given a local birth certificate with their names on it. As the Foreign and Commonwealth Office's guidance explains: 'even if your names appear on the local birth certificate, a baby born to a foreign national surrogate mother who is married will not be automatically eligible for British nationality'.[53]

In order to respond to the increasing number of foreign surrogacy cases which raise immigration issues, the UK Border Agency issued guidance on *Inter-Country Surrogacy and the Immigration Rules*.[54] In bold and underlined typeface, paragraph 6 warns:

Even if the surrogate mother's home country sees the commissioning couple as the 'parents' and issues documentation to this effect, UK law and the Immigration Rules will not view them as 'parents'.

The Foreign and Commonwealth Office (FCO) has also issued extensive guidance on the acquisition of British citizenship,[55] for children born as a result of overseas surrogacy. This warns prospective parents, again in bold typeface:

Please note, it can take several weeks, if not months, to process applications for children born through surrogacy overseas and you should be prepared for an extended stay overseas once your child is born.

---

[52] [2011] EWHC 921 (Fam).   [53] FCO, *Surrogacy Overseas* (FCO, 2014).
[54] Available at www.ukba.homeoffice.gov.uk/.   [55] FCO, *Surrogacy Overseas* (FCO, 2014).

Matters are simplest if the foreign surrogate mother is single when, provided that the commissioning father is British, has a genetic link to the child, and is able to pass on his nationality (ie he was born in Britain rather than qualifying for citizenship only by descent), the child has an automatic claim to British nationality, and the 'parents' can apply for a British passport for her. The FCO guidance, however, stresses the importance of being able to *prove* that the surrogate mother is, in fact, single. In practice, this can be extremely difficult.

The Foreign and Commonwealth Office[56]

For the application to be processed we will need to be completely satisfied that the surrogate mother is single. If there are any concerns as to surrogate mother's marital status, Her Majesty's Passport Office may need to complete additional checks and the passport application process may take longer. You should be prepared to provide documentary evidence of the surrogate mother's single status, including confirming that the surrogacy clinic or surrogate mother will be able to provide you with relevant and genuine documentation before you enter into the surrogacy arrangement. Please bear in mind that it may be difficult to prove the single status of the surrogate mother, particularly if she is claiming never to have married. Also, a divorcee or widow may have remarried, so a divorce decree or death certificate alone may not be sufficient proof.

If the foreign surrogate mother is married, the 'parents' will need to apply to register the child as a British citizen under section 3(1) of the British Nationality Act 1981, which allows children who are not automatically entitled to British citizenship at birth to be registered as British citizens at the discretion of the Home Secretary. According to FCO guidance, the Home Office must be satisfied that:

- at least one of the commissioning parents is a British Citizen
- the surrogate parents have consented
- had the child been born to the commissioning couple legitimately [sic], s/he would have had an automatic claim to British citizenship or would have qualified for registration under the British Nationality Act 1981.

To make matters more complicated still, the law in the surrogate mother's country of origin may place its own restrictions on surrogacy arrangements. So, for example, India no longer permits gay male couples to employ Indian surrogate mothers and it now requires all commissioning couples to obtain special medical visas; an almost complete ban is imminent. In 2015, Thailand banned commercial surrogacy, and prohibited foreigners from entering into surrogacy arrangements with Thai women. Because surrogacy inevitably takes place over a period of at least nine months, it is inevitable that some people will have already embarked on surrogacy arrangements when the rules change.

There is also, of course, the chance of unrest or political instability that may complicate arrangements. In *R v T*,[57] for example, twins were born to a Ukrainian surrogate mother around the time that a period of civil unrest started in Ukraine. As a result, the applicants' departure with the children was delayed for around six months and, as we saw earlier, it proved particularly difficult to locate the surrogate mother.

---

[56] Ibid.   [57] [2015] EWFC 22.

There might also be a clash between the steps that a couple are told to take in the country where the child is born and UK law. For example, in *Re G (Parental Orders)*, a British couple had entered into surrogacy arrangement in the US, and had been through a US adoption process. By doing so, they were potentially in violation of section 83 of the Adoption and Children Act 2002, which makes it a criminal offence for a person who is habitually resident in the British Isles to bring a child into the UK having adopted that child overseas, without first having obtained the approval of the Home Secretary, and complied with a series of other procedural requirements. As Theis J explained, the couple had been caught between a rock and a hard place, and the case illustrated the importance of securing expert legal advice in both jurisdictions.

Re G (Parental Orders)[58]

Theis J

This case provides yet another timely illustration of the legal minefield in international surrogacy arrangements. It underscores the critical importance of anyone considering this type of arrangement to secure expert advice, in particular legal advice in both jurisdictions at each stage of the process.

The applicants were clearly between a rock and a hard place. It is clear that from a welfare standpoint, and because of their obligations under the surrogacy agreement, the steps they took in the US were the right steps to take and were done with the best of intentions and with the children's welfare uppermost in their minds. They had no idea that by undertaking those steps, they would potentially be in breach of s.83.

Moylan J in *Re D (A Child) (Surrogacy)*, is not alone in suggesting that—in the light of increasing numbers of international surrogacy arrangements, and the clashes between jurisdictions which inevitably result—some sort of cross-national regulation would be desirable.

Re D (A Child) (Surrogacy)[59]

Moylan J

This case provides a clear example of the difficulties created as a result of surrogacy arrangements being subject to varying degrees of domestic regulation, from significant regulation to none at all, and also because of the existence of significant differences in the effect of such domestic regulation. There is, in my view, a compelling need for a uniform system of regulation to be created by an international instrument in order to make available an appropriate structure in respect of what can only be described as the surrogacy market.

Any cross-national regulation would have to happen at a relatively high level of abstraction: it is hard to imagine global agreement on acceptable levels of compensation, for example. Within the EU, states have a margin of appreciation on how to regulate surrogacy, although the European Court of Human Rights' (ECtHR) first decision in an international

[58] [2014] EWHC 1561 (Fam).   [59] [2014] EWHC 2121 (Fam).

surrogacy case made it clear that this does not extend to being able to deny the existence of a parent–child relationship between the commissioning parent(s) and their child.

In *Mennesson v France* and *Labassee v France*,[60] the ECtHR found that France's margin of appreciation did not permit it to refuse to issue birth certificates to children who had been born as a result of surrogacy arrangements in the US, and who were being brought up by their intended parents in France. Respect for the children's private life, under Article 8, required them to be able to establish their identity as a human being, and 'filiation' was an essential aspect of this. Denial of filiation led to legal uncertainty for the children; they would have no automatic inheritance rights and it also inaccurately represented their relationship with their biological father. France had therefore breached the children's Article 8 rights.

The Hague Conference on Private International Law, which has been responsible for drafting conventions on, for example, inter-country adoption and child abduction, has recently taken up the issue of international surrogacy arrangements, and in 2015, an Expert Group was set up in order to explore further the feasibility of drawing up a similar multilateral instrument to cover surrogacy.[61] While the most pressing issue was the plight of children whose legal parentage was left in limbo as a result of differences in the rules between states, this was by no means the only area of concern.

Hague Conference on Private International Law[62]

[T]he issues surrounding the legal status of children born to ISAs [International Surrogacy Arrangements], and in particular the need to eliminate 'limping' legal parentage and statelessness, were the most acute needs identified by States. However, in addition, many States mentioned the need to ensure respect for the rights and welfare of all parties to an ISA, including surrogate mothers and children, in any future international work. Indeed, as may be expected, the specific needs highlighted by States as those which should be addressed by future work echoed the areas of concern identified, i.e.: the need to ensure surrogate mothers' free and informed consent to ISAs; the need to ensure appropriate standards of medical care for surrogate mothers and children, including ensuring the surrogate mother's ability to retain decision-making over her own body; the need for some minimum checks concerning the intending parents' suitability to enter into the arrangement, and the need to establish standards concerning the child's right to know his/her genetic and birth origins.

(5) Informal Transfers

While parental orders and adoption are the only ways in which the commissioning couple can become the legal parents of a child born following a surrogacy arrangement, this does not mean that every surrogate birth is followed by a formal transfer of legal parenthood. A child may be handed over by the surrogate mother, and live with the commissioning couple without any legal formalities. For obvious reasons, it is impossible to tell how many unofficial transfers of children take place each year.

---

[60] *Mennesson v France* (Application no 61592/11), judgment of 26 June 2014; *Labassee v France* (Application no 65941/11), judgment of 26 June 2014.

[61] *Council on General Affairs and Policy of the Conference: Conclusions and Recommendations* (HCCH, 2015).

[62] *The Desirability and Feasibility of Further Work on the Parentage/Surrogacy Project* (HCCH, 2014).

It is indubitably not in a child's best interests for her 'parents' to have no legal relationship with her, while someone else, perhaps on another continent, retains legal parenthood. In *A v B*, Theis J spelled out the importance of seeking a parental order.

A v B[63]

Theis J

If such an order is not sought, one or both of them are not the legal parents of the child, which can have long term detrimental consequences. An obvious example is that testamentary provision for the child may be open to challenge.... Those who may maintain that a parental order is not required are not considering the best interests of the child who they care for and risk sleepwalking into future legal difficulties for the child, which can readily be avoided by a parental order being made.

The number of children in this sort of legal limbo has been described by Theis J, speaking extra-judicially, as 'a ticking legal timebomb',[64] a claim which is disputed by the Surrogacy UK Working Group on Surrogacy Law Reform, drawing in part upon their survey of UK surrogates and intended parents (IPs).

Surrogacy UK Working Group on Surrogacy Law Reform[65]

Anecdotal evidence from HMPO [Her Majesty's Passport Office] suggests that the majority of IPs who go overseas do in fact apply for POs [parental orders]. This is the same as suggested for both international and UK-based surrogacy in our survey. There is no evidence supporting concerns that POs are not generally sought, despite some claims to the contrary. . . .

104 (94.5%) of the surrogates say that the IPs they are working/have worked with will 'definitely' apply for a PO and a further 3 (2.7%) say they think so. No-one said 'no'. . . .

68 respondents in this IP group (36.4%) were already legal parents of their children, having completed the PO process, while a further 19 (10.2%) had the surrogate-born child(ren) living with them but no legal parenthood. 181 answered whether they had/would apply for a PO: 178 of these (98.3%) said they either had or would apply for a PO, while three (1.7%) said they would not.

(f) REFORM

As far back as 1997, the then Labour government appeared to accept the need for reform when it appointed a committee, chaired by Margaret Brazier, to review aspects of the regulation of surrogacy in the UK. The Brazier Committee's report was published in 1998,[66] but none of its recommendations—including a complete prohibition of any payments to surrogate mothers, other than compensation for specific expenses actually incurred as a result of the pregnancy—were ever implemented.

---

[63] [2015] EWHC 1059 (Fam).

[64] Quoted in Owen Bowcott, 'Unregistered surrogate-born children creating "legal timebomb", judge warns', *The Guardian*, 18 May 2015.

[65] *Surrogacy in the UK: Myth Busting and Reform* (Surrogacy UK, 2015).

[66] *Surrogacy: Review for Health Ministers of Current Arrangements for Payments and Regulation* (Cm 4068, 1998).

Nearly 20 years later, there continue to be multiple problems with the law governing surrogacy in the UK. First, as we have seen, the ban on commercialization is completely ineffective. If payments are to be permitted, it might be helpful for them to be prospectively regulated (as happens with egg donation, for example), rather than retrospectively authorized, which inevitably creates uncertainty for all involved.

Secondly, the Human Fertilisation and Embryology Act's fatherhood provisions are intended to cover cases in which donated sperm is used, and they apply awkwardly and inappropriately to surrogacy arrangements. Thirdly, even if the number of commissioning parents who do not acquire a formal relationship with 'their' child is low, this is very clearly not in a child's best interests. Fourthly, surrogacy agreements are often made without expert legal advice, with potentially disastrous consequences for all concerned.

Cross-national surrogacy arrangements can result in especially tricky legal problems. Although there are clearly difficulties in trying to regulate an international market in surrogacy, there is surely no excuse for leaving surrogacy in a regulatory vacuum within the UK.

So what form might law reform take? Perhaps the simplest change would be to enable people to apply for something akin to a parental order before the child is conceived. At the moment, as we have seen, the central problem with parental order applications is that by the time the case comes to court, the child has been born and has welfare needs that trump any other considerations. By having a mechanism through which a couple could be pre-authorized for a parental order, it might be possible to exercise some oversight and control over surrogacy agreements before a child exists. It would also mean that the child's parentage could be resolved before she is born, rather than leaving the child in an unsatisfactory legal limbo until parenthood is formally transferred.

Of course, in the case of partial surrogacy, it would be impossible to stop people entering into ill-advised arrangements and finding themselves embroiled in disputes that the court has to resolve after the event. But in the vast majority of surrogacy cases, the surrogate mother is happy to hand the child over at birth, and in these cases, pre-birth orders would have significant advantages for all parties.

In the next extract, Melissa Elsworth and Natalie Gamble argue that pre-birth orders would be the best way to avoid children born through surrogacy living in a potentially endless legal limbo.

Melissa Elsworth and Natalie Gamble[67]

Jessica Lee MP has proposed a system of contracts and pre-birth orders modelled on that of US states such as California, Texas, Utah, Virginia and Florida. This would enable surrogates and intended parents to enter into a surrogacy agreement at the outset to agree key issues (perhaps following counselling and medical/psychological clearance), and provide a system where a pre-birth order would be made by the family court to ratify that agreement before the child was born. Where there is no dispute (as in the overwhelming majority of cases), this would create a mechanism by which the intended parents would be recognised as the legal parents immediately upon their child's birth and named as such as on the birth certificate. It would bring the legal process forward and have the advantage of certainty in that the child would not be left in 'legal limbo' for many months between their birth and the granting of a parental order.

[67] 'Are contracts and pre-birth orders the way forward for UK surrogacy?' (2015) 2 International Family Law 101–96.

Of course, one of the issues which would have to be resolved is whether pre-birth orders would leave the current parentage rules intact, and would simply enable speedier transfer of parenthood once the child is born, or whether parentage would vest in the commissioning couple from birth. The latter is obviously more radical, since it could involve recognizing someone other than the child's birth mother as its mother from birth. If this were the effect of a pre-birth order, would it thereby eliminate the surrogate mother's right to change her mind and effectively make surrogacy contracts enforceable?

Some commentators would argue that surrogacy contracts' unenforceability is necessary in order to give adequate recognition to the 'gestational relationship'.

Rosemarie Tong[68]

The value of a 'change of heart' period is very important from a feminist point of view. First, it acknowledges a parental relationship whose moral significance traditional philosophy has ignored—namely, the gestational relationship . . . A second advantage of the 'change of heart' period is that it challenges the notion that contracts must be honored no matter what—as if contracts were more important than people . . .

A deal is not always a deal—at least not when one is trading in some of the deepest emotions human beings can ever feel. Any approach that *binds* women to reproductive decisions—as does the contract approach—must be regarded with deep suspicion.

Marjorie Shultz disagrees, and argues that giving women the right to change their mind reinforces damaging and sexist stereotypes.

Marjorie Shultz[69]

Once conception has taken place, reliance on the promises made is about as intense and significant as could be imagined. If intentions and the expectations and reliance that result are taken seriously, the unfairness of denying the equitable remedy [specific performance] becomes comparable to the hardship of granting it. . . .

In holding that surrogates but not other parties to the arrangement must have an opportunity to change their minds after giving birth, the court reinforces stereotypes of women as unstable, as unable to make decisions and stick to them, and as necessarily vulnerable to their hormones and emotions . . . In particular, it exalts a woman's experience of pregnancy and childbirth over her formation of emotional, intellectual and interpersonal decisions and expectations, as well as over others' reliance on the commitments she has earlier made.

In Israel, one of the only countries to have introduced a regulatory regime to approve surrogacy arrangements, the surrogate mother is only permitted to renege on her agreement if there has been a change of circumstances, and the welfare of the child would not be damaged. In the next extract, Rhona Schuz points out that the rigorous approval process that precedes any surrogacy arrangement in Israel minimizes the chance that the surrogate mother will in fact change her mind.

---

[68] 'Feminist Perspectives and Gestational Motherhood: The Search for a Unified Legal Focus' in J Callahan (ed), *Reproduction, Ethics and the Law: Feminist Responses* (Indiana UP: Bloomington, IN, 1995) 55–79.

[69] 'Reproductive Technology and Intention-Based Parenthood: An Opportunity for Gender Neutrality' (1990) 2 Wisconsin Law Review 297–398.

Rhona Schuz[70]

The Approvals Committee's guidelines for drawing up the surrogate motherhood agreement start with a clear statement that it is necessary to ensure, so far as is possible, that the birth mother understands the nature of the commitments involved in the agreement and agrees thereto voluntarily and without coercion. A number of the Approvals Committee's requirements are designed to further this end.

First, the physician who examines the birth mother has to declare that s/he has explained to the birth mother the consequences and significance of acting as a surrogate . . . Secondly, the Approvals Committee will not consider any application until it is satisfied that the birth mother has obtained independent legal advice from a lawyer who is an expert in surrogate motherhood agreements . . . Thirdly, the birth mother is interviewed separately by the Approvals Committee and will be asked questions designed to test whether her consent is voluntary and informed. Finally, the Approvals Committee's practice is only to approve birth mothers who have previously given birth . . .

We are not aware of any cases where the birth mother has requested to keep the child. One reason for this may be the screening by the Approvals Committee.

5 CONCLUSION

Although surrogacy arrangements can go disastrously wrong, this is the exception. Susan Imrie and Vasanti Jadva carried out interviews with surrogate mothers and found that the vast majority of surrogacy arrangements had been a positive experience (89 per cent; 8 per cent had had 'neutral' experiences; 5 per cent had had negative experiences, but most had also had positive experiences of surrogacy). Almost all surrogate mothers were happy with the ongoing contact they had with the child and their parents.

Susan Imrie and Vasanti Jadva[71]

Overall, in the majority of surrogacy arrangements surrogates remained in contact with surrogacy families, and viewed most of the relationships formed through surrogacy as positive. The variety of contact arrangements maintained, and surrogates' high levels of satisfaction with the amount of contact they had with surrogacy families, suggests that, in most cases, the parties involved in UK surrogacy arrangements managed to negotiate this potentially problematic relationship with a high degree of success and create relationships that were sustained over time and enjoyed.

As compared with conception involving donated gametes, and for obvious reasons (the arrival of a child without a pregnancy will have to be explained), openness tends to be the norm in families which have had children as a result of surrogacy.

---

[70] 'Surrogacy in Israel: An Analysis of the Law in Practice' in Rachel Cook, Shelley Day Sclater, with Felicity Kaganas (eds), *Surrogate Motherhood: International Perspectives* (Hart Publishing: Oxford, 2003) 35–53.

[71] 'The long-term experiences of surrogates: relationships and contact with surrogacy families in genetic and gestational surrogacy arrangements' (2014) 29 Reproductive BioMedicine Online 424–35.

V Jadva et al[72]

[M]ost children who are aware of their surrogacy conception are able to show some understanding of surrogacy by age 7 years. . . . For those who were in contact with their surrogate mother, the majority said that they liked her and most children were positive about their surrogacy birth at age 10 years . . . In contrast to families who use gamete donation to have a child, this study shows that families who use surrogacy are more open with their child about their use of assisted reproduction, with over 90% of families having explained surrogacy to their child.

But while surrogacy arrangements usually work well, the law on surrogacy is, in short, a mess. Since the first foreign surrogacy cases started to reach the UK courts in 2005, it would not be an overstatement to say that the floodgates have opened. Updating this chapter for the fourth edition, I was astonished by the number of new cases. And almost every judgment begins with a warning:

This case provides another cautionary tale of the difficulties that can be encountered in entering into foreign surrogacy arrangements.[73]

This case provides yet another timely illustration of the legal minefield in international surrogacy arrangements.[74]

Very sadly this case is another example of how 'agreements' between potential parents reached privately to conceive children to build a family go wrong and cause great distress to the biological parents and their spouses or partners.[75]

In the absence of clear prospective regulation, it is left to family judges to resolve *ex post facto* how to protect the best interests of the child born through surrogacy. As Kirsty Horsey and Sally Sheldon explain, the need for reform could not be more pressing.

Kirsty Horsey and Sally Sheldon[76]

The possibility of any oversight of the treatment of, say, an Indian surrogate, is highly limited, as is the possibility to protect the interests of the intending parents who have travelled out of the jurisdiction, and the children born within such arrangements. It seems to us that there is thus an overwhelming case for a fundamental review of the law of surrogacy. . . .

After all, the existence of cross-border provision should greatly heighten concerns regarding exploitation where surrogacy services are provided in countries where women may not have access to the same health services and legal protections as in the UK. Further, concerns

---

[72] 'Surrogacy families 10 years on: relationship with the surrogate, decisions over disclosure and children's understanding of their surrogacy origins' (2012) 27 Human Reproduction 3008–14.

[73] Per Theis J in *Re WT (Foreign Surrogacy)* [2014] EWHC 1303 (Fam).

[74] Per Theis J in *Re G (Parental Orders)* [2014] EWHC 1561 (Fam).

[75] Per Russell J in *Re M (A Child)* [2015] EWFC 36.

[76] 'Still Hazy After All These Years: The Law Regulating Surrogacy' (2012) 20 Medical Law Review 67–89.

regarding the possible harms suffered by intending parents are greater still where such individuals feel left with no alternative but to travel to other countries and navigate their way through foreign legal and health care systems and domestic immigration rules. Most crucially, if the central concern of a good law is to protect the welfare of the child, this is surely not best achieved by exporting surrogacy, yet this is the almost inevitable consequence of our current regime. While any changes to the UK law are unlikely to yield any means of overseeing surrogacy arrangements that occur oversees, it is at least possible that making surrogacy services more readily available in the UK would reduce the incidence of cross-border arrangements.

Finally, Kirsty Horsey and Katia Neofytou suggest that momentum for change is building.

Kirsty Horsey and Katia Neofytou[77]

Momentum for change is picking up, with increasing academic criticism mirrored by those experiencing surrogacy in day-to-day practice, and with surrogacy taken up as an issue in Parliament in October of 2014, with indications from the Minister for Public Health (Jane Ellison MP) that government will consider whether UK surrogacy law should be reviewed, after hearing opinions from other MPs.

FURTHER READING

Crawshaw, Marilyn, Purewal, Satvinder, and van den Akker, Olga, 'Working at the margins: the views and experiences of court social workers on parental orders work in surrogacy arrangements' (2012) 42 British Journal of Social Work 1–19.

Deomampo, Daisy, 'Transnational surrogacy in India' (2013) 34 Frontiers: A Journal of Women Studies 167–88.

Elsworth, Melissa and Gamble, Natalie, 'Are contracts and pre-birth orders the way forward for UK surrogacy?' (2015) 2 International Family Law 101–96.

Fenton-Glynn, Claire, 'The Difficulty of Enforcing Surrogacy Regulations' (2015) 74 Cambridge Law Journal 34–7.

Horsey, Kirsty and Sheldon, Sally, 'Still Hazy After All These Years: The Law Regulating Surrogacy' (2012) 20 Medical Law Review 67–89.

Imrie, Susan and Jadva, Vasanti, 'The long-term experiences of surrogates: relationships and contact with surrogacy families in genetic and gestational surrogacy arrangements' (2014) 29 Reproductive BioMedicine Online 424–35.

Jadva, Vasanti et al, 'Surrogacy families 10 years on: relationship with the surrogate, decisions over disclosure and children's understanding of their surrogacy origins' (2012) 27 Human Reproduction 3008–14.

Surrogacy UK Working Group on Surrogacy Law Reform, *Surrogacy in the UK: Myth Busting and Reform* (Surrogacy UK, 2015).

---

[77] 'The Fertility Treatment Time Forgot: What Should be Done About Surrogacy in the UK' in Kirsty Horsey (ed), *Revisiting the Regulation of Human Fertilisation and Embryology* (Routledge: Abingdon, 2015) 117–35.

17

END-OF-LIFE DECISIONS

CENTRAL ISSUES

1. Euthanasia involves a doctor deliberately killing a patient. In the UK, this would be murder, for which the only sentence is life imprisonment.

2. Assisted suicide is also a criminal offence, but the Director of Public Prosecutions (DPP) has discretion over the decision to prosecute. In response to the House of Lords' judgment in the *Purdy* case, the DPP has published the factors that will be taken into account when exercising this discretion.

3. It may be lawful to administer a dose of painkilling or sedative drugs that could shorten a patient's life, by virtue of the doctrine of double effect.

4. Competent adults have the right to refuse life-sustaining treatment, which in practice means a right to insist that doctors physically remove them from the mechanical ventilator or feeding tube which is keeping them alive.

5. The principal arguments in favour of legalizing assisted dying are respect for patient autonomy; compassion; the inconsistency of the line the law currently draws between lawful and unlawful life-shortening practices; and the benefits of openly regulating a practice which is otherwise shrouded in secrecy.

6. The arguments against legalization include respect for the sanctity of human life; the view that high-quality palliative care ought to make assisted dying unnecessary; the difficulty of ensuring that requests are genuine; the negative impact legalization might have on the doctor–patient relationship; and the dangers of the slippery slope.

7. Some other countries have legalized euthanasia and/or assisted suicide, but opinion differs over whether this has improved matters for patients, or made things worse.

8. In relation to patients who lack capacity, the courts have had to decide whether withdrawing or withholding life-saving treatment could ever be in a patient's best interests. Where life-prolonging measures are futile or overly burdensome, it can be lawful to withdraw treatment that is keeping the patient alive.

1 INTRODUCTION

(a) CONTROVERSY AT THE END OF LIFE

Although it will happen to all of us, no one knows what it is like to die. We may have watched life slip away from another person, and for some people, their religious faith means they have certain expectations about what happens after death. But when judging whether death could ever be preferable to continued life, we are all inevitably behind a 'veil of ignorance'.[1]

Interest in the legitimacy of taking steps to speed up the process of dying is not new. Some Greek and Roman philosophers, among them Seneca, believed that suicide was a rational response to extreme physical and mental deterioration:

> I shall not abandon old age, if old age preserves me intact as regards the better part of myself; but if old age begins to shatter my mind, and to pull its various faculties to pieces, if it leaves me, not life, but only the breath of life, I shall rush out of a house that is crumbling and tottering.[2]

For several reasons, the question of whether it could ever be legitimate for the medical profession to help patients to die has become more prominent in recent years. First, patients who would previously have died can now be kept alive using mechanical ventilators and artificially delivered nutrition and hydration. While initially developed to enable potentially curable patients to survive, despite a temporary inability to breathe or swallow, it is now possible to keep people alive when there is no prospect of recovery. New technologies have therefore forced us to think about the circumstances in which it might be legitimate to discontinue life-prolonging medical treatment.

Secondly, although life expectancy increased dramatically over the course of the twentieth century, medical progress has not been as successful in extending the period during which we are able to lead healthy, independent lives. As a result, many of us fear becoming increasingly dependent upon others, as our bodily functions fail.

Thirdly, as we have seen in previous chapters, the principle of patient autonomy is now dominant within medical law, raising the question of whether a patient's right to make decisions about her treatment should extend to being able to decide to end her life. Fourthly, when we looked at religious bioethics in Chapter 1, one common theme was the idea that life is not ours to dispose of as we please. In a secular society, less weight may be given to the proscription of suicide and euthanasia within religious teachings.

Fifthly, a number of high-profile legal cases, such as those brought by Debbie Purdy and Tony Nicklinson, have received intense media attention. There has also been considerable interest in the hundreds of UK citizens who have made the journey to Switzerland to access assisted suicide through Dignitas.

---

[1] John Rawls, *A Theory of Justice* (Harvard UP: Cambridge, MA, 1971).

[2] Seneca, *58th Letter to Lucilius* in TE Page et al (eds), *Seneca: Ad Lucilium Epistulae Morales*, vol I (trans Richard M Gummere) (Heinemann: London, 1961) 409.

(b) ORGANIZATION OF THIS CHAPTER

In this chapter, we are concerned with the legal status of practices that may result in life being shortened. We begin with the patient who has capacity. First, we look at the current law, distinguishing between lawful and unlawful life-shortening practices. Secondly, the arguments for and against the legalization of voluntary euthanasia and assisted suicide are set out, with extracts from both sides of this emotional and acrimonious debate. Next, we examine some other countries' experience with decriminalization.

In the second half of this chapter, our focus is on patients who lack capacity (see further Chapter 5). We start with children, discussing the application of the best interests test to non-treatment decisions, and we consider the extraordinary 'conjoined twins case', *Re A*.[3] In relation to adults, we begin with the House of Lords' groundbreaking decision that life-sustaining treatment could be withheld from Tony Bland, a patient in a permanent vegetative state.[4] We then consider how decisions about the withdrawal or the withholding of life-prolonging treatment from patients who lack capacity are taken under the Mental Capacity Act 2005.

(c) TERMINOLOGY

The word 'euthanasia' comes from the Greek words *eu* (good) and *thanatos* (death). In modern usage, it has developed a more specific meaning. Although most of us would agree that someone who dies peacefully and suddenly in her sleep, after a long and healthy life, has had a 'good death', we would not say that this was a case of euthanasia. The *Oxford English Dictionary*'s definition is 'a gentle and easy death, the bringing about of this, especially in the case of incurable and painful disease'. We would also usually confine the term 'euthanasia' to cases in which a doctor helps a patient to die: if someone kills a relative in order to relieve her suffering, we would tend to say that this was a 'mercy killing', rather than an example of euthanasia. In this chapter, I shall use the word 'euthanasia' to refer only to voluntary active euthanasia; that is, where a doctor deliberately acts to kill a patient at her request.

Euthanasia is not the same thing as assisted suicide. In euthanasia, it is the doctor's action that causes the patient's death. In a case of assisted suicide, the patient causes her own death, but someone else (often, but not necessarily, a doctor) has helped her, for example by prescribing a lethal dose of drugs. Assisted dying is a non-specific umbrella term that refers to both euthanasia and assisted suicide.

2 THE COMPETENT PATIENT

(a) THE CURRENT LAW

(1) Euthanasia

A doctor (or other health care professional) who deliberately ends the life of her patient is subject to the ordinary criminal law, and would often satisfy both the *actus reus* (proof of conduct, and proof that the conduct caused death) and the *mens rea* (the intention to kill or to cause grievous bodily harm) for the crime of murder. The doctor's motive and the consent of the victim are irrelevant, as is the fact that the patient would have died soon anyway.

---

[3] [2001] Fam 147 (CA). [4] *Airedale NHS Trust v Bland* [1993] AC 789 (HL).

Because murder carries a mandatory life sentence, the fact that the doctor acted for compassionate reasons cannot be taken into account in sentencing.

If someone who is suffering unbearably is killed by a friend or family member, it may be possible to reduce the charge to one of manslaughter on the grounds of diminished responsibility, thus allowing for some discretion, and hence leniency in sentencing. Under section 2 of the Homicide Act 1957, as amended by the Coroners and Justice Act 2009, the partial defence of diminished responsibility is available where someone is 'suffering from an abnormality of mental functioning' which—

> (a) arose from a recognised medical condition,
>
> (b) substantially impaired D's ability to do one or more of the things mentioned in subsection (1A), and
>
> (c) provides an explanation for D's acts and omissions in doing or being a party to the killing.
>
> (1A) Those things are—
>
> (a) to understand the nature of D's conduct;
>
> (b) to form a rational judgment;
>
> (c) to exercise self-control.

Whether or not mercy killers are actually suffering from 'abnormality of mental functioning', as opposed to making a rational decision, is open to question. There is some evidence that, in order to avoid the charge of murder, an inference is drawn that the defendant must have been suffering from a mental abnormality at the time of the offence, even though there is no sign of mental abnormality when the defendant is actually examined by a psychiatrist. Indeed, Dell goes so far as to say that mercy killers, in general, display a 'total lack of mental disorder'.[5] Nevertheless, there seems to be what has been described as a 'benign conspiracy' to use the partial defence of diminished responsibility in order to mitigate the harshness of applying the ordinary law of murder to mercy killers.[6]

In theory, this might be more difficult as a result of the 2009 reforms which introduced a new requirement for there to be a causal relationship between the abnormality of mental functioning and the killing. In practice, however, because so much depends upon juries' evaluation of the totality of the evidence, the 'benign conspiracy' is unlikely to disappear.

There have been cases where 'mercy killers' have chosen not to invoke their own mental disorder in order to explain their actions. In 2008, Kay Gilderdale had injected her adult daughter, Lynn Gilderdale, who was paralysed and unable to swallow, with morphine. Lynn had attempted to commit suicide, had a 'Do Not Resuscitate' order in place, and had been considering going to Dignitas in Switzerland to end her life. She had told her mother that she did not wish to continue living. Mrs Gilderdale wished to plead guilty to a charge of assisting her daughter's suicide, but she was charged with attempted murder instead. The jury refused to convict her, and the trial judge was critical of the decision to pursue a murder charge.

In contrast, at around the same time, another mother who had purchased enough heroin to kill her severely brain-damaged son was convicted of the full crime of murder. Frances Inglis did not plead the defence of diminished responsibility, even though she had been diagnosed with a depressive illness and post-traumatic stress disorder. She wished instead

---

5 S Dell, 'The mandatory sentence and section 2' (1986) 12 Journal of Medical Ethics 28–31.

6 The Law Commission, *Partial Defences to Murder* (Report No 290, 2004) para 2.34.

to plead not guilty, but given the clear evidence that she had taken her son's life, she was convicted of murder. In *R v Inglis*, her appeal against conviction was dismissed by the Court of Appeal.

R v Inglis[7]

Lord Judge CJ

[W]e must underline that the law of murder does not distinguish between murder committed for malevolent reasons and murder motivated by familial love. Subject to well established partial defences, like provocation or diminished responsibility, mercy killing is murder. The offences of which the appellant was convicted, and for which she fell to be sentenced, were attempted murder and murder. The sentence on conviction for murder is mandatory.

A health care professional who ends a patient's life will seldom be able to claim that she was suffering from an 'abnormality of mental functioning'.[8] Of course, when a doctor gives a fatal dose of drugs to a patient who is terminally ill, there may be some evidential difficulty in establishing that it was what the doctor did, rather than the pre-existing illness, that caused the patient's death. To be guilty of murder, the defendant's conduct must have 'contributed significantly' or been 'a substantial cause' of death; it need not, therefore, be the sole reason for the patient's death. If causation cannot be established, the doctor who administered a potentially lethal injection might be charged with attempted murder (as happened to Dr Cox, below).

While there have been prosecutions, no doctor who has complied with a patient's request to end her life has ever been convicted of the full offence of murder. As we can see in the following cases, both juries and the judiciary have tended to be lenient towards doctors whom they judge to have acted for compassionate reasons.

Dr Moor was arrested after taking part in a media debate about voluntary euthanasia, during which he admitted to having helped a number of his patients to die painlessly. In *R v Moor* he was prosecuted for the murder of George Liddell, an 85-year-old man who had been suffering from bowel cancer. Given the tone of Hooper J's direction to the jury, it is not surprising that the jury acquitted Dr Moor, reaching a unanimous verdict in less than an hour.

R v Moor[9]

Hooper J

You have heard that this defendant is a man of excellent character, not just in the sense that he has no previous convictions but how witnesses have spoken of his many admirable qualities. You may consider it a great irony that a doctor who goes out of his way to care for George Liddell ends up facing the charge that he does. You may also consider it another great irony that the doctor who takes time on his day off to tend to a dying patient ends up on this charge.

---

[7] [2010] EWCA Crim 2637. [8] Homicide Act 1957, s 2(1). [9] [1999] Crim LR 2000 Jul 568–90.

R v Cox is the only case to have resulted in a doctor's conviction, this time for attempted murder. It was impossible to establish exactly what had killed Mrs Boyes because her body had been cremated, so only the lesser charge of attempted murder was possible. Dr Cox had given Mrs Boyes a dose of potassium chloride that was guaranteed to kill her, so it was difficult to avoid the conclusion that he had intended to end her life, especially since potassium chloride is not a painkiller. Mrs Boyes was 70 years old and terminally ill; she had rheumatoid arthritis and had developed gastric ulcers, gangrene, and body sores. She suffered extreme pain, which could not be controlled by pain-killing drugs. There was evidence that she had repeatedly asked Dr Cox, a consultant rheumatologist who had been treating her for the last 13 years, and others, to kill her.

R v Cox[10]

Ognall J

There can be no doubt that the use of drugs to reduce pain and suffering will often be fully justified notwithstanding that it will, in fact hasten the moment of death, but please understand this, ladies and gentleman, what can never be lawful is the use of drugs with the primary purpose of hastening the moment of death. . . . [I]n the context of this case potassium chloride has no curative properties . . . it is not an analgesic. It is not used by the medical profession to relieve pain . . ., injected into a vein it is a lethal substance. One ampoule would certainly kill . . . the injection here was therefore twice that necessary to cause certain death.

Dr Cox was convicted of attempted murder, and was given a 12-month suspended prison sentence. It is noteworthy that in a separate General Medical Council (GMC) hearing, he was not struck off the medical register, and, after a formal reprimand, he returned to practise within a year of his conviction.

The only flexibility the law has been capable of exercising when dealing with cases of mercy killing has been to find a way to downgrade the charge from murder to one, like manslaughter or attempted murder, where there can be discretion in sentencing, or alternatively for juries to use their power to refuse to convict.

In 2012, Tony Nicklinson applied for a number of declarations which, if granted, would have a dramatic effect upon the prohibition of euthanasia in the UK. In his statement to the court, he explained his predicament:

Tony Nicklinson[11]

[The stroke] left me paralysed below the neck and unable to speak. I need help in almost every aspect of my life. I cannot scratch if I itch, I cannot pick my nose if it is blocked and I can only eat if I am fed like a baby—only I won't grow out of it, unlike the baby. I have no privacy or dignity left. I am washed, dressed and put to bed by carers who are, after all, still strangers. You try defecating to order whilst suspended in a sling over a commode and see how you get on.

---

[10] (1992) 12 BMLR 38.
[11] Quoted by Charles J in *Nicklinson v Ministry of Justice* [2012] EWHC 304 (QB).

> I am fed up with my life and don't want to spend the next 20 years or so like this. . . . I'm not depressed so do not need counselling. I have had over six years to think about my future and it does not look good. I have locked in syndrome and I can expect no cure or improvement in my condition as my muscles and joints seize up through lack of use. Indeed, I can expect to dribble my way into old age. If I am lucky I will acquire a life-threatening illness such as cancer so that I can refuse treatment and say no to those who would keep me alive against my will.
>
> By all means protect the vulnerable. By vulnerable I mean those who cannot make decisions for themselves just don't include me. I am not vulnerable, I don't need help or protection from death or those who would help me. If the legal consequences were not so huge i.e. life imprisonment, perhaps I could get someone to help me. As things stand, I can't get help.

Tony Nicklinson sought a declaration that it would not be unlawful, on the grounds of necessity, for his GP or another doctor to terminate or assist the termination of Mr Nicklinson's life. He also sought a declaration that by criminalizing euthanasia and assisted suicide, and by imposing a mandatory life sentence for cases of genuinely compassionate voluntary active euthanasia, the law was incompatible with his right to respect for his private life.

The *Nicklinson* case is complicated for several reasons. First, after the Divisional Court rejected his application for judicial review, he stopped eating and drinking and died six days later. His widow Jane was given permission to pursue an appeal in the Court of Appeal, and then in the Supreme Court and the European Court of Human Rights. Secondly, Tony Nicklinson's case was joined with those of two other men. First, and while Tony Nicklinson was still alive, it was joined with that of a man with locked-in syndrome, referred to only as 'Martin', whose claim was different and is considered later. After his death, his case was joined with that of Paul Lamb, whose predicament was similar. Thirdly, the arguments pursued differed substantially at different stages of the appeal. The Court of Appeal was the highest court to consider the question of whether there could be a common law defence to murder if Tony Nicklinson's or Paul Lamb's life was ended deliberately at their request. For four reasons, they rejected this part of their claim.

Nicklinson v Ministry of Justice[12]

Lord Dyson MR

In our view, this submission that the common law should recognise a defence of necessity to apply to certain cases of euthanasia is wholly unsustainable for a variety of reasons....

There is no self-evident reason why [the sanctity of life] should give way to the values of autonomy or dignity and there are cogent reasons why sensible people might properly think that it should not. So the mere fact that there may be rights to autonomy and to be treated with dignity does no more than raise the question whether they should be given priority in circumstances like this; it does not of itself carry the day.

Second ... it is wrong to say that there is a right to commit suicide; section 1 of the 1961 Act can more accurately be described as conferring an immunity from the criminal process for those who actually commit suicide. *A fortiori*, if there is no right to kill yourself, there can be no right, fundamental or otherwise, to require the State to allow others to assist you to die or to kill you....

---

[12] [2013] EWCA Civ 961.

> The third reason is that it is simply not appropriate for the court to fashion a defence of necessity in such a complex and controversial field; this is a matter for Parliament.... Parliament as the conscience of the nation is the appropriate constitutional forum, not judges who might be influenced by their own particular moral perspectives; the judicial process which has to focus on the particular facts and circumstances before the court is not one which is suited to enabling the judges to deal competently with the range of conflicting considerations and procedural requirements which a proper regulation of the field may require; and there is a danger that any particular judicial decision, influenced perhaps by particular sympathy for an individual claimant, may have unforeseen consequences, creating an unfortunate precedent binding in other contexts....
>
> Fourth, as we have already said, any defence provided to those who assist someone to die would have to apply not merely to euthanasia but also to assisted suicide. That immediately raises the question: how can the courts develop a defence to assisted suicide when Parliament has stated in unequivocal terms that it is a serious criminal offence carrying a maximum sentence of 14 years' imprisonment.... If a defence of necessity cannot be fashioned for assisted suicide, it certainly cannot for euthanasia.

In the Supreme Court, the applicants chose not to pursue their argument that the offence of murder, in the absence of a defence of necessity, was incompatible with their Article 8 rights. Their appeal to the Supreme Court focused exclusively on whether the prohibition on assisted suicide, discussed in the following section, was compatible with Article 8 of the Convention. We consider that judgment in Section 2(a)(2)(c). Paul Lamb sought to resurrect his complaint about the illegality of euthanasia before the European Court of Human Rights (ECtHR), but having not pursued this before the Supreme Court, the ECtHR rejected his claim as inadmissible.

(2) Assisted Suicide

At common law, suicide was regarded as self-murder, and was a criminal offence. According to Blackstone's *Commentaries*:

> The suicide is guilty of a double offence; one spiritual, in invading the prerogative of the Almighty, and rushing into his immediate presence uncalled for; the other temporal, against the King, who hath an interest in the preservation of all his subjects.[13]

Obviously, it was only those who had unsuccessfully tried to commit suicide who could actually be prosecuted for their attempted suicide. If the suicide had been successful, it was the relatives of the deceased who would suffer, through the confiscation of property and restrictions upon burial rites.

In 1961, suicide and attempted suicide were decriminalized, for compassionate reasons, by section 1 of the Suicide Act which states that: 'The rule of law whereby it is a crime for a person to commit suicide is hereby abrogated'. The fact that it is not now unlawful to commit, or attempt to commit, suicide does not, however, mean that there is a right to do so. The criminal offences of suicide and attempted suicide were not abolished in order to facilitate ending one's life, but rather to protect already distressed relatives from the imposition of

---

[13] *Commentaries on the Laws of England*, vol IV (1775).

additional hardship, and to ensure that people who had unsuccessfully attempted suicide could seek medical help, without fearing prosecution.

Despite suicide's decriminalization, under section 2(1) of the Suicide Act 1961, assisting another person to commit suicide is a criminal offence punishable by up to 14 years' imprisonment.

Suicide Act 1961 (as amended) section 2

2(1) A person ('D') commits an offence if—

(a) D does an act capable of encouraging or assisting the suicide or attempted suicide of another person, and

(b) D's act was intended to encourage or assist suicide or an attempt at suicide. . . .

(1C) An offence under this section is triable on indictment and a person convicted of such an offence is liable to imprisonment for a term not exceeding 14 years . . .

(4) No proceedings shall be instituted for an offence under this section except by or with the consent of the Director of Public Prosecutions.

While it is unusual for assisting a non-crime to itself be a criminal offence, there are undoubtedly sound public policy reasons for proscribing phony suicide pacts (when one person persuades another to take their own life first, in order to inherit their property), and for criminalizing the disgraceful 'egging on' of people with suicidal thoughts in internet chatrooms. As long ago as 1961, it was recognized that cases of assistance with suicide will vary, and that prosecution will not always be in the public interest; hence, section 2(4) provides that no prosecution can go ahead without the consent of the Director of Public Prosecutions.

Given that a person can commit suicide without committing any criminal offence, what reason would there be for choosing to implicate someone else in one's suicide attempt, and thereby exposing them to potential criminal charges? There are two principal reasons why people might need assistance in committing suicide. First, they may be physically incapable of arranging their own suicide. Secondly, patients may need expert advice on the combination and quantity of drugs needed to achieve a quick and painless death. Simply overdosing on painkillers can lead to a prolonged and agonizing death, or can leave someone alive but profoundly incapacitated.

In recent years, there has been growing pressure on the prohibition of assisted suicide, starting with the case of Dianne Pretty in 2002.[14] Mrs Pretty had been diagnosed with motor neurone disease, a progressive and degenerative terminal illness, during which the sufferer's mental faculties remain sharp while their body fails. Mrs Pretty's husband was willing to help her to commit suicide, but they were anxious that he might be prosecuted under section 2(1) of the Suicide Act 1961.

Because section 2(4) of the Suicide Act specifies that no proceedings can be brought without the consent of the Director of Public Prosecutions (DPP), Mrs Pretty asked the DPP to give an undertaking that he would not consent to Mr Pretty's prosecution. She then sought judicial review of his refusal, on the grounds that it violated her Convention rights, as incorporated in the Human Rights Act 1998.

---

[14] *R (on the application of Pretty) v Director of Public Prosecutions* [2001] UKHL 61; *Pretty v United Kingdom* (2002) 35 EHRR 1.

In *R (on the application of Pretty) v Director of Public Prosecutions*, the House of Lords found that there had been no prima facie violations of any of Mrs Pretty's Convention rights.

R (on the application of Pretty) v Director of Public Prosecutions[15]

Lord Steyn

The Director of Public Prosecutions may not under section 2(4) exercise his discretion to stop all prosecutions under section 2(1). It follows that he may only exercise his discretion, for or against a prosecution, in relation to the circumstances of a specific prosecution. His discretion can therefore only be exercised in respect of past events giving rise to a suspicion that a crime under section 2(1) has been committed. And then the exercise of this discretion will take into account whether there is a realistic prospect of securing a conviction and whether a prosecution would be in the public interest.

Mrs Pretty then appealed to the European Court of Human Rights (ECtHR). In *Pretty v United Kingdom,* the ECtHR was prepared to admit that Article 8 was engaged, but it nevertheless rejected her claim on the grounds that a complete prohibition of assisted suicide was not a disproportionate response to the state's concern to protect vulnerable members of society. Mrs Pretty died 12 days later.

Pretty v United Kingdom[16]

Judgment of the ECtHR

The applicant in this case is prevented by law from exercising her choice to avoid what she considers will be an undignified and distressing end to her life. The Court is not prepared to exclude that this constitutes an interference with her right to respect for private life as guaranteed under Article 8(1) of the Convention.

The law in issue in this case, section 2 of the 1961 Act, was designed to safeguard life by protecting the weak and vulnerable and especially those who are not in a condition to take informed decisions against acts intended to end life or to assist in ending life. Doubtless the condition of terminally ill individuals will vary. But many will be vulnerable and it is the vulnerability of the class which provides the rationale for the law in question. It is primarily for States to assess the risk and the likely incidence of abuse if the general prohibition on assisted suicides were relaxed or if exceptions were to be created. Clear risks of abuse do exist, notwithstanding arguments as to the possibility of safeguards and protective procedures. The Court does not consider therefore that the blanket nature of the ban on assisted suicide is disproportionate.

It was probably inevitable that Mrs Pretty's request for the DPP to issue a 'blank cheque', giving her husband future immunity from prosecution, would fail. If circumstances changed, for example, and Mrs Pretty had a change of heart, it would clearly be unacceptable for her husband to be immune from any future prosecution.

---

[15] [2001] UKHL 61.   [16] (2002) 35 EHRR 1.

(a) Debbie Purdy and the DPP's policy

A few years later Debbie Purdy, who suffered from primary progressive multiple sclerosis, mounted a different sort of argument. She did not ask for future immunity for her husband, Omar Puente, if he were to help her to travel to Switzerland in order to end her life. More modestly, Debbie Purdy argued that she and her husband should be entitled to know what factors the DPP would take into account when deciding whether to prosecute him.

Almost all of the UK citizens who have accessed assisted suicide at Dignitas in Switzerland have been helped by another person. Booking someone's flight; driving her to the airport, or taking her on her final journey could all be instances of assisting suicide. There have been police investigations when family members have returned from Switzerland—adding, inevitably, to the family's grief—but no one has yet faced prosecution.

Debbie Purdy's argument was that the DPP is plainly exercising his discretion not to prosecute in such cases, and that the criteria that are being used to make these decisions should be open and transparent. If the factors relevant to the DPP's decisions about prosecution were to be made public, Ms Purdy and Mr Puente could consider them before deciding whether he would accompany her to Switzerland, if her condition became unbearable. Ms Purdy said that unless she was able to weigh up the likelihood of prosecution in advance, she might have to go to Switzerland earlier than she would like, when she could still make the trip unaided.

At first instance, the court held that it was bound by the decision in *Pretty*, and that Ms Purdy's Article 8 rights were not engaged. Although this was sufficient to dismiss her claim, the court further held that even if her Article 8 rights had been engaged, the interference with them would have been both proportionate and justifiable.

Before Ms Purdy's case was heard by the Court of Appeal, the then DPP, Keir Starmer QC, published a detailed explanation of his decision not to prosecute the parents of Daniel James, a 23-year-old man who had been left paralysed after a rugby accident. Daniel James died at Dignitas in September 2008, accompanied by his parents. Although there was sufficient evidence to prosecute his parents, and a family friend who had booked his air ticket (and who had, in fact, booked a return flight for Daniel in the hope that he might be persuaded to change his mind), the DPP decided that the public interest would not be served by prosecution.[17]

When it handed down its judgment in the *Purdy* case, the Court of Appeal agreed that it was bound by the House of Lords' decision that Dianne Pretty's Article 8 rights were not engaged.[18] It was, however, noteworthy that the Court of Appeal implied that there was ample evidence, not least from the DPP's decision in relation to Daniel James's parents, upon which Debbie Purdy's legal advisers might base advice to her about the likelihood of her husband's prosecution. Without spelling it out explicitly, it was clear that the Court of Appeal thought that Mr Puente was unlikely to face prosecution if he accompanied his wife to Switzerland.

Debbie Purdy then appealed successfully to the House of Lords. In *R (on the application of Purdy) v Director of Public Prosecutions*, its last judgment before it was replaced by the Supreme Court, the House of Lords found that Ms Purdy's Article 8 rights were engaged by the DPP's refusal to give more specific guidance on how he exercised his discretion under section 2(4). The interference with her Article 8 rights could be justifiable under Article 8(2) only if the manner in which the DPP exercised his discretion was accessible and sufficiently

---

[17] 'DPP Decision On Prosecution—The Death by Suicide of Daniel James' (CPS, 2008).
[18] *R (on the application of Purdy) v Director of Public Prosecutions* [2009] EWCA Civ 92.

precise to enable a person to regulate her conduct accordingly. In order to be compliant with Article 8, the Lords agreed that there should be an offence-specific policy identifying the facts and circumstances that the DPP would take into account when deciding whether a prosecution was in the public interest.

The House of Lords also discussed whether section 2(1) of the Suicide Act 1961 applied to suicides that took place outside England and Wales.

R (on the application of Purdy) v Director of Public Prosecutions[19]

Lord Hope

[T]he language of the subsection suggests that it applies to any acts of the kind it describes that are performed within this jurisdiction irrespective of where the final act of suicide is to be committed, and that its application cannot be avoided by arranging for the final act of suicide to be performed on the high seas, for example, or in Scotland. Otherwise it would be all too easy to exclude the vulnerable or the easily led from its protection.

Baroness Hale

[A] major objective of the criminal law is to warn people that if they behave in a way which it prohibits they are liable to prosecution and punishment. People need and are entitled to be warned in advance so that, if they are of a law-abiding persuasion, they can behave accordingly. Hence the problem faced by Ms Purdy, her husband and other people who feel as she does:

> 'I want to avoid the situation where I am too unwell to terminate my life. I want to retain as much autonomy as possible. I want to make a choice about when the quality of my life is no longer adequate and to die a dignified death. The decision is of my own making. Nobody has suggested this to me or pressured me to reach this view. It is a decision that I have come to of my own free will.'

Lord Brown

Obviously no advance undertaking can be sought from the Director of Public Prosecutions that he will refuse consent to a prosecution in a particular case. He could never be sufficiently sure of the precise circumstances of the case and in any event, of course, circumstances can always change. It is perhaps unsurprising that Mrs Pretty's challenge failed at every stage. Surely, however, there can be no similar objection to the Director indicating in advance what will be his general approach towards the exercise of his discretion regarding the prosecution of this most sensitive and distressing class of case. . . .

I have concluded that, with the best will in the world, it is simply impossible to find in the Code [for Crown Prosecutors] itself enough to satisfy the article 8(2) requirements of accessibility and foreseeability in assessing how prosecutorial discretion is likely to be exercised in section 2(1) cases. I had thought at one stage of the argument that, deficient though the Code alone most certainly is, the Director, by publishing his decision in the *James* case, has now done enough to establish that the blanket ban on assisting suicides is being operated 'in accordance with the law'. In the end, however, I am persuaded that this is not so. Although generally helpful, the *James* decision itself, as stated, tends to perpetuate the unreality of

---

[19] [2009] UKHL 45.

attempting to consider the approach to section 2(1) under a Code that is substantially inapplicable to this type of case.

What to my mind is needed is a custom-built policy statement indicating the various factors for and against prosecution, many but not all of which are touched on in the *James* case, factors designed to distinguish between those situations in which, however tempted to assist, the prospective aider and abettor should refrain from doing so, and those situations in which he or she may fairly hope to be, if not commended, at the very least forgiven, rather than condemned, for giving assistance.

Following this decision, the DPP issued an interim offence-specific policy, and after a consultation process, the final policy was published in 2010.

DPP Policy for Prosecutors in Respect of Cases of Encouraging or Assisting Suicide[20]

43. Public interest factors tending in favour of prosecution

A prosecution is more likely to be required if:

- The victim was under 18 years of age.
- The victim did not have the capacity (as defined by the Mental Capacity Act 2005) to reach an informed decision to commit suicide.
- The victim had not reached a voluntary, clear, settled and informed decision to commit suicide.
- The victim had not clearly and unequivocally communicated his or her decision to commit suicide to the suspect.
- The victim did not seek the encouragement or assistance of the suspect personally or on his or her own initiative.
- The suspect was not wholly motivated by compassion; for example, the suspect was motivated by the prospect that he or she or a person closely connected to him or her stood to gain in some way from the death of the victim.
- The suspect pressured the victim to commit suicide.
- The suspect did not take reasonable steps to ensure that any other person had not pressured the victim to commit suicide.
- The suspect had a history of violence or abuse against the victim.
- The victim was physically able to undertake the act that constituted the assistance himself or herself.
- The suspect was unknown to the victim and encouraged or assisted the victim to commit or attempt to commit suicide by providing specific information via, for example, a website or publication.
- The suspect gave encouragement or assistance to more than one victim who were not known to each other.
- The suspect was paid by the victim or those close to the victim for his or her encouragement or assistance.

---

[20] (CPS, 2010).

- The suspect was acting in his or her capacity as a medical doctor, nurse, other healthcare professional, a professional carer (whether for payment or not), or as a person in authority, such as a prison officer, and the victim was in his or her care. **[NB this factor was revised in 2014, see the following section.]**
- The suspect was aware that the victim intended to commit suicide in a public place where it was reasonable to think that members of the public may be present.
- The suspect was acting in his or her capacity as a person involved in the management or as an employee (whether for payment or not) of an organisation or group, a purpose of which is to provide a physical environment (whether for payment or not) in which to allow another to commit suicide.

45. Public interest factors tending against prosecution

A prosecution is less likely to be required if:

- The victim had reached a voluntary, clear, settled and informed decision to commit suicide.
- The suspect was wholly motivated by compassion.
- The actions of the suspect, although sufficient to come within the definition of the crime, were of only minor encouragement or assistance.
- The suspect had sought to dissuade the victim from taking the course of action which resulted in his or her suicide.
- The actions of the suspect may be characterised as reluctant encouragement or assistance in the face of a determined wish on the part of the victim to commit suicide.
- The suspect reported the victim's suicide to the police and fully assisted them in their enquiries into the circumstances of the suicide or the attempt and his or her part in providing encouragement or assistance.

The policy focuses principally on the motive of the suspect, rather than on the condition of the victim(s). In the first case decided under the new policy—involving the deaths of Sir Edward and Lady Downes—the DPP explained that there was sufficient evidence to establish that their son, Mr Downes, had assisted his parents' suicide in Switzerland. He also stood to inherit from his parents. Being 'wholly motivated by compassion' appeared to operate as a trumping factor, however, weighing against prosecution even when a number of the factors in favour were present.

Keir Starmer QC[21]

There is information to suggest that Mr Downes has benefited financially from the death of his parents as a result of their wills. It might be said, as a result, that it is difficult to conclude that he was wholly motivated by compassion in giving his parents the assistance that he did . . . Having reviewed all the available information, we have concluded that this is a case where the only driving force behind Mr Downes' actions was compassion. . . . [W]e are sure that the public interest factors tending against prosecution outweigh those tending in favour.

---

[21] 'DPP Decision on Prosecution: The Death of Sir Edward and Lady Downes' (CPS, 2010).

It is also noteworthy that there is no requirement that the victim is terminally ill, nor that she is suffering unbearably. Instead, the policy operates to excuse—at the prosecutorial discretion stage—the commission of a criminal offence when the motive is wholly compassionate. The DPP's interim policy did originally contain, as a factor against prosecution, that the victim had a terminal illness, a severe and incurable physical illness, or a severe degenerative physical condition, but this was removed following pressure from disability activists. They claimed that including disability as a reason not to prosecute sent a message that their lives were less likely to be worth living.

The condition of the victim is not completely irrelevant, however. Being motivated by compassion will generally mean that relief of the victim's suffering is the suspect's principal reason for helping her to commit suicide. It is also a factor against prosecution that the victim had reached a settled and definite decision to die. If a person's decision to die is settled and definite, it is more likely to be a considered response to her bleak condition and prognosis.

(b) Professional vs Amateur Assisters?

It is noteworthy that several of the factors in favour of prosecution are essentially that the suspect was acting in a professional capacity, especially as a health care professional. This is significant for several reasons. First, there is a tension between this aspect of the policy and its focus on the suspect's motive. Professional assisters are less likely than relatives to have mixed or non-compassionate motives for acting. A professional assister is unlikely to profit from the person's death, for example, and nor will they wish to escape from the burdens of caring for her. In practice, most professional assisters are likely to be motivated solely by compassion.

Secondly, this aspect of the policy has made some health care professionals nervous about how they should react if a patient tells them that they are planning to travel to Dignitas. Might providing a patient with a copy of her medical records to take to Dignitas count as 'assistance', for example? Given that patients have a statutory right of access to their medical records, this is improbable, especially since we know that others who have played a far more active role in assisting relatives' suicides have escaped prosecution. Certainly, the GMC has taken the view that simply providing a patient who wished to have an assisted death with their records would not be sufficient to challenge a doctor's fitness to practise.

General Medical Council[22]

Allegations that will not normally give rise to a question of impaired fitness to practise

22 Some actions related to a person's decision to, or ability to, commit suicide are lawful, or will be too distant from the encouragement or assistance to raise a question about a doctor's fitness to practise. These include but are not limited to:

a. providing advice or information limited to the doctor's understanding of the law relating to encouraging or assisting suicide

b. providing access to a patient's records where a subject access request has been made in accordance with the terms of the Data Protection Act 1998

c. providing information or evidence in the context of legal proceedings relating to encouraging or assisting suicide.

[22] *Guidance for the Investigation Committee and Case Examiners When Considering Allegations About a Doctor's Involvement in Encouraging or Assisting Suicide* (GMC, 2013).

The decision of the DPP in the death of Raymond Cutkelvin suggests that the fact that someone has essentially acted as a professional assister will not necessarily lead to their prosecution. This case involved the pro-legalization campaigner, Dr Michael Irwin, who had been struck off the medical register for providing sleeping pills to a friend in order to help him to end his life. Dr Irwin was a member of Dignitas and had accompanied more than one person to Switzerland. In the case of Raymond Cutkelvin, Dr Irwin had not only accompanied him to Dignitas, but had also helped to pay for his assisted suicide. There were several factors in favour of prosecution, including that Dr Irwin was unknown to Mr Cutkelvin and had previously assisted others. The DPP nevertheless decided that these factors were outweighed by the factors against: Mr Cutkelvin had reached a voluntary, clear, settled, and informed decision to commit suicide, and Dr Irwin had fully assisted the police in their inquiries.[23]

Although this decision suggests that repeat or professional assisters will not necessarily face prosecution, some commentators have argued that it is odd that the policy explicitly favours amateur assisters. As Penney Lewis explains, the consequence could be more distressing assisted deaths.

Penney Lewis[24]

Unlike all of the other jurisdictions which permit assisted suicide (and in the Netherlands and Belgium, euthanasia as well), where the activity is carried out in whole or in part by physicians, the inclusion of these factors will discourage the involvement of healthcare professionals . . . The advantages of open medical involvement are manifold, and include a lower risk of botched suicides and suffering during the suicide or attempted suicide . . . and the possibility of screening for possibly hitherto unknown mental disorders including depression . . . By strongly discouraging medical involvement, the policy places a heavy burden on supportive friends and family . . .

Whether intentionally or not, these factors may keep the number of assisted suicides which take place entirely within the UK relatively low. Travel to a jurisdiction which does permit medical involvement will remain attractive to some, and this may have to be done earlier than the victim would otherwise wish. If travelling to a permissive jurisdiction is not possible, for financial or health reasons, then the burden of assisting the suicide will fall on someone with no experience and no access to relevant information . . . Without this knowledge, and without access to appropriate medications, the policy is likely to result in assisted suicides which are more difficult, less successful and more stressful for the victim and his or her friends and family (including the suspect) than would be the case if medical expertise were permitted in some form.

Clive Seale goes so far as to say the policy represents a halfway house that may be worse than both outright prohibition and permissive regulation.

Clive Seale[25]

Botched suicides assisted by amateurs and ill considered decisions to die by some of the most vulnerable people in society are the likely outcomes of the assisted dying policy of the director of public prosecutions (DPP) . . . It is a hard truth to face, but it takes expertise to achieve a humane assisted death. By ruling out medical involvement, the DPP policy ensures that no such expertise will accumulate.

---

[23] 'The Suicide of Mr Raymond Cutkelvin—Decision on Prosecution', CPS Press Release, 25 June 2010.
[24] 'Informal Legal Change on Assisted Suicide: The Policy for Prosecutors' (2011) 31 Legal Studies 119–34.
[25] 'Do it properly or not at all' (2010) 340 British Medical Journal 1719.

Swiss evidence shows what happens when terminal illness is not required as an essential factor for euthanasia, as in the DPP policy, seemingly because the DPP did not distinguish between disability and terminal illness. Swiss cases entail more women than men, and one in five has no fatal condition but rather, for example, arthritis, osteoporosis, 'general weakness,' blindness, or mental disorders, usually depression. Elderly women who are simply 'tired of life' can be assisted to die. This contrasts with cases in Oregon and the Netherlands, where attempts to regulate assisted dying are better (if not perfect).

To avoid these problems in the United Kingdom, either stick with the current legal ban and prosecute the well intentioned amateurs, or set up a properly regulated system, administered by experts, possibly members of the medical profession. Neither solution is perfect, but the current halfway house is worst of all.

A further problem with the preference for amateur assisters is that it may leave people without willing friends or family in a difficult position. In 2012, a man identified as 'Martin' applied for judicial review of the DPP's policy on the grounds that it did not provide sufficient clarity to someone like him, who did not know anyone who was willing to help him organize his assisted suicide. Martin had suffered a massive stroke in 2008, at the age of 43. As a result, he could not speak and could hardly move, communicating only through tiny movements of his head and eyes, and with the help of a computer that could detect where on the screen he was looking. His wife, who cared for him at home with the help of professional carers, did not agree with his decision to travel to Dignitas and was not prepared to assist him, although she had said that she would want to be there to provide comfort and to say goodbye.

Martin did not have any other family members he could ask, and he was concerned that if he sought assistance from a third party, they would be reluctant to help on the grounds that they might be more likely to face prosecution. Although it raised different issues, Martin's case was joined with that of Tony Nicklinson, discussed earlier. Martin's case was that the DPP's policy was defective because, in contrast to friends and family, there was a lack of clarity over whether a professional assister would face prosecution.

In the Court of Appeal, Lord Judge CJ dissented on Martin's appeal because he thought that the professional assister would only be more likely to face prosecution if he had abused a position of trust. The other judges in the Court of Appeal thought it was not possible to read this qualification into the very clear statement in the policy that acting in a professional capacity is a factor in favour of prosecution. However, the new DPP, Alison Saunders, agreed with Lord Judge CJ's interpretation. As a result, by the time Martin's case reached the Supreme Court, there was a discrepancy between what the policy said and what the DPP thought it should say. In *R (on the application of AM) v Director of Public Prosecutions*, the Supreme Court left it to her to resolve this.

R (on the application of AM) v Director of Public Prosecutions[26]

Lord Sumption

In summary, Lord Judge thought that factor 14 tending in favour of prosecution was concerned only with professionals who abused a position of trust arising from their professional relationship with the patient, for example by bringing undue influence to bear upon him. He thought that it did not extend to a 'professional carer who, with no earlier responsibility

---

[26] [2014] UKSC 38.

for the care of the victim, comes in from outside to help.' He would have regarded it as an 'extraordinary anomaly' that such a person should be more likely to be prosecuted than the family members who brought him in, at any rate if he was not 'profiteering'. This, in Lord Judge's view, was because such a person would be doing no more than (say) the patient's wife would do if she could....

Like Lord Neuberger, I do not think that this is what the Director's published policy says. On its face, it discloses a much more general principle that the professional character of an assister's involvement is in all circumstances a factor tending in favour of prosecution, although one whose weight will vary (like all the listed factors) according to the circumstances.

Nonetheless, in the course of argument, Counsel for the Director accepted, on her specific instructions, that ... Lord Judge's judgment correctly represented her policy. If this is so, and if, as I consider, the published policy as it stands says something different, then it is clear that the Director is bound to resolve the inconsistency one way or the other.

In 2014, the DPP amended the relevant factor in favour of prosecution (paragraph 14), so that it now reads as follows:

14. the suspect was acting in his or her capacity as a medical doctor, nurse, other health-care professional, a professional carer [whether for payment or not], or as a person in authority, such as a prison officer, **and the victim was in his or her care**.[1]

[1] This factor does not apply merely because someone was acting in a capacity described within it: it applies only where there was, in addition, a relationship of care between the suspect and the victims such that it will be necessary to consider whether the suspect may have exerted some influence on the victim.

(c) The Compatibility of section 2(1) with Article 8: R (Nicklinson and Another) v Ministry of Justice

As we saw earlier, once Tony Nicklinson and Paul Lamb's cases reached the Supreme Court, they were concerned with one question only: is section 2(1) of the Suicide Act compatible with Article 8 of the Convention? Nine Supreme Court Justices heard the appeal and, because each of them chose to deliver their own judgment, unpicking the decision is complicated.

To summarize very briefly: the Supreme Court was unanimous that the question of whether the current law on assisted suicide was incompatible with Article 8 lay within the UK's margin of appreciation, and was therefore for the UK to decide. On the case before them, five Justices (Lord Neuberger, Lady Hale, Lord Mance, Lord Kerr, and Lord Wilson) held that the Supreme Court had the constitutional authority to make a declaration that the prohibition on assisted suicide in section 2(1) was incompatible with Article 8. Of those five, Lords Neuberger, Mance, and Wilson declined to grant a declaration of incompatibility in these proceedings, whereas Lady Hale and Lord Kerr would have been prepared to do so.

Four Justices (Lord Clarke, Lord Sumption, Lord Reed, and Lord Hughes) concluded that this case involved the consideration of matters that parliament was better qualified to assess. Of those four, Lords Clarke and Sumption were prepared to countenance the future possibility of a declaration, but only if parliament abdicated its responsibility to consider the issue; whereas Lords Reed and Hughes were of the view that this was purely a matter for parliament.

In short, then, although their reasoning differed, a majority of the Supreme Court was not prepared to grant a declaration of incompatibility at this time.

R (Nicklinson and Another) v Ministry of Justice[27]

Lord Neuberger

The interference with Applicants' article 8 rights is grave, the arguments in favour of the current law are by no means overwhelming, the present official attitude to assisted suicide seems in practice to come close to tolerating it in certain situations, the appeal raises issues similar to those which the courts have determined under the common law, the rational connection between the aim and effect of section 2 is fairly weak, and no compelling reason has been made out for the court simply ceding any jurisdiction to Parliament.

Accordingly ... I am of the view that, provided that the evidence and the arguments justified such a conclusion, we could properly hold that section 2 infringed article 8....

However, I consider that ... it would not be appropriate to grant a declaration of incompatibility at this time. In my opinion, before making such a declaration, we should accord Parliament the opportunity of considering whether to amend section 2 so as to enable Applicants, and, quite possibly others, to be assisted in ending their lives, subject of course to such regulations and other protective features as Parliament thinks appropriate ...

There is a number of reasons which, when taken together, persuade me that it would be institutionally inappropriate at this juncture for a court to declare that section 2 is incompatible with article 8, as opposed to giving Parliament the opportunity to consider the position without a declaration. First, the question whether the provisions of section 2 should be modified raises a difficult, controversial and sensitive issue, with moral and religious dimensions, which undoubtedly justifies a relatively cautious approach from the courts. Secondly, this is not a case ... where the incompatibility is simple to identify and simple to cure: whether, and if so how, to amend section 2 would require much anxious consideration from the legislature; this also suggests that the courts should, as it were, take matters relatively slowly. Thirdly, section 2 has, as mentioned above, been considered on a number of occasions in Parliament, and it is currently due to be debated in the House of Lords in the near future; so this is a case where the legislature is and has been actively considering the issue. Fourthly, less than 13 years ago, the House of Lords in *R (Pretty) v Director of Public Prosecutions* gave Parliament to understand that a declaration of incompatibility in relation to section 2 would be inappropriate ... : a declaration of incompatibility on this appeal would represent an unheralded volte-face ...

Parliament now has the opportunity to address the issue of whether section 2 should be relaxed or modified, and if so how, in the knowledge that, if it is not satisfactorily addressed, there is a real prospect that a further, and successful, application for a declaration of incompatibility may be made....

Before we could uphold the contention that section 2 infringed the article 8 rights of Applicants, we would in my view have to have been satisfied that there was a physically and administratively feasible and robust system whereby Applicants could be assisted to kill themselves, and that the reasonable concerns expressed by the Secretary of State (particularly the concern to protect the weak and vulnerable) were sufficiently met so as to render the absolute ban on suicide disproportionate.

Lord Sumption

The question whether relaxing or qualifying the current absolute prohibition on assisted suicide would involve unacceptable risks to vulnerable people is in my view a classic example of the kind of issue which should be decided by Parliament. There are, I think, three main reasons. The first is that, as I have suggested, the issue involves a choice between two fundamental but mutually inconsistent moral values, upon which there is at present no consensus in our society. Such choices are inherently legislative in nature. The decision cannot fail to be strongly influenced by the decision-makers' personal opinions about the moral case for assisted suicide. This is entirely appropriate if the decision-makers are those who represent the community at large. It is not appropriate for professional judges. The imposition of their personal opinions on matters of this kind would lack all constitutional legitimacy.

Secondly, Parliament has made the relevant choice. It passed the Suicide Act in 1961, and as recently as 2009 amended section 2 without altering the principle. In recent years there have been a number of bills to decriminalise assistance to suicide, at least in part, but none has been passed into law.... Sometimes, parliamentary inaction amounts to a decision not to act. But this is not even an issue on which Parliament has been inactive. So far, there has simply not been enough parliamentary support for a change in the law. The reasons why this is so are irrelevant. That is the current position of the representative body in our constitution....

Third, the parliamentary process is a better way of resolving issues involving controversial and complex questions of fact arising out of moral and social dilemmas. The legislature has access to a fuller range of expert judgment and experience than forensic litigation can possibly provide. It is better able to take account of the interests of groups not represented or not sufficiently represented before the court in resolving what is surely a classic 'polycentric problem'.

Lady Hale

Why then is the present law incompatible? Not because it contains a general prohibition on assisting or encouraging suicide, but because it fails to admit of any exceptions....

The only legitimate aim which has been advanced for this interference [with article 8] is the protection of vulnerable people, those who feel that their lives are worthless or that they are a burden to others and therefore that they ought to end their own lives even though they do not really want to....

Is it then reasonably necessary to prohibit helping *everyone* who might want to end their own lives in order to protect those whom we regard as *vulnerable* to undue pressures to do so? ...

It would not be beyond the wit of a legal system to devise a process for identifying those people, those few people, who should be allowed help to end their own lives. There would be four essential requirements. They would firstly have to have the capacity to make the decision for themselves. They would secondly have to have reached the decision freely without undue influence from any quarter. They would thirdly have had to reach it with full knowledge of their situation, the options available to them, and the consequences of their decision ... And they would fourthly have to be unable, because of physical incapacity or frailty, to put that decision into effect without some help from others. I do not pretend that such cases would always be easy to decide, but the nature of the judgments involved would be no more difficult than those regularly required in the Court of Protection or the Family Division ...

To the extent that the current universal prohibition prevents those who would qualify under such a procedure from securing the help they need, I consider that it is a disproportionate interference with their right to choose the time and manner of their deaths. It goes much further than is necessary to fulfil its stated aim of protecting the vulnerable. It fails to strike a fair balance between the rights of those who have freely chosen to commit suicide but are unable to do so without some assistance and the interests of the community as a whole.

Several aspects of the judgments in *Nicklinson* are worth noting. First, the tone of almost all of the judgments is considerably more sympathetic towards the legalization of assisted suicide than any of the judgments in the cases that have preceded it. Only 12 years earlier, the House of Lords was of the view that Article 8 was not even engaged in Dianne Pretty's case. Now a majority in the Supreme Court not only believed it to be engaged, but appeared to be seriously concerned about whether section 2 of the Suicide Act is compatible with it.

Secondly, there is something curious about declining to make a declaration of incompatibility now, but being prepared to do so should parliament fail to act. All a declaration of incompatibility would do, as Lady Hale and Lord Kerr both pointed out, is invite parliament to consider whether to act. In the next extract, Elizabeth Wicks explains that a declaration of incompatibility certainly does not take the decision away from parliament.

Elizabeth Wicks[28]

[T]he majority approach seems to overlook, misconceive, or misrepresent the consequence of a declaration of incompatibility. The declaration has two elements that would be particularly useful in the context of this case: it is of declaratory effect only and it refers the matter back to Parliament. . . . It is this fact that renders so much of the judicial agonising about whether assisted dying is an issue for the courts or Parliament misguided and unnecessary. The declaration of incompatibility does not take the issue away from Parliament; it relinquishes the issue to it. . . .

Thus, the view of the majority of the Supreme Court judges that a declaration of incompatibility should not be made in relation to the statutory universal offence of assisted suicide, even if it is in the view of the court incompatible with Article 8, undermines the very nature of the HRA [Human Rights Act] scheme of protection for individual rights in domestic law. It ignores the fact that the declaratory power is one expressly granted by Parliament for the very purpose of the courts highlighting to Parliament laws that are incompatible with the Convention rights, and that a declaration does not have any legal effect, refers the issue back to Parliament, and leaves Parliament entirely free to retain the existing law.

Because those Justices who declined to make a declaration now referred to parliament's forthcoming opportunity to act, through debates on the Assisted Dying Bill (see Section 2(a)(2)(e)), and spelled out their willingness to intervene in the future, Mullock argues that, in practice, the majority judgments in *Nicklinson* could have much the same effect as an incompatibility declaration.

Alexandra Mullock[29]

While Lady Hale's and Lord Kerr's judgments seem comparatively radical, particularly in contrast to those colleagues who could see no future scope for challenging the legality of the blanket ban, the consequences of a declaration of incompatibility under section 4(2) HRA are, in fact, rather limited. The powers conferred to the court do no more than indicate to

---

[28] 'The Supreme Court Judgment in *Nicklinson*: One Step Forward on Assisted Dying; Two Steps Back on Human Rights' (2015) 23 Medical Law Review 144–56.

[29] 'The Supreme Court decision in *Nicklinson*: human rights, criminal wrongs and the dilemma of death' (2015) 31 Journal of Professional Negligence 18–28.

Parliament that they *should* review the relevant provision in order to reassess its compatibility with the Convention. . . . [T]he Supreme Court's warning (that a future declaration of incompatibility might follow Parliament's failure to consider this question) has arguably had a similar impact to an actual declaration. As the warning was so timely in the light of the Assisted Dying Bill, Parliament is conveniently presented with the opportunity to do just as Lord Neuberger has requested . . . In spite of the unwillingness of the majority to allow the main appeal, the remarkable judgment in *Nicklinson* distinguishes itself from other end-of-life decisions by strongly directing Parliament to address this issue in order to avoid a future declaration of incompatibility.

(d) Pressure on the status quo

In addition to the very clear signal the Supreme Court has sent to parliament that several of its members might be prepared to issue a declaration of incompatibility in the future, there are several other points of pressure on the status quo.

First, it could be said that the availability of assisted deaths at Dignitas acts as a 'safety valve' for UK citizens, who are able to access lawful assisted suicide provided that they are able and willing to travel to Zurich to do so. If Switzerland were to close this safety valve, there might be considerable pressure to reform the law in the UK, since citizens who might have had a reasonable expectation of being able to access an assisted death would no longer be able to do so.

Secondly, the Swiss option is only available to patients with considerable financial and social resources. In addition to the membership fee and the annual subscription, an assisted death at Dignitas costs around £7,700. That does not include travel and accommodation costs, which in the case of someone who is seriously incapacitated can be substantial. Comparatively few people will therefore be able to afford a Dignitas-assisted death. And it is not just a question of money; for older people who are unfamiliar with the internet, finding out how to join Dignitas may be difficult. Profoundly incapacitated people, like Martin, who do not have willing family or friends may also find it difficult to travel to Zurich unaided.

Thirdly, people seeking an assisted death in Switzerland must be physically fit enough to travel. In the final stages of a disease like cancer, this will often be impossible. As a result, it is not uncommon for people who are scared of what lies ahead of them to seek an assisted death at Dignitas sooner than they would wish, while they are still capable of making the journey. If assisted suicide were to be available in the UK, such individuals could wait until their condition became unbearable. In practice, many of them might never access an assisted death. It is therefore possible that some people who have died in Dignitas would have had longer lives, and experienced natural deaths, if assisted dying was lawful in the UK.

Fourthly, best practice in end-of-life care is to try to facilitate what most patients want, which is often to die in the comfort of their own home. For patients travelling to access an assisted death in Switzerland, not only can they not die at home, but they must die in a foreign country, far away from family, friends, and other sources of support and comfort such as their family doctor or spiritual adviser.

Fifthly, as we see later, there are comparatively few legal safeguards in Switzerland. Not only is the UK exporting assisted suicide, but it is doing so to a country in which the only legal restriction is that the assister's motive must not be selfish. Finally, as Charles Foster has pointed out, however convenient it might be, there is perhaps something dishonest and uncomfortable about outsourcing the 'dirty work' of assisted dying to Switzerland.

Charles Foster[30]

> If Switzerland is happy to continue providing the facility then, however intellectually dishonest it may be to allow her to siphon off all our own English pain, fear, angst and debate, it is likely to do less harm overall than introducing any conceivable assisted suicide law into England.
>
> There are two possible connections between suicide tourism and English policy. The first is the liberalisation of public opinion that comes naturally, if irrationally, with familiarity. And the second is the slowly growing public acknowledgement that there is something intellectually, if not morally, uncomfortable, about getting another country to do your dirty work. While both of these factors no doubt contribute to the DPP's view of whether it is in the public interest to prosecute cases of assisted suicide, and will certainly affect the legislature's view of assisted dying, neither has played any discernable part in the deliberations of English courts.

(e) The (latest) Assisted Dying Bill

There have been several unsuccessful attempts to introduce legislation to legalize assisted dying. The legislatures' hostility (so far) to assisted dying contrasts with the fairly stable and clear majority of the public, who say that they would support legalization, in strictly limited circumstances. A 2015 Populus opinion poll found that 82 per cent of respondents would be in favour of allowing assisted dying for terminally ill patients, provided that rigorous safeguards were in place.[31] While not disputing the apparent existence of a majority of public opinion in favour of assisted dying, Saunders argues that this may be due to the successful media strategy of pro-legalization campaigners and the result of inherent bias in some parts of the media.

Peter Saunders[32]

> Why is public opinion so much out of step with parliament and the institutions? One answer might be that whilst both parliament and the institutions tend to hear both sides of the argument most of the public do not. exposure solely to hard cases and emotive testimonies understandably induces support; and those trying to change the law will always attract more media interest than those working to preserve the status quo. [Dignity in Dying] has therefore built its media strategy around high-profile legal cases, personal interest stories and celebrity endorsement. Finding itself frustratingly blocked by parliament and the institutions it has turned to the courts and to the media in order to build pressure for change.

---

[30] 'Suicide tourism may change attitudes to assisted suicide, but not through the courts' (2015) 41 Journal of Medical Ethics 8.

[31] See further Populus.co.uk. See also Elizabeth Clery, Sheila McLean, and Miranda Phillips, 'Quickening Death: The Euthanasia Debate' in Alison Park, John, Curtice, Katarina Thomson, Miranda Phillips, and Mark Johnson (eds), *British Social Attitudes: The 23rd Report* (Sage: London, 2007).

[32] 'The Role of the Media in Shaping the UK Debate on "Assisted Dying"' (2011) 11 Medical Law International 239–56.

In 2012, the Commission on Assisted Dying, which had been chaired by Lord Falconer, published a report that concluded that the current legal status of assisted suicide was inadequate and incoherent.[33] With one dissenting voice, the Commission was of the view that it would be possible to devise a legal framework to protect potentially vulnerable people. Because it had received funding and support from people and organizations known to be in favour of legalization, the Commission's report was dismissed by some commentators, who questioned its claim to be independent.

The Commission's report led directly to the drafting of the latest Assisted Dying Bill, first introduced into the House of Lords by Lord Falconer in 2014. The Bill's progress was halted by the 2015 general election, and it was reintroduced into the Commons by Rob Marris MP.

Assisted Dying Bill 2015

1(1) Subject to the consent of the High Court (Family Division) pursuant to subsection (2), a person who is terminally ill may request and lawfully be provided with assistance to end his or her own life.

(2) Subsection (1) applies only if the High Court (Family Division), by order, confirms that it is satisfied that the person—

(a) has a voluntary, clear, settled and informed wish to end his or her own life;

(b) has made a declaration to that effect in accordance with section 3; and

(c) on the day the declaration is made—

(i) is aged 18 or over;

(ii) has the capacity to make the decision to end his or her own life; and

(iii) has been ordinarily resident in England and Wales for not less than one year.

(3) Upon receiving an application by the person, the High Court shall dispose of it within 14 days or as soon as reasonably practicable thereafter.

Under section 3, two doctors, who must be completely independent of each other, must separately examine the patient and her medical records, and each of them must independently be satisfied that the person is terminally ill; has the capacity to make the decision to end their own life; and 'has a clear and settled intention to end their own life which has been reached voluntarily, on an informed basis and without coercion or duress'. They must also be satisfied that the person seeking an assisted suicide 'has been fully informed of the palliative, hospice and other care which is available to that person'.

Terminal illness is defined in section 2 as 'an inevitably progressive condition which cannot be reversed by treatment', and 'as a consequence of that terminal illness, [the person] is reasonably expected to die within six months'. As Alexandra Mullock points out, some difficult questions of interpretation would remain: for example, if a patient exercises her right to refuse treatment that could reverse her condition, perhaps because the side effects are intolerable, would that make her ineligible for assisted dying?

---

[33] Commission on Assisted Dying, 'The Current Legal Status of Assisted Dying is Inadequate and Incoherent . . .' (Demos: London, 2011).

Alexandra Mullock[34]

> The bill goes on to explain in clause 2(2) that treatment that only temporarily relieves the symptoms of the inevitably progressive condition, without offering any reversal of that condition, is not to be regarded as a treatment which can reverse the condition. . . . Until science delivers immortality, even the most profoundly restorative treatment can serve only as a temporary prelude to death, and so questions of interpretation will be challenging. Moreover, a mentally competent adult has an inviolable right to refuse even life-sustaining treatment. Thus, the question of whether a patient who has refused a treatment (that might reverse or suspend the condition) is permitted to die via PAS [physician-assisted suicide] will be an obvious dilemma.

The Bill also illustrates neatly that there may be a tension between what is politically feasible, in terms of a change in the law, and what is intellectually defensible. Because public opinion surveys suggest that there is considerable support for legalized assisted dying for the terminally ill, confining access to the terminally ill might seem pragmatically sensible. On the other hand, we know that doctors' predictions of life expectancy are insufficiently accurate for 'having less than six months to live' to operate as a clear and precise boundary between those who should and those who should not have access to assisted dying.

In addition, unbearable suffering is not confined to those who are imminently dying, and it might even be argued that someone with longer to live will experience more suffering, in quantitative terms, than someone whose death is expected within days. Certainly three of the most vocal campaigners for assisted dying in recent years—Debbie Purdy, Tony Nicklinson, and Terry Pratchett—would not have been eligible for assistance under the Assisted Dying Bill. As Samantha Halliday explains, the 'terminal illness' restriction fails to capture the reason why people might seek assisted dying, which is not because they expect to die within six months, but because their suffering is unbearable and untreatable.

Samantha Halliday[35]

> The Bill's restrictive use of 'terminal illness' as a qualifying condition is nothing more than an artificial restriction upon assisted dying, which does not reflect any principled standpoint. It is merely a device intended to make the Bill appear more restrictive and thus more palatable, however, the illusion of control does not equate with true control. A more principled approach demands that access be provided to those suffering unbearably without prospect of improvement with robust safeguards to ensure assisted dying remains a last resort.

The competency requirement might appear less problematic: at first sight it seems obvious that anyone making such a profoundly important and final decision should have the capacity to do so. In practice, however, it might have unintended consequences. If mental capacity is a prerequisite, someone with a progressive, degenerative condition, who knows that they are likely to lose capacity at some point in the future, might opt for an assisted death earlier than they would like, fearing that if they leave it too long, they might lose capacity and become ineligible.

---

[34] 'The Assisted Dying Bill and the role of the physician' (2015) 41 Journal of Medical Ethics 621–4.
[35] 'Comparative reflections upon the Assisted Dying Bill 2013: a plea for a more European approach' (2013) 13 Medical Law International 135–67.

The proposal to legalize only assisted suicide (and not euthanasia) would also rule out access to assisted dying for patients who are incapable of completing the final act themselves. It might also create difficulties where the patient fails to ingest the whole lethal dose. If the patient is unable to swallow it all, or vomits, unless a doctor can take steps to end the patient's life, the patient might be left in a worse state than they were before.

In any event, in September 2015, the Assisted Dying Bill was defeated in the House of Commons by 330 votes to 118. Given his involvement in the formulation of the CPS policy on assisted suicide, it is interesting to note Keir Starmer MP's contribution to the debate.

Keir Starmer MP[36]

My experience is that there are two inherent limitations in the guidelines that I issued. . . . The first limitation is that, as a result, those who have reached a voluntary, clear, settled and informed decision to end their lives can now be confident of the compassionate assistance of loved ones without exposing them to the law, but they cannot have the assistance of professionals. They can have amateur assistance from nearest and dearest, but they cannot have professional help in fulfilling their desire unless they have the means and the physical ability to get to Dignitas. . . .

I understand those who say that we should revert to a position where nobody should be given any assistance at all, but we have arrived at a position where compassionate, amateur assistance from nearest and dearest is accepted but professional medical assistance is not, unless someone has the means and physical assistance to get to Dignitas. That to my mind is an injustice that we have trapped within our current arrangement.

On the second limitation in my guidelines, the only safeguard I could put into them was a requirement for an after-the-event investigation by the police into what had happened. Let me quote what the president of the Supreme Court said when he analysed that. This is what our most senior judge—not me—said:

'A system whereby a judge or other independent assessor is satisfied in advance that someone has a voluntary, clear, settled and informed wish to die and for his or her suicide then to be organised in an open and professional way would . . . provide greater and more satisfactory protection for the vulnerable, than a system which involves a lawyer from the DPP's office inquiring, after the event, whether the person who had killed himself or herself had such a wish'.

Opponents of the Bill, such as Liam Fox MP, were concerned with the slippery slope and the impact of legalization upon the vulnerable.

Liam Fox MP[37]

There is also a fundamental change in the doctors' relationship with patients. The No. 1 rule is 'Do no harm'. If a patient arrives unconscious or in a coma, their family needs to know—as the patient themselves would want to know—that the doctor will do them no harm and will not come under any pressure to do so for one reason or another. . . .

[36] Hansard 11 September 2015, col 674. [37] Hansard 11 September 2015, cols 679–80.

It was noted earlier that people feeling that they are a burden when making a decision to end their lives prematurely is only one factor, but that is one reason too many. The answer is not to make it easier to kill people; we need societal change to prevent people from feeling a burden in their elderly years. . . .

In practice it is impossible to differentiate between assisted dying and euthanasia. If we have one, because of the failures of process we will inevitably get the other. I do not believe that that is an improvement to our society. However well-meaning the proponents of this Bill may be, they will open a Pandora's box that will fundamentally change who we are, how we are as a society, and how we relate to the medical profession.

(3) Palliative Care that May Hasten Death: The Doctrine of Double Effect

Recall that in his summing up to the jury in *R v Cox*,[38] Ognall J said that there 'can be no doubt' that doctors are entitled to administer painkilling drugs, notwithstanding the fact that they may simultaneously hasten the moment of death. And it does appear to be an accepted and well-established principle of law that it can be lawful to administer painkilling or sedative drugs which might also 'hasten death' or 'shorten life'. In *Airedale NHS Trust v Bland*,[39] a case we consider later, Lord Goff referred to 'the established rule that a doctor may, when caring for a patient who is, for example, dying of cancer, lawfully administer painkilling drugs despite the fact that he knows that an incidental effect of that application will be to abbreviate the patient's life'.

This principle is the doctrine of double effect, which has its origins in Roman Catholic moral theology, and distinguishes between results that are intended and results that are foreseen as likely, but unintended, consequences of one's actions. So a doctor might give a patient a very large dose of an opioid drug, like diamorphine, in order to relieve her pain, even if this might shorten the patient's life.

Many palliative care specialists would challenge the idea that proper pain management could ever result in a patient's death. Nevertheless, according to the doctrine of double effect, a doctor who intends a good consequence (relieving pain) would not be guilty of murder just because she foresees, but does not intend, a bad consequence (death). But, while the doctrine of double effect may make sense when a procedure, such as surgery, carries a small risk to the patient's life, which is nevertheless worth taking in order to attempt to improve the patient's condition, in the context of palliative care, it has been invoked to excuse conduct where death is very likely indeed.

Despite its widespread acceptance, the doctrine of double effect may be at odds with ordinary principles of criminal law. To be guilty of murder, the patient's death does not have to be the sole purpose of the defendant's action. Instead, as we can see from the following quote from Lord Steyn's judgment in *R v Woollin*, the criminal law is clear that the jury may infer that a person has the requisite *mens rea* for murder if they engage in conduct which is virtually certain to cause death, even if this is not their primary purpose.

---

[38] (1992) 12 BMLR 38.   [39] [1993] AC 789.

R v Woollin[40]

Lord Steyn

Where a man realises that it is for all practical purposes inevitable that his actions will result in death or serious harm, the inference may be irresistible that he intended that result, however little he may have desired or wished it to happen.

In the next extract, Glanville Williams draws attention to the apparent discrepancy between the ordinary meaning of intention in the criminal law and the doctrine of double effect.

Glanville Williams[41]

There is no legal difference between desiring or intending a consequence as following from your conduct, and persisting in your conduct with a knowledge that the consequence will inevitably follow from it, though not desiring that consequence. When a result is foreseen as certain, it is the same as if it were desired or intended.

It is, however, worth noting that Lord Steyn in *Woollin* does not go so far as to say that where death is inevitable, the inference must be irresistible that he intended that result: rather, he merely suggests that in such cases the inference *may* be irresistible. Plainly, although Lord Steyn envisages that there will be times when intention may be inferred from the inevitability of death, by implication there could also be times when this may not be the case, and an example might plausibly be the provision of proper palliative care.

Regardless of the precise meaning of intention within the criminal law, when a doctor foresees that the dose of analgesics or sedatives that she is about to give to a particular patient may cause her death, she must have reached the conclusion that death has become an acceptable outcome. If a doctor were to give a healthy patient with a mild headache a life-threatening injection of diamorphine, her conduct would not be excused by the doctrine of double effect. She could not claim that her intention was merely to relieve pain, and that the patient's death was a foreseen but unintended side effect. Instead, while death may not be the principal purpose of a doctor who administers a potentially lethal dose of opioids, she must have decided that the patient's interest in pain relief now outweighs her interest in continued life.

In the next extract, Glanville Williams suggests that it is artificial for doctors to think only about one consequence of their action (relieving pain), while ignoring another (causing death).

Glanville Williams[42]

It is altogether too artificial to say that a doctor who gives an overdose of a narcotic having in the forefront of his mind the aim of ending his patient's existence is guilty of sin, while a doctor who gives the same overdose in the same circumstances in order to relieve pain is not guilty of sin, provided that he keeps his mind steadily off the consequence which his professional training teaches him is inevitable, namely the death of his patient. When you

---

[40] [1999] 1 AC 82 (HL).
[41] *Sanctity of Life and the Criminal Law* (Faber: London, 1957) 286.   [42] Ibid, 286.

> know that your conduct will have two consequences, one in itself good and one in itself evil, you are compelled as a moral agent to choose between acting and not acting by making a judgement of value, that is to say by deciding whether the good is more to be desired than the evil is to be avoided.

Stephen Wilkinson points out a further difficulty with the doctrine of double effect, namely that it relies upon knowledge of the doctor's primary intention.

Stephen Wilkinson[43]

> But *how do we know* what is intended and what is not? This question can arise from two different perspectives. First, from the 'first person' perspective, if a doctor administers diamorphine to relieve pain, but at the same time would be glad if the patient's death was hastened . . . , she may not be sure herself which effects she intends and which she doesn't. Second, from the 'third person' perspective, how are other professionals, relatives and the public to know what was going on 'in the doctor's head' when she administered the drug? How are they to know what she intends? This problem may render the doctrine unworkable in practice. Furthermore, it also opens up the possibility of health carers abusing the doctrine and using it as a way of 'smuggling in euthanasia by the back door'. In other words, the acceptance of the doctrine might make it possible to kill patients intentionally while *pretending* that their death is an unintended side-effect.

On the other hand, in the next extract, Douglas et al draw upon their interviews with clinicians to suggest that a degree of ambiguity in relation to what is intended may be helpful for doctors.

Charles Douglas, Ian Kerridge, and Rachel Ankeny[44]

> The most striking feature of these interviews is a sense of uncertainty and ambiguity with regard to intention . . . As almost all the respondents stated in one way or another, there is a 'grey area', where the intention is not explicitly to hasten death, but is no longer merely to palliate . . . Instead of always expressing discomfort or even displaying equanimity about the dual effects of AS [analgesics and sedatives], there was often a sense that the possibility of a double effect was a good thing, that both outcomes (an expedited death and relief of suffering) were desirable, but that only one needed to be the apparent intention.

In a similar vein, Alexander McCall Smith argues that we should be slow to deny doctors the 'comfort' they may gain from framing their actions in terms of helping, rather than killing.

---

[43] 'Palliative Care and the Doctrine of Double Effect' in Donna Dickenson, Malcolm Johnson, and Jeanne Samson Katz (eds), *Death, Dying and Bereavement*, 2nd edn (Sage: London, 2000) 299–302.

[44] 'Managing intentions: the end-of-life administration of analgesics and sedatives, and the possibility of slow euthanasia' (2008) 22 Bioethics 388–96.

Alexander McCall Smith[45]

Doctors know full well what they are doing when they increase a dose of diamorphine, but they need not describe their act, to themselves or to others as an act of killing. This approach has been described as hypocritical, but if it accords with a moral distinction which is meaningful for doctors, then why should they be denied the comfort it affords them?

Provided the drugs that caused a patient's death could plausibly be used as painkillers or sedatives, it would in practice be difficult to disprove a doctor's assertion that her principal aim was the relief of suffering. Hence, in *R v Adams*, it was possible for Dr Adams to argue that he had intended to relieve Mrs Morrell's pain by administering massive doses of morphine and diamorphine. In his summing up to the jury, Devlin J explained the doctrine of double effect.

R v Adams[46]

Devlin J

If the first purpose of medicine, the restoration of health, can no longer be achieved, there is still much for a doctor to do, and he is entitled to do all that is proper and necessary to relieve pain and suffering, even if the measures he takes may incidentally shorten life.

Many years after Dr Adams's acquittal for murder, Patrick Devlin, the judge in the case, wrote a book about the issues it had raised. In *Easing the Passing*, he explained how fine the line can be between lawful palliative care and murder.

Patrick Devlin[47]

If he really had an honest belief in easing suffering, Dr. Adams was on the right side of the law; if his purpose was simply to finish life, he was not . . . A narrow distinction. But in the law, as in all matters of principle, cases can be so close to each other that the gap can only be perceived theoretically.

In contrast, in *R v Cox*,[48] Dr Cox's use of potassium chloride (which has no analgesic properties) effectively ruled out the application of the doctrine of double effect. If Dr Cox had used morphine rather than potassium chloride to kill Lillian Boyes, he might plausibly have been able to argue that his primary intention was to relieve her suffering.

In addition to the administration of large, and potentially fatal, doses of analgesic drugs, palliative care can also involve the use of sedation. The distress caused by being unable to breathe or swallow may be relieved by sedatives, which can usually be titrated until a dosage is found that makes the patient comfortable. It has, however, been said

---

[45] 'Euthanasia: The Strengths of the Middle Ground' (1999) 7 Medical Law Review 194–207.
[46] Unreported, 8 April 1957.
[47] *Easing the Passing: The Trial of Doctor John Bodkin Adams* (Bodley Head: London, 1985).
[48] (1992) 12 BMLR 38.

that it could be lawful to sedate someone into unconsciousness, at which point—if they are not going to recover—the artificial nutrition and hydration which is keeping them alive might be removed, leading inevitably to the patient's death. It is not clear that this happens in practice in the UK—indeed many palliative care specialists are adamant that it does not—but, provided the principal purpose of giving the sedatives is to relieve pain and suffering, this might be lawful palliative care, justified by the doctrine of double effect.

From the patient's perspective, as Margaret Pabst Battin explains, 'terminal sedation' may be indistinguishable from being given a lethal injection.

Margaret Pabst Battin[49]

> Pain is not yet a 'thing of the past', nor are many associated kinds of physical distress. Some kinds of conditions, such as difficulty in swallowing, are still difficult to relieve without introducing other discomforting limitations. . . . Severe respiratory insufficiency may mean . . . 'a singularly terrifying and agonizing final few hours'.
>
> [O]f course, the patient can be sedated into unconsciousness; this does indeed end the pain. But in respect of the patient's experience, this is tantamount to causing death: the patient has no further conscious experience and thus can achieve no goods, experience no significant communication, satisfy no goals. Furthermore, adequate sedation, by depressing respiratory function, may hasten death. Thus, although it is always technically possible to achieve relief from pain, at least when the appropriate resources are available, the price may be functionally and practically equivalent, at least from the patient's point of view, to death.

A scenario that tests the limits of the doctrine of double effect to, or even perhaps beyond, breaking point is the use of muscle relaxants to stop the distressing gasping noise, sometimes referred to as 'agonal gasping', that is not uncommon immediately before death, and which can be very upsetting for relatives. A muscle relaxant will prevent the gasping noise, but only because it stops the patient's breathing. The dying person has by this stage lost consciousness and will be unaware that their life has been shortened by seconds or minutes. The muscle relaxant is not given to reduce their pain or suffering, because—despite the gasping sounds—by this stage there is none. Instead, as Govert den Hartogh explains, the muscle relaxant is given for the benefit of relatives, so that their loved one's death is as peaceful as possible.

Govert den Hartogh[50]

> Gasping is a normal phenomenon in all dying patients. It is the result of a beginning failure of the respiratory function, and hence by itself not a sign of suffering. . . . [A]t the stage of profound hypoxaemia which is also indicated to exist by the very phenomenon of gasping, it is unlikely that the dying person has any remnants of consciousness. . . . The standard view therefore is that gasping by itself is not a proper indication for the use of muscle relaxants.

---

[49] *The Least Worst Death: Essays in Bioethics on the End of Life* (OUP: Oxford, 1994).
[50] 'Comforting the parents by administering neuromuscular blockers to the dying child: a conflict between ethics and law?' (2014) 31 Journal of Applied Philosophy 91–103.

And from the descriptions we have of the practice it seems clear that the actual aim of this use . . . is not to alleviate any supposed suffering of the dying person, but to relieve or prevent the distress of her relatives.

Where a newborn baby is close to death, it is easy to see why a doctor might want to make her death as peaceful as possible for the benefit of her parents. A few years ago, Michael Munro, a neonatologist, who had given a muscle relaxant (in this case, pancuronium) to two dying babies had had his fitness to practise challenged by the GMC. Dr Munro told the fitness to practise panel that the parents 'were utterly distraught':

If you put yourself in their shoes, they have already said their last goodbyes to their baby, then suddenly there are these massive, racking agonal gasps that appeared to build up—they were utterly, utterly distraught. The parents were in tears, saying things like 'I can't take any more.' I took the decision then to administer pancuronium. I explained to the parents that this drug was to be used to ease the suffering but that one of the consequences of its use may be to hasten death. They were happy with that.[51]

Michael Munro was cleared of malpractice by the GMC fitness to practise panel. In the next extract, Anne Morris suggests that, as a result, the panel effectively condoned unlawful behaviour.

Anne Morris[52]

There is a good argument for saying that a doctor who cares about his patients as much as Dr Munro should not be punished. It is also arguable that he poses no threat to patients or public. Nevertheless, he admitted doing something which, on the face of it, could have led to criminal charges. Of course, a jury faced with the desperately sad facts in these cases might not have convicted. But that is evidence of the public attitude to what is acceptable treatment at the end of life. Sympathy for the doctor, parents and patients does not alter the law . . . [T]he failure of the GMC even to warn Dr Munro as to his future practice seems to invite the criticism that the profession is condoning (legally) questionable practice.

(4) Withdrawing and Withholding Life-Prolonging Treatment

(a) Contemporaneous refusal

As we saw in Chapter 5, competent adult patients have the right to refuse medical treatment, even if this refusal will result in their death. Although this right is not absolute, there are very few exceptions.[53] For the purposes of this chapter, the important point, as Lord Mustill explained in *Airedale NHS Trust v Bland*, is that doctors must comply with a competent adult's refusal of life-sustaining medical treatment.

---

[51] Owen Dyer, 'Doctor cleared of act "tantamount to euthanasia"' (2007) 335 British Medical Journal 67.

[52] 'Fitness to practise and the ethics of decision-making at the end of life: Dr Michael Munro' (2007) 23 Professional Negligence 228.

[53] An example would be s 63 of the Mental Health Act 1983, see further Chapter 6.

Airedale NHS Trust v Bland[54]

Lord Mustill

If the patient is capable of making a decision on whether to permit treatment and decides not to permit it his choice must be obeyed, even if on any objective view it is contrary to his best interests. A doctor has no right to proceed in the face of objection, even if it is plain to all, including the patient, that adverse consequences and even death will or may ensue.

Similarly, the British Medical Association's (BMA's) guidance to doctors explains that where a patient is competent, her right to refuse life-sustaining medical treatment must take priority over the doctors' duty to preserve life.

British Medical Association[55]

It is well established in law and ethics that competent adults have the right to refuse any medical treatment, even if that refusal results in their death. Patients are not obliged to justify their decisions but the health team usually wish to discuss the refusal with them in order to ensure that they have based their decisions on accurate information and to correct any misunderstandings. . . .

Health professionals can find it very difficult when a patient with capacity refuses treatment that they believe would provide a reasonable degree of recovery. While they may discuss their concern with patients, they must not put pressure on them to accept treatment. Ultimately the decision of whether to accept or reject the treatment offered rests with the patient.

One of the clearest illustrations of the robustness of the law's protection of a competent patient's right to insist on the withdrawal of life-prolonging medical treatment is *Re B (Adult: Refusal of Treatment)*. Ms B was tetraplegic, suffering complete paralysis from the neck down. She had respiratory problems, and was connected to a ventilator. She had repeatedly requested that she be removed from the ventilator, but the clinicians treating her were reluctant to comply with her wishes. Ms B sought, and was granted, a declaration that she had mental capacity and that, as a result, the doctors working for the NHS trust had been treating her unlawfully.

Re B (Adult: Refusal of Treatment)[56]

Dame Elizabeth Butler-Sloss P

Unless the gravity of the illness has affected the patient's capacity, a seriously disabled patient has the same rights as the fit person to respect for personal autonomy. There is a serious danger, exemplified in this case, of a benevolent paternalism which does not embrace recognition of the personal autonomy of the severely disabled patient. I do not

---

[54] [1993] AC 789.

[55] *Withholding and Withdrawing Life-Prolonging Medical Treatment: Guidance for Decision Making*, 3rd edn (BMA, 2007) para 25.5.

[56] [2002] EWHC 429 (Fam).

consider that either the lack of experience in a spinal rehabilitation unit and thereafter in the community or the unusual situation of being in an ICU for a year has had the effect of eroding Ms B's mental capacity to any degree whatsoever.

I am therefore entirely satisfied that Ms B is competent to make all relevant decisions about her medical treatment including the decision whether to seek to withdraw from artificial ventilation. Her mental competence is commensurate with the gravity of the decision she may wish to make. . . . I would like to add how impressed I am with her as a person, with the great courage, strength of will and determination she has shown in the last year, with her sense of humour, and her understanding of the dilemma she has posed to the Hospital. She is clearly a splendid person and it is tragic that someone of her ability has been struck down so cruelly. I hope she will forgive me for saying, diffidently, that if she did reconsider her decision, she would have a lot to offer the community at large.

In the light of my decision that the Claimant has mental capacity and has had such capacity since August 2001 I shall be prepared to grant the appropriate declarations. I also find that the Claimant has been treated unlawfully by the Trust since August.

It is worth noting that, despite the finding that they had been treating her unlawfully, the clinicians who had been caring for Ms B were not forced to participate in bringing about her death. Ms B was transferred to another hospital where she was removed from the artificial ventilator and died. I shall return to the significance of this later.

As we saw in Chapter 5, the competent patient's reasons for refusing treatment are irrelevant. As Lord Donaldson MR said in *Re T (Adult: Refusal of Treatment)*:[57] 'the patient's right of choice exists whether the reasons for making that choice are rational, irrational, unknown or even non-existent'. So, even if a patient refuses medical treatment *because* she wants to die, the doctor is still bound to comply with her wishes.

In *King's College NHS Foundation Trust v C*[58] a case we considered in Chapter 15, C, who had suffered kidney damage after taking an overdose, wished to refuse dialysis, even though she understood that this would lead to her death. Indeed, C was clear she did not want to go on living if this meant that she could no longer enjoy her previous 'sparkly' lifestyle, in which her appearance, material possessions, men, and alcohol had been especially important to her. Macdonald J held that she had capacity, and, as a result, she therefore had the right to refuse dialysis. C died two weeks later.

King's College NHS Foundation Trust v C[59]

MacDonald J

The decision C has reached to refuse dialysis can be characterised as an unwise one. That C considers that the prospect of growing old, the fear of living with fewer material possessions and the fear that she has lost, and will not regain, 'her sparkle' outweighs a prognosis that signals continued life will alarm and possibly horrify many, although I am satisfied that the ongoing discomfort of treatment, the fear of chronic illness and the fear of lifelong treatment and lifelong disability are factors that also weigh heavily in the balance for C. C's decision is certainly one that does not accord with the expectations of many in society. Indeed, others in society may consider C's decision to be unreasonable, illogical or even immoral within the context of the sanctity accorded to life by society in general. None of this however is evidence of a lack of capacity. The court being satisfied that, in accordance with the provisions of the Mental Capacity Act 2005, C has capacity to decide whether or not to accept treatment C is entitled to make her own decision on that question based on the things that are important to her, in keeping with her own personality and system of values and without conforming to society's expectation of what constitutes the 'normal' decision in this situation (if such a thing exists). As a capacitous individual C is, in respect of her own body and mind, sovereign.

If a doctor removes a feeding tube or a mechanical ventilator from a patient knowing that this is a course of conduct that will lead to the patient's death, could she satisfy both the *actus reus* and the *mens rea* of murder? If the withdrawal of medical treatment is an act done with the knowledge that it will cause the patient's death, then the patient's consent to the doctor's action is irrelevant, and the doctor might be guilty of murder. In order to avoid this conclusion, the withdrawal of life-prolonging medical treatment is described as an omission rather than an action.

It is possible to commit murder by omission, however, but only if the defendant was under a duty to act: an obvious example being a mother whose failure to feed her baby causes his death. Doctors are, of course, under a duty to care for their patients, so in theory, if a doctor's failure to provide medical treatment to a patient results in her death, a charge of murder is possible. Does this mean that doctors who respect their patients' refusals of life-sustaining treatment are potentially subject to prosecution for murder?

Almost certainly not. Because the patient's right to refuse unwanted intervention suspends the doctor's duty to provide medical treatment, the doctor's omission can no longer constitute the *actus reus* of murder. A doctor who maliciously unplugs the ventilator from a patient who is temporarily unconscious, but expected to make a full recovery, may be guilty of murder because she had a duty to provide life-prolonging treatment. In contrast, a doctor who respects a competent patient's refusal of further life-sustaining treatment no longer has a duty to provide that treatment—on the contrary, her duty is to comply with the patient's wishes—and she therefore acts lawfully by removing life support from the patient.

A further reason for treating the withdrawal of life support as an omission is that not starting life-sustaining treatment in the first place is plainly an omission, rather than an action. If doctors could be guilty of murder if they withdraw life-support, but not if they fail to initiate it, there would be a powerful incentive to withhold such treatment from patients altogether, which would clearly be undesirable.

The description of the removal of mechanical ventilation or an artificial feeding tube as an omission is, nevertheless, controversial.

Ian Kennedy[60]

[T]o describe turning off the machine as an omission does some considerable violence to the ordinary English usage. It represents an attempt to solve the problem by logic chopping. Such an approach may demonstrate to the satisfaction of some that no crime is involved, but it is surely most unsatisfactory to rest the response of the law to what is seen as a testing moral and philosophical issue on some semantic sleight of hand.

---

[60] *Treat Me Right: Essays in Medical Law and Ethics* (Clarendon Press: Oxford, 1998) 351.

Further evidence that it may be inappropriate, albeit convenient, to describe the withdrawal of life-prolonging treatment as an omission comes from the suggestion that doctors' conscientious objections to treatment withdrawal should be respected. The BMA's guidance to doctors, for example, states that: 'People who have a conscientious objection to withholding or withdrawing life-prolonging treatment should, wherever possible, be permitted to hand over care of the patient to a colleague'.[61]

As we saw earlier, the doctors who had been caring for Ms B were permitted to refuse to participate in the removal of the ventilator that was keeping her alive. Since it is hard to see how a doctor could have a conscientious objection to refraining from assaulting someone, it is surely more plausible to admit that doctors whose consciences prompt them to refuse to participate in the withdrawal of life-prolonging treatment are unwilling to act deliberately to cause their patients' deaths. As Dame Elizabeth Butler-Sloss P explained, this was certainly the perspective of the treating clinicians in *Re B (Adult: Refusal of Medical Treatment)*.

Re B (Adult: Refusal of Medical Treatment)[62]

Dame Elizabeth Butler-Sloss P

[Dr C] had studied and spent her professional life trying to do her best to improve and preserve life. She did not feel able to agree with simply switching off Ms B's ventilation. She would not be able to do it. She felt she was being asked to kill Ms B. . . .

They considered her to be competent to make decisions about her medical treatment. They could not, however, bring themselves to contemplate that they should be part of bringing Ms B's life to an end by the dramatic, (my word), step of turning off the ventilator. As I listened to the evidence of each of them I had the greatest possible sympathy for their position.

While lawyers may defend doctors' actions in withdrawing life support by pointing out the legal significance of the difference between acts and omissions, doctors are more likely to justify their conduct by drawing a distinction between 'killing' and 'letting die'. So a doctor who withdraws life support does not kill, she merely lets the patient die. This explanation undoubtedly has intuitive appeal, perhaps because we instinctively feel that acting deliberately to end someone's life is more reprehensible than letting her die.

In the next extract, Andrew McGee argues that there is also an important causal difference between euthanasia and treatment withdrawal.

Andrew McGee[63]

[I]n the case of withdrawal, the principle of the inviolability of life remains undisturbed. In withdrawal, we are not taking control of death in the way we do in the practice of euthanasia, because the issue in withdrawal is when we should stop artificially prolonging life and allow nature to take its course—to stop deferring what, at some point, is inevitable. In euthanasia, by contrast, we anticipate nature and override it by bringing about the patient's death before its time.

---

[61] *Withholding and Withdrawing Life-Prolonging Medical Treatment: Guidance for Decision Making*, 3rd edn (BMA, 2007) para 16.2.

[62] [2002] 1 FLR 1090.

[63] Finding a Way through the Ethic and Legal Maze: Withdrawal of Medical Treatment and Euthanasia' (2005) 13 Medical Law Review 357–85.

In contrast, Dan Brock argues that is not the simple fact that a doctor lets someone die that makes their act excusable: rather, it is the surrounding circumstances—such as the patient's request and their intolerable distress—that justify the doctor's conduct.

Dan W Brock[64]

Consider the case of a patient terminally ill with ALS [Amyotrophic Lateral Sclerosis] disease. She is completely respirator dependent with no hope of ever being weaned. She is unquestionably competent and persistently requests to be removed from the respirator and allowed to die. Most people and physicians would agree that the patient's physician should respect the patient's wishes and remove her from the respirator, though this will certainly cause the patient's death. . . .

Suppose the patient has a greedy and hostile son . . . Afraid that his inheritance will be dissipated by a long and expensive hospitalization, he enters his mother's room while she is sedated, extubates her, and she dies. Shortly thereafter the medical staff discovers what he has done and confronts the son. He replies, 'I didn't kill her. I merely allowed her to die. It was her ALS disease that caused her death.' I think this would rightly be dismissed as transparent sophistry—the son went into his mother's room and deliberately killed her. But, of course, the son performed just the same physical actions, did just the same thing, that the physician would have done. If that is so, then doesn't the physician also kill the patient when he extubates her?

I underline immediately that there are important ethical differences between what the physician and the greedy son do. First, the physician acts with the patient's consent whereas the son does not. Second, the physician acts with a good motive—to respect the patient's wishes and self-determination—whereas the son acts with a bad motive—to protect his own inheritance. Third, the physician acts in a social role through which he is legally authorized to carry out the patient's wishes regarding treatment whereas the son has no such authorization. These and perhaps other ethically important differences show that what the physician did was morally justified whereas what the son did was morally wrong. What they do not show, however, is that the son killed while the physician allowed to die. . . . Both the physician and the greedy son act in a manner intended to cause death, do cause death, and so both kill.

(b) Advance decisions to refuse treatment

As we saw in Chapter 5, advance decisions (ADs) may involve a patient prospectively refusing life-prolonging treatment. In theory, under the Mental Capacity Act (MCA) 2005, a valid and applicable advance refusal of medical treatment is as binding upon medical professionals as a contemporaneous refusal. In practice, however, while many of us will have expressed a vague preference for not being kept alive, few of us will have made recent, detailed, and specific refusals of life-prolonging treatment.

To be binding, the AD must be valid (ie still in force) and applicable (to the precise situation which has arisen), and importantly additional criteria apply to ADs which include the refusal of life-sustaining treatment. The person (referred to in the statute as P) must specifically acknowledge that they intend to refuse treatment even if this puts their life at risk; the decision must be in writing and signed by P or a representative in P's presence, and the signature must be witnessed.

[64] 'Voluntary active euthanasia' (1992) Hastings Center Report 10–22.

As we saw in Chapter 5, these additional criteria can operate harshly when someone has done their best to issue a binding advance refusal of life-prolonging treatment, but has not satisfied all of these procedural requirements. In *An NHS v D*,[65] the patient had gone so far as to write down precisely what treatment he wished to refuse and when. His AD was signed, but because his signature had not been witnessed, it was not binding (refer back to Chapter 5 for a full description of this case).

Because the patient now lacks capacity, it is not necessarily easy to tell whether she was competent when she made the directive, or to be sure she has not since had a change of heart. Where there is any doubt about the validity or applicability of an AD, under section 26(4) an application for a declaration can be made to the Court of Protection (again, see further Chapter 5). While the court's advice is being sought, under section 26(5) nothing in the advance decision should prevent the provision of life-sustaining treatment or steps to prevent deterioration in the P's condition.

If a patient has not made a binding AD, their wishes may nevertheless be taken into account when deciding whether to provide treatment, as we see in Section 3 when we consider patients who lack capacity.

(c) Do Not Attempt Cardio-Pulmonary Resuscitation Orders

What if the doctor recommends that life-prolonging treatment (such as cardiopulmonary resuscitation) should not be attempted if the patient suffers a respiratory or cardiac arrest? In 2002, in response to concern that hospitals were including Do Not Resuscitate orders in the medical notes of competent elderly patients without discussing them first, the BMA, the Resuscitation Council, and the Royal College of Nursing issued a joint statement on decisions relating to cardiopulmonary resuscitation. This guidance has since been updated, most recently in 2014. The term now used is 'Do Not *Attempt* Cardio-Pulmonary Resuscitation' (DNACPR) in order to make clear that resuscitation is not always successful. The guidance emphasizes that it is good practice to discuss DNACPR orders with competent adult patients, but stresses the need for sensitivity.

British Medical Association, Resuscitation Council, and the Royal College of Nursing[66]

6.3 Communication and discussion with patients with capacity

When a person with capacity is at foreseeable risk of cardiac or respiratory arrest, they should be offered information about CPR [Cardio-Pulmonary Resuscitation], about the local resuscitation policy and services, and about their role in decision-making in relation to CPR. In order to determine whether the benefits of CPR would be likely to outweigh the harms and burdens, or whether the level of recovery expected would be acceptable to the patient, there should be sensitive exploration of the patient's wishes, feelings, beliefs and values.

In practice, it is difficult to find a sensitive way to ask a patient who has just been admitted to hospital if she would wish to be resuscitated if she has a heart attack. An added difficulty

---

[65] [2012] EWHC 885 (COP).

[66] *Decisions Relating to Cardiopulmonary Resuscitation: Guidance from the British Medical Association, the Resuscitation Council (UK) and the Royal College of Nursing* (Resuscitation Council, 2014).

is that representations of CPR in the media, for example in TV hospital dramas, convey an unrealistic impression of CPR's success in reviving people whose hearts have stopped. In fact, CPR may just prolong the dying process; it works in only 10–15 per cent of patients, and it is not uncommon for patients to be left with serious brain damage.

The previously common practice of not discussing DNACPR orders with patients was challenged in *R (on the application of Tracey) v Cambridge NHS Foundation Trust*. Janet Tracey had been diagnosed with terminal lung cancer and was admitted to hospital after being seriously injured in a road traffic accident. Her condition deteriorated, and on two occasions DNACPR notices were issued, cancelled, and then reinstated before her death. She had expressed a wish to receive full active treatment and was not told about the first decision to include a DNACPR notice in her notes. The Court of Appeal found that this had breached her Article 8 rights.

R (on the application of Tracey) v Cambridge NHS Foundation Trust[67]

Lord Dyson MR

In my view, the court should be slow to give general guidance as to the circumstances in which it is not appropriate to consult a patient in relation to a DNACPR decision.... But I think it is right to say that, since a DNACPR decision is one which will potentially deprive the patient of life-saving treatment, there should be a presumption in favour of patient involvement. There need to be convincing reasons not to involve the patient.

There can be little doubt that it is inappropriate (and therefore not a requirement of article 8 to involve the patient in the process if the clinician considers that to do so is likely to cause her to suffer physical or psychological harm.... In my view, doctors should be wary of being too ready to exclude patients from the process on the grounds that their involvement is likely to distress them. Many patients may find it distressing to discuss the question whether CPR should be withheld from them in the event of a cardio-respiratory arrest. If however the clinician forms the view that the patient will not suffer harm if she is consulted, the fact that she may find the topic distressing is unlikely to make it inappropriate to involve her.

Lord Pannick submits that it is also inappropriate to involve the patient if the clinician forms the view that CPR would be futile even if he considers that involvement is unlikely to cause the patient harm. I would reject this submission for two reasons. First, a decision to deprive the patient of potentially life-saving treatment is of a different order of significance for the patient from a decision to deprive him or her of other kinds of treatment. It calls for particularly convincing justification. Prima facie, the patient is entitled to know that such an important clinical decision has been taken. The fact that the clinician considers that CPR will not work means that the patient cannot require him to provide it. It does not, however, mean that the patient is not entitled to know that the clinical decision has been taken. Secondly, if the patient is not told that the clinician has made a DNACPR decision, he will be deprived of the opportunity of seeking a second opinion....

[I]n my view there was a breach of the article 8 procedural obligation to involve Mrs Tracey before the first notice was completed and placed in her notes. The Trust has not demonstrated that there were convincing reasons in this case not to consult her before this step was taken.

[67] [2014] EWCA Civ 822.

Lord Dyson MR thus suggests that Article 8 creates a presumption of patient involvement in DNACPR decisions that can be rebutted only if involving the patient could cause her harm, and for these purposes 'harm' means more than that she might find the discussion distressing. Of course, this will require a line to be drawn between psychological harm and 'mere' distress, and if the doctor does not know the patient well, she may not know how the patient is likely to react to questions about resuscitation.

Patients cannot compel doctors to offer CPR where it would be futile, and the Court of Appeal decision in *Tracey* does not interfere with clinical judgement about CPR's appropriateness, but as Jo Samanta explains, the patient has the right to know that a decision as potentially significant as this has been taken.

Jo Samanta[68]

The judgment in *Tracey* confirms that if a doctor considers that resuscitation will be futile the patient cannot compel the doctor to provide CPR, a position that resonates with general principles of law. This does not mean, however, that the patient is not entitled to know that that clinical decision has been taken. . . .

DNACPR are clinical decisions to refrain from performing a medical intervention. Clinical decisions not to undertake other forms of intervention are not necessarily subject to patient consent, involvement or disclosure and it is questionable as to why this should apply uniquely to DNACPR decisions? For Lord Dyson, 'DNACPR decisions should be distinguished from other decisions to withhold life-saving treatment because they are taken in advance and therefore they present an opportunity for discussion with patients and their family members.' However, a range of decisions at end of life will similarly be taken in advance and ought therefore to present similar opportunities for patient involvement. Perhaps a better distinction is the level of finality that will inevitably accompany a DNACPR decision. . . . Doctors cannot be required to give treatment that is contrary to their clinical judgement, but should be willing to consider and discuss people's wishes to receive treatment, even if it offers only a very small chance of success or benefit.

Where the patient lacks capacity, as was the case in *Winspear v City Hospitals Sunderland NHS Foundation Trust*,[69] there is, as we saw in Chapter 5, a presumption of consultation with the family before a DNACPR decision is recorded.

(b) SHOULD EUTHANASIA AND/OR ASSISTED SUICIDE BE LEGALIZED?

As we have seen, the law draws a bright line between lawful practices that result in a patient's death (withholding/withdrawing life-prolonging medical treatment and providing palliative care which may, incidentally, shorten life), and unlawful practices which have the same effect (euthanasia and physician-assisted suicide). This means that doctors are allowed to help their patients to die provided that they happen to be connected to a ventilator or nasogastric feeding tube. They can also potentially shorten the lives of those who happen to require life-threatening doses of painkillers or sedatives. Some commentators argue that

---

[68] '*Tracey* and Respect for Autonomy: Will the Promise be Delivered?' (2015) 23 Medical Law Review 467–76.
[69] [2015] EWHC 3250 (QB).

access to medical assistance in dying should not depend upon a patient's fortuitous need for life support or substantial doses of diamorphine. Others believe that there is a fundamental difference between doctors letting their patients die and killing them, and that the integrity of the medical profession demands an absolute prohibition upon doctors acting deliberately to end their patients' lives. Who is right?

Before we review arguments for and against legalizing euthanasia and assisted suicide, it is worth pointing out that those who are for and against assisted dying are often talking past each other, by focusing their attention on different groups of people. Advocates of assisted dying are often concerned with the situation of individuals who might benefit from assisted dying, either because their suffering is unbearable or because they find it reassuring to know that there would be a way out if their suffering were to become intolerable. Indeed, Joseph Raz goes so far as to claim that legalized euthanasia might benefit an even wider class of people by enabling them to shape the way their life ends.

Joseph Raz[70]

The clear difference between what I called the narrow and the broad right to euthanasia is that the latter takes it to protect not only the option to escape certain undesirable conditions at the end of one's life, but also and primarily to protect an option to shape the way one's life ends, by deciding on its time and manner. And inevitably shaping one's dying contributes to giving shape, contributes to the form and meaning one's life has. Those who reflect, plan and decide on the manner of their dying make their dying part of their life. And if they do so well then by integrating their dying into their life they enrich their life. . . .

So, while the power to decide the time and manner of one's death, when wisely used, will contribute to the value of various episodes in one's life, the main positive effect I have in mind is of the full, guiltless acceptance of the power itself. It can transform one's perspective on one's life; reduce the aspects of it from which one is alienated, or those that inspire a sense of helplessness or terror. It is a change that makes one whole in generating a perspective, a way of conceiving oneself and one's life free from some of those negative aspects.

In contrast, opponents of assisted dying tend to focus on a different group in society: the vulnerable. They maintain that the interests of the most vulnerable in society would be positively harmed by legalization. John Finnis, for example, maintains that there is a strong public interest in an exceptionless ban on assisted dying.

John Finnis[71]

What received scant attention in the Lords' judgments [in *Purdy*] is the public interest in maintaining a clear and exceptionless prohibition of assisting suicide (along with a prosecutorial discretion which could accommodate many factors including compassion while creating no legitimate expectation of immunity, and thus leaving always in place precisely the deterrent effect so important for many and so objectionable to Purdy and other promoters of assisted suicide and euthanasia).

---

[70] 'Death in our life' (2013) 30 Journal of Applied Philosophy 1–11.
[71] John Finnis, 'The Lords' Eerie Swansong: A Note on *R (Purdy) v DPP*' (2009) Oxford Legal Studies Research Paper No 31/2009.

(1) Arguments For

(a) Autonomy

It is often assumed that one of the strongest arguments in favour of legalizing euthanasia and assisted suicide is respect for patient autonomy. It might be argued that a patient's right to make decisions about her medical treatment should extend to being able to decide when and how she dies. To die quickly and painlessly, perhaps at home and with people we love, is obviously preferable to a lonely, protracted, and frightening death. As Sylvia Law suggests, giving patients some control over how they die might then appear to be an especially important aspect of respect for autonomous decision-making.

Sylvia A Law[72]

> The dying patient has lost control of most significant aspects of his or her life. The assurance that assisted death is an option provides a measure of autonomy and control, however that autonomy is exercised. . . . [I]t is not easy to hasten death in a private, non-violent way. Bans on physician assistance, therefore, aggravate . . . suffering. It is, of course, possible to jump off a tall building or to leap in front of an oncoming train. But most terminally ill patients seek a death that is both more private and less violent.

In contrast, John Keown argues that a 'right to choose' is essentially meaningless and that an emphasis upon individualistic values such as autonomy marginalizes the impact our actions have upon others.

John Keown[73]

> The 'right to choose x' often serves as a slogan with powerful emotional appeal. But crude slogans are no substitute for rational reflection, and one can hardly sensibly assert a right to choose 'x' until one has considered whether it is right to choose 'x'; to do otherwise is simply to beg the question. Is there a 'right to choose . . . paedophilia'? Or a 'right to choose . . . cruelty to animals'? Does the mere fact that someone *wants* to blind ponies or to have sex with children carry any moral weight? The 'right to choose' only arguably makes any moral sense in the context of a moral framework which enables us to discern what it is *right* to choose and what choices will in fact promote human flourishing. And not only *our* flourishing, but that of others. For we do not live as atomised individuals, as much loose talk about absolute respect for personal autonomy appears to assume, but in community, where our choices can have profound effects not only on ourselves but on others.

For two reasons, autonomy could not be the only justification for legalization of assisted dying. First, few advocates of legalization would allow unrestricted access to medical assistance in dying. On the contrary, most would accept that a doctor should only be allowed to help a patient end her life in certain, limited circumstances. The fact that a person wants to die is not, on its own, a sufficient reason for a doctor to kill her. Although opinion differs over

---

[72] 'Physician-Assisted Death: An Essay on Constitutional Rights and Remedies' (1996) 55 Maryland Law Review 292.

[73] *Euthanasia, Ethics and Public Policy: An Argument against Legalisation* (CUP: Cambridge, 2002) 54.

whether terminal illness should be a prerequisite, most people would agree that a doctor should only act to bring about a patient's death in order to relieve her suffering. This would be inconsistent with an important feature of respect for autonomy, namely that doctors must respect patients' decisions even when they do not agree with them. As Butler-Sloss LJ memorably put it in *Re MB (Caesarean Section)*:[74] 'A mentally competent patient has an absolute right to refuse to consent to medical treatment for any reason, rational or irrational, or for no reason at all, even where that decision may lead to his or her own death'.

Secondly, as we saw in Chapter 5, a patient's right to make decisions about her medical treatment is usually confined to a right to refuse treatment. Patients do not have the right to demand that their doctors treat them in a particular way. So while the principle of autonomy requires doctors to respect a competent patient's refusal of life-prolonging medical treatment, it could not require doctors to comply with a request for euthanasia or assisted suicide.

In response, advocates of legalization accept that patients would not be entitled to demand that their doctors kill them. Rather, their right would be to ask for assistance in dying, a request which a doctor could legitimately turn down, either because she has a conscientious objection or because it would be incompatible with her duty of care. As the authors of the next extracts suggest, the purpose of legalization would simply be to allow doctors to act lawfully when they comply with a patient's request for assistance.

Ronald Dworkin, Thomas Nagel, Robert Nozick, John Rawls, Thomas Scanlon, and Judith Jarvis Thomson[75]

Most of us see death—whatever we think will follow it—as the final act of life's drama, and we want that last act to reflect our own convictions, those we have tried to live by, not the convictions of others forced on us in our most vulnerable moment . . .

Since patients have a right not to have life-support machinery attached to their bodies, they have, in principle, a right to compel its removal. But that is not true in the case of assisted suicide: patients in certain circumstances have a right that the state not forbid doctors to assist in their deaths, but they have no right to compel a doctor to assist them. The right in question, that is, is only a right to the help of a willing doctor.

David Orentlicher[76]

Some commentators distinguish the withdrawal of treatment from euthanasia/assisted suicide on the ground that a right to refuse treatment is a negative right to be left alone while a right to euthanasia or assisted suicide would be a positive right to command aid. This argument mischaracterizes the nature of a right to euthanasia or assisted suicide. Such a right would not mean that patients could require physicians to assist suicides or perform euthanasia. Rather, the right would prevent the state from interfering when a patient and physician voluntarily agree on a course of euthanasia/assisted suicide. Physicians would participate in euthanasia/assisted suicide only if they were willing to do so.

---

[74] [1997] 2 FLR 426.

[75] In two cases heard by the US Supreme Court at the same time (*Washington et al v Glucksberg* 117 S Ct 2258 (1997) and *Vacco v Quill* 117 S Ct 2293 (1997), these six distinguished philosophers presented an Amici Curiae Brief for Respondents—referred to as The Philosophers' Brief—to the Supreme Court.

[76] 'The Alleged Distinction between Euthanasia and the Withdrawal of Life-Sustaining Treatment: Conceptually Incoherent and Impossible to Maintain' (1998) University of Illinois Law Review 837.

(b) Compassion

A different sort of argument for legalization could be framed in terms of the principle of beneficence (see further Chapter 1). If a cure is no longer possible, the doctor's duty to 'do good' involves trying to relieve the patient's suffering. If the patient's suffering has become both unbearable and untreatable, might it be possible to argue that relieving suffering by ending the patient's life could be compatible with a doctor's duty to act beneficently?

In addition to helping individual patients whose suffering has become unbearable, the legalization of euthanasia might also benefit a wider group of patients by reassuring them that a doctor would be allowed to help them to die if their condition were to become intolerable. Some patients are so fearful of a protracted and distressing death that they take their own lives prematurely, while they are still capable of doing so. For such patients, the availability of legalized euthanasia would, in fact, prolong their lives. In *R (on the application of Purdy) v Director of Public Prosecutions*, Lord Hope explained that this was also the predicament in which Debbie Purdy found herself.

R (on the application of Purdy) v Director of Public Prosecutions[77]

Lord Hope

[T]he Director has declined to say what factors he will take into consideration in deciding whether or not it is in the public interest to prosecute those who assist people to end their lives in countries where assisted suicide is lawful. This presents her with a dilemma. If the risk of prosecution is sufficiently low, she can wait until the very last moment before she makes the journey. If the risk is too high she will have to make the journey unaided to end her life before she would otherwise wish to do so.

Using compassion or beneficence, rather than autonomy, as the justification for legalizing euthanasia and assisted suicide explains the restrictions that most people believe should be placed upon its use. A doctor would only be acting beneficently in helping a patient to die if she has reasonable grounds for believing that the patient's life has ceased to be a benefit to her.

Philippa Foot analyses euthanasia from the perspective of virtue ethics (considered in Chapter 1). She does not rule out the possibility that euthanasia might, in certain circumstances, be 'compatible with both justice and charity', but this would be the case only where its 'purpose is to benefit the one who dies'.

Philippa Foot[78]

Disease too can so take over a man's life that the normal human goods disappear. When a patient is so overwhelmed by pain or nausea that he cannot eat with pleasure, if he can eat at all, and is out of the reach of even the most loving voice, he no longer has ordinary human life in the sense in which the words are used here . . . crippling depression can destroy the enjoyment of ordinary goods as effectively as external circumstances can remove them.

---

[77] [2009] UKHL 45.   [78] 'Euthanasia' (1977) 6 Philosophy & Public Affairs 85–112.

(c) Inconsistency of the status quo

Another reason commonly given for legalizing assisted dying is that the line the law currently draws between lawful and unlawful life-shortening practices is incoherent and morally irrelevant.[79] On this view, if we are prepared to allow doctors to engage in some practices that will end their patients' lives (eg withdrawing life-prolonging medical treatment, or giving life-threatening doses of painkillers), there is no logical reason why we should not also allow doctors to give their patients lethal injections, particularly since dying from starvation or suffocation may be more protracted and distressing (both for the patient and her family) than the quick and painless death that would be induced by a single fatal injection. Paradoxically then, as James Rachels points out, the lawful means of hastening a patient's death may result in a more prolonged and less peaceful death than the unlawful means.

James Rachels[80]

Part of my point is that the process of being 'allowed to die' can be relatively slow and painful, whereas being given a lethal injection is relatively quick and painless . . . The doctrine that says that a baby may be allowed to dehydrate and wither, but may not be given an injection that would end its life without suffering, seems so patiently cruel as to require no further refutation.

The sort of death which most of us would prefer—quick and painless, at home, and holding the hand of someone we love—is not facilitated by any of the lawful means of hastening patients' deaths. On the contrary, the withdrawal of life-sustaining treatment will generally take place in hospital, and where artificial nutrition and hydration is withdrawn, the patient will slowly starve to death, albeit painlessly, over a period of about two weeks. The moment of death is unpredictable, and the patient's family may not be present.

If the patient is given life-threatening doses of painkilling drugs—justified by the doctrine of double effect—it will only be possible to ensure that her loved ones are present at the moment of her death if the doctor admits that she is killing her patient, rather than merely attempting to relieve her pain.

Voluntary euthanasia or assisted suicide, on the other hand, could be given to a patient in her home, in the presence of the people she loves. In Oregon, 89.5 per cent of patients who die as a result of physician-assisted suicide die at home.[81] Evidence from the Netherlands appears to indicate that the bereaved relatives of patients who die as a result of euthanasia cope better with bereavement, and suffer fewer post-traumatic stress reactions than the bereaved of comparable patients who die naturally.[82] The opportunity to say goodbye; being prepared for the time and manner of the death; and having talked openly about dying all appear to have a positive impact upon a family's ability to come to terms with a person's death.

Moreover, as RG Frey argues in the next extract, making the lawfulness of medical assistance in dying contingent upon whether a patient happens to be connected to a ventilator

---

[79] See further Emily Jackson, 'Whose Death is it Anyway? Euthanasia and the Medical Profession' (2004) 57 Current Legal Problems 415–42.

[80] 'Active and passive euthanasia' (1975) 292 New England Journal of Medicine 79–80.

[81] Oregon Health Authority, *Oregon's Death with Dignity Act—2014* (2015).

[82] Nikkie B Swarte et al, 'Effects of euthanasia on the bereaved family and friends: a cross sectional study' (2003) 327 British Medical Journal 189.

or a morphine drip could be said to discriminate against patients whose suffering may be equally unbearable, but whose illnesses deprive them of access to a lawful means of ending their life.

RG Frey[83]

It seems little short of incredible that the fact that a terminally ill patient is on a life-support system could so transform cases, morally, when both cases show quite clearly that patient and doctor are acting together to bring about the patient's death at the instigation of the patient . . . Withdrawing feeding tubes and starving the patient to death is permissible, supplying the patient with a pill that produces death is not. Yet both sorts of assistance assuredly produce death, and both sorts involve the patient and doctor acting together to produce that death.

To be prepared to see the patient dead; to take the step that will assuredly produce death; to know as a certainty that death will ensue or be hastened: is this not morally equivalent to intending the patient's death? If so, there is little difference here between the supply of pills and the withdrawal of feeding tubes, so far as intending the patient's death is concerned.

Sheila McLean agrees. In discussing the Ms B case, she says 'on all logic, Ms B's death was assisted', people who happen to need artificial ventilation can therefore 'orchestrate their deaths even when they need assistance in doing so'.[84]

A further argument from inconsistency is that, despite the illegality of assisted dying, prosecutions are rare, and convictions are rarer still. Cases of compassionate killing, whether by doctors or relatives, are not prosecuted or sentenced in the same way as other homicides. Sheila McLean asks 'what purpose is served by a law which technically criminalizes behaviour which it then effectively ignores and forgives?', and she further points out that this gap between the prohibition of assisted dying and its lenient treatment by prosecutors and the courts is 'an interesting indication of the law's actual rather than its theoretical approach to assisted dying'.[85]

As we saw earlier, the non-prosecution of relatives who have helped people to die in Dignitas offers an especially compelling illustration of the gulf between the law on the books—in which assisted suicide is a serious crime, punishable by 14 years in prison—and the reality, in which access to assisted suicide in Switzerland is relatively straightforward, and relatives are unlikely to be prosecuted.

(d) Benefits of regulation

If, despite its illegality, doctors do help their patients to die, it would obviously be better for it to be tightly regulated, rather than happening in a legal vacuum. Because UK doctors who admit to helping patients to die might be charged with murder or with assisting a suicide, it is virtually impossible to gather accurate information about their participation in life-shortening practices. However, it has been estimated that between 4 and 12 per cent of all doctors have assisted in bringing about a patient's death.[86]

---

[83] 'Distinctions in Death' in Gerald Dworkin, RG Frey, and Sissela Bok, *Euthanasia and Physician-Assisted Suicide: For and Against* (CUP: Cambridge, 1998) 36, 38.

[84] *Assisted Dying: Reflections on the Need for Law Reform* (Routledge-Cavendish: Abingdon, 2007) 84.

[85] Ibid, 144.

[86] House of Lords Select Committee, *Assisted Dying for the Terminally Ill Bill—First Report* (2005).

Some commentators have argued that if euthanasia is happening anyway, but in secret, legalization would enable it to be regulated. Not only are doctors unlikely to report instances of euthanasia, but the threat of prosecution means that they are deterred from consulting other colleagues. There are therefore no safeguards, such as seeking a second opinion or psychiatric assessment, and cases cannot be monitored to ensure that euthanasia was, in fact, justifiable. In the next extract, Margaret Pabst Battin argues that the purpose of legalization in the Netherlands was precisely to enable control to be exercised over an otherwise secretive practice.

Margaret Pabst Battin[87]

[For] the Dutch . . . bringing euthanasia and related practices out into the open is a way of gaining control. For the Dutch, this is a way of identifying a practice that, in the Netherlands as in every other country, has been going on undercover and entirely at the discretion of the physician. It brings the practice into public view, where it can be regulated by guidelines, judicial scrutiny, and the collection of objective data. It is not that the Dutch or anyone else have only recently begun to practise euthanasia for the dying patient, nor is this a new phenomenon in the last decade or so; rather, the Dutch are the first to try to assert formal public control over a previously hidden practice and, hence, to regulate it effectively.

In the next extract, Roger Magnusson draws upon his interviews with health care professionals to argue that we do not have a choice between legalized physician-assisted dying, where doctors help their patients to die, and illegal assisted dying, where it never happens. Rather, euthanasia's illegality instead means that it will instead be practised 'underground', which may be much more dangerous for patients.

Roger S Magnusson[88]

In *Angels of Death: Exploring the Euthanasia Underground*, I reported on 49 detailed, yet pseudonymous interviews with doctors, nurses, and therapists working in HIV/AIDS health care, principally in Sydney, Melbourne, and San Francisco. . . . Despite their mostly good intentions, interviewees painted a troubling picture of covert PAS/AE [physician-assisted suicide/active euthanasia] . . .

For me, the most striking feature of these accounts was the way they betrayed the absence of norms or principles for deciding when it was appropriate to proceed. One doctor injected a young man on the first occasion they met, despite concerns from close friends that the patient was depressed . . . In another case, a patient brought his death forward by a week so as not to interfere with the doctor's holiday plans . . .

It is important to remember that our ability to castigate the Dutch about their rates of non-compliance comes courtesy of the relative transparency created by the Dutch policy of legalisation. If we wish to make ambit claims about slippery slopes, it is only fair to point out that the reporting rate for Britain, Australia, and most other countries, is zero. Nevertheless, even partial compliance with statutory safeguards may represent an improvement on the kinds of clinical decisions that currently occur in secret.

[87] *The Least Worst Death: Essays in Bioethics on the End of Life* (OUP: Oxford, 1994) 141.
[88] 'Euthanasia: above ground, below ground' (2004) 30 Journal of Medical Ethics 441–6.

It might also be argued that legalization would facilitate the equal treatment of similarly situated patients. At present, as Charles Baron explains, a patient's access to euthanasia is contingent upon whether her doctor is willing to run the risk of life imprisonment. It has further been suggested that patients whose relationships with medical professionals are sufficiently close that they may be able to persuade them to act illegally are likely to be from the more privileged sections of society. Legalization would therefore enable access to euthanasia to depend upon need, rather than upon one's connections with members of the medical profession.

Charles Baron[89]

It is an open secret that such technically illegal practices take place, but prosecutions and disciplinary actions involving them have thus far been almost non-existent . . . Potential abuses are left completely without internal or external checks, and such a regime encourages the view that medical personnel may safely consider themselves 'above the law'. Patients are also denied equal protection of the law. Only patients with 'connections' are able to find physicians to assist them in dying—much as only women with 'connections' were able to obtain professional help in terminating pregnancies before abortion was legalized.

(2) Arguments Against

(a) Sanctity of life

The legalization of euthanasia and assisted suicide would necessarily involve accepting that death can rationally be preferred to life. According to Luke Gormally, this is inconsistent with the principle that all human life is intrinsically valuable.

Luke Gormally[90]

Euthanasiast killing, even when it is voluntary, involves denial of the ongoing worth of the lives of those reckoned to be candidates for euthanasia. It is a type of killing, therefore, which cannot be accommodated in a legal system for which belief in the worth and dignity of every human being is foundational . . . If the claim that a person lacks a worthwhile life is held to make killing lawful, then the state has ceased to recognize the innocent as having binding claims to protection. . . .

Those who attempt suicide are clearly moved by the (at least transient) belief that their lives are no longer worthwhile. Since just legal arrangements rest on a belief in the ineliminable worth of every human life, the law must reject the reasonableness of a choice which is so motivated.

Hence the law must also refuse to accommodate the behaviour of those who effectively endorse the choice of the suicide: for they too are acting on the view that the person they are helping no longer has a worthwhile life.

---

[89] 'Physician Assisted Suicide Should be Legalized and Regulated' (1997) 41 Boston Bar Journal 15.

[90] 'Euthanasia and Assisted Suicide: 7 Reasons Why They Should Not be Legalized' in Donna Dickenson, Malcolm Johnson, and Jeanne Samson Katz (eds), *Death, Dying and Bereavement*, 2nd edn (Sage: London, 2000) 286–90.

This sort of argument against legalization may derive from someone's religious belief that life is not ours to dispose of as we please. For human beings to choose the moment of their death and to take active steps to bring it about is—on this view—to usurp God's monopoly upon the power to give and to take life.

In the next extract, Margaret Otlowski suggests that this sort of argument is effectively a matter of private faith.

Margaret Otlowski[91]

Religious arguments will naturally be convincing to those who accept the religious viewpoint but they clearly do not have universal relevance. Religion is a matter of personal commitment, and objections to active voluntary euthanasia based purely on religious views should not dominate the law nor impinge on the freedoms of others. Whilst the convictions of believers must obviously be respected, it must be recognized that in a pluralistic and largely secular society, the freedom of conviction of non-believers must also be upheld.

(b) Legalization is unnecessary

For two different reasons, it is sometimes argued that the legalization of euthanasia is unnecessary. First, some would argue that the desire for euthanasia is evidence of our failure to provide sufficient hospice places and high-quality palliative care to terminally ill patients. If, so the argument goes, all patients were to be given optimum treatment at the end of life, none would request euthanasia, and the question of its legalization would be redundant. This is, to some extent, an empirical claim that might be substantiated by evidence that all suffering at the end of life can be adequately relieved by palliative care.

It is probably true that relatively few patients now have to endure unbearable levels of pain, but pain is seldom the principal reason for patients' requests for euthanasia. In both Oregon and Washington State in 2014, the principal reasons for requesting physician-assisted suicide were loss of autonomy (91 and 89 per cent respectively); decreasing ability to participate in activities that made life enjoyable (87 and 94 per cent), and loss of dignity (71 and 79 per cent); inadequate pain control was less commonly mentioned (31 and 41 per cent).[92]

Optimum palliative care may be able to minimize physical pain, but it is less clear that it can eradicate the helplessness and mental anguish that many people experience as a result of their bodies' progressive deterioration. In their interviews with 31 people in the Netherlands who had requested euthanasia, Dees et al found that it was the hopelessness of their condition which patients found unbearable.

Marianne K Dees et al[93]

All patients experienced existential suffering. There were four categories within this theme: loss of important and pleasurable activities, hopelessness, pointlessness and being tired of life. . . .

---

[91] *Voluntary Euthanasia and the Common Law* (OUP: Oxford, 2000) 216.

[92] Oregon Health Authority, *Oregon's Death with Dignity Act—2014* (2015); Washington State Department of Health, *2014 Death with Dignity Act Report* (2015).

[93] '"Unbearable suffering": a qualitative study on the perspectives of patients who request assistance in dying' (2011) 37 Journal of Medical Ethics 727–34.

> As an 80-year-old man, a former mathematics teacher and musician put it: 'I can't do anything anymore, I used to play music, participated in various clubs, all so very companionable, I had to say farewell to all of it. It feels so awful just waiting to become bedridden and then waiting to die'. All patients considered hopelessness to be a main factor in the perception of unbearableness. This is illustrated by a 55-year-old woman with nasopharyngeal cancer: 'You lie on a bed and none of the normal functions come back. They will never come back and it will only get worse' . . .
>
> In addition, patients placed unbearable suffering in the broader context of their personality characteristics. They explained how the irreversible consequences of disease or ageing resulted in loss of self, loss of autonomy and mental exhaustion until they felt themselves no longer the persons they used to be. This is exemplified by a 53-year-old woman with lung cancer: 'I lost my dignity, lying in bed in diapers, I am no longer the independent person I used to be'.

The second reason for arguing that the legalization of euthanasia is unnecessary derives from the recognition that, in practice, doctors do help their patients to die.

Martha Minow[94]

> For now, at least, it is better to live with the lie that prohibition prevents the practice than the lie that its approval would not cost all of us, deeply. It is better to live with the lie that prohibition works so that, at the margin, those who engage in it do so with trembling.

This sort of argument rests upon two different assumptions: first, that in individual cases euthanasia may be justifiable; and, secondly, that openly legalizing euthanasia might have negative consequences for society as a whole. Of course, these assumptions appear to pull in entirely different directions, and so the argument that we should retain euthanasia's illegality while acknowledging that some doctors will be justified in helping their patients to die is, as Kamisar admits, an attempt to have it both ways.

Yale Kamisar[95]

> I do not deny it is hard to defend an absolute prohibition when you not only expect the prohibition to be violated in certain situations, but you can visualize circumstances where you would understand and forgive the person who did so.

It could be argued that if we accept that euthanasia might be acceptable in some circumstances, retaining its absolute prohibition for symbolic reasons is disingenuous. If we think that doctors sometimes act properly in helping their patients to die, it seems unreasonable to expect them to expose themselves to the risk of life imprisonment.

---

[94] 'Which Question? Which Lie? Reflections on the Physician-Assisted Suicide Cases' (1997) 1 Supreme Court Review 30.

[95] 'Physician Assisted Suicide: The Problems Presented by the Compelling Heartwrenching Case' (1998) 88 Journal of Criminal Law and Criminology 1121, 1144.

(c) Difficulties in ensuring that a request has been made voluntarily

Obviously, if it were to be legalized, it would be important to ensure that patients' requests for euthanasia had been made voluntarily. For three reasons, some argue that this represents an insuperable obstacle to legalization. First, as Susan M Wolf explains, it is possible that the judgement of some patients who request euthanasia might be distorted by depression.

Susan M Wolf[96]

First, patients actually exercise little control over end-of-life care . . . In reality, patients are profoundly dependent on health professionals, with many patients reporting that they want their physician to make treatment decisions for them . . . The research shows . . . that depression is even more strongly correlated with requests for assisted suicide than pain is. Yet patients routinely face inadequate diagnosis and treatment of depression. Given these data, a patient requesting assisted suicide may actually be seeking relief from depression or pain . . .

Terminal patients are quite unlike independent rights-bearers freely negotiating in business transactions. Instead, they are profoundly dependent, often at the mercy of health professionals for everything from toileting to life-saving care, and may be experiencing too much pain, discomfort, or depression to make independent and truly voluntary decisions.

Diagnosis of depression in terminally ill patients is difficult because many of the symptoms of depression—such as weight loss, insomnia, loss of energy, and an inability to concentrate—may also be symptoms of conditions like cancer or the side effects of medication. Nevertheless, there have been attempts to use standardized diagnostic tests to work out the frequency of depression among those requesting assistance in dying. A recent study in Oregon suggests that the overwhelming majority of people who have died as a result of assisted suicide did not suffer from any sort of depressive disorder.[97] Levene and Parker's systematic review found that in the Netherlands there was a high incidence of depression in patients requesting euthanasia, but that most of these requests were turned down,[98] suggesting that doctors were generally able to spot when a request was prompted by depression.

Secondly, because the consequence of euthanasia will be the patient's death, there is no scope for correcting mistaken decisions if it subsequently emerges that the patient had in fact lacked capacity when she made the decision to die. Nor is there room for the correction of decisions made following a mistaken diagnosis of terminal illness. Given the finality of euthanasia and this inevitable risk of error, opponents of legalization have suggested that we could never be sufficiently certain that a person's request for euthanasia had been properly informed and competently made.

Thirdly, as we saw in Chapter 7, consultations between patients and their doctors are confidential. So while supporters of legalization often suggest that regulation would enable euthanasia to be scrutinized and monitored, in practice, as Callahan and White argue in the next extract, it might be difficult to exercise much control over doctors' oral discussions with their patients.

---

[96] 'Pragmatism in the Face of Death: The Role of Facts in the Assisted Suicide Debate' (1998) 82 Minnesota Law Review 1063.

[97] Linda Ganzini et al, 'Prevalence of depression and anxiety in patients requesting physicians' aid in dying: cross sectional survey' (2008) 337 British Medical Journal 1682.

[98] Ilana Levene and Michael Parker, 'Prevalence of depression in granted and refused requests for euthanasia and assisted suicide: a systematic review' (2011) 37 Journal of Medical Ethics 205–11.

Daniel Callahan and Margot White[99]

If it is true, as it indubitably is, that 'decisions about medical treatment are normally made in the privacy of the doctor–patient relationship', then an obvious question must be asked: how is it possible, or could it ever be possible, to monitor and regulate those decisions regarding physician-assisted suicide that occur within the ambit of that privacy? . . .

There are two possible ways to proceed here: either we can station a policeman in every doctor's office and next to every sickbed to monitor all conversations, or we can depend upon the individual physician to voluntarily reveal that he or she has been part of an agreement to pursue physician-assisted suicide. Since the former course would both violate doctor–patient confidentiality and be utterly impractical, only the latter option is available. But that course means, in effect, that any physician-assisted suicide regulation must, in the end, be physician self-regulated.

One response to these arguments against legalization might be that we already allow patients to make decisions that result in their deaths when we respect their refusals of life-prolonging medical treatment. Patients who are connected to mechanical ventilators may be depressed, and we may wrongly judge them to be competent, yet this risk of error, coupled with the finality of the outcome, does not persuade us that patients should be prevented from taking life-or-death decisions. Nor do we think that patient confidentiality represents an insurmountable obstacle to our ability to protect vulnerable patients from being pressurized into agreeing to the withdrawal of life-prolonging treatment.

Moreover, we should also be concerned about vulnerable patients who are physically capable of taking their own lives, and who may be temporarily depressed. While protecting the vulnerable is often cited as the main reason for a blanket ban on assisted dying, it offers rather haphazard protection in that only those who happen to be too physically incapacitated to commit suicide will be prevented from ending their lives precipitately.

(d) Risk of abuse

In a related argument, some commentators are concerned that if assisted dying were readily available, elderly patients would be pressurized into choosing a premature death. In some cases, pressure to opt for assisted dying might come from greedy relatives. But it is also common for elderly people to perceive themselves to be a burden to their family, and if death were an option, is there a danger that they might request euthanasia for altruistic reasons, despite their own desire to go on living? In the next extract, Hazel Biggs suggests that this desire to avoid becoming a burden is particularly acute for elderly women.

Hazel Biggs[100]

[M]any women feel vulnerable and concerned at the prospect of becoming the cared-for rather than the carer because society appears to no longer value them once they reach this state . . .

---

[99] 'The Legalization of Physician-Assisted Suicide: Creating a Regulatory Potemkin Village' (1996) 30 University of Richmond Law Review 1.

[100] 'I Don't Want to be a Burden! A Feminist Reflects on Women's Experiences of Death and Dying' in Sally Sheldon and Michael Thomson (eds), Feminist Perspectives on Health Care Law (Cavendish: London, 1998) 279–95.

[I]f active euthanasia were to be permitted as a right, what is to prevent the endorsement of this *right* being translated into a duty? How long will it be before those who seek euthanasia in order to avoid being a burden lose the right to continue living until the natural end of their lives? The experiences of women in the Cheyenne and Inuit societies who were expected to withdraw from their communities once they had outlived their usefulness as carers, are indicative of the dangers which could flow from laws permitting euthanasia. The introduction of legal euthanasia could alter social and personal expectations of old age beyond recognition, changing it from a time for relaxation and quiet enjoyment of the twilight years to a time for resisting pressure and the expectations of those who perceive that all useful life is over.

In countries that have legalized assisted dying, there is no evidence that women are more likely to request it than men. In Oregon, between 1998 and 2014, 53 per cent of those who had received assistance in dying were men.[101] In the Netherlands, too, it appears that men seek access to euthanasia slightly more frequently than women.[102]

Sheila McLean would question the assumption that there is something wrong with requesting euthanasia because one would prefer not to be a burden. Instead, she suggests that 'being a burden—rather than simply perceiving oneself to be one—is arguably a morally acceptable and perfectly reasonable factor to take into account when planning for the future'.[103] McLean argues that a competent adult, contemplating a future in which the costs of her care will eat away the inheritance she hopes to leave to her children, or in which her children's lives will be taken over with caring duties, might reasonably take these factors into account.

It is also possible that pressure to opt for an earlier death might come from the medical profession. Luke Gormally argues that because euthanasia would be cheaper than high-quality palliative care, it might seem like a cost-effective way to 'treat' the terminally ill.

Luke Gormally[104]

It is very important to bear in mind that a key element in the context of contemporary debates about legalizing euthanasia is the drive to reduce health care costs. One of the conspicuous dangers of legalization is that, before long, euthanasia would be seen as a convenient 'solution' to the heavy demands on care made by certain types of patient. Medicine would thereby be robbed of the incentive to find genuinely compassionate solutions to the difficulties presented by such patients. The kind of humane impulses which have sustained the development of hospice medicine and care would be undermined because too many would think euthanasia a cheaper and less personally demanding solution.

Of course, it would be unethical for doctors to try to persuade their patients to opt for euthanasia, but Kass and Lund argue that simply mentioning death as a treatment option might subtly influence patients' choices.

---

[101] Oregon Health Authority, *Oregon's Death with Dignity Act—2014* (2015).

[102] Margaret P Battin et al, 'Legal physician-assisted dying in Oregon and the Netherlands: evidence concerning the impact on patients in "vulnerable" groups' (2007) 33 Journal of Medical Ethics 591–7.

[103] *Assisted Dying: Reflections on the Need for Law Reform* (Routledge-Cavendish: Abingdon, 2007) 54.

[104] 'Euthanasia and Assisted Suicide: 7 Reasons Why They Should Not Be Legalized' in Donna Dickenson, Malcolm Johnson, and Jeanne Samson Katz (eds), *Death, Dying and Bereavement*, 2nd edn (Sage: London, 2000) 285, 287.

Leon R Kass and Nelson Lund[105]

With patients reduced—helpless in action and ambivalent about life—someone who will benefit from their death need not proceed by overt coercion. Rather, requests for assisted suicide can and will be subtly engineered. To alter and influence choices, physicians and families need not be driven entirely by base motives or even be consciously manipulative. Well-meaning and discreet suggestions, or even unconscious changes in expression, gesture, and tone of voice, can move a dependent and suggestible patient toward a choice for death. . . .

When the physician presents a depressed or frightened patient with a horrible prognosis and includes among the options the offer of a 'gentle quick release', what will the patient likely choose, especially in the face of a spiralling hospital bill or resentful children?

If we think that vulnerable patients need to be protected against choosing a premature death against their wishes, Orentlicher argues that we should also be concerned about refusals of life-prolonging treatment, where the decision must be respected even if it is wholly irrational.

David Orentlicher[106]

The law does not limit withdrawals of treatment only to cases in which a patient is irreversibly ill. Patients whose lives could be saved and who could be restored to very good health with the brief use of a ventilator or the transfusion of blood can still refuse the treatment . . . If the risks of . . . abuse are reason enough to condemn decisions to shorten a patient's life, they should lead a person to oppose treatment withdrawal as well as euthanasia and assisted suicide.

(e) Effect on the doctor–patient relationship

A further argument against legalization is that it would damage the doctor–patient relationship, and threaten the integrity of the medical profession. There are two interrelated aspects to this argument. First, from the point of view of the patient, it might be argued that knowing your doctor could legally kill you would reduce patient trust. Brian Simpson, for example, has argued that 'for a doctor to kill his own patients involves a peculiarly alarming breach of trust, and one that is dramatically incompatible with the role of a doctor'.[107] Whether or not patients share this assumption is unclear. According to a 2015 Populus opinion poll, 50 per cent of respondents said that the legalization of assisted suicide would not affect their trust in their doctors, while 37 per cent would trust their doctors more, and 12 per cent would trust their doctors less.[108]

Secondly, from the point of view of the doctor, if killing were to become a treatment option, it has been said that the ethical foundations of the medical profession would be

---

[105] 'Physician-Assisted Suicide, Medical Ethics and the Future of the Medical Profession' (1996) 35 Duquesne Law Review 395.

[106] 'The Alleged Distinction between Euthanasia and the Withdrawal of Life-Sustaining Treatment: Conceptually Incoherent and Impossible to Maintain' (1998) University of Illinois Law Review 837.

[107] 'Euthanasia for Sale?' (1986) 84 Michigan Law Review 807, 809.

[108] See further populus.co.uk.

undermined. The GMC took this view in their evidence to the House of Lords Select Committee on Assisted Dying:

> [A] change in the law to allow physician-assisted dying would have profound implications for the role and responsibilities of doctors and their relationships with patients. Acting with the primary intention to hasten a patient's death would be difficult to reconcile with the medical ethical principles of beneficence and non-maleficence.[109]

Of course, individual doctors would not be forced to participate in assisted dying: any statute legalizing the practice would inevitably include a 'conscientious objection' clause, in the same way as the Abortion Act. But, as Søren Holm explains, the right not to participate in assisted dying is insufficient to protect the views of doctors who do not wish this to be part of 'the context of their professional life'.

Søren Holm[110]

> Conscientious objection to PAD [physician-assisted death] is often assumed as 'the solution' to assuage the concerns of doctors and other healthcare professionals who do not want to participate in PAD or do not want PAD to be part of medical practice. But it is not obvious that conscientious objection adequately addresses the concerns, even in relation to those doctors who are in ignorance of the considerable philosophical literature arguing that conscientious objection should be abolished or curtailed in relation to the provision of elective abortion. The concerns doctors have may not only be personal or fully captured by 'I do not want to perform PAD'; they are often about a wider set of actions than direct performance, and often about changes in healthcare that will inevitably follow the introduction of PAD, and can perhaps be more accurately expressed as 'introducing PAD will inevitably make it part of the context of my professional life, and that worries me because it will change that life'.

In the next extract, Leon Kass and Nelson Lund suggest that an absolute 'taboo against medical killing' is also necessary to preserve patient trust in the medical profession.

Leon R Kass and Nelson Lund[111]

> Authorizing physician-assisted suicide would . . . overturn a centuries-old taboo against medical killing, a taboo understood by many to be one of the cornerstones of the medical ethic. . . .
>
> Just as patients necessarily divulge and reveal to the physician private and intimate details of their personal lives; just as patients necessarily expose their naked bodies to the physician's objectifying gaze and investigating hands; so patients necessarily expose and entrust the care of their very lives to the physician's skill, technique, judgment, and character. Mindful of the meaning of such exposure and vulnerability, and mindful too of their own human penchant for error and mischief, the Hippocratic physicians voluntarily set limits on their own conduct, pledging not to take advantage of or to violate the patient's intimacies, naked sexuality, or life itself.

[109] *Assisted Dying for the Terminally Ill Bill—First Report* (2005) 42.

[110] 'The debate about physician assistance in dying: 40 years of unrivalled progress in medical ethics?' (2015) 41 Journal of Medical Ethics 40–3.

[111] 'Physician-Assisted Suicide, Medical Ethics and the Future of the Medical Profession' (1996) 35 Duquesne Law Review 395.

(f) Slippery slope

It is important to remember that when someone invokes a slippery slope argument (see further Chapter 1), they are not arguing that there is something intrinsically wrong with doctors helping their patients to die. Of course, they may also believe this to be true, but this would not be a slippery slope claim. Rather, the slippery slope claim is that allowing some compassionate acts of killing would make it very difficult to prevent those with less benevolent motives from ending patients' lives.

It might, for example, be argued that it would be virtually impossible to police the boundary between acceptable and unacceptable medical killings. Carl Schneider has argued that there is also 'a psychological aspect of slippery slopes', namely that 'they work partly by domesticating one idea and thus making its nearest neighbor down the slope seem less extreme and unthinkable'.[112] It is this latter type of slippery slope argument that is invoked in the next extract by Dieter Giesen, who argues that allowing doctors to kill their patients would weaken the absolute prohibition upon the taking of innocent life, and that we would all therefore become progressively desensitized to the horror of murder.

Dieter Giesen[113]

Recent history shows us that once firm constraints against killing are removed, a general moral decline will result. The German experience of the Nazi euthanasia programme, during which 100,000 disabled persons were killed because they were classified as living 'lives not worth living', demonstrates the potential for perverse thinking and inhuman deeds once the first step upon the slippery slope is taken.

In some ways, as Dan Brock points out, a slippery slope argument is a straightforward empirical claim: does legalizing euthanasia make involuntary killing more likely?

Dan W Brock[114]

Slippery slope arguments . . . are the last refuge of conservative defenders of the status quo. When all the opponent's objections to the wrongness of euthanasia itself have been met, the opponent then shifts ground and acknowledges both that it is not in itself wrong and that a legal policy which resulted only in its being performed would not be bad. Nevertheless, the opponent maintains, it should still not be permitted because doing so would result in its being performed in other cases in which it is not voluntary and would be wrong. In this argument's most extreme form, permitting euthanasia is the first and fateful step down the slippery slope to Nazism. Once on the slope we will be unable to get off . . .

It must be relevant how likely it is that we will end with horrendous consequences and an unjustified practice of euthanasia. . . . Opponents of voluntary euthanasia on slippery slope grounds have not provided the data or evidence necessary to turn their speculative concerns into well-grounded likelihoods.

---

[112] 'Rights Discourse and Neonatal Euthanasia' (1988) 76 California Law Review 151, 168.

[113] 'Dilemmas at Life's End: A Comparative Legal Perspective' in John Keown (ed), *Euthanasia Examined* (CUP: Cambridge, 1995) 204.

[114] 'Voluntary active euthanasia' (1992) Hastings Centre Report 10–22.

Given their empirical nature, we might evaluate slippery slope claims by examining data from countries where legalization has taken place. But as we will see in the next section, the problem is that there are different (and often flatly contradictory) interpretations of the available data. John Keown and Dieter Giesen, for example, are convinced that the Dutch have already slid some way down the slope:

John Keown[115]

[T]he Dutch experience lends weighty support to the slippery slope argument ... Within a decade, the so-called strict safeguards against the slide have proved signally ineffectual; non-voluntary euthanasia is now widely practised and increasingly condoned in the Netherlands.

Dieter Giesen[116]

Experience in the Netherlands to date suggests that, in practice, no sharp distinction can be drawn between voluntary and non-voluntary euthanasia. Instead, commentators have documented a continuum of killing, from the (quite rare) paradigm case of informed and rational choice to frequent instances of familial and medical pressure, to the elimination of defenceless newborns, adjudged to be a burden upon society and to the purging of old people's homes.

In contrast, Helga Kuhse et al's confidential survey of 3,000 Australian doctors found that non-voluntary euthanasia is five times more common in Australia, where euthanasia is illegal, than it is in the Netherlands.[117] Australian doctors were far less likely than their Dutch counterparts to discuss the decision to hasten a patient's death with the patient herself, or to seek her consent. In their study of six European countries, Agnes van der Heide et al found that non-voluntary euthanasia was more than twice as common in Denmark as it was in the Netherlands.[118]

If patients' lives are ended in the absence of an explicit request with similar (or greater) frequency in countries that have not legalized euthanasia, it is not clear that the legalization of euthanasia in the Netherlands has caused any propensity to engage in non-voluntary euthanasia. Moreover, all of the Dutch data cited by those who claim that it proves the existence of a slippery slope was gathered after legalization. To have compelling evidence of a slippery slope, we would need to compare data from before and after legalization. Otherwise, evidence (if there is such evidence) that poor practices coexist with legalization could simply mean that poor practices existed anyway, and legalization made no difference.

---

[115] 'Euthanasia in the Netherlands: Sliding Down the Slippery Slope?' in John Keown (ed), *Euthanasia Examined* (CUP: Cambridge, 1995) 261–96.

[116] 'Dilemmas at Life's End: A Comparative Legal Perspective' in John Keown (ed), *Euthanasia Examined* (CUP: Cambridge, 1995) 204.

[117] Helga Kuhse et al, 'End-of-life decisions in Australian medical practice' (1997) 166 Medical Journal of Australia 191–6.

[118] Agnes van der Heide, Luc Deliens, Karin Faisst, Tore Nilstun, Michael Norup, Eugenio Paci, Gerrit van der Wal, and Paul J van der Maas, 'End-of-life decision-making in six European countries: descriptive study' (2003) 362 The Lancet 345–50.

Indeed, as Stephen Smith explains, even if it could be established that non-voluntary euthanasia has increased in the years following legalization, this does not necessarily provide evidence of a causal connection.

Stephen Smith[119]

The simple fact that something occurs after something else does not indicate, in any meaningful way, that the first action logically required the second to happen. Even if one can find a connection such that the first tends to precede the second, this will not provide evidence of a logical connection. Especially in the realm of human actions (as opposed to say the actions of physical laws), the preceding of an action by a first action does not indicate they must be connected in any logical way.

Let us consider a different claim in order to see what Smith means. There appears to be some evidence that palliative care provision in Oregon improved after the legalization of assisted suicide. This is not sufficient to prove that legalization *caused* palliative care to improve. We could use this evidence to show that legalization has not resulted in a decline in the provision of palliative care, but we could not use it to establish a causal relationship between legalization and better palliative care.

Even if we could establish that the slope is slippery and that it would be difficult to draw or police the line between acceptable and unacceptable instances of euthanasia, it is not obvious that an absolute prohibition is the optimum regulatory response.

Emily Jackson[120]

Let us apply slippery slope reasoning to a more mundane regulatory problem. Should I maintain an absolute prohibition on the late submission of essays on the grounds that giving an extension to student A who has a very compelling reason—say, the death of a close family member—might make it difficult for me to draw a line between her case and those of students B, C, D, and E who have progressively less persuasive grounds for late submission? An absolute prohibition would relieve me of the difficulty of drawing distinctions between borderline cases: perhaps student C's computer has stopped working, and student D left her essay on the bus. But I do a grave injustice to student A by preferring the simplicity of an absolute ban over the admittedly more time-consuming and complex task of drawing fine distinctions between serious and trivial excuses for late submission. . . .

Nor is it obvious that a blanket ban is the optimum response to concerns about a practice's potential misapplication. If we can imagine circumstances in which euthanasia might be legitimate, prohibiting it completely in order to prevent it being employed in other less compelling situations is a peculiarly blunt approach to regulation . . . It would be more logical to advocate regulations which confine access to euthanasia to patients whose circumstances lie at the top of the moral slope (whatever those might be), and prohibit it in all other cases.

---

[119] 'Fallacies of the Logical Slippery Slope in the Debate on Physician-Assisted Suicide and Euthanasia' (2005) 13 Medical Law Review 224.

[120] 'Whose Death is it Anyway? Euthanasia and the Medical Profession' (2004) 57 Current Legal Problems 415–42.

(3) A Third Way?

It would be a mistake to assume that there are only two options: legalization or criminalization. Rather, a different solution would be to treat euthanasia as a particular *type of killing*; less grave than murder, but not entirely non-criminal. In the next extract, Richard Huxtable explains that this sort of compromise would be more transparent than the status quo, in which the harsh consequences of euthanasia's illegality are mitigated by the leniency of judges, juries, and prosecutors.

Richard Huxtable[121]

As the law in operation in England demonstrates, stern pronouncements that assistance in dying is unlawful rarely translate into convictions for murder. Instead, ways are found to divert defendants from court, bring lesser charges, or impose mild non-custodial sentences. Such manoeuvres do, at least, signal that the law-in-action is capable of achieving a compromise. Yet this model of compromise seems to require subterfuge and to rely upon legal fictions, such as that the assistant must have acted with 'diminished responsibility'. The interests of clarity, consistency and fair labelling are surely better served by the creation of an explicit category of compassionate killing, which translates a shadowy, unpredictable and *ad hoc* compromise wrought in the law-in-action into an appropriately scrutinized, articulated and open component of the law-as-stated.

Heather Keating and Jo Bridgeman also advocate a middle-ground between criminalization and legalization. They argue that, in certain circumstances, the fact that a killing was compassionate should offer a partial defence to murder. This would not mean that someone who killed for compassionate reasons had done nothing wrong, but, like the partial defence of diminished responsibility, it would simply permit discretion in sentencing.

Heather Keating and Jo Bridgeman[122]

[W]e regard compassion as providing a (partial) excuse for killings which would otherwise be categorised as murder. The fact that the DPP's guidelines on assisting suicide suggest that it is inappropriate to prosecute someone who has been wholly motivated by compassion also supports the conclusion that an excusatory partial defence is the most appropriate way forward . . .

[W]e stress that there would need to be evidence that the deceased was experiencing extreme and unbearable suffering prior to death. It would not be enough for the accused to have an honest belief about the level of the suffering being experienced; it would need to be one based on reasonable grounds and thus a reasoned and caring response to the suffering of their loved one. In sum, the partial defence of compassionate killing we propose would be available to a relative or family member who had been fulfilling intensive caring responsibilities for the deceased and who, in response to an honest and reasonable belief that he or she had been experiencing extreme and unbearable suffering, ended the deceased's life in order to end his or her suffering.

---

[121] 'Splitting the difference? Principled compromise and assisted dying' (2014) 28 Bioethics 472–80.
[122] 'Compassionate Killings: The Case for a Partial Defence' (2012) 75 Modern Law Review 697–721.

(c) EXPERIENCE IN OTHER COUNTRIES

Clearly, it would be a mistake to ignore evidence from the handful of countries where euthanasia and/or assisted suicide have been treated more leniently than in the UK: ranging from overt legalization in the Netherlands to the de facto toleration of compassionately motivated assisted suicide in Switzerland. Yet, on the other hand, what happens in countries with different legal and health care systems and different cultural, religious, and social attitudes towards death, does not necessarily translate into compelling evidence of how legalized assisted dying would work, or not work, in the UK.

(1) The Netherlands

(a) The law

Although a statute specifically legalizing euthanasia was not introduced in the Netherlands until 2001, since 1973 the Dutch courts had gradually been developing exceptions to the express prohibitions on euthanasia and assisted suicide in the Dutch Penal Code (Articles 293 and 294). Through a series of court decisions, a set of guidelines had emerged which—if followed—protected doctors from criminal liability. To some extent, the 2001 statute simply formalized existing practice in the Netherlands.

The first important step was taken in the *Postma* case in 1973.[123] Dr Postma was prosecuted for giving a fatal dose of morphine to her mother who was very seriously disabled, had unsuccessfully attempted suicide, and repeatedly expressed her desire to die. There was widespread public sympathy for Dr Postma, and although the Leeuwarden District Court convicted her under Article 293, it imposed a symbolic suspended sentence of a week's imprisonment.

Furthermore, the court took the opportunity to indicate that, despite Article 293, euthanasia could be acceptable if performed in certain circumstances: (a) the patient should be incurably ill; (b) the patient should be experiencing unbearable suffering; (c) the patient should have requested that his or her life be terminated; and (d) the termination is performed by the patient's own doctor, or in consultation with him or her. In subsequent years, a number of other cases were brought before the Dutch courts and their decisions incrementally laid down a set of criteria that would exempt doctors from punishment.[124] These guidelines were then adopted by the public prosecutor's office as the criteria that determined whether or not cases of euthanasia or assisted suicide would be prosecuted.

The first case to come before the Dutch Supreme Court was the *Alkmaar* case in 1984.[125] Dr Schoonheim had given a lethal injection to a 95-year-old patient who had signed an advance declaration requesting euthanasia if her condition should deteriorate beyond a certain point, and who had more recently expressed a clear and unequivocal wish to die. Dr Schoonheim was initially convicted. On appeal, the Dutch Supreme Court ruled that there had been insufficient investigation of the possibility that the doctor had faced an irreconcilable conflict of duties. They invoked the *noodtoestand* or 'emergency' defence, which applies where the doctor's duty to preserve his patient's life may be outweighed by his duty to relieve suffering. The case was referred back to the Court of Appeal, and Dr Schoonheim was acquitted.

---

[123] *Nederlandse Jurisprudentie* 1973 No 183, District Court of Leeuwarden, 21 February 1973.
[124] Eg *Wertheim, Nederlandse Jurisprudentie* 1982 No 63, Rotterdam Criminal Court.
[125] *Nederlandse Jurisprudentie* 1985 No 106, Supreme Court, 27 November 1984.

Of course, the *noodtoestand* defence would only absolve doctors of criminal liability where the patient's suffering is so extreme that it overrides the doctor's normal duty to preserve life. The *noodtoestand* defence could exist where the person's suffering is mental rather than physical,[126] but this will be the case only where the patient's mental suffering results from a recognized psychiatric condition: it is not enough to simply be 'tired of life'.[127]

The Termination of Life on Request and Assisted Suicide (Review Procedures) Act 2001 amended Articles 293 and 294 of the Criminal Code, and came into force on 1 April 2002. Euthanasia and assisted suicide continue to be criminal offences under Articles 293(1) and 294(1). But exceptions are introduced in Article 293(2) and 294(2), which both now read:

> The act referred to in the first subsection shall not be an offence if it is committed by a physician who fulfils the due care criteria set out in Section 2 of the Termination of Life on Request and Assisted Suicide (Review Procedures) Act, and if the physician notifies the municipal pathologist of this act in accordance with the provisions of section 7, subsection 2 of the Burial and Cremation Act.

Under section 2, the requirements of due care are that the physician:

(a) holds the conviction that the request by the patient was voluntary and well considered;

(b) holds the conviction that the patient's suffering was lasting and unbearable;

(c) has informed the patient about the situation he was in and about his prospects;

(d) and the patient holds the conviction that there was no other reasonable solution for the situation he was in;

(e) has consulted at least one other independent physician who has seen the patient and has given his written opinion on the requirements of due care referred to in parts (a)–(d); and

(f) has terminated a life or assisted in a suicide with due care.

As the Ministry of Foreign Affairs makes clear, the doctor who carries out euthanasia must be the patient's own doctor. A British person could not travel to the Netherlands for an assisted death in the same way as they might travel to Dignitas in Switzerland.

Ministry of Foreign Affairs[128]

> An important, basic principle established in case law is the existence of a close doctor–patient relationship. A doctor may only perform euthanasia on a patient in his care. He must know the patient well enough to be able to assess whether the request for euthanasia is both voluntary and well-considered, and whether his suffering is unbearable and without prospect of improvement.

---

[126] The *Chabot* case (1994) No 656, Supreme Court.
[127] Tony Sheldon, 'Being "tired of life" is not grounds for euthanasia' (2003) 326 British Medical Journal 71.
[128] Q&A Euthanasia (Ministerie van Buitenlandse Zaken, 2008).

This point was stressed by a doctor who sat on one of the five regional assessment committees, in his evidence to a House of Lords Select Committee in 2005:

> [T]here is an absolute condition that [euthanasia] can only be done by the treating physician. It cannot be any other physician. We do not want to advertise 'euthanasia tourism'. What we insist on is that it only takes place within a meaningful medical relationship. That is an absolute condition.[129]

Two especially controversial aspects of the law are worth noting. First, the Act specifically allows for advance requests for euthanasia, with section 2(2) providing that doctors may comply with a request in a written declaration provided that the person was capable of making a reasonable appraisal of his own interests when the request was made. In practice, however, advance euthanasia directives are almost never implemented.[130]

Eva Elizabeth Bolt et al[131]

> [I]n case of advanced dementia, many physicians point out that it is impossible to determine whether a patient is suffering unbearably, due to a lack of meaningful communication. . . . Many elderly care physicians state that it is impossible to determine at what moment an advance euthanasia directive is to be carried out if the patient can no longer specify this. Also, it is probable that physicians cannot conceive of performing euthanasia in a patient with dementia who might not fully comprehend what is happening. Our study suggests that, in actual practice, physicians would rarely act upon an advance euthanasia directive in case of advanced dementia. People who write such directives are often unaware of this.

Secondly, children over the age of 12 may be entitled to request euthanasia or assisted suicide. A doctor is only allowed to comply with a request from a minor between the ages of 12 and 15 with parental consent. For children aged 16 and 17, parents should be consulted, but they do not have a right of veto. There have been very few cases of euthanasia in children, and no cases of assisted suicide.[132]

While the law specifically addresses the possibility of euthanasia for children over the age of 12, there is no provision for euthanasia in severely disabled newborn babies. In the next extract, Eduard Verhagen and Pieter Sauer suggest that, provided certain requirements are met, euthanasia in severely disabled neonates can be acceptable. The Groningen Protocol, named after the Dutch hospital that developed these guidelines and accepted as a national

[129] House of Lords Assisted Dying for the Terminally Ill Committee (2005) 175.

[130] Mette L Rurup et al, 'Physicians' experiences with demented patients with advance euthanasia directives in the Netherlands' (2005) 53 Journal of the American Geriatric Society 1138–44; CMPM Hertogh, 'The role of advance euthanasia directives as an aid to communication and shared decision-making in dementia' (2009) 35 Journal of Medical Ethics 100–3.

[131] 'Can physicians conceive of performing euthanasia in case of psychiatric disease, dementia or being tired of living?' (2015) 41 Journal of Medical Ethics 592–8.

[132] Margaret P Battin et al, 'Legal physician-assisted dying in Oregon and the Netherlands: evidence concerning the impact on patients in "vulnerable" groups' (2007) 33 Journal of Medical Ethics 591–7.

guideline by the Dutch Association of Pediatrics in 2005,[133] sets out five conditions which should be satisfied before doctors should proceed with euthanasia in newborn babies:

- The diagnosis and prognosis must be certain.

- Hopeless and unbearable suffering must be present.

- The diagnosis, prognosis, and unbearable suffering must be confirmed by at least one independent physician.

- Both parents must give informed consent.

- The procedure must be performed in accordance with the accepted medical standard.

Eduard Verhagen and Pieter Sauer[134]

We are convinced that life-ending measures can be acceptable in these cases under very strict conditions: the parents must agree fully, on the basis of a thorough explanation of the condition and prognosis; a team of physicians, including at least one who is not directly involved in the care of the patient, must agree; and the condition and prognosis must be very well defined. After the decision has been made and the child has died, an outside legal body should determine whether the decision was justified and all necessary procedures have been followed.

Alexander Kon disagrees. He argues that it is impossible to tell whether a baby's suffering is unbearable, and that neonatal euthanasia is therefore unacceptable.

Alexander A Kon[135]

Suffering, however, is wholly subjective and therefore can be gauged only by the individual. . . . [A]ny quantification of an individual's suffering that is not based on the personal report of that individual is unreliable. Certainly, parents and physicians may be very poor judges of the subjective experiences of infants. . . . Because we cannot accurately judge the subjective suffering of an infant, we cannot accurately determine if the burdens of living outweigh the benefits and therefore can never judge with certainty whether death is in the infant's best interest . . .

The Groningen Protocol could only be viable if physicians were able to accurately determine the subjective suffering of infants and were unbiased in their judgment of the quality of life of persons with special needs. Given that the former is impossible and the latter is currently untrue, the practice of neonatal euthanasia cannot be supported.

(b) Euthanasia in practice

Each case of euthanasia or assisted suicide is considered by a regional review committee, usually consisting of a lawyer, a doctor, and an ethicist. If the committee is satisfied that the criteria have been fulfilled, the case is closed without informing the public prosecutor,

---

[133] Nederlandse Vereniging voor Kindergeneeskunde (NVK).

[134] 'The Groningen Protocol—euthanasia in severely ill newborns' (2005) 352 New England Journal of Medicine 959–62.

[135] 'Neonatal euthanasia is unsupportable: the Groningen Protocol should be abandoned' (2007) 28 Theoretical Medicine and Bioethics 453.

who is notified only if the committee finds that the doctor did not fulfil the due care criteria. In about 6 per cent of cases each year, the regional review committee asks for more information, usually for further evidence that the patient's suffering was unbearable. Non-compliance with the 'due care' criteria is unusual, happening in less than 1 per cent of cases each year.

Initially, there was some concern that doctors were not reporting every case of euthanasia. Reporting rates are now much higher, and it is thought that the remaining gap between the number of euthanasia deaths calculated by national surveys and the number reported is not the result of doctors lying or concealing euthanasia deaths. Instead, there is some confusion over whether deaths which are preceded by palliative sedation or pain relief should be reported as euthanasia. It seems that many doctors do not consider these to be cases of euthanasia, and so do not report them as such, whereas they are classified as euthanasia by the officials who calculate euthanasia's frequency by examining death certificates.[136] The reporting rate for 2005 was 80 per cent, but when cases involving opioids (where this difference of opinion exists) were excluded, 99 per cent of cases were reported.[137]

Every five years, the Dutch national statistics authority produces statistics which set out how many deaths are preceded by a medical decision. As is evident, euthanasia and assisted suicide are much less common than deaths preceded by decisions to withhold treatment or to use 'intensifying' palliative care measures.

Deaths by medical end-of-life decision 2010[138]

	Total deaths	Percentage of deaths
Total deaths in 2010	136,058	100
Deaths without an end-of-life decision	57,331	42
Deaths with an end-of-life decision	78,727	58
Deaths preceded by withholding treatment while taking into account the possible hastening of death	10,713	7
Deaths preceded by withholding treatment with the explicit intention of hastening death	14,092	10
Deaths preceded by intensifying measures to alleviate pain or other symptoms while taking into account the possible hastening of death	47,957	35
Deaths preceded by intensifying measures to alleviate pain or other symptoms while partly intending the possible hastening of death	1,606	1
Euthanasia	3,859	3
Assisted suicide	192	0.1
Ending life without explicit request	310	0.2

---

[136] John Griffiths, Heleen Weyers, and Maurice Adams, *Euthanasia and Law in Europe* (Hart Publishing: Oxford, 2008) 203.

[137] Ibid, 204.

[138] *Deaths by medical end-of-life decision; age, cause of death* (Statistics Netherlands, 2012).

There is a consistent pattern of euthanasia being more common than assisted suicide. Cancer is by far the most common medical condition among those requesting euthanasia. It is also worth noting that a minority of patients who request euthanasia actually die assisted deaths. Most commonly this is because the patient dies first from her underlying condition.[139]

(c) Commentary

Unsurprisingly, there is considerable interest in how legalized euthanasia has worked in the Netherlands. The problem is that commentators cannot agree on what lessons we should learn as a result. John Keown has persistently warned that there is clear evidence of abuse, and that the Dutch are currently sliding down the slippery slope.

John Keown[140]

[T]he evidence points to the following three conclusions. First, voluntary active euthanasia is far from a rarity and is increasingly performed. Rather than being truly a 'last resort', it has quickly become an established part of mainstream Dutch medical practice to which doctors have resorted even when palliative care could have offered an alternative . . .

Secondly, despite the insistent claims by proponents of voluntary active euthanasia, inside and outside the Netherlands, that allowing it subject to 'safeguards' brings it from the shadows and 'into the open' where it can be controlled, the evidence indicates that such claims merit scepticism. The reality is that most cases of voluntary active euthanasia, until recently a substantial majority, have gone unreported and unchecked. In view of the intractable fact that in a clear majority of cases there has not even been an *opportunity* for official scrutiny, Dutch reassurances of effective regulation ring hollow.

In contrast, John Griffiths suggests that the Netherlands offers us an example of the benefits that flow from openly regulating euthanasia.

John Griffiths[141]

The Dutch data on medical practices which shorten life, in the cases of non-competent or of competent but not-consulted patients, are indeed a matter of concern. However, some differentiation is in order. Almost all of the behaviour concerned involves abstaining from or terminating life-prolonging treatment, or administration of heavy doses of painkillers, in circumstances in which remaining life expectancy was (very) short and the doctor's behaviour may, as far as we know, have been entirely appropriate. There is really not a shred of evidence that the frequency of this sort of behaviour is higher in the Netherlands than, for example, in the United States; the only thing that is clear is that more is known about it in the Netherlands. . . . [Those] who invoke the metaphor to criticise Dutch legal developments seem quite confused about the direction in which the 'slippery slope' is tilting . . . [T]he Dutch are busy trying to bring a number of socially dangerous medical practices which exist everywhere under a regime of effective societal control.

---

[139] *Euthanasia and Law in Europe* (Hart Publishing: Oxford, 2008) 157.
[140] *Euthanasia, Ethics and Public Policy: An Argument against Legalisation* (CUP: Cambridge, 2002).
[141] 'Assisted Suicide in the Netherlands: The *Chabot* Case' (1995) 58 Modern Law Review 232, 247–8.

A different argument, articulated here by Griffiths et al, is that distinctive features of Dutch society and, in particular, of the Dutch health care system reduce the international relevance of legalization in the Netherlands.

John Griffiths, Alex Bood, and Heleen Weyers[142]

A[n] important characteristic of Dutch society concerns the level of confidence in public institutions and in professions. It seems no accident that legalization of euthanasia is conceived in the United States, for example, in terms of the rights of *patients* (with doctors' organizations often prominent in opposition) whereas in the Netherlands the public discussion concerns the scope of the professional discretion of *doctors* (doctors have from the beginning been prominent in the movement for legalization). On the whole, the Dutch seem comfortable with the idea that doctors can be trusted with the discretion to perform euthanasia, so that the public debate largely concerns the boundaries of this professional discretion and the sorts of procedural controls to which it should be subjected.

(2) Oregon, Washington State, Vermont, California, and Montana

In the US, a distinction has been drawn between euthanasia—which is illegal throughout the US—and physician-assisted suicide, the legality of which is a matter for individual states. A decision of the Supreme Court in 1997 confirmed that there is no constitutional right to assisted suicide, but that legalization would not be unconstitutional.[143]

Oregon was the first state to vote in favour of the legalization of assisted suicide. The introduction of the Death with Dignity Act 1994 was delayed as a result of a series of legal challenges.[144] It came into force in 1998, and in its first year there were 15 assisted suicides in Oregon. Since then, the number of assisted suicides has increased, though the numbers remain fairly small: in 2014, 155 prescriptions were written under the Death with Dignity Act, and by the time of the publication of the Oregon Health Authority's annual report in 2015, 105 people had died as a result.[145]

The Death with Dignity Act provides that a physician may comply with a competent, terminally ill, adult patient's voluntary request for a prescription of drugs, which will allow her to end her life in a humane and dignified way. The Act only applies to residents of the state of Oregon. The patient must make an initial oral request, followed by a formal written request. At least 15 days after the written request, the patient must repeat their request orally, and a further 48 hours must elapse before the prescription can be filled. The patient's request must be witnessed by two people other than the doctor, at least one of whom must not be a relative, an heir, or an employee of the institution in which the patient is receiving care. The patient must be asked to notify her family. A second doctor must confirm the patient's diagnosis and that the patient is competent and acting voluntarily. The patient must have received complete information about her diagnosis, prognosis, and alternatives, such as hospice care and pain control. If there is any suggestion that the patient is depressed or has a psychiatric disorder, she must be referred to a psychiatrist or psychologist.

---

[142] *Euthanasia and Law in the Netherlands* (Amsterdam UP: Amsterdam, 1998) 304.
[143] *Washington et al v Glucksberg* 117 S Ct 2258 (1997) and *Vacco v Quill* 117 S Ct 2293 (1997).
[144] *Gonzales v Oregon* 546 US 243 (2006).
[145] Oregon Health Authority, *Oregon's Death with Dignity Act—2014* (2015).

In Oregon there were fears that PAS would be chosen by patients who did not have health insurance and could not afford high-quality palliative care, but the evidence does not bear this out. Indeed, there seems to be evidence that the quality of palliative care has improved in recent years.[146] In a study of all the physicians eligible to prescribe drugs under the Act, 30 per cent had increased their referrals to hospice care and 76 per cent reported that they made efforts to improve their knowledge of pain medication for the terminally ill. Sixty-nine per cent reported that they had sought to improve their recognition of psychiatric disorders, such as depression.[147]

The majority of patients who have sought PAS have been middle class and well educated.[148] In 2014, 48 per cent had been educated to degree level;[149] 94 per cent of the patients who died were enrolled in hospice care; and 100 per cent had some form of health care insurance, though a minority had private health insurance.[150] It seems clear those choosing PAS do not do so because of their lack of access to medical care or social support mechanisms.[151]

In the next extract, IG Finlay and R George query the use of Oregon's data to suggest that the vulnerable are not over-represented among those accessing PAS. They argue that the fact that people who ask for PAS are comparatively well educated and middle class may in fact establish that this socioeconomic group are more vulnerable in relation to assisted dying, since they may find dependency especially hard to bear.

IG Finlay and R George[152]

First, are people who are better educated more vulnerable, in the context of PAS, because illness and potential dependence are more frightening to them or because they have fewer psychosocial supports? Second, perhaps more interestingly, why did the finding that college graduates were 7.6 times more likely resort to PAS than others not lead Battin and her associates to question whether, if the less well educated are not especially vulnerable to PAS, perhaps the better educated are? There is a need to dig somewhat deeper in order to try and establish whether, for example, educated patients may resort more frequently to PAS because they are people who are familiar with the intricacies of the law and can argue more persuasively with their physicians . . .

We are told that 'death under the ODDA [Oregon Death with Dignity Act] was associated with having health insurance and with high educational status, both indirect indicators of affluence'. . . . Yet Battin *et al* do not reflect on the vulnerabilities that wealth may bring, for example, perceptions of suffering, dignity, control, or the stigmatisation of illness and disability.

[146] E Dahl and N Levy, 'The case for physician assisted suicide: how can it possibly be proven?' (2006) 32 Journal of Medical Ethics 335–8.

[147] Linda Ganzini et al, 'Oregon physician attitudes about and experiences with end of life care since the passage of the Death with Dignity Act' (2001) 285 Journal of the American Medical Association 2363–9.

[148] E Dahl and N Levy, 'The case for physician assisted suicide: how can it possibly be proven?' (2006) 32 Journal of Medical Ethics 335–8.

[149] Oregon Health Authority, *Oregon's Death with Dignity Act—2014* (2015).

[150] Ibid.

[151] Lois L Miller et al, 'Attitudes and experiences of Oregon hospice nurses and social workers regarding assisted suicide' (2004) 18 Palliative Medicine 685–91.

[152] 'Legal physician-assisted suicide in Oregon and the Netherlands: evidence concerning the impact on patients in vulnerable groups—another perspective on Oregon's data' (2011) 37 Journal of Medical Ethics 171–4.

As with the Netherlands, supporters and opponents of legalization offer different interpretations of the evidence from Oregon. In the next extract, Dan Brock argues that there has been no evidence of abuse in Oregon since the statute came into force.

Dan W Brock[153]

There is no evidence that any of the abuses feared by opponents of the Act have materialized in the first year of its operation. It has not led to unsuccessful suicide attempts; to assisted deaths accompanied by distress to the patient; to any influx of out-of-state residents seeking assisted death; to public deaths; to use of assisted death to avoid dealing with difficult symptoms or to reduce the financial costs of end-of-life care; to disproportionate use of assisted death for weak, vulnerable, or disabled patients or for women; or to increased suicide rates in the general population and especially among the young. On the contrary, the authors [of reports into how it has worked in practice] suggest several good consequences from the Act, including improvements in end-of-life care such as increased use of hospice . . . and several averted suicides or homicides.

Against this, Margot White and Daniel Callahan suggest that the lack of any reporting requirements casts doubt upon the reliability of the available evidence.

Margot White and Daniel Callahan[154]

The Oregon law does not require physicians or anyone else to report cases at all whether they follow the guidelines or depart from them. As a result, the probability of generating accurate and complete data about nonvoluntary or involuntary cases would appear to be virtually nil . . . The fact that no evidence is publicly available at this stage suggesting that the feared 'slippery slope' is at hand in Oregon does not alter the overall concern. It makes little sense to note that the abuse doesn't seem to have materialized if there is no mechanism in place for bringing it to anyone's attention or investigating it. If there is lack of clarity about abusive practices, responsibility for correcting this lies not with PAS opponents, but with the drafters of Oregon's Death with Dignity Act who chose to omit any obligations for health care professionals to report unlawful practices and to omit any sanctions for physicians who fail to report PAS cases in the first place.

In 2008, following a referendum, a similar statute was introduced in Washington State. Since 2009, the Death with Dignity Act has allowed Washington State residents with less than six months to live to request a prescription for lethal medication. In 2014, medication was dispensed under the Act to 176 individuals. Once again, most were well educated (50 per cent to degree level) and only 2 per cent did not have health insurance.[155] Vermont passed the Patient Choice and Control at End of Life Act in 2013 and became the third US state to legalize assisted suicide for terminally ill, competent adults, resident in Vermont. California passed a similar law, the End of Life Option Act, in 2015.

---

[153] 'Misconceived sources of opposition to physician-assisted suicide' (2000) 6 Psychology, Public Policy and Law 305.

[154] 'Oregon's first year: the medicalization of control' (2000) 6 Psychology, Public Policy and Law 331.

[155] Washington State Department of Health, *2014 Death with Dignity Act Report* (2015).

The state of Montana has not introduced specific legislation legalizing assisted suicide; rather, in *Montana v Baxter*,[156] its Supreme Court decided that 'physician aid in dying' was not contrary to public policy. Robert Baxter was 75 and had been suffering from lymphocytic leukaemia. He posthumously won his claim against the State of Montana that the right to die 'with dignity' should have extended to offering protection from liability under the state's homicide laws to a physician who prescribed him lethal medication.[157] Without prospective authorization of assisted suicide, however, this decision leaves the medical profession in Montana in limbo. Although it was decided *ex post facto* in Robert Baxter's case that there could have been no liability, doctors who help their patients to die still run the risk of prosecution.

(3) Belgium and Luxembourg

Belgium decriminalized euthanasia in 2002.[158] Originally the Euthanasia Act formally applied only to euthanasia and not to assisted suicide. However, in its first annual report, the Federal Control and Evaluation Commission accepted that assisted suicides also fall within the Act's scope.

To be eligible for euthanasia (or assisted suicide), the patient must have a serious and incurable mental or physical disorder, and must be suffering from persistent and unbearable pain or distress that cannot be alleviated. The physician must give the patient full information about her condition and about palliative care. A second doctor must examine the patient and confirm both that her suffering is unbearable, and that it cannot be alleviated. If the patient is not terminally ill, two additional requirements are imposed. First, the physician must consult two colleagues, one of whom must assess whether the request is voluntary, considered, and repeated and, secondly, at least a month must elapse between the request and the performance of euthanasia. As in the Netherlands, it is possible to make an AD requesting euthanasia: this must be in writing, signed by the patient, and witnessed by two adults, at least one of whom must have no material interest in the patient's death.

In 2014, access to euthanasia was extended to minors, provided that the minor's condition is terminal and incurable, their death imminent, and their unbearable suffering physical (rather than mental). The minor must be judged capable of making the decision, and have the agreement of their parents.

Doctors are not under a duty to comply with a patient's request for euthanasia; on the contrary, they are entitled to refuse on grounds of conscience or for medical reasons. There is, however, a duty to give reasons for the refusal.

The physician who has performed euthanasia or assisted a suicide must fill in a registration form and deliver it within four working days of the death to a national commission, whose members are doctors, lawyers, and palliative care experts. If the commission is satisfied that any of the criteria were not satisfied, the file will be sent to the public prosecutor. The commission reports to parliament on the implementation of the legislation. Since the law came into force, the number of cases of euthanasia has increased each year. Over the most recent two-year reporting period, there was an average of 1,619 cases of euthanasia each year.[159] Of these, 80 per cent involved individuals from Dutch-speaking Flanders, amongst

---

[156] 354 Mont 234 (2009).   [157] *Baxter v Montana* 224 P 3d 1211 (Mont Sup Ct 2009).

[158] *Loi relative l'euthanasie* (Act Concerning Euthanasia), 28 May 2002, in force 23 September 2002.

[159] Commission Fédérale de Contrôle et D'Évaluation de L'Euthanasie, Sixième Rapport Aux Chambres Législative Années 2012–2013 (2014).

whom euthanasia—perhaps as a result of cultural affinities with the Dutch—is much more common than in French–speaking Wallonia.

It is important to bear in mind, as Gastmans et al explain, that the legalization of euthanasia in Belgium took place within a context in which there is a strong emphasis upon the provision of palliative care, and where the first response to a request for euthanasia is extensive investigation of other palliative options.

C Gastmans, F Van Neste, and P Schotsmans[160]

[I]f euthanasia can ever be justified, it is necessary to provide good palliative care for all and to include in the euthanasia law a palliative filter—that is, a compulsory prior consultation with a specialised palliative care team . . .

The starting point of this clinical practice guideline is the principle that everything possible should be done to provide support and assistance to the competent, terminally ill person who asks for euthanasia, and his or her relatives. The aim is that such an active and integral palliative care approach can in many cases displace the request and allow the patient to die in a dignified manner without euthanasia. . . . In Belgium, the development of palliative care preceded the euthanasia debate. As a result, Belgian palliative care (for example, the Flemish Palliative Care Federation) played a very active role in the Belgian euthanasia debate. The Belgian euthanasia debate itself functioned as a lever that facilitated the further development of palliative care, as is illustrated by the new law on palliative care that was approved at the same time as the euthanasia law.

The decision-making process in Belgium does not just involve the patient and their doctor. Nurses and the patient's family also play an important role. Following a request for euthanasia, a palliative care nurse will spend time with the patient in order identify the reasons for the request.[161] Finding out why a patient wants to end their life helps the nurse to work out what palliative response might be able to alleviate the patient's underlying suffering. The legalization of euthanasia in Belgium rests upon the assumption that high-quality palliative care may be able to obviate most but not all requests for euthanasia. Euthanasia is a last resort and should be available only when other options have been exhausted.

Luxembourg passed similar legislation in 2009. Doctors in Luxembourg will not face penal sanctions for carrying out either euthanasia or assisted suicide provided that they consult a colleague to ensure that the competent adult patient has an incurable terminal illness, and is suffering unbearably—either physically or mentally—without any prospect of improvement. The patient's request must be made voluntarily, after reflection, and must not result from external pressure. As in Belgium, legislation to improve palliative care provision was passed at the same time.

Although the new law was supported by a majority of the population, it was vigorously opposed by the Catholic Church and by the Head of State, Grand Duke Henri, who refused to sign it into law. The constitution was amended in order to eliminate the monarch's veto. Because Luxembourg's population is so small, it is hard to draw conclusions from its

---

[160] 'Facing requests for euthanasia: a clinical practice guideline' (2004) 30 Journal of Medical Ethics 212–17.

[161] B Dierckx de Casterlé et al, 'Nurses' views on their involvement in euthanasia: a qualitative study in Flanders (Belgium)' (2006) 32 Journal of Medical Ethics 187–92.

National Commission's reports.[162] From 2009 to 2014, there were a total of 33 cases of euthanasia, almost all for patients with cancer.

(4) Switzerland

Assisting suicide is a criminal offence under Article 115 of the Swiss Penal Code, but only if the defendant's motive is 'selfish'. Article 115 does not specify that the suicide must be assisted by a doctor, nor does the patient have to be terminally ill or suffering unbearably. Provided that the person's motive for assisting the suicide is compassionate, no offence is committed.

According to the Swiss Academy of Medical Sciences, physicians whose consciences allow them to offer assistance in suicide are responsible for ensuring that additional criteria are met.

Swiss Academy of Medical Sciences[163]

[I]n the final phase of life, when the situation becomes intolerable for the patient he or she may ask for help in committing suicide and may persist in this wish.

In this borderline situation a very difficult conflict of interests can arise for the doctor. On the one hand assisted suicide is not part of a doctor's task, because this contradicts the aims of medicine. On the other hand, consideration of the patient's wishes is fundamental for the doctor–patient relationship. This dilemma requires a personal decision of conscience on the part of the doctor. The decision to provide assistance in suicide must be respected as such. In any case, the doctor has the right to refuse help in committing suicide. If he decides to assist a person to commit suicide, it is his responsibility to check the following preconditions:

- The patient's disease justifies the assumption that he is approaching the end of life.
- Alternative possibilities for providing assistance have been discussed and, if desired, have been implemented.
- The patient is capable of making the decision, his wish has been well thought out, without external pressure, and he persists in this wish. This has been checked by a third person, who is not necessarily a physician.
- The final action in the process leading to death must always be taken by the patient himself.

In Switzerland, assistance with suicide is generally provided by one of the 'right to die' societies, and these impose additional requirements. EXIT (Deutsche Schweiz) has over 90,000 members, and its affiliated francophone organization, EXIT (Romandie), has over 20,000 members. To be eligible for an assisted suicide with EXIT, a patient must be over the age of 18, mentally competent, and must have a 'hopeless' prognosis and/or be suffering unbearably/unacceptably. EXIT members must be either Swiss citizens or permanent residents.

Dignitas, a smaller organization set up in 1998, will assist non-Swiss residents to die. From 1998 to 2014, 273 UK citizens ended their lives with Dignitas's help. Dignitas will provide assisted suicides for members who are of sound judgement and possess a minimum level of physical mobility (sufficient to self-administer the drug). The person must also

---

[162] Commission Nationale de Contrôle et d'Évaluation de la loi du 16 mars 2009 sur l'euthanasie et l'assistance au suicide, *Troisième rapport à l'attention de la Chambre des Députés* (Années 2013 et 2014).
[163] *Care of Patients in the End of Life* (SAMS, 2013).

have a disease that will lead to death and/or an unendurable incapacitating disability and/or unbearable and uncontrollable pain.

Some in Switzerland are alarmed by its reputation as the destination for 'suicide tourism', and there have been attempts to prohibit foreigners from joining Swiss right to die societies, but none has been successful. In March 2011, 78 per cent of voters in a referendum in the canton of Zurich were in favour of continuing to allow foreigners to access assisted suicide.

(d) EUTHANASIA OR ASSISTED SUICIDE OR BOTH?

Some countries have formally only legalized euthanasia (Belgium), while other places have only legalized, specifically or de facto, assisted suicide (Oregon, Washington State, Vermont, and Switzerland). In the Netherlands, Luxembourg, and, in practice, Belgium both methods are lawful, but euthanasia is more common. What reasons might there be for preferring one technique rather than the other, or for legalizing both?

Doctors can end patients' lives more effectively than patients themselves, who might be unable to swallow the whole dose and be left both alive and severely injured by partially ingesting a lethal substance. If assisted suicide is more likely to go wrong, preferring it to euthanasia is justifiable only in order to provide an additional safeguard, or 'firewall'. As Dr Nick Gideonse, a general practitioner in Oregon, explained to the House of Lords Select Committee in 2005: 'The fact that the patient self-administers in a way that is not easy to do, drinking ounces of a bitter liquid, provides a final piece of clear evidence that this is completely volitional and self-administered.'[164] Against this, it might be argued that it is unfair to impose this unpleasant burden upon the patient, at a time when the emphasis should instead be on making her as comfortable as possible.

It could also be argued that allowing only euthanasia provides a different sort of control over the practice. If the doctor has to inject the medication, as opposed to simply writing a prescription for it, there is less chance that it will fall into the hands of a third party. In Oregon, in the six years between 1998 and 2014, a total of 1,327 people had prescriptions written under the Death with Dignity Act, and 859 patients died a result.[165] This statistic could be read in two ways. First, it might suggest that terminally ill patients do not, in practice, feel under pressure to complete their assisted suicide and that changing one's mind is not uncommon. Secondly, however, although most of the prescriptions which were issued were probably never filled, it is possible that the patient obtained the drugs but either chose not to use them or died first. The dangers of unused medication falling into the hands of others are obvious.

3 PATIENTS WHO LACK CAPACITY

In this chapter, because our interest is in practices that may result in a person's life being shortened, we are necessarily concerned with a very small subset of patients who lack capacity. As we saw in Chapter 5, the treatment of patients who lack capacity is governed by the best interests test, and usually it is obvious that it is in someone's best interests to be kept alive. There are, however, cases in which families, doctors, and courts have been faced with

---

[164] House of Lords, Assisted Dying for the Terminally Ill Committee (2005) 146.
[165] Oregon Health Authority, *Oregon's Death with Dignity Act—2014* (2015).

the question of whether it could ever be in the best interests of a patient who lacks capacity to withdraw or withhold life-prolonging treatment. We consider children and adults separately.

(a) CHILDREN

If doctors were always under a duty to prolong children's lives, then the non-treatment of severely disabled neonates would be murder. It is, however, widely agreed that doctors are not obliged to strive to maintain life at all costs. If treatment is futile (ie it is not going to lead to any improvement in the patient's condition), or overly burdensome, doctors may be entitled to withhold or discontinue it.

It would be a mistake to imagine that all cases involving decisions about withholding or withdrawing treatment come before the courts. On the contrary, in neonatal intensive care units (NICUs), decisions about withdrawing life-prolonging measures are not uncommon. It has been estimated that up to 70 per cent of deaths in NICUs are preceded by discussions about limiting or withholding treatment.[166] In paediatric intensive care wards between 43 per cent and 72 per cent of deaths result from decisions about treatment withdrawal.[167]

The Royal College of Paediatrics and Child Health has issued guidance about the circumstances when decisions to withhold or withdraw life-prolonging treatment are justifiable.

Royal College of Paediatrics and Child Health[168]

There are five situations where it may be ethical and legal to consider withholding or withdrawal of life-sustaining medical treatment:

1. *The 'Brain Dead' Child.* In the older child where criteria of brain-stem death are agreed by two practitioners in the usual way it may still be technically feasible to provide basal cardio-respiratory support by means of ventilation and intensive care. It is agreed within the profession that treatment in such circumstances is futile and the withdrawal of current medical treatment is appropriate.

2. *The 'Permanent Vegetative' State'.* The child who develops a permanent vegetative state following insults, such as trauma or hypoxia, is reliant on others for all care and does not react or relate with the outside world. It may be appropriate to withdraw or withhold life-sustaining treatment.

3. *The 'No Chance' Situation.* The child has such severe disease that life-sustaining treatment simply delays death without significant alleviation of suffering. Treatment to sustain life is inappropriate.

4. *The 'No purpose' Situation.* Although the patient may be able to survive with treatment, the degree of physical or mental impairment will be so great that it is unreasonable to expect them to bear it.

5. *The 'Unbearable' Situation.* The child and/or family feel that in the face of progressive and irreversible illness further treatment is more than can be borne. They wish to have a particular treatment withdrawn or to refuse further treatment irrespective of the medical opinion that it may be of some benefit.

---

[166] *Withholding or Withdrawing Life Sustaining Treatment in Children: A Framework for Practice,* 2nd edn (Royal College of Paediatrics and Child Health, 2004).
[167] Ibid.   [168] Ibid.

A very unusual case involving the first scenario arose in Manchester in 2015. In *Re A (A Child)*, A was 19 months old when he choked on the stalk of a satsuma. He lost consciousness, leading to cardiac arrest and profound and irreversible brain injury. Brain stem tests, carried out four days later, revealed that A had died. He was, however, still attached to a ventilator and his parents were unable to contemplate removing him from it. They wanted to take A, while still being ventilated, back to Saudi Arabia where life support cannot be withdrawn. A had been dead for 48 hours when the hospital applied for declarations that it would be lawful for him to be withdrawn from the ventilator. Hayden J granted the declarations sought.

Re A (A Child)[169]

Hayden J

Whilst expressing profound respect for the father's views, the time has now come to permit the ventilator to be turned off and to allow Child A, who died on 10th February, dignity in death. For those reasons, I propose to make the declarations sought by the Trust, with the indicated amendments, confident that this hospital will do everything they can to make this inevitably painful process as dignified as possible for all concerned. I would only add my profound condolences to Mr and Mrs A and to Child B and Child C.

More commonly, the cases that come before the courts tend to involve the last three situations ('no chance', 'no purpose', and 'unbearable'), and generally the courts only become involved in cases where the doctors and the parents cannot agree, or where the doctors are seeking reassurance that non-treatment would be lawful.

The most common sort of dispute arises when the doctors believe that life support should be withheld while the parents want treatment to continue, often as a result of their religious faith. In *King's College Hospital NHS Foundation Trust v T*, for example, Z was 17 months old and gravely ill. He had suffered a catastrophic irreversible hypoxic-ischemic injury to his brain, which had destroyed most of his brain tissue. There was no prospect of meaningful movement, vision, communication, engagement with others, or feeding, and indeed Z's condition was so poor that tests had been carried out in order to discover if he met the criteria for brain-stem death. Z was being kept alive on a mechanical ventilator, which the doctors now wished to withdraw, with the result that he would die within an hour. As committed and devout Christians, Z's parents believed that they did not have the right to agree to life-sustaining treatment being withdrawn. They also believed that, given time, God might work a miracle and Z might recover enough to participate more fully in life. Russell J granted permission for Z to be removed from the ventilator.

King's College Hospital NHS Foundation Trust v T[170]

Russell J

On balance I am driven to conclude that the mechanical ventilation is only just sustaining life with no other benefit. When I consider his best interests holistically, the life support confers little benefit as it prolongs all the likely discomfort and possible pain and increases

---

[169] [2015] EWHC 443 (Fam). [170] [2014] EWHC 3315 (Fam).

the probability of further infection leading to further invasive treatment and complications which will itself contribute to further physical deterioration without any real hope of restoring his health. His brain injuries are so profound, so catastrophic and the likelihood of further deterioration to his brain from hydrocephalus and the probability of lung infection and injury with continued ventilation all add to the conclusion that on balance not only is there no benefit, but in fact there is a strong probability of further pain, suffering and deterioration. Very sadly and with great reluctance I grant permission to withdraw the mechanically assisted ventilation.

When faced with an application for a declaration of the lawfulness of treatment withdrawal, the 'welfare principle' applies: that is, the child's best interests will be the court's paramount concern.[171] In applying the best interests test, the court is usually guided by medical evidence. Holman J's judgment in *An NHS Trust v B* is noteworthy for his decision to go against unanimous medical opinion, and the views of the guardian appointed to represent MB's interests, and order that certain types of life-prolonging treatment should be provided to MB, a terminally ill little boy.

MB suffered from Type 1 spinal muscular atrophy (SMA). He could barely move, could not breathe unaided, could not swallow, and suffered from epilepsy. The doctors treating him considered that MB's quality of life had become so poor and the burdens of treatment so great that it would be unethical to continue artificially to keep him alive. They sought a declaration that it would be lawful to withdraw his endotracheal tube, which would lead to his death within a few minutes. His parents disagreed, and wanted treatment to continue.

Holman J sided with the parents, and decided treatment should continue, although he did also recognize that there were some treatments, such as cardio-pulmonary resuscitation, which went beyond maintaining ventilation and which required the positive infliction of pain. If they became necessary, Holman J thought this would mean that MB had moved naturally towards his death, and that it would then be in MB's best interests to withhold those treatments.

In applying the best interests test, in *An NHS Trust v B*, Holman J drew up a 'balance sheet' with the benefits or advantages of treatment on one side, and the burdens or disadvantages of continuing or discontinuing treatment on the other side. On the benefits side were MB's capacity to gain pleasure from DVDs, CDs, and stories and, more importantly, from his relationship with his parents and family. The burdens were the discomfort, distress, or pain which accompanied the procedures to which he was subject, coupled with his inability to communicate his suffering. Holman J concluded that because MB's life did still contain benefits, treatment should continue.

An NHS Trust v B[172]

Holman J

I fully accept all the burdens of discomfort, distress and some pain to which M is daily subjected, but from which I would now specifically exclude, if the need arises, CPR and the other treatments I have just described. Even excluding these, I accept that there is almost relentless discomfort, periods of distress and relatively short episodes of pain (deep suctioning). It is indeed a helpless and sad life.

[171] Children Act 1989, s 1.   [172] [2006] EWHC 507 (Fam).

But that life does in my view include within it the benefits that I have tried to describe and will not repeat. Within those benefits, and central to them, is my view that on the available evidence I must proceed on the basis that M has age appropriate cognition, and does continue to have a relationship of value to him with his family, and does continue to gain other pleasures from touch, sight and sound. . . .

It is impossible to put a mathematical or any other value on the benefits. But they are precious and real and they are the benefits, and only benefits, that M was destined to gain from his life. I do not consider that from one day to the next all the routine discomfort, distress and pain that the doctors describe (but not the ones I have now excluded) outweigh those benefits so that I can say that it is in his best interests that those benefits, and life itself, should immediately end. On the contrary, I positively consider that as his life does still have benefits, and is his life, it should be enabled to continue, subject to excluding the treatment I have identified.

A year later, in *Re K (A Minor)*, Sir Mark Potter P distinguished K's situation from that of MB. She could gain no pleasure from life and, as a result, it would be in her best interests to cease to provide artificial feeding (known as total parenteral nutrition or TPN).

Re K (A Minor)[173]

Sir Mark Potter P

In this case K is less than 6 months old and has a developmental age of only 3 months. She has no accumulation of experiences and cognition comparable with that of MB. She is not, and with her short expectation of life is never likely to be, in a position to derive pleasure from DVDs or CDs and the only indication of real feelings of pleasure in her limited developmental state is enjoyment of a bath. On the evidence before me there is no realistic sense in which one can assign to her the simple pleasure of being alive or having other than a life dominated by regular pain, distress and discomfort and unrelieved by the pleasures of eating . . .

She has no prospect of relief from this pitiful existence before an end which is regarded as virtually certain by the age of one year and likely to be appreciably less. . . . In these circumstances, I have no doubt that it would not only be a mercy, but it is in her best interests, to cease to provide TPN while she is still clinically stable, so that she may die in peace and over a comparatively short space of time, relieved by the palliative treatment contemplated, which will cause her neither pain nor discomfort and will enable her to live out her short life in relative peace in the close care of her parents who love her.

Taken together, these two cases suggest that if the child has some meaningful cognitive development and awareness, the court may favour life-prolonging measures, even where these cause discomfort. But where that discomfort coexists with significantly impaired capacity to gain any pleasure from everyday life, life-prolonging treatment is less likely to be in a child's best interests.

In most of these cases, the courts are concerned to weigh up the burdens and the benefits of treatment. In cases where the baby is unconscious, invasive treatment will not be burdensome for her, but nor does it offer her any meaningful benefits, unless simply being alive,

---

[173] [2006] EWHC 1007 (Fam).

despite being wholly unaware of that fact, is regarded as a benefit. In such cases, the question will instead be whether the treatment is futile.

An example of such a case is *NHS Trust v Baby X*, in which the question for the court was whether baby X—who had suffered profound and irreversible brain damage—should be removed from a mechanical ventilator, with the expectation that he would die within minutes or hours. The staff in the children's hospital where X was being treated had concluded that it was no longer in X's best interests to remain on artificial ventilation: there was no prospect of any improvement and so continuing treatment would be futile. X's parents, on the other hand, wanted the treatment to continue. In part this was because they still believed that improvement was possible, but also their religious faith prevented them from consenting to a course of action which would result in X's death.

Hedley J accepted that treatment was not, in fact, burdensome for X because he had no awareness and could not experience pain. But since no improvement was possible, treatment would be futile, and Hedley J declared that it would be lawful to withdraw X from the ventilator.

NHS Trust v Baby X[174]

Hedley J

In the end I have to conclude that X's welfare requires his removal from ventilation on to palliative care. . . . The essence of the reasoning which supports this conclusion is as follows. First, I recognise the desire to preserve life as the proper starting point to which I add that X is very probably unaware of any burden in his continued existence. Against that, secondly, I have set both his unconsciousness or unawareness of self, others or surroundings and the evidence that any discernible improvement is an unrealistic aspiration. Thirdly, I have acknowledged his ability to continue for some time yet on ventilation but have balanced that with the risk of infection or other deterioration and the desire to avoid death in isolation from human contact. Fourthly, having accepted that treatment serves no purpose in terms of improvement and has no chance of effecting it, I have taken into account its persistent, intense and invasive nature. Fifthly, I have noted the treating consultant's view that X shows no desire to live or capacity to struggle to survive which are the conventional marks of a sick child; although I think that observation as such is correct, I would not want that to have significant let alone decisive weight in this balance.

Essentially for those reasons and on that balance I reach the conclusion that X should in future be treated on the basis of palliative care. This is, of course, not an order of the court. It is a declaration that so to treat would be lawful as being in X's best interests.

There have been cases, such as *Glass v United Kingdom*[175] and the prolonged litigation involving Charlotte Wyatt,[176] in which court proceedings over what should happen to a profoundly sick child sours the relationship between parents and clinicians, and makes an already traumatic situation worse. Litigation can also be extremely expensive: the six hearings in the Charlotte Wyatt case were estimated to have cost the public purse well over £500,000. As a result, and because court review happens only when there is a disagreement between parents

---

[174] [2012] EWHC 2188 (Fam).

[175] Application no 61827/00 (2004).

[176] *Portsmouth NHS Trust v Wyatt* [2004] EWHC 2247 (Fam); [2005] EWHC 117 (Fam); [2005] EWHC 693 (Fam); [2005] EWCA Civ 1181; [2006] EWHC 319 (Fam); [2006] EWCA Civ 529.

and doctors, the Nuffield Council on Bioethics has proposed two different approaches. First, instead of court involvement, it suggested that there could be routine review of non-treatment decisions by Clinical Ethics Committees (CECs). Secondly, the Nuffield Council recommended that mediation between parents and doctors should be attempted before resort to litigation.

Nuffield Council on Bioethics[177]

CECs could be charged to review all decisions made in relation to withdrawal of intensive care, whether such decisions are made by agreement between parents and professionals or not. Such a review would ensure an external and independent evaluation of a baby's interests. . . . Rapid advice would sometimes be required and mechanisms would be needed to achieve this. Such provision may well not be possible in all circumstances, for example with regard to decisions about resuscitation; however, one basis for such a mechanism would be for some members of existing CECs, or other facilitators, to be available on call to hospital staff . . .

When disagreements arise about the care of a very ill baby, there is rarely a 'right' answer and therefore the potential benefits of mediation merit examination. In the UK, mediation is increasingly used to assist parties in disputes that might otherwise be adjudicated in the courts. Mediation empowers the parties to a dispute to seek to resolve their disagreement themselves.

Indeed, it appears to be the case that where the parents and the medical team disagree, intensive efforts are made to reach a consensus before making an application to the court. Brierley et al's study of all deaths in the Great Ormond Street Paediatric Intensive Care Unit revealed that informal mediation, often with religious leaders, was often attempted when parents and doctors could not agree. Where the religious belief which prompted the parents' refusal to accept medical advice was fundamentalist in origin—and based upon a belief in miracles—Brierley et al suggest that there should be fast-track access to the courts.

Joe Brierley, Jim Linthicum, and Andy Petros[178]

During the 3-year period 203 children had withdrawal or limitation of invasive care recommended by the medical team and in 186 cases families agreed that this was in the child's best interests. However, in the remaining 17 cases agreement could not be achieved with the families. We reviewed the case notes and found a predominant theme of expression of strong religious belief influencing the family's response to the critical illness of their child. Of these 17 initial cases, 6 were resolved by considering the best interest of the child, further time for the families and ongoing multidisciplinary discussions. However, 11 (65%) involved challenging protracted discussions, largely based upon the belief in the sanctity of life as a result of the parents' religious convictions. . . .

For some religious groups with more fundamentalist beliefs, expectation of a miracle cure . . . is commonplace. Traditional mechanisms for resolution of end-of life disagreements

---

[177] *Critical Care Decisions in Fetal and Neonatal Medicine: Ethical Issues* (NCOB, 2006).
[178] 'Should religious beliefs be allowed to stonewall a secular approach to withdrawing and withholding treatment in children?' (2013) 29 Journal of Medical Ethics 574–7.

based upon local cultural, secular or religious values were not infrequently unsuccessful. Protracted dialogue was often unable to resolve these differences, while the child was subject to pain and discomfort from invasive ventilation, suctioning and multiple injections. We suggest it is time to reconsider current ethical and legal structures and facilitate rapid default access to courts in such situations when the best interests of the child are compromised in expectation of the miraculous.

(1) The 'Conjoined Twins Case' *Re A*

(a) Re A

As we have seen, the reason why doctors who discontinue life-prolonging treatment are not routinely charged with murder is that treatment withdrawal is treated in law as an omission. When the courts were first asked to authorize the separation of conjoined twins, a new problem arose. In *Re A (Children) (Conjoined Twins: Surgical Separation)*[179] the facts were that the weaker twin (known as Mary) would die if she was separated from the stronger twin (known as Jodie). If the twins were separated, Jodie would have a good chance of leading a normal life. Without an operation to separate the twins, Jodie's heart would be likely to fail within a few months, leading to the deaths of both babies. The parents, who were devout Roman Catholics from the Mediterranean island of Gozo, refused to consent to an operation that would kill one of their daughters. The hospital then applied for a declaration that it could lawfully carry out separation surgery.

At first instance, Johnson J attempted to justify the operation by describing it as an omission: the operation would, he said, interrupt or withdraw the blood supply which Mary was receiving from Jodie. This explanation was rejected by the Court of Appeal. Invasive surgery is unquestionably an action, and this meant that the doctors carrying out the operation would be guilty of murdering Mary, unless a defence was available.

Each of the four judges who heard the case started from the utilitarian presumption that saving one life must be preferable to losing two lives. The problem, of course, was that Jodie's life could only be saved by doing something that would kill Mary. So the judgments in *Re A (Children) (Conjoined Twins: Surgical Separation)* can be read as attempts to justify a course of action which, on the face of it, is impermissible in order to achieve 'the lesser of two evils', that is, the death of one child rather than two.

Re A (Children) (Conjoined Twins: Surgical Separation)[180]

Ward LJ

Just as the parents hold firm views worthy of respect, so every instinct of the medical team has been to save life where it can be saved. Despite such a professional judgment it would, nevertheless, have been a perfectly acceptable response for the hospital to bow to the weight of the parental wish however fundamentally the medical team disagreed with it. Other medical teams may well have accepted the parents' decision. Had St Mary's done so, there could not have been the slightest criticism of them for letting nature take its course in accordance with the parents' wishes. Nor should there be any criticism of the hospital for not bowing to the parents' choice.

---

[179] [2001] 1 FLR 267.   [180] [2001] 1 FLR 267.

Family Law

The question is whether this proposed operation is in Mary's best interests. It cannot be. It will bring her life to an end before it has run its natural span. It denies her inherent right to life. There is no countervailing advantage for her at all. It is contrary to her best interests. Looking at her position in isolation and ignoring, therefore, the benefit to Jodie, the court should not sanction the operation on her . . .

If the duty of the court is to make a decision which puts Jodie's interests paramount and that decision would be contrary to the paramount interests of Mary, then, for my part, . . . [g]iven the conflict of duty, I can see no other way of dealing with it than by choosing the lesser of the two evils and so finding the least detrimental alternative . . .

Mary may have a right to life, but she has little right to be alive. She is alive because and only because, to put it bluntly, but none the less accurately, she sucks the lifeblood of Jodie and she sucks the lifeblood out of Jodie. She will survive only so long as Jodie survives. Jodie will not survive long because constitutionally she will not be able to cope. Mary's parasitic living will be the cause of Jodie's ceasing to live. If Jodie could speak, she would surely protest, 'Stop it, Mary, you're killing me.' Mary would have no answer to that. Into my scales of fairness and justice between the children goes the fact that nobody but the doctors can help Jodie. Mary is beyond help.

Hence I am in no doubt at all that the scales come down heavily in Jodie's favour.

Criminal Law

I have to ask myself whether I am satisfied that the doctors recognise that death or serious harm will be virtually certain, barring some unforeseen intervention, to result from carrying out this operation. If so, the doctors intend to kill or to do that serious harm even though they may not have any desire to achieve that result. It is common ground that they appreciate that death to Mary would result from the severance of the common aorta. Unpalatable though it may be . . . to stigmatise the doctors with 'murderous intent', that is what in law they will have if they perform the operation and Mary dies as a result . . .

The reality here—harsh as it is to state it, and unnatural as it is that it should be happening—is that Mary is killing Jodie. . . . Mary uses Jodie's heart and lungs to receive and use Jodie's oxygenated blood. This will cause Jodie's heart to fail and cause Jodie's death as surely as a slow drip of poison. How can it be just that Jodie should be required to tolerate that state of affairs? . . . I can see no difference in essence between . . . resort to legitimate self-defence and the doctors coming to Jodie's defence and removing the threat of fatal harm to her presented by Mary's draining her lifeblood. The availability of such a plea of quasi-self-defence, modified to meet the quite exceptional circumstances nature has inflicted on the twins, makes intervention by the doctors lawful.

Brooke LJ

According to Sir James Stephen there are three necessary requirements for the application of the doctrine of necessity: (i) the act is needed to avoid inevitable and irreparable evil; (ii) no more should be done than is reasonably necessary for the purpose to be achieved; (iii) the evil inflicted must not be disproportionate to the evil avoided. Given that the principles of modern family law point irresistibly to the conclusion that the interests of Jodie must be preferred to the conflicting interests of Mary, I consider that all three of these requirements are satisfied in this case.

Robert Walker LJ

The surgery would plainly be in Jodie's best interests, and in my judgment it would be in the best interests of Mary also, since for the twins to remain alive and conjoined in the way they are would be to deprive them of the bodily integrity and human dignity which is the right of each of them . . .

The operation would give her, even in death, bodily integrity as a human being. She would die, not because she was intentionally killed, but because her own body cannot sustain her life . . . The proposed operation would not be unlawful. It would involve the positive act of invasive surgery and Mary's death would be foreseen as an inevitable consequence of an operation which is intended, and is necessary, to save Jodie's life. But Mary's death would not be the purpose or intention of the surgery, and she would die because tragically her body, on its own, is not and never has been viable.

In deciding whether the separation operation should take place despite the parents' objections, the court's paramount consideration had to be the children's best interests. But here there were two children whose best interests could not be reconciled. The operation was clearly in Jodie's best interests, because it was the only way in which she could survive. But—according to Ward and Brooke LJJ—it was equally clearly not in Mary's best interests, because it would kill her. Robert Walker LJ tried to argue that the operation would in fact be in Mary's best interests as well, because it would restore her bodily integrity, and allow her to die with the dignity of a separated body.

What should the court do when faced with two children whose interests are diametrically opposed? Ward and Brooke LJJ agreed that Jodie's interests should take priority because Mary was 'destined for death'. But while they believed that the operation would be consistent with family law principles, the problem that it might nevertheless be murder remained. Ward LJ's solution was to say that Mary was effectively killing Jodie, by 'draining her lifeblood', and that the operation could be justified as quasi self-defence. Brooke LJ, on the other hand, invoked the defence of necessity: here, he said, the doctors were entitled to operate because it was the lesser of two evils. Robert Walker LJ appeared to justify the operation through the doctrine of double effect: Mary's death is a foreseen but unintended consequence of saving Jodie's life.

Following the Court of Appeal's judgment, an appeal to the House of Lords was anticipated, and seven Law Lords were convened to hear the appeal. The parents had, however, had enough, and decided to accept the Court of Appeal's decision. The operation went ahead, leading to Mary's death and Jodie's survival. Jodie—whose real name is Gracie—returned to Gozo with her parents the following year where she was able to lead a healthy and active life.

(b) Commentary on Re A

Unsurprisingly *Re A* generated considerable academic controversy. In the next extract, John Harris rejects the Court of Appeal's reasoning and instead argues that the operation could be justified because Mary was not yet, and never would be, a 'person', and death would therefore not deprive her of a life that she would be capable of valuing.

John Harris[181]

> If we say that Mary is going to 'die anyway' we may not be concentrating on the *duration* of the life expectancy but on some other feature of that life expectancy. I believe that there is something about Mary's life expectancy that makes plausible the decision in *Re A* . . . It is that the life expectancy of Mary between the time when the operation would take place and her inevitable death, would not have been expectancy of what might be called 'biographical life', not the life of a person. Indeed neither Mary nor Jodie had started living biographical lives, neither were persons properly so called at the time of the operation. On this analysis, the life Mary would lose by the performance of the operation which would kill her, would not have been life from which she could benefit significantly, not life that could ethically be distinguished from her life *in utero*.

In the light of Harris's comments, it is interesting to contemplate whether the Court of Appeal would have made the same decision in a scenario with identical facts aside from the children's ages. Let us imagine that Jodie and Mary were in fact 10-year-old conjoined twins, with separate personalities, who had lived quite happily together, but whose health had suddenly deteriorated because their one heart could no longer support two bodies. In those circumstances, is it possible that the court might have given more weight to the parents' refusal to sign the consent form for an operation that would kill one of their daughters?

If, instead, the conjoined twins whose heart had started to fail had been adults who expressed a clear wish not to be separated, it is unimaginable that the defence of necessity would have been invoked to sanction the killing of one twin in order to save the other.

Even in the case of newborn babies, Raanan Gillon argues that the parents' view that it would be wrong to kill one daughter in order to save the other's life was not eccentric and should have been accorded greater respect.

Raanan Gillon[182]

> The parents were neither incompetent nor negligent—the standard justifications for depriving parents of such authority—and their reasoning was not eccentric or *merely* religious, but was widely acceptable moral reasoning—as was the contrary moral reasoning justifying an operation. The court should thus have declined to deprive the parents of their normal responsibilities and rights in order to impose its own preferred resolution of the moral dilemma, and should have allowed the parents to refuse medical intervention—while still ruling as it did, that such separation would not have been unlawful had the parents consented.

The Court of Appeal's preference for separation—articulated most strongly in Robert Walker's suggestion that an intact, albeit dead, body might be in Mary's best interests—is questioned from a different perspective by Bratton and Chetwynd. Drawing on evidence that suggests that conjoined twins who live long enough to express an opinion do not necessarily

---

[181] 'Human Beings, Persons and Conjoined Twins: An Ethical Analysis of the Judgment in *Re A*' (2001) 9 Medical Law Review 221–36.

[182] 'Imposed separation of conjoined twins—moral hubris by the English courts?' (2001) 27 Journal of Medical Ethics 3–4.

want to be separated, they question the Court of Appeal's presumption that separation is always in conjoined twins' best interests.

MQ Bratton and SB Chetwynd[183]

The ethical and legal thinking that treats conjoined twins as if they were physically separate entities who have unfortunately become entangled and need to have their separate existence restored, seems to have things the wrong way round. Conjoined twins are not separate and never have been. If we separate them, we should at the very least recognise that we are creating two new separate entities from two who were one, and that in doing so we are removing from each of them part of themselves. It may, of course, be a decision that we need to make for the benefit of both twins, but we should be wary of assuming that a physically separate existence is automatically in their best interests. If we are more comfortable faced by singletons, if they conform better to the hidden assumptions of our ethical, legal, and medical notions of what is normal and acceptable, that does not mean these are good enough reasons to change conjoined twins to fit.

Finally, Barbara Hewson draws attention to Ward LJ's observation that it would have been equally legitimate for the doctors to comply with the parents' wishes and let both children die. This comment may have been prompted by media interviews with paediatric surgeons from Great Ormond Street Hospital in London, who said that if the twins had been born there, the parents' wishes would have been respected. Hewson argues that Ward LJ's apparent willingness to condone an entirely different course of action undermines resort to the doctrine of necessity, since logically something cannot be both necessary and optional.

Barbara Hewson[184]

Thus the whole case turned on a contingency: the fact that the twins happened to be in Manchester, rather than London. On any view, this is arbitrary, and cannot but undermine the application of a doctrine of necessity. By definition, necessity cannot properly apply to a course of action which is entirely optional and which only comes into play if one happens to live in town A rather than in town B.

Another striking aspect of Ward LJ's judgment is his use of pejorative language, both about Mary and her parents. Initially, he cites a consultant's evidence that 'Mary does very little and her twin does all the work'. Subliminally, this description creates an impression of unworthiness. . . . Ward LJ seizes on these medical metaphors: 'She lives on borrowed time, all of which is borrowed from Jodie. It is a debt she can never repay.' This makes Mary seem positively culpable, in terms of conventional legal morality. By the end, in a logical leap, he portrays Mary as a killer: 'she sucks the lifeblood out of Jodie'. . . . Mary emerges from this forensic denunciation as akin to Dracula: not only monstrous, but also evil. Buoyed up by his disturbing metaphors, Ward LJ readily concludes that Mary 'has little right to be alive' . . .

Anatomically, Ward LJ's description was inaccurate: Mary was not sucking anything from Jodie. Rather the reverse: Jodie's heart was responsible for circulating blood around both of them. This was not Mary's fault.

---

[183] 'One into two will not go: conceptualising conjoined twins' (2004) 30 Journal of Medical Ethics 279–85.
[184] 'Killing Off Mary: Was the Court of Appeal Right?' (2001) 9 Medical Law Review 281–98.

(b) ADULTS

In Chapter 5 we saw that the Mental Capacity Act 2005 confirmed the common law position that an adult patient who lacks capacity should be treated in her best interests. Best interests is not confined to the patient's objectively-judged clinical interests, but encompasses their emotional and psychological interests, and is judged in the light of the patient's values, beliefs, and preferences.[185]

Usually, of course, it will be in the best interests of a patient who lacks capacity to receive life-prolonging medical treatment. The question of whether it could be in a patient's best interests to have life-prolonging treatment withdrawn first came before the House of Lords in *Airedale NHS Trust v Bland*. In what follows, we briefly consider the *Bland* case before moving on to see how the decisions about withholding or withdrawing life-prolonging treatment from patients who lack capacity are made under the Mental Capacity Act 2005.

(1) *Airedale NHS Trust v Bland*

Tony Bland had suffered serious brain damage in the Hillsborough football stadium disaster in 1989 and had been in a persistent vegetative state (PVS) for three years. Given that when he had set out for the FA Cup semi-final, Tony Bland had been a healthy teenager, it is not surprising that he had not expressed a view about how he would want to be treated if he was in a PVS. His father was nevertheless convinced that his son would not 'want to be left like that'.

With the agreement of his family, the trust responsible for the hospital where Tony Bland was being treated sought declarations that they could lawfully discontinue all life-sustaining treatment and medical support measures designed to keep him alive, including the termination of ventilation, nutrition, and hydration by artificial means.

The *Bland* case[186] raised several new legal and ethical questions. First, since the doctors were proposing to withhold artificial nutrition and hydration from Tony Bland, knowing that this would lead to his death, might they satisfy both the *actus reus* and *mens rea* of the crime of murder? Secondly, even if it might be permissible to withdraw futile medical treatment from patients, is artificial hydration and nutrition 'medical treatment', or is it more accurately described as basic care, which, by definition, cannot be futile? Thirdly, doctors must treat patients who lack capacity in their best interests, but since the result of the proposed course of action would be Tony Bland's death, could death be said to be in his best interests? Would withdrawing Tony Bland's feeding tube be tantamount to saying that his life has ceased to have any value, and is this compatible with respect for the sanctity of human life?

In *Airedale NHS Trust v Bland*, the House of Lords unanimously rejected the Official Solicitor's appeal, and confirmed that Airedale NHS Trust was entitled to the declarations that had been granted by Sir Stephen Brown P and upheld by the Court of Appeal.

Airedale NHS Trust v Bland[187]

Lord Keith

Given that existence in the persistent vegetative state is not a benefit to the patient, it remains to consider whether the principle of the sanctity of life, which it is the concern of the state, and the judiciary as one of the arms of the state, to maintain, requires this House to

---

[185] Mental Capacity Act 2005, s 4.   [186] [1993] AC 789 (HL).   [187] [1993] AC 789 (HL).

hold that the judgment of the Court of Appeal was incorrect. In my opinion it does not. The principle is not an absolute one . . . In my judgment it does no violence to the principle to hold that it is lawful to cease to give medical treatment and care to a PVS patient who has been in that state for over three years, considering that to do so involves invasive manipulation of the patient's body to which he has not consented and which confers no benefit upon him.

Lord Goff

I must however stress, at this point, that the law draws a crucial distinction between cases in which a doctor decides not to provide, or to continue to provide, for his patient treatment or care which could or might prolong his life, and those in which he decides, for example by administering a lethal drug, actively to bring his patient's life to an end. As I have already indicated, the former may be lawful . . . But it is not lawful for a doctor to administer a drug to his patient to bring about his death, even though that course is prompted by a humanitarian desire to end his suffering, however great that suffering may be . . . So to act is to cross the Rubicon which runs between on the one hand the care of the living patient and on the other hand euthanasia—actively causing his death to avoid or to end his suffering. . . .

It is true that the drawing of this distinction may lead to a charge of hypocrisy; because it can be asked why, if the doctor, by discontinuing treatment, is entitled in consequence to let his patient die, it should not be lawful to put him out of his misery straight away, in a more humane manner, by a lethal injection, rather than let him linger on in pain until he dies. . . .

I agree that the doctor's conduct in discontinuing life support can properly be categorised as an omission. It is true that it may be difficult to describe what the doctor actually does as an omission, for example where he takes some positive step to bring the life support to an end. But discontinuation of life support is, for present purposes, no different from not initiating life support in the first place. In each case, the doctor is simply allowing his patient to die in the sense that he is desisting from taking a step which might, in certain circumstances, prevent his patient from dying as a result of his pre-existing condition; and as a matter of general principle an omission such as this will not be unlawful unless it constitutes a breach of duty to the patient.

Lord Browne-Wilkinson

Where a case raises wholly new moral and social issues, in my judgment it is not for the judges to seek to develop new, all embracing, principles of law in a way which reflects the individual judges' moral stance when society as a whole is substantially divided on the relevant moral issues. Moreover, it is not legitimate for a judge in reaching a view as to what is for the benefit of the one individual whose life is in issue to take into account the wider practical issues as to allocation of limited financial resources or the impact on third parties of altering the time at which death occurs . . .

For these reasons, it seems to me imperative that the moral, social and legal issues raised by this case should be considered by Parliament. The judges' function in this area of the law should be to apply the principles which society, through the democratic process, adopts, not to impose their standards on society. If Parliament fails to act, then judge-made law will of necessity through a gradual and uncertain process provide a legal answer to each new question as it arises. But in my judgment that is not the best way to proceed . . .

Murder consists of causing the death of another with intent so to do. What is proposed in the present case is to adopt a course with the intention of bringing about Anthony Bland's death. As to the element of intention or mens rea, in my judgment there can be no real doubt that it is present in this case: the whole purpose of stopping artificial feeding is to bring about the death of Anthony Bland.

As to the guilty act, or actus reus, the criminal law draws a distinction between the commission of a positive act which causes death and the omission to do an act which would have prevented death. . . . Apart from the act of removing the nasogastric tube, the mere failure to continue to do what you have previously done is not, in any ordinary sense, to do anything positive: on the contrary it is by definition an omission to do what you have previously done. The positive act of removing the nasogastric tube presents more difficulty. It is undoubtedly a positive act, similar to switching off a ventilator in the case of a patient whose life is being sustained by artificial ventilation. But in my judgment in neither case should the act be classified as positive, since to do so would be to introduce intolerably fine distinctions. If, instead of removing the nasogastric tube, it was left in place but no further nutrients were provided for the tube to convey to the patient's stomach, that would not be an act of commission.

In my judgment, there is a further reason why the removal of the nasogastric tube in the present case could not be regarded as a positive act causing the death. The tube itself, without the food being supplied through it, does nothing. The removal of the tube by itself does not cause the death since by itself it did not sustain life . . .

Finally, the conclusion I have reached will appear to some to be almost irrational. How can it be lawful to allow a patient to die slowly, though painlessly, over a period of weeks from lack of food but unlawful to produce his immediate death by a lethal injection, thereby saving his family from yet another ordeal to add to the tragedy that has already struck them? I find it difficult to find a moral answer to that question. But it is undoubtedly the law.

Lord Mustill

The conclusion that the declarations can be upheld depends crucially on a distinction drawn by the criminal law between acts and omissions . . . The acute unease which I feel about adopting this way through the legal and ethical maze is I believe due in an important part to the sensation that however much the terminologies may differ the ethical status of the two courses of action is for all relevant purposes indistinguishable. By dismissing this appeal I fear that your Lordships' House may only emphasise the distortions of a legal structure which is already both morally and intellectually misshapen. Still, the law is there and we must take it as it stands . . .

The whole matter cries out for exploration in depth by Parliament and then for the establishment by legislation not only of a new set of ethically and intellectually consistent rules, distinct from the general criminal law, but also of a sound procedural framework within which the rules can be applied to individual cases. The rapid advance of medical technology makes this an ever more urgent task, and I venture to hope that Parliament will soon take it in hand . . .

The distressing truth which must not be shirked is that the proposed conduct is not in the best interests of Anthony Bland, for he has no best interests of any kind. . . Thus, although the termination of his life is not in the best interests of Anthony Bland, his best interests in being kept alive have also disappeared, taking with them the justification for the non-consensual regime and the co-relative duty to keep it in being . . . Since there is no longer a duty to provide nourishment and hydration a failure to do so cannot be a criminal offence . . .

I must recognise at once that this chain of reasoning makes an unpromising start by transferring the morally and intellectually dubious distinction between acts and omissions into a context where the ethical foundations of the law are already open to question.

Although there are some differences between the judgments (Lord Mustill, for example, was especially critical of the law he felt bound to apply), the points of agreement can be summarized as follows.

- First, the Lords were unanimous that the principle of the sanctity of life, while important, was not absolute.

- Secondly, artificial nutrition and hydration was agreed to be medical treatment and not basic care.

- Thirdly, the Lords accepted that withdrawing artificial nutrition and hydration was an omission rather than an action. Given that a majority accepted that the intention was to 'bring about the death of Anthony Bland',[188] had withdrawing the feeding tube been an act rather than an omission, this would have been a straightforward case of murder. Despite the importance of their reliance on the acts/omissions distinction, some members of the House of Lords were less than enthusiastic about it: Lord Mustill, for example, described it as 'intellectually and morally dubious'.

- Fourthly, treatment prolonging Tony Bland's life had ceased to be in his best interests.

- Fifthly, since treatment was no longer in his best interests, the doctor is no longer under a duty to prolong his life. Indeed, Lord Browne-Wilkinson and Lord Lowry went further and suggested that if continued treatment was not in Tony Bland's best interests, the doctor might be under a duty to cease treatment.

In one of the first cases to be brought after the Human Rights Act came into force, *NHS Trust A v MH*, the court was asked to consider whether the withdrawal of artificial nutrition and hydration from a PVS patient was compatible with his Convention rights.

NHS Trust A v MH[189]

Dame Elizabeth Butler-Sloss P

Article 2 . . . imposes a positive obligation to give life-sustaining treatment in circumstances where, according to responsible medical opinion, such treatment is in the best interests of the patient but does not impose an absolute obligation to treat if such treatment would be futile. This approach is entirely in accord with the principles laid down in *Airedale NHS Trust v Bland* . . . In a case where a responsible clinical decision is made to withhold treatment, on the grounds that it is not in the patient's best interests, and that clinical decision is made in accordance with a respectable body of medical opinion, the state's positive obligation under article 2 is, in my view, discharged.

Given that the sanctity of life had been a consideration in cases decided before the incorporation of the European Convention on Human Rights, Dame Elizabeth Butler-Sloss's conclusion that 'a reasonable clinical decision . . . to withhold treatment' could not violate Article 2 is not surprising.

(2) The Mental Capacity Act 2005

As we saw in Chapter 5, when a patient lacks capacity, decisions about her treatment must, in the absence of a valid and applicable advance directive, be taken in her best interests. Under section 4, the person making this decision must consider all relevant

---

[188] Per Lord Browne-Wilkinson; see also Lord Lowry: 'the intention to bring about the patient's death is there'; and Lord Mustill: 'the proposed conduct has the aim . . . of terminating the life of Anthony Bland'.
[189] [2001] Fam 348 (Fam Div).

circumstances including, under section 4(6), the patient's previous wishes, feelings, values, and beliefs.

Mental Capacity Act 2005

4(6) He must consider, so far as is reasonably ascertainable—

(a) the person's past and present wishes and feelings (and, in particular, any relevant written statement made by him when he had capacity),

(b) the beliefs and values that would be likely to influence his decision if he had capacity, and

(c) the other factors that he would be likely to consider if he were able to do so.

Section 4(7) further specifies that, so far as is practicable, 'anyone engaged in caring for the person or interested in his welfare' must be consulted about the matters in section 4(6).

When the Mental Capacity Act 2005 was debated in parliament, there was concern that, by placing advance refusals of life-prolonging treatment on a statutory footing, the Act would introduce 'euthanasia by the back door'. This concern was misplaced because the Act did not change the law relating to refusing life-prolonging treatment, and in fact introduced additional safeguards. Nevertheless, the government's response to this anxiety was a curious amendment to section 4:

4(5) Where the determination relates to life-sustaining treatment he must not, in considering whether the treatment is in the best interests of the person concerned, be motivated by a desire to bring about his death.

The use of the word 'desire' is odd, but the intention of this section is clear; namely, although the decision to withhold or withdraw life-sustaining treatment can be in a person's best interests, ending the patient's life must never be the doctor's sole intention.

Normally, of course, the preservation of their life will be in a patient's best interests, but the Mental Capacity Act Code of Practice makes clear that this is not always the case. Just as with children, where life-prolonging treatment would be futile, overly burdensome, or where there is no prospect of recovery, it may be withdrawn or withheld.

Mental Capacity Act Code of Practice paras 5.31 and 5.33[190]

5.31 All reasonable steps which are in the person's best interests should be taken to prolong their life. There will be a limited number of cases where treatment is futile, overly burdensome to the patient or where there is no prospect of recovery. In circumstances such as these, it may be that an assessment of best interests leads to the conclusion that it would be in the best interests of the patient to withdraw or withhold life-sustaining treatment, even if this may result in the person's death. The decision-maker must make a decision based on the best interests of the person who lacks capacity. They must not be motivated by a desire to bring about the person's death for whatever reason, even if this is from a sense of compassion . . .

5.33 Importantly, section 4(5) cannot be interpreted to mean that doctors are under an obligation to provide, or to continue to provide, life-sustaining treatment where that treatment is

---

[190] (DH, 2007).

> not in the best interests of the person, even where the person's death is foreseen. Doctors must apply the best interests' checklist and use their professional skills to decide whether life-sustaining treatment is in the person's best interests. If the doctor's assessment is disputed, and there is no other way of resolving the dispute, ultimately the Court of Protection may be asked to decide what is in the person's best interests.

For example, in *NHS Trust v L* the only treatment that had a very remote chance of saving L's life, force feeding, was judged to be both futile and overly burdensome. L had an extremely rare form of anorexia and was close to death. She lacked capacity in relation to decisions about force feeding, and Eleanor King J held that it would not be in her best interests: force feeding was unlikely to save her life, but was certain to cause her distress.

NHS Trust v L [191]

Eleanor King J

In carrying out the balancing exercise I bear in mind that our law contains a strong presumption that all steps will be taken to preserve life save in exceptional circumstances . . . In my judgment this is one of those few cases where the only possible treatment, namely force feeding under sedation, is not to be countenanced in Ms L's best interests: to do so would be futile, carrying with it a near certainty that it would cause her death in any event. Such a course would be overly burdensome in that every calorie that enters her body is an enemy to Ms L.

(a) The importance of the patient's wishes

While the patient's wishes were always part of the 'best interests' assessment—recall that Tony Bland's parents were asked whether he had ever given any indication of how he would want to be treated—the 'best interests' checklist in the MCA places doctors under a clear duty to take account of the patient's previous values and beliefs. This means that a patient's previously expressed desire to have life-prolonging measures continued must be taken into account, although, unlike a valid and applicable advance refusal of treatment, it is not determinative.

This issue arose in the first Supreme Court case to consider the Mental Capacity Act 2005, *Aintree University Hospitals Foundation Trust v James*.[192] David James was 68 years old and suffered from multiple co-morbidities. His condition fluctuated and he had been receiving treatment for stroke, cardiac arrest, recurring infections, and multiple organ failure. The trust where he was being treated had sought declarations that Mr James lacked capacity (which was uncontentious), and that it would be lawful to discontinue or withhold CPR, renal replacement therapy, and invasive therapy for low blood pressure. Mr James's family wanted treatment to continue.

Peter Jackson J declined to make the declarations sought, on the ground that he was not satisfied that these treatments had become futile. The trust appealed. By the time the case was heard by the Court of Appeal, Mr James's condition had deteriorated, the declarations were granted and Mr James died. Because of a difference between the way in which Peter Jackson J and the Court of Appeal applied the best interests test, Mr James's widow was given leave to appeal to the Supreme Court.

---

[191] [2012] EWHC 2741 (COP). [192] [2013] UKSC 67.

In the Court of Appeal, Sir Alan Ward, with whom Laws LJ agreed, had held that Mr James's wishes, 'if they were to be the product of full informed thought', would have to recognize the futility of treatment, its burdensome nature, and the fact that he would never go home:

> One is driven to conclude that his wish to survive was unattainable.... In the overall assessment, therefore, of where his best interests lie, I respect his wishes but in my judgment they must give way to what is best in his medical interests.[193]

Arden LJ had reasoned that if the court had any doubt as to an individual's wishes, it should proceed on the basis that the individual would act as a reasonable person would act. Essentially, then, the Court of Appeal had suggested that when assessing a patient's best interests, if his condition was hopeless or there was any room for doubt about his wishes, they could be overridden by what was judged objectively to be in his best medical interests.

In *Aintree University Hospitals Foundation Trust v James*, the Supreme Court held that the question for the court was not whether it would be in David James's best interests to withhold treatment, but rather whether it would be in his best interests to give him treatment. If it was not in his best interests to receive treatment, the court could not consent to it on his behalf, and it would therefore be lawful to withhold or withdraw it.

The Supreme Court then unanimously decided that Peter Jackson J's approach had been the right one. Best interests must be judged subjectively, with treatment only being judged futile if this patient would consider continued existence to be futile. Given the change of facts when it heard the case, however, the Court of Appeal had been right to grant the declarations sought, albeit not for the reasons it had given.

Aintree University Hospitals Foundation Trust v James[194]

Baroness Hale (with whom the other Justices agreed)

The most that can be said, therefore, is that in considering the best interests of this particular patient at this particular time, decision-makers must look at his welfare in the widest sense, not just medical but social and psychological; they must consider the nature of the medical treatment in question, what it involves and its prospects of success; they must consider what the outcome of that treatment for the patient is likely to be; they must try and put themselves in the place of the individual patient and ask what his attitude to the treatment is or would be likely to be; and they must consult others who are looking after him or interested in his welfare, in particular for their view of what his attitude would be ...

The purpose of the best interests test is to consider matters from the patient's point of view. That is not to say that his wishes must prevail, any more than those of a fully capable patient must prevail. We cannot always have what we want. Nor will it always be possible to ascertain what an incapable patient's wishes are. Even if it is possible to determine what his views were in the past, they might well have changed in the light of the stresses and strains of his current predicament. In this case, the highest it could be put was, as counsel had agreed, that 'It was likely that Mr James would want treatment up to the point where it became hopeless'. But in so far as it is possible to ascertain the patient's wishes and feelings,

---

[193] [2013] EWCA Civ 65.   [194] [2013] UKSC 67.

> his beliefs and values or the things which were important to him, it is those which should be taken into account because they are a component in making the choice which is right for him as an individual human being.

Aintree was followed in *St George's Healthcare NHS Trust v P*, where Newton J took P's previously expressed wishes and religious faith into account when deciding whether he, rather than the population in general, would regard his continued existence as worthwhile.

St George's Healthcare NHS Trust v P[195]

Newton J

Mr Moore pointed to the most undignified existence that a patient must necessarily have when nursed in ICU [intensive care unit] and suggested that that was not an existence that most people would tolerate, let alone welcome, when there is so little prospect of functional recovery.

In looking at those aspects and as to whether or not P would assess his life as being regarded as worthwhile I attach far more weight to the relevant expressions of his articulate and well informed family members and friends who have direct knowledge of P's pre-injury knowledge, understanding and philosophy, in particular those who know about his beliefs and values.

In the light of his previously expressed strong views, coupled with his strong religious beliefs, the weight of the evidence all falls heavily to one side which is that the preservation of any life would be considered by P to be of significant value. His present circumstances are a life which P would find worthwhile, even though I entirely accept many others would not adopt the same position.

Post-*Aintree*, it is also clear that a patient's clear preference for no treatment, even if it has not been set out in a binding advance directive, should carry very considerable weight. In *Sheffield Teaching Hospitals NHS Foundation Trust v TH*, a heavy drinker had been very clear with his ex-wife and his friends that he did not want to receive any more treatment in hospital. Hayden J bluntly summed up his situation.

Sheffield Teaching Hospitals NHS Foundation Trust v TH[196]

Hayden J

He declined all support. He wished for no intervention from outside services. He was frustrated and angry with his disabilities. As he was never going to improve, he would rather die young and drink to the end he said. He expressed it uncompromisingly. 'My brain is fucked, I am fucked and I want to drink as it's the only thing I enjoy.' ...

I have no doubt that he would wish to leave the hospital and go to the home of his ex-wife and his mate's Spud and end his days quietly there and with dignity as he sees it. Privacy, personal autonomy and dignity have not only been features of TH's life, they have been the

---

[195] [2015] EWCOP 42.   [196] [2014] EWCOP 4.

creed by which he has lived it. He may not have prepared a document that complies with the criteria of section 24, giving advance directions to refuse treatment but he has in so many oblique and tangential ways over so many years communicated his views so uncompromisingly and indeed bluntly that none of his friends are left in any doubt what he would want in his present situation.

(b) Withdrawal of assisted nutrition and hydration from patients in a persistent vegetative state or a minimally conscious state

Practice Direction 9E, issued under the Court of Protection Rules 2007, specifies that certain cases must be brought before the Court of Protection:

Cases involving any of the following decisions . . . should be brought to the court:

(a) decisions about the proposed withholding or withdrawal of artificial nutrition and hydration from a person in a permanent vegetative state or a minimally conscious state.[197]

Both Practice Direction 9E and the Mental Capacity Act Code of Practice continue to insist that PVS cases should be brought before the court. Judicial oversight continues to be necessary notwithstanding the fact that, provided the diagnosis of PVS is accurate, a declaration of the legality of treatment withdrawal now appears to be automatic. In *A Primary Care Trust v CW*, for example, Ryder J explained that if CW's diagnosis of PVS was correct, treatment would be futile.

A Primary Care Trust v CW[198]

Ryder J

It should be noted that for the dicta [from *Bland*] to apply a patient must have a clear diagnosis of PVS . . . In essence medical treatment is of no benefit to a person in a PVS because they are not sensient and have no prospect of recovery. Thus, whether or not the withdrawal of life-sustaining treatment measures is in CW's best interests will depend upon whether or not his diagnosis of PVS is correct. If it is correct, in other words if he has no awareness of self or environment and no prospect of recovery, then the provision of any treatment is futile and cannot be in his best interests.

If a declaration that withdrawal is lawful follows automatically from an accurate diagnosis of PVS, it is worth asking what, if any, purpose is served by insisting upon court approval of decisions to withdraw treatment from PVS patients? As Penney Lewis has put it:

The judicial decision simply rubber-stamps the decision reached by the medical staff and the patient's family, having confirmed the diagnosis of PVS. The need to go court may cause distress to the patient's family and is expensive for the NHS.[199]

---

[197] Para 5. See also para 6.18 of the Mental Capacity Act Code of Practice.
[198] [2010] EWHC 3448 (Fam).
[199] Penney Lewis, 'Withdrawal of Treatment from a Patient in a Permanent Vegetative State: Judicial Involvement and Innovative "Treatment"' (2007) 15 Medical Law Review 392.

Halliday et al have calculated that, on average, each of these cases costs about £122,000 (£53,000 in litigation costs and £69,000 in ongoing care costs). They also found mixed evidence as to whether the need for court approval was stressful or reassuring for families.

Simon Halliday, Adam Formby, and Richard Cookson[200]

First, we can see that the declaratory relief judgments often operate as memorials of the living dead that anticipate the funerals that will follow in due course. The judgment of the court performs a function of ceremonially moving the family on from a state of limbo. Second, it also offers the family a formal affirmation of the extreme difficulty of their situation and the reality of their suffering. . . . There is evidence of the comfort and reassurance that these judgments can give . . . [T]he judgments often stress the appropriateness of letting the patient die. Research shows that family members often do not want to seek withdrawal of CANH [clinically assisted nutrition and hydration]. . . . For such relatives, the jurisdiction of the court can help them not to feel responsible for the patient's death. . . .

Interview data certainly confirm that the declaratory relief process carries potential emotional burdens for families. First, for some relatives, the prospect of declaratory relief may be distressing because they feel that the court is an illegitimate forum for such decisions to be made. For some relatives, the requirement to go to court is an unwelcome legal intrusion into the family domain . . . Second, some relatives, like many lay people who face the prospect of involvement in court procedure, feel some anxiety about the formalities of the process. . . . Finally, the delay to the ending of the patient's life caused by the court process can be very upsetting for some families.

Even if families do benefit from a formal process through which the decision to withdraw assisted nutrition and hydration (ANH) is taken, this does not necessarily have to take the form of a court hearing, which in practice simply confirms the diagnosis. Rather Halliday et al suggest that a formal 'best interests meeting' might serve a similar purpose, without the opportunity cost that this litigation has for other patients.

The Court of Protection has recently had to consider whether it could be lawful to withdraw life support from someone in a minimally conscious state (MCS). 'Minimal consciousness', in which a person has some awareness of her environment but lacks full consciousness, covers a wider spectrum of patients than 'permanently vegetative'. It can be the result of sudden trauma and sudden onset, but it might also describe someone's lack of capacity towards the end of a degenerative illness.

The first MCS case was that of *Re M (Adult Patient) (Minimally Conscious State: Withdrawal of Treatment).*[201] M had been about to go on a skiing holiday when she became drowsy and confused and lapsed into a coma, leaving her with extensive and irreparable brain damage. It was initially thought that M was in a PVS, but investigations revealed that her condition was instead one of minimal consciousness.

Unlike Tony Bland, it appeared that M could experience some pain and discomfort: she made a loud noise when her incontinence pads needed changing, for example. It might be thought that the fact that M had negative sensory experiences and that she might have some limited insight into her condition, would be worse than being in a PVS, in which someone is

---

[200] 'An Assessment of the Court's Role in the Withdrawal of Clinically Assisted Nutrition and Hydration from Patients in the Permanent Vegetative State' (2015) 23 Medical Law Review.
[201] [2011] EWHC 2443 (Fam).

completely unaware of what has happened to them. L Syd M Johnson, for example, has said that 'many persons prospectively considering the possibility of living in a MCS—of being permanently and profoundly disabled, unable to interact meaningfully, but consciously aware—might view it as a fate worse than the vegetative state, and indeed, a fate worse than death'.[202]

Nevertheless, in *Re M*, Baker J decided that, because M could also experience comfort and even small pleasures, such as turning her face towards the sun, the principle of the preservation of life took priority. A DNACPR order was to remain in force, but the positive withdrawal of life support was held not to be in M's best interests.

Baker J's pre-*Aintree* decision in *Re M (Adult Patient) (Minimally Conscious State: Withdrawal of Treatment)* is noteworthy for the comparative lack of weight he attached to the views of M's family's about her wishes and beliefs. When her maternal grandmother had gone to live in a nursing home, M had said she did not want to be looked after in that way. When her father became ill and had to go into a care home, M had said 'Don't ever put me in a place like that'; she had said that she wanted to 'be off quick and not dependent on others'. When she saw television reports about the Tony Bland case, M had said 'it would be better to allow him to die'. M's partner of 30 years said she would have been 'horrified' by the thought of living in her present condition. In contrast, her professional carers believed that M did have positive experiences, and their accounts carried more weight with Baker J.

Re M (Adult Patient) (Minimally Conscious State: Withdrawal of Treatment)[203]

Baker J

The first principle is the right to life . . . The principle of the right to life is simply stated but of the most profound importance. It needs no further elucidation. It carries very great weight in any balancing exercise.

The second factor requires more extensive analysis. As set out above, section 4(6) of the 2005 Act requires the court to consider, so far as reasonably ascertainable, M's past and present wishes and feelings. Even though M made no formal advance decision as to medical treatment, it is said on behalf of the applicant that she expressed wishes and feelings about the matter which should be give significant weight when deciding whether ANH should now be withdrawn. . . . M's family feel strongly that she would have rejected her current treatment and the rationale for this application is fundamentally based on M's perceived wishes and feelings. . . .

It is unclear whether M ever had a detailed understanding of Tony Bland's condition, but it does not follow from the fact that she indicated that she would not wish to be continue living in a vegetative state that she would have wished to have ANH withdrawn when she was conscious, albeit minimally. In addition, I have to take into account the fact that M has lived in her current minimally conscious state for many years. We have no way of knowing how she now feels about her current life. In those circumstances, the court must be particularly cautious about attaching significant weight to statements she made before her collapse. . . .

On one view, the pleasures of life in such circumstances may appear smaller, but that does not mean they can be disregarded. I do not accept the submission that the absence of

---

[202] 'The right to die in the minimally conscious state' (2011) 37 Journal of Medical Ethics 175–8.
[203] [2011] EWHC 2443 (Fam).

> pain or discomfort is not in itself a positive feature of life. Comfort and contentment can be, in my view, profoundly positive sensations…. Having considered the evidence of the carers, however, I find that M does enjoy some aspects of her life. I do not accept that her experiences are wholly, or even on balance, negative….
>
> On this aspect of the case, I accept the evidence of the carers, who have far greater experience of living with M in recent years than do members of her family whose visits have become less frequent as time has gone by.

Although each case is decided on its particular facts, in the MCS cases that have been decided post-*Aintree*, considerable weight has been attached to the family's views as to what the patient would have wanted. In *United Lincolnshire Hospitals NHS Trust v N*, N was a woman in her fifties, who had sustained significant brain damage following a haemorrhage in her brain. She was now in a MCS, and had persistently pulled out her feeding tubes. The question for the court was whether a percutaneous endoscopic gastrostomy (PEG) tube should be reinserted so that she could continue to be fed. Although successful reinsertion of a PEG tube would enable her to be kept alive, and perhaps to 'return to a relatively comfortable state at her care home where she was excellently cared for', this was outweighed by her family's account of what she would have wanted.

United Lincolnshire Hospitals NHS Trust v N [204]

Pauffley J

[B]eing allowed to die would accord with N's reported comment made prior to her brain injury as to her wishes and feelings should she be incapacitated in the context of a road traffic accident; by authorising the non-replacement of the PEG tube or other methods of providing artificial nutrition and thereby allowing N to 'die with dignity', the court would be acting in accordance with what family members believe she would have wanted.

There is no evidence that N has made any advance refusal of treatment directly applicable to the circumstances in which she now finds herself, namely in a minimally conscious state facing the prospect of no further provision of nutrition. However, what the views of the patient might be, and what the views of the family are, are highly material factors when considering best interests, although not determinative.

Hayden J's 2015 judgment in *M v N* is notable for the emphasis he placed upon the patient's wishes and feelings, and the weight he attached to her family's opinion as to whether ANH was in her best interests. Mrs N was 68, and profoundly incapacitated by multiple sclerosis. She was minimally conscious, although one of the experts believed that she satisfied the criteria for a diagnosis of PVS. When her own parents had dementia and had had to go into a home, she could not bear to visit them, and had said to her children: 'if I ever get like that shoot me!' Interestingly, the Official Solicitor had originally opposed the application for a declaration that it would be lawful to discontinue ANH, on the grounds that 'the strong presumption in favour of the benefit of the continuance of life had not been displaced'. After hearing the family's evidence, and following consultation with counsel, he changed his mind, and decided it would be wrong for him to continue to oppose the application. Given

---

[204] [2014] EWCOP 16.

the importance of the decision, Hayden J nevertheless delivered a lengthy judgment that is striking in its respect for the person that Mrs N was.

M v N[205]

Hayden J

For one who has set such store by outward appearance and who has been so attentive to the impression she created on others, her decline, in the way I have outlined, is particularly poignant. Some might well have endured all that Mrs. N has with phlegmatism and fortitude. Mrs. N is simply not such a person. I am satisfied, as the family say, that some considerable time ago now she had simply had enough and that, as they see it, to force nutrition and hydration upon her is to fail to respect the person she is and the code by which she has lived her life….

As is clear from the above analysis this case is not concerned with a right to die. No such right exists. What is in focus here is Mrs. N's right to live her life at the end of her days in the way that she would have wished. I am required to evaluate the 'inviolability of life' as an ethical concept and to weigh that against an individual's right to self determination or personal autonomy. Not only do these principles conflict, they are of a fundamentally different complexion. The former is an ideological imperative found in most civilised societies and in all major religions, the latter requires an intense scrutiny of an individual's circumstances, views and attitudes. The exercise is almost a balance of opposites: the philosophical as against the personal. For this reason, as I have already indicated, I consider that a formulaic 'balance sheet' approach to Mrs. N's best interests is artificial.

As I have already set out and at some length, I am entirely satisfied that Mrs. N's views find real and authoritative expression through her family in this courtroom. I start with the assumption that an instinct for life beats strongly in all human beings. However, I am entirely satisfied that Mrs. N would have found her circumstances to be profoundly humiliating and that *she* would have been acutely alert to the distress caused to her family, which *she* would very much have wanted to avoid. LR told me that Mrs. N would not have wanted to have been a burden; that I also believe to be entirely reliable.

There is an innate dignity in the life of a human being who is being cared for well, and who is free from pain. There will undoubtedly be people who for religious or cultural reasons or merely because it accords with the behavioural code by which they have lived their life prefer to, or think it morally right to, hold fast to life no matter how poor its quality or vestigial its nature. Their choice must be respected. But choice where rational, informed and un-coerced is the essence of autonomy. It follows that those who would not wish to live in this way must have their views respected too.

I am entirely satisfied that there is no prospect of her achieving a life that *she* would consider to be meaningful, worthwhile or dignified…. Quite simply, I have come to the conclusion that it would be disrespectful to Mrs. N to preserve her further in a manner I think *she* would regard as grotesque.

In relation to both PVS and MCS patients, palliative care will be given at the same time as the withdrawal of ANH in order to ensure that the patient's death is pain-free and peaceful. However, the withdrawal of ANH may nevertheless be extremely distressing for relatives: the deliberate decision to starve someone to death is clearly inconsistent

---

[205] [2015] EWCOP 76.

with our most basic need to care for those we love. Celia and Jenny Kitzinger's research with family members of patients with disorders of consciousness suggests that it was not uncommon for them to contemplate mercy killing in preference to the withdrawal of ANH.

Celia Kitzinger and Jenny Kitzinger[206]

Failing to feed (or to provide water) to a loved one via whatever route (orally or by tube)—even because of the conviction that they would prefer to be dead—is a highly emotive issue with deep cultural resonance. . . . Interviewees were often concerned that, even with a confirmed VS [vegetative state] diagnosis, it was possible that their relative would experience pain and suffering and there was a widespread perception that lethal injections would be more humane, compassionate and dignified than 'death from neglect' as a result of treatment withdrawal. . . . If you've made that decision, you might as well do it as humanely as you possibly can. . . . To starve somebody to death seems a particularly cruel thing to do.

Even when families were told by clinicians that the person would receive palliative care, they still found ANH withdrawal unacceptable—if not for the patient, then for the rest of the family. One mother says: We hated it. They reassured us that, you know, 'oh he would be sedated, he wouldn't feel any pain.' But we would have to sit there for up to three weeks to, basically, watch him die . . . Many interviewees had thought about killing the patient themselves—with varying levels of seriousness. . . . Although, in the end, each of these interviewees had decided that carrying out a 'mercy killing' was not the answer, they were angry that the current system had, they felt, forced them into the position where they were contemplating it, and some felt guilty at their failure to carry through.

4 CONCLUSION

As we have seen in this chapter, end-of-life decisions raise some extraordinarily difficult and ethically contentious questions. It is, however, interesting to contrast concern about the possible abuse of vulnerable patients if euthanasia were to be legalized, with the relative lack of interest in the much more common and lawful ways in which doctors are involved routinely in end-of-life decision-making. If a doctor is contemplating giving a patient steadily increasing doses of diamorphine, in the knowledge that this may shorten her life, there is no need for the patient's agreement. When ANH or ventilation is withdrawn from a patient who lacks capacity, the patient dies slowly if painlessly from dehydration, starvation, or suffocation. Could it plausibly be argued that the lawful ways in which doctors may shorten their patients lives are not only more common, but also might be more open to abuse and be likely to lead to more protracted deaths than assisted dying?

On the other hand, others, like the Archbishop of Canterbury Justin Welby, argue that to sanction assisted dying 'would be to cross a fundamental legal and ethical rubicon'.

[206] 'Withdrawing artificial nutrition and hydration from minimally conscious and vegetative patients: family perspectives' (2015) 41 Journal of Medical Ethics 157–60.

Justin Welby[207]

[W]e need to reflect on what sort of society we might become if we were to permit assisted suicide. At present, we can show love, care and compassion to those who at all ages and stages of life are contemplating suicide. We can try to intervene, to support them to embrace life once more. We can do all in our power to surround those who are terminally ill with the best possible palliative care, including physical, emotional and spiritual support. We can redouble our efforts to alleviate suffering. We can show that we love even when people have given up on caring for themselves. We can support our doctors and nurses as they act consistently in the best interests of their patients, affirming life and caring for the vulnerable.

We risk all this for what? Becoming a society where each life is no longer seen as worth protecting, worth honouring, worth fighting for? The current law and the guidelines for practice work; compassion is shown, the vulnerable are protected. In spite of individual celebrity opinions and the 'findings' of snap opinion polls (that cannot hope to do justice to the intricacies of the issue) the current law is not 'broken'. There is no need to fix it.

FURTHER READING

Battin, Margaret Pabst, *Ending Life: Ethics and the Way We Die* (OUP: Oxford, 2005).

Bolt, Eva Elizabeth et al, 'Can physicians conceive of performing euthanasia in case of psychiatric disease, dementia or being tired of living?' (2015) 41 Journal of Medical Ethics 592–8.

Commission on Assisted Dying, *The Current Legal Status of Assisted Dying is Inadequate and Incoherent . . .* (Demos: London, 2011).

Foster, Charles, 'Suicide tourism may change attitudes to assisted suicide, but not through the courts' (2015) 41 Journal of Medical Ethics 620.

Halliday, Simon, Formby, Adam, and Cookson, Richard, 'An Assessment of the Court's Role in the Withdrawal of Clinically Assisted Nutrition and Hydration from Patients in the Permanent Vegetative State' (2015) 23 Medical Law Review 556–87.

Holm, Søren, 'The debate about physician assistance in dying: 40 years of unrivalled progress in medical ethics?' (2015) 41 Journal of Medical Ethics 40–3.

Huxtable, Richard, 'Splitting the difference? Principled compromise and assisted dying' (2014) 28 Bioethics 472–80.

Jackson, Emily, 'Whose Death is it Anyway? Euthanasia and the Medical Profession' (2004) 57 Current Legal Problems 415–42.

Jackson, Emily and Keown, John, *Debating Euthanasia* (Hart Publishing: Oxford, 2011).

Keown, John, *Euthanasia, Ethics and Public Policy: An Argument against Legalisation* (CUP: Cambridge, 2002).

Kitzinger, Celia and Kitzinger, Jenny, 'Withdrawing artificial nutrition and hydration from minimally conscious and vegetative patients: family perspectives' (2015) 41 Journal of Medical Ethics 157–60.

---

[207] 'Why I believe assisting people to die would dehumanise our society for ever', *The Guardian*, 5 September 2015.

Levene, Ilana and Parker, Michael, 'Prevalence of depression in granted and refused requests for euthanasia and assisted suicide: a systematic review' (2011) 37 Journal of Medical Ethics 205–11.

Lewis, Penney, 'Informal Legal Change on Assisted Suicide: The Policy for Prosecutors' (2011) 31 Legal Studies 119–34.

Magnusson, RS, 'Euthanasia: above ground, below ground' (2004) 30 Journal of Medical Ethics 441–6.

Mullock, Alexandra, 'The Supreme Court decision in *Nicklinson*: human rights, criminal wrongs and the dilemma of death' (2015) 31 Journal of Professional Negligence 18–28.

Wicks, Elizabeth, 'The Supreme Court Judgment in *Nicklinson*: One Step Forward on Assisted Dying; Two Steps Back on Human Rights' (2015) 23 Medical Law Review 144–56.

INDEX